# ROAD ATLAS

# 2025 EASY TO READ BRITAIN

## CONTENTS




**www.philips-maps.co.uk**

First published in 2020 by Philip's
a division of Octopus Publishing Group Ltd
www.octopusbooks.co.uk
Carmelite House, 50 Victoria Embankment
London EC4Y 0DZ
An Hachette UK Company
www.hachette.co.uk

Fifth edition 2024
First impression 2024

ISBN 978-1-84907-666-1 spiral-bound
ISBN 978-1-84907-665-4 perfect-bound

Cartography by Philip's




Information for National Parks, Areas of Outstanding Natural Beauty, National Trails and Country Parks in Wales supplied by the Countryside Council for Wales.

Information for National Parks, Areas of Outstanding Natural Beauty, National Trails and Country Parks in England supplied by Natural England. Data for Regional Parks, Long Distance Footpaths and Country Parks in Scotland provided by Scottish Natural Heritage.

Gaelic name forms used in the Western Isles provided by Comhairle nan Eilean.

Data for the National Nature Reserves in England provided by Natural England. Data for the National Nature Reserves in Wales provided by Countryside Council for Wales. Darparwyd data'n ymwneud â Gwarchodfeydd Natur Cenedlaethol Cymru gan Gyngor Cefn Gwlad Cymru.

Information on the location of National Nature Reserves in Scotland was provided by Scottish Natural Heritage.





Printed in China

*Data from Nielsen Total Consumer Market 2023 weeks 1–39

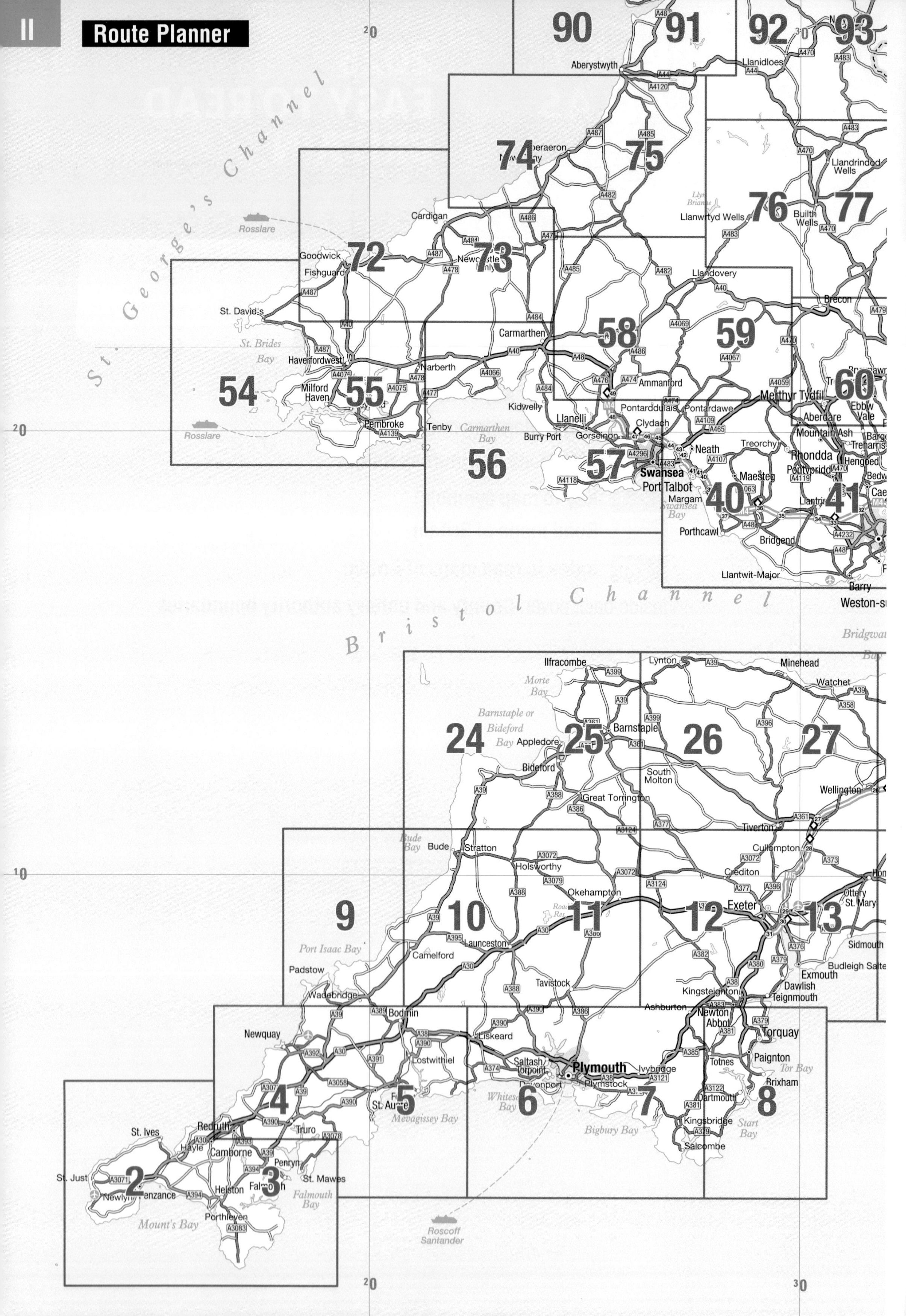

90
91
92
93
74
75
76
77
72
73
58
59
60
54
55
56
57
40
41
24
25
26
27
9
10
11
12
13
4
5
6
7
8
2
3
St. George's Channel
Bristol Channel
Aberystwyth
Llanidloes
Aberaeron
Llandrindod Wells
Llanwrtyd Wells
Builth Wells
Cardigan
Rosslare
Goodwick
Fishguard
Newcastle Emlyn
Llandovery
Brecon
St. David's
St. Brides Bay
Haverfordwest
Carmarthen
Narberth
Ammanford
Milford Haven
Pembroke
Kidwelly
Llanelli
Pontarddulais
Pontardawe
Merthyr Tydfil
Ebbw Vale
Aberdare
Mountain Ash
Treharris
Tenby
Carmarthen Bay
Burry Port
Gorseinon
Clydach
Neath
Treorchy
Rhondda
Pontypridd
Hengoed
Swansea
Port Talbot
Maesteg
Margam
Swansea Bay
Porthcawl
Bridgend
Llantwit-Major
Barry
Ilfracombe
Lynton
Minehead
Watchet
Morte Bay
Barnstaple or Bideford Bay
Barnstaple
Appledore
Bideford
South Molton
Great Torrington
Wellington
Tiverton
Bude Bay
Bude
Stratton
Holsworthy
Cullompton
Crediton
Okehampton
Exeter
Ottery St. Mary
Sidmouth
Port Isaac Bay
Launceston
Camelford
Padstow
Tavistock
Budleigh Salterton
Exmouth
Dawlish
Teignmouth
Kingsteignton
Wadebridge
Ashburton
Newton Abbot
Bodmin
Torquay
Newquay
Liskeard
Lostwithiel
Paignton
Saltash
Torpoint
Plymouth
Ivybridge
Plymstock
Devonport
Totnes
Tor Bay
Brixham
Whitesand Bay
Dartmouth
St. Austell
Mevagissey Bay
Bigbury Bay
Kingsbridge
Start Bay
Salcombe
St. Ives
Redruth
Truro
Hayle
Camborne
Penryn
St. Just
St. Mawes
Newlyn
Penzance
Helston
Falmouth
Falmouth Bay
Mount's Bay
Porthleven
Roscoff
Santander

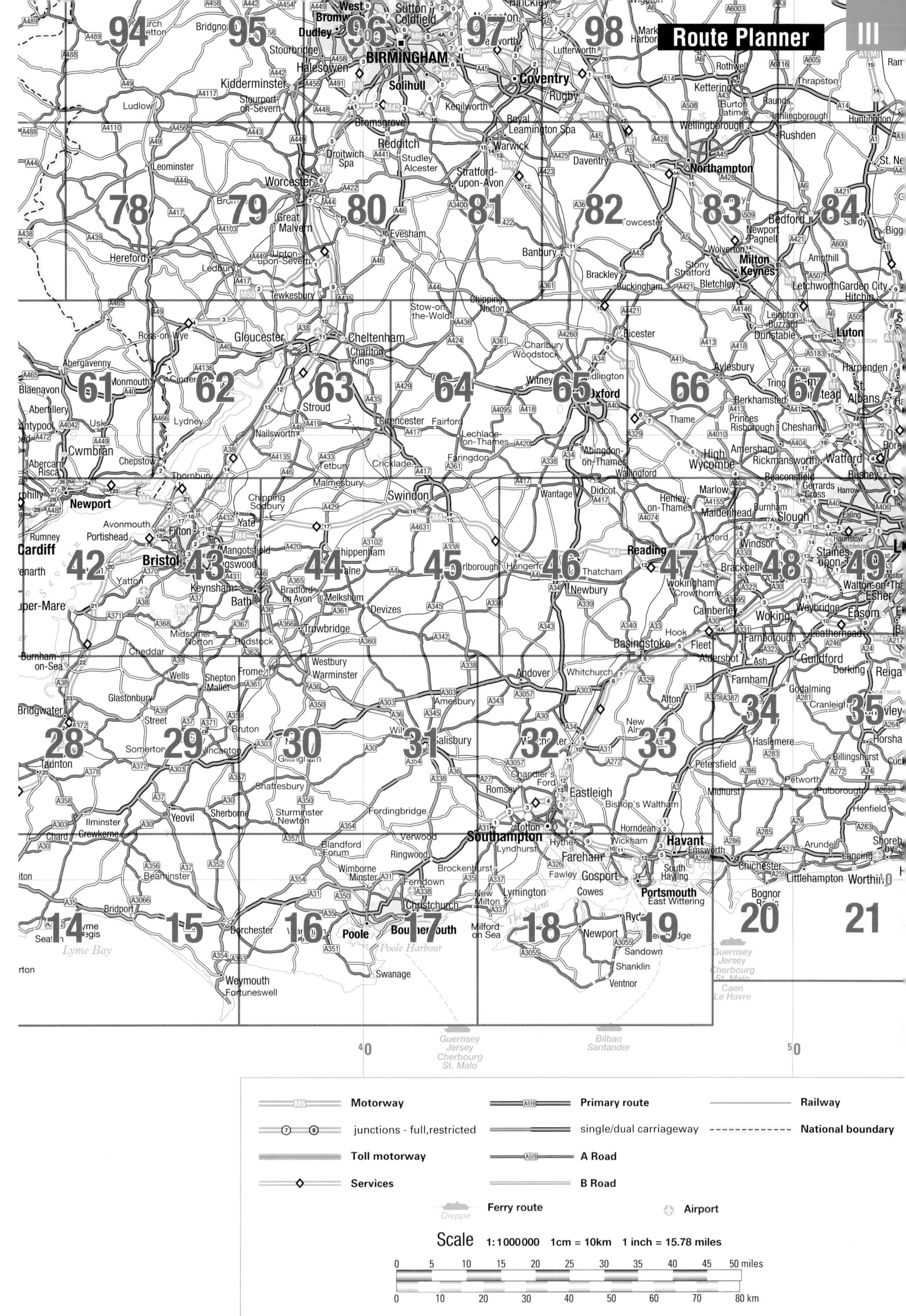
Route Planner
III
BIRMINGHAM
Coventry
Northampton
Milton Keynes
Worcester
Gloucester
Cheltenham
Oxford
Luton
Newport
Cardiff
Bristol
Bath
Swindon
Reading
Slough
Basingstoke
Salisbury
Southampton
Portsmouth
Bournemouth
Poole
Weymouth
Lyme Bay
The Solent
Poole Harbour
Guernsey
Jersey
Cherbourg
St. Malo
Bilbao
Santander
Caen
Le Havre
Motorway
Primary route
Railway
junctions - full,restricted
single/dual carriageway
National boundary
Toll motorway
A Road
Services
B Road
Ferry route
Dieppe
Airport
Scale 1:1000000 1cm = 10km 1 inch = 15.78 miles
0 5 10 15 20 25 30 35 40 45 50 miles
0 10 20 30 40 50 60 70 80 km

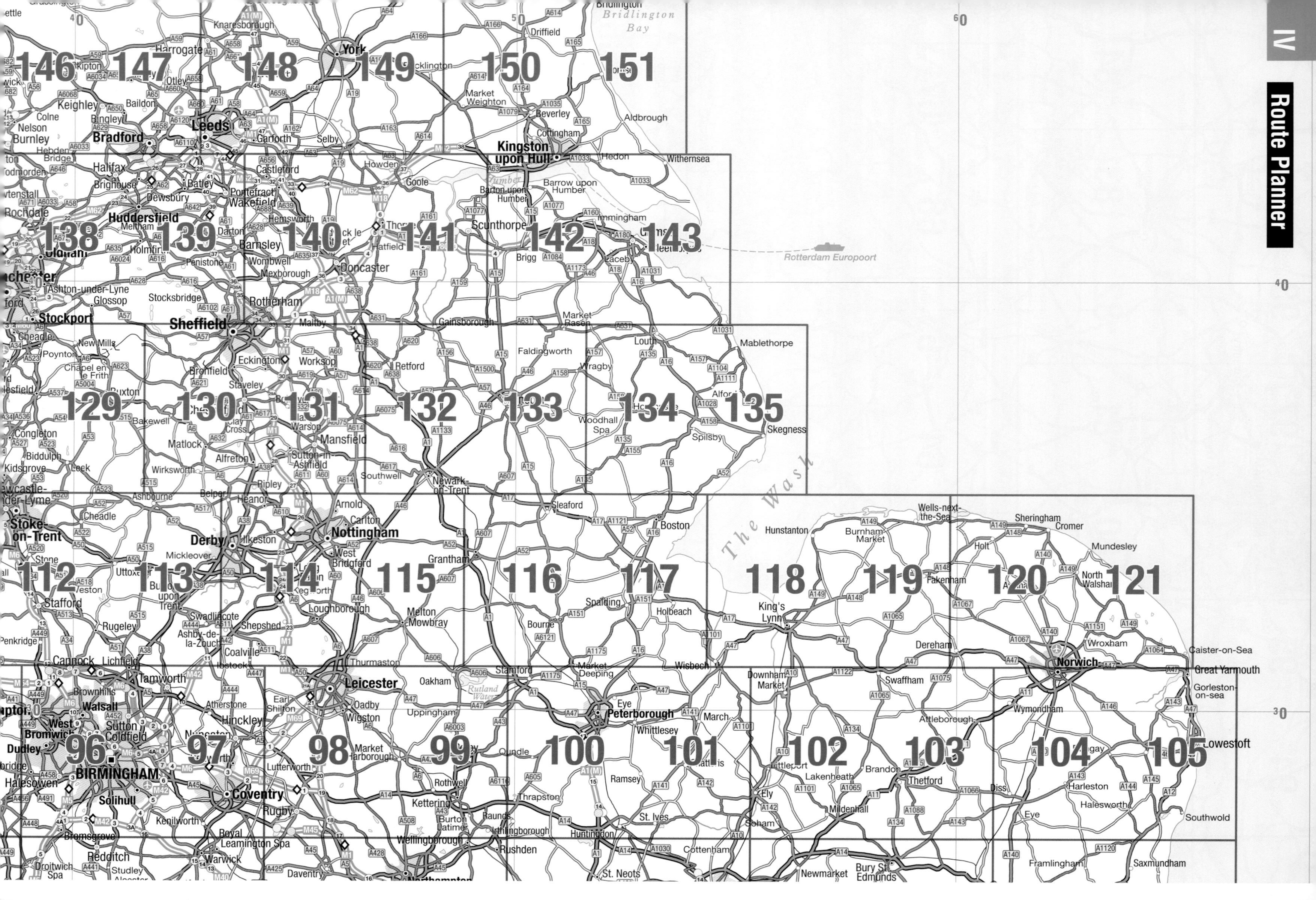

Bridlington Bay
The Wash
Rotterdam Europoort
York
Leeds
Bradford
Huddersfield
Sheffield
Stockport
Kingston upon Hull
Scunthorpe
Doncaster
Nottingham
Derby
Leicester
Coventry
BIRMINGHAM
Peterborough
Norwich
Great Yarmouth
Lowestoft
King's Lynn
Boston
Skegness
Cromer
146
147
148
149
150
151
138
139
140
141
142
143
129
130
131
132
133
134
135
112
113
114
115
116
117
118
119
120
121
96
97
98
99
100
101
102
103
104
105

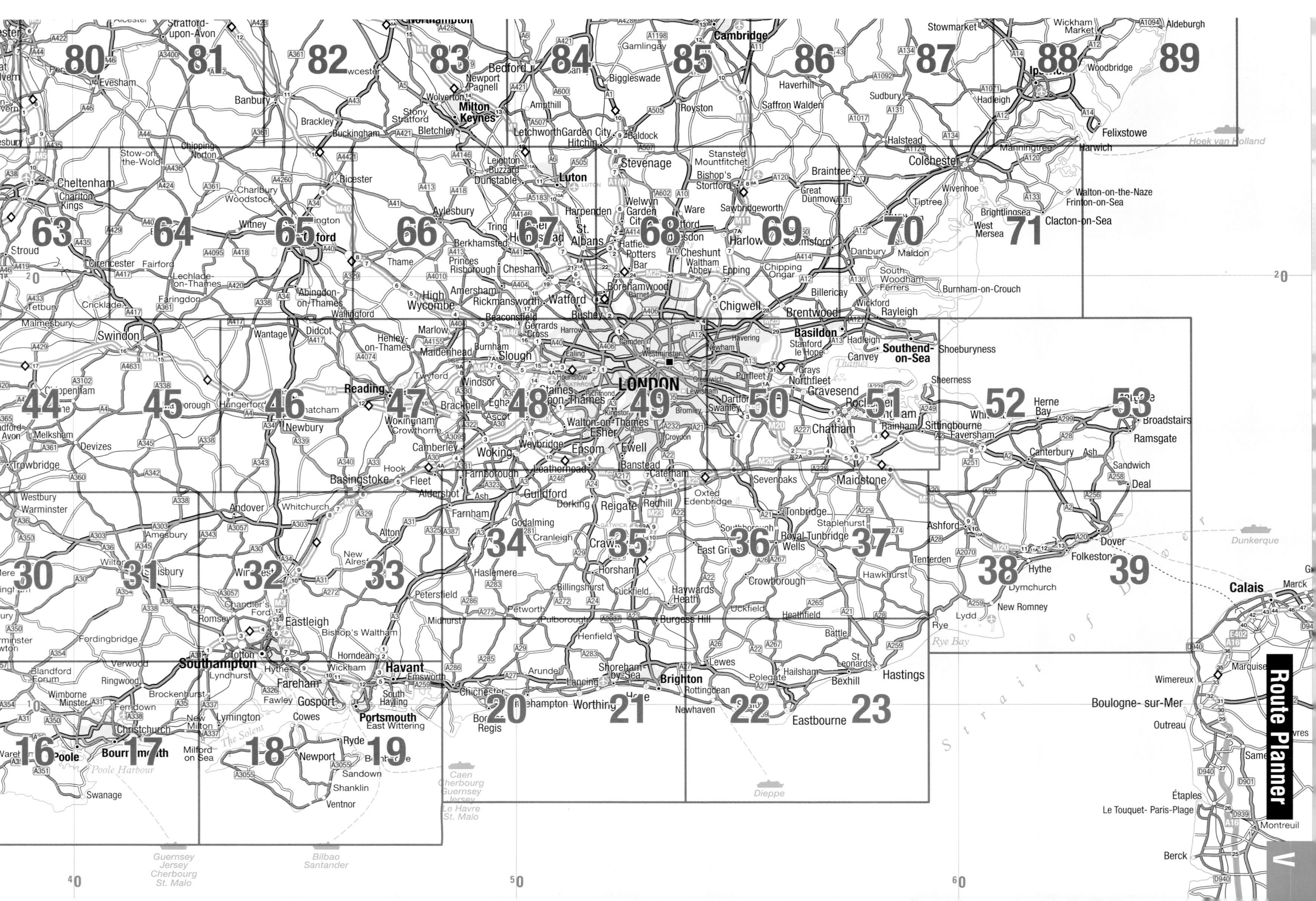
LONDON
Calais
Boulogne-sur-Mer
Dunkerque
Le Touquet- Paris-Plage
Étaples
Berck
Wimereux
Outreau
Marquise
Montreuil
Marck
Hoek van Holland
Dieppe
Caen Cherbourg Guernsey Jersey
Le Havre St. Malo
Bilbao Santander
Guernsey Jersey Cherbourg St. Malo
Rye Bay
Poole Harbour
The Solent
Aldeburgh
Woodbridge
Felixstowe
Harwich
Wickham Market
Walton-on-the-Naze
Frinton-on-Sea
Clacton-on-Sea
Manningtree
Brightlingsea
West Mersea
Colchester
Wivenhoe
Tiptree
Maldon
Burnham-on-Crouch
Stowmarket
Hadleigh
Sudbury
Halstead
Braintree
Great Dunmow
Haverhill
Saffron Walden
Cambridge
Royston
Baldock
Biggleswade
Gamlingay
Stevenage
Letchworth Garden City
Hitchin
Luton
Harpenden
St. Albans
Welwyn Garden City
Potters Bar
Borehamwood
Watford
Rickmansworth
Chesham
Amersham
Beaconsfield
High Wycombe
Marlow
Maidenhead
Slough
Windsor
Bracknell
Ascot
Wokingham
Crowthorne
Camberley
Farnborough
Fleet
Aldershot
Farnham
Guildford
Woking
Weybridge
Walton-on-Thames
Esher
Epsom
Ewell
Leatherhead
Dorking
Reigate
Redhill
Banstead
Caterham
Oxted
Edenbridge
Sevenoaks
Tonbridge
Royal Tunbridge Wells
Crowborough
Uckfield
Heathfield
Hailsham
Polegate
Eastbourne
Lewes
Newhaven
Rottingdean
Brighton
Lancing
Worthing
Arundel
Chichester
Emsworth
Havant
Portsmouth
East Wittering
Gosport
Fareham
Fawley
Cowes
Newport
Ryde
Sandown
Shanklin
Ventnor
Eastleigh
Bishop's Waltham
Horndean
Wickham
Southampton
Lyndhurst
Romsey
Lymington
Christchurch
Poole
Swanage
Ferndown
Ringwood
Verwood
Fordingbridge
Amesbury
Andover
Whitchurch
Basingstoke
Hook
Alton
Petersfield
Haslemere
Godalming
Cranleigh
Midhurst
Petworth
Pulborough
Billingshurst
Horsham
Cuckfield
Burgess Hill
Henfield
Hawkhurst
Tenterden
Ashford
Staplehurst
Maidstone
Chatham
Gravesend
Northfleet
Swanley
Bromley
Croydon
Sutton
Kingston
Richmond
Ealing
Harrow
Camden
Westminster
Greenwich
Lewisham
Newham
Havering
Barnet
Chigwell
Epping
Harlow
Sawbridgeworth
Bishop's Stortford
Stansted Mountfitchet
Ware
Cheshunt
Waltham Abbey
Chipping Ongar
Brentwood
Billericay
Wickford
Rayleigh
South Woodham Ferrers
Danbury
Basildon
Stanford le Hope
Grays
Purfleet
Canvey
Southend-on-Sea
Shoeburyness
Sheerness
Sittingbourne
Faversham
Herne Bay
Canterbury
Broadstairs
Ramsgate
Sandwich
Deal
Dover
Hythe
Dymchurch
New Romney
Lydd
Rye
Hastings
St. Leonards
Bexhill
Battle
Reading
Twyford
Henley-on-Thames
Wallingford
Didcot
Abingdon-on-Thames
Wantage
Newbury
Hungerford
Swindon
Devizes
Melksham
Trowbridge
Westbury
Warminster
Malmesbury
Tetbury
Cirencester
Fairford
Lechlade-on-Thames
Faringdon
Cricklade
Stroud
Cheltenham
Charlton Kings
Witney
Woodstock
Charlbury
Chipping Norton
Stow-on-the-Wold
Banbury
Brackley
Bicester
Buckingham
Thame
Princes Risborough
Aylesbury
Tring
Berkhamsted
Leighton Buzzard
Dunstable
Bletchley
Milton Keynes
Newport Pagnell
Wolverton
Stony Stratford
Bedford
Ampthill
Stratford-upon-Avon
Evesham

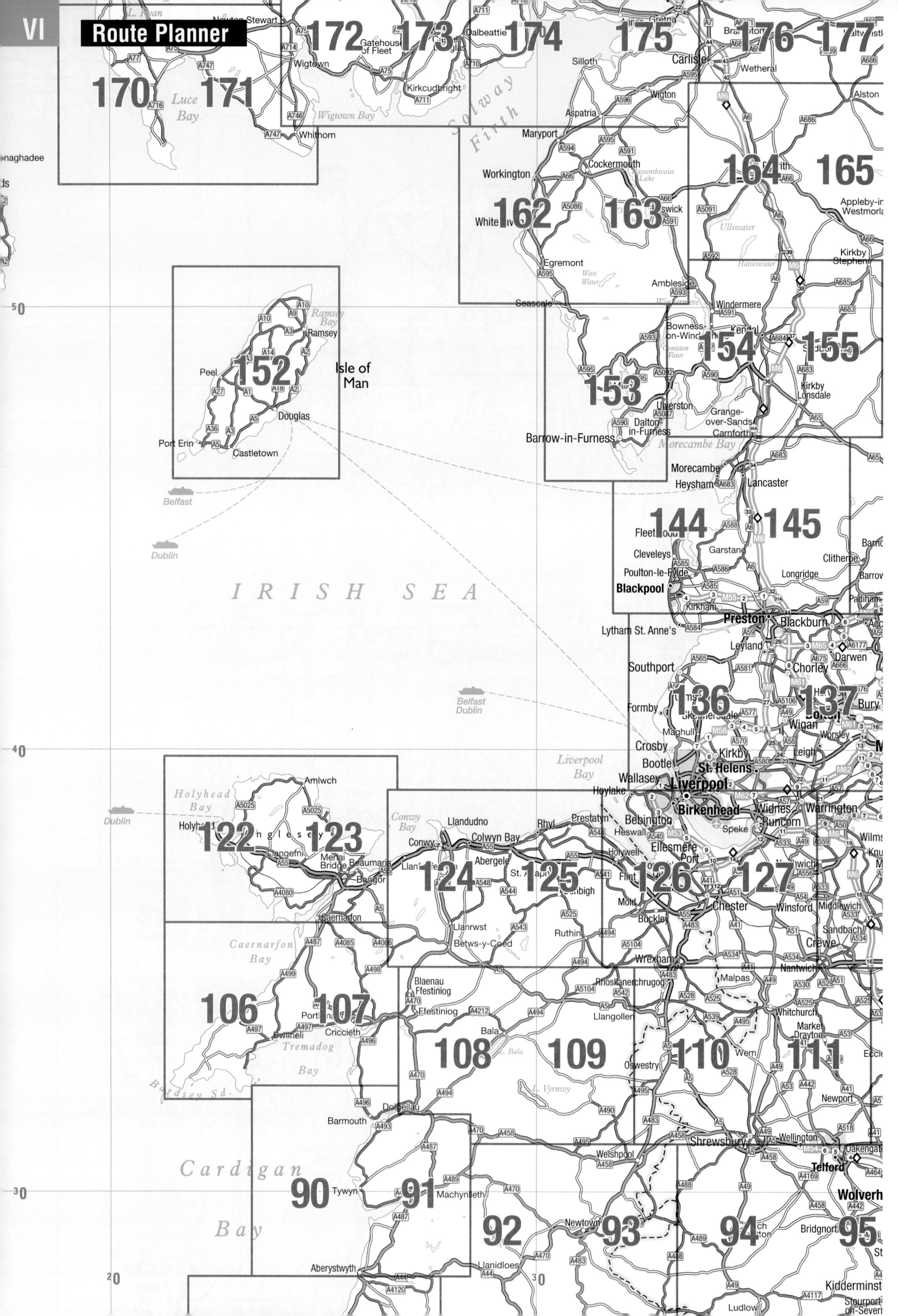
170
171
172
173
174
175
176
177
Newton Stewart
Gatehouse of Fleet
Dalbeattie
Gretna
Carlisle
Wetheral
Wigtown
Kirkcudbright
Luce Bay
Wigtown Bay
Whithorn
Solway Firth
Silloth
Wigton
Aspatria
Alston
Maryport
Workington
Cockermouth
Bassenthwaite Lake
162
163
164
165
Whitehaven
Appleby-in-Westmorland
Ullswater
Kirkby Stephen
Haweswater
Egremont
Wast Water
Ambleside
Seascale
Windermere
Bowness-on-Windermere
Kendal
Coniston Water
154
155
Kirkby Lonsdale
152
Ramsey Bay
Ramsey
Peel
Isle of Man
Douglas
Port Erin
Castletown
153
Ulverston
Grange-over-Sands
Carnforth
Dalton-in-Furness
Barrow-in-Furness
Morecambe Bay
Morecambe
Heysham
Lancaster
Belfast
144
145
Garstang
Dublin
Cleveleys
Clitheroe
Poulton-le-Fylde
Longridge
Blackpool
IRISH SEA
Kirkham
Preston
Blackburn
Lytham St. Anne's
Leyland
Darwen
Southport
Chorley
Belfast
Dublin
136
137
Formby
Bury
Wigan
Maghull
Worsley
Crosby
Kirkby
Leigh
Bootle
St. Helens
Liverpool Bay
Wallasey
Liverpool
Holyhead Bay
Amlwch
Hoylake
Birkenhead
Warrington
Dublin
Holyhead
122
123
Anglesey
Conwy Bay
Llandudno
Rhyl
Prestatyn
Bebington
Widnes
Runcorn
Speke
Heswall
Ellesmere Port
Colwyn Bay
Conwy
Llangefni
Menai Bridge
Beaumaris
Abergele
Holywell
124
125
126
127
Bangor
Flint
Denbigh
Mold
Chester
Winsford
Middlewich
Caernarfon
Buckley
Llanrwst
Ruthin
Sandbach
Caernarfon Bay
Betws-y-Coed
Crewe
Wrexham
Nantwich
Blaenau Ffestiniog
Rhosllanerchrugog
Malpas
106
107
Porthmadog
Ffestiniog
Llangollen
Whitchurch
Market Drayton
Pwllheli
Criccieth
Bala
Tremadog Bay
108
109
110
111
L. Bala
Oswestry
Wem
Bardsey Sd.
L. Vyrnwy
Newport
Dolgellau
Barmouth
Shrewsbury
Wellington
Welshpool
Telford
Oakengates
Cardigan Bay
90
91
92
93
94
95
Tywyn
Machynlleth
Newtown
Bridgnorth
Wolverhampton
Aberystwyth
Llanidloes
Kidderminster
Ludlow
Stourport-on-Severn
50
40
30
20

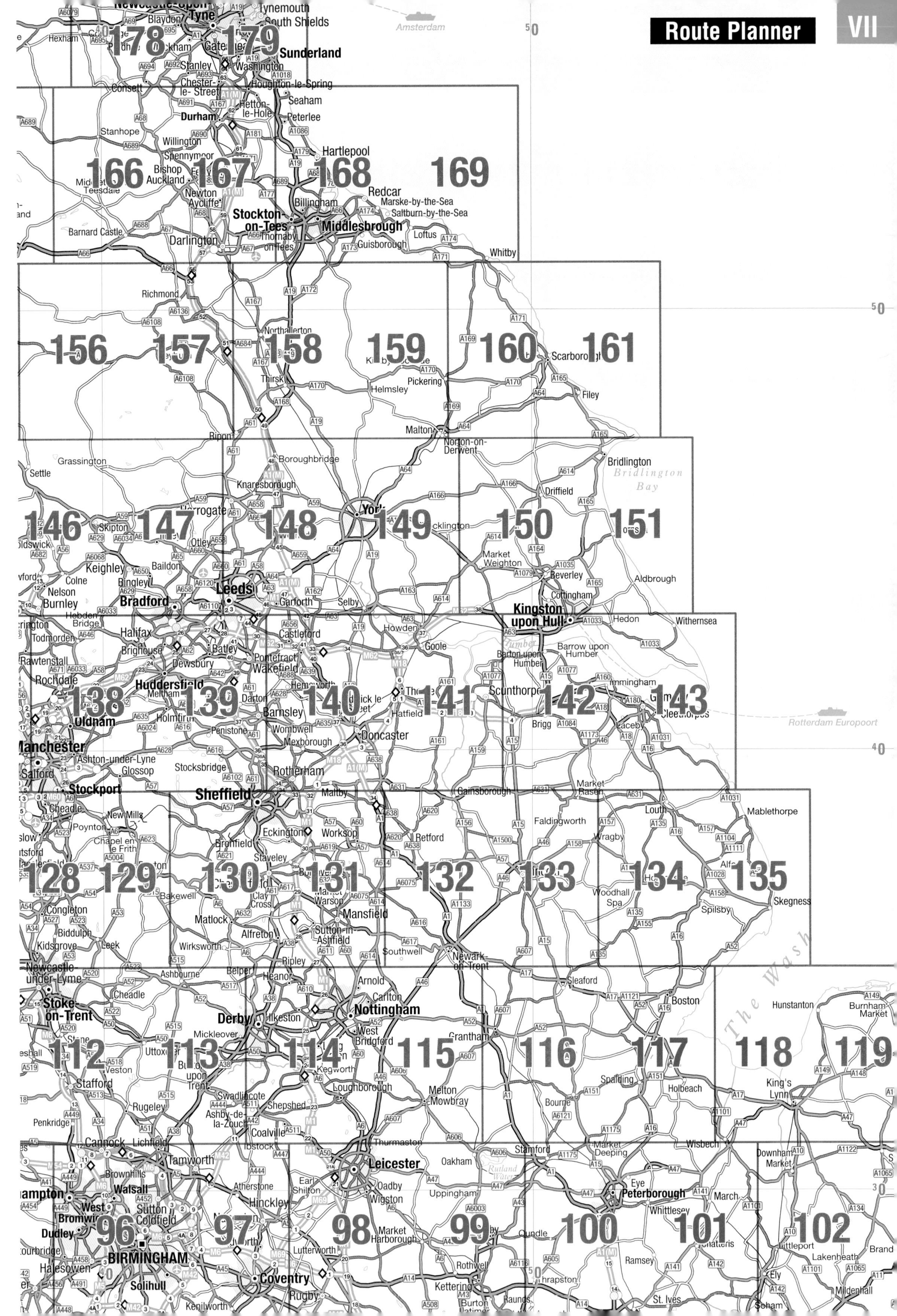
Tynemouth
South Shields
Sunderland
Amsterdam
178
179
Hexham
Blaydon
Stanley
Washington
Houghton-le-Spring
Consett
Chester-le-Street
Seaham
Durham
Hetton-le-Hole
Peterlee
Stanhope
Willington
Spennymoor
Hartlepool
166
167
168
169
Bishop Auckland
Newton Aycliffe
Redcar
Marske-by-the-Sea
Saltburn-by-the-Sea
Stockton-on-Tees
Middlesbrough
Barnard Castle
Darlington
Thornaby-on-Tees
Guisborough
Loftus
Whitby
Richmond
Northallerton
156
157
158
159
160
161
Scarborough
Pickering
Helmsley
Thirsk
Filey
Malton
Norton-on-Derwent
Ripon
Grassington
Settle
Boroughbridge
Knaresborough
Bridlington
Bridlington Bay
Driffield
146
147
148
149
150
151
Skipton
Otley
York
Market Weighton
Keighley
Baildon
Bingley
Colne
Nelson
Burnley
Bradford
Leeds
Garforth
Selby
Beverley
Cottingham
Aldbrough
Kingston upon Hull
Hedon
Withernsea
Hebden Bridge
Halifax
Todmorden
Brighouse
Batley
Castleford
Howden
Goole
Dewsbury
Pontefract
Wakefield
Barrow upon Humber
Barton-upon-Humber
Rawtenstall
Rochdale
Huddersfield
Meltham
Hemsworth
Scunthorpe
Immingham
138
139
140
141
142
143
Oldham
Holmfirth
Barnsley
Hatfield
Brigg
Cleethorpes
Rotterdam Europoort
Penistone
Wombwell
Mexborough
Doncaster
Manchester
Ashton-under-Lyne
Salford
Glossop
Stocksbridge
Rotherham
Stockport
Sheffield
Maltby
Gainsborough
Market Rasen
Louth
Mablethorpe
Cheadle
New Mills
Poynton
Chapel en le Frith
Eckington
Worksop
Retford
Faldingworth
Wragby
Dronfield
Staveley
128
129
130
131
132
133
134
135
Bakewell
Mansfield
Woodhall Spa
Skegness
Spilsby
Congleton
Biddulph
Kidsgrove
Leek
Matlock
Alfreton
Sutton-in-Ashfield
Southwell
Newark-on-Trent
Wirksworth
Ripley
Newcastle-under-Lyme
Ashbourne
Belper
Heanor
Arnold
Carlton
Sleaford
Boston
The Wash
Hunstanton
Burnham Market
Stoke-on-Trent
Cheadle
Derby
Ilkeston
Nottingham
West Bridgford
Grantham
Mickleover
112
113
114
115
116
117
118
119
Uttoxeter
Stafford
Kegworth
Loughborough
Melton Mowbray
Spalding
Holbeach
King's Lynn
Rugeley
Swadlincote
Shepshed
Bourne
Penkridge
Ashby-de-la-Zouch
Coalville
Cannock
Lichfield
Thurmaston
Stamford
Market Deeping
Wisbech
Downham Market
Tamworth
Ibstock
Leicester
Oakham
Rutland Water
Brownhills
Walsall
Atherstone
Earl Shilton
Oadby
Wigston
Uppingham
Eye
Peterborough
March
Hinckley
Whittlesey
West Bromwich
Sutton Coldfield
Dudley
96
97
98
99
100
101
102
Market Harborough
Oundle
Chatteris
Littleport
Lakenheath
Brand
Halesowen
BIRMINGHAM
Lutterworth
Ramsey
Ely
Solihull
Coventry
Rugby
Kettering
Mildenhall
Kenilworth
Burton Latimer
St. Ives
Soham

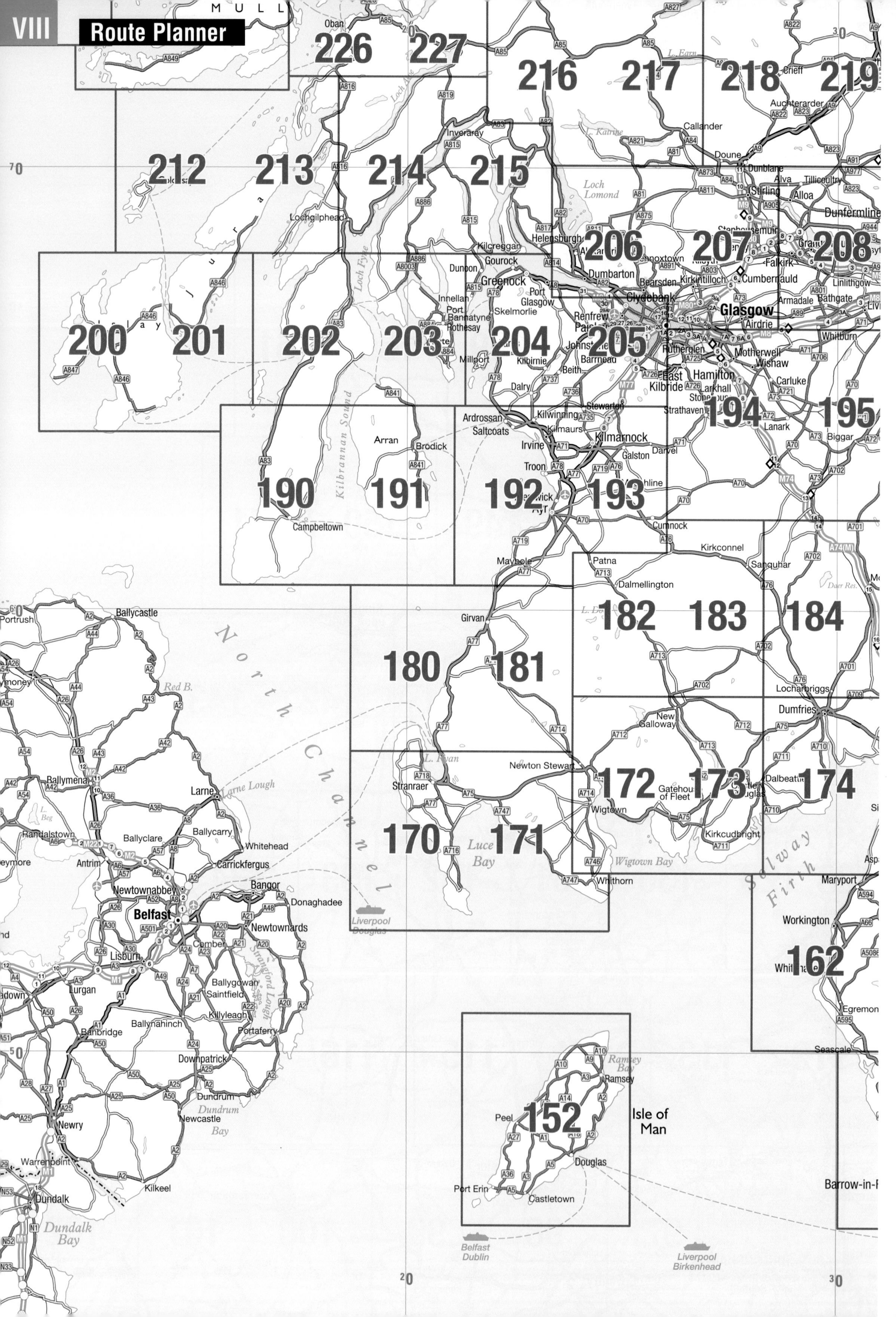
226
227
216
217
218
219
212
213
214
215
206
207
208
200
201
202
203
204
205
190
191
192
193
194
195
180
181
182
183
184
170
171
172
173
174
162
152
Oban
Inveraray
Lochgilphead
Helensburgh
Dumbarton
Greenock
Gourock
Dunoon
Rothesay
Clydebank
Glasgow
Stirling
Falkirk
Dunfermline
Paisley
Kilmarnock
Irvine
Ayr
Troon
Campbeltown
Arran
Brodick
Girvan
Stranraer
Newton Stewart
Dumfries
Kirkcudbright
Wigtown
Whithorn
Workington
Maryport
Belfast
Larne
Bangor
Lisburn
Newry
Dundalk
Downpatrick
Isle of Man
Douglas
Peel
Ramsey
Castletown
Port Erin
North Channel
Solway Firth
Luce Bay
Wigtown Bay
Dundalk Bay
Belfast Dublin
Liverpool Birkenhead
Liverpool Douglas
Barrow-in-F

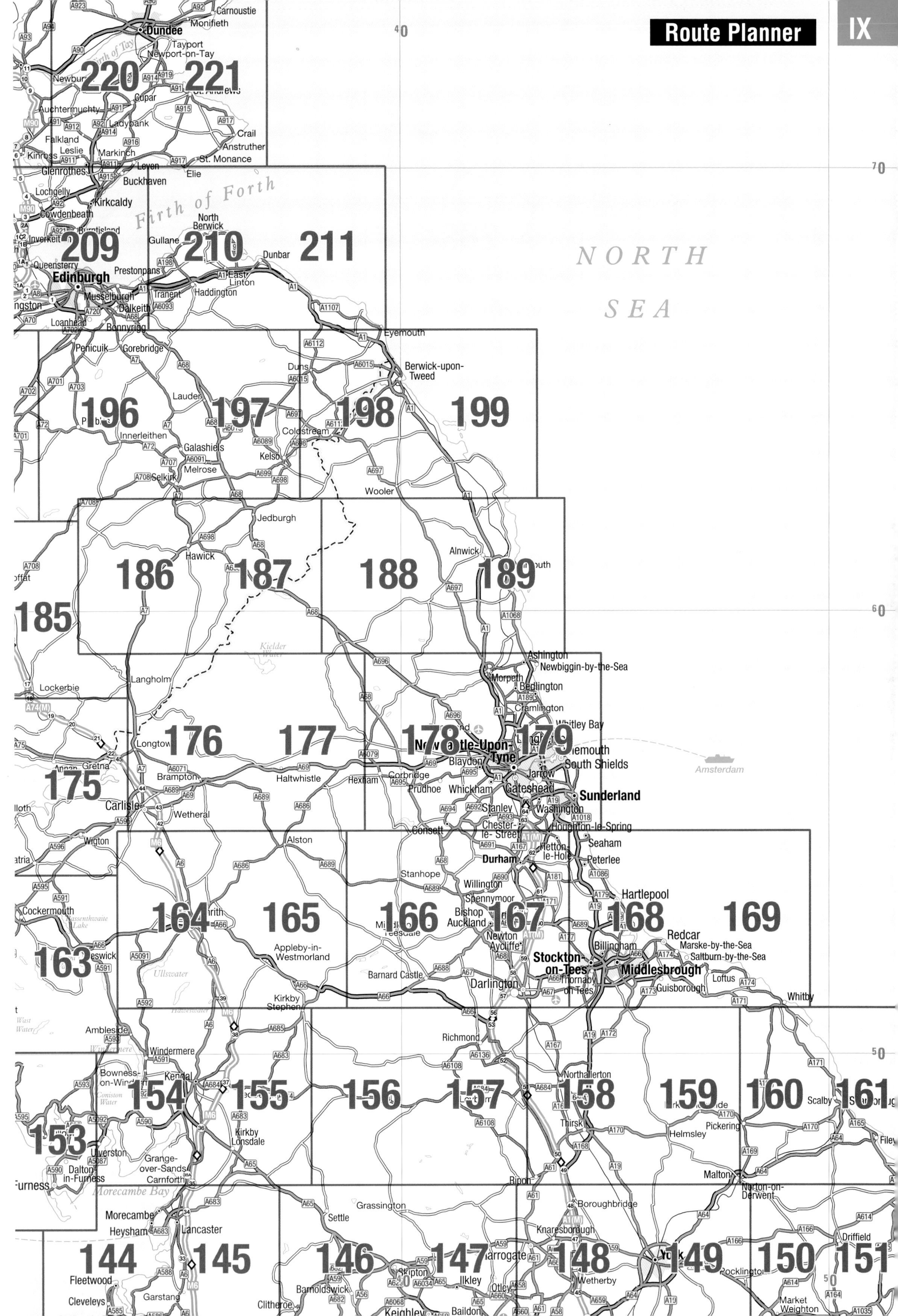
NORTH
SEA
Firth of Forth
Dundee
Edinburgh
Newcastle-Upon-Tyne
Sunderland
Middlesbrough
Durham
Carlisle
Berwick-upon-Tweed
Stockton-on-Tees
Hartlepool
Darlington
York
Lancaster
Kendal
Amsterdam

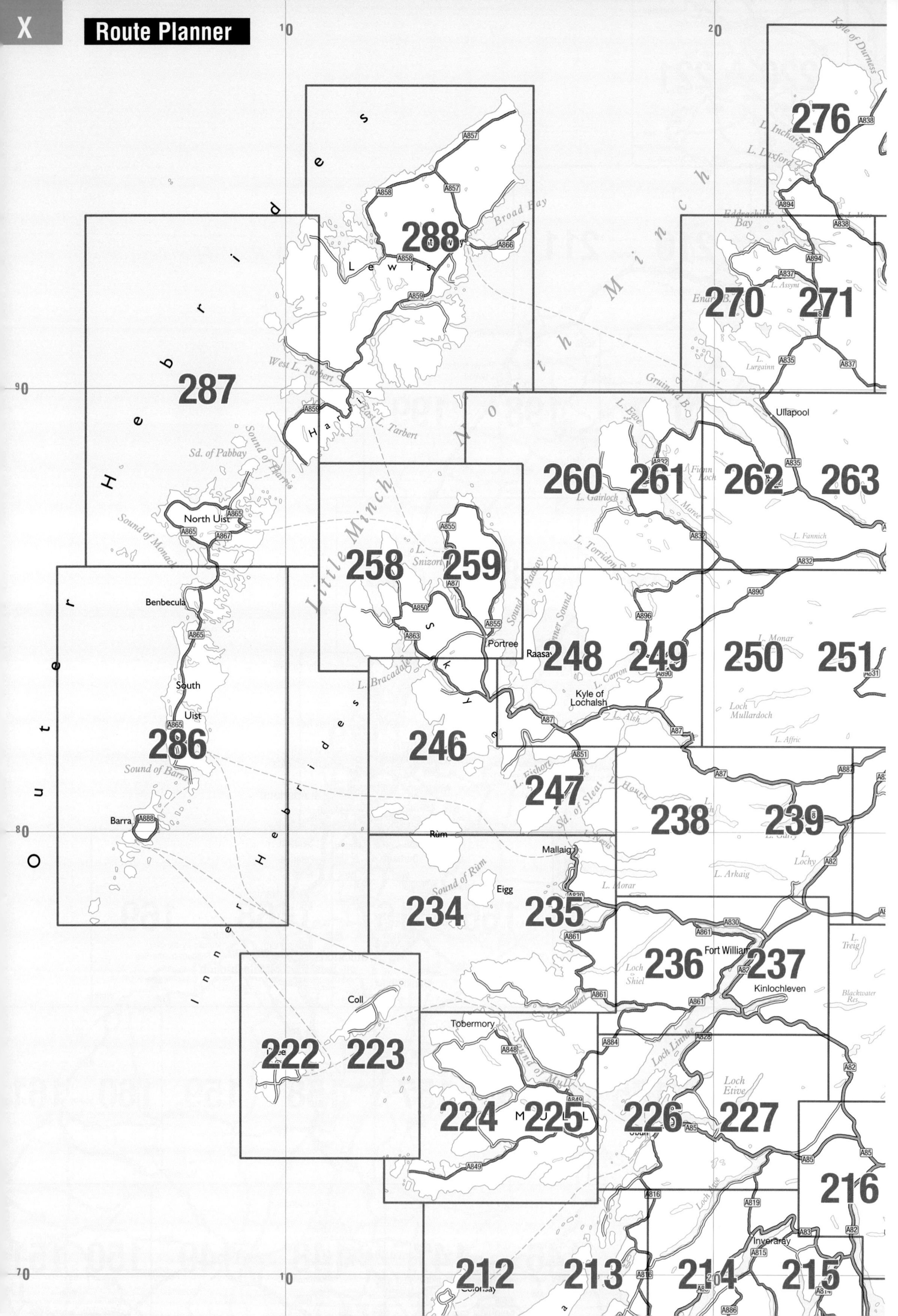
Outer Hebrides
Inner Hebrides
Lewis
Harris
North Uist
Benbecula
South Uist
Barra
Sd. of Pabbay
Sound of Harris
Sound of Monach
Sound of Barra
West L. Tarbert
East L. Tarbert
Broad Bay
North Minch
Little Minch
Skye
L. Snizort
L. Bracadale
Portree
Raasay
Sound of Raasay
Inner Sound
Kyle of Lochalsh
L. Alsh
L. Carron
L. Torridon
L. Gairloch
L. Maree
L. Ewe
Fionn Loch
Gruinard B.
Ullapool
L. Fannich
L. Monar
Loch Mullardoch
L. Affric
Eddrachillis Bay
L. Assynt
L. Lurgainn
L. Inchard
L. Laxford
Kyle of Durness
L. Eishort
Sd. of Sleat
L. Hourn
L. Nevis
L. Morar
L. Arkaig
L. Garry
L. Lochy
Mallaig
Rùm
Sound of Rùm
Eigg
Fort William
Kinlochleven
Loch Shiel
L. Treig
Blackwater Res.
Coll
Tobermory
Sound of Mull
Mull
Loch Linnhe
Loch Etive
Inveraray
Colonsay
A857
A858
A859
A866
A865
A867
A888
A855
A87
A850
A863
A890
A896
A832
A835
A837
A838
A894
A831
A851
A887
A82
A830
A861
A884
A848
A849
A828
A85
A816
A819
A815
A83
A814
A886
287
288
286
258
259
260
261
262
263
270
271
276
248
249
250
251
246
247
238
239
234
235
236
237
222
223
224
225
226
227
216
212
213
214
215
10
20
90
80
70

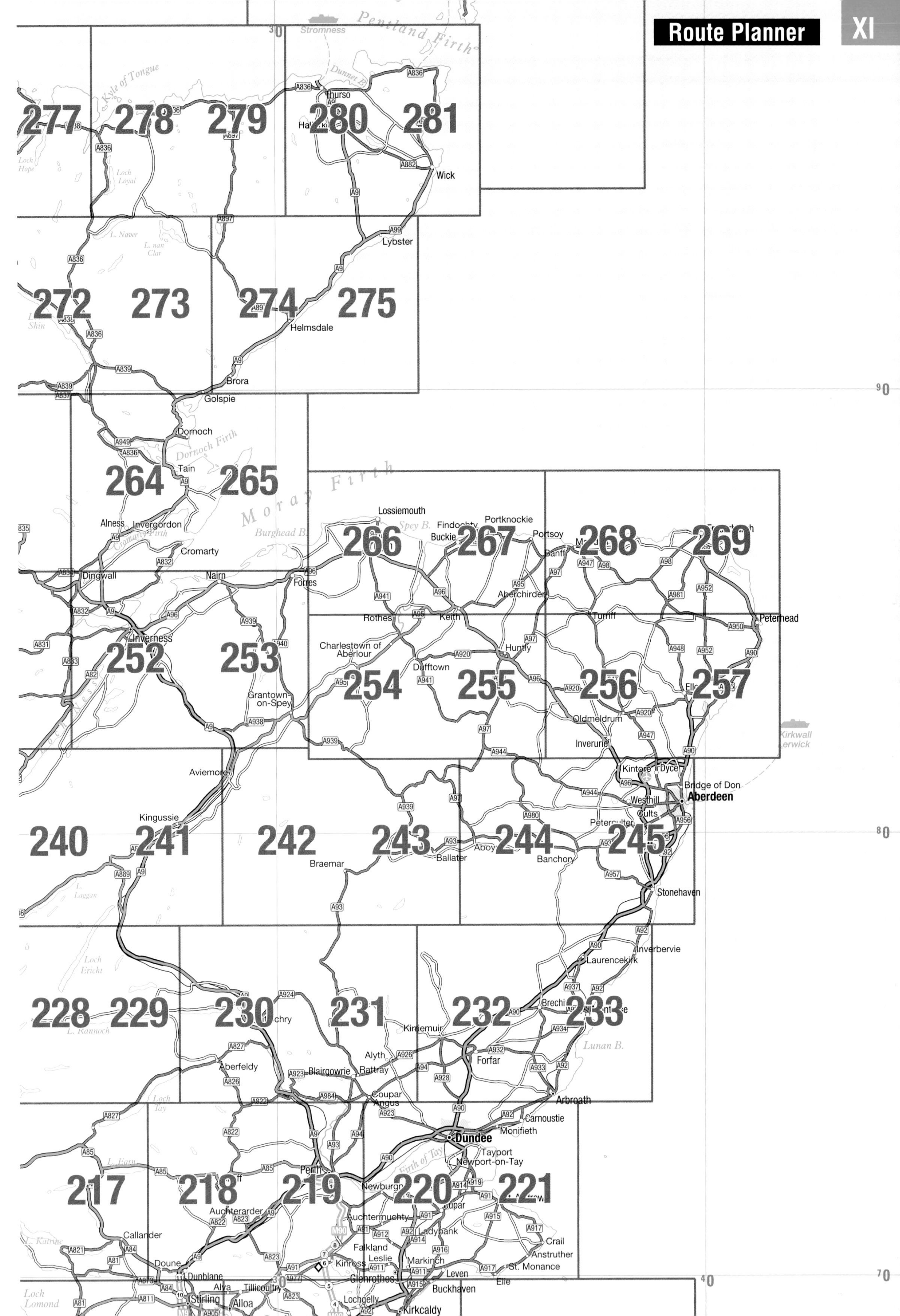
Pentland Firth
Stromness
Kyle of Tongue
Dunnet B.
Thurso
Wick
277
278
279
280
281
Loch Hope
Loch Loyal
L. Naver
L. nan Clar
Lybster
272
273
274
275
Shin
Helmsdale
Brora
Golspie
Dornoch
Dornoch Firth
Tain
264
265
Moray Firth
Lossiemouth
Spey B.
Findochty
Portknockie
Buckie
Portsoy
Banff
Burghead B.
266
267
268
269
Alness
Invergordon
Cromarty Firth
Cromarty
Dingwall
Nairn
Forres
Aberchirder
Rothes
Keith
Turriff
Peterhead
Inverness
Charlestown of Aberlour
Huntly
252
253
Dufftown
254
255
256
257
Grantown-on-Spey
Oldmeldrum
Inverurie
Kirkwall
Lerwick
Kintore
Dyce
Bridge of Don
Aberdeen
Aviemore
Westhill
Cults
Kingussie
Peterculter
240
241
242
243
244
245
Braemar
Ballater
Banchory
Stonehaven
L. Laggan
Inverbervie
Laurencekirk
Loch Ericht
228
229
230
231
232
233
L. Rannoch
Kirriemuir
Lunan B.
Alyth
Forfar
Aberfeldy
Blairgowrie
Rattray
Arbroath
Loch Tay
Coupar Angus
Carnoustie
Dundee
Monifieth
Tayport
Newport-on-Tay
Firth of Tay
L. Earn
Perth
217
218
219
220
221
Newburgh
Cupar
Auchterarder
Auchtermuchty
Callander
Ladybank
Crail
L. Katrine
Falkland
Anstruther
Kinross
Leslie
Markinch
St. Monance
Doune
Dunblane
Glenrothes
Leven
Elie
Alva
Tillicoultry
Buckhaven
Loch Lomond
Stirling
Alloa
Lochgelly
Kirkcaldy
A836
A9
A882
A99
A897
A838
A839
A837
A949
A832
A96
A941
A95
A97
A98
A947
A981
A952
A950
A948
A90
A831
A833
A82
A939
A940
A920
A938
A944
A93
A980
A956
A957
A889
A92
A937
A934
A924
A827
A826
A926
A923
A928
A932
A933
A984
A822
A85
A94
A914
A919
A91
A915
A917
A912
A916
A911
A823
A821
A84
A81
A873
A811
A905
A977
M90
M9
30
40
90
80
70

# Distance table

## How to use this table

Distances are shown in miles and kilometres with estimated journey times in hours and minutes.

For example: the distance between Dover and Fishguard is 331 miles or 533 kilometres with an estimated journey time of 6 hours, 20 minutes.

| | Fishguard | Exeter | Edinburgh | Dundee | Dover |
|---|---|---|---|---|---|
| Dundee | | | | | 523 / 842 / 9:10 |
| Edinburgh | | | | 56 / 90 / 1:30 | 462 / 744 / 8:10 |
| Exeter | | | 450 / 724 / 8:00 | 518 / 834 / 9:10 | 248 / 399 / 4:40 |
| Fishguard | | 230 / 370 / 4:30 | 399 / 642 / 7:30 | 460 / 740 / 8:30 | 331 / 533 / 6:20 |
| Fort William | 486 / 782 / 9:30 | 560 / 901 / 10:20 | 144 / 232 / 3:30 | 127 / 204 / 3:10 | 596 / 959 / 11:00 |

Estimated driving times are based on an average speed of 60mph on Motorways and 40mph on other roads. Drivers should allow extra time when driving at peak periods or through areas likely to be congested.



Supporting THINK!

Travel safe – Don't drive tired

Each cell: miles / kilometres / journey time.

| | Swansea | Stranraer | Southampton | Shrewsbury | Sheffield | Portsmouth | Plymouth | Oxford | Oban | Nottingham | Norwich | Newcastle upon Tyne | Manchester | Liverpool | Lincoln | Leicester | Leeds | Land's End | Kyle of Lochalsh | Kingston upon Hull | John o' Groats | Inverness | Holyhead | Harwich | Great Yarmouth | Gloucester | Glasgow | Fort William | Fishguard | Exeter | Edinburgh | Dundee | Dover | Doncaster | Carlisle | Cardiff | Cambridge | Bristol | Brighton | Braemar | Bournemouth | Blackpool | Birmingham | Berwick-upon-Tweed | Ayr | Aberystwyth | Aberdeen | London |
|---|---|---|---|---|---|---|---|---|---|---|---|---|---|---|---|---|---|---|---|---|---|---|---|---|---|---|---|---|---|---|---|---|---|---|---|---|---|---|---|---|---|---|---|---|---|---|---|---|
| Aberdeen | | | | | | | | | | | | | | | | | | | | | | | | | | | | | | | | | | | | | | | | | | | | | | | | 517 / 832 / 11:20 |
| Aberystwyth | | | | | | | | | | | | | | | | | | | | | | | | | | | | | | | | | | | | | | | | | | | | | | | 445 / 716 / 8:40 | 211 / 340 / 4:40 |
| Ayr | | | | | | | | | | | | | | | | | | | | | | | | | | | | | | | | | | | | | | | | | | | | | | 317 / 510 / 6:10 | 183 / 295 / 4:20 | 394 / 634 / 7:20 |
| Berwick-upon-Tweed | | | | | | | | | | | | | | | | | | | | | | | | | | | | | | | | | | | | | | | | | | | | | 134 / 216 / 3:00 | 311 / 501 / 6:20 | 182 / 293 / 4:40 | 352 / 567 / 7:30 |
| Birmingham | | | | | | | | | | | | | | | | | | | | | | | | | | | | | | | | | | | | | | | | | | | | 274 / 441 / 5:30 | 289 / 465 / 5:30 | 114 / 183 / 2:50 | 420 / 676 / 8:30 | 117 / 188 / 2:50 |
| Blackpool | | | | | | | | | | | | | | | | | | | | | | | | | | | | | | | | | | | | | | | | | | | 123 / 198 / 2:40 | 181 / 291 / 3:50 | 180 / 290 / 3:30 | 153 / 246 / 3:20 | 308 / 496 / 6:20 | 226 / 364 / 4:30 |
| Bournemouth | | | | | | | | | | | | | | | | | | | | | | | | | | | | | | | | | | | | | | | | | | 270 / 435 / 5:00 | 147 / 237 / 3:10 | 412 / 663 / 7:50 | 436 / 702 / 8:00 | 207 / 333 / 4:30 | 564 / 908 / 10:20 | 107 / 172 / 2:40 |
| Braemar | | | | | | | | | | | | | | | | | | | | | | | | | | | | | | | | | | | | | | | | | 524 / 843 / 9:30 | 281 / 452 / 5:20 | 385 / 620 / 7:10 | 148 / 238 / 3:20 | 143 / 230 / 3:00 | 405 / 652 / 7:50 | 59 / 95 / 1:30 | 482 / 776 / 10:30 |
| Brighton | | | | | | | | | | | | | | | | | | | | | | | | | | | | | | | | | | | | | | | | 534 / 859 / 9:40 | 92 / 148 / 2:10 | 286 / 460 / 5:20 | 163 / 262 / 3:20 | 409 / 658 / 7:40 | 446 / 718 / 8:00 | 253 / 407 / 5:10 | 573 / 922 / 10:30 | 52 / 84 / 1:50 |
| Bristol | | | | | | | | | | | | | | | | | | | | | | | | | | | | | | | | | | | | | | | 147 / 237 / 4:10 | 477 / 768 / 8:40 | 82 / 132 / 2:30 | 204 / 328 / 3:50 | 81 / 130 / 2:00 | 362 / 583 / 6:50 | 370 / 595 / 6:40 | 125 / 201 / 3:00 | 493 / 793 / 9:10 | 122 / 196 / 2:50 |
| Cambridge | | | | | | | | | | | | | | | | | | | | | | | | | | | | | | | | | | | | | | 169 / 272 / 3:10 | 116 / 187 / 2:20 | 438 / 705 / 7:50 | 154 / 248 / 3:00 | 208 / 335 / 3:50 | 100 / 161 / 2:10 | 306 / 493 / 5:40 | 357 / 575 / 6:20 | 214 / 344 / 4:20 | 471 / 758 / 10:00 | 54 / 87 / 1:30 |
| Cardiff | | | | | | | | | | | | | | | | | | | | | | | | | | | | | | | | | | | | | 190 / 306 / 3:30 | 45 / 72 / 1:20 | 182 / 293 / 3:40 | 483 / 778 / 8:40 | 117 / 188 / 3:00 | 209 / 336 / 4:00 | 103 / 166 / 2:20 | 368 / 592 / 7:00 | 382 / 615 / 7:00 | 105 / 169 / 2:40 | 505 / 813 / 9:20 | 157 / 253 / 3:20 |
| Carlisle | | | | | | | | | | | | | | | | | | | | | | | | | | | | | | | | | | | | 289 / 465 / 5:20 | 264 / 425 / 4:40 | 277 / 446 / 5:00 | 370 / 596 / 6:40 | 196 / 316 / 3:50 | 343 / 552 / 6:20 | 87 / 140 / 1:50 | 196 / 315 / 3:50 | 87 / 140 / 2:10 | 93 / 150 / 2:00 | 224 / 360 / 4:30 | 221 / 356 / 4:30 | 301 / 484 / 5:40 |
| Doncaster | | | | | | | | | | | | | | | | | | | | | | | | | | | | | | | | | | | 142 / 229 / 3:00 | 209 / 336 / 4:00 | 116 / 187 / 2:10 | 175 / 282 / 3:20 | 236 / 380 / 4:30 | 310 / 499 / 5:40 | 235 / 378 / 4:20 | 94 / 151 / 1:50 | 94 / 151 / 2:00 | 184 / 296 / 3:50 | 235 / 378 / 4:20 | 176 / 283 / 3:40 | 344 / 554 / 6:50 | 171 / 275 / 3:30 |
| Dover | | | | | | | | | | | | | | | | | | | | | | | | | | | | | | | | | | 242 / 390 / 4:30 | 389 / 626 / 7:00 | 238 / 383 / 4:30 | 125 / 201 / 2:30 | 202 / 325 / 3:50 | 82 / 132 / 2:20 | 553 / 890 / 9:50 | 174 / 280 / 4:30 | 312 / 502 / 5:40 | 194 / 312 / 3:50 | 424 / 683 / 7:50 | 478 / 769 / 8:30 | 297 / 478 / 5:50 | 588 / 947 / 10:40 | 71 / 114 / 2:00 |
| Dundee | | | | | | | | | | | | | | | | | | | | | | | | | | | | | | | | | 523 / 842 / 9:10 | 275 / 443 / 5:00 | 152 / 245 / 3:00 | 441 / 710 / 8:00 | 406 / 654 / 7:10 | 430 / 692 / 7:40 | 517 / 832 / 9:10 | 52 / 84 / 1:20 | 495 / 797 / 8:50 | 239 / 385 / 4:30 | 349 / 562 / 6:20 | 113 / 182 / 2:40 | 117 / 188 / 2:30 | 376 / 605 / 7:10 | 67 / 108 / 1:50 | 448 / 721 / 8:40 |
| Edinburgh | | | | | | | | | | | | | | | | | | | | | | | | | | | | | | | | 56 / 90 / 1:30 | 462 / 744 / 8:10 | 219 / 352 / 4:00 | 96 / 154 / 2:00 | 385 / 620 / 7:00 | 345 / 555 / 6:10 | 373 / 600 / 6:50 | 456 / 734 / 8:20 | 91 / 146 / 2:10 | 439 / 707 / 8:00 | 183 / 295 / 3:30 | 292 / 470 / 5:30 | 57 / 92 / 1:40 | 73 / 117 / 1:50 | 320 / 515 / 6:20 | 125 / 201 / 3:10 | 390 / 628 / 7:20 |
| Exeter | | | | | | | | | | | | | | | | | | | | | | | | | | | | | | | 450 / 724 / 8:00 | 518 / 834 / 9:10 | 248 / 399 / 4:40 | 251 / 404 / 4:30 | 353 / 568 / 6:20 | 121 / 195 / 2:30 | 249 / 401 / 4:30 | 76 / 122 / 1:40 | 184 / 296 / 5:00 | 550 / 885 / 9:40 | 82 / 132 / 2:20 | 282 / 454 / 5:10 | 157 / 253 / 3:10 | 428 / 689 / 7:50 | 446 / 718 / 7:50 | 201 / 323 / 4:10 | 569 / 916 / 10:20 | 181 / 291 / 3:40 |
| Fishguard | | | | | | | | | | | | | | | | | | | | | | | | | | | | | | 230 / 370 / 4:30 | 399 / 642 / 7:30 | 460 / 740 / 8:30 | 331 / 533 / 6:20 | 247 / 398 / 4:50 | 297 / 478 / 5:40 | 112 / 180 / 2:40 | 270 / 435 / 5:10 | 154 / 248 / 3:20 | 291 / 468 / 5:40 | 493 / 794 / 9:10 | 222 / 357 / 4:40 | 209 / 336 / 4:10 | 170 / 274 / 3:40 | 371 / 597 / 7:20 | 373 / 600 / 7:00 | 56 / 90 / 1:30 | 504 / 811 / 10:10 | 260 / 418 / 5:20 |
| Fort William | | | | | | | | | | | | | | | | | | | | | | | | | | | | | 486 / 782 / 9:30 | 560 / 901 / 10:20 | 144 / 232 / 3:30 | 127 / 204 / 3:10 | 596 / 959 / 11:00 | 357 / 575 / 7:00 | 206 / 332 / 4:30 | 485 / 781 / 9:10 | 479 / 771 / 9:00 | 486 / 782 / 9:10 | 575 / 926 / 10:50 | 125 / 201 / 3:10 | 539 / 867 / 10:10 | 296 / 476 / 6:00 | 392 / 631 / 7:40 | 190 / 306 / 4:40 | 133 / 214 / 3:20 | 430 / 692 / 8:40 | 149 / 240 / 3:50 | 510 / 821 / 9:50 |
| Glasgow | | | | | | | | | | | | | | | | | | | | | | | | | | | | 101 / 163 / 2:50 | 376 / 605 / 7:10 | 449 / 723 / 8:00 | 44 / 71 / 1:20 | 83 / 134 / 2:00 | 488 / 786 / 8:40 | 249 / 401 / 4:40 | 96 / 154 / 2:10 | 385 / 620 / 7:00 | 372 / 599 / 6:40 | 373 / 600 / 6:50 | 468 / 753 / 8:30 | 110 / 177 / 2:30 | 439 / 707 / 8:00 | 183 / 295 / 3:40 | 292 / 470 / 5:30 | 101 / 163 / 2:40 | 33 / 53 / 1:10 | 320 / 515 / 6:20 | 145 / 233 / 3:30 | 397 / 639 / 7:30 |
| Gloucester | | | | | | | | | | | | | | | | | | | | | | | | | | | 346 / 557 / 6:10 | 454 / 731 / 8:30 | 153 / 246 / 3:10 | 111 / 179 / 2:10 | 349 / 562 / 6:10 | 410 / 660 / 7:10 | 191 / 307 / 3:30 | 150 / 241 / 2:50 | 247 / 398 / 4:20 | 56 / 90 / 1:20 | 123 / 198 / 2:20 | 35 / 56 / 1:00 | 159 / 256 / 3:10 | 443 / 713 / 8:00 | 99 / 159 / 2:40 | 174 / 280 / 3:10 | 56 / 90 / 1:20 | 318 / 512 / 6:00 | 330 / 531 / 5:50 | 102 / 164 / 2:30 | 468 / 753 / 8:30 | 109 / 175 / 2:30 |
| Great Yarmouth | | | | | | | | | | | | | | | | | | | | | | | | | | 225 / 362 / 4:40 | 419 / 674 / 8:00 | 527 / 848 / 10:20 | 366 / 589 / 7:20 | 335 / 539 / 6:30 | 386 / 621 / 7:30 | 484 / 779 / 9:00 | 185 / 298 / 4:00 | 167 / 269 / 3:40 | 320 / 515 / 6:20 | 284 / 457 / 5:50 | 82 / 132 / 2:10 | 275 / 443 / 5:40 | 180 / 290 / 4:10 | 477 / 768 / 9:10 | 240 / 386 / 5:00 | 252 / 406 / 5:10 | 180 / 290 / 4:10 | 345 / 555 / 7:00 | 402 / 647 / 7:40 | 294 / 473 / 6:20 | 517 / 832 / 10:50 | 128 / 206 / 3:40 |
| Harwich | | | | | | | | | | | | | | | | | | | | | | | | | 82 / 132 / 2:10 | 196 / 316 / 4:00 | 432 / 695 / 8:10 | 543 / 874 / 10:30 | 337 / 542 / 6:40 | 279 / 449 / 5:20 | 413 / 665 / 7:40 | 469 / 755 / 8:40 | 125 / 201 / 2:50 | 194 / 312 / 4:00 | 336 / 541 / 6:20 | 246 / 396 / 5:00 | 67 / 108 / 1:50 | 217 / 349 / 4:30 | 128 / 206 / 3:00 | 504 / 811 / 9:20 | 187 / 301 / 4:00 | 275 / 443 / 5:20 | 167 / 269 / 3:40 | 372 / 599 / 7:20 | 425 / 684 / 8:00 | 281 / 452 / 5:50 | 535 / 861 / 11:20 | 76 / 122 / 2:20 |
| Holyhead | | | | | | | | | | | | | | | | | | | | | | | | 349 / 562 / 7:10 | 334 / 538 / 7:00 | 191 / 307 / 4:00 | 330 / 531 / 6:40 | 438 / 705 / 8:50 | 167 / 269 / 4:00 | 282 / 454 / 5:40 | 333 / 536 / 6:40 | 394 / 634 / 7:30 | 360 / 580 / 7:00 | 181 / 291 / 3:50 | 231 / 372 / 4:50 | 216 / 348 / 5:40 | 270 / 435 / 5:20 | 206 / 332 / 4:30 | 334 / 538 / 6:40 | 426 / 686 / 8:20 | 288 / 463 / 5:50 | 141 / 227 / 3:20 | 148 / 238 / 3:30 | 311 / 501 / 6:30 | 305 / 491 / 6:10 | 111 / 179 / 2:50 | 439 / 707 / 8:40 | 269 / 433 / 5:40 |
| Inverness | | | | | | | | | | | | | | | | | | | | | | | 474 / 763 / 9:40 | 569 / 916 / 11:00 | 553 / 890 / 11:00 | 504 / 811 / 9:30 | 166 / 267 / 4:00 | 66 / 106 / 1:40 | 542 / 872 / 10:30 | 618 / 995 / 11:30 | 158 / 254 / 3:50 | 132 / 212 / 3:20 | 622 / 1001 / 11:30 | 383 / 617 / 7:30 | 262 / 422 / 5:30 | 549 / 884 / 10:20 | 505 / 813 / 9:30 | 539 / 867 / 10:10 | 617 / 993 / 11:30 | 75 / 121 / 2:00 | 597 / 961 / 11:20 | 348 / 560 / 7:00 | 458 / 737 / 9:00 | 215 / 346 / 5:10 | 199 / 320 / 4:30 | 486 / 782 / 9:40 | 105 / 169 / 2:50 | 550 / 885 / 10:40 |
| John o' Groats | | | | | | | | | | | | | | | | | | | | | | 129 / 208 / 3:20 | 603 / 970 / 12:40 | 693 / 1116 / 14:00 | 677 / 1090 / 14:00 | 628 / 1011 / 12:30 | 295 / 475 / 7:10 | 195 / 314 / 5:00 | 671 / 1080 / 13:40 | 744 / 1197 / 14:30 | 285 / 459 / 7:00 | 259 / 417 / 6:30 | 746 / 1201 / 14:40 | 507 / 816 / 10:30 | 391 / 629 / 8:40 | 680 / 1094 / 13:30 | 630 / 1014 / 12:30 | 668 / 1075 / 13:20 | 741 / 1193 / 14:40 | 202 / 325 / 5:00 | 724 / 1165 / 14:20 | 478 / 769 / 10:00 | 574 / 924 / 11:50 | 342 / 550 / 8:10 | 328 / 528 / 7:40 | 601 / 967 / 12:40 | 232 / 373 / 5:50 | 663 / 1067 / 13:30 |
| Kingston upon Hull | | | | | | | | | | | | | | | | | | | | | 518 / 834 / 10:50 | 394 / 634 / 7:50 | 231 / 372 / 4:50 | 196 / 316 / 4:10 | 207 / 333 / 5:20 | 169 / 272 / 3:10 | 254 / 409 / 4:50 | 369 / 594 / 7:20 | 280 / 451 / 5:30 | 309 / 497 / 5:40 | 234 / 377 / 4:30 | 295 / 475 / 5:30 | 256 / 412 / 4:50 | 47 / 76 / 1:10 | 158 / 254 / 3:00 | 244 / 393 / 4:40 | 139 / 224 / 3:10 | 233 / 375 / 4:20 | 245 / 394 / 4:40 | 327 / 526 / 6:10 | 264 / 425 / 5:00 | 127 / 204 / 2:30 | 134 / 216 / 2:50 | 185 / 298 / 3:50 | 251 / 404 / 4:40 | 223 / 359 / 4:40 | 364 / 586 / 7:20 | 184 / 296 / 3:50 |
| Kyle of Lochalsh | | | | | | | | | | | | | | | | | | | | 445 / 716 / 9:00 | 189 / 304 / 4:40 | 84 / 135 / 2:10 | 514 / 827 / 10:40 | 611 / 983 / 12:10 | 602 / 969 / 12:10 | 528 / 850 / 10:20 | 179 / 288 / 4:40 | 76 / 122 / 1:50 | 567 / 913 / 11:20 | 628 / 1011 / 12:00 | 216 / 348 / 5:20 | 186 / 299 / 4:40 | 671 / 1080 / 12:50 | 432 / 695 / 8:40 | 275 / 443 / 6:10 | 564 / 908 / 11:10 | 555 / 893 / 10:50 | 552 / 888 / 10:50 | 651 / 1048 / 12:40 | 159 / 256 / 4:00 | 618 / 995 / 12:10 | 372 / 599 / 7:50 | 471 / 758 / 9:40 | 263 / 423 / 6:20 | 212 / 341 / 5:10 | 499 / 803 / 10:20 | 189 / 304 / 4:50 | 586 / 943 / 11:40 |
| Land's End | | | | | | | | | | | | | | | | | | | 763 / 1228 / 15:10 | 421 / 678 / 8:20 | 868 / 1397 / 17:20 | 741 / 1193 / 14:20 | 405 / 652 / 8:30 | 390 / 628 / 8:00 | 446 / 718 / 9:10 | 235 / 378 / 5:00 | 573 / 922 / 10:50 | 686 / 1104 / 13:20 | 353 / 568 / 7:20 | 123 / 198 / 3:20 | 574 / 924 / 10:50 | 642 / 1033 / 12:00 | 381 / 613 / 7:40 | 374 / 602 / 7:20 | 477 / 768 / 9:10 | 245 / 394 / 5:20 | 374 / 602 / 7:20 | 200 / 322 / 4:40 | 308 / 496 / 7:50 | 665 / 1070 / 12:30 | 205 / 330 / 5:20 | 405 / 652 / 8:00 | 281 / 452 / 6:00 | 552 / 888 / 10:40 | 570 / 917 / 10:50 | 313 / 504 / 6:50 | 692 / 1114 / 13:10 | 297 / 478 / 6:30 |
| Leeds | | | | | | | | | | | | | | | | | | 405 / 652 / 8:00 | 394 / 634 / 8:20 | 55 / 89 / 1:30 | 487 / 784 / 10:20 | 360 / 579 / 7:10 | 176 / 283 / 4:00 | 223 / 359 / 4:30 | 196 / 315 / 4:20 | 174 / 280 / 3:20 | 215 / 346 / 4:10 | 329 / 530 / 6:40 | 237 / 381 / 4:40 | 270 / 435 / 5:00 | 202 / 325 / 4:00 | 258 / 415 / 4:50 | 260 / 418 / 4:50 | 29 / 47 / 0:50 | 119 / 192 / 2:30 | 232 / 373 / 4:20 | 145 / 233 / 2:50 | 194 / 312 / 3:50 | 260 / 419 / 5:00 | 293 / 472 / 5:30 | 255 / 410 / 4:50 | 72 / 116 / 1:40 | 113 / 182 / 2:30 | 156 / 251 / 3:20 | 212 / 341 / 4:00 | 169 / 272 / 3:40 | 327 / 526 / 6:50 | 189 / 304 / 3:50 |
| Leicester | | | | | | | | | | | | | | | | | 95 / 153 / 2:00 | 320 / 515 / 6:30 | 500 / 805 / 9:50 | 102 / 164 / 2:10 | 588 / 947 / 11:50 | 461 / 742 / 8:50 | 190 / 306 / 4:00 | 147 / 237 / 3:10 | 140 / 225 / 3:20 | 85 / 137 / 1:40 | 314 / 505 / 5:40 | 422 / 679 / 8:00 | 209 / 336 / 4:10 | 196 / 315 / 3:40 | 296 / 476 / 5:20 | 349 / 562 / 6:20 | 185 / 298 / 3:30 | 74 / 119 / 1:30 | 206 / 332 / 3:50 | 154 / 248 / 3:00 | 68 / 109 / 1:20 | 120 / 193 / 2:30 | 166 / 267 / 3:20 | 389 / 626 / 7:00 | 158 / 254 / 3:10 | 140 / 225 / 2:40 | 39 / 63 / 1:10 | 252 / 406 / 5:00 | 299 / 481 / 5:20 | 153 / 246 / 3:20 | 414 / 666 / 7:40 | 97 / 156 / 2:20 |
| Lincoln | | | | | | | | | | | | | | | | 51 / 82 / 1:20 | 68 / 109 / 1:50 | 371 / 597 / 7:30 | 476 / 766 / 9:40 | 44 / 71 / 1:20 | 554 / 892 / 11:30 | 427 / 687 / 8:30 | 216 / 348 / 4:40 | 155 / 249 / 3:30 | 128 / 206 / 3:20 | 159 / 256 / 3:10 | 291 / 468 / 5:30 | 399 / 642 / 7:50 | 272 / 438 / 5:30 | 247 / 398 / 4:40 | 258 / 415 / 5:00 | 314 / 505 / 5:50 | 202 / 325 / 4:00 | 39 / 63 / 1:10 | 191 / 307 / 3:40 | 208 / 335 / 4:10 | 85 / 137 / 2:20 | 183 / 295 / 3:40 | 197 / 317 / 4:00 | 357 / 575 / 6:40 | 209 / 336 / 4:10 | 128 / 206 / 2:40 | 90 / 145 / 2:10 | 224 / 360 / 4:40 | 274 / 441 / 5:10 | 199 / 320 / 4:20 | 383 / 616 / 7:20 | 131 / 211 / 3:10 |
| Liverpool | | | | | | | | | | | | | | | 129 / 208 / 2:50 | 130 / 209 / 2:40 | 75 / 121 / 1:50 | 361 / 581 / 7:20 | 407 / 655 / 8:30 | 130 / 209 / 2:40 | 511 / 822 / 10:40 | 382 / 615 / 7:40 | 102 / 164 / 2:40 | 265 / 427 / 5:20 | 240 / 386 / 5:00 | 140 / 225 / 2:40 | 216 / 348 / 4:10 | 329 / 530 / 6:40 | 160 / 257 / 3:30 | 237 / 381 / 4:30 | 216 / 348 / 4:10 | 286 / 460 / 5:20 | 299 / 481 / 5:30 | 86 / 138 / 1:50 | 120 / 193 / 2:30 | 169 / 272 / 3:20 | 194 / 312 / 3:40 | 161 / 259 / 3:10 | 272 / 438 / 5:10 | 318 / 512 / 6:00 | 234 / 377 / 4:30 | 49 / 79 / 1:20 | 93 / 150 / 2:10 | 219 / 352 / 4:30 | 213 / 343 / 4:10 | 104 / 167 / 2:40 | 341 / 549 / 6:40 | 202 / 325 / 4:10 |
| Manchester | | | | | | | | | | | | | | 35 / 56 / 1:10 | 84 / 135 / 2:00 | 92 / 148 / 2:00 | 40 / 64 / 1:10 | 361 / 581 / 7:20 | 406 / 654 / 8:30 | 95 / 153 / 2:10 | 500 / 805 / 10:30 | 373 / 600 / 7:30 | 124 / 200 / 3:00 | 228 / 367 / 4:40 | 212 / 341 / 4:30 | 126 / 203 / 2:30 | 215 / 346 / 4:10 | 329 / 530 / 6:40 | 197 / 317 / 4:00 | 236 / 380 / 4:20 | 215 / 346 / 4:10 | 285 / 459 / 5:20 | 276 / 444 / 5:10 | 61 / 98 / 1:30 | 119 / 192 / 2:30 | 183 / 295 / 3:40 | 165 / 266 / 3:10 | 161 / 259 / 3:10 | 257 / 414 / 4:50 | 318 / 512 / 6:00 | 227 / 365 / 4:20 | 48 / 77 / 1:20 | 80 / 129 / 2:00 | 196 / 315 / 4:00 | 212 / 341 / 4:00 | 129 / 208 / 3:00 | 340 / 547 / 6:30 | 185 / 298 / 3:50 |
| Newcastle upon Tyne | | | | | | | | | | | | | 132 / 212 / 2:50 | 168 / 270 / 3:20 | 159 / 256 / 3:20 | 187 / 301 / 3:40 | 92 / 148 / 2:10 | 498 / 802 / 9:40 | 318 / 512 / 7:00 | 132 / 212 / 2:50 | 395 / 636 / 8:50 | 268 / 431 / 5:40 | 272 / 438 / 5:40 | 308 / 496 / 6:00 | 281 / 452 / 5:40 | 266 / 428 / 4:50 | 148 / 238 / 3:10 | 253 / 407 / 5:20 | 329 / 529 / 6:20 | 364 / 586 / 6:30 | 110 / 177 / 2:20 | 166 / 267 / 3:20 | 358 / 576 / 6:30 | 114 / 183 / 2:20 | 57 / 92 / 1:50 | 325 / 523 / 6:00 | 241 / 388 / 4:20 | 299 / 481 / 5:30 | 352 / 567 / 6:30 | 201 / 323 / 4:00 | 347 / 558 / 6:30 | 129 / 208 / 2:40 | 207 / 333 / 4:10 | 64 / 103 / 1:50 | 149 / 240 / 3:00 | 257 / 414 / 5:20 | 235 / 378 / 4:50 | 286 / 460 / 5:40 |
| Norwich | | | | | | | | | | | | 264 / 425 / 5:20 | 185 / 298 / 4:30 | 220 / 354 / 4:40 | 105 / 169 / 2:50 | 119 / 192 / 3:20 | 176 / 283 / 3:50 | 421 / 678 / 8:40 | 582 / 937 / 11:50 | 149 / 240 / 4:00 | 654 / 1053 / 13:30 | 529 / 852 / 10:30 | 311 / 501 / 6:40 | 73 / 117 / 2:00 | 20 / 32 / 0:40 | 204 / 328 / 4:10 | 385 / 620 / 9:00 | 504 / 811 / 10:00 | 343 / 552 / 7:00 | 308 / 496 / 6:00 | 366 / 589 / 7:00 | 422 / 679 / 8:00 | 174 / 280 / 3:50 | 147 / 237 / 3:20 | 289 / 465 / 5:40 | 262 / 422 / 5:20 | 62 / 100 / 1:50 | 252 / 406 / 5:10 | 175 / 282 / 4:00 | 457 / 735 / 8:40 | 214 / 344 / 4:40 | 232 / 373 / 4:50 | 166 / 267 / 3:50 | 328 / 528 / 6:40 | 382 / 615 / 7:20 | 276 / 444 / 6:00 | 496 / 798 / 9:40 | 114 / 183 / 3:30 |
| Nottingham | | | | | | | | | | | 130 / 209 / 3:40 | 157 / 253 / 3:10 | 73 / 118 / 1:40 | 98 / 158 / 2:10 | 35 / 56 / 1:10 | 25 / 40 / 0:50 | 70 / 113 / 1:40 | 345 / 555 / 7:00 | 479 / 771 / 9:40 | 90 / 145 / 2:00 | 557 / 896 / 11:30 | 430 / 692 / 8:20 | 185 / 298 / 4:00 | 150 / 241 / 3:20 | 153 / 246 / 3:30 | 110 / 177 / 2:10 | 293 / 472 / 5:30 | 401 / 646 / 7:50 | 220 / 354 / 4:30 | 221 / 356 / 4:10 | 262 / 422 / 4:50 | 328 / 528 / 6:00 | 205 / 330 / 3:50 | 43 / 69 / 1:10 | 194 / 312 / 3:40 | 172 / 277 / 3:20 | 83 / 134 / 1:40 | 145 / 233 / 3:00 | 193 / 311 / 3:50 | 353 / 568 / 6:30 | 183 / 295 / 3:40 | 111 / 179 / 2:20 | 50 / 80 / 1:20 | 221 / 356 / 4:30 | 274 / 441 / 5:10 | 164 / 264 / 3:40 | 393 / 633 / 7:30 | 122 / 196 / 2:40 |
| Oban | | | | | | | | | | 390 / 628 / 7:30 | 492 / 792 / 9:40 | 233 / 375 / 4:50 | 307 / 494 / 6:00 | 308 / 496 / 6:10 | 387 / 623 / 7:30 | 419 / 674 / 7:50 | 307 / 494 / 6:00 | 665 / 1070 / 12:50 | 128 / 206 / 3:10 | 346 / 557 / 6:40 | 244 / 393 / 6:10 | 117 / 188 / 3:00 | 427 / 687 / 8:30 | 524 / 843 / 10:00 | 515 / 829 / 10:00 | 441 / 710 / 8:10 | 92 / 148 / 2:30 | 49 / 79 / 1:20 | 481 / 774 / 9:10 | 549 / 884 / 10:00 | 123 / 198 / 3:00 | 117 / 188 / 2:50 | 585 / 942 / 10:40 | 346 / 557 / 6:40 | 188 / 303 / 4:00 | 477 / 768 / 9:00 | 468 / 753 / 8:40 | 465 / 748 / 8:40 | 565 / 910 / 10:30 | 141 / 227 / 3:30 | 530 / 853 / 9:50 | 285 / 459 / 5:40 | 384 / 618 / 7:30 | 180 / 290 / 4:20 | 94 / 151 / 2:20 | 412 / 663 / 8:10 | 178 / 286 / 4:20 | 499 / 803 / 9:30 |
| Oxford | | | | | | | | | 462 / 744 / 8:30 | 109 / 175 / 2:10 | 145 / 233 / 3:50 | 260 / 418 / 4:50 | 144 / 232 / 2:50 | 172 / 277 / 3:20 | 137 / 221 / 2:50 | 73 / 117 / 1:30 | 168 / 270 / 3:10 | 274 / 441 / 5:40 | 550 / 885 / 10:40 | 192 / 309 / 3:40 | 656 / 1056 / 13:00 | 532 / 856 / 10:00 | 238 / 383 / 4:50 | 145 / 233 / 3:10 | 200 / 322 / 4:20 | 52 / 84 / 1:30 | 356 / 573 / 6:30 | 472 / 760 / 9:00 | 205 / 330 / 4:10 | 156 / 251 / 3:00 | 372 / 599 / 6:40 | 433 / 697 / 7:40 | 141 / 227 / 2:50 | 145 / 233 / 2:40 | 260 / 418 / 4:40 | 108 / 174 / 2:20 | 83 / 134 / 1:40 | 74 / 119 / 1:40 | 108 / 174 / 2:20 | 465 / 749 / 8:20 | 90 / 145 / 2:00 | 187 / 301 / 3:30 | 64 / 103 / 1:30 | 324 / 521 / 6:10 | 353 / 568 / 6:20 | 154 / 248 / 3:20 | 483 / 777 / 8:50 | 57 / 92 / 1:40 |
| Plymouth | | | | | | | | 199 / 320 / 4:00 | 587 / 945 / 11:00 | 267 / 430 / 5:10 | 343 / 552 / 7:00 | 410 / 660 / 7:40 | 283 / 455 / 5:30 | 283 / 455 / 5:30 | 293 / 472 / 5:50 | 242 / 389 / 4:40 | 316 / 509 / 6:00 | 89 / 143 / 2:20 | 674 / 1085 / 13:10 | 355 / 571 / 6:40 | 790 / 1271 / 15:40 | 664 / 1069 / 12:30 | 328 / 528 / 6:40 | 309 / 497 / 6:10 | 365 / 588 / 7:20 | 157 / 253 / 3:20 | 495 / 797 / 9:10 | 595 / 958 / 11:20 | 264 / 425 / 5:30 | 46 / 74 / 1:30 | 496 / 798 / 9:00 | 552 / 888 / 10:00 | 300 / 483 / 5:50 | 297 / 478 / 5:40 | 399 / 642 / 7:20 | 167 / 269 / 3:40 | 293 / 472 / 5:30 | 122 / 196 / 2:50 | 224 / 361 / 6:00 | 587 / 945 / 10:40 | 128 / 206 / 3:30 | 328 / 528 / 6:10 | 203 / 327 / 4:20 | 474 / 763 / 9:00 | 492 / 792 / 9:00 | 237 / 382 / 5:10 | 615 / 990 / 11:20 | 218 / 351 / 4:40 |
| Portsmouth | | | | | | | 176 / 283 / 4:50 | 77 / 124 / 1:40 | 545 / 877 / 10:00 | 191 / 307 / 3:40 | 207 / 333 / 4:20 | 337 / 542 / 6:10 | 236 / 380 / 4:30 | 254 / 409 / 4:50 | 201 / 323 / 4:00 | 162 / 261 / 3:10 | 257 / 414 / 4:50 | 259 / 417 / 5:40 | 633 / 1019 / 12:10 | 269 / 433 / 5:00 | 737 / 1186 / 14:30 | 613 / 987 / 11:30 | 311 / 501 / 6:10 | 166 / 267 / 3:40 | 221 / 356 / 4:40 | 119 / 192 / 3:00 | 448 / 721 / 8:10 | 555 / 893 / 10:20 | 251 / 404 / 5:00 | 135 / 217 / 2:40 | 453 / 729 / 8:10 | 514 / 827 / 9:00 | 130 / 209 / 2:50 | 234 / 377 / 4:20 | 348 / 560 / 6:10 | 142 / 229 / 3:00 | 144 / 232 / 2:50 | 97 / 156 / 2:10 | 48 / 77 / 1:40 | 547 / 881 / 9:50 | 52 / 84 / 1:30 | 264 / 425 / 4:50 | 141 / 227 / 3:00 | 401 / 645 / 7:30 | 430 / 692 / 7:40 | 222 / 357 / 4:40 | 560 / 901 / 10:10 | 70 / 113 / 2:00 |
| Sheffield | | | | | | 230 / 370 / 4:20 | 283 / 455 / 5:30 | 135 / 217 / 2:40 | 339 / 546 / 6:30 | 37 / 60 / 1:00 | 146 / 235 / 3:20 | 125 / 201 / 2:40 | 38 / 61 / 1:00 | 72 / 116 / 1:40 | 46 / 74 / 1:20 | 62 / 100 / 1:20 | 33 / 53 / 1:00 | 361 / 581 / 7:10 | 427 / 687 / 8:40 | 65 / 105 / 1:30 | 520 / 837 / 10:50 | 393 / 632 / 7:40 | 168 / 270 / 3:40 | 187 / 301 / 3:50 | 166 / 267 / 3:40 | 126 / 203 / 2:20 | 248 / 399 / 4:40 | 348 / 560 / 6:50 | 215 / 346 / 4:20 | 237 / 381 / 4:20 | 235 / 378 / 4:20 | 291 / 468 / 5:20 | 245 / 394 / 4:30 | 18 / 29 / 0:40 | 152 / 245 / 3:00 | 194 / 312 / 3:40 | 120 / 193 / 2:20 | 161 / 259 / 3:10 | 226 / 364 / 4:20 | 320 / 515 / 6:00 | 216 / 348 / 4:10 | 86 / 138 / 1:50 | 76 / 122 / 1:50 | 190 / 306 / 4:00 | 245 / 394 / 4:30 | 159 / 256 / 3:30 | 360 / 579 / 6:50 | 159 / 256 / 3:20 |
| Shrewsbury | | | | | 82 / 132 / 2:10 | 207 / 333 / 3:50 | 225 / 362 / 4:40 | 106 / 171 / 2:10 | 364 / 586 / 7:00 | 93 / 150 / 2:00 | 205 / 330 / 4:20 | 201 / 323 / 3:50 | 69 / 111 / 1:40 | 58 / 93 / 1:50 | 133 / 214 / 2:50 | 84 / 135 / 1:40 | 109 / 175 / 2:20 | 303 / 488 / 6:10 | 451 / 726 / 9:00 | 169 / 272 / 3:10 | 567 / 912 / 11:30 | 438 / 705 / 8:20 | 113 / 182 / 2:50 | 240 / 386 / 4:40 | 225 / 362 / 4:40 | 77 / 124 / 1:30 | 272 / 438 / 5:00 | 382 / 615 / 7:20 | 145 / 233 / 3:10 | 179 / 288 / 3:20 | 274 / 441 / 5:00 | 330 / 531 / 6:00 | 251 / 404 / 4:30 | 109 / 175 / 2:10 | 176 / 283 / 3:20 | 111 / 179 / 2:20 | 159 / 256 / 3:00 | 103 / 166 / 2:50 | 226 / 364 / 4:20 | 371 / 597 / 6:50 | 185 / 298 / 3:40 | 98 / 158 / 2:00 | 45 / 72 / 1:20 | 265 / 426 / 5:10 | 269 / 433 / 5:00 | 77 / 124 / 2:10 | 399 / 642 / 7:30 | 160 / 258 / 3:20 |
| Southampton | | | | 185 / 298 / 4:10 | 199 / 320 / 3:40 | 21 / 34 / 0:50 | 151 / 243 / 4:10 | 64 / 103 / 1:30 | 530 / 853 / 9:40 | 176 / 283 / 3:20 | 206 / 332 / 4:20 | 324 / 521 / 5:50 | 221 / 356 / 4:10 | 239 / 385 / 4:30 | 204 / 328 / 4:00 | 137 / 220 / 2:40 | 232 / 373 / 4:20 | 228 / 367 / 5:00 | 618 / 995 / 12:00 | 256 / 412 / 4:40 | 723 / 1164 / 14:10 | 598 / 963 / 11:10 | 293 / 472 / 5:50 | 164 / 264 / 3:30 | 220 / 354 / 4:40 | 105 / 169 / 2:40 | 433 / 697 / 7:40 | 541 / 871 / 10:00 | 233 / 375 / 4:40 | 105 / 169 / 3:00 | 438 / 705 / 7:50 | 500 / 805 / 8:50 | 143 / 230 / 2:50 | 209 / 336 / 3:50 | 324 / 521 / 5:50 | 121 / 195 / 2:30 | 148 / 238 / 2:50 | 76 / 122 / 2:20 | 61 / 98 / 1:50 | 532 / 856 / 9:30 | 31 / 50 / 1:00 | 251 / 404 / 4:40 | 128 / 206 / 2:40 | 388 / 624 / 7:10 | 417 / 671 / 7:30 | 201 / 323 / 4:10 | 547 / 880 / 10:00 | 77 / 124 / 2:00 |
| Stranraer | | | 445 / 716 / 8:20 | 277 / 446 / 5:30 | 263 / 423 / 5:20 | 461 / 742 / 8:40 | 500 / 805 / 9:40 | 379 / 610 / 7:10 | 148 / 238 / 3:40 | 290 / 467 / 5:50 | 403 / 649 / 8:10 | 158 / 254 / 3:40 | 220 / 354 / 4:40 | 221 / 356 / 4:40 | 298 / 480 / 6:00 | 330 / 531 / 6:20 | 220 / 354 / 4:40 | 585 / 942 / 11:30 | 263 / 423 / 6:30 | 259 / 417 / 5:20 | 379 / 610 / 9:00 | 262 / 422 / 6:00 | 338 / 544 / 7:00 | 410 / 660 / 8:10 | 426 / 686 / 8:40 | 343 / 552 / 6:30 | 84 / 135 / 2:30 | 195 / 314 / 4:50 | 392 / 631 / 7:50 | 454 / 731 / 8:30 | 124 / 200 / 3:00 | 167 / 269 / 3:40 | 496 / 798 / 9:10 | 257 / 414 / 5:10 | 101 / 163 / 2:40 | 390 / 628 / 7:30 | 379 / 610 / 7:10 | 378 / 608 / 7:20 | 475 / 765 / 9:00 | 194 / 312 / 4:20 | 444 / 715 / 8:30 | 188 / 303 / 4:00 | 297 / 478 / 6:00 | 170 / 274 / 4:10 | 51 / 82 / 1:20 | 325 / 523 / 6:50 | 228 / 367 / 5:10 | 402 / 647 / 7:50 |
| Swansea | | 417 / 671 / 7:50 | 161 / 259 / 3:00 | 118 / 190 / 2:20 | 217 / 349 / 4:00 | 182 / 293 / 3:30 | 206 / 332 / 4:10 | 141 / 227 / 2:40 | 506 / 815 / 9:20 | 192 / 309 / 3:40 | 301 / 485 / 6:00 | 347 / 559 / 6:20 | 187 / 301 / 3:30 | 195 / 314 / 3:40 | 233 / 375 / 4:30 | 177 / 285 / 3:20 | 248 / 399 / 4:40 | 285 / 459 / 6:00 | 594 / 956 / 11:30 | 264 / 425 / 4:50 | 696 / 1120 / 13:40 | 572 / 921 / 10:40 | 184 / 296 / 4:50 | 267 / 430 / 5:10 | 329 / 530 / 6:30 | 89 / 143 / 1:50 | 409 / 658 / 7:20 | 496 / 798 / 9:20 | 67 / 108 / 1:50 | 161 / 259 / 3:00 | 412 / 663 / 7:20 | 473 / 761 / 8:20 | 274 / 441 / 5:00 | 232 / 373 / 4:10 | 309 / 497 / 5:30 | 41 / 66 / 1:10 | 227 / 365 / 4:10 | 85 / 137 / 1:50 | 222 / 357 / 4:20 | 505 / 813 / 9:00 | 167 / 269 / 3:20 | 216 / 348 / 4:00 | 119 / 192 / 2:30 | 383 / 616 / 7:10 | 379 / 610 / 6:50 | 73 / 117 / 2:00 | 507 / 816 / 9:20 | 194 / 312 / 4:00 |
| York | 272 / 438 / 5:10 | 222 / 357 / 4:40 | 258 / 415 / 5:10 | 133 / 214 / 2:40 | 52 / 84 / 1:20 | 278 / 448 / 5:10 | 333 / 536 / 6:20 | 181 / 291 / 3:20 | 309 / 497 / 6:00 | 77 / 124 / 1:40 | 181 / 291 / 4:20 | 84 / 135 / 2:20 | 64 / 103 / 1:30 | 99 / 159 / 2:10 | 75 / 121 / 1:50 | 108 / 174 / 2:10 | 24 / 39 / 0:50 | 411 / 661 / 8:00 | 407 / 655 / 8:20 | 37 / 60 / 1:10 | 479 / 771 / 10:10 | 352 / 566 / 7:00 | 204 / 328 / 4:20 | 228 / 367 / 4:40 | 201 / 323 / 4:20 | 189 / 304 / 3:30 | 217 / 349 / 4:10 | 330 / 531 / 6:30 | 261 / 420 / 5:10 | 287 / 462 / 5:10 | 194 / 312 / 3:40 | 250 / 402 / 4:40 | 282 / 454 / 5:10 | 34 / 55 / 1:00 | 121 / 195 / 2:30 | 244 / 393 / 4:40 | 165 / 266 / 3:10 | 222 / 357 / 4:10 | 275 / 443 / 5:10 | 285 / 459 / 5:20 | 269 / 433 / 5:00 | 96 / 154 / 2:00 | 130 / 209 / 2:40 | 148 / 238 / 3:10 | 214 / 344 / 4:00 | 195 / 314 / 4:10 | 319 / 513 / 6:10 | 207 / 333 / 4:10 |

# Road map symbols

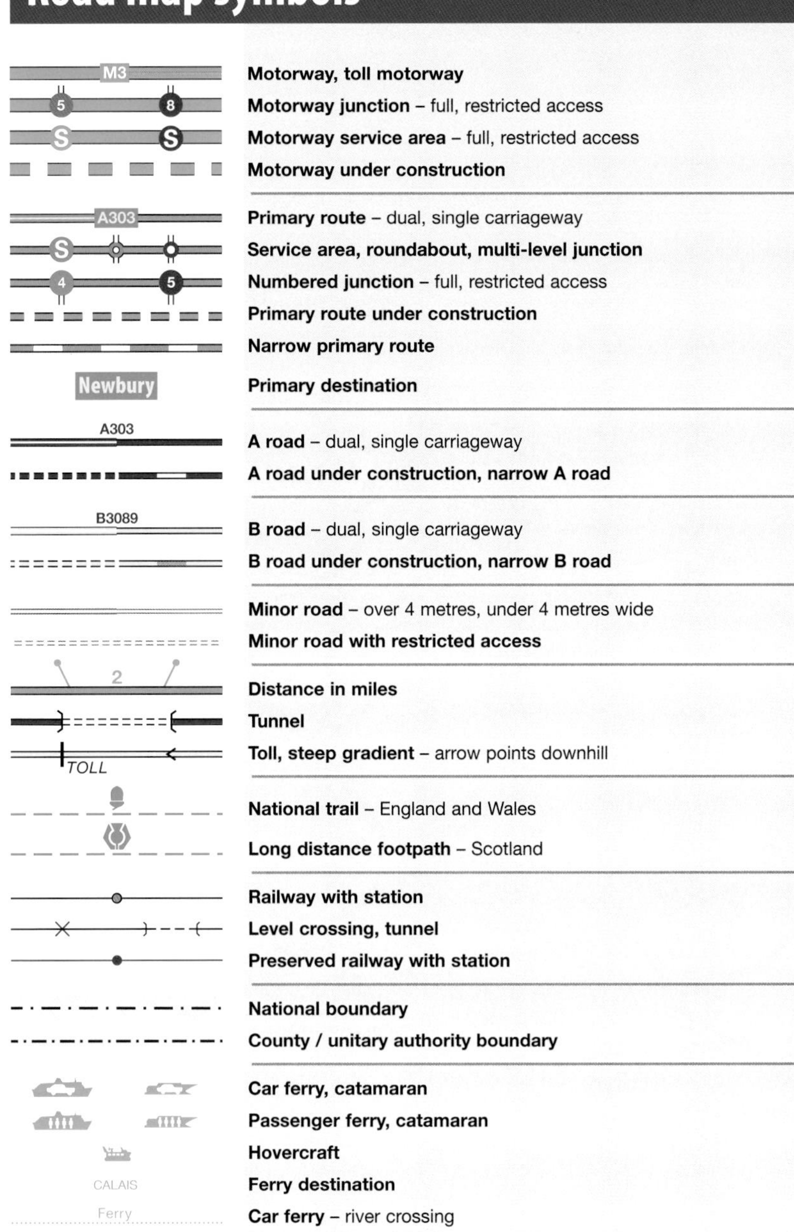


**Motorway, toll motorway**
**Motorway junction** – full, restricted access
**Motorway service area** – full, restricted access
**Motorway under construction**

**Primary route** – dual, single carriageway
**Service area, roundabout, multi-level junction**
**Numbered junction** – full, restricted access
**Primary route under construction**
**Narrow primary route**
**Primary destination**

**A road** – dual, single carriageway
**A road under construction, narrow A road**

**B road** – dual, single carriageway
**B road under construction, narrow B road**

**Minor road** – over 4 metres, under 4 metres wide
**Minor road with restricted access**

**Distance in miles**
**Tunnel**
**Toll, steep gradient** – arrow points downhill

**National trail** – England and Wales
**Long distance footpath** – Scotland

**Railway with station**
**Level crossing, tunnel**
**Preserved railway with station**

**National boundary**
**County / unitary authority boundary**

**Car ferry, catamaran**
**Passenger ferry, catamaran**
**Hovercraft**
**Ferry destination**
**Car ferry** – river crossing
**Principal airport, other airport**

**National Park, National Landscape** – England and Wales
**National Scenic Area** – Scotland
**forest park / regional park / national forest**

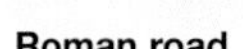

**Beach**
**Linear antiquity**
**Roman road**
**Hillfort, battlefield** – with date
**Viewpoint, nature reserve, spot height** – in metres
**Golf course, youth hostel, sporting venue**
**Camp site, caravan site, camping and caravan site**
**Shopping village, park and ride**

**Adjoining page number** – road maps

# Tourist information

**Abbey, cathedral or priory**
**Ancient monument**
**Aquarium**
**Art gallery**
**Bird collection or aviary**
**Castle**
**Church**
**Country park**
England and Wales
Scotland
**Farm park**
**Garden**
**Historic ship**
**House**
**House and garden**
**Motor racing circuit**
**Museum**
**Picnic area**
**Preserved railway**
**Race course**
**Roman antiquity**
**Safari park**
**Theme park**
**Tourist information**
**Zoo**
**Other place of interest**

## Road map scale

1: 150 000 • 1 cm = 1.5 km • 1 inch = 2·37 miles

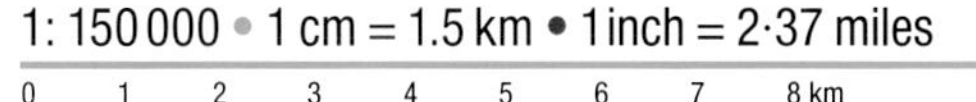
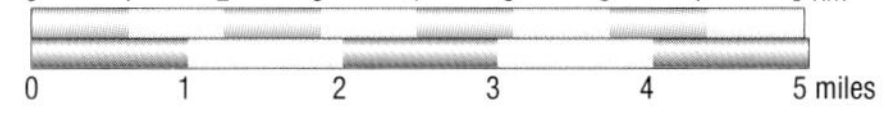


## Outer Hebrides, Orkney and Shetland:

1: 303 000 • 1 cm = 3.0 km • 1 inch = 4.78 miles

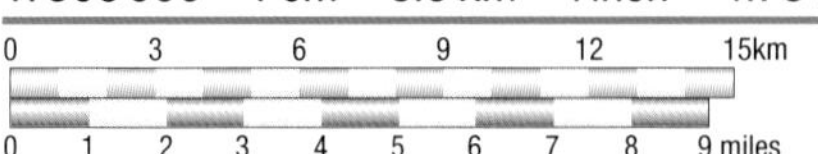

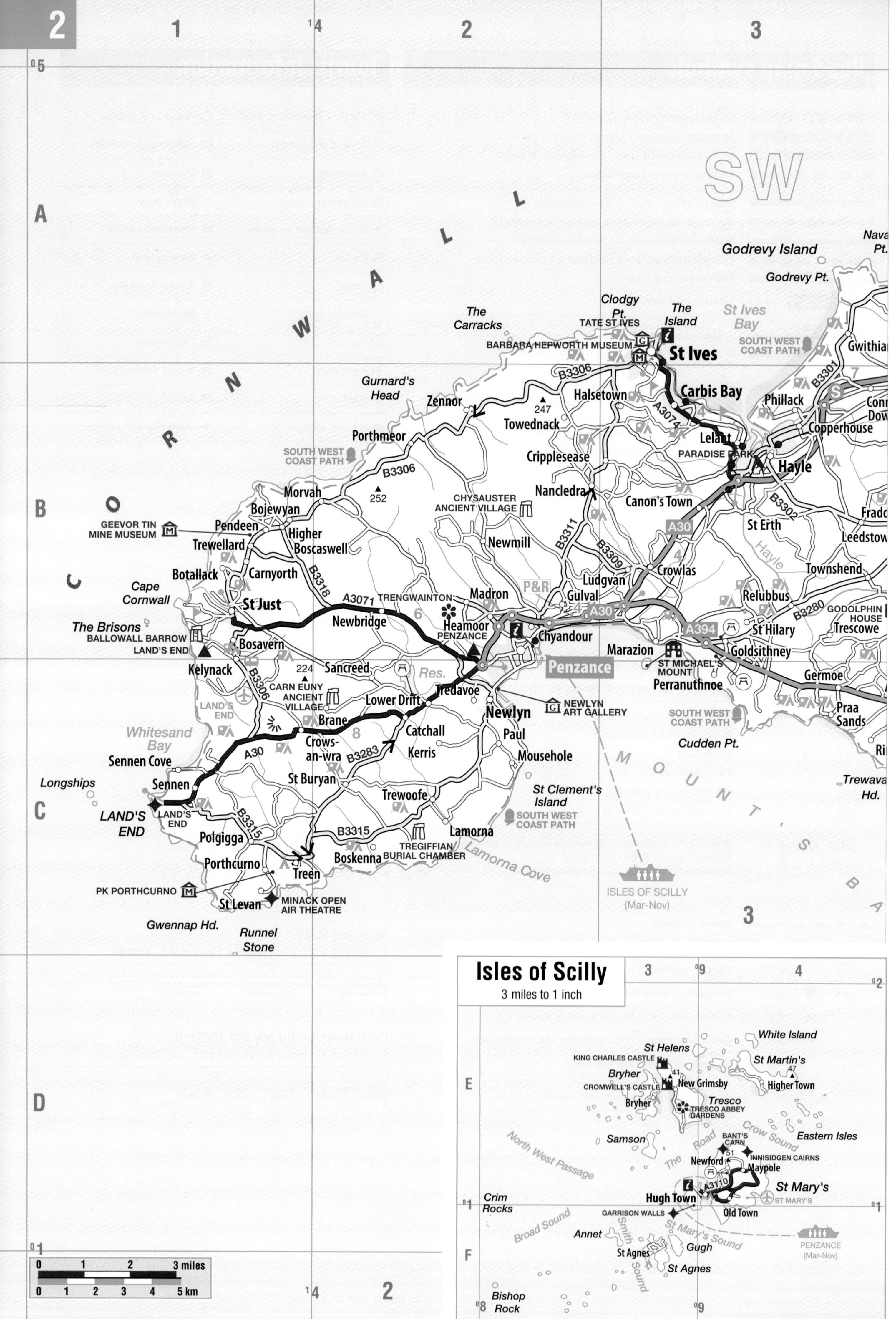
CORNWALL
SW
Godrevy Island
Godrevy Pt.
St Ives Bay
The Island
St Ives
TATE ST IVES
BARBARA HEPWORTH MUSEUM
Clodgy Pt.
The Carracks
Gurnard's Head
Zennor
Towednack
Halsetown
Carbis Bay
Lelant
PARADISE PARK
Hayle
Phillack
Copperhouse
Gwithian
St Erth
Canon's Town
Nancledra
Cripplesease
Porthmeor
SOUTH WEST COAST PATH
Morvah
Bojewyan
Pendeen
GEEVOR TIN MINE MUSEUM
Trewellard
Higher Boscaswell
Botallack
Carnyorth
Cape Cornwall
St Just
The Brisons
BALLOWALL BARROW
LAND'S END
Bosavern
Kelynack
CHYSAUSTER ANCIENT VILLAGE
Newmill
Madron
TRENGWAINTON
Heamoor
PENZANCE
Gulval
Ludgvan
Crowlas
Chyandour
Penzance
Marazion
ST MICHAEL'S MOUNT
Perranuthnoe
Relubbus
St Hilary
Goldsithney
GODOLPHIN HOUSE
Trescowe
Townshend
Leedstown
Germoe
Praa Sands
Newbridge
Sancreed
CARN EUNY ANCIENT VILLAGE
Lower Drift
Tredavoe
Newlyn
NEWLYN ART GALLERY
Brane
Catchall
Crows-an-wra
Kerris
Paul
Mousehole
St Buryan
Trewoofe
Lamorna
TREGIFFIAN BURIAL CHAMBER
Boskenna
Lamorna Cove
Whitesand Bay
Sennen Cove
Sennen
Longships
LAND'S END
Polgigga
Porthcurno
PK PORTHCURNO
Treen
St Levan
MINACK OPEN AIR THEATRE
Gwennap Hd.
Runnel Stone
St Clement's Island
Cudden Pt.
Trewavas Hd.
MOUNT'S BAY
ISLES OF SCILLY (Mar-Nov)
A30
A3071
A3074
A394
B3306
B3318
B3315
B3283
B3311
B3309
B3302
B3280
B3301
P&R
Res.
Isles of Scilly
3 miles to 1 inch
White Island
St Helens
KING CHARLES CASTLE
St Martin's
Higher Town
Bryher
CROMWELL'S CASTLE
New Grimsby
Tresco
TRESCO ABBEY GARDENS
Eastern Isles
Crow Sound
Samson
North West Passage
The Road
BANT'S CARN
INNISIDGEN CAIRNS
Newford
Maypole
St Mary's
A3110
Hugh Town
ST MARY'S
Old Town
GARRISON WALLS
Crim Rocks
Broad Sound
Annet
Smith Sound
St Mary's Sound
St Agnes
Gugh
Bishop Rock
PENZANCE (Mar-Nov)
0 1 2 3 miles
0 1 2 3 4 5 km

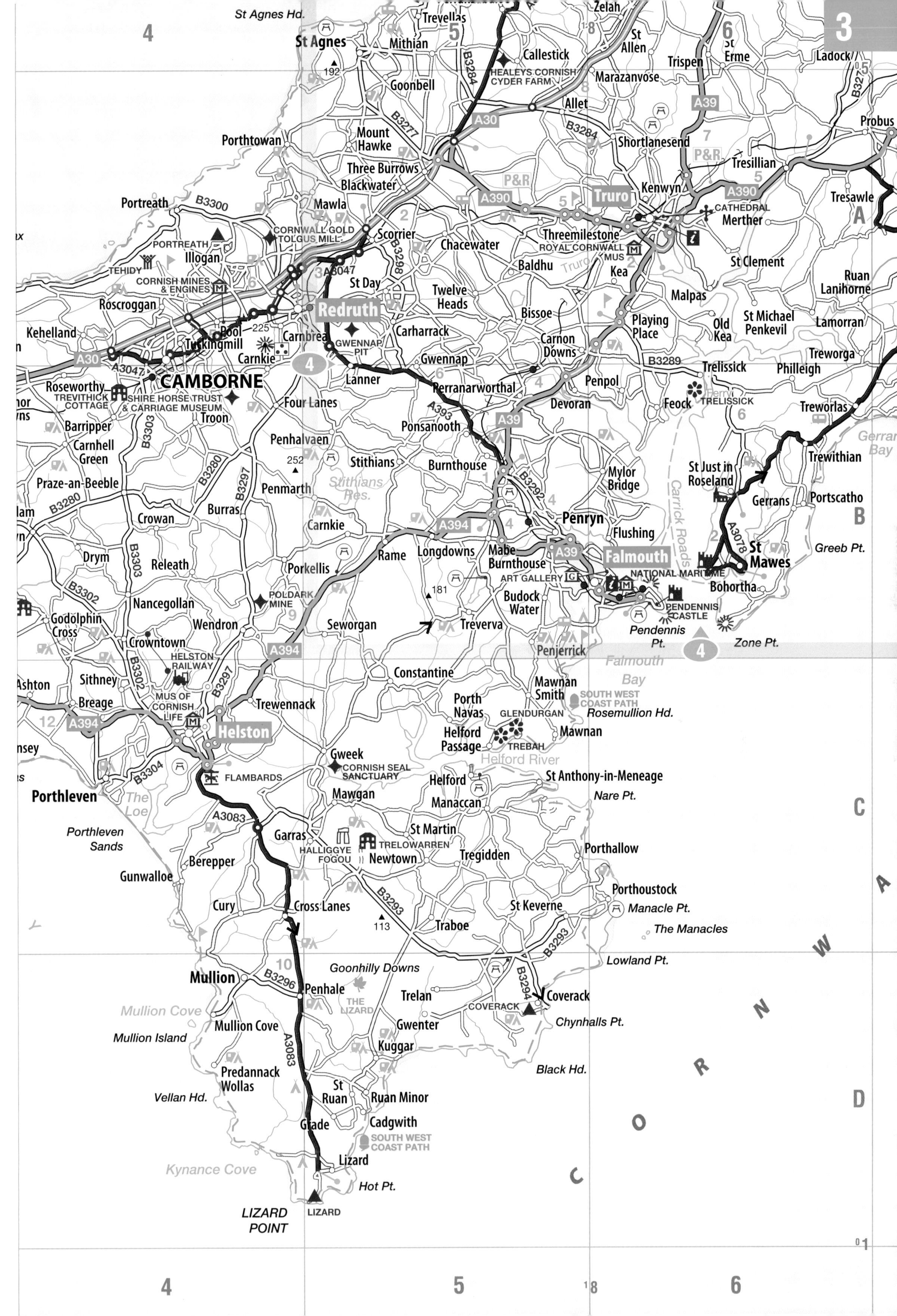
3
4
5
6
A
B
C
D
St Agnes Hd.
St Agnes
192
Trevellas
Mithian
Zelah
St Allen
St Erme
Trispen
Ladock
Callestick
HEALEYS CORNISH CYDER FARM
Marazanvose
Goonbell
Allet
B3284
B3277
A30
A39
Probus
Porthtowan
Mount Hawke
Shortlanesend
Tresillian
Three Burrows
Blackwater
P&R
A390
Truro
Kenwyn
CATHEDRAL
Merther
Tresawle
Portreath
B3300
Mawla
CORNWALL GOLD TOLGUS MILL
Scorrier
Chacewater
Threemilestone
ROYAL CORNWALL MUS
St Clement
PORTREATH
Illogan
TEHIDY
B3298
Baldhu
Truro
Kea
CORNISH MINES & ENGINES
A3047
St Day
Ruan Lanihorne
Roscroggan
Redruth
Twelve Heads
Malpas
Bissoe
Playing Place
Old Kea
St Michael Penkevil
Lamorran
Kehelland
Pool
225
Carnbrea
Carharrack
Tuckingmill
GWENNAP PIT
Carnon Downs
Carnkie
Gwennap
B3289
Trelissick
Treworga
Philleigh
A30
A3047
CAMBORNE
Lanner
Penpol
Roseworthy
TREVITHICK COTTAGE
SHIRE HORSE TRUST & CARRIAGE MUSEUM
Four Lanes
Perranarworthal
Devoran
Feock
Ferry
TRELISSICK
Treworlas
Troon
A393
Ponsanooth
B3303
Barripper
Penhalvaen
Carnhell Green
252
Stithians
Burnthouse
Mylor Bridge
St Just in Roseland
Trewithian
Gerrans Bay
Praze-an-Beeble
B3280
Penmarth
Stithians Res.
B3292
Carrick Roads
Gerrans
Portscatho
B3280
Burras
B3297
Crowan
Penryn
Flushing
Carnkie
A394
A3078
St Mawes
Greeb Pt.
Drym
Releath
Rame
Longdowns
Mabe Burnthouse
Falmouth
B3302
Porkellis
ART GALLERY
NATIONAL MARITIME
Bohortha
181
Budock Water
Nancegollan
POLDARK MINE
PENDENNIS CASTLE
Godolphin Cross
Wendron
Seworgan
Treverva
Pendennis Pt.
Zone Pt.
Crowntown
HELSTON RAILWAY
Penjerrick
Falmouth Bay
Sithney
Constantine
Ashton
Breage
MUS OF CORNISH LIFE
Trewennack
Porth Navas
Mawnan Smith
SOUTH WEST COAST PATH
GLENDURGAN
Rosemullion Hd.
Helston
Helford Passage
TREBAH
Mawnan
Helford River
Gweek
CORNISH SEAL SANCTUARY
Helford
St Anthony-in-Meneage
FLAMBARDS
B3304
Porthleven
The Loe
Mawgan
Manaccan
Nare Pt.
A3083
Porthleven Sands
Garras
HALLIGGYE FOGOU
TRELOWARREN
St Martin
Newtown
Tregidden
Porthallow
Berepper
Gunwalloe
B3293
Porthoustock
Cury
Cross Lanes
St Keverne
Manacle Pt.
113
Traboe
The Manacles
Lowland Pt.
Goonhilly Downs
B3296
Mullion
Penhale
THE LIZARD
Trelan
B3294
Coverack
COVERACK
Mullion Cove
Mullion Island
Mullion Cove
Gwenter
Chynhalls Pt.
Kuggar
Predannack Wollas
Black Hd.
Vellan Hd.
St Ruan
Ruan Minor
Grade
Cadgwith
SOUTH WEST COAST PATH
Kynance Cove
Lizard
Hot Pt.
LIZARD
LIZARD POINT
CORNWALL

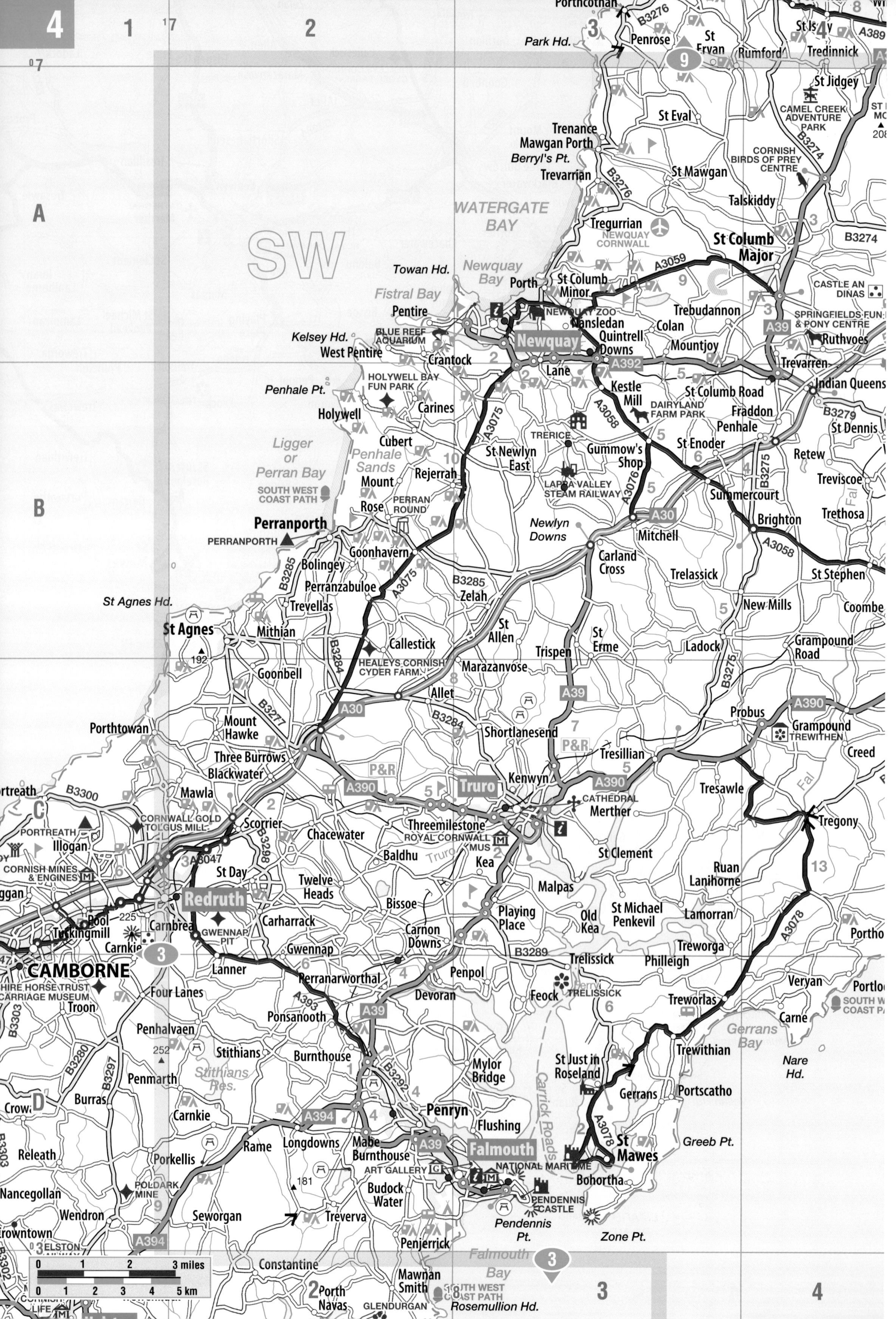

4
1
2
3
4
A
B
C
D
SW
Porthcothan
Park Hd.
B3276
Penrose
St Ervan
Rumford
St Issey
Tredinnick
A389
St Jidgey
CAMEL CREEK ADVENTURE PARK
St Eval
Trenance
Mawgan Porth
Berryl's Pt.
Trevarrian
St Mawgan
CORNISH BIRDS OF PREY CENTRE
B3274
Talskiddy
WATERGATE BAY
Tregurrian
NEWQUAY CORNWALL
St Columb Major
B3274
CASTLE AN DINAS
Towan Hd.
Newquay Bay
Porth
St Columb Minor
A3059
Fistral Bay
Pentire
NEWQUAY ZOO
Trebudannon
SPRINGFIELDS FUN & PONY CENTRE
Kelsey Hd.
BLUE REEF AQUARIUM
Newquay
Nansledan
Colan
Ruthvoes
West Pentire
Crantock
Quintrell Downs
Mountjoy
A39
Lane
A392
Trevarren
Indian Queens
Penhale Pt.
HOLYWELL BAY FUN PARK
Kestle Mill
St Columb Road
Holywell
Carines
DAIRYLAND FARM PARK
Fraddon
B3279
Penhale
St Dennis
A3075
A3058
TRERICE
Cubert
St Enoder
Ligger or Perran Bay
Penhale Sands
St Newlyn East
Gummow's Shop
Retew
Rejerrah
SOUTH WEST COAST PATH
Mount
LAPPA VALLEY STEAM RAILWAY
A3076
B3275
Treviscoe
Summercourt
Rose
PERRAN ROUND
Fal
Perranporth
Brighton
Trethosa
PERRANPORTH
A30
Mitchell
Newlyn Downs
Goonhavern
Carland Cross
A3058
Bolingey
B3285
Trelassick
St Stephen
Perranzabuloe
B3285
Zelah
St Agnes Hd.
Trevellas
New Mills
Coombe
St Agnes
Mithian
St Allen
St Erme
Ladock
Grampound Road
192
B3284
Callestick
HEALEYS CORNISH CYDER FARM
Trispen
Marazanvose
Goonbell
A39
B3275
Allet
Probus
A390
Porthtowan
Mount Hawke
B3277
A30
B3284
Shortlanesend
Grampound
TREWITHEN
P&R
Tresillian
Creed
Three Burrows
Blackwater
P&R
Truro
Kenwyn
Tresawle
Fal
rtreath
B3300
Mawla
A390
A390
CATHEDRAL
Merther
PORTREATH
CORNWALL GOLD TOLGUS MILL
Scorrier
Chacewater
Threemilestone
Tregony
Illogan
ROYAL CORNWALL MUS
B3298
A3047
St Day
Baldhu
Truro
St Clement
CORNISH MINES & ENGINES
Kea
Ruan Lanihorne
Redruth
Twelve Heads
Malpas
ggan
Pool
225
Bissoe
Playing Place
St Michael Penkevil
Lamorran
A3078
Tuckingmill
Carnbrea
GWENNAP PIT
Carharrack
Old Kea
Portho
Carnkie
Carnon Downs
B3289
Treworga
CAMBORNE
Gwennap
Trelissick
Philleigh
Lanner
Penpol
TRELISSICK
Veryan
Portlo
SHIRE HORSE TRUST CARRIAGE MUSEUM
Four Lanes
Perranarworthal
Feock
Troon
Devoran
Treworlas
SOUTH W COAST P
A393
Ponsanooth
Carne
B3303
A39
Gerrans Bay
Penhalvaen
Nare Hd.
252
Stithians
Burnthouse
Mylor Bridge
St Just in Roseland
Trewithian
B3280
B3292
Stithians Res.
Carrick Roads
Penmarth
Gerrans
Portscatho
B3297
Crow
Burras
Penryn
Carnkie
A394
Flushing
A3078
St Mawes
Greeb Pt.
B3303
Releath
Rame
Longdowns
Mabe Burnthouse
A39
Falmouth
Porkellis
NATIONAL MARITIME
Bohortha
ART GALLERY
181
Nancegollan
POLDARK MINE
Budock Water
PENDENNIS CASTLE
Wendron
Seworgan
Treverva
Pendennis Pt.
Zone Pt.
rowntown
ELSTON
A394
Penjerrick
Falmouth Bay
3
B3302
0 1 2 3 miles
0 1 2 3 4 5 km
Constantine
Mawnan Smith
SOUTH WEST COAST PATH
Porth Navas
GLENDURGAN
Rosemullion Hd.

Egloshayle
Burlawn
Pencarrow House
Helland
Washaway
Bodmin Forest
A389
A30
Millpool
Maidenwell
Warleggan
Commonmoor
Golitha Falls
King Doniert's Stone
St Cleer
Breock Downs
Cardinham
St Neot
Mount
Bodmin
Bodmin Town Museum
Nanstallon
Ruthernbridge
Rosenannon
St Lawrence
Withiel
St Wenn
Bodmin and Wenford Railway
Ley
Carnglaze Slate Caverns
Fowey
Dobwalls
Doublebois
A38
Tregonetha
Lanivet
Lanhydrock House
West Taphouse
East Taphouse
A390
St Pinnock
Cornwall Services
Trebyan
227
Belowda
Victoria
Restormel Castle
Sweethouse
Braddock
Lockengate
Redmoor
B3269
B3268
Herodsfoot
St Keyne
Tregoss
Goss Moor
Roche
Bilberry
Lostwithiel
Trewidland
Trezaise
Bugle
Lanlivery
Couch's Mill
208
B3274
A391
B3374
Milltown
Duloe
B3254
Hensbarrow Downs
312
Luxulyan
Lerryn
Bocaddon
Whitemoor
Stenalees
Penwithick
Penpillick
B3359
Sandplace
Lanreath
Nanpean
Carthew
Muchlarnick
Wheal Martyn China Clay Ctry Park & Mus
Trethurgy
St Blazey
Golant
St Veep
Pelynt
Foxhole
Eden Project
Penpoll
High Street
B3279
Carclaze
Tywardreath
Looe
Boscoppa
Lanteglos Highway
Trenewan
St Austell
Par
West Looe
Trewoon
Holmbush
A3082
Polkerris
Bodinnick
Porthallow
St Mewan
Shipwreck Treasure Mus
Charlestown
Menabilly
Fowey
Ferry
Lansallos
St Austell Brewery
St Catherine's Castle
Polruan
Polperro
Talland Bay
Heritage Mus of Smuggling & Fishing
Sticker
Polgooth
Porthpean
St. Austell Bay
South West Coast Path
Pencarrow Hd.
Hewas Water
Gribbin Hd.
Trenarren
B3273
Black Hd.
SX
The Lost Gardens of Heligan
Pentewan
(Apr-Oct)
St Ewe
Mevagissey Bay
B3287
Kestle
Polmassick
World of Model Railways
Mevagissey
Portmellon
Trevarrick
Chapel Pt.
Gorran Churchtown
St Michael Caerhays
Gorran Haven
Boswinger
Penare
114
Veryan Bay
Dodman Pt.
A
B
C
D
4
5
6
7
20
22
03

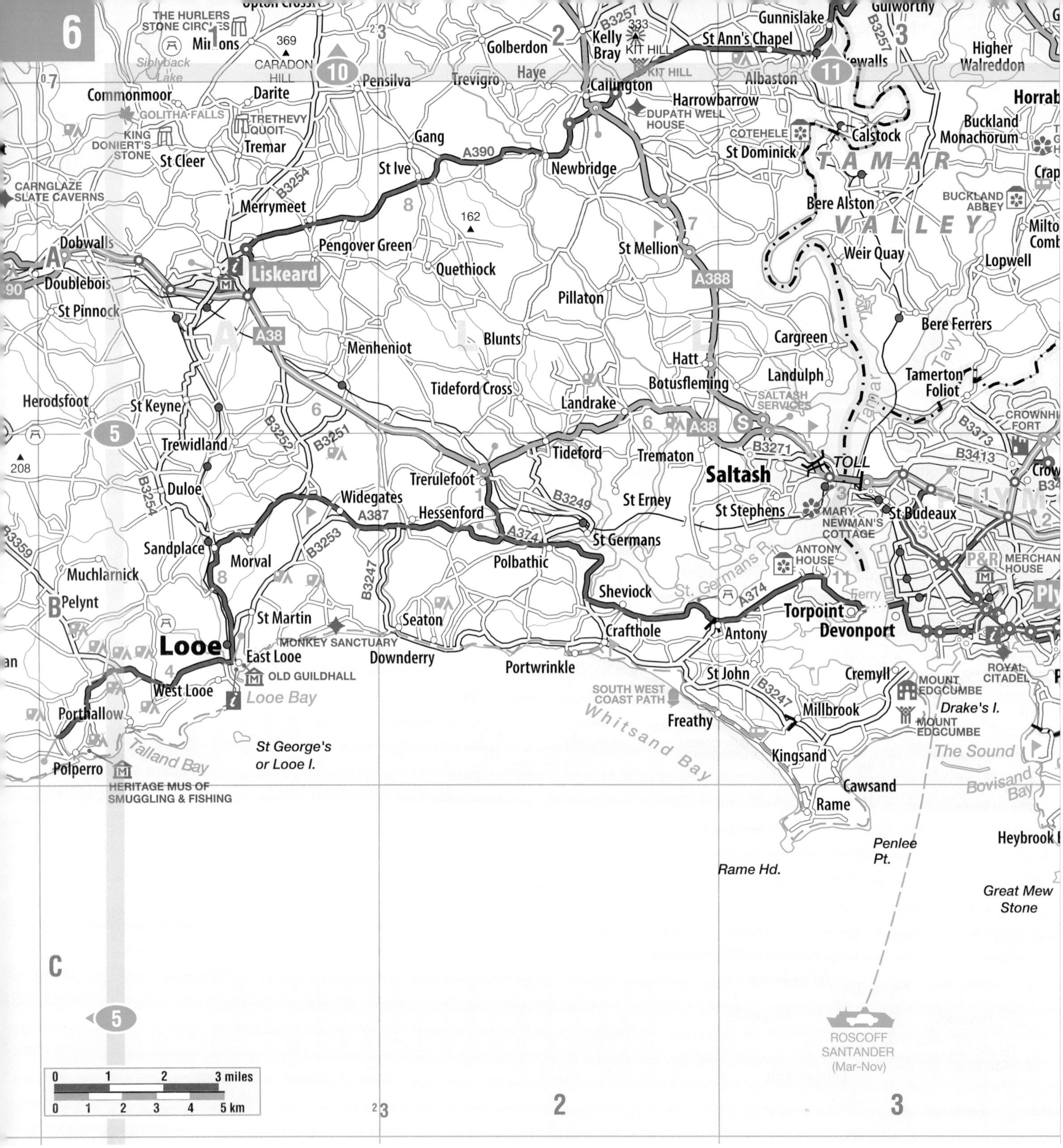

THE HURLERS STONE CIRCLES
Minions
369
CARADON HILL
Siblyback Lake
10
Pensilva
Golberdon
Trevigro
Haye
Kelly Bray
333
KIT HILL
St Ann's Chapel
Gunnislake
Gulworthy
Albaston
11
Higher Walreddon
Callington
Harrowbarrow
DUPATH WELL HOUSE
Horrabridge
Commonmoor
GOLITHA FALLS
KING DONIERT'S STONE
TRETHEVY QUOIT
Darite
Tremar
St Cleer
Gang
A390
St Ive
Newbridge
COTEHELE
St Dominick
Calstock
Buckland Monachorum
TAMAR VALLEY
CARNGLAZE SLATE CAVERNS
B3254
Merrymeet
8
162
BUCKLAND ABBEY
Bere Alston
Milton Combe
Dobwalls
Doublebois
Pengover Green
Liskeard
Quethiock
St Mellion
Weir Quay
Lopwell
A388
St Pinnock
A38
Pillaton
Menheniot
Blunts
Cargreen
Bere Ferrers
Hatt
Herodsfoot
St Keyne
Tideford Cross
Landrake
Botusfleming
Landulph
SALTASH SERVICES
Tamerton Foliot
Tavy
Tamar
5
208
Trewidland
B3252
B3251
6
Tideford
Trematon
Saltash
B3271
TOLL
CROWNHILL FORT
B3373
B3413
Duloe
B3254
Trerulefoot
Widegates
A387
Hessenford
B3249
St Erney
St Stephens
MARY NEWMAN'S COTTAGE
St Budeaux
B3359
Sandplace
B3253
A374
St Germans
Polbathic
Morval
B3247
ANTONY HOUSE
St. Germans R.
P&R
MERCHANT'S HOUSE
Muchlarnick
Sheviock
A374
Pelynt
St Martin
Seaton
Torpoint
Ferry
Devonport
Plymouth
MONKEY SANCTUARY
Crafthole
Antony
Looe
East Looe
Downderry
Portwrinkle
OLD GUILDHALL
St John
Cremyll
MOUNT EDGCUMBE
ROYAL CITADEL
West Looe
Looe Bay
SOUTH WEST COAST PATH
B3247
Millbrook
Drake's I.
Portwallow
Freathy
Whitsand Bay
St George's or Looe I.
Kingsand
The Sound
Polperro
Talland Bay
HERITAGE MUS OF SMUGGLING & FISHING
Cawsand
Rame
Bovisand Bay
Penlee Pt.
Rame Hd.
Heybrook Bay
Great Mew Stone
C
5
ROSCOFF SANTANDER (Mar-Nov)

| 0 | 1 | 2 | 3 miles |
|---|---|---|---|

| 0 | 1 | 2 | 3 | 4 | 5 km |
|---|---|---|---|---|---|

2 3 | 2 | 3

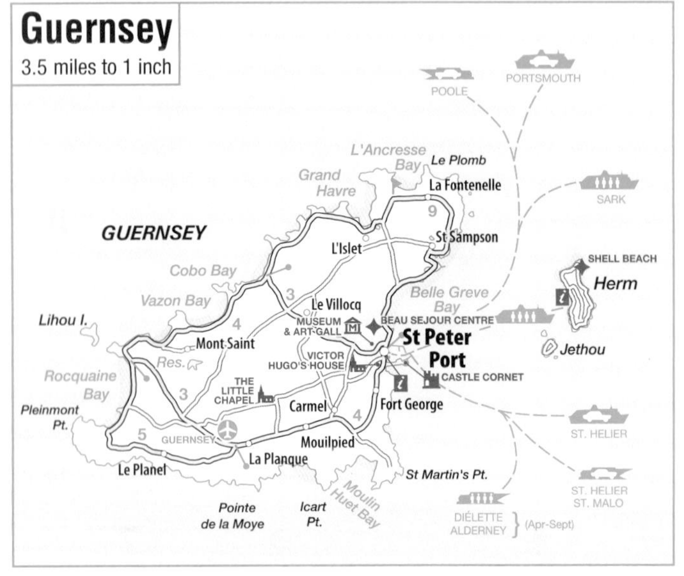


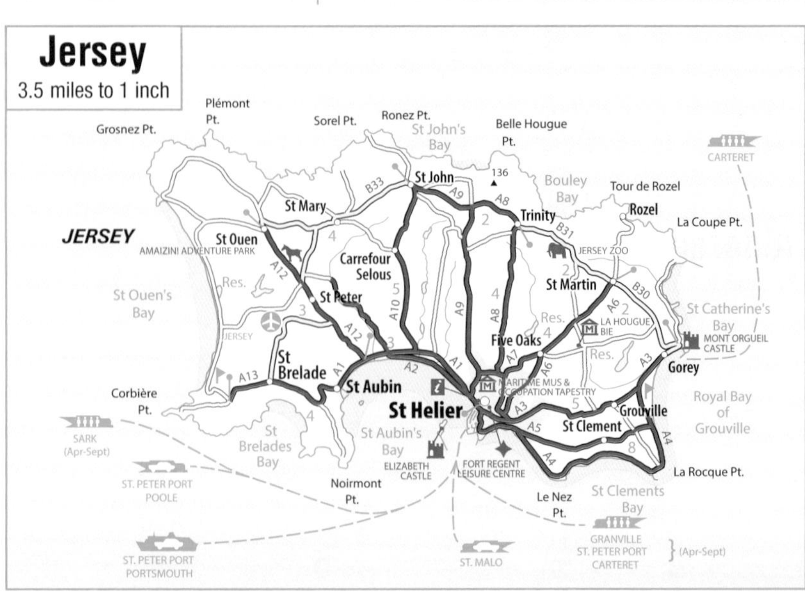

Poundsgate
Whiteworks
Walkhampton
Dousland
Burrator Res.
Sheepstor
Yelverton
Meavy
UPPER PLYM VALLEY
Clearbrook
Shaugh Prior
Bickleigh
Roborough
Wotter
Lee Moor
Plym Forest
Drakeland Corner
Lutton
Cornwood
Harford
DARTMOOR ZOOLOGICAL PARK
Eggbuckland
PLYM VALLEY RAILWAY
Plympton
Sparkwell
Lee Mill
Ivybridge
SALTRAM
Plymstock
Elburton
Hooe
Staddiscombe
Down Thomas
Knighton
Wembury
Wembury Bay
Worswell
Noss Mayo
Newton Ferrers
Battisborough Cross
Mothecombe
Holbeton
Luson
Brixton
Yealmpton
Ermington
Westlake
Modbury
Kingston
Ringmore
SOUTH WEST COAST PATH
Stoke Pt.
SX
Bigbury on Sea
Burgh I.
BIGBURY BAY
Bantham
Thurlestone
Buckland
Bigbury
St Ann's Chapel
Aveton Gifford
Churchstow
West Alvington
South Milton
Kingsbridge
Galmpton
Hope
Bolt Tail
Bolberry
Salcombe
Soar
SALCOMBE
OVERBECKS MUSEUM AND GARDEN
Bolt Hd.
East Portlemouth
East Prawle
Prawle Pt.
Malborough
Woolston
Charleton
Frogmore
Chillington
Stokenham
Kernborough
South Pool
Kellaton
South Allington
Sherford
Goveton
East Allington
Woodleigh
Loddiswell
Millcombe
Woodford
Halwell
Moreleigh
WOODLANDS FAMILY THEME PARK
Curtisknowle
Brownston
Crabadon
Harbertonford
Harberton
Diptford
Lincombe
Avonwick
North Huish
Ugborough
THE DONKEY SANCTUARY
Bittaford
Cheston
UGBOROUGH BEACON
South Brent
Tigley
Rattery
Didworthy
Ugborough Moor
Dean Prior
PENNYWELL FARM
DARTINGTON CIDER PRESS CENTRE
Dartington
Shinner's B
Cott
Dean
Buckfastleigh
Buckfast
BUCKFAST ABBEY
Landscove
BUCKFAST BUTTERFLIES & DARTMOOR OTTER SANCTUARY
Forder Grn.
Woodland
Ashburton
Holne
RIVER DART ADVENTURES
RYDER'S HILL
SHELL TOP
DENDLES WOOD
Alderney
3.5 miles to 1 inch
DIÉLETTE
ST. PETER PORT (Apr-Sept)
Quesnard Pt.
Braye
Brehou
Clonque Bay
Longis Bay
St Anne
ALDERNEY
Telegraph Bay
SOUTH

NEWTON ABBOT
West Ogwell
East Ogwell
Bradley
Wolborough
Decoy
Combeinteignhead
Netherton
Stokeinteignhead
Shaldon Wildlife Trust
South West Coast Path
Plant World
Babbacombe Bay
Coffinswell
Kingskerswell
Maidencombe
Abbotskerswell
Woodland
Denbury
Forder Grn.
Torbryan
Ipplepen
North Whilborough
Barton
Watcombe
Model Village
Babbacombe
Landscove
Broadhempston
Buckfast Butterflies & Dartmoor Otter Sanctuary
Shiphay
Compton
Compton Castle
Torquay
Kent's Cavern Prehistoric Caves
Staverton
Cockington
Torre
Torre Abbey
Wellswood
Hope's Nose
Dartington
Dartington Hall
Littlehempston
Marldon
Hollicombe
Dartington Cider Press Centre
Shinner's Bridge
Berry Pomeroy Castle
South Devon Railway
Blagdon
Torbay
Rattery
Cott
Totnes
Berry Pomeroy
Kirkham
Paignton
Castle
Tigley
Belsford
Collaton St Mary
Zoo
Dartmouth Steam Railway
TORBAY
Tor Bay
Harberton
Dart
Goodrington
Golden Hind
Ashprington
Brixham
Berry Head
Harbertonford
Stoke Gabriel
Galmpton
Churston Ferrers
Tuckenhay
Cornworthy
Greenway
St Mary's Bay
Crabadon
Washbourne
Dittisham
River Dart
Sharkham Pt.
Halwell
Allaleigh
Capton
Hillhead
SX
SY
Moreleigh
Woodlands Family Theme Park
Ferry
Dartmouth
Newcomen Engine House
Woodford
Blackawton
Kingswear
Scabbacombe Hd.
Millcombe
Warfleet
Coleton Fishacre
Bayards Cove Fort
Bowden
Dartmouth Castle
Mew Stone
East Allington
Stoke Fleming
Blackpool
Strete
Goveton
South West Coast Path
Harleston
Slapton
Sherford
Kingsbridge
Frittiscombe
Slapton Ley
Stokenham
Slapton Sands
Frogmore
Chillington
Torcross
Start Bay
Kernborough
Beeson
South Pool
Beesands
Kellaton
East Portlemouth
Hallsands
South Allington
Start Point
East Prawle
Lannacombe Bay
Prawle Pt.
Devon
A38
A383
A379
A3022
A380
A384
A381
A385
A3122
B3205
P&R
0 1 2 3 miles
0 1 2 3 4 5 km

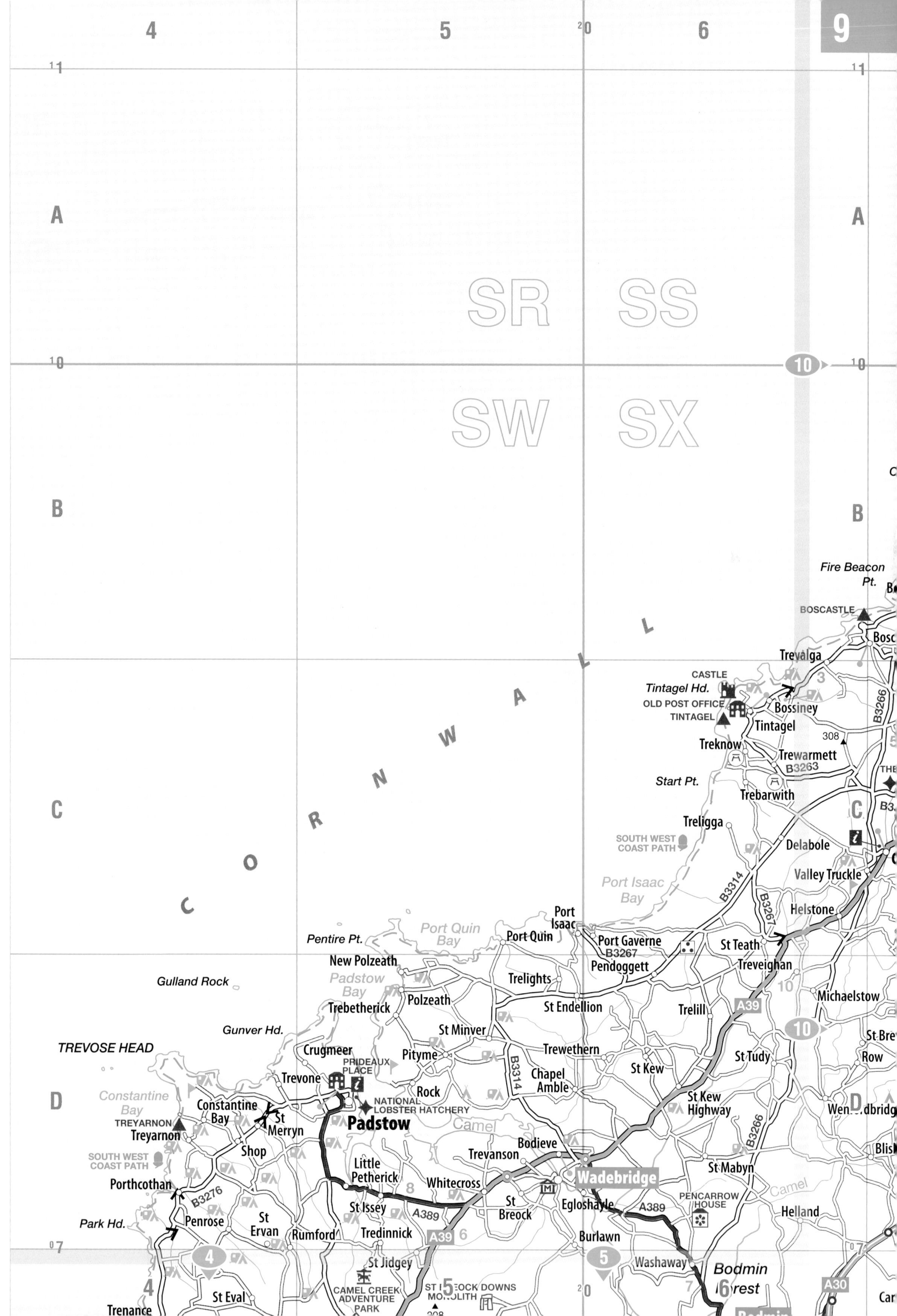

4
5
6
A
B
C
D
SR
SS
SW
SX
10
CORNWALL
Fire Beacon Pt.
BOSCASTLE
Trevalga
CASTLE
Tintagel Hd.
OLD POST OFFICE
TINTAGEL
Bossiney
Tintagel
Treknow
Trewarmett
B3263
B3266
Start Pt.
Trebarwith
Treligga
SOUTH WEST COAST PATH
Delabole
Valley Truckle
Port Isaac Bay
B3314
B3267
Helstone
Port Isaac
Port Quin Bay
Port Quin
Port Gaverne
Pendoggett
St Teath
Treveighan
Pentire Pt.
New Polzeath
Padstow Bay
Trelights
Gulland Rock
Polzeath
St Endellion
Trelill
A39
Michaelstow
Trebetherick
Gunver Hd.
St Minver
TREVOSE HEAD
Crugmeer
Pityme
Trewethern
St Kew
St Tudy
Row
PRIDEAUX PLACE
Trevone
Rock
Chapel Amble
B3314
Constantine Bay
NATIONAL LOBSTER HATCHERY
St Kew Highway
TREYARNON
Constantine Bay
St Merryn
Padstow
Camel
Treyarnon
Shop
Bodieve
Trevanson
SOUTH WEST COAST PATH
Little Petherick
Wadebridge
St Mabyn
Porthcothan
Whitecross
Egloshayle
PENCARROW HOUSE
B3276
St Issey
A389
St Breock
Helland
Park Hd.
Penrose
St Ervan
Rumford
Tredinnick
Burlawn
A39
Washaway
Bodmin Forest
St Jidgey
CAMEL CREEK ADVENTURE PARK
St Eval
Trenance
A30
308

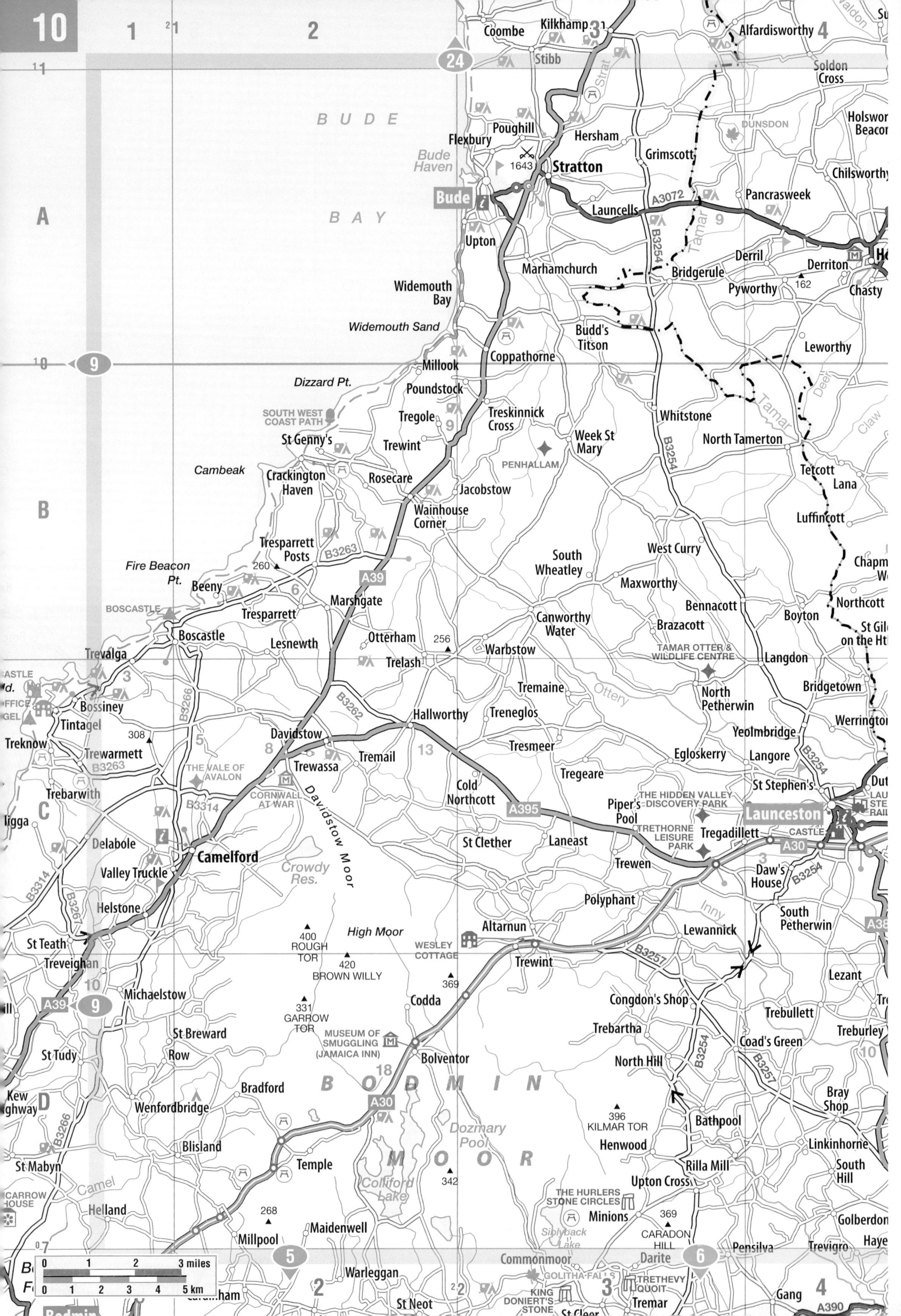

Coombe
Kilkhampton
Alfardisworthy
Stibb
Soldon Cross
BUDE
Poughill
Flexbury
Hersham
Grimscott
DUNSDON
Holsworthy Beacon
Bude Haven
1643
Stratton
Chilsworthy
Bude
Launcells
A3072
Pancrasweek
BAY
Tamar
Upton
B3254
Derril
Marhamchurch
Bridgerule
Derriton
Pyworthy
162
Chasty
Widemouth Bay
Widemouth Sand
Budd's Titson
Leworthy
Millook
Coppathorne
Dizzard Pt.
Poundstock
SOUTH WEST COAST PATH
Tregole
Treskinnick Cross
Whitstone
St Genny's
Trewint
Week St Mary
North Tamerton
Cambeak
PENHALLAM
Crackington Haven
Rosecare
Tetcott
Lana
Jacobstow
Wainhouse Corner
Luffincott
South Wheatley
West Curry
Trespartett Posts
B3263
Fire Beacon Pt.
260
Beeny
A39
Maxworthy
BOSCASTLE
Trespartett
Marshgate
Bennacott
Northcott
Canworthy Water
Boyton
Brazacott
Boscastle
Lesnewth
Otterham
256
Warbstow
TAMAR OTTER & WILDLIFE CENTRE
Trevalga
Trelash
Langdon
Tremaine
Bossiney
B3266
North Petherwin
Bridgetown
Tintagel
B3262
Hallworthy
Treneglos
Ottery
Treknow
308
Davidstow
Yeolmbridge
Werrington
Trewarmett
B3263
Tremail
Tresmeer
Egloskerry
Langore
Trewassa
THE VALE OF AVALON
Tregeare
B3254
Trebarwith
CORNWALL AT WAR
Davidstow Moor
Cold Northcott
THE HIDDEN VALLEY DISCOVERY PARK
St Stephen's
B3314
Piper's Pool
A395
Launceston
TRETHORNE LEISURE PARK
Tregadillett
CASTLE
Delabole
St Clether
Laneast
A30
Camelford
Crowdy Res.
Trewen
Daw's House
Valley Truckle
B3254
B3314
Polyphant
South Petherwin
Helstone
B3267
Inny
St Teath
High Moor
Altarnun
Lewannick
400 ROUGH TOR
WESLEY COTTAGE
Treveighan
420 BROWN WILLY
Trewint
B3257
Lezant
369
Michaelstow
A39
331 GARROW TOR
Codda
Congdon's Shop
Trebullett
St Breward
MUSEUM OF SMUGGLING (JAMAICA INN)
Trebartha
Treburley
St Tudy
Row
Bolventor
Coad's Green
North Hill
B3254
B3257
BODMIN
Bradford
Bray Shop
Kew Highway
Wenfordbridge
A30
396 KILMAR TOR
Bathpool
B3266
Dozmary Pool
Henwood
Linkinhorne
Blisland
MOOR
St Mabyn
Temple
Rilla Mill
South Hill
342
Colliford Lake
Upton Cross
Camel
THE HURLERS STONE CIRCLES
Helland
268
Minions
369
Golberdon
Maidenwell
CARADON HILL
Millpool
Siblyback Lake
Pensilva
Trevigro
Commonmoor
Darite
Warleggan
GOLITHA FALLS
TRETHEVY QUOIT
KING DONIERT'S STONE
Tremar
St Neot
Gang
A390
0 1 2 3 miles
0 1 2 3 4 5 km

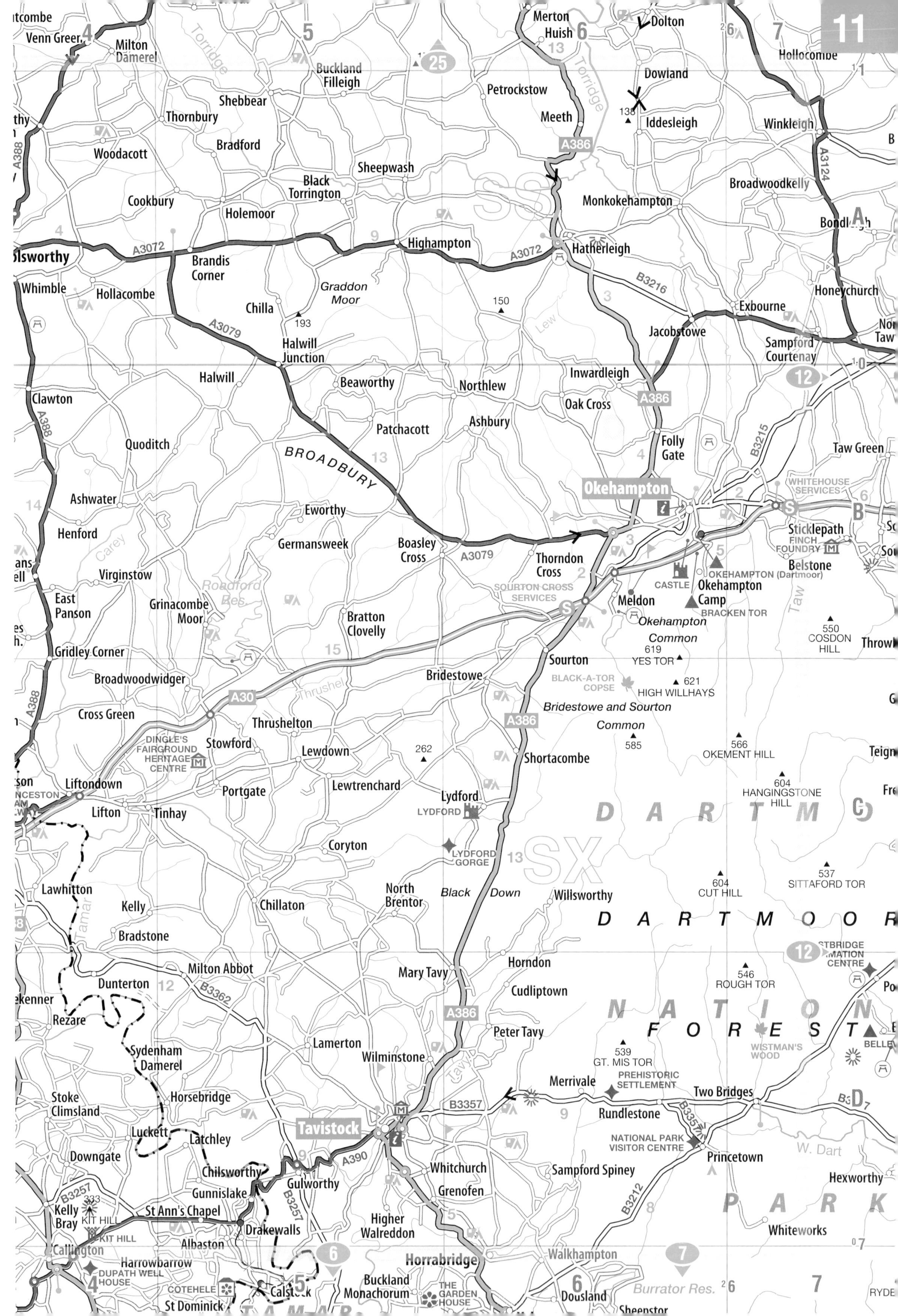

Merton
Huish
Dolton
Hollocombe
Milton Damerel
Venn Green
Buckland Filleigh
Petrockstow
Dowland
Shebbear
Thornbury
Meeth
Iddesleigh
Winkleigh
Bradford
Woodacott
Sheepwash
Black Torrington
Broadwoodkelly
Cookbury
Holemoor
Monkokehampton
Bondleigh
Highampton
Hatherleigh
Brandis Corner
Whimble
Hollacombe
Graddon Moor
Chilla
Exbourne
Honeychurch
Jacobstowe
Halwill Junction
Sampford Courtenay
Halwill
Beaworthy
Northlew
Inwardleigh
Clawton
Oak Cross
Patchacott
Ashbury
Quoditch
Folly Gate
BROADBURY
Taw Green
Okehampton
Ashwater
Eworthy
WHITEHOUSE SERVICES
Henford
Germansweek
Boasley Cross
Sticklepath
FINCH FOUNDRY
Thorndon Cross
Belstone
Virginstow
Roadford Res.
SOURTON CROSS SERVICES
CASTLE
OKEHAMPTON (Dartmoor)
East Panson
Grinacombe Moor
Bratton Clovelly
Meldon
Okehampton Camp
BRACKEN TOR
Okehampton Common
Gridley Corner
COSDON HILL
YES TOR
Sourton
Broadwoodwidger
Bridestowe
BLACK-A-TOR COPSE
HIGH WILLHAYS
Thrushel
Cross Green
Bridestowe and Sourton Common
Thrushelton
DINGLE'S FAIRGROUND HERITAGE CENTRE
Stowford
Lewdown
Shortacombe
OKEMENT HILL
Liftondown
Portgate
Lewtrenchard
Lydford
HANGINGSTONE HILL
Lifton
Tinhay
LYDFORD
DARTMOOR
Coryton
LYDFORD GORGE
Lawhitton
Tamar
Chillaton
North Brentor
Black Down
Wilsworthy
CUT HILL
SITTAFORD TOR
Kelly
Bradstone
Horndon
Milton Abbot
Dunterton
Mary Tavy
ROUGH TOR
Cudliptown
Rezare
NATIONAL FOREST PARK
Sydenham Damerel
Lamerton
Peter Tavy
Wilminstone
GT. MIS TOR
WISTMAN'S WOOD
Merrivale
PREHISTORIC SETTLEMENT
Two Bridges
Stoke Climsland
Horsebridge
Tavistock
Rundlestone
Luckett
Latchley
NATIONAL PARK VISITOR CENTRE
Downgate
Whitchurch
Sampford Spiney
Princetown
W. Dart
Chilsworthy
Gulworthy
Hexworthy
Grenofen
Gunnislake
Kelly Bray
KIT HILL
St Ann's Chapel
Drakewalls
Higher Walreddon
Whiteworks
Albaston
Callington
Harrowbarrow
DUPATH WELL HOUSE
Horrabridge
Walkhampton
Burrator Res.
COTEHELE
Calstock
Buckland Monachorum
THE GARDEN HOUSE
Dousland
Sheepstor
St Dominick
SS
SX
A386
A3072
A3079
A30
A388
A3124
B3216
B3215
B3362
B3357
B3212
B3257
A390

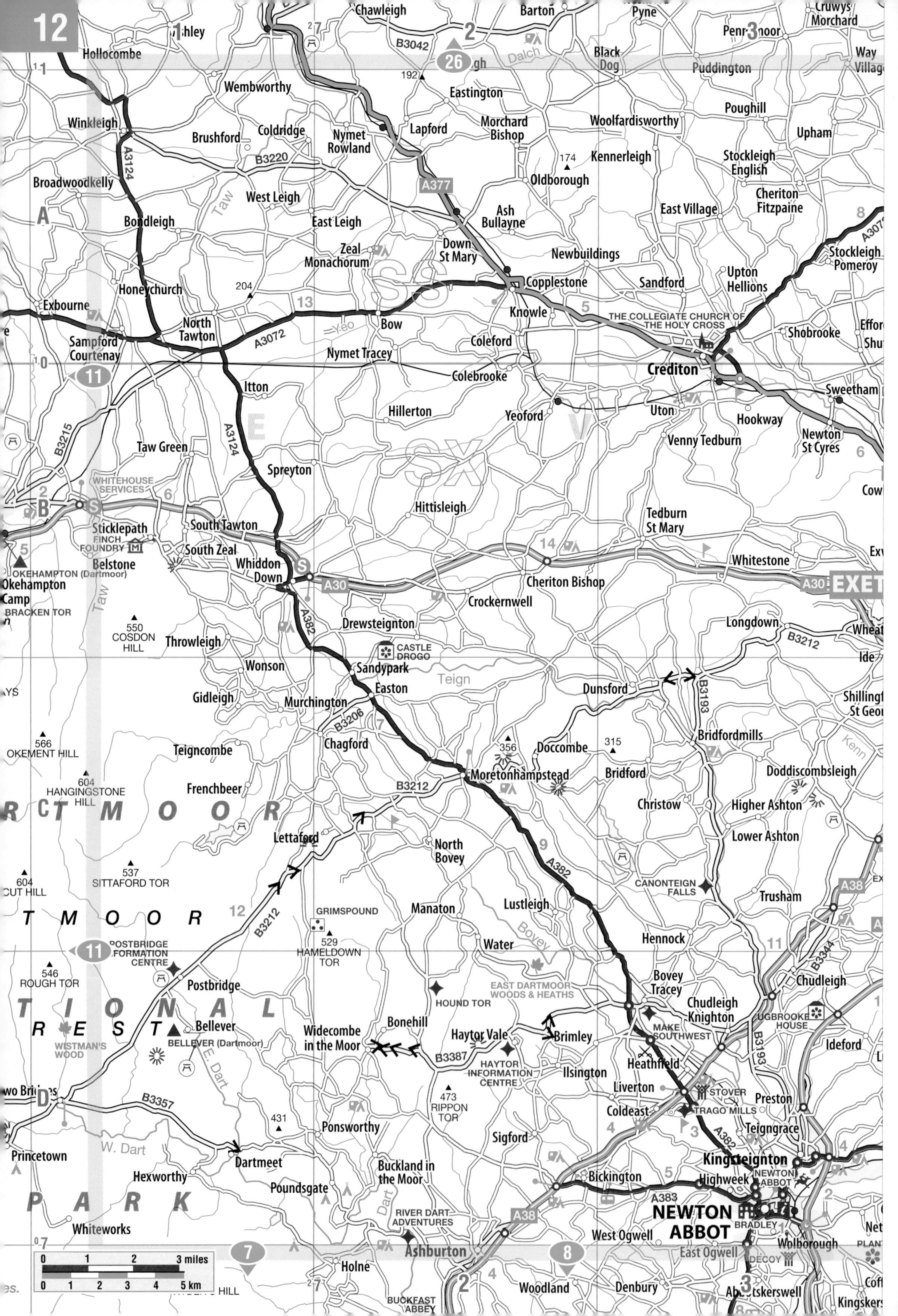
Chawleigh
Barton
Pyne
Cruwys Morchard
Hollocombe
B3042
26
Dalch
Black Dog
Puddington
Way Village
Wembworthy
Eastington
Poughill
Winkleigh
Brushford
Coldridge
Nymet Rowland
Lapford
Morchard Bishop
Woolfardisworthy
Upham
B3220
A3124
174
Kennerleigh
Stockleigh English
Broadwoodkelly
West Leigh
Taw
A377
Oldborough
Cheriton Fitzpaine
Bondleigh
East Leigh
Ash Bullayne
East Village
Zeal Monachorum
Down St Mary
Newbuildings
Stockleigh Pomeroy
A3072
Honeychurch
204
Copplestone
Sandford
Upton Hellions
Exbourne
13
Knowle
THE COLLEGIATE CHURCH OF THE HOLY CROSS
Shobrooke
North Tawton
Bow
Yeo
Sampford Courtenay
A3072
Coleford
Nymet Tracey
Crediton
Colebrooke
11
Sweetham
Itton
Hillerton
Yeoford
Uton
Hookway
B3215
A3124
Venny Tedburn
Newton St Cyres
Taw Green
SX
Spreyton
WHITEHOUSE SERVICES
Hittisleigh
Sticklepath
FINCH FOUNDRY
South Tawton
Tedburn St Mary
South Zeal
Belstone
Whiddon Down
14
Whitestone
OKEHAMPTON (Dartmoor)
Okehampton Camp
A30
Cheriton Bishop
EXETER
Crockernwell
BRACKEN TOR
Drewsteignton
Longdown
550 COSDON HILL
Throwleigh
A382
CASTLE DROGO
B3212
Ide
Wonson
Sandypark
Teign
Gidleigh
Easton
Dunsford
Murchington
B3193
Shillingford St George
B3206
566 OKEMENT HILL
Teigncombe
Chagford
356
Doccombe
315
Bridfordmills
Kenn
604 HANGINGSTONE HILL
Frenchbeer
Moretonhampstead
Bridford
Doddiscombsleigh
B3212
DARTMOOR
Christow
Higher Ashton
Lettaford
North Bovey
Lower Ashton
537 SITTAFORD TOR
604 CUT HILL
A382
CANONTEIGN FALLS
A38
Trusham
GRIMSPOUND
Manaton
Lustleigh
12
B3212
529 HAMELDOWN TOR
Water
Bovey
Hennock
POSTBRIDGE INFORMATION CENTRE
B3344
546 ROUGH TOR
Postbridge
EAST DARTMOOR WOODS & HEATHS
Bovey Tracey
Chudleigh
HOUND TOR
Chudleigh Knighton
NATIONAL PARK
FOREST
Bellever
UGBROOKE HOUSE
WISTMAN'S WOOD
BELLEVER (Dartmoor)
Widecombe in the Moor
Bonehill
Haytor Vale
Brimley
MAKE SOUTHWEST
Ideford
E. Dart
B3387
HAYTOR INFORMATION CENTRE
Ilsington
Heathfield
B3193
Two Bridges
473 RIPPON TOR
Liverton
STOVER
Preston
B3357
TRAGO MILLS
431
Coldeast
Ponsworthy
Teigngrace
Princetown
W. Dart
Sigford
A382
Dartmeet
Kingsteignton
Hexworthy
Buckland in the Moor
Bickington
Highweek
NEWTON ABBOT
Poundsgate
A383
PARK
Dart
RIVER DART ADVENTURES
A38
NEWTON ABBOT
Whiteworks
BRADLEY
7
Ashburton
8
West Ogwell
Wolborough
East Ogwell
DECOY
Holne
0 1 2 3 miles
0 1 2 3 4 5 km
Woodland
Denbury
Abbotskerswell
BUCKFAST ABBEY
Kingskerswell

Cotteylands
Tiverton
Ash Thomas
Craddock
HACKPEN HILL
Smithincott
Ashill
Bolham Water
Abbey
Smeatharpe
Well Town
Willand
Blackborough
Cadeleigh
Butterleigh
BICKLEIGH MILL
DEVON RAILWAY CENTRE
BICKLEIGH CASTLE
Bickleigh
CULLOMPTON SERVICES
Cullompton
A373
Kentisbeare
Sheldon
Dunkeswell
Upottery
BLACK DOWN
Luppitt
Rawridge
Cadbury
FURSDON HOUSE
Colebrook
Dulford
Kerswell
Beacon
Mutterton
Bradninch
Westcott
Norman's Green
Broadhembury
Wick
Monkton
Silverton
Thorverton
Up Exe
Hele
Langford
Clyst Hydon
Plymtree
Payhembury
Combe Raleigh
Ellerhayes
Tale
Awliscombe
Nether Exe
Colestocks
Buckerell
Clyst St Lawrence
KILLERTON HOUSE
Honiton
Offwell
Brampford Speke
Rewe
Budlake
Westwood
Talaton
Feniton
A30
WILDWOOD ESCOT
Fenny Bridges
Gittisham
Alfington
Stoke Canon
M5
Broadclyst
Whimple
Upton Pyne
Poltimore
Fairmile
Church Green
Dog Village
Jack in the Green
Ottery St Mary
North
Cranbrook
Rockbeare
B3174
Farway
Pinhoe
Clyst Honiton
EXETER INTERNATIONAL
West Hill
Broad Down
Whipton
CATHEDRAL
Marsh Green
Wiggaton
Heavitree
Sowton
EXETER SERVICES
Tipton St John
Sidbury
BLACKBURY CAMP
St Thomas
Clyst St Mary
Aylesbeare
Venn Ottery
Countess Wear
Farringdon
Harcombe
Alphington
CREALY GREAT ADVENTURE PARK
Harpford
Bowd
Sidford
BEER QUARRY CAVES
Clyst St George
Woodbury Salterton
Newton Poppleford
Weston
Vicarage
THE DONKEY SANCTUARY
Hawkerland
Sid
Salcombe Regis
Branscombe
Topsham
MUS.
Ebford
Woodbury
Cotmaton
Exminster
Colaton Raleigh
DORSET & EAST DEVON COAST WORLD HERITAGE SITE
Kennford
Exton
Sidmouth
BICTON PARK
River Exe
Kenn
BLACK HILL
Yettington
Otterton
Ladram Bay
Powderham
Lympstone
OTTERTON MILL
East Budleigh
POWDERHAM CASTLE
Kenton
Withycombe Raleigh
Knowle
SOUTH WEST COAST PATH
Starcross
Budleigh Salterton
Danger Pt.
Littleham
FAIRLYNCH ARTS CENTRE AND MUSEUM
Cockwood
Exmouth
WORLD OF COUNTRY LIFE
Ashcombe
DAWLISH WARREN
DAWLISH
Straight Pt.
Dawlish Warren
SX
Dawlish
Little Haldon
SY
Holcombe
Bishopsteignton
Teignmouth
Teign
Shaldon
SHALDON WILDLIFE TRUST
Combeinteignhead
SOUTH WEST COAST PATH
Stokeinteignhead
BABBACOMBE BAY
Maidencombe

Bolham Water
Smeatharpe
Abbey
Marsh
Whitestaunton
Combe St Nicholas
Wadeford
Cricket Malherbie
Chillington
Cudworth
St George
A303
28
Newcott
Howley
A30
Chaffcombe
Cricket St Thomas
Crewkerne
Hewish
B3165
Dunkeswell
Yarcombe
Wambrook
Chard
Upottery
261
B3162
Whatley
Wayford
Forton
Winsham
Clapton
Luppitt
Rawridge
A30
Tatworth
Seaborough
H I L L S
Beacon
South Chard
Drimpton
A
Stockland
Furley
FORDE ABBEY AND GARDENS
Millhayes
Chardstock
B3167
Wick
261
Tytherleigh
Thorncombe
Burstock
Monkton
Membury
B3162
Combe Raleigh
Heathstock
Alston
Holditch
Cotleigh
Churchill
A358
REDLANDS YARD
Ham
218
Yarty
B3165
277
Dalwood
Smallridge
Birdsmoorgate
B3164
Hawkchurch
Wilmington
Axe
Marshalsea
Bettiscombe
Honiton
Offwell
BURROW FARM
Weycroft
13
254
AXE VALLEY WILDLIFE PARK
Axminster
Marshwood
Pilsdon
A35
223
256
A375
Shute
Kilmington
B3261
Broad Oak
Church Green
A358
Wootton Fitzpaine
Whitchurch Canonicorum
Northleigh
Farway
Whitford
E A S T D E V O N
Ryall
Char
B
Musbury
Morcombelake
Southleigh
Colyton
B3165
Broad Down
Charmouth
Symondsbury
Uplyme
Colyford
Combpyne
CHARMOUTH HERITAGE COAST CENTRE
A35
Chideock
BLACKBURY CAMP
A3052
Lyme Regis
B3172
Eype
Axmouth
Rousdon
AQUARIUM
Seatown
Harcombe
SEATON TRAMWAY
DINOSAURLAND
155
SOUTH WEST COAST PATH
B3174
dford
A3052
AXMOUTH TO LYME REGIS UNDERCLIFFS
BEER QUARRY CAVES
BEER
Charlton Bay
Weston
Vicarage
Seaton
THE DONKEY SANCTUARY
SOUTH WEST COAST PATH
Beer
MARINE HOUSE
L Y M E B A Y
Salcombe Regis
Branscombe
Seaton Bay
DORSET & EAST DEVON COAST WORLD HERITAGE SITE
Beer Hd.
uth
C
13
D
0 1 2 3 miles
0 1 2 3 4 5 km
2
3
4

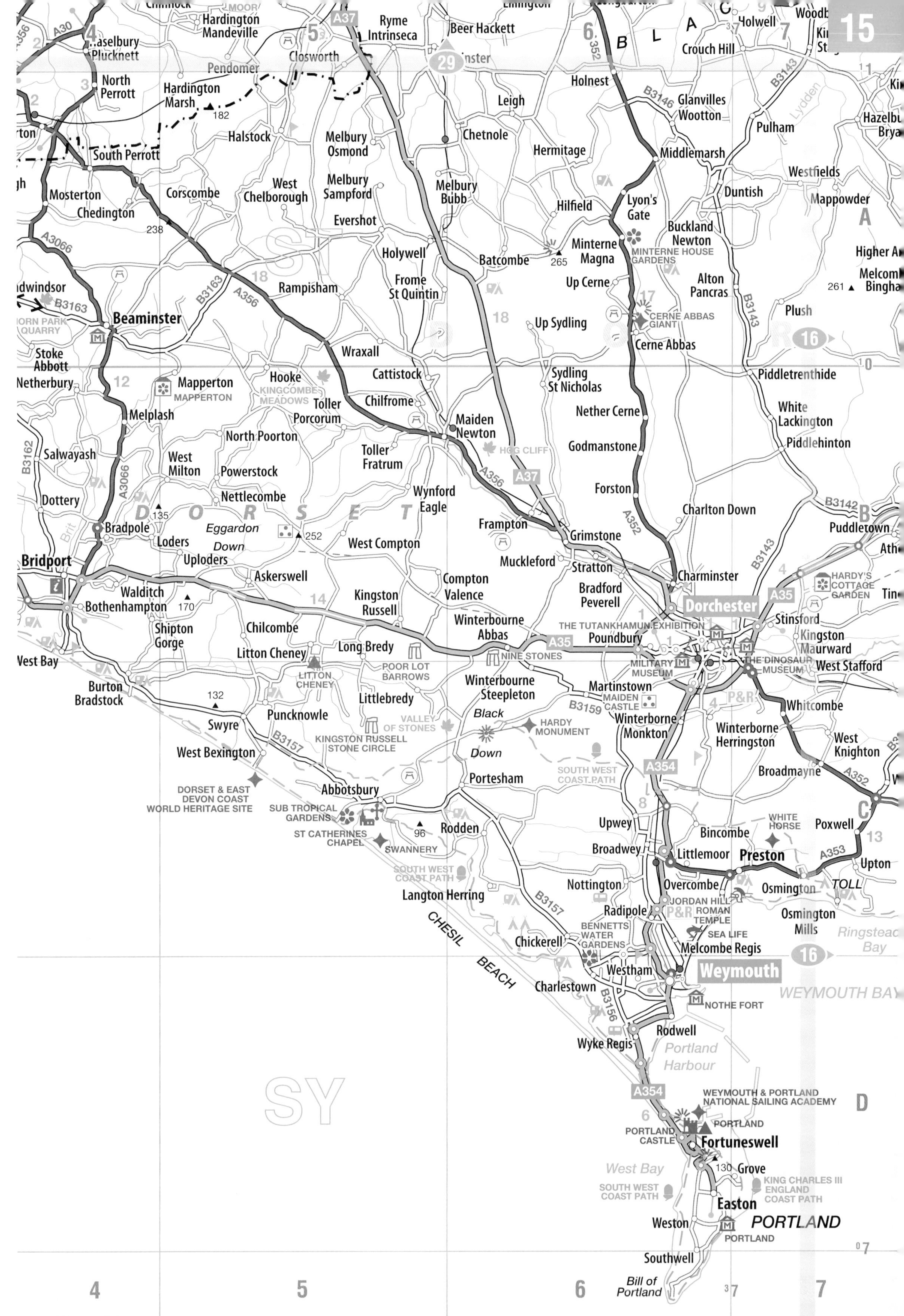
Hardington Mandeville
Ryme Intrinseca
Beer Hackett
Holwell
Crouch Hill
Haselbury Plucknett
Closworth
North Perrott
Hardington Marsh
Pendomer
Holnest
Leigh
Glanvilles Wootton
Pulham
Halstock
Melbury Osmond
Chetnole
Hermitage
Middlemarsh
South Perrott
Mosterton
Corscombe
West Chelborough
Melbury Sampford
Melbury Bubb
Hilfield
Lyon's Gate
Duntish
Westfields
Mappowder
Chedington
Evershot
Buckland Newton
Minterne Magna
MINTERNE HOUSE GARDENS
Holywell
Batcombe
Higher Ansty
Alton Pancras
Up Cerne
Frome St Quintin
Rampisham
Beaminster
Plush
Up Sydling
CERNE ABBAS GIANT
Cerne Abbas
Stoke Abbott
Wraxall
Netherbury
Mapperton
MAPPERTON
Hooke
KINGCOMBE MEADOWS
Cattistock
Sydling St Nicholas
Piddletrenthide
Toller Porcorum
Chilfrome
Melplash
Maiden Newton
Nether Cerne
White Lackington
North Poorton
Salwayash
West Milton
Powerstock
Toller Fratrum
HOG CLIFF
Godmanstone
Piddlehinton
Dottery
Nettlecombe
Wynford Eagle
Forston
Charlton Down
DORSET
Bradpole
Eggardon Down
Frampton
Puddletown
Loders
Grimstone
Uploders
West Compton
Bridport
Askerswell
Muckleford
Stratton
Charminster
Walditch
Compton Valence
Kingston Russell
Bradford Peverell
HARDY'S COTTAGE GARDEN
Bothenhampton
Dorchester
Shipton Gorge
Chilcombe
Winterbourne Abbas
THE TUTANKHAMUN EXHIBITION
Stinsford
Poundbury
Kingston Maurward
West Bay
Litton Cheney
Long Bredy
NINE STONES
POOR LOT BARROWS
MILITARY MUSEUM
THE DINOSAUR MUSEUM
West Stafford
Burton Bradstock
LITTON CHENEY
Littlebredy
Winterbourne Steepleton
Martinstown
MAIDEN CASTLE
Whitcombe
Swyre
Puncknowle
VALLEY OF STONES
Black Down
HARDY MONUMENT
Winterborne Monkton
Winterborne Herrington
West Knighton
West Bexington
KINGSTON RUSSELL STONE CIRCLE
SOUTH WEST COAST PATH
Broadmayne
Portesham
DORSET & EAST DEVON COAST WORLD HERITAGE SITE
Abbotsbury
SUB TROPICAL GARDENS
Upwey
WHITE HORSE
Poxwell
ST CATHERINES CHAPEL
SWANNERY
Rodden
Bincombe
Broadwey
Littlemoor
Preston
Upton
Nottington
Overcombe
Osmington
TOLL
Langton Herring
JORDAN HILL ROMAN TEMPLE
Radipole
Osmington Mills
CHESIL BEACH
BENNETTS WATER GARDENS
Chickerell
SEA LIFE
Ringstead Bay
Melcombe Regis
Westham
Weymouth
Charlestown
WEYMOUTH BAY
NOTHE FORT
Rodwell
Wyke Regis
Portland Harbour
SY
WEYMOUTH & PORTLAND NATIONAL SAILING ACADEMY
PORTLAND
PORTLAND CASTLE
Fortuneswell
West Bay
Grove
KING CHARLES III ENGLAND COAST PATH
Easton
Weston
PORTLAND
Southwell
Bill of Portland
A37
A356
A3066
A35
A352
A354
A353
B3163
B3162
B3146
B3143
B3142
B3159
B3157
B3156
29
16

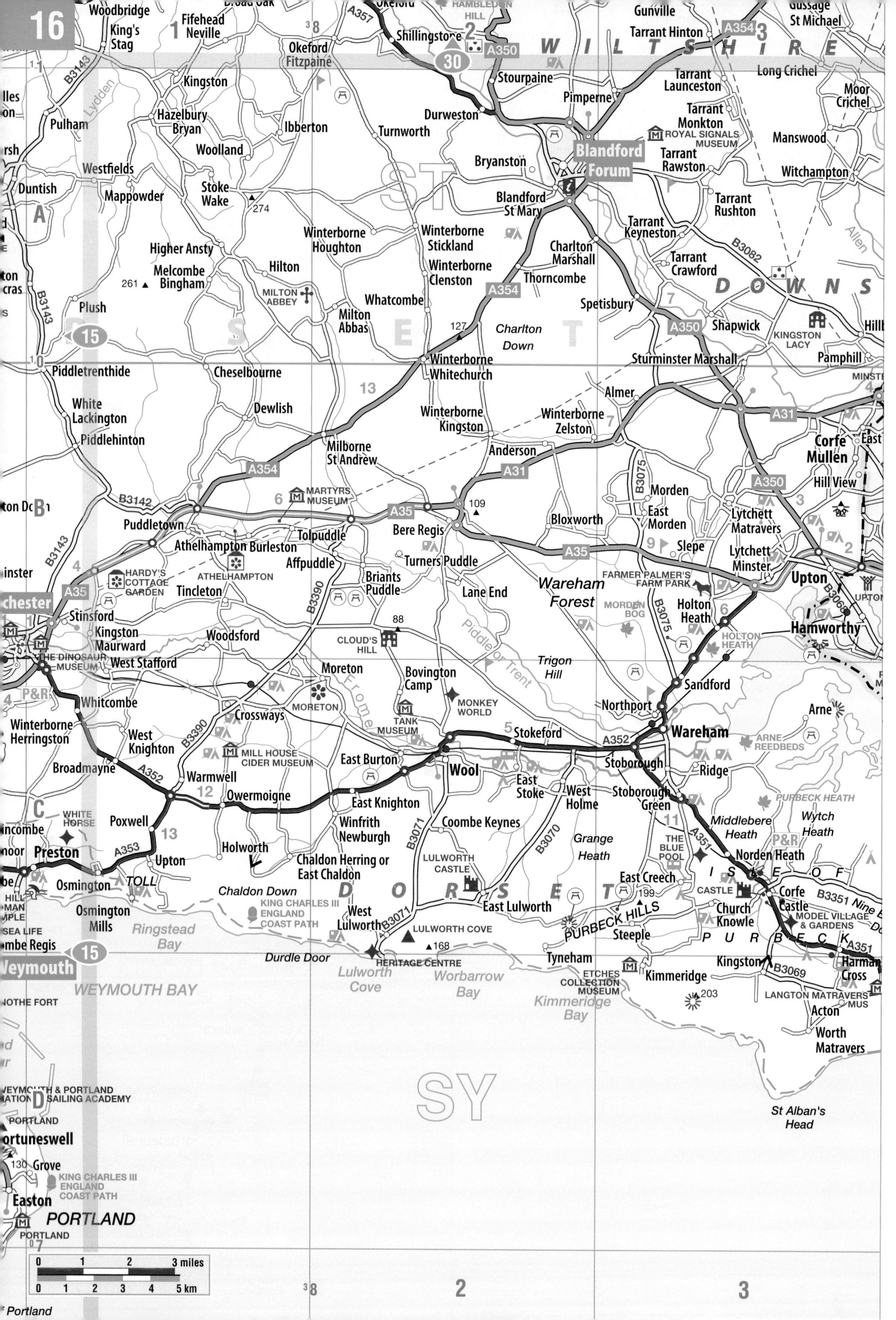
Woodbridge
King's Stag
Fifehead Neville
Okeford Fitzpaine
Shillingstone
HAMBLEDON HILL
Gunville
Tarrant Hinton
Gussage St Michael
W I L T S H I R E
A357
A350
A354
30
Kingston
Stourpaine
Tarrant Launceston
Long Crichel
Moor Crichel
B3143
Lydden
Pulham
Hazelbury Bryan
Ibberton
Turnworth
Durweston
Pimperne
Tarrant Monkton
ROYAL SIGNALS MUSEUM
Manswood
Woolland
Bryanston
Blandford Forum
Tarrant Rawston
Witchampton
Westfields
Duntish
Mappowder
Stoke Wake
274
Blandford St Mary
Tarrant Rushton
Winterborne Houghton
Winterborne Stickland
Tarrant Keyneston
Higher Ansty
Charlton Marshall
Allen
Melcombe Bingham
Hilton
Winterborne Clenston
Tarrant Crawford
B3082
261
Thorncombe
MILTON ABBEY
Whatcombe
Spetisbury
D O W N S
Plush
Milton Abbas
Charlton Down
127
Shapwick
KINGSTON LACY
15
Winterborne Whitechurch
Sturminster Marshall
Pamphill
Piddletrenthide
Cheselbourne
13
White Lackington
Dewlish
Almer
Winterborne Kingston
Winterborne Zelston
A31
Corfe Mullen
Piddlehinton
Milborne St Andrew
Anderson
B3075
Hill View
MARTYRS MUSEUM
109
Morden
B3142
A35
Puddletown
Bloxworth
East Morden
Lytchett Matravers
Tolpuddle
Bere Regis
Athelhampton
Burleston
Slepe
Lytchett Minster
Affpuddle
Turners Puddle
HARDY'S COTTAGE GARDEN
ATHELHAMPTON
Briants Puddle
Wareham Forest
FARMER PALMER'S FARM PARK
Upton
Tincleton
Lane End
Stinsford
B3390
88
MORDEN BOG
Holton Heath
Hamworthy
Kingston Maurward
Woodsford
CLOUD'S HILL
Piddle or Trent
HOLTON HEATH
THE DINOSAUR MUSEUM
West Stafford
Trigon Hill
Moreton
Bovington Camp
Sandford
P&R
Whitcombe
MORETON
MONKEY WORLD
Northport
Arne
Crossways
TANK MUSEUM
Frome
Winterborne Herrington
West Knighton
Stokeford
Wareham
A352
ARNE REEDBEDS
MILL HOUSE CIDER MUSEUM
East Burton
Wool
Stoborough
Ridge
Broadmayne
Warmwell
East Stoke
West Holme
Stoborough Green
PURBECK HEATH
Owermoigne
East Knighton
WHITE HORSE
Poxwell
Winfrith Newburgh
Coombe Keynes
Middlebere Heath
Wytch Heath
B3071
B3070
Grange Heath
THE BLUE POOL
A351
Preston
A353
Upton
Holworth
Chaldon Herring or East Chaldon
LULWORTH CASTLE
Norden Heath
Osmington
TOLL
East Creech
Chaldon Down
CASTLE
Corfe Castle
D O R S E T
199
B3351
Osmington Mills
KING CHARLES III ENGLAND COAST PATH
West Lulworth
East Lulworth
PURBECK HILLS
Church Knowle
MODEL VILLAGE & GARDENS
Ringstead Bay
LULWORTH COVE
Steeple
P U R B E C K
SEA LIFE
168
Tyneham
Kingston
A351
Weymouth
Durdle Door
HERITAGE CENTRE
B3069
Harmans Cross
WEYMOUTH BAY
Lulworth Cove
Worbarrow Bay
ETCHES COLLECTION MUSEUM
Kimmeridge
203
LANGTON MATRAVERS MUS
NOTHE FORT
Kimmeridge Bay
Acton
Worth Matravers
SY
WEYMOUTH & PORTLAND NATIONAL SAILING ACADEMY
St Alban's Head
PORTLAND
130
Grove
KING CHARLES III ENGLAND COAST PATH
Easton
PORTLAND
0 1 2 3 miles
0 1 2 3 4 5 km
38
2
3
Portland

17
St Giles
Cripplestyle
Edmondsham Ho
Edmondsham
Charing Cross
Hungerford
North Gorley
South Gorley
Broomy Lodge
Stoney Cross
Minstead
Newtown
Knowlton Church
Gussage All Saints
Dorset Heavy Horse Farm Park
Knowlton
Verwood
Ibsley
Mockbeggar
Linwood
Woodlands
Ringwood Forest
Moyles Court
Rockford
Emery Down
Forest
Horton
Chalbury Common
Chalbury
Blashford
Linford
New Forest Reptile Centre
Bank
Mannington
Three Legged Cross
Moors Valley
Picket Post
Burley Lodge
Hinton Martell
Gaunt's Common
Ashley
Ringwood
Stanbridge
Holt
Holt Heath
Ashley Heath
St Ives
St Leonards Services
Moortown
Liberty's Owl, Raptor & Reptile Centre
Burley Street
New Forest
Burley
Bisterne Close
New Park
Lymington
Broom Hill
West Moors
Avon Heath
St Leonards
Brockenhurst
Clapgate
Colehill
Canford Bottom
Matchams
Kingston
Kingston Great Common
Walford Mill
Wimborne Minster
Stapehill
Trickett's Cross
Knoll Gdns
Ferndown
Hampreston
Longham
West Parley
Thorney Hill
Avon
Ripley
Sway
Wootton
Oakley
Canford Magna
Merley
Bournemouth
Parley Cross
Bransgore
Bashley
Bearwood
Bear Cross
Hurn
Adventure Wonderland
Kinson
Ensbury
Sopley
Neacroft
Beckley
Golden Hill
Mount Pleasant
Hordle
Buckland
Broadstone
Canford Heath
Holdenhurst
Winkton
Godwinscroft
Hinton
New Milton
Sammy Miller's Motorcycle Mus
Bournemouth, Christchurch & Poole
Moordown
Jumpers Green
Burton
Walkford
Highcliffe
Ashley
Everton
Lymington
Waterloo
Talbot Village
Newtown
Winton
Red House Mus
Somerford
Old Milton
Downton
Lymore
Branksome
Pokesdown
Purewell
Highcliffe Castle
Barton on Sea
Christchurch
Priory Church
Wick
Mudeford
Parkstone
Westbourne
Boscombe
Southbourne
Christchurch Bay
Milford on Sea
Lilliput
Branksome Park
Russell-Cotes Mus
Poole
Poole Museum
Bournemouth
Visitor Centre
Hengistbury Head
Canford Cliffs
Compton Acres
Oceanarium
Poole Harbour
Brownsea I.
Brownsea Island
Sandbanks
Poole Bay
Ferry
Toll
Totland Bay
Studland Beach and Nature Reserve
Studland Bay
SZ
Alum Bay
The Needles
The Needles Old Battery
Newton Heath
Purbeck Heath
Studland
The Foreland
South West Coast Path
Ulwell
New Swanage
Cherbourg
Swanage Bay
Swanage
Swanage Railway
Langton Matravers
Peveril Pt.
Swanage
Durlston
Durlston Head
Guernsey Jersey St. Malo
Tilly Whim Caves
D
4
5
6

SOUTHAMPTON
32
Minstead
Woodlands
Ashurst
Newtown
LONGDOWN ACTIVITY FARM
Pooksgreen
SEA CITY MUS
Northam
TOLL
Sholing
Itchen
Woolston
Hamble
MANOR FARM
Burridge
Curbridge
WHITELEY VILLAGE
Old Netley
Lowford
NETLEY ABBEY
Bursledon
Lower Swanwick
Swanwick
Netley
Hound
HOLLY HILL WOODLAND PARK
Park Gate
Locks Heath
ABBEY
ROYAL VICTORIA
Hamble-le-Rice
ST ANDREWS
Warsash
Titchfield
Newtown
NEW FOREST WILDLIFE PARK
Emery Down
Lyndhurst
NEW FOREST CENTRE
NEW FOREST REPTILE CENTRE
Clayhill
Bank
Denny Lodge
Dibden
Hythe
Dibden Purlieu
SOUTHAMPTON WATER
Buttsash
Hardley
Holbury
Beaulieu Heath
New Park
Balmerlawn
Hill Top
Fawley
Ashlett
PALACE HO
NATIONAL MOTOR MUS
ABBEY
Beaulieu
Blackfield
Fawley Waterside
CALSHOT CASTLE
CALSHOT ACTIVITIES CENTRE
Calshot
Langley
Hill Head
Lee-on-the-Solent
TITCHFIELD HAVEN
Brockenhurst
Hatchet Gate
East Boldre
Setley
Beaulieu Heath
EXBURY
Exbury
Bucklers Hard
MARITIME MUSEUM
LEPE
Lepe
Stone Pt.
Battramsley
Bull Hill
Sway
Boldre
Pilley
Norleywood
East End
Portmore
Mount Pleasant
NORTH SOLENT
Needs Ore Pt.
Golden Hill
Hordle
Buckland
Walhampton
LYMINGTON
Pennington
Waterford
Woodside
Everton
Milton
Downton
BRAXTON
Lymore
Lower Pennington
KEYHAVEN & PENNINGTON MARSHES
Milford on Sea
Keyhaven
HURST CASTLE
Sconce Pt.
FORT VICTORIA
ISLAND PLANETARIUM
Colwell Bay
Norton
Yarmouth
Totland
Totland Bay
TOTLAND BAY
Pound Green
Norton Green
Freshwater
Freshwater Bay
Afton
DIMBOLA LODGE
Alum Bay
The Needles
THE NEEDLES PARK
THE NEEDLES OLD BATTERY
Freshwater Bay
Hamstead
Cranmore
Thorley Street
Ningwood
Wellow
Newbridge
CALBOURNE WATER MILL
Calbourne
Shalcombe
OLD TOWN HALL
Newtown
Shalfleet
NEWTOWN HARBOUR
Newtown Bay
Porchfield
Cowes
MARITIME MUSEUM
East Cowes
OSBORNE HOUSE
Gurnard Bay
Gurnard
Rew Street
Northwood
Thorness Bay
Whippingham
Medina
Parkhurst
Parkhurst Forest
Wootton Bridge
Wootton Common
BUTTERFLY WORLD
Staplers
Hunny Hill
NEWPORT
ROMAN VILLA
Shide
Gunville
Carisbrooke
Clatterford
CARISBROOKE CASTLE
Bowcombe
ARRETON MANOR
Blackwater
Merstone
Rookley
Gatcombe
Chillerton
AMAZON WORLD
ISLE OF WIGHT
Brightstone Forest
Hulverstone
Brook
Mottistone
Moortown
The Undercliff
Shorwell
Limerstone
Brighstone
BRIGHSTONE
Thorncross
Yafford
Kingston
Godshill
MODEL VILLAGE
Little Atherfield
Brighstone Bay
Roud
Pyle
Chale Green
Atherfield Pt.
Stenbury Down
Chale
ST CATHERINE'S ORATORY
Whitwell
Chale Bay
Blackgang
Niton
Blackgang Chine
BLACKGANG CHINE
St Catherine's Point
A337
A35
A326
B3056
B3054
B3055
B3053
A3025
A27
B3397
A337
B3058
A3054
B3401
B3399
A3055
A3020
A3021
A3056
B3323
17
0 1 2 3 miles
0 1 2 3 4 5 km
2
3
4
C
D

Wickham
Hundred Acres
North Boarhunt
Denmead
FOREST OF BERE
Cowplain
A3(M)
33
TAUNTON
Rowland's Castle
Forestside
Stoughton
STANSTED PARK
Walderton
206 BOW HILL
Waterlooville
Southwick
SOUTHWICK BREWHOUSE
Funtley
Boarhunt
FORT NELSON
Ports Down
131
Leigh Park
Stockheath
Westbourne
Woodend
West Stoke
Mid Lavant
East Ashling
Funtington
Woodmancote
West Ashling
Summersdale
Purbrook
Bedhampton
HAVANT
Warblington
Hermitage
Hambrook
Nutbourne
M27
Wallington
Wymering
Fareham
Portchester
Fleetlands
PORTCHESTER CAS.
Drayton
Cosham
Hilsea
Langstone
FARLINGTON MARSHES
THE SPRING
Emsworth
Southbourne
Broadbridge
Fishbourne
Chichester
Peel Common
Bridgemary
PORTSMOUTH
Portsmouth Harbour
Northney
Thorney I.
CHICHESTER
Chidham
Bosham
BOSHAM WALK
FISHBOURNE PALACE
Apuldram
FORT BROCKHURST
Brockhurst
Hardway
North End
Langstone Harbour
Stoke
North Hayling
West Thorney
Donnington
Hunston
SOLENT
1642 LIVING HISTORY VILLAGE
EXPLOSION
HMS VICTORY, MARY ROSE
GUNWHARF QUAYS
DICKENS BIRTHPLACE
Fleet
West Itchenor
HARBOUR
Shipton Green
Portsea
PORTSMOUTH
HAYLING ISLAND
Chichester Harbour
GOSPORT
CATHEDRAL
Fratton
West Town
Birdham
Milton
SUBMARINE
FORT
Eastney
ROYAL MARINES MUSEUM
South Hayling
Eastoke
West Wittering
Acre Street
Somerley
Highleigh
Stokes Bay
Alverstoke
BLUE REEF AQUARIUM
Southsea
SOUTHSEA CASTLE
HAYLING SEASIDE RAILWAY
East Wittering
Earnley
Bracklesham
Gilkicker Pt.
SPITHEAD
Norton
RYDE
Selsey
Binstead
Nettlestone Pt.
Elmfield
Seaview
Nettlestone
Havenstreet
ISLE OF WIGHT STEAM RAILWAY
St Helens
Bembridge
Foreland
Lane End
WINDMILL
Brading
Steyne Cross
Hillway
Whitecliff Bay
ROMAN VILLA
Alverstone
DINOSAUR ISLE
104
CAEN ST. MALO
BILBAO SANTANDER
Newchurch
WIGHT AVIATION
Yaverland
Culver Cliff
ISLE OF WIGHT ZOO
Winford
Sandown
Lake
Apse Heath
Sandown Bay
GUERNSEY JERSEY
CHERBOURG (SEASONAL)
Shanklin
SHANKLIN CHINE
Whiteley Bank
235
Luccombe Village
Luccombe Chine
Wroxall
Dunnose
Bonchurch
Ventnor
BOTANIC GARDEN & VISITOR CENTRE
SZ
A
B
C
D
4
5
6
7
20

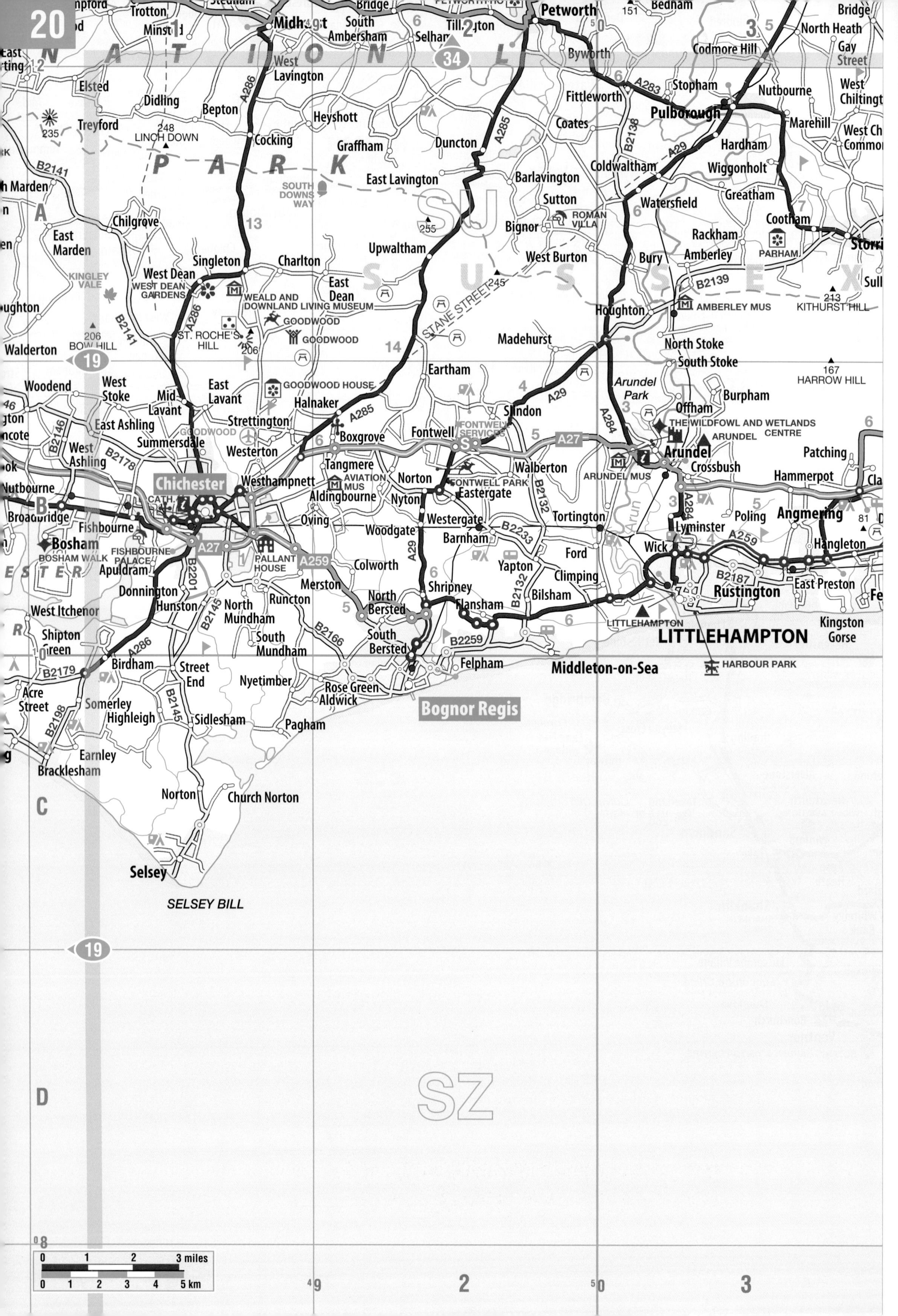
Trotton
Midhurst
South Ambersham
Selham
Tillington
Petworth
Bedham
Bridge
North Heath
Gay Street
Codmore Hill
Byworth
34
NATIONAL PARK
West Lavington
Elsted
Didling
Bepton
Heyshott
Stopham
Nutbourne
West Chiltington
Fittleworth
Pulborough
Coates
Marehill
West Chiltington Common
Treyford
235
248
LINCH DOWN
Cocking
Graffham
Duncton
A285
A286
B2138
A29
Hardham
Wiggonholt
Coldwaltham
B2141
SOUTH DOWNS WAY
East Lavington
Barlavington
Greatham
Watersfield
Sutton
ROMAN VILLA
Bignor
Cootham
Rackham
Amberley
PARHAM
Storrington
Chilgrove
East Marden
255
13
Upwaltham
West Burton
Bury
Singleton
Charlton
SU
SUSSEX
KINGLEY VALE
West Dean
WEST DEAN GARDENS
East Dean
WEALD AND DOWNLAND LIVING MUSEUM
245
B2139
213
KITHURST HILL
AMBERLEY MUS
Houghton
GOODWOOD
STANE STREET
ST. ROCHE'S HILL
206
BOW HILL
Walderton
19
14
Madehurst
North Stoke
South Stoke
167
HARROW HILL
Woodend
West Stoke
Mid Lavant
East Lavant
GOODWOOD HOUSE
Eartham
Arundel Park
Burpham
Halnaker
A285
Slindon
A29
A284
Offham
THE WILDFOWL AND WETLANDS CENTRE
ARUNDEL
Strettington
East Ashling
B2146
Summersdale
Westerton
Boxgrove
Fontwell
FONTWELL SERVICES
A27
Arundel
Patching
West Ashling
B2178
Tangmere
AVIATION MUS
Norton
Walberton
ARUNDEL MUS
Crossbush
Hammerpot
Chichester
Westhampnett
CATH
Aldingbourne
FONTWELL PARK
Eastergate
B2132
Nutbourne
Broadbridge
Fishbourne
Oving
Nyton
Westergate
Woodgate
Barnham
B2233
Tortington
Arun
Poling
Angmering
Lyminster
A259
Bosham
BOSHAM WALK
FISHBOURNE PALACE
Apuldram
A27
PALLANT HOUSE
A259
Colworth
Ford
Yapton
Wick
Hangleton
Climping
B2187
East Preston
Donnington
B2201
Hunston
B2145
North Mundham
Runcton
Merston
North Bersted
Shripney
Flansham
Bilsham
Rustington
West Itchenor
Shipton Green
South Mundham
B2166
South Bersted
B2259
LITTLEHAMPTON
Kingston Gorse
Birdham
A286
Street End
Felpham
Middleton-on-Sea
HARBOUR PARK
B2179
Acre Street
Nyetimber
Rose Green
Aldwick
Bognor Regis
Somerley
Highleigh
Sidlesham
Pagham
B2198
Earnley
Bracklesham
C
Norton
Church Norton
Selsey
SELSEY BILL
19
D
SZ
0 1 2 3 miles
0 1 2 3 4 5 km
49
2
50
3

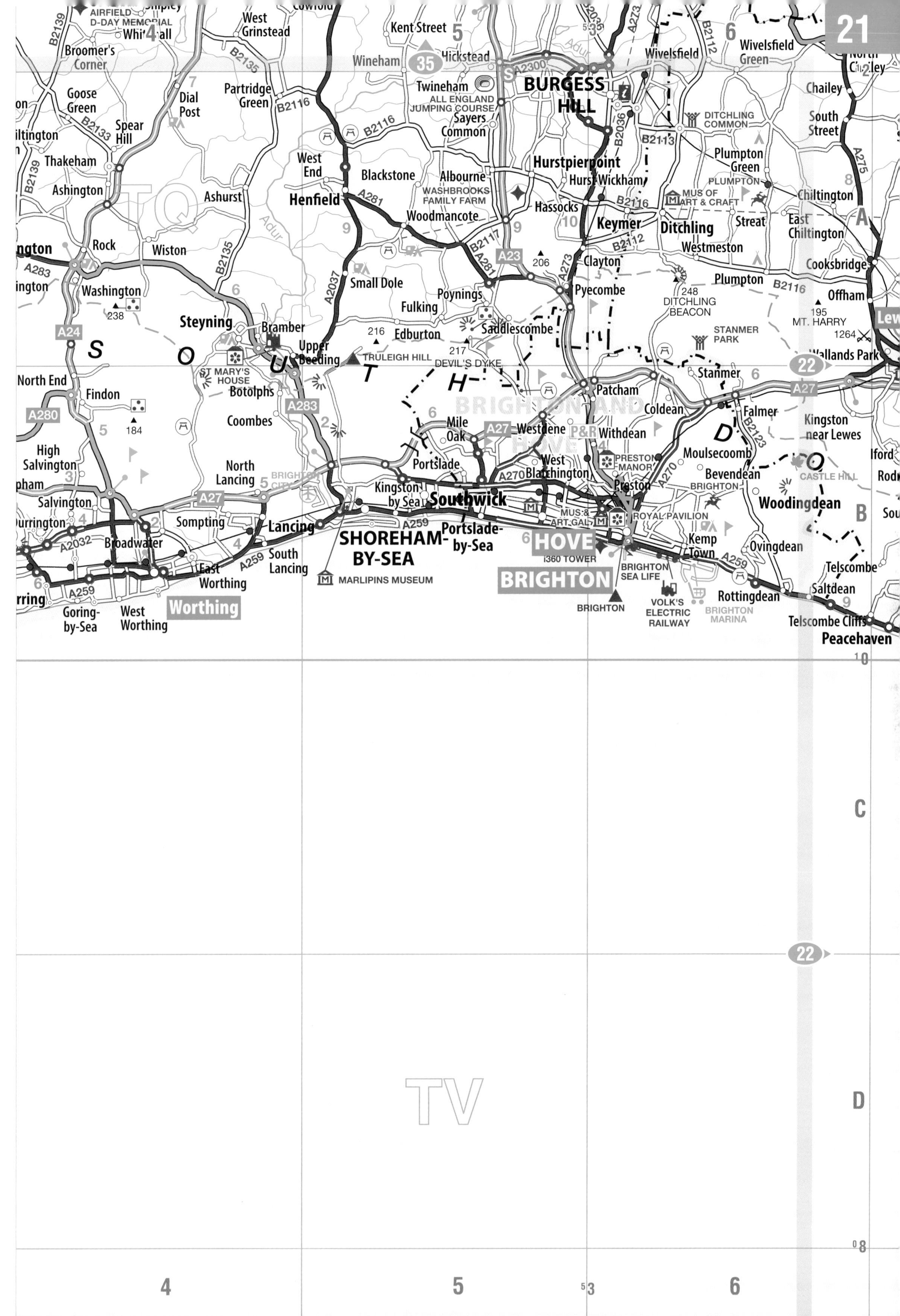
AIRFIELD
D-DAY MEMORIAL
West Grinstead
Kent Street
Wivelsfield
Wivelsfield Green
Broomer's Corner
Wineham
35
Hickstead
A2300
BURGESS HILL
Twineham
ALL ENGLAND JUMPING COURSE
Sayers Common
Goose Green
Dial Post
Partridge Green
B2116
B2133
Spear Hill
Thakeham
Ashington
Ashurst
West End
Blackstone
Albourne
WASHBROOKS FAMILY FARM
Henfield
A281
Woodmancote
Hurstpierpoint
Hurst Wickham
Hassocks
Keymer
Ditchling
Westmeston
B2113
DITCHLING COMMON
Plumpton Green
PLUMPTON
MUS OF ART & CRAFT
Streat
Chailey
South Street
Chiltington
East Chiltington
Cooksbridge
A275
TQ
Rock
Wiston
B2135
A283
Washington
238
Steyning
Bramber
Upper Beeding
A2037
Small Dole
Fulking
Poynings
Edburton
216
Saddlescombe
A23
206
Clayton
Pyecombe
A273
B2112
248
DITCHLING BEACON
Plumpton
B2116
Offham
195
MT. HARRY
1264
Wallands Park
STANMER PARK
Stanmer
TRULEIGH HILL
217
DEVIL'S DYKE
A24
S
O
U
T
H
D
O
ST MARY'S HOUSE
Botolphs
North End
Findon
A280
A283
Coombes
184
High Salvington
Salvington
Durrington
North Lancing
BRIGHTON CITY
A27
Mile Oak
Portslade
Westdene
Withdean
Patcham
Coldean
Falmer
Kingston near Lewes
B2123
Moulsecoomb
Bevendean
CASTLE HILL
Woodingdean
BRIGHTON AND HOVE
P&R
PRESTON MANOR
West Blatchington
A270
Preston
ROYAL PAVILION
MUS & ART GAL
Kingston by Sea
Southwick
Sompting
Lancing
A2032
Broadwater
SHOREHAM-BY-SEA
Portslade-by-Sea
A259
HOVE
i360 TOWER
Kemp Town
Ovingdean
Telscombe
Saltdean
East Worthing
South Lancing
MARLIPINS MUSEUM
BRIGHTON
BRIGHTON SEA LIFE
VOLK'S ELECTRIC RAILWAY
BRIGHTON MARINA
Rottingdean
Telscombe Cliffs
Peacehaven
Goring-by-Sea
West Worthing
Worthing
22
TV
A
B
C
D
4
5
6

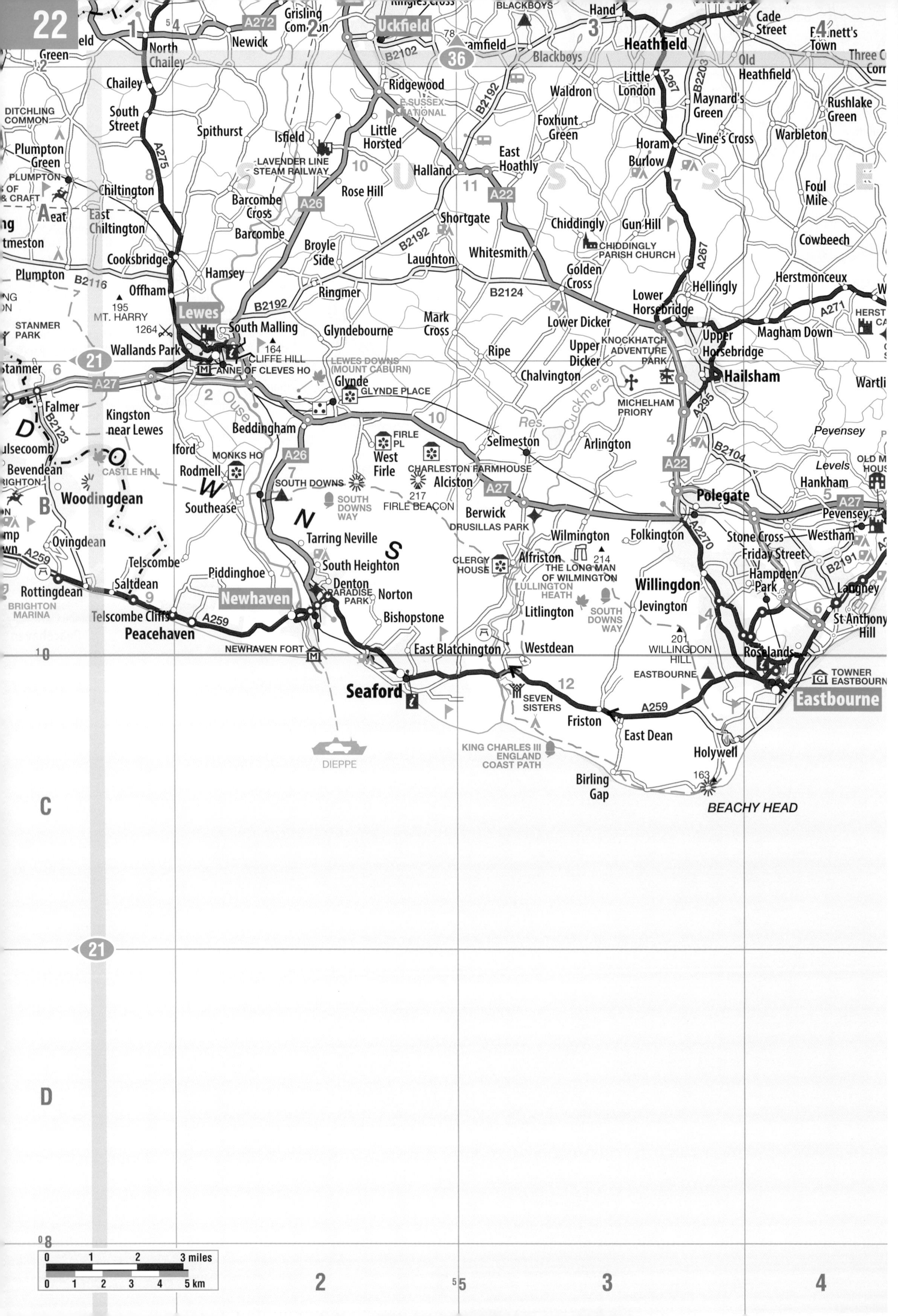
North Chailey
Newick
A272
Grisling Common
Uckfield
Framfield
Blackboys
BLACKBOYS
Hand
Heathfield
Cade Street
Punnett's Town
Three Cups Corner
Old Heathfield
Chailey
Ridgewood
E.SUSSEX NATIONAL
B2102
36
B2192
Waldron
Little London
A267
B2203
Maynard's Green
Rushlake Green
DITCHLING COMMON
South Street
Spithurst
Isfield
Little Horsted
Foxhunt Green
Horam
Vine's Cross
Warbleton
Plumpton Green
PLUMPTON
LAVENDER LINE STEAM RAILWAY
A275
Halland
East Hoathly
Burlow
Foul Mile
Chiltington
Rose Hill
Barcombe Cross
A26
A22
East Chiltington
Barcombe
Shortgate
Chiddingly
Gun Hill
Cowbeech
Broyle Side
B2192
Whitesmith
CHIDDINGLY PARISH CHURCH
Cooksbridge
Hamsey
Laughton
Plumpton
B2116
Offham
Ringmer
Golden Cross
Hellingly
Herstmonceux
195
MT. HARRY
B2192
B2124
Lower Horsebridge
A271
STANMER PARK
1264
Lewes
South Malling
Glyndebourne
Mark Cross
Lower Dicker
Magham Down
HERSTMONCEUX CASTLE
Wallands Park
164
CLIFFE HILL
Ripe
Upper Dicker
KNOCKHATCH ADVENTURE PARK
Upper Horsebridge
21
Stanmer
ANNE OF CLEVES HO
LEWES DOWNS (MOUNT CABURN)
Chalvington
Hailsham
A27
Glynde
GLYNDE PLACE
Cuckmere
MICHELHAM PRIORY
Wartling
Falmer
Kingston near Lewes
Ouse
Beddingham
A295
B2123
Res.
Pevensey
Bulsecoomb
Iford
FIRLE PL
West Firle
Selmeston
Arlington
B2104
Levels
OLD MINT HOUSE
Bevendean
MONKS HO
A26
Rodmell
CASTLE HILL
CHARLESTON FARMHOUSE
A22
BRIGHTON
SOUTH DOWNS
Alciston
A27
Hankham
Polegate
Woodingdean
Southease
SOUTH DOWNS WAY
217
FIRLE BEACON
Berwick
DRUSILLAS PARK
Pevensey
Wilmington
Folkington
A2270
Stone Cross
Westham
Ovingdean
Tarring Neville
Friday Street
A259
Telscombe
South Heighton
CLERGY HOUSE
Alfriston
214
THE LONG MAN OF WILMINGTON
Hampden Park
B2191
Piddinghoe
Saltdean
Denton
LULLINGTON HEATH
Willingdon
Langney
Rottingdean
Newhaven
PARADISE PARK
Norton
BRIGHTON MARINA
Jevington
St Anthony's Hill
Telscombe Cliffs
Litlington
SOUTH DOWNS WAY
Bishopstone
Peacehaven
A259
201
WILLINGDON HILL
NEWHAVEN FORT
East Blatchington
Westdean
Roselands
EASTBOURNE
TOWNER EASTBOURNE
Seaford
SEVEN SISTERS
Eastbourne
A259
Friston
East Dean
DIEPPE
KING CHARLES III ENGLAND COAST PATH
Holywell
Birling Gap
163
BEACHY HEAD
0 1 2 3 miles
0 1 2 3 4 5 km

Brightling
Darwell Hole
Mountfield
Dallington
Netherfield
Whatlington
Canadia
Penhurst
Battle
Ponts Green
1066 ABBEY
Telham
Bodle Street Green
Catsfield
Henley's Down
Crowhurst
Windmill Hill
Ninfield
Boreham Street
HERSTMONCEUX CASTLE
OBSERVATORY SCIENCE CENTRE
Lunsford's Cross
Hooe Common
Hooe
Little Common
Sidley
Cooden
BEXHILL
DE LA WARR PAVILION
PEVENSEY LEVELS
PEVENSEY SERVICES
Norman's Bay
Pevensey Bay
TQ
TV
John's Cross
Vinehall Street
Cripp's Corner
Sedlescombe
Sedlescombe Street
BREDE STEAM GIANTS
Kent Street
Hollington
COMBE VALLEY
Silverhill
St Leonards
Bulverhythe
West Marina
Hastings
Baldslow
Westfield
Broad Oak
Brede
Horns Cross
Broadland Row
Udimore
Guestling Thorn
Three Oaks
Icklesham
Winchelsea
WINCHELSEA COURT HALL MUSEUM
Pett
Guestling Green
Cliff End
St Helen's
Ore
Fairlight
Fairlight Cove
HASTINGS
ST CLEMENT'S CAVES
FISHERMEN'S & SHIPWRECK MUSEUMS
HASTINGS AQUARIUM
Rye
Rye Foreign
Playden
RYE HERITAGE CENTRE
Rye Harbour
CAMBER CASTLE
Winchelsea Beach
A
B
C
D
4
5
6
7

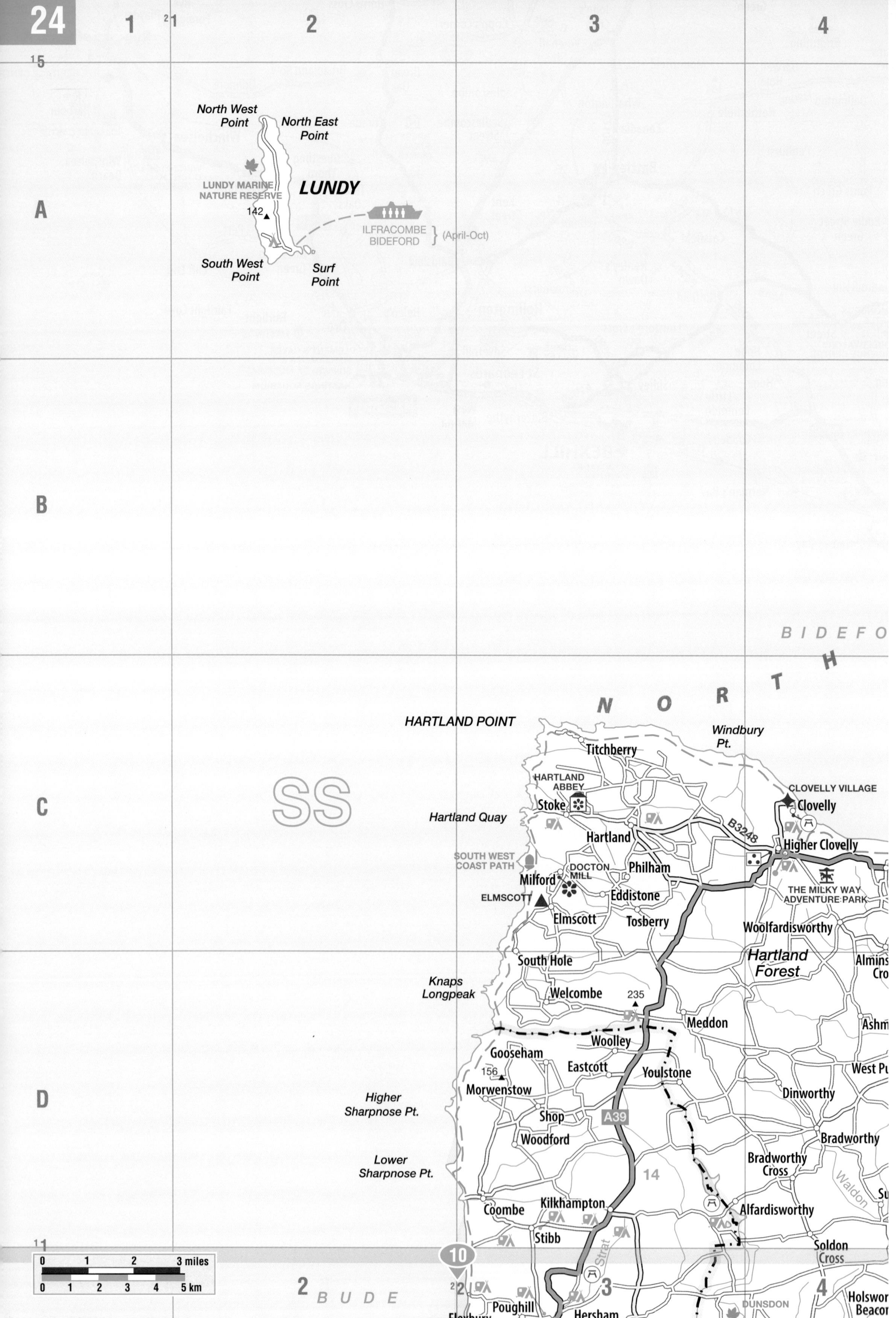
1
2
3
4
A
B
C
D
North West Point
North East Point
LUNDY MARINE NATURE RESERVE
LUNDY
142
ILFRACOMBE BIDEFORD
(April-Oct)
South West Point
Surf Point
BIDEFO
N O R T H
HARTLAND POINT
Windbury Pt.
Titchberry
HARTLAND ABBEY
CLOVELLY VILLAGE
Stoke
Clovelly
SS
Hartland Quay
Hartland
B3248
Higher Clovelly
SOUTH WEST COAST PATH
DOCTON MILL
Philham
Milford
THE MILKY WAY ADVENTURE PARK
ELMSCOTT
Eddistone
Elmscott
Tosberry
Woolfardisworthy
South Hole
Hartland Forest
Almins Cro
Knaps Longpeak
Welcombe
235
Meddon
Ashm
Woolley
Gooseham
Eastcott
Youlstone
156
West Pu
Morwenstow
Dinworthy
Higher Sharpnose Pt.
Shop
A39
Woodford
Bradworthy
Lower Sharpnose Pt.
Bradworthy Cross
14
Waldon
Coombe
Kilkhampton
Alfardisworthy
Stibb
Soldon Cross
Strat
0 1 2 3 miles
0 1 2 3 4 5 km
10
2
BUDE
3
4
Poughill
Hersham
DUNSDON
Holswor Beacon
Flexbury

4
5
6
7
HELE CORN MILL
Rillage Pt.
Combe Martin Bay
LUNDY (April-Oct)
Ilfracombe
ILFRACOMBE MUSEUM
Hele
WATERMOUTH CASTLE
Girt Down
Trentishoe
Heale
349
Bull Pt.
Rockham Bay
Lee
206
Berrynarbor
Combe Martin
Mortehoe
Whitestone
Slade
A361
B3230
Sterridge
WILDLIFE & DINOSAUR PARK
A399
Morte Point
269
A3123
Woolacombe
MORTE BAY
Trimstone
Berry Down Cross
Kentisbury
B3343
Cheglinch
Berry Down
B3229
Patchole
Kentisbury Ford
210
Dean
Woolacombe Sand
SOUTH WEST COAST PATH
Bittadon
West Down
East Down
North Buckland
EXMOOR ZOO
Pickwell
Churchill
Arlington
Baggy Pt.
Putsborough
B3230
ARLINGTON COURT
26
Georgeham
Nethercott
Croyde Bay
Halsinger
Milltown
Croyde
Darracott
A39
Loxhore
Knightacott
Muddiford
B3231
158
Lobb
Knowle
Marwood
Guineaford
Shirwell
Bratton Fleming
Saunton
Pippacott
Kingsheanton
198
Braunton
MARWOOD HILL GARDENS
BROOMHILL
Shirwell Cross
Stoke Rivers
Benton
ELLIOT GALLERY
Heanton Punchardon
Prixford
Saunton Sands
Wrafton
Ashford
Burridge
TOLL
A361
Braunton Burrows
Chivenor
Barnstaple
Goodleigh
DEVON
Gunn
Taw
Pilton
LUNDY (April-Oct)
MUSEUM OF BARNSTAPLE & NORTH DEVON
Fremington
Westacott
Yelland
B3233
Bickleton
Bickington
P&R
Newport
NORTH DEVON MARITIME MUSEUM
A39
Bishops Tawton
Landkey
West Buckland
NORTHAM BURROWS
Instow
Swimbridge Newland
Appledore
Tawstock
Swimbridge
Westward Ho!
TAPELEY PARK GDNS
Westleigh
A386
Torridge
Northam
Horwood
Newton Tracey
Orchard Hill
Eastleigh
THE BIG SHEEP
Bideford
Ensis
Herner
Cobbaton
Abbotsham
BURTON ART GALL & MUS
East-the -Water
Hiscott
Chapelton
East Stowford
COBBATON COMBAT COLLECTION
Woodtown
A39
Handy Cross
Alverdiscott
Fishleigh Barton
AFFINITY DEVON
Fairy Cross
Buck's Mills
Horns Cross
Ford
Landcross
A377
Woodtown
B3232
Umberleigh
Yarnscombe
Atherington
Littleham
Goldworthy
Warkleigh
Buck's Cross
A386
Langridge Ford
B3217
Weare Giffard
Chittlehamholt
Parkham
High Bickington
Monkleigh
Sherwood Green
Buckland Brewer
B3227
High Bullen
DARTINGTON CRYSTAL
Parkham Ash
26
216
St Giles in the Wood
Frithelstock
Great Torrington
Frithelstock Stone
Taddiport
Tythecott
A388
B3227
Kingscott
Roborough
R.H.S. GARDEN ROSEMOOR
Little Torrington
205
Burrington
East Putford
Langtree
Beaford
A3124
Riddlecombe
Bulkworthy
Stibb Cross
Peters Marland
Ashreigney
Abbots Bickington
Newton St Petrock
Woollaton
Winswell
B3217
Merton
Dolton
Venn Green
Milton Damerel
Huish
Torridge
Hollocombe
170
Buckland Filleigh
Dowland
Torridge
11
Petrockstow
Shebbear
Thornbury
138
Iddesleigh
Winkleigh

1
2
3
Highveer Pt.
Foreland Pt.
Lynmouth Bay
Woody Bay
CLIFF RAILWAY
TOLL
Lynmouth
Countisbury
Lynton
WATERSMEET HOUSE
Trentishoe
Martinhoe
Porlock Bay
Porlock Weir
Bossington
CULBONE HILL
413
TOLL
Malmsmead
Brendon
Oare
B3225
TOLL
Porlock
Heale
349
LYNTON AND BARNSTAPLE RLY
A39
Barbrook
East Ilkerton
Cheriton
Martinhoe Cross
WILDLIFE & DINOSAUR PARK
A399
Parracombe
West Lyn
Furzehill
B3223
Shallowford
E X M O O R
Brendon Common
HAWKCOMBE WOODS
Holnicote Estate
Kentisbury
B3229
Blackmoor Gate
EXMOOR FOREST
465
Patchole
Kentisbury Ford
Challacombe Common
Pinkworthy Pond
487
PINKERY CENTRE FOR OUTDOOR LEARNING
THE DUNKERY & HORNER WOOD
DUNKERY BEACON
519
Down
25
EXMOOR ZOO
B3358
Challacombe
Exe Plain
Arlington
ARLINGTON COURT
Exe
N A T I O N A L
329
Shoulsbarrow Common
Simonsbath
B3223
Edgcott
B3224
A39
Loxhore
Knightacott
Leworthy
Exford
EXFORD
Shirwell
Bray
Yeo
Bratton Fleming
Barle
Shirwell Cross
Stoke Rivers
Benton
A399
Lydcott
493
B3223
443
HORSEN HILL
Withypool
Withypool Common
WINSFORD HILL
B
Goodleigh
13
North Radworthy
Brayford
High Bray
Gunn
265
North Heasley
P A R K
426
ARNSTAPLE
Charles
Liscombe
TARR STEPS WOODLAND
TARR STEPS
West Buckland
Heasley Mill
South Radworthy
Dane's Brook
377
Molland Common
Hawkridge
East Buckland
224
Swimbridge
10
A361
North Molton
Twitchen
Anstey Common
Filleigh
Mole
Molland
West Anstey
EXMOOR VISITOR CENTRE
QUINCE HONEY FARM
SS
Cobbaton
East Anstey
East Stowford
B3227
Yeo
Yeo Mill
COBBATON COMBAT COLLECTION
Chittlehampton
B3226
South Molton
Bish Mill
Newtown
B3227
Oldways End
C
A377
Umberleigh
Clapworthy
173
Bishops Nympton
Ash Mill
Knowstone
Roachill
Warkleigh
George Nympton
Alswear
Satterleigh
B3217
Mariansleigh
Rose Ash
17
Chittlehamholt
High Bickington
Taw
25
Romansleigh
Meshaw
A361
King's Nympton
238
Creacombe
STOODLEIGH BEACON
301
B3137
Rackenford
205
Burrington
26
Cadbury Barton
Week
Dart
Queen Dart
Elstone
Little
Lutworthy
D
Witheridge
Templeton Bridge
Riddlecombe
B3096
Chulmleigh
West Worlington
East Worlington
Templeton
Cheldon
Drayford
Nomansland
Ashreigney
B3042
B3137
Thelbridge Barton
Washford Pyne
Cruwys Morchard
Chawleigh
Ashley
Pennymoor
B3042
Dalch
Black Dog
Way Village
Hollocombe
Filleigh
Puddington
12
Wembworthy
0 1 2 3 miles
0 1 2 3 4 5 km
Eastington
Woolfardisworthy
Winkleigh
Lapford
Morchard Bishop
Coldridge

4
30
5
31
6
15
BRIDGWATER
BAY
ST
EXMOOR OWL & HAWK CENTRE
SOUTH WEST COAST PATH
SELWORTHY BEACON
308
Allerford
Selworthy
Woodcombe
Minehead
WEST SOMERSET RAILWAY
BUTLINS
Alcombe
Periton
A39
Luccombe
Marsh Street
MINEHEAD
DOLL COLLECTION
Dunster
MILL & YARN MARKET
DUNKERY VINEYARD
Wootton Courtenay
Cowbridge
DUNSTER CASTLE
Carhampton
Timberscombe
Blue Anchor Bay
Blue Anchor
B3191
Old Cleeve
MARKET HOUSE MUS
Watchet
TROPIQUARIA
Williton
West Quantoxhead
East Quantoxhead
KING CHARLES III ENGLAND COAST PATH
Lilstock
Kilton
Burton
Kilve
Stringston
Hinkley Point Power Station
A
Withycombe
Bilbrook
CLEEVE ABBEY
Washford
Sampford Brett
Staple
QUANTOCK HILLS
Holford
18
28
Nether Stowey
BRENDON FOREST
CROYDON HILL
365
A396
Rodhuish
Bicknoller
COLERIDGE COTTAGE
Cutcombe
Wheddon Cross
Roadwater
Yard
B3188
Vellow
358
Over Stowey
Luxborough
423
LYPE HILL
Kingsbridge
290
Monksilver
Stogumber
WEST SOMERSET RAILWAY
A358
QUANTOCK FOREST
Crowcombe
B3224
BRENDON HILLS
Treborough
412
B3190
Flaxpool
Elworthy
Lower Vexford
384
West Bagborough
B
Exton
B3224
Willett
Lydeard St Lawrence
16
Bridgetown
Withiel Florey
Clatworthy Res.
Tolland
B3224
Brompton Regis
Brompton Ralph
East Combe
Combe Florey
Cothelstone
27
Clatworthy
Tarr
Cushuish
Wimbleball Lake
Langley Marsh
Ash Priors
A396
Upton
Huish Champflower
Bishops Lydeard
355
HADDON HILL
B3222
Maundown
B3188
Fitzhead
A358
HEYDON HILL
338
Wiveliscombe
Halse
Bury
Skilgate
Chipstable
VALE OF TAUNTON DEANE
Barle
B3190
Preston Bowyer
B3227
Heathfield
Milverton
Hillcommon
Norton Fitzwarren
Brushford
Morebath
Waterrow
Oake
Bishop's Hull
C
Petton
B3227
B3187
Hillfarance
Exebridge
267
Bathealton
239
Shillingford
East Nynehead
Bradford-on-Tone
Bampton
Clayhanger
Langford Budville
Nynehead
SHEPPY'S CIDER
A38
6
Oakford
Kittisford
Runnington
Appley
Wellington
West Buckland
TAUNTON DEANE SERVICES
Huntsham
Ashbrittle
Thorne St Margaret
Rockwell Green
26
28
Hockworthy
Holywell Lake
Cove
286
9
A396
Holcombe Rogus
Sampford Arundel
Stoodleigh
8
Wrangway
Ford Street
Angersleigh
EXE VALLEY
Westleigh
East Mere
BLACKDOWN HILLS
Nicholashayne
Washfield
Chevithorne
Whitnage
Burlescombe
Clayhidon
KNIGHTSHAYES COURT
Uplowman
A38
Rosemary Lane
D
Bolham
Chettiscombe
7
Appledore
Calverleigh
A361
27
Culm Valley
Culmstock
TIVERTON CASTLE
Sampford Peverell
Stapley
Halberton
Uffculme
B3391
Hemyock
Cowleymoor
GRAND WESTERN CANAL
TIVERTON SERVICES
COLDHARBOUR MILL
258
HACKPEN HILL
Cotteylands
Tiverton
B3440
Craddock
Bolham Water
237
Ash Thomas
Smithincott
Ashill
5
4
Abbey
Smeatharpe
Well Town
Willand
13
A396
Blackborough
4
30
CULLOMPTON SERVICES
5
31
6
Cadeleigh
Butterleigh
BICKLEIGH MILL
Cullompton
28
Sheldon
Dunkeswell
Kentisbeare

Gore Sands
Berrow
Burnham-on-Sea
STERT FLATS
Highbridge
HINKLEY POINT POWER STATION
BRIDGWATER BAY
Stolford
Steart
Huntspill
WWT STEART MARSHES NAT RESERVE
Lilstock
Kilton
Burton
Shurton
Stockland Bristol
Stretcholt
Stogursey
Kilve
Stringston
Otterhampton
Combwich
Pawlett
Holford
Nether Stowey
Fiddington
Dunball
Puriton
Woolavington
Cossington
Chilton Polden
Edington
Rodway
Cannington
CANNINGTON COLLEGE
COLERIDGE COTTAGE
Over Stowey
Chilton Trinity
BLAKE MUS
Bawdrip
POLDEN HILLS
Catcott
Stawell
Shapwick
SHAPWICK HEATH
Charlynch
Wembdon
BRIDGWATER AND TAUNTON CANAL AND DOCKS
Chedzoy
Moorlinch
Sutton Mallet
Greinton
Pedwell
Spaxton
QUANTOCK FOREST
Crowcombe
Four Forks
Durleigh
Bridgwater
Flaxpool
Lower Aisholt
Enmore
BRIDGWATER SERVICES
Westonzoyland
West Bagborough
Courtway
Goathurst
North Petherton
Huntworth
King's Sedge Moor
SOMERSET LEVELS
TEMPLE OF HARMONY
WESTONZOYLAND PUMPING STATION
FYNE COURT
Broomfield
Middlezoy
East Combe
Cothelstone
Northmoor Green or Moorland
Henley
Othery
Pathe
High Ham
Cushuish
North Newton
STEMBRIDGE
Ash Priors
Fulford
Kingston St Mary
Thurloxton
BRIDGWATER & TAUNTON CANAL MAUNSEL LOCKS
Lyng
Burrow-bridge
Stathe
Aller
Low Ham
Bishops Lydeard
Pickney
HESTERCOMBE GARDENS
Hedging
Athelney
West Monkton
Nailsbourne
Durston
West Lyng
Halse
DEANE
Cheddon Fitzpaine
Monkton Heathfield
Creech Heathfield
Stoke St Gregory
Langport
Heathfield
Staplegrove
Bathpool
North End
Meare Green
West Sedge Moor
Huish Episcopi
Hillcommon
Norton Fitzwarren
COATES ENGLISH WILLOW VISITOR CENTRE
Knapp
Curry Rivel
Oake
Bishop's Hull
Creech St Michael
North Curry
Muchelney
Hillfarance
Ruishton
SOMERSET CRICKET MUS
Drayton
ABBEY
East Nynehead
Bradford-on-Tone
Taunton
Henlade
Thornfalcon
Fivehead
SHEPPY'S CIDER
Trull
Stoke St Mary
Staplehay
TAUNTON
Wrantage
Curry Mallet
Isle Brewers
TAUNTON DEANE SERVICES
West Buckland
Orchard Portman
West Hatch
Thurlbear
Hatch Beauchamp
Isle Abbotts
Hambridge
Kingsbury Episcopi
Pitminster
Corfe
Beercrocombe
Westport
East Lambrook
West Lambrook
Staple Fitzpaine
Hatch Green
Angersleigh
Blagdon Hill
Puckington
BARRINGTON COURT
E. LAMBROOK MANOR
Ford Street
Bickenhall
Ilton
Barrington
South Petherton
BLACKDOWN HILLS
BARRINGTON HILL
Ashill
Curland
STAPLE HILL
Stocklinch
ILMINSTER SERVICES
Shepton Beauchamp
Windmill Hill
Clayhidon
Broadway
Ashwell
Seavington St Michael
Over Stratton
Horton
Ilminster
Churchstanton
Fyfett
Seavington St Mary
Lopen
Rosemary Lane
Buckland St Mary
Donyatt
PERRYS CIDER
BLACKDOWN
Crock Street
Kingstone
Dinnington
Hemyock
Stapley
Churchinford
Dowlish Wake
Hinton St George
Bishopswood
Combe St Nicholas
Bolham Water
Cricket Malherbie
Marsh
Whitestaunton
Chillington
HORNSBURY MILL
Abbey
Smeatharpe
Wadeford
Cudworth
Chaffcombe
Newcott
Howley
Cricket St Thomas
Crewkerne
Yarcombe
Wambrook
Chard
Hewish
Dunkeswell
Misterton
East Brent
Rooks Bridge
Badgworth
Brent Knoll
Stone Allerton
Chapel Allerton
ASHTON WINDMILL
Edithmead
Cocklake
West Stoughton
Mark Causeway
Mark
Blackford
Wedmore
Watchfield
Westham
Bason Bridge
Heath House
SECRET WORLD WILDLIFE RESCUE
East Huntspill
HUNTSPILL RIVER
Burtle
Brue
Westhay
Huntspill
Parrett
Tone
Isle
A38
A39
A372
A361
A358
A378
A303
A30
M5
B3140
B3139
B3141
B3151
B3227
B3170
B3168
B3165
0 1 2 3 miles
0 1 2 3 4 5 km

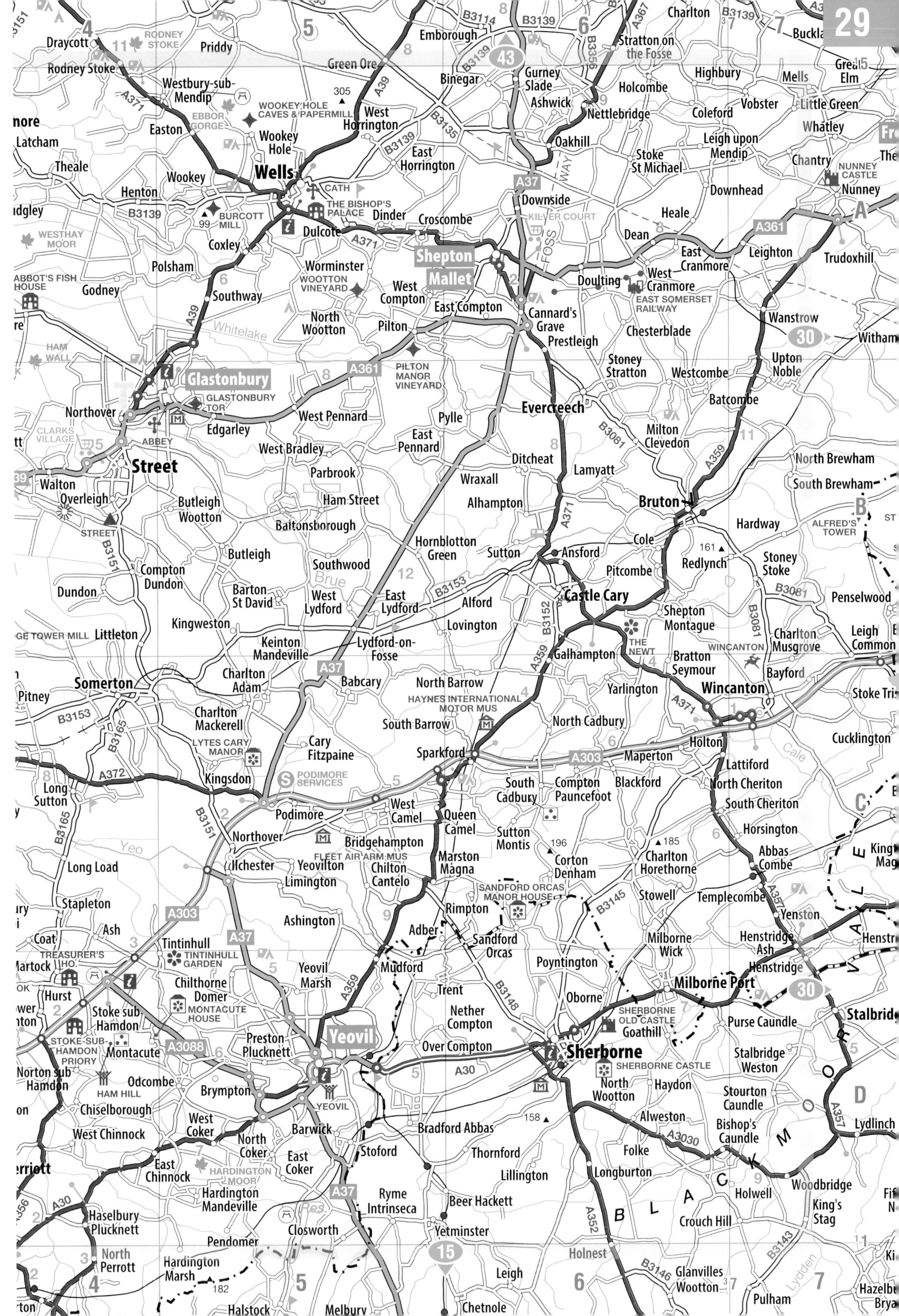
Draycott
Rodney Stoke
Priddy
Emborough
Green Ore
Binegar
Gurney Slade
Ashwick
Stratton on the Fosse
Charlton
Holcombe
Highbury
Mells
Great Elm
Vobster
Little Green
Coleford
Whatley
Nettlebridge
Oakhill
Leigh upon Mendip
Stoke St Michael
Chantry
Nunney Castle
Nunney
Downhead
Westbury-sub-Mendip
Wookey Hole Caves & Papermill
Ebbor Gorge
Easton
Wookey Hole
West Horrington
East Horrington
Latcham
Theale
Wookey
Wells
Henton
Cath
The Bishop's Palace
Dinder
Croscombe
Downside
Kilver Court
Heale
Burcott Mill
Westhay Moor
Dulcote
Coxley
Polsham
Worminster
Wootton Vineyard
Shepton Mallet
Dean
East Cranmore
West Cranmore
Leighton
Trudoxhill
Doulting
East Somerset Railway
Abbot's Fish House
Godney
Southway
West Compton
East Compton
North Wootton
Pilton
Cannard's Grave
Prestleigh
Chesterblade
Wanstrow
Witham
Whitelake
Ham Wall
Pilton Manor Vineyard
Glastonbury
Glastonbury Tor
Stoney Stratton
Westcombe
Upton Noble
Batcombe
Northover
Edgarley
West Pennard
Pylle
Evercreech
Milton Clevedon
Clarks Village
Abbey
Street
West Bradley
East Pennard
Ditcheat
Lamyatt
North Brewham
South Brewham
Walton
Overleigh
Butleigh Wootton
Parbrook
Ham Street
Wraxall
Alhampton
Bruton
Hardway
Alfred's Tower
Baltonsborough
Street
Hornblotton Green
Sutton
Ansford
Cole
Redlynch
Stoney Stoke
Butleigh
Southwood
Brue
Pitcombe
Compton Dundon
Dundon
Barton St David
West Lydford
East Lydford
Alford
Castle Cary
Penselwood
Kingweston
Lovington
Shepton Montague
The Newt
Charlton Musgrove
Leigh Common
Littleton
Keinton Mandeville
Lydford-on-Fosse
Galhampton
Wincanton
Bratton Seymour
Bayford
Somerton
Charlton Adam
Babcary
North Barrow
Yarlington
Haynes International Motor Mus
Pitney
Charlton Mackerell
South Barrow
North Cadbury
Stoke Trister
Cary Fitzpaine
Lytes Cary Manor
Sparkford
Maperton
Holton
Cucklington
Kingsdon
Podimore Services
Lattiford
Long Sutton
South Cadbury
Compton Pauncefoot
Blackford
North Cheriton
South Cheriton
Podimore
West Camel
Queen Camel
Sutton Montis
Horsington
Northover
Bridgehampton
Fleet Air Arm Mus
Corton Denham
Charlton Horethorne
Abbas Combe
Yeo
Long Load
Ilchester
Yeovilton
Limington
Chilton Cantelo
Marston Magna
Sandford Orcas Manor House
Stowell
Templecombe
Stapleton
Rimpton
Yenston
Ash
Ashington
Adber
Sandford Orcas
Milborne Wick
Henstridge Ash
Henstridge
Coat
Tintinhull
Tintinhull Garden
Treasurer's Ho.
Martock
Yeovil Marsh
Mudford
Poyntington
Milborne Port
Chilthorne Domer
Trent
Oborne
Hurst
Stoke sub Hamdon
Montacute House
Nether Compton
Sherborne Old Castle
Goathill
Purse Caundle
Stalbridge
Stoke-sub-Hamdon Priory
Montacute
Preston Plucknett
Yeovil
Over Compton
Sherborne
Sherborne Castle
Stalbridge Weston
Norton sub Hamdon
Odcombe
Ham Hill
Brympton
North Wootton
Haydon
Stourton Caundle
Chiselborough
Yeovil
West Coker
Barwick
Bradford Abbas
Alweston
Bishop's Caundle
Lydlinch
West Chinnock
North Coker
East Coker
Stoford
Thornford
Folke
East Chinnock
Hardington Moor
Hardington Mandeville
Ryme Intrinseca
Lillington
Longburton
Holwell
Woodbridge
Haselbury Plucknett
Beer Hackett
Crouch Hill
King's Stag
Closworth
Yetminster
Blackmore Vale
Pendomer
Holnest
North Perrott
Hardington Marsh
Leigh
Glanvilles Wootton
Pulham
Halstock
Melbury
Chetnole
Lydden
Res.
WAY
FOSS

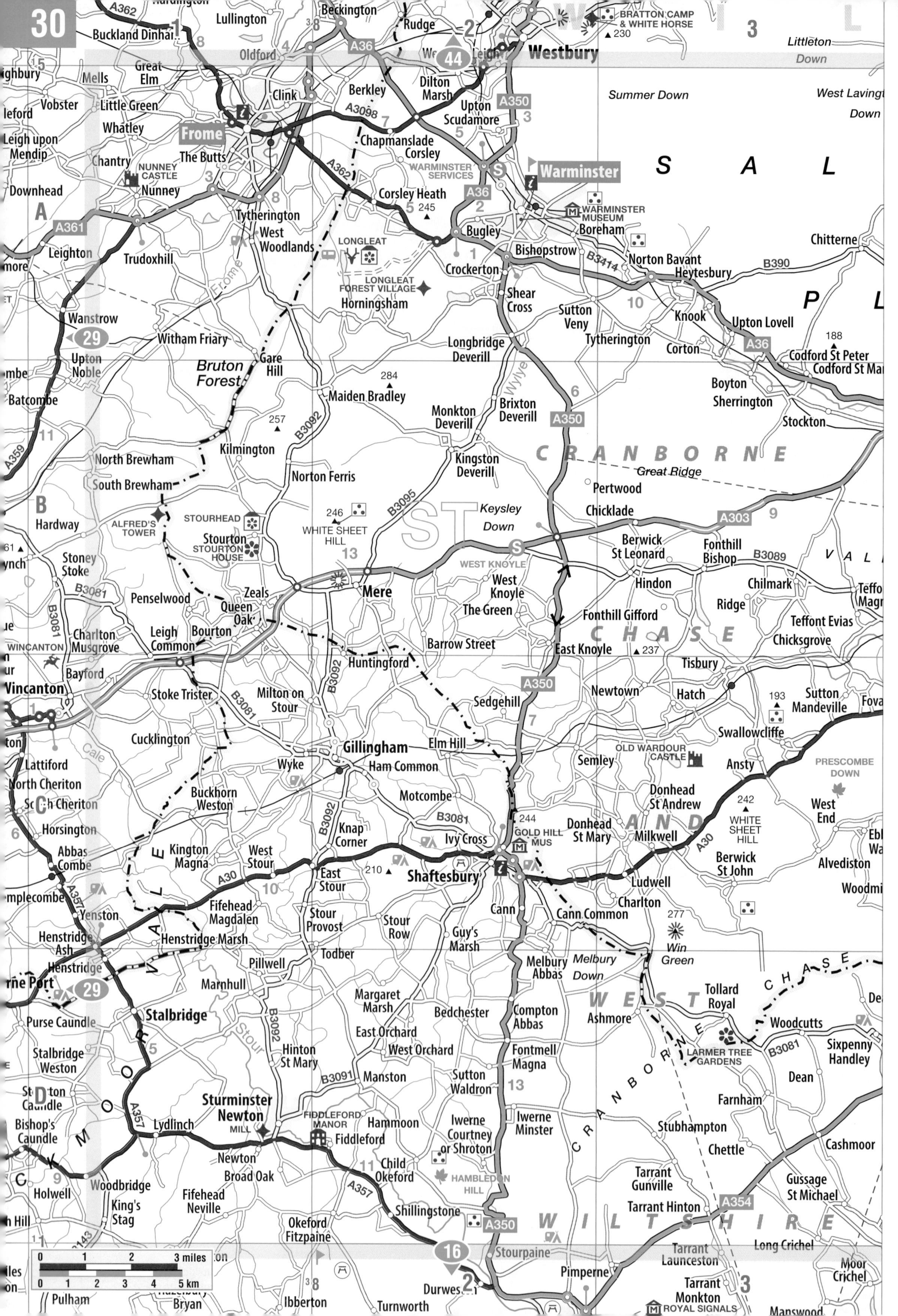
A362
Beckington
Rudge
BRATTON CAMP & WHITE HORSE
230
Littleton Down
Buckland Dinham
Lullington
Oldford
A36
44
Leigh
Westbury
Mells
Great Elm
Clink
Berkley
Dilton Marsh
Summer Down
West Lavington Down
Vobster
Little Green
A3098
Upton Scudamore
A350
Whatley
Frome
Chapmanslade
Corsley
Leigh upon Mendip
Chantry
NUNNEY CASTLE
The Butts
A362
WARMINSTER SERVICES
Warminster
S A L
Downhead
Nunney
Corsley Heath
245
A36
WARMINSTER MUSEUM
A361
Tytherington
West Woodlands
LONGLEAT
Bugley
Boreham
Leighton
Trudoxhill
Bishopstrow
Norton Bavant
Chitterne
B3414
Crockerton
Heytesbury
B390
LONGLEAT FOREST VILLAGE
Horningsham
Shear Cross
Sutton Veny
Knook
P L
Wanstrow
Upton Lovell
29
Witham Friary
Tytherington
Corton
A36
188
Upton Noble
Gare Hill
Longbridge Deverill
Codford St Peter
Codford St Mary
Bruton Forest
284
Maiden Bradley
Boyton
Batcombe
Sherrington
Monkton Deverill
Brixton Deverill
257
B3092
A350
Stockton
A359
Kilmington
CRANBORNE
North Brewham
Kingston Deverill
Great Ridge
Norton Ferris
South Brewham
Pertwood
Hardway
ALFRED'S TOWER
STOURHEAD
246
B3095
Keysley Down
Chicklade
A303
Stourton
STOURTON HOUSE
WHITE SHEET HILL
Berwick St Leonard
Fonthill Bishop
B3089
Stoney Stoke
WEST KNOYLE
West Knoyle
Hindon
Chilmark
Teffont Magna
B3081
Penselwood
Zeals
Mere
The Green
Queen Oak
Ridge
Fonthill Gifford
Teffont Evias
Charlton Musgrove
Leigh Common
Bourton
CHASE
WINCANTON
Barrow Street
East Knoyle
237
Chicksgrove
Huntingford
Bayford
Tisbury
Vincanton
Stoke Trister
Milton on Stour
B3092
A350
Newtown
Hatch
193
Sutton Mandeville
Sedgehill
Cucklington
Elm Hill
Swallowcliffe
Gillingham
Lattiford
Wyke
Ham Common
OLD WARDOUR CASTLE
Semley
Ansty
PRESCOMBE DOWN
North Cheriton
Buckhorn Weston
Motcombe
Donhead St Andrew
South Cheriton
B3081
244
West End
Horsington
Knap Corner
B3092
Ivy Cross
GOLD HILL MUS
Donhead St Mary
Milkwell
242
WHITE SHEET HILL
Abbas Combe
Kington Magna
West Stour
A30
Berwick St John
Alvediston
210
East Stour
Shaftesbury
Templecombe
A357
A30
Ludwell
Charlton
Fifehead Magdalen
Cann
Cann Common
277
Yenston
Stour Provost
Stour Row
Guy's Marsh
Win Green
Henstridge Ash
Henstridge Marsh
Todber
Melbury Abbas
Melbury Down
Henstridge
Pillwell
29
Marnhull
Margaret Marsh
Tollard Royal
WEST
CHASE
Stalbridge
B3092
Bedchester
Compton Abbas
Ashmore
Woodcutts
Purse Caundle
East Orchard
Fontmell Magna
Sixpenny Handley
Stalbridge Weston
Hinton St Mary
West Orchard
LARMER TREE GARDENS
B3081
Stourton Caundle
B3091
Manston
Sutton Waldron
Dean
A357
Sturminster Newton
CRANBORNE
Farnham
Bishop's Caundle
Lydlinch
FIDDLEFORD MANOR
MILL
Hammoon
Iwerne Courtney or Shroton
Iwerne Minster
Stubhampton
Fiddleford
Cashmoor
Chettle
Newton
Child Okeford
Holwell
Woodbridge
Broad Oak
A357
HAMBLEDON HILL
Tarrant Gunville
Gussage St Michael
King's Stag
Fifehead Neville
Shillingstone
Tarrant Hinton
A354
WILTSHIRE
A350
Okeford Fitzpaine
Long Crichel
16
Stourpaine
Tarrant Launceston
Moor Crichel
0 1 2 3 miles
0 1 2 3 4 5 km
Pimperne
Durweston
Tarrant Monkton
Pulham
Bryan
Ibberton
Turnworth
ROYAL SIGNALS
Manswood

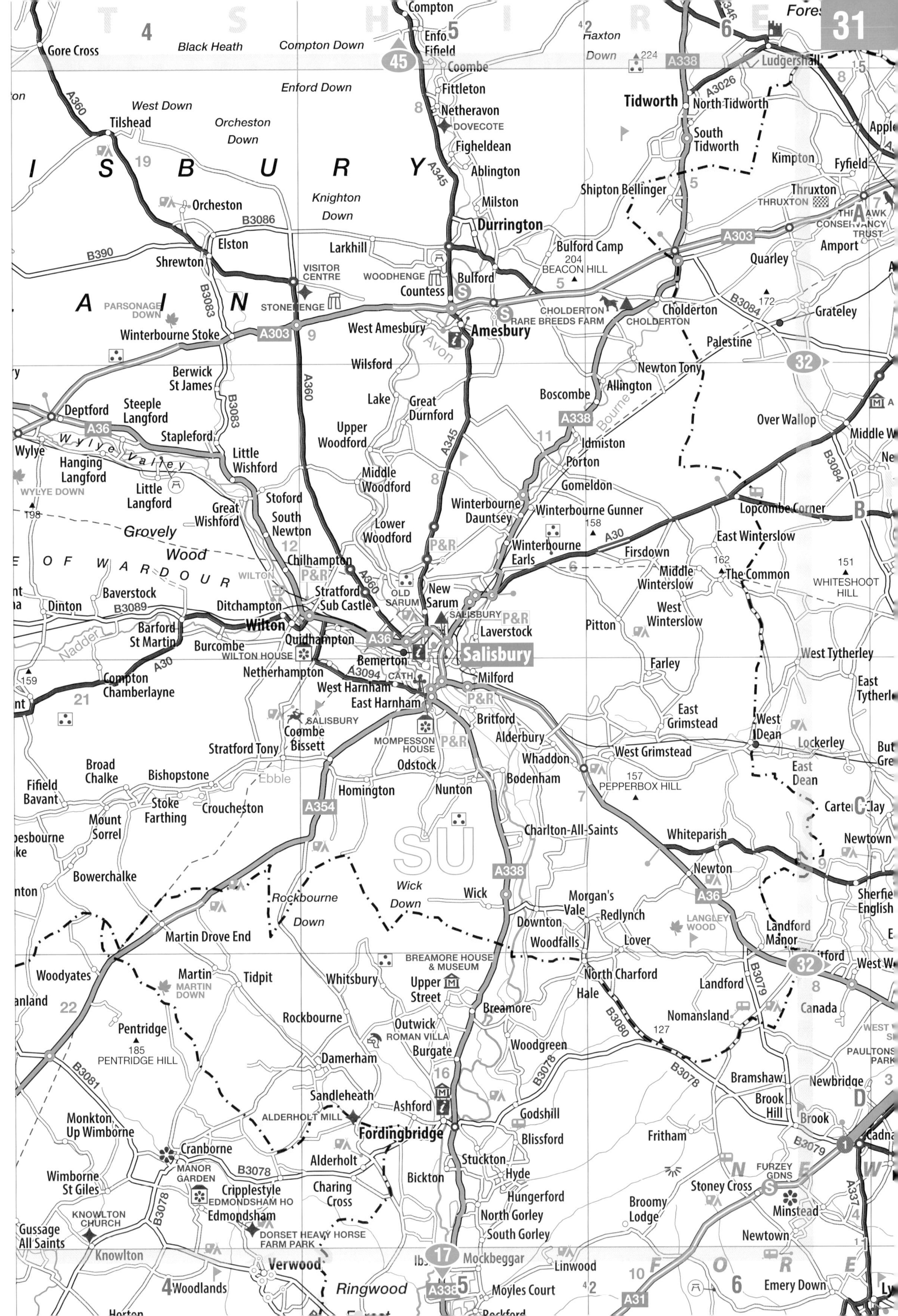
Gore Cross
Black Heath
Compton Down
Compton
Enford
Fifield
Coombe
Haxton
Down
Ludgershall
A338
A360
Enford Down
Fittleton
Netheravon
DOVECOTE
West Down
Tilshead
Orcheston
Down
Tidworth
North Tidworth
A3026
South
Tidworth
Figheldean
Ablington
A345
Appleshaw
Kimpton
Fyfield
S
B
U
R
Y
Knighton
Down
Orcheston
Milston
Durrington
Shipton Bellinger
Thruxton
THRUXTON
THE HAWK
CONSERVANCY
TRUST
Amport
Quarley
B3086
B390
Elston
Shrewton
Larkhill
VISITOR
CENTRE
WOODHENGE
Bulford Camp
204
BEACON HILL
Bulford
Countess
A303
B3083
A
I
N
PARSONAGE
DOWN
STONEHENGE
CHOLDERTON
RARE BREEDS FARM
CHOLDERTON
Cholderton
B3084
Grateley
Winterbourne Stoke
West Amesbury
Amesbury
Avon
Palestine
32
Wilsford
Newton Tony
Allington
Boscombe
Berwick
St James
Deptford
Steeple
Langford
Lake
Great
Durnford
Upper
Woodford
Over Wallop
Middle Wallop
A36
Stapleford
Wylye
Wylye Valley
Hanging
Langford
Little
Wishford
Little
Langford
Middle
Woodford
Idmiston
Porton
Gomeldon
WYLYE DOWN
198
Great
Wishford
Stoford
South
Newton
Winterbourne
Dauntsey
Winterbourne Gunner
158
Lopcombe Corner
East Winterslow
Grovely
Wood
Lower
Woodford
A30
Firsdown
Winterbourne
Earls
P&R
OF WARDOUR
WILTON
Chilhampton
Middle
Winterslow
162
The Common
151
WHITESHOOT
HILL
Baverstock
Dinton
B3089
Ditchampton
Stratford
Sub Castle
OLD
SARUM
New
Sarum
SALISBURY
West
Winterslow
Pitton
Barford
St Martin
Wilton
Laverstock
Nadder
Burcombe
Quidhampton
WILTON HOUSE
Salisbury
Bemerton
CATH
Netherhampton
A3094
West Harnham
East Harnham
Milford
Farley
West Tytherley
East
Tytherley
159
Compton
Chamberlayne
SALISBURY
Coombe
Bissett
Britford
East
Grimstead
West
Dean
Lockerley
MOMPESSON
HOUSE
Alderbury
Stratford Tony
Whaddon
West Grimstead
Broad
Chalke
Bishopstone
Odstock
Bodenham
157
PEPPERBOX HILL
East
Dean
Fifield
Bavant
Ebble
Homington
Nunton
Stoke
Farthing
Croucheston
A354
Mount
Sorrel
Charlton-All-Saints
Carter's Clay
Whiteparish
Newtown
Bowerchalke
SU
A338
Newton
Rockbourne
Down
Wick
Down
Wick
Morgan's
Vale
Redlynch
A36
Sherfield
English
Martin Drove End
Downton
Woodfalls
LANGLEY
WOOD
Lover
Landford
Manor
BREAMORE HOUSE
& MUSEUM
North Charford
West Wellow
Woodyates
Martin
MARTIN
DOWN
Tidpit
Whitsbury
Upper
Street
Hale
Landford
B3079
Canada
Breamore
B3080
Nomansland
127
Pentridge
185
PENTRIDGE HILL
Rockbourne
Outwick
ROMAN VILLA
Burgate
Woodgreen
PAULTONS
PARK
B3081
Damerham
B3078
Bramshaw
Newbridge
16
Sandleheath
Ashford
Brook
Hill
Brook
Monkton
Up Wimborne
ALDERHOLT MILL
Fordingbridge
Godshill
Blissford
Fritham
B3079
Cadnam
Cranborne
MANOR
GARDEN
Alderholt
Stuckton
Wimborne
St Giles
B3078
Cripplestyle
EDMONDSHAM HO
Charing
Cross
Bickton
Hyde
FURZEY
GDNS
Stoney Cross
Broomy
Lodge
Minstead
A337
Hungerford
KNOWLTON
CHURCH
Edmondsham
North Gorley
Gussage
All Saints
DORSET HEAVY HORSE
FARM PARK
South Gorley
Newtown
Knowlton
Verwood
17
Mockbeggar
Linwood
F
O
R
E
Woodlands
Ringwood
A338
Moyles Court
A31
Emery Down
Horton
Rockford

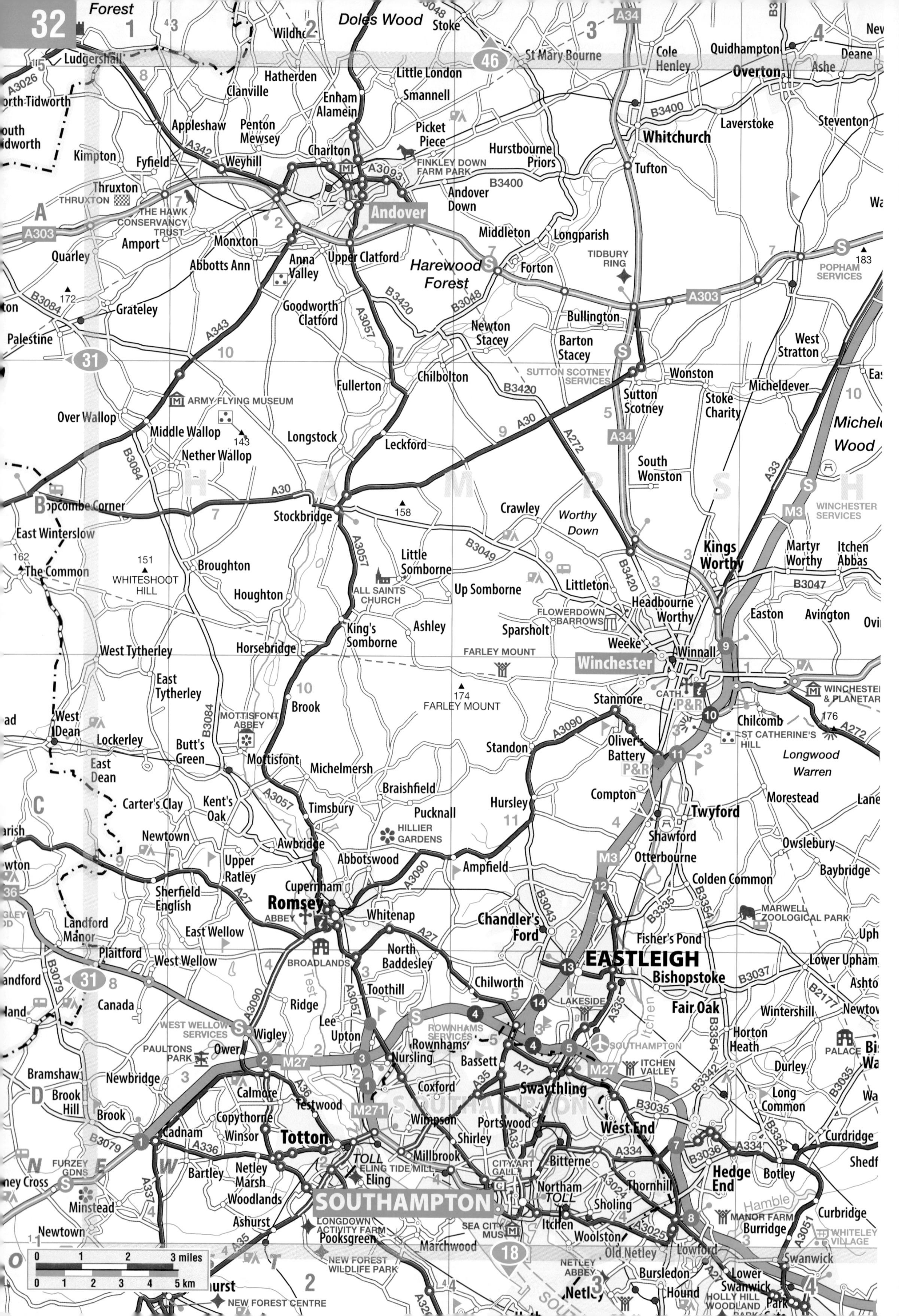
Forest
Ludgershall
Wildhern
Doles Wood
Stoke
St Mary Bourne
Cole Henley
Quidhampton
Deane
Overton
Ashe
Hatherden
Little London
Clanville
Enham Alamein
Smannell
North Tidworth
South Tidworth
Appleshaw
Penton Mewsey
Picket Piece
Whitchurch
Laverstoke
Steventon
Kimpton
Fyfield
Weyhill
Charlton
FINKLEY DOWN FARM PARK
Hurstbourne Priors
Tufton
Thruxton
THRUXTON
THE HAWK CONSERVANCY TRUST
Andover
Andover Down
Quarley
Amport
Monxton
Abbotts Ann
Anna Valley
Upper Clatford
Harewood Forest
Middleton
Longparish
Forton
TIDBURY RING
POPHAM SERVICES
Grateley
Goodworth Clatford
Bullington
Palestine
Newton Stacey
Barton Stacey
West Stratton
Fullerton
Chilbolton
SUTTON SCOTNEY SERVICES
Wonston
Sutton Scotney
Stoke Charity
Micheldever
ARMY FLYING MUSEUM
Over Wallop
Middle Wallop
Nether Wallop
Longstock
Leckford
South Wonston
Micheldever Wood
Stockbridge
Crawley
Worthy Down
WINCHESTER SERVICES
East Winterslow
The Common
WHITESHOOT HILL
Broughton
Little Somborne
Kings Worthy
Martyr Worthy
Itchen Abbas
Houghton
ALL SAINTS CHURCH
Up Somborne
Littleton
Headbourne Worthy
Easton
Avington
FLOWERDOWN BARROWS
King's Somborne
Ashley
Sparsholt
West Tytherley
Horsebridge
FARLEY MOUNT
Weeke
Winnall
Winchester
East Tytherley
Brook
Stanmore
CATH.
Chilcomb
WINCHESTER & PLANETARIUM
West Dean
MOTTISFONT ABBEY
Lockerley
Butt's Green
Mottisfont
Standon
Oliver's Battery
ST CATHERINE'S HILL
Longwood Warren
East Dean
Michelmersh
Braishfield
Compton
Carter's Clay
Kent's Oak
Timsbury
Pucknall
Hursley
Twyford
Morestead
Newtown
HILLIER GARDENS
Shawford
Owslebury
Awbridge
Upper Ratley
Abbotswood
Ampfield
Otterbourne
Baybridge
Cupernham
Colden Common
Sherfield English
Romsey
ABBEY
Whitenap
Chandler's Ford
MARWELL ZOOLOGICAL PARK
Landford Manor
East Wellow
North Baddesley
Fisher's Pond
Plaitford
West Wellow
BROADLANDS
EASTLEIGH
Bishopstoke
Lower Upham
Canada
Toothill
Chilworth
Fair Oak
Ridge
LAKESIDE
Wintershill
WEST WELLOW SERVICES
Wigley
Lee
Upton
ROWNHAMS SERVICES
Rownhams
SOUTHAMPTON
Horton Heath
PAULTONS PARK
Ower
Nursling
Bassett
ITCHEN VALLEY
Durley
Bramshaw
Newbridge
Calmore
Coxford
Swaythling
Long Common
Brook Hill
Brook
Testwood
Copythorne
Wimpson
Portswood
West End
Cadnam
Winsor
Totton
Shirley
Curdridge
FURZEY GDNS
Millbrook
Bitterne
Hedge End
Botley
Bartley
Netley Marsh
ELING TIDE MILL
Eling
CITY ART GALL.
Northam
Thornhill
Minstead
Woodlands
SOUTHAMPTON
Sholing
MANOR FARM
Curbridge
Newtown
Ashurst
LONGDOWN ACTIVITY FARM
Pooksgreen
SEA CITY MUS.
Itchen
Woolston
Burridge
WHITELEY VILLAGE
Marchwood
Old Netley
Lowford
NEW FOREST WILDLIFE PARK
NETLEY ABBEY
Bursledon
Swanwick
Lower Swanwick
Netley
Hound
HOLLY HILL WOODLAND PARK
NEW FOREST CENTRE
3 miles
5 km

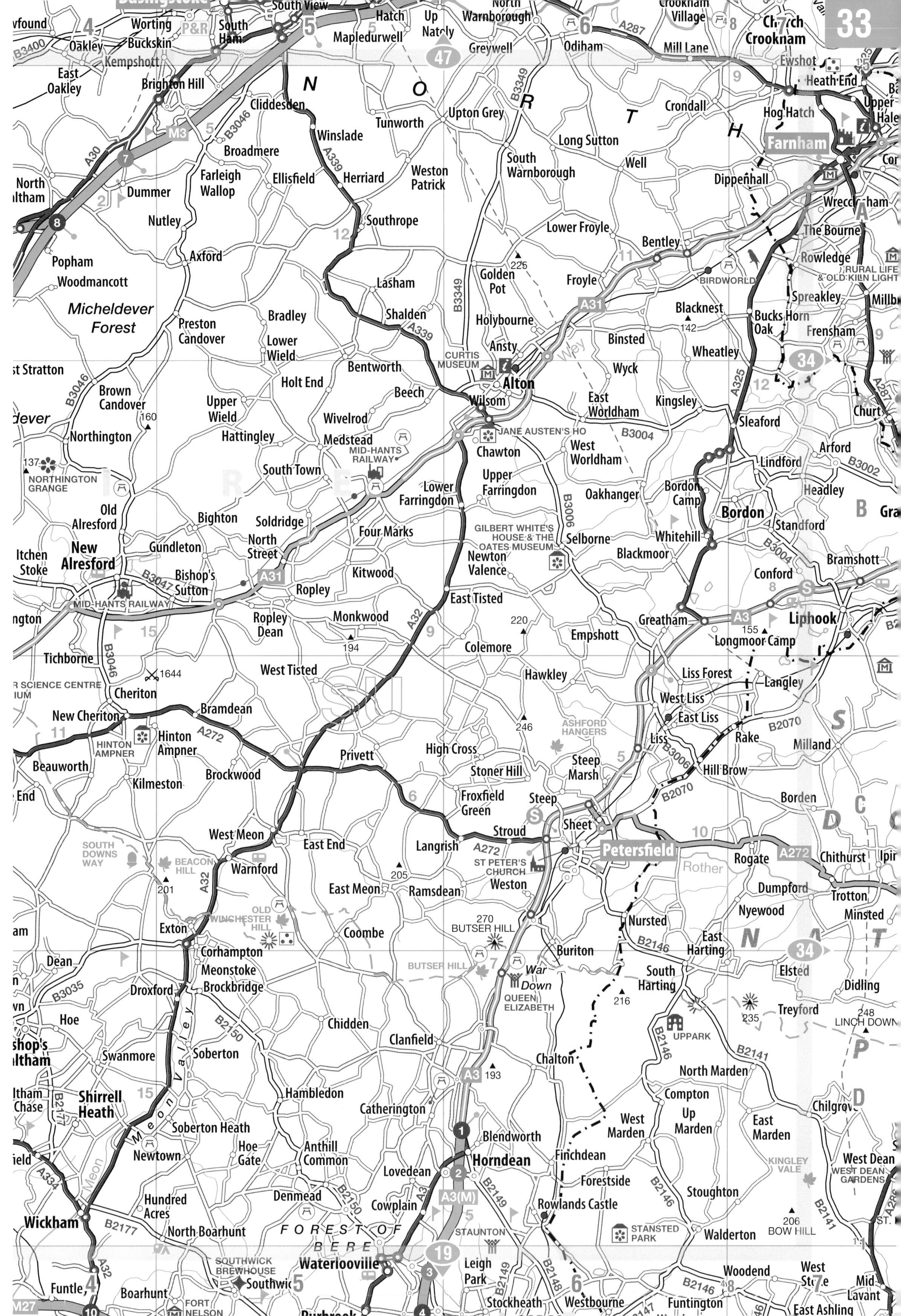
Basingstoke
South View
Hatch
Up Natoly
North Warnborough
Crookham Village
Church Crookham
Worting
South Ham
Mapledurwell
Greywell
Odiham
Mill Lane
Oakley
Buckskin
Kempshott
Ewshot
East Oakley
Brighton Hill
Heath End
Cliddesden
Upton Grey
Crondall
Hog Hatch
Upper Hale
Winslade
Tunworth
Long Sutton
Farnham
Broadmere
South Warnborough
Well
Farleigh Wallop
Ellisfield
Herriard
Weston Patrick
Dippenhall
North Waltham
Dummer
Wrecclesham
Nutley
Southrope
Lower Froyle
The Bourne
Bentley
Rowledge
Axford
Popham
Golden Pot
Froyle
BIRDWORLD
RURAL LIFE & OLD KILN LIGHT
Woodmancott
Lasham
Spreakley
Micheldever Forest
Blacknest
Preston Candover
Bradley
Shalden
Holybourne
Bucks Horn Oak
Frensham
Lower Wield
Ansty
Binsted
Wheatley
CURTIS MUSEUM
Alton
Wyck
East Stratton
Bentworth
Holt End
Brown Candover
Beech
Wilson
East Worldham
Kingsley
Upper Wield
Wivelrod
Sleaford
Micheldever
Northington
Hattingley
Medstead
JANE AUSTEN'S HO
Chawton
West Worldham
Arford
MID-HANTS RAILWAY
Lindford
NORTHINGTON GRANGE
South Town
Upper Farringdon
Headley
Lower Farringdon
Oakhanger
Bordon Camp
Bordon
Old Alresford
Bighton
Soldridge
Standford
Four Marks
GILBERT WHITE'S HOUSE & THE OATES MUSEUM
Whitehill
Itchen Stoke
New Alresford
Gundleton
North Street
Selborne
Blackmoor
Bramshott
Newton Valence
Bishop's Sutton
Kitwood
Conford
Ropley
MID-HANTS RAILWAY
East Tisted
Liphook
Itchen Abbas
Ropley Dean
Monkwood
Greatham
Empshott
Longmoor Camp
Tichborne
Colemore
West Tisted
Liss Forest
Hawkley
Langley
SCIENCE CENTRE
Cheriton
West Liss
East Liss
New Cheriton
Bramdean
ASHFORD HANGERS
Rake
HINTON AMPNER
Hinton Ampner
Liss
Milland
Beauworth
Privett
High Cross
Steep Marsh
Brockwood
Stoner Hill
Hill Brow
Kilmeston
Froxfield Green
Steep
Borden
Stroud
Sheet
West Meon
Langrish
Petersfield
East End
Rogate
Chithurst
SOUTH DOWNS WAY
BEACON HILL
Warnford
ST PETER'S CHURCH
Weston
Rother
East Meon
Ramsdean
Dumpford
Trotton
OLD WINCHESTER HILL
Nyewood
Minsted
Nursted
Exton
Coombe
BUTSER HILL
Corhampton
Buriton
East Harting
Dean
Meonstoke
BUTSER HILL
War Down
South Harting
Elsted
Droxford
Brockbridge
QUEEN ELIZABETH
Didling
Hoe
Treyford
LINCH DOWN
Chidden
UPPARK
Clanfield
Bishop's Waltham
Swanmore
Soberton
Chalton
North Marden
Meon Valley
Waltham Chase
Shirrell Heath
Hambledon
Compton
Chilgrove
Catherington
Up Marden
West Marden
East Marden
Soberton Heath
Blendworth
Hoe Gate
Anthill Common
Finchdean
West Dean
Newtown
WEST DEAN GARDENS
Horndean
KINGLEY VALE
Lovedean
Forestside
Denmead
Stoughton
Cowplain
Hundred Acres
Rowlands Castle
Wickham
BOW HILL
North Boarhunt
FOREST OF BERE
STAUNTON
STANSTED PARK
Walderton
Waterlooville
SOUTHWICK BREWHOUSE
Leigh Park
West Stoke
Southwick
Woodend
Mid Lavant
Funtley
Boarhunt
Stockheath
Westbourne
Funtington
East Ashling
FORT NELSON
Purbrook
NORTH
HAMPSHIRE
SOUTH
DOWNS
SU
A30
M3
B3046
A339
B3349
A31
A325
B3004
B3002
A287
B3006
B3047
A32
A272
A3
B2070
B2146
B2150
B3035
B2177
A334
A3(M)
B2149
B2148
B2141
M27
47
34
19

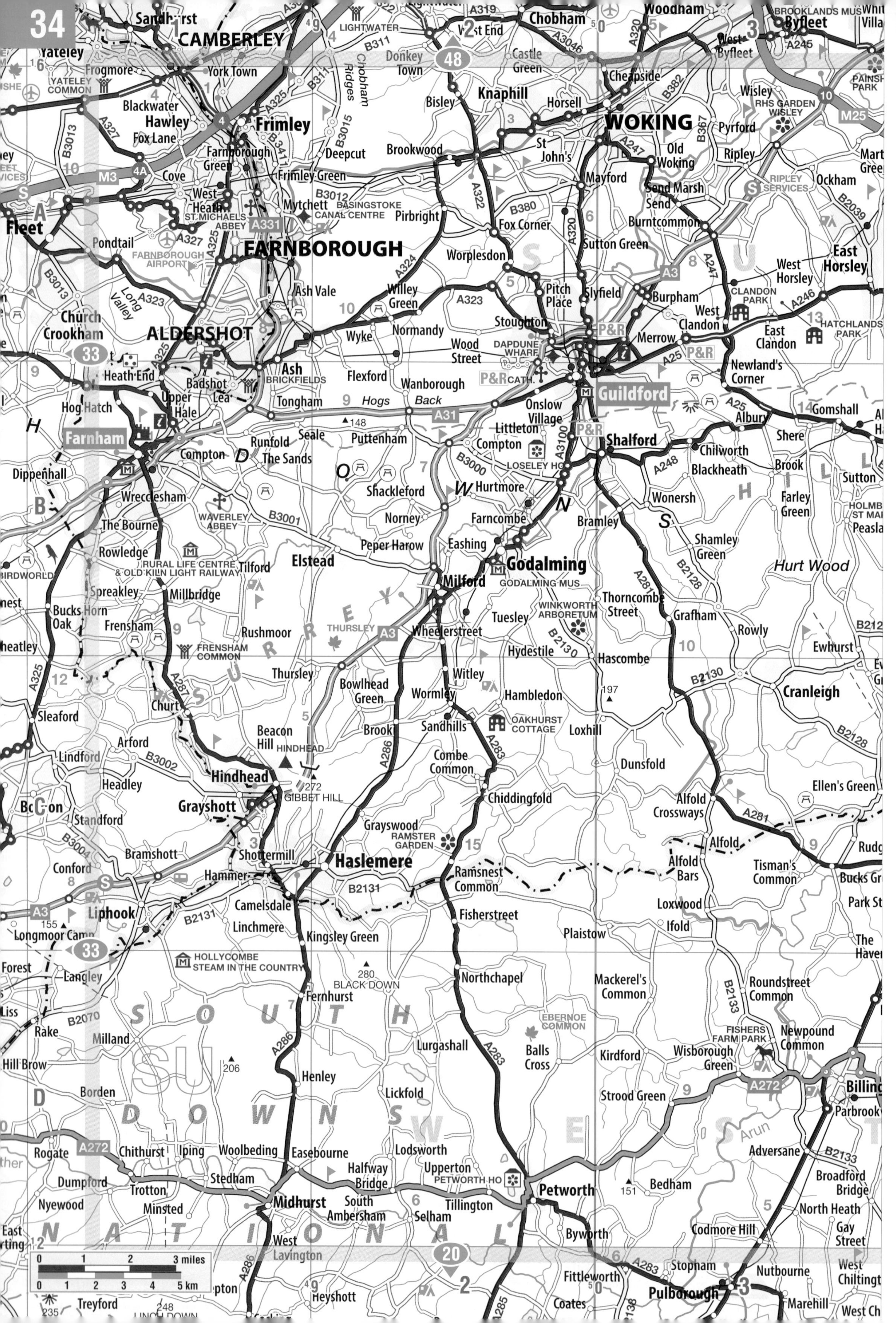
Sandhurst
CAMBERLEY
Yateley
Frogmore
YATELEY COMMON
York Town
Blackwater
Hawley
Fox Lane
Frimley
Farnborough Green
Cove
West Heath
ST MICHAELS ABBEY
Fleet
Pondtail
FARNBOROUGH AIRPORT
FARNBOROUGH
Deepcut
Frimley Green
Mytchett
BASINGSTOKE CANAL CENTRE
Pirbright
Brookwood
Bisley
LIGHTWATER
West End
Donkey Town
Chobham Ridges
Chobham
Castle Green
Knaphill
Horsell
Woodham
Cheapside
WOKING
St John's
Old Woking
Mayford
Byfleet
West Byfleet
BROOKLANDS MUS
Wisley
RHS GARDEN WISLEY
Pyrford
Ripley
RIPLEY SERVICES
Ockham
PAINSHILL PARK
Send Marsh
Send
Burntcommon
Fox Corner
Sutton Green
Worplesdon
Pitch Place
Slyfield
Burpham
West Horsley
East Horsley
CLANDON PARK
West Clandon
East Clandon
HATCHLANDS PARK
Merrow
Newland's Corner
Ash Vale
Long Valley
Church Crookham
ALDERSHOT
Willey Green
Wyke
Normandy
Stoughton
Wood Street
DAPDUNE WHARF
Ash
BRICKFIELDS
Flexford
Wanborough
CATH.
Guildford
Heath End
Badshot Lea
Upper Hale
Hog Hatch
Farnham
Tongham
Hogs Back
Onslow Village
Littleton
Compton
LOSELEY HO
Shalford
Chilworth
Albury
Gomshall
Shere
Brook
Blackheath
Sutton
Farley Green
Runfold
Seale
Puttenham
The Sands
Dippenhall
Shackleford
Hurtmore
Wrecclesham
WAVERLEY ABBEY
The Bourne
Norney
Farncombe
Bramley
Wonersh
Shamley Green
Rowledge
Peper Harow
Eashing
Godalming
GODALMING MUS
BIRDWORLD
RURAL LIFE CENTRE & OLD KILN LIGHT RAILWAY
Tilford
Elstead
Milford
Hurt Wood
Spreakley
Millbridge
Bucks Horn Oak
Frensham
Rushmoor
THURSLEY
Wheelerstreet
Tuesley
WINKWORTH ARBORETUM
Thorncombe Street
Grafham
Rowly
Ewhurst
FRENSHAM COMMON
Hydestile
Hascombe
Thursley
Witley
Hambledon
Bowlhead Green
Wormley
Cranleigh
Sleaford
Churt
Sandhills
OAKHURST COTTAGE
Loxhill
Arford
Beacon Hill
HINDHEAD
Brook
Combe Common
Dunsfold
Lindford
Hindhead
GIBBET HILL
Chiddingfold
Headley
Grayshott
Alfold Crossways
Ellen's Green
Standford
Grayswood
RAMSTER GARDEN
Alfold
Bramshott
Shottermill
Haslemere
Alfold Bars
Tisman's Common
Conford
Hammer
Ramsnest Common
Camelsdale
Loxwood
Liphook
Longmoor Camp
Linchmere
Fisherstreet
Ifold
Plaistow
Kingsley Green
HOLLYCOMBE STEAM IN THE COUNTRY
Langley
BLACK DOWN
Northchapel
Mackerel's Common
Roundstreet Common
Fernhurst
Liss
Rake
Milland
EBERNOE COMMON
FISHERS FARM PARK
Newpound Common
Lurgashall
Balls Cross
Kirdford
Wisborough Green
Hill Brow
Henley
Borden
Lickfold
Strood Green
Billingshurst
Parbrook
SOUTH DOWNS
Rogate
Chithurst
Iping
Woolbeding
Easebourne
Lodsworth
Adversane
Halfway Bridge
Upperton
PETWORTH HO
Petworth
Bedham
Broadford Bridge
Dumpford
Trotton
Stedham
Nyewood
Minsted
Midhurst
South Ambersham
Selham
Tillington
North Heath
Byworth
Codmore Hill
Gay Street
West Lavington
Stopham
Nutbourne
Fittleworth
Pulborough
Heyshott
Coates
Treyford
Marehill
0 1 2 3 miles
0 1 2 3 4 5 km

WORLD OF ADVENTURES
Belmont
Purley
Sanderstead
Cobham
Oxshott
EPSOM
ASHTEAD COMMON
Woodmansterne
Hamsey Green
Farleigh
BIGGIN HILL MEMORIAL
Stoke D'Abernon
Wood Field
BANSTEAD
Kenley
Coulsdon
Warlingham
Downside
Great Burgh
Burgh Heath
Chipstead
Whyteleafe
Leatherhead Common
Ashtead
EPSOM DOWNS
Old Coulsdon
COBHAM SERVICES
Fetcham
Leatherhead
Tadworth
Kingswood
Hooley
SOUTH LONDON DOWNS
Woldingham
Little Bookham
Walton on the Hill
Chaldon
CATERHAM
Effingham
BOCKETTS FARM PARK
Headley
Lower Kingswood
Great Bookham
WALTON HEATH
Mickleham
Limpsfield
POLESDEN LACEY
Merstham
Brewer Street
Godstone
Oxted
Westhumble
BOX HILL
TANNERS HATCH SURREY HILLS
Church Town
Ranmore Common
Dorking
Buckland
REDHILL
Nutfield
Pixham
Tandridge
Betchworth
Bletchingley
GODSTONE FARM
Earlswood
Brockham
Reigate
South Nutfield
NORTH DOWNS WAY
Crowhurst Lane End
Westcott
Strood Green
Doversgreen
Ridge Green
REDHILL
South Godstone
Wotton
North Holmwood
Sidlow
Salfords
Crowhurst
Leigh
Abinger Common
Blindley Heath
HAXTED WATERMILL
Nalderswood
Outwood
South Holmwood
Meath Green
Horne
Holmbury St Mary
Coldharbour
Parkgate
Norwood Hill
Weatherhill
Lingfield
LEITH HILL
Beare Green
Hookwood
Horley
Smallfield
LINGFIELD PARK
Newdigate
GATWICK AIRPORT
LONDON GATWICK
Newchapel
Charlwood
Burstow
Forest Green
Felcourt
Capel
Copthorne
Ockley
Clark's Green
Felbridge
Walliswood
County Oak
East Grinstead
Ifield
Three Bridges
Crawley Down
Oakwoodhill
Rusper
Lambs Green
Kingsfold
IFIELD WATERMILL
Pound Hill
Worth
Sunnyside
Turners Hill
Crawley
Saint Hill
STANE STREET
Rowhook
Faygate
HOLMBUSH FARM
Broadfield
Tilgate
Warnham
BUCHAN
Selsfield Common
Pease Pottage
PEASE POTTAGE SERVICES
TILGATE
West Hoathly
Strood Green
Roffey
Colgate
Tilgate Forest Row
Balcombe Lane
Sharpthorne
Broadbridge Heath
PRIEST HOUSE
St Leonard's Forest
THE HIGH BEECHES
WAKEHURST PLACE
Slinfold
Horsham
Balcombe
Highbrook
WINGS MUS
Handcross
NYMANS GARDEN
Ashfold Crossways
Ardingly
Horsted Keynes
Itchingfield
Staplefield
Five Oaks
Mannings Heath
Southwater Street
Monk's Gate
Slaugham
Barns Green
Lower Beeding
Brook Street
BORDE HILL GARDEN
Nuthurst
Slough Green
Southwater
Warninglid
HEAVEN FARM
SOUTHWATER
Whitemans Green
Brooks Green
Copsale
Crabtree
LEONARDSLEE LAKES & GDNS
Cuckfield
Lindfield
HAYWARDS HEATH
Coneyhurst
Maplehurst
Ansty
Scayne's Hill
Bolney
Coolham
COOLHAM AIRFIELD D-DAY MEMORIAL
Shipley
Cowfold
Whitehall
West Grinstead
Kent Street
Wivelsfield Green
Broomer's Corner
Wineham
Hickstead
Wivelsfield
North Chailey
BURGESS HILL
Goose Green
Dial Post
Partridge Green
Chailey
JUMPING
DITCHLING COMMON
South Street
Spear Hill
Sayers Common
A3
A243
A240
A24
A217
A23
M25
A25
A246
A2003
A29
A264
A281
A272
A22
B2028
B2036
A2300
49
36
21

Leaves Green
Downe
DARWIN MUSEUM
Pratt's Bottom
Badger's Mount
Halstead
Shoreham
Fairseat
Hamsey Green
Farleigh
BIGGIN HILL
BIGGIN HILL MEMORIAL
Biggin Hill
Cudham
Knockholt Pound
Otford
Warlingham
Knockholt
Kemsing
Heaverham
Wrotham
South Street
Chevening
M26
Borough Green
Tatsfield
NORTH DOWNS WAY
Dunton Green
Seal
Platt
Woldingham
B2024
Chipstead
Riverhead
Ightham
GREAT COMP
Crouch
CLACKET LANE SERVICES
Sundridge
Stone Street
Claygate Cross
Titsey
Brasted
Sevenoaks
KNOLE
Ivy Hatch
Plaxtol
Westerham
QUEBEC HO
Brasted Chart
IGHTHAM MOTE
OLD SOAR MANOR
Limpsfield
The Chart
Cross Keys
Dunk's Green
Limpsfield Chart
Whitley Row
Underriver
West Peckham
Oxted
EMMETTS
CHARTWELL
Church Town
Crockham Hill
Ide Hill
Shipbourne
Tandridge
Toy's Hill
Sevenoaks Weald
Oakhurst
Coldharbour
BROADVIEW GARDEN
Pittswood
Hadlow
GODSTONE FARM
Pootings
Crowhurst Lane End
Marlpit Hill
Four Elms
Hildenborough
Higham Wood
Hilden Park
South Godstone
Golden Green
Crowhurst
Crouch House Green
B2027
Chiddingstone Causeway
TONBRIDGE CASTLE
Medway
Blindley Heath
HAXTED WATERMILL
Edenbridge
How Green
Bough Beech
Leigh
Brook Street
TONBRIDGE
Five Oak Green
CHIDDINGSTONE CASTLE
Hever
Chiddingstone
Tudeley
Lingfield
Marsh Green
HEVER CASTLE AND GARDENS
PENSHURST PLACE
HAYSDEN
ALL SAINTS CHURCH
B2028
Penshurst
Bidborough
LINGFIELD PARK
Markbeech
B2176
Dormansland
Newchapel
Chiddingstone Hoath
Southborough
High Brooms
Felcourt
Speldhurst
Pembury
Cowden
MUS & ART GALL
Lullenden
Hammerwood
Blackham
Fordcombe
Rusthall
Felbridge
A264
ROYAL TUNBRIDGE WELLS
Blackwell
Ashurst
Langton Green
East Grinstead
HAMMERWOOD PARK
Hawkenbury
Crawley Down
Sunnyside
Ashurstwood
SPA VALLEY RAILWAY
Bells Yew Green
Groombridge
B2110
Hartfield
B2169
Saint Hill
STANDEN
Forest Row
FOREST WAY
Withyham
Eridge Green
Frant
Upper Hartfield
Lye Green
B2099
West Hoathly
Coleman's Hatch
BOWLES OUTDOOR CENTRE
Wood's Green
Sharpthorne
Friar's Gate
Boarshead
PRIEST HOUSE
Durgates
Wych Cross
Mark Cross
B2100
Bestbeech Hill
Chelwood Gate
Crowborough
Riseden
Highbrook
ASHDOWN FOREST
Poundfield
Town Row
Shover's Green
Horsted Keynes
Chelwood Common
Rotherfield
Tidebrook
Jarvis Brook
Danehill
Nutley
Duddleswell
Coggins Mill
HEAVEN FARM
Cackle Street
Fairwarp
High Hurstwood
Mayfield
Lindfield
Sheffield Green
Butcher's Cross
HAYWARDS HEATH
Splayne's Green
Five Ashes
Rother
SHEFFIELD PARK
Maresfield
Hadlow Down
Pound Green
Fletching
A272
BLUEBELL RAILWAY
Buxted
Scayne's Hill
Burwash Weald
Ringles Cross
Cross in Hand
Broad Oak
Grisling Common
BLACKBOYS
Cade Street
Newick
Uckfield
Wivelsfield Green
North Chailey
Framfield
Heathfield
Punnett's Town
Blackboys
Old Heathfield
B2102
Ridgewood
Little London
Waldron
Maynard's Green
Rushlake Green
E SUSSEX NATIONAL
Foxhunt Green
Spithurst
Little
0 1 2 3 miles
0 1 2 3 4 5 km
DITCH COMMON

Snodland
Birling
Ryarsh
KIT'S COTY HOUSE
LEYBOURNE LAKE
Eccles
New Hythe
THE FRIARS
Aylesford
TYLAND BARN
Boxley
Bredhurst
Stockbury
South Green
Bredgar
BREDGAR & WORMSHILL LT RLY
Bicknor
Swanton Street
Milstead
Tunstall
Highsted
DODDINGTON PLACE
Doddington
M2
M20
A249
51
188
WOOD
Addington
Leybourne
West Malling
Ditton
British Legion Village
Sandling
KENT LIFE
Detling
Thurnham
Hucking
Wormshill
Frinsted
Offham
East Malling
MANOR PARK
TOWER
P&R
NEWNHAM COURT
Broad Street
BEARSTED MAIDSTONE SERVICES
197
Wichling
Kent Street
King's Hill
Maidstone
East Barming
Roseacre
Bearsted
Hollingbourne
Eyhorne Street
West Street
A228
A26
A20
Teston
Wateringbury
Tovil
East Farleigh
West Farleigh
B2010
Shepway
Otham
STONEACRE
Leeds
LEEDS CASTLE
Broomfield
Harrietsham
NORTH DOWNS WAY
Warren Street
A229
A274
B2163
Nettlestead
Nettlestead Green
Loose
Boughton Monchelsea
Langley
Langley Heath
Kingswood
Lenham
Sandway
Lenham Heath
B2015
B2010
B2163
Coxheath
Yalding
Hunton
Linton
Chart Corner
Chart Sutton
123
Warmlake
Sutton Valence
Grafty Green
Boughton Malherbe
Charing Heath
38
Hale Street
Peckham
Benover
Laddingford
B2162
Chainhurst
Beult
Rabbit's Cross
Ulcombe
Egerton
Beltring
THE HOP FARM
Queen Street
Collier Street
13
Cross-at-Hand
Milebush
TQ
Southernden
Egerton Forstal
Little Chart
Pluckley
Pluckley Thorne
Paddock Wood
B2161
Claygate
Marden
Hawkenbury
Headcorn
Staplehurst
HEADCORN
Maltman's Hill
Castle Hill
Marden Beech
Marden Thorn
FARM MUS
Sinkhurst Green
Smarden Bell
B2079
IDEN CROFT HERBS
Knox Bridge
Frittenden
Smarden
Haffenden Quarter
Wissenden
B2160
Brenchley
Petteridge
Horsmonden
Winchet Hill
Curtisden Green
Lashenden
Bethersden
Hazel Street
Collier's Green
Cranbrook Common
Standen
Three Chimneys
SISSINGHURST CASTLE
A262
Biddenden
Tanden
A28
Shadoxhurst
B2162
Goudhurst
Iden Green
Wilsley Pound
Sissinghurst
High Halden
Lamberhurst
CRANBROOK MUSEUM
UNION MILL
BIDDENDEN VINEYARDS
SCOTNEY CASTLE
Kilndown
B2085
Cranbrook
East End
St Michael's
Shirkoak
B2100
Cousley Wood
Hartley
KENT & EAST SUSSEX RAILWAY
Parkgate
Woodchurch
B2079
BEDGEBURY PINETUM
Bedgebury Forest
A229
B2086
Tenterden
Brook Street
Bewl Water
Benenden
CM BOOTH COLLECTION
Leigh Green
Kenardington
Three Leg Cross
Gill's Green
COLONEL STEPHENS RAILWAY MUSEUM
B2080
Flimwell
High Street
Iden Green
Dingleden
Rolvenden
B2082
Small Hythe
Reading Street
Appledore Heath
B2099
Union Street
Hawkhurst
Four Throws
A268
Wallcrouch
Ticehurst
Horns Corner
A21
The Moor
Rolvenden Layne
SMALLHYTHE PLACE
ISLE OF OXNEY
Appledore
PASHLEY MANOR GARDENS
Peening Quarter
Stonegate
Swiftsden
Sandhurst
Linkhill
Stone
Hurst Green
Sandhurst Cross
Newenden
Wittersham
B2244
Rother
ROTHER LEVELS
The Stocks
Ham Green
Witherenden Hill
Etchingham
A265
Bodiam
GREAT DIXTER
Northbridge Street
Northiam
Burwash
BATEMAN'S
Salehurst
Ewhurst Green
Beckley
Four Oaks
Robertsbridge
ROTHER VALLEY RLY
Millcorner
Clayhill
Iden
Houghton Green
B2165
Staple Cross
Peasmarsh
Oxley's Green
Horns Cross
Rye Foreign
Playden
East Guldeford
John's Cross
80
Cripp's Corner
B2089
Vinehall Street
197
Brightling
Res.
Mountfield
Darwell Hole
Rye
Tillingham
RYE HERITAGE CENTRE
23
Broad Oak
Broadland Row
Udimore
164
Dallington
B2096
Netherfield
Whatlington
Sedlescombe
Sedlescombe Street
Brede
Rye Harbour
CAMBER CASTLE
Canadia

Lenham Heath
Charing
Charing Heath
Egerton
Egerton Forstal
Little Chart
Pluckley
Pluckley Thorne
Maltman's Hill
Wissenden
Bethersden
Tanden
High Halden
Woodchurch
Brook Street
Leigh Green
Reading Street
SMALLHYTHE PLACE
ISLE OF OXNEY
Peening Quarter
Ham Green
The Stocks
Iden
Houghton Green
Playden
Rye
RYE HERITAGE CENTRE
Rye Harbour
CAMBER CASTLE
Rye Bay
Winchelsea Beach
WINCHELSEA COURT HALL MUSEUM
Westwell Leacon
Westwell
Ram Lane
Hothfield
GODINTON HOUSE
Great Chart
Ashford
Willesborough
Sevington
Kingsnorth
Stubbs Cross
Shadoxhurst
Henghurst
Shirkoak
Orlestone
SOUTH OF ENGLAND RARE BREEDS CEN
Kenardington
Warehorne
Appledore Heath
HORNE'S PLACE CHAPEL
Appledore
Stone
Snargate
Brenzett
AERONAUTICAL MUSEUM
Brookland
Walland Marsh
East Guldeford
Camber
Challock
Molash
NORTH DOWNS WAY
Bilting
Boughton Aluph
Boughton Lees
Goat Lees
Kennington
CONNINGBROOK LAKES
Wye
WYE CROWN
Brook
Hastingleigh
Hinxhill
Willesborough Lees
Mersham
Cheeseman's Green
Bromley Green
Aldington Frith
Bonnington
Ham Street Woods
Ruckinge
Hamstreet
Bilsington
Royal Military Canal
Snave
ROMNEY MARSH
Ivychurch
ROMNEY WARREN
ROMNEY MARSH VISITOR CENTRE
Old Romney
New Romney
Lydd
LYDD (LONDON ASHFORD)
Denge Marsh
LYDD INTERNATIONAL RACEWAY
DUNGENESS
Denge Beach
THE OLD LIGHTHOUSE
Godmersham
Petham
Sole Street
Crundale
Waltham
Hassell Street
Bodsham
Elmsted
Lymbridge Green
Brabourne
Stowting
Brabourne Lees
Smeeth
Sellindge
Sellindge Lees
STOP 24 SERVICES
E. Stour
Clap Hill
Aldington
Court-at-Street
PORT LYMPNE WILD ANIMAL PARK AND GARDENS
Lympne
West Hythe
Newingreen
Burmarsh
Newchurch
ROMNEY, HYTHE AND DYMCHURCH RAILWAY
Dymchurch
MARTELLO TOWER
St Mary in the Marsh
St Mary's Bay
Littlestone on Sea
Romney Sands
Greatstone on Sea
Lydd on Sea
Kingston
Upper Hardres Court
Bossingham
Derringstone
Stelling Minnis
ELHAM VALLEY VINEYARD
Lyminge Forest
Elham
Rhodes Minnis
Ottinge
KENT BATTLE OF BRITAIN MUSEUM
Lyminge
Etchinghill
Postling
Paddlesworth
Beachborough
Stanford
Newington
CHANNEL TUNNEL
Pedlinge
ELHAM VALLEY RLY MUS
Cheriton
Saltwood
BROCKHILL
Hythe
Palmarsh
NORTH DOWNS WAY
A20
A252
A28
A251
A2070
B2067
B2080
B2082
B2089
A259
B2075
A261
B2068
M20
0 1 2 3 miles
0 1 2 3 4 5 km

Nonington
Northbourne
DEAL CASTLE
THE DOWNS
Tilmanstone
Elvington
Great Mongeham
Walmer
WALMER CASTLE AND GARDENS
Womenswold
Barfrestone
EAST KENT RLY
Ripple
Sutton
Woolage Green
Eythorne
East Studdal
West Langdon
Ringwould
Kingsdown
Coxhill
Shepherdswell
Martin
Denton
LYDDEN
Coldred
East Langdon
Martin Mill
Wootton
Whitfield
Guston
Selsted
Lydden
LYDDEN TEMPLE EWELL
St Margaret's at Cliffe
ST JOHN'S COMMANDERY
Temple Ewell
ST MARGARET'S MUS
Ewell Minnis
West Cliffe
St Margaret's Bay
Swingfield Street
CRABBLE CORN MILL
THE PINES GARDEN
Buckland
SOUTH FORELAND
Swingfield Minnis
Alkham
ROMAN PAINTED HOUSE
WHITE CLIFFS
CALAIS DUNKERQUE
Densole
Drellingore
Maxton
CASTLE & HELLFIRE CORNER
Farthingloe
West Hougham
DOVER
Hawkinge
Aycliff
DE BRADELEI WHARF
Capel le Ferne
SAMPHIRE HOE
EAST CLIFF & WARREN
East Wear Bay
Folkestone
CLIFF LIFT
ndgate
CHANNEL TUNNEL
TR
ENGLISH CHANNEL
A2
A256
A258
A260
A20
B2011
A
B
C
D
4
5
6

Pontardawe
Clydach
Ynystawe
Glais
Alltwen
Trebanos
Rhyd-y-fro
Cilybebyll
Gellinudd
Rhôs
Crynant
Morfa Glas
Blaengwrach
Cwmgwrach
Resolven
RESOLVEN MTN.
Rhigos
Cwm-hwnt
ZIP WORLD TOWER
VALE OF NEATH
CWM NEDD
Melincourt
Clyne
Cilfrew
Aberdulais
Tonna
Cadoxton-Juxta-Neath
NEATH MUSEUM
Neath
(CASTELL-NEDD)
NEATH PORT TALBOT
(CASTELL-NEDD PORT TALBOT)
Blaenrhondda
Tynewydd
Treherbert
Glyncorrwg
Blaen-gwynfi
Aber-gwynfi
Cwm-parc
Morriston
Llansamlet
Skewen
Birchgrove
Bryn-coch
Rhydding
Neath Abbey
Heol-las
Cwm
Bon-y-maen
Pentre-dwr
Llandarcy
Swansea
(ABERTAWE)
PLANTASIA
Port Tennant
SWANSEA MUSEUM
NATIONAL WATERFRONT MUSEUM
Foxhole
Cimla
GNOLL
Briton Ferry
Pontrhydyfen
Baglan
Pwll-y-glaw
Brynbryddan
MYNYDD DINAS
528
Cwmafan
Aberavon
Port Talbot
Taibach
Goytre
Margam
Groes
MARGAM
MARGAM ABBEY AND STONES MUSEUM
VISITOR CENTRE
AFAN FOREST PARK
SOUTH WALES MINERS MUSEUM
Duffryn
Cymer
Croeserw
Caerau
Spelter
Dyffryn
FOEL Y DYFFRYN
366
Bryn
Nantyffyllon
MAESTEG
Cwmfelin
Garth
Llangynwyd
Blaengarw
Pontycymer
568 WERFA
Nant-y-moel
Wyndham
Price Town
Ogmore Vale
Pont Rhyd-y-cyff
344 MYNYDD MARGAM
319 MOEL TON-MAWR
BRIDGEND
(PEN-Y-BONT AR OGWR)
Bettws
Llangeinor
Blackmill
Coytrahen
Tondu
Aberkenfig
Brynmenyn
Bryncethin
BRYNGARW
BEDFORD
Kenfig Hill
Cefn Cross
Cefn Cribbwr
SARN PARK SERVICES
Sarn
Pen-y-fai
Pendre
Coity
COITY CASTLE
Bridgend
(Pen-y-bont ar Ogwr)
NEWCASTLE
Laleston
Coychurch
Kenfig
Mawdlam
KENFIG POOL AND DUNES
Kenfig Burrows
North Cornelly
Pyle
(Y Pîl)
South Cornelly
ROYAL PORTHCAWL
Nottage
Hutchwns
Newton
Clevis
Porthcawl
CONEY BEACH
Tythegston
Merthyr Mawr
OGMORE CASTLE
MERTHYR MAWR WARREN
Ogmore
Ewenny
Corntown
Treoes
Ogmore-by-Sea
St Brides Major
Colwinston
Penuchadre
Southerndown
GLAMORGAN HERITAGE COAST CENTRE
WALES COAST PATH
Wick
Broughton
Monknash
Marcross
St Donat's
Nash Pt.
Trwyn yr As
Tusker Rock
SWANSEA BAY
BAE ABERTAWE
SS
M4
A465
A4109
A474
A483
A4107
A48
A4241
A4229
A4106
A473
A4063
A4064
A4061
A4065
B4283
B4281
B4282
B4286
B4287
B4290
B4434
B4242
B4603
B4291
B4524
B4265
0 1 2 3 miles
0 1 2 3 4 5 km

Hirwaun
Tre-Gibbon
Gellideg
Pen-yr-Heolgerrig
Merthyr Tydfil
(Merthyr Tudful)
YNYSFACH ENGINE HOUSE
Pentrebach
Abercanaid
Troedyrhiw
60
PARC CWM DARREN
Tirphil
(Rhymni)
Pontlottyn
Abertysswg
New Tredegar
(Tredegar Newydd)
Waunlwyd
East
Cwmtillery
Abertillery
(Abertyleri)
Talywain
Cwm
Man-moel
Hollybush
Aberbeeg
St Illtyd
Brynithel
Llanhilleth
(Llanhiledd)
Penywaun
Trecynon
Llwydcoed
Cwmdare
ABERDARE
(ABERDÂR)
DARE VALLEY
Aber-nant
Cwmbâch
Aberaman
Cwmaman
MOUNTAIN ASH
(ABERPENNAR)
Penrhiwceiber
Deri
Bedlinog
Cwmfelin
Aberfan
Merthyr Vale
Markham
PEN-Y-FAN POND
Trinant
ABERBARGOED GRASSLANDS
Bargoed
(Bargod)
Argoed
TAF BARGOED
Gilfach
61
Crumlin
(Crymlyn)
Newbridge
Maerdy
Treorchy
(Treorci)
Pentre
Ferndale
St Gwynno Forest
Treharris
Trelewis
Gelligaer
LLANCAIACH FAWR MANOR
Nelson
PARCPENALLTA
Pengam
Blackwood
(Coed Duon)
Oakdale
Pontllanfraith
Lanfach
RHONDDA
Ton-Pentre
Ystrad
Gelli
Tylorstown
Pont-y-gwaith
Wattstown
Ynysboeth
Abercynon
Hengoed
Ystrad-mynach
Maesy-cwmmer
Wyllie
Ynysddu
Abercarn
Cwmcarn
FOREST
Clydach Vale
CLYDACH VALE
Llwynypia
Trealaw
Ynyshir
Ynysybwl
Rhymney Valley
Sirhowy Valley
Pontywaun
Crosskeys
Cwmfelinfach
Risca
(Rhisga)
SIRHOWY VALLEY
Tonypandy
Penygraig
Porth
A WELSH COAL MINING EXPERIENCE
Glyncoch
Cilfynydd
Trehafod
PONTYPRIDD
Trebanog
Senghenydd
Abertridwr
Llanbradach
Bedwas
Machen
Lower Machen
Evanstown
Gilfach Goch
Bryn Golau
Tonyrefail
Pen-y-coedcae
Treforest
Glyntaff
Rhydyfelin
Penyrheol
Trecenydd
Hendreforgan
Glynogwr
Hawthorn
CAERPHILLY
(CAERFFILI)
Rudry
Rhiwderin
Castellau
Upper Church Village
Llantwit Fardre
Coedely
THE ROYAL MINT EXPERIENCE
Church Village
Nantgarw
MYNYDD MAENDY
Beddau
Thornhill
PARC CEFN ONN
CARDIFF GATE SERVICES
Machen y-Fedw
Efail Isaf
Llantrisant
Taff's Well
CASTELL COCH
Tongwynlais
Lisvane
Llanedeyrn
Brynna
Llanharan
Talbot Green
Cross Inn
Creigiau
Llanishen
Pencoed
Bryncae
Dolau
Pontyclun
Pentyrch
Rhiwbina
Cyncoed
St Mellons
Llanrumney
Llanilid
Llanharry
Brynsadler
Miskin
Groes-faen
Capel Llanilltern
FOREST FARM
Radyr
Whitchurch
Rumney
Tâlygarn
LLANERCH VINEYARD
CARDIFF WEST SERVICES
Birchgrove
Heath
Mary Hill
Craig Penllyn
St Brides-super-Ely
NATIONAL MUS OF HISTORY
Llandaff
Roath
Newton
Llangan
Llansannor
Ystradowen
Peterston-super-Ely
St George's
St Fagans
Canton
CATH.
Cathays
Ely
NAT MUS OF WALES
PRINCIPALITY STADIUM
CARDIFF
(CAERDYDD)
Pentre Meyrick
Penllyn
Maendy
Aberthin
Welsh St Donats
Pendoylan
Michaelston-super-Ely
Caerau
Butetown
Grangetown
Cowbridge
(Y Bont-Faen)
Llanblethian
Llandough
St Nicholas
Leckwith
MILLENNIUM CENTRE
Michaelston-le-Pit
TECHNIQUEST
St Hilary
Llantrithyd
Bonvilston
Wallston
St Lythans
Wenvoe
Llandough
Cogan
CARDIFF BAY BARRAGE
42
Llanmihangel
St Mary Church
OLD BEAUPRE CASTLE
DYFFRYN GARDENS
St Andrew's Major
TURNER HOUSE GALLERY
Sigingstone
Walterston
Dinas Powys
PENARTH
Flemingston
Moulton
Cadoxton
COSMESTON LAKES
Lower Penarth
Llanmaes
Eglwys-Brewis
Llanbethêry
Llancarfan
Colcot
Merthyr-Dyfan
Penmark
Sully
MEDIEVAL VILLAGE
Llantwit Major
Boverton
St Athan
CARDIFF (MAES AWYR CAERDYDD-CYMRU)
PORTHKERRY
BARRY
(Y BARRI)
Barry Island
BARRY ISLAND PLEASURE PARK
Lavernock Pt.
Trwyn Larnog
Sully Island
Ynys Sili
Gileston
East Aberthaw
Rhoose
(Y Rhws)
Porthkerry
Breaksea Pt.
Trwyn Breaksea
Flat Holm
CYNON
CAERPHILLY
RHONDDA CYNON TAF
CARDIFF
VALE OF GLAMORGAN
(BRO MORGANNWG)
A465
A470
A4054
A469
A4046
A467
A472
A4048
A4049
A4059
B4275
A4233
A4058
A4119
B5464
A4093
A473
A4222
A48
B4270
B4268
B4265
A4226
B4266
A4050
A4231
A4055
B4267
A4160
A4232
A48(M)
M4
B4600
A468
B4263
B4562
B4487
B4251
B4255
B4254
B4273
B4595
B4276
A4119
A4233
A4054
4
5
6
7
A
B
C
D
E

Risca
(Rhisga)
Machen
Lower Machen
Rogerstone
Rhiwderin
Pentre-poeth
Bassaleg
Rudry
Michaelston-y-Fedw
Castleton
Coedkernew
Marshfield
Blacktown
St Brides Wentlooge
Peterstone Wentlooge
St Mellons
Llanrumney
Rumney
Lisvane
Llanedeyrn
Roath
Newton
CARDIFF
(CAERDYDD)
MILLENNIUM CENTRE
CARDIFF BAY BARRAGE
TURNER HOUSE GALLERY
PENARTH
Lavernock Pt.
Flat Holm
Steep Holm
Malpas
Bettws
Christchurch
Maindee
Newport
(Casnewydd)
MUS & GALLERY
TREDEGAR HOUSE
Duffryn
FOURTEEN LOCKS
Seymour
Llanvaches
Penhow
Llanbeder
Langstone
Llanmartin
Llanwern
Bishton
Wilcrick
St Bride's Netherwent
MAGOR SERVICES
Magor
Llandevenny
GERAINT THOMAS NAT VELODROME OF WALES
Llanfihangel-Rogiet
Rogiet
Caldicot
Undy
Crick
Caerwent
Highmoor Hill
RUNSTON CHAPEL
Summerleaze
Redwick
Caldicot Level
WALES COAST PATH
NEWPORT
(CASNEWYDD)
Pye Corner
Nash
Goldcliff
Whitson
NEWPORT WETLANDS
Usk (Wysg)
MOUTH OF THE SEVERN
ABER HAFREN
ST
Battery Pt.
Portishead
West Hill
Redcliff Bay
Sheepway
Weston-in-Gordano
Clapton-in-Gordano
Walton-in-Gordano
GORDANO VALLEY
NOAH'S ARK ZOO FARM
Clevedon
CLEVEDON COURT
Stone-edge Batch
Tickenham
Nailsea
NORTH SOMERSET
West End
East End
Farleigh
Kenn
Kingston Seymour
North End
Claverham
Chelvey
Brockley
West Town
Yatton
Cleeve
Sand Pt.
Wick St Lawrence
Bourton
Sand Bay
Kewstoke
Worle
Milton
Hewish
Puxton
Congresbury
Wrington
PUXTON PARK
NORTH SOMERSET
Weston-super-Mare
Weston Bay
West Wick
Brinsea
Lower Langford
COURT FARM COUNTRY PARK
HELICOPTER MUS
Locking
Hutton
Banwell
Churchill
Sandford
Burrington
Blagdon
Brean Down
Uphill
BLEADON HILL
Christon
Bleadon
Winscombe
Star
Sidcot
Shipham
Brean
Compton Bishop
Loxton
Charterhouse
BERROW FLATS
BREAN LEISURE PARK
Eastertown
Cross
KING JOHN'S HUNTING LODGE
Lympsham
Lower Weare
Axbridge
Cheddar Res.
CHEDDAR CAVES & GORGE
Cheddar
SEDGEMOOR SERVICES
Biddisham
Weare
Gore Sands
East Brent
Rooks Bridge
Badgworth
Berrow
Brent Knoll
Stone Allerton
Chapel Allerton
ASHTON WINDMILL
Clewer
Draycott
Rodney Stoke
Edithmead
Cocklake
West Stoughton
Mark Causeway
Mark
Blackford
Wedmore
Burnham-on-Sea
STERT FLATS
M4
M48
M5
A48
A48(M)
A4810
A468
A467
B4591
B4239
B4487
A369
B3124
B3130
B3133
A370
A371
A368
A38
B3440
B3140
B3135
B3151
0 1 2 3 miles
0 1 2 3 4 5 km

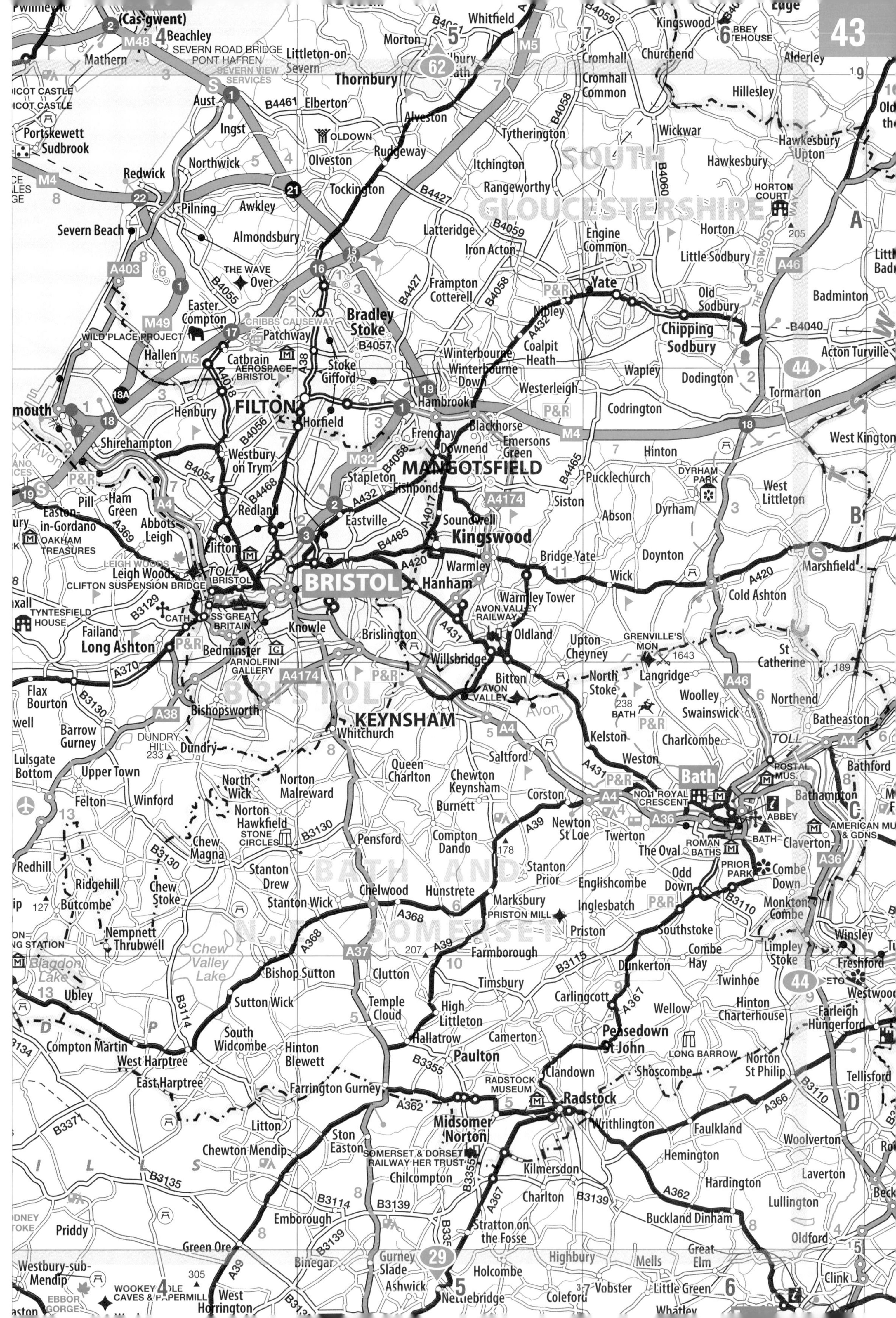
(Cas-gwent)
Beachley
SEVERN ROAD BRIDGE
PONT HAFREN
Mathern
SEVERN VIEW SERVICES
Littleton-on-Severn
Morton
Whitfield
Thornbury
Kingswood
Churchend
Cromhall
Cromhall Common
Alderley
Hillesley
Aust
Ingst
Elberton
Alveston
OLDOWN
Tytherington
Wickwar
Portskewett
Sudbrook
Northwick
Olveston
Rudgeway
Itchington
SOUTH GLOUCESTERSHIRE
Hawkesbury Upton
Hawkesbury
Redwick
Tockington
Rangeworthy
HORTON COURT
Pilning
Awkley
Severn Beach
Almondsbury
Latteridge
Iron Acton
Engine Common
Horton
Little Sodbury
THE WAVE
Over
Frampton Cotterell
Yate
Old Sodbury
Badminton
Easter Compton
CRIBBS CAUSEWAY
Bradley Stoke
Patchway
WILD PLACE PROJECT
Hallen
Catbrain
AEROSPACE BRISTOL
Stoke Gifford
Nibley
Coalpit Heath
Chipping Sodbury
Winterbourne
Winterbourne Down
Wapley
Dodington
Acton Turville
Westerleigh
Tormarton
Henbury
FILTON
Horfield
Hambrook
Codrington
Shirehampton
Frenchay
Blackhorse
Emersons Green
Downend
West Kington
Westbury on Trym
Stapleton
MANGOTSFIELD
Hinton
Pucklechurch
DYRHAM PARK
Fishponds
West Littleton
Pill
Ham Green
Easton-in-Gordano
Redland
Siston
Dyrham
OAKHAM TREASURES
Abbots Leigh
Eastville
Soundwell
Kingswood
Abson
Clifton
LEIGH WOODS
Leigh Woods
TOLL
BRISTOL
CLIFTON SUSPENSION BRIDGE
Bridge Yate
Doynton
Warmley
Wick
Marshfield
Hanham
Cold Ashton
TYNTESFIELD HOUSE
CATH
SS GREAT BRITAIN
Warmley Tower
AVON VALLEY RAILWAY
Failand
Long Ashton
Knowle
Brislington
Oldland
Upton Cheyney
GRENVILLE'S MON
Bedminster
ARNOLFINI GALLERY
Willsbridge
St Catherine
Langridge
North Stoke
Bitton
AVON VALLEY
Woolley
Swainswick
Flax Bourton
Northend
Batheaston
Bishopsworth
KEYNSHAM
Whitchurch
Kelston
Charlcombe
DUNDRY HILL
Dundry
Barrow Gurney
Lulsgate Bottom
Upper Town
Queen Charlton
Saltford
Weston
Bath
Bathford
POSTAL MUS.
Chewton Keynsham
North Wick
Norton Malreward
Corston
NO.1 ROYAL CRESCENT
Bathampton
Felton
Winford
Burnett
Norton Hawkfield
STONE CIRCLES
Newton St Loe
Twerton
ABBEY
AMERICAN MUS & GDNS
Chew Magna
Pensford
Compton Dando
The Oval
ROMAN BATHS
Claverton
Redhill
Stanton Drew
BATH AND N.E. SOMERSET
Stanton Prior
Englishcombe
Odd Down
PRIOR PARK
Combe Down
Ridgehill
Chew Stoke
Chelwood
Hunstrete
Marksbury
Inglesbatch
Monkton Combe
Butcombe
Stanton Wick
PRISTON MILL
Priston
Southstoke
Winsley
Nempnett Thrubwell
Farmborough
Combe Hay
Limpley Stoke
Freshford
Chew Valley Lake
Blagdon Lake
Bishop Sutton
Clutton
Timsbury
Dunkerton
Twinhoe
Ubley
Sutton Wick
Temple Cloud
High Littleton
Carlingcott
Wellow
Hinton Charterhouse
Farleigh Hungerford
Westwood
South Widcombe
Hinton Blewett
Hallatrow
Camerton
Peasedown St John
Compton Martin
West Harptree
Paulton
LONG BARROW
Norton St Philip
East Harptree
RADSTOCK MUSEUM
Clandown
Shoscombe
Tellisford
Farrington Gurney
Radstock
Litton
Midsomer Norton
Writhlington
Faulkland
Woolverton
Ston Easton
Chewton Mendip
SOMERSET & DORSET RAILWAY HERITAGE TRUST
Kilmersdon
Hemington
Laverton
Chilcompton
Charlton
Hardington
Lullington
Emborough
Buckland Dinham
Priddy
Stratton on the Fosse
Oldford
Green Ore
Great Elm
Westbury-sub-Mendip
Binegar
Gurney Slade
Highbury
Mells
Ashwick
Holcombe
Clink
WOOKEY HOLE CAVES & PAPERMILL
West Horrington
Nettlebridge
Coleford
Vobster
Little Green
EBBOR GORGE
M48
M4
M49
M5
M32
A403
A4018
A38
A4
A369
A370
A4174
A432
A4017
A420
A431
A46
A39
A36
A368
A37
A362
A367
A366
B4461
B4427
B4059
B4058
B4060
B4055
B4057
B4056
B4054
B4468
B4465
B3129
B3130
B3114
B3115
B3110
B3355
B3139
B3135
B3371
B4040
62
44
29
THE COTSWOLD WAY

Alderley
Leighterton
Long Newnton
Doughton
Shipton Moyne
Brokenborough
Hankerton
Upper Minety
Minety
Hillesley
WESTONBIRT ARBORETUM
Oldbury on the Hill
Westonbirt
Filands
Perry Green
Charlton
Garsdon
Hawkesbury Upton
Hawkesbury
Didmarton
Easton Grey
Malmesbury
Queen Street
Sopworth
Sherston
Foxley
Lea
Cleverton
The Common
HORTON COURT
Horton
Norton
Corston
Little Somerford
Brinkworth
Callow Hill
Little Badminton
Luckington
Rodbourne
Dauntsey
Old Sodbury
Badminton
Alderton
Hullavington
Startley
Great Somerford
Grittenham
Lower Stanton St Quintin
Lower Seagry
Tockenham Wick
Acton Turville
Littleton Drew
Grittleton
Stanton St Quintin
Upper Seagry
Leigh Delamere
Tormarton
Burton
Sutton Benger
Christian Malford
Bradenstoke
Lyneham
Church End
LEIGH DELAMERE SERVICES
Kington St Michael
Nettleton
West Kington
Castle Combe
Yatton Keynell
Kington Langley
Foxham
Preston
Goatacre
CASTLE COMBE
CEPEN PARK
Langley Burrell
West End
Spirthill
West Littleton
North Wraxall
Ford
Hardenhuish
CHIPPENHAM MUS
East Tytherton
West Tytherton
Hilmarton
Slaughterford
Biddestone
Chippenham
Marshfield
Bremhill
Compton Bassett
Cold Ashton
Thickwood
Studley
Colerne
Corsham
CORSHAM COURT
Easton
Calne
Cherhill
St Catherine
Alcombe
Notton
LACKHAM
Derry Hill
BOWOOD HOUSE
Mile Elm
Quemerford
Hawthorn
Northend
Gastard
LACOCK ABBEY
Sandy Lane
Calstone Wellington
Blackland
Batheaston
Box
Neston
Lacock
FOX TALBOT MUS
Bowden Hill
Stockley
TOLL
Bathford
Whitley
Chittoe
MORGAN'S HILL
POSTAL MUS
Bathampton
Atworth
Shaw
Beanacre
Heddington
Bath
Monkton Farleigh
Norrington Common
Sandridge
Bromham
Bishops Cannings
ABBEY
AMERICAN MUS & GDNS
Broughton Common
St Edith's
ROUNDWAY HILL
ROMAN BATHS
Claverton
South Wraxall
Melksham
Broughton Gifford
PRIOR PARK
Combe Down
Bradford Leigh
GREAT CHALFIELD MANOR
Bowerhill
Rowde
Roundway
CANAL
Bradford-on-Avon
Holt
Sells Green
Monkton Combe
THE COURTS
Seend Cleeve
Devizes
Winsley
Turleigh
Staverton
Kennet & Avon Canal
Semington
Seend
BROADLEAS GARDENS
Limpley Stoke
Freshford
TITHE BARN
BARTON FARM
Hilperton
Poulshot
Twinhoe
PETO
Trowle Common
Great Hinton
Stert
Hinton Charterhouse
Westwood
WESTWOOD MANOR
Ashton Common
Potterne
Farleigh Hungerford
Keevil
Bulkington
Worton
Wedhampton
Trowbridge
Steeple Ashton
Potterne Wick
Urchfont
BARROW
Norton St Philip
Wingfield
Marston
Tellisford
Southwick
West Ashton
Eastcott
Faulkland
North Bradley
Yarnbrook
Great Cheverell
Littleton Pannell
Easterton
Woolverton
Hawkeridge
Heywood
Coulston
Market Lavington
Rode
BROKERSWOOD
Erlestoke
Little Cheverell
West Lavington
Laverton
Edington
Hardington
Bratton
Beckington
BRATTON CAMP & WHITE HORSE
Lullington
Rudge
Littleton Down
Dinham
Gore Cross
Oldford
Westbury Leigh
Westbury
Great Elm
Dilton Marsh
Summer Down
West Lavington Down
Upton Scudamore
Tilshead
0 1 2 3 miles
0 1 2 3 4 5 km

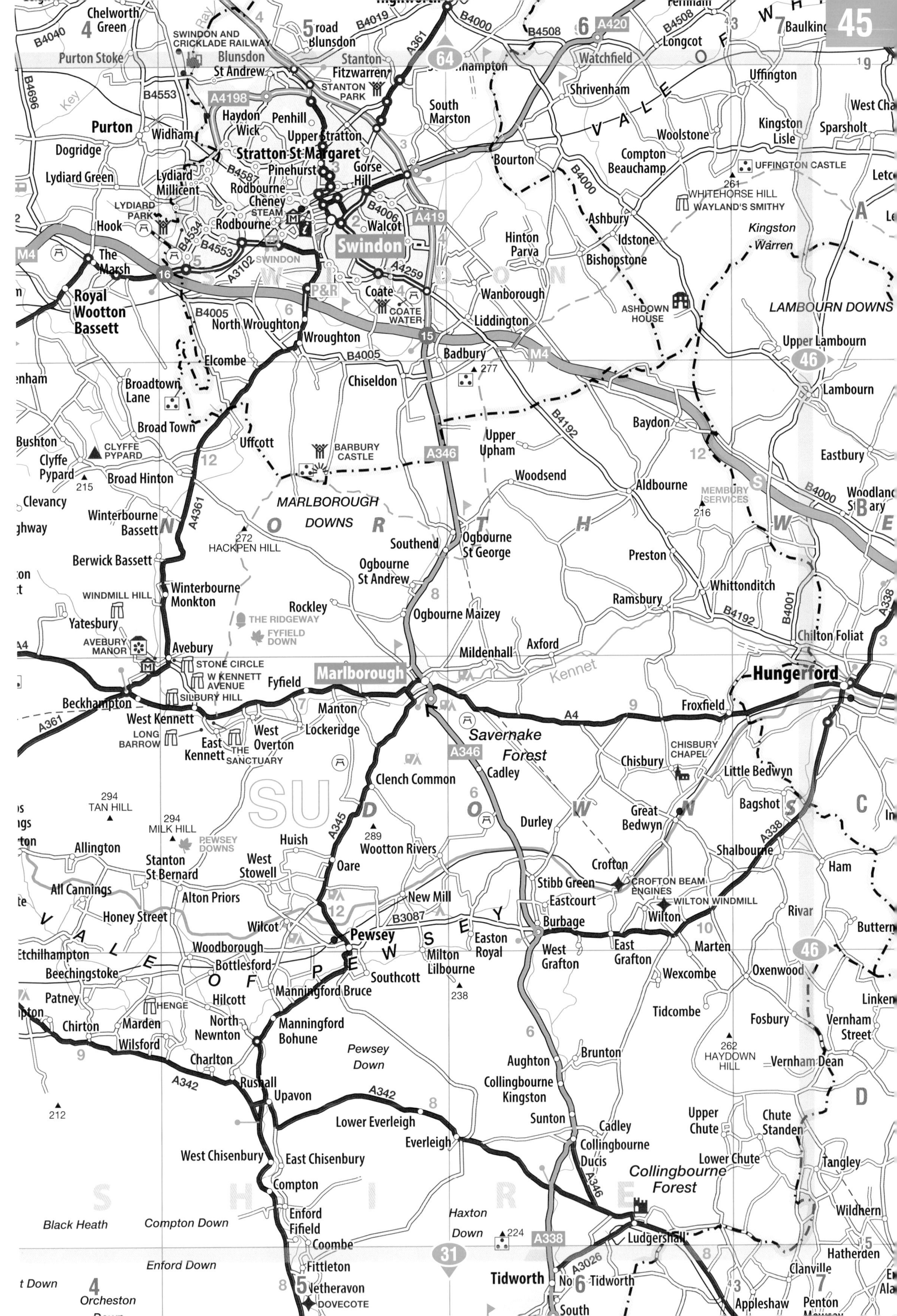
Chelworth Green
SWINDON AND CRICKLADE RAILWAY
Blunsdon St Andrew
Broad Blunsdon
Stanton Fitzwarren
STANTON PARK
Purton Stoke
Purton
Widham
Haydon Wick
Penhill
Upper Stratton
Stratton St Margaret
Dogridge
Lydiard Green
Lydiard Millicent
LYDIARD PARK
Rodbourne Cheney
Pinehurst
Gorse Hill
Hook
Rodbourne
STEAM
Walcot
Swindon
The Marsh
Royal Wootton Bassett
SWINDON
Coate
COATE WATER
North Wroughton
Wroughton
Elcombe
Broadtown Lane
Broad Town
Chiseldon
Badbury
Liddington
Wanborough
Hinton Parva
South Marston
Bourton
Shrivenham
Watchfield
Longcot
Uffington
Woolstone
Compton Beauchamp
Kingston Lisle
Sparsholt
UFFINGTON CASTLE
WHITEHORSE HILL
WAYLAND'S SMITHY
Kingston Warren
Ashbury
Idstone
Bishopstone
ASHDOWN HOUSE
LAMBOURN DOWNS
Upper Lambourn
Lambourn
Baydon
Eastbury
Aldbourne
MEMBURY SERVICES
Woodsend
Upper Upham
Bushton
Clyffe Pypard
CLYFFE PYPARD
Broad Hinton
Uffcott
BARBURY CASTLE
MARLBOROUGH DOWNS
Clevancy
Winterbourne Bassett
HACKPEN HILL
Southend
Ogbourne St George
Ogbourne St Andrew
Ogbourne Maizey
Berwick Bassett
Preston
Whittonditch
Ramsbury
Chilton Foliat
Winterbourne Monkton
WINDMILL HILL
Yatesbury
Rockley
THE RIDGEWAY
FYFIELD DOWN
AVEBURY MANOR
Avebury
STONE CIRCLE
W KENNETT AVENUE
SILBURY HILL
Fyfield
Marlborough
Mildenhall
Axford
Kennet
Hungerford
Froxfield
Beckhampton
West Kennett
LONG BARROW
East Kennett
THE SANCTUARY
West Overton
Manton
Lockeridge
Savernake Forest
Chisbury
CHISBURY CHAPEL
Little Bedwyn
Clench Common
Cadley
TAN HILL
MILK HILL
PEWSEY DOWNS
Huish
Wootton Rivers
Durley
Great Bedwyn
Bagshot
Shalbourne
Ham
Allington
Stanton St Bernard
West Stowell
Oare
Crofton
CROFTON BEAM ENGINES
WILTON WINDMILL
Stibb Green
Eastcourt
Wilton
Rivar
All Cannings
Alton Priors
Honey Street
New Mill
Wilcot
Pewsey
Burbage
Easton Royal
Milton Lilbourne
West Grafton
East Grafton
Marten
Oxenwood
Etchilhampton
Woodborough
Bottlesford
Beechingstoke
Southcott
Wexcombe
Manningford Bruce
Patney
Hilcott
HENGE
Chirton
Marden
North Newnton
Manningford Bohune
Tidcombe
Fosbury
Vernham Street
Wilsford
Charlton
Pewsey Down
Aughton
Brunton
HAYDOWN HILL
Vernham Dean
Rushall
Upavon
Collingbourne Kingston
Lower Everleigh
Sunton
Upper Chute
Chute Standen
Everleigh
Cadley
Collingbourne Ducis
West Chisenbury
East Chisenbury
Lower Chute
Tangley
Collingbourne Forest
Compton
Enford
Fifield
Wildhern
Black Heath
Compton Down
Haxton Down
Ludgershall
Coombe
Enford Down
Fittleton
Tidworth
North Tidworth
Clanville
Hatherden
Netheravon
DOVECOTE
Orcheston
Appleshaw
Penton
South
VALE OF WHITE HORSE
SWINDON
NORTH WESSEX DOWNS
VALE OF PEWSEY
WILTSHIRE
SU
M4
A4
A420
A419
A4259
A4361
A346
A345
A342
A338
A3026
A361
A3102
A4198
B4000
B4001
B4005
B4006
B4019
B4040
B4192
B4508
B4534
B4553
B4587
B4696
B3087
64
46
31
15
16

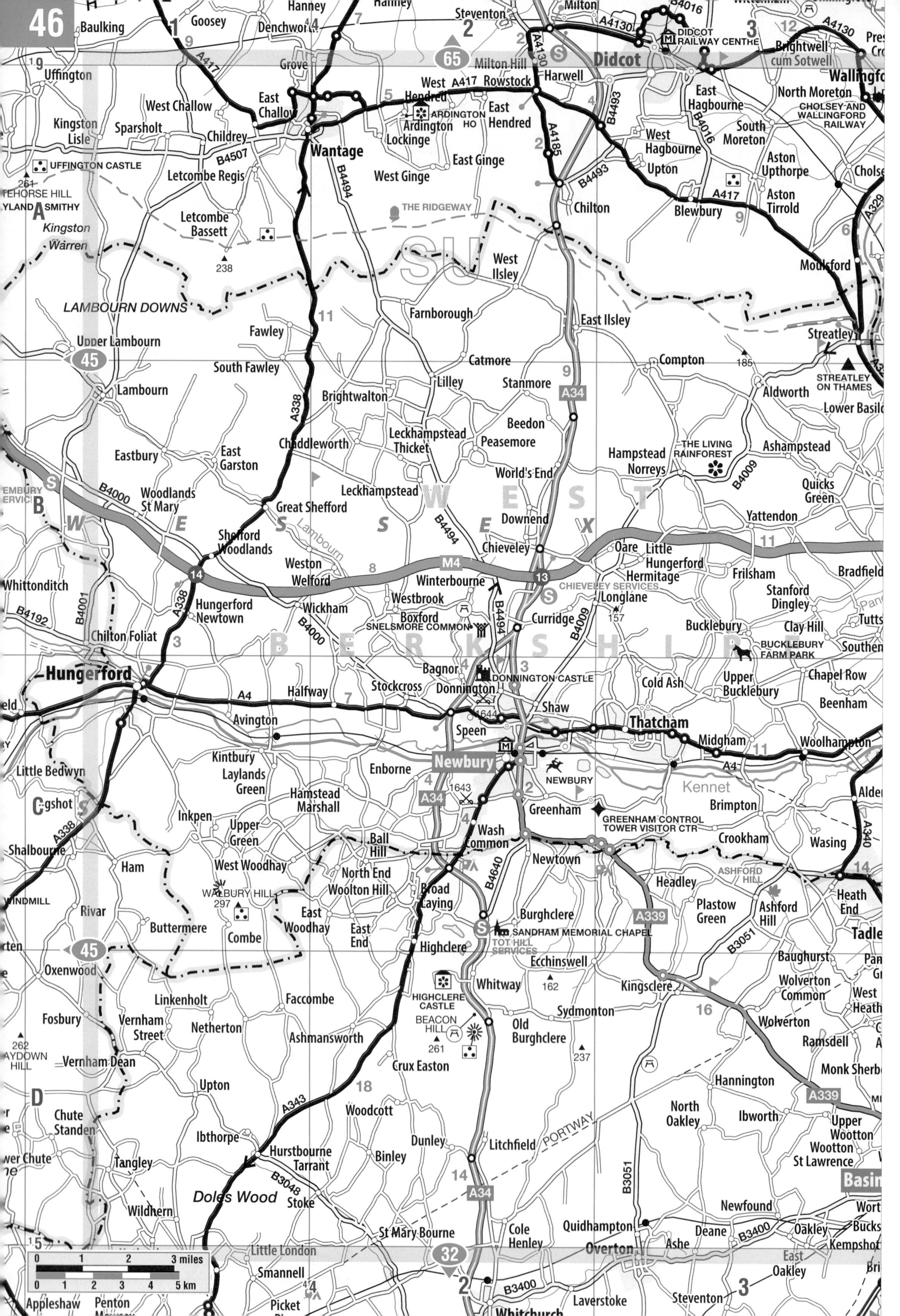
Baulking
Goosey
Hanney
Denchworth
Steventon
Milton
DIDCOT RAILWAY CENTRE
Didcot
Brightwell cum Sotwell
Uffington
Grove
Milton Hill
Harwell
Rowstock
West Hendred
East Hendred
East Hagbourne
North Moreton
CHOLSEY AND WALLINGFORD RAILWAY
West Challow
East Challow
ARDINGTON HO
Ardington
Lockinge
Kingston Lisle
Sparsholt
Childrey
Wantage
West Hagbourne
South Moreton
UFFINGTON CASTLE
Letcombe Regis
East Ginge
West Ginge
Upton
Aston Upthorpe
Chilton
Blewbury
Aston Tirrold
THE RIDGEWAY
Kingston Warren
Letcombe Bassett
238
SU
West Ilsley
Moulsford
LAMBOURN DOWNS
Farnborough
East Ilsley
Upper Lambourn
Fawley
Streatley
Compton
Catmore
185
South Fawley
Lambourn
Lilley
Stanmore
STREATLEY ON THAMES
Aldworth
Brightwalton
Lower Basildon
Beedon
Leckhampstead Thicket
Peasemore
Chaddleworth
Hampstead Norreys
THE LIVING RAINFOREST
Ashampstead
Eastbury
East Garston
World's End
Woodlands St Mary
Leckhampstead
Quicks Green
Great Shefford
W E S S E X
Downend
Yattendon
Shefford Woodlands
Lambourn
Chieveley
Oare
Little Hungerford
Hermitage
Weston
Welford
Winterbourne
Frilsham
Bradfield
Whittonditch
CHIEVELEY SERVICES
Longlane
Stanford Dingley
Hungerford Newtown
Westbrook
Wickham
Boxford
SNELSMORE COMMON
Curridge
157
Bucklebury
Clay Hill
Chilton Foliat
B E R K S H I R E
BUCKLEBURY FARM PARK
Bagnor
DONNINGTON CASTLE
Chapel Row
Hungerford
Halfway
Stockcross
Donnington
Cold Ash
Upper Bucklebury
Beenham
Avington
Shaw
Thatcham
Speen
Midgham
Woolhampton
Kintbury
Newbury
NEWBURY
Little Bedwyn
Laylands Green
Enborne
Kennet
1643
Hamstead Marshall
Greenham
Brimpton
Inkpen
Upper Green
GREENHAM CONTROL TOWER VISITOR CTR
Crookham
Wasing
Shalbourne
Ball Hill
Wash Common
Ham
West Woodhay
Newtown
North End
ASHFORD HILL
Woolton Hill
Headley
WALBURY HILL
297
Broad Laying
Plastow Green
Ashford Hill
Heath End
Rivar
Burghclere
East Woodhay
Buttermere
Combe
East End
SANDHAM MEMORIAL CHAPEL
TOT HILL SERVICES
Highclere
Ecchinswell
Baughurst
Oxenwood
Whitway
162
Kingsclere
Wolverton Common
Linkenholt
Faccombe
HIGHCLERE CASTLE
Sydmonton
Wolverton
Fosbury
Vernham Street
Netherton
BEACON HILL
261
Old Burghclere
Ramsdell
Ashmansworth
237
262
Vernham Dean
Crux Easton
Monk Sherborne
Upton
Hannington
Woodcott
North Oakley
Ibworth
Chute Standen
Ibthorpe
Upper Wootton
Wootton St Lawrence
Tangley
Hurstbourne Tarrant
Dunley
Binley
Litchfield
PORTWAY
Doles Wood
Stoke
Wildhern
Newfound
St Mary Bourne
Cole Henley
Quidhampton
Deane
Oakley
Kempshott
Ashe
Overton
Little London
East Oakley
Smannell
Laverstoke
Steventon
Appleshaw
Penton
Picket
0 1 2 3 miles
0 1 2 3 4 5 km
M4
A34
A338
A4
A339
A343
A417
A4130
A4185
B4494
B4000
B4009
B4493
B4016
B4507
B4001
B4192
B4640
B3051
B3048
B3400
65
45
32

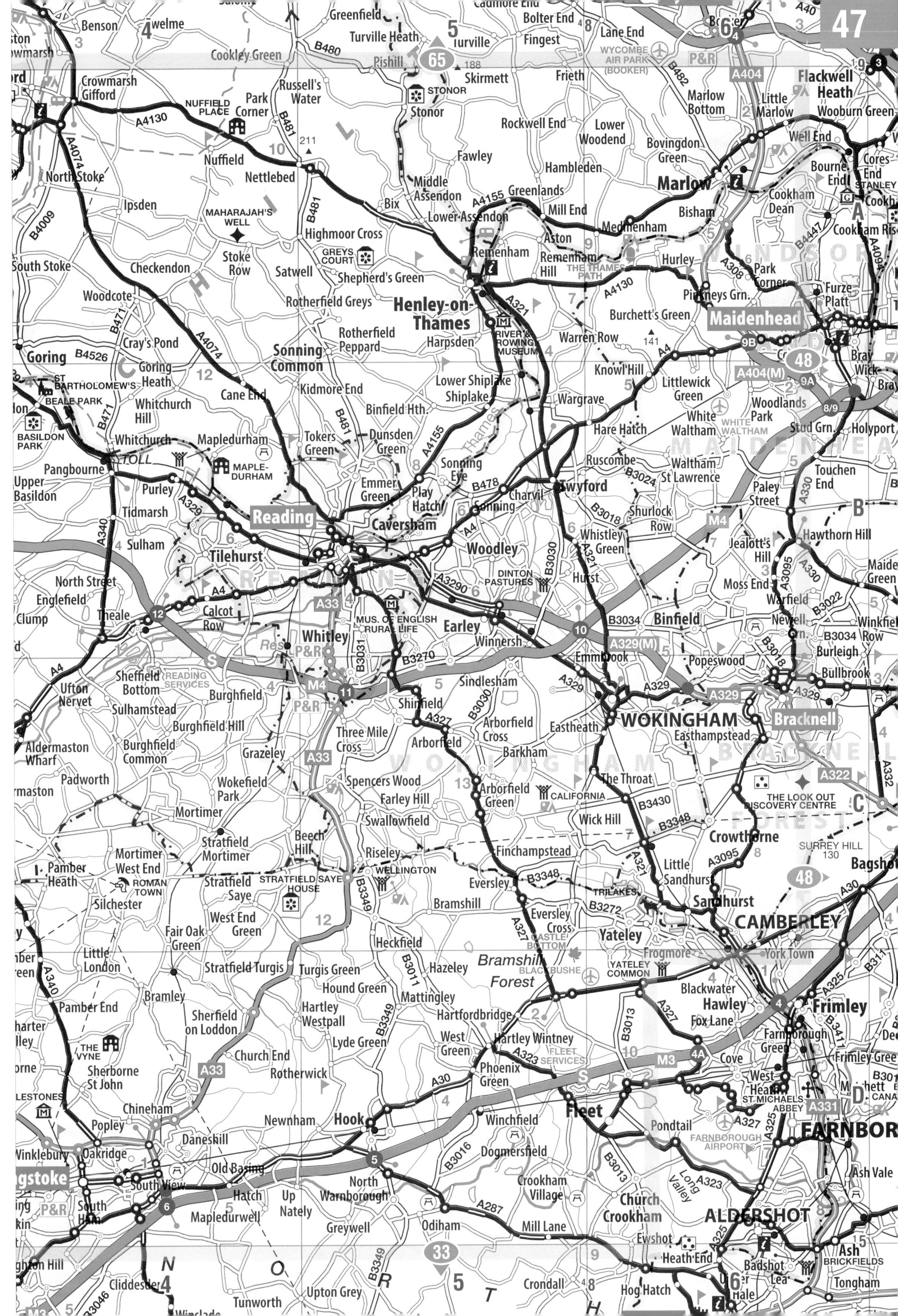
Benson
Greenfield
Turville Heath
Turville
Bolter End
Lane End
Fingest
Cookley Green
Pishill
65
Skirmett
Frieth
WYCOMBE AIR PARK (BOOKER)
Crowmarsh Gifford
Russell's Water
Stonor
Flackwell Heath
Little Marlow
Wooburn Green
Marlow Bottom
Nuffield Place
Park Corner
Nuffield
Nettlebed
Rockwell End
Lower Woodend
Bovingdon Green
Fawley
Hambleden
Marlow
North Stoke
Ipsden
Middle Assendon
Bix
Lower Assendon
Greenlands
Mill End
Medmenham
Bisham
Cookham Dean
Maharajah's Well
Highmoor Cross
Aston
Remenham
Remenham Hill
Hurley
South Stoke
Checkendon
Stoke Row
Greys Court
Satwell
Shepherd's Green
The Thames Path
Pinkneys Grn.
Park Corner
Furze Platt
Woodcote
Rotherfield Greys
Henley-on-Thames
Burchett's Green
Maidenhead
Rotherfield Peppard
Harpsden
River & Rowing Museum
Warren Row
Cray's Pond
Goring
Goring Heath
Sonning Common
Knowl Hill
48
Bray Wick
Cane End
Kidmore End
Lower Shiplake
Shiplake
Littlewick Green
St Bartholomew's
Beale Park
Whitchurch Hill
Binfield Hth.
Wargrave
White Waltham
Woodlands Park
Basildon Park
Whitchurch
Mapledurham
Tokers Green
Dunsden Green
Hare Hatch
Stud Grn.
Holyport
Pangbourne
Maple-Durham
Sonning Eye
Ruscombe
Waltham St Lawrence
Upper Basildon
Purley
Emmer Green
Play Hatch
Charvil
Sonning
Twyford
Paley Street
Touchen End
Tidmarsh
Reading
Caversham
Shurlock Row
Sulham
Tilehurst
Woodley
Whistley Green
Jealott's Hill
Hawthorn Hill
North Street
Dinton Pastures
Hurst
Moss End
Warfield
Englefield
Theale
Calcot Row
Mus. of English Rural Life
Earley
Binfield
Newell Grn.
Winkfield Row
Whitley
Winnersh
Emmbrook
Popeswood
Burleigh
Bullbrook
Sheffield Bottom
Reading Services
Sindlesham
Ufton Nervet
Burghfield
Shinfield
Wokingham
Bracknell
Sulhamstead
Arborfield Cross
Eastheath
Easthampstead
Burghfield Hill
Three Mile Cross
Arborfield
Barkham
Aldermaston Wharf
Burghfield Common
Grazeley
Padworth
Wokefield Park
Spencers Wood
The Throat
The Look Out Discovery Centre
Farley Hill
Arborfield Green
California
Mortimer
Swallowfield
Wick Hill
Stratfield Mortimer
Beech Hill
Crowthorne
Surrey Hill 130
Mortimer West End
Riseley
Finchampstead
Pamber Heath
Roman Town
Stratfield Saye
Stratfield Saye House
Wellington
Little Sandhurst
Bagshot
Silchester
Eversley
Trilakes
Sandhurst
West End Green
Bramshill
Eversley Cross
Camberley
Fair Oak Green
Castle Bottom
Yateley
Heckfield
Little London
Bramshill Forest
Blackbushe
Yateley Common
Frogmore
York Town
Stratfield Turgis
Turgis Green
Hazeley
Hound Green
Mattingley
Blackwater
Frimley
Bramley
Pamber End
Hartley Westpall
Hartfordbridge
Hawley
Fox Lane
Sherfield on Loddon
Lyde Green
Farnborough Green
West Green
Hartley Wintney
The Vyne
Church End
Fleet Services
Cove
Frimley Green
Sherborne St John
Rotherwick
Phoenix Green
West Heath
St Michael's Abbey
Chineham
Fleet
Newnham
Hook
Winchfield
Pondtail
Farnborough
Popley
Daneshill
Dogmersfield
Farnborough Airport
Winklebury
Oakridge
Long Valley
Ash Vale
Old Basing
South View
North Warnborough
Crookham Village
Church Crookham
Aldershot
South Ham
Hatch
Up Nately
Mapledurwell
Greywell
Odiham
Mill Lane
Ewshot
Heath End
Ash
Badshot Lea
Ash Brickfields
33
Crondall
Hog Hatch
Hale
Tongham
Cliddesden
Tunworth
Upton Grey
Winslade
North
Wokingham
Windsor
Maidenhead
Bracknell Forest

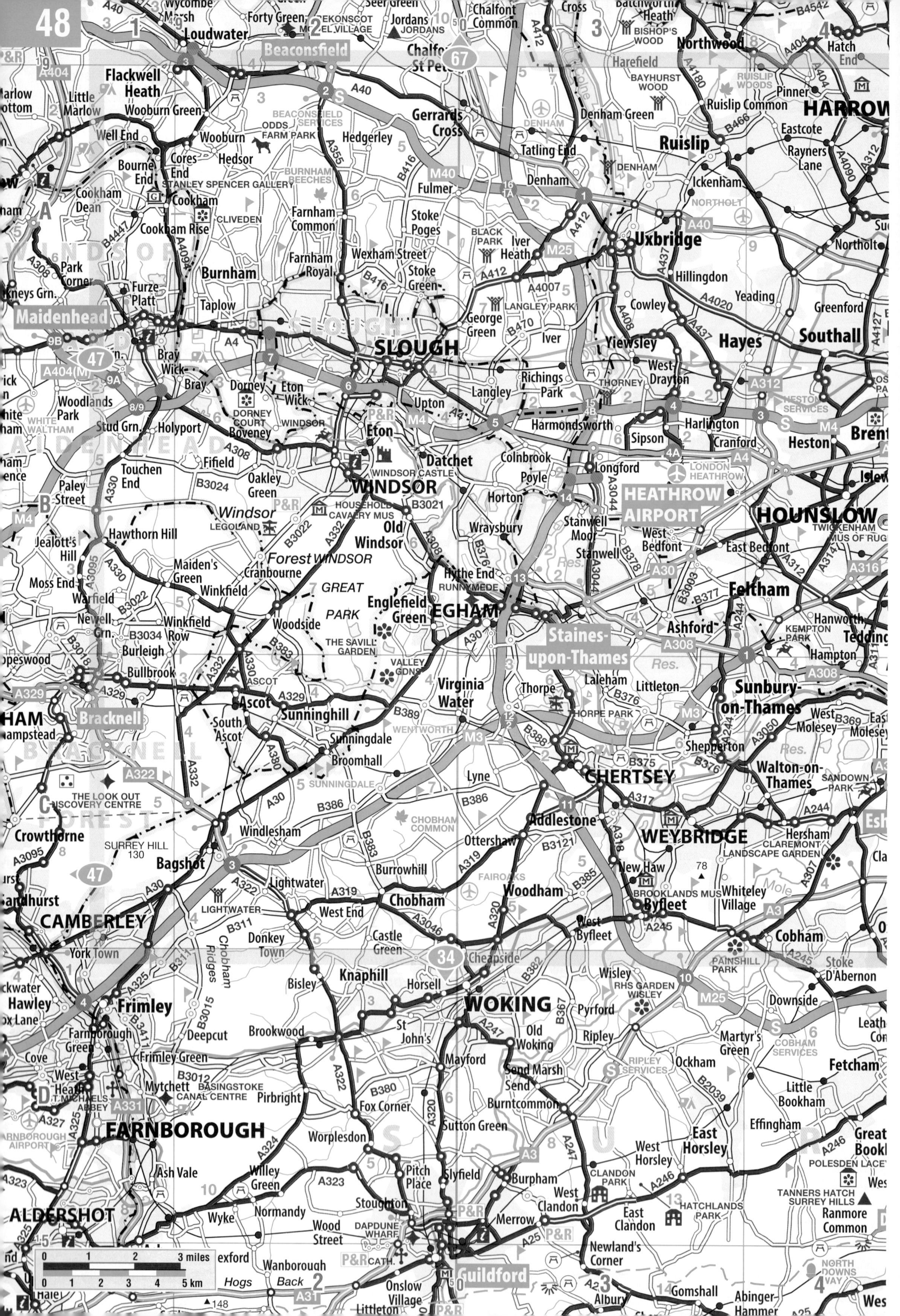
Loudwater
Forty Green
Jordans
Chalfont Common
Beaconsfield
Chalfont St Peter
67
Northwood
Hatch End
Harefield
Bayhurst Wood
Ruislip Woods
Pinner
Harrow
Flackwell Heath
Little Marlow
Wooburn Green
Beaconsfield Services
Odds Farm Park
Gerrards Cross
Hedgerley
Denham Green
Ruislip Common
Ruislip
Eastcote
Rayners Lane
Well End
Wooburn
Cores End
Hedsor
Bourne End
Stanley Spencer Gallery
Burnham Beeches
Fulmer
Tatling End
Denham
Ickenham
Cookham Dean
Cookham
Cliveden
Farnham Common
Stoke Poges
Black Park
Iver Heath
Northolt
Uxbridge
Windsor
Cookham Rise
Wexham Street
Farnham Royal
Stoke Green
Hillingdon
Park Corner
Burnham
Langley Park
Cowley
Yeading
Greenford
Furze Platt
Taplow
George Green
Iver
Maidenhead
Slough
Yiewsley
Hayes
Southall
47
Bray Wick
Bray
Dorney
Eton Wick
Richings Park
West Drayton
Woodlands Park
Dorney Court
Windsor
Upton
Langley
Thorney
Harlington
Heston Services
White Waltham
Stud Grn.
Holyport
Boveney
Eton
Harmondsworth
Sipson
Cranford
Heston
Brent
Datchet
Colnbrook
Longford
London Heathrow
Fifield
Touchen End
Oakley Green
Windsor Castle
Windsor
Poyle
Paley Street
Horton
Heathrow Airport
Household Cavalry Mus
Hounslow
Windsor
Legoland
Old Windsor
Wraysbury
Stanwell Moor
West Bedfont
Twickenham Mus of Rugby
Hawthorn Hill
Jealott's Hill
Stanwell
East Bedfont
Forest Windsor
Maiden's Green
Cranbourne
Hythe End
Runnymede
Moss End
Winkfield
Great Park
Feltham
Warfield
Englefield Green
Egham
Newell Grn.
Winkfield Row
Woodside
Ashford
Hanworth
Kempton Park
Teddington
Burleigh
The Savill Garden
Staines-upon-Thames
Valley Gdns
Hampton
Bullbrook
Ascot
Virginia Water
Laleham
Thorpe
Littleton
Sunbury-on-Thames
Bracknell
Sunninghill
Thorpe Park
Wentworth
West Molesey
East Molesey
Easthampstead
South Ascot
Sunningdale
Shepperton
Broomhall
Chertsey
Walton-on-Thames
Sandown Park
The Look Out Discovery Centre
Sunningdale
Lyne
Addlestone
Weybridge
Hersham
Chobham Common
Claremont Landscape Garden
Crowthorne
Windlesham
Surrey Hill 130
Ottershaw
Bagshot
Burrowhill
Fairoaks
Woodham
New Haw
Lightwater
Chobham
Brooklands Mus
Byfleet
Whiteley Village
Sandhurst
West End
Camberley
Donkey Town
Castle Green
West Byfleet
Cobham
York Town
Chobham Ridges
34
Cheapside
Painshill Park
Stoke D'Abernon
Hawley
Bisley
Knaphill
Horsell
Wisley
RHS Garden Wisley
Frimley
Woking
Pyrford
Downside
Farnborough Green
Deepcut
Brookwood
St John's
Old Woking
Ripley
Martyr's Green
Cobham Services
Leatherhead Common
Cove
Frimley Green
Mayford
Ripley Services
Ockham
Fetcham
West Heath
Mytchett
Basingstoke Canal Centre
Pirbright
Send Marsh
Send
St Michael's Abbey
Fox Corner
Burntcommon
Little Bookham
Farnborough
Sutton Green
Effingham
Farnborough Airport
Worplesdon
West Horsley
East Horsley
Great Bookham
Ash Vale
Willey Green
Pitch Place
Slyfield
Burpham
Clandon Park
Polesden Lacey
Stoughton
West Clandon
Hatchlands Park
Tanners Hatch
Surrey Hills
Aldershot
Wyke
Normandy
Wood Street
Dapdune Wharf
Merrow
East Clandon
Ranmore Common
Newlands Corner
North Downs Way
Wanborough
Cath.
Guildford
Hogs Back
Onslow Village
Gomshall
Abinger Hammer
Albury
Littleton
148
0 1 2 3 miles
0 1 2 3 4 5 km

Edgware
Harrow Weald
Mill Hill
Finchley
Wood Green
Tottenham
Woodford
Wealdstone
Kingsbury
Hendon
Hornsey
Walthamstow
Barkingside
Greenhill
Harrow on the Hill
Golders Green
Highgate
Leytonstone
Wanstead
Seven Kings
Stoke Newington
Leyton
Ilford
Wembley
Cricklewood
Hampstead
Forest Gate
Manor Park
Willesden
Hackney
Alperton
Harlesden
Kilburn
Camden
Islington
Bethnal Green
Stratford
East Ham
Perivale
Regents Park
Shoreditch
Finsbury
West Ham
Holborn
Poplar
Beckton
EALING
Paddington
City
Hanwell
Acton
Kensington
Hyde Park
Tower
The O2
London City
North Woolwich
Woolwich Ferry
Blackwall Tunnel
Westminster
Southwark
Bermondsey
Chiswick
Hammersmith
Chelsea
Lambeth
Greenwich
Woolwich
Plumstead
Kew
Kew Br.
Fulham
Battersea
Peckham
Deptford
Charlton
Camberwell
New Cross
Kidbrooke
Putney
Mortlake
Clapham
Lewisham
Richmond
Brixton
Dulwich
Hither Green
Eltham
Roehampton
Wandsworth
Catford
New Eltham
Twickenham
Balham
Streatham
Grove Park
Mottingham
Ham
Kingston Vale
Upper Tooting
West Norwood
Sydenham
Chislehurst
Merton
Wimbledon
Penge
BROMLEY
Bushy Park
Raynes Park
South Norwood
Beckenham
Kingston upon Thames
Mitcham
Thornton Heath
Elmers End
Bickley
Petts Wood
Thames Ditton
Morden
Surbiton
New Malden
Selhurst
Eden Park
West Wickham
Hayes
Bromley Common
Long Ditton
Tolworth
Worcester Park
St Helier
Addiscombe
Hackbridge
Shirley
Hook
Carshalton
Croydon
Keston
Cheam
Beddington
Addington
Farnborough
Chessington
Sutton
Wallington
South Croydon
New Addington
Ewell
Belmont
Selsdon
Leaves Green
Downe
Purley
Sanderstead
EPSOM
Woodmansterne
Hamsey Green
Farleigh
Biggin Hill
Cudham
Kenley
Wood Field
BANSTEAD
Coulsdon
Great Burgh
Burgh Heath
Whyteleafe
Warlingham
Ashtead
Chipstead
Old Coulsdon
South Street
Tatsfield
Leatherhead
Tadworth
Hooley
Kingswood
Woldingham
Walton on the Hill
Chaldon
CATERHAM
Headley
Lower Kingswood
Titsey
Westerham
Mickleham
Merstham
Limpsfield
Limpsfield Chart
Brewer Street
Godstone
Oxted
Church Town
Buckland
REDHILL
Nutfield
Tandridge
Crockham Hill
Pixham
Betchworth
Bletchingley
Earlswood
Brockham
Reigate
South Nutfield
Crowhurst Lane End
Marlpit Hill
Strood
Doversgreen
Ridge Green

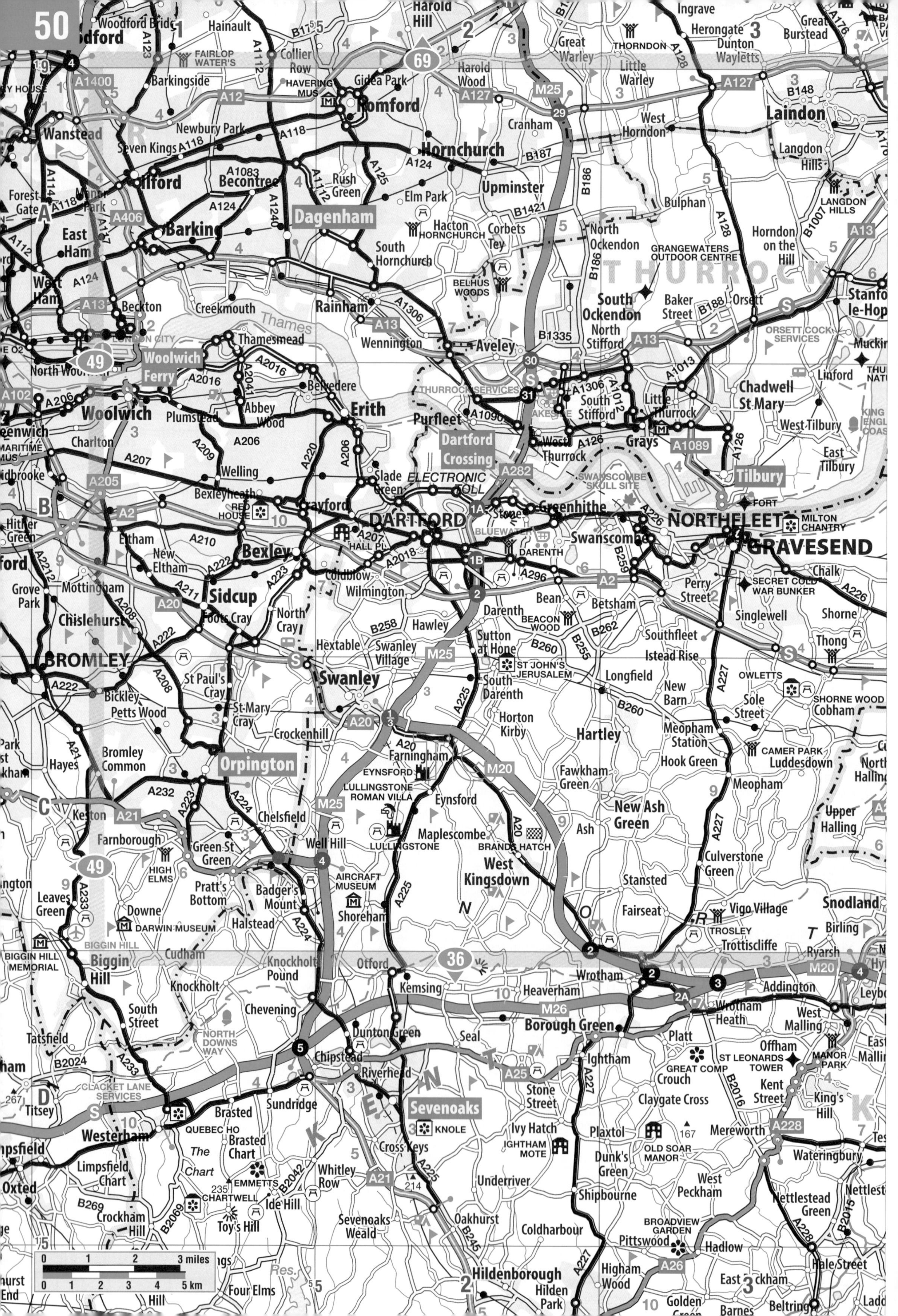
Woodford Bridge
Hainault
Harold Hill
Ingrave
Herongate
Dunton Wayletts
Great Burstead
Fairlop Water's
Collier Row
Havering Mus
Gidea Park
Romford
Harold Wood
Thorndon
Great Warley
Little Warley
Barkingside
Newbury Park
Seven Kings
Wanstead
Hornchurch
Cranham
West Horndon
Laindon
Langdon Hills
Langdon Hills
Ilford
Becontree
Rush Green
Upminster
Elm Park
Dagenham
Forest Gate
Manor Park
East Ham
Barking
Hacton
Hornchurch
Corbets Tey
North Ockendon
Bulphan
Horndon on the Hill
Grangewaters Outdoor Centre
South Hornchurch
Thurrock
West Ham
Beckton
Creekmouth
Rainham
Belhus Woods
South Ockendon
North Stifford
Baker Street
Orsett
Orsett Cock Services
Stanford-le-Hope
Mucking
Thames
London City
Thamesmead
Wennington
Aveley
North Woolwich
Woolwich Ferry
Woolwich
Plumstead
Abbey Wood
Belvedere
Erith
Thurrock Services
Purfleet
Dartford Crossing
South Stifford
Lakeside
Little Thurrock
Grays
West Thurrock
Chadwell St Mary
Linford
West Tilbury
East Tilbury
Tilbury
Fort
Greenwich
Charlton
Maritime Mus
Welling
Bexleyheath
Red House
Slade Green
Electronic Toll
Swanscombe Skull Site
Stone
Greenhithe
Northfleet
Milton Chantry
Gravesend
Blackheath
Hither Green
Eltham
New Eltham
Bexley
Crayford
Dartford
Hall Pl
Bluewater
Darenth
Swanscombe
Chalk
Secret Cold War Bunker
Perry Street
Singlewell
Shorne
Grove Park
Mottingham
Sidcup
Foots Cray
Coldblow
Wilmington
Bean
Betsham
Chislehurst
North Cray
Hawley
Darenth
Beacon Wood
Sutton at Hone
Southfleet
Thong
Istead Rise
Bromley
Hextable
Swanley Village
St John's Jerusalem
Longfield
Owletts
St Paul's Cray
Swanley
South Darenth
New Barn
Sole Street
Shorne Wood
Cobham
Bickley
Petts Wood
St Mary Cray
Crockenhill
Horton Kirby
Hartley
Meopham Station
Camer Park
Luddesdown
Hayes
Bromley Common
Orpington
Farningham
Eynsford
Lullingstone Roman Villa
Fawkham Green
Hook Green
Meopham
North Halling
Upper Halling
Keston
Farnborough
Chelsfield
Eynsford
Maplescombe
Brands Hatch
Ash
New Ash Green
Green St Green
High Elms
Well Hill
Lullingstone
Aircraft Museum
West Kingsdown
Culverstone Green
Stansted
Leaves Green
Pratt's Bottom
Badger's Mount
Downe
Darwin Museum
Halstead
Shoreham
Fairseat
Vigo Village
Trosley
Snodland
Birling
Trottiscliffe
Ryarsh
Biggin Hill
Biggin Hill Memorial
Cudham
Knockholt Pound
Otford
Kemsing
Wrotham
Addington
Knockholt
Heaverham
Leybourne
Tatsfield
South Street
Chevening
North Downs Way
Seal
Borough Green
Wrotham Heath
West Malling
Dunton Green
Platt
Offham
Chipstead
Ightham
St Leonards Tower
Great Comp
Manor Park
East Malling
Riverhead
Crouch
Kent Street
Titsey
Clacket Lane Services
Sundridge
Sevenoaks
Stone Street
Claygate Cross
King's Hill
Westerham
Quebec Ho
Brasted
Knole
Ivy Hatch
Plaxtol
Mereworth
Limpsfield
Brasted Chart
The Chart
Cross Keys
Ightham Mote
Old Soar Manor
Wateringbury
Oxted
Limpsfield Chart
Emmetts
Whitley Row
Dunk's Green
West Peckham
Chartwell
Ide Hill
Underriver
Shipbourne
Nettlestead
Crockham Hill
Toy's Hill
Sevenoaks Weald
Oakhurst
Coldharbour
Broadview Garden
Nettlestead Green
Pittswood
Hadlow
Hale Street
Hildenborough
Hilden Park
Higham Wood
East Peckham
Four Elms
Hill
Beltring
Golden Green
Barnes
Ladd
Res.
0 1 2 3 miles
0 1 2 3 4 5 km
M25
M26
M20
A13
A2
A20
A21
A25
A127
A12
A406
A282
A226
A227
A228
A225
A224
A223
A222
A232
A233
A124
A118
A1306
A1089
A126
A1013
A1012
A206
A207
A208
A209
A210
A211
A220
A2016
A2041
A2018
A296
B186
B187
B1335
B1421
B148
B188
B258
B259
B260
B262
B2024
B2042
B2069
B269
B245
B2016
B2015
B1007
A1400
A1083
A1112
A1240
A1153
A1090
A102
A205
A2212
69
49
36
30
31
29
1A
1B
2
3
4
5
2A
B
C
D
A
K
E
N
T
O
R
S

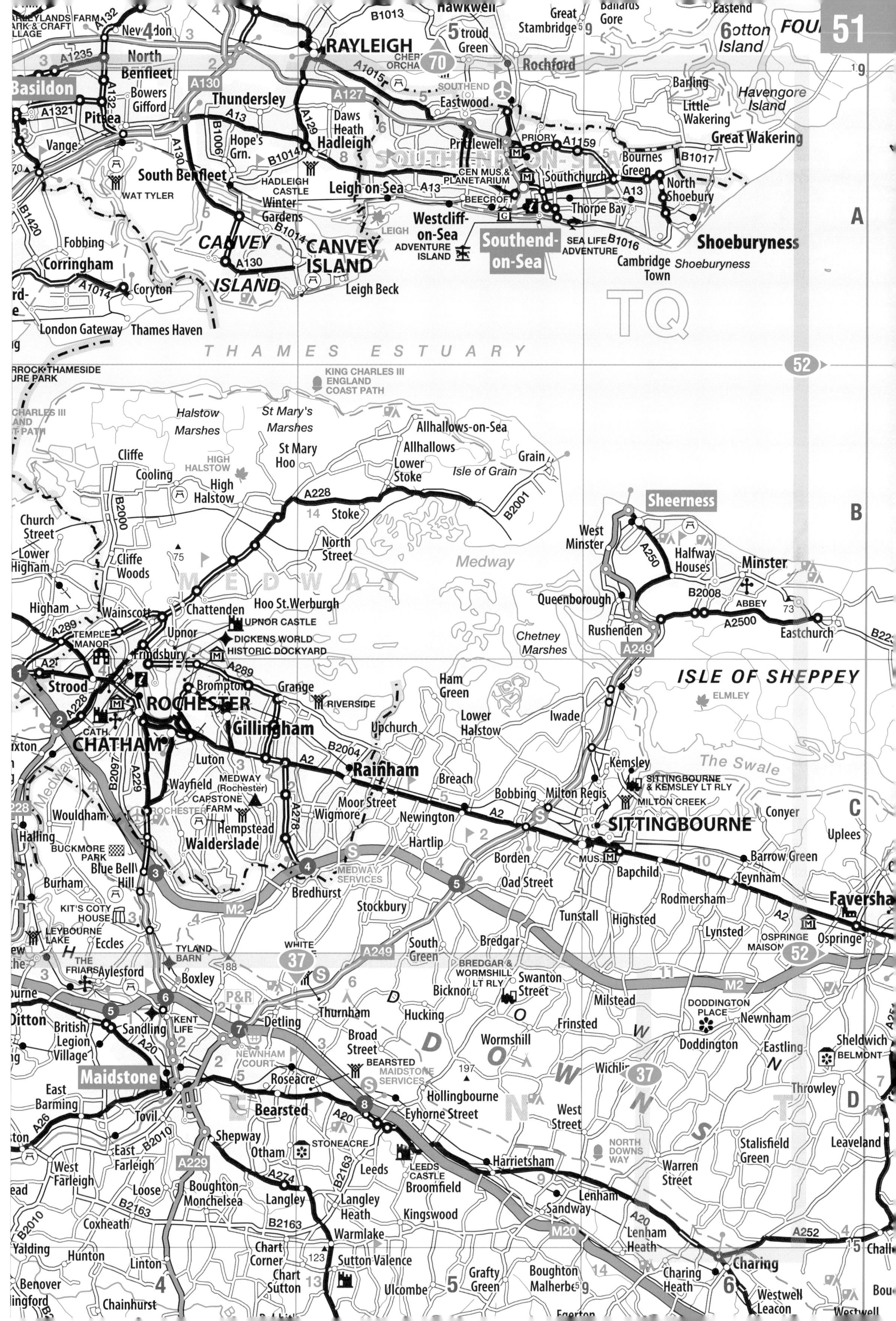

RAYLEIGH
Hawkwell
Rochford
Great Stambridge
Ballards Gore
Eastend
Potton Island
North Benfleet
Basildon
Bowers Gifford
Pitsea
Vange
Thundersley
Daws Heath
Hadleigh
Hope's Grn.
South Benfleet
WAT TYLER
HADLEIGH CASTLE
Leigh on Sea
Eastwood
SOUTHEND
Prittlewell
PRIORY
SOUTHEND-ON-SEA
CEN MUS.& PLANETARIUM
Southchurch
Barling
Havengore Island
Little Wakering
Great Wakering
Bournes Green
North Shoebury
Thorpe Bay
BEECROFT
Westcliff-on-Sea
ADVENTURE ISLAND
Southend-on-Sea
SEA LIFE ADVENTURE
Shoeburyness
Cambridge Town
Winter Gardens
CANVEY ISLAND
Leigh Beck
Fobbing
Corringham
Coryton
London Gateway
Thames Haven
TQ
THAMES ESTUARY
KING CHARLES III ENGLAND COAST PATH
Halstow Marshes
St Mary's Marshes
Allhallows-on-Sea
Allhallows
St Mary Hoo
Lower Stoke
Grain
Isle of Grain
Cliffe
HIGH HALSTOW
Cooling
High Halstow
Stoke
Church Street
Lower Higham
Cliffe Woods
North Street
Medway
MEDWAY
Sheerness
West Minster
Halfway Houses
Minster
Queenborough
ABBEY
Rushenden
Eastchurch
Higham
Wainscott
Chattenden
Hoo St.Werburgh
UPNOR CASTLE
Upnor
TEMPLE MANOR
DICKENS WORLD
HISTORIC DOCKYARD
Frindsbury
Chetney Marshes
Strood
Brompton
ROCHESTER
Grange
RIVERSIDE
Ham Green
ISLE OF SHEPPEY
ELMLEY
CATH.
CHATHAM
Gillingham
Upchurch
Lower Halstow
Iwade
Luton
Rainham
Kemsley
The Swale
Wayfield
MEDWAY (Rochester)
Breach
Bobbing
Milton Regis
SITTINGBOURNE & KEMSLEY LT RLY
MILTON CREEK
CAPSTONE FARM
ROCHESTER
Moor Street
Newington
Wouldham
Hempstead
Wigmore
SITTINGBOURNE
Conyer
Halling
Walderslade
Hartlip
Borden
Uplees
BUCKMORE PARK
MEDWAY SERVICES
MUS.
Bapchild
Barrow Green
Blue Bell Hill
Burham
Bredhurst
Oad Street
Teynham
Rodmersham
Faversham
KIT'S COTY HOUSE
Stockbury
Tunstall
Highsted
LEYBOURNE LAKE
Eccles
Lynsted
OSPRINGE MAISON
Ospringe
TYLAND BARN
South Green
Bredgar
THE FRIARS
Aylesford
BREDGAR & WORMSHILL LT RLY
Swanton Street
Boxley
Bicknor
Milstead
DODDINGTON PLACE
Ditton
KENT LIFE
Sandling
Thurnham
Detling
Hucking
Newnham
British Legion Village
Frinsted
Wormshill
Doddington
Eastling
Sheldwich
BELMONT
NEWNHAM COURT
Broad Street
D O W N S
Maidstone
Roseacre
BEARSTED
MAIDSTONE SERVICES
Wichling
Throwley
East Barming
Bearsted
Hollingbourne
Eyhorne Street
West Street
Tovil
Shepway
STONEACRE
Otham
NORTH DOWNS WAY
Stalisfield Green
Leaveland
East Farleigh
West Farleigh
Harrietsham
Leeds
LEEDS CASTLE
Broomfield
Warren Street
Loose
Boughton Monchelsea
Langley
Lenham
Sandway
Langley Heath
Kingswood
Coxheath
Warmlake
Lenham Heath
Yalding
Hunton
Chart Corner
Chart Sutton
Sutton Valence
Linton
Grafty Green
Boughton Malherbe
Charing
Charing Heath
Benover
Ulcombe
Westwell
Chainhurst
Westwell Leacon

FOULNESS ISLAND
Potton Island
Eastend
MAPLIN SANDS
Barling
Havengore Island
Little Wakering
Great Wakering
A1159
Bournes Green
B1017
A13
North Shoebury
Thorpe Bay
SEA LIFE ADVENTURE
B1016
Shoeburyness
Cambridge Town
71
51
TQ
Sheerness
West Minster
A250
Halfway Houses
Minster
ABBEY
B2008
A2500
Eastchurch
B2231
Warden Pt.
Warden
Leysdown-on-Sea
Rushenden
A249
ISLE OF SHEPPEY
ELMLEY
Isle of Harty
THE SWALE
Shell Ness
The Swale
Kemsley
SITTINGBOURNE & KEMSLEY LT RLY
MILTON CREEK
SITTINGBOURNE
Conyer
Uplees
KING CHARLES III ENGLAND COAST PATH
WHITSTABLE
Tankerton
Swalecliffe
HERNE BAY
MUSEUM & GALLERY
Seasalter
A2990
Chestfield
Greenhill
Herne
South Street
Yorkletts
A290
Calcott
A291
Barrow Green
Teynham
Bapchild
Rodmersham
Tunstall
Highsted
Lynsted
Oare
Faversham
CHART GUNPOWDER MILLS
FLEUR DE LIS HERITAGE CENTRE
Graveney
Goodnestone
A299
Dargate
66
Honey Hill
Broadoak
Tyler Hill
Sturry
Hales Place
Fordwich
OSPRINGE MAISON DIEU
Ospringe
Preston
Hernhill
MOUNT EPHRAIM
BLEAN WOODS
Blean
Rough Common
Boughton Street
Dunkirk
M2
A2
GATE SERVICES
Canterbury
A257
ST AUGUSTINE'S ABBEY
Milstead
DODDINGTON PLACE
Newnham
Doddington
North Street
A251
Sheldwich
BELMONT
South Street
123
Oversland
Harbledown
Chartham Hatch
Thanington
CANTERBURY ROMAN MUS.
P&R
A2050
Frinsted
Wichling
Eastling
Throwley
Selling
Old Wives Lees
A28
Chartham
West Street
NORTH DOWNS WAY
Stalisfield Green
Leaveland
Badlesmere
Shottenden
Chilham
Shalmsford Street
Nackington
Street End
Bridge
Garlinge Green
Lower Hardres
Bishopsbourne
Warren Street
A252
Molash
B2068
Petham
Kingston
Upper Hardres Court
Lenham
A20
Lenham Heath
A252
Challock
NORTH DOWNS WAY
Godmersham
Sole Street
38
Bossingham
Derringston
Crundale
Waltham
ELHAM VALLEY VINEYARD
Boughton Aluph
Westwell Leacon
Westwell
Stelling
0 1 2 3 miles
0 1 2 3 4 5 km

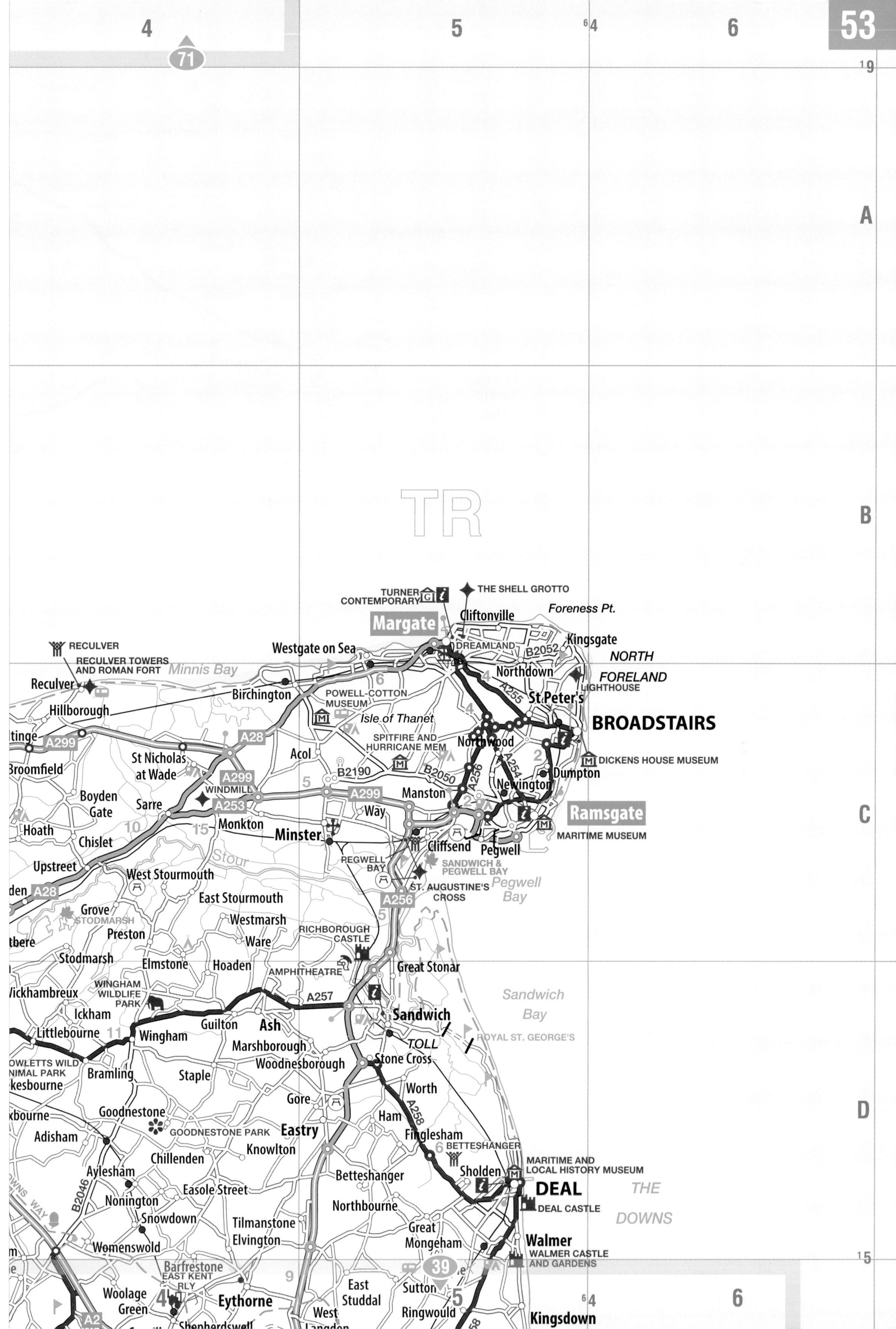
4
5
6
71
A
B
C
D
TR
TURNER CONTEMPORARY
THE SHELL GROTTO
Foreness Pt.
Margate
Cliftonville
Kingsgate
DREAMLAND
B2052
NORTH
FORELAND
LIGHTHOUSE
RECULVER
RECULVER TOWERS AND ROMAN FORT
Minnis Bay
Westgate on Sea
Northdown
Reculver
Birchington
POWELL-COTTON MUSEUM
A255
St. Peter's
BROADSTAIRS
Hillborough
Isle of Thanet
A299
A28
SPITFIRE AND HURRICANE MEM
Northwood
St Nicholas at Wade
Acol
DICKENS HOUSE MUSEUM
Broomfield
A254
Dumpton
B2190
B2050
A256
Newington
Boyden Gate
Sarre
WINDMILL
Manston
Ramsgate
A253
Way
MARITIME MUSEUM
Hoath
Monkton
Chislet
Minster
Cliffsend
Pegwell
Upstreet
Stour
PEGWELL BAY
SANDWICH & PEGWELL BAY
West Stourmouth
ST. AUGUSTINE'S CROSS
Pegwell Bay
East Stourmouth
Grove
STODMARSH
Westmarsh
Preston
RICHBOROUGH CASTLE
Ware
Stodmarsh
Elmstone
Hoaden
AMPHITHEATRE
Great Stonar
WINGHAM WILDLIFE PARK
A257
Sandwich Bay
Ickham
Sandwich
Guilton
Ash
Littlebourne
Wingham
TOLL
ROYAL ST. GEORGE'S
Marshborough
Stone Cross
Bramling
Woodnesborough
Staple
Worth
Gore
Goodnestone
Ham
A258
Adisham
GOODNESTONE PARK
Eastry
Finglesham
BETTESHANGER
Knowlton
Chillenden
Aylesham
Betteshanger
Sholden
MARITIME AND LOCAL HISTORY MUSEUM
DEAL
THE
Easole Street
Nonington
Northbourne
DEAL CASTLE
B2046
Snowdown
DOWNS
Tilmanstone
Great Mongeham
Elvington
Walmer
Womenswold
WALMER CASTLE AND GARDENS
Barfrestone
EAST KENT RLY
39
East Studdal
Woolage Green
Eythorne
Sutton
West Langdon
Ringwould
Kingsdown
Shepherdswell
A2

1 2 3 4
A B C D E
PEMBROKESHIRE
ARFORDIR P
Ynysduellyn
Penclegyr
Porthgain
Trefin
Abereiddy
Llanrhian
Croes-goch
ST. DAVID'S HEAD
PENMAEN DEWI
Tretio
Treffynnon
Treleddyd-fawr
Carnhedryn
Treglemais
Whitesand Bay
Porth-mawr
ST DAVID'S
Rhodiad
Caerfarchell
BISHOP'S PALACE
B4583
A487
Rhosson
Whitchurch
Middle Mill
Ramsey Sound
CATHEDRAL
Ramsey Island
Ynys Dewi
RAMSEY ISLAND
St David's
(Tyddewi)
Nine Wells
Solva
ST. BRIDES
BAY
BAE SAIN FFRAID
SM
PEMBROKESHIRE COAST PATH
LLWYBR ARFORDIR PENFRO
BROAD
Broad Haven
Little Haven
Talbenny
Tower Point
Trwyn Tŵr
St Bride's
NATIONAL NATURE RESERVE
Wooltack Point
Trwyn Wooltack
GRASSHOLM ISLAND
Skomer Island
Ynys Skomer
SKOMER ISLAND
Marloes
B4327
Hasguard
MARLOES SANDS
Broad Sound
Sandy Haven
St Ishmael's
Gateholm Island
Ynys Gateholm
Dale
MILFORD
ABERDAUG
Skokholm Island
Ynys Skokholm
St Ann's Hd.
Pentir St. Ann
ROSSLARE
Sheep Island
Ynys y Defaid
PEMBROKESHIRE
PARFORDIR P
181
79
82
71
0 1 2 3 miles
0 1 2 3 4 5 km

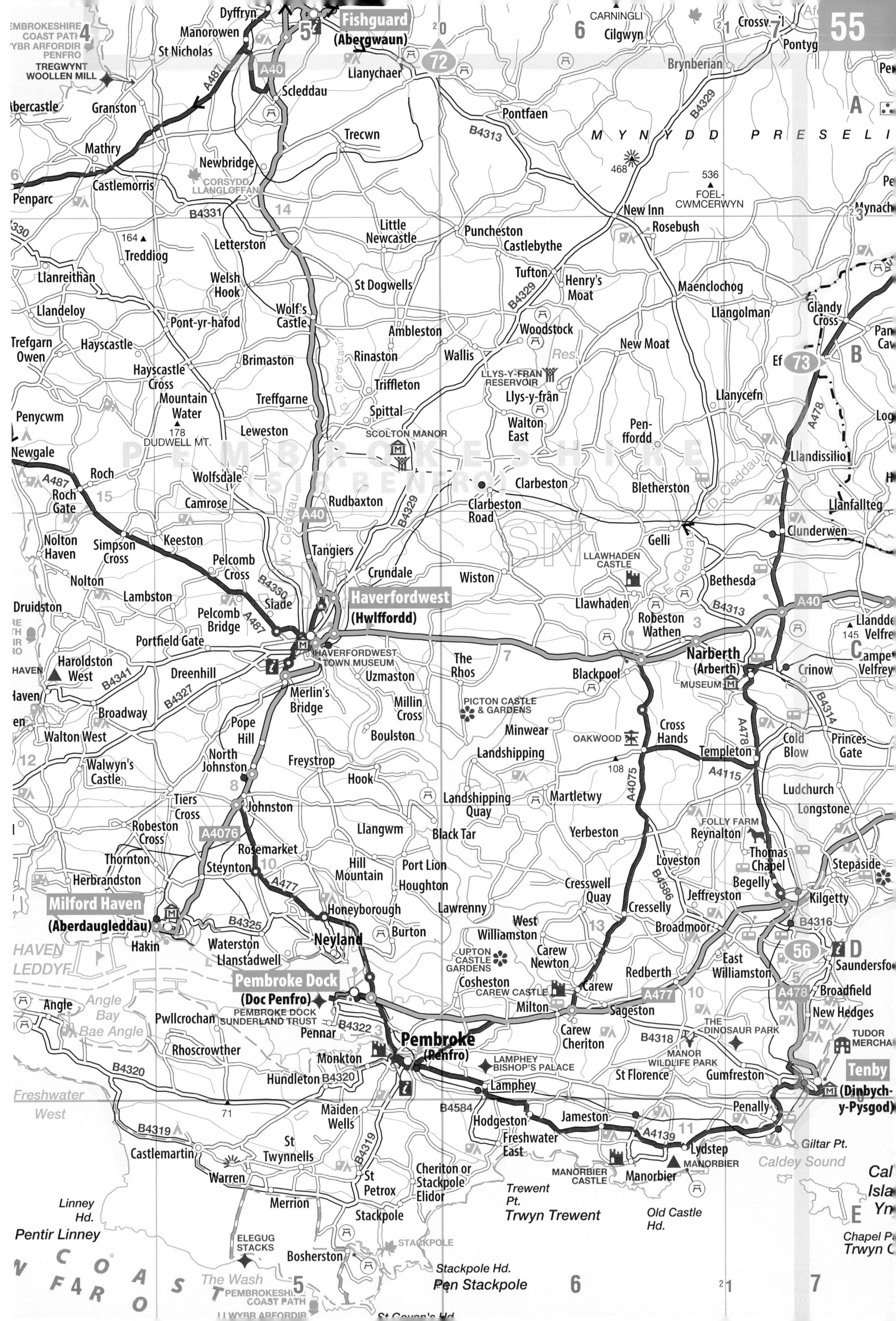
PEMBROKESHIRE COAST PATH
LLWYBR ARFORDIR PENFRO
4
5
6
7
Dyffryn
Manorowen
Fishguard
(Abergwaun)
CARNINGLI
Cilgwyn
Crossway
Pontyglasier
St Nicholas
Llanychaer
72
Brynberian
TREGWYNT WOOLLEN MILL
A40
A487
Scleddau
Abercastle
Granston
Pontfaen
B4329
A
MYNYDD PRESELI
B4313
Trecwn
Mathry
Newbridge
468
536
FOEL-CWMCERWYN
CORSYDD LLANGLOFFAN
Castlemorris
Penparc
B4331
14
New Inn
Rosebush
Mynachlog-ddu
B4330
164
Treddiog
Letterston
Little Newcastle
Puncheston
Castlebythe
Llanreithan
Welsh Hook
St Dogwells
Tufton
Henry's Moat
Maenclochog
Llandeloy
Wolf's Castle
Ambleston
Woodstock
Llangolman
Glandy Cross
Pont-yr-hafod
Trefgarn Owen
Hayscastle
Brimaston
Rinaston
Wallis
New Moat
Res.
Efailwen
73
B
Hayscastle Cross
LLYS-Y-FRAN RESERVOIR
Llys-y-frân
Triffleton
Llanycefn
Mountain Water
Treffgarne
Spittal
Walton East
A478
178
DUDWELL MT.
Penycwm
Leweston
SCOLTON MANOR
Pen-ffordd
Newgale
PEMBROKESHIRE (SIR BENFRO)
Llandissilio
Roch
Wolfsdale
Clarbeston
Bletherston
A487
Roch Gate
15
Camrose
Rudbaxton
Clarbeston Road
Llanfallteg
A40
Clunderwen
Nolton Haven
Simpson Cross
Keeston
Tangiers
Gelli
W. Cleddau
E. Cleddau
SN
LLAWHADEN CASTLE
Pelcomb Cross
Crundale
Wiston
Bethesda
Nolton
B4330
Haverfordwest
(Hwlffordd)
Lambston
Slade
Llawhaden
Robeston Wathen
A40
Druidston
Pelcomb Bridge
B4313
Llanddewi Velfrey
145
Portfield Gate
3
Narberth
(Arberth)
C
HAVERFORDWEST TOWN MUSEUM
The Rhos
7
Haroldston West
Dreenhill
Uzmaston
Blackpool
MUSEUM
Crinow
Lampeter Velfrey
B4341
B4327
Merlin's Bridge
Millin Cross
PICTON CASTLE & GARDENS
B4314
Broadway
Pope Hill
Boulston
Minwear
OAKWOOD
Cross Hands
Cold Blow
Princes Gate
Walton West
A478
North Johnston
Freystrop
Landshipping
Templeton
12
108
A4115
Walwyn's Castle
Hook
Ludchurch
8
Landshipping Quay
Martletwy
A4075
Tiers Cross
Johnston
Longstone
Robeston Cross
Llangwm
Black Tar
Yerbeston
FOLLY FARM
A4076
Reynalton
Thornton
Rosemarket
Thomas Chapel
Loveston
Stepaside
Herbrandston
Steynton
10
Hill Mountain
Port Lion
Begelly
A477
Houghton
Cresswell Quay
B4586
Jeffreyston
Kilgetty
Milford Haven
(Aberdaugleddau)
Honeyborough
Lawrenny
Cresselly
B4325
West Williamston
13
Broadmoor
B4316
Hakin
Neyland
Burton
D
Waterston
Carew Newton
56
HAVEN
Llanstadwell
UPTON CASTLE GARDENS
East Williamston
Saundersfoot
Redberth
Pembroke Dock
(Doc Penfro)
Cosheston
Carew
CAREW CASTLE
10
A478
Broadfield
Angle
Angle Bay
Bae Angle
A477
Milton
PEMBROKE DOCK SUNDERLAND TRUST
Sageston
New Hedges
Pwllcrochan
Pennar
B4322
Carew Cheriton
THE DINOSAUR PARK
TUDOR MERCHANT'S HOUSE
Rhoscrowther
Pembroke
(Penfro)
B4318
MANOR WILDLIFE PARK
Monkton
LAMPHEY BISHOP'S PALACE
Tenby
B4320
St Florence
Gumfreston
Hundleton
B4320
Freshwater West
Lamphey
(Dinbych-y-Pysgod)
71
Maiden Wells
B4584
Jameston
Penally
Hodgeston
B4319
A4139
11
St Twynnells
Freshwater East
Giltar Pt.
Castlemartin
B4319
Lydstep
MANORBIER
Caldey Sound
Warren
St Petrox
Cheriton or Stackpole Elidor
MANORBIER CASTLE
Manorbier
Trewent Pt.
Trwyn Trewent
Caldey Island
Ynys Bŷr
E
Linney Hd.
Merrion
Old Castle Hd.
Pentir Linney
Stackpole
ELEGUG STACKS
STACKPOLE
Chapel Pt.
Trwyn Capel
Bosherston
The Wash
PEMBROKESHIRE COAST PATH
LLWYBR ARFORDIR
Stackpole Hd.
Pen Stackpole
St Govan's Hd.
5
6
21
7

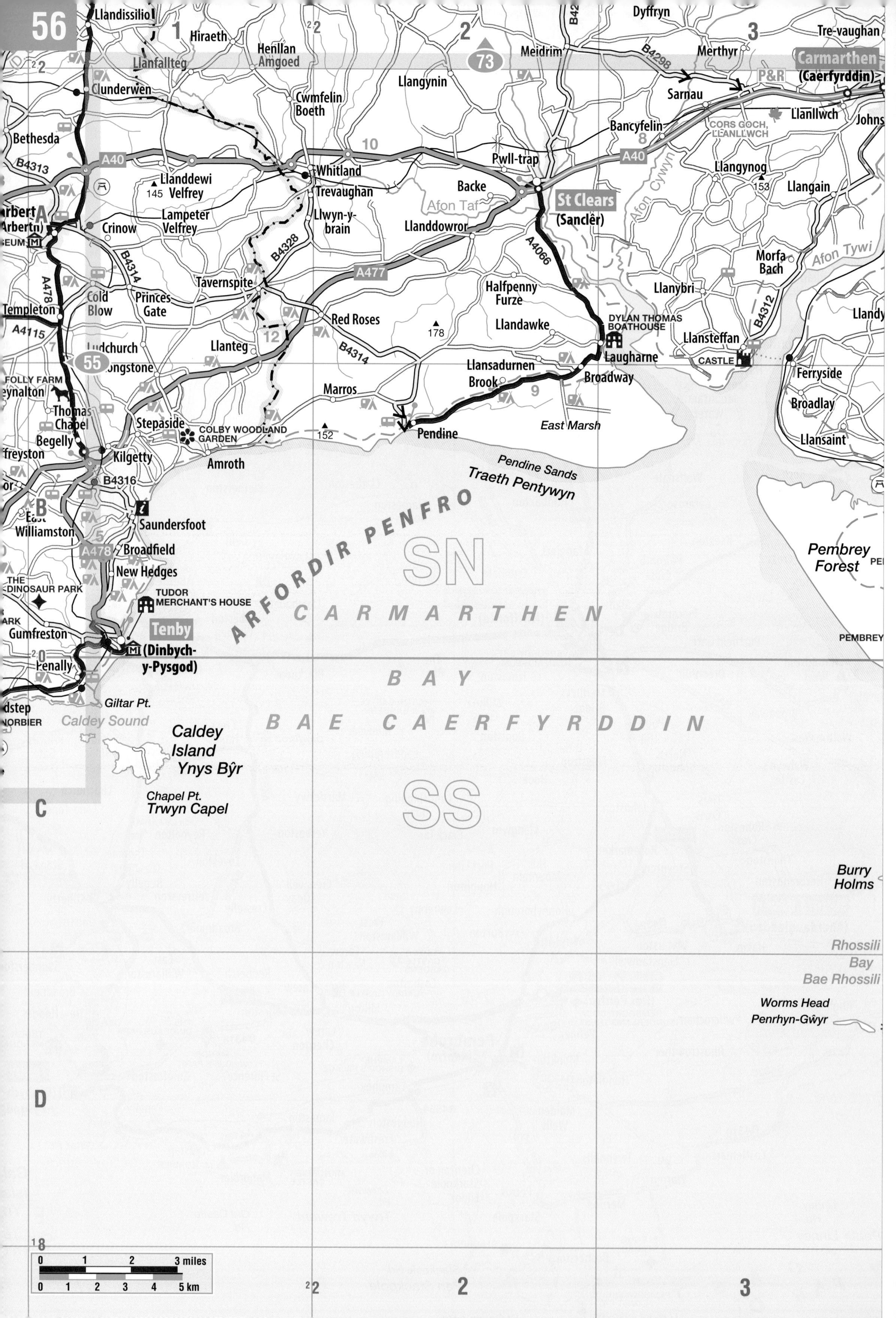
Llandissilio
Hiraeth
Henllan Amgoed
Llanfallteg
Meidrim
Dyffryn
Merthyr
Tre-vaughan
Carmarthen (Caerfyrddin)
P&R
73
B4298
Llangynin
Sarnau
Llanllwch
Johns
Clunderwen
Cwmfelin Boeth
Bancyfelin
CORS GOCH, LLANLLWCH
Bethesda
B4313
A40
Whitland
Pwll-trap
Llangynog
153
Llangain
Llanddewi Velfrey
145
Trevaughan
Backe
St Clears (Sanclêr)
Afon Taf
Afon Cywyn
Narberth (Arberth)
Crinow
Lampeter Velfrey
Llwyn-y-brain
Llanddowror
A4066
Morfa Bach
Afon Tywi
B4314
B4328
A477
A478
Templeton
Cold Blow
Princes Gate
Tavernspite
Halfpenny Furze
Llanybri
B4312
A4115
Red Roses
178
Llandawke
DYLAN THOMAS BOATHOUSE
Llansteffan
Llandy
Ludchurch
Longstone
Llanteg
B4314
Laugharne
CASTLE
55
Llansadurnen
Brook
Broadway
Ferryside
FOLLY FARM
Reynalton
Marros
Broadlay
Thomas Chapel
Stepaside
COLBY WOODLAND GARDEN
152
Pendine
East Marsh
Llansaint
Begelly
Kilgetty
Amroth
Pendine Sands
Traeth Pentywyn
B4316
ARFORDIR PENFRO
East Williamston
Saundersfoot
A478
Broadfield
New Hedges
SN
Pembrey Forest
THE DINOSAUR PARK
TUDOR MERCHANT'S HOUSE
CARMARTHEN
Gumfreston
Tenby (Dinbych-y-Pysgod)
PEMBREY
Penally
BAY
Giltar Pt.
Caldey Sound
BAE CAERFYRDDIN
NORBIER
Caldey Island Ynys Bŷr
Chapel Pt. Trwyn Capel
SS
Burry Holms
Rhossili Bay Bae Rhossili
Worms Head Penrhyn-Gŵyr
A
B
C
D
1
2
3
0 1 2 3 miles
0 1 2 3 4 5 km

Llandeilo
Ffairfach
Pont-ar-gothi
Nantgaredig
Llanegwad
Dryslwyn
Cilsan
ABERGLASNEY
GELLI AUR
Golden Grove
CARMARTHENSHIRE COUNTY MUS
Llangunnor
Capel Dewi
Llanarthne
Pensarn
Nantycaws
THE NATIONAL BOTANIC GARDEN OF WALES
Penrhiwgoch
Trapp
CARREG CENNEN CASTLE & FARM
Cwmffrwd
Llanddarog
Maesybont
Temple Bar
Milo
Llandyfan
CARMEL
Carmel
Croesyceiliog
Idole
Cwmisfael
Porthyrhyd
LLYN LLECH OWAIN
Pentre-Gwenlais
Llandybie
Dre-fach
Bancycapel
Foel-gastell
Cefneithin
Caer-bryn
Twynmynydd
Llangendeirne
Gwendraeth Fach
Gorslas
Glanaman
Afon Aman
Crwbin
Drefach
Cwm-y-glo
Pen-y-groes
Tir-y-dail
Morfa
Saron
Pontamman
Garnant
Pontantwn
Bancffosfelen
Cwm-mawr
Cross Hands
Ammanford
Betws (Rhydaman)
Gwaun-Cae-Gurwen
Pontyberem
Tumble
Penybanc
Pentre
Capel Hendre
Cwmgwili
Pantyffynnon
Tycroes
Meinciau
Four Roads
Pont-Henri
Greynor
Garnswllt
Mynyddygarreg
Pontyates
Llannon
Mynydd y Gwair
Cynheidre
Llwyn-têg
PONT ABRAHAM SERVICES
Kidwelly (Cydweli)
Sylen
Llanedi
276
GRAIG FAWR
Carway
FFOS LAS
Five Roads
Horeb
Lliedi Resrs.
Sardis
Pentrebach
Trimsaran
Fforest
Pontarddulais
Pinged
Waun-y-clyn
Hendy
Cwm-Dulais
Rhyd-y-gwin
Craig-cefn-parc
Rhyd-y-pandy
Felindre
Pontardawe
Cwmbach
Felinfoel
Allt
Llangennech
Faerdre
Pembrey
Achddu
Pwll
Furnace
Dafen
Waungron
Pontlliw
Clydach
Ynystawe
Burry Port (Porth Tywyn)
Sandy
Bryn
Grovesend
SWANSEA WEST SERVICES
Pant-lasau
Llwynhendy
Bynea
Yspitty
Penllergaer
Llangyfelach
Llanelli
Morfa
Machynys
WILDFOWL AND WETLANDS TRUST
Loughor
Gorseinon
Morriston
Heol-las
Cadle
Llansamlet
Whiteford Pt.
Trwyn Whiteford
WHITEFORD
Llanrhidian Sands
Traeth Llanrhidian
Pen-clawdd
Gowerton
Fforest-fâch
Landore
Pentre-dwr
Pentre-chwyth
Cwm Bon-y-maen
Crofty
Blue Anchor
Waunarlwydd
Wernffrwd
Llanmorlais
Three Crosses
Cwmdu
Foxhole
Swansea (ABERTAWE)
Dunvant
PLANTASIA
Port Tennant
Cheriton
Llanmadoc
Landimore
WEOBLEY CASTLE
Killay
Sketty
SWANSEA (ABERTAWE)
Brynmill
SWANSEA MUSEUM
Burry Green
Llanrhidian
Llethrid
Upper Killay
CLYNE VALLEY
NATIONAL WATERFRONT MUSEUM
Llangennith
SWANSEA
Ilston
Mayals
Burry
Reynoldston
GOWER
Bishopston
Black Pill
West Cross
THE BEACON
Llanddewi
Lunnon
Kittle
Mansfelfield
SWANSEA BAY
GOWER HERITAGE CENTRE
Parkmill
LOVESPOON GALLERY
OYSTERMOUTH CASTLE
Rhossili
Knelston
Nicholaston
Penmaen
Pennard
Oldway
Newton
The Mumbles (Y Mwmbwls)
BAE ABERTAWE
Middleton
Scurlage
Penrice
OXWICH
Southgate
GOWER COAST
Pilton Green
Oxwich Bay
Bae Oxwich
Mumbles Hd.
Trwyn yr Mwmbwls
Horton
Oxwich
OXWICH CASTLE
Pwlldu Hd.
Pen Pwlldu
Overton
Port-Eynon
Port Eynon Bay
Bae Port Eynon
Port Eynon Pt.
Trwyn Port Eynon
A40
A48
A476
A483
A474
A484
A4138
A4240
A4118
A4067
A4217
A4603
M4
B4300
B4310
B4297
B4556
B4306
B4309
B4317
B4308
B4311
B4296
B4489
B4620
B4295
B4271
B4247
58
59
40
A
B
C
D
4
5
6

Llanwnnen
Cwmann
Pentre-bâch
Cwmsychpant
Ram
Tregroes
Rhydowen
Dre-fach
Alltyblaca
A485
Pencarreg
Parc-y-rhôs
Llanycrwys
Ffarmers
Prengwyn
Brynteg
Llanybydder
Ffaldybrenin
258
Capel Dewi
Rhuddlan
Glan-Duar
Ty Mawr
415
Mynydd Pencarreg
Harford
B4476
Maesycrugiau
Llandysul
Llandre
Esgairdawe
Aber-Giâr
Pumsaint
DOLAUCOTHI GOLD MINES
Llanfihangel-ar-arth
Llanllwni
408
B4337
Caio
B4336
Rhydcymerau
Bancyffordd
Crugybar
16
Lllidiad Nenog
New Inn
73
Llansawel
A482
Pencader
B4302
Edwinsford
Gwyddgrug
B4310
Abergorlech
Dolgran
Gwernogle
Afon Cothi
TALLEY ABBEY
B4459
23
329
CYNROS
Talley
314
355
MYNYDD RHOS-WEN
Brechfa Forest
Nant-y-ffin
Cwm-byr
Waunclunda
Pen-y-garn
Alltwalis
Llansadwrn
A485
Cwmdu
Halfway
Brechfa
Felindre
192
Llanllawddog
Llanpumsaint
CARMARTHENSHIRE
(SIR GAERFYRDDIN)
Soar
Ashfield
Horeb
Hermon
Pontarsais
Llanfynydd
Capel Isaac
B4301
B4310
Manordeilo
Felindre
Pant-glas
Afon Duad
Salem
Cwmifor
8
Rhydargaeau
GWILI RAILWAY
Pant-teg
Pantgwyn
Felingwm uchaf
Felingwm isaf
Rhosmaen
Bethlehem
Pen-y-banc
Peniel
Llanfihangel-uwch-Gwili
Bronwydd Arms
Pentrefelin
Capel Gwyn
Broad Oak
Court Henry
DINEFWR PARK
VALE OF TYWI
DYFFRYN TYWI
Pontbren Araeth
Ffynnon ddrain
White Mill
15
Pont-ar-gothi
Llangathen
A40
Cilsan
Llandeilo
Abergwili
Tanerdy
Nantgaredig
Felindre
ABERGLASNEY
B4300
Ffairfach
CARMARTHENSHIRE COUNTY MUS
Llanegwad
Dryslwyn
B4300
GELLI AUR
Llangunnor
Capel Dewi
Llanarthne
57
Afon Tywi
Golden Grove
Pensarn
Trapp
CARREG CENNEN CASTLE & FARM
B4310
Nantycaws
Johnstown
THE NATIONAL BOTANIC GARDEN OF WALES
Penrhiwgoch
A476
12
A48
9
Temple Bar
Milo
A483
Llandyfan
Cwmffrwd
CARMEL
B4297
Llanddarog
Maesybont
Carmel
8
Croesyceiliog
Pentre-Gwenlais
Dre-fach
Cwmisfael
LLYN LLECH OWAIN
272
Llandybie
Idole
Porthyrhyd
Bancycapel
Foel-gastell
Twynmynydd
B4306
Gwendraeth Fach
Caer-bryn
Gorslas
B4556
Llangendeirne
Cefneithin
Glanaman
262
Pen-y-groes
Tir-y-dail
A484
Crwbin
Drefach
Cwm-y-glo
Morfa
A474
10
Saron
Pontamman
Garnant
Pontantwn
Bancffosfelen
Cwm-mawr
B4310
Cross Hands
Llandyfaelog
Penybanc
Ammanford
11
Betws (Rhydaman)
Gwaun-Cae-Gurwen
B4309
Pontyberem
Tumble
4
Capel Hendre
Pantyffynnon
Pentre
Cwmgwili
5
Tycroes
Meinciau
B4317
B4306
57
Pont-Henri
A48
A483
Greynor
Four Roads
Garnswllt
374
Pontyates
284
Llannon
Mynyddygarreg
B4297
Mynydd y Gwair
Cynheidre
Llwyn-têg
Loughor (Llwchwr)
Sylen
49
PONT ABRAHAM SERVICES
Kidwelly (Cydweli)
B4309
A476
Llanedi
276
GRAIG FAWR
Carway
FFOS LAS
B4306
Sardis
Pentrebach
Five Roads
Horeb
Lliedi Resrs.
10
Fforest
193
3
Trimsaran
Pontarddulais
2
Hendy
3
Rhyd-y-gwin
Craig-cefn-parc
Cwm-Dulais
48
Waun-y-clyn
0 1 2 3 miles
0 1 2 3 4 5 km

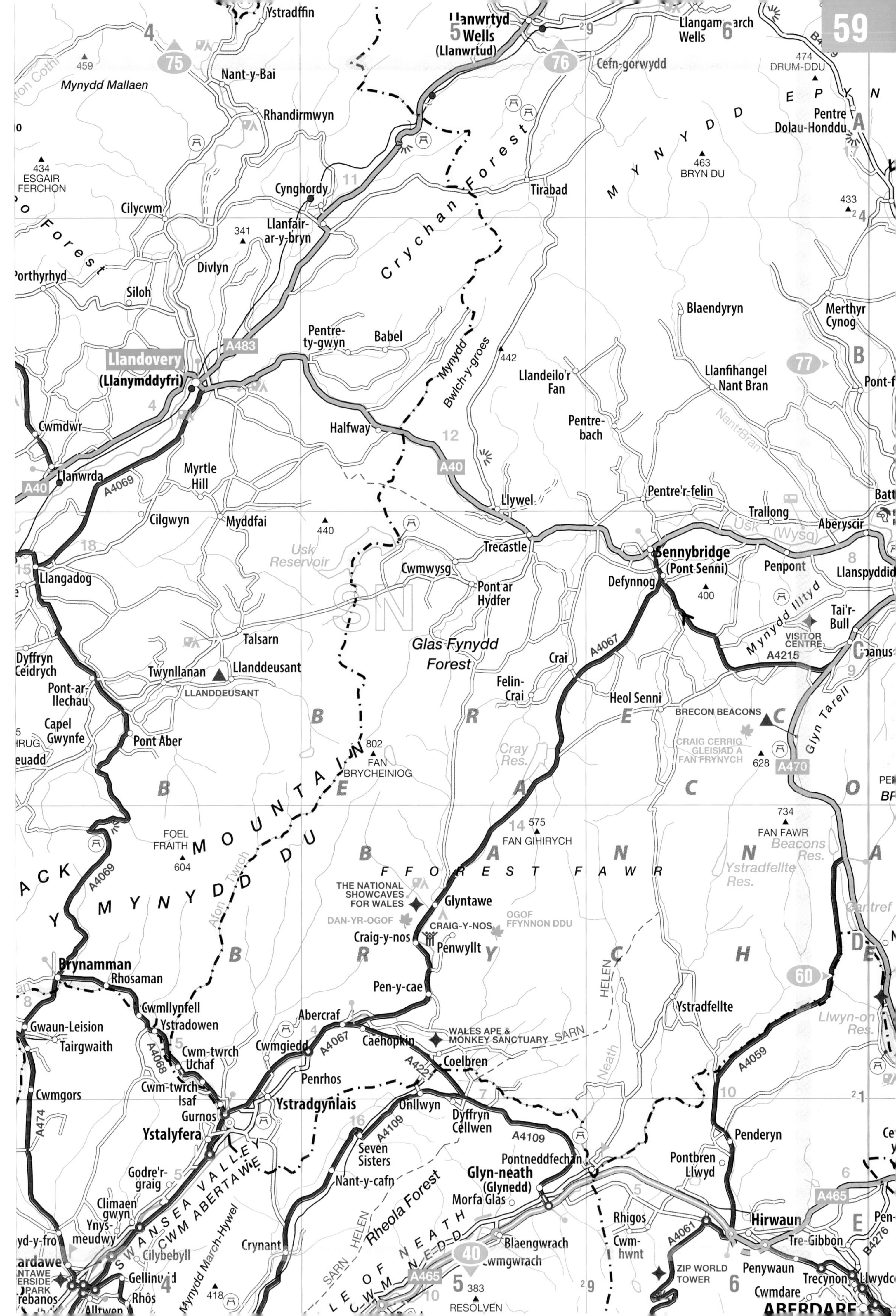
Ystradffin
Llanwrtyd Wells (Llanwrtud)
Llangammarch Wells
Mynydd Mallaen
Nant-y-Bai
Cefn-gorwydd
474 DRUM-DDU
Rhandirmwyn
M Y N Y D D E P Y N T
Pentre Dolau-Honddu
434 ESGAIR FERCHON
463 BRYN DU
Cynghordy
Tirabad
Cilycwm
Llanfair-ar-y-bryn
Crychan Forest
341
Divlyn
Porthyrhyd
Siloh
Blaendyryn
Merthyr Cynog
Pentre-ty-gwyn
Babel
Llandovery (Llanymddyfri)
A483
Mynydd Bwlch-y-groes
442
Llandeilo'r Fan
Llanfihangel Nant Bran
Pentre-bach
Halfway
Cwmdwr
Llanwrda
A40
A4069
Myrtle Hill
Llywel
Pentre'r-felin
Trallong
Cilgwyn
Myddfai
440
Usk Reservoir
Trecastle
Sennybridge (Pont Senni)
Aberyscir
Llangadog
Cwmwysg
Penpont
Llanspyddid
Defynnog
Pont ar Hydfer
400
Mynydd Illtyd
Tai'r-Bull
VISITOR CENTRE
Talsarn
Glas Fynydd Forest
Dyffryn Ceidrych
Twynllanan
Llanddeusant
LLANDDEUSANT
Crai
A4067
A4215
Pont-ar-llechau
Felin-Crai
Heol Senni
Capel Gwynfe
Pont Aber
BRECON BEACONS
802 FAN BRYCHEINIOG
Cray Res.
CRAIG CERRIG GLEISIAD A FAN FRYNYCH
628
A470
Glyn Tarell
734 FAN FAWR
575 FAN GIHIRYCH
FOEL FRAITH 604
MOUNTAIN
Y MYNYDD DU
F F O R E S T F A W R
Beacons Res.
Ystradfellte Res.
THE NATIONAL SHOWCAVES FOR WALES
Glyntawe
Afon Twrch
DAN-YR-OGOF
CRAIG-Y-NOS
OGOF FFYNNON DDU
Craig-y-nos
Penwyllt
Brynamman
Rhosaman
Pen-y-cae
HELEN
Ystradfellte
Llwyn-on Res.
Cwmllynfell
Ystradowen
Gwaun-Leision
Tairgwaith
Abercraf
WALES APE & MONKEY SANCTUARY
SARN
Cwm-twrch Uchaf
Cwmgiedd
Caehopkin
Coelbren
A4068
A4221
Neath
A4059
Cwm-twrch Isaf
Cwmgors
Penrhos
Ystradgynlais
Onllwyn
Gurnos
Dyffryn Cellwen
A474
Ystalyfera
A4109
Seven Sisters
Penderyn
Godre'r-graig
Pontneddfechan
Pontbren Llwyd
Nant-y-cafn
Glyn-neath (Glynedd)
SWANSEA VALLEY CWM ABERTAWE
Climaen gwyn
Rheola Forest
Morfa Glas
Rhigos
A465
Hirwaun
Ynys-meudwy
SARN HELEN
VALE OF NEATH CWM NEDD
Blaengwrach
Cwm-hwnt
A4061
Tre-Gibbon
Cilybebyll
Crynant
Cwmgwrach
ZIP WORLD TOWER
Penywaun
Trecynon
Gellinudd
Mynydd March-Hywel
383 RESOLVEN
Cwmdare
Rhôs
418
ABERDARE
Alltwen
Cwm Tawe
Cantref
75
76
77
60
40
SN

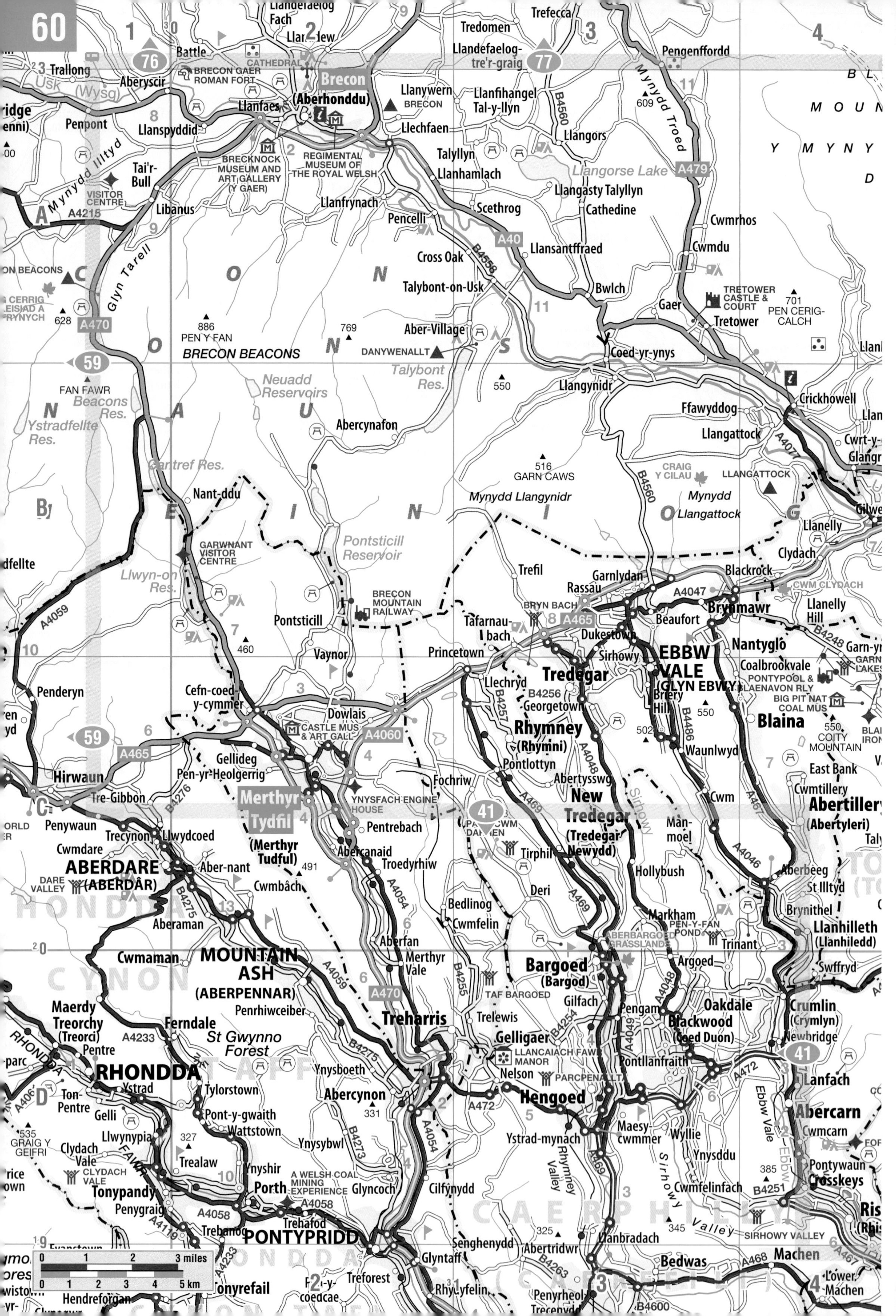
Brecon
(Aberhonddu)
Battle
Trallong
Aberyscir
Usk (Wysg)
BRECON GAER ROMAN FORT
CATHEDRAL
Llanfaes
Penpont
Llanspyddid
BRECKNOCK MUSEUM AND ART GALLERY (Y GAER)
REGIMENTAL MUSEUM OF THE ROYAL WELSH
Llanywern
BRECON
Llechfaen
Tredomen
Trefecca
Llandefaelog-tre'r-graig
Pengenffordd
Llanfihangel Tal-y-llyn
Llangors
Mynydd Troed
609
Talyllyn
Llanhamlach
Llangorse Lake
Llangasty Talyllyn
Cathedine
Scethrog
Llanfrynach
Pencelli
Cwmrhos
Cwmdu
Llansantffraed
Cross Oak
Talybont-on-Usk
Bwlch
Gaer
TRETOWER CASTLE & COURT
Tretower
701
PEN CERIG-CALCH
BLACK MOUNTAINS
Y MYNYDD DU
Mynydd Illtyd
VISITOR CENTRE
Tai'r-Bull
Libanus
A4215
Glyn Tarell
A470
628
886
PEN Y FAN
BRECON BEACONS
769
DANYWENALLT
Aber-Village
Coed-yr-ynys
Talybont Res.
550
Llangynidr
Crickhowell
FAN FAWR
Beacons Res.
Ystradfellte Res.
Neuadd Reservoirs
Abercynafon
Ffawyddog
Llangattock
Cantref Res.
516
GARN CAWS
Mynydd Llangynidr
CRAIG Y CILAU
LLANGATTOCK
Mynydd Llangattock
Nant-ddu
GARWNANT VISITOR CENTRE
Pontsticill Reservoir
Llanelly
Clydach
Llwyn-on Res.
Trefil
Garnlydan
Rassau
Blackrock
A4047
CWM CLYDACH
Llanelly Hill
BRECON MOUNTAIN RAILWAY
BRYN BACH
A465
Pontsticill
Tafarnaubach
Beaufort
Brynmawr
Dukestown
Nantyglo
460
Vaynor
Princetown
Sirhowy
EBBW VALE
(GLYN EBWY)
Tredegar
Coalbrookvale
PONTYPOOL & BLAENAVON RLY
BIG PIT NAT COAL MUS
Penderyn
Cefn-coed-y-cymmer
Dowlais
Llechryd
B4256
Georgetown
Briery Hill
B4486
550
Blaina
CASTLE MUS & ART GALL
A4060
Rhymney
(Rhymni)
502
550
COITY MOUNTAIN
Hirwaun
Gellideg
Pen-yr-Heolgerrig
Pontlottyn
Waunlwyd
Abertysswg
East Bank
Cwmtillery
Tre-Gibbon
Merthyr Tydfil
(Merthyr Tudful)
Fochriw
YNYSFACH ENGINE HOUSE
New Tredegar
(Tredegar Newydd)
Cwm
Abertillery
(Abertyleri)
Penywaun
Llwydcoed
Pentrebach
Man-moel
Trecynon
Cwmdare
Abercanaid
Tirphil
Aberbeeg
ABERDARE
(ABERDÂR)
Aber-nant
491
Troedyrhiw
Hollybush
St Illtyd
DARE VALLEY
Cwmbâch
Deri
Brynithel
Aberaman
Bedlinog
Cwmfelin
Markham
PEN-Y-FAN POND
Llanhilleth
(Llanhiledd)
Aberfan
ABERBARGOED GRASSLANDS
Trinant
Cwmaman
MOUNTAIN ASH
(ABERPENNAR)
Merthyr Vale
Bargoed
(Bargod)
Argoed
Swffryd
TAF BARGOED
Gilfach
Oakdale
Crumlin
(Crymlyn)
Maerdy
Treorchy
(Treorci)
Ferndale
Penrhiwceiber
Treharris
Trelewis
Pengam
Blackwood
(Coed Duon)
Newbridge
A4233
St Gwynno Forest
Gelligaer
LLANCAIACH FAWR MANOR
Pontllanfraith
Pentre
RHONDDA
Ynysboeth
Nelson
PARC PENALLTA
A472
Ton-Pentre
Ystrad
Tylorstown
Abercynon
331
Hengoed
Llanfach
Gelli
Pont-y-gwaith
Ynysybwl
Maesycwmmer
Wyllie
Abercarn
Cwmcarn
535
GRAIG Y GEIFRI
Llwynypia
327
Wattstown
B4273
Ystrad-mynach
Rhymney Valley
Sirhowy
Ynysddu
Ebbw Vale
Clydach Vale
Trealaw
Ynyshir
A WELSH COAL MINING EXPERIENCE
Glyncoch
Cilfynydd
Cwmfelinfach
385
B4251
Pontywaun
Crosskeys
CLYDACH VALE
Tonypandy
Porth
A4058
Penygraig
Trehafod
CAERPHILLY
345
Sirhowy Valley
SIRHOWY VALLEY
Trebanog
PONTYPRIDD
Senghenydd
325
Abertridwr
Llanbradach
Machen
Glyntaff
Bedwas
A468
Treforest
Rhydyfelin
Penyrheol
Lower Machen
Tonyrefail
Hendreforgan
B4600
B4263
A4054
A4059
B4275
B4255
B4254
A4049
A4048
A469
A467
A4046
B4257
B4276
B4248
B4560
B4558
A40
A479
A4077
A4061
A4119
0 1 2 3 miles
0 1 2 3 4 5 km

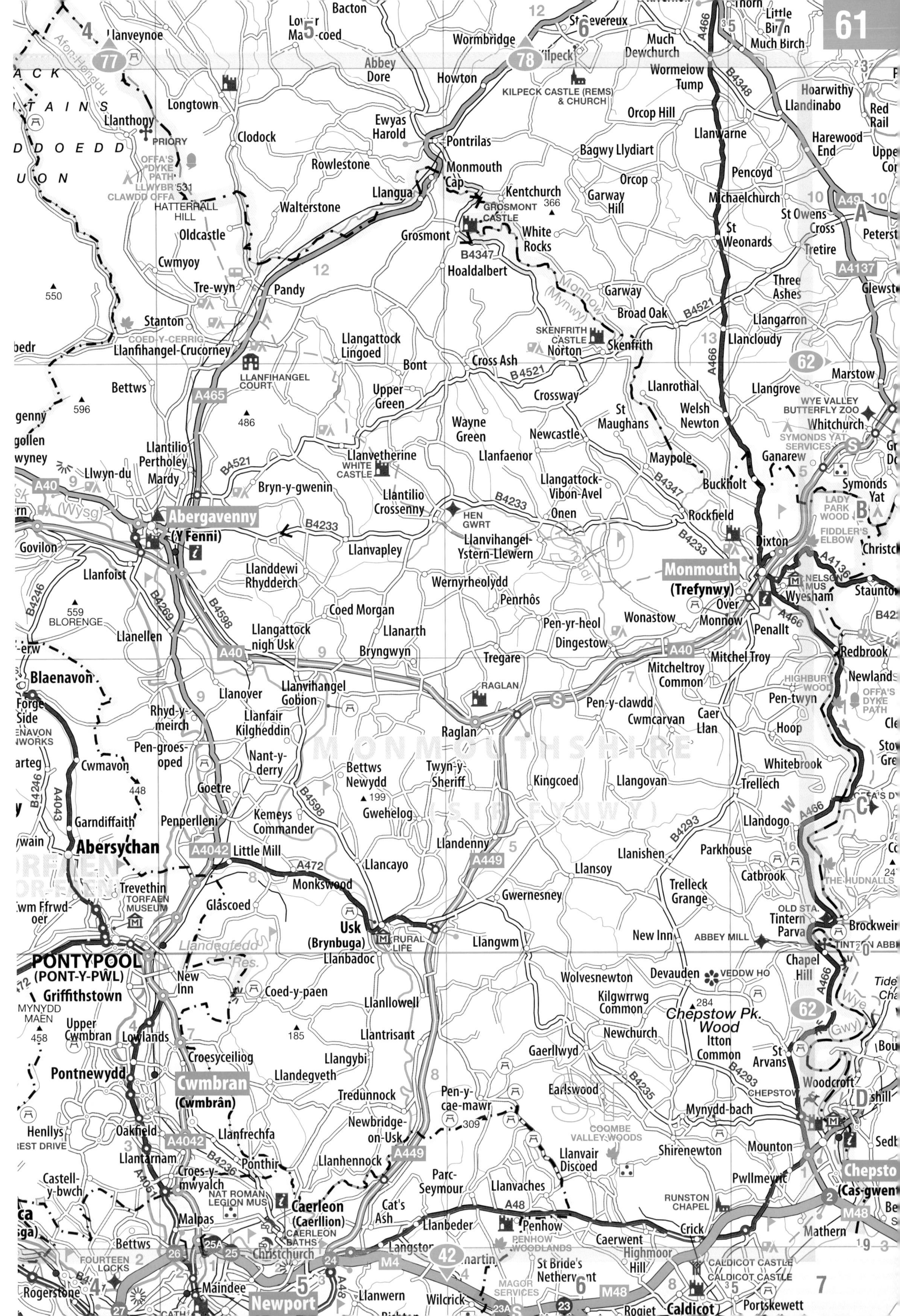
Llanveynoe
Bacton
Lower Maescoed
Wormbridge
St Devereux
Much Dewchurch
Little Birch
Much Birch
Kilpeck
KILPECK CASTLE (REMS) & CHURCH
Abbey Dore
Howton
Wormelow Tump
Hoarwithy
Llandinabo
Red Rail
Longtown
Llanthony
PRIORY
Clodock
Ewyas Harold
Pontrilas
Orcop Hill
Llanwarne
Harewood End
OFFA'S DYKE PATH
LLWYBR CLAWDD OFFA
HATTERRALL HILL
Rowlestone
Monmouth Cap
Bagwy Llydiart
Orcop
Pencoyd
Llangua
Kentchurch
Garway Hill
Michaelchurch
Walterstone
GROSMONT CASTLE
St Owens Cross
Oldcastle
Grosmont
White Rocks
St Weonards
Tretire
Cwmyoy
B4347
Hoaldalbert
Tre-wyn
Pandy
Monnow (Mynwy)
Garway
Three Ashes
Broad Oak
B4521
Stanton
SKENFRITH CASTLE
Llangarron
COED-Y-CERRIG
Llanfihangel-Crucorney
Llangattock Lingoed
Norton
Skenfrith
Llancloudy
LLANFIHANGEL COURT
Bont
Cross Ash
Marstow
Bettws
A465
Upper Green
Crossway
Llanrothal
Llangrove
WYE VALLEY BUTTERFLY ZOO
Wayne Green
St Maughans
Welsh Newton
Whitchurch
Llantilio Pertholey
Newcastle
SYMONDS YAT SERVICES
Llwyn-du
Mardy
Llanvetherine
WHITE CASTLE
Llanfaenor
Maypole
Ganarew
A40
Bryn-y-gwenin
Llangattock-Vibon-Avel
Buckholt
Symonds Yat
Abergavenny
(Y Fenni)
Llantilio Crossenny
HEN GWRT
B4233
Onen
Rockfield
LADY PARK WOOD
Govilon
Llanvapley
Llanvihangel-Ystern-Llewern
Dixton
FIDDLER'S ELBOW
Llanfoist
Llanddewi Rhydderch
Wernyrheolydd
Monmouth
(Trefynwy)
B4246
B4269
B4598
Penrhôs
NELSON MUS
Wyesham
Coed Morgan
Over Monnow
BLORENGE
Llanellen
Llangattock nigh Usk
Llanarth
Pen-yr-heol
Wonastow
Penallt
Dingestow
Redbrook
Blaenavon
Bryngwyn
Tregare
Mitchel Troy
Mitcheltroy Common
Newland
HIGHBURY WOOD
Forge Side
Llanover
Llanvihangel Gobion
RAGLAN
Pen-y-clawdd
Pen-twyn
Rhyd-y-meirch
Llanfair Kilgheddin
Raglan
Cwmcarvan
Caer Llan
Hoop
Pen-groes-oped
Nant-y-derry
MONMOUTHSHIRE
(SIR FYNWY)
Kingcoed
Llangovan
Whitebrook
Cwmavon
Bettws Newydd
Twyn-y-Sheriff
A4043
Goetre
Trellech
Garndiffaith
Penperlleni
Kemeys Commander
Gwehelog
B4293
Llandogo
A466
Abersychan
A4042
Little Mill
Llandenny
Llanishen
Parkhouse
A472
A449
Llancayo
Llansoy
Catbrook
Trevethin
TORFAEN MUSEUM
Monkswood
THE HUDNALLS
Trelleck Grange
Glascoed
Gwernesney
Usk
(Brynbuga)
RURAL LIFE
OLD STA. Tintern Parva
Brockweir
New Inn
ABBEY MILL
Llandegfedd Res.
Llangwm
PONTYPOOL
(PONT-Y-PŴL)
Llanbadoc
Chapel Hill
New Inn
Wolvesnewton
Devauden
Griffithstown
Coed-y-paen
Kilgwrrwg Common
MYNYDD MAEN
Llanllowell
Chepstow Pk. Wood
Itton Common
Upper Cwmbran
Lowlands
Llantrisant
Newchurch
St Arvans
Croesyceiliog
Gaerllwyd
Pontnewydd
Llangybi
B4235
Llandegveth
Cwmbran
(Cwmbrân)
Tredunnock
Pen-y-cae-mawr
Earlswood
Woodcroft
CHEPSTOW
Newbridge-on-Usk
Mynydd-bach
Henllys
Oakfield
COOMBE VALLEY WOODS
Llanfrechfa
Shirenewton
Mounton
Llantarnam
Llanvair Discoed
B4236
Ponthir
Llanhennock
Chepstow
(Cas-gwent)
Castell-y-bwch
Croes-y-mwyalch
Parc-Seymour
Llanvaches
Pwllmeyric
A4051
NAT ROMAN LEGION MUS
Caerleon
(Caerllion)
RUNSTON CHAPEL
Malpas
Cat's Ash
A48
Llanbeder
Penhow
Crick
Mathern
CAERLEON BATHS
PENHOW WOODLANDS
Caerwent
M48
Bettws
Christchurch
Langstone
Highmoor Hill
CALDICOT CASTLE
FOURTEEN LOCKS
M4
St Bride's Netherwent
Rogerstone
Maindee
MAGOR SERVICES
Newport
Llanwern
Wilcrick
Caldicot
Portskewett
Rogiet

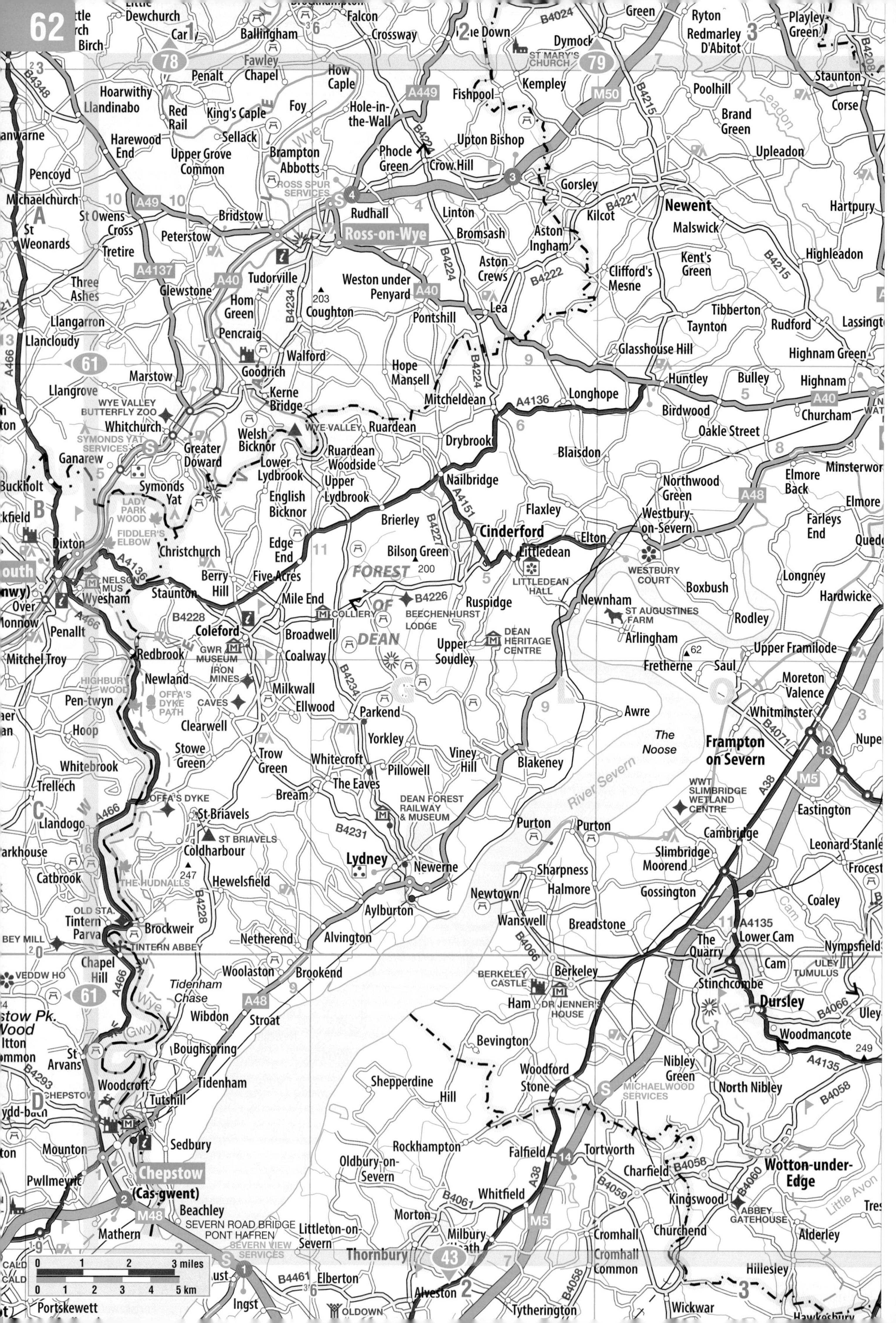

Dewchurch
Birch
Ballingham
Falcon
Crossway
Green
Ryton
Playley Green
Redmarley D'Abitot
78
Fawley Chapel
How Caple
Penalt
Hoarwithy
Llandinabo
Red Rail
King's Caple
Foy
Hole-in-the-Wall
Fishpool
Kempley
Dymock
ST MARY'S CHURCH
79
M50
B4024
B4215
Poolhill
Brand Green
Staunton
Corse
Leadon
Llanwarne
Harewood End
Upper Grove Common
Sellack
Brampton Abbotts
ROSS SPUR SERVICES
Phocle Green
Crow Hill
Upton Bishop
Upleadon
Pencoyd
Michaelchurch
A49
St Owens Cross
Bridstow
Peterstow
Ross-on-Wye
Rudhall
Linton
Gorsley
Kilcot
Newent
Malswick
Hartpury
St Weonards
Tretire
Bromsash
Aston Ingham
Aston Crews
B4221
B4222
Highleadon
Three Ashes
A4137
Glewstone
A40
Tudorville
Hom Green
Weston under Penyard
Coughton
203
B4234
Clifford's Mesne
Kent's Green
B4224
Pontshill
Lea
Tibberton
Tayton
Rudford
Lassington
Llangarron
Llancloudy
Pencraig
Walford
Glasshouse Hill
Highnam Green
61
A466
Marstow
Goodrich
Hope Mansell
Huntley
Bulley
Highnam
Llangrove
Kerne Bridge
Mitcheldean
Longhope
WYE VALLEY BUTTERFLY ZOO
A4136
Birdwood
Churcham
Whitchurch
WYE VALLEY
Ruardean
Drybrook
Oakle Street
SYMONDS YAT SERVICES
Welsh Bicknor
Greater Doward
Ruardean Woodside
Blaisdon
Ganarew
Lower Lydbrook
Upper Lydbrook
Nailbridge
Northwood Green
Elmore Back
Minsterworth
A48
Buckholt
Symonds Yat
English Bicknor
LADY PARK WOOD
A4151
Flaxley
Elmore
Brierley
Westbury-on-Severn
Farleys End
FIDDLER'S ELBOW
B4227
Cinderford
Dixton
Christchurch
Edge End
Bilson Green
Littledean
Elton
FOREST
200
WESTBURY COURT
Boxbush
Longney
NELSON MUS
Wyesham
Staunton
Berry Hill
Five Acres
LITTLEDEAN HALL
Mile End
B4226
Ruspidge
Newnham
Hardwicke
Over Monnow
OF
COLLIERY
BEECHENHURST LODGE
ST AUGUSTINES FARM
Rodley
B4228
Coleford
Broadwell
DEAN
Upper Soudley
DEAN HERITAGE CENTRE
Arlingham
Penallt
GWR MUSEUM
Coalway
62
Upper Framilode
Mitchel Troy
Redbrook
IRON MINES
Fretherne
Saul
Newland
Milkwall
Moreton Valence
HIGHBURY WOOD
OFFA'S DYKE PATH
CAVES
Ellwood
Parkend
Awre
Whitminster
Pen-twyn
Clearwell
The Noose
Frampton on Severn
Hoop
Yorkley
B4071
Stowe Green
Trow Green
Viney Hill
Blakeney
Nupend
Whitebrook
Whitecroft
Pillowell
13
Trellech
The Eaves
River Severn
M5
OFFA'S DYKE
Bream
WWT SLIMBRIDGE WETLAND CENTRE
A38
St Briavels
DEAN FOREST RAILWAY & MUSEUM
Eastington
Llandogo
ST BRIAVELS
B4231
Purton
Cambridge
Leonard Stanley
Coldharbour
Lydney
Slimbridge
Moorend
Catbrook
Sharpness
247
Newerne
Frocester
THE HUDNALLS
Hewelsfield
Halmore
Newtown
Gossington
Coaley
OLD STA. Tintern
Aylburton
Tintern Parva
Brockweir
Wanswell
Breadstone
A4135
Netherend
Alvington
Lower Cam
BEY MILL
B4066
The Quarry
Nympsfield
TINTERN ABBEY
Cam
Chapel Hill
Woolaston
Brookend
Berkeley
ULEY TUMULUS
VEDDW HO
BERKELEY CASTLE
Stinchcombe
Tidenham Chase
Dursley
DR JENNER'S HOUSE
Ham
Uley
Wibdon
Stroat
Woodmancote
Boughspring
Bevington
249
St Arvans
Nibley Green
Woodford
Shepperdine
Stone
North Nibley
B4058
Woodcroft
Tidenham
Hill
MICHAELWOOD SERVICES
Tutshill
Sedbury
Mounton
Rockhampton
Falfield
Tortworth
Oldbury-on-Severn
Charfield
Wotton-under-Edge
Chepstow
(Cas-gwent)
B4059
B4060
Pwllmeyric
Whitfield
Kingswood
Little Avon
Beachley
B4061
ABBEY GATEHOUSE
Mathern
M48
SEVERN ROAD BRIDGE
PONT HAFREN
Littleton-on-Severn
Morton
Churchend
Alderley
SEVERN VIEW SERVICES
Milbury Heath
Cromhall
Thornbury
43
Cromhall Common
Hillesley
B4461
Elberton
Alveston
Wickwar
Portskewett
Ingst
OLDOWN
Tytherington
Hawkesbury
0 1 2 3 miles
0 1 2 3 4 5 km

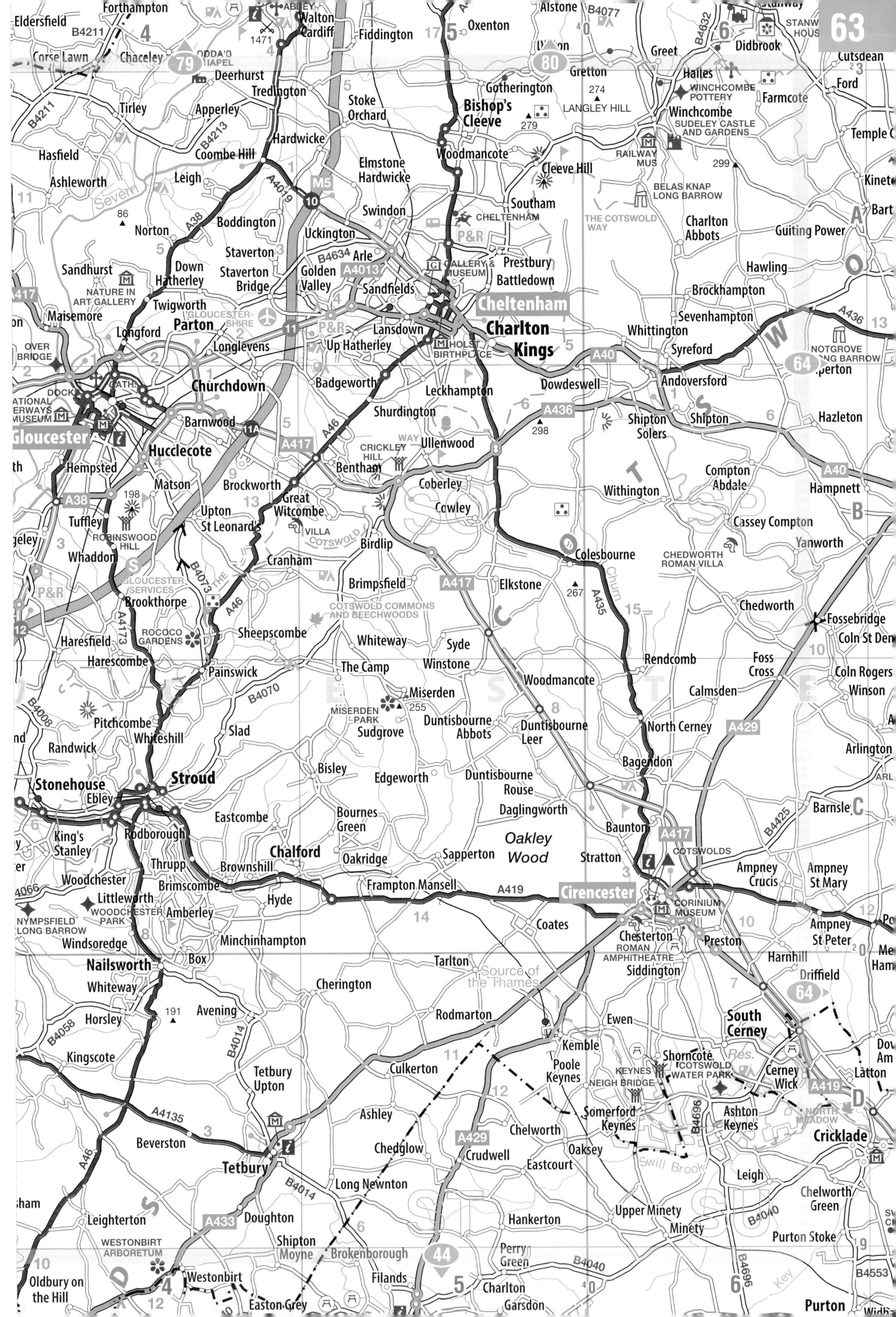

Eldersfield
Forthampton
Walton Cardiff
Fiddington
Oxenton
Alstone
Greet
Didbrook
Cutsdean
Ford
Corse Lawn
Chaceley
Deerhurst
Tredington
Gretton
Hailes
Stoke Orchard
Gotherington
LANGLEY HILL
WINCHCOMBE POTTERY
Farmcote
Tirley
Apperley
Bishop's Cleeve
Winchcombe
SUDELEY CASTLE AND GARDENS
Temple
Hardwicke
Hasfield
Coombe Hill
Woodmancote
RAILWAY MUS
Elmstone Hardwicke
Cleeve Hill
Ashleworth
Leigh
Severn
M5
BELAS KNAP LONG BARROW
Kineton
Swindon
Southam
Bartonsham
Norton
Boddington
Uckington
CHELTENHAM
THE COTSWOLD WAY
Charlton Abbots
Guiting Power
Staverton
Arle
Sandhurst
Down Hatherley
Staverton Bridge
Golden Valley
GALLERY & MUSEUM
Prestbury
Battledown
Hawling
NATURE IN ART GALLERY
Sandfields
Brockhampton
Twigworth
Cheltenham
Maisemore
GLOUCESTER-SHIRE
Charlton Kings
Sevenhampton
Longford
Parton
Lansdown
Whittington
OVER BRIDGE
Longlevens
Up Hatherley
HOLST BIRTHPLACE
Syreford
NOTGROVE LONG BARROW
Churchdown
Badgeworth
Dowdeswell
Andoversford
Leckhampton
DOCK
NATIONAL WATERWAYS MUSEUM
CATH.
Shurdington
Barnwood
Shipton Solers
Shipton
Hazleton
Gloucester
Ullenwood
Hucclecote
CRICKLEY HILL
Bentham
Compton Abdale
Hempsted
Matson
Brockworth
Coberley
Withington
Hampnett
Tuffley
Upton St Leonard's
Great Witcombe
Cowley
Cassey Compton
ROBINSWOOD HILL
VILLA
COTSWOLD
Birdlip
Whaddon
Cranham
Colesbourne
CHEDWORTH ROMAN VILLA
Yanworth
GLOUCESTER SERVICES
Brimpsfield
Elkstone
Brookthorpe
COTSWOLD COMMONS AND BEECHWOODS
Churn
Chedworth
Fossebridge
Haresfield
ROCOCO GARDENS
Sheepscombe
Whiteway
Syde
Coln St Dennis
Harescombe
The Camp
Winstone
Rendcomb
Foss Cross
Coln Rogers
Painswick
Woodmancote
Calmsden
Winson
Miserden
MISERDEN PARK
Pitchcombe
Whiteshill
Slad
Sudgrove
Duntisbourne Abbots
Duntisbourne Leer
North Cerney
Randwick
Arlington
Bisley
Bagendon
Stonehouse
Stroud
Edgeworth
Duntisbourne Rouse
Ebley
Daglingworth
Barnsley
Eastcombe
Bournes Green
Oakley Wood
Baunton
King's Stanley
Rodborough
Chalford
Oakridge
Sapperton
Stratton
COTSWOLDS
Ampney Crucis
Ampney St Mary
Thrupp
Brownshill
Woodchester
Brimscombe
Frampton Mansell
Cirencester
Littleworth
Hyde
CORINIUM MUSEUM
NYMPSFIELD LONG BARROW
WOODCHESTER PARK
Amberley
Coates
Chesterton
Ampney St Peter
Windsoredge
Minchinhampton
ROMAN AMPHITHEATRE
Preston
Nailsworth
Box
Tarlton
Source of the Thames
Siddington
Harnhill
Whiteway
Cherington
Driffield
Horsley
Avening
Rodmarton
Ewen
South Cerney
Kemble
Kingscote
Culkerton
Poole Keynes
Shorncote
Res.
Cerney Wick
Tetbury Upton
KEYNES COTSWOLD WATER PARK
NEIGH BRIDGE
Latton
Ashley
Somerford Keynes
Ashton Keynes
NORTH MEADOW
Beverston
Chelworth
Cricklade
Chedglow
Crudwell
Oaksey
Tetbury
Eastcourt
Swill Brook
Leigh
Long Newnton
Chelworth Green
Leighterton
Doughton
Hankerton
Upper Minety
Minety
WESTONBIRT ARBORETUM
Shipton Moyne
Brokenborough
Purton Stoke
Perry Green
Oldbury on the Hill
Westonbirt
Filands
Charlton
Easton Grey
Garsdon
Purton
B4211
B4213
A4019
A38
B4634
A4013
A40
A436
A46
A417
B4073
A4173
B4070
B4008
A435
A429
A419
B4425
B4066
B4058
B4014
A4135
A433
B4040
B4696
B4553
B4077
B4632

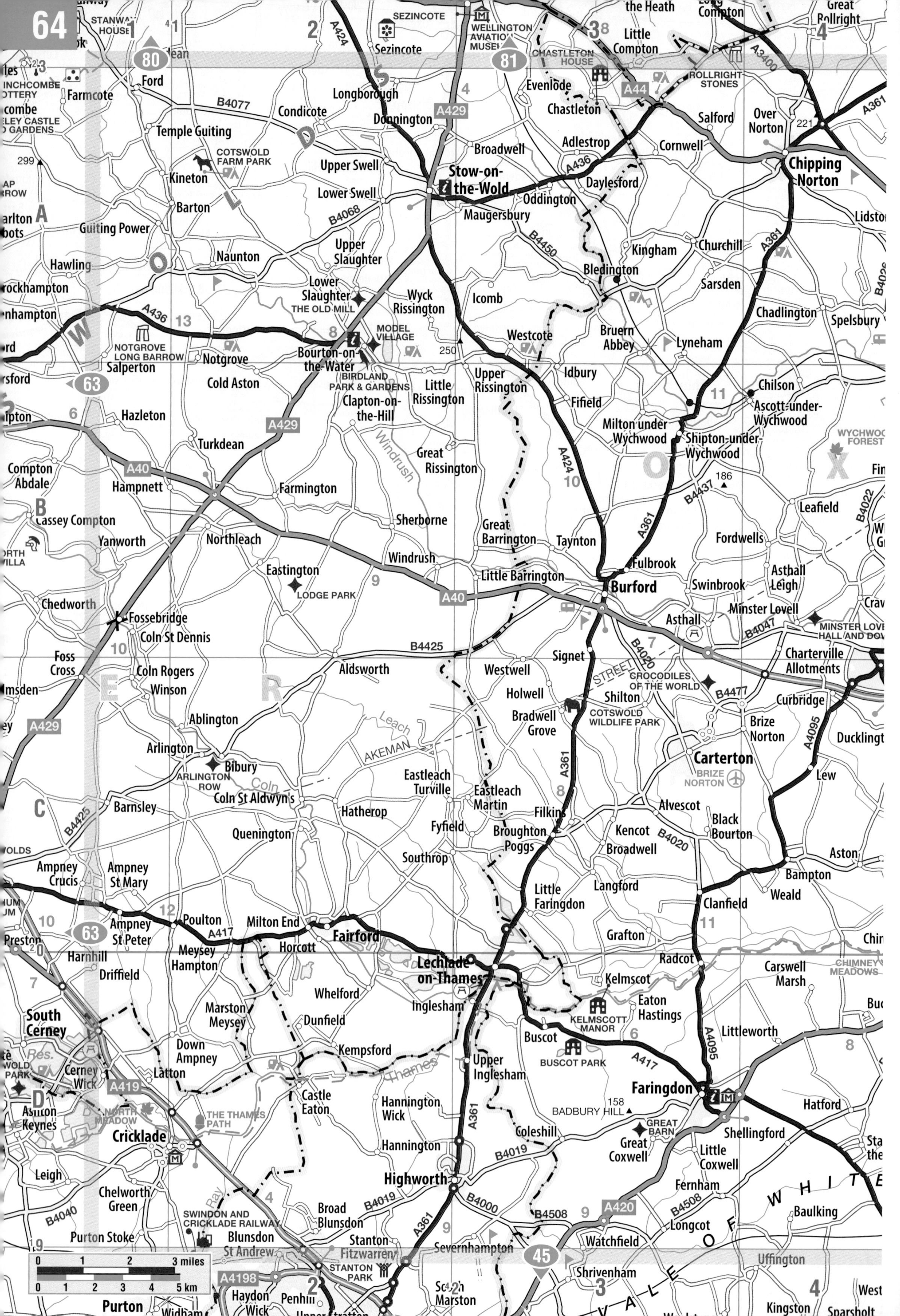
80
81
63
45
SEZINCOTE
Sezincote
WELLINGTON AVIATION MUSEUM
CHASTLETON HOUSE
the Heath
Little Compton
Great Rollright
ROLLRIGHT STONES
INCHCOMBE
Farmcote
Ford
B4077
Condicote
Longborough
Donnington
A424
A429
A44
A3400
A361
Evenlode
Chastleton
Temple Guiting
COTSWOLD FARM PARK
Kineton
Upper Swell
Broadwell
Adlestrop
Cornwell
Salford
Over Norton
Chipping Norton
Stow-on-the-Wold
A436
Daylesford
Oddington
Lower Swell
Maugersbury
Barton
B4068
Guiting Power
B4450
Kingham
Churchill
Naunton
Upper Slaughter
Hawling
Bledington
Sarsden
Lower Slaughter
THE OLD MILL
Wyck Rissington
Icomb
Bruern Abbey
Chadlington
Spelsbury
MODEL VILLAGE
Westcote
Lyneham
NOTGROVE LONG BARROW
Notgrove
Bourton-on-the-Water
BIRDLAND PARK & GARDENS
Salperton
Cold Aston
Little Rissington
Upper Rissington
Idbury
Fifield
Chilson
Clapton-on-the-Hill
Ascott-under-Wychwood
Hazleton
Milton under Wychwood
Shipton-under-Wychwood
WYCHWOOD FOREST
Turkdean
Windrush
Great Rissington
Compton Abdale
A40
Hampnett
Farmington
Leafield
Cassey Compton
Sherborne
Great Barrington
Taynton
Fordwells
Yanworth
Northleach
Windrush
Fulbrook
Eastington
LODGE PARK
Little Barrington
Burford
Swinbrook
Asthall Leigh
Chedworth
Minster Lovell
Asthall
MINSTER LOVELL HALL AND DOVECOTE
Fossebridge
Coln St Dennis
B4425
B4047
Foss Cross
Coln Rogers
Aldsworth
Westwell
Signet
Charterville Allotments
Winson
Holwell
CROCODILES OF THE WORLD
Shilton
B4477
Curbridge
Ablington
Bradwell Grove
COTSWOLD WILDLIFE PARK
Brize Norton
Ducklington
Arlington
Bibury
ARLINGTON ROW
Leach
AKEMAN
Carterton
BRIZE NORTON
A4095
Lew
Eastleach Turville
Eastleach Martin
Coln
Coln St Aldwyn's
Barnsley
Hatherop
Filkins
Alvescot
Black Bourton
Fyfield
Broughton Poggs
Kencot
B4020
Quenington
Broadwell
Aston
B4425
Southrop
Ampney Crucis
Ampney St Mary
Bampton
Little Faringdon
Langford
Weald
Clanfield
Poulton
Ampney St Peter
A417
Milton End
Fairford
Grafton
Meysey Hampton
Horcott
Harnhill
Driffield
Lechlade-on-Thames
Radcot
Carswell Marsh
CHIMNEY MEADOWS
Kelmscot
Eaton Hastings
Whelford
Inglesham
KELMSCOTT MANOR
South Cerney
Marston Meysey
Dunfield
Buscot
Littleworth
Down Ampney
Kempsford
BUSCOT PARK
A4095
Upper Inglesham
Thames
Cerney Wick
Latton
A419
Faringdon
Castle Eaton
Hatford
Ashton Keynes
NORTH MEADOW
THE THAMES PATH
Hannington Wick
BADBURY HILL
GREAT BARN
Shellingford
Cricklade
Coleshill
Great Coxwell
Little Coxwell
Leigh
Hannington
B4019
Highworth
Fernham
Chelworth Green
B4000
A420
Baulking
B4508
B4040
SWINDON AND CRICKLADE RAILWAY
Broad Blunsdon
Ray
Longcot
Purton Stoke
Blunsdon St Andrew
Stanton Fitzwarren
STANTON PARK
Sevenhampton
Watchfield
Uffington
Shrivenham
A4198
Haydon Wick
Penhill
South Marston
Kingston
Sparsholt
Purton
VALE OF WHITE HORSE
COTSWOLDS
OX
0 1 2 3 miles
0 1 2 3 4 5 km

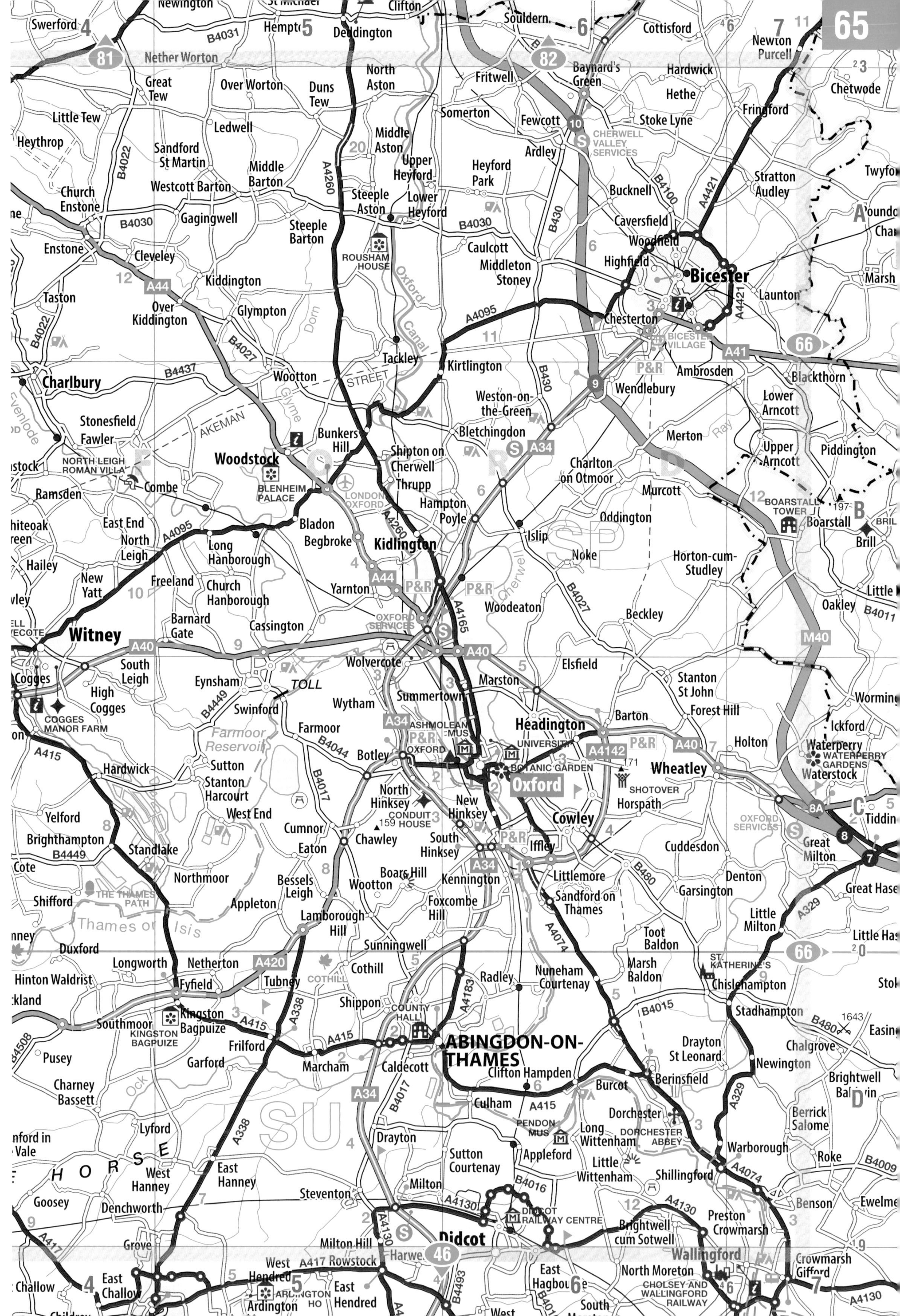
Swerford
Newington
Hempton
Deddington
Clifton
Souldern
Cottisford
Newton Purcell
B4031
Nether Worton
81
82
Great Tew
Over Worton
Duns Tew
North Aston
Fritwell
Baynard's Green
Hardwick
Hethe
Chetwode
Little Tew
Somerton
Fewcott
Stoke Lyne
Fringford
Heythrop
Sandford St Martin
Ledwell
Middle Aston
Upper Heyford
Ardley
CHERWELL VALLEY SERVICES
B4022
Middle Barton
A4260
Heyford Park
Bucknell
B4100
A4421
Stratton Audley
Twyford
Church Enstone
Westcott Barton
Steeple Aston
Lower Heyford
B4030
Caversfield
Poundon
Gagingwell
Steeple Barton
Woodfield
Enstone
Cleveley
ROUSHAM HOUSE
Caulcott
Highfield
Bicester
Middleton Stoney
Marsh
Kiddington
Oxford Canal
Tasten
A44
Over Kiddington
Glympton
A4095
Chesterton
Launton
BICESTER VILLAGE
A41
66
B4027
Dorn
Tackley
Kirtlington
Charlbury
B4437
Wootton
STREET
Ambrosden
Blackthorn
Wendlebury
B430
Lower Arncott
Evenlode
Stonesfield
Fawler
AKEMAN
Glyme
Weston-on-the-Green
Bunkers Hill
Bletchingdon
Merton
Ray
Upper Arncott
Piddington
NORTH LEIGH ROMAN VILLA
Woodstock
Shipton on Cherwell
Charlton on Otmoor
A34
BLENHEIM PALACE
Combe
Ramsden
Thrupp
LONDON OXFORD
Murcott
Hampton Poyle
BOARSTALL TOWER
Boarstall
Brill
Oddington
East End
Bladon
Islip
North Leigh
Begbroke
Kidlington
Hailey
Long Hanborough
Noke
Horton-cum-Studley
New Yatt
Freeland
Church Hanborough
Yarnton
P&R
Cherwell
Woodeaton
Oakley
B4011
Little
Barnard Gate
OXFORD SERVICES
A4165
Beckley
Witney
Cassington
M40
A40
Wolvercote
Elsfield
South Leigh
Eynsham
Marston
Stanton St John
Cogges
High Cogges
TOLL
Summertown
COGGES MANOR FARM
B4449
Swinford
Wytham
Headington
Barton
Forest Hill
Ickford
Farmoor
A4142
Holton
Waterperry
WATERPERRY GARDENS
Waterstock
Farmoor Reservoir
B4044
ASHMOLEAN MUS
UNIVERSITY
Botley
A415
Hardwick
Sutton
OXFORD
BOTANIC GARDEN
Oxford
Wheatley
SHOTOVER
Stanton Harcourt
B4017
North Hinksey
New Hinksey
Horspath
8A
Yelford
West End
Cumnor
CONDUIT HOUSE
Cowley
OXFORD SERVICES
Tiddington
Brighthampton
Chawley
South Hinksey
Eaton
Iffley
Cuddesdon
Great Milton
B4449
Standlake
Cote
Boars Hill
Littlemore
B480
Northmoor
Bessels Leigh
Wootton
Kennington
Denton
Great Haseley
Shifford
THE THAMES PATH
Appleton
Foxcombe Hill
Sandford on Thames
Garsington
Little Milton
A329
Thames or Isis
Lamborough Hill
A4074
Toot Baldon
Little Haseley
Duxford
Sunningwell
Marsh Baldon
ST. KATHERINE'S
Longworth
Netherton
A420
Cothill
Radley
Nuneham Courtenay
Chiselhampton
Hinton Waldrist
Fyfield
Tubney
COTHILL
A4183
Stadhampton
Stoke
Shippon
Kingston Bagpuize
COUNTY HALL
B4015
B480
Easington
Southmoor
KINGSTON BAGPUIZE
A338
ABINGDON-ON-THAMES
Drayton St Leonard
Chalgrove
Pusey
Frilford
Newington
Garford
Marcham
Caldecott
Clifton Hampden
Berinsfield
Brightwell Baldwin
Charney Bassett
Ock
Burcot
A34
B4017
Culham
Dorchester
Berrick Salome
SU
PENDON MUS
DORCHESTER ABBEY
Lyford
Long Wittenham
Warborough
Roke
Drayton
Sutton Courtenay
Appleford
B4009
HORSE
West Hanney
East Hanney
Little Wittenham
Shillingford
A4074
Milton
B4016
Benson
Ewelme
Goosey
Denchworth
Steventon
A4130
DIDCOT RAILWAY CENTRE
Brightwell cum Sotwell
Preston Crowmarsh
Grove
Milton Hill
Didcot
Harwell
46
Wallingford
Crowmarsh Gifford
A417
West Hendred
A417 Rowstock
North Moreton
East Challow
Challow
ARDINGTON HO
East Hendred
B4493
East Hagbourne
CHOLSEY AND WALLINGFORD RAILWAY
Ardington
South
West

Gawcott
Singleborough
Barton Hartshorn
Preston Bissett
Padbury
Adstock
Great Horwood
Little Horwood
Newton Longville
Chetwode
Fringford
Addington
Hillesden
Drayton Parslow
Stoke Hammond
Mursley
Winslow
Swanbourne
North End
Soulbury
Steeple Claydon
Twyford
Stratton Audley
Poundon
Middle Claydon
CLAYDON HOUSE
East Claydon
Granborough
Hoggeston
Stewkley
South End
Charndon
Calvert
Botolph Claydon
Dunton
Burcott
B U C K I N G H A M
Bicester
Marsh Gibbon
Launton
Edgcott
North Marston
Creslow
Wing
ASCOTT
Grendon Underwood
QUAINTON WINDMILL
187
Quainton
Oving
Whitchurch
Cublington
Aston Abbotts
Pitchcott
Blackthorn
Lower Arncott
Upper Arncott
Kingswood
BUCKINGHAMSHIRE RAILWAY CENTRE
Hardwick
Wingrave
Ludgershall
Westcott
Waddesdon
Weedon
Rowsham
Piddington
Wotton Underwood
WADDESDON MANOR
AKEMAN STREET
Berryfields
Hulcott
Long Marston
BOARSTALL TOWER
Boarstall
197
BRILL WINDMILL
Brill
Dorton
Ashendon
147
Upper Winchendon
Upper Pollicott
1642
Bierton
Aylesbury
Puttenham
NATIONAL PARALYMPIC HERITAGE CTR
Wilstone
Stone
Southcourt
Buckland
Little London
NETHER WINCHENDON HOUSE
Lower Winchendon
Weston Turville
Aston Clinton
Oakley
Chilton
Cuddington
Dinton
Easington
Chearsley
Westlington
Stoke Mandeville
Halton
Bishopstone
Townsend
Ford
Worminghall
Long Crendon
Haddenham
Kimble Wick
North Lee
Terrick
Nash Lee
Wendover
Ickford
Aston Sandford
Holton
Waterperry
WATERPERRY GARDENS
Waterstock
Shabbington
Little Kimble
Butler's Cross
St Leon
Owlswick
Ellesborough
Meadle
Kingsey
Great Kimble
Thame
Ilmer
Askett
RYCOTE CHAPEL
Towersey
Longwick
Dunsmore
The Lee
OXFORD SERVICES
Tiddington
Moreton
Monks Risborough
Great Milton
Pitch Green
Little Hampden
Emmington
Henton
Bledlow
Princes Risborough
Denton
Great Haseley
Tetsworth
Sydenham
Saunderton
Great Hampden
Little Milton
Chinnor
Loosley Row
Oakley
Prestwood
Little Haseley
CHINNOR & PRINCES RISBOROUGH RAILWAY
ST. KATHERINE'S
Chislehampton
Postcombe
Crowell
Lacey Green
Speen
Little Kingshill
Stoke Talmage
Kingston Blount
246
Great Kingshill
Adwell
Aston Rowant
Bledlow Ridge
Walters Ash
Upper North Dean
Stadhampton
South Weston
Radnage
Cryers Hill
1643
Easington
Lewknor
ASTON ROWANT
BRADENHAM
Bradenham
Widmer End
Chalgrove
The City
Naphill
Newington
Stokenchurch
Hughenden Valley
187
Brightwell Baldwin
Pyrton
Shirburn
HUGHENDEN MANOR
255
West Wycombe
WEST WYCOMBE CAVES
Downley
Berrick Salome
Cuxham
Beacon's Bottom
Watlington
Christmas Common
WEST WYCOMBE PARK
Tylers Green
Warborough
Ibstone
High Wycombe
Roke
THE RIDGEWAY
Northend
Britwell Salome
Cadmore End
Benson
Ewelme
Greenfield
Bolter End
Booker
Preston Crowmarsh
Turville Heath
Turville
Fingest
Lane End
Cookley Green
WYCOMBE AIR PARK (BOOKER)
Pishill
188
Skirmett
Frieth
Flackwell Heath
Russell's Water
Park Corner
STONOR
Stonor
Marlow Bottom
Little Marlow
FFIELD PLACE
Rockwell End
Lower
Wooburn
0 1 2 3 miles
0 1 2 3 4 5 km
82
83
65
47
A41
A413
A418
A4129
A4010
A4009
A329
A40
M40
A4074
A404
A4146
A4421
A4157
B4033
B4032
B4011
B4012
B4445
B4443
B480
B4009
B481
B482
A4128
Ray
Thame
Ouse
Chase

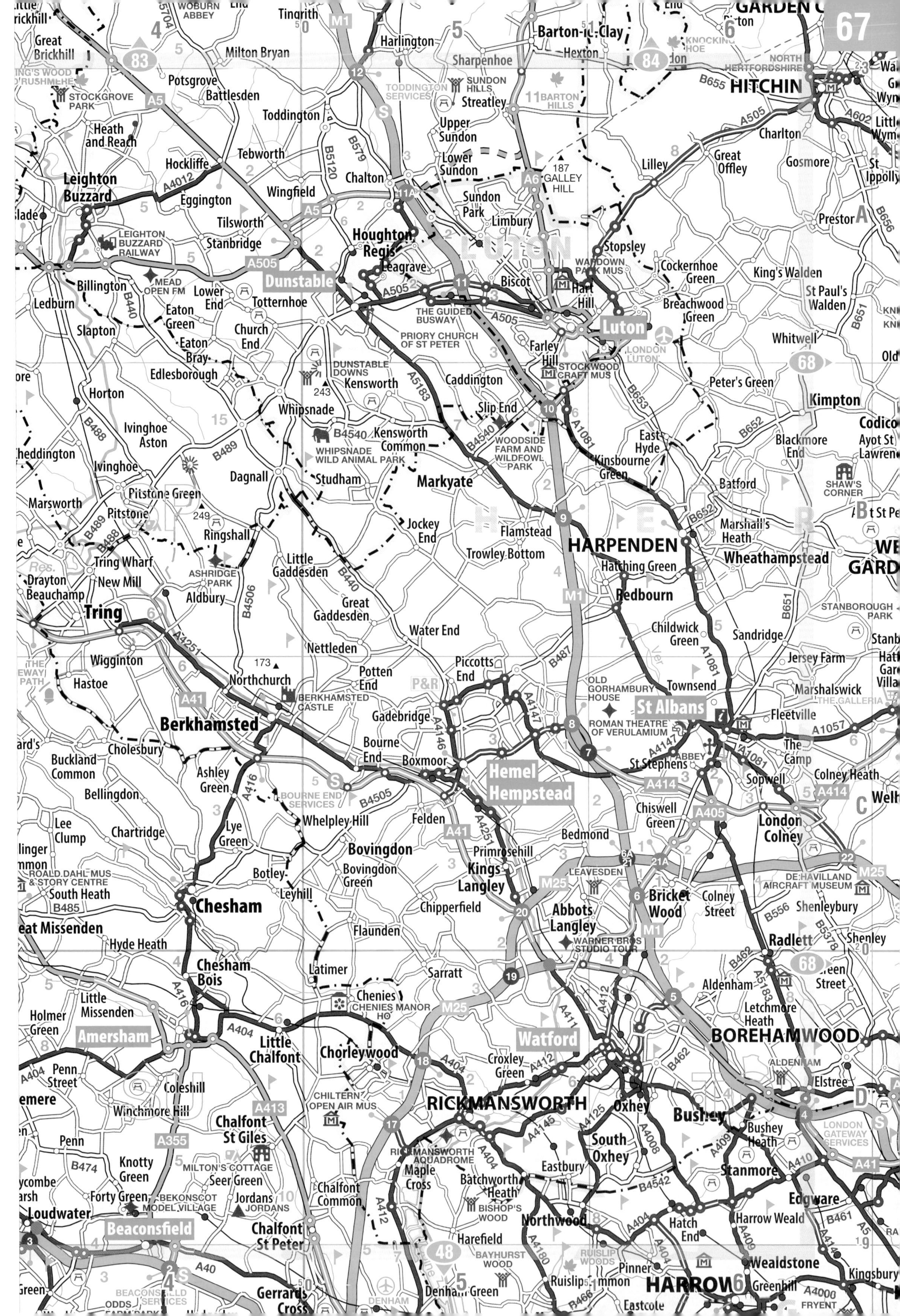

Woburn Abbey
Tingrith
Harlington
Barton-le-Clay
Hexton
Garden City
Great Brickhill
Milton Bryan
Sharpenhoe
Knocking Hoe
North Hertfordshire
Hitchin
Potsgrove
Battlesden
Toddington Services
Sundon Hills
Streatley
Barton Hills
Stockgrove Park
Toddington
Upper Sundon
Charlton
Heath and Reach
Lower Sundon
Great Offley
Gosmore
Tebworth
Lilley
St Ippolyts
Hockliffe
Chalton
187 Galley Hill
Leighton Buzzard
Wingfield
Sundon Park
Eggington
Limbury
Prestor
Tilsworth
Houghton Regis
Luton
Stopsley
Leighton Buzzard Railway
Stanbridge
Leagrave
Wardown Park Mus
Cockernhoe Green
King's Walden
Billington
Mead Open Fm
Dunstable
Biscot
Hart Hill
St Paul's Walden
Ledburn
Lower End
Totternhoe
The Guided Busway
Breachwood Green
Eaton Green
Church End
Priory Church of St Peter
Farley Hill
Whitwell
Slapton
London Luton
Eaton Bray
Dunstable Downs
Stockwood Craft Mus
Edlesborough
Kensworth
Caddington
Peter's Green
Horton
243
Kimpton
Whipsnade
Slip End
Codicote
Ivinghoe Aston
Kensworth Common
East Hyde
Blackmore End
Ayot St Lawrence
Cheddington
Whipsnade Wild Animal Park
Woodside Farm and Wildfowl Park
Kinsbourne Green
Ivinghoe
Dagnall
Studham
Markyate
Batford
Shaw's Corner
Marsworth
Pitstone Green
Pitstone
249
Jockey End
Marshall's Heath
Ringshall
Flamstead
Harpenden
Wheathampstead
Tring Wharf
Trowley Bottom
Ashridge Park
Little Gaddesden
Hatching Green
Drayton Beauchamp
New Mill
Aldbury
Redbourn
Great Gaddesden
Stanborough Park
Tring
Childwick Green
Sandridge
Water End
Nettleden
Wigginton
Piccotts End
Jersey Farm
Hastoe
173
Northchurch
Potten End
Townsend
Marshalswick
Old Gorhambury House
The Galleria
Berkhamsted Castle
St Albans
Fleetville
Gadebridge
Roman Theatre of Verulamium
Berkhamsted
Cholesbury
Bourne End
Boxmoor
Abbey
The Camp
Buckland Common
St Stephens
Hemel Hempstead
Sopwell
Colney Heath
Ashley Green
Bellingdon
Bourne End Services
Chiswell Green
London Colney
Whelpley Hill
Felden
Bedmond
Lee Clump
Lye Green
Chartridge
Bovingdon
Primrose Hill
Roald Dahl Mus & Story Centre
Bovingdon Green
Kings Langley
Leavesden
De Havilland Aircraft Museum
Botley
South Heath
Leyhill
Bricket Wood
Colney Street
Chesham
Chipperfield
Abbots Langley
Shenleybury
Great Missenden
Flaunden
Radlett
Hyde Heath
Warner Bros Studio Tour
Shenley
Chesham Bois
Latimer
Sarratt
Green Street
Aldenham
Little Missenden
Chenies
Chenies Manor Ho
Letchmore Heath
Holmer Green
Amersham
Little Chalfont
Chorleywood
Watford
Borehamwood
Croxley Green
Aldenham
Penn Street
Elstree
Coleshill
Rickmansworth
Oxhey
Bushey
Winchmore Hill
Chalfont St Giles
Chiltern Open Air Mus
London Gateway Services
South Oxhey
Bushey Heath
Penn
Rickmansworth Aquadrome
Eastbury
Stanmore
Knotty Green
Milton's Cottage
Maple Cross
Seer Green
Batchworth Heath
Chalfont Common
Edgware
Forty Green
Bekonscot Model Village
Jordans
Bishop's Wood
Loudwater
Northwood
Hatch End
Harrow Weald
Beaconsfield
Chalfont St Peter
Harefield
Ruislip Woods
Wealdstone
Bayhurst Wood
Pinner
Kingsbury
Beaconsfield Services
Gerrards Cross
Denham
Denham Green
Ruislip Common
Harrow
Greenhill
Eastcote
Fryent
M1
M25
A5
A505
A4012
A6
A5183
A4540
B4540
A1081
B653
B652
B651
A602
A505
B655
B656
B440
B488
B489
B4506
B487
A4146
A4147
A4251
A41
A416
B4505
A414
A405
A1057
A4147
B485
A404
A355
A413
B474
A40
A412
A411
A4145
A4125
A4008
A409
A410
B462
B5378
B556
B4542
A4180
B466
A5120
B579
B5120
83
84
68
48

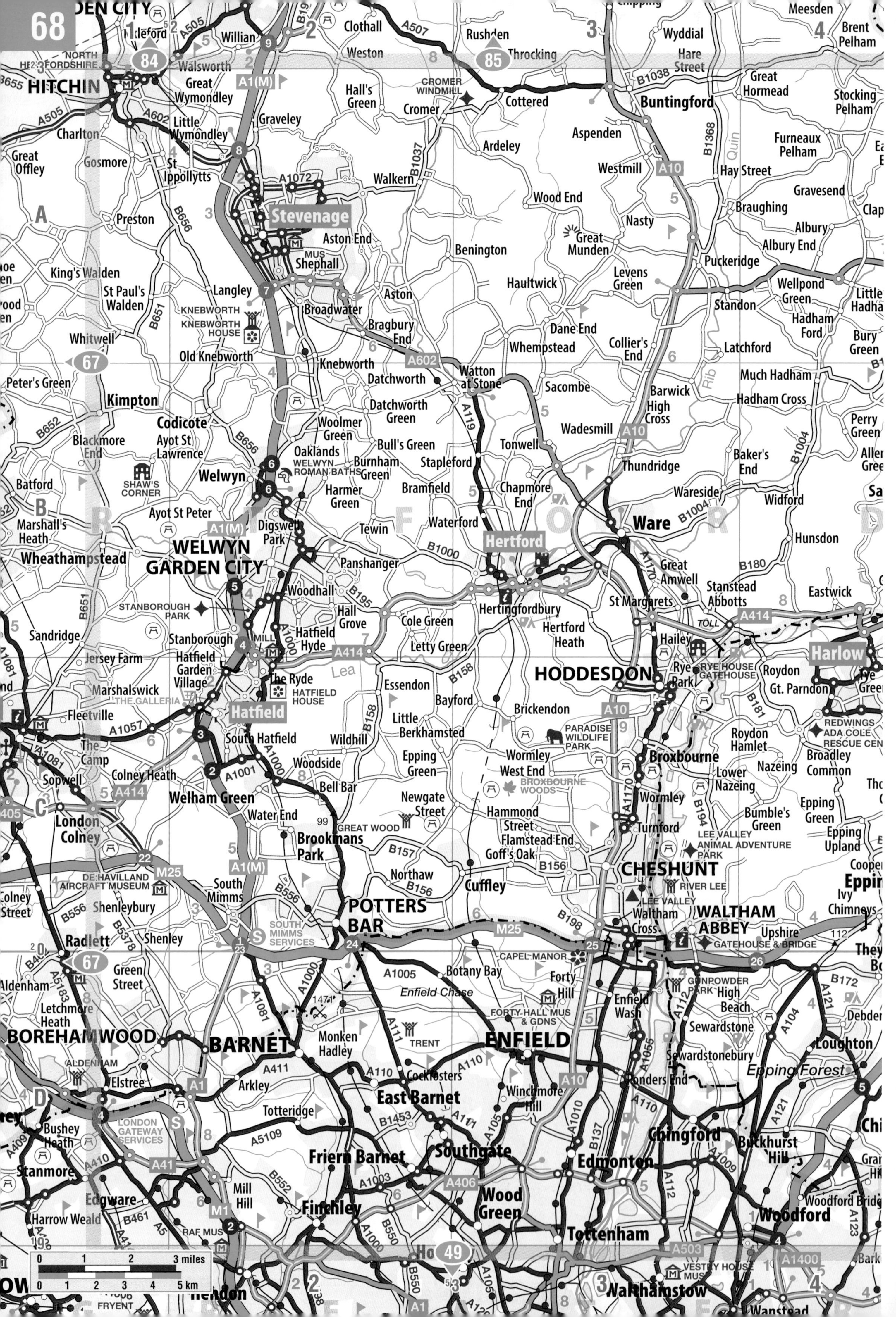
Ickleford
Willian
Clothall
Rushden
Meesden
Wyddial
Brent Pelham
84
85
Walsworth
Weston
Throcking
Hare Street
NORTH HERTFORDSHIRE
HITCHIN
Great Wymondley
A1(M)
Hall's Green
CROMER WINDMILL
Cromer
Cottered
Buntingford
Great Hormead
Stocking Pelham
Charlton
Little Wymondley
Graveley
Ardeley
Aspenden
Furneaux Pelham
Great Offley
Gosmore
St Ippollytts
Walkern
Westmill
Hay Street
Wood End
Gravesend
Preston
Stevenage
Nasty
Braughing
Aston End
Great Munden
Albury
Benington
Albury End
King's Walden
Shephall
Puckeridge
St Paul's Walden
Langley
Haultwick
Levens Green
Wellpond Green
Aston
Standon
Broadwater
KNEBWORTH
KNEBWORTH HOUSE
Bragbury End
Dane End
Hadham Ford
Whitwell
Whempstead
Collier's End
Latchford
Bury Green
67
Old Knebworth
Knebworth
Datchworth
Watton at Stone
Much Hadham
Peter's Green
Sacombe
Barwick
Kimpton
Datchworth Green
High Cross
Hadham Cross
Codicote
Woolmer Green
Wadesmill
Perry Green
Blackmore End
Ayot St Lawrence
Bull's Green
Tonwell
Oaklands
Burnham Green
Stapleford
Baker's End
Thundridge
WELWYN ROMAN BATHS
Welwyn
Batford
SHAW'S CORNER
Harmer Green
Bramfield
Chapmore End
Wareside
Widford
Ayot St Peter
Marshall's Heath
Digswell Park
Tewin
Waterford
Ware
Hertford
Hunsdon
Wheathampstead
WELWYN GARDEN CITY
Panshanger
Great Amwell
Woodhall
St Margarets
Stanstead Abbotts
Eastwick
STANBOROUGH PARK
Hertingfordbury
Sandridge
Hall Grove
Cole Green
Hertford Heath
Hailey
Harlow
Stanborough
Hatfield Hyde
Letty Green
Jersey Farm
Hatfield Garden Village
Rye Park
RYE HOUSE GATEHOUSE
Roydon
HODDESDON
The Ryde
Essendon
Gt. Parndon
Marshalswick
THE GALLERIA
HATFIELD HOUSE
Bayford
Brickendon
Fleetville
Hatfield
Little Berkhamsted
PARADISE WILDLIFE PARK
REDWINGS ADA COLE RESCUE CENTRE
The Camp
South Hatfield
Wildhill
Roydon Hamlet
Broxbourne
Epping Green
Wormley West End
Broadley Common
Sopwell
Colney Heath
Woodside
Lower Nazeing
Nazeing
BROXBOURNE WOODS
Welham Green
Bell Bar
Wormley
London Colney
Water End
Newgate Street
Hammond Street
Bumble's Green
Epping Green
GREAT WOOD
Turnford
Brookmans Park
Flamstead End
LEE VALLEY ANIMAL ADVENTURE PARK
Epping Upland
Goff's Oak
DE HAVILLAND AIRCRAFT MUSEUM
South Mimms
Northaw
Cuffley
CHESHUNT
RIVER LEE
Colney Street
Shenleybury
POTTERS BAR
LEE VALLEY
Waltham Cross
WALTHAM ABBEY
Ivy Chimneys
SOUTH MIMMS SERVICES
M25
Upshire
Radlett
Shenley
GATEHOUSE & BRIDGE
CAPEL MANOR
Botany Bay
Green Street
Forty Hill
Aldenham
Enfield Chase
GUNPOWDER PARK
High Beach
Letchmore Heath
Enfield Wash
FORTY HALL MUS & GDNS
Sewardstone
BOREHAMWOOD
BARNET
Monken Hadley
TRENT
ENFIELD
Loughton
ALDENHAM
Sewardstonebury
Elstree
Arkley
Cockfosters
Ponders End
Epping Forest
East Barnet
Winchmore Hill
Bushey Heath
LONDON GATEWAY SERVICES
Totteridge
Chingford
Buckhurst Hill
Stanmore
Friern Barnet
Southgate
Edmonton
Edgware
Mill Hill
Wood Green
Woodford
Finchley
Woodford Bridge
Harrow Weald
RAF MUS
Tottenham
49
VESTRY HOUSE MUS
Walthamstow
Hendon
FRYENT
0 1 2 3 miles
0 1 2 3 4 5 km

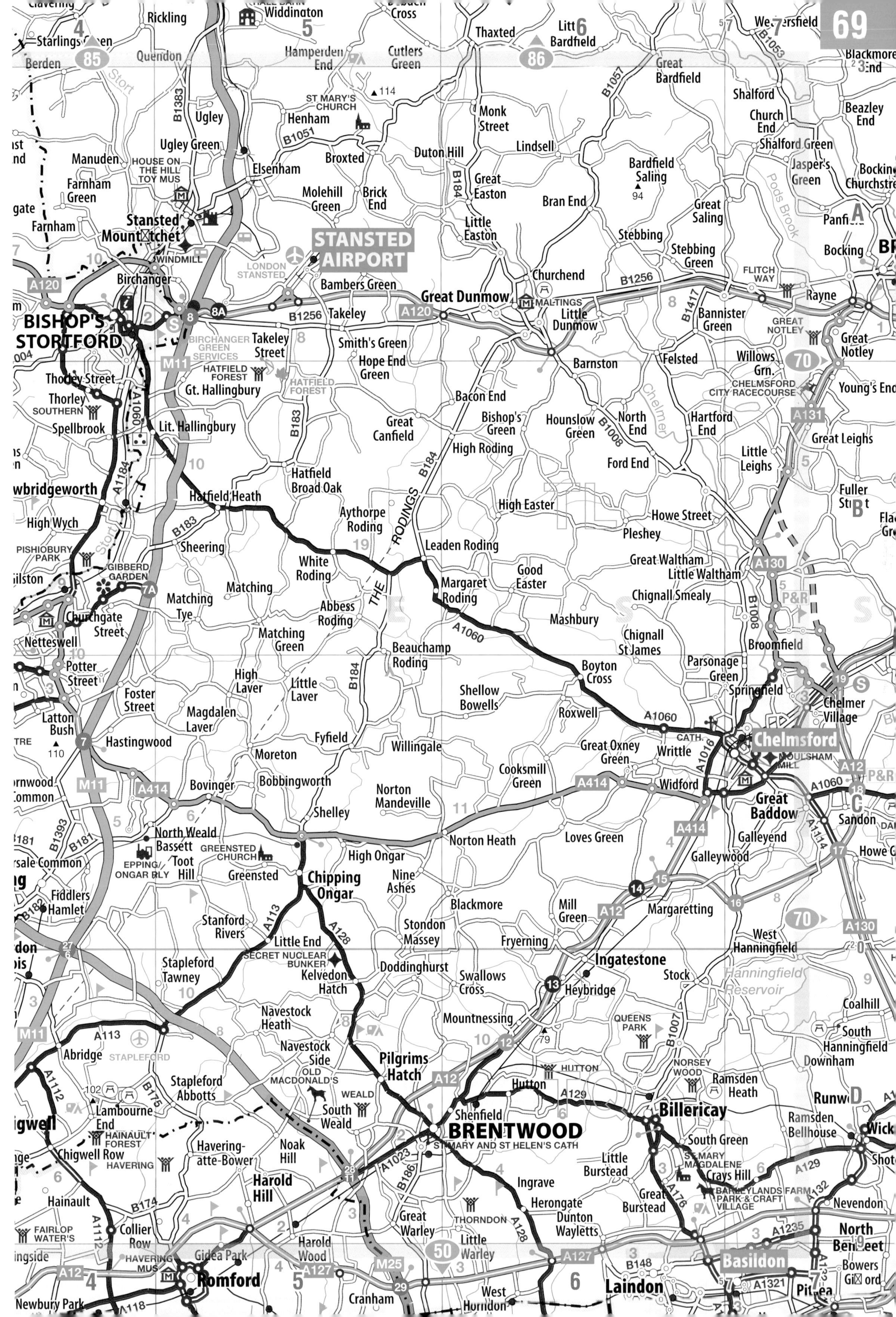
Rickling
Widdington
Thaxted
Little Bardfield
Wethersfield
Starlings Green
Berden
Quendon
Hamperden End
Cutlers Green
Great Bardfield
Blackmore End
Ugley
ST MARY'S CHURCH
Henham
Monk Street
Shalford
Church End
Beazley End
Ugley Green
B1051
Broxted
Duton Hill
Lindsell
Shalford Green
Manuden
HOUSE ON THE HILL TOY MUS
Elsenham
Bardfield Saling
Jasper's Green
Bocking Churchstreet
Farnham Green
Molehill Green
Brick End
Great Easton
Bran End
Great Saling
Farnham
Stansted Mountfitchet
STANSTED AIRPORT
Little Easton
Stebbing
Stebbing Green
Pods Brook
Panfield
Bocking
WINDMILL
LONDON STANSTED
Birchanger
Churchend
FLITCH WAY
B1256
Bambers Green
Great Dunmow
MALTINGS
Little Dunmow
Rayne
BISHOP'S STORTFORD
Takeley
A120
Bannister Green
GREAT NOTLEY
Great Notley
BIRCHANGER GREEN SERVICES
Takeley Street
Smith's Green
Hope End Green
Barnston
Felsted
Willows Grn.
CHELMSFORD CITY RACECOURSE
Young's End
Thorley Street
HATFIELD FOREST
Gt. Hallingbury
Thorley
SOUTHERN
Spellbrook
Bacon End
Chelmer
Lit. Hallingbury
Great Canfield
Bishop's Green
Hounslow Green
North End
Hartford End
A131
Great Leighs
High Roding
B1008
Ford End
Little Leighs
Hatfield Broad Oak
Sawbridgeworth
Hatfield Heath
High Easter
Fuller Street
Aythorpe Roding
Howe Street
High Wych
THE RODINGS
Pleshey
Sheering
Leaden Roding
PISHIOBURY PARK
GIBBERD GARDEN
White Roding
Great Waltham
Little Waltham
Good Easter
A130
Matching
Margaret Roding
Chignall Smealy
Matching Tye
Abbess Roding
Churchgate Street
Mashbury
P&R
Netteswell
Matching Green
A1060
Chignall St James
Broomfield
Beauchamp Roding
Potter Street
High Laver
Boyton Cross
Parsonage Green
Little Laver
Shellow Bowells
Springfield
Foster Street
Chelmer Village
Magdalen Laver
Roxwell
Latton Bush
Fyfield
Chelmsford
Hastingwood
CATH.
Willingale
Great Oxney Green
Writtle
MOULSHAM MILL
Moreton
Cooksmill Green
A12
M11
A414
Bovinger
Bobbingworth
Norton Mandeville
Widford
A1060
Great Baddow
Shelley
Sandon
North Weald Bassett
Norton Heath
Loves Green
Galleyend
Howe Green
EPPING/ONGAR RLY
GREENSTED CHURCH
Toot Hill
High Ongar
Galleywood
Greensted
Chipping Ongar
Nine Ashes
Fiddlers Hamlet
Blackmore
Mill Green
Margaretting
Stanford Rivers
Stondon Massey
A128
Fryerning
West Hanningfield
Little End
Ingatestone
SECRET NUCLEAR BUNKER
Stapleford Tawney
Kelvedon Hatch
Doddinghurst
Swallows Cross
Stock
Hanningfield Reservoir
Heybridge
Navestock Heath
Mountnessing
Coalhill
QUEENS PARK
South Hanningfield
A113
Abridge
STAPLEFORD
Navestock Side
Pilgrims Hatch
Downham
OLD MACDONALD'S
HUTTON
NORSEY WOOD
Ramsden Heath
Stapleford Abbotts
WEALD
Hutton
Lambourne End
South Weald
Shenfield
Billericay
Runwell
HAINAULT FOREST
BRENTWOOD
Ramsden Bellhouse
Wickford
ST MARY AND ST HELEN'S CATH
South Green
Chigwell
Chigwell Row
Havering-atte-Bower
Noak Hill
HAVERING
Little Burstead
ST MARY MAGDALENE
Crays Hill
Harold Hill
Ingrave
Great Burstead
BARLEYLANDS FARM PARK & CRAFT VILLAGE
Hainault
Herongate
Nevendon
Dunton Wayletts
FAIRLOP WATER'S
Great Warley
THORNDON
Collier Row
North Benfleet
Harold Wood
Little Warley
Gidea Park
HAVERING MUS
Basildon
Romford
M25
Laindon
Bowers Gifford
Cranham
West Horndon
Pitsea
Newbury Park
A127
A1235

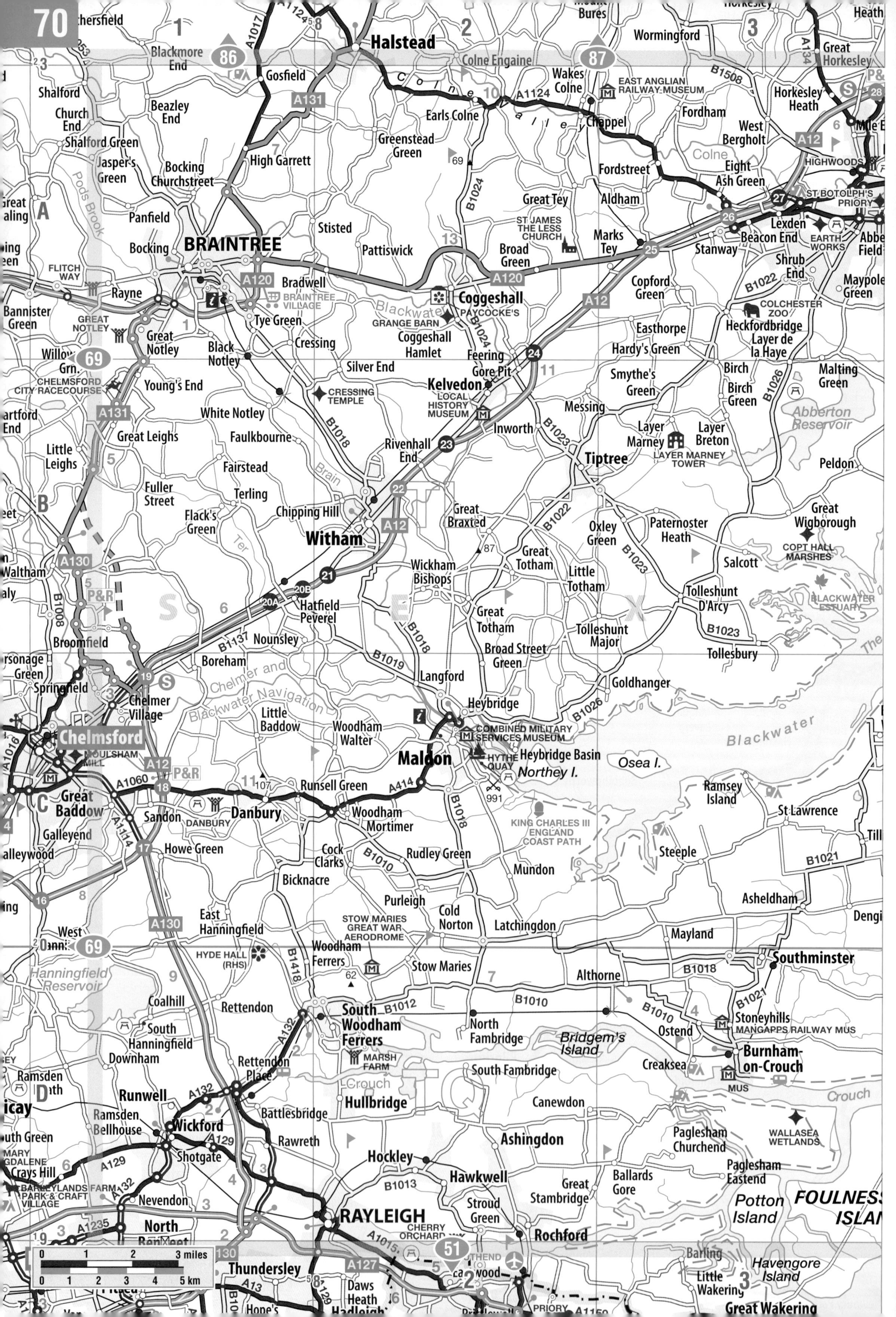
Halstead
Bures
Wormingford
Heath
Great Horkesley
Blackmore End
86
87
Gosfield
Colne Engaine
Wakes Colne
EAST ANGLIAN RAILWAY MUSEUM
Shalford
Beazley End
Earls Colne
Chappel
Fordham
Horkesley Heath
Church End
Shalford Green
Greenstead Green
West Bergholt
Jasper's Green
Bocking Churchstreet
High Garrett
Fordstreet
Eight Ash Green
HIGHWOODS
Great Tey
Aldham
ST BOTOLPH'S PRIORY
Panfield
Stisted
Lexden
ST JAMES THE LESS CHURCH
Marks Tey
Beacon End
EARTH WORKS
Bocking
BRAINTREE
Pattiswick
Broad Green
Stanway
Shrub End
FLITCH WAY
Bradwell
Copford Green
Maypole Green
Rayne
BRAINTREE VILLAGE
Coggeshall
COLCHESTER ZOO
Bannister Green
GREAT NOTLEY
Tye Green
Blackwater
PAYCOCKE'S
GRANGE BARN
Eastthorpe
Heckfordbridge
Great Notley
Cressing
Coggeshall Hamlet
Hardy's Green
Layer de la Haye
Willow Grn.
69
Black Notley
Feering
Gore Pit
Silver End
Smythe's Green
Birch
Malting Green
CHELMSFORD CITY RACECOURSE
Young's End
CRESSING TEMPLE
Kelvedon
Birch Green
LOCAL HISTORY MUSEUM
Messing
Abberton Reservoir
White Notley
Inworth
Layer Marney
Layer Breton
Great Leighs
Faulkbourne
Rivenhall End
LAYER MARNEY TOWER
Tiptree
Little Leighs
Fairstead
Peldon
Fuller Street
Terling
Great Braxted
Chipping Hill
Flack's Green
Great Wigborough
Paternoster Heath
Oxley Green
Witham
COPT HALL MARSHES
Great Totham
Wickham Bishops
Salcott
Little Totham
Tolleshunt D'Arcy
BLACKWATER ESTUARY
Hatfield Peverel
Great Totham
Tolleshunt Major
Broomfield
Nounsley
Boreham
Broad Street Green
Tollesbury
Springfield
Langford
Goldhanger
Chelmer Village
Chelmer and Blackwater Navigation
Heybridge
Little Baddow
Woodham Walter
COMBINED MILITARY SERVICES MUSEUM
Chelmsford
MOULSHAM MILL
Maldon
HYTHE QUAY
Heybridge Basin
Osea I.
Northey I.
Great Baddow
Runsell Green
Ramsey Island
Sandon
DANBURY
Danbury
Woodham Mortimer
St Lawrence
Galleyend
KING CHARLES III ENGLAND COAST PATH
Howe Green
Cock Clarks
Rudley Green
Steeple
Mundon
Bicknacre
Purleigh
Cold Norton
Asheldham
East Hanningfield
STOW MARIES GREAT WAR AERODROME
Latchingdon
Mayland
West Hanningfield
Woodham Ferrers
HYDE HALL (RHS)
Stow Maries
Southminster
Hanningfield Reservoir
Althorne
Coalhill
Rettendon
South Woodham Ferrers
North Fambridge
Stoneyhills
MANGAPPS RAILWAY MUS
South Hanningfield
Bridgem's Island
Ostend
Downham
Rettendon Place
MARSH FARM
Burnham-on-Crouch
Ramsden Heath
Creaksea
South Fambridge
MUS
Runwell
Crouch
Hullbridge
Canewdon
Ramsden Bellhouse
Wickford
Battlesbridge
Shotgate
Rawreth
Ashingdon
Paglesham Churchend
WALLASEA WETLANDS
Crays Hill
Hockley
BARLEYLANDS FARM PARK & CRAFT VILLAGE
Hawkwell
Ballards Gore
Paglesham Eastend
Nevendon
Great Stambridge
Potton Island
FOULNESS
Stroud Green
North
RAYLEIGH
CHERRY ORCHARD
Rochford
51
Barling
Havengore Island
Thundersley
Little Wakering
Daws Heath
Great Wakering
0 1 2 3 miles
0 1 2 3 4 5 km

Dedham
MUNNINGS ART MUSEUM
Langham
Lawford
Mistley
Parkeston
HARWICH REDOUBT FORT
Dovercourt
Upper Dovercourt
Bradfield
Wrabness
Ramsey
Manningtree
Ardleigh
Bradfield Heath
Horsleycross Street
Little Bromley
Horsley Cross
Wix
Little Oakley
Great Oakley
Parsons Heath
Fox Street
Crockleford Heath
Great Bromley
Tendring Green
Stone's Green
Little Bentley
Colchester
Elmstead Market
Beaumont
Horsey Island
The Naze
Hare Green
Balls Green
Tendring
Thorpe Green
HAMFORD WATER
Old Heath
Wivenhoe Cross
BETH CHATTO GDNS
BOURNE MILL
Frating Green
Great Bentley
Thorpe-le-Soken
Kirby-le-Soken
Blackheath
Wivenhoe
Weeley
Weeley Heath
Rowhedge
Alresford
Aingers Green
Walton-on-the-Naze
Kirby Cross
Fingringhoe
Thorrington
Row Heath
Frinton-on-Sea
CLACTON VILLAGE
Little Clacton
Abberton
Great Holland
Langenhoe
St Osyth Heath
HOLLAND HAVEN
River Colne
Brightlingsea
ST OSYTH PRIORY
St Osyth
Holland-on-Sea
Great Clacton
Mersea Island
East Mersea
CUDMORE GROVE
Point Clear
Clacton-on-Sea
Blue Row
COLNE ESTUARY
Jaywick
West Mersea
MERSEA MUSEUM
Colne Pt.
Nass
Virley Channel
Sales Pt.
ST PETERS ON THE WALL
Bradwell Waterside
KING CHARLES III ENGLAND COAST PATH
Bradwell on Sea
TM
DENGIE
Ray Sand
Montsale
Deal Hall
Foulness Sand
Foulness Pt.
TR
Courtsend
Churchend
MAPLIN SANDS
A120
A133
A137
A1232
B1029
B1028
B1027
B1025
B1035
B1033
B1034
B1414
B1352
B1032
B1336
87
88
52
53
A
B
C
D
4
5
6

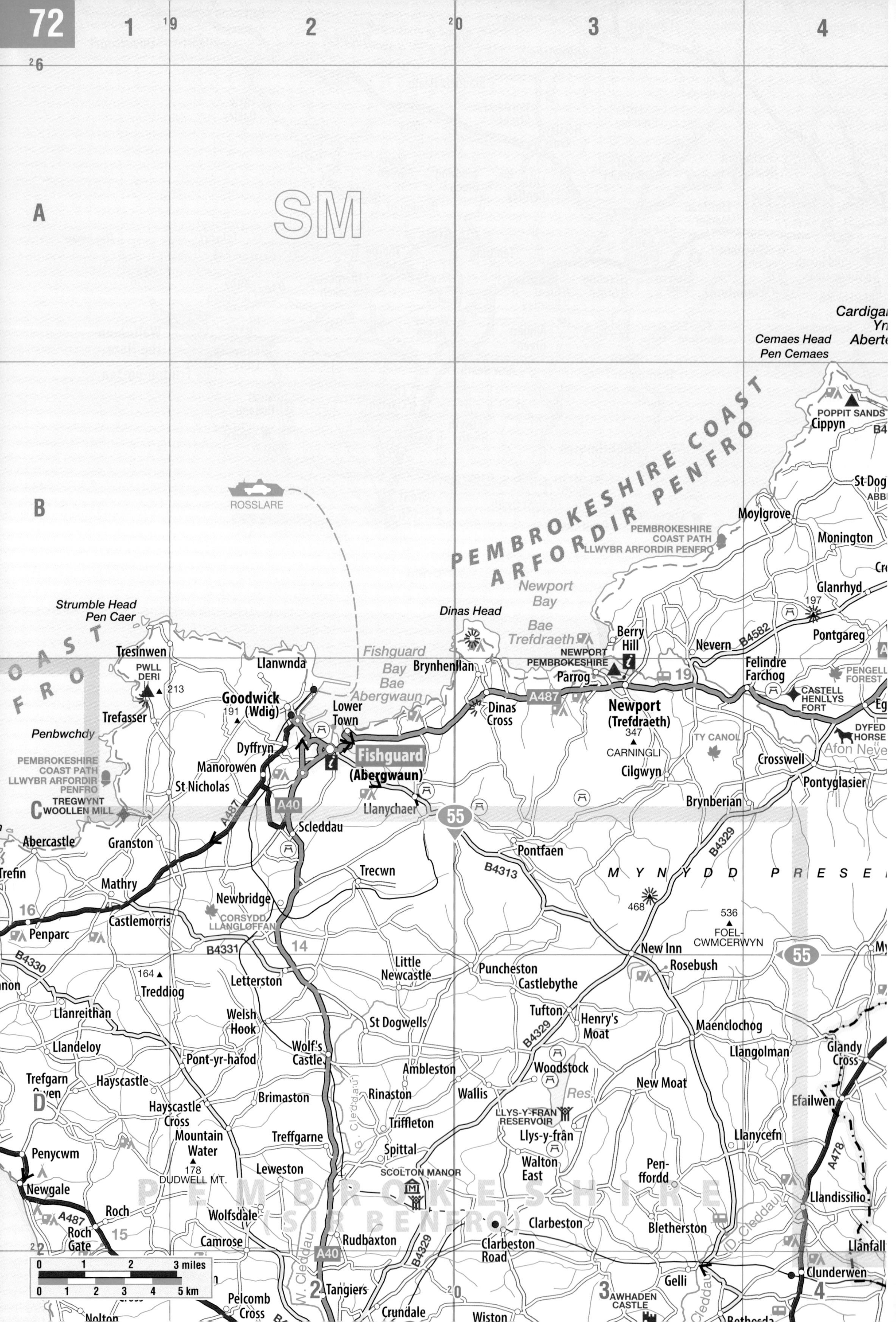
1
2
3
4
A
B
C
D
SM
Cardigan
Cemaes Head
Pen Cemaes
POPPIT SANDS
Cippyn
St Dogmaels
Moylgrove
Monington
Glanrhyd
197
Pontgareg
PEMBROKESHIRE COAST
ARFORDIR PENFRO
PEMBROKESHIRE COAST PATH
LLWYBR ARFORDIR PENFRO
ROSSLARE
Newport Bay
Bae Trefdraeth
Dinas Head
Berry Hill
NEWPORT PEMBROKESHIRE
Parrog
Nevern
B4582
Felindre Farchog
CASTELL HENLLYS FORT
PENGELLI FOREST
DYFED SHIRE HORSE
Afon Nevern
Strumble Head
Pen Caer
Tresinwen
PWLL DERI
213
Llanwnda
Fishguard Bay
Bae Abergwaun
Brynhenllan
Goodwick
(Wdig)
191
Lower Town
Dinas Cross
A487
Newport
(Trefdraeth)
347
CARNINGLI
TY CANOL
Crosswell
Pontyglasier
Trefasser
Penbwchdy
Dyffryn
Manorowen
Fishguard
(Abergwaun)
Cilgwyn
Brynberian
PEMBROKESHIRE COAST PATH
LLWYBR ARFORDIR PENFRO
St Nicholas
TREGWYNT WOOLLEN MILL
A40
Llanychaer
55
Scleddau
Abercastle
Granston
Pontfaen
B4329
Trefin
Mathry
Trecwn
B4313
MYNYDD PRESELI
468
536
FOEL-CWMCERWYN
Newbridge
16
Penparc
Castlemorris
CORSYDD LLANGLOFFAN
B4331
14
B4330
New Inn
Rosebush
Little Newcastle
Puncheston
Castlebythe
164
Treddiog
Letterston
Llanreithan
Welsh Hook
Tufton
Henry's Moat
St Dogwells
Maenclochog
Llandeloy
Wolf's Castle
Woodstock
Llangolman
Glandy Cross
Pont-yr-hafod
Ambleston
New Moat
Trefgarn Owen
Hayscastle
Rinaston
Wallis
Res.
Efailwen
Brimaston
LLYS-Y-FRAN RESERVOIR
Hayscastle Cross
Triffleton
Llys-y-frân
Mountain Water
Treffgarne
Llanycefn
Spittal
A478
Penycwm
178
DUDWELL MT.
Leweston
Walton East
Pen-ffordd
SCOLTON MANOR
Newgale
PEMBROKESHIRE
(SIR BENFRO)
Llandissilio
Roch
Wolfsdale
Clarbeston
A487
Roch Gate
15
Camrose
Rudbaxton
Clarbeston Road
Bletherston
Llanfall
W. Cleddau
A40
B4329
E. Cleddau
Clunderwen
0 1 2 3 miles
0 1 2 3 4 5 km
Tangiers
Gelli
AWHADEN CASTLE
Pelcomb Cross
Crundale
Wiston
Nolton

4
5
6
7
74
SN
New Quay
(Ceinewydd)
Cei-bach
Maen-y-groes
Gilfachrheda
Cwmtudu
Cwmtydu
Cross Inn
Llanarth
Nanternis
Caerwedros
Ynys-Lochtyn
169
Blaencelyn
Llwyndafydd
A487
Synod Inn
Llangrannog
Pontgarreg
B4334
B4321
Plwmp
Pentregat
B4338
Penbryn
Penmorfa
Tresaith
Parcllyn
MWNT
Felinwynt
Aberporth
Brynhoffnant
Sarnau
Talgarreg
Gwbert
151
16
ABERPORTH
WEST WALES
AIRPORT
B4548
Y Ferwig
Blaenannerch
Tremain
Tan-y-groes
Glynarthen
Capel
Cynon
314
RHOS LLAWR
CWRT
Bwlch-
y-fadfa
Castell-
Howell
Blaenporth
Penparc
Cardigan
(Aberteifi)
CASTLE
Bettws
Ifan
B4333
Rhydlewis
Ffostrasol
Hawen
Beulah
14
Pantgwyn
Maesymeillion
B4459
Pont-siân
19
Bridgend
B4570
Llangoedmor
185
Ponthirwaun
Bryngwyn
Brongest
Troedyraur
Penrhiw-pâl
Coed-y-bryn
A486
Tregroes
A484
Llechryd
COEDMOR
CILGERRAN
CASTLE
Llandygwydd
Capel
Tygwydd
Maesllyn
Croes-lan
Prengwyn
258
Pen-y-
bryn
Afon Teifi
Cilgerran
B4571
Horeb
B4476
Bridell
Carreg-wen
11
Cwm-cou
Llandyfriog
Aber-banc
A475
Penrhiw-llan
Llantood
A478
NATIONAL CORACLE
CENTRE
Cenarth
Newcastle
Emlyn
(Castell Newydd
Emlyn)
TEIFI VALLEY RAILWAY
Llandysul
Abercych
Pentrecagal
Henllan
487
Rhos-hill
Llanfihangel-
ar-arth
Newchapel
CLYNFYW
Aber-
Arad
NATIONAL
WOOL
MUSEUM
Llangeler
Drefach
A486
B4336
B4332
Cilwendeg
Penrherber
B4333
Felindre
Pentre-cwrt
Boncath
CHEESE
FARM
Saron
Bancyffordd
Llanfair-
Nant-Gwyn
Blaenffos
Cwmhiraeth
Drefelin
Cwmpengraig
Bwlchygroes
Cwmcych
Capel Iwan
Eglwyswen
335
MOELFRE
Rhôs
Penygroes
395
Star
Clydey
Cwmorgan
Tanglwst
Dolgran
B4459
C
Crymych
Tegryn
A484
314
B4299
Bryn-Iwan
247
Pentre-galar
Hermon
Hen-feddau
fawr
Cwmduad
Hermon
B4333
Llanfyrnach
Trelech
Dinas
58
192
A485
20
Afon Taf
Llanpumsaint
Glandwr
289
20
Pontarsais
Hebron
Blaen-
waun
Pen-y-bont
Blaen-y-
coed
Cynwyl
Elfed
Pant-y-
Caws
Llanglydwen
Cwmbach
Llanwinio
14
Afon Duad
Rhydargaeau
Cefn-y-pant
Talog
GWILI
RAILWAY
D
B4301
Bwlchnewydd
Ty-hen
200
Cwmfelin
Mynach
Maesgwynne
Login
Cross-
hands
189
Llanboidy
Gellywen
Abernant
Newchurch
179
Bronwydd
Arms
Peniel
Ffynnon
ddrain
B4299
Dyffryn
White Mill
Hiraeth
Tre-vaughan
Tanerdy
Abergwili
Henllan
Amgoed
Meidrim
Merthyr
Carmarthen
(Caerfyrddin)
B4298
P&R
56
Llangynin
Sarnau
6
Llangunnor
Cwmfelin
Boeth
4
5
Llanllwch
Johnstown
Pensarn
7
Bancyfelin
CORS GOCH,
LLANLLWCH
Alltwalis
Blaen-
Eglwyswrw

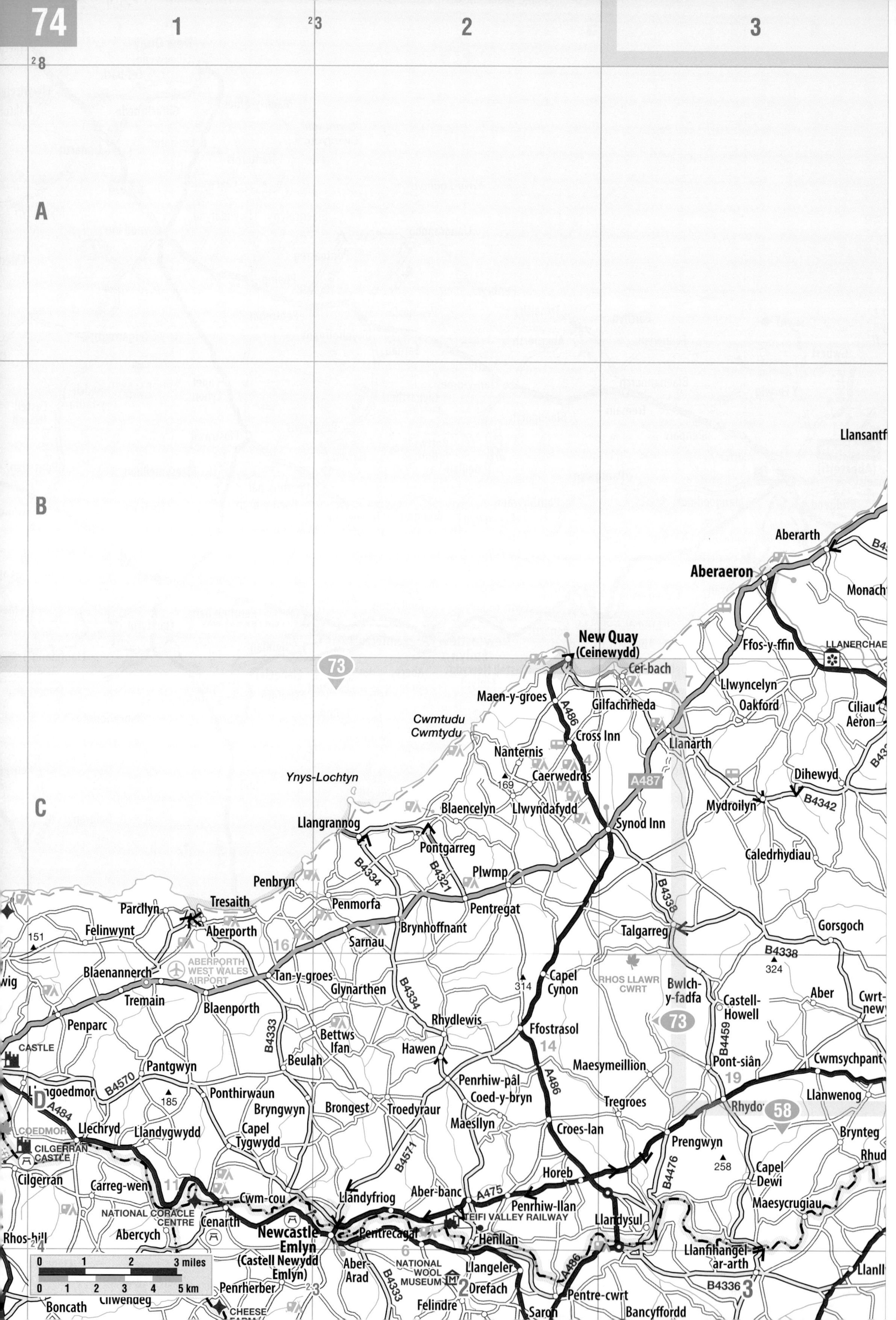
1
2
3
A
B
C
D
Llansantf
Aberarth
Aberaeron
Monacht
New Quay
(Ceinewydd)
Cei-bach
Ffos-y-ffin
LLANERCHAE
Llwyncelyn
Oakford
Ciliau
Aeron
Maen-y-groes
Gilfachrheda
Cwmtudu
Cwmtydu
Cross Inn
Llanarth
Nanternis
Caerwedros
169
Dihewyd
A486
A487
Ynys-Lochtyn
Blaencelyn
Llwyndafydd
Mydroilyn
B4342
Llangrannog
Synod Inn
Pontgarreg
Caledrhydiau
Penbryn
B4334
B4321
Plwmp
B4338
Tresaith
Penmorfa
Pentregat
Parcllyn
Aberporth
Brynhoffnant
Talgarreg
Gorsgoch
151
Felinwynt
Sarnau
16
B4338
324
ABERPORTH
WEST WALES
AIRPORT
Blaenannerch
Tan-y-groes
Capel
Cynon
314
RHOS LLAWR
CWRT
Bwlch-
y-fadfa
Castell-
Howell
Aber
Cwrt-
newy
Tremain
Blaenporth
Glynarthen
73
Penparc
B4333
Bettws
Ifan
Rhydlewis
Ffostrasol
CASTLE
Hawen
14
B4459
Beulah
Maesymeillion
Pont-siân
Cwmsychpant
Pantgwyn
19
B4570
185
Penrhiw-pâl
Llangoedmor
Ponthirwaun
Coed-y-bryn
A486
Llanwenog
A484
Bryngwyn
Brongest
Troedyraur
Tregroes
Rhydo
58
COEDMOR
Llechryd
Llandygwydd
Capel
Tygwydd
Maesllyn
Croes-lan
Brynteg
CILGERRAN
CASTLE
Prengwyn
B4571
B4476
258
Rhud
Cilgerran
Capel
Dewi
Carreg-wen
11
Horeb
Cwm-cou
Llandyfriog
Aber-banc
A475
Penrhiw-llan
Maesycrugiau
NATIONAL CORACLE
CENTRE
TEIFI VALLEY RAILWAY
Cenarth
Newcastle
Emlyn
(Castell Newydd
Emlyn)
Llandysul
Rhos-hill
Abercych
Pentrecagal
Henllan
6
Llanfihangel-
ar-arth
Aber-
Arad
NATIONAL
WOOL
MUSEUM
Llangeler
A486
Llanll
0 1 2 3 miles
0 1 2 3 4 5 km
Penrherber
B4333
2
Drefach
B4336
3
Boncath
Cilwendeg
CHEESE
Felindre
Saron
Pentre-cwrt
Bancyffordd

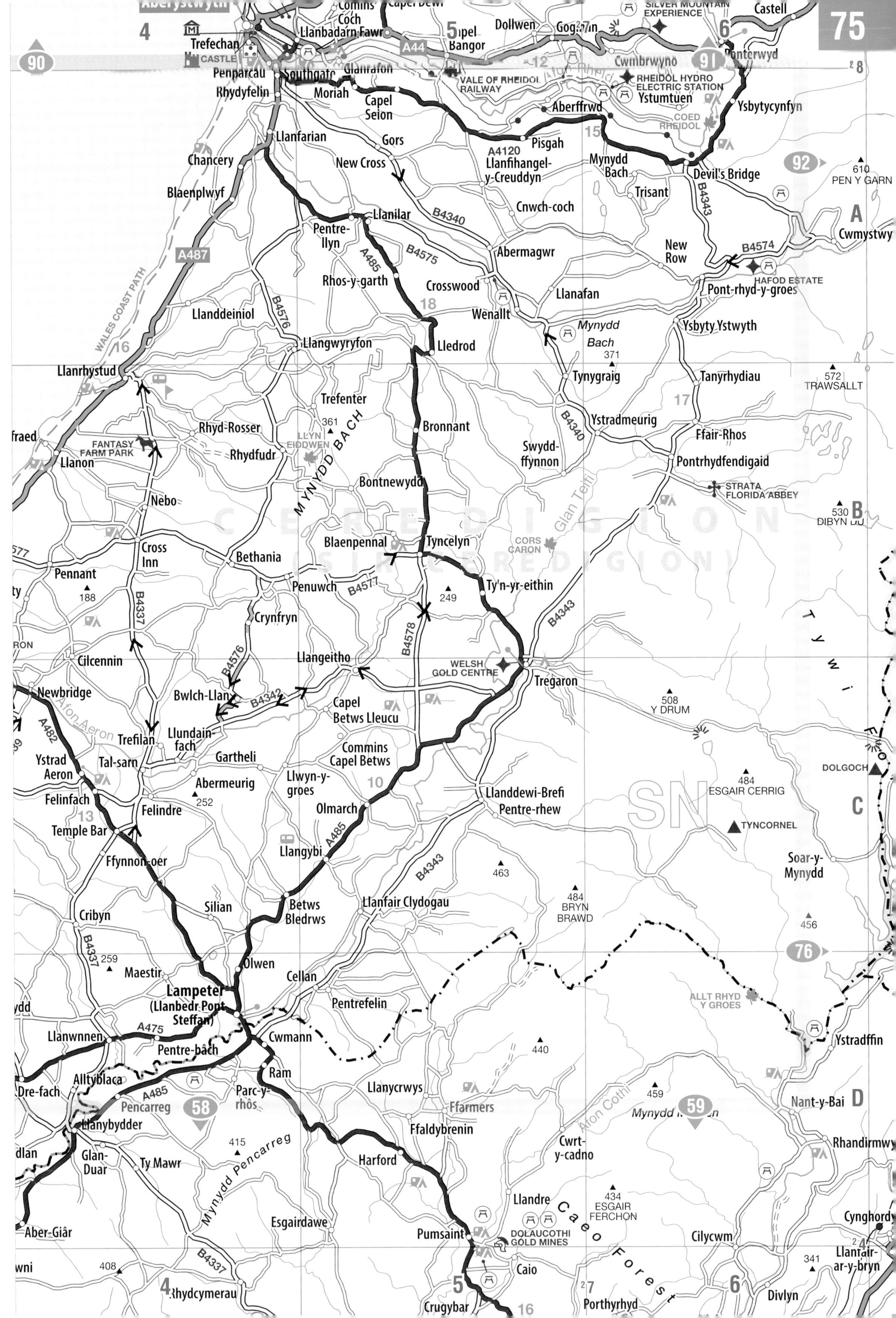
75
90
91
92
76
58
59
Aberystwyth
Trefechan
CASTLE
Penparcau
Southgate
Rhydyfelin
Comins Coch
Llanbadarn Fawr
Glanrafon
Moriah
Capel Seion
Capel Bangor
Dollwen
Goginan
SILVER MOUNTAIN EXPERIENCE
Castell
Ponterwyd
Cwmbrwyno
VALE OF RHEIDOL RAILWAY
RHEIDOL HYDRO ELECTRIC STATION
Ystumtuen
Aberffrwd
COED RHEIDOL
Ysbytycynfyn
A44
A4120
Pisgah
Llanfihangel-y-Creuddyn
Mynydd Bach
Trisant
Devil's Bridge
B4343
610
PEN Y GARN
Llanfarian
Gors
New Cross
Chancery
Blaenplwyf
Llanilar
Pentre-llyn
B4340
Cnwch-coch
Abermagwr
A485
B4575
New Row
B4574
Cwmystwyth
HAFOD ESTATE
Pont-rhyd-y-groes
A487
Rhos-y-garth
Crosswood
WALES COAST PATH
Llanddeiniol
B4576
Wenallt
Llanafan
Mynydd Bach
Ysbyty Ystwyth
371
Lledrod
Llangwyryfon
Llanrhystud
Tynygraig
Tanyrhydiau
572
TRAWSALLT
Trefenter
LLYN EIDDWEN
361
MYNYDD BACH
Bronnant
Ystradmeurig
Ffair-Rhos
Rhyd-Rosser
FANTASY FARM PARK
Llanon
Rhydfudr
Swydd-ffynnon
Pontrhydfendigaid
STRATA FLORIDA ABBEY
Bontnewydd
Nebo
CEREDIGION
(SIR CEREDIGION)
Glan Teifi
530
DIBYN DU
CORS CARON
Blaenpennal
Tyncelyn
Cross Inn
Bethania
Pennant
188
Penuwch
B4577
249
Ty'n-yr-eithin
Crynfryn
B4343
TYWI FOREST
B4337
B4578
Cilcennin
B4576
Llangeitho
WELSH GOLD CENTRE
Tregaron
Newbridge
Bwlch-Llan
B4342
Capel Betws Lleucu
508
Y DRUM
Afon Aeron
A482
Trefilan
Llundain-fach
Ystrad Aeron
Tal-sarn
Gartheli
Commins Capel Betws
Abermeurig
252
Llwyn-y-groes
DOLGOCH
Llanddewi-Brefi
Pentre-rhew
484
ESGAIR CERRIG
SN
Felinfach
Felindre
Olmarch
Temple Bar
TYNCORNEL
Ffynnon-oer
Llangybi
463
Soar-y-Mynydd
B4343
484
BRYN BRAWD
Cribyn
Silian
Betws Bledrws
Llanfair Clydogau
456
259
Maestir
Olwen
Cellan
Lampeter (Llanbedr Pont Steffan)
Pentrefelin
ALLT RHYD Y GROES
Llanwnnen
A475
Cwmann
440
Ystradffin
Pentre-bâch
Alltyblaca
Ram
Dre-fach
A485
Parc-y-rhôs
Llanycrwys
459
Pencarreg
Ffarmers
Afon Cothi
Nant-y-Bai
Llanybydder
Ffaldybrenin
Mynydd
415
Cwrt-y-cadno
Rhandirmwyn
Glan-Duar
Ty Mawr
Mynydd Pencarreg
Harford
434
ESGAIR FERCHON
Llandre
Caeo Forest
Cynghordy
Aber-Giâr
Esgairdawe
Pumsaint
DOLAUCOTHI GOLD MINES
Cilycwm
408
B4337
Caio
341
Llanfair-ar-y-bryn
Rhydcymerau
Porthyrhyd
Divlyn
Crugybar
A
B
C
D
4
5
6

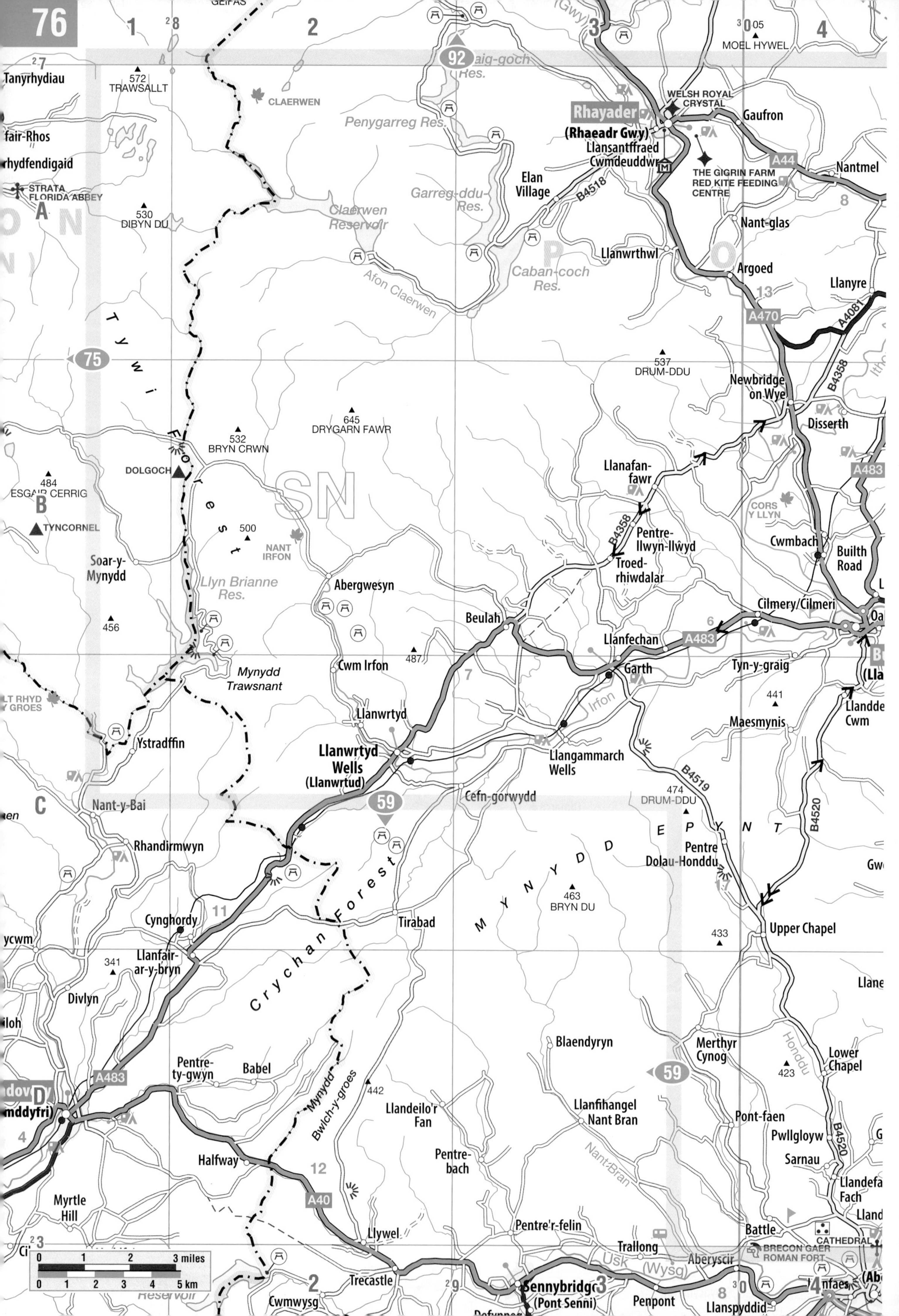

Tanyrhydiau
572 TRAWSALLT
CLAERWEN
Penygarreg Res.
92
Rhayader
(Rhaeadr Gwy)
WELSH ROYAL CRYSTAL
Gaufron
Llansantffraed Cwmdeuddwr
THE GIGRIN FARM RED KITE FEEDING CENTRE
Nantmel
A44
Elan Village
B4518
Garreg-ddu Res.
Claerwen Reservoir
STRATA FLORIDA ABBEY
530 DIBYN DU
Nant-glas
Llanwrthwl
Argoed
Caban-coch Res.
Afon Claerwen
Llanyre
A470
A4081
75
537 DRUM-DDU
Newbridge on Wye
B4358
Disserth
645 DRYGARN FAWR
532 BRYN CRWN
Tywi Forest
DOLGOCH
484 ESGAIR CERRIG
TYNCORNEL
SN
Llanafan-fawr
A483
CORS Y LLYN
Pentre-llwyn-llwyd
Cwmbach
Builth Road
500
NANT IRFON
Soar-y-Mynydd
Llyn Brianne Res.
Abergwesyn
Troed-rhiwdalar
Cilmery/Cilmeri
456
Beulah
Llanfechan
Garth
Tyn-y-graig
487
Cwm Irfon
Mynydd Trawsnant
Irfon
441
Llanwrtyd
Maesmynis
Llanddewi Cwm
Ystradffin
Llanwrtyd Wells (Llanwrtud)
Llangammarch Wells
59
Cefn-gorwydd
B4519
474 DRUM-DDU
Nant-y-Bai
Rhandirmwyn
B4520
Mynydd Epynt
Pentre Dolau-Honddu
Crychan Forest
463 BRYN DU
Cynghordy
Tirabad
433
Upper Chapel
Llanfair-ar-y-bryn
341
Divlyn
Blaendyryn
Merthyr Cynog
Honddu
Lower Chapel
423
Pentre-ty-gwyn
Babel
A483
Mynydd Bwlch-y-groes
442
Llandeilo'r Fan
Llanfihangel Nant Bran
Pont-faen
Pwllgloyw
Pentre-bach
Nant Bran
Sarnau
Halfway
A40
Llandefaelog Fach
Myrtle Hill
Pentre'r-felin
Llywel
Battle
CATHEDRAL
Trallong
BRECON GAER ROMAN FORT
Usk (Wysg)
Aberyscir
Trecastle
Sennybridge (Pont Senni)
Penpont
Llanspyddid
Cwmwysg
0 1 2 3 miles
0 1 2 3 4 5 km

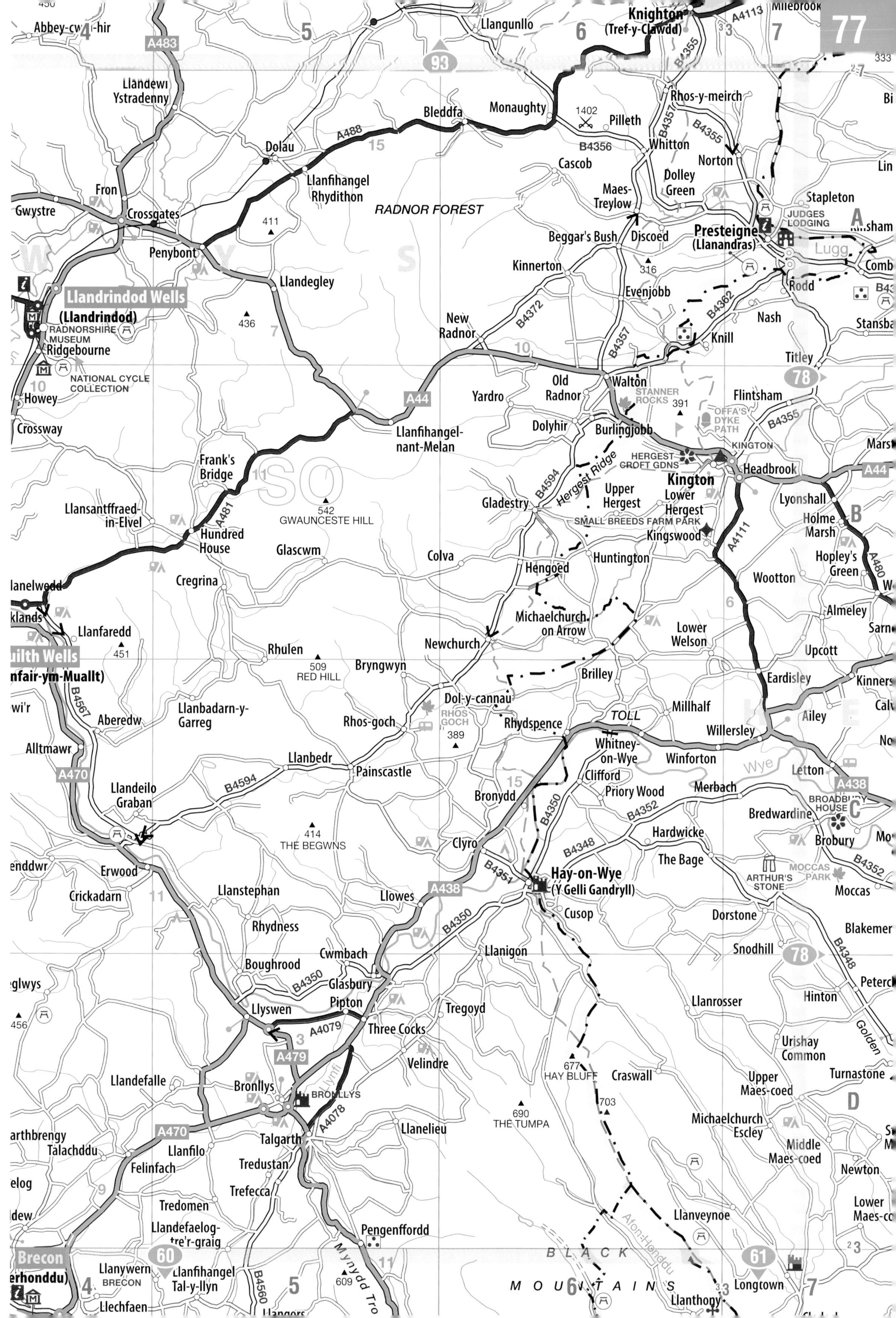
77
Abbey-cwm-hir
Llangunllo
Knighton
(Tref-y-Clawdd)
Milebrook
A483
93
Llandewi
Ystradenny
Bleddfa
Monaughty
1402
Pilleth
Rhos-y-meirch
B4356
Whitton
B4355
B4357
A488
Dolau
Cascob
Norton
Llanfihangel
Rhydithon
Maes-
Treylow
Dolley
Green
Fron
Stapleton
Gwystre
Crossgates
RADNOR FOREST
411
JUDGES
LODGING
Presteigne
(Llanandras)
Beggar's Bush
Discoed
Lugg
Penybont
Kinnerton
316
Rodd
Llandegley
Evenjobb
Llandrindod Wells
(Llandrindod)
RADNORSHIRE
MUSEUM
Ridgebourne
436
New
Radnor
B4372
B4362
Nash
Knill
NATIONAL CYCLE
COLLECTION
Titley
Howey
Old
Radnor
Walton
78
Yardro
STANNER
ROCKS
391
Flintsham
A44
OFFA'S
DYKE
PATH
Crossway
Llanfihangel-
nant-Melan
Dolyhir
Burlingjobb
B4355
KINGTON
Frank's
Bridge
HERGEST
CROFT GDNS
Headbrook
SO
Hergest Ridge
Kington
A44
Llansantffraed-
in-Elvel
542
GWAUNCESTE HILL
Gladestry
B4594
Upper
Hergest
Lower
Hergest
Lyonshall
A481
SMALL BREEDS FARM PARK
Holme
Marsh
Hundred
House
Kingswood
Glascwm
Colva
Huntington
A4111
Hopley's
Green
Hengoed
A480
Cregrina
Wootton
Llanelwedd
Michaelchurch-
on-Arrow
Almeley
Llanfaredd
451
Lower
Welson
Rhulen
Newchurch
509
RED HILL
Bryngwyn
Upcott
Builth Wells
(Llanfair-ym-Muallt)
Brilley
Eardisley
Dol-y-cannau
B4567
Llanbadarn-y-
Garreg
RHOS
GOCH
Millhalf
Aberedw
Rhos-goch
Rhydspence
389
TOLL
Ailey
Willersley
Alltmawr
Whitney-
on-Wye
Winforton
Llanbedr
Painscastle
Wye
Letton
A470
Clifford
A438
Llandeilo
Graban
B4594
Priory Wood
Merbach
Bronydd
BROADBURY
HOUSE
B4352
Bredwardine
B4350
414
THE BEGWNS
Hardwicke
Clyro
Brobury
B4348
The Bage
Erwood
B4351
Hay-on-Wye
(Y Gelli Gandryll)
MOCCAS
PARK
ARTHUR'S
STONE
B4352
Crickadarn
A438
Moccas
Llowes
Cusop
Dorstone
Llanstephan
Rhydness
B4350
Blakemere
Llanigon
Snodhill
78
Boughrood
Cwmbach
B4348
B4350
Glasbury
Llanrosser
Pipton
Hinton
456
Llyswen
Tregoyd
A4079
Three Cocks
A479
Velindre
Urishay
Common
677
HAY BLUFF
Craswall
Golden
Turnastone
Llandefalle
Bronllys
BRONLLYS
Upper
Maes-coed
Llynfi
703
690
THE TUMPA
Michaelchurch
Escley
A470
A4078
Talgarth
Llanelieu
Middle
Maes-coed
Talachddu
Llanfilo
Felinfach
Tredustan
Newton
Trefecca
Tredomen
Lower
Maes-coed
Llanveynoe
Llandefaelog-
tre'r-graig
Pengenffordd
Afon Honddu
Brecon
60
BLACK
61
Llanywern
BRECON
Llanfihangel
Tal-y-llyn
B4560
609
Mynydd Troed
MOUNTAINS
Longtown
Llanthony
Llechfaen

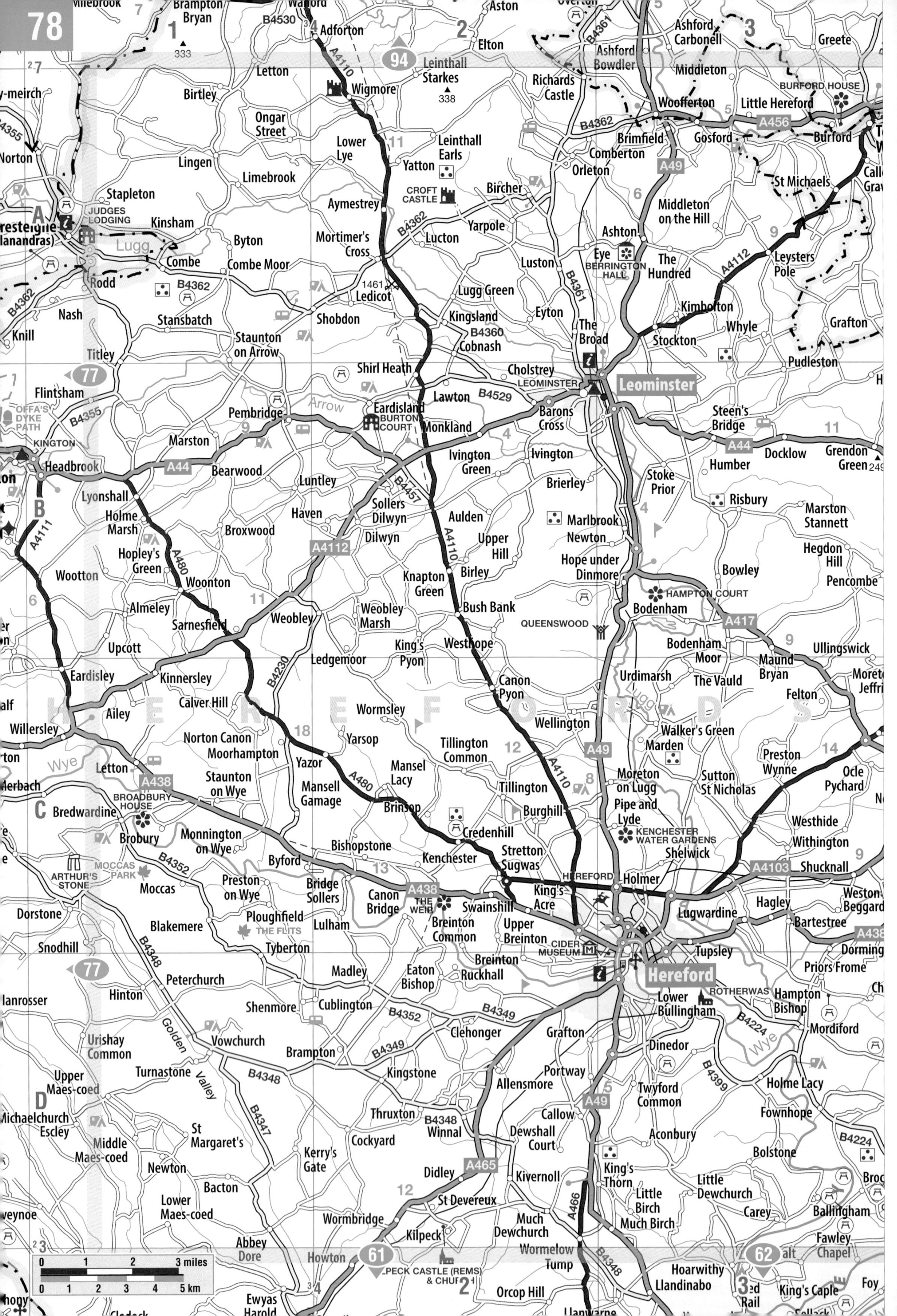
Brampton Bryan
Wigmore
Adforton
Aston
Elton
Ashford Carbonell
Greete
333
Leinthall Starkes
338
94
Ashford Bowdler
Letton
Richards Castle
Middleton
Birtley
BURFORD HOUSE
Woofferton
Little Hereford
Ongar Street
B4530
A4110
B4361
Lower Lye
Leinthall Earls
B4362
A456
Brimfield
Gosford
Burford
Norton
Lingen
Yatton
Comberton
Orleton
A49
Limebrook
CROFT CASTLE
Bircher
St Michaels
Stapleton
JUDGES LODGING
Aymestrey
Middleton on the Hill
Presteigne (Llanandras)
Kinsham
Yarpole
Ashton
Mortimer's Cross
Lucton
Byton
Eye
BERRINGTON HALL
Leysters Pole
Lugg
Combe
Combe Moor
Luston
The Hundred
Rodd
A4112
B4362
1461
Ledicot
Lugg Green
Kimbolton
Nash
Stansbatch
Shobdon
Kingsland
Eyton
The Broad
Whyle
Grafton
Knill
B4360
Cobnash
Stockton
Staunton on Arrow
Pudleston
Titley
77
Shirl Heath
Cholstrey
LEOMINSTER
Leominster
Flintsham
Lawton
B4529
OFFA'S DYKE PATH
Eardisland
Arrow
Pembridge
B4355
BURTON COURT
Monkland
Barons Cross
Steen's Bridge
KINGTON
Marston
Docklow
Grendon Green
249
Headbrook
A44
Bearwood
Ivington Green
Ivington
Humber
Luntley
Stoke Prior
Lyonshall
Brierley
B4457
Risbury
Marston Stannett
Sollers Dilwyn
Holme Marsh
Haven
Aulden
Marlbrook
Broxwood
Newton
A4111
Dilwyn
A4112
A4110
Upper Hill
Hegdon Hill
Hopley's Green
Hope under Dinmore
Bowley
Wootton
A480
Knapton Green
Birley
Pencombe
Woonton
HAMPTON COURT
Almeley
Weobley Marsh
Bush Bank
Bodenham
Sarnesfield
Weobley
QUEENSWOOD
A417
Upcott
King's Pyon
Westhope
Bodenham Moor
Ullingswick
Ledgemoor
B4230
Maund Bryan
Eardisley
Kinnersley
Canon Pyon
Urdimarsh
The Vauld
Felton
Calver Hill
Ailey
Wormsley
Wellington
Willersley
HEREFORDSHIRE
Walker's Green
Yarsop
Norton Canon
Tillington Common
Marden
Preston Wynne
Letton
Moorhampton
Ocle Pychard
Wye
Yazor
Mansel Lacy
Staunton on Wye
A438
Moreton on Lugg
Sutton St Nicholas
Mansell Gamage
Tillington
BROADBURY HOUSE
Bredwardine
A4110
Brinsop
Burghill
Pipe and Lyde
Westhide
Withington
Monnington on Wye
Credenhill
KENCHESTER WATER GARDENS
Brobury
Bishopstone
Shelwick
MOCCAS PARK
B4352
ARTHUR'S STONE
Kenchester
Stretton Sugwas
Shucknall
Byford
A4103
Moccas
HEREFORD
Holmer
Preston on Wye
Bridge Sollers
Canon Bridge
King's Acre
Weston Beggard
THE WEIR
Swainshill
Hagley
Dorstone
Lugwardine
Ploughfield
Breinton Common
Upper Breinton
Blakemere
THE FLITS
Lulham
Bartestree
Snodhill
Tyberton
CIDER MUSEUM
Tupsley
Dormington
Breinton
Madley
Eaton Bishop
Ruckhall
Hereford
Priors Frome
Peterchurch
Hinton
ROTHERWAS
Lower Bullingham
Hampton Bishop
B4348
Shenmore
Cublington
B4352
B4349
Mordiford
Urishay Common
Golden Valley
Vowchurch
Clehonger
Grafton
B4224
Wye
Brampton
B4349
Dinedor
Upper Maes-coed
Turnastone
B4348
Kingstone
Portway
Allensmore
B4399
Holme Lacy
Twyford Common
A49
Michaelchurch Escley
Callow
Fownhope
Thruxton
B4348
Winnal
Dewshall Court
St Margaret's
B4347
Cockyard
Aconbury
B4224
Middle Maes-coed
Kerry's Gate
Bolstone
King's Thorn
Newton
Didley
A465
Kivernoll
Little Birch
Little Dewchurch
Bacton
St Devereux
A466
Carey
Ballingham
Lower Maes-coed
Much Birch
Much Dewchurch
Wormbridge
Kilpeck
Fawley Chapel
Abbey Dore
Wormelow Tump
B4348
Howton
61
62
PECK CASTLE (REMS) & CHURCH
Hoarwithy
Llandinabo
King's Caple
Foy
Orcop Hill
Ewyas Harold
0 1 2 3 miles
0 1 2 3 4 5 km

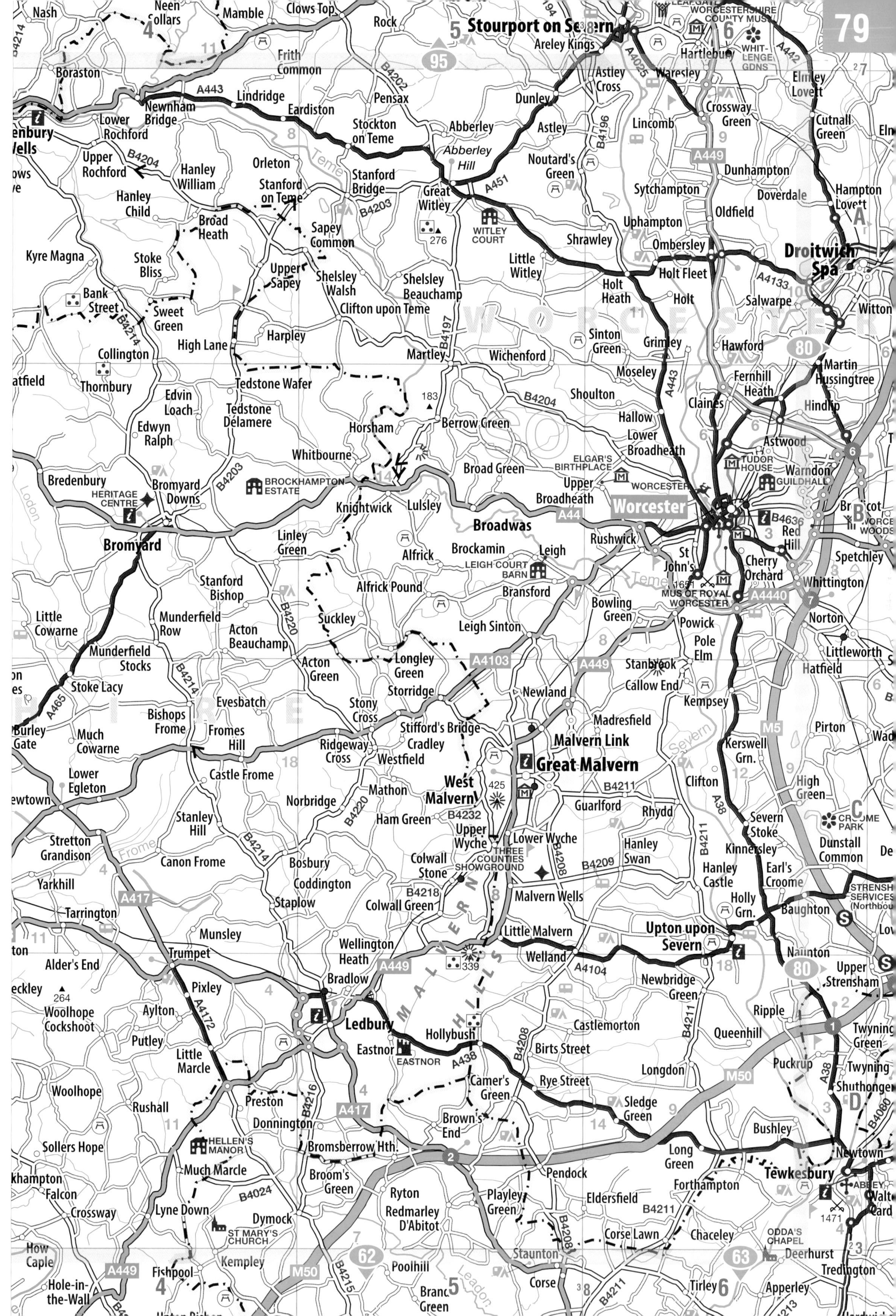
Stourport on Severn
Areley Kings
Worcestershire County Museum
Hartlebury
Whitlenge Gdns
Elmley Lovett
Rock
Clows Top
Mamble
Neen Sollars
Nash
Boraston
Frith Common
Lindridge
Eardiston
Pensax
Newnham Bridge
Lower Rochford
Tenbury Wells
Upper Rochford
Hanley William
Hanley Child
Orleton
Stanford on Teme
Stockton on Teme
Stanford Bridge
Abberley
Abberley Hill
Great Witley
Witley Court
Dunley
Astley
Astley Cross
Waresley
Crossway Green
Cutnall Green
Lincomb
Noutard's Green
Dunhampton
Sytchampton
Oldfield
Hampton Lovett
Doverdale
Uphampton
Ombersley
Droitwich Spa
Holt Fleet
Holt Heath
Holt
Salwarpe
Witton
Shrawley
Little Witley
Sapey Common
Broad Heath
Kyre Magna
Stoke Bliss
Upper Sapey
Shelsley Walsh
Shelsley Beauchamp
Clifton upon Teme
Bank Street
Sweet Green
Harpley
High Lane
Collington
Thornbury
Martley
Wichenford
Sinton Green
Grimley
Hawford
Martin Hussingtree
Worcester
Moseley
Fernhill Heath
Claines
Hindlip
Tedstone Wafer
Tedstone Delamere
Edvin Loach
Edwyn Ralph
Shoulton
Hallow
Lower Broadheath
Horsham
Berrow Green
Astwood
Whitbourne
Broad Green
Elgar's Birthplace
Tudor House
Warndon
Guildhall
Bredenbury
Heritage Centre
Bromyard Downs
Brockhampton Estate
Knightwick
Lulsley
Upper Broadheath
Worcester
Bromyard
Broadwas
Rushwick
Red Hill
Worcs Woods
Linley Green
Alfrick
Brockamin
Leigh
Leigh Court Barn
St John's
Cherry Orchard
Spetchley
Whittington
Stanford Bishop
Alfrick Pound
Bransford
Mus of Royal Worcester
Little Cowarne
Munderfield Row
Suckley
Bowling Green
Powick
Norton
Acton Beauchamp
Leigh Sinton
Pole Elm
Littleworth
Munderfield Stocks
Acton Green
Longley Green
Stanbrook
Hatfield
Callow End
Stoke Lacy
Storridge
Newland
Kempsey
Evesbatch
Stony Cross
Madresfield
Bishops Frome
Stifford's Bridge
Burley Gate
Much Cowarne
Fromes Hill
Ridgeway Cross
Cradley
Malvern Link
Kerswell Grn.
Pirton
Westfield
Great Malvern
Castle Frome
Lower Egleton
West Malvern
Clifton
High Green
Newtown
Mathon
Norbridge
Guarlford
Rhydd
Stanley Hill
Ham Green
Upper Wyche
Severn Stoke
Croome Park
Lower Wyche
Stretton Grandison
Hanley Swan
Kinnersley
Dunstall Common
Three Counties Showground
Canon Frome
Bosbury
Colwall Stone
Hanley Castle
Earl's Croome
Yarkhill
Coddington
Holly Grn.
Strensham Services (Northbound)
Malvern Wells
Staplow
Colwall Green
Baughton
Tarrington
Munsley
Little Malvern
Upton upon Severn
Wellington Heath
Trumpet
Welland
Naunton
Alder's End
Upper Strensham
Newbridge Green
Bradlow
Pixley
Ripple
Woolhope Cockshoot
Aylton
Ledbury
Hollybush
Castlemorton
Twyning Green
Putley
Eastnor
Eastnor
Queenhill
Little Marcle
Birts Street
Puckrup
Twyning
Longdon
Camer's Green
Rye Street
Shuthonger
Woolhope
Preston
Rushall
Sledge Green
Donnington
Brown's End
Bushley
Hellen's Manor
Sollers Hope
Bromsberrow Hth.
Long Green
Newtown
Much Marcle
Pendock
Tewkesbury
Broom's Green
Forthampton
Falcon
Ryton
Playley Green
Eldersfield
Abbey
Crossway
Lyne Down
Dymock
Redmarley D'Abitot
Walton Cardiff
St Mary's Church
Corse Lawn
Chaceley
Odda's Chapel
How Caple
Kempley
Staunton
Deerhurst
Tredington
Hole-in-the-Wall
Fishpool
Poolhill
Corse
Tirley
Apperley
Branch Green
Worcester
Severn
Teme
Frome
Leadon
Lodon
Malvern Hills
A443
A449
A451
A44
A4103
A4104
A417
A438
A4172
A465
A4440
A4133
A4025
A442
A38
M5
M50
B4202
B4203
B4204
B4196
B4197
B4220
B4214
B4232
B4211
B4208
B4209
B4218
B4216
B4024
B4215
B4636
B4080
95
80
62
63
276
183
425
339
264
1651
1471

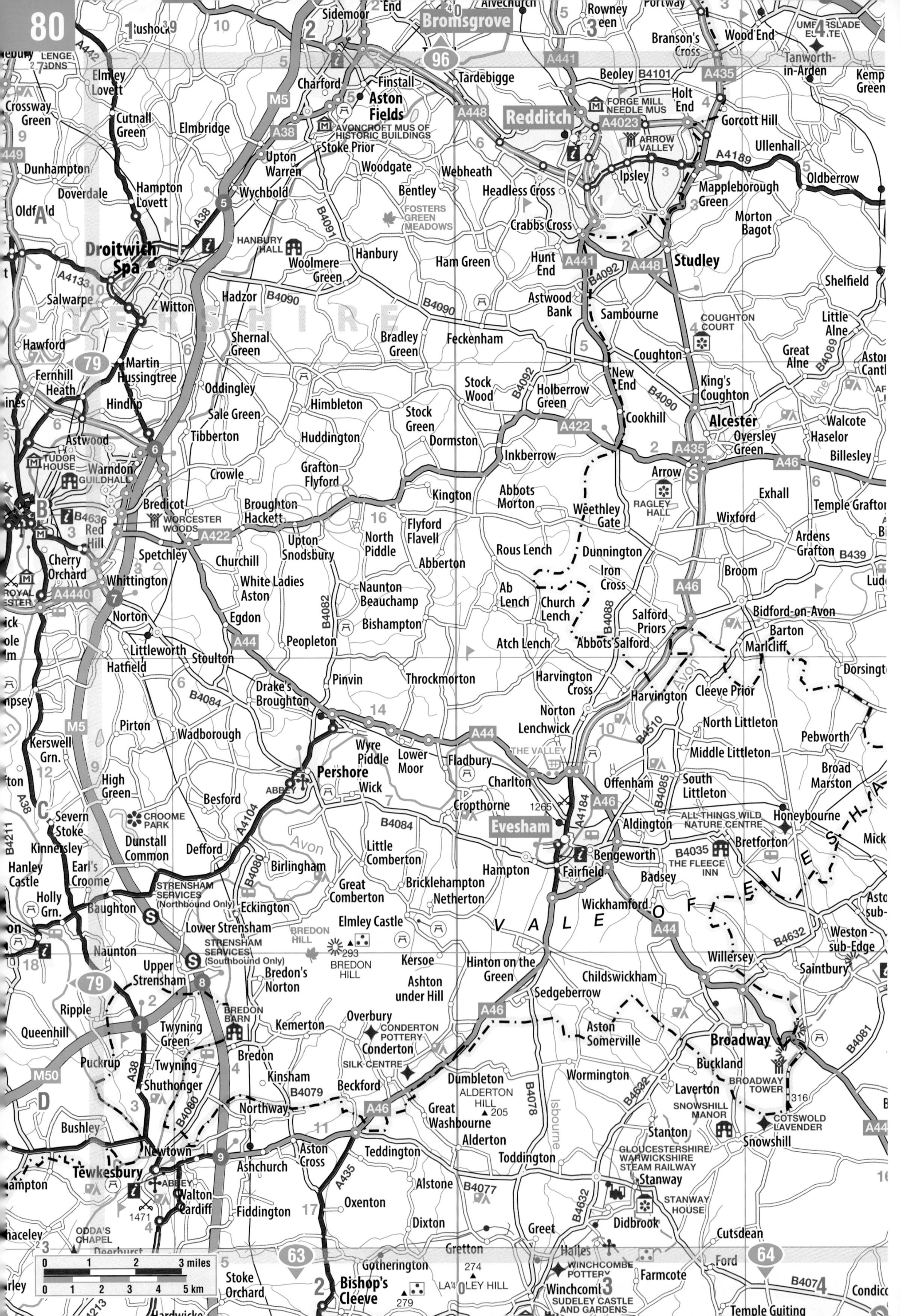

Sidemoor
Bromsgrove
96
Alvechurch
Rowney Green
Portway
Wood End
Branson's Cross
UMBERSLADE ESTATE
Tanworth-in-Arden
Kemp Green
Elmley Lovett
Crossway Green
Cutnall Green
Elmbridge
Charford
Finstall
Aston Fields
Tardebigge
Beoley
Holt End
Redditch
FORGE MILL NEEDLE MUS
Gorcott Hill
AVONCROFT MUS OF HISTORIC BUILDINGS
Stoke Prior
ARROW VALLEY
Ullenhall
Upton Warren
Woodgate
Webheath
Ipsley
Oldberrow
Dunhampton
Hampton Lovett
Doverdale
Wychbold
Bentley
Headless Cross
Mappleborough Green
Morton Bagot
FOSTERS GREEN MEADOWS
Crabbs Cross
HANBURY HALL
Hanbury
Droitwich Spa
Woolmere Green
Ham Green
Hunt End
Studley
Salwarpe
Witton
Hadzor
Astwood Bank
Sambourne
Shelfield
COUGHTON COURT
Little Alne
Hawford
Shernal Green
Bradley Green
Feckenham
Great Alne
Coughton
Martin Hussingtree
Fernhill Heath
79
Oddingley
Stock Wood
New End
Holberrow Green
King's Coughton
Hindlip
Himbleton
Stock Green
Cookhill
Alcester
Walcote
Astwood
Sale Green
Tibberton
Huddington
Dormston
Oversley Green
Haselor
TUDOR HOUSE
Warndon
GUILDHALL
Crowle
Grafton Flyford
Inkberrow
Arrow
Billesley
Bredicot
Broughton Hackett
Kington
Abbots Morton
RAGLEY HALL
Exhall
Temple Grafton
WORCESTER WOODS
Red Hill
Spetchley
Upton Snodsbury
North Piddle
Flyford Flavell
Weethley Gate
Wixford
Ardens Grafton
Cherry Orchard
Churchill
Rous Lench
Dunnington
Broom
White Ladies Aston
Naunton Beauchamp
Abberton
Iron Cross
ROYAL WORCESTER
Whittington
Norton
Egdon
Bishampton
Ab Lench
Church Lench
Salford Priors
Bidford-on-Avon
Barton
Peopleton
Littleworth
Stoulton
Atch Lench
Abbots Salford
Marlcliff
Hatfield
Pinvin
Throckmorton
Harvington Cross
Dorsington
Drake's Broughton
Harvington
Cleeve Prior
Norton
Pirton
Wadborough
Wyre Piddle
Lenchwick
North Littleton
Pebworth
Kerswell Grn.
Lower Moor
Fladbury
THE VALLEY
Middle Littleton
Pershore
Charlton
Offenham
South Littleton
Broad Marston
High Green
Besford
ABBEY
Wick
Cropthorne
Severn Stoke
CROOME PARK
Evesham
Aldington
ALL THINGS WILD NATURE CENTRE
Honeybourne
Kinnersley
Dunstall Common
Defford
Birlingham
Little Comberton
Bengeworth
Bretforton
Hanley Castle
Earl's Croome
Hampton
Fairfield
THE FLEECE INN
Badsey
Great Comberton
Bricklehampton
Netherton
Holly Grn.
STRENSHAM SERVICES (Northbound Only)
Baughton
Eckington
Wickhamford
Lower Strensham
Elmley Castle
VALE OF EVESHAM
BREDON HILL
STRENSHAM SERVICES (Southbound Only)
Weston-sub-Edge
Naunton
293
BREDON HILL
Kersoe
Hinton on the Green
Willersey
Saintbury
Upper Strensham
Bredon's Norton
Ashton under Hill
Childswickham
Ripple
Sedgeberrow
BREDON BARN
Overbury
Queenhill
Twyning Green
Kemerton
CONDERTON POTTERY
Aston Somerville
Broadway
Conderton
Bredon
Puckrup
Twyning
SILK CENTRE
Kinsham
Dumbleton
Wormington
Buckland
Shuthonger
ALDERTON HILL
205
BROADWAY TOWER
Beckford
Laverton
316
Northway
Great Washbourne
SNOWSHILL MANOR
COTSWOLD LAVENDER
Bushley
Stanton
Alderton
Snowshill
Newtown
Aston Cross
Teddington
Toddington
GLOUCESTERSHIRE WARWICKSHIRE STEAM RAILWAY
Tewkesbury
Ashchurch
Stanway
ABBEY
Walton Cardiff
Alstone
STANWAY HOUSE
Fiddington
Oxenton
Didbrook
1471
Dixton
Greet
Cutsdean
ODDA'S CHAPEL
Gretton
Hailes
Deerhurst
63
64
Gotherington
274
WINCHCOMBE POTTERY
Farmcote
Ford
Stoke Orchard
Bishop's Cleeve
LANGLEY HILL
Winchcombe
279
SUDELEY CASTLE AND GARDENS
Temple Guiting
Condicote
0 1 2 3 miles
0 1 2 3 4 5 km
M5
M50
A38
A441
A435
A448
A4023
A4189
B4101
B4091
B4090
B4092
A422
B4089
A44
A46
B4088
B4082
B4084
B4510
B4085
A4184
B4035
A4104
B4080
B4211
A4440
B4636
A4133
B4079
B4080
B4078
B4632
B4077
B4081
A442
B4439
A435

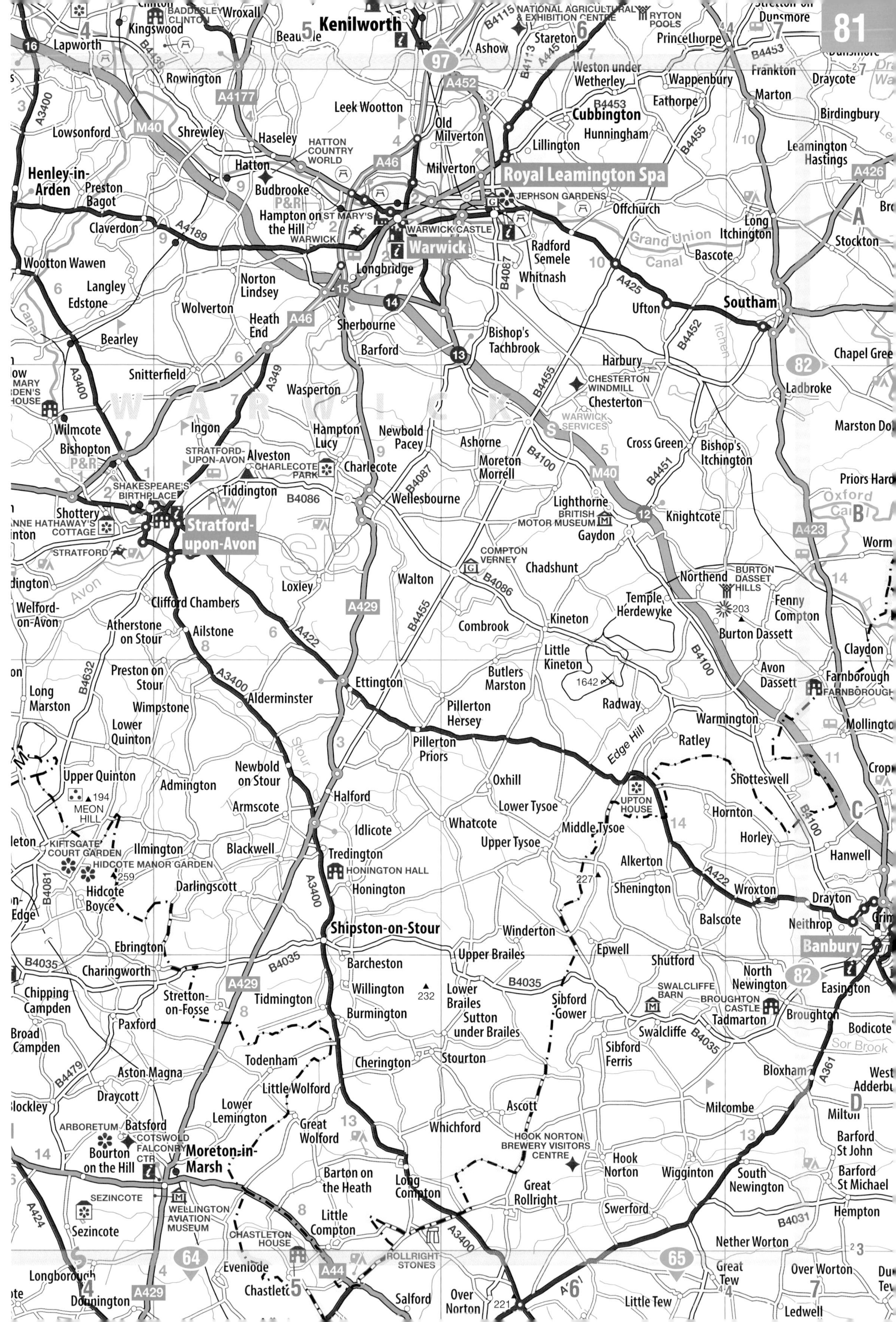

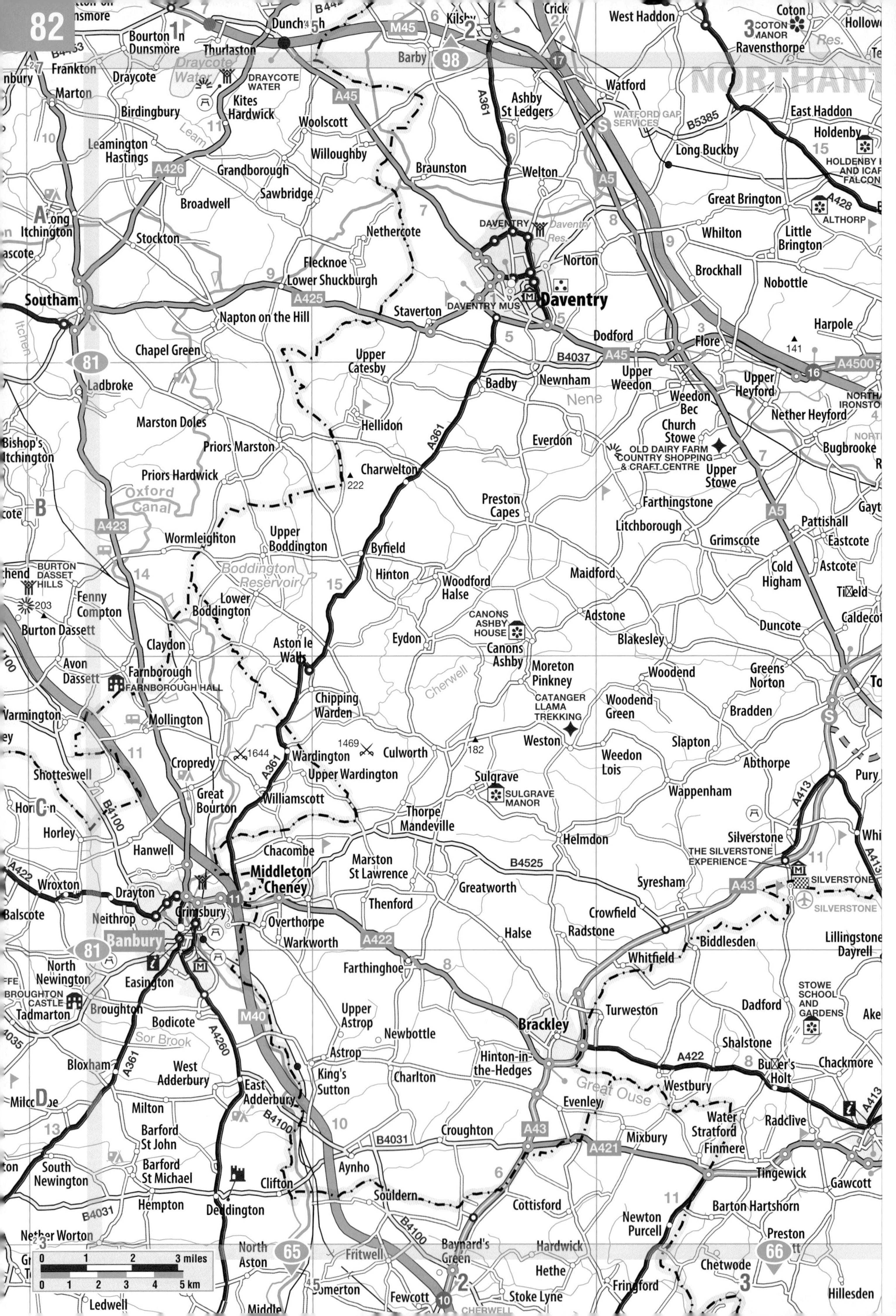
Bourton on Dunsmore
Thurlaston
Dunchurch
Kilsby
Crick
West Haddon
Coton
COTON MANOR
Ravensthorpe
M45
Barby
98
17
Frankton
Draycote
Draycote Water
DRAYCOTE WATER
Kites Hardwick
Marton
Birdingbury
A45
Woolscott
A361
Ashby St Ledgers
Watford
WATFORD GAP SERVICES
B5385
East Haddon
Holdenby
HOLDENBY HOUSE AND ICARUS FALCONRY
Leamington Hastings
Leam
Willoughby
Long Buckby
A426
Grandborough
Braunston
Welton
A5
Sawbridge
Broadwell
Great Brington
A428
ALTHORP
Long Itchington
Nethercote
DAVENTRY
Daventry Res.
Whilton
Little Brington
Stockton
Norton
Flecknoe
Lower Shuckburgh
Brockhall
Nobottle
Southam
A425
DAVENTRY MUS
Daventry
Napton on the Hill
Staverton
Dodford
Harpole
Flore
141
A4500
Itchen
Chapel Green
B4037
81
Upper Catesby
Badby
Newnham
Upper Weedon
Weedon Bec
Upper Heyford
16
Ladbroke
Nene
NORTHAMPTON IRONSTONE
Nether Heyford
Marston Doles
Hellidon
Church Stowe
A361
Everdon
OLD DAIRY FARM COUNTRY SHOPPING & CRAFT CENTRE
Bugbrooke
Bishop's Itchington
Priors Marston
Upper Stowe
Priors Hardwick
Charwelton
222
Oxford Canal
Preston Capes
Farthingstone
Litchborough
Pattishall
A423
Wormleighton
Upper Boddington
Byfield
Grimscote
Eastcote
BURTON DASSET HILLS
Boddington Reservoir
Hinton
Woodford Halse
Maidford
Cold Higham
Astcote
Fenny Compton
203
Lower Boddington
Adstone
Burton Dassett
CANONS ASHBY HOUSE
Canons Ashby
Eydon
Blakesley
Duncote
Claydon
Aston le Walls
Avon Dassett
Farnborough
FARNBOROUGH HALL
Moreton Pinkney
Cherwell
Woodend
Greens Norton
Chipping Warden
CATANGER LLAMA TREKKING
Woodend Green
Bradden
Warmington
Mollington
Weston
Slapton
1469
Culworth
182
Wardington
Weedon Lois
1644
Cropredy
Abthorpe
Shotteswell
Upper Wardington
Sulgrave
SULGRAVE MANOR
Great Bourton
Wappenham
Williamscott
A413
Thorpe Mandeville
Horley
B4100
Silverstone
Helmdon
Hanwell
Chacombe
THE SILVERSTONE EXPERIENCE
B4525
Marston St Lawrence
A422
Middleton Cheney
Wroxton
Greatworth
Syresham
SILVERSTONE
Drayton
A43
Thenford
Balscote
Neithrop
Grimsbury
Overthorpe
Crowfield
Banbury
Halse
Radstone
Biddlesden
Lillingstone Dayrell
Warkworth
North Newington
Farthinghoe
Whitfield
BROUGHTON CASTLE
Easington
Tadmarton
Broughton
Upper Astrop
Turweston
Dadford
STOWE SCHOOL AND GARDENS
Bodicote
M40
Newbottle
Brackley
Sor Brook
A4260
Shalstone
Astrop
Hinton-in-the-Hedges
Bloxham
West Adderbury
King's Sutton
Charlton
Westbury
Chackmore
East Adderbury
Great Ouse
Evenley
Milton
Water Stratford
Radclive
Barford St John
B4031
Croughton
Mixbury
A421
Finmere
South Newington
Barford St Michael
Aynho
Tingewick
Gawcott
Clifton
Souldern
Cottisford
Hempton
Deddington
Newton Purcell
Barton Hartshorn
B4100
Nether Worton
Preston Bissett
North Aston
65
Baynard's Green
Hardwick
Fritwell
66
Chetwode
Hethe
0 1 2 3 miles
0 1 2 3 4 5 km
Somerton
Fewcott
Stoke Lyne
Fringford
Hillesden
Ledwell
CHERWELL

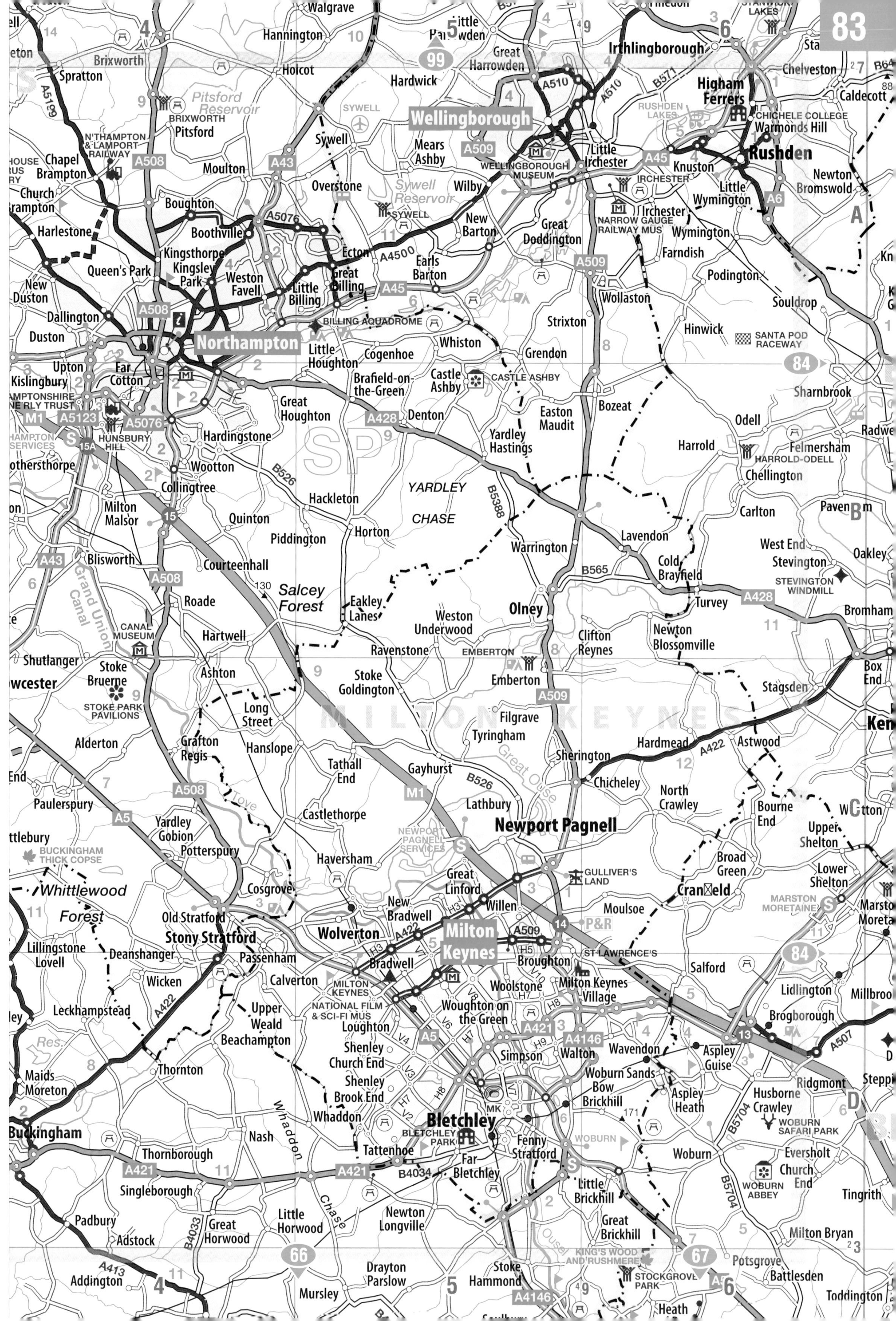
Walgrave
Hannington
Little
Harrowden
99
Great
Harrowden
Irthlingborough
Higham
Ferrers
Chelveston
Caldecott
Brixworth
Spratton
Holcot
Hardwick
Pitsford
Reservoir
BRIXWORTH
Pitsford
SYWELL
Sywell
Wellingborough
Mears
Ashby
A509
WELLINGBOROUGH
MUSEUM
Little
Irchester
A45
Knuston
Rushden
CHICHELE COLLEGE
Warmonds Hill
RUSHDEN
LAKES
Newton
Bromswold
N'THAMPTON
& LAMPORT
RAILWAY
Chapel
Brampton
Church
Brampton
Harlestone
A508
Moulton
A43
Overstone
Sywell
Reservoir
SYWELL
Wilby
IRCHESTER
Irchester
NARROW GAUGE
RAILWAY MUS
Little
Wymington
A6
Wymington
Boughton
Boothville
A5076
New
Barton
Great
Doddington
Farndish
Kingsthorpe
Kingsley
Park
Weston
Favell
Ecton
A4500
Earls
Barton
Queen's Park
New
Duston
Great
Billing
Little
Billing
A45
A509
Wollaston
Podington
Souldrop
Dallington
A508
BILLING AQUADROME
Strixton
Hinwick
SANTA POD
RACEWAY
Duston
Northampton
Little
Houghton
Whiston
Grendon
Upton
Kislingbury
Far
Cotton
Cogenhoe
Brafield-on-
the-Green
Castle
Ashby
CASTLE ASHBY
84
Sharnbrook
Great
Houghton
A428
Denton
Easton
Maudit
Bozeat
Odell
Radwell
M1
A5123
A5076
HUNSBURY
HILL
Hardingstone
SP
Yardley
Hastings
Harrold
Felmersham
HARROLD-ODELL
Wootton
B526
Chellington
Collingtree
Hackleton
YARDLEY
CHASE
B5388
Carlton
Pavenham
Milton
Malsor
Quinton
Horton
Piddington
Warrington
Lavendon
West End
Stevington
Oakley
Blisworth
A43
Courteenhall
B565
Cold
Brayfield
STEVINGTON
WINDMILL
A508
Salcey
Forest
Eakley
Lanes
Olney
Turvey
A428
Roade
Bromham
CANAL
MUSEUM
Grand Union
Canal
Hartwell
Weston
Underwood
Clifton
Reynes
Newton
Blossomville
Ravenstone
EMBERTON
Shutlanger
Stoke
Bruerne
Ashton
Emberton
Box
End
Stoke
Goldington
A509
Stagsden
STOKE PARK
PAVILIONS
Long
Street
MILTON KEYNES
Filgrave
Tyringham
Alderton
Grafton
Regis
Hanslope
Hardmead
A422
Astwood
Sherington
Tathall
End
Gayhurst
Great Ouse
Chicheley
North
Crawley
A508
Paulerspury
M1
B526
Lathbury
Bourne
End
Wootton
A5
Yardley
Gobion
Castlethorpe
Newport Pagnell
Upper
Shelton
NEWPORT
PAGNELL
SERVICES
BUCKINGHAM
THICK COPSE
Potterspury
Haversham
Broad
Green
Lower
Shelton
GULLIVER'S
LAND
Whittlewood
Forest
Cosgrove
Great
Linford
Cranfield
MARSTON
MORETAINE
Marston
Moretaine
New
Bradwell
Willen
Moulsoe
Old Stratford
Stony Stratford
Wolverton
A422
Milton
Keynes
A509
P&R
H5
Lillingstone
Lovell
Deanshanger
Passenham
H3
Bradwell
Broughton
ST LAWRENCE'S
Salford
Wicken
Calverton
MILTON
KEYNES
NATIONAL FILM
& SCI-FI MUS
Woolstone
Milton Keynes
Village
Lidlington
Millbrook
Leckhampstead
A422
Upper
Weald
Woughton on
the Green
A421
Brogborough
Beachampton
Loughton
A5
A4146
Wavendon
Aspley
Guise
A507
Res.
Thornton
Shenley
Church End
Simpson
Walton
Maids
Moreton
Shenley
Brook End
Woburn Sands
Bow
Brickhill
Aspley
Heath
Ridgmont
Husborne
Crawley
Steppingley
Buckingham
Whaddon
Whaddon
Nash
Bletchley
BLETCHLEY
PARK
Fenny
Stratford
WOBURN
WOBURN
SAFARI PARK
Thornborough
Tattenhoe
Far
Bletchley
Woburn
Eversholt
Church
End
A421
A421
B4034
Little
Brickhill
WOBURN
ABBEY
B5704
B5704
Singleborough
Chase
Padbury
Little
Horwood
Newton
Longville
Great
Brickhill
Tingrith
Great
Horwood
Milton Bryan
Adstock
B4033
Ouzel
KING'S WOOD
AND RUSHMERE
66
67
Potsgrove
A413
Drayton
Parslow
Stoke
Hammond
STOCKGROVE
PARK
Battlesden
Addington
Mursley
A4146
Toddington
Heath

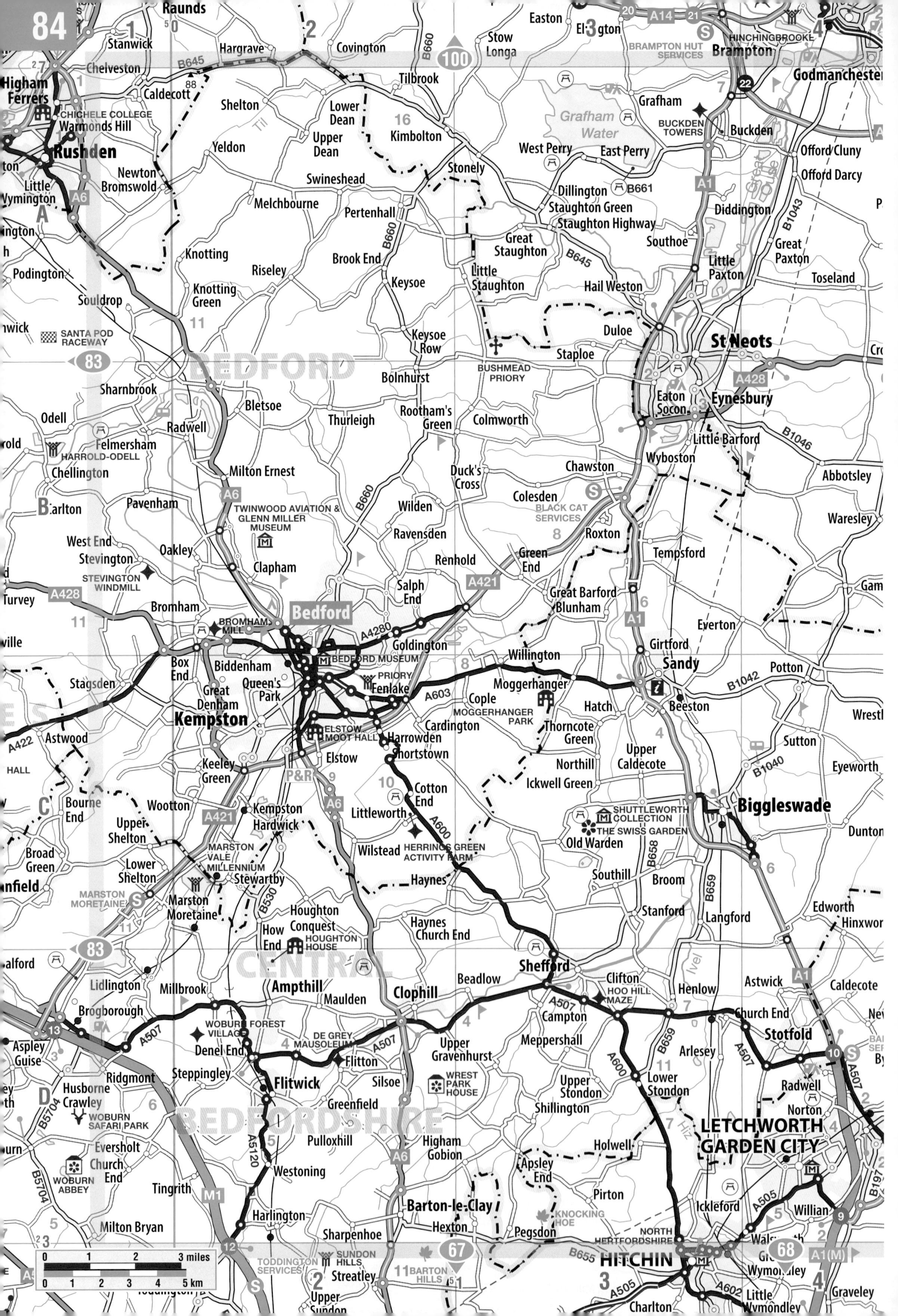
Raunds
Stanwick
Hargrave
Covington
Easton
Ellington
A14
Brampton Hut Services
Hinchingbrooke
Brampton
Godmanchester
Stow Longa
100
B660
Chelveston
B645
Tilbrook
Higham Ferrers
Caldecott
Shelton
Lower Dean
Grafham
Buckden Towers
Buckden
Chichele College
Warmonds Hill
Grafham Water
Upper Dean
Kimbolton
Rushden
Yeldon
West Perry
East Perry
Offord Cluny
Offord Darcy
Newton Bromswold
Stonely
Little Irchester
Wymington
A6
Swineshead
Dillington
B661
Melchbourne
Pertenhall
Staughton Green
Staughton Highway
Diddington
A1
B1043
Great Ouse
Great Staughton
Southoe
Great Paxton
Podington
Knotting
Riseley
Brook End
Keysoe
B645
Little Staughton
Little Paxton
Toseland
Hail Weston
Souldrop
Knotting Green
Duloe
Santa Pod Raceway
Keysoe Row
St Neots
Staploe
83
BEDFORD
Bushmead Priory
Sharnbrook
Bolnhurst
Eaton Socon
Eynesbury
A428
Odell
Bletsoe
Thurleigh
Rootham's Green
Colmworth
Radwell
Little Barford
B1046
Harrold
Felmersham
Harrold-Odell
Wyboston
Chellington
Milton Ernest
Duck's Cross
Chawston
Abbotsley
Carlton
Pavenham
Colesden
Black Cat Services
Twinwood Aviation & Glenn Miller Museum
Wilden
Waresley
West End
Roxton
Ravensden
Stevington
Oakley
Tempsford
Green End
Renhold
Stevington Windmill
Clapham
Salph End
A421
Great Barford
Gamlingay
Turvey
A428
Blunham
Bromham
Bedford
Bromham Mill
A4280
Everton
Goldington
Girtford
Biddenham
Bedford Museum
Willington
Sandy
Potton
Box End
Priory
B1042
Stagsden
Queen's Park
Fenlake
Moggerhanger
Great Denham
A603
Cople
Hatch
Beeston
Kempston
Moggerhanger Park
Wrestlingworth
Cardington
Thorncote Green
Astwood
Elstow Moot Hall
Harrowden
A422
Shortstown
Upper Caldecote
Sutton
Keeley Green
Elstow
Northill
B1040
Eyeworth
P&R
Ickwell Green
Bourne End
Cotton End
Wootton
Kempston Hardwick
Biggleswade
Shuttleworth Collection
Upper Shelton
Littleworth
The Swiss Garden
Dunton
A600
Old Warden
Broad Green
Wilstead
Herring's Green Activity Farm
Lower Shelton
Marston Vale Millennium
B658
Southill
Cranfield
Stewartby
Haynes
Broom
Marston Moretaine Services
Marston Moretaine
B530
B659
Houghton Conquest
Stanford
Langford
Edworth
Hinxworth
How End
Houghton House
Haynes Church End
CENTRAL
Salford
Shefford
Ivel
Lidlington
Millbrook
Ampthill
Beadlow
Clifton
Henlow
Astwick
Caldecote
Maulden
Clophill
Hoo Hill Maze
Brogborough
A507
Campton
Church End
Woburn Forest Village
Stotfold
Aspley Guise
De Grey Mausoleum
Upper Gravenhurst
Meppershall
Arlesey
Denel End
Flitton
Ridgmont
Steppingley
Wrest Park House
Lower Stondon
Upper Stondon
Radwell
Husborne Crawley
Flitwick
Silsoe
Woburn Safari Park
Greenfield
Shillington
Norton
BEDFORDSHIRE
Letchworth Garden City
Eversholt
Pulloxhill
Higham Gobion
Holwell
A5120
Church End
Westoning
Apsley End
Woburn Abbey
Tingrith
M1
Barton-le-Clay
Pirton
B5704
Knocking Hoe
Ickleford
A505
Willian
Harlington
Milton Bryan
Hexton
Pegsdon
Sharpenhoe
North Hertfordshire
67
Toddington Services
Sundon Hills
Barton Hills
B655
Hitchin
68
Wymondley
Streatley
A1(M)
A602
Little Wymondley
Graveley
Upper Sundon
Charlton
0 1 2 3 miles
0 1 2 3 4 5 km

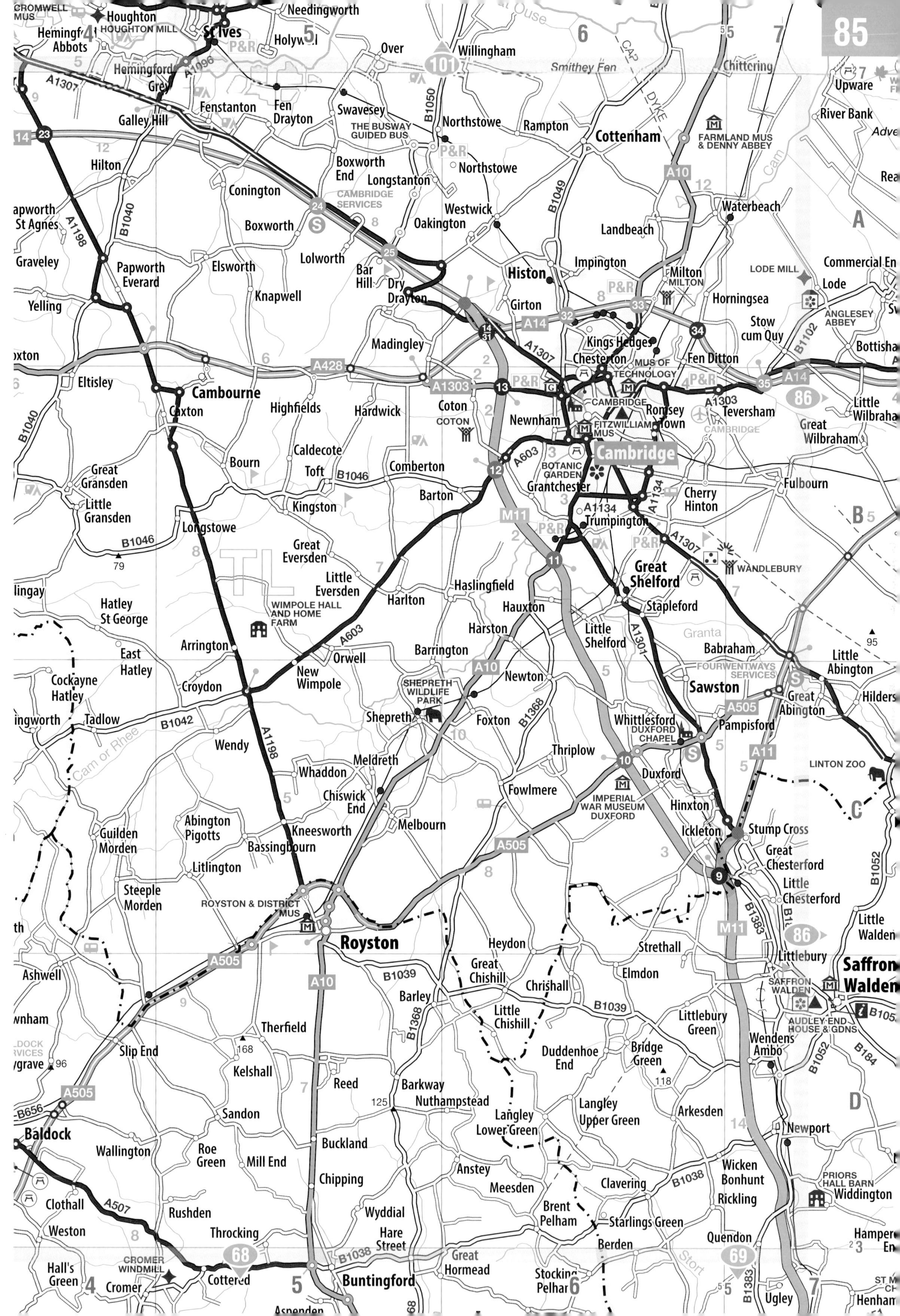
85
Cromwell Mus
Houghton
Houghton Mill
Hemingford Abbots
St Ives
Needingworth
Holywell
Over
Willingham
Smithey Fen
Chittering
Upware
River Bank
Hemingford Grey
A1096
A1307
Fenstanton
Fen Drayton
Swavesey
The Busway Guided Bus
B1050
Northstowe
Rampton
Cottenham
Car Dyke
Farmland Mus & Denny Abbey
Galley Hill
Hilton
Conington
Boxworth End
Longstanton
Cambridge Services
Northstowe
B1049
A10
Waterbeach
Papworth St Agnes
A1198
B1040
Boxworth
Westwick
Oakington
Landbeach
Graveley
Papworth Everard
Elsworth
Lolworth
Bar Hill
Dry Drayton
Histon
Impington
Milton
Milton
Lode Mill
Lode
Commercial End
Horningsea
Yelling
Knapwell
Girton
A14
Stow cum Quy
Anglesey Abbey
B1102
Bottisham
Madingley
Kings Hedges
Chesterton
Fen Ditton
Mus of Technology
A428
Eltisley
Cambourne
Caxton
Highfields
Hardwick
A1303
Coton
Coton
Newnham
Cambridge
Romsey Town
Teversham
Fitzwilliam Mus
Cambridge
Little Wilbraham
Great Wilbraham
B1040
Bourn
Caldecote
Toft
B1046
Comberton
A603
Botanic Garden
Grantchester
Cambridge
Fulbourn
Great Gransden
Little Gransden
Kingston
Barton
Cherry Hinton
A1134
Trumpington
M11
Longstowe
B1046
79
Great Eversden
Little Eversden
Great Shelford
A1307
Wandlebury
Gamlingay
Hatley St George
Wimpole Hall and Home Farm
Harlton
Haslingfield
Hauxton
Stapleford
Harston
Little Shelford
A1301
Granta
Babraham
95
East Hatley
Arrington
Orwell
Barrington
Fourwentways Services
Little Abington
Cockayne Hatley
Croydon
New Wimpole
Shepreth Wildlife Park
Newton
Sawston
Great Abington
Hildersham
Wrestlingworth
Tadlow
B1042
Shepreth
Foxton
B1368
Whittlesford
Duxford Chapel
A505
Pampisford
Cam or Rhee
Wendy
Meldreth
Thriplow
A11
Whaddon
Duxford
Linton Zoo
Chiswick End
Fowlmere
Imperial War Museum Duxford
Hinxton
Abington Pigotts
Guilden Morden
Kneesworth
Melbourn
Ickleton
Stump Cross
Bassingbourn
Great Chesterford
Litlington
Steeple Morden
Royston & District Mus
Little Chesterford
B1052
B1383
Little Walden
Royston
Heydon
Strethall
Ashwell
Great Chishill
Elmdon
Littlebury
Saffron Walden
B1039
Barley
Chrishall
Saffron Walden
Audley End House & Gdns
Newnham
Little Chishill
B1039
Littlebury Green
Therfield
Slip End
168
Duddenhoe End
Bridge Green
Wendens Ambo
Baldock Services
Bygrave
96
Kelshall
118
B184
Reed
Barkway
Nuthampstead
125
Langley Upper Green
Arkesden
Sandon
Langley Lower Green
Newport
Baldock
Buckland
Wallington
Roe Green
Mill End
Anstey
Wicken Bonhunt
Chipping
Clavering
B1038
Priors Hall Barn
Clothall
A507
Meesden
Rickling
Widdington
Rushden
Wyddial
Brent Pelham
Starlings Green
Weston
Throcking
Hare Street
Quendon
Hampers End
Berden
Hall's Green
Cromer Windmill
Cottered
Buntingford
B1038
Great Hormead
Stocking Pelham
Stort
Cromer
Ugley
Henham
Aspenden
86
68
69
101

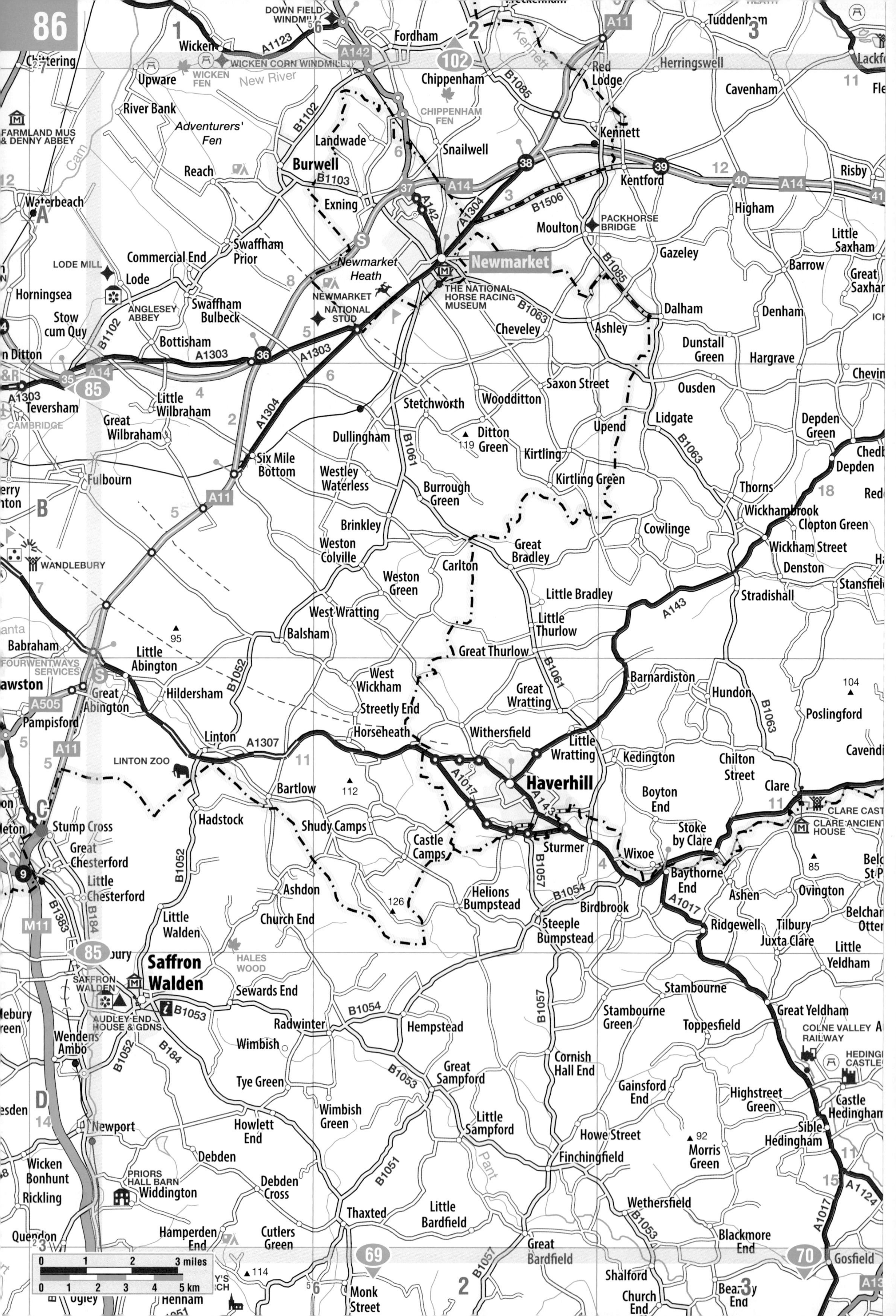
86
DOWN FIELD WINDMILL
Fordham
Tuddenham
Wicken
A1123
A142
Chippenham
102
Red Lodge
Herringswell
Lackford
Chittering
Upware
WICKEN CORN WINDMILL
WICKEN FEN
New River
Kennett
B1085
Cavenham
River Bank
CHIPPENHAM FEN
Adventurers' Fen
B1102
Landwade
Kennett
FARMLAND MUS & DENNY ABBEY
Cam
Snailwell
Reach
Burwell
B1103
38
39
Kentford
12
40
A14
Risby
Waterbeach
Exning
37
A14
A142
A1304
B1506
Higham
Moulton
PACKHORSE BRIDGE
Little Saxham
Commercial End
Swaffham Prior
Newmarket Heath
Newmarket
Gazeley
Barrow
LODE MILL
Lode
NEWMARKET
THE NATIONAL HORSE RACING MUSEUM
B1085
Great Saxham
Horningsea
Swaffham Bulbeck
NATIONAL STUD
B1063
Dalham
Denham
Stow cum Quy
ANGLESEY ABBEY
Cheveley
Ashley
Bottisham
A1303
Dunstall Green
Hargrave
B1102
A1303
36
Fen Ditton
A14
35
85
Saxon Street
Ousden
Chevington
A1303
Teversham
Little Wilbraham
Woodditton
Stetchworth
CAMBRIDGE
Great Wilbraham
A1304
Lidgate
Depden Green
Dullingham
Ditton Green
Upend
Kirtling
B1063
Chedburgh
Depden
Six Mile Bottom
Westley Waterless
B1061
Kirtling Green
Fulbourn
Burrough Green
Thorns
18
A11
Wickhambrook
Clopton Green
Brinkley
Cowlinge
Weston Colville
Great Bradley
Wickham Street
Denston
WANDLEBURY
Carlton
Weston Green
Stansfield
Little Bradley
Stradishall
A143
West Wratting
Little Thurlow
Balsham
95
Babraham
Great Thurlow
Little Abington
FOURWENTWAYS SERVICES
B1061
Barnardiston
104
West Wickham
Hundon
Sawston
Great Abington
Hildersham
B1052
Great Wratting
A505
B1063
Streetly End
Poslingford
Pampisford
Horseheath
Withersfield
Linton
A1307
Little Wratting
Cavendish
A11
LINTON ZOO
Kedington
Chilton Street
Haverhill
Boyton End
Clare
Bartlow
112
A1017
A143
CLARE CASTLE
Stump Cross
Hadstock
CLARE ANCIENT HOUSE
Shudy Camps
Stoke by Clare
Castle Camps
Sturmer
Great Chesterford
Wixoe
85
Belchamp St Paul
B1052
Baythorne End
Little Chesterford
Ashdon
B1057
Helions Bumpstead
B1054
Ashen
Ovington
A1017
Birdbrook
126
Belchamp Otten
B1383
B184
Church End
Little Walden
Steeple Bumpstead
Ridgewell
Tilbury Juxta Clare
M11
85
Saffron Walden
HALES WOOD
Little Yeldham
SAFFRON WALDEN
Stambourne
Sewards End
B1057
B1053
B1054
Stambourne Green
Great Yeldham
AUDLEY END HOUSE & GDNS
Radwinter
Hempstead
Toppesfield
COLNE VALLEY RAILWAY
Wendens Ambo
Wimbish
B184
HEDINGHAM CASTLE
B1052
Cornish Hall End
B1053
Great Sampford
Gainsford End
Tye Green
Castle Hedingham
Highstreet Green
Wimbish Green
Little Sampford
Sible Hedingham
Newport
Howlett End
Howe Street
92
Morris Green
Wicken Bonhunt
Debden
Finchingfield
Pant
B1051
PRIORS HALL BARN
Widdington
Rickling
Debden Cross
Wethersfield
A1124
Thaxted
Little Bardfield
B1053
A1017
Quendon
Hamperden End
Cutlers Green
Blackmore End
Great Bardfield
69
B1057
70
Gosfield
114
Shalford
Monk Street
Church End
Beazley End
3 miles
5 km

Bury St Edmunds
Stowmarket
Needham Market
Hadleigh
Sudbury
Halstead
Lavenham
Long Melford
Ixworth
Woolpit
Elmswell
Haughley
Bacton
Capel St Mary
East Bergholt
Dedham
Lawford
Nayland
Bures
Boxford
Kersey
Bildeston
Chelsworth
Great Cornard
Glemsford
Clare
Horringer
Ickworth House
Cathedral and Abbey Ruins
Melford Hall
Kentwell Hall
Guildhall
Gainsborough's Ho
Woolpit & District Museum
The Museum of Food
Wattisham Station Heritage Mus
Wolves Wood RSPB Reserve
Bridge Cottage
The Munnings Art Museum
East Anglian Railway Museum
Haughley Park
Bradfield Woods
Needham Lake
St James's Chapel
St Peter & St Paul
Abbey (Rem)
Dedham Vale
Colne Valley
Stour
Gipping
Brett
A14
A134
A143
A1141
A1071
A1092
A131
A12
A137
A1088
A1101
B1066
B1065
B1064
B1071
B1115
B1106
B1113
B1078
B1070
B1068
B1087
B1508
B1029
B1115
88
70
71
103
TL

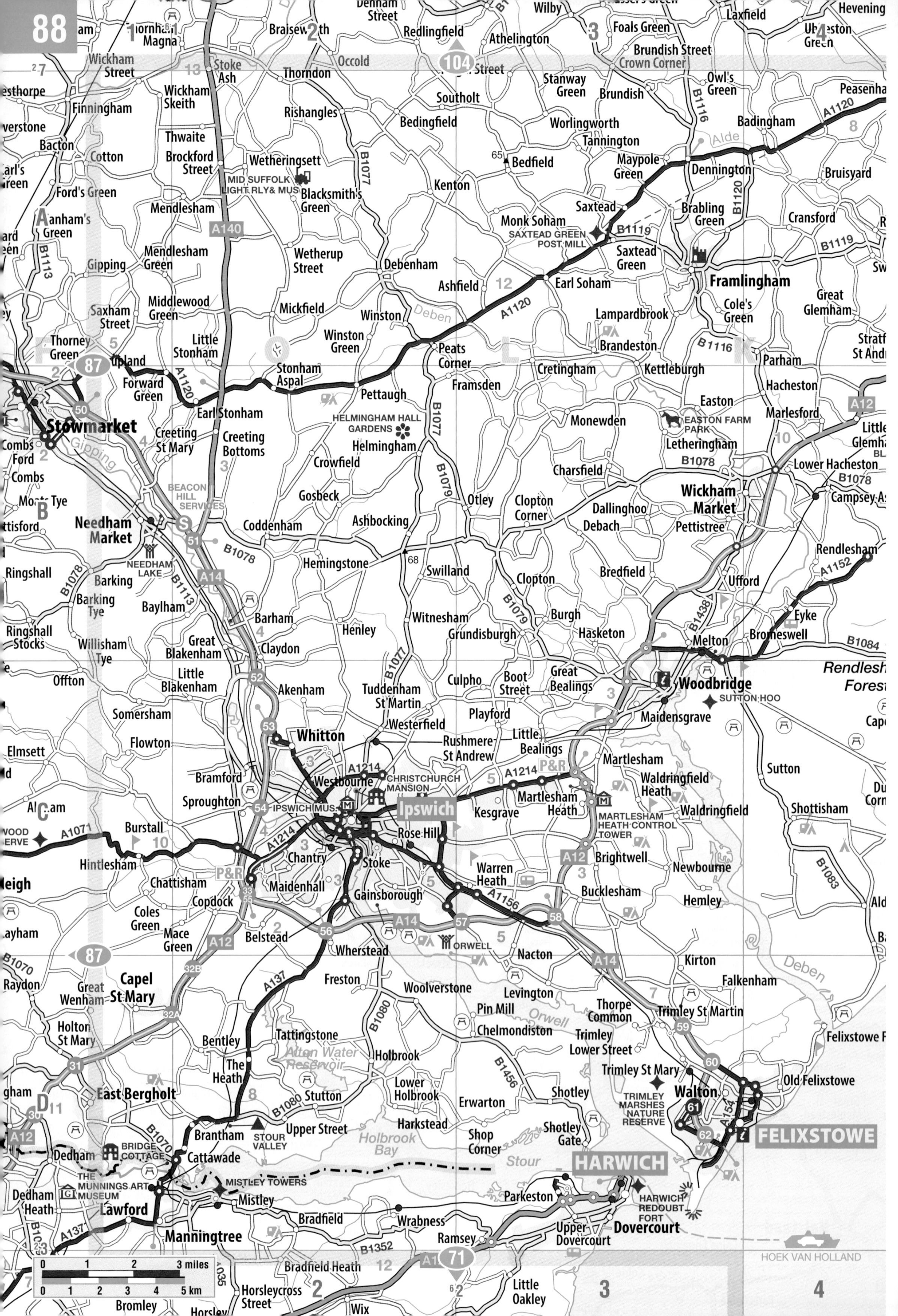
Thornham Magna
Braiseworth
Denham Street
Redlingfield
Wilby
Laxfield
Hevening
Foals Green
Ubbeston Green
Wickham Street
Occold
Athelington
Brundish Street
Crown Corner
Stoke Ash
Thorndon
Owl's Green
Peasenhall
Finningham
Wickham Skeith
Southolt
Stanway Green
Brundish
Rishangles
Bedingfield
Worlingworth
Badingham
Thwaite
Tannington
Alde
Bacton
Cotton
Brockford Street
Wetheringsett
Bedfield
Maypole Green
Dennington
Bruisyard
MID SUFFOLK LIGHT RLY & MUS
Kenton
Ford's Green
Blacksmith's Green
Saxtead
Brabling Green
Cransford
Mendlesham
Monk Soham
Wickham Skeith
SAXTEAD GREEN POST MILL
Saxtead Green
Mendlesham Green
Gipping
Wetherup Street
Debenham
Framlingham
Earl Soham
Ashfield
Great Glemham
Middlewood Green
Saxham Street
Mickfield
Winston
Deben
Lampardbrook
Cole's Green
Thorney Green
Little Stonham
Winston Green
Peats Corner
Brandeston
Parham
Upland
Forward Green
Stonham Aspal
Framsden
Cretingham
Kettleburgh
Stratford St Andrew
Stowmarket
Earl Stonham
Pettaugh
Hacheston
Easton
Creeting St Mary
Creeting Bottoms
HELMINGHAM HALL GARDENS
Helmingham
Monewden
EASTON FARM PARK
Marlesford
Combs Ford
Combs
Gipping
Crowfield
Letheringham
Little Glemham
Charsfield
Lower Hacheston
BEACON HILL SERVICES
Gosbeck
Wickham Market
Campsey Ash
Needham Market
Otley
Clopton Corner
Dallinghoo
Debach
Pettistree
Coddenham
Ashbocking
Rendlesham
NEEDHAM LAKE
Ringshall
Barking
Hemingstone
Swilland
Clopton
Bredfield
Ufford
Barking Tye
Baylham
Barham
Henley
Witnesham
Grundisburgh
Burgh
Hasketon
Eyke
Ringshall Stocks
Willisham Tye
Great Blakenham
Claydon
Melton
Bromeswell
Offton
Little Blakenham
Akenham
Tuddenham St Martin
Culpho
Boot Street
Great Bealings
Woodbridge
Rendlesham Forest
SUTTON HOO
Somersham
Playford
Maidensgrave
Westerfield
Whitton
Flowton
Rushmere St Andrew
Little Bealings
Elmsett
Martlesham
Sutton
Bramford
Westbourne
CHRISTCHURCH MANSION
Waldringfield Heath
Sproughton
IPSWICH MUS.
Ipswich
Kesgrave
Martlesham Heath
MARTLESHAM HEATH CONTROL TOWER
Waldringfield
Shottisham
Burstall
Rose Hill
Hintlesham
Chantry
Stoke
Brightwell
Warren Heath
Newbourne
Chattisham
Maidenhall
Gainsborough
Bucklesham
Copdock
Hemley
Coles Green
Mace Green
Belstead
Wherstead
ORWELL
Nacton
Raydon
Capel St Mary
Great Wenham
Freston
Woolverstone
Levington
Kirton
Falkenham
Deben
Pin Mill
Thorpe Common
Trimley St Martin
Holton St Mary
Chelmondiston
Orwell
Tattingstone
Bentley
Trimley Lower Street
Felixstowe Ferry
Alton Water Reservoir
Holbrook
The Heath
Trimley St Mary
East Bergholt
Stutton
Lower Holbrook
Erwarton
Shotley
Walton
Old Felixstowe
TRIMLEY MARSHES NATURE RESERVE
Brantham
STOUR VALLEY
Upper Street
Harkstead
Shotley Gate
Holbrook Bay
Shop Corner
FELIXSTOWE
Dedham
BRIDGE COTTAGE
Cattawade
Stour
HARWICH
THE MUNNINGS ART MUSEUM
MISTLEY TOWERS
Dedham Heath
Lawford
Mistley
Parkeston
HARWICH REDOUBT FORT
Bradfield
Wrabness
Upper Dovercourt
Dovercourt
Manningtree
Ramsey
HOEK VAN HOLLAND
Bradfield Heath
Horsleycross Street
Little Oakley
Bromley
Wix
0 1 2 3 miles
0 1 2 3 4 5 km

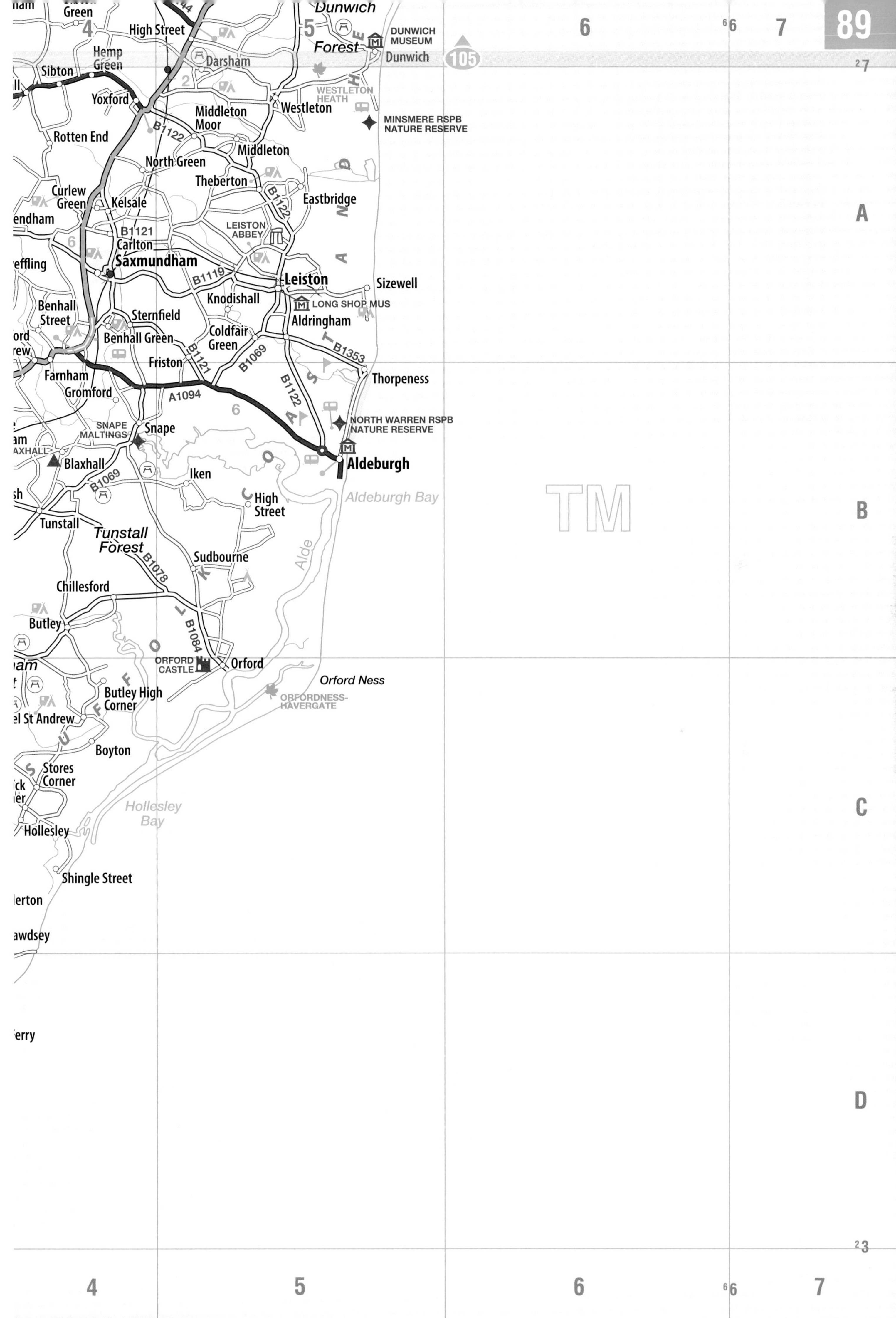
Dunwich
Forest
DUNWICH MUSEUM
Dunwich
105
High Street
Hemp Green
Darsham
Sibton
Yoxford
WESTLETON HEATH
Westleton
MINSMERE RSPB NATURE RESERVE
Middleton Moor
B1122
Rotten End
Middleton
North Green
Theberton
Eastbridge
Curlew Green
Kelsale
LEISTON ABBEY
B1121
Carlton
Saxmundham
B1119
Leiston
Sizewell
Knodishall
LONG SHOP MUS
Benhall Street
Sternfield
Aldringham
Coldfair Green
Benhall Green
B1353
B1069
Friston
Farnham
Thorpeness
Gromford
A1094
SNAPE MALTINGS
Snape
NORTH WARREN RSPB NATURE RESERVE
Blaxhall
Aldeburgh
Iken
Aldeburgh Bay
High Street
Tunstall
Tunstall Forest
TM
B1078
Sudbourne
Alde
Chillesford
Butley
B1084
ORFORD CASTLE
Orford
Orford Ness
Butley High Corner
ORFORDNESS-HAVERGATE
Boyton
Stores Corner
Hollesley Bay
Hollesley
Shingle Street
A
B
C
D
4
5
6
7

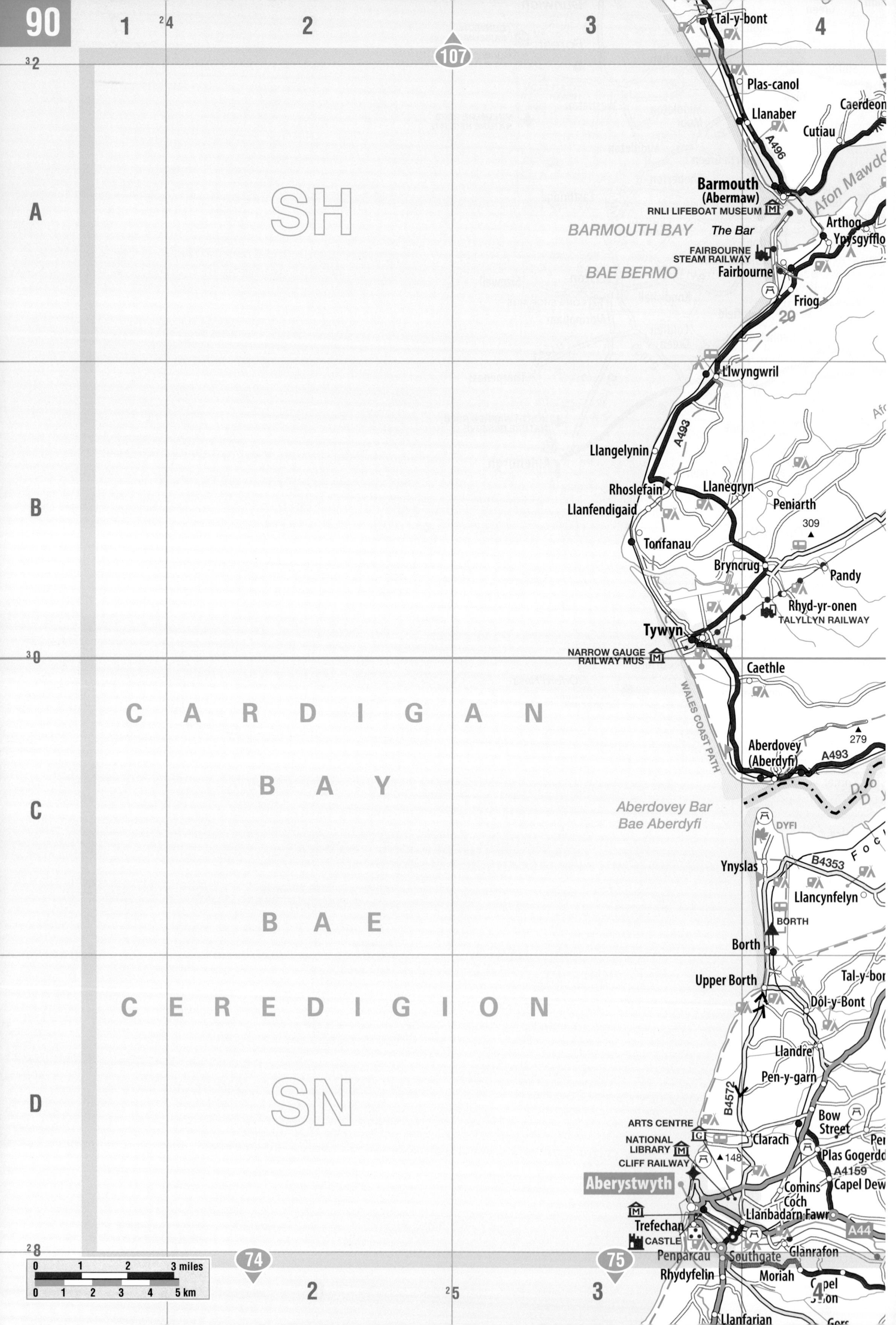

1
2
3
4
107
A
B
C
D
SH
SN
Tal-y-bont
Plas-canol
Llanaber
Caerdeon
Cutiau
A496
Barmouth
(Abermaw)
RNLI LIFEBOAT MUSEUM
Afon Mawdd
BARMOUTH BAY
The Bar
Arthog
Ynysgyfflo
FAIRBOURNE
STEAM RAILWAY
BAE BERMO
Fairbourne
Friog
20
Llwyngwril
A493
Llangelynin
Rhoslefain
Llanegryn
Llanfendigaid
Peniarth
309
Tonfanau
Bryncrug
Pandy
Rhyd-yr-onen
TALYLLYN RAILWAY
Tywyn
NARROW GAUGE
RAILWAY MUS
Caethle
WALES COAST PATH
C A R D I G A N
B A Y
B A E
C E R E D I G I O N
Aberdovey
(Aberdyfi)
279
A493
Aberdovey Bar
Bae Aberdyfi
DYFI
Ynyslas
B4353
Llancynfelyn
BORTH
Borth
Upper Borth
Tal-y-bon
Dôl-y-Bont
Llandre
Pen-y-garn
B4572
ARTS CENTRE
NATIONAL
LIBRARY
CLIFF RAILWAY
Bow
Street
Clarach
148
Plas Gogerdd
A4159
Aberystwyth
Comins
Coch
Capel Dew
Llanbadarn Fawr
A44
Trefechan
CASTLE
Glanrafon
Penparcau
Southgate
Rhydyfelin
Moriah
Capel
Seion
Llanfarian
74
75
0 1 2 3 miles
0 1 2 3 4 5 km

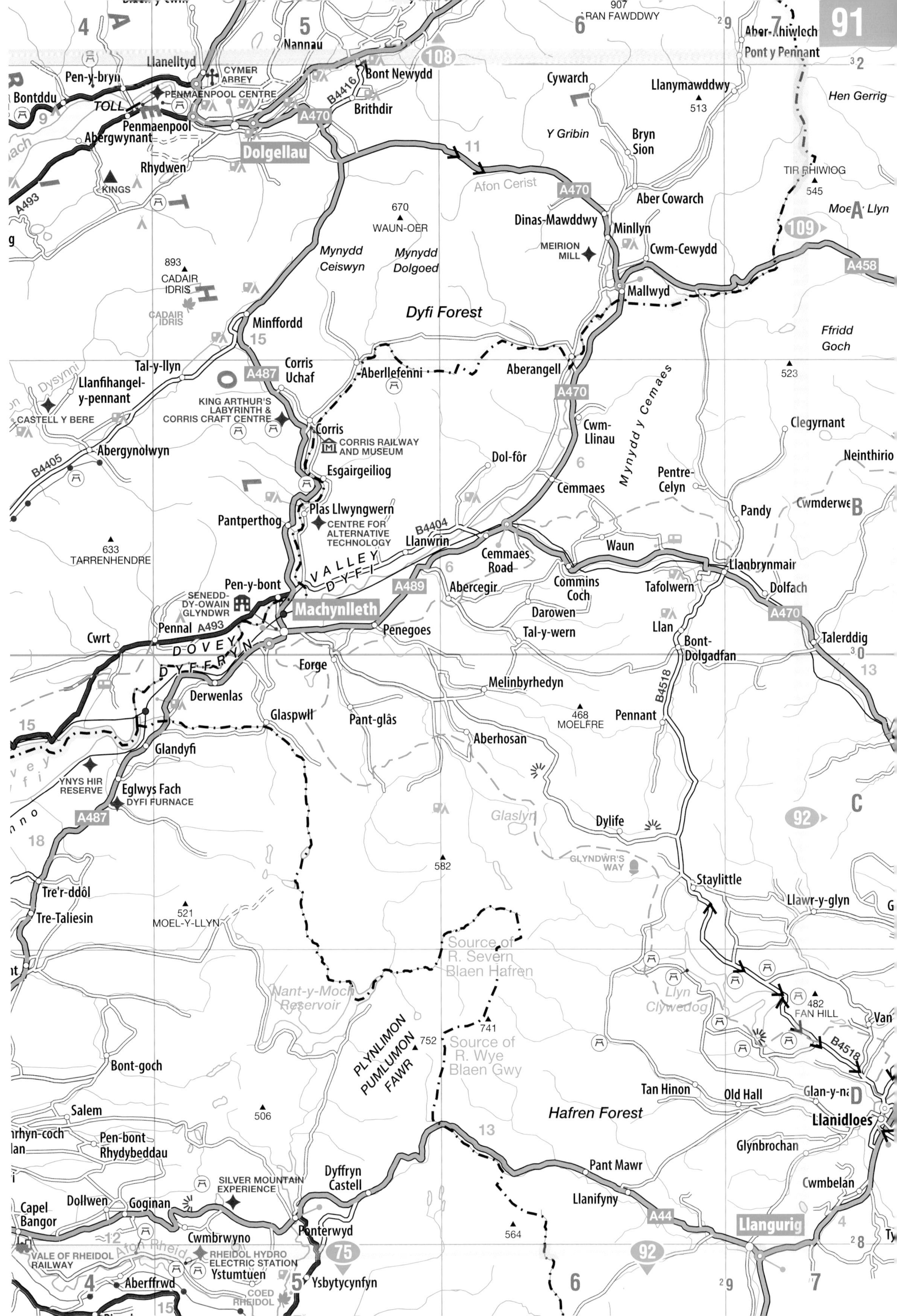

Nannau
Llanelltyd
CYMER ABBEY
Pen-y-bryn
Bontddu
PENMAENPOOL CENTRE
TOLL
Penmaenpool
Abergwynant
Dolgellau
Rhydwen
KINGS
Bont Newydd
Brithdir
B4416
A470
108
907
RAN FAWDDWY
Aber-Rhiwlech
Pont y Pennant
Cywarch
Llanymawddwy
513
Hen Gerrig
Y Gribin
Bryn Sion
TIR RHIWIOG
545
Afon Cerist
A470
Aber Cowarch
Dinas-Mawddwy
Minllyn
Moel Llyn
109
670
WAUN-OER
Mynydd Ceiswyn
Mynydd Dolgoed
MEIRION MILL
Cwm-Cewydd
A458
893
CADAIR IDRIS
Mallwyd
Dyfi Forest
Minffordd
Ffridd Goch
Tal-y-llyn
Corris Uchaf
Aberllefenni
Aberangell
523
Dysynni
Llanfihangel-y-pennant
A487
A470
KING ARTHUR'S LABYRINTH & CORRIS CRAFT CENTRE
CASTELL Y BERE
Corris
Cwm-Llinau
Mynydd y Cemaes
Clegyrnant
CORRIS RAILWAY AND MUSEUM
Abergynolwyn
Dol-fôr
Neinthirio
B4405
Esgairgeiliog
Pentre-Celyn
Cemmaes
Cwmderwen
Plas Llwyngwern
Pandy
Pantperthog
CENTRE FOR ALTERNATIVE TECHNOLOGY
B4404
Llanwrin
633
TARRENHENDRE
Cemmaes Road
Waun
Llanbrynmair
VALLEY
DYFI
Pen-y-bont
A489
Abercegir
Commins Coch
Tafolwern
Dolfach
SENEDD-DY-OWAIN GLYNDWR
Machynlleth
Darowen
A470
Pennal
A493
Llan
Cwrt
Penegoes
Tal-y-wern
Talerddig
DOVEY
DYFFRYN
Bont-Dolgadfan
Forge
Melinbyrhedyn
Derwenlas
B4518
Glaspwll
Pant-glâs
468
MOELFRE
Pennant
Aberhosan
Glandyfi
Dovey
Dyfi
YNYS HIR RESERVE
Eglwys Fach
DYFI FURNACE
A487
Glaslyn
Dylife
92
582
GLYNDWR'S WAY
Tre'r-ddôl
Staylittle
Llawr-y-glyn
Tre-Taliesin
521
MOEL-Y-LLYN
Source of R. Severn
Blaen Hafren
Nant-y-Moch Reservoir
Llyn Clywedog
482
FAN HILL
741
PLYNLIMON
PUMLUMON FAWR
752
Source of R. Wye
Blaen Gwy
B4518
Bont-goch
Tan Hinon
Old Hall
Glan-y-nant
Salem
506
Hafren Forest
Llanidloes
Pen-bont Rhydybeddau
13
Glynbrochan
Dyffryn Castell
Pant Mawr
SILVER MOUNTAIN EXPERIENCE
Cwmbelan
Capel Bangor
Dollwen
Goginan
Llanifyny
A44
Llangurig
Ponterwyd
Cwmbrwyno
VALE OF RHEIDOL RAILWAY
Afon Rheidol
RHEIDOL HYDRO ELECTRIC STATION
75
92
564
Aberffrwd
Ystumtuen
Ysbytycynfyn
COED RHEIDOL

Dyfi Forest
Corris Uchaf
Aberllefenni
Aberangell
A470
Mynydd y Cemaes
Ffridd Goch
523
Foel
109
Llangadfan
330
Pen Coed
GLYNDŴR'S WAY
Llanerfyl
Corris
CORRIS RAILWAY AND MUSEUM
Cwm-Llinau
Clegyrnant
Dolwen
Sychtyn
Melin-y-grug
Esgairgeiliog
Dol-fôr
Neinthirion
Pentre-Celyn
Cemmaes
Plas Llwyngwern
CENTRE FOR ALTERNATIVE TECHNOLOGY
Pandy
Cwmderwen
Mynydd Waun Fawr
B4404
Llanwrin
Waun
DYFI VALLEY
Cemmaes Road
Llanbrynmair
A489
Abercegir
Commins Coch
Tafolwern
Dolfach
440
Machynlleth
Darowen
Llan
A470
Penegoes
Tal-y-wern
Bont-Dolgadfan
Talerddig
Rhyd
Forge
Melinbyrhedyn
B4518
13
Glaspwll
Pant-glâs
468 MOELFRE
Pennant
91
Aberhosan
Carno
458
B
Glaslyn
Clatter
Dylife
398
Llanwnog
582
GLYNDŴR'S WAY
Staylittle
Caersws
Llawr-y-glyn
Gleiniant
B4569
Source of R. Severn Blaen Hafren
Trefeglwys
Nant-y-Moch Reservoir
Llyn Clywedog
482 FAN HILL
Little London
741
PLYNLIMON PUMLUMON FAWR
752
Van
Oakley Park
307
Llandinam
Source of R. Wye Blaen Gwy
B4518
SN
Severn (Hafren)
C
A470
Tan Hinon
Old Hall
Glan-y-nant
Hafren Forest
Llanidloes
13
Glynbrochan
Newchapel
Pant Mawr
Dyffryn Castell
Cwmbelan
Llanifyny
GLYNDŴR'S WAY
A44
Llangurig
Ponterwyd
564
91
Tylwch
584
Ysbytycynfyn
David's
75
610 PEN Y GARN
Nantgwyn
Devil's Bridge
B4343
B4518
Blaenycwm
D
A470
Pant-y-dwr
Cwmystwyth
B4574
Bwlch-y-sarnau
498
HAFOD ESTATE
Wye (Gwy)
St Harmon
Pont-rhyd-y-groes
571 GEIFAS
Ysbyty Ystwyth
505 MOEL HYWEL
Craig-goch Res.
76
0 1 2 3 miles
0 1 2 3 4 5 km
CLAERWEN
WELSH ROYAL CRYSTAL
Rhayader (Rhaeadr Gwy)
Gaufron
Penygarreg Res.
Pont-rhyd-y-groes

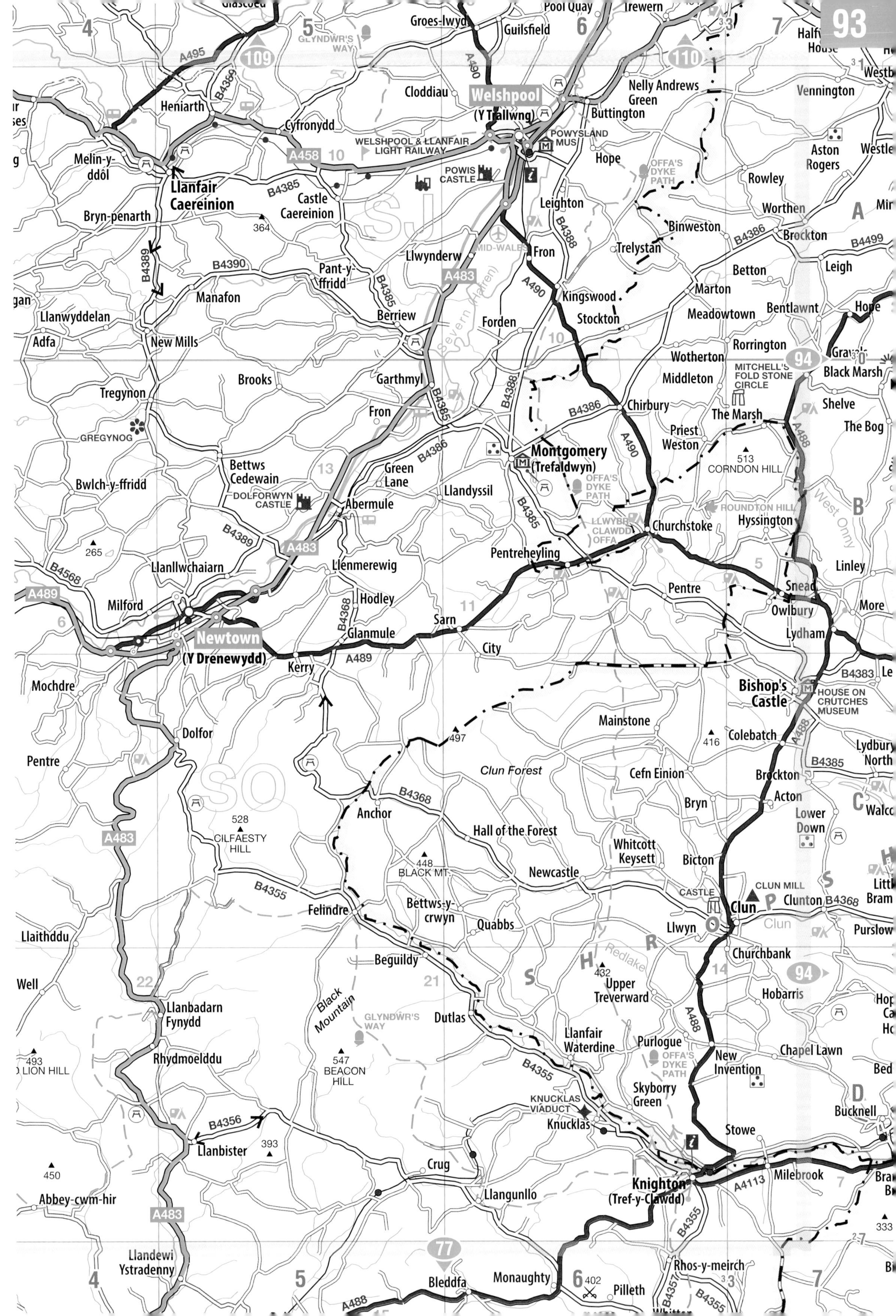
Groes-lwyd
Pool Quay
Trewern
Guilsfield
GLYNDŴR'S WAY
109
110
A495
A490
B4392
Cloddiau
Welshpool
(Y Trallwng)
Nelly Andrews Green
Buttington
Vennington
Heniarth
Cyfronydd
WELSHPOOL & LLANFAIR LIGHT RAILWAY
POWYSLAND MUS
Hope
Aston Rogers
Melin-y-ddôl
A458
Llanfair Caereinion
POWIS CASTLE
OFFA'S DYKE PATH
Rowley
B4385
Castle Caereinion
Leighton
Worthen
Bryn-penarth
364
SJ
Binweston
B4386
Brockton
B4499
B4389
B4390
Llwynderw
MID-WALES
Fron
B4388
Trelystan
Leigh
Pant-y-ffridd
A483
Severn (Hafren)
Betton
Manafon
B4385
Kingswood
Marton
Llanwyddelan
Berriew
Forden
Stockton
Meadowtown
Bentlawnt
Hope
Adfa
New Mills
Rorrington
Wotherton
94
Black Marsh
Brooks
Garthmyl
Middleton
MITCHELL'S FOLD STONE CIRCLE
Tregynon
Fron
B4388
B4365
B4386
Chirbury
Shelve
The Marsh
GREGYNOG
Priest Weston
The Bog
A488
Bettws Cedewain
B4386
Green Lane
Montgomery (Trefaldwyn)
A490
513
CORNDON HILL
Bwlch-y-ffridd
DOLFORWYN CASTLE
Abermule
Llandyssil
OFFA'S DYKE PATH
B4385
ROUNDTON HILL
Hyssington
West Onny
B
265
B4389
A483
LLWYBR CLAWDD OFFA
Churchstoke
Llanllwchaiarn
Llanmerewig
Pentreheyling
Linley
B4568
A489
Hodley
Pentre
Snead
Milford
B4368
Owlbury
More
Sarn
Lydham
Newtown
(Y Drenewydd)
Glanmule
A489
City
Kerry
B4383
Mochdre
Bishop's Castle
HOUSE ON CRUTCHES MUSEUM
Mainstone
Dolfor
497
416
Colebatch
Pentre
A488
Lydbury North
B4385
SO
Clun Forest
Cefn Einion
Brockton
B4368
Acton
Anchor
Bryn
C
Lower Down
528
CILFAESTY HILL
Hall of the Forest
A483
Whitcott Keysett
448
BLACK MT.
Bicton
Newcastle
B4355
CLUN MILL
Felindre
Bettws-y-crwyn
CASTLE
Clun
Clunton
B4368
Quabbs
Clun
Llwyn
Llaithddu
Redlake
Churchbank
Purslow
Beguildy
432
Upper Treverward
94
Well
Black Mountain
Hobarris
Llanbadarn Fynydd
GLYNDŴR'S WAY
Dutlas
A488
Llanfair Waterdine
Purlogue
Chapel Lawn
493
LION HILL
Rhydmoelddu
547
BEACON HILL
B4355
OFFA'S DYKE PATH
New Invention
KNUCKLAS VIADUCT
Skyborry Green
D
Bucknell
B4356
Knucklas
Stowe
Llanbister
393
Crug
450
Milebrook
A4113
Knighton
(Tref-y-Clawdd)
Abbey-cwm-hir
Llangunllo
A483
B4355
333
Llandewi Ystradenny
77
Rhos-y-meirch
Bleddfa
Monaughty
402
Pilleth
B4357
B4355
A488
4
5
6
7
A
S
H
R
O
P

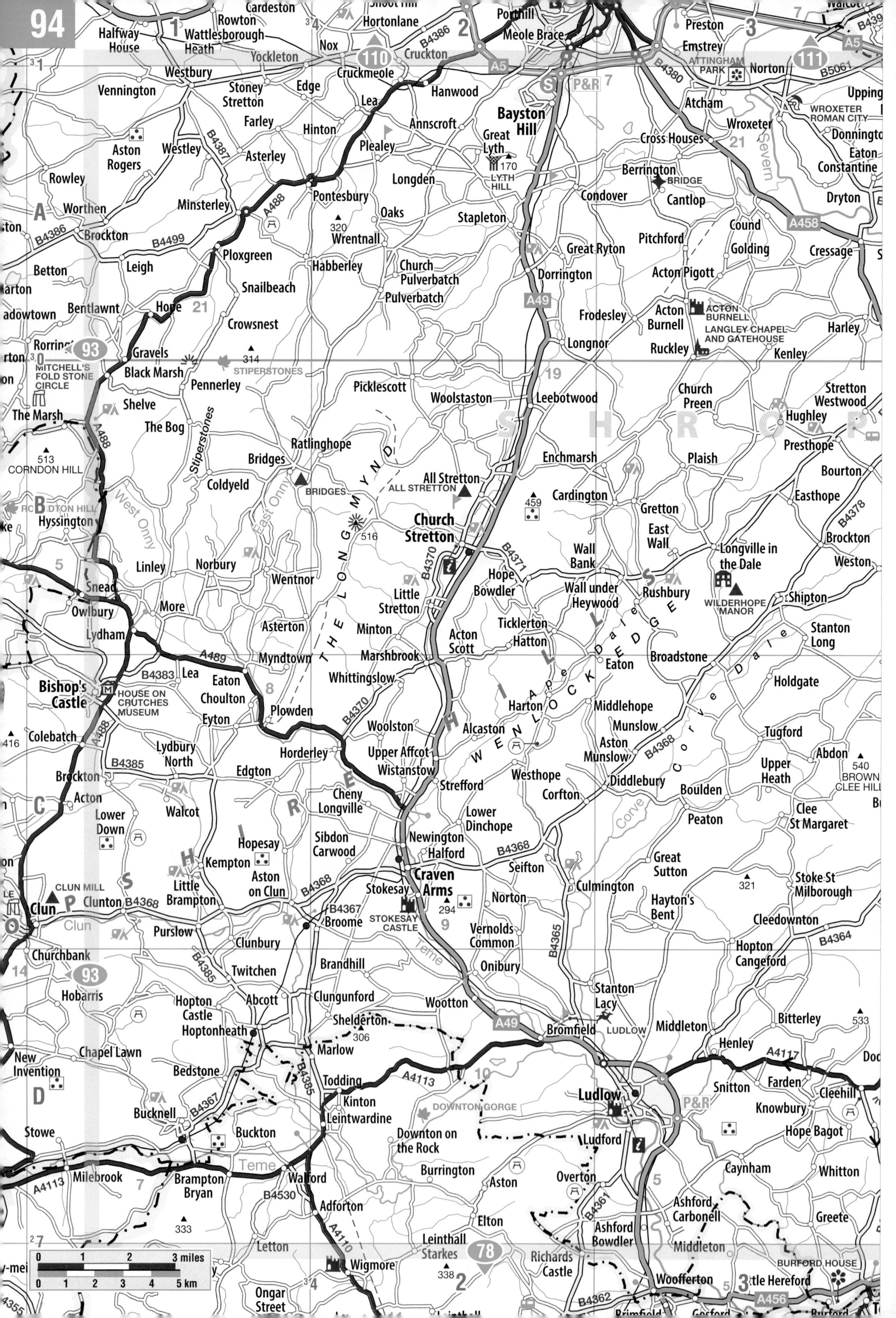
Cardeston
Rowton
Halfway House
Wattlesborough Heath
Hortonlane
Porthill
Meole Brace
Preston
Emstrey
Nox
Cruckton
Yockleton
110
111
ATTINGHAM PARK
Norton
A5
B4386
B4380
B5061
Westbury
Vennington
Stoney Stretton
Edge
Cruckmeole
Hanwood
P&R
Bayston Hill
Atcham
Uppington
WROXETER ROMAN CITY
Wroxeter
Farley
Lea
Hinton
Annscroft
Great Lyth
Cross Houses
Donnington
Aston Rogers
Westley
B4387
Asterley
Plealey
Eaton Constantine
Rowley
Longden
170
LYTH HILL
Berrington
BRIDGE
Severn
Minsterley
Pontesbury
Condover
Cantlop
Dryton
Worthen
A488
Oaks
Stapleton
Cound
A458
B4386
Brockton
320
Wrentnall
Pitchford
B4499
Golding
Cressage
Ploxgreen
Great Ryton
Betton
Leigh
Habberley
Church Pulverbatch
Dorrington
Acton Pigott
Snailbeach
Pulverbatch
A49
Bentlawnt
Hope
Frodesley
Acton Burnell
ACTON BURNELL
LANGLEY CHAPEL AND GATEHOUSE
Harley
Crowsnest
93
Gravels
314
Longnor
Ruckley
Kenley
MITCHELL'S FOLD STONE CIRCLE
Black Marsh
STIPERSTONES
Pennerley
Picklescott
19
Church Preen
Stretton Westwood
Woolstaston
Leebotwood
The Marsh
Shelve
Stiperstones
Hughley
The Bog
SHROPSHIRE
Ratlinghope
Presthope
513
CORNDON HILL
Bridges
Enchmarsh
Plaish
Bourton
Coldyeld
BRIDGES
All Stretton
ALL STRETTON
459
Cardington
Easthope
West Onny
East Onny
THE LONG MYND
Gretton
B4378
Hyssington
516
Church Stretton
East Wall
Brockton
Wall Bank
B4371
Longville in the Dale
Weston
Linley
Norbury
B4370
Snead
Wentnor
Hope Bowdler
Wall under Heywood
Rushbury
Owlbury
Little Stretton
WILDERHOPE MANOR
Shipton
More
Lydham
Asterton
Minton
Acton Scott
Ticklerton
Hatton
WENLOCK EDGE
Stanton Long
A489
Myndtown
Marshbrook
Eaton
Broadstone
Bishop's Castle
B4383
Lea
Eaton
Whittingslow
Ape Dale
Corve Dale
Holdgate
HOUSE ON CRUTCHES MUSEUM
Choulton
Plowden
Harton
Middlehope
Eyton
Munslow
416
Colebatch
Woolston
Alcaston
Tugford
Lydbury North
Horderley
Upper Affcot
Aston Munslow
B4368
Abdon
B4385
Wistanstow
540
BROWN CLEE HILL
Brockton
Edgton
Strefford
Westhope
Diddlebury
Upper Heath
Acton
Cheny Longville
Boulden
Walcot
Lower Dinchope
Corfton
Lower Down
Corve
Clee St Margaret
Hopesay
Newington
Peaton
Sibdon Carwood
Halford
B4368
Kempton
Aston on Clun
Craven Arms
Seifton
Great Sutton
CLUN MILL
Little Brampton
Stokesay
Culmington
321
Stoke St Milborough
Clun
Clunton
B4367
Broome
294
Norton
Hayton's Bent
Clun
STOKESAY CASTLE
Purslow
Vernolds Common
B4365
Cleedownton
Clunbury
Churchbank
Teme
Hopton Cangeford
B4364
Brandhill
Onibury
Twitchen
Hobarris
Clungunford
Hopton Castle
Abcott
Stanton Lacy
Wootton
Bitterley
Sheldrton
Hoptonheath
306
A49
Bromfield
LUDLOW
Middleton
533
New Invention
Chapel Lawn
Marlow
Henley
A4117
Bedstone
Snitton
Farden
Todding
A4113
Cleehill
Ludlow
Kinton
DOWNTON GORGE
Knowbury
Bucknell
B4367
Leintwardine
Buckton
Hope Bagot
Stowe
Downton on the Rock
Ludford
Teme
Caynham
Whitton
Milebrook
Brampton Bryan
Walford
Burrington
Aston
Overton
A4113
Bryan
B4530
Adforton
B4361
Ashford Carbonell
Greete
A4110
Elton
333
Ashford Bowdler
Letton
Leinthall Starkes
78
Richards Castle
Middleton
BURFORD HOUSE
Wigmore
338
Woofferton
Little Hereford
A456
Ongar Street
B4362
3 miles
5 km

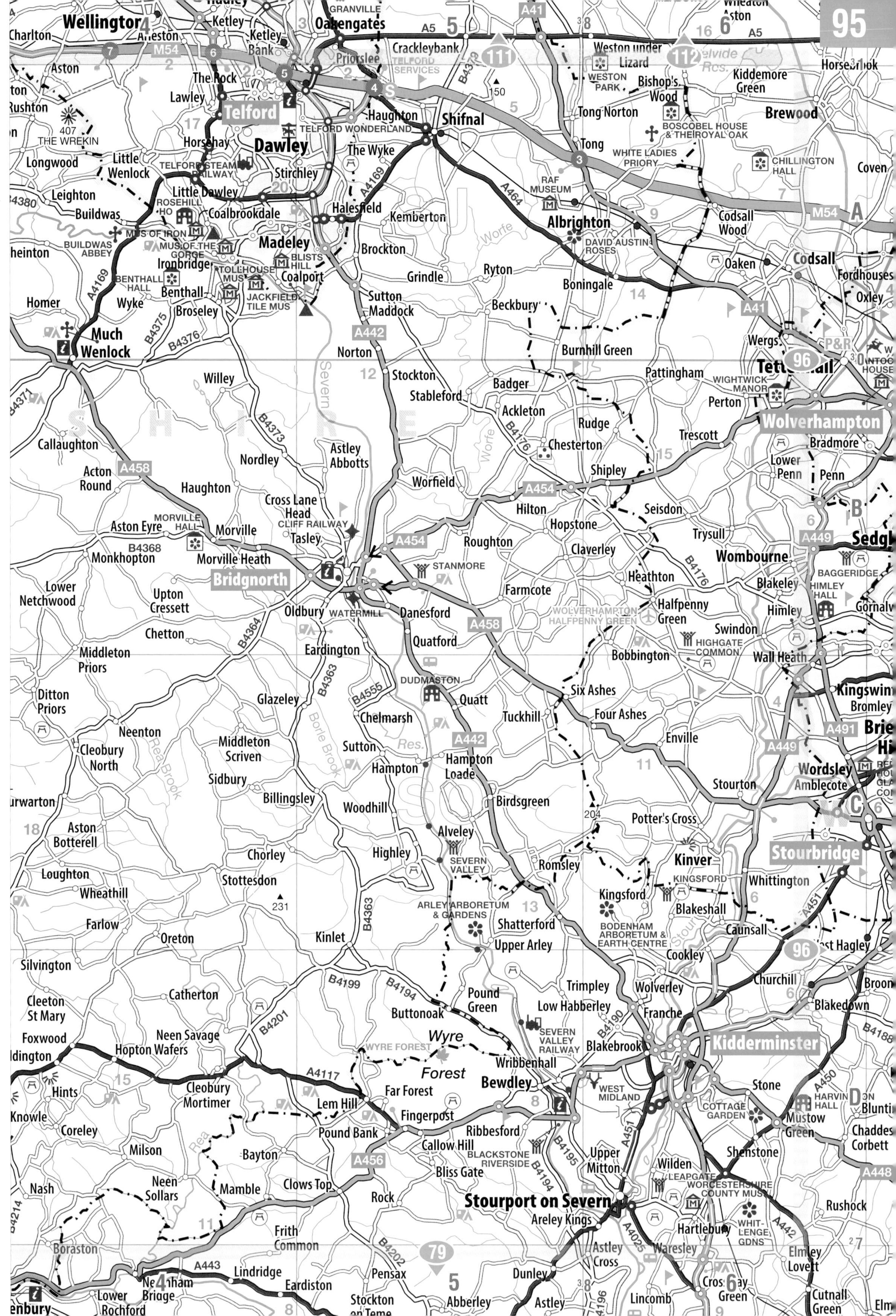
Wellington
Charlton
Arleston
Ketley
Ketley Bank
GRANVILLE
Oakengates
Priorslee
TELFORD SERVICES
Crackleybank
A5
A41
Weston under Lizard
WESTON PARK
Wheaton Aston
Horsebrook
Kiddemore Green
Bishop's Wood
Brewood
M54
111
112
Aston
Rushton
The Rock
Lawley
Telford
407
THE WREKIN
Horsehay
Dawley
TELFORD WONDERLAND
Haughton
Shifnal
Tong Norton
BOSCOBEL HOUSE & THE ROYAL OAK
Tong
WHITE LADIES PRIORY
CHILLINGTON HALL
Coven
Longwood
Little Wenlock
TELFORD STEAM RAILWAY
Stirchley
The Wyke
A4169
Little Dawley
Leighton
Buildwas
ROSEHILL HO
Coalbrookdale
Halesfield
Kemberton
A464
RAF MUSEUM
Albrighton
Codsall Wood
Codsall
Oaken
MUS OF IRON
MUS OF THE GORGE
Madeley
BLISTS HILL
Ironbridge
BUILDWAS ABBEY
Sheinton
Brockton
Worfe
DAVID AUSTIN ROSES
Fordhouses
BENTHALL HALL
TOLLHOUSE MUS
Coalport
Grindle
Ryton
Boningale
Oxley
Homer
Wyke
Benthall
JACKFIELD TILE MUS
Sutton Maddock
Beckbury
Broseley
B4375
B4376
Much Wenlock
A442
Norton
Wergs
Burnhill Green
P&R
Tettenhall
96
Willey
Stockton
Stableford
Badger
Pattingham
WIGHTWICK MANOR
Perton
Severn
Ackleton
Rudge
Wolverhampton
SHROPSHIRE
B4373
B4176
Chesterton
Trescott
Bradmore
Callaughton
Nordley
Astley Abbotts
Lower Penn
Penn
Acton Round
A458
Haughton
Worfield
Shipley
A454
Cross Lane Head
Hilton
Seisdon
MORVILLE HALL
Aston Eyre
CLIFF RAILWAY
Morville
Hopstone
Trysull
B4368
Tasley
Roughton
Claverley
Sedgley
Monkhopton
Morville Heath
STANMORE
Wombourne
BAGGERIDGE
Bridgnorth
Heathton
Lower Netchwood
Farmcote
Blakeley
HIMLEY HALL
Upton Cressett
Oldbury
WATERMILL
Danesford
WOLVERHAMPTON HALFPENNY GREEN
Halfpenny Green
Himley
Gornal
B4364
Chetton
Eardington
Quatford
Bobbington
Swindon
HIGHGATE COMMON
Wall Heath
Middleton Priors
DUDMASTON
B4363
B4555
Six Ashes
Kingswinford
Bromley
Ditton Priors
Glazeley
Quatt
Tuckhill
Four Ashes
Neenton
Borle Brook
Chelmarsh
Brierley Hill
A491
Cleobury North
Rea Brook
Middleton Scriven
Sutton
Res.
Enville
A449
Hampton Loade
Hampton
Wordsley
Amblecote
Sidbury
Burwarton
Billingsley
Woodhill
Birdsgreen
Stourton
Aston Botterell
204
Potter's Cross
Alveley
Loughton
Chorley
Highley
SEVERN VALLEY
Romsley
Kinver
Stourbridge
Wheathill
Stottesdon
KINGSFORD
Whittington
231
Kingsford
ARLEY ARBORETUM & GARDENS
Blakeshall
Farlow
Oreton
Shatterford
BODENHAM ARBORETUM & EARTH CENTRE
Caunsall
Kinlet
Upper Arley
A451
Stour
West Hagley
Silvington
Cookley
B4199
B4194
Trimpley
Churchill
Cleeton St Mary
Catherton
Pound Green
Wolverley
Broome
Low Habberley
Blakedown
Buttonoak
Franche
B4190
Foxwood
Neen Savage
B4201
Wyre
SEVERN VALLEY RAILWAY
Blakebrook
Kidderminster
B4188
Hopton Wafers
WYRE FOREST
Wribbenhall
A4117
Forest
Hints
Cleobury Mortimer
Far Forest
Bewdley
Stone
HARVINGTON HALL
A450
WEST MIDLAND
Knowle
Lem Hill
Fingerpost
COTTAGE GARDEN
Mustow Green
Coreley
Pound Bank
Ribbesford
Chaddesley Corbett
Callow Hill
Milson
BLACKSTONE RIVERSIDE
B4195
Bayton
A456
Upper Mitton
Shenstone
Bliss Gate
Wilden
A448
Neen Sollars
Nash
Mamble
Clows Top
LEAPGATE
WORCESTERSHIRE COUNTY MUS
Rock
Stourport on Severn
Rushock
Areley Kings
Hartlebury
WHITLENGE GDNS
A4025
Frith Common
Boraston
79
B4202
Astley Cross
Waresley
Elmley Lovett
A443
Lindridge
Newnham Bridge
Eardiston
Pensax
Dunley
Crossway Green
Lower Rochford
Stockton on Teme
Abberley
Astley
B4196
Lincomb
Cutnall Green

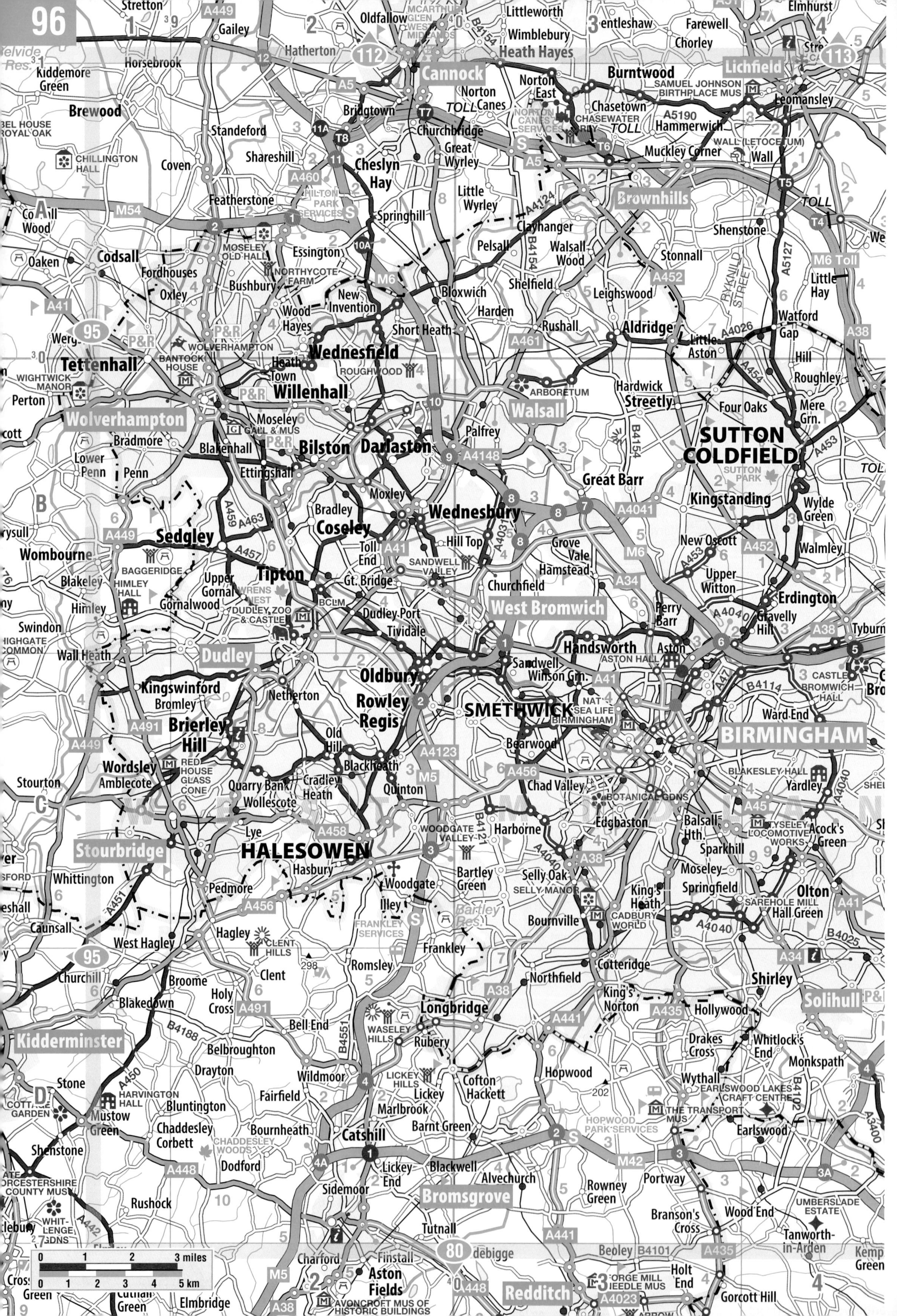
Stretton
Gailey
Oldfallow
Littleworth
Elmhurst
Farewell
Chorley
Wimblebury
Heath Hayes
Hatherton
Cannock
Lichfield
Kiddemore Green
Horsebrook
Brewood
Norton East
Norton Canes
Burntwood
SAMUEL JOHNSON BIRTHPLACE MUS
Leomansley
Chasetown
Hammerwich
CHASEWATER
Bridgtown
Churchbridge
Standeford
CHILLINGTON HALL
Shareshill
Coven
Cheslyn Hay
Great Wyrley
Muckley Corner
Wall
Little Wyrley
Brownhills
Featherstone
Springhill
Clayhanger
Shenstone
Codsall
Oaken
MOSELEY OLD HALL
Essington
Pelsall
Walsall Wood
Stonnall
Fordhouses
NORTHYCOTE FARM
Bushbury
Oxley
Shelfield
Leighswood
Little Hay
New Invention
Bloxwich
Wood Hayes
Harden
Short Heath
Rushall
Aldridge
Watford Gap
Little Aston
Wednesfield
Tettenhall
WOLVERHAMPTON
BANTOCK HOUSE
Heath Town
ROUGHWOOD
WIGHTWICK MANOR
Willenhall
Hardwick
Streetly
Four Oaks
Roughley
Perton
Wolverhampton
Moseley
ARBORETUM
Walsall
Mere Grn.
Palfrey
Bradmore
Blakenhall
Bilston
Darlaston
SUTTON COLDFIELD
Lower Penn
Penn
Ettingshall
Great Barr
Kingstanding
Moxley
Bradley
Wednesbury
Wylde Green
Coseley
Sedgley
Toll End
Hill Top
Grove Vale
New Oscott
Walmley
Wombourne
BAGGERIDGE
Tipton
SANDWELL VALLEY
Hamstead
Upper Witton
Blakeley
HIMLEY HALL
Upper Gornal
Gt. Bridge
Churchfield
Erdington
Himley
Gornalwood
DUDLEY ZOO & CASTLE
Dudley Port
West Bromwich
Perry Barr
Gravelly Hill
Swindon
Tividale
Tyburn
Wall Heath
Dudley
Handsworth
Aston
ASTON HALL
Oldbury
Sandwell
Winson Grn.
CASTLE BROMWICH HALL
Kingswinford
Netherton
Bromley
Rowley Regis
SMETHWICK
NAT SEA LIFE BIRMINGHAM
Ward End
Brierley Hill
Old Hill
BIRMINGHAM
Bearwood
Wordsley
RED HOUSE GLASS CONE
Blackheath
Stourton
Amblecote
Quarry Bank
Cradley Heath
Quinton
Chad Valley
BLAKESLEY HALL
Yardley
Wollescote
BOTANICAL GDNS
Lye
WOODGATE VALLEY
Harborne
Edgbaston
Balsall Hth.
TYSELEY LOCOMOTIVE WORKS
Acock's Green
Stourbridge
HALESOWEN
Sparkhill
Hasbury
Bartley Green
Moseley
Whittington
Pedmore
Woodgate
Selly Oak
SELLY MANOR
Springfield
Olton
Illey
King's Heath
SAREHOLE MILL
Hall Green
Caunsall
FRANKLEY SERVICES
Bournville
CADBURY WORLD
Hagley
CLENT HILLS
Frankley
West Hagley
Romsley
Cotteridge
Shirley
Churchill
Clent
Broome
Northfield
Holy Cross
King's Norton
Solihull
Blakedown
Longbridge
Hollywood
WASELEY HILLS
Kidderminster
Bell End
Rubery
Drakes Cross
Whitlock's End
Belbroughton
Monkspath
Drayton
Hopwood
Wildmoor
LICKEY HILLS
Cofton Hackett
Stone
Lickey
Wythall
EARLSWOOD LAKES CRAFT CENTRE
HARVINGTON HALL
Bluntington
Fairfield
Marlbrook
COTTAGE GARDEN
Mustow Green
THE TRANSPORT MUS
Barnt Green
HOPWOOD PARK SERVICES
Earlswood
Chaddesley Corbett
Bournheath
Catshill
Shenstone
CHADDESLEY WOODS
Dodford
Lickey End
Blackwell
Alvechurch
Portway
Rowney Green
WORCESTERSHIRE COUNTY MUS
Sidemoor
Rushock
Bromsgrove
Wood End
Branson's Cross
UMBERSLADE ESTATE
WHITLENGE GDNS
Tutnall
Tanworth-in-Arden
Charford
Finstall
Beoley
Holt End
Aston Fields
FORGE MILL NEEDLE MUS
Redditch
Gorcott Hill
Elmbridge
AVONCROFT MUS OF HISTORIC BUILDINGS
0 1 2 3 miles
0 1 2 3 4 5 km

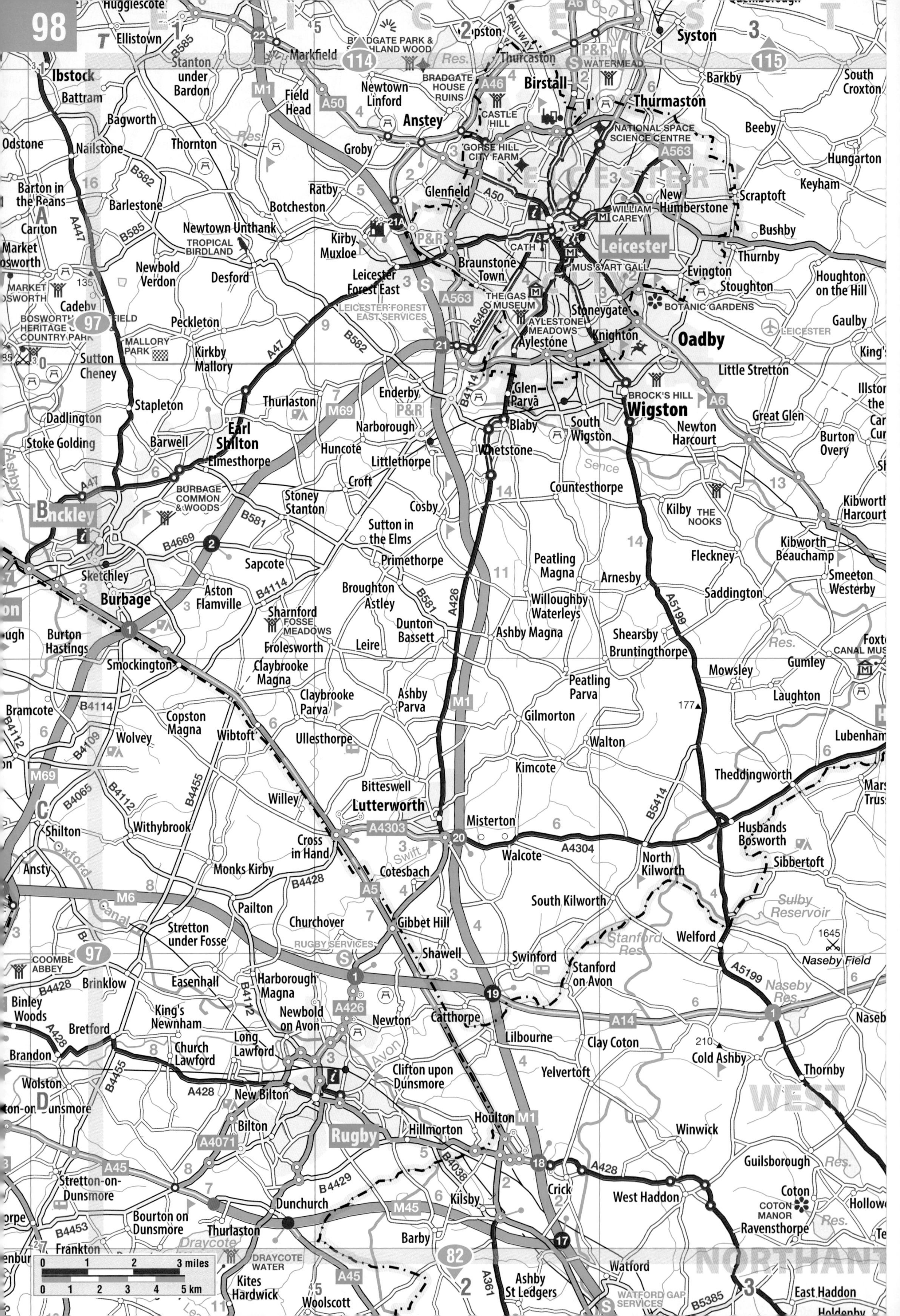
Hugglescote
Ellistown
Stanton under Bardon
Markfield
BRADGATE PARK & SWITHLAND WOOD
114
Newtown Linford
BRADGATE HOUSE RUINS
Thurcaston
Birstall
WATERMEAD
Syston
115
Barkby
South Croxton
Ibstock
Battram
Field Head
Anstey
CASTLE HILL
Thurmaston
Beeby
Bagworth
Odstone
Nailstone
Thornton
Groby
GORSE HILL CITY FARM
NATIONAL SPACE SCIENCE CENTRE
Hungarton
Barton in the Beans
Barlestone
Ratby
Glenfield
Botcheston
LEICESTER
New Humberstone
WILLIAM CAREY
Scraptoft
Keyham
Carlton
Market Bosworth
Newtown Unthank
TROPICAL BIRDLAND
Kirby Muxloe
CATH
Leicester
MUS & ART GALL
Bushby
Thurnby
Newbold Verdon
Desford
Leicester Forest East
Braunstone Town
THE GAS MUSEUM
Evington
Stoughton
Houghton on the Hill
MARKET BOSWORTH
Cadeby
BOSWORTH FIELD HERITAGE & COUNTRY PARK
97
Peckleton
LEICESTER FOREST EAST SERVICES
AYLESTONE MEADOWS
Stoneygate
BOTANIC GARDENS
Knighton
Aylestone
Oadby
LEICESTER
Gaulby
MALLORY PARK
Sutton Cheney
Kirkby Mallory
Little Stretton
Enderby
Glen Parva
BROCK'S HILL
Wigston
Illston on the Hill
Stapleton
Thurlaston
Dadlington
Earl Shilton
Narborough
Blaby
South Wigston
Newton Harcourt
Great Glen
Stoke Golding
Barwell
Elmesthorpe
Huncote
Littlethorpe
Whetstone
Burton Overy
Croft
Countesthorpe
Sence
BURBAGE COMMON & WOODS
Stoney Stanton
Cosby
Kilby
THE NOOKS
Kibworth Harcourt
Hinckley
Sutton in the Elms
Kibworth Beauchamp
Fleckney
Sapcote
Primethorpe
Peatling Magna
Arnesby
Smeeton Westerby
Sketchley
Burbage
Aston Flamville
Broughton Astley
Saddington
Willoughby Waterleys
Sharnford
FOSSE MEADOWS
Dunton Bassett
Ashby Magna
Shearsby
Bruntingthorpe
Burton Hastings
Frolesworth
Leire
Foxton
CANAL MUS
Smockington
Claybrooke Magna
Mowsley
Gumley
Peatling Parva
Claybrooke Parva
Ashby Parva
Laughton
Bramcote
Copston Magna
Gilmorton
177
Wolvey
Wibtoft
Ullesthorpe
Walton
Lubenham
Kimcote
Theddingworth
Bitteswell
Willey
Lutterworth
Marston Trussell
Shilton
Withybrook
Misterton
Husbands Bosworth
Cross in Hand
Swift
Walcote
North Kilworth
Ansty
Oxford Canal
Monks Kirby
Cotesbach
Sibbertoft
Pailton
South Kilworth
Sulby Reservoir
Churchover
Stretton under Fosse
Gibbet Hill
Stanford Res
Welford
RUGBY SERVICES
Shawell
Swinford
1645
Naseby Field
COOMBE ABBEY
97
Brinklow
Easenhall
Harborough Magna
Stanford on Avon
Naseby Res
Binley Woods
King's Newnham
Newbold on Avon
Newton
Catthorpe
Naseby
Bretford
Church Lawford
Long Lawford
Lilbourne
Clay Coton
210
Cold Ashby
Brandon
Avon
Clifton upon Dunsmore
Yelvertoft
Thornby
Wolston
New Bilton
Ryton-on-Dunsmore
Bilton
Houlton
WEST
Rugby
Hillmorton
Winwick
Stretton-on-Dunsmore
Guilsborough
Crick
West Haddon
Coton
COTON MANOR
Dunchurch
Kilsby
Bourton on Dunsmore
Thurlaston
Barby
Ravensthorpe
Frankton
Draycote Water
DRAYCOTE WATER
Watford
NORTHANTS
82
Kites Hardwick
Woolscott
Ashby St Ledgers
WATFORD GAP SERVICES
East Haddon
Holdenby
A447
B585
B582
A47
A50
A46
A563
A5460
B4114
B581
B4669
M69
A426
M1
A5199
B5414
A4304
A4303
A5
M6
B4428
B4112
B4109
B4065
B4455
A428
A426
A14
A4071
A45
B4429
B4038
M45
B4453
A361
B5385
A6
0 1 2 3 miles
0 1 2 3 4 5 km

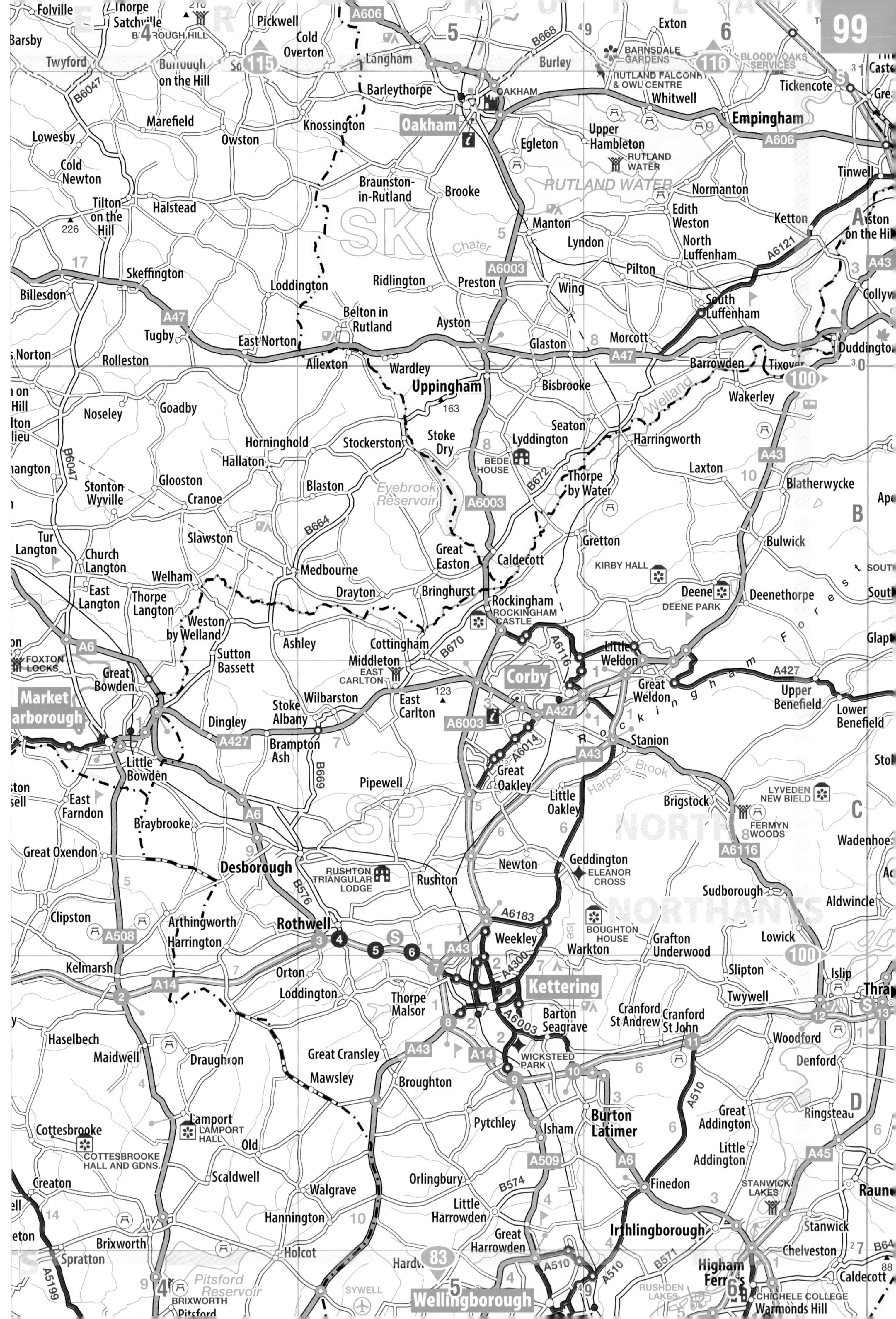
Folville
Thorpe Satchville
BURROUGH HILL
Pickwell
A606
Cold Overton
Langham
Exton
BARNSDALE GARDENS
116
BLOODY OAKS SERVICES
Barsby
Twyford
Burrough on the Hill
115
B668
Burley
RUTLAND FALCONRY & OWL CENTRE
Tickencote
B6047
Barleythorpe
OAKHAM
Whitwell
Empingham
Marefield
Knossington
Oakham
Lowesby
Owston
Egleton
Upper Hambleton
A606
Cold Newton
RUTLAND WATER
Tinwell
Braunston-in-Rutland
Brooke
Normanton
Tilton on the Hill
Halstead
226
Manton
Edith Weston
Ketton
SK
Lyndon
North Luffenham
Chater
A6121
Skeffington
Loddington
Ridlington
Preston
A6003
Pilton
Billesdon
Wing
South Luffenham
A43
Belton in Rutland
A47
Tugby
Ayston
East Norton
Glaston
Morcott
Rolleston
Allexton
A47
Barrowden
Tixover
Duddington
Wardley
Uppingham
Bisbrooke
Welland
100
Wakerley
163
Noseley
Goadby
Seaton
Horninghold
Stockerston
Stoke Dry
Lyddington
Harringworth
BEDE HOUSE
Hallaton
B6047
Laxton
Thorpe by Water
A43
Stonton Wyville
Glooston
B672
Blatherwycke
Cranoe
Blaston
Eyebrook Reservoir
A6003
B664
Slawston
Gretton
Bulwick
Tur Langton
Church Langton
Great Easton
Caldecott
Medbourne
KIRBY HALL
Welham
East Langton
Drayton
Bringhurst
Deene
Deenethorpe
Thorpe Langton
Rockingham
ROCKINGHAM CASTLE
DEENE PARK
Weston by Welland
Ashley
Cottingham
A6116
A6
FOXTON LOCKS
Sutton Bassett
B670
Little Weldon
Middleton
EAST CARLTON
Corby
A427
Great Bowden
Great Weldon
Upper Benefield
Lower Benefield
Market Harborough
Wilbarston
East Carlton
123
Stoke Albany
A6003
A427
Dingley
A427
Brampton Ash
A6014
Stanion
Rockingham Forest
A43
Little Bowden
B669
Harper's Brook
Pipewell
Great Oakley
Little Oakley
Brigstock
LYVEDEN NEW BIELD
East Farndon
SP
NORTH
FERMYN WOODS
Braybrooke
A6
Great Oxendon
Desborough
RUSHTON TRIANGULAR LODGE
Newton
Geddington
ELEANOR CROSS
A6116
Wadenhoe
Rushton
B576
Sudborough
Aldwincle
Clipston
Arthingworth
NORTHANTS
A6183
BOUGHTON HOUSE
Rothwell
Weekley
A508
Harrington
Warkton
Grafton Underwood
Lowick
A43
Kelmarsh
Orton
A4300
Kettering
Slipton
Islip
A14
Loddington
Twywell
Thorpe Malsor
Barton Seagrave
Cranford St Andrew
Cranford St John
A6003
Haselbech
A43
A14
WICKSTEED PARK
Woodford
Maidwell
Draughton
Great Cransley
Denford
Mawsley
Broughton
Burton Latimer
Great Addington
Ringstead
A510
Lamport
LAMPORT HALL
Pytchley
Isham
Cottesbrooke
COTTESBROOKE HALL AND GDNS.
Old
Little Addington
A45
A509
A6
Scaldwell
Orlingbury
Creaton
Finedon
Walgrave
B574
STANWICK LAKES
Little Harrowden
Hannington
Irthlingborough
Stanwick
Brixworth
Great Harrowden
Chelveston
Spratton
Holcot
83
A510
B571
A510
Higham Ferrers
Caldecott
A5199
Pitsford Reservoir
SYWELL
Wellingborough
RUSHDEN LAKES
CHICHELE COLLEGE
BRIXWORTH
Warmonds Hill

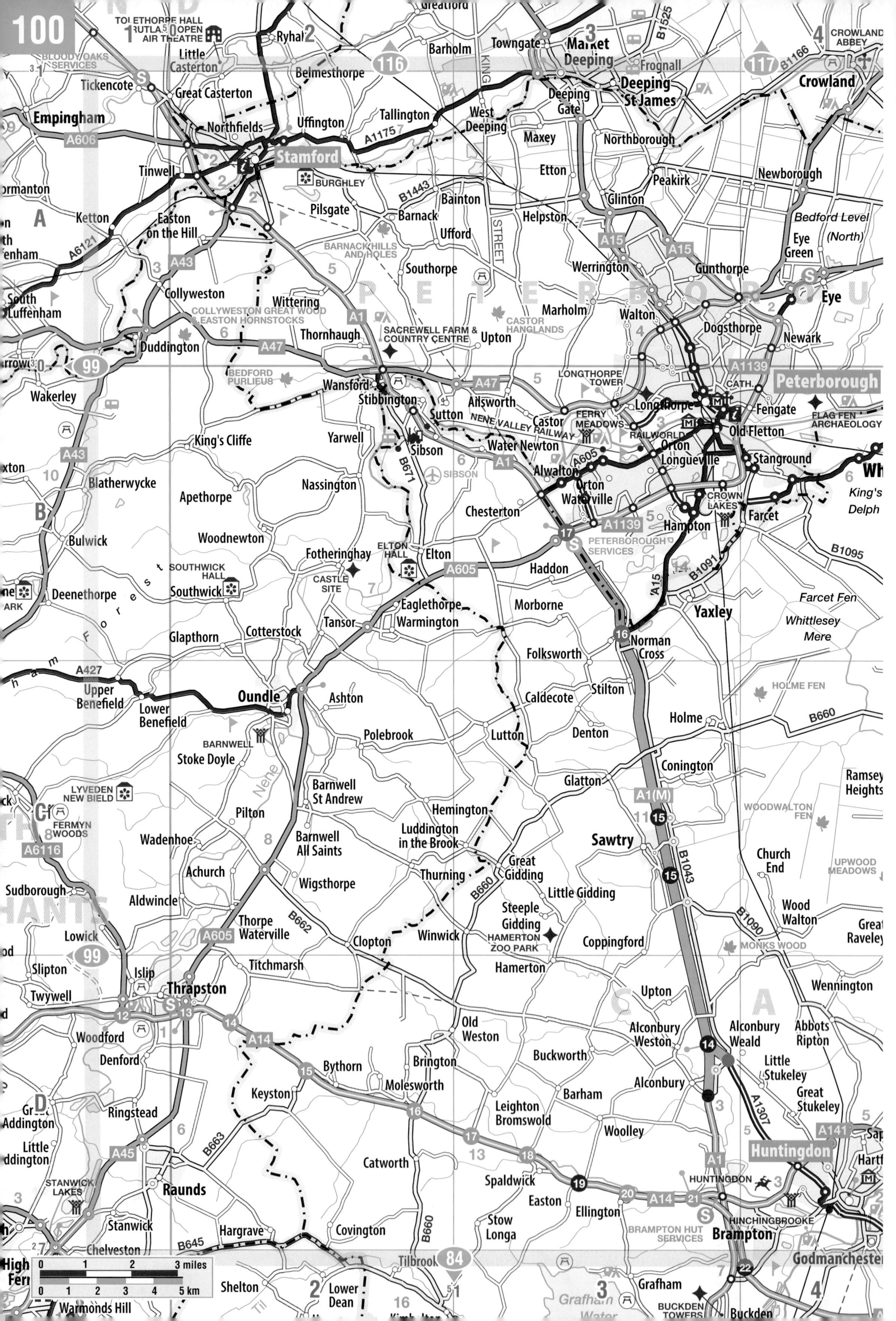
Stamford
Peterborough
Huntingdon
Market Deeping
Deeping St James
Crowland
Empingham
Tickencote
Great Casterton
Little Casterton
Ryhall
Belmesthorpe
Barholm
Towngate
Frognall
Uffington
Tallington
West Deeping
Deeping Gate
Maxey
Northborough
Newborough
Peakirk
Glinton
Etton
Helpston
Bainton
Barnack
Ufford
Pilsgate
Burghley
Tinwell
Ketton
Easton on the Hill
Collyweston
Wittering
Duddington
South Luffenham
Wakerley
Southorpe
Barnack Hills and Holes
Thornhaugh
Sacrewell Farm & Country Centre
Upton
Castor Hanglands
Marholm
Werrington
Walton
Gunthorpe
Eye
Eye Green
Bedford Level (North)
Dogsthorpe
Newark
Wansford
Stibbington
Sutton
Ailsworth
Castor
Longthorpe Tower
Longthorpe
Ferry Meadows
Nene Valley Railway
Railworld
Cath.
Fengate
Flag Fen Archaeology
Old Fletton
Stanground
Orton Longueville
Orton Waterville
Alwalton
Water Newton
Sibson
Yarwell
King's Cliffe
Blatherwycke
Apethorpe
Nassington
Chesterton
Crown Lakes
Hampton
Farcet
King's Delph
Peterborough Services
Bulwick
Woodnewton
Fotheringhay
Elton Hall
Elton
Haddon
Southwick Hall
Southwick
Deenethorpe
Castle Site
Eaglethorpe
Warmington
Tansor
Morborne
Yaxley
Farcet Fen
Whittlesey Mere
Glapthorn
Cotterstock
Norman Cross
Folksworth
Upper Benefield
Lower Benefield
Oundle
Ashton
Caldecote
Stilton
Holme Fen
Holme
Barnwell
Stoke Doyle
Polebrook
Lutton
Denton
Conington
Glatton
Ramsey Heights
Lyveden New Bield
Barnwell St Andrew
Pilton
Fermyn Woods
Hemington
Luddington in the Brook
Woodwalton Fen
Sawtry
Wadenhoe
Barnwell All Saints
Achurch
Wigsthorpe
Thurning
Great Gidding
Church End
Upwood Meadows
Little Gidding
Sudborough
Aldwincle
Steeple Gidding
Wood Walton
Thorpe Waterville
Winwick
Hamerton Zoo Park
Coppingford
Great Raveley
Monks Wood
Lowick
Clopton
Hamerton
Slipton
Islip
Titchmarsh
Twywell
Thrapston
Upton
Wennington
Old Weston
Alconbury Weston
Alconbury Weald
Abbots Ripton
Woodford
Denford
Brington
Buckworth
Little Stukeley
Bythorn
Molesworth
Alconbury
Great Stukeley
Keyston
Barham
Great Addington
Ringstead
Leighton Bromswold
Woolley
Little Addington
Catworth
Stanwick Lakes
Raunds
Spaldwick
Easton
Ellington
Huntingdon
Hinchingbrooke
Stanwick
Hargrave
Covington
Stow Longa
Brampton Hut Services
Brampton
Chelveston
Tilbrook
Godmanchester
Higham Ferrers
Shelton
Lower Dean
Grafham
Grafham Water
Buckden Towers
Buckden
Warmonds Hill
Rockingham Forest
Nene
King Street
Peterborough
Cambs
Northants
Toll Bar
Tolethorpe Hall Rutland Open Air Theatre
Bloody Oaks Services
Collyweston Great Wood & Easton Hornstocks
Bedford Purlieus
Sibson
A1
A1(M)
A14
A15
A43
A45
A47
A605
A606
A6121
A6116
A1139
A1175
A141
A1307
A427
B1443
B1525
B1166
B1095
B1091
B1043
B1090
B660
B662
B663
B645
B671
116
117
99
84
0 1 2 3 miles
0 1 2 3 4 5 km

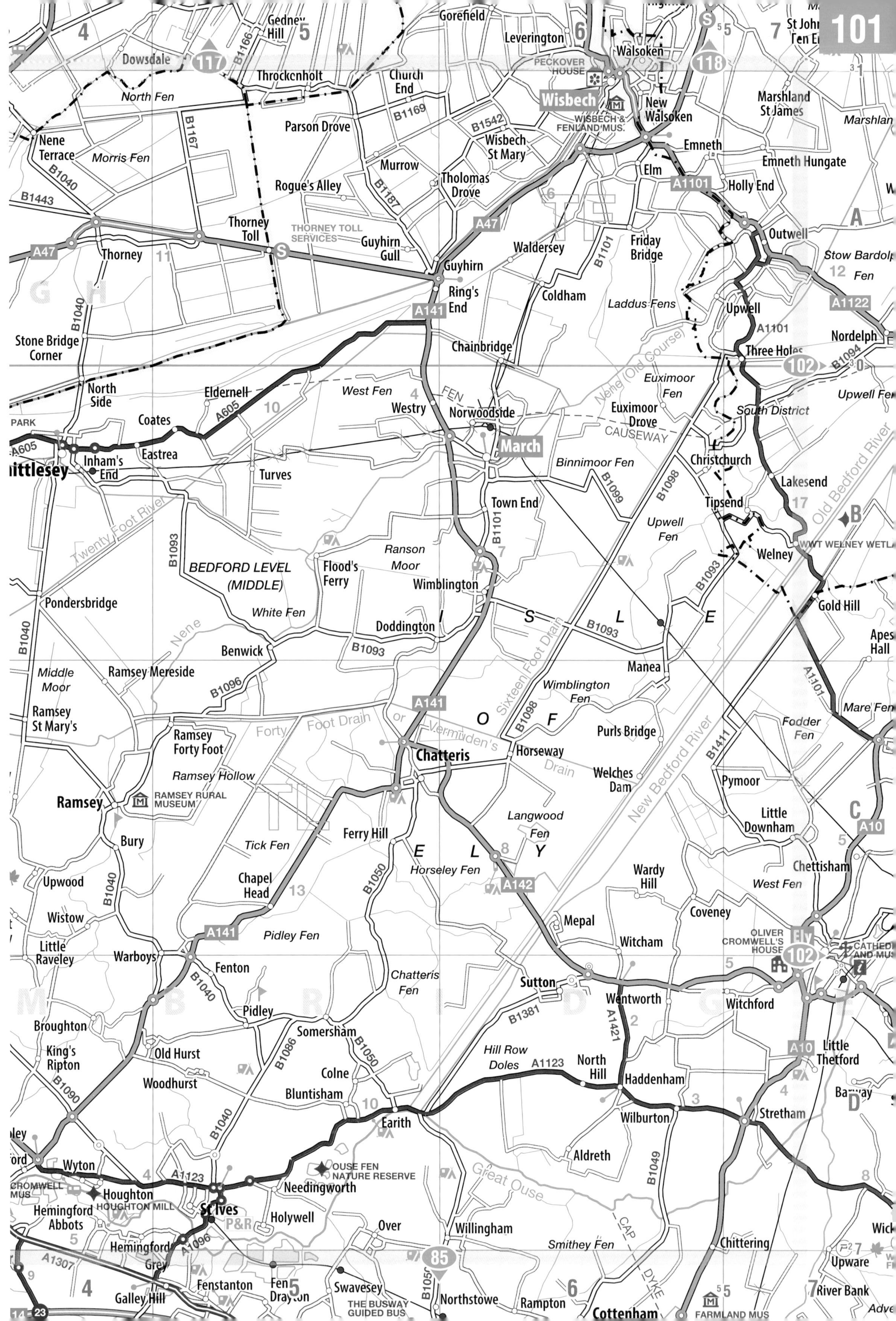
Gedney Hill
Dowsdale
117
B1166
Throckenholt
Gorefield
Leverington
Church End
PECKOVER HOUSE
Walsoken
118
St John's Fen End
Wisbech
WISBECH & FENLAND MUS.
New Walsoken
Marshland St James
North Fen
B1167
Parson Drove
B1169
B1542
Wisbech St Mary
Emneth
Emneth Hungate
Nene Terrace
Morris Fen
B1040
Murrow
Tholomas Drove
Elm
A1101
Holly End
B1443
Rogue's Alley
B1187
Thorney Toll
THORNEY TOLL SERVICES
Guyhirn Gull
A47
Waldersey
Friday Bridge
B1101
Outwell
Stow Bardolph Fen
A47
Thorney
Guyhirn
Coldham
Laddus Fens
Ring's End
A141
Upwell
A1122
Stone Bridge Corner
Chainbridge
A1101
Nordelph
Three Holes
102
B1094
Nene (Old Course)
Euximoor Fen
Upwell Fen
North Side
Eldernell
West Fen
FEN
Westry
Norwoodside
Euximoor Drove
South District
A605
CAUSEWAY
PARK
Coates
March
A605
Eastrea
Inham's End
Whittlesey
Turves
Binnimoor Fen
Christchurch
B1099
B1098
Lakesend
Town End
Tipsend
Old Bedford River
Twenty Foot River
Upwell Fen
Ranson Moor
B1093
BEDFORD LEVEL (MIDDLE)
Flood's Ferry
B1101
Welney
WWT WELNEY WETLANDS
Wimblington
B1093
Pondersbridge
White Fen
Gold Hill
B1040
Doddington
B1093
Apes Hall
Nene
Benwick
B1093
Manea
Middle Moor
Ramsey Mereside
A1101
B1096
Wimblington Fen
Sixteen Foot Drain
Ramsey St Mary's
A141
Mare Fen
B1098
Ramsey Forty Foot
Forty Foot Drain or Vermuden's Drain
Purls Bridge
Fodder Fen
Chatteris
Horseway
B1411
Ramsey Hollow
Welches Dam
Pymoor
Ramsey
RAMSEY RURAL MUSEUM
New Bedford River
Langwood Fen
Little Downham
A10
Bury
Ferry Hill
Tick Fen
Horseley Fen
A142
Wardy Hill
Chettisham
Upwood
B1040
Chapel Head
B1050
West Fen
Wistow
Mepal
Coveney
A141
Pidley Fen
Witcham
OLIVER CROMWELL'S HOUSE
Ely
CATHEDRAL AND MUS
102
Little Raveley
Warboys
Fenton
Chatteris Fen
Sutton
B1040
Wentworth
Witchford
Pidley
B1381
A1421
Broughton
Somersham
B1050
Little Thetford
A10
King's Ripton
Old Hurst
Hill Row Doles
A1123
North Hill
B1086
Colne
Haddenham
B1090
Woodhurst
Bluntisham
Barway
Earith
Wilburton
Stretham
B1040
Wyton
OUSE FEN NATURE RESERVE
Aldreth
CROMWELL MUS
A1123
Needingworth
Houghton
HOUGHTON MILL
Great Ouse
B1049
Hemingford Abbots
St Ives
P&R
Holywell
Over
CAR DYKE
Willingham
Chittering
A1096
Hemingford Grey
Smithey Fen
Upware
A1307
85
Fenstanton
Fen Drayton
Swavesey
B1050
Northstowe
Rampton
River Bank
Galley Hill
THE BUSWAY GUIDED BUS
Cottenham
FARMLAND MUS

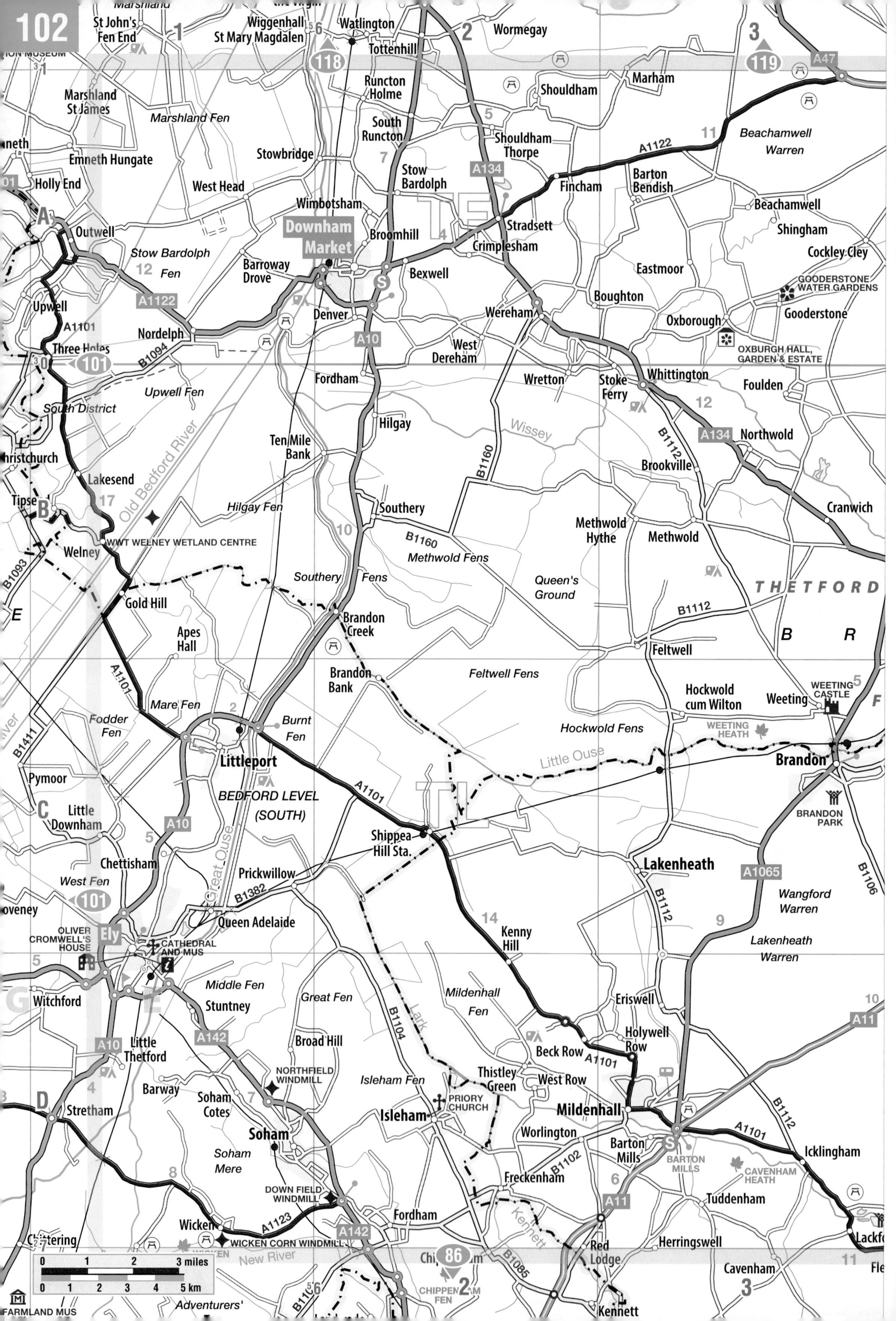
St John's Fen End
Wiggenhall St Mary Magdalen
Watlington
Wormegay
Tottenhill
118
119
A47
Marham
Runcton Holme
Shouldham
Marshland St James
Marshland Fen
South Runcton
Shouldham Thorpe
Beachamwell Warren
A1122
Emneth Hungate
Stowbridge
Stow Bardolph
A134
Fincham
Barton Bendish
Holly End
West Head
Wimbotsham
Beachamwell
Outwell
Downham Market
Broomhill
Stradsett
Shingham
Stow Bardolph Fen
Crimplesham
Cockley Cley
Barroway Drove
Bexwell
Eastmoor
Upwell
A1122
Denver
Wereham
Boughton
GOODERSTONE WATER GARDENS
Gooderstone
A1101
Nordelph
Oxborough
Three Holes
A10
West Dereham
OXBURGH HALL, GARDEN & ESTATE
101
B1094
Fordham
Wretton
Stoke Ferry
Whittington
Foulden
Upwell Fen
South District
Hilgay
A134
Northwold
Old Bedford River
Wissey
Ten Mile Bank
B1112
Brookville
B1160
Christchurch
Lakesend
Southery
Cranwich
Tipps End
Hilgay Fen
Methwold Hythe
Methwold
WWT WELNEY WETLAND CENTRE
B1160
Methwold Fens
Welney
B1093
Southery
Fens
Queen's Ground
THETFORD
Gold Hill
Brandon Creek
B1112
Apes Hall
Feltwell
Brandon Bank
Feltwell Fens
A1101
Hockwold cum Wilton
Weeting
WEETING CASTLE
Mare Fen
Burnt Fen
Fodder Fen
Hockwold Fens
WEETING HEATH
B1411
Little Ouse
Brandon
Littleport
Pymoor
BEDFORD LEVEL (SOUTH)
A1101
Little Downham
A10
BRANDON PARK
Shippea Hill Sta.
Chettisham
Great Ouse
Prickwillow
Lakenheath
A1065
West Fen
B1106
101
B1382
B1112
Wangford Warren
Coveney
Queen Adelaide
OLIVER CROMWELL'S HOUSE
Ely
CATHEDRAL AND MUS
Kenny Hill
Lakenheath Warren
Middle Fen
Mildenhall Fen
Witchford
Stuntney
Great Fen
Eriswell
B1104
Lark
A142
A11
Holywell Row
Beck Row
A1101
Broad Hill
Little Thetford
A10
NORTHFIELD WINDMILL
Isleham Fen
Thistley Green
West Row
Barway
PRIORY CHURCH
Soham Cotes
Stretham
Isleham
Mildenhall
B1112
Soham
Worlington
Barton Mills
A1101
Icklingham
BARTON MILLS
Soham Mere
B1102
CAVENHAM HEATH
Freckenham
DOWN FIELD WINDMILL
A11
Tuddenham
A1123
Fordham
Wicken
Kennett
WICKEN CORN WINDMILL
A142
Red Lodge
Herringswell
Lackford
Chittering
New River
86
Chippenham
B1085
Cavenham
CHIPPENHAM FEN
0 1 2 3 miles
0 1 2 3 4 5 km
Adventurers'
FARMLAND MUS
Kennett

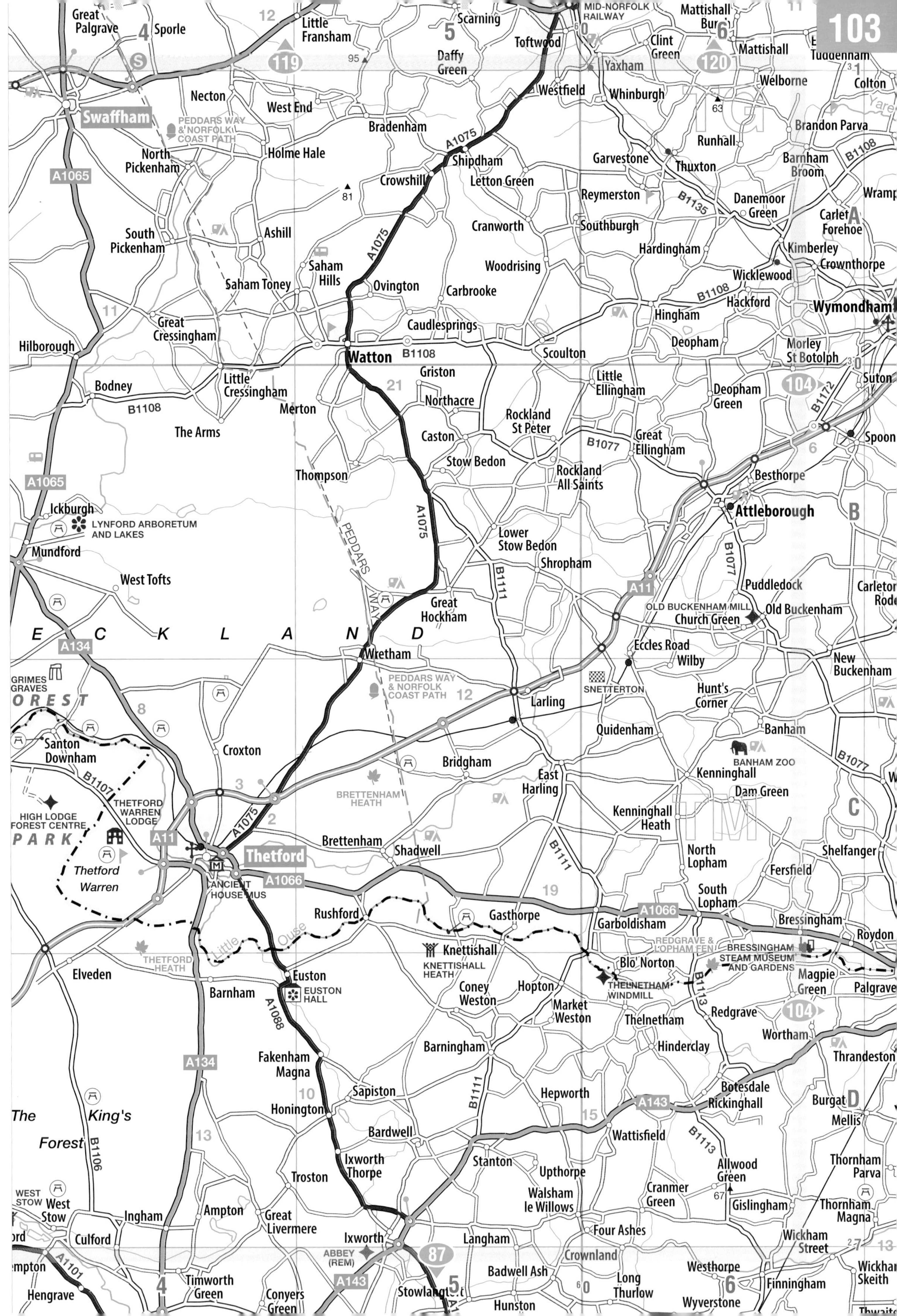
Great Palgrave
Sporle
Little Fransham
Scarning
MID-NORFOLK RAILWAY
Mattishall Burgh
Toftwood
Clint Green
Mattishall
Tuddenham
Daffy Green
Yaxham
Colton
Necton
Westfield
Whinburgh
Welborne
Swaffham
West End
PEDDARS WAY & NORFOLK COAST PATH
Bradenham
Brandon Parva
A1075
Runhall
North Pickenham
Holme Hale
Shipdham
Garvestone
Thuxton
Barnham Broom
B1108
A1065
Crowshill
Letton Green
Reymerston
Danemoor Green
B1135
Carleton Forehoe
South Pickenham
Ashill
Cranworth
Southburgh
Hardingham
Kimberley
Saham Hills
Woodrising
Crownthorpe
Saham Toney
Ovington
Carbrooke
Wicklewood
Hackford
Wymondham
Great Cressingham
Caudlesprings
Hingham
Hilborough
Scoulton
Deopham
Morley St Botolph
Watton
Griston
Little Ellingham
Suton
Bodney
Little Cressingham
Merton
Northacre
Deopham Green
Rockland St Peter
B1172
The Arms
Caston
B1077
Great Ellingham
Spooner
Stow Bedon
Rockland All Saints
Thompson
Besthorpe
Ickburgh
Attleborough
LYNFORD ARBORETUM AND LAKES
PEDDARS WAY
Lower Stow Bedon
Mundford
B1111
Shropham
West Tofts
Puddledock
Carleton Rode
A11
Great Hockham
OLD BUCKENHAM MILL
Old Buckenham
Church Green
E C K L A N D
A134
Wretham
Eccles Road
Wilby
New Buckenham
GRIMES GRAVES
SNETTERTON
Hunt's Corner
FOREST
Larling
Santon Downham
Quidenham
Banham
Croxton
BANHAM ZOO
Bridgham
Kenninghall
B1107
East Harling
Dam Green
THETFORD WARREN LODGE
BRETTENHAM HEATH
HIGH LODGE FOREST CENTRE
Kenninghall Heath
PARK
Brettenham
Shadwell
North Lopham
Shelfanger
Thetford
Thetford Warren
Fersfield
ANCIENT HOUSE MUS
A1066
South Lopham
Rushford
Gasthorpe
Garboldisham
Bressingham
Roydon
REDGRAVE & LOPHAM FEN
BRESSINGHAM STEAM MUSEUM AND GARDENS
Knettishall
Little Ouse
THETFORD HEATH
KNETTISHALL HEATH
Blo' Norton
Elveden
Euston
THELNETHAM WINDMILL
Magpie Green
Palgrave
EUSTON HALL
Coney Weston
Hopton
Barnham
Market Weston
Redgrave
A1088
Thelnetham
Wortham
B1113
Hinderclay
Thrandeston
Fakenham Magna
Barningham
Botesdale
Burgate
Rickinghall
Sapiston
Hepworth
A143
Mellis
The King's Forest
Honington
Wattisfield
B1106
Bardwell
Thornham Parva
Stanton
Allwood Green
Ixworth Thorpe
Upthorpe
Troston
Cranmer Green
Walsham le Willows
WEST STOW
West Stow
Ampton
Gislingham
Thornham Magna
Ingham
Great Livermere
Four Ashes
Wickham Street
Culford
Langham
Ixworth
ABBEY (REM)
Crownland
A1101
Westhorpe
Wickham Skeith
Timworth Green
Badwell Ash
Long Thurlow
Finningham
Hengrave
Conyers Green
Stowlangtoft
Hunston
Wyverstone
TG
TM

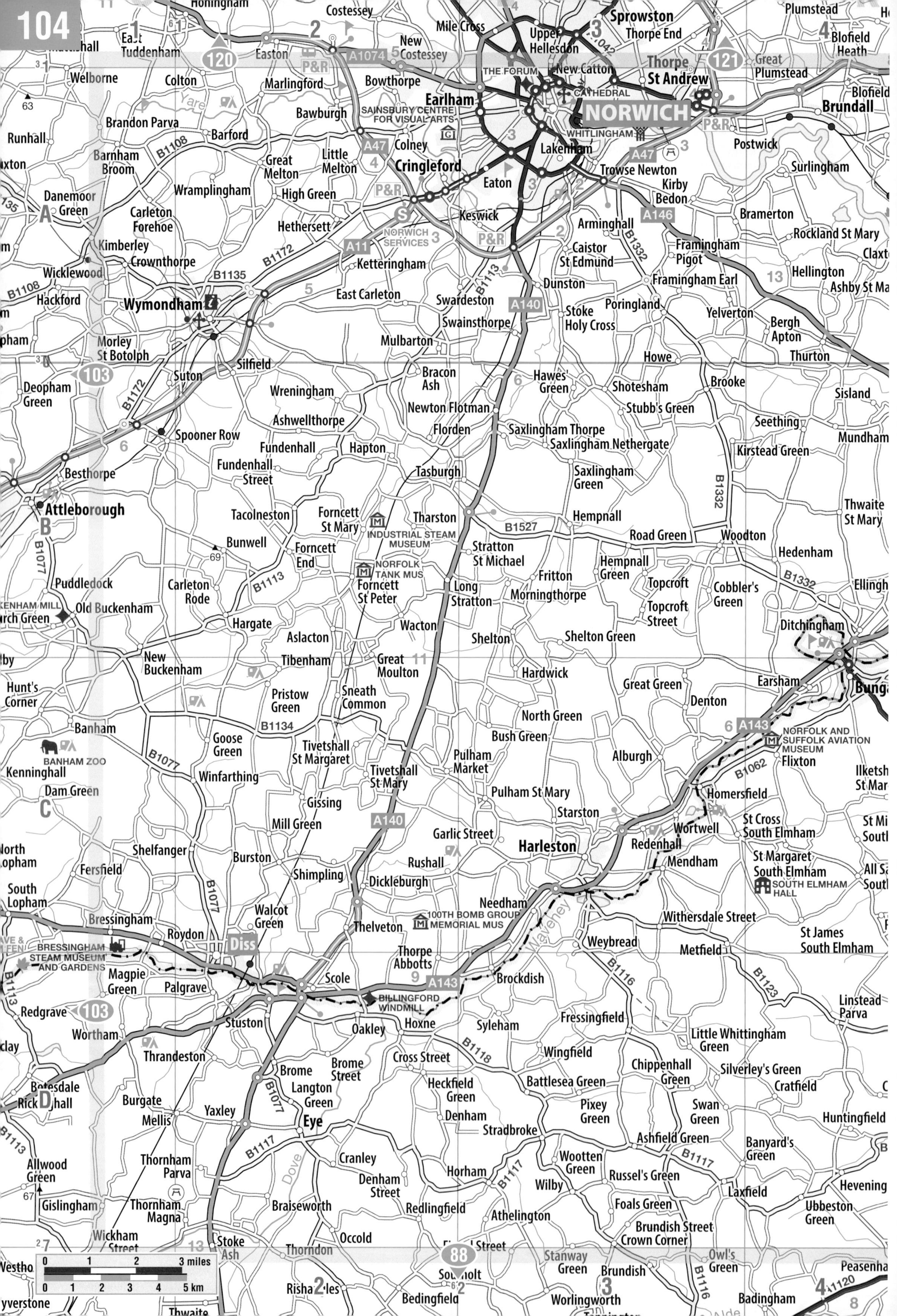
Honingham
Costessey
Mile Cross
Sprowston
Plumstead
East Tuddenham
Easton
New Costessey
Upper Hellesdon
Thorpe End
Blofield Heath
120
A1074
P&R
THE FORUM
New Catton
Thorpe St Andrew
121
Great Plumstead
Welborne
Colton
Marlingford
Bowthorpe
CATHEDRAL
Blofield
Yare
Earlham
NORWICH
Brundall
Brandon Parva
Bawburgh
SAINSBURY CENTRE FOR VISUAL ARTS
Runhall
Barford
WHITLINGHAM
Postwick
Barnham Broom
B1108
Great Melton
Little Melton
A47
Colney
Lakenham
Cringleford
Eaton
Trowse Newton
Surlingham
Wramplingham
High Green
Kirby Bedon
Danemoor Green
Carleton Forehoe
Keswick
Bramerton
Hethersett
Arminghall
A146
Rockland St Mary
NORWICH SERVICES
A11
Caistor St Edmund
B1332
Framingham Pigot
Kimberley
Crownthorpe
Ketteringham
Hellington
Wicklewood
B1172
B1135
Framingham Earl
Ashby St Mary
Hackford
East Carleton
Swardeston
Dunston
Poringland
Yelverton
Wymondham
A140
Stoke Holy Cross
Swainsthorpe
Bergh Apton
Morley St Botolph
Mulbarton
Howe
Thurton
Silfield
Suton
103
Bracon Ash
Hawes' Green
Shotesham
Brooke
Sisland
Deopham Green
Wreningham
Newton Flotman
Stubb's Green
Ashwellthorpe
Florden
Saxlingham Thorpe
Seething
Spooner Row
Saxlingham Nethergate
Mundham
Fundenhall
Hapton
Kirstead Green
Besthorpe
Fundenhall Street
Tasburgh
Saxlingham Green
Attleborough
Tacolneston
Forncett St Mary
Tharston
Hempnall
Thwaite St Mary
INDUSTRIAL STEAM MUSEUM
B1527
Road Green
Woodton
Bunwell
Forncett End
Stratton St Michael
Hedenham
B1077
NORFOLK TANK MUS
Hempnall Green
Fritton
Topcroft
Cobbler's Green
B1113
Forncett St Peter
Long Stratton
Puddledock
Carleton Rode
Morningthorpe
Topcroft Street
Old Buckenham
Hargate
Wacton
Ditchingham
Aslacton
Shelton
Shelton Green
New Buckenham
Tibenham
Great Moulton
Hardwick
Earsham
Hunt's Corner
Pristow Green
Sneath Common
Great Green
Denton
North Green
A143
Banham
B1134
Goose Green
Bush Green
NORFOLK AND SUFFOLK AVIATION MUSEUM
BANHAM ZOO
Tivetshall St Margaret
Pulham Market
Alburgh
Flixton
Kenninghall
Winfarthing
Tivetshall St Mary
B1062
Dam Green
Pulham St Mary
Homersfield
Gissing
Starston
St Cross South Elmham
Mill Green
Wortwell
Garlic Street
Redenhall
Harleston
Shelfanger
Burston
Rushall
Mendham
St Margaret South Elmham
Fersfield
Shimpling
Dickleburgh
SOUTH ELMHAM HALL
South Lopham
Needham
Walcot Green
100TH BOMB GROUP MEMORIAL MUS
Withersdale Street
Bressingham
Roydon
Diss
Thelveton
Waveney
St James South Elmham
BRESSINGHAM STEAM MUSEUM AND GARDENS
Weybread
Metfield
Thorpe Abbotts
Magpie Green
Palgrave
Scole
Brockdish
B1116
B1123
BILLINGFORD WINDMILL
Redgrave
Linstead Parva
Wortham
Stuston
Oakley
Hoxne
Syleham
Fressingfield
Little Whittingham Green
Thrandeston
Cross Street
B1118
Wingfield
Brome
Brome Street
Chippenhall Green
Silverley's Green
Botesdale
Heckfield Green
Battlesea Green
Cratfield
Rickinghall
Burgate
Langton Green
Pixey Green
Swan Green
Yaxley
Denham
Huntingfield
Mellis
Eye
Stradbroke
Ashfield Green
B1117
Banyard's Green
Thornham Parva
Cranley
Wootten Green
Allwood Green
Dove
Horham
Wilby
Russel's Green
Denham Street
Laxfield
Hevening
Gislingham
Thornham Magna
Braiseworth
Redlingfield
Athelington
Foals Green
Ubbeston Green
Wickham Street
Stoke Ash
Occold
Thorndon
Brundish Street
Crown Corner
88
Stanway Green
Brundish
Owl's Green
Peasenhall
Southolt
Rishangles
Bedingfield
Worlingworth
Badingham
Thwaite
3 miles
5 km

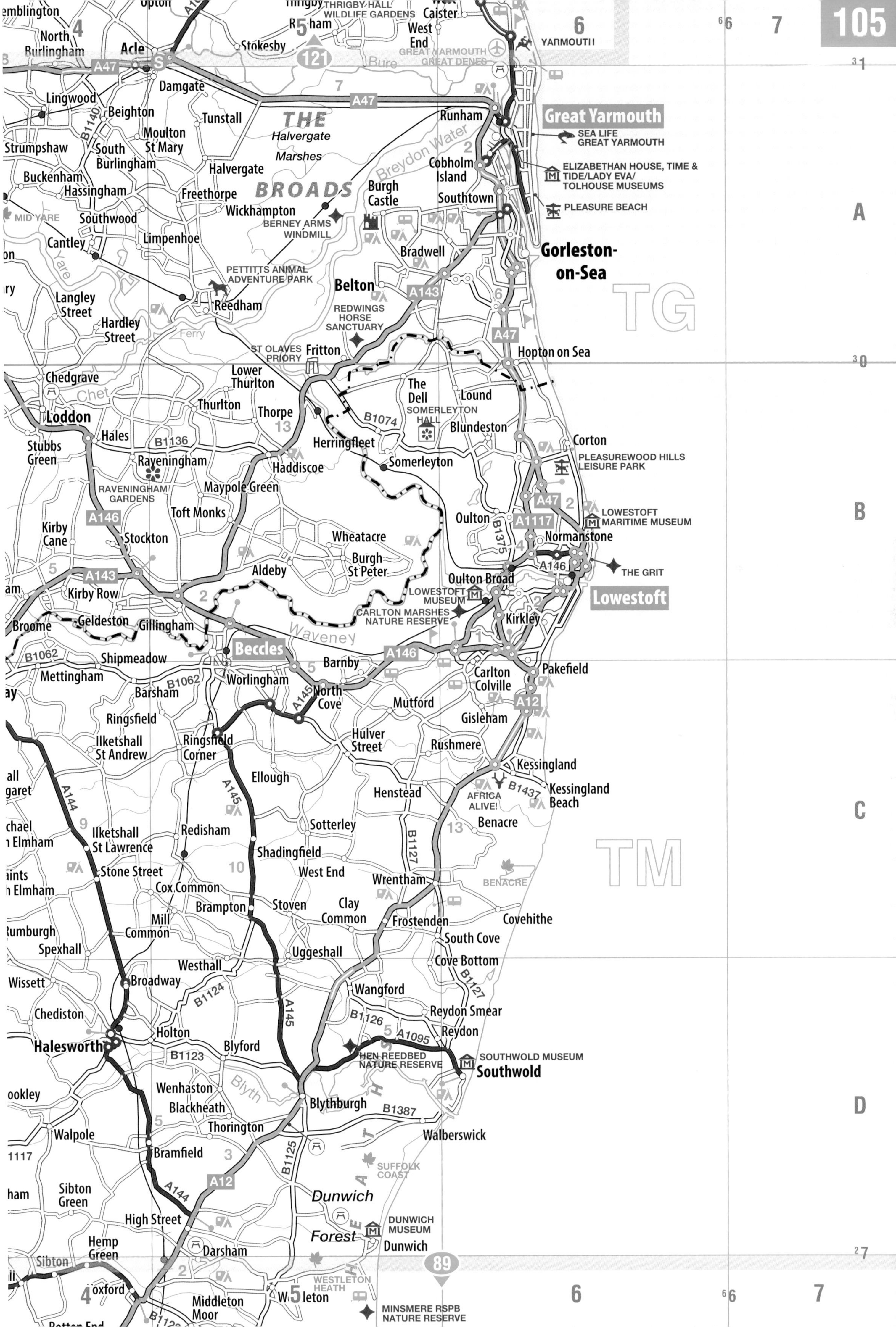
Great Yarmouth
SEA LIFE GREAT YARMOUTH
ELIZABETHAN HOUSE, TIME & TIDE/LADY EVA/ TOLHOUSE MUSEUMS
PLEASURE BEACH
Gorleston-on-Sea
THE BROADS
Halvergate Marshes
BERNEY ARMS WINDMILL
PETTITTS ANIMAL ADVENTURE PARK
REDWINGS HORSE SANCTUARY
ST OLAVES PRIORY
SOMERLEYTON HALL
PLEASUREWOOD HILLS LEISURE PARK
LOWESTOFT MARITIME MUSEUM
THE GRIT
Lowestoft
LOWESTOFT MUSEUM
CARLTON MARSHES NATURE RESERVE
RAVENINGHAM GARDENS
Beccles
AFRICA ALIVE!
BENACRE
HEN REEDBED NATURE RESERVE
SOUTHWOLD MUSEUM
Southwold
SUFFOLK COAST
Dunwich Forest
DUNWICH MUSEUM
WESTLETON HEATH
MINSMERE RSPB NATURE RESERVE
Halesworth
Loddon
Acle
TG
TM
A47
A143
A146
A12
A144
A145
A1117
B1074
B1136
B1062
B1127
B1126
A1095
B1124
B1123
B1387
B1125
B1437
B1375
B1140
121
89

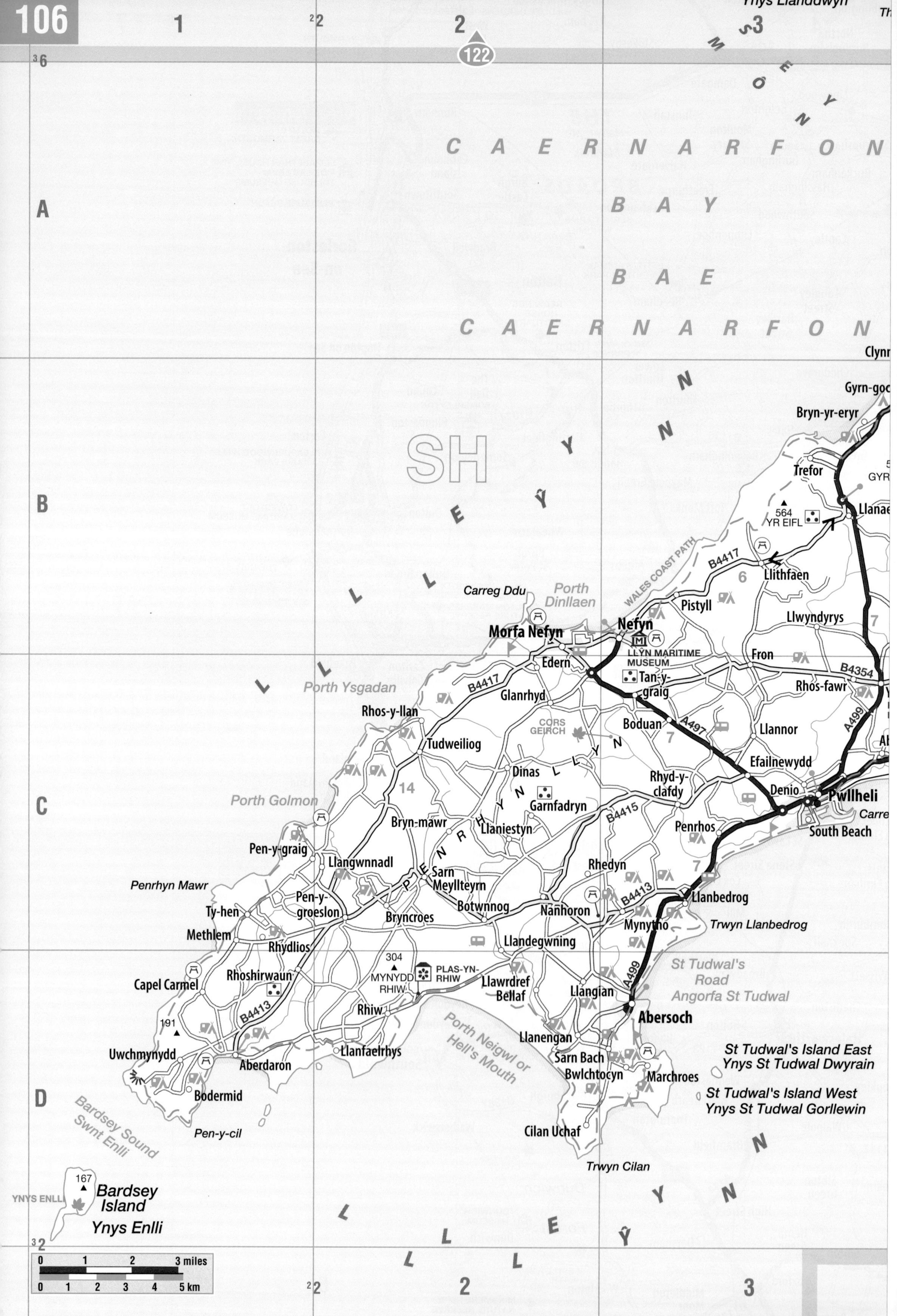

1
2
3
122
Ynys Llanddwyn
CAERNARFON BAY
BAE CAERNARFON
SH
LLEYN
PENRHYN LLYN
Clynnog
Gyrn-goch
Bryn-yr-eryr
Trefor
Llanaelhaearn
564 YR EIFL
B4417
WALES COAST PATH
Llithfaen
Pistyll
Llwyndyrys
Carreg Ddu
Porth Dinllaen
Morfa Nefyn
Nefyn
LLYN MARITIME MUSEUM
Edern
Fron
B4354
Rhos-fawr
Tan-y-graig
Glanrhyd
Porth Ysgadan
Rhos-y-llan
CORS GEIRCH
Boduan
A497
A499
Llannor
Tudweiliog
Efailnewydd
Dinas
Rhyd-y-clafdy
Denio
Pwllheli
Porth Golmon
Garnfadryn
B4415
South Beach
Bryn-mawr
Llaniestyn
Penrhos
Pen-y-graig
Llangwnnadl
Rhedyn
Penrhyn Mawr
Sarn Meyllteyrn
B4413
Llanbedrog
Ty-hen
Pen-y-groeslon
Botwnnog
Nanhoron
Methlem
Bryncroes
Mynytho
Trwyn Llanbedrog
Rhydlios
Llandegwning
304 MYNYDD RHIW
PLAS-YN-RHIW
St Tudwal's Road
Angorfa St Tudwal
Capel Carmel
Rhoshirwaun
Llawrdref Bellaf
Llangian
Abersoch
Rhiw
191
Porth Neigwl or Hell's Mouth
Llanengan
Uwchmynydd
Aberdaron
Llanfaelrhys
Sarn Bach
St Tudwal's Island East
Ynys St Tudwal Dwyrain
Bwlchtocyn
Marchroes
Bodermid
St Tudwal's Island West
Ynys St Tudwal Gorllewin
Bardsey Sound
Swnt Enlli
Pen-y-cil
Cilan Uchaf
Trwyn Cilan
167
YNYS ENLLI
Bardsey Island
Ynys Enlli
A
B
C
D
0 1 2 3 miles
0 1 2 3 4 5 km

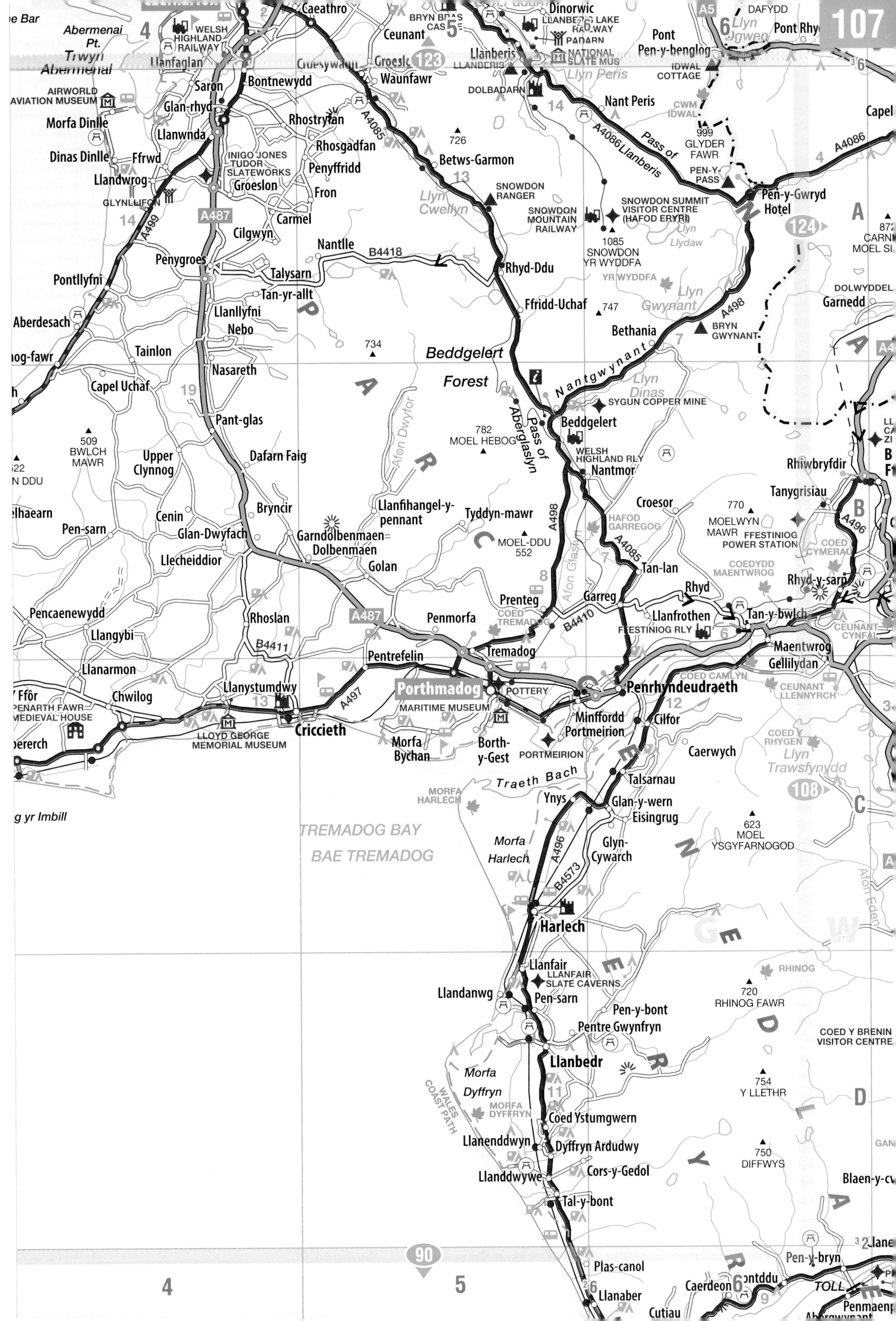
Caeathro
BRYN BRAS CASTLE
Dinorwic
LLANBERIS LAKE RAILWAY
PADARN
DAFYDD
Pont Pen-y-benglog
Pont Rhyd
Abermenai Pt.
Trwyn Abermenai
WELSH HIGHLAND RAILWAY
Llanfaglan
Ceunant
Groeslon
Waunfawr
Llanberis
NATIONAL SLATE MUS
LLANBERIS
Llyn Peris
IDWAL COTTAGE
Llyn Ogwen
AIRWORLD AVIATION MUSEUM
Saron
Bontnewydd
DOLBADARN
Nant Peris
CWM IDWAL
Capel
Morfa Dinlle
Glan-rhyd
Rhostryfan
A4085
726
A4086
Pass of Llanberis
999 GLYDER FAWR
Llanwnda
Rhosgadfan
Betws-Garmon
PEN-Y-PASS
Dinas Dinlle
Ffrwd
INIGO JONES TUDOR SLATEWORKS
Penyffridd
Pen-y-Gwryd Hotel
Llandwrog
Groeslon
Fron
SNOWDON RANGER
GLYNLLIFON
A487
Llyn Cwellyn
SNOWDON MOUNTAIN RAILWAY
SNOWDON SUMMIT VISITOR CENTRE (HAFOD ERYRI)
Carmel
A499
Cilgwyn
1085 SNOWDON YR WYDDFA
Llyn Llydaw
124
872 CARNEDD MOEL SIABOD
Nantlle
B4418
Penygroes
Talysarn
Rhyd-Ddu
YR WYDDFA
Llyn Gwynant
Pontllyfni
Tan-yr-allt
Ffridd-Uchaf
747
A498
DOLWYDDELAN
Garnedd
Aberdesach
Llanllyfni
Nebo
Bethania
BRYN GWYNANT
734
Beddgelert Forest
Tainlon
Nasareth
Nantgwynant
Capel Uchaf
Llyn Dinas
SYGUN COPPER MINE
Pass of Aberglaslyn
Beddgelert
Pant-glas
509 BWLCH MAWR
782 MOEL HEBOG
Afon Dwyfor
WELSH HIGHLAND RLY
Upper Clynnog
Dafarn Faig
Nantmor
Rhiwbryfdir
Tanygrisiau
Bryncir
Croesor
770 MOELWYN MAWR
FFESTINIOG POWER STATION
Pen-sarn
Cenin
Llanfihangel-y-pennant
Tyddyn-mawr
HAFOD GARREGOG
A496
Glan-Dwyfach
Garndolbenmaen
Dolbenmaen
MOEL-DDU 552
A4085
COED CYMERAU
Llecheiddior
Golan
Tan-lan
COEDYDD MAENTWROG
Rhyd-y-sarn
Prenteg
Afon Glaslyn
Rhyd
Garreg
Pencaenewydd
Rhoslan
A487
Penmorfa
COED TREMADOG
B4410
Llanfrothen
Tan-y-bwlch
FFESTINIOG RLY
CEUNANT CYNFAL
Llangybi
B4411
Tremadog
Maentwrog
Gellilydan
Llanarmon
Pentrefelin
COED CAMLYN
Llanystumdwy
Porthmadog
Penrhyndeudraeth
Chwilog
POTTERY
CEUNANT LLENNYRCH
PENARTH FAWR MEDIEVAL HOUSE
A497
MARITIME MUSEUM
Minffordd
Cilfor
Criccieth
LLOYD GEORGE MEMORIAL MUSEUM
Portmeirion
Morfa Bychan
Borth-y-Gest
PORTMEIRION
Caerwych
COED Y RHYGEN
Llyn Trawsfynydd
Traeth Bach
Talsarnau
108
MORFA HARLECH
Ynys
Glan-y-wern
Eisingrug
TREMADOG BAY
BAE TREMADOG
623 MOEL YSGYFARNOGOD
Morfa Harlech
Glyn-Cywarch
A496
B4573
Afon Eden
Harlech
Llanfair
LLANFAIR SLATE CAVERNS
RHINOG
Llandanwg
Pen-sarn
720 RHINOG FAWR
Pen-y-bont
Pentre Gwynfryn
COED Y BRENIN VISITOR CENTRE
Llanbedr
Morfa Dyffryn
WALES COAST PATH
754 Y LLETHR
MORFA DYFFRYN
Coed Ystumgwern
Llanenddwyn
Dyffryn Ardudwy
750 DIFFWYS
Llanddwywe
Cors-y-Gedol
Blaen-y-cwm
Tal-y-bont
Pen-y-bryn
90
Plas-canol
Caerdeon
Bontddu
TOLL
Llanaber
Cutiau
Penmaenpool
4
5
6
PARC CENEDLAETHOL ERYRI
SNOWDONIA NATIONAL PARK

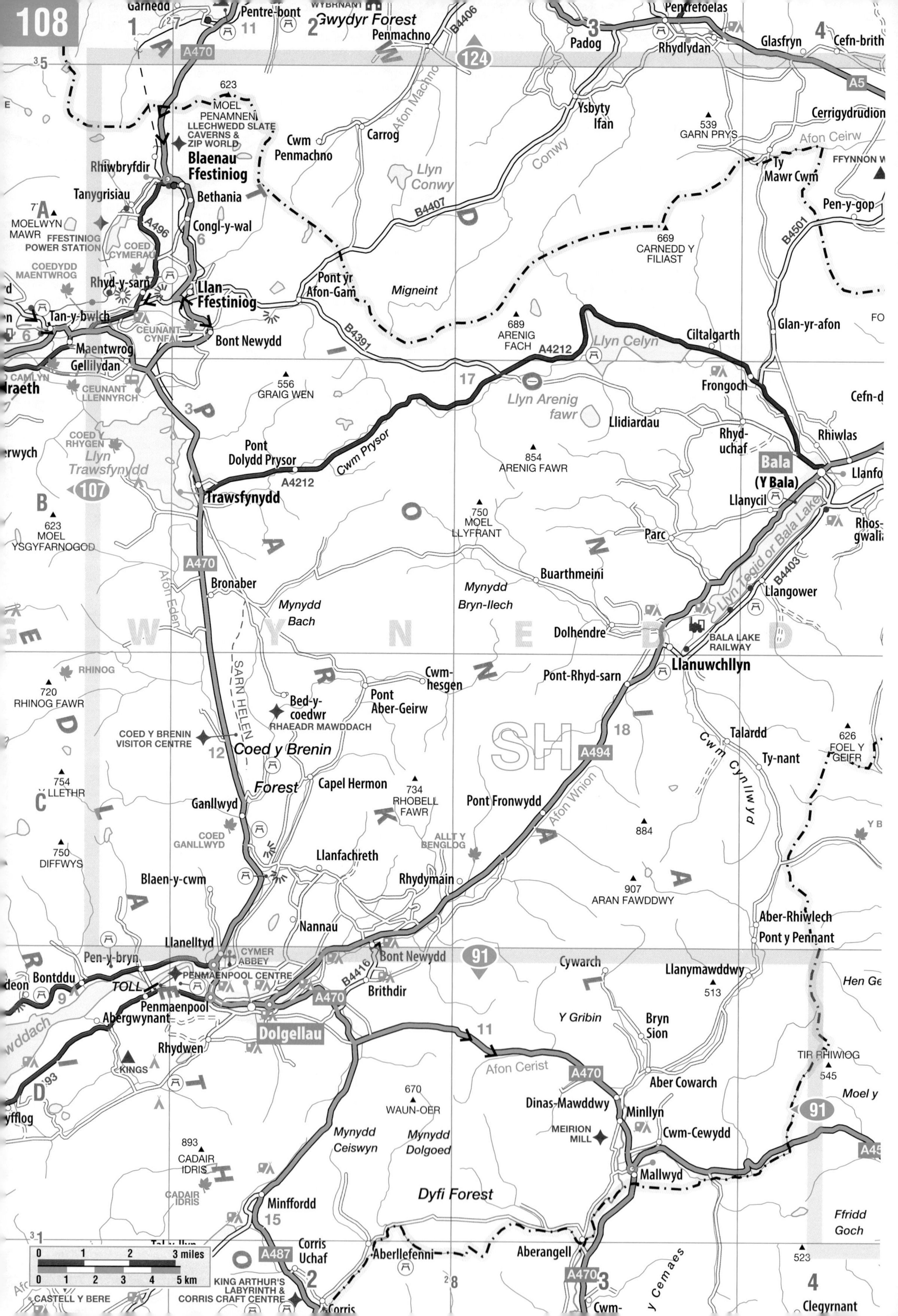
Garnedd
Pentre-bont
Gwydyr Forest
Penmachno
B4406
124
Pentrefoelas
Padog
Rhydlydan
Glasfryn
Cefn-brith
A5
A470
623
MOEL PENAMNEN
LLECHWEDD SLATE CAVERNS & ZIP WORLD
Blaenau Ffestiniog
Rhiwbryfdir
Tanygrisiau
Bethania
Congl-y-wal
A496
MOELWYN MAWR
FFESTINIOG POWER STATION
COED CYMERAU
COEDYDD MAENTWROG
Rhyd-y-sarn
Llan-Ffestiniog
Tan-y-bwlch
Maentwrog
Gellilydan
CEUNANT CYNFAL
Bont Newydd
CEUNANT LLENNYRCH
Cwm Penmachno
Carrog
Afon Machno
Llyn Conwy
B4407
Conwy
Ysbyty Ifan
539
GARN PRYS
Cerrigydrudion
Afon Ceirw
FFYNNON W
Ty Mawr Cwm
Pen-y-gop
B4501
669
CARNEDD Y FILIAST
Pont yr Afon-Gam
Migneint
B4391
689
ARENIG FACH
A4212
Llyn Celyn
Ciltalgarth
Glan-yr-afon
Frongoch
17
556
GRAIG WEN
Llyn Arenig fawr
Llidiardau
Rhyd-uchaf
Rhiwlas
Bala
(Y Bala)
Llanfor
Llanycil
COED Y RHYGEN
Llyn Trawsfynydd
107
Pont Dolydd Prysor
Cwm Prysor
A4212
854
ARENIG FAWR
Trawsfynydd
623
MOEL YSGYFARNOGOD
750
MOEL LLYFRANT
Parc
Rhos-gwalia
Llyn Tegid or Bala Lake
B4403
Buarthmeini
Llangower
A470
Bronaber
Afon Eden
Mynydd Bach
Mynydd Bryn-llech
Dolhendre
BALA LAKE RAILWAY
Llanuwchllyn
RHINOG
720
RHINOG FAWR
SARN HELEN
Cwm-hesgen
Pont-Rhyd-sarn
Pont Aber-Geirw
Bed-y-coedwr
RHAEADR MAWDDACH
COED Y BRENIN VISITOR CENTRE
12
Coed y Brenin Forest
18
SH
A494
Talardd
626
FOEL Y GEIFR
Ty-nant
Cwm Cynllwyd
754
LLETHR
Capel Hermon
734
RHOBELL FAWR
Ganllwyd
Pont Fronwydd
Afon Wnion
884
COED GANLLWYD
ALLT Y BENGLOG
750
DIFFWYS
Llanfachreth
Blaen-y-cwm
Rhydymain
907
ARAN FAWDDWY
Nannau
Aber-Rhiwlech
Pont y Pennant
Llanelltyd
CYMER ABBEY
Pen-y-bryn
Bont Newydd
91
Cywarch
Llanymawddwy
513
Hen Ge
Bontddu
PENMAENPOOL CENTRE
TOLL
B4416
Brithdir
A470
Penmaenpool
Abergwynant
Dolgellau
Y Gribin
Bryn Sion
11
Rhydwen
KINGS
Afon Cerist
TIR RHIWIOG
545
Moel y
A470
Aber Cowarch
670
WAUN-OER
Dinas-Mawddwy
Minllyn
91
MEIRION MILL
Cwm-Cewydd
Mynydd Ceiswyn
Mynydd Dolgoed
893
CADAIR IDRIS
Mallwyd
CADAIR IDRIS
Dyfi Forest
Minffordd
15
Ffridd Goch
Corris Uchaf
A487
Aberllefenni
Aberangell
523
A470
Cwm Cemaes
KING ARTHUR'S LABYRINTH & CORRIS CRAFT CENTRE
CASTELL Y BERE
Corris
Clegyrnant
0 1 2 3 miles
0 1 2 3 4 5 km

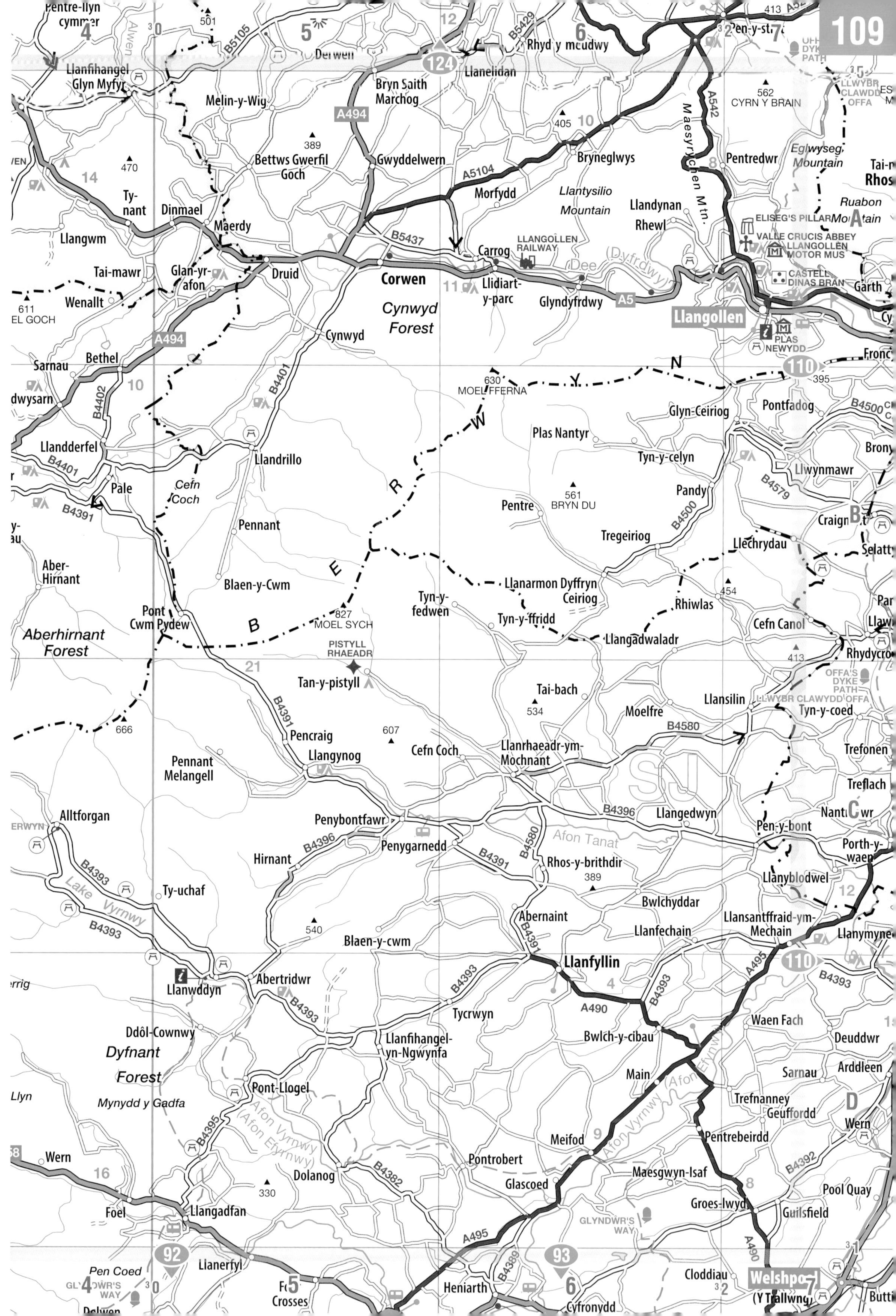
Pentre-llyn cymmer
Alwen
Derwen
Rhyd y meudwy
Pen-y-stryt
Llanfihangel Glyn Myfyr
Llanelidan
Bryn Saith Marchog
Melin-y-Wig
A494
562 CYRN Y BRAIN
LLWYBR CLAWDD OFFA
Maesyrychen Mtn.
A542
Bettws Gwerfil Goch
Gwyddelwern
Bryneglwys
Pentredwr
Eglwyseg Mountain
A5104
Morfydd
Llantysilio Mountain
Llandynan
Rhewl
Ruabon Mountain
Ty-nant
Dinmael
Maerdy
ELISEG'S PILLAR
VALLE CRUCIS ABBEY
LLANGOLLEN MOTOR MUS
Llangwm
B5437
Carrog
LLANGOLLEN RAILWAY
Dee (Dyfrdwy)
CASTELL DINAS BRAN
Garth
Tai-mawr
Glan-yr-afon
Druid
Corwen
Llidiart-y-parc
Glyndyfrdwy
A5
Wenallt
611 EL GOCH
Cynwyd Forest
Llangollen
PLAS NEWYDD
Cynwyd
Sarnau
Bethel
A494
B4401
630 MOEL FFERNA
BERWYN
Glyn-Ceiriog
Pontfadog
B4500
B4402
Plas Nantyr
Tyn-y-celyn
Llandderfel
Llandrillo
Llwynmawr
B4401
Cefn Coch
561 BRYN DU
Pandy
B4579
Pale
Pentre
B4391
Pennant
Tregeiriog
Llechrydau
Aber-Hirnant
Llanarmon Dyffryn Ceiriog
454
Blaen-y-Cwm
Tyn-y-fedwen
Rhiwlas
Pont Cwm Pydew
827 MOEL SYCH
Tyn-y-ffridd
Cefn Canol
Aberhirnant Forest
Llangadwaladr
PISTYLL RHAEADR
413
Rhydycroesau
Tan-y-pistyll
OFFA'S DYKE PATH
Tai-bach
534
Llansilin
LLWYBR CLAWDD OFFA
Tyn-y-coed
666
B4391
Moelfre
B4580
607
Pencraig
Pennant Melangell
Llangynog
Cefn Coch
Llanrhaeadr-ym-Mochnant
Trefonen
SJ
Treflach
Alltforgan
B4396
Llangedwyn
Penybontfawr
Afon Tanat
Pen-y-bont
B4396
Penygarnedd
B4580
Porth-y-waen
B4393
Hirnant
B4391
Rhos-y-brithdir
Lake Vyrnwy
Ty-uchaf
389
Llanyblodwel
Bwlchyddar
B4393
540
Abernaint
Llansantffraid-ym-Mechain
B4391
Llanfechain
Blaen-y-cwm
Llanymynech
Llanwddyn
Abertridwr
Llanfyllin
B4393
A495
B4393
A490
B4393
Ddôl-Cownwy
Tycrwyn
Waen Fach
Dyfnant Forest
Llanfihangel-yn-Ngwynfa
Bwlch-y-cibau
Deuddwr
Arddleen
Sarnau
Main
Afon Efyrnwy
Llyn
Pont-Llogel
Trefnanney
Mynydd y Gadfa
Geufford
Afon Vyrnwy (Afon Efyrnwy)
Afon Vyrnwy
Wern
B4395
Meifod
Pentrebeirdd
Wern
Pontrobert
B4382
Maesgwyn-Isaf
B4392
Dolanog
330
Glascoed
Pool Quay
Foel
Llangadfan
Groes-lwyd
Guilsfield
GLYNDWR'S WAY
A495
A490
Pen Coed
Llanerfyl
B4389
Cloddiau
Welshpool (Y Trallwng)
Foel Crosses
Heniarth
Cyfronydd
Dolwen
Butt

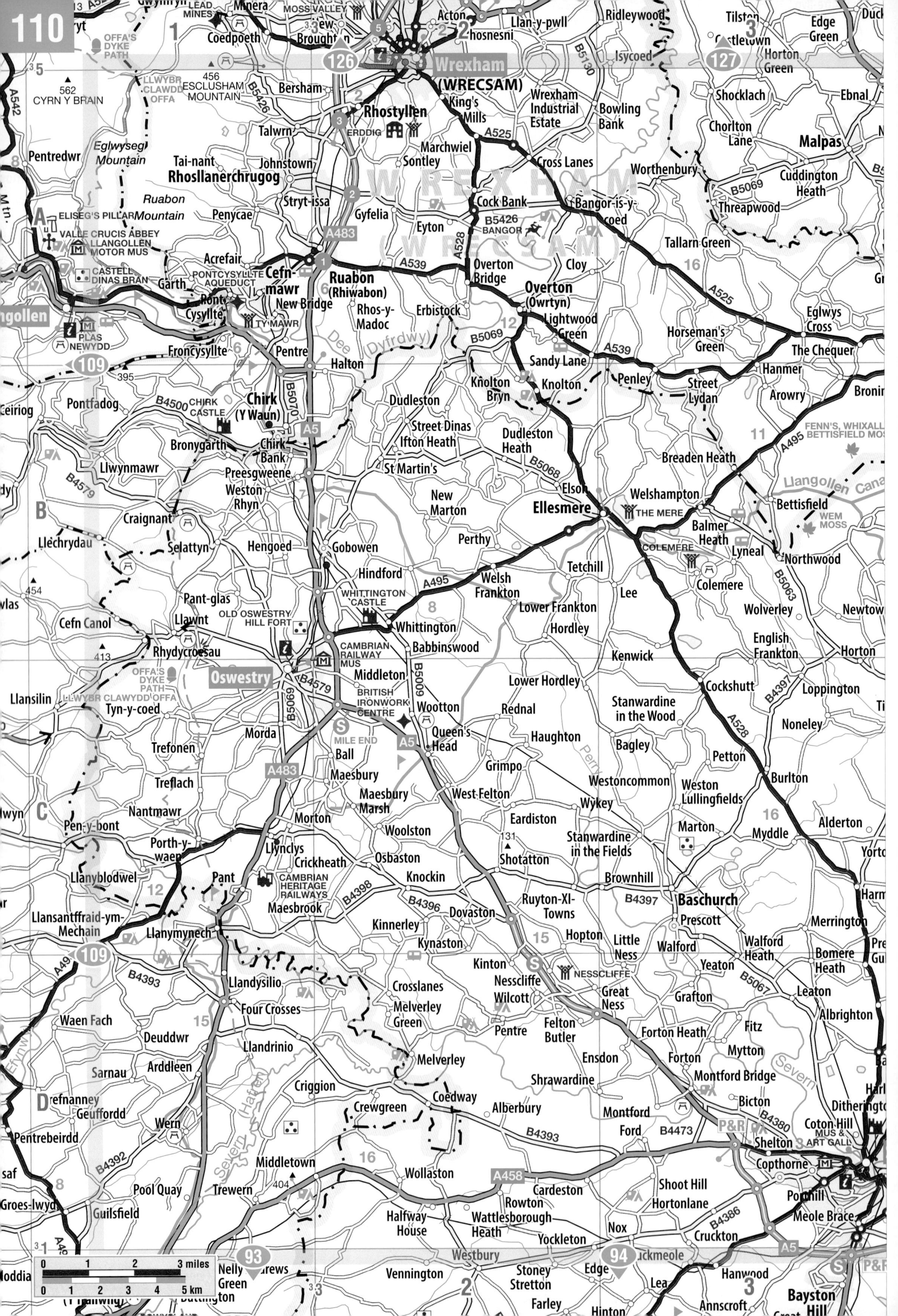

Wrexham
(WRECSAM)
Rhostyllen
Rhosllanerchrugog
Ruabon
(Rhiwabon)
Cefn-mawr
Chirk
(Y Waun)
Overton
(Owrtyn)
Ellesmere
Oswestry
Baschurch
Malpas
Llangollen
WREXHAM
(WRECSAM)
Minera
Coedpoeth
Bersham
Broughton
Acton
Llan-y-pwll
Ridleywood
Isycoed
Tilston
Castletown
Edge Green
Horton Green
Shocklach
Ebnal
Chorlton Lane
Cuddington Heath
Threapwood
Worthenbury
Bangor-is-y-coed
Tallarn Green
Cross Lanes
Bowling Bank
Wrexham Industrial Estate
King's Mills
Marchwiel
Sontley
Johnstown
Talwrn
ERDDIG
Tai-nant
Stryt-issa
Gyfelia
Eyton
Cock Bank
BANGOR
Penycae
Acrefair
Garth
Pontcysyllte
PONTCYSYLLTE AQUEDUCT
New Bridge
Rhos-y-Madoc
Erbistock
Overton Bridge
Cloy
Lightwood Green
Horseman's Green
Eglwys Cross
The Chequer
Hanmer
Sandy Lane
Penley
Street Lydan
Arowry
Knolton
Knolton Bryn
Froncysyllte
Pentre
Halton
TY MAWR
PLAS NEWYDD
CASTELL DINAS BRAN
VALLE CRUCIS ABBEY
LLANGOLLEN MOTOR MUS
ELISEG'S PILLAR
Ruabon Mountain
Eglwyseg Mountain
Pentredwr
ESCLUSHAM MOUNTAIN
CYRN Y BRAIN
OFFA'S DYKE PATH
LLWYBR CLAWDD OFFA
LEAD MINES
MOSS VALLEY
Pontfadog
CHIRK CASTLE
Ceiriog
Bronygarth
Chirk Bank
Llwynmawr
Preesgweene
Weston Rhyn
St Martin's
Dudleston
Street Dinas
Ifton Heath
Dudleston Heath
Elson
Welshampton
Breaden Heath
FENN'S, WHIXALL & BETTISFIELD MOSSES
Bettisfield
Llangollen Canal
WEM MOSS
THE MERE
Balmer Heath
COLEMERE
Colemere
Lyneal
Northwood
Craignant
Selattyn
Llechrydau
Hengoed
Gobowen
New Marton
Perthy
Tetchill
Hindford
WHITTINGTON CASTLE
Welsh Frankton
Lower Frankton
Lee
Wolverley
Newtown
Pant-glas
Llawnt
OLD OSWESTRY HILL FORT
Cefn Canol
Rhydycroesau
Whittington
Babbinswood
CAMBRIAN RAILWAY MUS
Hordley
Kenwick
English Frankton
Horton
Middleton
BRITISH IRONWORK CENTRE
Wootton
Lower Hordley
Stanwardine in the Wood
Cockshutt
Loppington
Llansilin
Tyn-y-coed
Morda
Trefonen
MILE END
Ball
Queen's Head
Rednal
Haughton
Bagley
Noneley
Petton
Treflach
Maesbury
Grimpo
Westoncommon
Weston Lullingfields
Burlton
Nantmawr
Maesbury Marsh
West Felton
Wykey
Eardiston
Marton
Alderton
Pen-y-bont
Morton
Woolston
Shotatton
Stanwardine in the Fields
Myddle
Porth-y-waen
Llynclys
Crickheath
Osbaston
Knockin
Brownhill
Llanyblodwel
Pant
CAMBRIAN HERITAGE RAILWAYS
Maesbrook
Dovaston
Ruyton-XI-Towns
Prescott
Merrington
Llansantffraid-ym-Mechain
Llanymynech
Kinnerley
Kynaston
Hopton
Little Ness
Walford
Walford Heath
Bomere Heath
Kinton
Nesscliffe
NESSCLIFFE
Yeaton
Wilcott
Great Ness
Grafton
Leaton
Llandysilio
Crosslanes
Melverley Green
Four Crosses
Pentre
Felton Butler
Albrighton
Waen Fach
Deuddwr
Forton Heath
Fitz
Llandrinio
Mytton
Melverley
Ensdon
Forton
Sarnau
Arddleen
Shrawardine
Montford Bridge
Criggion
Coedway
Bicton
Drefnanney
Geuffordd
Crewgreen
Alberbury
Montford
Dithering
Wern
Ford
Coton Hill
MUS & ART GALL
Shelton
Pentrebeirdd
Severn (Hafren)
Middletown
Wollaston
Copthorne
Trewern
Cardeston
Shoot Hill
Porthill
Pool Quay
Rowton
Hortonlane
Guilsfield
Groes-lwyd
Halfway House
Wattlesborough Heath
Nox
Meole Brace
Yockleton
Cruckton
Westbury
Nelly Andrews Green
Vennington
Stoney Stretton
Edge
Annscroft
Hanwood
Bayston Hill
Farley
Hinton
Duddlestone
Cuckmeole
Lea
Efyrnwy
3 miles
5 km
A483
A539
A528
A525
A5
A495
B5069
B5070
B5426
B5130
B5068
B5063
B4500
B4579
B4397
B5009
B4398
B4396
B4393
B4392
B4380
B4473
B4386
A458
A49
A542
B5067
P&R

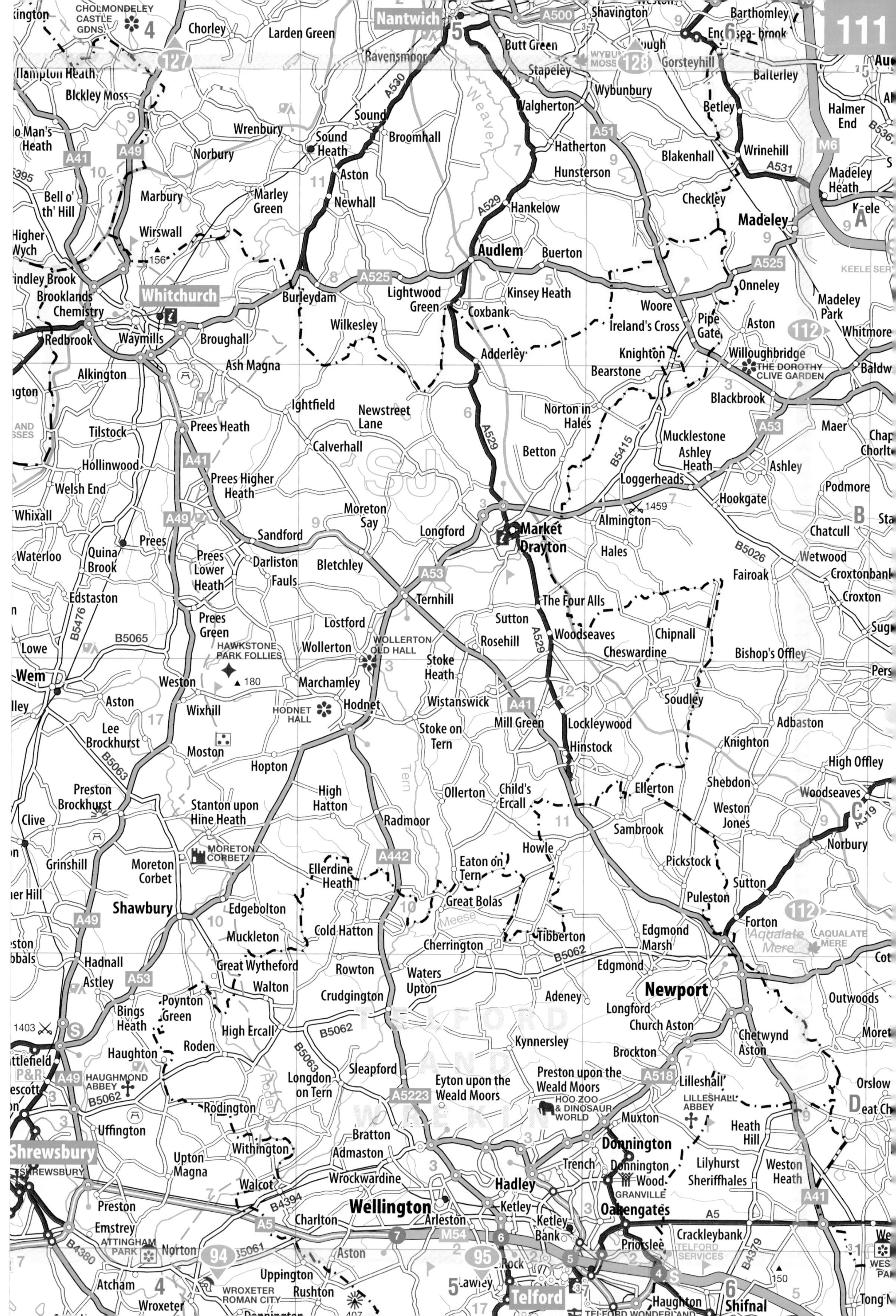
111
CHOLMONDELEY CASTLE GDNS
Chorley
Larden Green
Nantwich
A500
Shavington
Barthomley
Engelsea-brook
Butt Green
Ravensmoor
Wybunbury Moss
Gorsteyhill
Stapeley
Balterley
Hampton Heath
Bickley Moss
A530
Wybunbury
Walgherton
Betley
Halmer End
Weaver
Sound
Wrenbury
Broomhall
Sound Heath
Hatherton
A51
Wrinehill
Man's Heath
A41
A49
Norbury
Aston
Blakenhall
A531
M6
Hunsterson
Madeley Heath
Bell o' th' Hill
Marbury
Marley Green
Newhall
A529
Hankelow
Checkley
Madeley
Keele
Higher Wych
Wirswall
156
Audlem
Buerton
A525
Onneley
Fiddley Brook
Brooklands
Chemistry
Whitchurch
Burleydam
A525
Lightwood Green
Kinsey Heath
Madeley Park
Coxbank
Woore
Redbrook
Waymills
Broughall
Wilkesley
Ireland's Cross
Pipe Gate
Aston
Whitmore
Knighton
Willoughbridge
THE DOROTHY CLIVE GARDEN
Adderley
Bearstone
Baldwin
Ash Magna
Alkington
Blackbrook
Ightfield
Newstreet Lane
Norton in Hales
Tilstock
Prees Heath
A53
Maer
Mucklestone
Ashley Heath
Calverhall
Betton
B5415
A41
Hollinwood
Ashley
Prees Higher Heath
Loggerheads
Welsh End
Podmore
Hookgate
Moreton Say
1459
Whixall
A49
Almington
Chatcull
Sandford
Longford
Market Drayton
Prees
Quina Brook
Waterloo
Prees Lower Heath
Hales
B5026
Darliston
Bletchley
Wetwood
Fauls
A53
Fairoak
Croxtonbank
Edstaston
Ternhill
The Four Alls
Croxton
B5476
Prees Green
Lostford
Sutton
Woodseaves
Chipnall
Lowe
B5065
Rosehill
Cheswardine
Wollerton
WOLLERTON OLD HALL
Bishop's Offley
HAWKSTONE PARK FOLLIES
Stoke Heath
Wem
Weston
180
Marchamley
A529
Aston
HODNET HALL
Hodnet
Wistanswick
A41
Soudley
Wixhill
Lee Brockhurst
Mill Green
Lockleywood
Adbaston
Stoke on Tern
Knighton
Moston
Hinstock
B5063
Hopton
High Offley
Tern
Preston Brockhurst
Stanton upon Hine Heath
High Hatton
Ollerton
Child's Ercall
Ellerton
Shebdon
Woodseaves
Clive
Radmoor
Weston Jones
Sambrook
A519
MORETON CORBET
Howle
Norbury
Grinshill
Moreton Corbet
A442
Eaton on Tern
Pickstock
Ellerdine Heath
Sutton
Shawbury
Edgebolton
Great Bolas
Puleston
A49
Meese
Forton
Muckleton
Cold Hatton
Tibberton
Edgmond Marsh
AQUALATE MERE
Aqualate Mere
Cherrington
Hadnall
Great Wytheford
B5062
Edgmond
Rowton
Waters Upton
Astley
A53
Walton
Newport
Outwoods
Poynton Green
Crudgington
Adeney
Longford
TELFORD AND WREKIN
Bings Heath
1403
Church Aston
Chetwynd Aston
High Ercall
B5062
Roden
Kynnersley
Haughton
B5063
Brockton
Sleapford
Preston upon the Weald Moors
A518
Lilleshall
Orslow
HAUGHMOND ABBEY
A49
Longdon on Tern
Eyton upon the Weald Moors
A5223
B5062
P&R
LILLESHALL ABBEY
HOO ZOO & DINOSAUR WORLD
Rodington
Muxton
Uffington
Heath Hill
Bratton
Donnington
Shrewsbury
Withington
Upton Magna
Admaston
Trench
Lilyhurst
Weston Heath
SHREWSBURY
Donnington Wood
Sheriffhales
Walcot
Wrockwardine
Hadley
GRANVILLE
B4394
Wellington
Ketley
Oakengates
A41
Preston
Charlton
Arleston
Ketley Bank
A5
A5
M54
Crackleybank
Emstrey
ATTINGHAM PARK
Norton
94
Aston
95
Priorslee
TELFORD SERVICES
B4380
B5061
Rock
B4379
Atcham
Wroxeter
WROXETER ROMAN CITY
Uppington
Rushton
Lawley
150
Telford
Haughton
Shifnal
TELFORD WONDERLAND
127
128
112

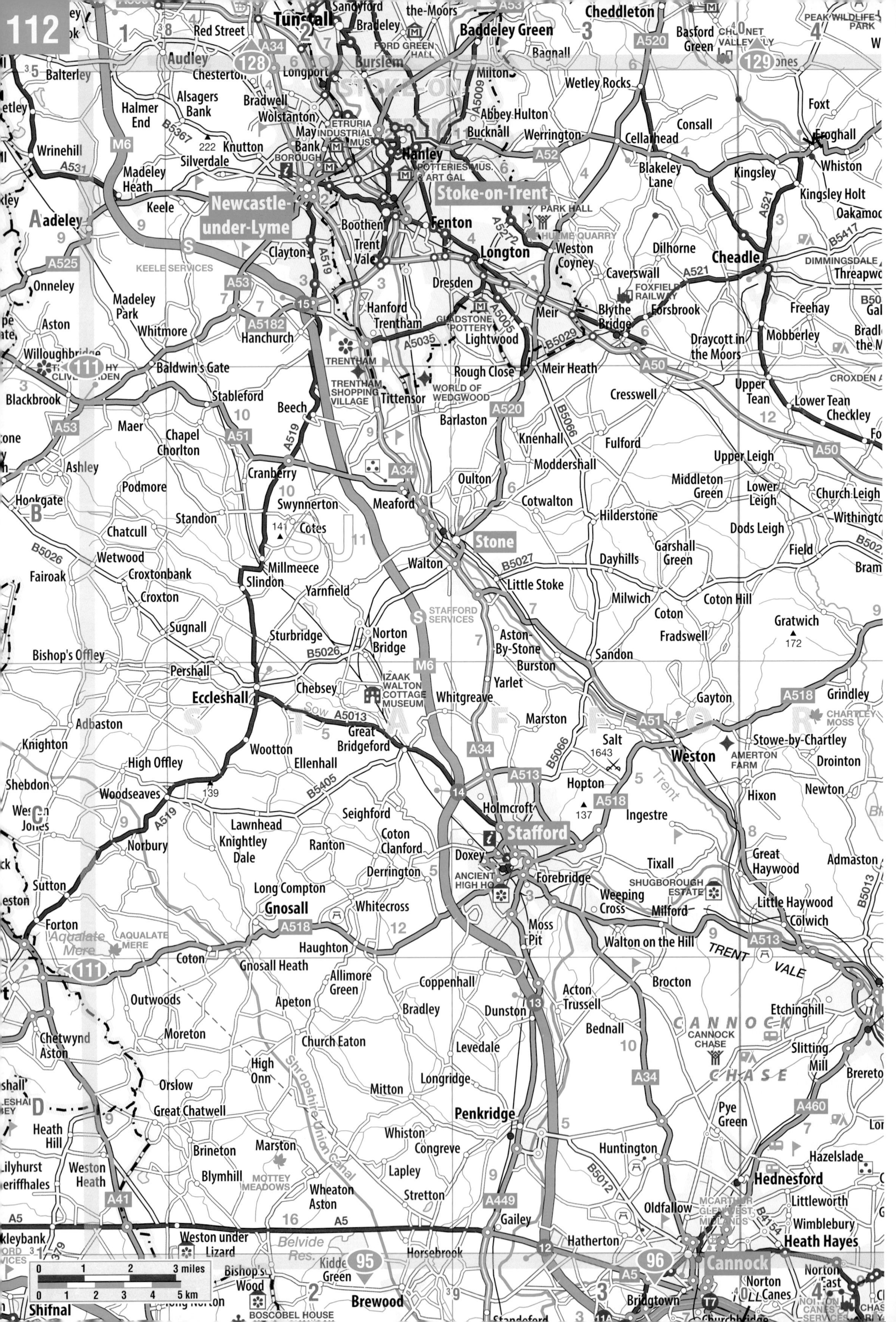

Red Street
Tunstall
Sandyford
Bradeley
the-Moors
Baddeley Green
Cheddleton
Basford Green
Bagnall
Audley
Balterley
Chesterton
Longport
Burslem
Milton
Wetley Rocks
Foxt
Halmer End
Alsagers Bank
Bradwell
Wolstanton
Abbey Hulton
Consall
Froghall
Wrinehill
Knutton
May Bank
Bucknall
Werrington
Cellarhead
Whiston
Madeley Heath
Silverdale
Hanley
Blakeley Lane
Kingsley
Kingsley Holt
Keele
Newcastle-under-Lyme
Stoke-on-Trent
Oakamoor
Madeley
Boothen
Fenton
Park Hall
Longton
Dilhorne
Cheadle
Trent Vale
Clayton
Weston Coyney
Caverswall
Keele Services
Onneley
Madeley Park
Whitmore
Hanford
Trentham
Dresden
Lightwood
Meir
Blythe Bridge
Forsbrook
Freehay
Aston
Hanchurch
Gladstone Pottery
Foxfield Railway
Draycott in the Moors
Mobberley
Willoughbridge
Baldwin's Gate
Trentham
Rough Close
Meir Heath
Blackbrook
Stableford
Beech
Trentham Shopping Village
Tittensor
World of Wedgwood
Cresswell
Upper Tean
Lower Tean
Checkley
Maer
Chapel Chorlton
Barlaston
Knenhall
Fulford
Ashley
Moddershall
Upper Leigh
Podmore
Cranberry
Oulton
Middleton Green
Lower Leigh
Church Leigh
Hookgate
Swynnerton
Meaford
Cotwalton
Hilderstone
Standon
Chatcull
Cotes
Stone
Dods Leigh
Wetwood
Millmeece
Walton
Garshall Green
Dayhills
Field
Fairoak
Croxtonbank
Slindon
Little Stoke
Croxton
Yarnfield
Milwich
Coton Hill
Coton
Stafford Services
Sugnall
Sturbridge
Norton Bridge
Aston-By-Stone
Fradswell
Gratwich
Bishop's Offley
Sandon
Burston
Pershall
Yarlet
Eccleshall
Chebsey
Izaak Walton Cottage Museum
Whitgreave
Gayton
Grindley
Chartley Moss
Adbaston
Marston
Great Bridgeford
Salt
Stowe-by-Chartley
Knighton
Wootton
Weston
Amerton Farm
Drointon
Ellenhall
High Offley
Hopton
Shebdon
Woodseaves
Holmcroft
Hixon
Newton
Ingestre
Seighford
Lawnhead
Knightley Dale
Ranton
Coton Clanford
Stafford
Norbury
Doxey
Tixall
Great Haywood
Admaston
Derrington
Ancient High House
Forebridge
Shugborough Estate
Sutton
Long Compton
Weeping Cross
Milford
Little Haywood
Colwich
Gnosall
Whitecross
Forton
Aqualate Mere
Moss Pit
Walton on the Hill
Trent Vale
Haughton
Coton
Gnosall Heath
Brocton
Allimore Green
Coppenhall
Acton Trussell
Etchinghill
Outwoods
Apeton
Bradley
Dunston
Bednall
Cannock Chase
Chetwynd Aston
Moreton
Church Eaton
Levedale
Slitting Mill
High Onn
Brereton
Shropshire Union Canal
Longridge
Orslow
Mitton
Penkridge
Pye Green
Great Chatwell
Heath Hill
Whiston
Congreve
Huntington
Hazelslade
Brineton
Marston
Weston Heath
Blymhill
Lapley
Hednesford
Mottey Meadows
Wheaton Aston
Stretton
Oldfallow
Littleworth
Wimblebury
Weston under Lizard
Gailey
Heath Hayes
Belvide Res.
Hatherton
Horsebrook
Kiddemore Green
Cannock
Norton East
Bishop's Wood
Norton Canes
Brewood
Bridgtown
Shifnal
Boscobel House
M6
A34
A53
A520
A50
A52
A5009
A521
B5417
A525
A5182
A5035
A5005
B5029
A5272
A519
A51
B5066
B5026
B5027
B5405
A5013
A518
A513
B5013
A41
A5
A449
B5012
B4154
A460
0 1 2 3 miles
0 1 2 3 4 5 km

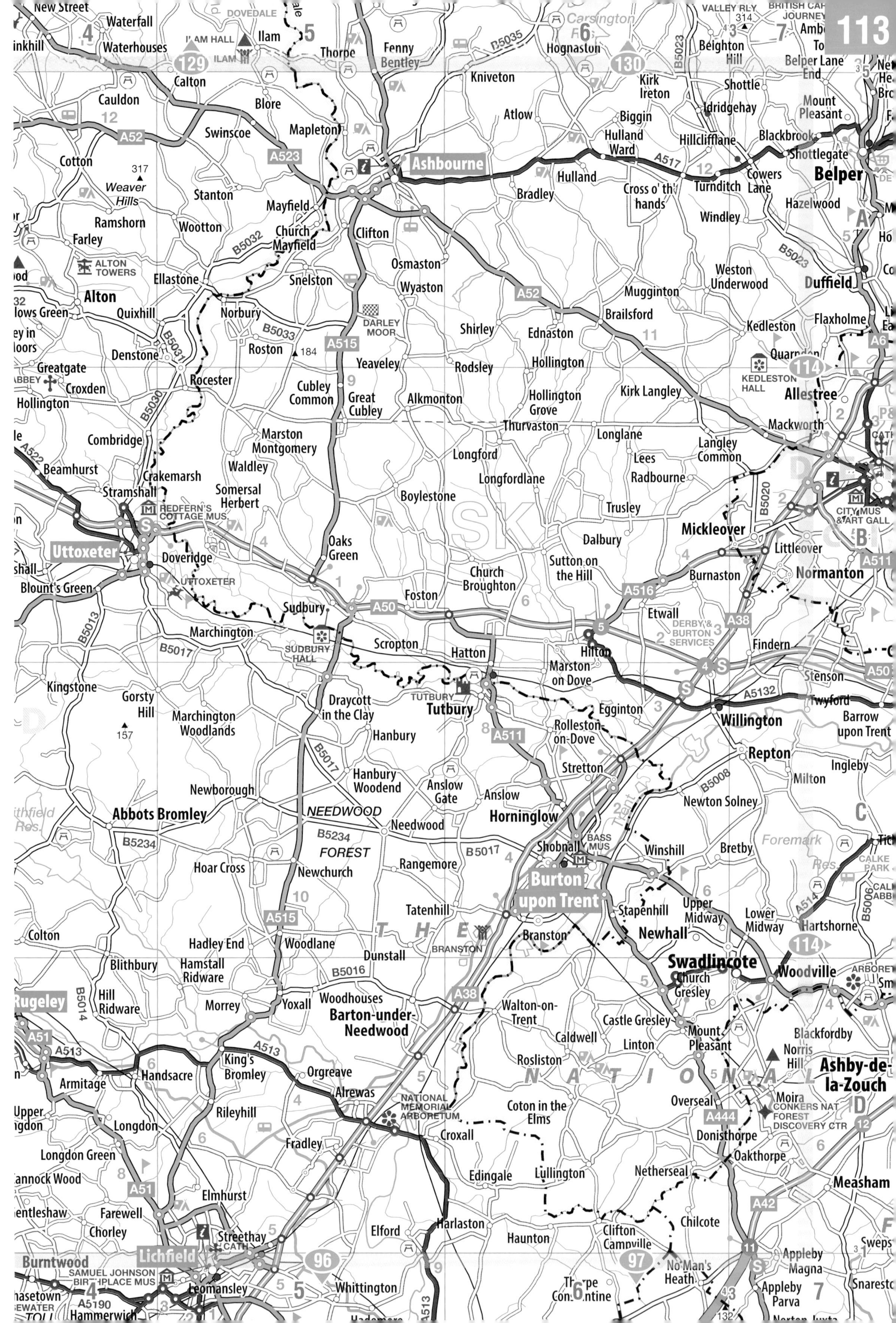

Ashbourne
Uttoxeter
Burton upon Trent
Swadlincote
Lichfield
Belper
Rugeley
Burntwood
Ashby-de-la-Zouch
Abbots Bromley
Barton-under-Needwood
Tutbury
Mickleover
Normanton
Allestree
Duffield
Willington
Repton
Newhall
Woodville
Measham
Horninglow
Alton
NEEDWOOD FOREST
NATIONAL
SK

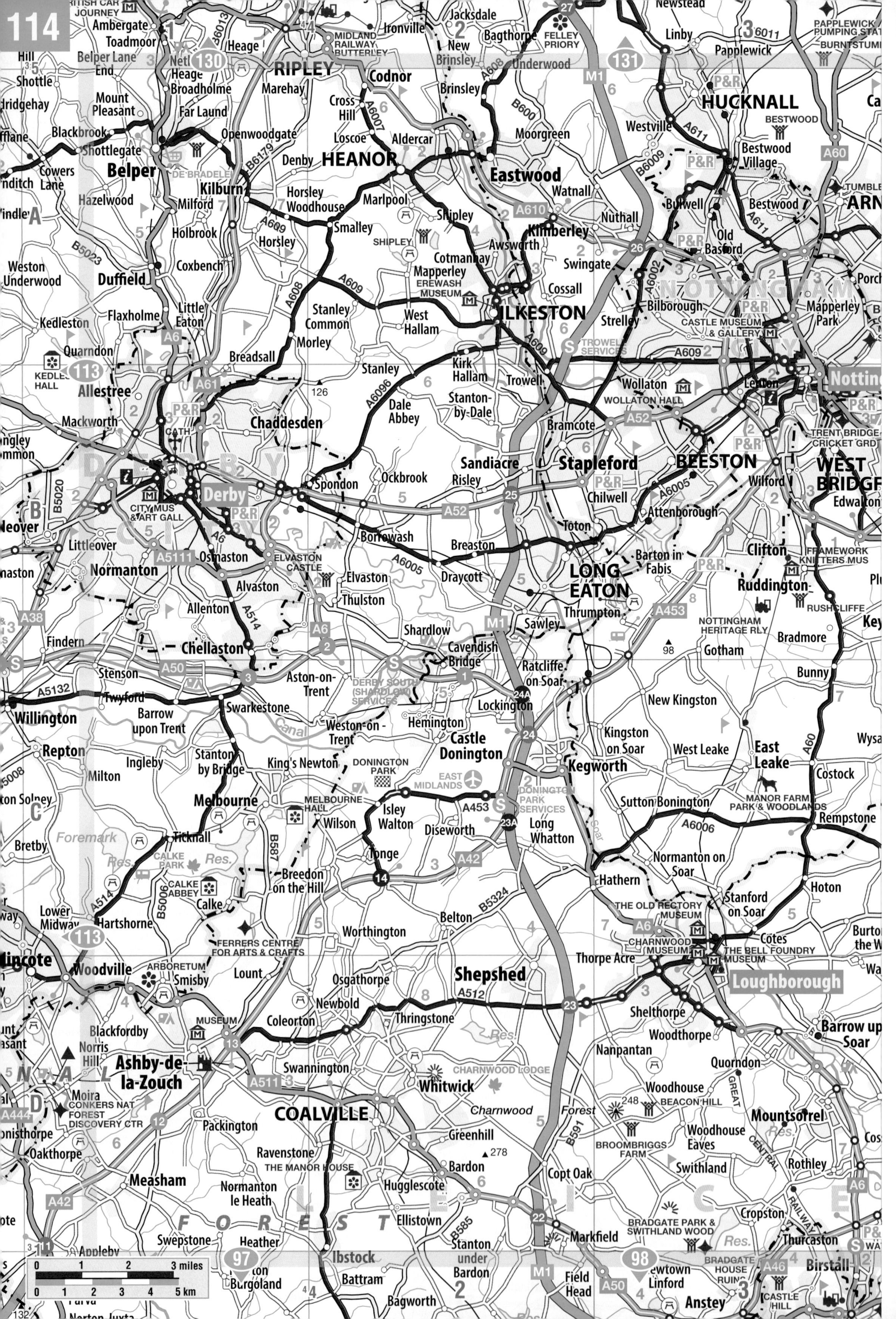
Ambergate
Toadmoor
Belper Lane End
Heage
Nether Heage
Broadholme
RIPLEY
Codnor
Marehay
Ironville
Jacksdale
New Brinsley
Bagthorpe
Felley Priory
Underwood
Newstead
Linby
Papplewick
Papplewick Pumping Station
Shottle
Mount Pleasant
Far Laund
Cross Hill
Brinsley
HUCKNALL
Bestwood
Blackbrook
Shottlegate
Openwoodgate
Loscoe
Aldercar
Moorgreen
Westville
Bestwood Village
Cowers Lane
Belper
De Bradelei
Denby
HEANOR
Eastwood
Watnall
Kilburn
Horsley Woodhouse
Marlpool
Bulwell
Hazelwood
Milford
Shipley
Nuthall
Kimberley
Holbrook
Smalley
Horsley
Old Basford
Shipley
Awsworth
Cotmanhay
Swingate
Weston Underwood
Duffield
Coxbench
Mapperley
Erewash Museum
Cossall
NOTTINGHAM
Porchester
Kedleston
Flaxholme
Little Eaton
Stanley Common
West Hallam
ILKESTON
Strelley
Bilborough
Mapperley Park
Castle Museum & Gallery
Quarndon
Kedleston Hall
Morley
Trowell Services
Breadsall
Stanley
Kirk Hallam
Trowell
Allestree
Wollaton
Wollaton Hall
Lenton
Nottingham
Mackworth
Chaddesden
Dale Abbey
Stanton-by-Dale
Bramcote
Trent Bridge Cricket Grd
DERBY
Derby
Spondon
Ockbrook
Sandiacre
Risley
Stapleford
BEESTON
WEST BRIDGFORD
Wilford
Chilwell
Attenborough
Edwalton
City Mus & Art Gall
Littleover
Osmaston
Borrowash
Breaston
Toton
Normanton
Elvaston Castle
Elvaston
Draycott
Barton in Fabis
Clifton
Framework Knitters Mus
LONG EATON
Alvaston
Thulston
Ruddington
Rushcliffe
Allenton
Thrumpton
Shardlow
Sawley
Nottingham Heritage Rly
Findern
Chellaston
Cavendish Bridge
Gotham
Bradmore
Stenson
Aston-on-Trent
Ratcliffe on Soar
Bunny
Derby South (Shardlow) Services
Twyford
Willington
Barrow upon Trent
Swarkestone
Lockington
Weston-on-Trent
Hemington
New Kingston
Castle Donington
Kingston on Soar
West Leake
East Leake
Repton
Ingleby
Stanton by Bridge
King's Newton
Donington Park
Kegworth
Costock
Milton
East Midlands
Donington Park Services
Sutton Bonington
Manor Farm Park & Woodlands
Melbourne
Melbourne Hall
Isley Walton
Rempstone
Bretby
Foremark
Wilson
Diseworth
Long Whatton
Ticknall
Tonge
Normanton on Soar
Calke Park
Breedon on the Hill
Hathern
Hoton
Calke Abbey
Calke
The Old Rectory Museum
Stanford on Soar
Lower Midway
Hartshorne
Belton
Worthington
Charnwood Museum
The Bell Foundry Museum
Cotes
Ferrers Centre for Arts & Crafts
Thorpe Acre
Woodville
Arboretum
Lount
Osgathorpe
Shepshed
Loughborough
Smisby
Newbold
Shelthorpe
Coleorton
Thringstone
Barrow upon Soar
Blackfordby
Museum
Woodthorpe
Norris Hill
Nanpantan
Ashby-de-la-Zouch
Swannington
Charnwood Lodge
Quorndon
Whitwick
Woodhouse
Moira
Conkers Nat Forest Discovery Ctr
Charnwood
Forest
Beacon Hill
COALVILLE
Mountsorrel
Packington
Greenhill
Broombriggs Farm
Woodhouse Eaves
Oakthorpe
Ravenstone
Swithland
Rothley
The Manor House
Bardon
Copt Oak
Measham
Normanton le Heath
Hugglescote
Cropston
Bradgate Park & Swithland Wood
Ellistown
Thurcaston
Swepstone
Heather
Stanton under Bardon
Markfield
Appleby
Ibstock
Newton Linford
Bradgate House Ruins
Birstall
Field Head
Battram
Burgoland
Bagworth
Anstey
Castle Hill
0 1 2 3 miles
0 1 2 3 4 5 km

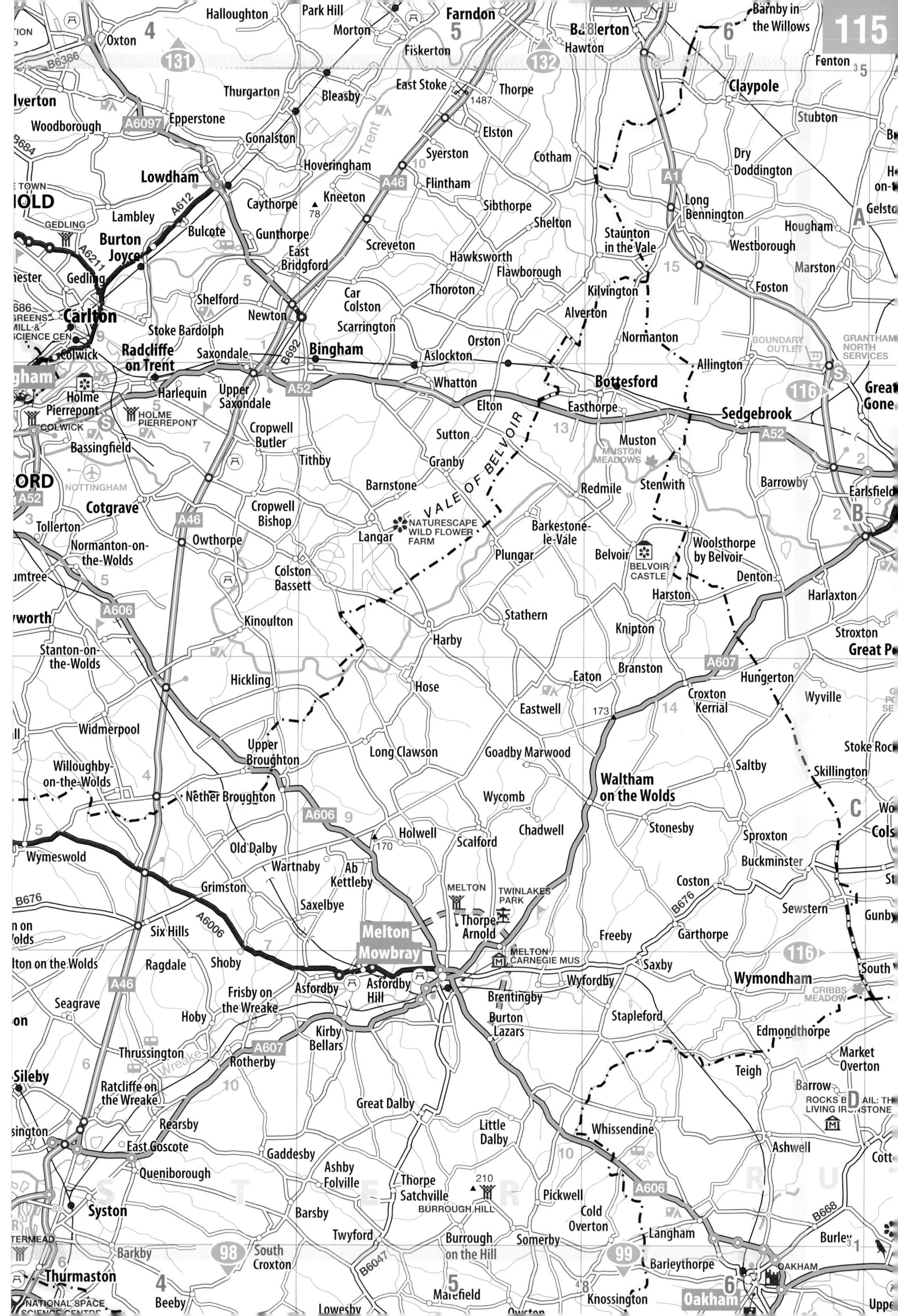
Halloughton
Park Hill
Morton
Farndon
Balderton
Hawton
Barnby in the Willows
Oxton
Fiskerton
Fenton
Thurgarton
Bleasby
East Stoke
Thorpe
Claypole
Calverton
Woodborough
Epperstone
Elston
Stubton
Gonalston
Syerston
Cotham
Dry Doddington
Lowdham
Hoveringham
Flintham
Long Bennington
Lambley
Caythorpe
Kneeton
Sibthorpe
Shelton
Gelston
Hougham
Burton Joyce
Bulcote
Gunthorpe
East Bridgford
Screveton
Hawksworth
Staunton in the Vale
Westborough
Gedling
Flawborough
Marston
Thoroton
Kilvington
Foston
Carlton
Shelford
Newton
Car Colston
Alverton
Stoke Bardolph
Scarrington
Normanton
Radcliffe on Trent
Saxondale
Bingham
Orston
Aslockton
Allington
Colwick
Holme Pierrepont
Harlequin
Upper Saxondale
Whatton
Bottesford
Sedgebrook
Great Gonerby
Elton
Easthorpe
Bassingfield
Cropwell Butler
Sutton
Muston
Muston Meadows
Tithby
Granby
Stenwith
Barrowby
Earlsfield
Redmile
Barnstone
Cotgrave
Cropwell Bishop
Vale of Belvoir
Naturescape Wild Flower Farm
Barkestone-le-Vale
Woolsthorpe by Belvoir
Tollerton
Normanton-on-the-Wolds
Owthorpe
Langar
Plungar
Belvoir
Belvoir Castle
Denton
Colston Bassett
Harston
Harlaxton
Kinoulton
Stathern
Knipton
Stroxton
Stanton-on-the-Wolds
Harby
Hickling
Eaton
Branston
Hungerton
Hose
Eastwell
Croxton Kerrial
Wyville
Widmerpool
Upper Broughton
Long Clawson
Goadby Marwood
Saltby
Stoke Rochford
Willoughby-on-the-Wolds
Nether Broughton
Waltham on the Wolds
Skillington
Wycomb
Chadwell
Stonesby
Sproxton
Holwell
Scalford
Old Dalby
Buckminster
Wymeswold
Wartnaby
Ab Kettleby
Coston
Grimston
Melton
Twinlakes Park
Sewstern
Saxelbye
Thorpe Arnold
Gunby
Melton Mowbray
Freeby
Garthorpe
Six Hills
Ragdale
Shoby
Melton Carnegie Mus
Saxby
Wymondham
Asfordby
Asfordby Hill
Wyfordby
Frisby on the Wreake
Brentingby
Cribbs Meadow
Seagrave
Hoby
Burton Lazars
Stapleford
Kirby Bellars
Edmondthorpe
Thrussington
Rotherby
Wreake
Market Overton
Sileby
Teigh
Ratcliffe on the Wreake
Barrow
Rocks by Rail: The Living Ironstone
Great Dalby
Rearsby
Little Dalby
Whissendine
East Goscote
Ashwell
Gaddesby
Queniborough
Ashby Folville
Thorpe Satchville
Burrough Hill
Pickwell
Cold Overton
Syston
Barsby
Twyford
Langham
Burley
Barkby
South Croxton
Burrough on the Hill
Somerby
Barleythorpe
Oakham
Thurmaston
Beeby
Marefield
Knossington
National Space Science Centre
Nottingham
Trent
Eye
A6097
A612
A6211
A46
B692
A52
A606
A607
A1
B676
A6006
B6047
B668
B6386
131
132
116
98
99

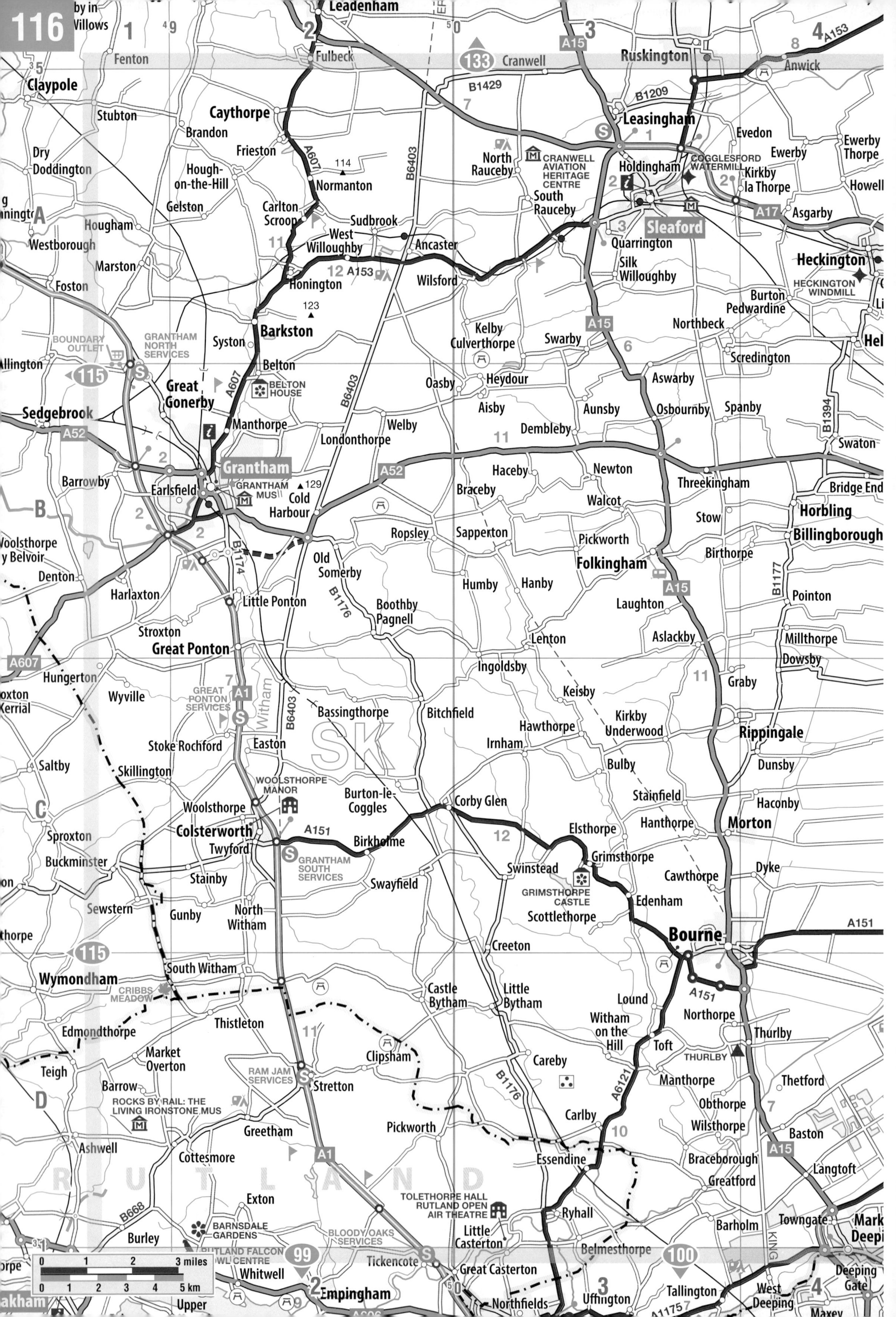
Leadenham
Fulbeck
Cranwell
Ruskington
Anwick
Fenton
Claypole
Stubton
Caythorpe
Brandon
Frieston
Dry Doddington
Hough-on-the-Hill
Normanton
Leasingham
Holdingham
Evedon
Ewerby
Ewerby Thorpe
North Rauceby
CRANWELL AVIATION HERITAGE CENTRE
South Rauceby
COGGLESFORD WATERMILL
Kirkby la Thorpe
Howell
Asgarby
Sleaford
Gelston
Carlton Scroop
Sudbrook
West Willoughby
Ancaster
Quarrington
Hougham
Westborough
Marston
Honington
Wilsford
Silk Willoughby
Heckington
HECKINGTON WINDMILL
Foston
Barkston
Syston
Kelby
Culverthorpe
Swarby
Northbeck
Burton Pedwardine
Scredington
BOUNDARY OUTLET
GRANTHAM NORTH SERVICES
Belton
BELTON HOUSE
Great Gonerby
Oasby
Heydour
Aswarby
Aisby
Aunsby
Osbournby
Spanby
Sedgebrook
Manthorpe
Welby
Londonthorpe
Dembleby
Swaton
Grantham
Barrowby
Earlsfield
GRANTHAM MUS
Cold Harbour
Haceby
Newton
Threekingham
Bridge End
Braceby
Walcot
Horbling
Billingborough
Woolsthorpe by Belvoir
Ropsley
Sapperton
Pickworth
Stow
Birthorpe
Old Somerby
Folkingham
Denton
Harlaxton
Little Ponton
Humby
Hanby
Pointon
Boothby Pagnell
Laughton
Stroxton
Great Ponton
Lenton
Aslackby
Millthorpe
Dowsby
Ingoldsby
Hungerton
Graby
Wyville
GREAT PONTON SERVICES
Keisby
Bassingthorpe
Bitchfield
Kirkby Underwood
Hawthorpe
Rippingale
Stoke Rochford
Easton
Irnham
Saltby
Skillington
Bulby
Dunsby
WOOLSTHORPE MANOR
Burton-le-Coggles
Stainfield
Haconby
Woolsthorpe
Corby Glen
Colsterworth
Hanthorpe
Morton
Sproxton
Twyford
Birkholme
Elsthorpe
Grimsthorpe
Buckminster
GRANTHAM SOUTH SERVICES
Stainby
Swinstead
Cawthorpe
Dyke
Swayfield
GRIMSTHORPE CASTLE
Edenham
Sewstern
Gunby
North Witham
Scottlethorpe
Bourne
Creeton
South Witham
Wymondham
CRIBBS MEADOW
Castle Bytham
Little Bytham
Lound
Northorpe
Thistleton
Witham on the Hill
Thurlby
Edmondthorpe
Toft
Clipsham
Market Overton
THURLBY
Teigh
Careby
Thetford
Barrow
RAM JAM SERVICES
Stretton
Manthorpe
Obthorpe
ROCKS BY RAIL: THE LIVING IRONSTONE MUS
Carlby
Wilsthorpe
Baston
Greetham
Pickworth
Ashwell
Cottesmore
Essendine
Braceborough
Langtoft
Greatford
RUTLAND
Exton
TOLETHORPE HALL RUTLAND OPEN AIR THEATRE
Ryhall
Towngate
Barholm
Burley
BARNSDALE GARDENS
Little Casterton
BLOODY OAKS SERVICES
RUTLAND FALCONRY & OWL CENTRE
Belmesthorpe
Tickencote
Great Casterton
Whitwell
Empingham
Tallington
West Deeping
Deeping Gate
Uffington
Northfields
Upper
Maxey
SK
Witham
KING STREET
A15
A153
A17
A607
B1429
B1209
B6403
A52
B1394
B1174
B1176
B1177
A1
A151
A6121
B668
A606
133
115
99
100
3 miles
5 km

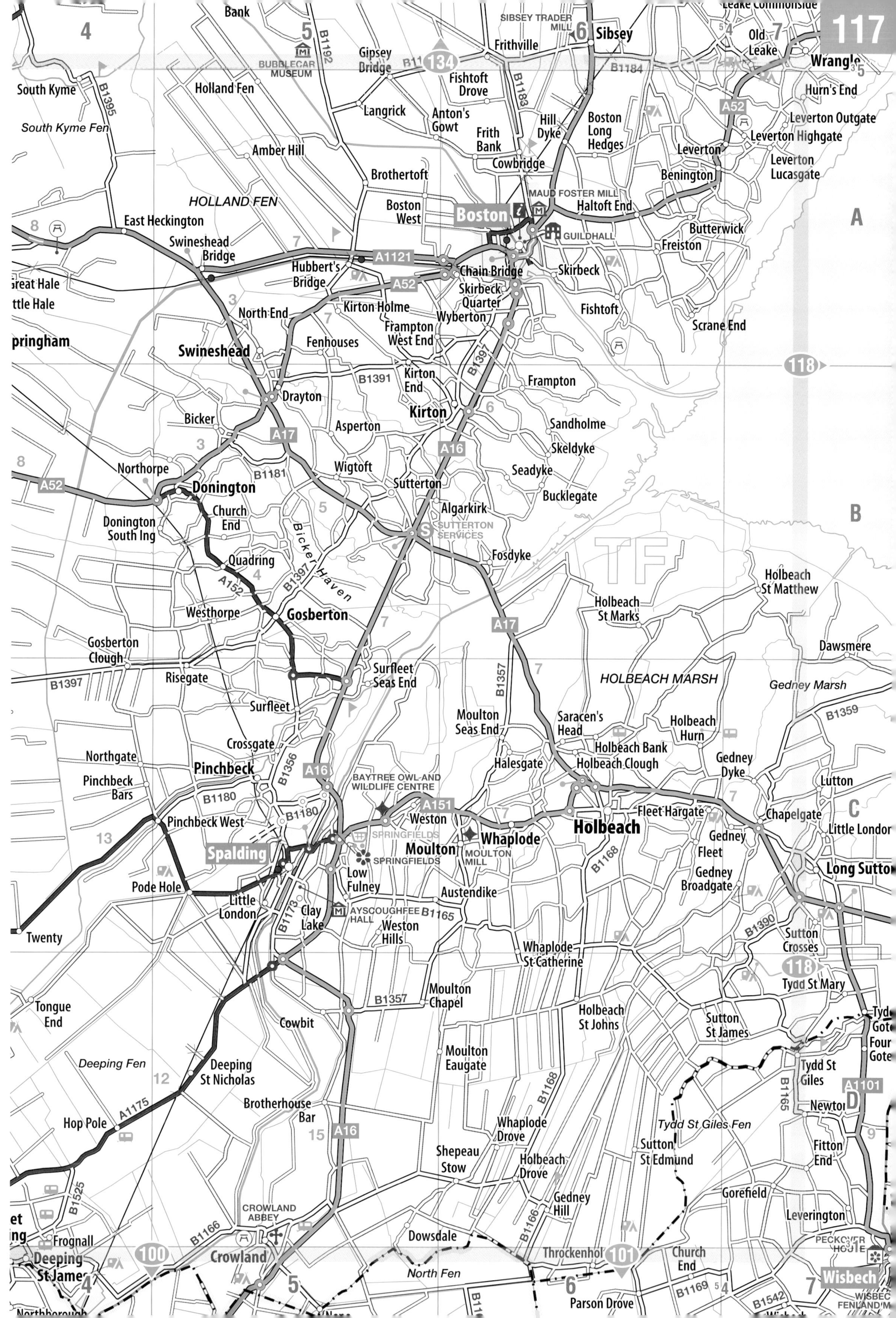
117
A
B
C
D
TF
134
118
118
100
101
Bank
Sibsey Trader Mill
Sibsey
Frithville
Old Leake
Wrangle
Bubblecar Museum
Gipsey Bridge
Fishtoft Drove
South Kyme
South Kyme Fen
Holland Fen
Langrick
Anton's Gowt
Frith Bank
Hill Dyke
Boston Long Hedges
Hurn's End
Leverton Outgate
Leverton Highgate
Leverton
Leverton Lucasgate
Benington
Amber Hill
Brothertoft
Cowbridge
Maud Foster Mill
Haltoft End
HOLLAND FEN
Boston West
Boston
East Heckington
Guildhall
Butterwick
Freiston
Swineshead Bridge
Hubbert's Bridge
Chain Bridge
Skirbeck
Skirbeck Quarter
Fishtoft
Scrane End
Great Hale
Little Hale
North End
Kirton Holme
Wyberton
Frampton West End
Fenhouses
Swineshead
Kirton End
Frampton
Drayton
Kirton
Sandholme
Bicker
Asperton
Skeldyke
Northorpe
Wigtoft
Seadyke
Donington
Sutterton
Bucklegate
Church End
Algarkirk
Donington South Ing
Sutterton Services
Bicker Haven
Quadring
Fosdyke
Holbeach St Matthew
Holbeach St Marks
Westhorpe
Gosberton
Gosberton Clough
Dawsmere
Risegate
Surfleet Seas End
HOLBEACH MARSH
Gedney Marsh
Surfleet
Moulton Seas End
Saracen's Head
Holbeach Hurn
Crossgate
Holbeach Bank
Northgate
Halesgate
Holbeach Clough
Gedney Dyke
Pinchbeck
Lutton
Pinchbeck Bars
Baytree Owl and Wildlife Centre
Fleet Hargate
Chapelgate
Pinchbeck West
Weston
Whaplode
Holbeach
Little London
Spalding
Springfields
Moulton
Moulton Mill
Gedney
Fleet
Long Sutton
Gedney Broadgate
Low Fulney
Pode Hole
Austendike
Little London
Clay Lake
Ayscoughfee Hall
Weston Hills
Sutton Crosses
Twenty
Whaplode St Catherine
Tydd St Mary
Tongue End
Moulton Chapel
Holbeach St Johns
Sutton St James
Cowbit
Tydd Gote
Four Gotes
Deeping Fen
Moulton Eaugate
Deeping St Nicholas
Tydd St Giles
Brotherhouse Bar
Newton
Hop Pole
Whaplode Drove
Tydd St Giles Fen
Shepeau Stow
Sutton St Edmund
Fitton End
Holbeach Drove
Gedney Hill
Gorefield
Leverington
Frognall
Crowland Abbey
Dowsdale
Peckover House
Deeping St James
Crowland
Throckenholt
Church End
Wisbech
North Fen
Parson Drove
Wisbech Fenland M
A52
A1121
A17
A16
A152
A151
A1175
A1101
B1192
B1184
B1183
B1395
B1391
B1397
B1181
B1357
B1359
B1356
B1180
B1168
B1165
B1173
B1390
B1525
B1166
B1169
B1542

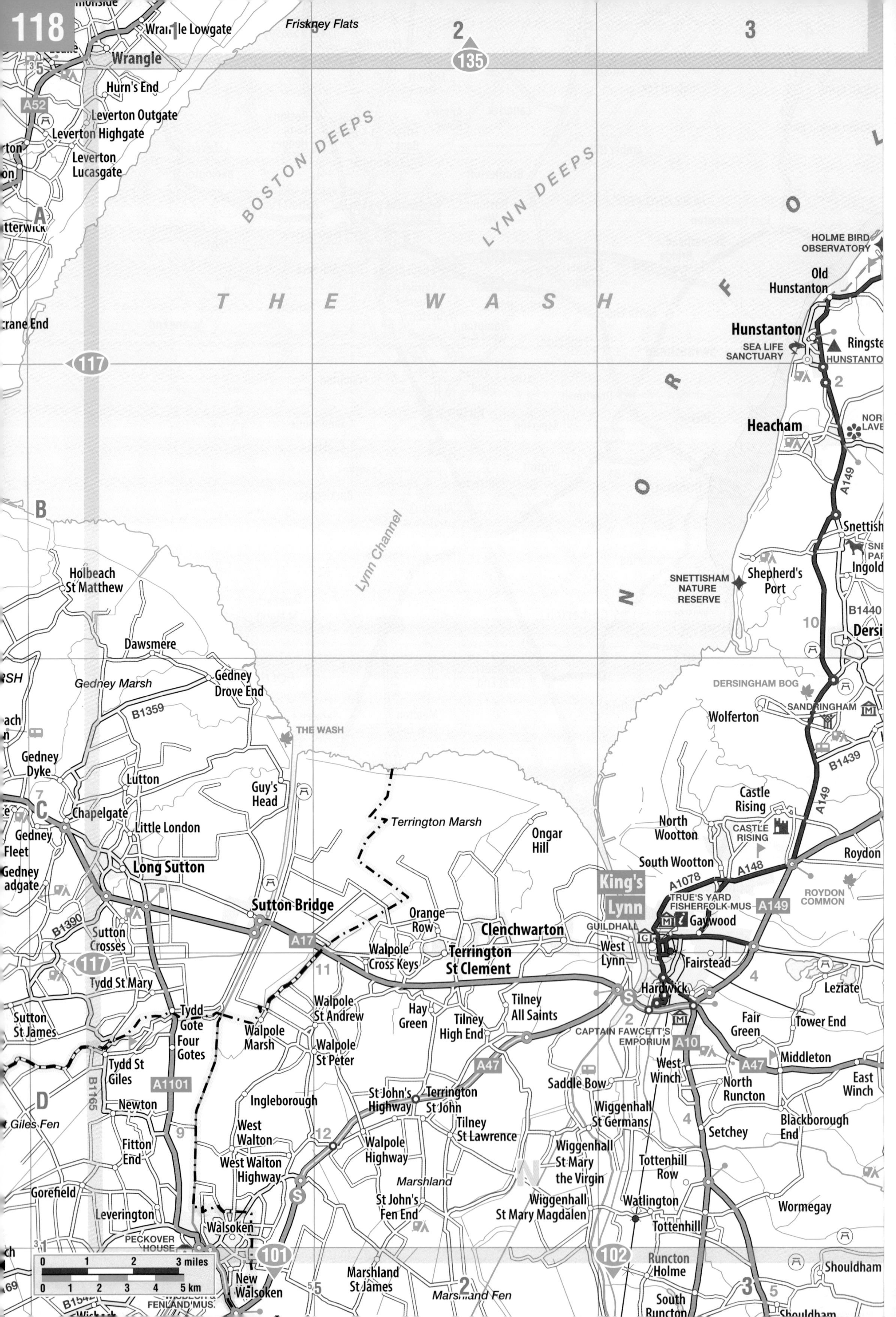
Friskney Flats
Wrangle Lowgate
Wrangle
Hurn's End
Leverton Outgate
Leverton Highgate
Leverton Lucasgate
A52
BOSTON DEEPS
LYNN DEEPS
THE WASH
NORFOLK
117
135
HOLME BIRD OBSERVATORY
Old Hunstanton
Hunstanton
SEA LIFE SANCTUARY
Heacham
A149
Lynn Channel
SNETTISHAM NATURE RESERVE
Shepherd's Port
B1440
DERSINGHAM BOG
SANDRINGHAM
Wolferton
B1439
Castle Rising
CASTLE RISING
North Wootton
South Wootton
Roydon
ROYDON COMMON
Holbeach St Matthew
Dawsmere
Gedney Marsh
Gedney Drove End
B1359
THE WASH
Gedney Dyke
Lutton
Guy's Head
Chapelgate
Little London
Terrington Marsh
Ongar Hill
Gedney Fleet
Long Sutton
King's Lynn
A1078
A148
TRUE'S YARD FISHERFOLK MUS
A149
Gaywood
Sutton Bridge
B1390
Sutton Crosses
A17
Orange Row
Clenchwarton
GUILDHALL
West Lynn
Walpole Cross Keys
Terrington St Clement
Fairstead
Leziate
Tydd St Mary
Hardwick
Sutton St James
Tydd Gote
Walpole St Andrew
Hay Green
Tilney All Saints
Tilney High End
Fair Green
Tower End
Walpole Marsh
Four Gotes
Walpole St Peter
CAPTAIN FAWCETT'S EMPORIUM
A10
West Winch
A47
Middleton
Tydd St Giles
B1165
A1101
Saddle Bow
North Runcton
East Winch
Newton
Ingleborough
St John's Highway
Terrington St John
Wiggenhall St Germans
Giles Fen
Tilney St Lawrence
Setchey
Blackborough End
West Walton
Fitton End
Walpole Highway
Wiggenhall St Mary the Virgin
West Walton Highway
Tottenhill Row
Marshland
Gorefield
St John's Fen End
Wiggenhall St Mary Magdalen
Watlington
Wormegay
Leverington
Walsoken
Tottenhill
PECKOVER HOUSE
101
102
Runcton Holme
Shouldham
Marshland St James
New Walsoken
Marshland Fen
South Runcton
0 1 2 3 miles
0 1 2 3 4 5 km

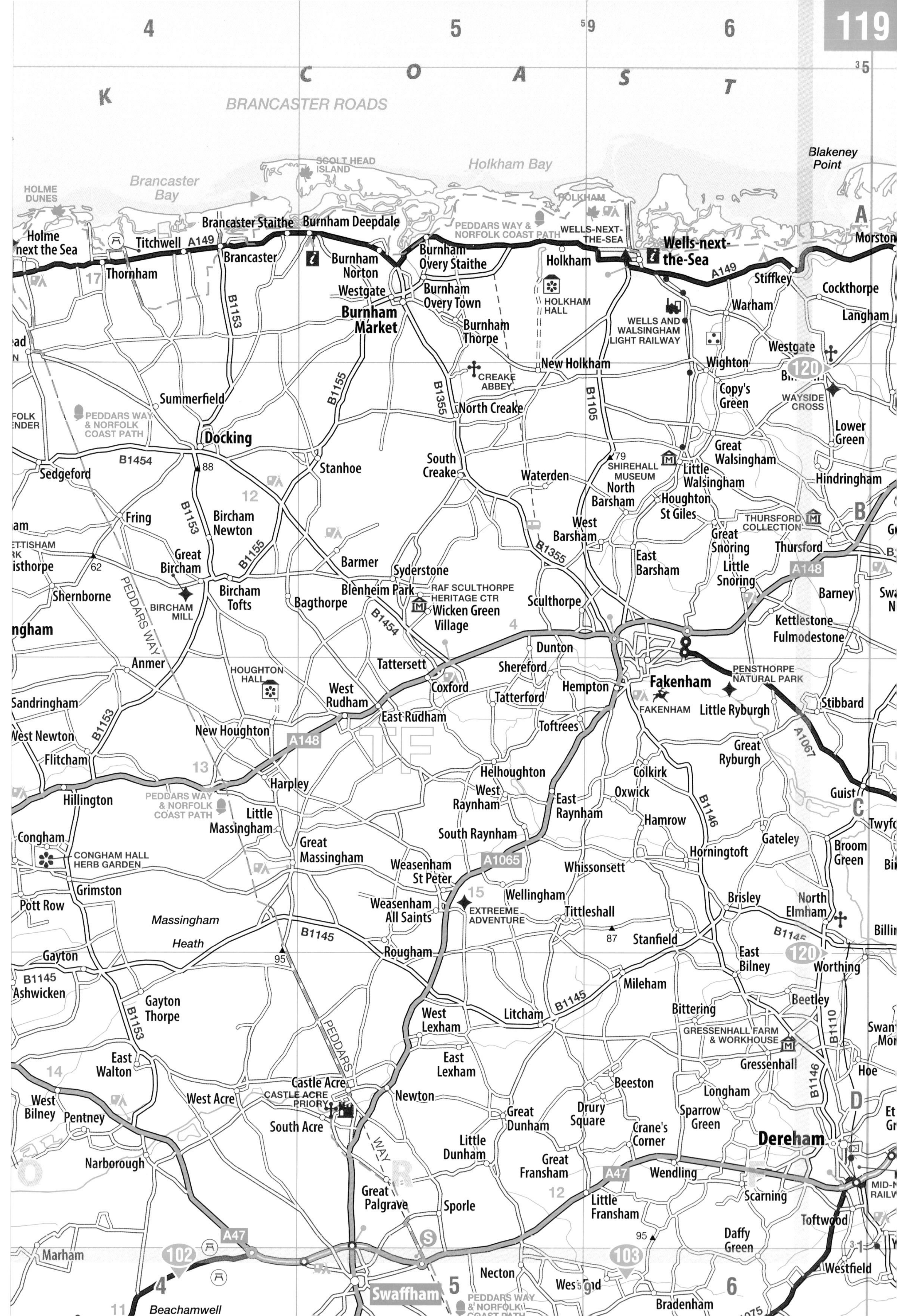

4
5
6
COAST
BRANCASTER ROADS
Holkham Bay
Brancaster Bay
HOLME DUNES
SCOLT HEAD ISLAND
HOLKHAM
Blakeney Point
Holme next the Sea
Titchwell
A149
Brancaster Staithe
Burnham Deepdale
PEDDARS WAY & NORFOLK COAST PATH
WELLS-NEXT-THE-SEA
Wells-next-the-Sea
Morston
Thornham
Brancaster
Burnham Norton
Burnham Overy Staithe
Holkham
Stiffkey
Cockthorpe
Westgate
Burnham Overy Town
HOLKHAM HALL
WELLS AND WALSINGHAM LIGHT RAILWAY
Warham
Langham
Burnham Market
Burnham Thorpe
B1153
Westgate
Wighton
120
CREAKE ABBEY
New Holkham
Summerfield
B1155
B1355
B1105
Copy's Green
WAYSIDE CROSS
PEDDARS WAY & NORFOLK COAST PATH
North Creake
Lower Green
Docking
Great Walsingham
B1454
Sedgeford
88
Stanhoe
South Creake
Waterden
79
SHIREHALL MUSEUM
Little Walsingham
Hindringham
North Barsham
Houghton St Giles
Fring
Bircham Newton
12
West Barsham
THURSFORD COLLECTION
Great Snoring
Thursford
Great Bircham
62
Barmer
Syderstone
East Barsham
Little Snoring
A148
Shernborne
Bircham Tofts
Blenheim Park
RAF SCULTHORPE HERITAGE CTR
Bagthorpe
Sculthorpe
Barney
BIRCHAM MILL
Wicken Green Village
PEDDARS WAY
Kettlestone
Fulmodestone
Dunton
Anmer
HOUGHTON HALL
Tattersett
Shereford
Fakenham
PENSTHORPE NATURAL PARK
West Rudham
Coxford
Hempton
Sandringham
Tatterford
FAKENHAM
Little Ryburgh
Stibbard
East Rudham
West Newton
New Houghton
Toftrees
A148
TF
Great Ryburgh
A1067
Flitcham
13
Helhoughton
Colkirk
Harpley
Guist
West Raynham
Oxwick
Hillington
PEDDARS WAY & NORFOLK COAST PATH
Little Massingham
East Raynham
B1146
Hamrow
Congham
South Raynham
Great Massingham
Gateley
Broom Green
CONGHAM HALL HERB GARDEN
Weasenham St Peter
A1065
Whissonsett
Horningtoft
Grimston
15
Wellingham
Brisley
Pott Row
Weasenham All Saints
EXTREEME ADVENTURE
Tittleshall
North Elmham
Massingham Heath
87
Stanfield
B1145
B1145
Rougham
East Bilney
Worthing
Gayton
95
120
B1145
Ashwicken
Mileham
Beetley
Gayton Thorpe
West Lexham
Litcham
B1145
Bittering
B1110
B1153
GRESSENHALL FARM & WORKHOUSE
PEDDARS
East Lexham
Gressenhall
East Walton
14
Hoe
Castle Acre
CASTLE ACRE PRIORY
Beeston
Longham
B1146
West Bilney
West Acre
Newton
Pentney
Great Dunham
Drury Square
Sparrow Green
South Acre
Crane's Corner
WAY
Dereham
Little Dunham
Great Fransham
Narborough
A47
Wendling
12
Great Palgrave
Little Fransham
Scarning
MID-N RAILW
Sporle
Toftwood
A47
95
Daffy Green
Marham
102
103
Westfield
4
Necton
Swaffham
5
6
Wesfield
PEDDARS WAY & NORFOLK COAST PATH
Bradenham
11
Beachamwell
A
B
C
D

1
2
3
4
A
B
C
D
Blakeney Point
BLAKENEY
GUILDHALL
CLEY MILL
Cley next the Sea
PEDDARS WAY AND NORFOLK COAST PATH
NORTH NORFOLK RAILWAY (THE POPPY LINE)
Sheringham
PRIORY MAZE & GARDENS
HILLSIDE SHIRE HORSE SANCTUARY
CROMER MUSEUM
Cromer
Morston
Blakeney
Wiveton
Newgate
Salthouse
Kelling
MUCKLEBURGH COLLECTION
Weybourne
SHERINGHAM PARK
SHERINGHAM
Upper Sheringham
Beeston Regis
West Runton
East Runton
Stiffkey
Cockthorpe
Warham
Langham
NORFOLK
Glandford
High Kelling
Bodham
East Beckham
Aylmerton
Felbrigg
Northrepps
Wighton
Westgate
Binham
Copy's Green
WAYSIDE CROSS
Saxlingham
Letheringsett
Holt
THE GALLERY
LETHERINGSETT WATERMILL
HOLT
West Beckham
FELBRIGG HALL
Crossdale Street
Field Dalling
Lower Green
Bale
Sharrington
Hempstead
BACONSTHORPE CASTLE
Baconsthorpe
Gresham
Sustead
Roughton
Frogshall
Great Walsingham
Hindringham
Thornage
Brinton
Hunworth
Bessingham
Hanworth
THURSFORD COLLECTION
Stody
Edgefield
Plumstead
Matlaske
Thurgarton
Alby Hill
Great Snoring
Thursford
Gunthorpe
Briningham
Aldborough
Little Snoring
Barney
Swanton Novers
Melton Constable
Briston
Edgefield Street
Little Barningham
Wickmere
Erpingham
Antingham
Suffield
ALBY CRAFTS & GARDENS
MANNINGTON GARDENS
Calthorpe
Colby
Kettlestone
Fulmodestone
Corpusty
Saxthorpe
Itteringham
PENSTHORPE NATURAL PARK
Little Ryburgh
Stibbard
Hindolveston
Thurning
BLICKLING HALL
Ingworth
Banningham
Blickling
Oulton
Wood Norton
Norton Corner
Silvergate
Dunkirk
Great Ryburgh
Guestwick
Heydon
Oulton Street
Aylsham
Tuttington
Guestwick Green
Wood Dalling
Burgh next Aylsham
Guist
Salle
Southgate
Fengate
Twyford
Foulsham
Themelthorpe
Marsham
Brampton
Gateley
Broom Green
Cawston
Little London
BURE VALLEY RAILWAY
Horningtoft
Bintree
FOXLEY WOOD
Reepham
Booton
Eastgate
Buxton
Foxley
Whitwell Street
The Heath
Brisley
North Elmham
Brandiston
Billingford
Bawdeswell
Haveringland
Hevingham
Stratton Strawless
East Bilney
Sparham
Worthing
Swannington
Waterloo
Beetley
Alderford
Mill Street
Upgate
New Hainford
Hainford
Lenwade
Wensum
ROARR!
GRESSENHALL FARM & WORKHOUSE
Swanton Morley
Lyng
Elsing
Felthorpe
Gressenhall
Morton
Attlebridge
Newton St Faith
Hoe
Primrose Green
Horsford
Woodgate
Weston Longville
CITY OF NORWICH AVIATION MUSEUM
Horsham St Faith
Longham
Thorpe Marriot
Etling Green
North Tuddenham
Weston Green
Ringland
Drayton
Dereham
Taverham
NORWICH INTERNATIONAL
Hockering
Tud
Hellesdon
Old Catton
MID-NORFOLK RAILWAY
Scarning
Mattishall Burgh
Honingham
Costessey
Mile Cross
Toftwood
Clint Green
Mattishall
East Tuddenham
Easton
New Costessey
Upper Hellesdon
Daffy Green
Yaxham
Welborne
P&R
Marlingford
Bowthorpe
THE FORUM
New Catton
Earlham
SAINSBURY CENTRE FOR VISUAL ARTS
Bawburgh
Yare
Brandon Parva
Barford
A149
A148
A1082
B1156
B1110
B1354
B1149
B1436
A140
B1145
A1067
B1146
A47
B1535
A1270
A1074
B1150
119
104
Glaven
Bure
0 1 2 3 miles
0 1 2 3 4 5 km

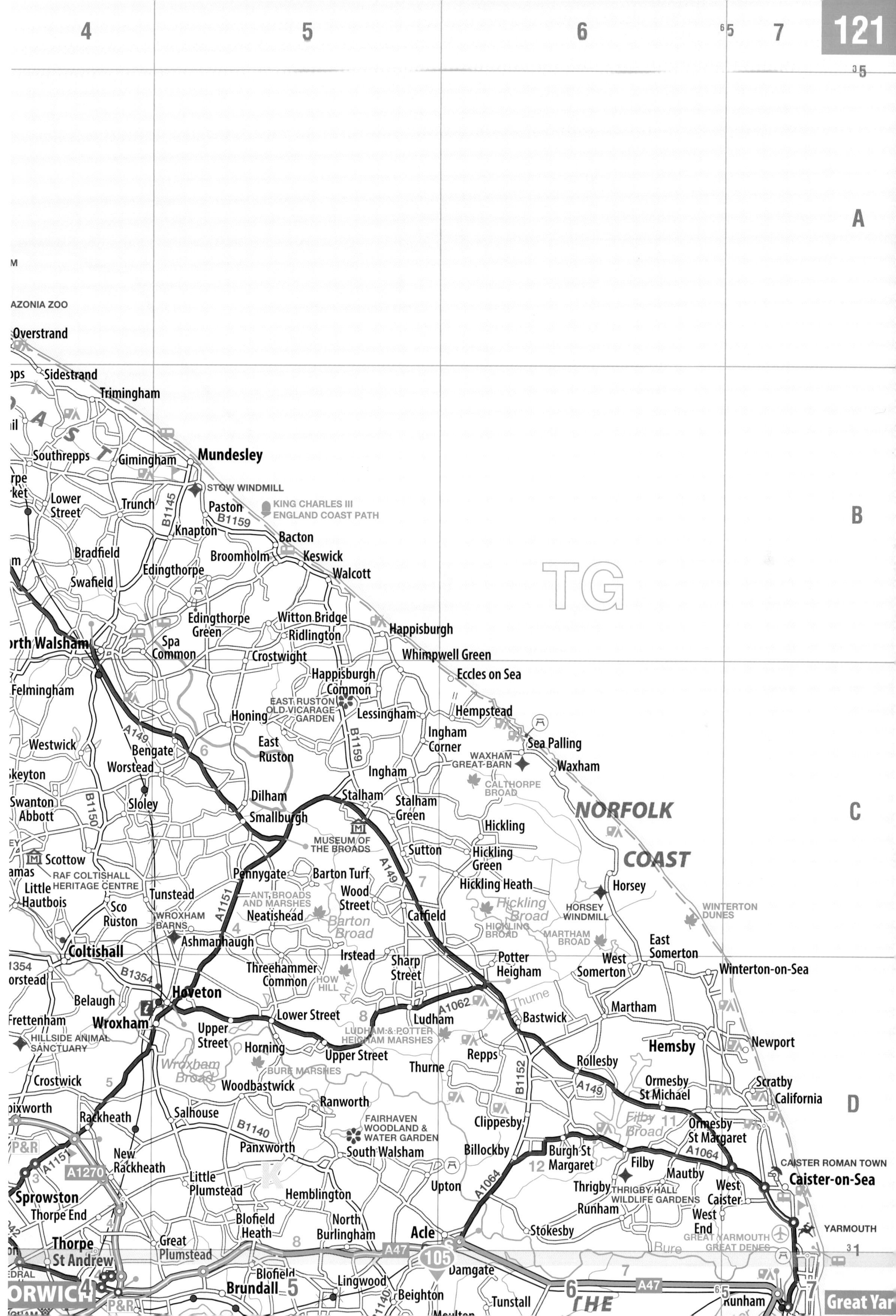

4
5
6
7
A
B
C
D
AZONIA ZOO
Overstrand
Sidestrand
Trimingham
Southrepps
Gimingham
Mundesley
STOW WINDMILL
Lower Street
Trunch
Paston
KING CHARLES III ENGLAND COAST PATH
Knapton
Bacton
Bradfield
Broomholm
Keswick
Edingthorpe
Walcott
Swafield
TG
Edingthorpe Green
Witton Bridge
Happisburgh
Ridlington
Spa Common
Crostwight
Whimpwell Green
Happisburgh Common
Eccles on Sea
Felmingham
EAST RUSTON OLD VICARAGE GARDEN
Lessingham
Hempstead
Honing
Ingham Corner
Sea Palling
Westwick
Bengate
East Ruston
WAXHAM GREAT BARN
Waxham
Worstead
Ingham
CALTHORPE BROAD
Swanton Abbott
Sloley
Dilham
Stalham
Stalham Green
NORFOLK
Smallburgh
Hickling
MUSEUM OF THE BROADS
Scottow
Sutton
Hickling Green
COAST
RAF COLTISHALL HERITAGE CENTRE
Pennygate
Barton Turf
Little Hautbois
Tunstead
Hickling Heath
Horsey
ANT BROADS AND MARSHES
Wood Street
Sco Ruston
Neatishead
Barton Broad
Catfield
Hickling Broad
HORSEY WINDMILL
WINTERTON DUNES
WROXHAM BARNS
HICKLING BROAD
MARTHAM BROAD
Ashmanhaugh
East Somerton
Coltishall
Irstead
Sharp Street
Potter Heigham
West Somerton
Winterton-on-Sea
Threehammer Common
HOW HILL
Belaugh
Hoveton
Thurne
Martham
Frettenham
Wroxham
Lower Street
Ludham
Bastwick
Upper Street
LUDHAM & POTTER HEIGHAM MARSHES
HILLSIDE ANIMAL SANCTUARY
Horning
Upper Street
Repps
Hemsby
Newport
Rollesby
Thurne
Crostwick
Wroxham Broad
BURE MARSHES
Woodbastwick
Ormesby St Michael
Scratby
California
Ranworth
Rackheath
Salhouse
Clippesby
Filby Broad
Ormesby St Margaret
FAIRHAVEN WOODLAND & WATER GARDEN
Panxworth
South Walsham
Billockby
Burgh St Margaret
Filby
CAISTER ROMAN TOWN
New Rackheath
Caister-on-Sea
Little Plumstead
Mautby
Sprowston
Thrigby
THRIGBY HALL WILDLIFE GARDENS
West Caister
Hemblington
Upton
Thorpe End
Runham
Blofield Heath
North Burlingham
West End
YARMOUTH
Acle
Stokesby
Thorpe St Andrew
Great Plumstead
GREAT YARMOUTH GREAT DENES
Bure
Damgate
Blofield
Lingwood
Brundall
Beighton
Tunstall
Runham
THE
Great Yar
A149
A1151
A1062
A1064
A47
A1270
B1145
B1159
B1150
B1354
B1152
B1140
105

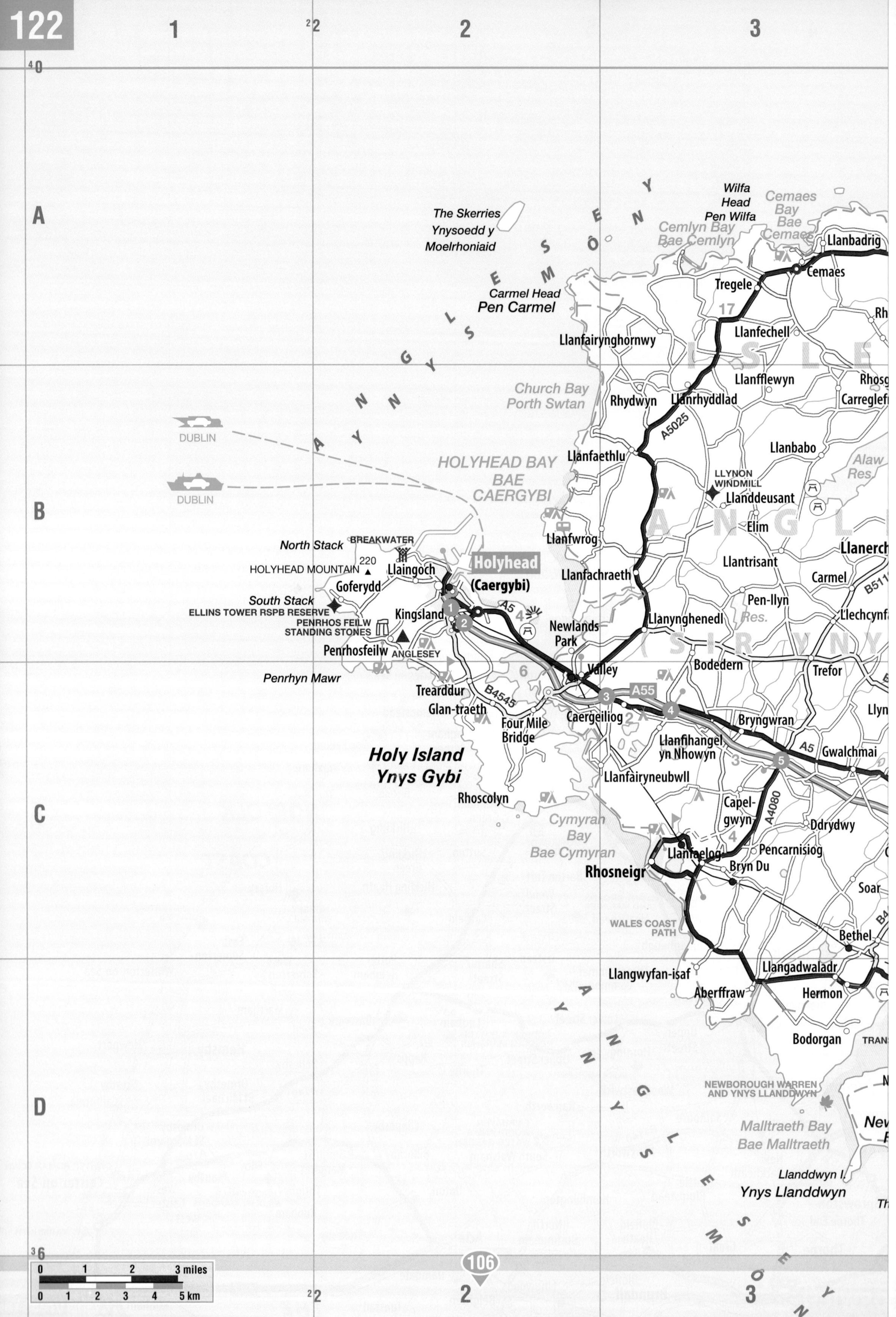
The Skerries
Ynysoedd y Moelrhoniaid
Wilfa Head
Pen Wilfa
Cemaes Bay
Bae Cemaes
Cemlyn Bay
Bae Cemlyn
Llanbadrig
Cemaes
Tregele
Carmel Head
Pen Carmel
Llanfechell
Llanfairynghornwy
Llanfflewyn
Church Bay
Porth Swtan
Rhydwyn
Llanrhyddlad
A5025
Llanbabo
Alaw Res.
DUBLIN
DUBLIN
HOLYHEAD BAY
BAE CAERGYBI
Llanfaethlu
LLYNON WINDMILL
Llanddeusant
Elim
Llanfwrog
North Stack
BREAKWATER
HOLYHEAD MOUNTAIN 220
Llaingoch
Holyhead
(Caergybi)
Llantrisant
Llanfachraeth
Carmel
Goferydd
South Stack
ELLINS TOWER RSPB RESERVE
Kingsland
PENRHOS FEILW STANDING STONES
Penrhosfeilw
ANGLESEY
Newlands Park
Llanynghenedl
Pen-llyn Res.
Llechcynfa
Bodedern
Trefor
Penrhyn Mawr
Valley
A5
A55
B4545
Trearddur
Glan-traeth
Four Mile Bridge
Caergeiliog
Bryngwran
Llanfihangel yn Nhowyn
Gwalchmai
Holy Island
Ynys Gybi
Llanfairyneubwll
Rhoscolyn
Capel-gwyn
A4080
Ddrydwy
Cymyran Bay
Bae Cymyran
Llanfaelog
Pencarnisiog
Rhosneigr
Bryn Du
Soar
WALES COAST PATH
Bethel
Llangwyfan-isaf
Llangadwaladr
Aberffraw
Hermon
Bodorgan
NEWBOROUGH WARREN AND YNYS LLANDDWYN
Malltraeth Bay
Bae Malltraeth
Llanddwyn I.
Ynys Llanddwyn
ANGLESEY (SIR YNYS MÔN)
YNYS MÔN
0 1 2 3 miles
0 1 2 3 4 5 km

106

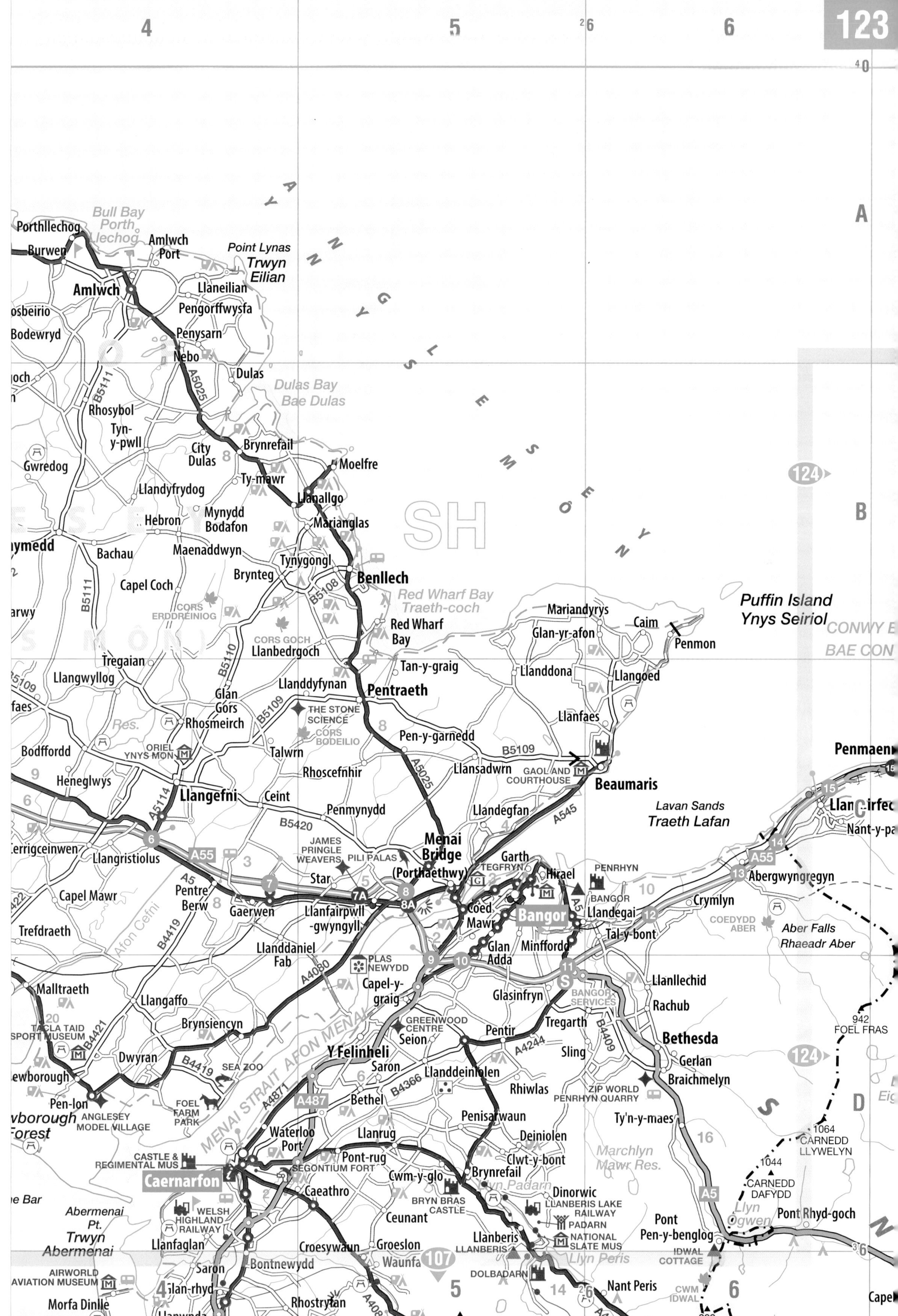

4
5
6
A
B
D
Porthllechog
Bull Bay
Porth Llechog
Amlwch Port
Point Lynas
Trwyn Eilian
Burwen
Amlwch
Llaneilian
Pengorffwysfa
Bodewryd
Penysarn
Nebo
Dulas
A5025
B5111
Rhosybol
Dulas Bay
Bae Dulas
Tyn-y-pwll
City Dulas
Brynrefail
Moelfre
Gwredog
Ty-mawr
Llandyfrydog
Llanallgo
Hebron
Mynydd Bodafon
Marianglas
SH
Bachau
Maenaddwyn
Tynygongl
Capel Coch
Brynteg
Benllech
B5108
CORS ERDDREINIOG
Red Wharf Bay
Traeth-coch
Mariandyrys
Caim
Puffin Island
Ynys Seiriol
CONWY B
BAE CON
Glan-yr-afon
Penmon
CORS GOCH
Llanbedrgoch
Red Wharf Bay
B5110
Tan-y-graig
Tregaian
Llanddona
Llangoed
Llangwyllog
Llanddyfnan
Pentraeth
Glan Gors
B5109
THE STONE SCIENCE
Llanfaes
Res.
Rhosmeirch
CORS BODEILIO
Pen-y-garnedd
Bodffordd
ORIEL YNYS MON
Talwrn
B5109
Penmaen
Heneglwys
Rhoscefnhir
Llansadwrn
GAOL AND COURTHOUSE
Beaumaris
Llangefni
A5114
Ceint
Lavan Sands
Traeth Lafan
Penmynydd
Llandegfan
A545
B5420
Menai Bridge
(Porthaethwy)
Cerrigceinwen
Llangristiolus
A55
JAMES PRINGLE WEAVERS
PILI PALAS
Garth
Hirael
PENRHYN
Star
TEGFRYN
A55
Abergwyngregyn
Pentre Berw
A5
Capel Mawr
Gaerwen
Llanfairpwll -gwyngyll
Coed Mawr
Bangor
BANGOR
Llandegai
Crymlyn
Trefdraeth
Afon Cefni
B4419
Tal-y-bont
COEDYDD ABER
Aber Falls
Rhaeadr Aber
Llanddaniel Fab
Glan Adda
Minffordd
PLAS NEWYDD
A4080
Malltraeth
Capel-y-graig
Llanllechid
Llangaffo
Glasinfryn
BANGOR SERVICES
Rachub
TACLA TAID SPORT MUSEUM
Brynsiencyn
Tregarth
942 FOEL FRAS
B4421
GREENWOOD CENTRE
Pentir
Seion
A4244
B4409
Bethesda
Dwyran
MENAI STRAIT AFON MENAI
Sling
B4419
SEA ZOO
Y Felinheli
Gerlan
Newborough
Saron
Llanddeiniolen
Braichmelyn
Pen-lon
A4871
A487
B4366
Rhiwlas
ZIP WORLD PENRHYN QUARRY
Newborough Forest
ANGLESEY MODEL VILLAGE
FOEL FARM PARK
Bethel
Penisarwaun
Ty'n-y-maes
Waterloo Port
Llanrug
Deiniolen
Marchlyn Mawr Res.
1064 CARNEDD LLYWELYN
CASTLE & REGIMENTAL MUS
Pont-rug
Clwt-y-bont
1044
Caernarfon
SEGONTIUM FORT
Cwm-y-glo
Brynrefail
Llyn Padarn
CARNEDD DAFYDD
Caeathro
Dinorwic
LLANBERIS LAKE RAILWAY
A5
Abermenai Pt.
Trwyn Abermenai
WELSH HIGHLAND RAILWAY
BRYN BRAS CASTLE
PADARN
Llyn Ogwen
Pont Rhyd-goch
Ceunant
Pont Pen-y-benglog
Llanfaglan
Croesywaun
Groeslon
Llanberis
NATIONAL SLATE MUS
LLANBERIS
IDWAL COTTAGE
Saron
Bontnewydd
Waunfa
Llyn Peris
AIRWORLD AVIATION MUSEUM
DOLBADARN
CWM IDWAL
Dinas Dinlle
Morfa Dinlle
Rhostryfan
Nant Peris
Llanwnda

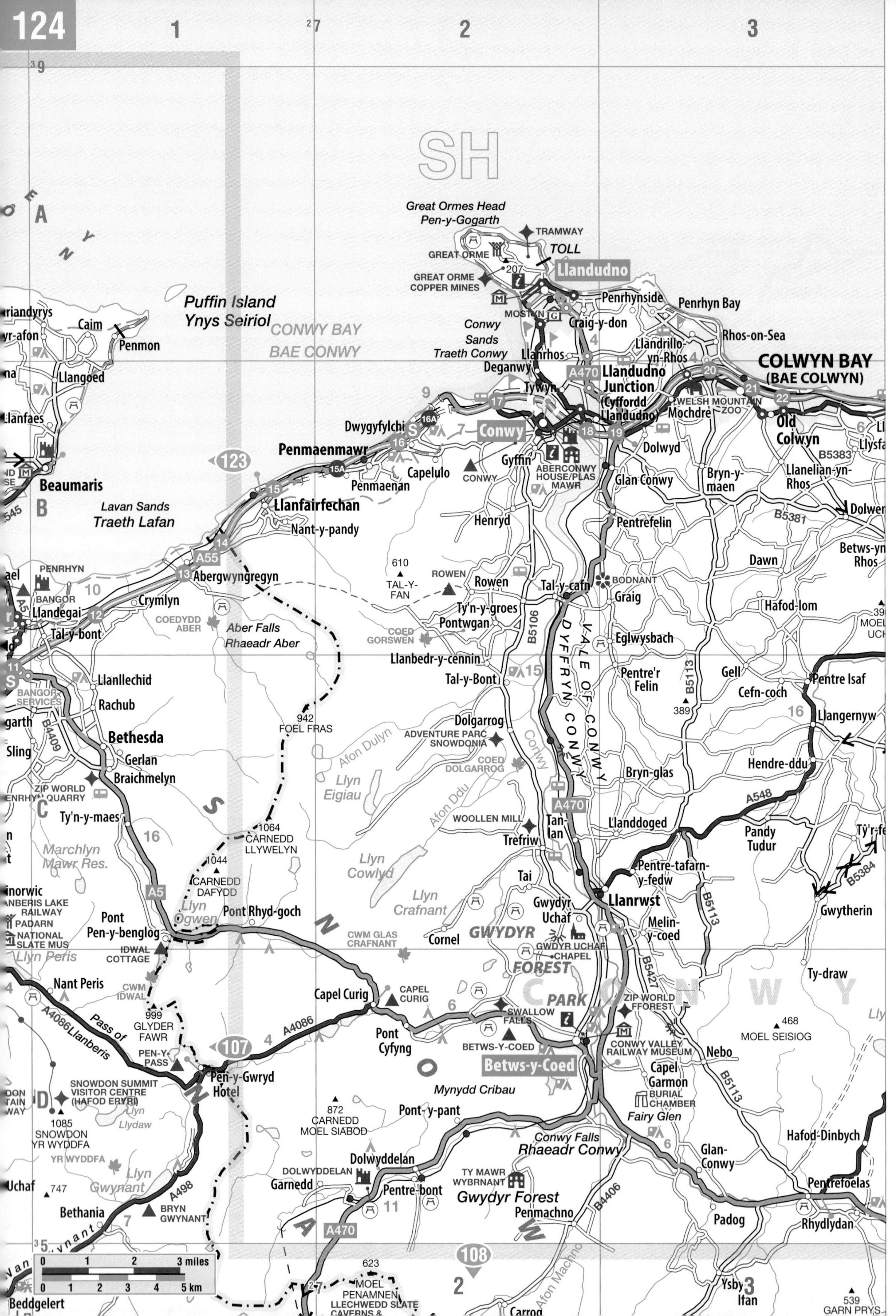
1
2
3
SH
Great Ormes Head
Pen-y-Gogarth
TRAMWAY
TOLL
GREAT ORME
207
Llandudno
GREAT ORME COPPER MINES
Puffin Island
Ynys Seiriol
CONWY BAY
BAE CONWY
Penrhynside
Penrhyn Bay
Rhos-on-Sea
MOSTYN
Craig-y-don
Conwy Sands
Traeth Conwy
Llanrhos
Llandrillo-yn-Rhos
Deganwy
A470
Llandudno Junction
(Cyffordd Llandudno)
COLWYN BAY
(BAE COLWYN)
Tywyn
WELSH MOUNTAIN ZOO
Mochdre
Old Colwyn
Llysfaen
Dwygyfylchi
Conwy
Penmaenmawr
Capelulo
Penmaenan
CONWY
Gyffin
ABERCONWY HOUSE/PLAS MAWR
Dolwyd
Glan Conwy
Bryn-y-maen
Llanelian-yn-Rhos
B5383
B5381
Dolwen
Llanfairfechan
Nant-y-pandy
Henryd
Pentrefelin
Betws-yn-Rhos
Caim
Penmon
Llangoed
Llanfaes
Beaumaris
Lavan Sands
Traeth Lafan
A55
Abergwyngregyn
610
TAL-Y-FAN
ROWEN
Rowen
Ty'n-y-groes
Pontwgan
Tal-y-cafn
BODNANT
Graig
Dawn
Hafod-lom
PENRHYN
BANGOR
Llandegai
Crymlyn
Tal-y-bont
COEDYDD ABER
Aber Falls
Rhaeadr Aber
COED GORSWEN
Llanbedr-y-cennin
B5106
Eglwysbach
VALE OF CONWY
DYFFRYN CONWY
Tal-y-Bont
Pentre'r Felin
B5113
Gell
Pentre Isaf
Cefn-coch
BANGOR SERVICES
Llanllechid
Rachub
B4409
Bethesda
Gerlan
Braichmelyn
942
FOEL FRAS
Dolgarrog
ADVENTURE PARC SNOWDONIA
389
Llangernyw
Afon Dulyn
COED DOLGARROG
Llyn Eigiau
Bryn-glas
Hendre-ddu
ZIP WORLD PENRHYN QUARRY
Ty'n-y-maes
Afon Ddu
A548
WOOLLEN MILL
Tan-lan
Llanddoged
Pandy Tudur
Marchlyn Mawr Res.
1064
CARNEDD LLYWELYN
Trefriw
Llyn Cowlyd
1044
CARNEDD DAFYDD
Tai
Pentre-tafarn-y-fedw
B5384
Llanrwst
B5113
Gwydyr Uchaf
Gwytherin
A5
Dinorwic
LLANBERIS LAKE RAILWAY
PADARN
NATIONAL SLATE MUS
Pont Pen-y-benglog
Llyn Ogwen
Pont Rhyd-goch
Llyn Crafnant
Melin-y-coed
CWM GLAS CRAFNANT
Cornel
GWYDYR
GWDYR UCHAF CHAPEL
FOREST
PARK
B5427
Ty-draw
IDWAL COTTAGE
Llyn Peris
Nant Peris
CWM IDWAL
Capel Curig
CAPEL CURIG
ZIP WORLD FFOREST
999
GLYDER FAWR
SWALLOW FALLS
468
MOEL SEISIOG
A4086
Llanberis
Pass of
Pont Cyfyng
BETWS-Y-COED
CONWY VALLEY RAILWAY MUSEUM
Nebo
PEN-Y-PASS
Pen-y-Gwryd Hotel
Betws-y-Coed
Capel Garmon
BURIAL CHAMBER
B5113
SNOWDON SUMMIT VISITOR CENTRE (HAFOD ERYRI)
Llyn Llydaw
Mynydd Cribau
1085
SNOWDON
YR WYDDFA
872
CARNEDD MOEL SIABOD
Pont-y-pant
Fairy Glen
Conwy Falls
Rhaeadr Conwy
Hafod-Dinbych
Glan-Conwy
YR WYDDFA
Llyn Gwynant
Dolwyddelan
DOLWYDDELAN
Garnedd
Pentre-bont
TY MAWR WYBRNANT
Gwydyr Forest
Penmachno
B4406
Pentrefoelas
747
Uchaf
A498
BRYN GWYNANT
Bethania
A470
Padog
Rhydlydan
Afon Machno
108
107
123
623
MOEL PENAMNEN
LLECHWEDD SLATE CAVERNS &
Ysbyty Ifan
539
GARN PRYS
Carrog
Beddgelert
0 1 2 3 miles
0 1 2 3 4 5 km

4
30
5
31
6
39
SJ
West Hoyle Bank
Hilbre I.
West Kirby
Welsh Channel
Point of Ayr
Yr Parlwr Du
Talacre
River Dee
Afon Dyfrdwy
A
SEAQUARIUM
Y-Ffrith
RHYL
(Y RHYL)
Gronant
Gwespyr
Prestatyn
Gwaenysgor
Ffynnongroyw
Picton
Meliden
Llanasa
Mostyn Quay
OFFA'S DYKE PATH
LLWYBR CLAWDD OFFA
Mostyn
Kinmel Bay
B5119
250
Axton
Trelogan
Abergele Roads
Angorfa
Abergele
COLWYN BAY
Towyn
A525
A547
Trelawnyd
126
Glan-y-don
Pensarn
A548
Rhuddlan
Dyserth
A5151
Whitford
Llanddulas
Abergele
Cwm
Greenfield
Carmel
A547
A55
Pant-y-Wacco
Gorsedd
Rhŷd-y-foel
Bodelwyddan
Clwyd
B5429
Holywell
(Treffynnon)
St George
Rhuallt
Pen-y-cefn
A548
B5381
St Asaph
(Llanelwy)
Brynford
Glascoed
398
Tremeirchion
Babell
Groesffordd Marli
Waen
Goleugoed
B5122
Caerwys
B5121
317
MOELFRE ISAF
ST. ASAPH CATHEDRAL
AFONWEN CRAFT AND ANTIQUE CENTRE
Pentre Halkyn
Elwy
Graig
Ysceifiog
Afon-wen
Plas-yn-Cefn
VALE OF CLWYD
DYFFRYN CLWYD
Lixwm
Halkyn Mountain
Llanfair Talhaiarn
Llannefydd
Bont-newydd
Trefnant
Bodfari
Rhes-y-cae
Nannerch
Bryn-nantllech
A544
Cefn Berain
B5428
A541
Castell
OFFA'S DYKE PATH
LLWYBR CLAWDD OFFA
Green
Bryn Rhyd-yr-Arian
A543
Henllan
B5382
Rhosesmor
Hendre
FLINTSHIRE
(SIR Y FFLINT)
B5382
Llansannan
Denbigh
(Dinbych)
Fron
13
Waen
Llangwyfan
400
A543
CASTLE & TOWN WALLS
Llandyrnog
465
MOEL LLYS-Y-COED
Cilcain
Pantymwyn
Gwernaffield
Tan-y-fron
Groes
B5429
Llangynhafal
MOEL FAMAU
554
elin-isaf
Clwt-grugoer
B4501
Llanrhaeadr
A525
LOGGERHEADS
Bylchau
Waen
Peniel
Prion
Llanynys
Gellifor
MOEL FAMAU
Tafarn-y-gelyn
B5435
Nantglyn
Pentre Llanrhaeadr
CLWYDIAN RANGE
BRYNIAU CLWYD
Saron
Hirwaen
Rhewl
126
Llanferres
BRYN TRILLYN
496
518
GORSEDD BRAN
Meifod
Llanbedr-Dyffryn-Clwyd
511
CRAFT CENTRE
Llanfwrog
Ruthin
(Rhuthun)
A494
B4501
Cyffylliog
Bontuchel
Aled
467
Llyn Alwen
A543
Tai-Ucha
DENBIGHSHIRE
(SIR DDINBYCH)
Mynydd Hiraethog
Llanarmon-yn-Iâl
B5430
Graianrhyd
Brenig Res.
Nant Uchaf
Efenechtyd
Llanfair-Dyffryn-Clwyd
Nilig
Alwen Reservoir
HAFOD ELWY MOOR
Pwll-glas
B5431
D
B4501
LLYN BRENIG VISITOR CENTRE
Pennant
Clocaenog
A525
Graig-fechan
532
Mwdwl-eithin
Clocaenog Forest
Clawdd-newydd
Pentre-celyn
Llandegla
Pentre-llyn cymmer
Afon Alwen
501
12
B5429
Glasfryn
Cefn-brith
B5105
Derwen
Rhyd-y-meudwy
Llanfihangel Glyn Myfyr
109
Llanelidan
A5
Bryn Saith Marchog
Cerrigydrudion
Melin-y-Wig
A494
405
A542
CYR
Maes

LIVERPOOL
Wallasey
Birkenhead
BEBINGTON
HOYLAKE
West Kirby
Everton
Seacombe
Poulton
Bidston
Edge Hill
Claughton
Toxteth
Wavertree
Mossley Hill
Dingle
Rock Ferry
Tranmere
Prenton
LADY LEVER ART GALLERY
Aigburth
Grassendale
New Ferry
PORT SUNLIGHT MUS
Port Sunlight
Storeton
Garston
Meols
Moreton
Upton
Greasby
Grange
Woodchurch
Frankby
ARROWE
Caldy
Irby
Thurstaston
Thingwall
Barnston
Brimstage
Pensby
WIRRAL
Heswall
Thornton Hough
Bromborough
EASTHAM
Eastham Ferry
Eastham
Gayton
Raby
Parkgate
Hinderton
Willaston
Hooton
Childer Thornton
RIVACRE
Overpool
Little Sutton
Great Sutton
Neston
Little Neston
Ness
NESS BOTANIC GARDENS
Burton
Two Mills
Capenhurst
Ledsham
Backford Cross
Puddington
Shotwick
Mollington
Saughall
Sealand
Blacon
Chester
CHESTER
Saltney
Bretton
Broughton
HAWARDEN
Hawarden (Penarlâg)
Mancot
Sandycroft
Queensferry
Garden City
Connah's Quay
Shotton
Ewloe
Ewloe Grn.
Buckley (Bwcle)
Drury
Northop Hall
Northop
Flint (Y Fflint)
Oakenholt
Flint Mountain
Mount Pleasant
West Hoyle Bank
Hilbre I.
Welsh Channel
Point of Ayr
Yr Parlwr Du
River Dee
Afon Dyfrdwy
Dawpool Bank
Gayton Sands
Holywell Bank
Talacre
Gwespyr
Ffynnongroyw
Picton
Llanasa
Mostyn Quay
Mostyn
Axton
Trelogan
Glan-y-don
Whitford
Greenfield
GREENFIELD VALLEY HERITAGE PARK
Walwen
Carmel
Pant-y-Wacco
Gorsedd
Holywell (Treffynnon)
Bagillt
Dolphin
Brynford
Babell
Caerwys
Pentre Halkyn
Halkyn
Halkyn Mountain
AFONWEN CRAFT AND ANTIQUE CENTRE
Ysceifiog
Afon-wen
Lixwm
Rhes-y-cae
Nannerch
Castell
OFFA'S DYKE PATH
LLWYBR CLAWDD OFFA
Rhosesmor
Hendre
Rhydymwyn
FLINTSHIRE (SIR Y FFLINT)
Soughton
New Brighton
Cilcain
Pantymwyn
Gwernaffield
Mold (Yr Wyddgrug)
Mynydd Isa
Llong
Spon Green
Penyffordd
Lower Kinnerton
Dodleston
Balderton
Higher Kinnerton
Cadole
LOGGERHEADS
MOEL LLYS-Y-COED
MOEL FAMAU
Tafarn-y-gelyn
Gwernymynydd
Maeshafn
Nercwys
Pontblyddyn
Leeswood
Coed-Talon
Llanferres
Waen
Llangwyfan
Llangynhafal
Llanynys
Gellifor
Hirwaen
Rhewl
Llanbedr-Dyffryn-Clwyd
CRAFT CENTRE
Llanfwrog
Ruthin (Rhuthun)
Eryrys
Treuddyn
WAUN-Y-LLYN
Caergwrle
Hope (Yr Hôb)
Burton Green
Pulford
Lavister
Rossett
Trevalyn
Marford
Llay
Gresford
Cefn-y-bedd
Llanfynydd
Llanarmon-yn-Iâl
Graianrhyd
Efenechtyd
Llanfair-Dyffryn-Clwyd
Graig-fechan
DENBIGHSHIRE (SIR DDINBYCH)
Pentre-celyn
Rhydtalog
Ffrith
Brymbo
ALYN WATERS
Moss
Gwersyllt
Bwlchgwyn
Four Crosses
Llandegla
Gwynfryn
LEAD MINES
Minera
MOSS VALLEY
Rhosrobin
Borras Head
Garden Village
Acton
Llan-y-pwll
Rhosnesni
New Broughton
Coedpoeth
Pen-y-stryt
Rhyd-y-meudwy
Llanelidan
Wrexham (WRECSAM)
Bersham
Rhostyllen
Wrexham Industrial Estate
CYRN Y BRAIN
ESCLUSHAM MOUNTAIN
Talwrn
WALES COAST PATH
0 1 2 3 miles
0 1 2 3 4 5 km

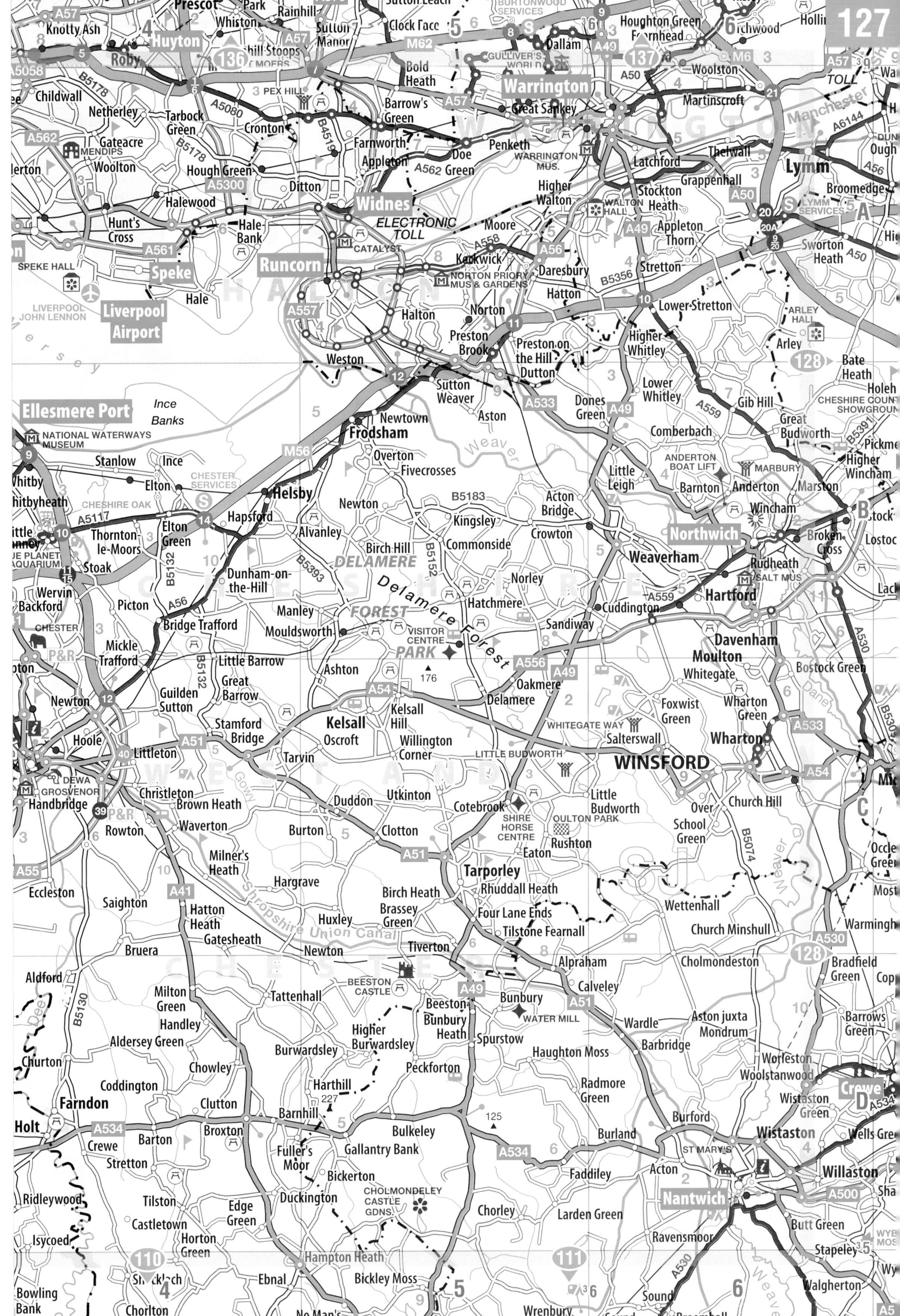
Prescot
Park
Rainhill
Sutton Leach
BURTONWOOD SERVICES
Houghton Green
Fearnhead
Knotty Ash
Huyton
Whiston
Sutton Manor
Clock Face
Dallam
Richwood
Hollins
Roby
136
Whiston
Bold Heath
GULLIVER'S WORLD
137
Woolston
TOLL
Childwall
Netherley
Tarbock Green
PEX HILL
Barrow's Green
Warrington
Great Sankey
Martinscroft
Manchester
Gateacre
MENDIPS
Cronton
Farnworth
Doe Green
Penketh
WARRINGTON MUS.
Thelwall
Lymm
Woolton
Hough Green
Appleton
Latchford
Grappenhall
Broomedge
Halewood
Ditton
Widnes
Higher Walton
Stockton Heath
LYMM SERVICES
Hunt's Cross
Hale Bank
ELECTRONIC TOLL
Moore
WALTON HALL
Appleton Thorn
Swarton Heath
CATALYST
SPEKE HALL
Speke
Runcorn
Keckwick
Daresbury
Stretton
NORTON PRIORY MUS & GARDENS
HALTON
Hale
Hatton
Lower Stretton
LIVERPOOL JOHN LENNON
Liverpool Airport
Halton
Norton
ARLEY HALL
Preston Brook
Preston on the Hill
Higher Whitley
Arley
Weston
Dutton
128
Bate Heath
Sutton Weaver
Lower Whitley
Gib Hill
Holeh
Ellesmere Port
Ince Banks
Dones Green
Aston
CHESHIRE COUNTY SHOWGROUND
Newtown
Great Budworth
NATIONAL WATERWAYS MUSEUM
Frodsham
Comberbach
Overton
ANDERTON BOAT LIFT
Stanlow
Ince
Fivecrosses
Weaver
MARBURY
Higher Wincham
Elton
CHESTER SERVICES
Little Leigh
Barnton
Anderton
Marston
Whitby
Whitbyheath
Helsby
Newton
Acton Bridge
Wincham
CHESHIRE OAK
Kingsley
Hapsford
Alvanley
Crowton
Northwich
Broken Cross
Lostock
Thornton-le-Moors
Elton Green
Birch Hill
Commonside
Weaverham
DELAMERE
Rudheath
SALT MUS
Stoak
Dunham-on-the-Hill
Norley
Hartford
Wervin
Backford
Picton
Delamere Forest
Hatchmere
Cuddington
CHESTER
Bridge Trafford
Manley
FOREST
Sandiway
Davenham
Mouldsworth
VISITOR CENTRE
PARK
Moulton
Mickle Trafford
Little Barrow
Ashton
176
Whitegate
Bostock Green
Great Barrow
Oakmere
Guilden Sutton
Delamere
Foxwist Green
Wharton Green
Newton
Kelsall Hill
Kelsall
WHITEGATE WAY
Stamford Bridge
Oscroft
Salterswall
Wharton
Willington Corner
Hoole
Littleton
Tarvin
LITTLE BUDWORTH
WINSFORD
DEWA
GROSVENOR
Christleton
Brown Heath
Duddon
Utkinton
Little Budworth
Over
Church Hill
Handbridge
Cotebrook
SHIRE HORSE CENTRE
OULTON PARK
School Green
Rowton
Waverton
Burton
Clotton
Rushton
Milner's Heath
Eaton
Tarporley
Eccleston
Hargrave
Rhuddall Heath
Birch Heath
Saighton
Brassey Green
Wettenhall
Hatton Heath
Four Lane Ends
Shropshire Union Canal
Huxley
Tilstone Fearnall
Church Minshull
Gatesheath
Bruera
Newton
Tiverton
Alpraham
Cholmondeston
Bradfield Green
Aldford
BEESTON CASTLE
Calveley
Milton Green
Tattenhall
Bunbury
Beeston
Bunbury Heath
WATER MILL
Wardle
Aston juxta Mondrum
Barrows Green
Handley
Higher Burwardsley
Aldersey Green
Spurstow
Barbridge
Burwardsley
Haughton Moss
Churton
Chowley
Worleston
Woolstanwood
Peckforton
Coddington
Harthill
Radmore Green
Crewe
Farndon
Clutton
227
Wistaston Green
Barnhill
125
Holt
Burford
Broxton
Bulkeley
Crewe
Barton
Burland
Wistaston
Wells Green
Stretton
Fuller's Moor
Gallantry Bank
ST MARY'S
Faddiley
Acton
Willaston
Bickerton
Ridleywood
Tilston
Duckington
CHOLMONDELEY CASTLE GDNS
Nantwich
Edge Green
Chorley
Larden Green
Butt Green
Castletown
Horton Green
Ravensmoor
Isycoed
110
Hampton Heath
111
Stapeley
Bowling Bank
Ebnal
Bickley Moss
Walgherton
Chorlton
No Man's
Wrenbury
Sound
Broomhall

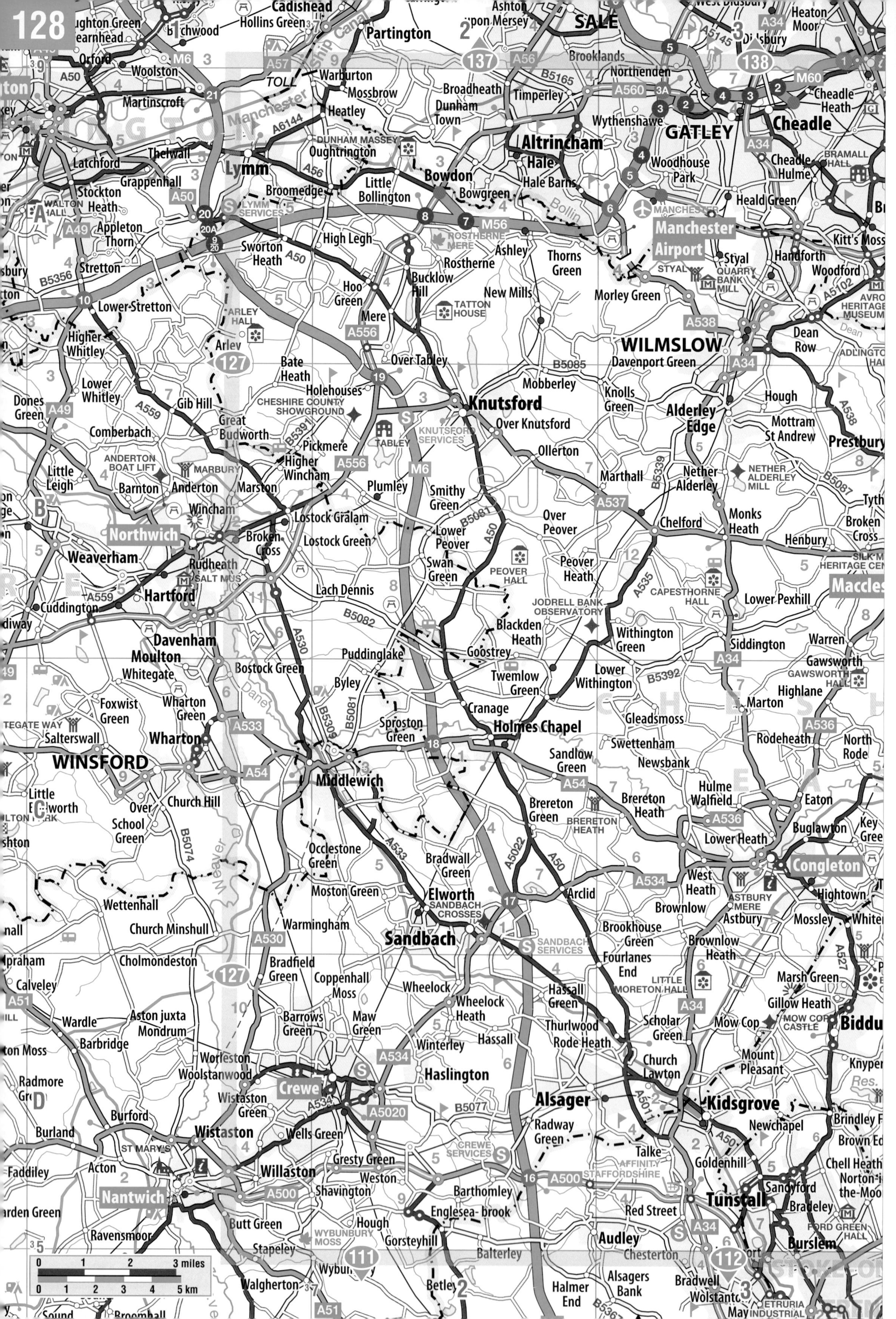
Cadishead
Hollins Green
Partington
SALE
Brooklands
Heaton Moor
Didsbury
Orford
Woolston
Warburton
Mossbrow
Heatley
Broadheath
Dunham Town
Timperley
Northenden
Wythenshawe
GATLEY
Cheadle
Cheadle Heath
Martinscroft
Thelwall
Latchford
Lymm
Oughtrington
DUNHAM MASSEY
Altrincham
Hale
Hale Barns
Woodhouse Park
Cheadle Hulme
BRAMALL HALL
Grappenhall
Stockton Heath
WALTON HALL
Appleton Thorn
Broomedge
Little Bollington
Bowdon
Bowgreen
Heald Green
MANCHESTER
Manchester Airport
LYMM SERVICES
Swarton Heath
High Legh
Rostherne Mere
Rostherne
Ashley
Thorns Green
Styal
STYAL
QUARRY BANK MILL
Handforth
Kitt's Moss
Woodford
Stretton
Lower Stretton
Hoo Green
Bucklow Hill
New Mills
TATTON HOUSE
Morley Green
AVRO HERITAGE MUSEUM
ARLEY HALL
Higher Whitley
Arley
Mere
WILMSLOW
Dean Row
Davenport Green
ADLINGTON HALL
Bate Heath
Holehouses
Over Tabley
Knutsford
Mobberley
Knolls Green
Hough
Lower Whitley
Dones Green
Gib Hill
CHESHIRE COUNTY SHOWGROUND
TABLEY
KNUTSFORD SERVICES
Over Knutsford
Alderley Edge
Mottram St Andrew
Prestbury
Comberbach
Great Budworth
Pickmere
Higher Wincham
Ollerton
ANDERTON BOAT LIFT
MARBURY
Little Leigh
Barnton
Anderton
Marston
Plumley
Smithy Green
Marthall
Nether Alderley
NETHER ALDERLEY MILL
Wincham
Lostock Gralam
Monks Heath
Northwich
Broken Cross
Lostock Green
Lower Peover
Over Peover
Chelford
Henbury
Tytherington
Weaverham
Rudheath
SALT MUS
Swan Green
PEOVER HALL
Peover Heath
CAPESTHORNE HALL
SILK M HERITAGE CEN
Macclesfield
Hartford
Cuddington
Lach Dennis
JODRELL BANK OBSERVATORY
Lower Pexhill
Davenham
Moulton
Blackden Heath
Withington Green
Siddington
Warren
Whitegate
Puddinglake
Goostrey
Bostock Green
Twemlow Green
Lower Withington
Gawsworth
GAWSWORTH HALL
Foxwist Green
Wharton Green
Byley
Cranage
Highlane
Marton
VALE ROYAL ABBEY / TEGATE WAY
Salterswall
Wharton
Sproston Green
Holmes Chapel
Gleadsmoss
Swettenham
Rodeheath
North Rode
WINSFORD
Middlewich
Sandlow Green
Newsbank
Little Budworth
Over
Church Hill
Brereton Green
BRERETON HEATH
Brereton Heath
Hulme Walfield
Eaton
School Green
Buglawton
Lower Heath
Occlestone Green
Bradwall Green
West Heath
Congleton
Moston Green
Elworth
SANDBACH CROSSES
Arclid
Brownlow
ASTBURY MERE
Astbury
Hightown
Mossley
Wettenhall
Church Minshull
Warmingham
Sandbach
SANDBACH SERVICES
Brookhouse Green
Brownlow Heath
Cholmondeston
Bradfield Green
Coppenhall Moss
Fourlanes End
LITTLE MORETON HALL
Marsh Green
Calveley
Wheelock
Wheelock Heath
Hassall Green
Gillow Heath
Biddulph
Wardle
Aston juxta Mondrum
Barrows Green
Maw Green
Thurlwood
Rode Heath
Scholar Green
Mow Cop
MOW COP CASTLE
Barbridge
Winterley
Hassall
Mount Pleasant
Knypersley
Worleston
Woolstanwood
Haslington
Church Lawton
Radmore Green
Crewe
Wistaston Green
Alsager
Kidsgrove
Newchapel
Brindley Ford
Burford
Wells Green
Radway Green
Brown Edge
Burland
Wistaston
ST MARY'S
Gresty Green
CREWE SERVICES
Talke
Goldenhill
Chell Heath
Faddiley
Acton
Willaston
Weston
AFFINITY STAFFORDSHIRE
Sandyford
Norton-in-the-Moors
Nantwich
Shavington
Barthomley
Tunstall
Bradeley
Englesea-brook
Red Street
FORD GREEN HALL
Butt Green
Hough
Ravensmoor
WYBUNBURY MOSS
Gorsteyhill
Audley
Burslem
Stapeley
Balterley
Chesterton
Wybunbury
Walgherton
Betley
Halmer End
Alsagers Bank
Bradwell
Wolstanton
ETRURIA INDUSTRIAL
STOKE-ON-TRENT
0 1 2 3 miles
0 1 2 3 4 5 km

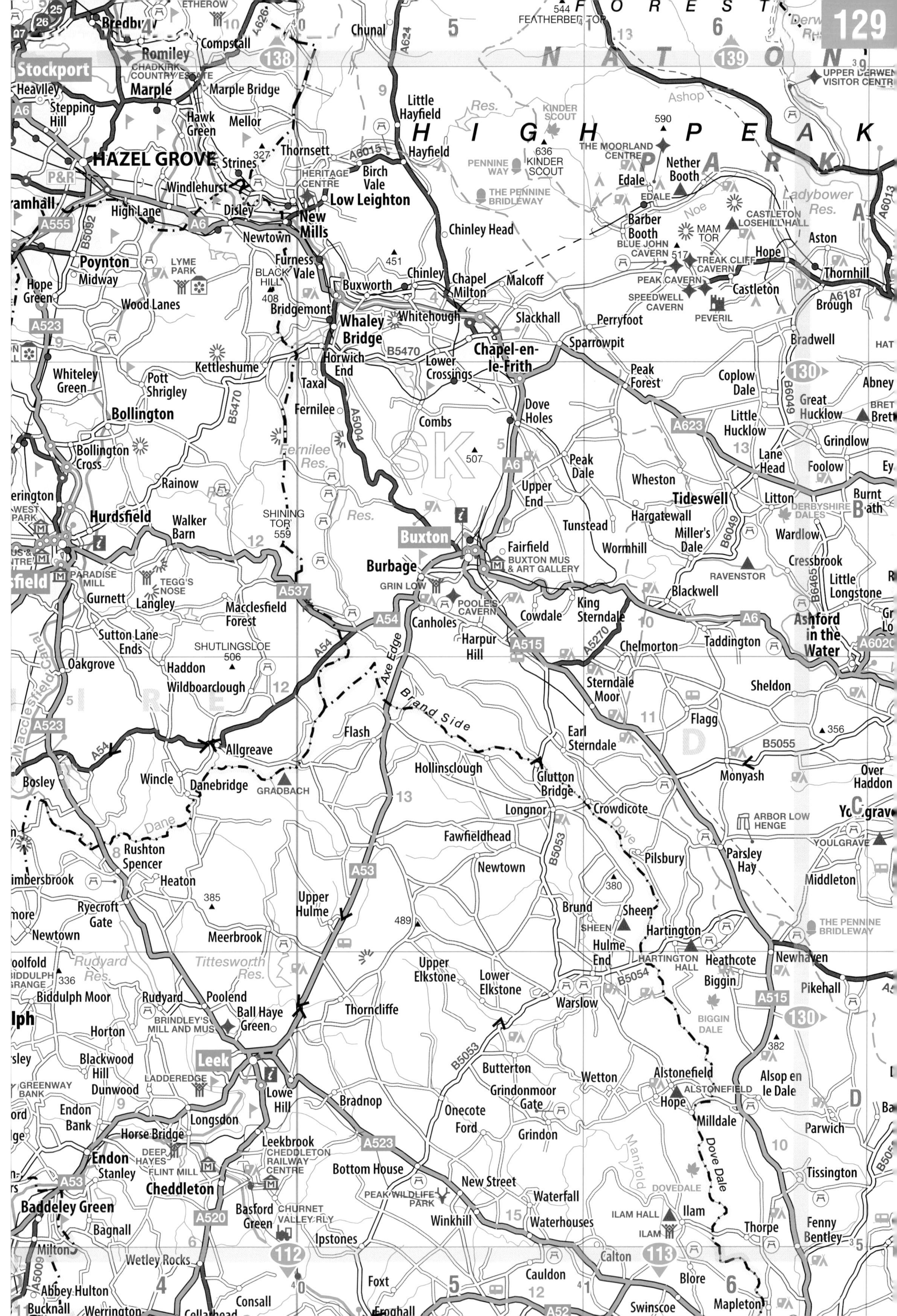
FOREST
FEATHERBED TOP
544
NATIONAL
Bredbury
Romiley
Compstall
Chunal
138
139
Stockport
CHADKIRK COUNTRY ESTATE
Heaviley
Marple
Marple Bridge
Stepping Hill
Hawk Green
Mellor
Little Hayfield
Res.
KINDER SCOUT
590
UPPER DERWENT VISITOR CENTRE
Ashop
HIGH PEAK
HAZEL GROVE
Strines
327
Thornsett
Hayfield
636
KINDER SCOUT
PENNINE WAY
THE MOORLAND CENTRE
Nether Booth
HERITAGE CENTRE
Birch Vale
Windlehurst
Edale
EDALE
THE PENNINE BRIDLEWAY
Ladybower Res.
Bramhall
High Lane
Disley
New Mills
Low Leighton
Noe
Barber Booth
CASTLETON LOSEHILL HALL
Aston
A555
B5092
A6
Newtown
Chinley Head
MAM TOR
BLUE JOHN CAVERN
517
TREAK CLIFF CAVERN
Hope
Poynton
LYME PARK
Furness Vale
451
Midway
BLACK HILL
408
Buxworth
Chinley
Chapel Milton
Malcoff
PEAK CAVERN
SPEEDWELL CAVERN
Castleton
PEVERIL
Thornhill
Brough
A6187
Hope Green
Wood Lanes
Bridgemont
Whaley Bridge
Whitehough
Slackhall
Perryfoot
A523
Sparrowpit
Bradwell
Horwich End
B5470
Lower Crossings
Chapel-en-le-Frith
Kettleshume
Peak Forest
Coplow Dale
130
Abney
Whiteley Green
Pott Shrigley
Taxal
Great Hucklow
Bollington
B5470
Fernilee
Combs
Dove Holes
Little Hucklow
B6049
A623
Grindlow
Bollington Cross
A5004
Fernilee Res.
SK
507
Peak Dale
Lane Head
Foolow
Rainow
Wheston
Upper End
Tideswell
Litton
Burnt Bath
DERBYSHIRE DALES
Hurdsfield
Walker Barn
SHINING TOR
559
Res.
Hargatewall
Tunstead
Miller's Dale
Wardlow
Buxton
Fairfield
Wormhill
B6049
Burbage
BUXTON MUS & ART GALLERY
RAVENSTOR
Cressbrook
PARADISE MILL
TEGG'S NOSE
GRIN LOW
Blackwell
Little Longstone
Macclesfield
Gurnett
Langley
Macclesfield Forest
A537
POOLE'S CAVERN
King Sterndale
Cowdale
Ashford in the Water
A6
B6465
Sutton Lane Ends
A54
Canholes
Harpur Hill
A515
A5270
Chelmorton
Taddington
A6020
SHUTLINGSLOE
506
Oakgrove
Haddon
A54
Axe Edge
Wildboarclough
Sterndale Moor
Sheldon
Brand Side
Macclesfield Canal
A523
Flash
Earl Sterndale
Flagg
356
B5055
A54
Allgreave
Hollinsclough
Glutton Bridge
Monyash
Over Haddon
Bosley
Wincle
Danebridge
GRADBACH
Longnor
Crowdicote
ARBOR LOW HENGE
Youlgrave
Dane
Fawfieldhead
Dove
Pilsbury
Parsley Hay
YOULGRAVE
Rushton Spencer
Newtown
B5053
Heaton
A53
380
Middleton
Timbersbrook
385
Upper Hulme
Ryecroft Gate
Brund
Sheen
THE PENNINE BRIDLEWAY
489
SHEEN
Hartington
Newtown
Meerbrook
Hulme End
HARTINGTON HALL
Heathcote
Newhaven
Rudyard Res.
Tittesworth Res.
Upper Elkstone
Lower Elkstone
B5054
Biggin
BIDDULPH GRANGE
336
Biddulph Moor
Rudyard
Poolend
Thorncliffe
Warslow
A515
Pikehall
Ball Haye Green
130
BRINDLEY'S MILL AND MUS
BIGGIN DALE
382
Horton
Leek
B5053
Blackwood Hill
LADDEREDGE
Butterton
Wetton
Alstonefield
Alsop en le Dale
GREENWAY BANK
Dunwood
Lowe Hill
Grindonmoor Gate
ALSTONEFIELD
Hope
Bradnop
Endon Bank
Onecote Ford
Milldale
Parwich
Longsdon
Grindon
Horse Bridge
Leekbrook
Dove Dale
Manifold
Endon
DEEP HAYES
CHEDDLETON RAILWAY CENTRE
A523
Tissington
Stanley
FLINT MILL
Bottom House
A53
Cheddleton
New Street
DOVEDALE
Baddeley Green
PEAK WILDLIFE PARK
Waterfall
Basford Green
CHURNET VALLEY RLY
A520
ILAM HALL
Ilam
Thorpe
Fenny Bentley
Winkhill
Waterhouses
Bagnall
ILAM
Milton
Ipstones
112
113
Wetley Rocks
Calton
A5009
Abbey Hulton
Foxt
Cauldon
Blore
Consall
Mapleton
Bucknall
Werrington
Froghall
A52
Swinscoe

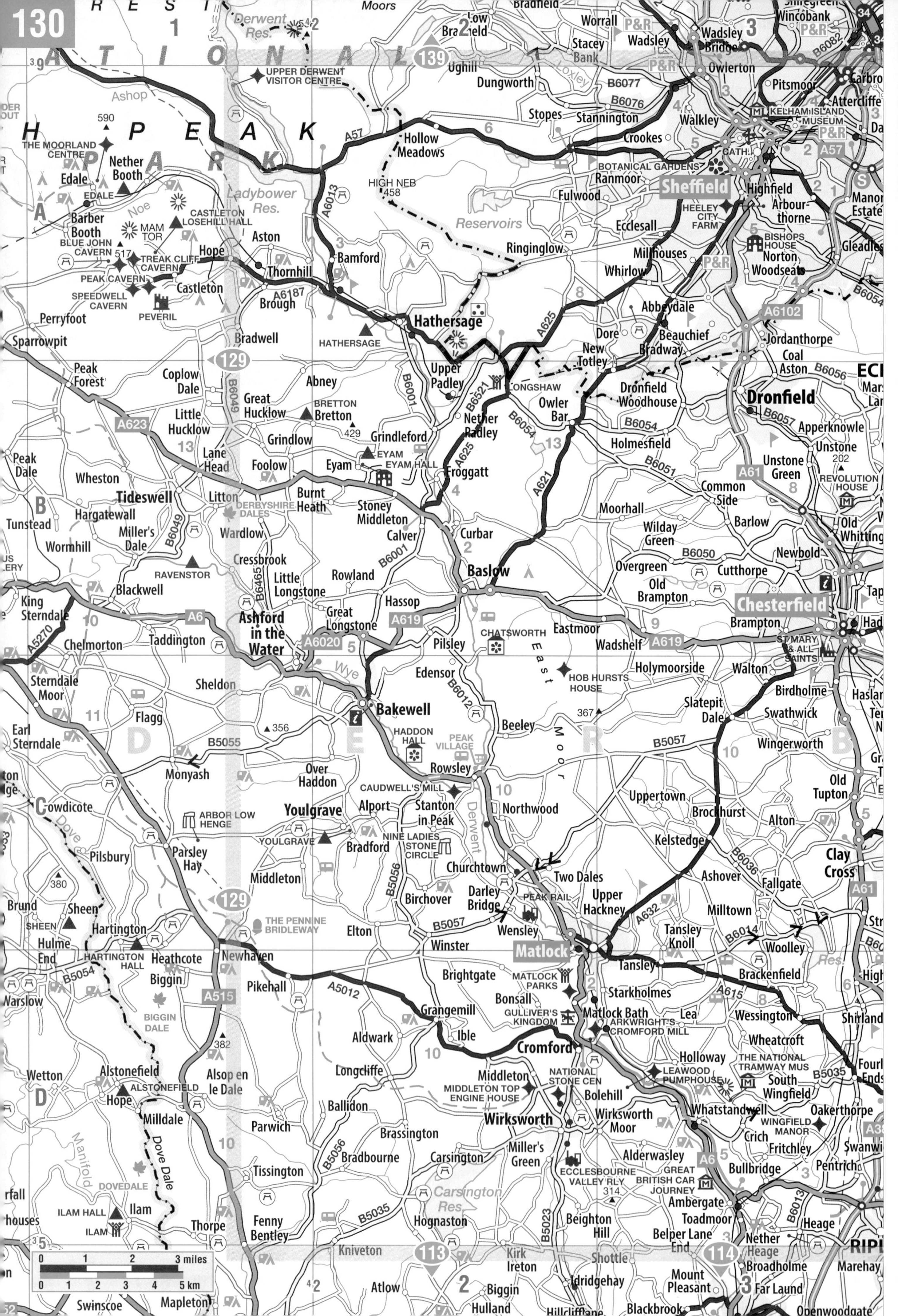

PEAK NATIONAL PARK
DERBYSHIRE DALES
Moors
Derwent Res.
UPPER DERWENT VISITOR CENTRE
Ashop
590
THE MOORLAND CENTRE
Edale
Nether Booth
EDALE
Noe
Barber Booth
BLUE JOHN CAVERN
517
MAM TOR
CASTLETON LOSEHILL HALL
TREAK CLIFF CAVERN
PEAK CAVERN
SPEEDWELL CAVERN
PEVERIL
Castleton
Hope
Aston
Thornhill
Ladybower Res.
Brough
A6187
Bamford
A6013
A57
Hollow Meadows
HIGH NEB 458
Reservoirs
Ringinglow
Hathersage
HATHERSAGE
Perryfoot
Sparrowpit
Bradwell
129
Peak Forest
Coplow Dale
Abney
Upper Padley
B6001
B6049
Great Hucklow
BRETTON
Bretton
429
Little Hucklow
A623
Grindlow
Grindleford
EYAM
EYAM HALL
Eyam
Foolow
Lane Head
Peak Dale
Wheston
Tideswell
Litton
Burnt Heath
Stoney Middleton
Calver
Froggatt
Nether Padley
LONGSHAW
B6521
A625
B6054
Owler Bar
A621
Tunstead
Hargatewall
Miller's Dale
Wormhill
Wardlow
Cressbrook
RAVENSTOR
Blackwell
B6465
Little Longstone
Rowland
Hassop
Baslow
Curbar
King Sterndale
A5270
A6
Ashford in the Water
Great Longstone
A619
A6020
Chelmorton
Taddington
Pilsley
CHATSWORTH
Edensor
Wye
Sterndale Moor
Sheldon
Bakewell
B6012
HADDON HALL
PEAK VILLAGE
Flagg
Earl Sterndale
356
B5055
Monyash
Over Haddon
Rowsley
CAUDWELL'S MILL
Youlgrave
Alport
Stanton in Peak
Derwent
Northwood
Cowdicote
Dove
ARBOR LOW HENGE
YOULGRAVE
NINE LADIES STONE CIRCLE
Bradford
Pilsbury
Parsley Hay
Middleton
B5056
Churchtown
Two Dales
380
Brund
Sheen
SHEEN
Hartington
HARTINGTON HALL
Heathcote
THE PENNINE BRIDLEWAY
Elton
Birchover
Darley Bridge
PEAK RAIL
Wensley
B5057
Winster
Matlock
Hulme End
B5054
Biggin
Newhaven
Pikehall
A5012
Brightgate
MATLOCK PARKS
Bonsall
GULLIVER'S KINGDOM
Matlock Bath
ARKWRIGHT'S CROMFORD MILL
Warslow
A515
BIGGIN DALE
Grangemill
Ible
Aldwark
Cromford
382
Wetton
Alstonefield
ALSTONEFIELD
Hope
Alsop en le Dale
Longcliffe
Middleton
MIDDLETON TOP ENGINE HOUSE
NATIONAL STONE CEN
Bolehill
Milldale
Manifold
Dove Dale
Ballidon
Parwich
Wirksworth
Wirksworth Moor
Brassington
Miller's Green
Bradbourne
Carsington
Tissington
DOVEDALE
Carsington Res
ECCLESBOURNE VALLEY RLY
314
ILAM HALL
Ilam
ILAM
Thorpe
Fenny Bentley
B5035
Hognaston
B5023
Beighton Hill
Kniveton
113
Kirk Ireton
Shottle
Idridgehay
Atlow
Biggin
Hulland
Swinscoe
Mapleton
Hillcliffane
Blackbrook
Low Bradfield
Bradfield
139
Ughill
Dungworth
Worrall
Stacey Bank
Loxley
Wadsley
Wadsley Bridge
Owlerton
Wincobank
B6082
Pitsmoor
Carbrook
Attercliffe
B6077
B6076
Stopes
Stannington
Walkley
KELHAM ISLAND MUSEUM
Crookes
CATH.
BOTANICAL GARDENS
Ranmoor
Sheffield
Highfield
Fulwood
HEELEY CITY FARM
Arbourthorne
Manor Estate
Ecclesall
BISHOPS HOUSE
Norton
Woodseats
Gleadless
Millhouses
Whirlow
Abbeydale
A6102
Dore
Beauchief
Bradway
Jordanthorpe
B6054
Coal Aston
B6056
Totley
New Totley
Dronfield Woodhouse
Dronfield
B6057
Apperknowle
Holmesfield
Unstone
202
Unstone Green
REVOLUTION HOUSE
A61
B6051
Common Side
Barlow
Moorhall
Wilday Green
B6050
Old Whittington
Newbold
Overgreen
Cutthorpe
Old Brampton
Chesterfield
Brampton
Eastmoor
Wadshelf
ST MARY & ALL SAINTS
HOB HURSTS HOUSE
Holymoorside
Walton
East Moor
Birdholme
367
Slatepit Dale
Swathwick
Beeley
Wingerworth
B5057
Uppertown
Brockhurst
Alton
Old Tupton
Kelstedge
B6036
Ashover
Fallgate
Clay Cross
Upper Hackney
A632
Milltown
Tansley Knoll
B6014
Woolley
Tansley
Brackenfield
Res.
A615
Starkholmes
Lea
Wessington
Shirland
Holloway
Wheatcroft
THE NATIONAL TRAMWAY MUS
LEAWOOD PUMPHOUSE
South Wingfield
B5035
Fourlane Ends
Whatstandwell
Oakerthorpe
WINGFIELD MANOR
Crich
Fritchley
Swanwick
Alderwasley
GREAT BRITISH CAR JOURNEY
Bullbridge
Pentrich
A6
Ambergate
Toadmoor
B6013
Heage
Belper Lane End
Nether Heage
114
Broadholme
Marehay
Mount Pleasant
Far Laund
Openwoodgate
0 1 2 3 miles
0 1 2 3 4 5 km

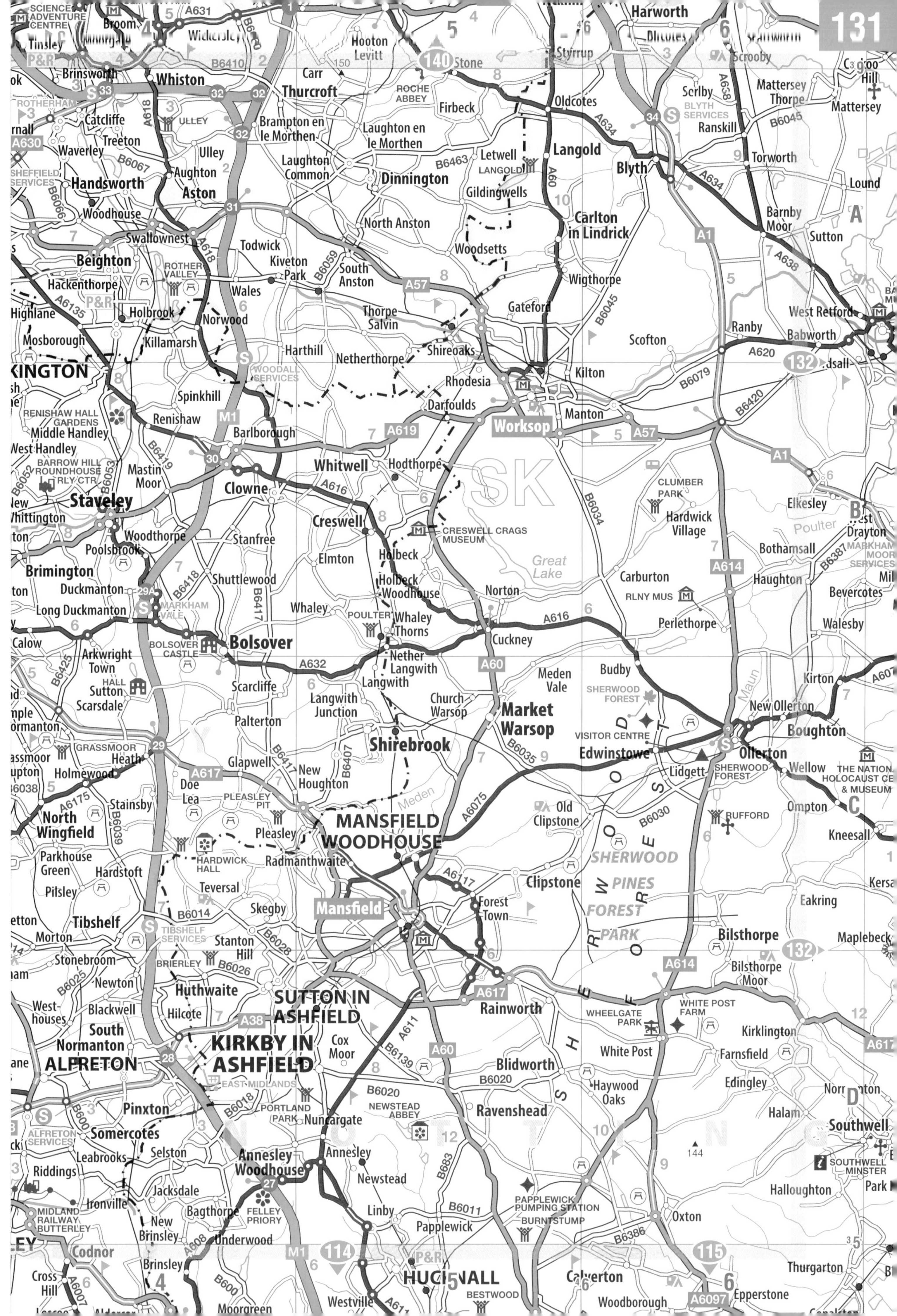
Harworth
Hooton Levitt
Stone
Styrrup
Scrooby
Brinsworth
Whiston
Carr
Thurcroft
ROCHE ABBEY
Firbeck
Oldcotes
Serlby
BLYTH SERVICES
Mattersey Thorpe
Mattersey
Catcliffe
ULLEY
Brampton en le Morthen
Laughton en le Morthen
Langold
Ranskill
Treeton
Waverley
Ulley
Letwell
LANGOLD
Blyth
Torworth
Handsworth
Aughton
Laughton Common
Dinnington
Gildingwells
Lound
Aston
Woodhouse
North Anston
Carlton in Lindrick
Barnby Moor
Sutton
Swallownest
Todwick
Woodsetts
Beighton
ROTHER VALLEY
Kiveton Park
South Anston
Wigthorpe
Hackenthorpe
Wales
Gateford
West Retford
Highlane
Holbrook
Norwood
Thorpe Salvin
Ranby
Babworth
Mosborough
Killamarsh
Harthill
Netherthorpe
Shireoaks
Scofton
WOODALL SERVICES
Rhodesia
Kilton
Spinkhill
Darfoulds
Worksop
Manton
RENISHAW HALL GARDENS
Renishaw
Middle Handley
West Handley
Barlborough
Whitwell
Hodthorpe
BARROW HILL ROUNDHOUSE RLY CTR
Mastin Moor
Clowne
CLUMBER PARK
Elkesley
Staveley
Hardwick Village
Creswell
CRESWELL CRAGS MUSEUM
Woodthorpe
Stanfree
Poolsbrook
Holbeck
Great Lake
Brimington
Elmton
Carburton
Haughton
Bothamsall
MARKHAM MOOR SERVICES
Duckmanton
Shuttlewood
Holbeck Woodhouse
Norton
RLNY MUS
Bevercotes
Long Duckmanton
MARKHAM VALE
Whaley
POULTER
Whaley Thorns
Perlethorpe
Walesby
Calow
Arkwright Town
BOLSOVER CASTLE
Bolsover
Cuckney
Nether Langwith
Budby
Kirton
Sutton Scarsdale
HALL
Scarcliffe
Langwith
Meden Vale
SHERWOOD FOREST
Langwith Junction
Church Warsop
Market Warsop
New Ollerton
Boughton
Palterton
VISITOR CENTRE
Edwinstowe
Ollerton
Shirebrook
GRASSMOOR
Heath
Glapwell
New Houghton
Lidgett
SHERWOOD FOREST
Wellow
THE NATIONAL HOLOCAUST CENTRE & MUSEUM
Holmewood
Doe Lea
PLEASLEY PIT
Old Clipstone
Ompton
Stainsby
North Wingfield
MANSFIELD WOODHOUSE
RUFFORD
Pleasley
Kneesall
Parkhouse Green
HARDWICK HALL
Radmanthwaite
SHERWOOD
Hardstoft
Clipstone
PINES
Pilsley
Teversal
Forest Town
FOREST
Eakring
Mansfield
Tibshelf
Skegby
Morton
TIBSHELF SERVICES
Stanton Hill
PARK
Bilsthorpe
Maplebeck
Stonebroom
BRIERLEY
Bilsthorpe Moor
Newton
Huthwaite
SUTTON IN ASHFIELD
Rainworth
West-houses
Blackwell
WHITE POST FARM
Hilcote
WHEELGATE PARK
Kirklington
South Normanton
KIRKBY IN ASHFIELD
Cox Moor
White Post
Farnsfield
ALFRETON
Blidworth
Haywood Oaks
Edingley
EAST MIDLANDS
NEWSTEAD ABBEY
Pinxton
PORTLAND PARK
Nuncargate
Ravenshead
Halam
Southwell
ALFRETON SERVICES
Somercotes
Selston
Annesley
SOUTHWELL MINSTER
Leabrooks
Annesley Woodhouse
Riddings
Newstead
Park
Jacksdale
Halloughton
Ironville
MIDLAND RAILWAY BUTTERLEY
Bagthorpe
FELLEY PRIORY
Linby
PAPPLEWICK PUMPING STATION
Oxton
New Brinsley
BURNTSTUMP
Papplewick
Underwood
Codnor
Brinsley
Calverton
Thurgarton
Hucknall
Cross Hill
BESTWOOD
Epperstone
Westville
Woodborough
Moorgreen
SK
Maun
Meden
Poulter
Great Lake

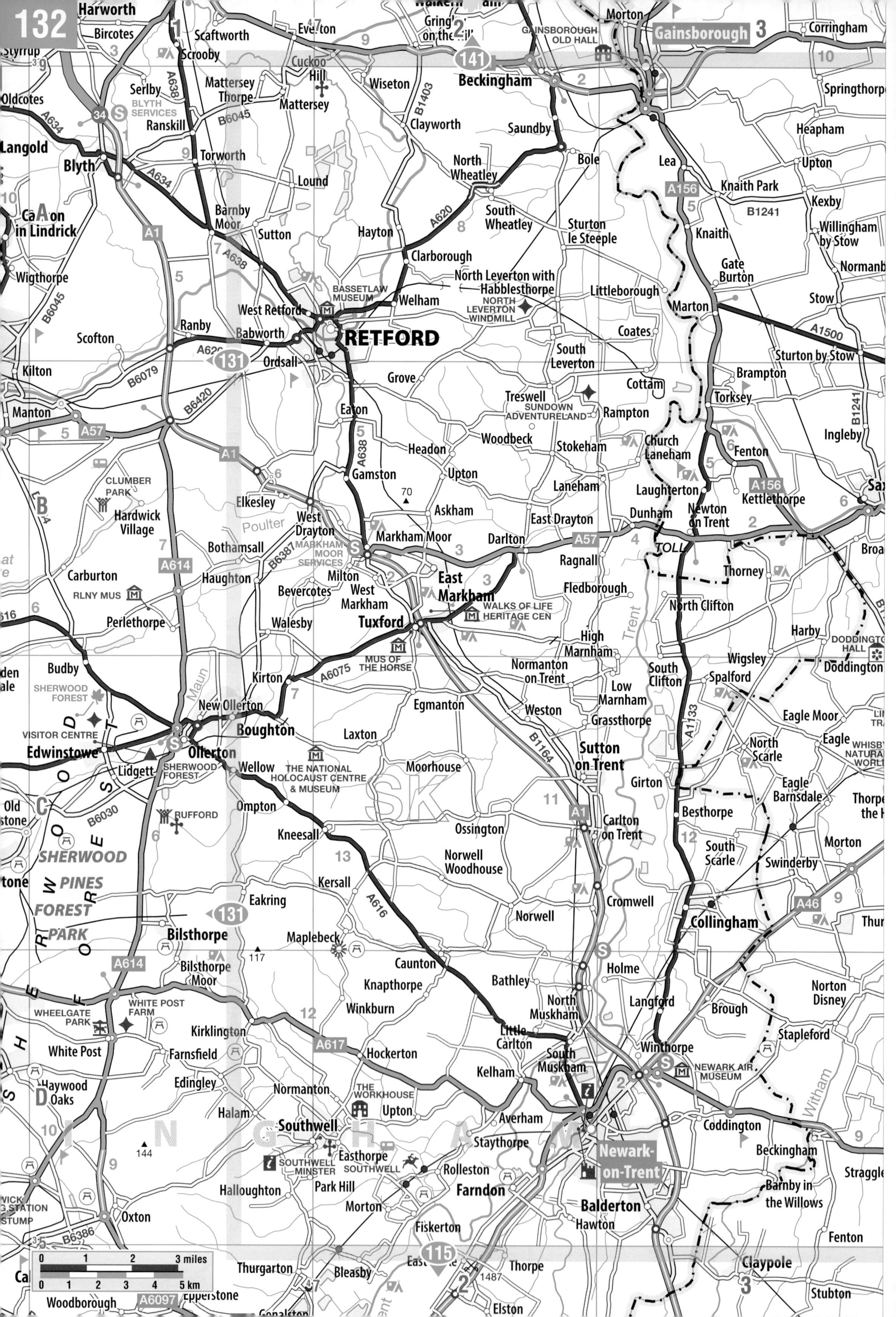
Harworth
Bircotes
Scaftworth
Everton
Gainsborough
Corringham
Morton
GAINSBOROUGH OLD HALL
Scrooby
Cuckoo Hill
Beckingham
Wiseton
Springthorpe
Serlby
Mattersey Thorpe
Mattersey
Oldcotes
BLYTH SERVICES
Ranskill
Clayworth
Saundby
Heapham
Langold
Torworth
Bole
Lea
Blyth
Upton
North Wheatley
Knaith Park
Lound
Kexby
Carlton in Lindrick
Barnby Moor
Sutton
Hayton
South Wheatley
Sturton le Steeple
Knaith
Willingham by Stow
Clarborough
Gate Burton
Wigthorpe
North Leverton with Habblesthorpe
Littleborough
Marton
Stow
BASSETLAW MUSEUM
Welham
NORTH LEVERTON WINDMILL
West Retford
Ranby
Scofton
Babworth
RETFORD
Coates
South Leverton
Sturton by Stow
Ordsall
Kilton
Grove
Cottam
Brampton
Torksey
Manton
Treswell
SUNDOWN ADVENTURELAND
Rampton
Eaton
Woodbeck
Headon
Stokeham
Church Laneham
Ingleby
Fenton
CLUMBER PARK
Gamston
Upton
Laneham
Laughterton
Kettlethorpe
Elkesley
Hardwick Village
Askham
East Drayton
Dunham
Newton on Trent
Poulter
West Drayton
Markham Moor
Darlton
MARKHAM MOOR SERVICES
Bothamsall
Ragnall
TOLL
Thorney
Carburton
Haughton
Milton
East Markham
Fledborough
Bevercotes
West Markham
RLNY MUS
WALKS OF LIFE HERITAGE CEN
North Clifton
Perlethorpe
Walesby
Tuxford
High Marnham
Harby
Trent
DODDINGTON HALL
MUS OF THE HORSE
Normanton on Trent
Wigsley
Budby
Kirton
South Clifton
Doddington
SHERWOOD FOREST
Spalford
Low Marnham
Egmanton
New Ollerton
Weston
Grassthorpe
Eagle Moor
VISITOR CENTRE
Boughton
Laxton
Edwinstowe
Ollerton
Sutton on Trent
Eagle
North Scarle
Lidgett
SHERWOOD FOREST
Wellow
THE NATIONAL HOLOCAUST CENTRE & MUSEUM
Moorhouse
Girton
Eagle Barnsdale
RUFFORD
Ompton
Besthorpe
Carlton on Trent
SHERWOOD
Kneesall
Ossington
South Scarle
Morton
Norwell Woodhouse
Swinderby
PINES
Kersall
FOREST
Eakring
Cromwell
Collingham
PARK
Norwell
Bilsthorpe
Maplebeck
Holme
Bilsthorpe Moor
Caunton
Bathley
Norton Disney
Knapthorpe
North Muskham
Langford
WHITE POST FARM
WHEELGATE PARK
Winkburn
Brough
Kirklington
Little Carlton
Stapleford
White Post
Farnsfield
Hockerton
Winthorpe
South Muskham
NEWARK AIR MUSEUM
Haywood Oaks
Edingley
Kelham
Normanton
THE WORKHOUSE
Halam
Upton
Averham
Southwell
Coddington
Staythorpe
Newark-on-Trent
Beckingham
Easthorpe
SOUTHWELL MINSTER
SOUTHWELL
Rolleston
Barnby in the Willows
Halloughton
Park Hill
Farndon
Morton
Balderton
Oxton
Hawton
Fiskerton
Fenton
Thurgarton
Bleasby
Thorpe
Claypole
Woodborough
Epperstone
Elston
Stubton
Witham
Maun
A1
A57
A614
A616
A617
A620
A631
A634
A638
A6075
A6097
A156
A1133
A1500
A46
B1164
B1241
B1403
B6045
B6079
B6030
B6386
B6387
B6420
SK
0 1 2 3 miles
0 1 2 3 4 5 km

133
Hemswell
Spital in the Street
Bishop Norton
Glentham
Bishopbridge
Kirkby
Walesby
Tealby
West Rasen
Middle Rasen
Market Rasen
North Willingham
Harpswell
Hemswell Cliff
Caenby Corner
Caenby
Normanby-by-Spital
Toft next Newton
Glentworth
CAENBY CORNER SERVICES
MARKET RASEN
WILD PINES PARK
Owmby-by-Spital
Newton by Toft
Sixhills
Linwood
Fillingham
Saxby
Buslingthorpe
Legsby
Spridlington
Faldingworth
Bleasby
Hainton
South Willingham
Friesthorpe
Cold Hanworth
Lissington
East Torrington
West Torrington
Ingham
Hackthorn
Wickenby
Holton cum Beckering
Cammeringham
Snarford
Thorpe in the Fallows
Welton Hill
Brattleby
East Barkwith
West Barkwith
Aisthorpe
RAF SCAMPTON HERITAGE CENTRE
Welton
Snelland
Fulnetby
Scampton
Dunholme
Rand
RAND FARM PARK
Sotby
Bransby
Stainton by Langworth
Wragby
Panton
Broxholme
North Carlton
Scothern
Bullington
Langworth
WOODSIDE WILDLIFE PARK
Hatton
South Carlton
Sudbrooke
Langton by Wragby
Riseholme
Nettleham
Apley
Kingthorpe
Odder
Burton
MUSEUM OF LINCOLNSHIRE LIFE
Reepham
Low Barlings
Minting
Bunker's Hill
North Greetwell
Cherry Willingham
Ermine
ELLIS MILL
Skellingthorpe
St Giles
CATH
Fiskerton
Stainfield
Gautby
Lincoln
Washingborough
Young Wood
New Boultham
Birchwood
Boultham
HARTSHOLME
Canwick
Branston Booths
Bardney
Heighington
INT BOMBER COMMAND CTR
Bucknall
Horsington
LINCOLNSHIRE ROAD TRANSPORT MUSEUM
Bracebridge
Whisby
Bracebridge Heath
Branston
Potterhanworth Booths
BARDNEY LIMEWOODS
Southrey
Bracebridge Low Fields
Potterhanworth
Stixwould
North Hykeham
River Witham
Wasps Nest
Sots Hole
South Hykeham
Waddington
Nocton
COTTAGE MUSEUM
Haddington
Dunston
Woodhall Spa
Kirkstead
Aubourn
Harmston
Metheringham
Martin Dales
Coleby
Martin
Bassingham
Blankney
METHERINGHAM AIRFIELD VISITOR CENTRE
Boothby Graffoe
Scopwick
TATTERSHALL COLLEGE
Tattershall
Navenby
Timberland
Carlton le Moorland
Kirkby Green
Thorpe Tilney
Walcott
Tattershall Bridge
Wellingore
Rowston
Ashby de la Launde
Brant
Dogdyke
Billinghay
Welbourn
Digby
Chapel Hill
Brant Broughton
Bloxholm
NORTH INGS FARM MUSEUM
Dorrington
North Kyme
Leadenham
ERMINE
STREET
Fulbeck
Ruskington
Anwick
Cranwell
South Kyme
Caythorpe
Leasingham
Brandon
South Kyme Fen
A15
A1103
A631
A46
A57
A158
A1434
A607
A17
A153
A157
B1202
B1398
B1399
B1190
B1188
B1178
B1189
B1191
B1429
B1209
B1395
142
134
116
TF

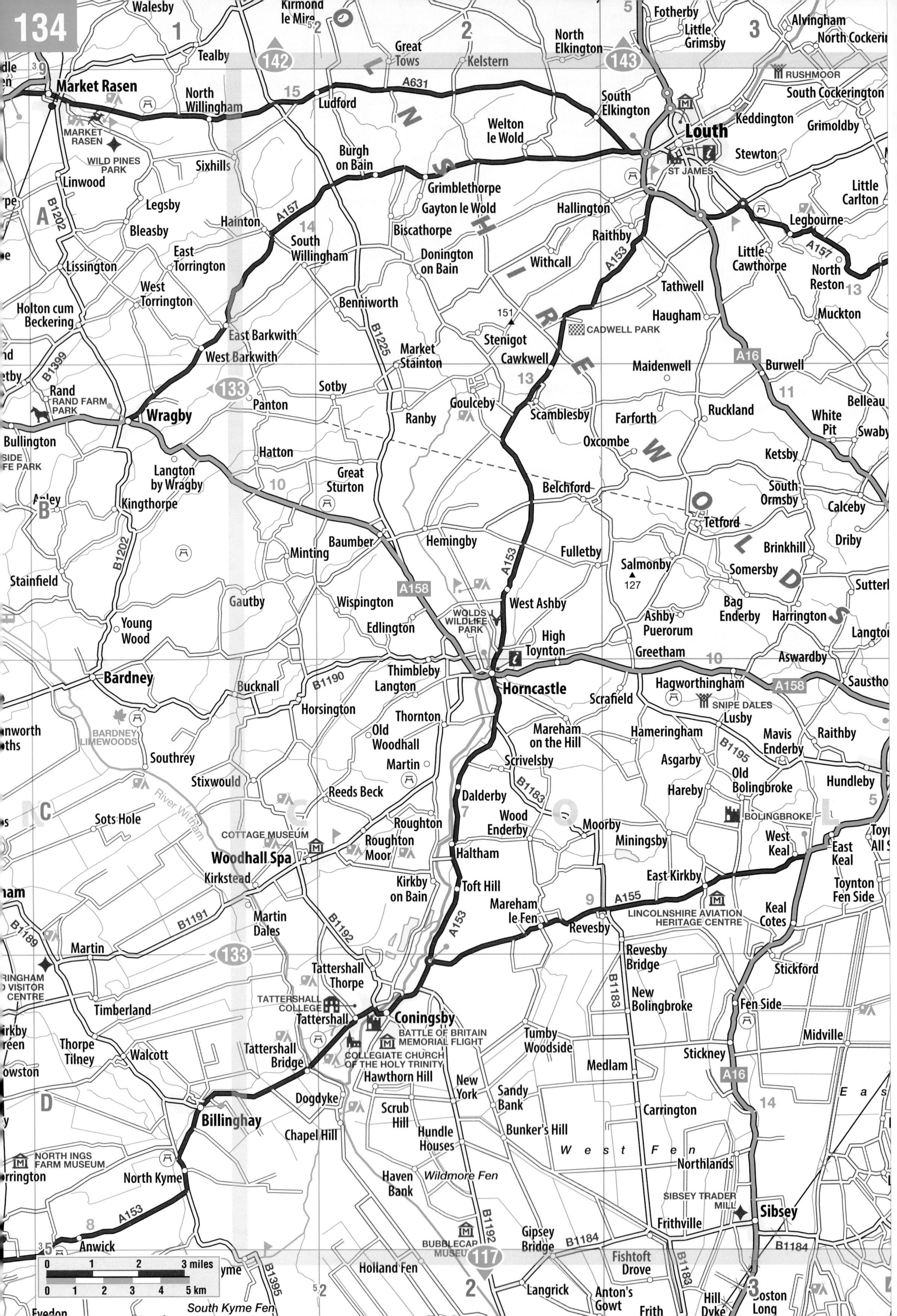
Walesby
Kirmond le Mire
Fotherby
Little Grimsby
Alvingham
North Cockerington
142
143
Great Tows
Kelstern
North Elkington
Tealby
Market Rasen
North Willingham
A631
Ludford
South Elkington
Louth
RUSHMOOR
South Cockerington
Keddington
Grimoldby
MARKET RASEN
WILD PINES PARK
Sixhills
Burgh on Bain
Welton le Wold
Stewton
ST JAMES
Linwood
Legsby
Grimblethorpe
Gayton le Wold
Hallington
Little Carlton
B1202
A157
Hainton
Bleasby
Biscathorpe
Raithby
Legbourne
South Willingham
Donington on Bain
Withcall
A153
Little Cawthorpe
North Reston
Lissington
East Torrington
West Torrington
Tathwell
Holton cum Beckering
Benniworth
151
Haugham
Muckton
CADWELL PARK
East Barkwith
West Barkwith
B1225
Market Stainton
Stenigot
Cawkwell
A16
Burwell
Maidenwell
B1399
Rand
RAND FARM PARK
Sotby
133
Panton
Wragby
Ranby
Goulceby
Scamblesby
Farforth
Ruckland
Belleau
White Pit
Swaby
Bullington
Oxcombe
Hatton
Langton by Wragby
Great Sturton
Belchford
Ketsby
South Ormsby
Calceby
Apley
Kingthorpe
Tetford
Baumber
Hemingby
Minting
Brinkhill
Driby
Fulletby
Salmonby
127
Somersby
B1202
Stainfield
A158
Wispington
A153
West Ashby
Gautby
Bag Enderby
Harrington
Ashby Puerorum
Young Wood
WOLDS WILDLIFE PARK
Edlington
High Toynton
Greetham
Aswardby
Bardney
Thimbleby
Langton
Horncastle
Bucknall
B1190
Scrafield
Hagworthingham
A158
Sausthorpe
Horsington
SNIPE DALES
Lusby
Thornton
Old Woodhall
Mareham on the Hill
Hameringham
Mavis Enderby
Raithby
BARDNEY LIMEWOODS
Southrey
Scrivelsby
B1195
Asgarby
Martin
Old Bolingbroke
Hundleby
Stixwould
Reeds Beck
B1183
Dalderby
Hareby
Sots Hole
River Witham
Wood Enderby
BOLINGBROKE
Roughton
Moorby
COTTAGE MUSEUM
Roughton Moor
Miningsby
West Keal
East Keal
Woodhall Spa
Haltham
Kirkstead
Kirkby on Bain
Toft Hill
East Kirkby
Toynton Fen Side
Mareham le Fen
A155
Revesby
LINCOLNSHIRE AVIATION HERITAGE CENTRE
Keal Cotes
Martin Dales
B1191
B1192
A153
B1189
Martin
133
Revesby Bridge
Stickford
Tattershall Thorpe
B1183
New Bolingbroke
TATTERSHALL COLLEGE
Fen Side
Timberland
Tattershall
Coningsby
BATTLE OF BRITAIN MEMORIAL FLIGHT
Tumby Woodside
Midville
Thorpe Tilney
Walcott
Tattershall Bridge
COLLEGIATE CHURCH OF THE HOLY TRINITY
Stickney
Medlam
Hawthorn Hill
A16
New York
Sandy Bank
Dogdyke
Scrub Hill
Carrington
Billinghay
Chapel Hill
Hundle Houses
Bunker's Hill
West Fen
Northlands
NORTH INGS FARM MUSEUM
Haven Bank
Wildmore Fen
North Kyme
SIBSEY TRADER MILL
Sibsey
A153
Frithville
Anwick
BUBBLECAR MUSEUM
B1192
Gipsey Bridge
B1184
B1184
117
Fishtoft Drove
B1183
Holland Fen
B1395
Langrick
Anton's Gowt
Frith
Hill Dyke
Boston Long
South Kyme Fen
0 1 2 3 miles
0 1 2 3 4 5 km

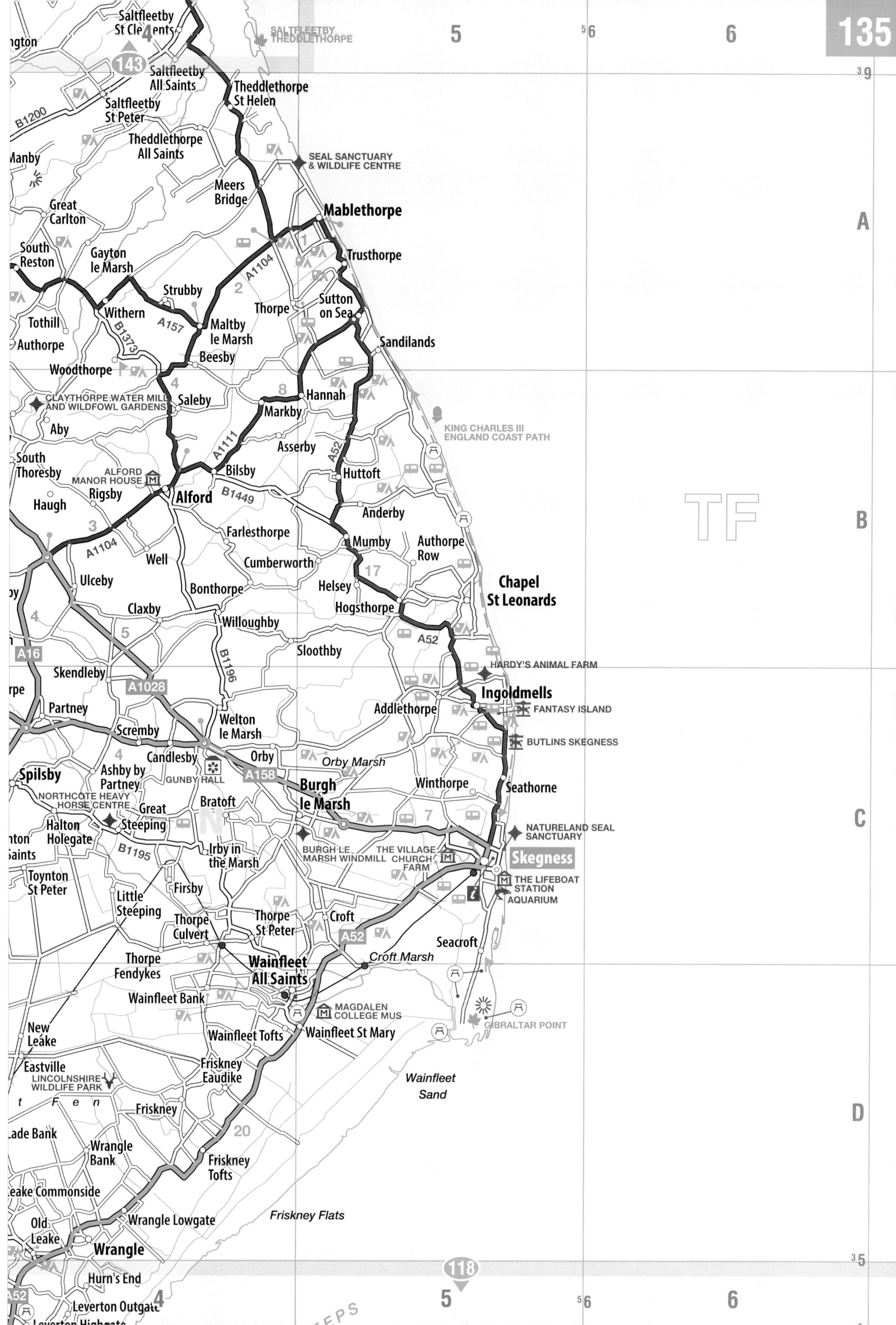

4
5
6
A
B
C
D
TF
Saltfleetby St Clements
SALTFLEETBY THEDDLETHORPE
143
Saltfleetby All Saints
Theddlethorpe St Helen
Saltfleetby St Peter
B1200
Theddlethorpe All Saints
SEAL SANCTUARY & WILDLIFE CENTRE
Meers Bridge
Great Carlton
Mablethorpe
South Reston
Gayton le Marsh
A1104
Trusthorpe
Strubby
Thorpe
Sutton on Sea
Tothill
Withern
A157
Maltby le Marsh
Sandilands
Authorpe
B1373
Beesby
Woodthorpe
Saleby
Hannah
CLAYTHORPE WATER MILL AND WILDFOWL GARDENS
Markby
Aby
KING CHARLES III ENGLAND COAST PATH
Asserby
A1111
A52
South Thoresby
ALFORD MANOR HOUSE
Bilsby
Huttoft
Rigsby
Alford
B1449
Haugh
Anderby
Farlesthorpe
Mumby
Authorpe Row
A1104
Well
Cumberworth
Chapel St Leonards
Ulceby
Helsey
Bonthorpe
Hogsthorpe
Claxby
Willoughby
A52
A16
Sloothby
HARDY'S ANIMAL FARM
Skendleby
B1196
A1028
Ingoldmells
Partney
Addlethorpe
FANTASY ISLAND
Welton le Marsh
Scremby
BUTLINS SKEGNESS
Candlesby
Orby
Orby Marsh
Spilsby
Ashby by Partney
GUNBY HALL
A158
Winthorpe
Seathorne
NORTHCOTE HEAVY HORSE CENTRE
Burgh le Marsh
Bratoft
Great Steeping
Halton Holegate
NATURELAND SEAL SANCTUARY
B1195
Irby in the Marsh
BURGH LE MARSH WINDMILL
THE VILLAGE CHURCH FARM
Skegness
Toynton St Peter
THE LIFEBOAT STATION
Firsby
AQUARIUM
Little Steeping
Thorpe Culvert
Thorpe St Peter
Croft
A52
Seacroft
Thorpe Fendykes
Wainfleet All Saints
Croft Marsh
Wainfleet Bank
MAGDALEN COLLEGE MUS
GIBRALTAR POINT
New Leake
Wainfleet Tofts
Wainfleet St Mary
Eastville
Friskney Eaudike
Wainfleet Sand
LINCOLNSHIRE WILDLIFE PARK
Friskney
Wrangle Bank
Friskney Tofts
Wrangle Lowgate
Friskney Flats
Old Leake
Wrangle
118
Hurn's End
Leverton Outgate

Squires Gate
Westby
Wrea Green
Moss Side
Dowbridge
Lea Town
Ingol
Cadley
Fulwood
BLACKPOOL
Higher Ballam
Newton
Scales
Clifton
Preston
ROYAL LYTHAM & ST ANNES
LYTHAM HALL
Ansdell
Lytham
St Annes
Lytham St Anne's
Fairhaven
Salters Bank
Warton
Freckleton
A584
RIBBLE STEAM RAILWAY
Bottom of Hutton
Higher Penwortham
Walton le-Dale
Middleforth Green
Hutton
Longton
Lostock Hall
New Longton
Farington
Ribble
RIBBLE ESTUARY
KING CHARLES III ENGLAND COAST PATH
Banks Sands
Great Bank
RIBBLE MARSHES
WEST LANCASHIRE LIGHT RAILWAY
Hesketh Bank
Walmer Bridge
Midge Hall
BRITISH COMMERCIAL VEHICLE MUS
Much Hoole
Becconsall
LEYLAND
Hundred End
Banks
Tarleton
Broadfield
SOUTH RIBBLE MUSEUM & EXHIBITION CENTRE
WORDEN PARK
Horse Bank
Bretherton
Crossens
Marshside
Sollom
Croston
Ulnes Walton
Shaw Green
ECO VISITOR CENTRE
Southport
Churchtown
Mere Brow
Yarrow
THE ATKINSON
Holmeswood
Eccleston
Blowick
WINDMILL ANIMAL FARM
RUFFORD OLD HALL
Rufford
MARTIN MERE WILDFOWL AND WETLAND CENTRE
Mawdesley
Heskin Green
Birkdale
Brown Edge
Tarlscough
Snape Green
Bescar
Hillside
ROYAL BIRKDALE
Scarisbrick
New Lane
Bispham Green
Wrightington Bar
Ainsdale-on-Sea
Shirdley Hill
Hill Dale
Mossy Lea
Ainsdale
Burscough Bridge
KING CHARLES III ENGLAND COAST PATH
Woodvale
Pinfold
Liverpool
Burscough
Dangerous Corner
Parbold
Formby Hills
Halsall
Newburgh
AINSDALE SAND DUNES
Barton
Haskayne
ORMSKIRK
Appley Bridge
Shevington
Dalton
BEACON
Freshfield
Westhead
Roby Mill
Formby
Downholland Cross
Stanley
Formby Pt.
Aughton Park
Blaguegate
Skelmersdale
Gathurst
Little Altcar
Great Altcar
Orrell
CABIN HILL
Digmoor
Up Holland
Stanley Gate
Aughton
Royal Oak
Hightown
Ince Blundell
Lydiate
Bickerstaffe
Rainford Junction
Higher End
Maghull
Barrow Nook
Crawford
Longshaw
Lunt
Little Crosby
Melling Mount
Rainford
Sefton
Billinge
Thornton
Netherton
Melling
Garswood
Great Crosby
Kirkby
Crank
BELFAST
Chadwick Green
ANTONY GORMLEY SCULPTURES
AINTREE
Aintree
Moss Bank
Crosby Channel
LITHERLAND
Southdene
DOUGLAS (Nov-March) DUBLIN
Waterloo
Seaforth
Orrell
Fazakerley
Denton's Green
Knowsley
Blackbrook
Bootle
Gillar's Green
St Helens
Eccleston
DOUGLAS (March-Nov)
New Brighton
Norris Green
KNOWSLEY SAFARI PARK
Peasley Cross
Walton
CROXTETH
Sutton
MERSEYSIDE
Kirkdale
Mockbeggar Wharf
Liscard
Egremont
Anfield
West Derby
Thatto Heath
Eccleston Park
WALKER GALL
Everton
Longview
Prescot
Rainhill
Sutton Leach
Wallasey
Whiston
Clock Face
Leasowe
Seacombe
LIVERPOOL
Knotty Ash
Huyton
Sutton Manor
Moreton
Poulton
MARITIME MUS
Edge Hill
Roby
Rainhill Stoops
Bidston
Bold Heath
TATE
Wavertree
Childwall
Netherley
PEX HILL
Barrow's Green
Toxteth
Farbock Green
Cronton
Greasby
0 1 2 3 miles
0 1 2 3 4 5 km

Ribbleton
Brockholes Nature Reserve
Samlesbury Hall
Samlesbury
Mellor Brook
Osbaldeston
Mellor
Wilpshire
Brownhill
Rishton
Clayton-le-Moors
Huncoat
Lane Ends
Rose Hill
Pleckgate
Beardwood
Higher Walton
Coup Green
Samlesbury Bottoms
Hoghton Tower
Blackburn
Blackburn Mus & Art Gallery
Milnshaw
Church
ACCRINGTON
Clow Bridge
Dunnockshaw
Love Clough
West End
Scaitcliffe
Oswaldtwistle
Bamber Bridge
Gregson Lane
Feniscliffe
Witton
Pleasington
Riley Green
Hoghton
Shadsworth
Guide
Lower Darwen
Ewood
Earcroft
Feniscowles
Baxenden
Rising Bridge
Acre
Goodshaw
Goodshaw Chapel
Forest of Rossendale
Water
Crawshawbooth
Whitewell Bottom
Clayton Green
Brindle
Higher Wheelton
Abbey Village
Tockholes
Blackburn with Darwen
Belthorn
Waterside
Haslingden
The Whitaker
Lane Side
RAWTENSTALL
Edgeside
Clayton-le-Woods
Whittle-le-Woods
Withnell
Brinscall
Sunnyhurst
Ryal Fold
DARWEN
Hoddlesden
Bent Gate
Waterfoot
Helmshore
Cowpe
Buckshaw Village
Euxton
Wheelton
Whitehall
Turton Moor
Whittlestone Head
Edenfield
Turn
White Coppice
Anglezarke Moor
Anglezarke Reservoir
Cadshaw
Stubbins
CHORLEY
Cowling
Ramsbottom
Edgworth
Turton Bottoms
Charnock Richard
Weld Bank
Charnock Richard Services
Yarrow Valley
Chapeltown
Turton Tower
Egerton
Belmont
Rivington
Winter Hill
Woodhey
Greenmount
Summerseat
Burrs
Norden
Coppull
Adlington
Grimeford Village
Toppings
Jumbles
Tottington
Walmersley
Limefield
Bamford
Coppull Moor
Shevington Moor
Standish
Rivington Services
Horwich
Smithills Hall
Astley Bridge
Bradshaw
East Lancashire Railway
Bury
HEYWOOD
Blackrod
Bottom o' th' Moor
Halliwell
Bolton
Harwood
Walshaw
The Fusilier Mus
Ainsworth
Breightmet
Broadfield
Boars Head
Red Rock
Haigh
Haigh Hall
Lostock Junction
Darcy Lever
Redvales
Black Lane
Hollins
Birch Services
Beech Hill
Aspull
Deane
Moses Gate
Marylebone
Wingates
Daubhill
Great Lever
Little Lever
Radcliffe
Whitefield
Wigan
WESTHOUGHTON
Hart Common
Water's Nook
Over Hulton
Highfield
FARNWORTH
Kearsley
Stand
Clifton
Rhodes
Middleton
Heaton Hall
Ince in Makerfield
Daisy Hill
Hindley
Hindley Green
Cutacre
Blackleach
Little Hulton
Walkden
Goose Green
Platt Bridge
Flashes of Wigan & Leigh
ATHERTON
Tyldesley
Clifton Green
PRESTWICH
Pendlebury
Swinton
Bickershaw
Howe Bridge
Bryn Gates
Abram
Crank Wood
Westleigh
Leigh Guided Busway
Worsley
Broughton Park
Crumpsall
Mus of Transport
Bryn
Leigh
Lancashire Mining Mus
RHS Bridgewater
Charlestown
ASHTON-IN-MAKERFIELD
Pennington Flash
Plank Lane
Pennington
Astley Green
SALFORD
Haydock Park
Lowton Common
Lately Common
City (Barton)
Eccles
Imp War Mus North
The Lowry
Golborne
Lowton
Haydock
Twiss Green
Glazebury
Chat Moss
The Trafford Centre
Trafford Park
Hulme
Old Trafford
Lane Head
Fowley Common
Davyhulme
Whitworth
Newton-le-Willows
New Lane End
Croft
Culcheth
Irlam
URMSTON
Stretford
Flixton
Chorlton cum Hardy
Withington
Burtonwood
Winwick
Glazebrook
Carrington
Ashton upon Mersey
West Didsbury
Burtonwood Services
Risley
Birchwood
Cadishead
Hollins Green
SALE
Didsbury
Houghton Green
Fearnhead
Partington
Brooklands
Northenden
Dallam
Gulliver's World
Orford
Woolston
Warburton
Manchester Ship Canal
Toll
Timperley
Warrington
Martinscroft
Mossbrow
Broadheath
Great Sankey
Heatley
Dunham Town
Wythenshawe
GATLEY

Rose Hill
Brunshaw
Worsthorne
Hurstwood
Walk Mill
Mereclough
WEAVERS TRIANGLE
146
Heptonstall Moor
Warley Moor Res.
Dean Head Res.
147
Clough
Causeway Foot
Queensbury
TOWNELEY HALL
Clow Bridge
GTON
Holme Chapel
Colden
Pecket Well
Illingworth
Dunnockshaw
Love Clough
A646
Blackshaw Head
Heptonstall
Chiserley
Wainstalls
Hebden Bridge
Mount Tabor
449
THIEVELEY PIKE
Mytholm
Charlestown
Booth
Ovenden
Midgley
Wheatley
Forest of Rossendale
Cornholme
Lydgate
WALKLEY CLOGS
Goodshaw
GOODSHAW CHAPEL
Water
Portsmouth
Mytholmroyd
A646
Luddenden
Luddenden Foot
Pellon
Acre
Crawshawbooth
Weir
Eastwood
Savile Park
Whitewell Bottom
Clough Foot
THE WHITAKER
Todmorden
MANKINHOLES
Mankinholes
Lane Side
RAWTENSTALL
Greave
Bacup
A681
Shade
Walsden
Cragg Vale
Sowerby
Triangle
Sowerby Bridge
Edgeside
Res.
Waterfoot
A681
Nun Hills
A6066
Britannia
Lumb
Reservoirs
Mill Bank
Shawforth
A6033
Warland
B6138
A672
B6113
Greetland
Cowpe
137
Edenfield
Facit
PENNINE WAY
Soyland Moor
Ripponden
B6114
Barkisland
Stainland
Holywell Green
Whitworth
Turn
468
Calderbrook
11
Rishworth
Sowood
Outlane
A58
23
SD
Wardle
Rishworth Moor
Booth Wood
Scapegoat Hill
Resvrs.
HEALEY DELL
Broadley
Healey
472
Littleborough
COLNE VALLEY MUSEUM
A680
Syke
Smallbridge
Hollingworth Lake
Rakewood
Res.
Golcar
Summers
BURRS
Norden
Cutgate
Rochdale
M62
22
Moss Moor
Bradshaw
A640
Wilberlee
HOLLINGWORTH LAKE
Slaithwaite
Walmersley
Bamford
Firgrove
453
Limefield
EAST LANCASHIRE RAILWAY
B6222
Milnrow
466
Res.
STANDEDGE VISITOR CENTRE
Lingards Wood
Bury
Marland
Lower Place
21
Haugh
Newhey
A640
A62
Marsden
B6107
HEYWOOD
Castleton
Res.
A58
B6194
Denshaw
B6197
Meltham
M66
Broadfield
Hopwood
20
Summit
Bleak Hey Nook
Slattocks
Res.
500
Redvales
Lane
Hollins
BIRCH SERVICES
19
TANDLE HILL
Shaw
A672
Res.
Res.
18
ROYTON
Heyside
Diggle
Wessenden Moor
Ratcliffe
Whitefield
Top of Hebers
Birch
A627(M)
Long Sight
Moorside
Delph
Flush
Dobcross
A635
Chadderton Fold
Middleton
A62
Uppermill
15
Holme
18
Rhodes
OLDHAM
Saddleworth
Chadderton
Lees
Grasscroft
Greenfield
Moor
A669
Tunstead
A664
17
HEATON HALL
Oldham
582
BLACK HILL
M60
A6104
M60
A62
Dove Stone Res.
PRESTWICH
Blackley
21
Hathershaw
308
A635
A670
PENNINE WAY
Crumpsall
22
Mossley
469
Chew Res.
Pendlebury
A56
Moston
Hollinwood
THE PENNINE BRIDLEWAY
Broughton Park
MUS OF TRANSPORT
Harpurhey
A663
A627
Failsworth
DAISY NOOK
B6194
B6175
A6024
Waterloo
Ashton-under-Lyne
Charlestown
Newton Heath
Hazelhurst
CROWDEN
137
MANCHESTER
MUS OF THE MANCHESTERS
STALYBRIDGE
Crowden
A628
SALFORD
NATIONAL SQUASH
MANCHESTER VELODROME
STALYBRIDGE
LONGDENDALE
ASTLEY CHEETHAM
Droylsden
23
Reservoirs
THE LOWRY
A635
Audenshaw
Dukinfield
Tintwistle
B6105
Ardwick
Hulme
Gorton
Newton
Mottram in Longdendale
A6018
Hadfield
Padfield
Old Trafford
Trafford Park
A57
1A
2
M67
PENNINE WAY
Rusholme
WHITWORTH
Hollingworth
633
BLEAKLOW
Stretford
A5103
Denton
Hyde
Godley
Warhill
Gamesley
Old Glossop
Levenshulme
M60
A560
Broadbottom
A6010
REDDISH VALE
WERNETH LOW
Simmondley
GLOSSOP
Shelf Moor
Fallowfield
Chorlton cum Hardy
Withington
HIGHFIELD
Reddish
Haughton Grn.
Gee Cross
Charlestown
A6
Woodley
Chisworth
Charlesworth
A57
M60
West Didsbury
25
ETHEROW
544
FEATHERBED
SALE
Heaton Moor
A34
26
Bredbury
A626
Chunal
A5145
Didsbury
27
Compstall
A624
Brooklands
Romiley
Northenden
CHADKIRK COUNTRY ESTATE
M60
128
Stockport
129
0 1 2 3 miles
0 1 2 3 4 5 km
Cheadle Heath
Heaviley
Marple
Marple Bridge
Stepping Hill
Little Hayfield
Res.
KINDER SCOUT
Wythenshawe
GATLEY
Cheadle
Hawk Green
Mellor

Clayton
Great Horton
Horton
Bowling
Holme Wood
Farnley
Wortley
Hunslet
NATIONAL SCIENCE & MEDIA MUSEUM
West Bowling
BOLLING HALL
New Farnley
Beeston
THWAITE MILLS INDUSTRIAL MUS
TEMPLE NEWSAM
Swillington
147
148
Tong
A647
A6110
A63
A650
A58
A62
Bierley
Buttershaw
Wibsey
Low Moor
Birkenshaw
Drighlington
Churwell
Gildersome
M621
A653
MIDDLETON RAILWAY
Rothwell
Haigh
ROTHWELL COLLIERY
Woodlesford
Great Preston
Shelf
A6036
Stone Chair
Northowram
SHIBDEN HALL
M606
Oakenshaw
Adwalton
Bruntcliffe
Rothwell
Robin Hood
Oulton
Wyke
OAKWELL HALL
Birstall
MORLEY
Middleton
Carlton
Methley
Mickletown
Halifax
A58
Hipperholme
Scholes
Gomersal
BAGSHAW MUS
BATLEY
M62
Tingley
East Ardsley
Lofthouse
PIECE HALL ART GALLERY
Southowram
A649
HARTSHEAD MOOR SERVICES
A643
Cleckheaton
THE MILL
Woodkirk
Haigh Moor
Stanley
B6135
Bottom Boat
Altofts
EUREKA!
BRIGHOUSE
Liversedge
Roberttown
Heckmondwike
Mount Pleasant
Chidswell
Kirkhamgate
Outwood
A6025
Rastrick
Hartshead
Dewsbury
Gawthorpe
Wrenthorpe
Normanton
Ackton
Elland
A644
Dewsbury Moor
A638
Earlsheaton
Flanshaw
Wakefield
Woodhouse
Bradley
Ravensthorpe
OSSETT
WAKEFIELD CATHEDRAL
Warmfield
Deighton
Mirfield
Calder
Lupset
HEPWORTH GALLERY
140
Common
Birchencliffe
Fartown
Thornhill Lees
Thornhill
Horbury
Sharlston
Lindley
TOLSON
Upper Hopton
Thornhill Edge
NATIONAL COAL MINING MUS FOR ENGLAND
A642
Sandal Magna
A640
Oakes
Kirkheaton
Whitley Lower
Middlestown
Durkar
Crofton
Foulby
Leymoor
Tandem
Grange Moor
Overton
Netherton
Crigglestone
Walton
ANGLERS
Wragby
Huddersfield
Moldgreen
Fenay Bridge
A637
Midgley
Great Cliff
Hill Top
Wintersett
Fitzwilliam
Lockwood
Almondbury
Lepton
Flockton
West Bretton
Hall Green
Ryhill
Newsome
Rowley Hill
YORKSHIRE SCULPTURE PARK
WOOLLEY EDGE SERVICES
NEWMILLERDAM
Linthwaite
JUBILEE TOWER
Highburton
Emley
Woolley
Havercroft
Netherton
Kirkburton
BRETTON
B6132
South Hiendley
Farnley Tyas
A629
Roydhouse
WHISTLESTOP VALLEY
Notton
Felkirk
Honley
Haigh
Royston
Shelley
Clayton West
High Hoyland
Shafton
Brockholes
Thurstonland
B6116
Darton
B6428
Netherthong
Thongsbridge
Shepley
Lower Cumberworth
Skelmanthorpe
Kexbrough
Staincross
Carlton
Wooldale
Lane Head
CANNON HALL
Dearne
A628
Upperthong
New Mill
Denby Dale
Barugh
Monk Bretton
Cudworth
HOLMFIRTH
Upper Cumberworth
A635
Cawthorne
DEARNE VALLEY
Burnlee
Scholes
Birds Edge
Tivy Dale
M1
Barnsley
Hepworth
Upper Denby
Gawber
MONK BRETTON PRIORY
Holmbridge
Silkstone
Ardsley
Longley
Ingbirchworth
Noblethorpe
Kendray
Victoria
Crow Edge
Hoylandswaine
Dodworth
Worsbrough Common
Darfield
Hade Edge
B6106
A616
Thurlstone
B6449
Silkstone Common
Carlecotes
Millhouse Green
Penistone
Spring Vale
Hood Green
Worsbrough
MILL MUSEUM
WIGFIELD FARM
Platts Common
A6195
Townhead
Cubley
Oxspring
Crane Moor
Birdwell
Dunford Bridge
B6462
Thurgoland
Jump
A628
Langsett
Res.
A616
Snowden Hill
Pilley
Tankersley
Hoyland
Elsecar
ELSECAR HERITAGE CENTRE
Midhopestones
Wortley
A61
Harley
PEAK
B6088
Midhope Moors
Stocksbridge
WESTWOOD
Howbrook
High Green
B6090
Wentworth
Deepcar
Derwent
Howden Moors
Bolsterstone
Ewden Village
Chapeltown
Wigtwizzle
Wharncliffe Wood
Burncross
Thorpe Hesley
546
Broomhead Moor
Wharncliffe Side
DISTRICT
Grenoside
HOPE
Howden Res.
Oughtibridge
Ecclesfield
Kimberworth
Reservoirs
Bradfield Moors
High Bradfield
A6102
Parson Cross
FOREST
Derwent Res.
538
Low Bradfield
Worrall
Shiregreen
Wincobank
Wadsley
Wadsley Bridge
Stacey Bank
NATIONAL
129
130
UPPER DERWENT VISITOR CENTRE
Ughill
Dungworth
Loxley
B6077
Owlerton
Pitsmoor
Carbrook
Ashop
B6076
Attercliffe
590
Stopes
Stannington
Walkley
KELHAM ISLAND MUSEUM
Darnall
PEAK

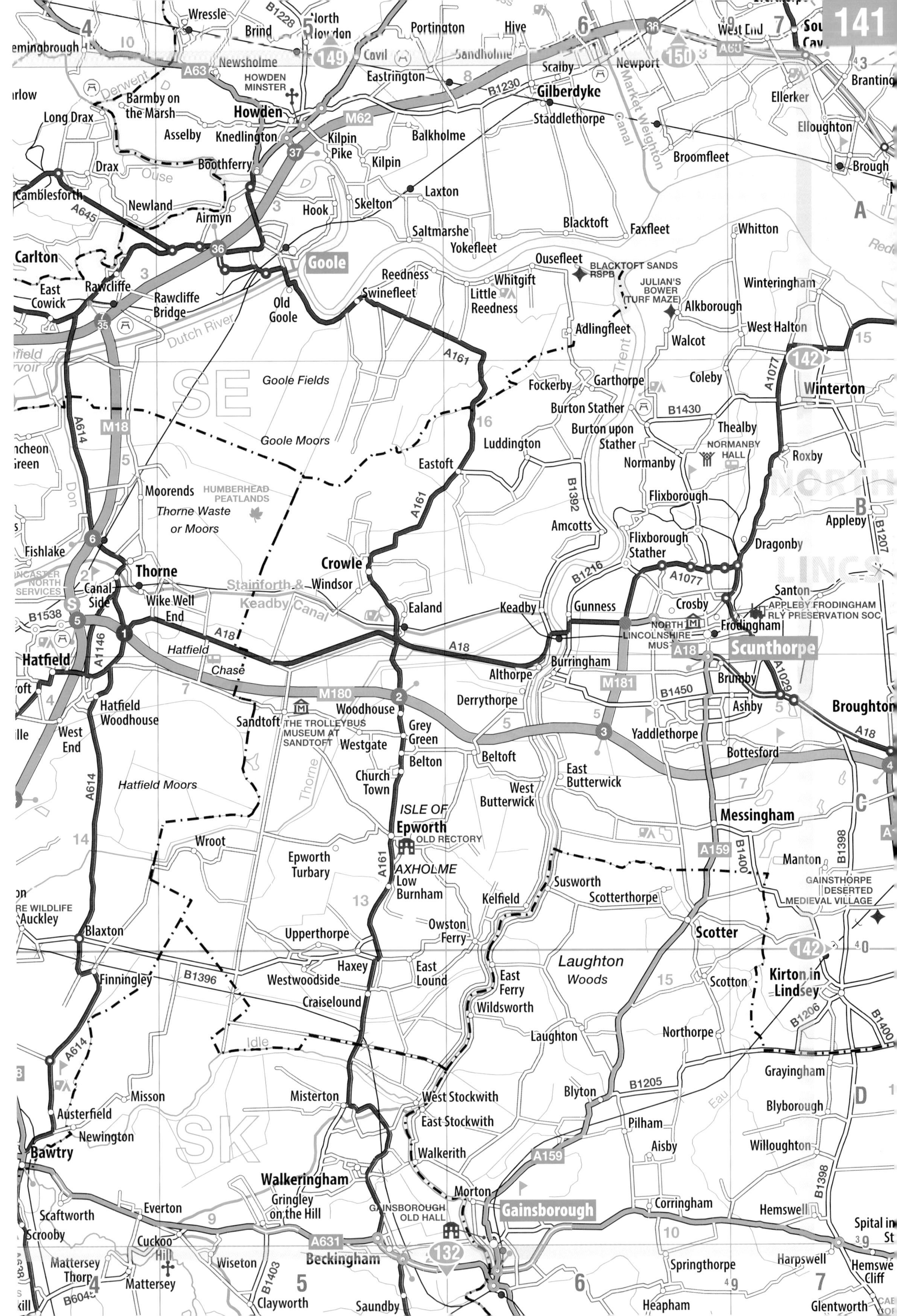
Wressle
Brind
North Howden
Portington
Hive
West End
Hemingbrough
Newsholme
Cavil
Sandholme
Scalby
Newport
HOWDEN MINSTER
Eastrington
Gilberdyke
Ellerker
Brantingham
Barlow
Barmby on the Marsh
Howden
Staddlethorpe
Elloughton
Long Drax
Asselby
Knedlington
Kilpin Pike
Balkholme
Kilpin
Broomfleet
Brough
Drax
Boothferry
Market Weighton Canal
Camblesforth
Newland
Airmyn
Hook
Skelton
Laxton
Saltmarshe
Blacktoft
Faxfleet
Whitton
Yokefleet
Carlton
Goole
Ousefleet
BLACKTOFT SANDS RSPB
JULIAN'S BOWER (TURF MAZE)
Reedness
Whitgift
Winteringham
East Cowick
Rawcliffe
Rawcliffe Bridge
Swinefleet
Little Reedness
Alkborough
Old Goole
Dutch River
Adlingfleet
West Halton
Walcot
Goole Fields
Fockerby
Garthorpe
Coleby
Winterton
Burton Stather
Burton upon Stather
Thealby
Goole Moors
Luddington
Normanby
NORMANBY HALL
Roxby
Eastoft
Moorends
HUMBERHEAD PEATLANDS
Thorne Waste or Moors
Flixborough
Appleby
Amcotts
Flixborough Stather
Dragonby
Fishlake
Thorne
Crowle
Canal Side
Stainforth & Keadby Canal
Windsor
Santon
APPLEBY FRODINGHAM RLY PRESERVATION SOC
Wike Well End
Ealand
Keadby
Gunness
Crosby
Frodingham
NORTH LINCOLNSHIRE MUS
Scunthorpe
Hatfield
Hatfield Chase
Burringham
Althorpe
Brumby
Derrythorpe
Ashby
Broughton
Hatfield Woodhouse
Woodhouse
Sandtoft
THE TROLLEYBUS MUSEUM AT SANDTOFT
Grey Green
Westgate
Yaddlethorpe
West End
Belton
Beltoft
Bottesford
Church Town
East Butterwick
West Butterwick
Hatfield Moors
ISLE OF AXHOLME
Epworth
OLD RECTORY
Messingham
Wroot
Epworth Turbary
Low Burnham
Manton
Susworth
Scotterthorpe
GAINSTHORPE DESERTED MEDIEVAL VILLAGE
Kelfield
Auckley
Blaxton
Owston Ferry
Upperthorpe
Scotter
Laughton Woods
Haxey
East Lound
Finningley
Westwoodside
East Ferry
Scotton
Kirton in Lindsey
Craiselound
Wildsworth
Laughton
Northorpe
Idle
Grayingham
Misson
Misterton
West Stockwith
Blyton
Austerfield
East Stockwith
Pilham
Blyborough
Newington
Bawtry
Walkerith
Aisby
Willoughton
Walkeringham
Morton
Gainsborough
Corringham
Hemswell
Scaftworth
Everton
Gringley on the Hill
GAINSBOROUGH OLD HALL
Scrooby
Cuckoo Hill
Springthorpe
Harpswell
Mattersey Thorpe
Mattersey
Wiseton
Beckingham
Clayworth
Saundby
Heapham
Glentworth
Hemswell Cliff
Spital in the Street
SE
SK
NORTH LINCS
Derwent
Ouse
Trent
Don
Thorne
Eau
A63
M62
B1228
B1230
A645
A614
M18
A161
A1077
B1430
B1392
B1216
A18
M180
M181
B1450
A1029
B1538
A1146
A159
B1400
B1398
B1396
B1206
B1205
A631
B1403
B6045
149
150
142
132

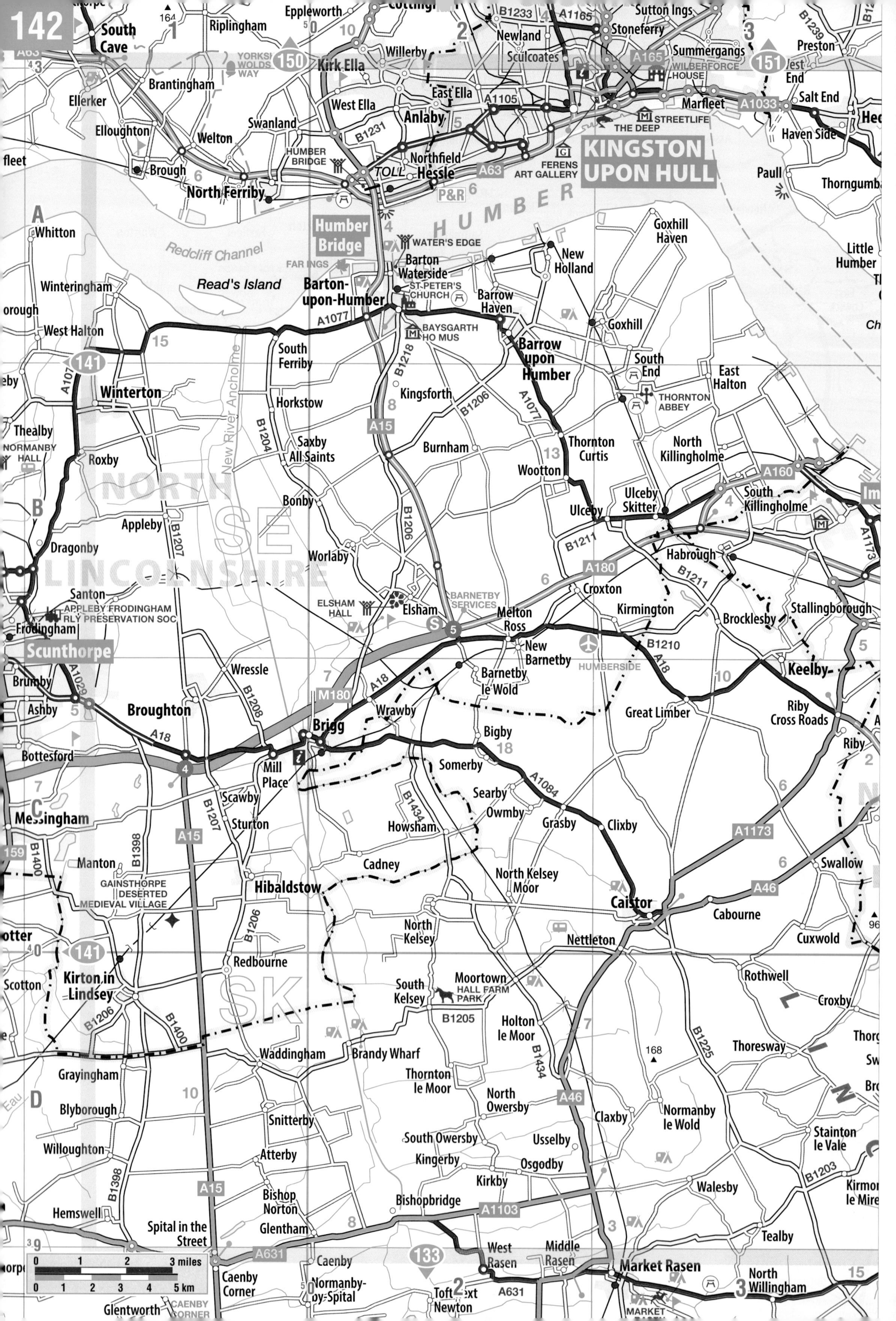
South Cave
Riplingham
Eppleworth
Newland
Stoneferry
Sutton Ings
Preston
Sculcoates
Summergangs
Willerby
Kirk Ella
YORKSHIRE WOLDS WAY
150
151
WILBERFORCE HOUSE
Brantingham
Ellerker
East Ella
West Ella
Anlaby
Marfleet
Salt End
Elloughton
Welton
Swanland
THE DEEP
STREETLIFE
Haven Side
KINGSTON UPON HULL
HUMBER BRIDGE
Northfield
Hessle
FERENS ART GALLERY
Paull
Brough
North Ferriby
TOLL
P&R
Thorngumbald
HUMBER
Whitton
Humber Bridge
WATER'S EDGE
Goxhill Haven
New Holland
Little Humber
Redcliff Channel
FAR INGS
Barton Waterside
Read's Island
Winteringham
Barton-upon-Humber
ST PETER'S CHURCH
Barrow Haven
Goxhill
West Halton
A1077
BAYSGARTH HO MUS
Barrow upon Humber
141
South Ferriby
South End
East Halton
Winterton
Kingsforth
THORNTON ABBEY
Horkstow
B1206
B1218
A15
A1077
Thealby
NORMANBY HALL
Saxby All Saints
Burnham
Thornton Curtis
North Killingholme
Roxby
New River Ancholme
Wootton
NORTH
A160
SE
Bonby
Ulceby Skitter
South Killingholme
Ulceby
Appleby
B1207
B1206
Dragonby
Worlaby
B1211
Habrough
LINCOLNSHIRE
A180
Croxton
Santon
ELSHAM HALL
Elsham
BARNETBY SERVICES
Melton Ross
Kirmington
Stallingborough
APPLEBY FRODINGHAM RLY PRESERVATION SOC
Brocklesby
Frodingham
New Barnetby
B1210
Scunthorpe
HUMBERSIDE
Keelby
Wressle
Barnetby le Wold
Brumby
A1029
B1208
A18
Ashby
Broughton
M180
Wrawby
Great Limber
Riby Cross Roads
Brigg
A18
Bigby
Riby
Bottesford
Somerby
Mill Place
A1084
Searby
Messingham
Scawby
Owmby
B1207
B1434
Howsham
Grasby
Clixby
Sturton
A15
A1173
159
B1398
Manton
Cadney
Swallow
B1400
GAINSTHORPE DESERTED MEDIEVAL VILLAGE
Hibaldstow
North Kelsey Moor
Caistor
A46
Cabourne
North Kelsey
Nettleton
Cuxwold
B1206
Redbourne
Kirton in Lindsey
Moortown
HALL FARM PARK
Rothwell
Scotton
South Kelsey
Croxby
SK
B1205
B1206
B1400
Holton le Moor
Waddingham
Brandy Wharf
B1434
B1225
Thoresway
Grayingham
Thornton le Moor
A46
North Owersby
Claxby
Normanby le Wold
Blyborough
Snitterby
Stainton le Vale
South Owersby
Usselby
Willoughton
Atterby
Kingerby
Osgodby
B1203
Kirkby
Walesby
Bishop Norton
B1398
Bishopbridge
A1103
Hemswell
Glentham
Spital in the Street
Tealby
West Rasen
Middle Rasen
A15
A631
Caenby
133
Market Rasen
North Willingham
Caenby Corner
Normanby-by-Spital
Toft next Newton
A631
Glentworth
CAENBY CORNER
MARKET RASEN
0 1 2 3 miles
0 1 2 3 4 5 km

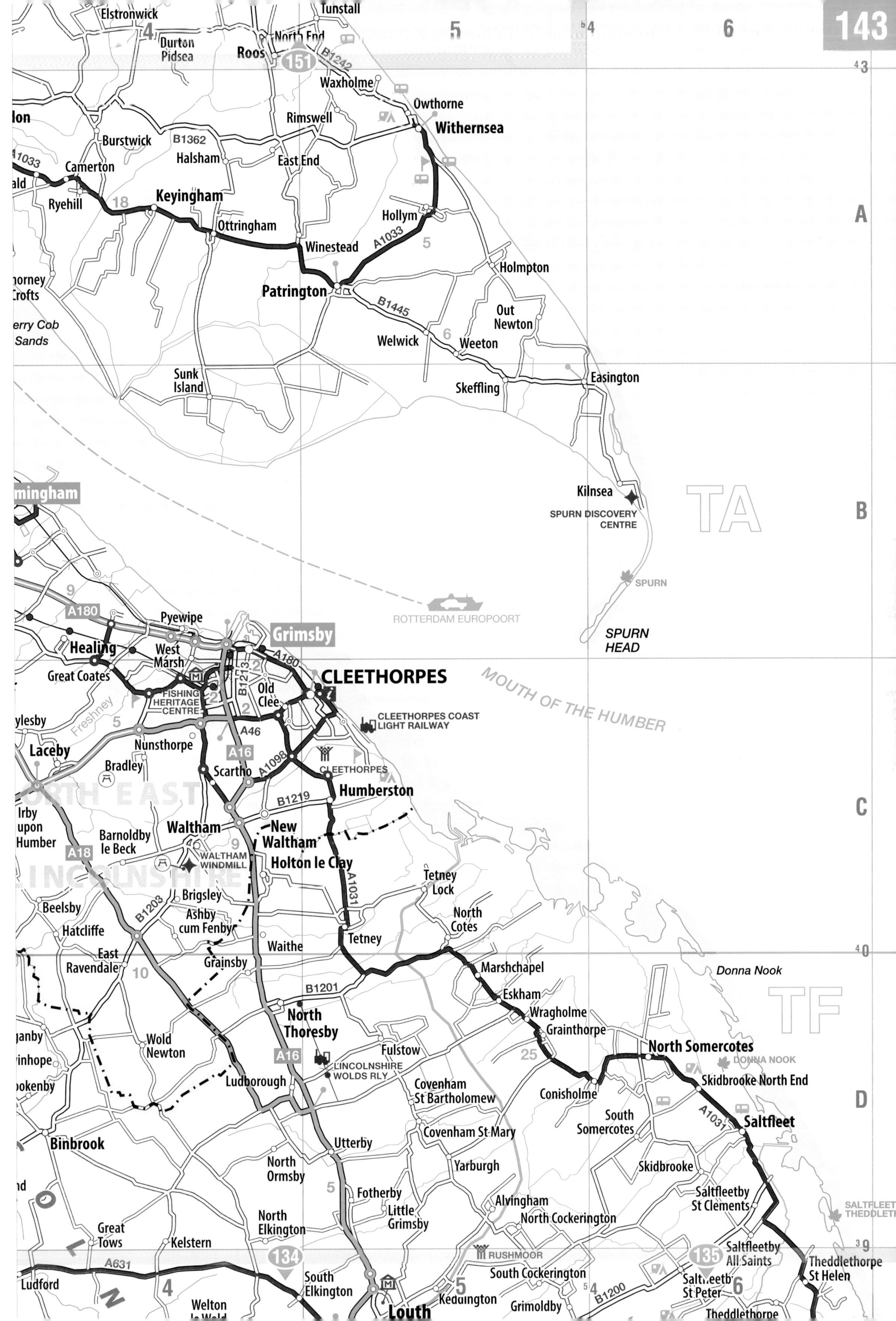

Elstronwick
Tunstall
Durton
Pidsea
Roos
North End
151
B1242
Waxholme
Owthorne
Withernsea
Rimswell
Burstwick
B1362
Halsham
East End
Camerton
Ryehill
Keyingham
Ottringham
Hollym
A1033
Winestead
Holmpton
Patrington
B1445
Out
Newton
Welwick
Weeton
Sunk
Island
Skeffling
Easington
Kilnsea
SPURN DISCOVERY
CENTRE
TA
SPURN
ROTTERDAM EUROPOORT
SPURN
HEAD
A180
Pyewipe
Grimsby
Healing
West
Marsh
Great Coates
FISHING
HERITAGE
CENTRE
B1213
Old
Clee
CLEETHORPES
MOUTH OF THE HUMBER
CLEETHORPES COAST
LIGHT RAILWAY
Laceby
Nunsthorpe
A46
A16
Bradley
Scartho
A1098
CLEETHORPES
Humberston
B1219
Irby
upon
Humber
Barnoldby
le Beck
Waltham
New
Waltham
WALTHAM
WINDMILL
Holton le Clay
A18
LINCOLNSHIRE
A1031
Tetney
Lock
Beelsby
B1203
Brigsley
Ashby
cum Fenby
North
Cotes
Hatcliffe
Tetney
East
Ravendale
Waithe
Grainsby
Marshchapel
Donna Nook
TF
B1201
Eskham
Wragholme
North
Thoresby
Grainthorpe
Wold
Newton
Fulstow
North Somercotes
A16
DONNA NOOK
LINCOLNSHIRE
WOLDS RLY
Skidbrooke North End
Ludborough
Covenham
St Bartholomew
Conisholme
South
Somercotes
Saltfleet
Binbrook
Utterby
Covenham St Mary
Yarburgh
Skidbrooke
North
Ormsby
Fotherby
Saltfleetby
St Clements
Alvingham
Little
Grimsby
North Cockerington
North
Elkington
Great
Tows
Kelstern
Saltfleetby
All Saints
134
135
A631
RUSHMOOR
South Cockerington
Theddlethorpe
St Helen
Ludford
South
Elkington
Keddington
B1200
Welton
le Wold
Louth
Grimoldby
Theddlethorpe

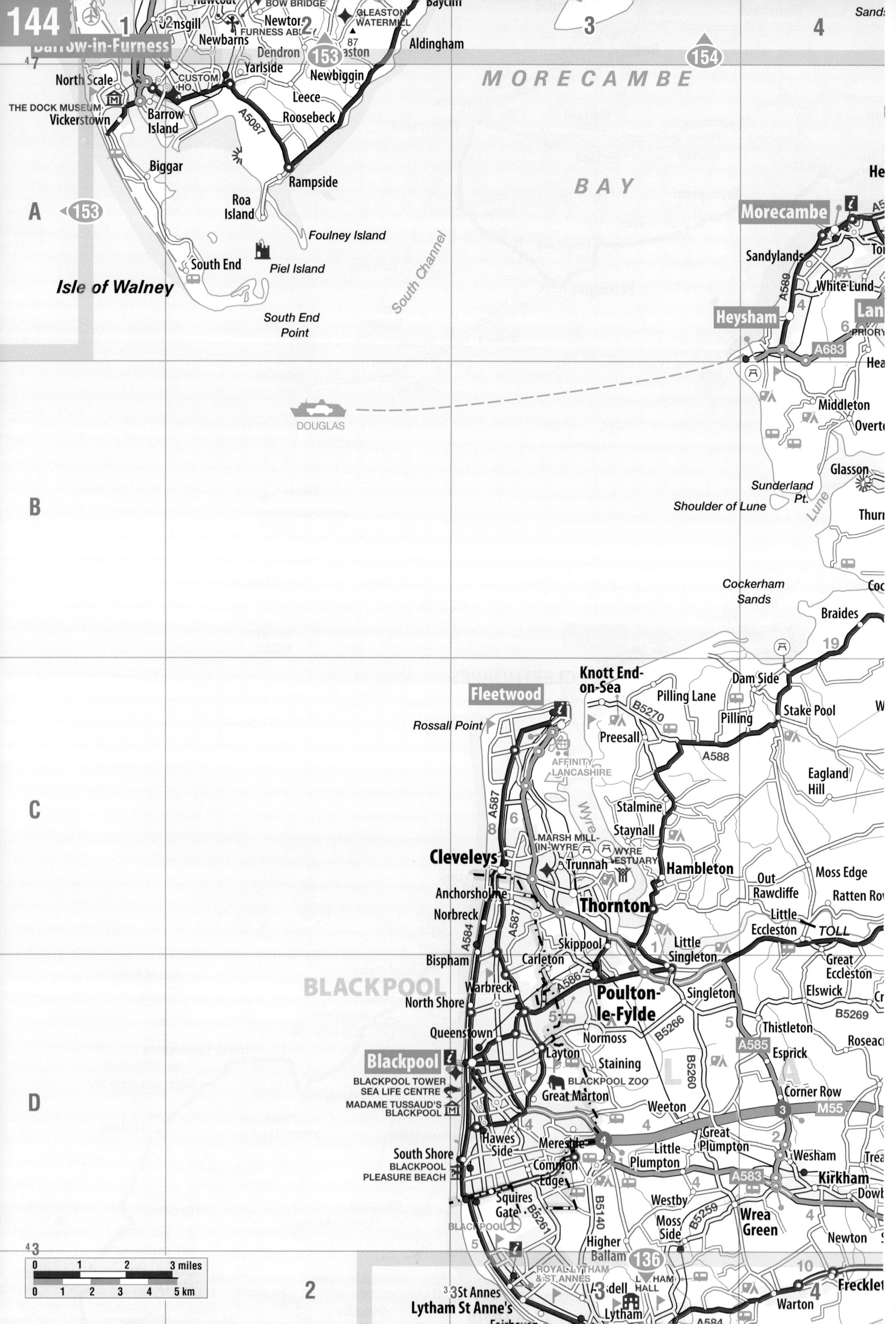
Barrow-in-Furness
North Scale
THE DOCK MUSEUM
Vickerstown
Barrow Island
Newbarns
Newton
FURNESS ABBEY
BOW BRIDGE
GLEASTON WATERMILL
Aldingham
Dendron
Yarlside
Newbiggin
Leece
Roosebeck
Biggar
Rampside
Roa Island
Foulney Island
Piel Island
South End
Isle of Walney
South End Point
South Channel
MORECAMBE
BAY
Morecambe
Sandylands
White Lund
Heysham
PRIORY
Middleton
Glasson
Sunderland Pt.
Shoulder of Lune
Lune
Cockerham Sands
Braides
DOUGLAS
Knott End-on-Sea
Fleetwood
Rossall Point
Pilling Lane
Dam Side
Pilling
Stake Pool
Preesall
AFFINITY LANCASHIRE
Eagland Hill
Stalmine
Staynall
Wyre
MARSH MILL-IN-WYRE
WYRE ESTUARY
Trunnah
Hambleton
Cleveleys
Anchorsholme
Norbreck
Thornton
Out Rawcliffe
Moss Edge
Little Eccleston
TOLL
Skippool
Little Singleton
Bispham
Carleton
Great Eccleston
Elswick
BLACKPOOL
Warbreck
Poulton-le-Fylde
Singleton
North Shore
Thistleton
Queenstown
Normoss
Esprick
Blackpool
Layton
Staining
BLACKPOOL TOWER
SEA LIFE CENTRE
MADAME TUSSAUD'S BLACKPOOL
BLACKPOOL ZOO
Great Marton
Weeton
Corner Row
Hawes Side
Marton Moss
Great Plumpton
Little Plumpton
South Shore
BLACKPOOL PLEASURE BEACH
Common Edge
Wesham
Kirkham
Squires Gate
Westby
Wrea Green
Moss Side
BLACKPOOL
Higher Ballam
Newton
ROYAL LYTHAM & ST. ANNES
St Annes
Lytham St Anne's
Lytham
Warton
A5087
A589
A683
A588
B5270
A587
A584
A586
B5266
B5260
A585
B5269
M55
A583
B5140
B5261
B5259
153
154
136
0 1 2 3 miles
0 1 2 3 4 5 km

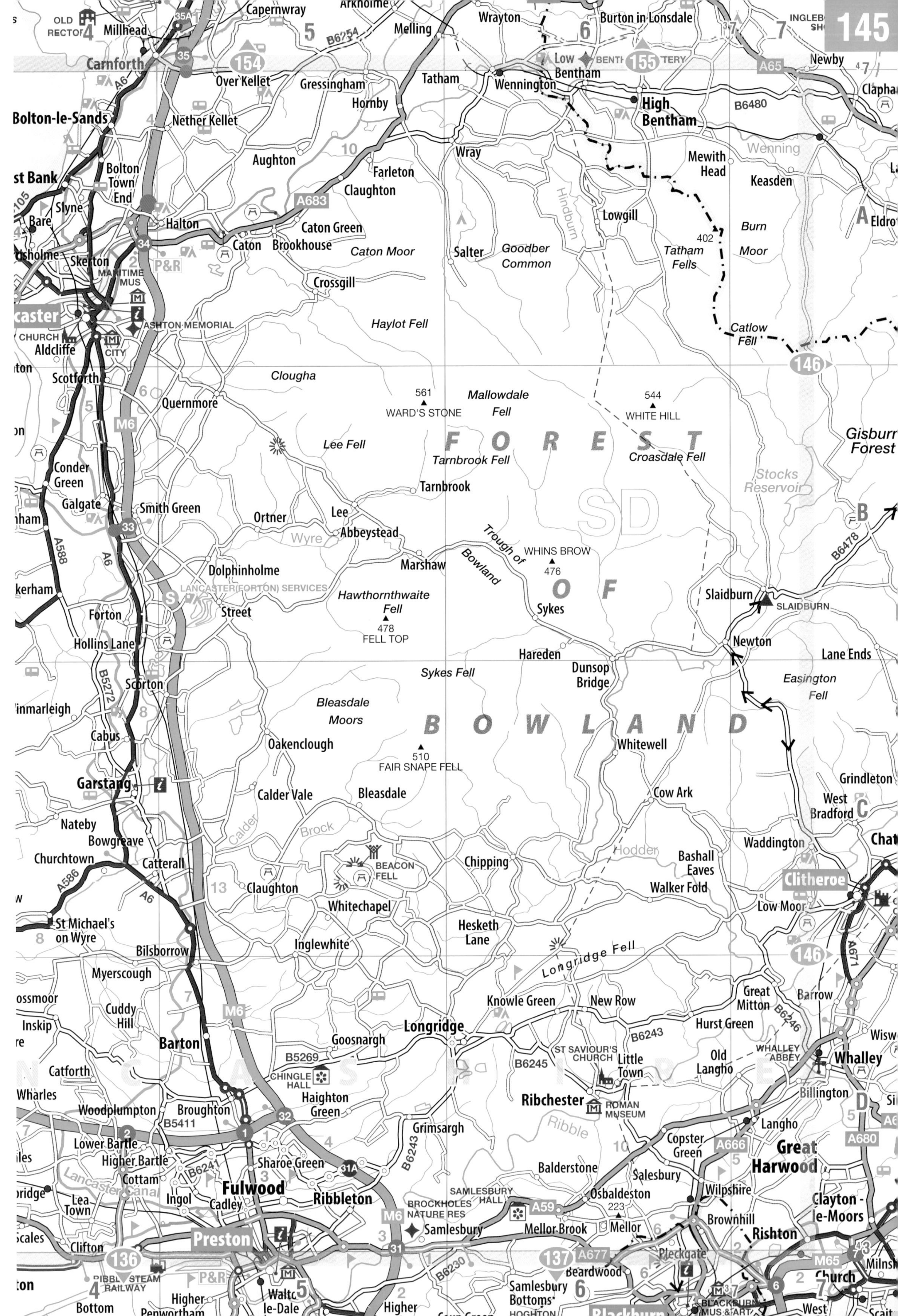

Carnforth
Bolton-le-Sands
Lancaster
Galgate
Garstang
Longridge
Fulwood
Preston
Ribchester
High Bentham
Clitheroe
Whalley
Great Harwood
Slaidburn
Dunsop Bridge
Chipping
FOREST OF BOWLAND
SD
Trough of Bowland
WARD'S STONE
WHITE HILL
WHINS BROW
FELL TOP
FAIR SNAPE FELL
Longridge Fell
ASHTON MEMORIAL
LANCASTER(FORTON) SERVICES
BEACON FELL
ROMAN MUSEUM
SAMLESBURY HALL
BROCKHOLES NATURE RES
WHALLEY ABBEY
M6
A6
A683
A59
B6243
B6245

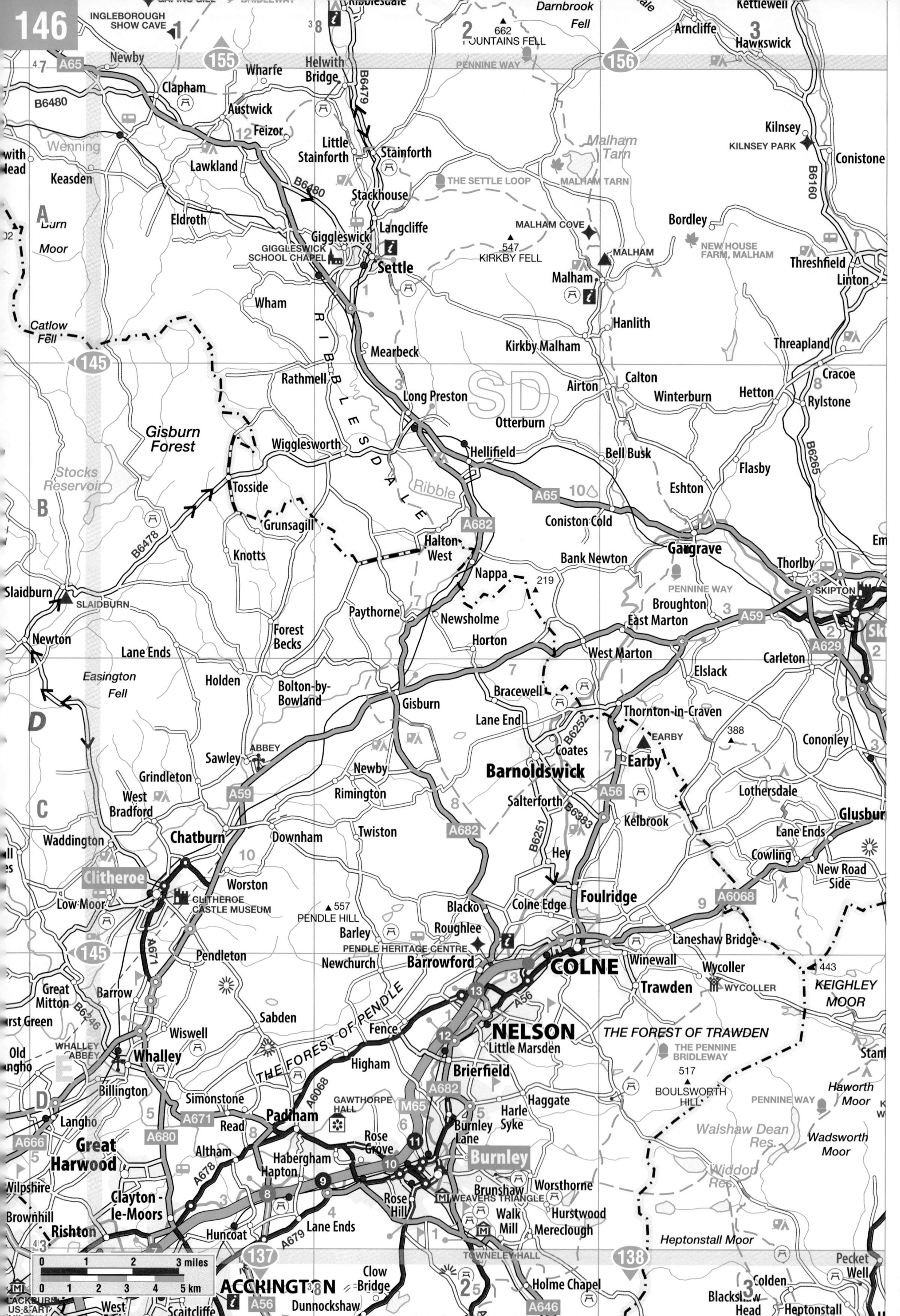

INGLEBOROUGH SHOW CAVE
Ribblesdale
Darnbrook Fell
662 FOUNTAINS FELL
Kettlewell
Arncliffe
Hawkswick
155
156
Newby
A65
Wharfe
Helwith Bridge
B6479
PENNINE WAY
Clapham
B6480
Austwick
Feizor
Little Stainforth
Stainforth
Malham Tarn
Kilnsey
KILNSEY PARK
Conistone
Wenning
Lawkland
Keasden
B6480
THE SETTLE LOOP
MALHAM TARN
B6160
Stackhouse
Burn Moor
Eldroth
Giggleswick
Langcliffe
MALHAM COVE
547 KIRKBY FELL
Bordley
GIGGLESWICK SCHOOL CHAPEL
Settle
MALHAM
NEW HOUSE FARM, MALHAM
Threshfield
Linton
Malham
Wham
RIBBLESDALE
Catlow Fell
Hanlith
145
Mearbeck
Kirkby Malham
Threapland
Rathmell
Long Preston
SD
Airton
Calton
Cracoe
Winterburn
Hetton
Rylstone
Otterburn
Gisburn Forest
Wigglesworth
Hellifield
Bell Busk
B6265
Stocks Reservoir
Flasby
Tosside
Ribble
A65
Eshton
Grunsagill
Coniston Cold
A682
B6478
Halton West
Knotts
Bank Newton
Gargrave
Thorlby
Nappa
219
PENNINE WAY
SKIPTON
Slaidburn
SLAIDBURN
Paythorne
Broughton
Newsholme
East Marton
A59
Newton
Forest Becks
Horton
A629
Lane Ends
West Marton
Carleton
Easington Fell
Holden
Elslack
Bolton-by-Bowland
Bracewell
Gisburn
Lane End
Thornton-in-Craven
388
EARBY
B6252
Coates
Cononley
Sawley
ABBEY
Newby
Earby
Barnoldswick
Grindleton
A59
Rimington
Salterforth
A56
West Bradford
Lothersdale
B6383
Kelbrook
Glusburn
Waddington
Chatburn
Downham
Twiston
A682
Lane Ends
B6251
Hey
Cowling
Clitheroe
New Road Side
Worston
A6068
Foulridge
Low Moor
CLITHEROE CASTLE MUSEUM
557 PENDLE HILL
Blacko
Colne Edge
Barley
Roughlee
Laneshaw Bridge
145
A671
PENDLE HERITAGE CENTRE
Pendleton
Newchurch
Barrowford
COLNE
Winewall
Wycoller
443
Trawden
WYCOLLER
KEIGHLEY MOOR
Great Mitton
Barrow
A56
B6246
THE FOREST OF PENDLE
Sabden
NELSON
Wiswell
Fence
Little Marsden
THE FOREST OF TRAWDEN
WHALLEY ABBEY
Whalley
THE PENNINE BRIDLEWAY
Higham
Brierfield
517 BOULSWORTH HILL
Haworth Moor
Billington
A6068
A682
Simonstone
GAWTHORPE HALL
M65
Harle Syke
Haggate
PENNINE WAY
Langho
A671
Read
Padiham
Burnley Lane
Walshaw Dean Res.
Wadsworth Moor
A666
Great Harwood
A680
Altham
Rose Grove
Burnley
Habergham
Hapton
Widdop Res.
Wilpshire
A678
Clayton-le-Moors
Brunshaw
Worsthorne
Rose Hill
WEAVERS TRIANGLE
Brownhill
Walk Mill
Hurstwood
Rishton
Huncoat
Lane Ends
A679
Mereclough
Heptonstall Moor
TOWNELEY HALL
Pecket Well
137
138
ACCRINGTON
Clow Bridge
Holme Chapel
Colden
Blackshaw Head
Heptonstall
A56
Dunnockshaw
A646
Scaitcliffe
West
0 1 2 3 miles
0 1 2 3 4 5 km

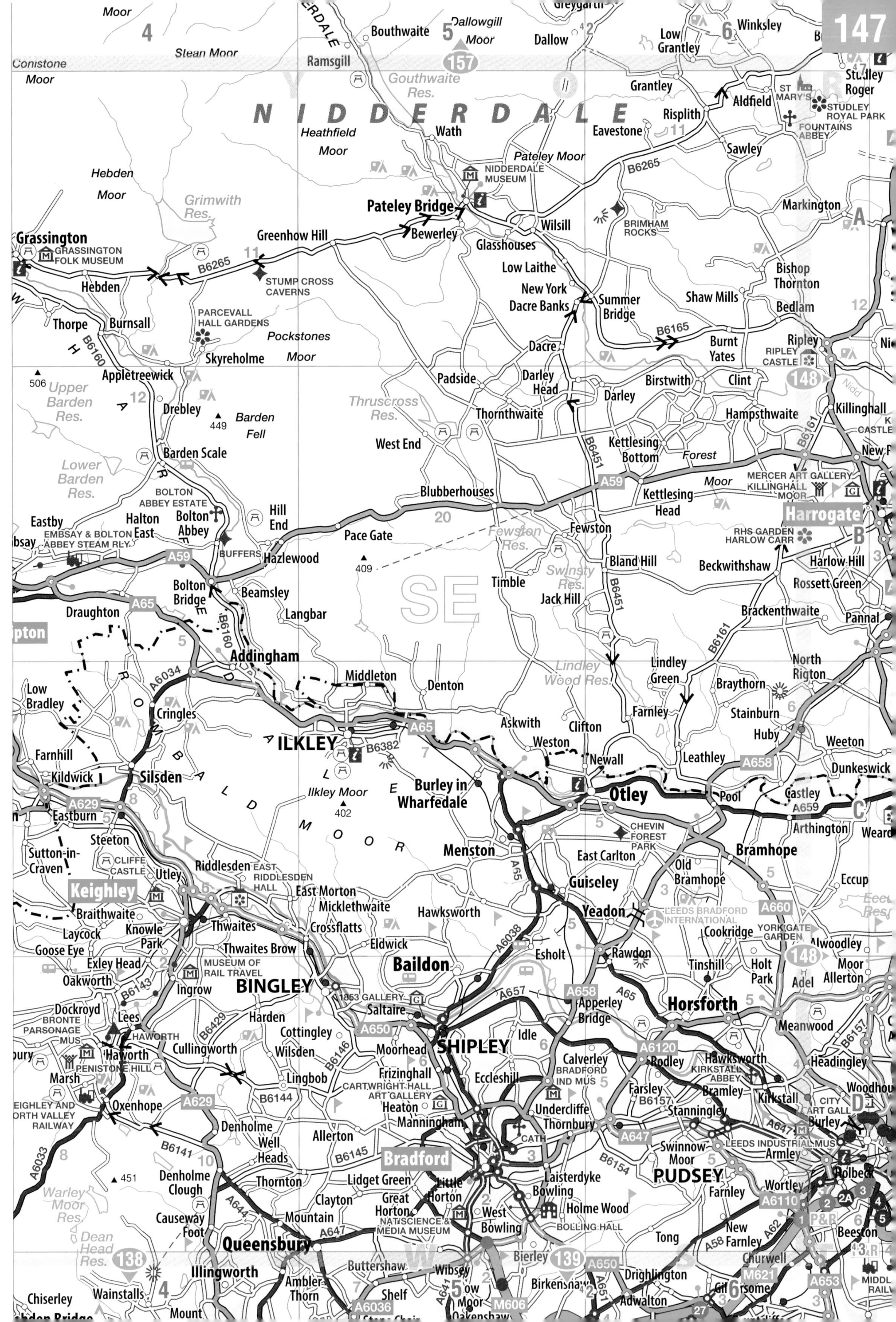
Moor
4
Stean Moor
Conistone
Moor
Ramsgill
Bouthwaite
5
Dallowgill
Moor
157
Dallow
Greygarth
Low
Grantley
6
Winksley
Goulthwaite
Res.
Grantley
Studley
Roger
ST
MARY'S
Aldfield
STUDLEY
ROYAL PARK
FOUNTAINS
ABBEY
NIDDERDALE
Heathfield
Moor
Wath
Eavestone
Risplith
Sawley
Pateley Moor
B6265
NIDDERDALE
MUSEUM
Hebden
Moor
Grimwith
Res.
Pateley Bridge
Markington
Grassington
GRASSINGTON
FOLK MUSEUM
Greenhow Hill
Bewerley
Glasshouses
Wilsill
BRIMHAM
ROCKS
11
B6265
STUMP CROSS
CAVERNS
Hebden
Low Laithe
Bishop
Thornton
New York
Summer
Bridge
Shaw Mills
Dacre Banks
Bedlam
12
Thorpe
Burnsall
PARCEVALL
HALL GARDENS
Pockstones
Moor
B6165
Burnt
Yates
Ripley
RIPLEY
CASTLE
Dacre
B6160
Skyreholme
Appletreewick
506
Upper
Barden
Res.
12
Drebley
449
Barden
Fell
Padside
Darley
Head
Darley
Birstwith
Clint
148
Killinghall
Thruscross
Res.
Thornthwaite
Hampsthwaite
B6161
West End
Kettlesing
Bottom
Forest
B6451
Barden Scale
Lower
Barden
Res.
A59
Moor
MERCER ART GALLERY
KILLINGHALL
MOOR
Blubberhouses
BOLTON
ABBEY ESTATE
Kettlesing
Head
Hill
End
Bolton
Abbey
Halton
East
Eastby
EMBSAY & BOLTON
ABBEY STEAM RLY
20
Harrogate
Pace Gate
Fewston
Res.
Fewston
RHS GARDEN
HARLOW CARR
B
BUFFERS
Hazlewood
409
Bland Hill
Beckwithshaw
Harlow Hill
A59
Swinsty
Res.
Timble
Jack Hill
Rossett Green
Bolton
Bridge
Beamsley
SE
B6451
A65
Draughton
Langbar
Brackenthwaite
Pannal
B6160
5
B6161
Addingham
Lindley
Wood Res.
Lindley
Green
North
Rigton
A6034
Middleton
Denton
Low
Bradley
Braythorn
Askwith
Clifton
Farnley
Stainburn
Cringles
6
Huby
A65
ILKLEY
B6382
Weston
Weeton
Farnhill
Newall
Leathley
A658
Dunkeswick
Kildwick
Silsden
7
Otley
Pool
Castley
Ilkley Moor
Burley in
Wharfedale
A629
402
A659
C
Eastburn
Arthington
Weardley
5
CHEVIN
FOREST
PARK
Steeton
Menston
Bramhope
East Carlton
Sutton-in-
Craven
CLIFFE
CASTLE
Riddlesden
EAST
RIDDLESDEN
HALL
Old
Bramhope
Utley
5
Eccup
Keighley
A65
Guiseley
3
East Morton
Micklethwaite
A660
Braithwaite
Yeadon
LEEDS BRADFORD
INTERNATIONAL
Hawksworth
Laycock
Knowle
Park
Thwaites
Crossflatts
YORKGATE
GARDEN
5
Cookridge
Alwoodley
Goose Eye
Thwaites Brow
Eldwick
A6038
Esholt
Rawdon
148
Exley Head
2
MUSEUM OF
RAIL TRAVEL
Baildon
Tinshill
Holt
Park
Moor
Allerton
Oakworth
Adel
BINGLEY
A657
A658
B6143
Ingrow
1853 GALLERY
Saltaire
Apperley
Bridge
A65
Horsforth
5
Dockroyd
BRONTE
PARSONAGE
MUS
B6429
Harden
Meanwood
Lees
A650
Idle
B6157
HAWORTH
Cottingley
Haworth
Cullingworth
Wilsden
Moorhead
SHIPLEY
6
A6120
Rodley
Hawksworth
Headingley
PENISTONE HILL
B6146
Calverley
KIRKSTALL
ABBEY
4
BRADFORD
IND MUS
Marsh
Lingbob
Frizinghall
Eccleshill
5
Farsley
Bramley
Kirkstall
Woodhouse
CARTWRIGHT HALL
ART GALLERY
B6144
B6157
CITY
ART GALL
KEIGHLEY AND
WORTH VALLEY
RAILWAY
Oxenhope
A629
Heaton
Undercliffe
Stanningley
Burley
D
Denholme
Manningham
Thornbury
A647
8
CATH
A647
LEEDS INDUSTRIAL MUS
Allerton
Well
Heads
Swinnow
Moor
Armley
A6033
B6141
10
B6145
Bradford
3
B6154
5
Holbeck
451
Denholme
Clough
Thornton
Lidget Green
Little
Horton
Laisterdyke
PUDSEY
Farnley
Wortley
Warley
Moor
Res.
Clayton
Great
Horton
Bowling
A6110
2
2A
3
A644
Holme Wood
NAT SCIENCE &
MEDIA MUSEUM
West
Bowling
BOLLING HALL
4
Causeway
Foot
Mountain
A62
P&R
6
5
Dean
Head
Res.
A647
Queensbury
New
Farnley
Tong
A58
Beeston
138
Bierley
139
Churwell
43
Illingworth
Buttershaw
Wibsey
A650
Drighlington
M621
Ambler
Thorn
7
Shelf
A641
5
Low
Moor
Birkenshaw
A651
2
Gildersome
6
A653
MIDDL
RAIL
Chiserley
Wainstalls
4
A6036
M606
27
Adwalton
Mount
Oakenshaw

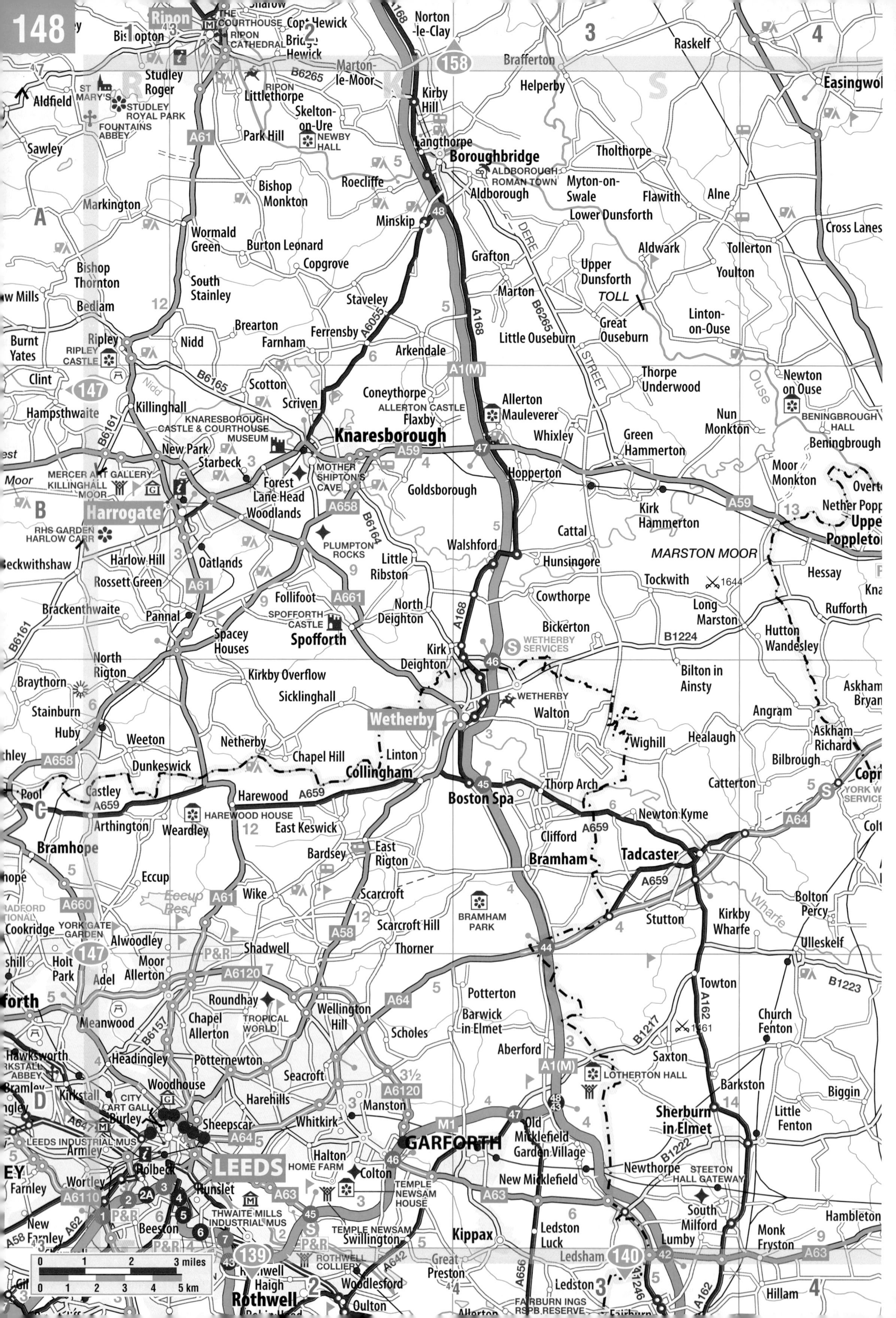
Ripon
THE COURTHOUSE
RIPON CATHEDRAL
Copt Hewick
Bridge Hewick
Norton -le-Clay
158
Brafferton
Raskelf
Easingwold
Marton-le-Moor
B6265
Studley Roger
Aldfield
ST MARY'S
STUDLEY ROYAL PARK
FOUNTAINS ABBEY
RIPON
Littlethorpe
Kirby Hill
Helperby
Skelton-on-Ure
NEWBY HALL
Park Hill
A61
Sawley
Langthorpe
Boroughbridge
ALDBOROUGH ROMAN TOWN
Aldborough
Tholthorpe
Bishop Monkton
Roecliffe
Myton-on-Swale
Flawith
Alne
Markington
Minskip
Lower Dunsforth
Cross Lanes
Wormald Green
Burton Leonard
Grafton
DERE STREET
Aldwark
Tollerton
Bishop Thornton
Copgrove
Upper Dunsforth
Youlton
South Stainley
TOLL
Staveley
Marton
Bedlam
Great Ouseburn
Linton-on-Ouse
A168
B6265
Brearton
Ferrensby
A6055
Burnt Yates
Ripley
RIPLEY CASTLE
Nidd
Farnham
Arkendale
Little Ouseburn
A1(M)
Clint
147
Nidd
B6165
Scotton
Coneythorpe
Thorpe Underwood
Newton on Ouse
Ouse
Hampsthwaite
Killinghall
Scriven
ALLERTON CASTLE
Allerton Mauleverer
Flaxby
Nun Monkton
BENINGBROUGH HALL
B6161
KNARESBOROUGH CASTLE & COURTHOUSE MUSEUM
Knaresborough
Whixley
Green Hammerton
Beningbrough
New Park
Starbeck
A59
Hopperton
Moor Monkton
Overton
MERCER ART GALLERY
KILLINGHALL MOOR
MOTHER SHIPTON'S CAVE
Forest Lane Head
Goldsborough
Kirk Hammerton
A59
Nether Poppleton
Upper Poppleton
Harrogate
Woodlands
A658
B6164
RHS GARDEN HARLOW CARR
PLUMPTON ROCKS
Walshford
Cattal
MARSTON MOOR
Beckwithshaw
Harlow Hill
Oatlands
Little Ribston
Hunsingore
Hessay
Rossett Green
A61
Follifoot
A661
Cowthorpe
Tockwith
1644
Long Marston
Rufforth
Brackenthwaite
Pannal
SPOFFORTH CASTLE
Spofforth
North Deighton
A168
Bickerton
Hutton Wandesley
B6161
Spacey Houses
WETHERBY SERVICES
B1224
Kirk Deighton
North Rigton
Bilton in Ainsty
Braythorn
Kirkby Overflow
Sicklinghall
WETHERBY
Askham Bryan
Stainburn
Wetherby
Walton
Angram
Huby
Weeton
Netherby
Wighill
Healaugh
Askham Richard
A658
Dunkeswick
Chapel Hill
Linton
Bilbrough
Collingham
Pool
Castley
Harewood
A659
Boston Spa
Thorp Arch
Catterton
A659
YORK SERVICES
HAREWOOD HOUSE
Newton Kyme
A64
Arthington
Weardley
East Keswick
Clifford
A659
Bramhope
Bardsey
East Rigton
Tadcaster
Bramham
Eccup
Eccup Res
A61
Wike
Scarcroft
A659
A660
BRAMHAM PARK
Bolton Percy
Kirkby Wharfe
Stutton
Wharfe
Cookridge
YORKGATE GARDEN
A58
Scarcroft Hill
Alwoodley
Shadwell
Thorner
Ulleskelf
147
P&R
Holt Park
Moor Allerton
A6120
B1223
Adel
Towton
Roundhay
Potterton
A162
TROPICAL WORLD
Wellington Hill
A64
Chapel Allerton
Barwick in Elmet
Church Fenton
Meanwood
B6157
Scholes
1461
B1217
Aberford
Hawksworth
KIRKSTALL ABBEY
Headingley
Potternewton
Saxton
Seacroft
A1(M)
LOTHERTON HALL
Barkston
Bramley
Kirkstall
Woodhouse
Harehills
A6120
Biggin
CITY ART GALL
Manston
Sherburn in Elmet
Little Fenton
Burley
Sheepscar
Whitkirk
M1
Old Micklefield
A647
LEEDS INDUSTRIAL MUS
A64
GARFORTH
Micklefield Garden Village
B1222
Armley
Halton
HOME FARM
Colton
Newthorpe
STEETON HALL GATEWAY
Farnley
Holbeck
LEEDS
Wortley
Hunslet
TEMPLE NEWSAM HOUSE
New Micklefield
A6110
A63
A63
South Milford
Hambleton
New Farnley
A62
Beeston
THWAITE MILLS INDUSTRIAL MUS
TEMPLE NEWSAM
Swillington
Kippax
Ledston Luck
Lumby
Monk Fryston
A58
P&R
139
ROTHWELL COLLIERY
A642
Great Preston
Ledsham
140
A63
Rothwell Haigh
Woodlesford
A656
Ledston
A1246
A162
Hillam
Rothwell
Oulton
FAIRBURN INGS RSPB RESERVE
0 1 2 3 miles
0 1 2 3 4 5 km

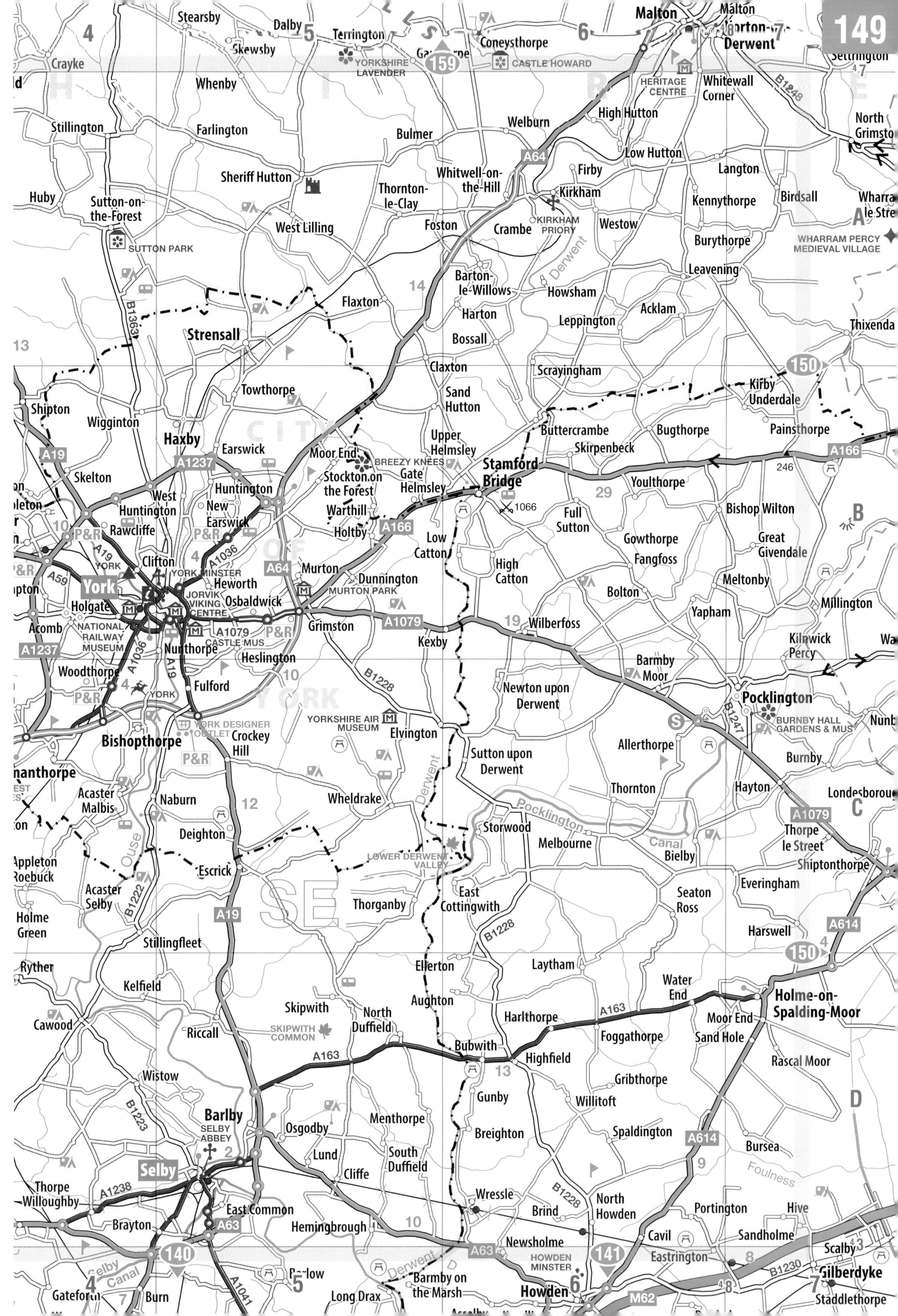
Stearsby
Dalby
Terrington
Coneysthorpe
Malton
Malton
Norton-on-Derwent
Skewsby
Crayke
YORKSHIRE LAVENDER
159
CASTLE HOWARD
Settrington
Whenby
HERITAGE CENTRE
Whitewall Corner
B1248
High Hutton
Stillington
Farlington
Welburn
Bulmer
North Grimston
Low Hutton
A64
Firby
Langton
Sheriff Hutton
Whitwell-on-the-Hill
Thornton-le-Clay
Kirkham
Huby
Sutton-on-the-Forest
Kennythorpe
Birdsall
Foston
Crambe
KIRKHAM PRIORY
Westow
West Lilling
SUTTON PARK
Burythorpe
WHARRAM PERCY MEDIEVAL VILLAGE
Leavening
Barton-le-Willows
Derwent
Howsham
Flaxton
Harton
Acklam
B1363
Strensall
Leppington
Thixendale
Bossall
Claxton
Scrayingham
150
Kirby Underdale
Towthorpe
Sand Hutton
Shipton
Wigginton
Buttercrambe
Bugthorpe
Painsthorpe
Upper Helmsley
Haxby
Earswick
CITY OF YORK
Skirpenbeck
A19
Moor End
BREEZY KNEES
Stamford Bridge
A166
A1237
Stockton on the Forest
Gate Helmsley
Youlthorpe
Skelton
Huntington
West Huntington
New Earswick
Warthill
1066
Full Sutton
Bishop Wilton
Rawcliffe
P&R
Holtby
Low Catton
Gowthorpe
Great Givendale
Fangfoss
A1036
A19
A59
Clifton
A64
Murton
YORK MINSTER
High Catton
York
Heworth
Dunnington
Meltonby
Bolton
JORVIK VIKING CENTRE
MURTON PARK
Millington
Holgate
Osbaldwick
Yapham
Acomb
NATIONAL RAILWAY MUSEUM
Grimston
A1079
Wilberfoss
Kilnwick Percy
A1237
A1079
CASTLE MUS
Kexby
Nunthorpe
Heslington
Barmby Moor
Woodthorpe
Fulford
B1228
Newton upon Derwent
YORK
Pocklington
YORKSHIRE AIR MUSEUM
BURNBY HALL GARDENS & MUS
YORK DESIGNER OUTLET
Crockey Hill
Elvington
B1247
Bishopthorpe
Allerthorpe
Sutton upon Derwent
Burnby
Bilbrough
Copmanthorpe
Acaster Malbis
Naburn
Wheldrake
Thornton
Hayton
Pocklington Canal
Londesborough
A1079
Deighton
Storwood
Melbourne
Thorpe le Street
Bielby
Appleton Roebuck
Ouse
Escrick
LOWER DERWENT VALLEY
Shiptonthorpe
Everingham
Acaster Selby
East Cottingwith
Seaton Ross
B1222
SE
Thorganby
Holme Green
A19
B1228
A614
Harswell
Stillingfleet
150
Ryther
Ellerton
Laytham
Water End
Kelfield
Holme-on-Spalding-Moor
Aughton
A163
Skipwith
North Duffield
Moor End
Cawood
Harlthorpe
Foggathorpe
SKIPWITH COMMON
Sand Hole
Riccall
Bubwith
Rascal Moor
A163
Highfield
Gribthorpe
Wistow
Gunby
Willitoft
B1223
Barlby
Menthorpe
SELBY ABBEY
Osgodby
Breighton
Spaldington
A614
Selby
Lund
South Duffield
Bursea
Cliffe
Foulness
Thorpe Willoughby
A1238
Wressle
North Howden
East Common
Brind
B1228
Portington
Hive
Brayton
Hemingbrough
Cavil
Sandholme
A63
Newsholme
Scalby
140
A63
HOWDEN MINSTER
141
Eastrington
B1230
Gilberdyke
Selby Canal
Derwent
Barmby on the Marsh
Howden
Gateforth
Burn
Long Drax
M62
Staddlethorpe

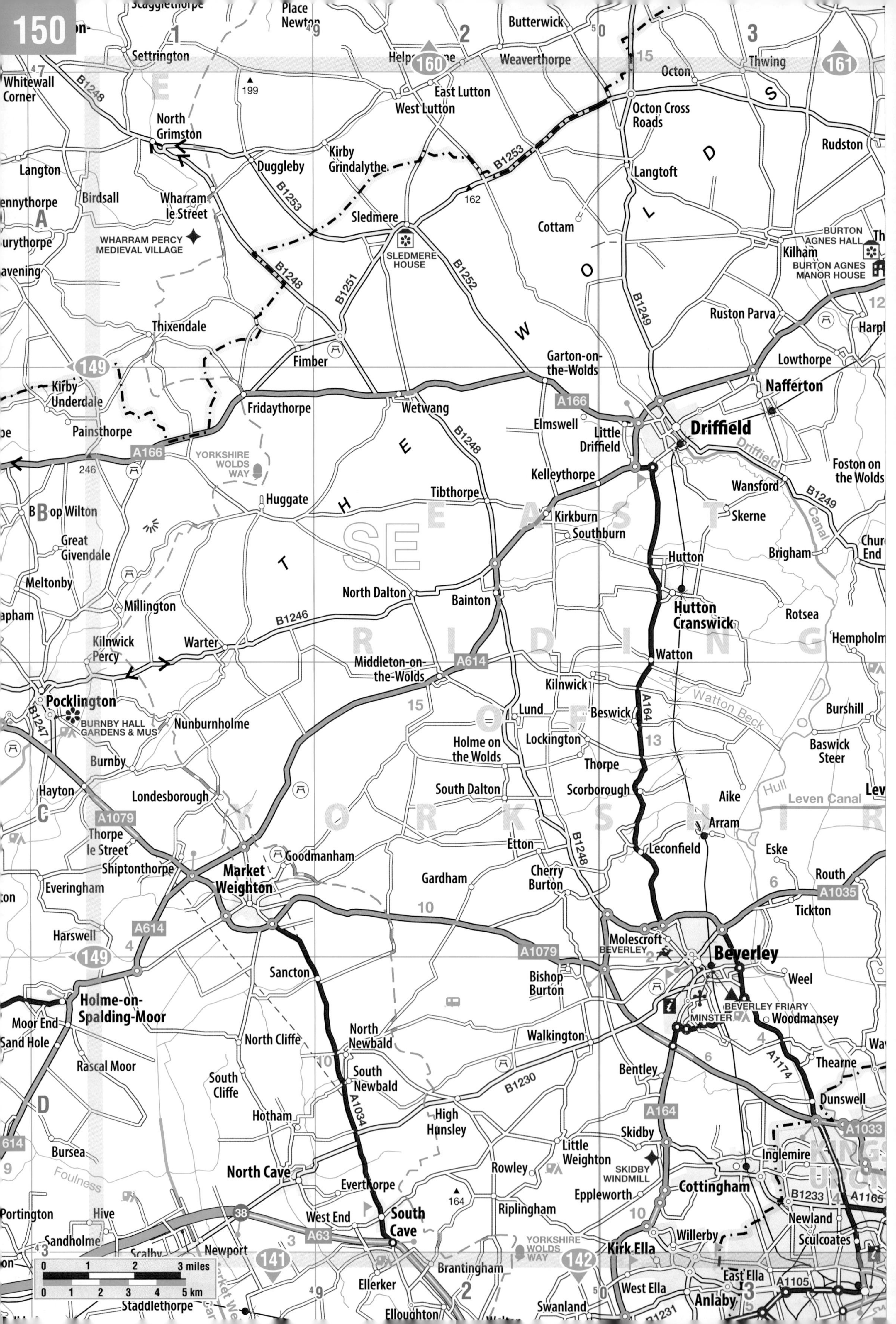
Settrington
Whitewall Corner
North Grimston
Langton
Birdsall
Wharram le Street
WHARRAM PERCY MEDIEVAL VILLAGE
Duggleby
Kirby Grindalythe
Sledmere
SLEDMERE HOUSE
Helperthorpe
Weaverthorpe
Butterwick
East Lutton
West Lutton
Octon
Thwing
Octon Cross Roads
Rudston
Langtoft
Cottam
Kilham
BURTON AGNES HALL
BURTON AGNES MANOR HOUSE
Ruston Parva
Lowthorpe
Nafferton
Thixendale
Fimber
Kirby Underdale
Fridaythorpe
Wetwang
Painsthorpe
Garton-on-the-Wolds
Elmswell
Little Driffield
Driffield
Kelleythorpe
Wansford
Foston on the Wolds
Skerne
YORKSHIRE WOLDS WAY
Huggate
Tibthorpe
Kirkburn
Southburn
Great Givendale
Meltonby
Millington
North Dalton
Bainton
Hutton
Hutton Cranswick
Brigham
Rotsea
Kilnwick Percy
Warter
Middleton-on-the-Wolds
Watton
Kilnwick
Pocklington
BURNBY HALL GARDENS & MUS
Nunburnholme
Lund
Beswick
Watton Beck
Burshill
Hempholme
Holme on the Wolds
Lockington
Thorpe
Baswick Steer
Burnby
Hayton
Londesborough
South Dalton
Scorborough
Aike
Arram
Leven Canal
Thorpe le Street
Goodmanham
Etton
Leconfield
Eske
Shiptonthorpe
Market Weighton
Everingham
Gardham
Cherry Burton
Routh
Tickton
Harswell
Molescroft
BEVERLEY
Beverley
Bishop Burton
Weel
Holme-on-Spalding-Moor
Sancton
BEVERLEY FRIARY
MINSTER
Woodmansey
Moor End
Sand Hole
North Cliffe
North Newbald
Walkington
Rascal Moor
South Cliffe
South Newbald
Bentley
Thearne
Dunswell
Hotham
High Hunsley
Skidby
Bursea
Little Weighton
SKIDBY WINDMILL
Inglemire
North Cave
Rowley
Cottingham
Everthorpe
Eppleworth
Riplingham
Newland
Portington
Hive
South Cave
West End
Willerby
Sculcoates
Sandholme
Newport
Kirk Ella
Brantingham
East Ella
Ellerker
West Ella
Anlaby
Staddlethorpe
Swanland
Elloughton
THE WOLDS
EAST RIDING OF YORKSHIRE
0 1 2 3 miles
0 1 2 3 4 5 km

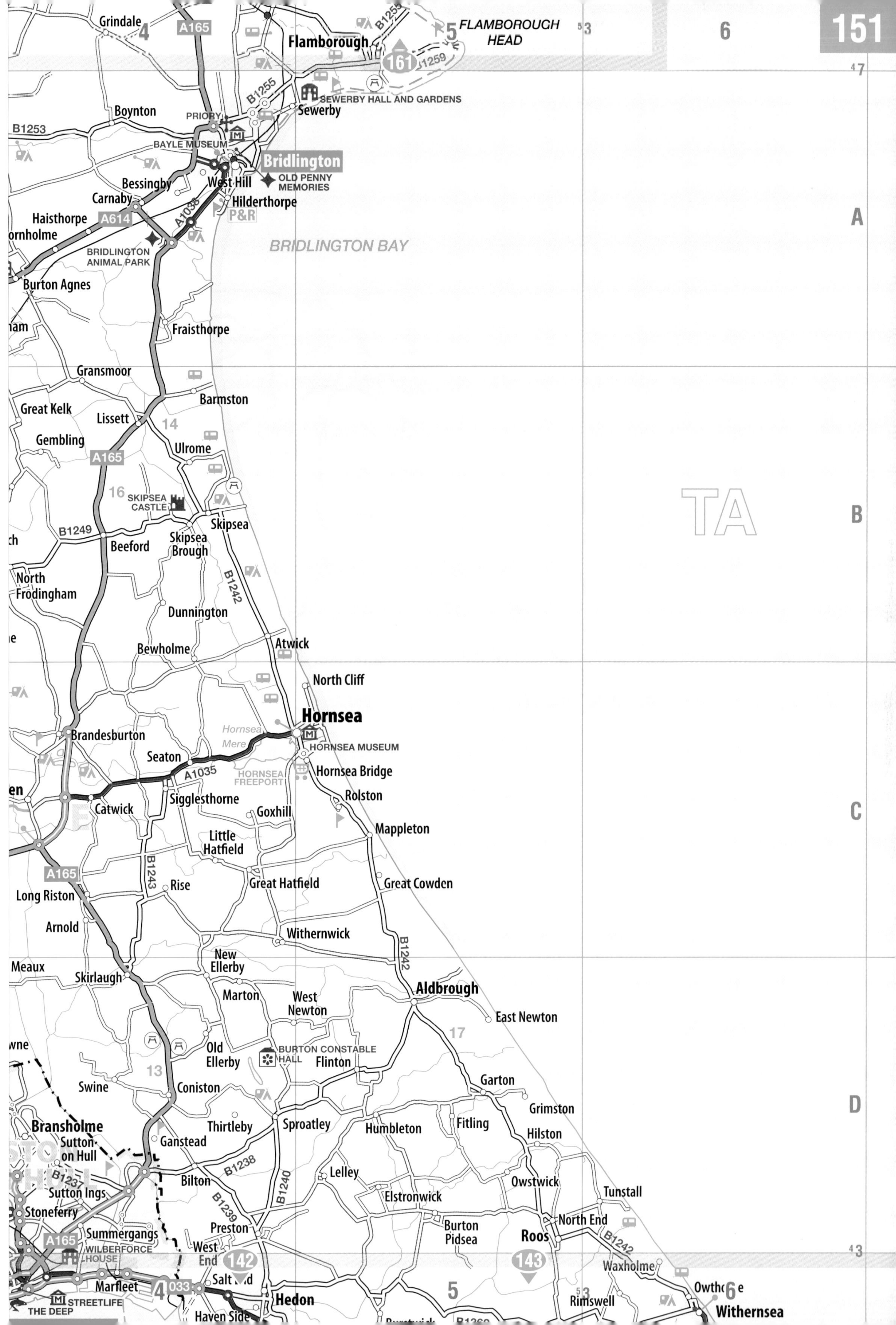
4
5
6
A
B
C
D
FLAMBOROUGH HEAD
Grindale
A165
Flamborough
B1255
B1259
161
SEWERBY HALL AND GARDENS
Sewerby
Boynton
PRIORY
B1253
BAYLE MUSEUM
Bridlington
OLD PENNY MEMORIES
Bessingby
West Hill
Carnaby
Hilderthorpe
Haisthorpe
A614
A1038
P&R
BRIDLINGTON BAY
BRIDLINGTON ANIMAL PARK
Burton Agnes
Fraisthorpe
Gransmoor
Barmston
Great Kelk
Lissett
14
Gembling
A165
Ulrome
16
SKIPSEA CASTLE
TA
B1249
Skipsea
Beeford
Skipsea Brough
North Frodingham
B1242
Dunnington
Bewholme
Atwick
North Cliff
Hornsea
Hornsea Mere
HORNSEA MUSEUM
Brandesburton
Seaton
A1035
HORNSEA FREEPORT
Hornsea Bridge
Rolston
Sigglesthorpe
Catwick
Goxhill
Mappleton
Little Hatfield
A165
B1243
Rise
Great Hatfield
Great Cowden
Long Riston
Arnold
Withernwick
B1242
New Ellerby
Meaux
Skirlaugh
Aldbrough
Marton
West Newton
East Newton
17
Old Ellerby
BURTON CONSTABLE HALL
Flinton
13
Swine
Coniston
Garton
Grimston
Bransholme
Thirtleby
Sproatley
Humbleton
Fitling
Sutton-on Hull
Ganstead
Hilston
B1238
Lelley
Owstwick
B1237
Bilton
Tunstall
Sutton Ings
B1240
Elstronwick
B1239
North End
Stoneferry
Preston
Burton Pidsea
Roos
B1242
A165
Summergangs
WILBERFORCE HOUSE
West End
142
143
Waxholme
Marfleet
Salt End
5
Owthorne
6
Hedon
Rimswell
A1033
STREETLIFE
THE DEEP
Haven Side
Withernsea

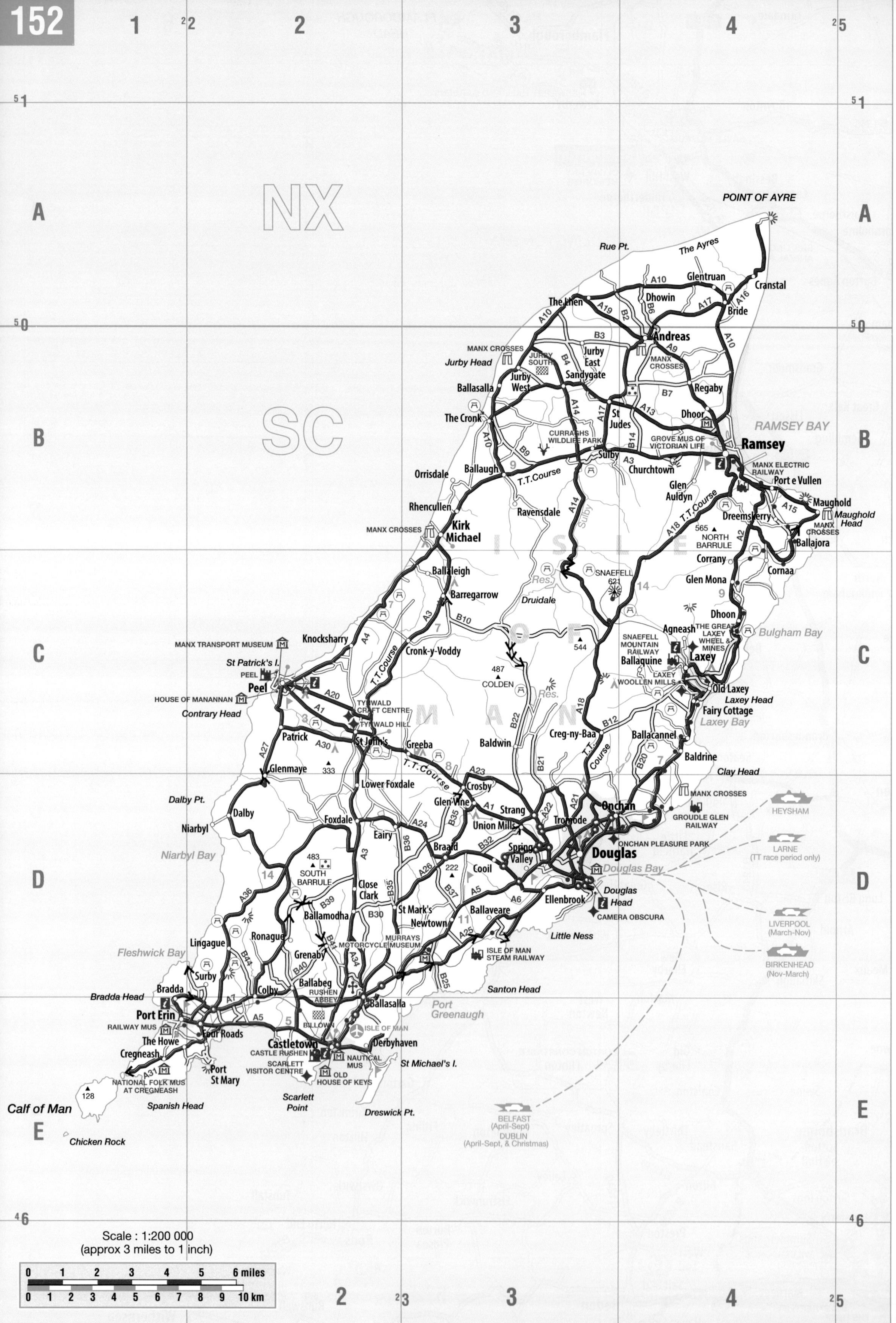
NX
SC
POINT OF AYRE
Rue Pt.
The Ayres
Glentruan
Cranstal
Dhowin
The Lhen
Bride
Andreas
MANX CROSSES
Jurby Head
Jurby East
Jurby West
Sandygate
Ballasalla
Regaby
St Judes
The Cronk
Dhoor
CURRAGHS WILDLIFE PARK
GROVE MUS OF VICTORIAN LIFE
RAMSEY BAY
Ramsey
Sulby
Churchtown
MANX ELECTRIC RAILWAY
Port e Vullen
Orrisdale
Ballaugh
T.T.Course
Glen Auldyn
Maughold
Maughold Head
Rhencullen
Ravensdale
Dreemskerry
Kirk Michael
NORTH BARRULE
Ballajora
ISLE OF MAN
Corrany
Cornaa
Ballaleigh
SNAEFELL
Glen Mona
Barregarrow
Druidale
Dhoon
Bulgham Bay
MANX TRANSPORT MUSEUM
Knocksharry
Agneash
THE GREAT LAXEY WHEEL & MINES
SNAEFELL MOUNTAIN RAILWAY
Cronk-y-Voddy
Ballaquine
Laxey
St Patrick's I.
PEEL
Peel
COLDEN
LAXEY WOOLLEN MILLS
Old Laxey
HOUSE OF MANANNAN
Laxey Head
Contrary Head
TYNWALD CRAFT CENTRE
TYNWALD HILL
Fairy Cottage
Laxey Bay
Patrick
St John's
Greeba
Baldwin
Creg-ny-Baa
Ballacannel
Baldrine
Glenmaye
Clay Head
Lower Foxdale
Crosby
MANX CROSSES
HEYSHAM
Dalby Pt.
Glen Vine
Strang
Onchan
GROUDLE GLEN RAILWAY
Niarbyl
Dalby
Foxdale
Union Mills
Tromode
ONCHAN PLEASURE PARK
LARNE
(TT race period only)
Eairy
Braaid
Spring Valley
Douglas
Niarbyl Bay
SOUTH BARRULE
Cooil
Douglas Bay
Close Clark
Douglas Head
Ellenbrook
CAMERA OBSCURA
Ballamodha
St Mark's
Newtown
Ballaveare
LIVERPOOL
(March-Nov)
Ronague
Little Ness
Lingague
MURRAYS MOTORCYCLE MUSEUM
Fleshwick Bay
Grenaby
ISLE OF MAN STEAM RAILWAY
BIRKENHEAD
(Nov-March)
Surby
Ballabeg
Bradda
Colby
RUSHEN ABBEY
Santon Head
Bradda Head
Ballasalla
Port Erin
Port Greenaugh
RAILWAY MUS
Four Roads
BILLOWN
ISLE OF MAN
The Howe
Castletown
Derbyhaven
Cregneash
CASTLE RUSHEN
NAUTICAL MUS
SCARLETT VISITOR CENTRE
St Michael's I.
Port St Mary
OLD HOUSE OF KEYS
NATIONAL FOLK MUS AT CREGNEASH
Scarlett Point
Calf of Man
Spanish Head
Dreswick Pt.
BELFAST
(April-Sept)
DUBLIN
(April-Sept, & Christmas)
Chicken Rock
Scale : 1:200 000
(approx 3 miles to 1 inch)
0 1 2 3 4 5 6 miles
0 1 2 3 4 5 6 7 8 9 10 km

153
FURNESS FELLS
Seascale
Santon Bridge
Eskdale Green
Beckfoot
Boot
HARDKNOTT FORT
Hard Knott Pass
Wrynose Pass
Cockley Beck
Eskdale
162
163
HALLSENNA MOOR
Irt
Holmrook
B5344
Drigg
Mite
Esk
231
649
HARTER FELL
Seathwaite Tarn
CONISTON COPPERMINES
CONISTON HOLLY HOW
801
THE OLD MAN OF CONISTON
Bowmanstead
Birker Fell
Devoke Water
Saltcoats
RAVENGLASS AND ESKDALE RAILWAY & MUS
Ravenglass
BATH HOUSE
MUNCASTER CASTLE & HAWK & OWL CENTRE
Woodend
Hall Dunnerdale
Seathwaite
Duddon
Ulpha Fell
Broad Oak
Newbiggin
Lane End
572
WHITFELL
529
CAW
Ulpha
Hoses
Torver
Coniston Water
A595
Corney Fell
Stub Place
Corney
Broughton Mills
A593
A5084
154
Selker Bay
Hycemoor
Bootle
Duddon Bridge
Lower Hawthwaite
Water Yeat
Blawith
High Nibthwaite
Broughton in Furness
Black Combe
600
Lowick Bridge
Lowick Green
Hallthwaites
DUDDON MOSSES
Foxfield
Grizebeck
A5092
Gawthwaite
Whitbeck
The Green
The Hill
333
B5281
KING CHARLES III ENGLAND COAST PATH
Kirkby-in-Furness
Beck Side
Penny Bridge
Broughton Beck
Greenodd
Silecroft
Whicham
A5093
Arrad Foot
Mansriggs
Kirksanton
Millom
MILLOM HERITAGE & ARTS CENTRE
Soutergate
LAUREL & HARDY MUS
Haverigg
Ulverston
DUDDON SANDS
Askam in Furness
Ireleth
Pennington
Swarthmoor
Lindal in Furness
A5087
SD
SAFARI ZOO CUMBRIA
SANDSCALE HAWS
Great Urswick
Bardsea
A590
DALTON CASTLE
Dalton-in-Furness
Little Urswick
NORTH WALNEY
Stainton with Adgarley
Scales
BARROW (WALNEY ISLAND)
Hawcoat
BOW BRIDGE
Baycliff
GLEASTON WATERMILL
Ormsgill
Newton
FURNESS ABBEY
87
Newbarns
Barrow-in-Furness
Aldingham
Dendron
Gleaston
North Scale
CUSTOM HO
Newbiggin
144
THE DOCK MUSEUM
Leece
Vickerstown
Barrow Island
Roosebeck
Biggar
Rampside
Roa Island
Foulney Island
South End
Piel Island
Isle of Walney
South Channel
South End Point
0 1 2 3 miles
0 1 2 3 4 5 km

LAKE DISTRICT NATIONAL PARK
ULLSCARF
HIGH WHITE STONES
762
Easedale Tarn
GRASMERE THORNEY HOW
GRASMERE BUTHARLYP HOWE
DOVE COTTAGE AND WORDSWORTH MUSEUM
Grasmere
Rydal
RYDAL MOUNT
Rydal Water
Langdale Pikes
Stickle Tarn
B5343
Chapel Stile
902
OW FELL
163
ELTERWATER
Elterwater
LANGDALE
Ambleside
Little Langdale
Clappersgate
Waterhead
ROMAN FORT
STAGSHAW GARDENS
Skelwith Bridge
Brathay
Wrynose Pass
Cockley Beck
322
B5286
AMBLESIDE
BROCKHOLE - NAT PK VISITOR CENTRE
BLELHAM BOG
Low Wray
A591
A593
FURNESS FELLS
Seathwaite Tarn
CONISTON COPPERMINES
HAWKSHEAD COURTHOUSE
Outgate
High Wray
Hawkshead Hill
Colthouse
WINDERMERE STEAMBOATS & MUS.
CONISTON HOLLY HOW
801
THE OLD MAN OF CONISTON
Coniston
BEATRIX POTTER GALLERY
Hawkshead
Esthwaite Water
B5285
GONDOLA
BRANTWOOD
HAWKSHEAD
Bowmanstead
Near Sawrey
THE WORLD OF BEATRIX POTTER
Grizedale Forest
GRIZEDALE FOREST PARK VISITOR CENTRE
Grizedale
HILL TOP
Far Sawrey
Torver
GRIZEDALE FOREST PARK
Coniston Water
A5084
Satterthwaite
335
Force Mills
FOREST SPINNERS
GRAYTHWAITE HALL
153
Water Yeat
Blawith
High Nibthwaite
FURNESS FELLS
Rusland
RUSLAND MOSS
STOTT PARK BOBBIN MILL
Finsthwaite
Oxen Park
Lakeside
LAKES AQUARIUM
Lowick Bridge
Colton
Bouth
Lowick Green
Grizebeck
A5092
Spark Bridge
LAKESIDE AND HAVERTHWAITE RAILWAY
Newby Bridge
Gawthwaite
Backbarrow
333
B5281
Penny Bridge
Haverthwaite
Broughton Beck
Greenodd
Arrad Foot
Mansriggs
A590
ROUDSEA WOOD AND MOSSES
LAUREL & HARDY MUS
Ulverston
Pennington
Swarthmoor
A5087
CONISHEAD PRIORY & MANJUSHRI KADAMPA MEDITATION CENTRE
Cartmel Sands
Great Urswick
Bardsea
Little Urswick
Stainton with Adgarley
Scales
Baycliff
GLEASTON WATERMILL
87
Gleaston
Aldingham
Roosebeck
Lee
MORECAMBE
144
145
Windermere
Inn
Kirkstone Pass
776
828 HIGH STREET
164
774
HARTER FELL
Shap Fells
Sadgill
Long Sleddale
Kentmere
530
A592
Troutbeck
TOWNEND
WINDERMERE
HOLEHIRD GARDENS
Troutbeck Bridge
Elfhowe
Lowbridge House
Garnett Bridge
Ings
Staveley
Watchgate
Bowness-on-Windermere
Bowston
Garth Row
Ferney Green
B5284
Burneside
Meal Bank
LAKELAND CLIMBING CENTRE
Crook
Storrs
Winster
Underbarrow
Kendal
KENDAL
229
Crosthwaite
Gregg Hall
A5074
Gilpin
A6
Oxenholme
Brigsteer
Natland
Middleshaw
Barrows Green
Bowland Bridge
Row
Cartmel Fell
The Howe
SIZERGH
Sedgwick
Cotes
FELL FOOT
WHITBARROW
Levens
Stainton
A65
Sampool Bridge
Staveley
Hincaster
Endmoor
LEVENS HALL
Witherslack
Mill Side
Crooklands
Leasgill
High Newton
Town End
Ayside
Heversham
Low Newton
B6385
Milnthorpe
Field Broughton
Meathop
B6384
Lindale
Farleton
Storth
B5271
A6070
CARTMEL PRIORY
Beetham
HERON CORN MILL
CARTMEL
Cartmel
B5278
ARNSIDE
B5282
Holme
Arnside
HOLKER HALL
LAKELAND WILDLIFE OASIS
Holker
Allithwaite
Grange-over-Sands
GAIT BARROWS
Clawthorpe
Burton-in-Kendal
Cark
B5277
Kents Bank
Yealand Redmayne
Flookburgh
Ravenstown
Silverdale
ARNSIDE AND SILVERDALE
Yealand Conyers
M6
Priest Hutton
LEIGHTON HALL
Humphrey Head Pt.
Warton Sands
Warton
Borwick
OLD RECTORY
Millhead
Capernwray
35A
35
36
Carnforth
Over Kellet
Nether Kellet
Bolton-le-Sands
0 1 2 3 miles
0 1 2 3 4 5 km

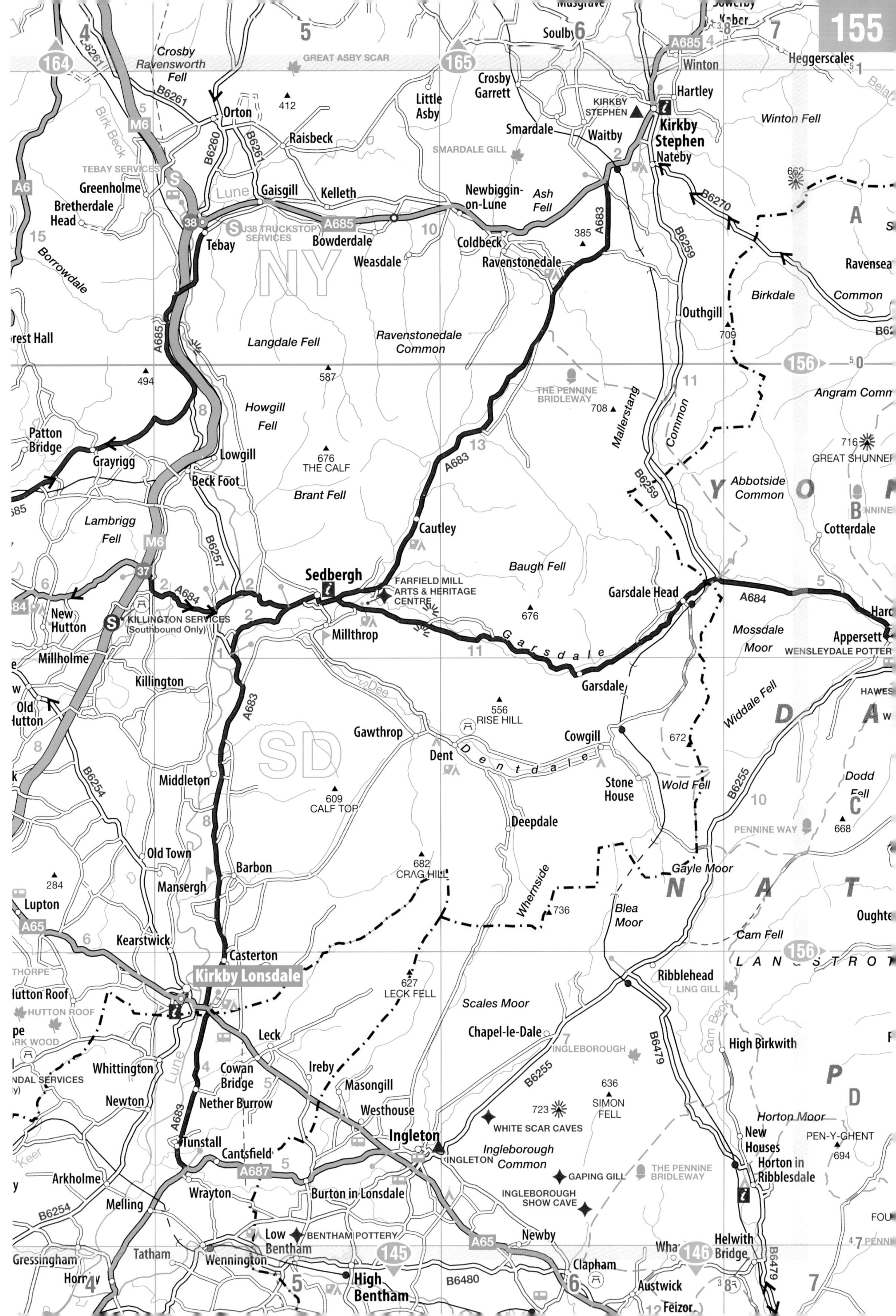
Crosby Ravensworth Fell
GREAT ASBY SCAR
Soulby
Winton
Heggerscales
Crosby Garrett
Little Asby
Orton
Raisbeck
Hartley
KIRKBY STEPHEN
Kirkby Stephen
Smardale
Waitby
Winton Fell
Nateby
SMARDALE GILL
TEBAY SERVICES
Greenholme
Bretherdale Head
Gaisgill
Kelleth
Newbiggin-on-Lune
Ash Fell
J38 TRUCKSTOP SERVICES
Tebay
Bowderdale
Weasdale
Coldbeck
Ravenstonedale
Borrowdale
Birkdale
Common
Ravenseat
Outhgill
Langdale Fell
Ravenstonedale Common
Howgill Fell
THE PENNINE BRIDLEWAY
Mallerstang
Common
Angram Common
Patton Bridge
Grayrigg
Lowgill
THE CALF
Beck Foot
Brant Fell
Abbotside Common
GREAT SHUNNER
Lambrigg Fell
Cautley
Cotterdale
Baugh Fell
Sedbergh
FARFIELD MILL ARTS & HERITAGE CENTRE
Garsdale Head
New Hutton
KILLINGTON SERVICES (Southbound Only)
Millthrop
Garsdale
Mossdale Moor
Appersett
WENSLEYDALE POTTER
Millholme
Killington
Old Hutton
Widdale Fell
HAWES
RISE HILL
Gawthrop
Dent
Dentdale
Cowgill
Middleton
CALF TOP
Stone House
Wold Fell
Dodd Fell
Deepdale
PENNINE WAY
Old Town
Barbon
CRAG HILL
Mansergh
Gayle Moor
Whernside
Lupton
Blea Moor
Kearstwick
Oughte
Cam Fell
Casterton
Kirkby Lonsdale
Ribblehead
LING GILL
THORPE
Hutton Roof
HUTTON ROOF
LECK FELL
Scales Moor
Leck
Chapel-le-Dale
INGLEBOROUGH
High Birkwith
Whittington
Cowan Bridge
Ireby
Masongill
Newton
Nether Burrow
SIMON FELL
Westhouse
WHITE SCAR CAVES
Horton Moor
PEN-Y-GHENT
New Houses
Tunstall
Cantsfield
Ingleton
Ingleborough Common
INGLETON
Horton in Ribblesdale
GAPING GILL
THE PENNINE BRIDLEWAY
Arkholme
Wrayton
Burton in Lonsdale
INGLEBOROUGH SHOW CAVE
Melling
Low Bentham
BENTHAM POTTERY
Newby
Gressingham
Tatham
Wennington
Helwith Bridge
High Bentham
Clapham
Austwick
Feizor
NY
SD
YORKSHIRE DALES NATIONAL PARK
M6
A6
A65
A683
A684
A685
A687
B6254
B6255
B6257
B6259
B6260
B6261
B6270
B6479
B6480
164
165
156
145
146

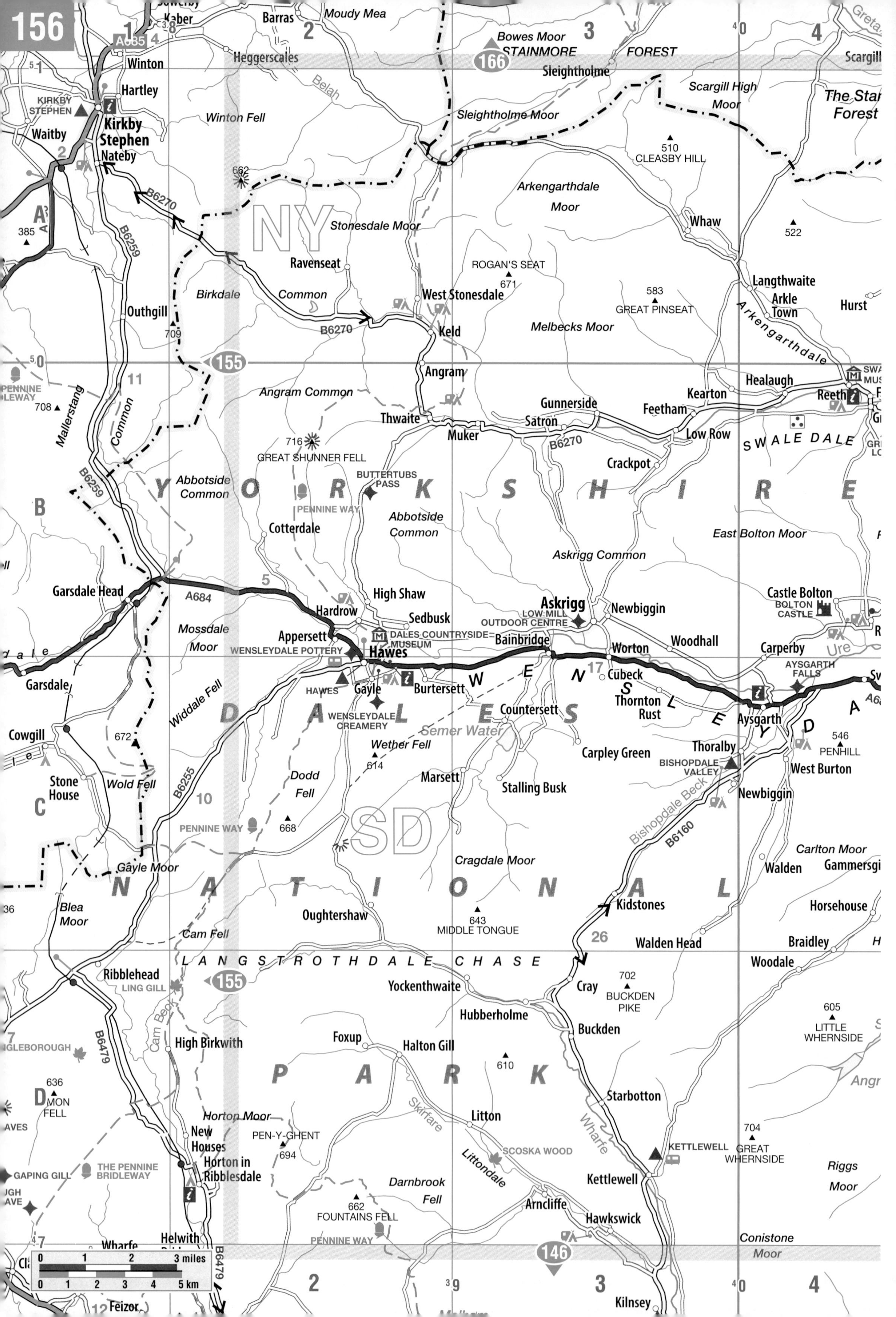
Kaber
Barras
Moudy Mea
Bowes Moor
STAINMORE
FOREST
166
Heggerscales
Winton
Sleightholme
Scargill
Hartley
KIRKBY STEPHEN
Kirkby Stephen
Winton Fell
Sleightholme Moor
Scargill High Moor
The Stang Forest
Waitby
Nateby
662
510
CLEASBY HILL
B6270
Arkengarthdale Moor
NY
Stonesdale Moor
Whaw
385
B6259
522
Ravenseat
ROGAN'S SEAT
671
Birkdale
Common
West Stonesdale
583
GREAT PINSEAT
Langthwaite
Arkle Town
Hurst
Outhgill
Keld
Melbecks Moor
Arkengarthdale
709
155
PENNINE BRIDLEWAY
Angram
Healaugh
Reeth
708
Mallerstang
Common
Angram Common
Gunnerside
Kearton
Feetham
Thwaite
Satron
Muker
Low Row
716
GREAT SHUNNER FELL
SWALE DALE
Crackpot
BUTTERTUBS PASS
Abbotside Common
YORKSHIRE
PENNINE WAY
Cotterdale
East Bolton Moor
Askrigg Common
Garsdale Head
A684
High Shaw
Hardrow
Sedbusk
Askrigg
Newbiggin
Castle Bolton
BOLTON CASTLE
Mossdale Moor
LOW MILL OUTDOOR CENTRE
Appersett
DALES COUNTRYSIDE MUSEUM
Bainbridge
Woodhall
Worton
Carperby
Ure
WENSLEYDALE POTTERY
Hawes
Cubeck
AYSGARTH FALLS
Garsdale
HAWES
Gayle
Burtersett
Thornton Rust
Aysgarth
Widdale Fell
WENSLEYDALE
Countersett
Cowgill
672
WENSLEYDALE CREAMERY
Semer Water
Wether Fell
614
Carpley Green
Thoralby
546
PENHILL
BISHOPDALE VALLEY
West Burton
Stone House
Wold Fell
Dodd Fell
Marsett
Stalling Busk
Bishopdale Beck
Newbiggin
B6255
B6160
668
SD
Carlton Moor
Cragdale Moor
Walden
Gammersgill
Gayle Moor
NATIONAL
Blea Moor
Oughtershaw
643
MIDDLE TONGUE
Kidstones
Horsehouse
Cam Fell
Walden Head
Braidley
LANGSTROTHDALE CHASE
Woodale
Ribblehead
LING GILL
702
BUCKDEN PIKE
Yockenthwaite
Cray
Hubberholme
605
LITTLE WHERNSIDE
Buckden
INGLEBOROUGH
B6479
Cam Beck
High Birkwith
Foxup
Halton Gill
610
PARK
636
SIMON FELL
Starbotton
Skirfare
Wharfe
Horton Moor
Litton
New Houses
PEN-Y-GHENT
694
704
GREAT WHERNSIDE
KETTLEWELL
SCOSKA WOOD
Littondale
Riggs Moor
GAPING GILL
THE PENNINE BRIDLEWAY
Horton in Ribblesdale
Kettlewell
Darnbrook Fell
662
FOUNTAINS FELL
Arncliffe
Hawkswick
Conistone Moor
PENNINE WAY
Helwith Bridge
146
0 1 2 3 miles
0 1 2 3 4 5 km
Feizor
Kilnsey

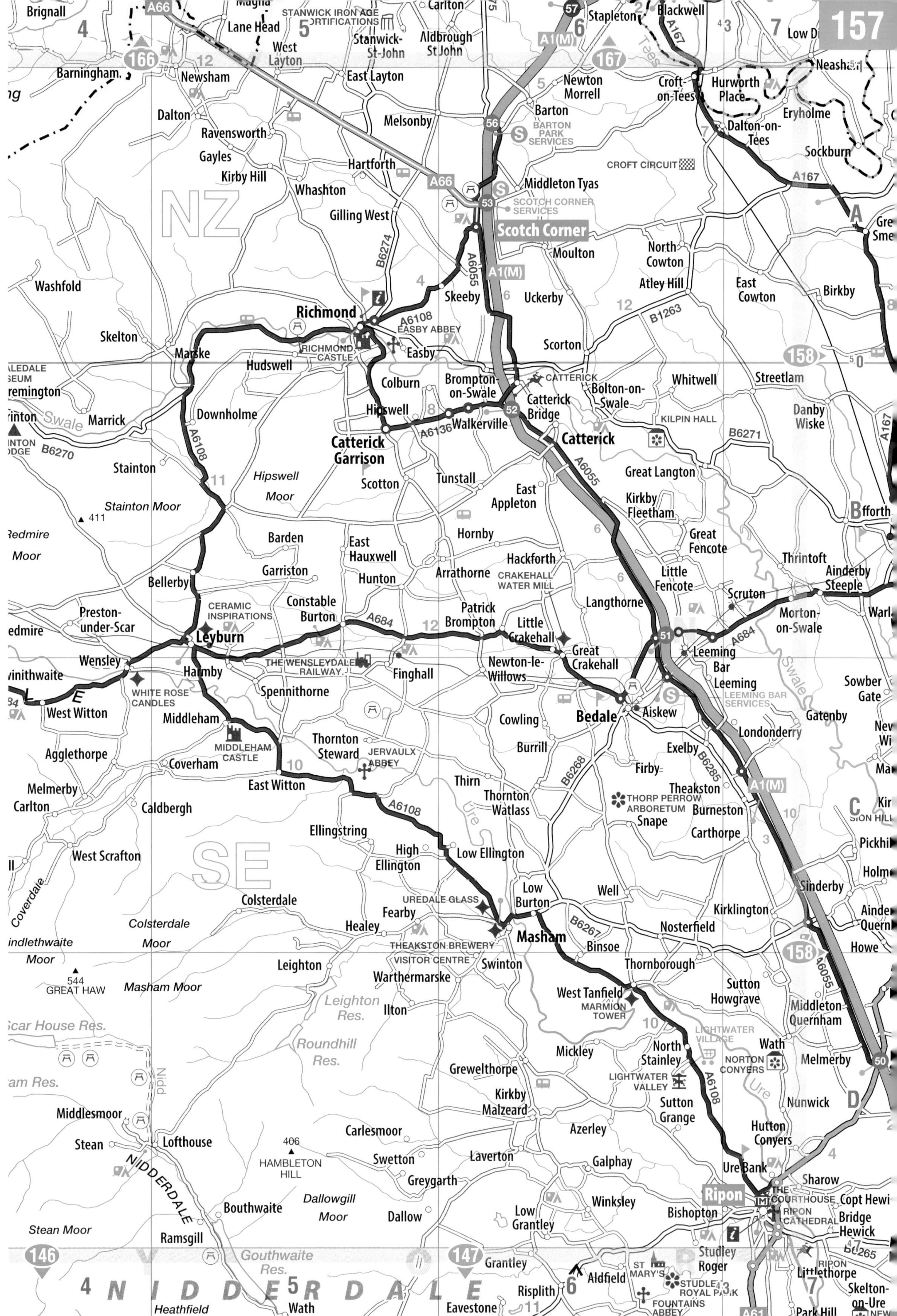
Brignall
Barningham
Newsham
Dalton
Ravensworth
Gayles
Kirby Hill
Lane Head
West Layton
STANWICK IRON AGE FORTIFICATIONS
Stanwick-St-John
Carlton
Aldbrough St John
East Layton
Melsonby
Hartforth
Whashton
Gilling West
Stapleton
Blackwell
Newton Morrell
Barton
BARTON PARK SERVICES
Croft-on-Tees
Hurworth Place
Neasham
Eryholme
Dalton-on-Tees
Sockburn
CROFT CIRCUIT
Middleton Tyas
SCOTCH CORNER SERVICES
Scotch Corner
Moulton
North Cowton
Atley Hill
East Cowton
Birkby
Uckerby
Skeeby
Scorton
NZ
Washfold
Skelton
Richmond
RICHMOND CASTLE
EASBY ABBEY
Easby
Marske
Hudswell
Colburn
Brompton-on-Swale
CATTERICK
Bolton-on-Swale
Whitwell
Streetlam
Catterick Bridge
Catterick
KILPIN HALL
Danby Wiske
Marrick
Downholme
Hipswell
Walkerville
Catterick Garrison
Stainton
Hipswell Moor
Scotton
Tunstall
Great Langton
East Appleton
Kirkby Fleetham
Stainton Moor
411
Redmire Moor
Barden
Hornby
Great Fencote
Little Fencote
East Hauxwell
Garriston
Hunton
Arrathorne
Hackforth
CRAKEHALL WATER MILL
Thrintoft
Ainderby Steeple
Scruton
Morton-on-Swale
Bellerby
Preston-under-Scar
CERAMIC INSPIRATIONS
Constable Burton
Patrick Brompton
Little Crakehall
Langthorne
Leyburn
Great Crakehall
Leeming Bar
Leeming
LEEMING BAR SERVICES
Wensley
THE WENSLEYDALE RAILWAY
Finghall
Newton-le-Willows
Harmby
Spennithorne
Bedale
Aiskew
Sowber Gate
Gatenby
West Witton
WHITE ROSE CANDLES
Middleham
MIDDLEHAM CASTLE
Cowling
Londonderry
Exelby
Agglethorpe
Coverham
Thornton Steward
JERVAULX ABBEY
Burrill
Firby
Melmerby
Carlton
East Witton
Thirn
Thornton Watlass
Theakston
THORP PERROW ARBORETUM
Snape
Burneston
Carthorpe
Caldbergh
Ellingstring
High Ellington
Low Ellington
West Scrafton
SE
Coverdale
Colsterdale
Low Burton
Well
Sinderby
Kirklington
Fearby
Healey
UREDALE GLASS
Masham
THEAKSTON BREWERY VISITOR CENTRE
Nosterfield
Binsoe
Colsterdale Moor
Thornborough
Swinton
Leighton
Warthermarske
544 GREAT HAW
Masham Moor
West Tanfield
MARMION TOWER
Sutton Howgrave
Middleton Quernham
Leighton Res.
Ilton
Scar House Res.
Roundhill Res.
North Stainley
LIGHTWATER VILLAGE
Wath
Mickley
NORTON CONYERS
Melmerby
Grewelthorpe
LIGHTWATER VALLEY
Kirkby Malzeard
Sutton Grange
Nunwick
Middlesmoor
Stean
Lofthouse
NIDDERDALE
406 HAMBLETON HILL
Carlesmoor
Azerley
Hutton Conyers
Swetton
Laverton
Galphay
Ure Bank
Sharow
Greygarth
Ripon
THE COURTHOUSE
RIPON CATHEDRAL
Copt Hewick
Bridge Hewick
Bouthwaite
Dallowgill Moor
Dallow
Low Grantley
Winksley
Bishopton
Stean Moor
Ramsgill
Goutháwaite Res.
Grantley
Studley Roger
ST MARY'S
STUDLEY ROYAL PARK
Aldfield
Littlethorpe
Risplith
FOUNTAINS ABBEY
Skelton-on-Ure
Heathfield
Wath
Eavestone
Park Hill
NIDDERDALE
A66
A1(M)
A167
A6055
A6108
A6136
A684
B6274
B1263
B6271
B6270
B6268
B6285
B6267
B6265
Swale
Tees
Ure
Nidd

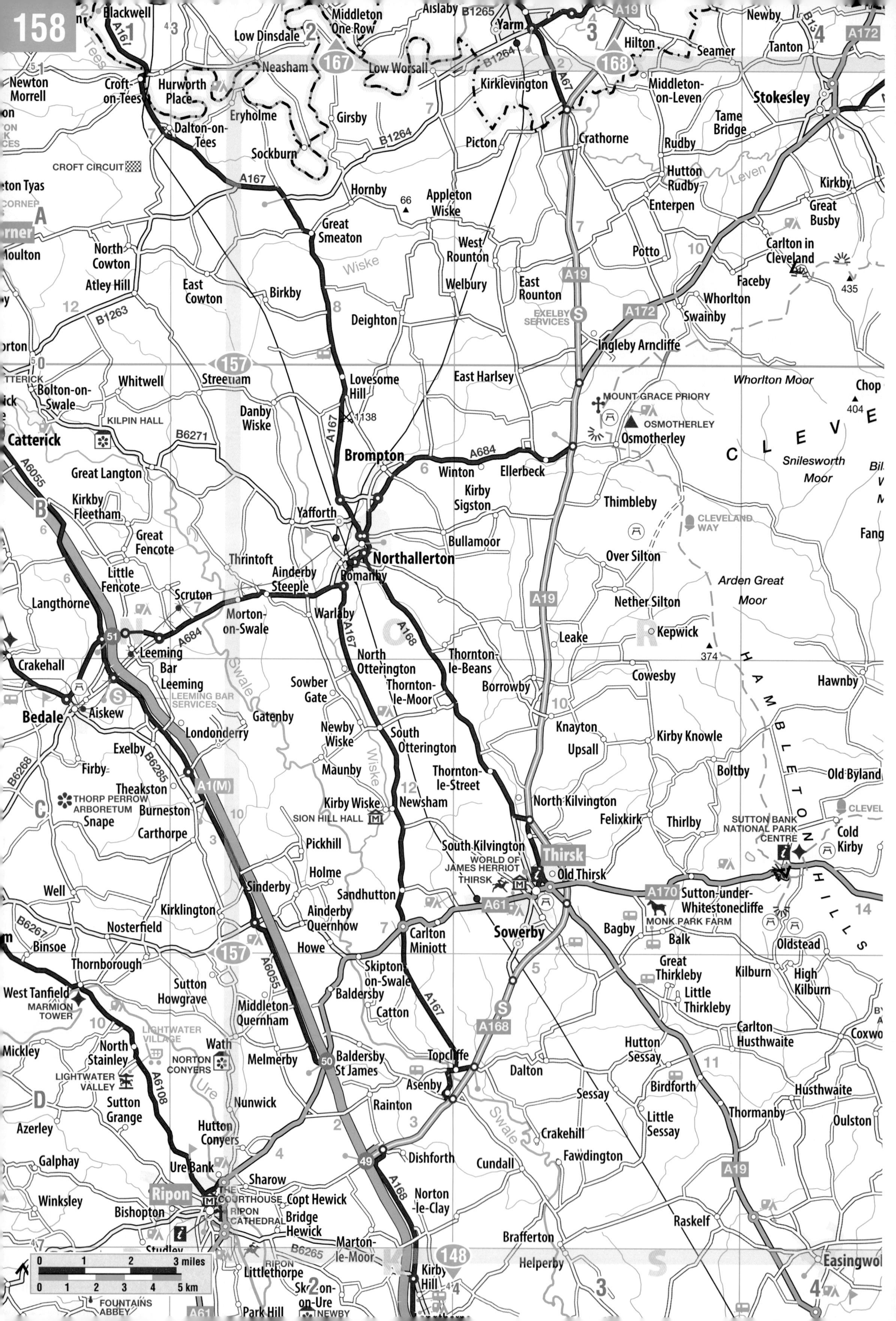
Blackwell
Middleton One Row
Aislaby
B1265
Yarm
A19
Newby
Tanton
A172
Low Dinsdale
Hilton
Seamer
167
168
Tees
Neasham
Low Worsall
B1264
Newton Morrell
Croft-on-Tees
Hurworth Place
Kirklevington
Middleton-on-Leven
Stokesley
Eryholme
Girsby
Dalton-on-Tees
Crathorne
Tame Bridge
B1264
Picton
Rudby
Sockburn
CROFT CIRCUIT
A167
Hutton Rudby
Leven
Hornby
Appleton Wiske
Enterpen
Kirkby
Great Busby
Great Smeaton
West Rounton
Potto
Carlton in Cleveland
Moulton
North Cowton
Wiske
Faceby
East Cowton
Atley Hill
Welbury
East Rounton
Birkby
Whorlton
435
B1263
Deighton
EXELBY SERVICES
A172
Swainby
Ingleby Arncliffe
157
Streetlam
Lovesome Hill
East Harlsey
Whorlton Moor
Whitwell
Chop
Bolton-on-Swale
MOUNT GRACE PRIORY
404
KILPIN HALL
Danby Wiske
1138
OSMOTHERLEY
Osmotherley
Catterick
B6271
A684
C L E V E
Snilesworth Moor
Brompton
Winton
Ellerbeck
A6055
Great Langton
Kirby Sigston
Kirkby Fleetham
Thimbleby
Yafforth
CLEVELAND WAY
Great Fencote
Bullamoor
Fang
Northallerton
Over Silton
Thrintoft
Little Fencote
Ainderby Steeple
Romanby
Arden Great Moor
Scruton
Langthorne
Morton-on-Swale
Warlaby
A19
Nether Silton
A167
A168
Leake
Kepwick
Leeming Bar
A684
North Otterington
Thornton-le-Beans
374
Crakehall
Leeming
Swale
Sowber Gate
Thornton-le-Moor
Borrowby
Cowesby
Hawnby
LEEMING BAR SERVICES
H A M B L E T O N H I L L S
Bedale
Aiskew
Gatenby
Newby Wiske
South Otterington
Knayton
Londonderry
Kirby Knowle
Exelby
Upsall
Upsall
B6285
Maunby
Wiske
Thornton-le-Street
Boltby
Firby
Old Byland
B6268
Theakston
A1(M)
THORP PERROW ARBORETUM
Kirby Wiske
Newsham
North Kilvington
Felixkirk
Burneston
Snape
SION HILL HALL
Thirlby
SUTTON BANK NATIONAL PARK CENTRE
Cold Kirby
Carthorpe
Pickhill
South Kilvington
WORLD OF JAMES HERRIOT
Thirsk
Holme
Old Thirsk
Well
Sinderby
Sandhutton
A170
Sutton-under-Whitestonecliffe
Kirklington
A61
Ainderby Quernhow
MONK PARK FARM
Nosterfield
B6267
Carlton Miniott
Sowerby
Bagby
Balk
Binsoe
Howe
157
Oldstead
Thornborough
Skipton-on-Swale
Great Thirkleby
Kilburn
High Kilburn
Sutton Howgrave
A6055
Baldersby
Little Thirkleby
West Tanfield
MARMION TOWER
Middleton Quernham
Catton
A167
A168
Carlton Husthwaite
Coxwold
LIGHTWATER VILLAGE
Wath
Hutton Sessay
Mickley
North Stainley
NORTON CONYERS
Melmerby
Baldersby St James
Topcliffe
Dalton
LIGHTWATER VALLEY
A6108
Ure
Asenby
Sessay
Birdforth
Husthwaite
Sutton Grange
Nunwick
Rainton
Thormanby
Azerley
Hutton Conyers
Swale
Little Sessay
Oulston
Crakehill
Galphay
Ure Bank
Dishforth
Cundall
Fawdington
A19
Sharow
Ripon
A168
Winksley
Bishopton
THE COURTHOUSE
Copt Hewick
Norton-le-Clay
RIPON CATHEDRAL
Bridge Hewick
Raskelf
Brafferton
Studley
Marton-le-Moor
B6265
148
Easingwold
Littlethorpe
Helperby
RIPON
Kirby Hill
Skelton-on-Ure
0 1 2 3 miles
0 1 2 3 4 5 km
FOUNTAINS ABBEY
Park Hill
NEWBY
A61

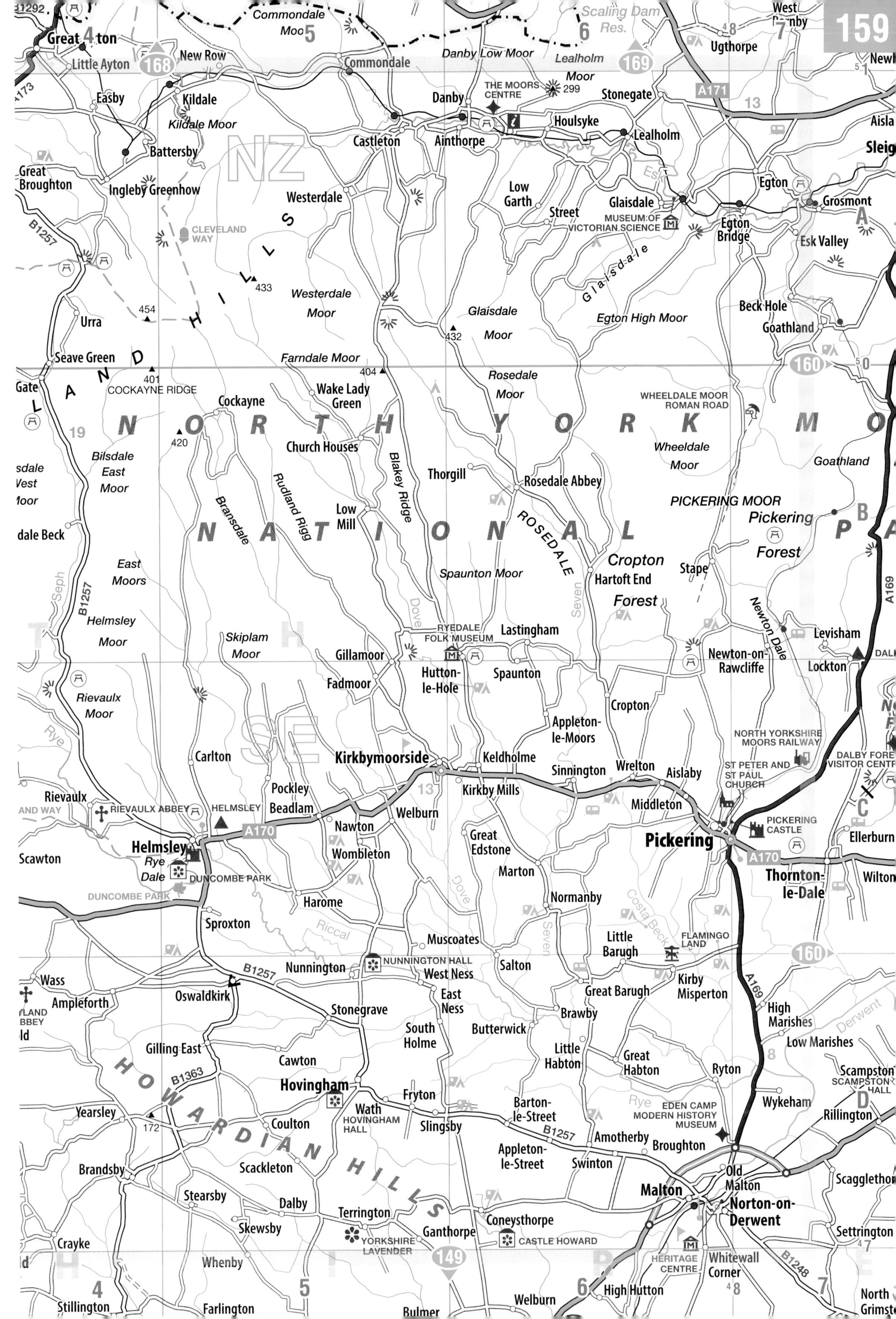
Commondale Moor
Scaling Dam Res.
West Danby
Ugthorpe
Great Ayton
Little Ayton
168
New Row
Commondale
Danby Low Moor
Lealholm Moor
169
299
THE MOORS CENTRE
Easby
Kildale
Kildale Moor
Danby
Stonegate
A171
Castleton
Ainthorpe
Houlsyke
Lealholm
Battersby
NZ
Great Broughton
Ingleby Greenhow
Westerdale
Low Garth
Street
Glaisdale
MUSEUM OF VICTORIAN SCIENCE
Egton
Egton Bridge
Grosmont
Esk Valley
CLEVELAND WAY
B1257
433
Glaisdale
Westerdale Moor
Glaisdale Moor
Egton High Moor
Beck Hole
Goathland
454
Urra
432
Seave Green
Farndale Moor
404
401
COCKAYNE RIDGE
Wake Lady Green
Rosedale Moor
WHEELDALE MOOR ROMAN ROAD
CLEVELAND HILLS
Cockayne
NORTH YORK MOORS NATIONAL PARK
420
Church Houses
Wheeldale Moor
Goathland
Bilsdale East Moor
Thorgill
Rosedale Abbey
PICKERING MOOR
Bransdale
Rudland Rigg
Blakey Ridge
Low Mill
ROSEDALE
Pickering Forest
Cropton Forest
Hartoft End
Stape
East Moors
Spaunton Moor
A169
Helmsley Moor
Newton Dale
RYEDALE FOLK MUSEUM
Lastingham
Levisham
Skiplam Moor
Gillamoor
Newton-on-Rawcliffe
Lockton
Hutton-le-Hole
Spaunton
Fadmoor
Rievaulx Moor
Cropton
Appleton-le-Moors
NORTH YORKSHIRE MOORS RAILWAY
Carlton
Kirkbymoorside
Keldholme
ST PETER AND ST PAUL CHURCH
DALBY FOREST VISITOR CENTRE
Sinnington
Wrelton
Aislaby
Pockley
Kirkby Mills
Rievaulx
RIEVAULX ABBEY
HELMSLEY
Beadlam
Middleton
Welburn
Nawton
A170
PICKERING CASTLE
Great Edstone
Pickering
Ellerburn
Helmsley
Wombleton
Scawton
Rye Dale
Thornton-le-Dale
Wilton
DUNCOMBE PARK
Marton
Harome
Normanby
Sproxton
Muscoates
Little Barugh
FLAMINGO LAND
160
Salton
Nunnington
NUNNINGTON HALL
B1257
Wass
West Ness
Kirby Misperton
Great Barugh
Ampleforth
Oswaldkirk
East Ness
Stonegrave
Brawby
High Marishes
South Holme
Butterwick
Low Marishes
Gilling East
Little Habton
Great Habton
Cawton
Ryton
Scampston
SCAMPSTON HALL
B1363
Hovingham
HOWARDIAN HILLS
Fryton
Wykeham
Yearsley
Wath
HOVINGHAM HALL
Barton-le-Street
EDEN CAMP MODERN HISTORY MUSEUM
Rillington
172
Coulton
Slingsby
Amotherby
Broughton
Appleton-le-Street
Swinton
Brandsby
Scackleton
Old Malton
Scagglethorpe
Malton
Stearsby
Dalby
Norton-on-Derwent
Terrington
Coneysthorpe
Skewsby
Ganthorpe
CASTLE HOWARD
Settrington
Crayke
YORKSHIRE LAVENDER
HERITAGE CENTRE
Whitewall Corner
B1248
Whenby
149
Stillington
Farlington
Bulmer
Welburn
High Hutton
North Grimston

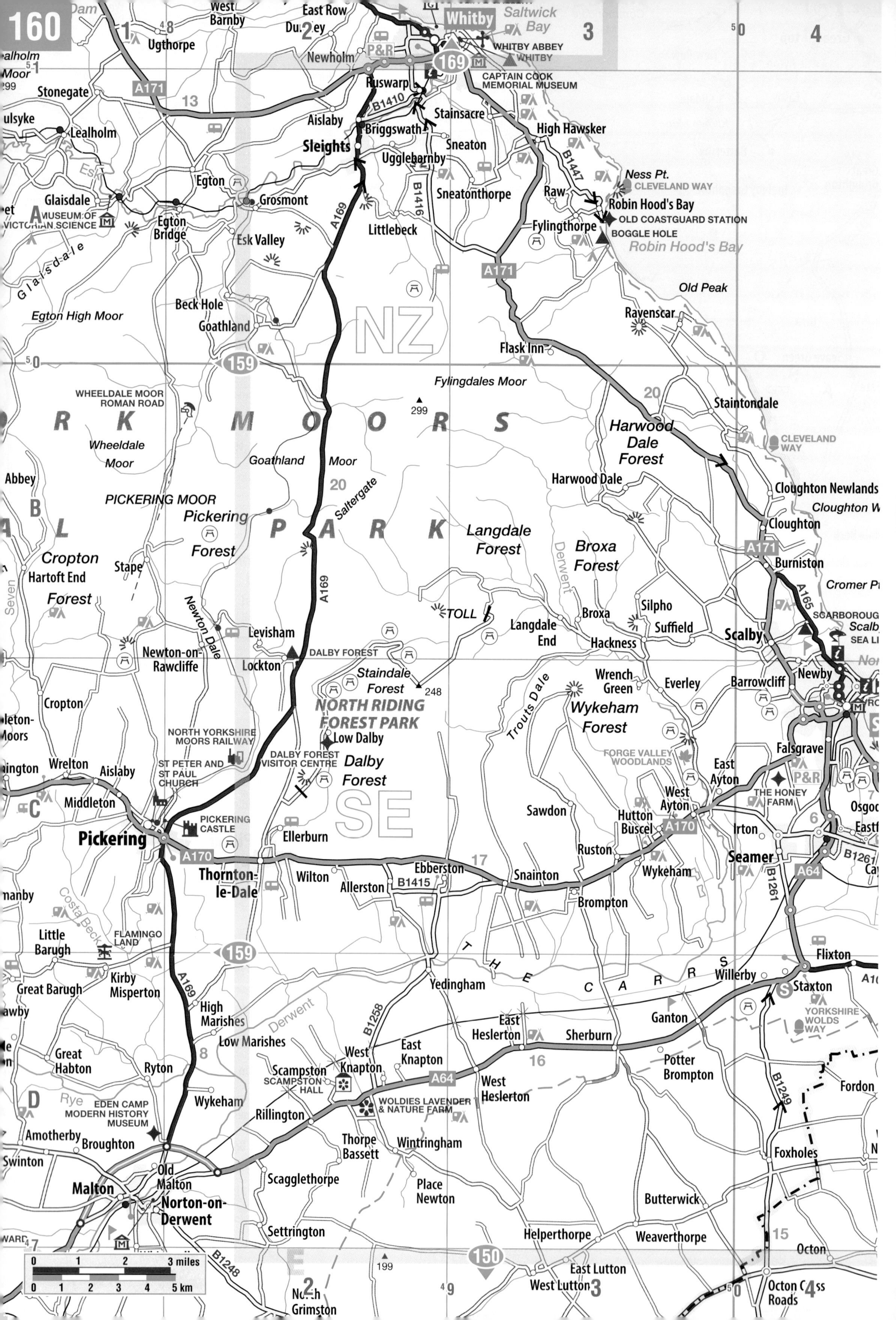
Ugthorpe
West Barnby
East Row
Whitby
Saltwick Bay
WHITBY ABBEY
WHITBY
Newholm
P&R
169
CAPTAIN COOK MEMORIAL MUSEUM
Stonegate
A171
13
Ruswarp
B1410
Stainsacre
Aislaby
Briggswath
High Hawsker
Lealholm
Sleights
Sneaton
Ugglebarnby
B1447
Ness Pt.
CLEVELAND WAY
Egton
B1416
Sneatonthorpe
Raw
Glaisdale
Grosmont
Robin Hood's Bay
MUSEUM OF VICTORIAN SCIENCE
OLD COASTGUARD STATION
Egton Bridge
A169
Littlebeck
Fylingthorpe
BOGGLE HOLE
Esk Valley
Robin Hood's Bay
Glaisdale
A171
Old Peak
Egton High Moor
Beck Hole
Ravenscar
Goathland
NZ
Flask Inn
159
Fylingdales Moor
WHEELDALE MOOR ROMAN ROAD
20
299
Staintondale
R K M O O R S
Harwood Dale Forest
Wheeldale Moor
CLEVELAND WAY
Goathland
Moor
Abbey
20
Harwood Dale
Saltergate
Cloughton Newlands
PICKERING MOOR
Pickering Forest
Cloughton
P A R K
Langdale Forest
Broxa Forest
Derwent
A171
Cropton
Burniston
Hartoft End
Stape
Forest
Seven
Newton Dale
A169
A165
Silpho
Suffield
TOLL
Broxa
Scalby
Levisham
Langdale End
Hackness
DALBY FOREST
Newton-on-Rawcliffe
Lockton
Staindale Forest
Wrench Green
Everley
Barrowcliff
Newby
248
Trouts Dale
Cropton
NORTH RIDING FOREST PARK
Wykeham Forest
NORTH YORKSHIRE MOORS RAILWAY
Low Dalby
FORGE VALLEY WOODLANDS
Falsgrave
Wrelton
Aislaby
ST PETER AND ST PAUL CHURCH
DALBY FOREST VISITOR CENTRE
Dalby Forest
East Ayton
P&R
West Ayton
THE HONEY FARM
Middleton
SE
Sawdon
Hutton Buscel
PICKERING CASTLE
A170
Irton
Pickering
Ellerburn
Ruston
Seamer
A170
17
Thornton-le-Dale
Wilton
Allerston
Ebberston
Snainton
Wykeham
B1261
A64
B1415
Brompton
Costa Beck
FLAMINGO LAND
Little Barugh
159
T H E C A R R S
Flixton
Kirby Misperton
Yedingham
Willerby
Staxton
Great Barugh
A169
High Marishes
Derwent
East Heslerton
Sherburn
Ganton
YORKSHIRE WOLDS WAY
B1258
Low Marishes
8
West Knapton
East Knapton
16
Potter Brompton
Great Habton
Ryton
Scampston
SCAMPSTON HALL
A64
West Heslerton
B1249
Fordon
Rye
EDEN CAMP MODERN HISTORY MUSEUM
Wykeham
WOLDIES LAVENDER & NATURE FARM
Rillington
Amotherby
Broughton
Thorpe Bassett
Wintringham
Foxholes
Swinton
Old Malton
Scagglethorpe
Malton
Place Newton
Butterwick
Norton-on-Derwent
Settrington
Helperthorpe
Weaverthorpe
15
Octon
B1248
150
199
East Lutton
West Lutton
Octon Cross Roads
North Grimston
0 1 2 3 miles
0 1 2 3 4 5 km

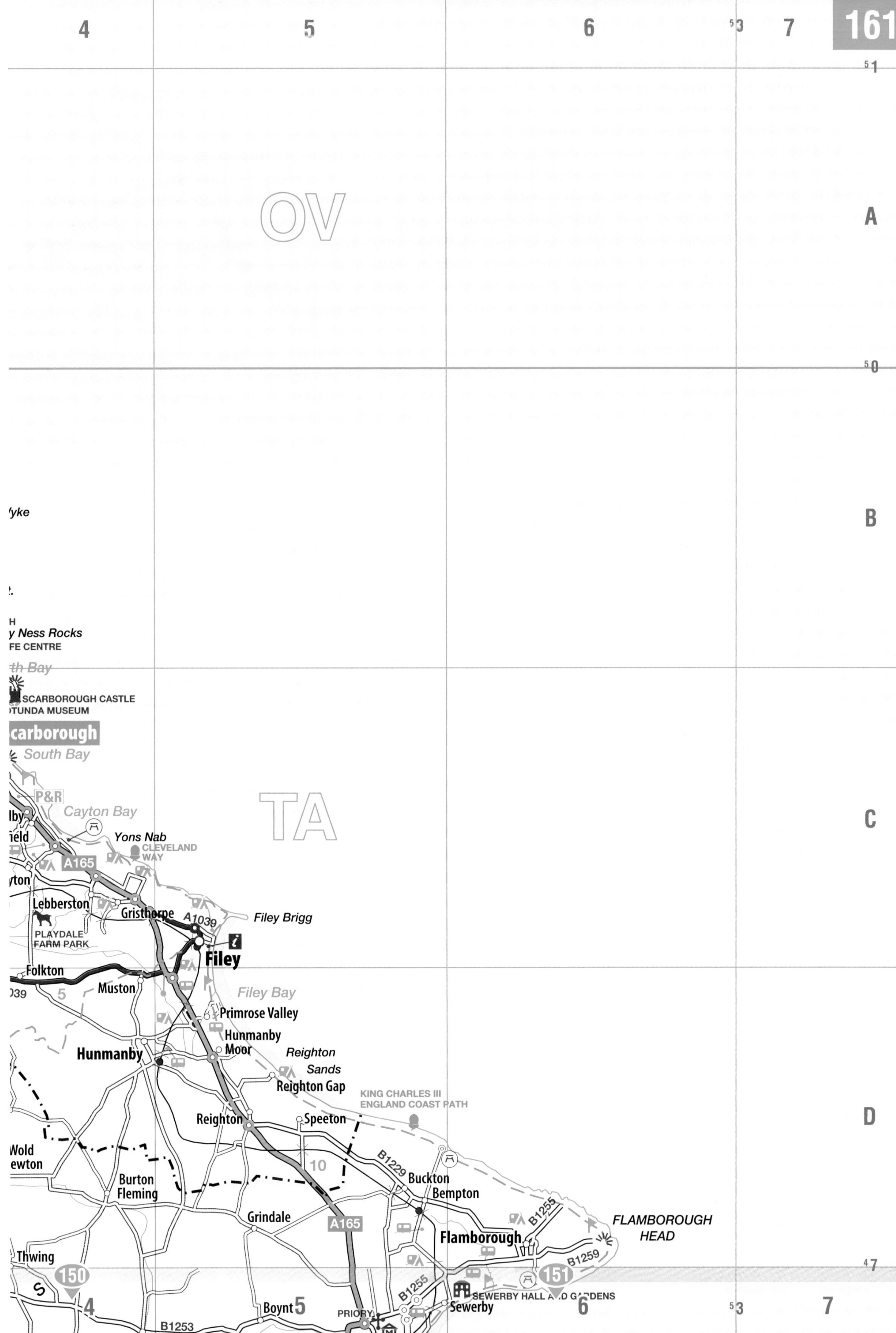
4
5
6
53
7
51
A
OV
50
B
/yke
y Ness Rocks
FE CENTRE
th Bay
SCARBOROUGH CASTLE
)TUNDA MUSEUM
carborough
South Bay
P&R
Cayton Bay
C
TA
Yons Nab
CLEVELAND WAY
A165
Lebberston
Gristhorpe
A1039
Filey Brigg
PLAYDALE FARM PARK
Filey
Folkton
Muston
Filey Bay
Primrose Valley
Hunmanby Moor
Hunmanby
Reighton Sands
Reighton Gap
KING CHARLES III ENGLAND COAST PATH
D
Reighton
Speeton
Wold Newton
B1229
Buckton
Bempton
Burton Fleming
10
Grindale
A165
B1255
FLAMBOROUGH HEAD
Flamborough
B1259
47
Thwing
150
151
Sewerby
SEWERBY HALL AND GARDENS
Boynt
PRIORY
B1253
B1255

Allonby Bay
Allerby
Crosscanonby
Crosby
MARYPORT MARITIME MUSEUM
Maryport
Dearham
A594
Flimby
Dovenby
Broughton Moor
Standingstone
A596
Great Broughton
Little Broughton
Siddick
Camerton
Seaton
Derwent
Great Clifton
Bridgefoot
North Side
Stainburn
Greysouthen
Workington
HELENA THOMPSON MUS
Little Clifton
Westfield
A595
Eaglesfield
Mossbay
A596
Deanscales
Winscales
Harrington
High Harrington
Dean
Branthwaite
NX
Distington
Ullock
Lowca
Pica
Moresby
247
Asby
Parton
Moresby Parks
Arlecdon
Bransty
A5086
THE RUM STORY
WALK MILL
Rowrah
HIGH LEYS
Kirkland
Whitehaven
Frizington
B5294
Hensingham
Saltom Bay
Cleator Moor
Mirehouse
Ennerdale Bridge
Sandwith
ST BEES HEAD
A595
Moor Row
B5295
Wath Brow
A5086
Rottington
Cleator
LONGLANDS LAKE
St Bees
Egremont
Wilton
B5345
Coulderton
Thornhill
Middletown
Haile
Calder
322
Nethertown
Beckermet
Calder Bridge
Braystones
A595
High Sellafield
Wellington
Calder Hall
Gosforth
B5344
Seascale
HALLSENNA MOOR
Holmrook
B5344
Drigg
Irt
173
174
153
0 1 2 3 miles
0 1 2 3 4 5 km

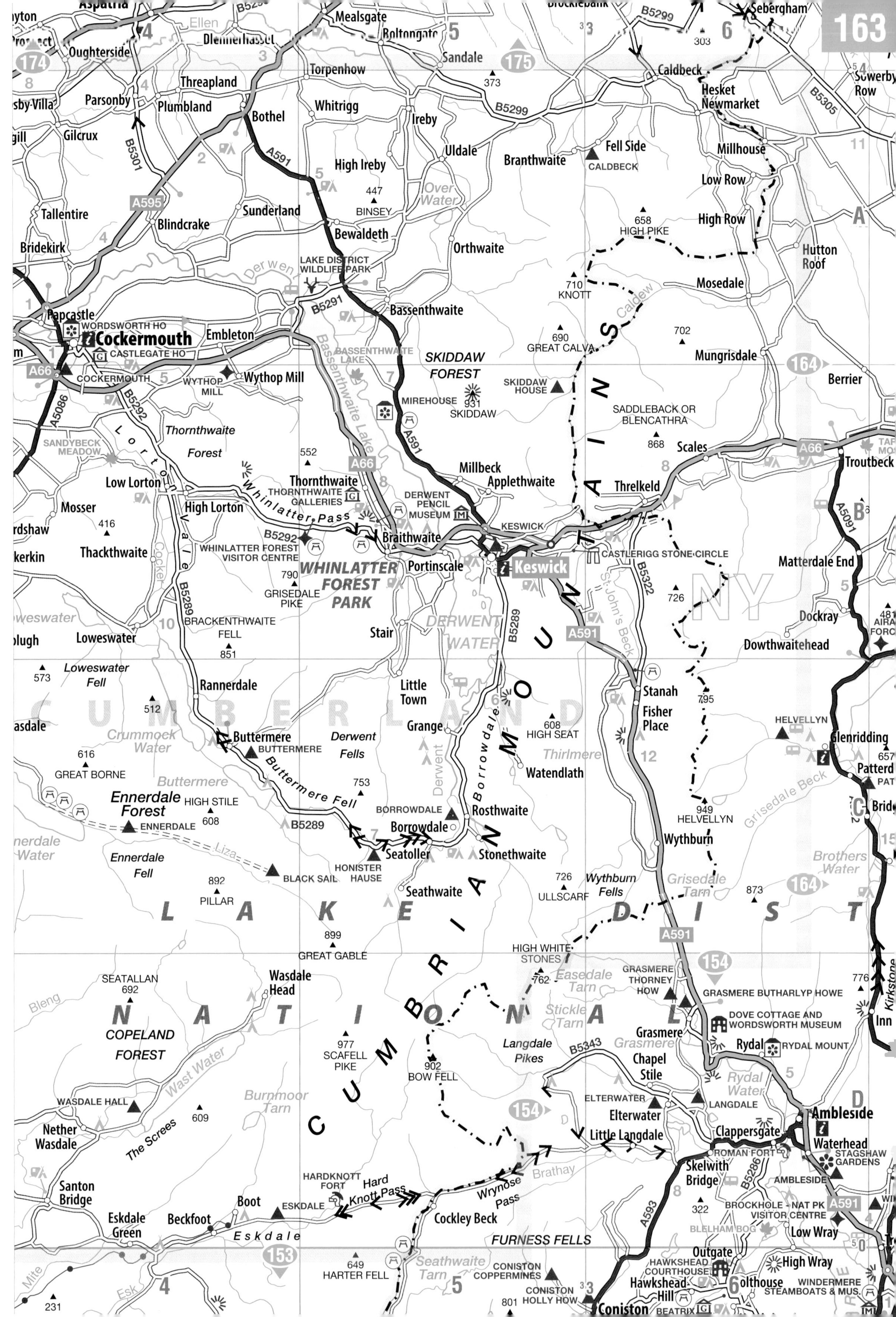

Mealsgate
Boltongate
Sebergham
Oughterside
Dlennerhasset
174
175
Sandale
Torpenhow
Caldbeck
Hesket Newmarket
Sowerby Row
Threapland
Parsonby
Plumbland
Bothel
Whitrigg
Ireby
B5299
B5305
Gilcrux
B5301
A591
High Ireby
Uldale
Branthwaite
Fell Side
CALDBECK
Millhouse
Low Row
Over Water
447
BINSEY
Tallentire
A595
Blindcrake
Sunderland
Bewaldeth
Orthwaite
658
HIGH PIKE
High Row
Hutton Roof
Bridekirk
Derwent
LAKE DISTRICT WILDLIFE PARK
710
KNOTT
Mosedale
Caldew
Papcastle
WORDSWORTH HO
Cockermouth
CASTLEGATE HO
Embleton
B5291
Bassenthwaite
690
GREAT CALVA
702
Mungrisdale
164
Berrier
A66
COCKERMOUTH
WYTHOP MILL
Wythop Mill
BASSENTHWAITE LAKE
Bassenthwaite Lake
SKIDDAW FOREST
SKIDDAW HOUSE
MIREHOUSE
931
SKIDDAW
SADDLEBACK OR BLENCATHRA
868
Scales
A5086
B5292
SANDYBECK MEADOW
Lorton
Thornthwaite Forest
552
Thornthwaite
THORNTHWAITE GALLERIES
Millbeck
Applethwaite
Threlkeld
Troutbeck
Low Lorton
Mosser
High Lorton
Whinlatter Pass
DERWENT PENCIL MUSEUM
A5091
416
Thackthwaite
WHINLATTER FOREST VISITOR CENTRE
Braithwaite
KESWICK
CASTLERIGG STONE CIRCLE
Keswick
Matterdale End
WHINLATTER FOREST PARK
Portinscale
790
GRISEDALE PIKE
Cocker
Vale
B5289
B5322
726
NY
Dockray
Loweswater
BRACKENTHWAITE FELL
Stair
DERWENT WATER
St John's Beck
A591
Dowthwaitehead
851
Loweswater Fell
573
Rannerdale
Little Town
Stanah
Fisher Place
795
512
CUMBERLAND
Buttermere
BUTTERMERE
Grange
608
HIGH SEAT
Derwent Fells
Borrowdale
Thirlmere
HELVELLYN
Glenridding
Crummock Water
Watendlath
Patterdale
616
GREAT BORNE
Buttermere Fell
753
Buttermere
Ennerdale Forest
HIGH STILE
BORROWDALE
Rosthwaite
949
HELVELLYN
Grisedale Beck
ENNERDALE
B5289
Borrowdale
Wythburn
Ennerdale Water
Liza
Seatoller
Stonethwaite
Brothers Water
Ennerdale Fell
BLACK SAIL
HONISTER HAUSE
726
ULLSCARF
Wythburn Fells
Grisedale Tarn
892
PILLAR
Seathwaite
873
LAKE DISTRICT
899
GREAT GABLE
HIGH WHITE STONES
154
SEATALLAN
692
Wasdale Head
762
Easedale Tarn
GRASMERE THORNEY HOW
GRASMERE BUTHARLYP HOWE
776
Bleng
NATIONAL
CUMBRIAN MOUNTAINS
Stickle Tarn
DOVE COTTAGE AND WORDSWORTH MUSEUM
Kirkstone
Inn
COPELAND FOREST
977
SCAFELL PIKE
Langdale Pikes
Grasmere
B5343
Rydal
RYDAL MOUNT
902
BOW FELL
Chapel Stile
Rydal Water
Wast Water
Burnmoor Tarn
WASDALE HALL
609
ELTERWATER
Elterwater
LANGDALE
Ambleside
Nether Wasdale
The Screes
Little Langdale
Clappersgate
Waterhead
ROMAN FORT
STAGSHAW GARDENS
Brathay
Skelwith Bridge
B5286
AMBLESIDE
HARDKNOTT FORT
Hard Knott Pass
Wrynose Pass
Santon Bridge
Boot
ESKDALE
A593
322
BROCKHOLE - NAT PK VISITOR CENTRE
Eskdale Green
Beckfoot
Cockley Beck
BLELHAM BOG
Low Wray
Eskdale
FURNESS FELLS
Outgate
153
649
HARTER FELL
Seathwaite Tarn
CONISTON COPPERMINES
HAWKSHEAD COURTHOUSE
High Wray
Hawkshead
Hawkshead Hill
Colthouse
WINDERMERE STEAMBOATS & MUS.
Mite
Esk
231
CONISTON HOLLY HOW
801
Coniston
BEATRIX

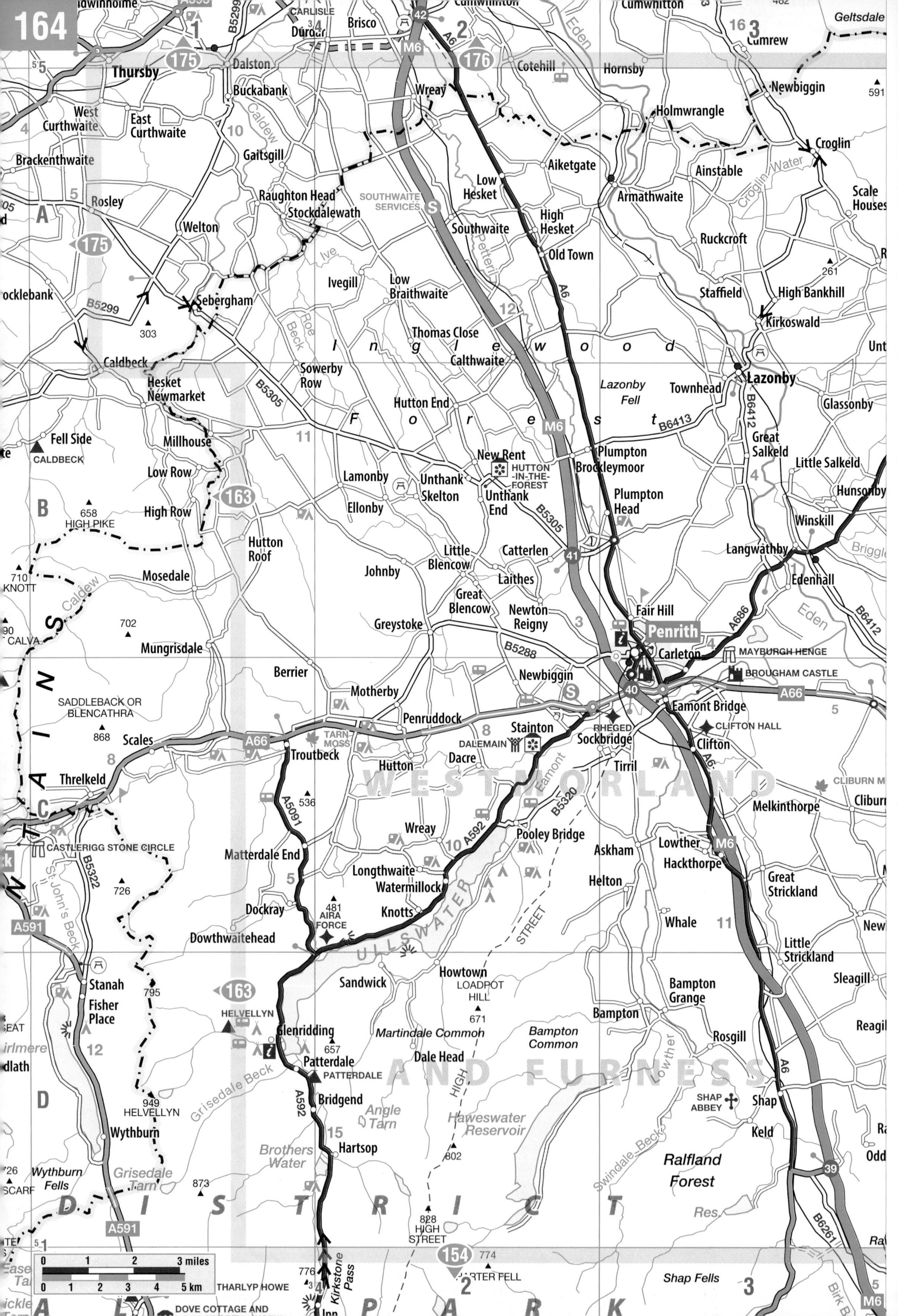


175
176
163
154

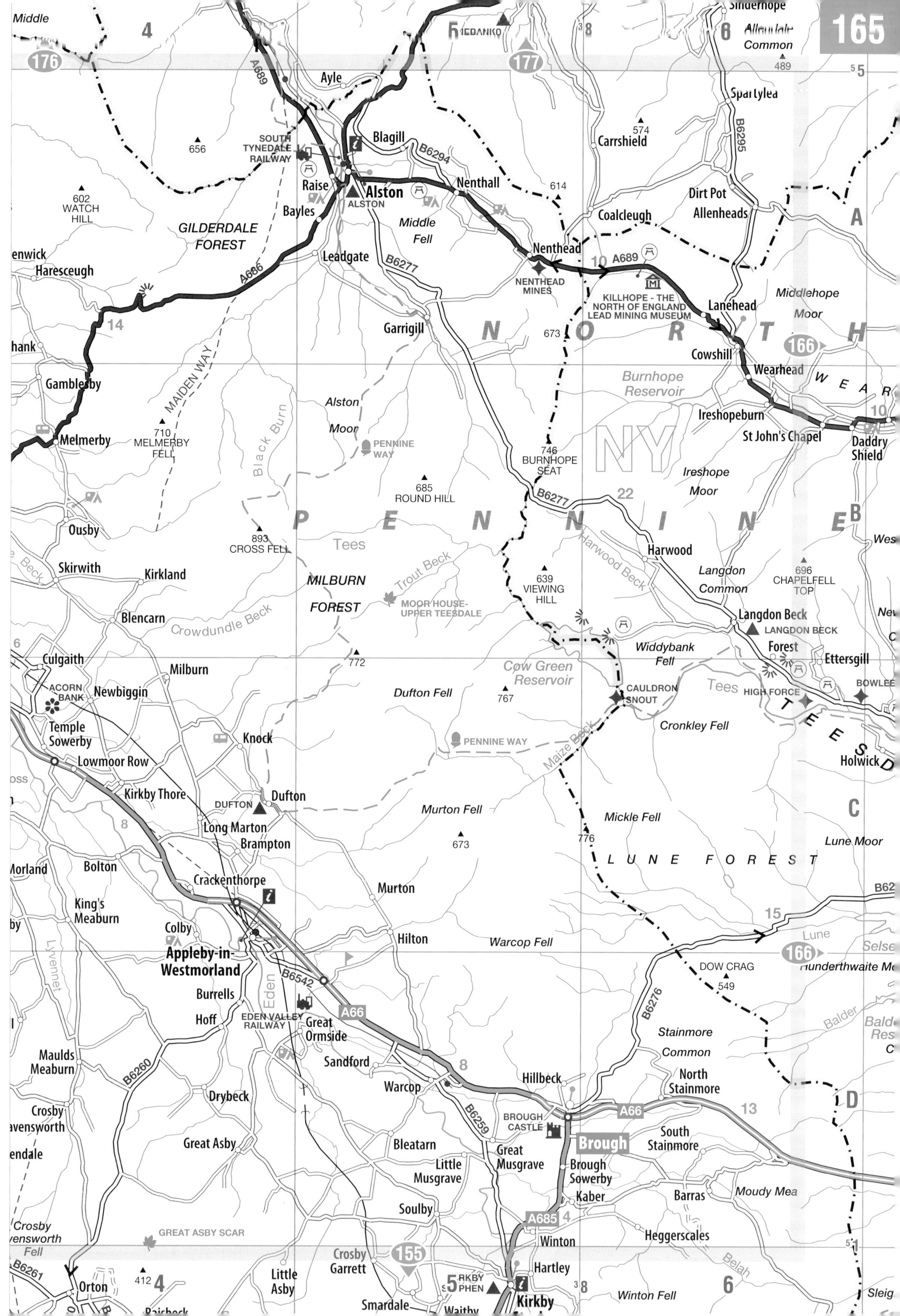
Middle
4
5
6
176
177
Allendale Common
489
Ayle
A689
Spartylea
B6295
574
Carrshield
656
SOUTH TYNEDALE RAILWAY
Blagill
B6294
Nenthall
614
602 WATCH HILL
Raise
Alston
ALSTON
Bayles
Middle Fell
Dirt Pot
Allenheads
Coalcleugh
GILDERDALE FOREST
Nenthead
Leadgate
B6277
A686
10
NENTHEAD MINES
KILLHOPE - THE NORTH OF ENGLAND LEAD MINING MUSEUM
Harescugh
14
Garrigill
Lanehead
Middlehope Moor
673
NORTH
166
Cowshill
Wearhead
WEAR
Gamblesby
MAIDEN WAY
Burnhope Reservoir
Alston Moor
Ireshopeburn
St John's Chapel
Daddry Shield
Melmerby
710 MELMERBY FELL
Black Burn
PENNINE WAY
746 BURNHOPE SEAT
NY
Ireshope Moor
685 ROUND HILL
B6277
22
Ousby
PENNINE
893 CROSS FELL
Tees
Harwood
Harwood Beck
Langdon Common
696 CHAPELFELL TOP
Skirwith
Kirkland
MILBURN FOREST
Trout Beck
639 VIEWING HILL
MOOR HOUSE-UPPER TEESDALE
Blencarn
Crowdundle Beck
Langdon Beck
LANGDON BECK
Forest
Widdybank Fell
Ettersgill
Culgaith
772
Milburn
Cow Green Reservoir
ACORN BANK
Newbiggin
Dufton Fell
767
CAULDRON SNOUT
Tees
HIGH FORCE
BOWLEES
Temple Sowerby
Cronkley Fell
TEESDALE
Knock
PENNINE WAY
Maize Beck
Lowmoor Row
Holwick
Kirkby Thore
DUFTON
Dufton
Murton Fell
C
8
Long Marton
Brampton
Mickle Fell
Lune Moor
673
776
Bolton
LUNE FOREST
Crackenthorpe
Murton
King's Meaburn
B62
15
Colby
Hilton
Appleby-in-Westmorland
Warcop Fell
Lune
166
Lyvennet
Eden
B6542
DOW CRAG 549
Hunderthwaite Moor
Burrells
B6276
Hoff
EDEN VALLEY RAILWAY
A66
Great Ormside
Stainmore Common
Maulds Meaburn
Sandford
8
Hillbeck
North Stainmore
B6260
Warcop
Drybeck
B6259
BROUGH CASTLE
A66
13
D
Great Asby
Brough
South Stainmore
Bleatarn
Great Musgrave
Little Musgrave
Brough Sowerby
Kaber
Barras
Moudy Mea
Soulby
A685
Crosby Ravensworth Fell
GREAT ASBY SCAR
Winton
Heggerscales
Crosby Garrett
155
Hartley
Belah
B6261
412
Little Asby
KIRKBY STEPHEN
Kirkby
Winton Fell
Orton
Smardale
Waitby
Sleightholme

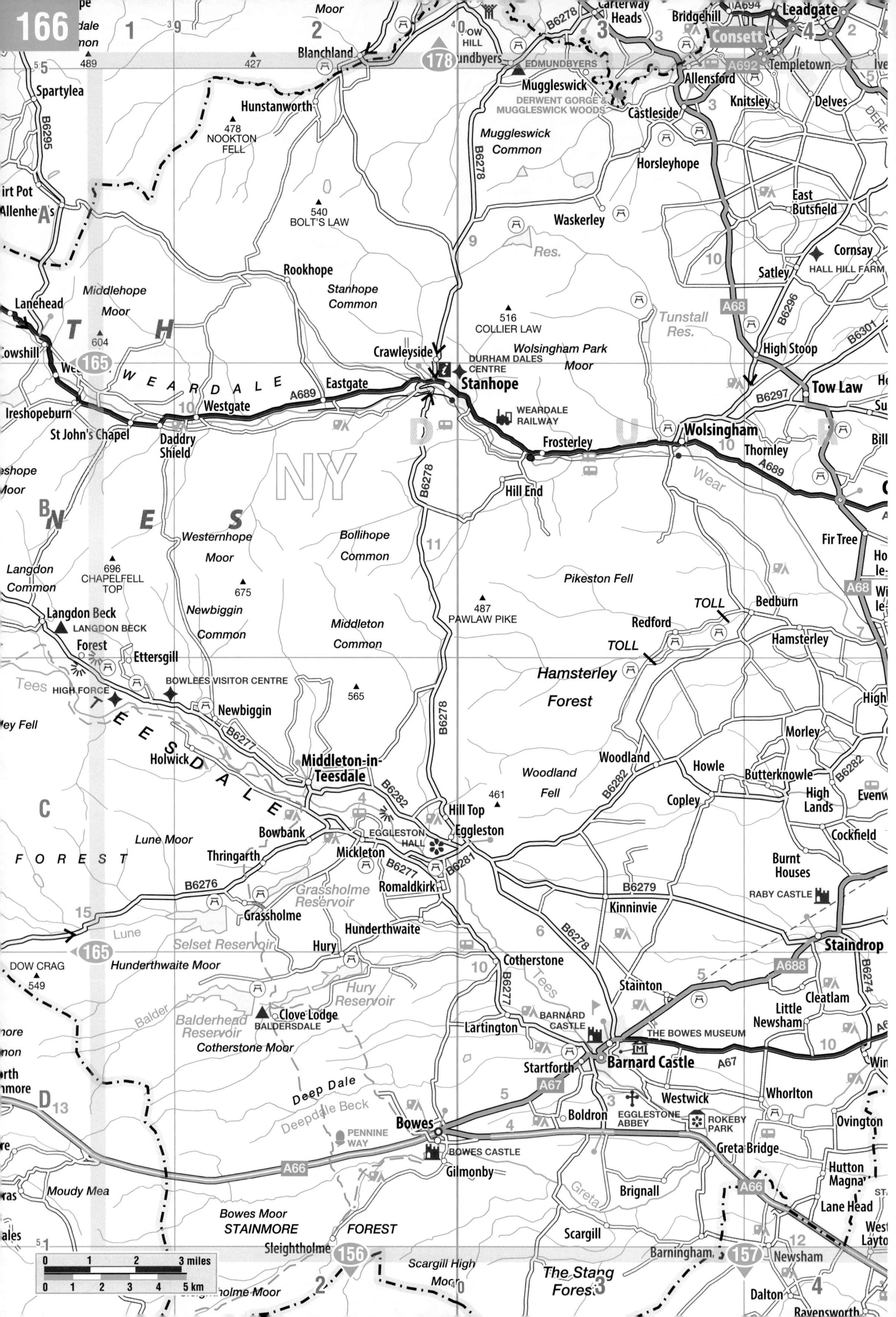

Moor
Blanchland
489
427
Spartylea
B6295
Hunstanworth
478
NOOKTON
FELL
Allenheads
540
BOLT'S LAW
Rookhope
Stanhope
Common
Middlehope
Moor
Lanehead
604
Cowshill
165
WEARDALE
Eastgate
A689
Westgate
Ireshopeburn
St John's Chapel
Daddry
Shield
Crawleyside
DURHAM DALES
CENTRE
Stanhope
WEARDALE
RAILWAY
Frosterley
Hill End
B6278
NY
Westernhope
Moor
Bollihope
Common
Langdon
Common
696
CHAPELFELL
TOP
675
Newbiggin
Common
Middleton
Common
Langdon Beck
LANGDON BECK
Forest
Ettersgill
BOWLEES VISITOR CENTRE
Tees
HIGH FORCE
565
Newbiggin
B6277
TEESDALE
Holwick
Middleton-in-
Teesdale
B6282
Bowbank
Lune Moor
Thringarth
FOREST
Mickleton
EGGLESTON
HALL
Eggleston
Hill Top
Romaldkirk
B6281
B6276
Grassholme
Reservoir
Grassholme
Hunderthwaite
Hury
Lune
Selset Reservoir
DOW CRAG
549
Hunderthwaite Moor
Hury
Reservoir
Balder
Balderhead
Reservoir
Clove Lodge
BALDERSDALE
Cotherstone Moor
Cotherstone
Deep Dale
Deepdale Beck
PENNINE
WAY
Bowes
BOWES CASTLE
Gilmonby
A66
Moudy Mea
Bowes Moor
STAINMORE
FOREST
Sleightholme
156
Scargill High
Moor
Muggleswick
DERWENT GORGE &
MUGGLESWICK WOODS
EDMUNDBYERS
178
Edmundbyers
Muggleswick
Common
B6278
Carterway
Heads
Bridgehill
A694
Leadgate
Consett
A692
Templetown
Allensford
Castleside
Knitsley
Delves
Horsleyhope
Waskerley
Res.
East
Butsfield
Cornsay
HALL HILL FARM
Satley
516
COLLIER LAW
Wolsingham Park
Moor
Tunstall
Res.
A68
B6296
High Stoop
B6301
Tow Law
B6297
Wolsingham
Thornley
A689
Wear
Fir Tree
Pikeston Fell
487
PAWLAW PIKE
TOLL
Bedburn
Redford
TOLL
Hamsterley
Hamsterley
Forest
Morley
Woodland
Woodland
Fell
461
Howle
Butterknowle
B6282
Copley
High
Lands
Cockfield
Burnt
Houses
B6279
RABY CASTLE
Kinninvie
B6278
Staindrop
A688
B6274
B6277
Tees
Stainton
Cleatlam
Little
Newsham
BARNARD
CASTLE
Lartington
THE BOWES MUSEUM
Barnard Castle
A67
Startforth
A67
Westwick
Whorlton
Boldron
EGGLESTONE
ABBEY
ROKEBY
PARK
Ovington
Greta Bridge
Hutton
Magna
Greta
Brignall
A66
Lane Head
Scargill
Barningham
157
Newsham
The Stang
Forest
Dalton
Ravensworth
0 1 2 3 miles
0 1 2 3 4 5 km

The Middles
Grange Villa
CHESTER-LE-STREET
Herrington
Doxford Park
Burdon
Annfield Plain
Craghead
THE ANKERS HOUSE
Bournmoor
Newbottle
THE FARM
Fence Houses
Seaton
Northlea
SEAHAM
Maiden Law
Waldridge
Chester Moor
Great Lumley
Colliery Row
HOUGHTON-LE-SPRING
West Lea
Burnhope
Edmondsley
WALDRIDGE FELL
East Rainton
Dalton-le-Dale
Lanchester
Nettlesworth
Plawsworth
West Rainton
Hetton-le-Hole
Cold Hesledon
BROOM HOUSE FARM
Sacriston
Kimblesworth
FINCHALE PRIORY
Leamside
Murton
DALTON PARK
Witton Gilbert
Pity Me
Low Moorsley
Easington Lane
Hawthorn
DIGGERLAND
Framwellgate Moor
Pittington
South Hetton
Langley Park
Carrville
Littletown
Easington
Esh
Bearpark
Haswell
Cornsay Colliery
Quebec
Durham
Sherburn
Sherburn Hill
Haswell Plough
Ushaw Moor
Broompark
DURHAM CITY
DURHAM CATH
Shotton Colliery
Horden
Waterhouses
Esh Winning
New Brancepeth
DURHAM UNIV ORIENTAL MUS
Shadforth
Ludworth
Shincliffe
PETERLEE
East Hedleyhope
Brandon
Old Cassop
Thornley
Shotton
CASTLE EDEN DENE
Wheatley Hill
193
Cassop
Castle Eden
Brancepeth
Bowburn
Old Quarrington
CASSOP VALE
Hesleden
Sunderland Bridge
DURHAM SERVICES
Wingate
Croxdale
Hett
Quarrington Hill
Deaf Hill
Station Town
Oakenshaw
Page Bank
Kelloe
Helmington Row
Tudhoe
Trimdon Grange
Hutton Henry
Crook
Willington
Coxhoe
Trimdon Colliery
Sheraton
Cornforth
Trimdon
Byers Green
Spennymoor
Ferryhill
THRISLINGTON
Ferryhill Station
Newfield
Middlestone Moor
Fishburn
Hunwick
Kirk Merrington
High Grange
Binchester Blocks
BINCHESTER FORT
Mainsforth
Westerton
Bishop Middleham
Witton Park
Toronto
AUCKLAND CASTLE
Middlestone
Chilton Lane
Butterwick
ESCOMB CHURCH
Escomb
Coundon
Leasingthorne
Low Etherley
Chilton
HARDWICK HALL
Bishop Auckland
Sedgefield
Etherley
Rushyford
Toft Hill
Eldon
Bradbury
ST HELEN'S
Coundon Grange
Old Eldon
SEDGEFIELD
Shildon
Wynyard Village
St Helen Auckland
Middridge
NEWTON AYCLIFFE
Mordon
West Auckland
LOCOMOTION
Thorpe Larches
WYNYARD WOODLAND
222
Bildershaw
Evenwood Gate
Royal Oak
Foxton
Stillington
Redworth
Aycliffe
Thorpe Thewles
Wackerfield
Bolam
Heighington
Elstob
Whitton
Hilton
Great Stainton
Redmarshall
Carlton
Norton
Houghton-le-Side
Brafferton
Roseworth
Ingleton
Bishopton
Killerby
Walworth Gate
Coatham Mundeville
Little Stainton
Fairfield
Langton
Denton
Skerne
Stockton-on-Tees
Headlam
Summerhouse
Walworth
Beaumont Hill
Barmpton
Hartburn
Gainford
Harrowgate Hill
Great Burdon
Sadberge
Elton
Thornaby-on-Tees
High Coniscliffe
DARLINGTON
Longnewton
PRESTON PARK MUS & GROUNDS
Piercebridge
HEAD OF STEAM
Haughton-le-Skerne
Urlay Nook
Egglescliffe
ROMAN BRIDGE
Low Coniscliffe
Caldwell
Manfield
Darlington
Middleton St George
TEESSIDE INTERNATIONAL AIRPORT
Eaglescliffe
Ingleby Barwick
Eppleby
Cleasby
Forcett
High Leven
Carlton
Stapleton
Blackwell
Middleton One Row
Aislaby
STANWICK IRON AGE FORTIFICATIONS
Yarm
Stanwick-St-John
Aldbrough St John
Low Dinsdale
Neasham
Low Worsall
Kirklevington
East Layton
Newton Morrell
Croft-on-Tees
Hurworth Place
Melsonby
Barton
BARTON PARK
Eryholme
Girsby
Dalton-on-Tees

178
179
168
157
158

SEAHAM
179
HOUGHTON-LE-SPRING
Hetton-le-Hole
Murton
DALTON PARK
Easington Lane
South Hetton
Seaton
Northlea
Burdon
Doxford Park
West Lea
Dalton-le-Dale
Cold Hesledon
Hawthorn
Beacon Pt.
Easington Colliery
Easington
Haswell
Haswell Plough
Shotton Colliery
Horden
Ludworth
167
PETERLEE
Thornley
Wheatley Hill
Shotton
CASTLE EDEN DENE
Blackhall Colliery
Blackhall Rocks
Castle Eden
Hesleden
High Hesleden
DURHAM COAST
CASSOP VALE
Wingate
Deaf Hill
Station Town
Kelloe
Trimdon Grange
Trimdon Colliery
Trimdon
Hutton Henry
Sheraton
Hart Station
Hart
High Throston
ST HILDA'S PARISH CHURCH
THE NATIONAL MUS OF THE ROYAL NAVY
Hartlepool Bay
Hartlepool
Fishburn
Elwick
West Park
SUMMERHILL
HARTLEPOOL
Dalton Piercy
Rift House
Seaton Carew
Butterwick
HARDWICK HALL
SEDGEFIELD
Tees Bay
Greatham
Graythorp
Wynyard Village
Thorpe Larches
WYNYARD WOODLAND
Newton Bewley
COWPEN BEWLEY
Wolviston
Cowpen Bewley
TEESMOUTH
Salt Scar
REDCAR
Coatham
Foxton
Stillington
BILLINGHAM ART GALLERY
BILLINGHAM
Thorpe Thewles
Haverton Hill
Port Clarence
Dormanstown
REDCAR
KIRKLEATHAM OLD HALL MUSEUM
Marske-by-the-Sea
Whitton
Redmarshall
STOCKTON-ON-TEES
Norton
Roseworth
BILLINGHAM BECK
TOLL
South Bank
Grangetown
Kirkleatham
Yearby
New Marske
Bishopton
Little Stainton
Fairfield
North Ormesby
Lazenby
KIRKLEATHAM GARDEN
Wilton
Upleatham
Stockton-on-Tees
Middlesbrough
DORMAN MUSEUM
Eston
Dunsdale
TOCKETTS WATER MILL
Skelt
Hartburn
Normanby
MIDDLESBROUGH
Sadberge
Elton
Thornaby-on-Tees
Acklam
Park End
Ormesby
FLATTS LANE WOODLAND
242
REDCAR
GUISBOROUGH PRIORY
Longnewton
PRESTON PARK MUS & GROUNDS
Marton
ORMESBY HALL
Guisborough
Charltons
Urlay Nook
Eaglescliffe
CAPTAIN COOK BIRTHPLACE
Coulby Newham
GUISBOROUGH FOREST
Hutton Gate
CLEVELAND
Egglescliffe
Ingleby Barwick
Stainton
Thornton
Hemlington
Nunthorpe
Hutton Village
Gisborough Moor
Middleton St George
TEESSIDE INTERNATIONAL AIRPORT
High Leven
Maltby
Newton under Roseberry
329
Middleton One Row
Aislaby
Yarm
Newby
Common Moor
Hilton
Seamer
Tanton
Great Ayton
Little Ayton
New Row
Low Worsall
Kirklevington
Middleton-on-Leven
158
Stokesley
Easby
159
Kildale
Kildale Moor
Tame Bridge
Crathorne
0 1 2 3 miles
0 1 2 3 4 5 km
A19
A179
A689
A177
A178
A1185
A1086
A1049
A66
A1053
A174
A171
A1043
A172
A173
A1032
A1044
A67
A135
A1027
A1046
A182
A181
A1085
A1042
B1404
B1285
B1287
B1283
B1432
B1280
B1281
B1278
B1276
B1277
B1275
B1269
B1380
B1365
B1292
B1264
B1265

4
5
6
7
A
B
C
D
NZ
MINIATURE RAILWAY
Saltburn-by-the-Sea
166
Brotton
Skinningrove
KING CHARLES III ENGLAND COAST PATH
Boulby
Staithes
Carlin How
Loftus
A174
North Skelton
Kilton Thorpe
Easington
Port Mulgrave
Runswick Bay
Hinderwell
Lingdale
Margrove Park
Stanghow
Liverton
Roxby
Runswick Bay
Kettleness
Newton Mulgrave
Goldsborough
Moorsholm
B1366
Ellerby
Scaling
A174
Lythe
Sandsend
B1266
Sandsend Wyke
SUTCLIFFE GALLERY
Mickleby
East Barnby
West Barnby
East Row
Dunsley
Whitby
Saltwick Bay
Scaling Dam Res.
Ugthorpe
WHITBY ABBEY
WHITBY
Danby Low Moor
Lealholm Moor
299
Commondale
Newholm
P&R
CAPTAIN COOK MEMORIAL MUSEUM
159
160
Ruswarp
Danby
Stonegate
A171
13
Houlsyke
Aislaby
B1410
High Hawsker
Briggswath

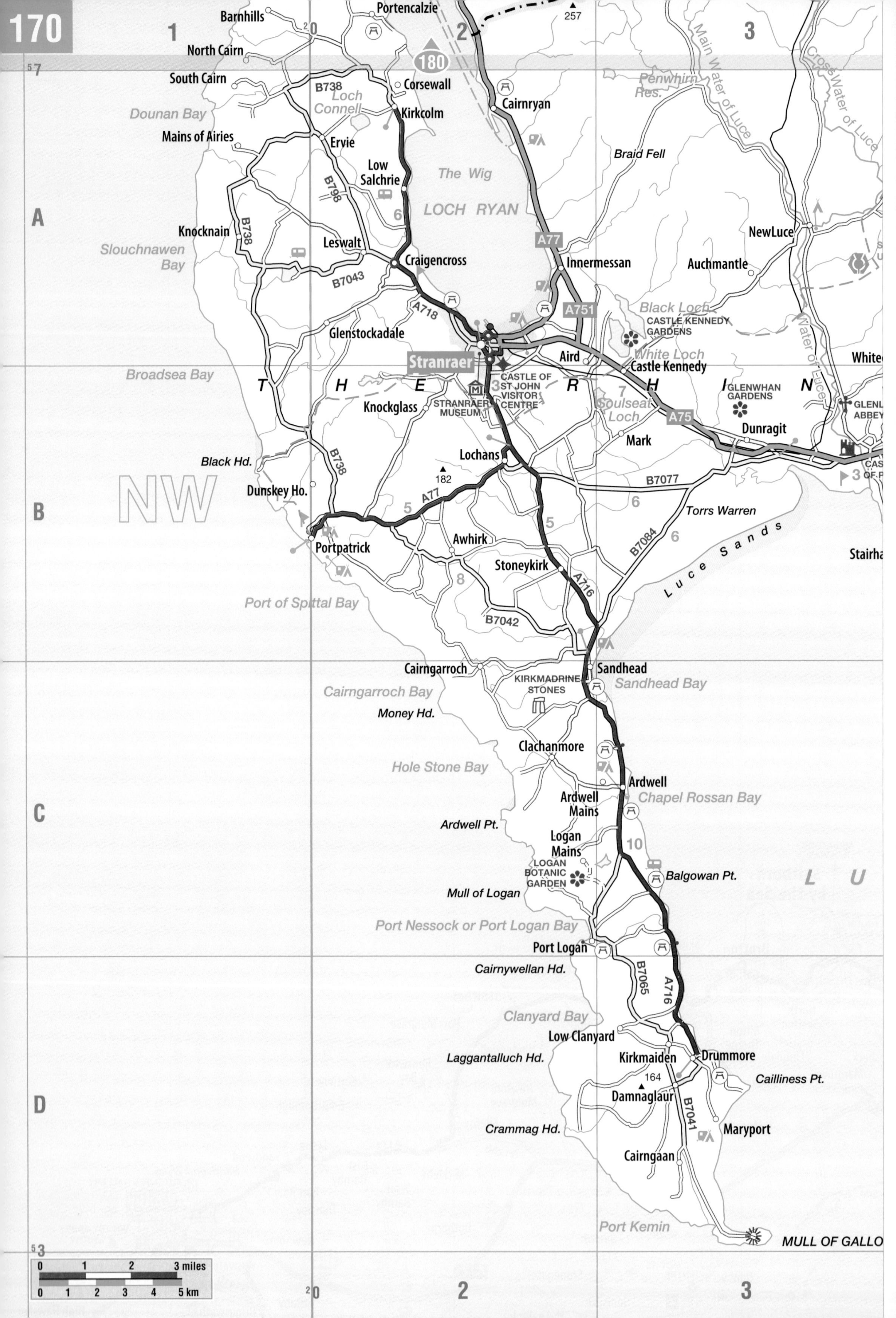
Barnhills
Portencalzie
North Cairn
South Cairn
Corsewall
Loch Connell
Kirkcolm
Dounan Bay
Mains of Airies
Ervie
Low Salchrie
The Wig
LOCH RYAN
Knocknain
Slouchnawen Bay
Leswalt
Craigencross
Cairnryan
Penwhirn Res.
Main Water of Luce
Cross Water of Luce
Braid Fell
NewLuce
Auchmantle
Innermessan
Black Loch
CASTLE KENNEDY GARDENS
White Loch
Castle Kennedy
Water of Luce
Glenstockadale
Stranraer
Aird
Broadsea Bay
THE RHINNS
Knockglass
STRANRAER MUSEUM
CASTLE OF ST JOHN VISITOR CENTRE
Soulseat Loch
GLENWHAN GARDENS
Dunragit
GLENLUCE ABBEY
Mark
Lochans
Black Hd.
Dunskey Ho.
NW
B7077
Torrs Warren
Luce Sands
Portpatrick
Awhirk
Stoneykirk
Port of Spittal Bay
B7042
B7084
Cairngarroch
Sandhead
Sandhead Bay
KIRKMADRINE STONES
Cairngarroch Bay
Money Hd.
Clachanmore
Hole Stone Bay
Ardwell
Chapel Rossan Bay
Ardwell Mains
Ardwell Pt.
Logan Mains
LOGAN BOTANIC GARDEN
Balgowan Pt.
Mull of Logan
Port Nessock or Port Logan Bay
Port Logan
Cairnywellan Hd.
B7065
Clanyard Bay
Low Clanyard
Laggantalluch Hd.
Kirkmaiden
Drummore
Cailliness Pt.
Damnaglaur
B7041
Crammag Hd.
Maryport
Cairngaan
Port Kemin
MULL OF GALLO
B738
B798
B7043
A718
A77
A751
A75
A716
180
257
182
164
0 1 2 3 miles
0 1 2 3 4 5 km

Newton Stewart
Wigtown
Whithorn
Glenluce
Port William
Isle of Whithorn
Penninghame Forest
THE MACHARS
Kirkcowan
Creetown
Garlieston
Monreith
Sorbie
Kirkinner
Glasserton
Burrow Head
Luce Bay
Monreith Bay
Auchenmalg Bay
Wigtown Sands
Baldoon Sands
Port Castle Bay
Barsalloch Pt.
Milton Pt.
Cairn Hd.
Port Allen
Portyerrock
Eggerness
Knock Moss
Torhousemuir
Scotland's Book Town
Visitor Centre
Kirroughtree Visitor Centre
Gem Rock Museum
Torhouse Stone Circle
Chapel Finian
Mote of Druchtag
Drumtroddan Stones
Barsalloch Fort
Priory and Museum
Whithorn Trust Discovery Centre
St Ninian's Cave
Fell of Carleton
Galloway House Gardens
Cruggleton
Wild Goat Park
Laggangairn Standing Stones
Artfield Fell
Challoch
Minnigaff
Creebridge
Benfield
Shennanton
Palnure
Baltersan
Causeway End
Carsegowan
Spittal
High Mindork
Craighlaw Mains
Carscreugh
Drumphail
Black Loch
Loch Heron
Loch Ronald
Dernaglar Loch
Whitefield Loch
Castle Loch
Fell Loch
Mochrum Loch
Culmazie
Bladnoch
Braehead
Culshabbin
Alticry
Auchenmalg
Milton
Loch Head
Barrachan
Elrig
Mochrum
Whauphill
Airyhassen
Drumtroddan
Drummoddie
Monreith Mains
Moor of Ravenstone
Bishopton
Cults
Cutcloy
Carsluith
A75
A714
A712
A747
A746
B7027
B733
B735
B7005
B7052
B7085
B7004
B7021
B7063
181
172
NX

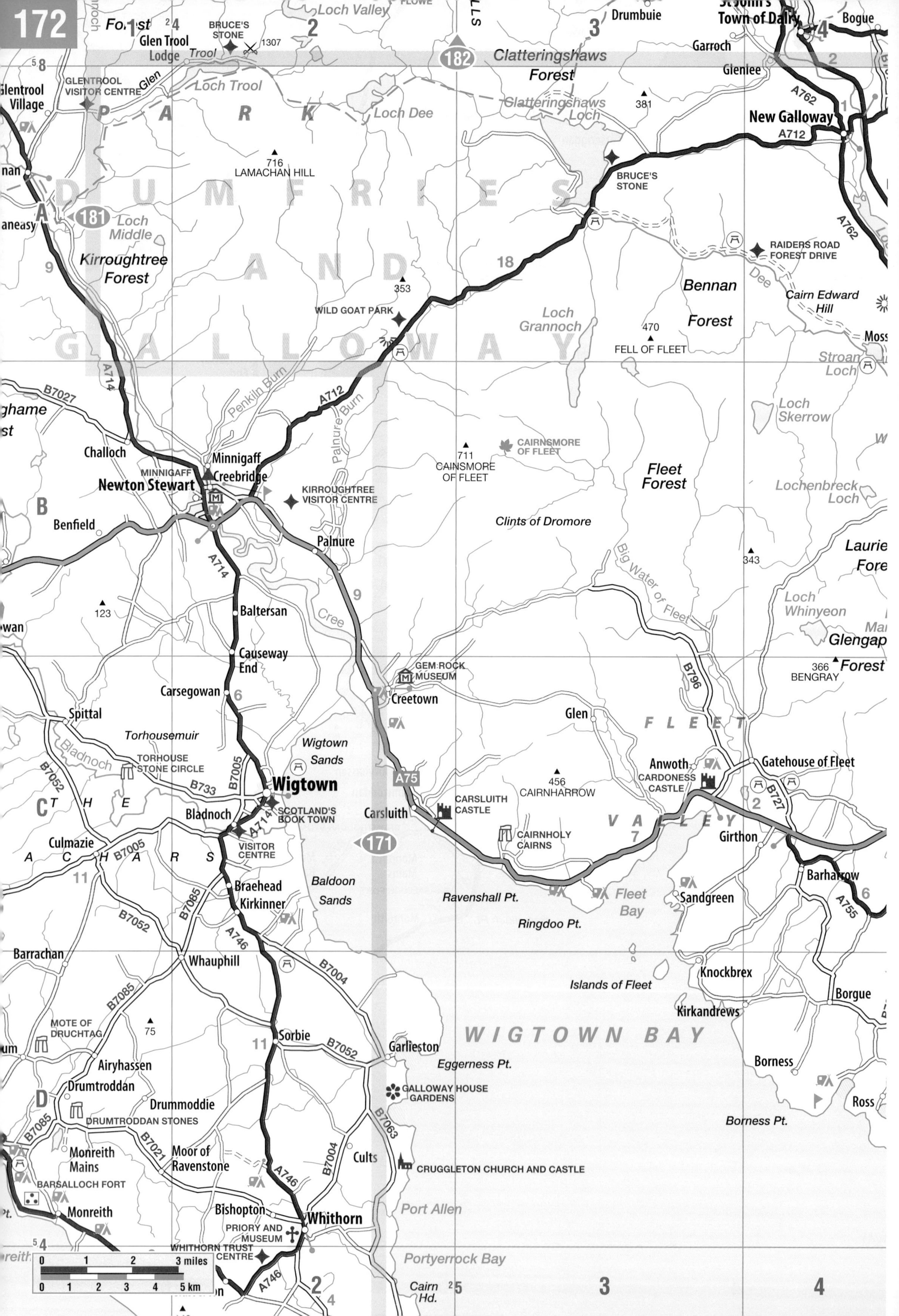
Glen Trool Lodge
BRUCE'S STONE
1307
Loch Valley
Drumbuie
Town of Dalry
Bogue
Garroch
182
Clatteringshaws Forest
Glenlee
Trool
Loch Trool
GLENTROOL VISITOR CENTRE
Glentrool Village
Glen
P A R K
Loch Dee
Clatteringshaws Loch
381
A762
New Galloway
A712
716
LAMACHAN HILL
BRUCE'S STONE
D U M F R I E S
A N D
G A L L O W A Y
181
Loch Middle
Kirroughtree Forest
RAIDERS ROAD FOREST DRIVE
A762
18
353
Bennan
Dee
Cairn Edward Hill
WILD GOAT PARK
Loch Grannoch
470
FELL OF FLEET
Forest
Stroan Loch
A714
B7027
Penkiln Burn
A712
Palnure Burn
Loch Skerrow
711
CAIRNSMORE OF FLEET
Challoch
Minnigaff
MINNIGAFF
Creebridge
Newton Stewart
KIRROUGHTREE VISITOR CENTRE
Fleet Forest
Lochenbreck Loch
Benfield
Clints of Dromore
Palnure
A714
Big Water of Fleet
343
Laurie
123
Baltersan
Cree
9
Loch Whinyeon
Glengap
Causeway End
366
BENGRAY
Forest
GEM ROCK MUSEUM
Carsegowan
6
B796
Creetown
Glen
Spittal
Torhousemuir
F L E E T
Wigtown Sands
Bladnoch
TORHOUSE STONE CIRCLE
Anwoth
Gatehouse of Fleet
B7052
B733
B7005
Wigtown
CARDONESS CASTLE
456
CAIRNHARROW
A75
B727
SCOTLAND'S BOOK TOWN
Carsluith
CARSLUITH CASTLE
Bladnoch
V A L L E Y
A714
7
Girthon
CAIRNHOLY CAIRNS
171
VISITOR CENTRE
Culmazie
A C H A R S
B7005
Barharrow
11
Braehead
Baldoon Sands
Ravenshall Pt.
Fleet Bay
Sandgreen
Kirkinner
B7065
B7052
Ringdoo Pt.
A755
A746
Barrachan
Whauphill
B7004
Knockbrex
Islands of Fleet
Borgue
B7085
Kirkandrews
MOTE OF DRUCHTAG
75
W I G T O W N   B A Y
Sorbie
11
B7052
Garlieston
Airyhassen
Eggerness Pt.
Borness
Drumtroddan
GALLOWAY HOUSE GARDENS
Drummoddie
Ross
DRUMTRODDAN STONES
B7063
Borness Pt.
B7085
B7021
Monreith Mains
Moor of Ravenstone
B7004
Cults
CRUGGLETON CHURCH AND CASTLE
A746
BARSALLOCH FORT
Monreith
Bishopton
Port Allen
Whithorn
PRIORY AND MUSEUM
WHITHORN TRUST CENTRE
Portyerrock Bay
A746
Cairn Hd.
0 1 2 3 miles
0 1 2 3 4 5 km
1
2
3
4
B
C
D

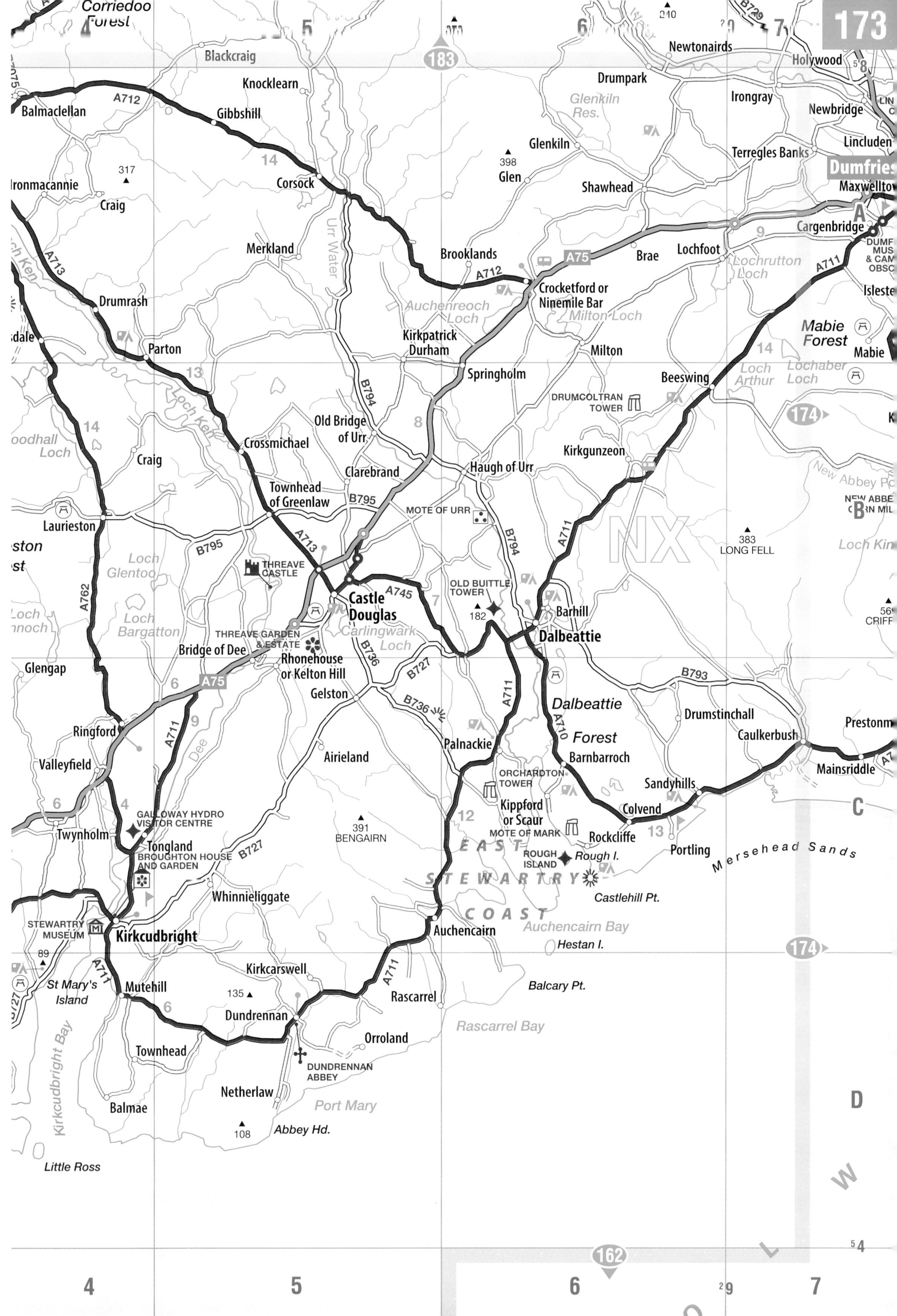

Corriedoo Forest
Blackcraig
Knocklearn
Gibbshill
Balmaclellan
A712
Newtonairds
Holywood
Drumpark
Irongray
Newbridge
Glenkiln Res.
Glenkiln
398
Glen
Lincluden
Terregles Banks
Dumfries
Maxwelltown
Shawhead
Corsock
317
Craig
Urr Water
Merkland
Brooklands
A75
Brae
Lochfoot
Cargenbridge
Lochrutton Loch
A711
A713
Drumrash
Crocketford or Ninemile Bar
Milton Loch
Auchenreoch Loch
Kirkpatrick Durham
Parton
Milton
Mabie Forest
Mabie
Springholm
Beeswing
Loch Arthur
Lochaber Loch
Loch Ken
B794
DRUMCOLTRAN TOWER
Old Bridge of Urr
Crossmichael
Craig
Kirkgunzeon
Clarebrand
Haugh of Urr
Townhead of Greenlaw
B795
MOTE OF URR
Laurieston
383 LONG FELL
Loch Glentoo
THREAVE CASTLE
A762
OLD BUITTLE TOWER
A745
182
Barhill
Castle Douglas
Loch Bargatton
THREAVE GARDEN & ESTATE
Carlingwark Loch
Dalbeattie
Bridge of Dee
Rhonehouse or Kelton Hill
B736
Glengap
B727
B793
Gelston
Dalbeattie Forest
Drumstinchall
Ringford
A710
Caulkerbush
Palnackie
Barnbarroch
Airieland
Valleyfield
Mainsriddle
ORCHARDTON TOWER
Sandyhills
Colvend
Kippford or Scaur
GALLOWAY HYDRO VISITOR CENTRE
391 BENGAIRN
MOTE OF MARK
Twynholm
Rockcliffe
Tongland
Portling
BROUGHTON HOUSE AND GARDEN
ROUGH ISLAND
Rough I.
Mersehead Sands
EAST STEWARTRY COAST
Whinnieliggate
Castlehill Pt.
STEWARTRY MUSEUM
Auchencairn
Kirkcudbright
Auchencairn Bay
Hestan I.
89
Kirkcarswell
St Mary's Island
Mutehill
Rascarrel
Balcary Pt.
135
Dundrennan
Rascarrel Bay
Townhead
Orroland
DUNDRENNAN ABBEY
Kirkcudbright Bay
Netherlaw
Port Mary
Balmae
108
Abbey Hd.
Little Ross
NX
183
174
162

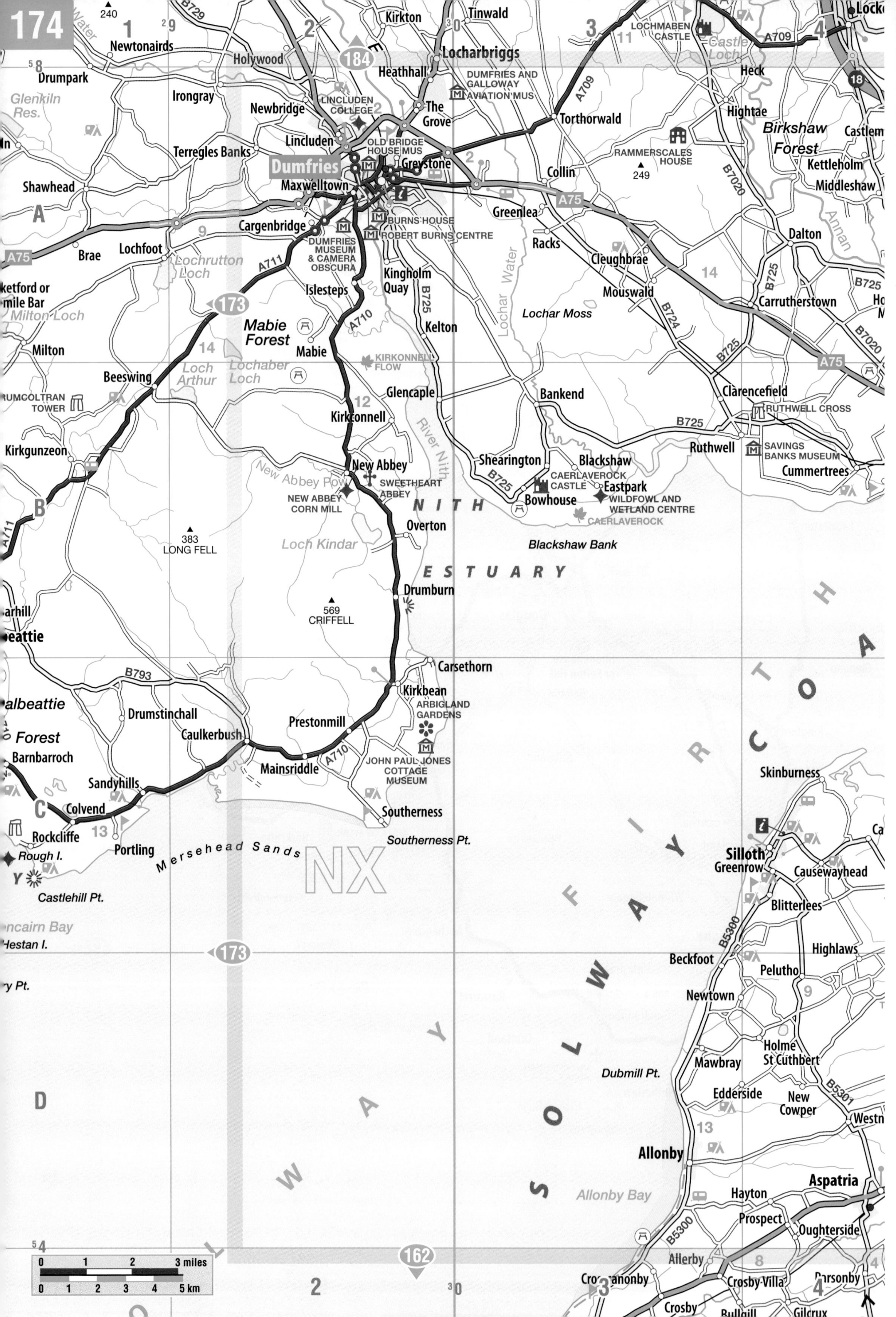
Newtonairds
Drumpark
Holywood
Kirkton
Tinwald
Locharbriggs
Heathhall
LOCHMABEN CASTLE
Castle Loch
A709
Heck
Hightae
Birkshaw Forest
Kettleholm
Middleshaw
Glenkiln Res.
Irongray
Newbridge
LINCLUDEN COLLEGE
The Grove
DUMFRIES AND GALLOWAY AVIATION MUS
Torthorwald
Lincluden
OLD BRIDGE HOUSE MUS
Terregles Banks
Dumfries
Greystone
RAMMERSCALES HOUSE
249
Collin
Shawhead
Maxwelltown
A75
Greenlea
BURNS HOUSE
ROBERT BURNS CENTRE
Cargenbridge
DUMFRIES MUSEUM & CAMERA OBSCURA
Brae
Lochfoot
Lochrutton Loch
Racks
Cleughbrae
Dalton
Annan
Kingholm Quay
A711
Islesteps
Mousswald
Carrutherstown
Milton Loch
Milton
Mabie Forest
Mabie
A710
B725
Kelton
Lochar Water
Lochar Moss
B724
B7020
KIRKCONNELL FLOW
Loch Arthur
Lochaber Loch
Beeswing
Glencaple
Bankend
Clarencefield
RUTHWELL CROSS
Kirkconnell
River Nith
Ruthwell
SAVINGS BANKS MUSEUM
Cummertrees
Kirkgunzeon
New Abbey
New Abbey Pow
SWEETHEART ABBEY
NEW ABBEY CORN MILL
Shearington
Blackshaw
CAERLAVEROCK CASTLE
Eastpark
Bowhouse
WILDFOWL AND WETLAND CENTRE
CAERLAVEROCK
NITH ESTUARY
383 LONG FELL
Loch Kindar
Overton
Blackshaw Bank
Drumburn
569 CRIFFELL
Carsethorn
Kirkbean
ARBIGLAND GARDENS
B793
Drumstinchall
Caulkerbush
Prestonmill
Mainsriddle
JOHN PAUL JONES COTTAGE MUSEUM
Barnbarroch
Sandyhills
Colvend
Rockcliffe
Rough I.
Portling
Southerness
Southerness Pt.
Mersehead Sands
Castlehill Pt.
NX
Hestan I.
SOLWAY FIRTH
Skinburness
Silloth
Greenrow
Causewayhead
Blitterlees
B5300
Beckfoot
Highlaws
Pelutho
Newtown
Holme St Cuthbert
Mawbray
Dubmill Pt.
Edderside
New Cowper
B5301
Allonby
Allonby Bay
Hayton
Aspatria
Prospect
Oughterside
Allerby
Crosby Villa
Parsonby
Crosby
0 1 2 3 miles
0 1 2 3 4 5 km

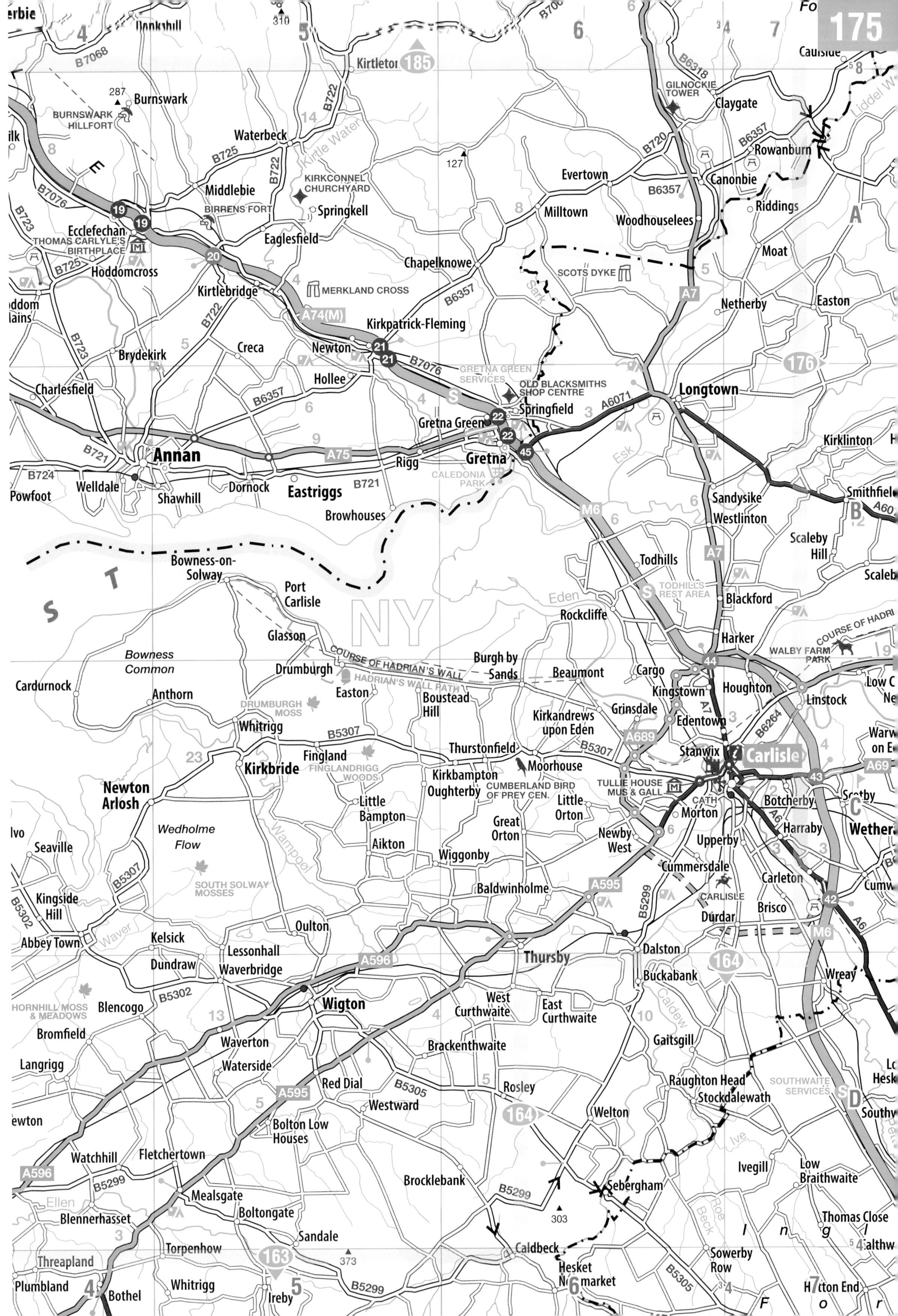
Kirtleton
185
Burnswark
BURNSWARK HILLFORT
Waterbeck
Middlebie
BIRRENS FORT
KIRKCONNEL CHURCHYARD
Springkell
Ecclefechan
THOMAS CARLYLE'S BIRTHPLACE
Eaglesfield
Hoddomcross
Kirtlebridge
MERKLAND CROSS
Chapelknowe
Evertown
Milltown
Woodhouselees
SCOTS DYKE
GILNOCKIE TOWER
Claygate
Rowanburn
Canonbie
Riddings
Moat
Netherby
Easton
Kirkpatrick-Fleming
Newton
Creca
Brydekirk
Charlesfield
Hollee
GRETNA GREEN SERVICES
OLD BLACKSMITHS SHOP CENTRE
Springfield
Gretna Green
Gretna
Longtown
176
Annan
Rigg
CALEDONIA PARK
Welldale
Powfoot
Shawhill
Dornock
Eastriggs
Browhouses
Kirklinton
Smithfield
Sandysike
Westlinton
Scaleby Hill
Todhills
TODHILLS REST AREA
Blackford
Bowness-on-Solway
Port Carlisle
Glasson
Rockcliffe
Harker
Bowness Common
Cardurnock
Anthorn
Drumburgh
COURSE OF HADRIAN'S WALL
HADRIAN'S WALL PATH
Easton
Burgh by Sands
Beaumont
Cargo
Kingstown
Houghton
WALBY FARM PARK
Linstock
Boustead Hill
Grinsdale
Kirkandrews upon Eden
Edentown
DRUMBURGH MOSS
Whitrigg
Fingland
FINGLANDRIGG WOODS
Thurstonfield
Moorhouse
Stanwix
Carlisle
Kirkbride
Kirkbampton
Oughterby
CUMBERLAND BIRD OF PREY CEN.
TULLIE HOUSE MUS & GALL
CATH
Newton Arlosh
Little Bampton
Great Orton
Little Orton
Morton
Botcherby
Harraby
Wetheral
Wedholme Flow
Aikton
Wiggonby
Newby West
Upperby
Seaville
Cummersdale
Carleton
SOUTH SOLWAY MOSSES
Baldwinholme
CARLISLE
Kingside Hill
Durdar
Brisco
Abbey Town
Kelsick
Oulton
Lessonhall
Dundraw
Waverbridge
Thursby
Dalston
164
Buckabank
Wreay
HORNHILL MOSS & MEADOWS
Blencogo
Wigton
West Curthwaite
East Curthwaite
Bromfield
Waverton
Brackenthwaite
Gaitsgill
Langrigg
Waterside
Red Dial
Westward
Rosley
Raughton Head
Stockdalewath
SOUTHWAITE SERVICES
Bolton Low Houses
Welton
164
Watchhill
Fletchertown
Ivegill
Low Braithwaite
Brocklebank
Sebergham
Mealsgate
Blennerhasset
Boltongate
Thomas Close
Sandale
Caldbeck
Sowerby Row
Torpenhow
Threapland
163
Hesket Newmarket
Plumbland
Bothel
Whitrigg
Ireby
Hutton End
A74(M)
A75
A7
A6071
M6
A689
A69
A6
A595
A596
B7068
B7076
B725
B722
B723
B721
B724
B6357
B7076
B6318
B720
B6264
B5307
B5302
B5299
B5305
NY
Solway
Eden
Esk
Sark
Wampool
Waver
Caldew
Ellen
Ivegill
Roe Beck

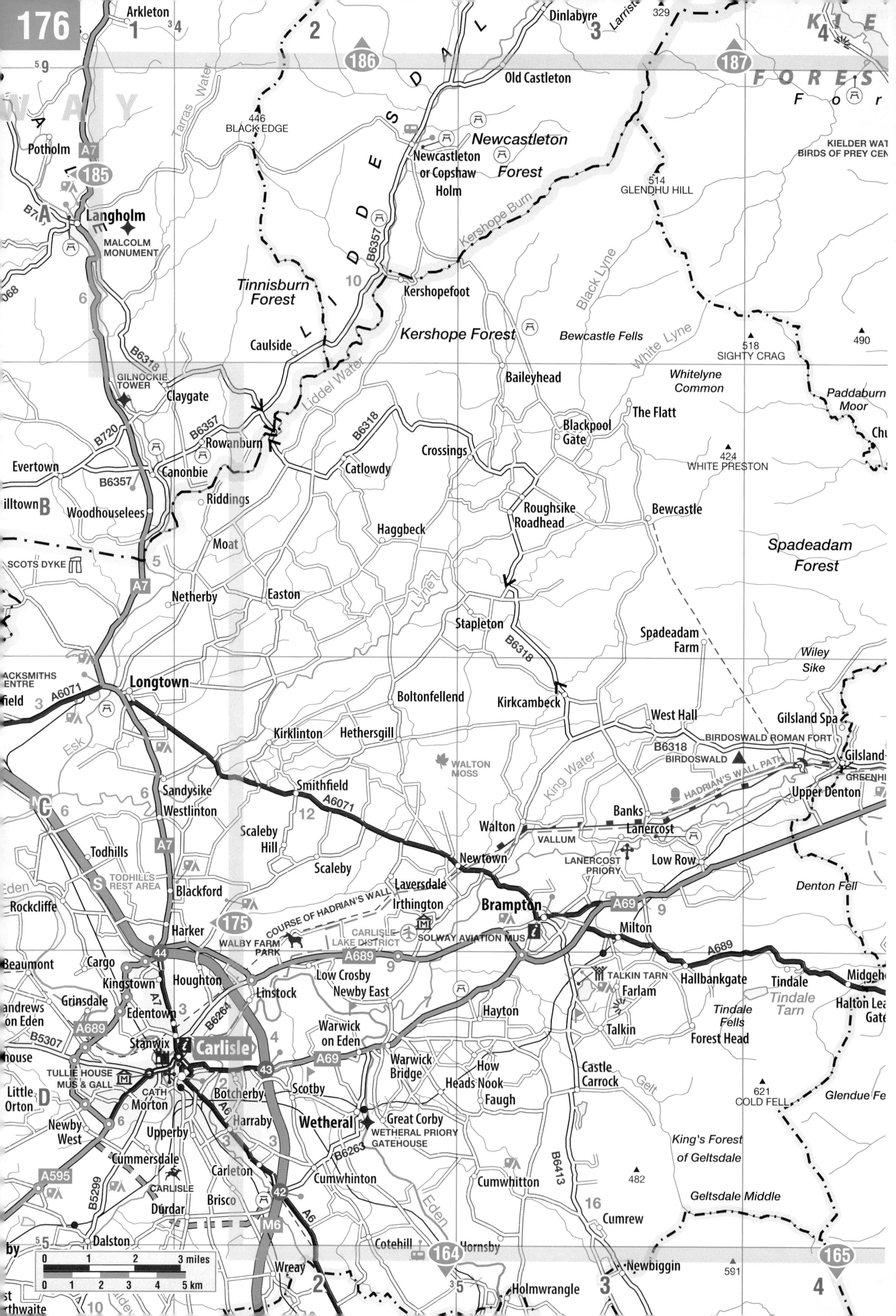
Arkleton
Dinlabyre
Old Castleton
BLACK EDGE
Newcastleton
Newcastleton or Copshaw Holm
Forest
Potholm
Langholm
MALCOLM MONUMENT
GLENDHU HILL
Kershope Burn
Black Lyne
Tinnisburn Forest
Kershopefoot
Kershope Forest
Bewcastle Fells
White Lyne
SIGHTY CRAG
Caulside
Liddel Water
GILNOCKIE TOWER
Claygate
Baileyhead
Whitelyne Common
Paddaburn Moor
The Flatt
Blackpool Gate
Crossings
Rowanburn
Catlowdy
WHITE PRESTON
Evertown
Canonbie
Riddings
Woodhouselees
Roughsike
Roadhead
Bewcastle
Haggbeck
Moat
Spadeadam Forest
SCOTS DYKE
Netherby
Easton
Lyne
Stapleton
Spadeadam Farm
Wiley Sike
BLACKSMITHS CENTRE
Longtown
Boltonfellend
Kirkcambeck
West Hall
Gilsland Spa
Kirklinton
Hethersgill
BIRDOSWALD ROMAN FORT
BIRDOSWALD
Gilsland
WALTON MOSS
King Water
HADRIAN'S WALL PATH
Sandysike
Smithfield
Upper Denton
Westlinton
Banks
Scaleby Hill
Walton
Lanercost
VALLUM
Todhills
TODHILLS REST AREA
Scaleby
Newtown
LANERCOST PRIORY
Low Row
Rockcliffe
Blackford
Laversdale
Denton Fell
COURSE OF HADRIAN'S WALL
Irthington
Brampton
Harker
CARLISLE LAKE DISTRICT
SOLWAY AVIATION MUS
Milton
WALBY FARM PARK
Beaumont
Cargo
Kingstown
Houghton
Low Crosby
TALKIN TARN
Hallbankgate
Tindale
Midgeholm
Linstock
Newby East
Farlam
Tindale Tarn
Tindale Fells
Grinsdale
Edentown
Hayton
Halton Lea Gate
Warwick on Eden
Talkin
Forest Head
Stanwix
Carlisle
Warwick Bridge
How
Castle Carrock
TULLIE HOUSE MUS & GALL
Heads Nook
Gelt
Little Orton
CATH
Botcherby
Scotby
Faugh
COLD FELL
Glendue Fell
Morton
Newby West
Harraby
Wetheral
Great Corby
WETHERAL PRIORY GATEHOUSE
Upperby
King's Forest of Geltsdale
Cummersdale
Carleton
Cumwhinton
Cumwhitton
CARLISLE
Durdar
Brisco
Geltsdale Middle
Cumrew
Dalston
Cotehill
Hornsby
Wreay
Newbiggin
Holmwrangle
Eden
3 miles
5 km

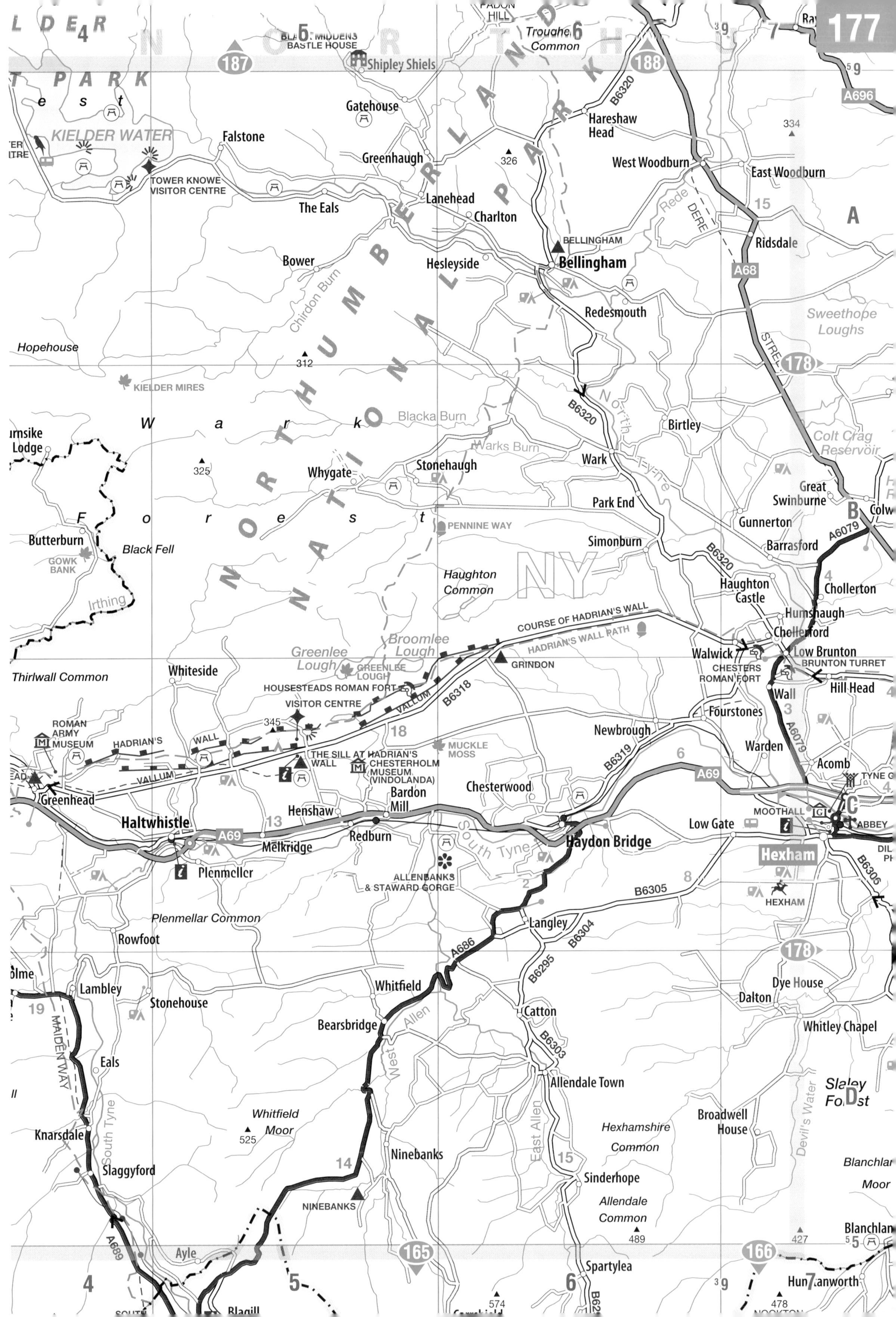

177
KIELDER WATER
TOWER KNOWE
VISITOR CENTRE
BLACK MIDDENS
BASTLE HOUSE
Shipley Shiels
187
188
Trough Common
Gatehouse
Falstone
Greenhaugh
Hareshaw Head
B6320
West Woodburn
East Woodburn
334
326
A696
Lanehead
The Eals
Charlton
NORTHUMBERLAND NATIONAL PARK
BELLINGHAM
Bellingham
Bower
Hesleyside
Rede
DERE
Ridsdale
A68
15
A
Redesmouth
Chirdon Burn
Sweethope Loughs
Hopehouse
312
178
KIELDER MIRES
Wark Forest
Blacka Burn
North Tyne
Birtley
Colt Crag Reservoir
Warks Burn
325
Whygate
Stonehaugh
Wark
Park End
Great Swinburne
Gunnerton
PENNINE WAY
Butterburn
Black Fell
GOWK BANK
Simonburn
Barrasford
A6079
B
Haughton Common
NY
Haughton Castle
Chollerton
Irthing
COURSE OF HADRIAN'S WALL
HADRIAN'S WALL PATH
Humshaugh
Chollerford
Broomlee Lough
Greenlee Lough
GREENLEE LOUGH
GRINDON
Walwick
Low Brunton
BRUNTON TURRET
CHESTERS ROMAN FORT
Thirlwall Common
Whiteside
HOUSESTEADS ROMAN FORT
VALLUM
B6318
Hill Head
Wall
VISITOR CENTRE
Fourstones
345
18
ROMAN ARMY MUSEUM
HADRIAN'S WALL
MUCKLE MOSS
Newbrough
Warden
THE SILL AT HADRIAN'S WALL
CHESTERHOLM MUSEUM (VINDOLANDA)
B6319
6
Acomb
TYNE GREEN
A69
Greenhead
Bardon Mill
Chesterwood
Henshaw
C
MOOTHALL
ABBEY
Haltwhistle
13
Low Gate
Melkridge
Redburn
South Tyne
Haydon Bridge
Hexham
Plenmeller
ALLEN BANKS & STAWARD GORGE
B6305
8
HEXHAM
Plenmellar Common
Langley
B6304
Rowfoot
A686
B6295
Whitfield
Dye House
Lambley
Dalton
Stonehouse
19
MAIDEN WAY
Catton
Bearsbridge
West Allen
Whitley Chapel
B6303
Eals
Allendale Town
Slaley Forest
D
Whitfield Moor
525
Hexhamshire Common
Broadwell House
Devil's Water
Knarsdale
East Allen
South Tyne
Ninebanks
15
Slaggyford
14
Sinderhope
Blanchland Moor
Allendale Common
NINEBANKS
489
427
Blanchland
A689
Ayle
165
166
Spartylea
4
5
6
7
Hunstanworth
574
478
Blagill

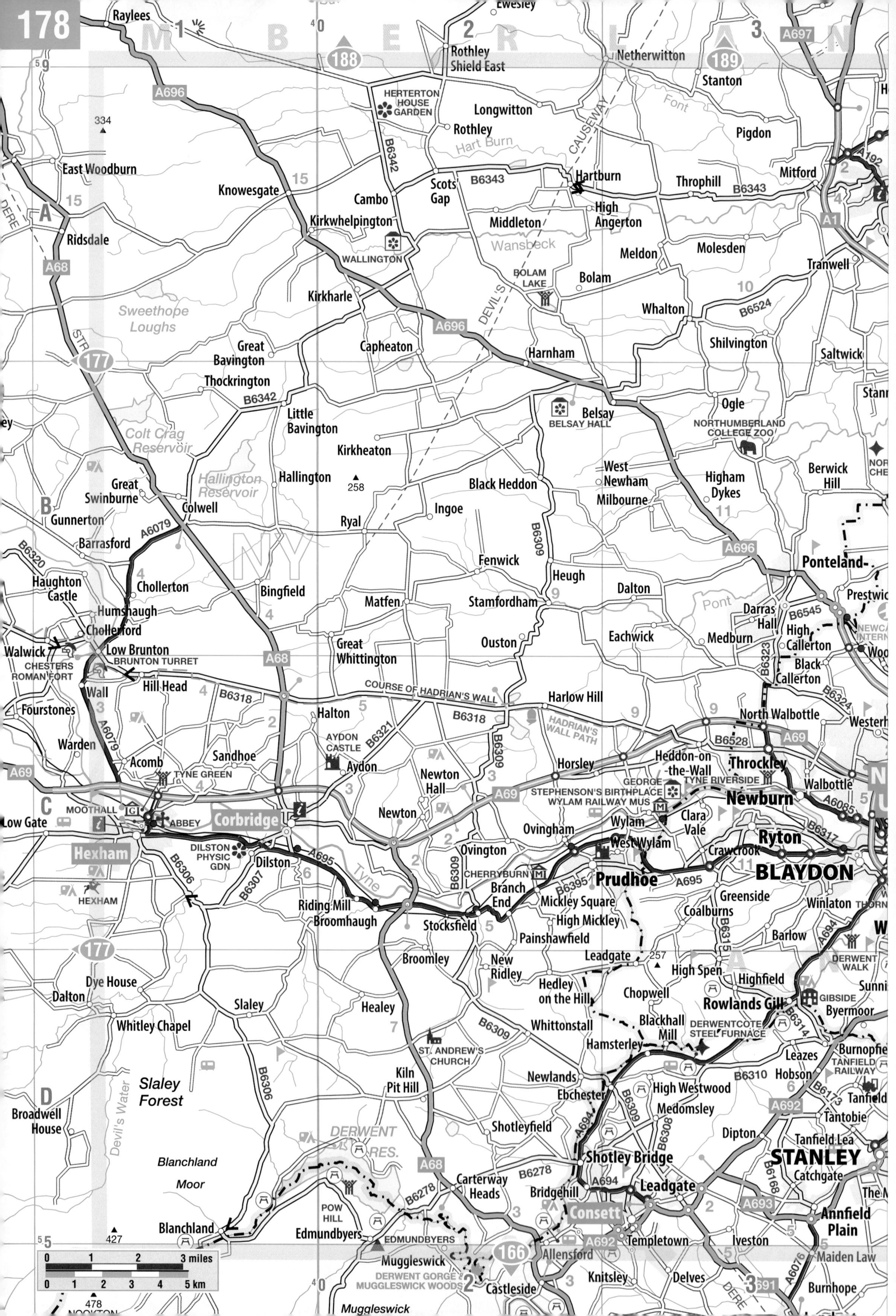
Raylees
Rothley Shield East
Netherwitton
Stanton
188
189
A697
A696
HERTERTON HOUSE GARDEN
Longwitton
Rothley
Hart Burn
Font
Pigdon
334
East Woodburn
Knowesgate
B6342
Scots' Gap
B6343
Hartburn
Throphill
Mitford
A192
Cambo
High Angerton
A1
Ridsdale
Kirkwhelpington
Middleton
Wansbeck
Meldon
Molesden
Tranwell
A68
WALLINGTON
BOLAM LAKE
Bolam
Whalton
B6524
Kirkharle
DEVIL'S CAUSEWAY
Sweethope Loughs
Capheaton
Harnham
Shilvington
Saltwick
177
Great Bavington
Thockrington
Little Bavington
Belsay
BELSAY HALL
Ogle
NORTHUMBERLAND COLLEGE ZOO
Colt Crag Reservoir
Kirkheaton
Hallington Reservoir
Hallington
258
Black Heddon
West Newham
Milbourne
Higham Dykes
Berwick Hill
Great Swinburne
Colwell
Gunnerton
Ingoe
Ryal
A6079
Barrasford
B6320
B6309
Fenwick
A696
Ponteland
Haughton Castle
Chollerton
Bingfield
Matfen
Heugh
Dalton
Prestwick
Stamfordham
Darras Hall
B6545
Humshaugh
Chollerford
Walwick
Low Brunton
BRUNTON TURRET
CHESTERS ROMAN FORT
Great Whittington
Ouston
Eachwick
Medburn
High Callerton
B6323
Black Callerton
Wall
Hill Head
B6318
COURSE OF HADRIAN'S WALL
Harlow Hill
Fourstones
Halton
AYDON CASTLE
B6321
HADRIAN'S WALL PATH
North Walbottle
B6324
Warden
Acomb
Sandhoe
Aydon
Newton Hall
Horsley
Heddon-on-the-Wall
B6528
A69
Throckley
TYNE GREEN
GEORGE STEPHENSON'S BIRTHPLACE
WYLAM RAILWAY MUS
TYNE RIVERSIDE
Walbottle
Newburn
MOOTHALL
ABBEY
Corbridge
Newton
Ovingham
Wylam
Clara Vale
A6085
Low Gate
Hexham
DILSTON PHYSIC GDN
Dilston
A695
Tyne
Ovington
West Wylam
Crawcrook
Ryton
B6317
BLAYDON
B6306
B6307
CHERRYBURN
Prudhoe
HEXHAM
Riding Mill
Broomhaugh
Branch End
B6395
Mickley Square
Greenside
Coalburns
Winlaton
High Mickley
Stocksfield
Painshawfield
B6315
Barlow
Broomley
New Ridley
Leadgate
257
High Spen
Dye House
Dalton
Hedley on the Hill
Chopwell
Highfield
DERWENT WALK
Slaley
Healey
Rowlands Gill
GIBSIDE
Byermoor
Whitley Chapel
B6309
Whittonstall
Blackhall Mill
DERWENTCOTE STEEL FURNACE
B6314
ST. ANDREW'S CHURCH
Hamsterley
Burnopfield
Leazes
TANFIELD RAILWAY
Slaley Forest
Kiln Pit Hill
Newlands
B6310
Hobson
Broadwell House
Ebchester
High Westwood
B6173
Tanfield
Devil's Water
Medomsley
A692
Tantobie
Shotleyfield
A694
Dipton
DERWENT RES.
B6308
Tanfield Lea
Blanchland Moor
Shotley Bridge
STANLEY
A68
B6278
Carterway Heads
Bridgehill
Leadgate
Catchgate
B6168
POW HILL
Consett
A693
Annfield Plain
427
Blanchland
Edmundbyers
EDMUNDBYERS
166
Templetown
Iveston
Muggleswick
Allensford
Knitsley
Maiden Law
DERWENT GORGE & MUGGLESWICK WOODS
Castleside
Delves
A6076
Burnhope
478
Muggleswick
0 1 2 3 miles
0 1 2 3 4 5 km

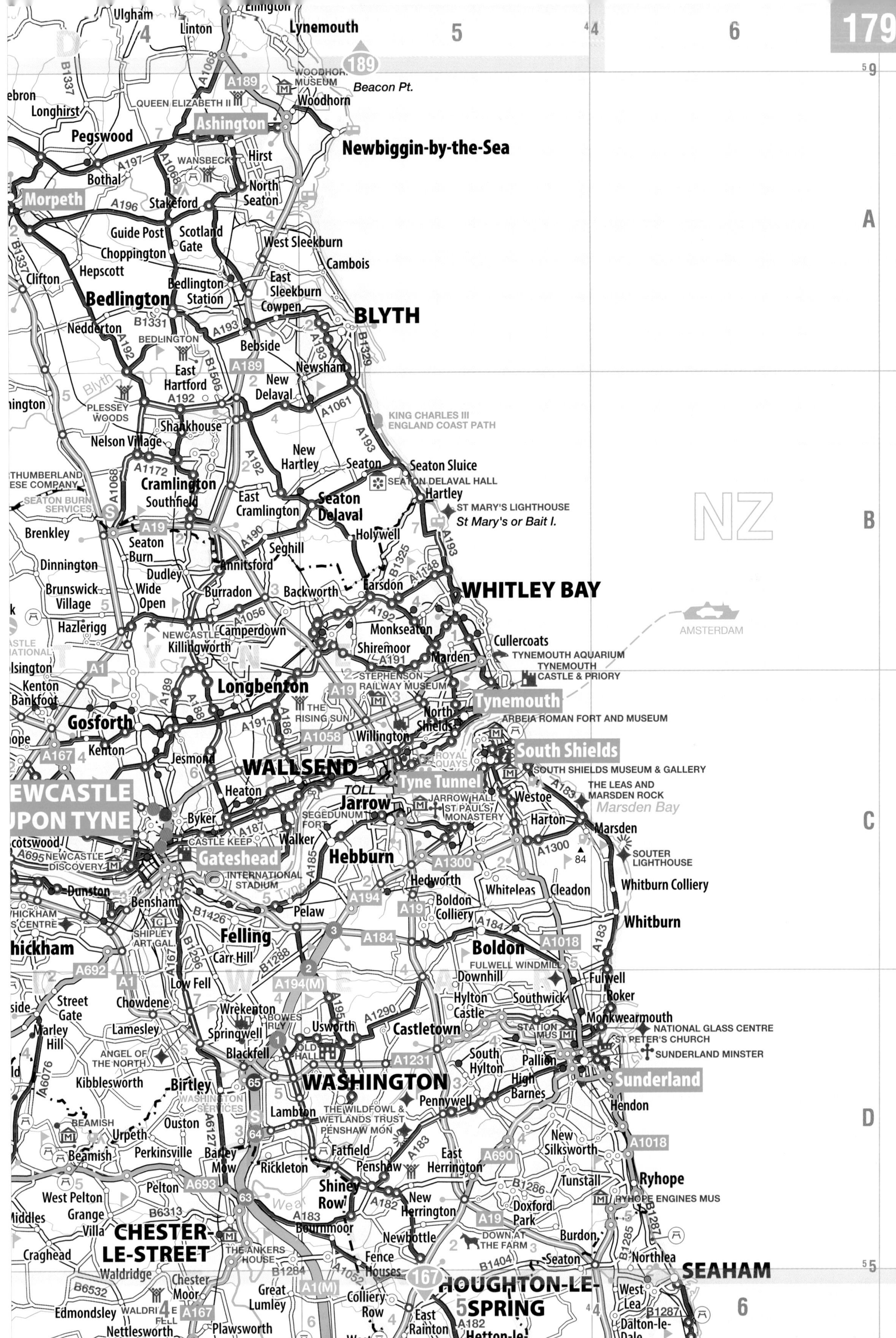
4
5
6
A
B
C
D
NZ
Ulgham
Linton
Ellington
Lynemouth
189
Woodhorn Museum
Beacon Pt.
Woodhorn
Queen Elizabeth II
Longhirst
Pegswood
Ashington
Newbiggin-by-the-Sea
Wansbeck
Hirst
Bothal
Morpeth
North Seaton
Stakeford
Guide Post
Scotland Gate
Choppington
Hepscott
West Sleekburn
Cambois
Clifton
Bedlington Station
East Sleekburn
Bedlington
Cowpen
BLYTH
Nedderton
Bedlington
Bebside
Newsham
East Hartford
New Delaval
Plessey Woods
Shankhouse
King Charles III England Coast Path
Nelson Village
New Hartley
Seaton
Seaton Sluice
Cramlington
Seaton Delaval Hall
Southfield
East Cramlington
Seaton Delaval
Hartley
St Mary's Lighthouse
St Mary's or Bait I.
Seaton Burn Services
Brenkley
Seaton Burn
Holywell
Seghill
Dinnington
Annitsford
Dudley
Earsdon
Brunswick Village
Wide Open
Burradon
Backworth
WHITLEY BAY
Amsterdam
Hazlerigg
Camperdown
Monkseaton
Newcastle Killingworth
Shiremoor
Cullercoats
Marden
Tynemouth Aquarium
Tynemouth Castle & Priory
Stephenson Railway Museum
Longbenton
Tynemouth
Kenton Bankfoot
The Rising Sun
North Shields
Arbeia Roman Fort and Museum
Gosforth
Willington
Kenton
Jesmond
WALLSEND
Royal Quays
South Shields
South Shields Museum & Gallery
NEWCASTLE UPON TYNE
Heaton
Toll
Tyne Tunnel
The Leas and Marsden Rock
Jarrow
Jarrow Hall
St Paul's Monastery
Westoe
Marsden Bay
Byker
Segedunum Fort
Harton
Marsden
Castle Keep
Walker
Newcastle Discovery
Gateshead
Hebburn
Souter Lighthouse
International Stadium
Dunston
Hedworth
Whiteleas
Cleadon
Whitburn Colliery
Bensham
Boldon Colliery
Whickham
Pelaw
Whitburn
Shipley Art Gal.
Felling
Boldon
Whickham
Carr Hill
Fulwell Windmill
Downhill
Fulwell
Low Fell
Roker
Street Gate
Chowdene
Hylton Castle
Southwick
Monkwearmouth
Wrekenton
National Glass Centre
Marley Hill
Lamesley
Bowes Rly
Springwell
Usworth
Castletown
Station Mus
St Peter's Church
Angel of the North
Blackfell
Old Hall
South Hylton
Pallion
Sunderland Minster
Kibblesworth
Birtley
WASHINGTON
High Barnes
Sunderland
Washington Services
Pennywell
Hendon
Beamish
Ouston
Lambton
The Wildfowl & Wetlands Trust
Penshaw Mon
Urpeth
Perkinsville
Barley Mow
Fatfield
East Herrington
New Silksworth
Beamish
Rickleton
Penshaw
Tunstall
Ryhope
Shiney Row
Ryhope Engines Mus
Wear
West Pelton
Pelton
New Herrington
Doxford Park
Middles
Grange Villa
CHESTER-LE-STREET
Bournmoor
Newbottle
Down at the Farm
Burdon
Craghead
The Ankers House
Fence Houses
Seaton
Northlea
Waldridge
Chester Moor
Great Lumley
SEAHAM
HOUGHTON-LE-SPRING
Colliery Row
West Lea
Edmondsley
Waldridge Fell
Nettlesworth
Plawsworth
East Rainton
Dalton-le-Dale
A189
A1068
A197
A196
B1337
A193
B1331
A192
B1505
B1329
A1061
A1172
A19
A190
B1325
A1148
A1056
A191
A1
A188
A186
A1058
A167
A187
A1300
A695
B1426
A194
A185
A184
A1018
B1296
B1288
A183
A692
A194(M)
A195
A1290
A1231
A6076
A6127
A182
A693
B6313
A690
B1286
B1285
B1287
B1404
A1(M)
B1284
A1052
B6532
A182
65
64
63
167
84
Tyne
Blyth

NW
191
192
170
Turnberry Bay
Turnberry
Brest Rocks
Ailsa Craig
338
Girvan
Glendoune
B7035
Woodland Bay
A77
Pinn
A714
Kennedy's Pass
297
GREY HILL
12
Straid
Currarie
Lendalfoot
CARLETON CASTLE
260
Poundland
B734
Bennane Hd.
9
Colmonell
265
Knockdolian
Ballantrae Bay
Heronsford
Glen Tig
Water of Tig
Ballantrae
Balkissock
Downan Pt.
Auchencrosh
Arecleoch Forest
439
BENERAIRD
BELFAST
LARNE
Mark
Glen App
Milleur Pt.
Miltonise
Corsewall Pt.
17
Portencalzie
Barnhills
257
North Cairn
Main Water of Luce
Cross Water of Luce
South Cairn
B738
Loch Connell
Corsewall
Penwhirn Res.
Cairnryan
Dounan Bay
Kirkcolm
Mains of Airies
Ervie
Braid Fell
Low Salchrie
The Wig
B798
LOCH RYAN
6
B738
Leswalt
NewLuce
Craigencr
Innermessan
Auchmant
B7043
0 1 2 3 miles
0 1 2 3 4 5 km
A B C D E
1 2 3

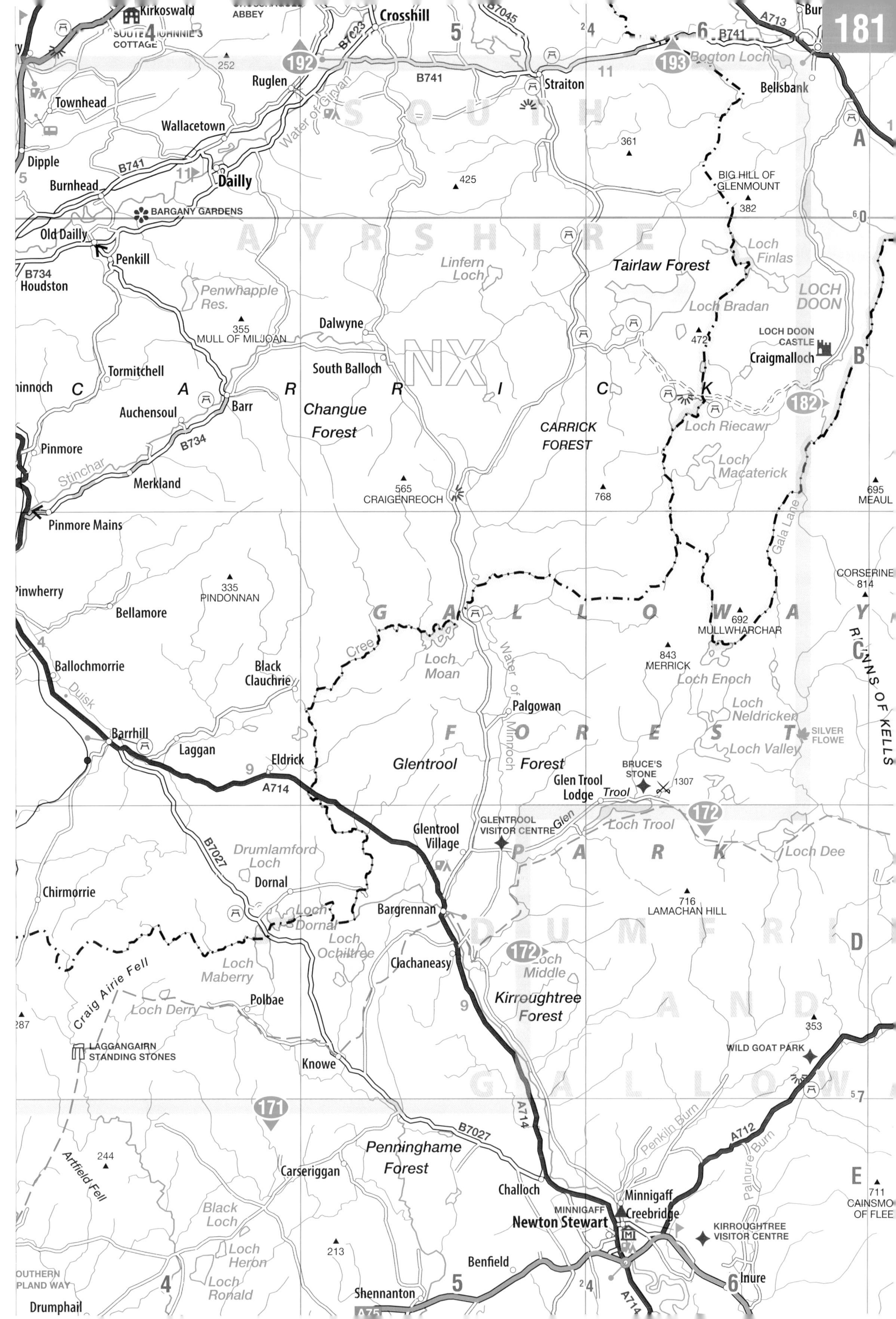
Kirkoswald
ABBEY
Crosshill
B7045
B7023
SOUTER JOHNNIE'S COTTAGE
252
192
Ruglen
B741
Straiton
11
193
Bogton Loch
B741
A713
Bellsbank
Townhead
Wallacetown
Water of Girvan
SOUTH
361
A
Dipple
B741
Burnhead
Daily
425
BIG HILL OF GLENMOUNT
382
BARGANY GARDENS
Old Dailly
AYRSHIRE
Penkill
Linfern Loch
Loch Finlas
Tairlaw Forest
B734
Houdston
Penwhapple Res.
Loch Bradan
LOCH DOON
355
MULL OF MILJOAN
Dalwyne
472
LOCH DOON CASTLE
Craigmalloch
B
South Balloch
NX
Tormitchell
CARRICK
Barr
Auchensoul
Changue Forest
182
Loch Riecawr
CARRICK FOREST
Pinmore
B734
Stinchar
Merkland
Loch Macaterick
565
CRAIGENREOCH
768
695
MEAUL
Pinmore Mains
Gala Lane
Pinwherry
335
PINDONNAN
CORSERINE
814
Bellamore
GALLOWAY
692
MULLWHARCHAR
Cree
Loch Moan
843
MERRICK
Ballochmorrie
Black Clauchrie
Water of Minnoch
Loch Enoch
RHINNS OF KELLS
Duisk
Palgowan
Loch Neldricken
Barrhill
Laggan
FOREST
SILVER FLOWE
Loch Valley
Eldrick
Glentrool
Forest
BRUCE'S STONE
1307
Glen Trool Lodge
Trool
A714
172
GLENTROOL VISITOR CENTRE
Glen
Loch Trool
Glentrool Village
PARK
Loch Dee
B7027
Drumlamford Loch
Dornal
Chirmorrie
716
LAMACHAN HILL
Bargrennan
Loch Dornal
DUMFRIES
D
Loch Ochiltree
Clachaneasy
172
Loch Middle
Loch Maberry
Craig Airie Fell
Kirroughtree Forest
AND
Polbae
Loch Derry
287
353
LAGGANGAIRN STANDING STONES
WILD GOAT PARK
Knowe
GALLOWAY
171
A714
B7027
Penkiln Burn
A712
Palnure Burn
244
Artfield Fell
Penninghame Forest
Carseriggan
Challoch
Minnigaff
E
711
CAIRNSMORE OF FLEET
Black Loch
MINNIGAFF
Creebridge
Newton Stewart
KIRROUGHTREE VISITOR CENTRE
213
Loch Heron
SOUTHERN UPLAND WAY
Benfield
Loch Ronald
Inure
Drumphail
Shennanton
A75
A714
4
5
6

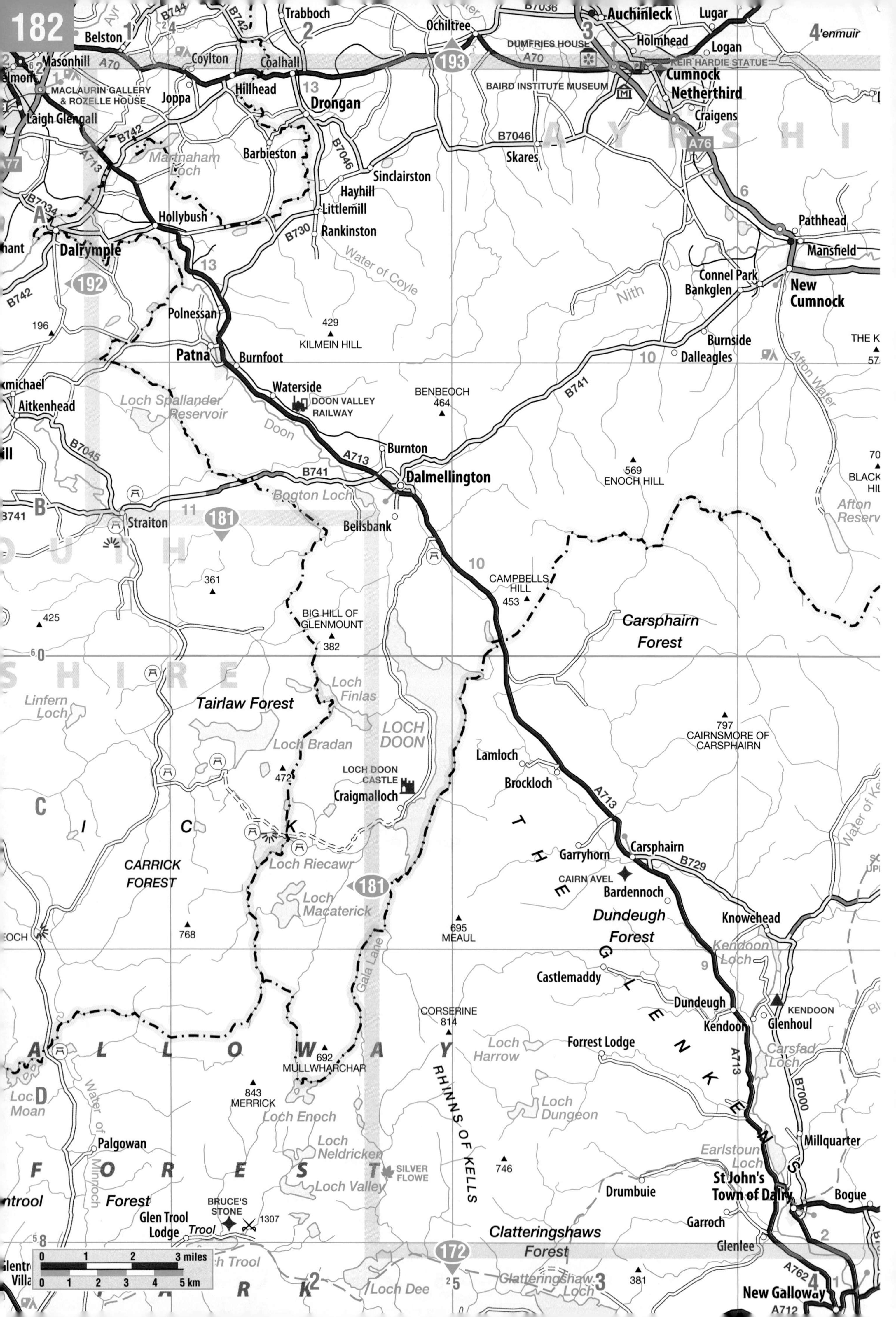

Auchinleck
Ochiltree
Trabboch
Belston
Coylton
Coalhall
Masonhill
MACLAURIN GALLERY & ROZELLE HOUSE
Joppa
Hillhead
Drongan
Laigh Glengall
Martnaham Loch
Barbieston
Sinclairston
Hayhill
Littlemill
Rankinston
Hollybush
Dalrymple
Water of Coyle
Polnessan
Patna
Burnfoot
KILMEIN HILL
Waterside
DOON VALLEY RAILWAY
Loch Spallander Reservoir
Aitkenhead
BENBEOCH
Burnton
Dalmellington
Bogton Loch
Bellsbank
Straiton
CAMPBELLS HILL
BIG HILL OF GLENMOUNT
Carsphairn Forest
Tairlaw Forest
Loch Finlas
Loch Bradan
LOCH DOON
LOCH DOON CASTLE
Craigmalloch
Lamloch
Brockloch
Linfern Loch
Loch Riecawr
CARRICK FOREST
Loch Macaterick
Carsphairn
Garryhorn
CAIRN AVEL
Bardennoch
Dundeugh Forest
Knowehead
MEAUL
Kendoon Loch
Castlemaddy
Dundeugh
Kendoon
Glenhoul
KENDOON
CORSERINE
Forrest Lodge
Loch Harrow
Carsfad Loch
MULLWHARCHAR
MERRICK
Loch Enoch
Loch Dungeon
Loch Moan
Palgowan
Loch Neldricken
SILVER FLOWE
Loch Valley
RHINNS OF KELLS
Earlstoun Loch
Millquarter
St John's Town of Dalry
Drumbuie
Bogue
Garroch
Glenlee
BRUCE'S STONE
Glen Trool Lodge
Clatteringshaws Forest
Clatteringshaw Loch
Loch Dee
New Galloway
Lugar
Holmhead
Logan
DUMFRIES HOUSE
KEIR HARDIE STATUE
Cumnock
Netherthird
BAIRD INSTITUTE MUSEUM
Craigens
Skares
Pathhead
Mansfield
Connel Park
Bankglen
New Cumnock
Nith
Burnside
Dalleagles
Afton Water
ENOCH HILL
CAIRNSMORE OF CARSPHAIRN
THE GLENKENS
AYRSHIRE
SOUTH AYRSHIRE
GALLOWAY FOREST PARK

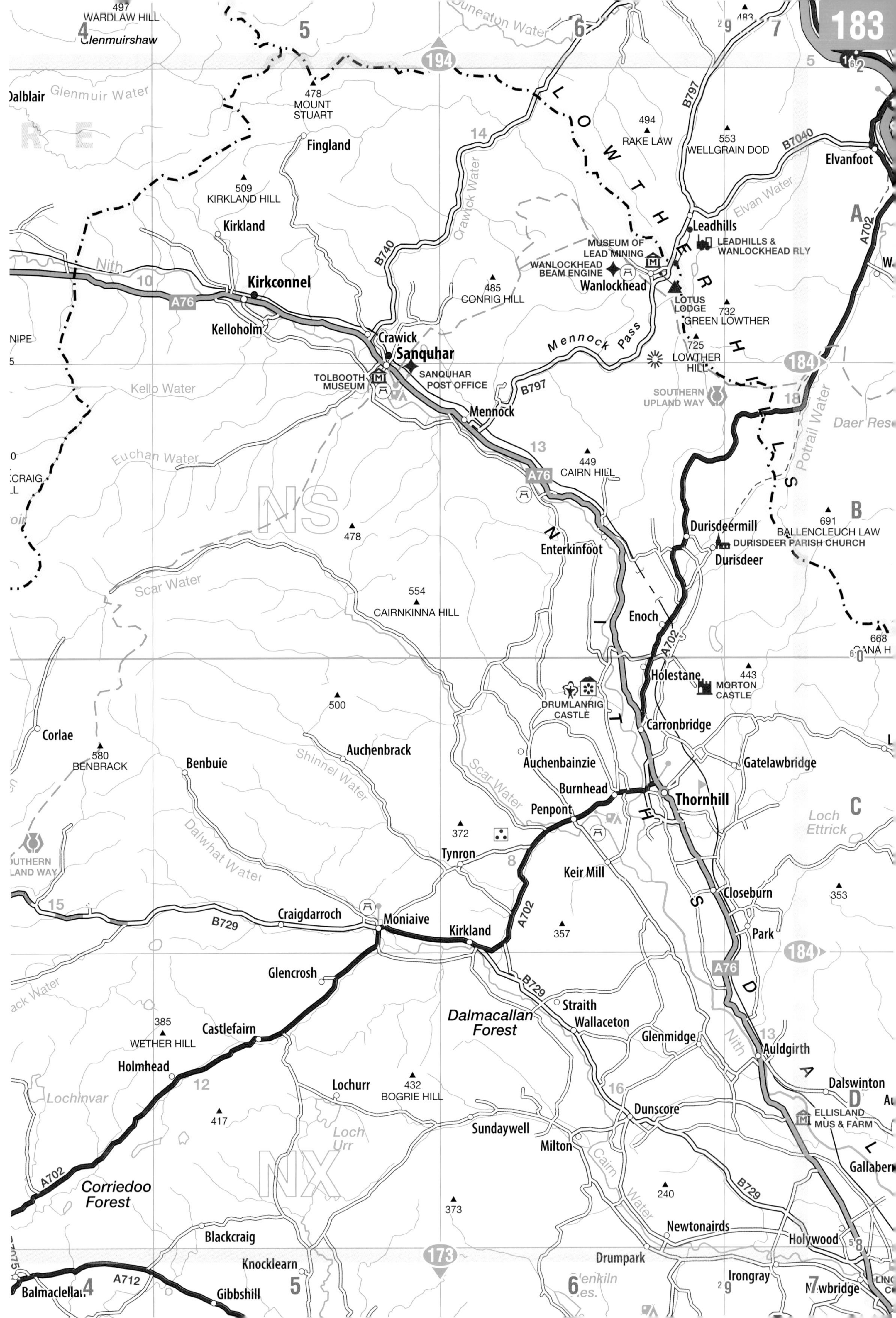


194
184
184
173

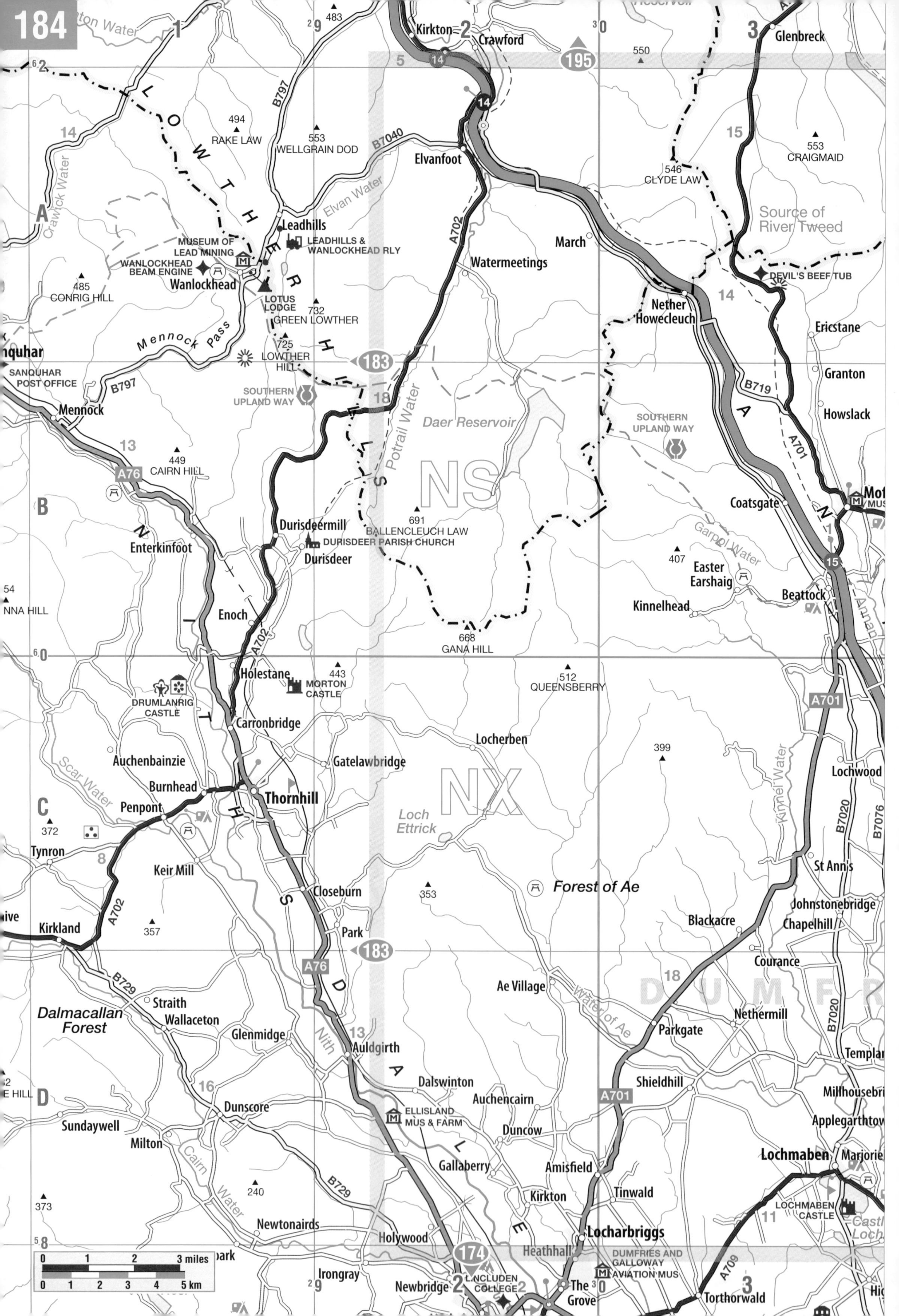
Kirkton
Crawford
Glenbreck
195
183
174
RAKE LAW
WELLGRAIN DOD
Elvanfoot
CLYDE LAW
CRAIGMAID
Source of River Tweed
LOWTHER HILLS
Leadhills
LEADHILLS & WANLOCKHEAD RLY
MUSEUM OF LEAD MINING
WANLOCKHEAD BEAM ENGINE
Wanlockhead
CONRIG HILL
LOTUS LODGE
GREEN LOWTHER
LOWTHER HILL
Mennock Pass
March
Watermeetings
DEVIL'S BEEF TUB
Nether Howecleuch
Ericstane
Granton
Howslack
SANQUHAR POST OFFICE
Mennock
SOUTHERN UPLAND WAY
Daer Reservoir
Potrail Water
Elvan Water
Crawick Water
CAIRN HILL
Durisdeermill
DURISDEER PARISH CHURCH
Durisdeer
BALLENCLEUCH LAW
Enterkinfoot
Coatsgate
Garpol Water
Easter Earshaig
Beattock
Kinnelhead
Enoch
GANA HILL
QUEENSBERRY
Holestane
MORTON CASTLE
DRUMLANRIG CASTLE
Carronbridge
Locherben
Auchenbainzie
Gatelawbridge
Lochwood
Scar Water
Burnhead
Thornhill
Penpont
Loch Ettrick
Kinnel Water
Tynron
Keir Mill
St Ann's
Closeburn
Forest of Ae
Johnstonebridge
Chapelhill
Kirkland
Park
Blackacre
Courance
NITHSDALE
DUMFR
Ae Village
Water of Ae
Straith
Wallaceton
Dalmacallan Forest
Glenmidge
Parkgate
Nethermill
Auldgirth
Nith
Templand
Dalswinton
Shieldhill
Millhousebri
Auchencairn
ELLISLAND MUS & FARM
Dunscore
Sundaywell
Milton
Cairn Water
Duncow
Applegarthtow
Gallaberry
Amisfield
Lochmaben
Marjorie
Kirkton
Tinwald
LOCHMABEN CASTLE
Newtonairds
Holywood
Locharbriggs
Heathhall
DUMFRIES AND GALLOWAY AVIATION MUS
Irongray
Newbridge
LINCLUDEN COLLEGE
The Grove
Torthorwald
NS
NX
A76
A702
A701
A709
B797
B7040
B719
B729
B7020
B7076
0 1 2 3 miles
0 1 2 3 4 5 km

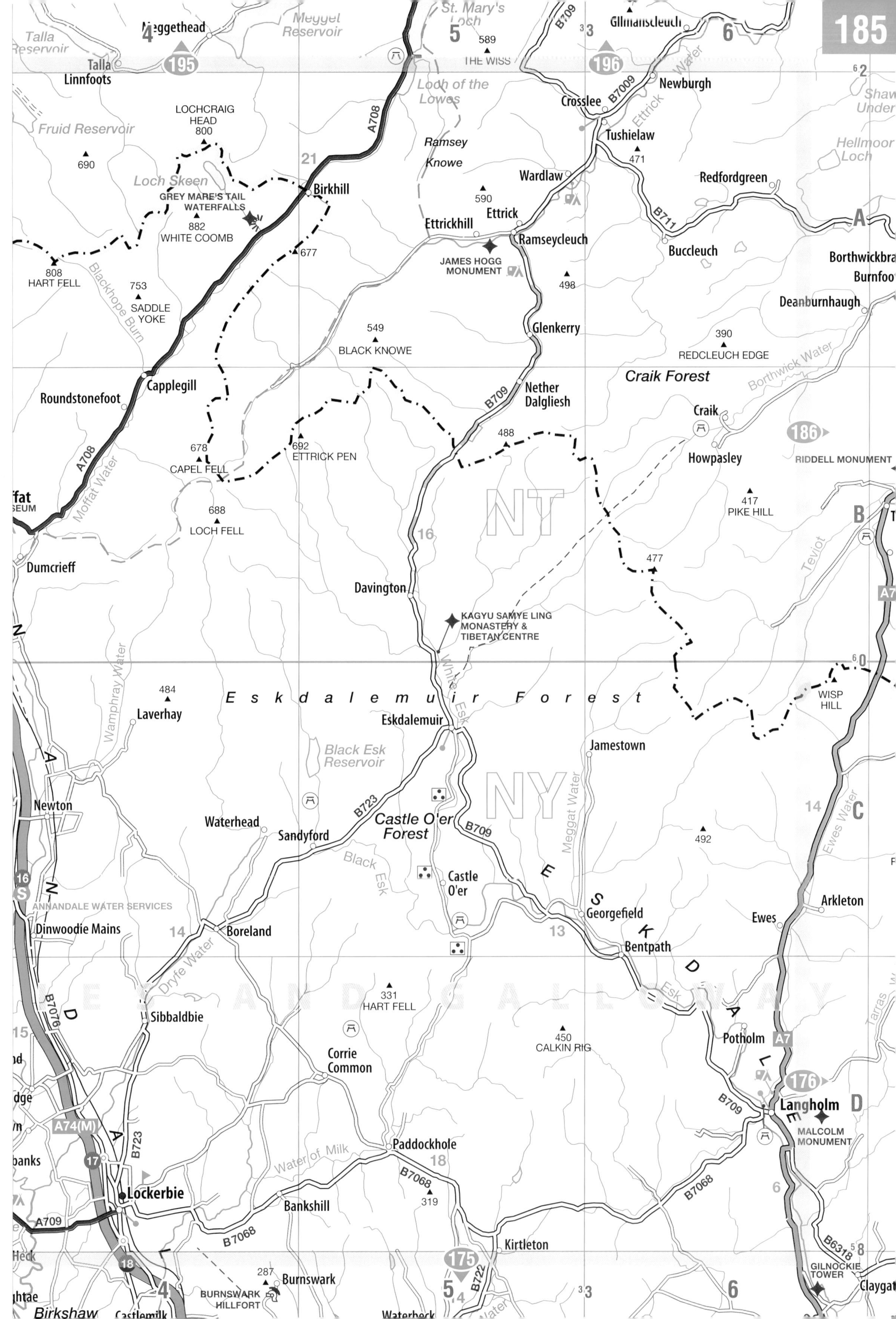
Meggethead
Talla Reservoir
Talla
Linnfoots
Megget Reservoir
St. Mary's Loch
589
THE WISS
Gilmanscleuch
195
196
Loch of the Lowes
Newburgh
Crosslee
B7009
Ettrick Water
Tushielaw
Fruid Reservoir
LOCHCRAIG HEAD
800
690
A708
Ramsey Knowe
Hellmoor Loch
471
Redfordgreen
Loch Skeen
Birkhill
GREY MARE'S TAIL WATERFALLS
882
WHITE COOMB
Wardlaw
590
Ettrick
Ettrickhill
Ramseycleuch
B711
Buccleuch
677
JAMES HOGG MONUMENT
808
HART FELL
Blackhope Burn
753
SADDLE YOKE
498
Borthwickbra
Burnfoo
Deanburnhaugh
549
BLACK KNOWE
Glenkerry
390
REDCLEUCH EDGE
Craik Forest
Borthwick Water
Capplegill
Roundstonefoot
Nether Dalgliesh
B709
Craik
186
488
Howpasley
RIDDELL MONUMENT
678
CAPEL FELL
692
ETTRICK PEN
Moffat Water
fat
SEUM
688
LOCH FELL
NT
417
PIKE HILL
16
Dumcrieff
477
Teviot
Davington
KAGYU SAMYE LING MONASTERY & TIBETAN CENTRE
Wamphray Water
White Esk
484
Laverhay
Eskdalemuir Forest
WISP HILL
Eskdalemuir
Jamestown
Black Esk Reservoir
NY
Meggat Water
Newton
B723
Castle O'er Forest
Waterhead
Sandyford
B709
14
492
Ewes Water
Black Esk
Castle O'er
16
ANNANDALE WATER SERVICES
ESKDALE
Arkleton
Georgefield
Ewes
Dinwoodie Mains
Boreland
13
Dryfe Water
Bentpath
331
HART FELL
Esk
B7076
Sibbaldbie
450
CALKIN RIG
Tarras
Potholm
A7
Corrie Common
176
Langholm
MALCOLM MONUMENT
A74(M)
B709
B723
Paddockhole
Water of Milk
18
17
Lockerbie
B7068
319
Bankshill
A709
B7068
Kirtleton
B6318
175
GILNOCKIE TOWER
18
287
Burnswark
BURNSWARK HILLFORT
B722
Claygat
Birkshaw
Castlemilk
Waterbeck

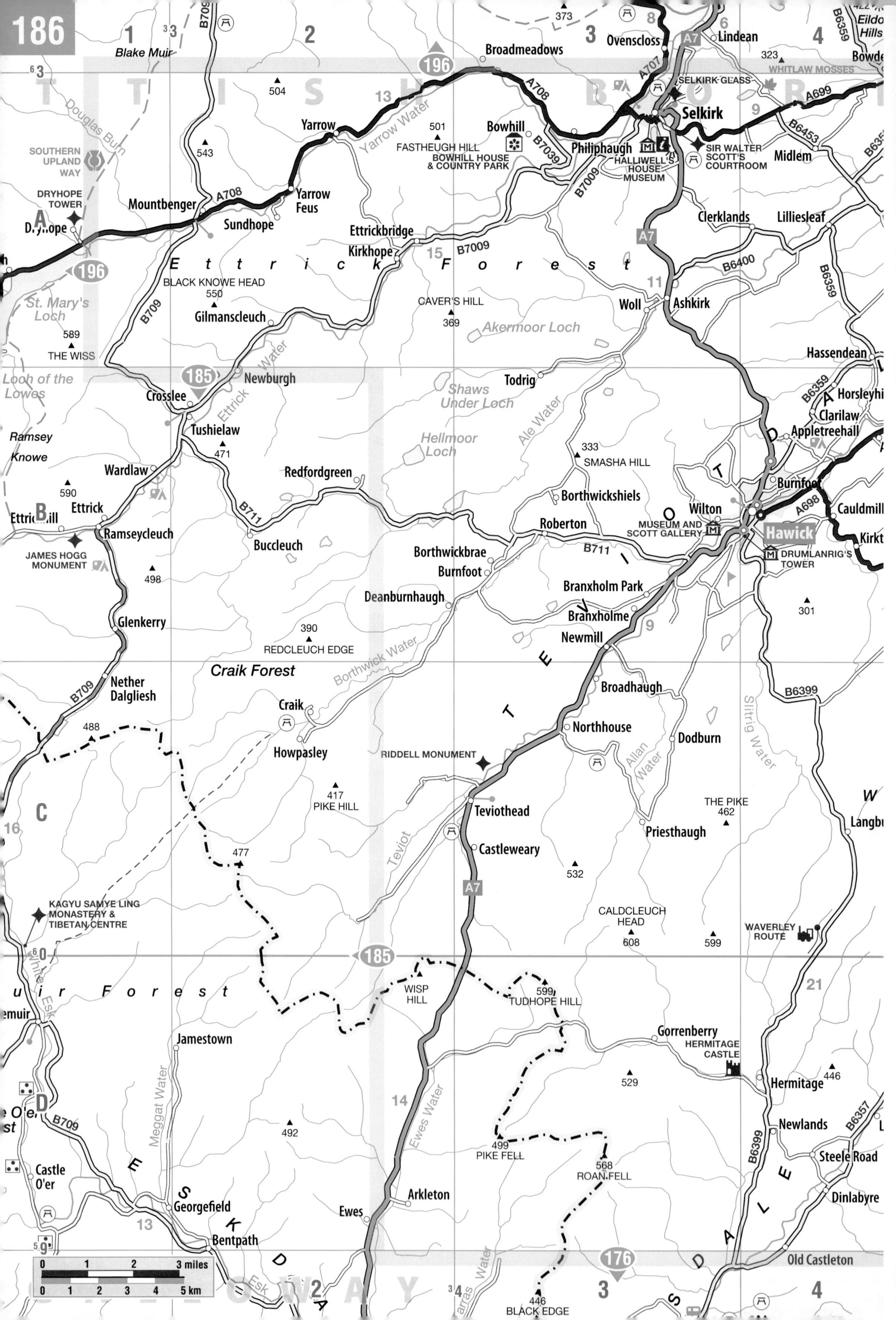
Blake Muir
Broadmeadows
Ovenscloss
Lindean
Eildon Hills
Bowden
196
373
323
WHITLAW MOSSES
SELKIRK GLASS
Selkirk
504
Douglas Burn
Yarrow
Yarrow Water
501
FASTHEUGH HILL
Bowhill
BOWHILL HOUSE & COUNTRY PARK
Philiphaugh
HALLIWELL'S HOUSE MUSEUM
SIR WALTER SCOTT'S COURTROOM
Midlem
SOUTHERN UPLAND WAY
543
DRYHOPE TOWER
Dryhope
Mountbenger
Yarrow Feus
Sundhope
Ettrickbridge
Kirkhope
Clerklands
Lilliesleaf
Ettrick Forest
BLACK KNOWE HEAD
550
St. Mary's Loch
Gilmanscleuch
CAVER'S HILL
369
Akermoor Loch
Woll
Ashkirk
589
THE WISS
Hassendean
Loch of the Lowes
185
Newburgh
Crosslee
Ettrick Water
Todrig
Shaws Under Loch
Horsleyhill
Clarilaw
Appletreehall
Ramsey Knowe
Tushielaw
471
Hellmoor Loch
Ale Water
333
SMASHA HILL
Wardlaw
Redfordgreen
Borthwickshiels
Burnfoot
590
Ettrick
Ettrick Hill
Ramseycleuch
JAMES HOGG MONUMENT
Buccleuch
Robertson
Wilton
MUSEUM AND SCOTT GALLERY
Hawick
Cauldmill
Kirkton
Borthwickbrae
Burnfoot
DRUMLANRIG'S TOWER
498
Deanburnhaugh
Branxholm Park
Branxholme
301
Glenkerry
390
REDCLEUCH EDGE
Newmill
Nether Dalgliesh
Craik Forest
Borthwick Water
Broadhaugh
Craik
488
B6399
Slitrig Water
Northhouse
Dodburn
Howpasley
RIDDELL MONUMENT
Allan Water
417
PIKE HILL
Teviothead
THE PIKE
462
Langburnshiels
Priesthaugh
Teviot
Castleweary
477
532
KAGYU SAMYE LING MONASTERY & TIBETAN CENTRE
CALDCLEUCH HEAD
608
599
WAVERLEY ROUTE
White Esk
Eskdalemuir Forest
WISP HILL
599
TUDHOPE HILL
Gorrenberry
HERMITAGE CASTLE
Jamestown
529
Hermitage
446
Meggat Water
Ewes Water
492
Newlands
499
PIKE FELL
568
ROAN FELL
Steele Road
Castle O'er
Arkleton
Dinlabyre
Georgefield
Ewes
Bentpath
ESKDALE
TEVIOTDALE
LIDDESDALE
DUMFRIES AND GALLOWAY
Tarras Water
176
Old Castleton
446
BLACK EDGE
3 miles
5 km

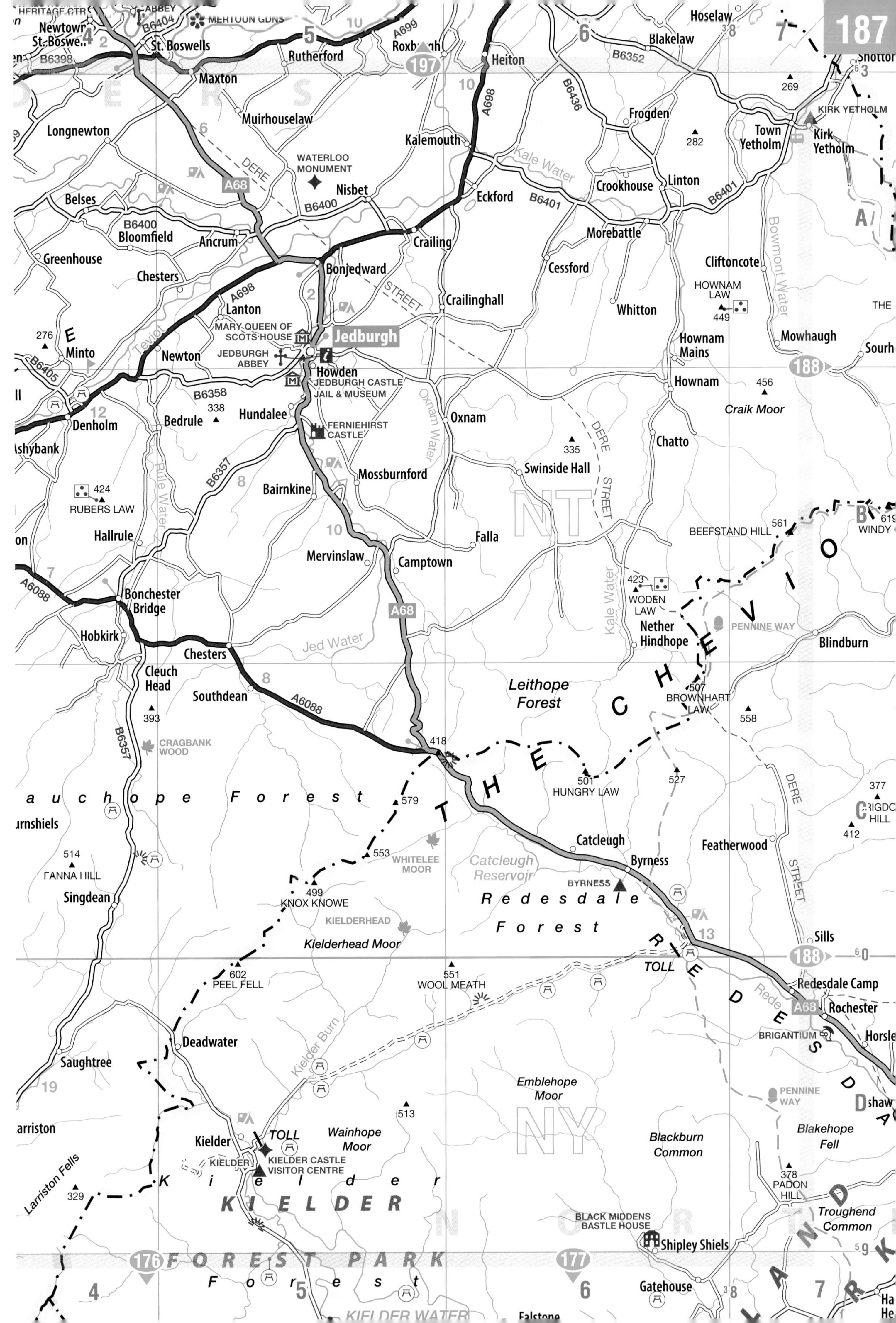

Newtown St. Boswells
St. Boswells
Maxton
Rutherford
Roxburgh
197
Heiton
Hoselaw
Blakelaw
Town Yetholm
Kirk Yetholm
KIRK YETHOLM
Frogden
Longnewton
Muirhouselaw
Kalemouth
WATERLOO MONUMENT
Nisbet
Eckford
Crookhouse
Linton
Belses
Bloomfield
Ancrum
Crailing
Morebattle
Greenhouse
Chesters
Bonjedward
Cessford
Cliftoncote
Lanton
Crailinghall
Whitton
HOWNAM LAW
MARY QUEEN OF SCOTS HOUSE
Jedburgh
JEDBURGH ABBEY
Howden
JEDBURGH CASTLE JAIL & MUSEUM
Minto
Newton
Hownam Mains
Mowhaugh
Hownam
188
Craik Moor
Denholm
Bedrule
Hundalee
Oxnam
FERNIEHIRST CASTLE
Ashybank
Chatto
Swinside Hall
Mossburnford
Bairnkine
RUBERS LAW
Hallrule
Falla
Mervinslaw
Camptown
BEEFSTAND HILL
WINDY
Bonchester Bridge
WODEN LAW
Nether Hindhope
PENNINE WAY
Blindburn
Hobkirk
Chesters
Cleuch Head
Southdean
Leithope Forest
BROWNHART LAW
CRAGBANK WOOD
HUNGRY LAW
Wauchope Forest
Catcleugh
Byrness
Featherwood
WHITELEE MOOR
Catcleugh Reservoir
BYRNESS
KNOX KNOWE
Singdean
TANNA HILL
KIELDERHEAD
Kielderhead Moor
Redesdale Forest
Sills
PEEL FELL
WOOL MEATH
TOLL
Redesdale Camp
Rochester
BRIGANTIUM
Deadwater
Saughtree
Kielder Burn
Emblehope Moor
Larriston Fells
Kielder
KIELDER
KIELDER CASTLE VISITOR CENTRE
Wainhope Moor
Blackburn Common
Blakehope Fell
PADON HILL
Troughend Common
KIELDER FOREST PARK
BLACK MIDDENS BASTLE HOUSE
Shipley Shiels
Gatehouse
THE CHEVIOT
REDESDALE
NORTHUMBERLAND PARK
KIELDER WATER
Falstone
176
177
Dere Street
Kale Water
Oxnam Water
Rule Water
Jed Water
Teviot
Bowmont Water
Rede

Shotton
Westnewton
Lanton
Newtown
West Horton
Hazelrigg
East Horton
Weetwood Hall
Kirknewton
Akeld
Humbleton
Wooler
Chatton
Greendikes
KIRK YETHOLM
Town Yetholm
Kirk Yetholm
Hethpool
College Burn
Earle
Haugh Head
CHILLINGHAM CASTLE
Chillingham
WILD CATTLE OF CHILLINGHAM
Middleton Hall
Newtown
PENNINE WAY
COLD LAW
North Middleton
Lilburn Tower
East Lilburn
Hepburn
South Middleton
DEVIL'S CAUSEWAY
Cliftoncote
Bowmont Water
MOUNTHOOLEY
THE SCHIL
Ilderton
Old Bewick
Langleeford
Roseden
Mowhaugh
Sourhope
Roddam
Wooperton
New Bewick
AUCHOPE CAIRN
THE CHEVIOT
Harthope Burn
Craik Moor
NT
DUNMOOR HILL
Brandon
Beanley
Greensidehill
Powburn
Breamish
Ingram
Branton
Shill Moor
Glanton
WINDY GYLE
CHEVIOT HILLS
NORTHUMBERLAND NATIONAL PARK
Glanton Pike
CUSHAT LAW
Great Ryle
Prendwick
Kidland Forest
Usway
Whittingham
PENNINE WAY
Barrowburn
Alnham
Aln
Thrunton
Blindburn
Little Ryle
Yetlington
Scrainwood
Callaly
Thrunton Wood
Biddlestone
Alwin
Netherton
Lorbottle Hall
Shillmoor
Lorbottle
Alwinton
Burradon
Linshiels
High Trewhitt
CRIGDON HILL
DERE STREET
Coquet
Cartington
Harbottle
Sharperton
eatherwood
LADY'S WELL
Warton
Snitter
WATTY BELL'S CAIRN
Holystone
Flotterton
Rothbury
CRAGSIDE HOUSE
Caistron
Thropton
Hepple
Newtown
Sills
Whitton
Great Tosson
Redesdale Camp
Rochester
NY
Rede
BRIGANTIUM
Horsley
TOSSON HILL
ROTHBURY FOREST
Low
Forestburn Gate
Otterburn Camp
PENNINE WAY
Elishaw
Harwood Forest
Blakehope Fell
REDESDALE
Otterburn
Elsdon
Fallowlees Burn
Fontburn Res.
Nunnykirk
PADON HILL
Raylees
Ewesley
Troughend Common
NORTHUMBERLAND
Rothley Shield East
HERTERTON HOUSE GARDEN
Longwitton
Rothley
0 1 2 3 miles
0 1 2 3 4 5 km

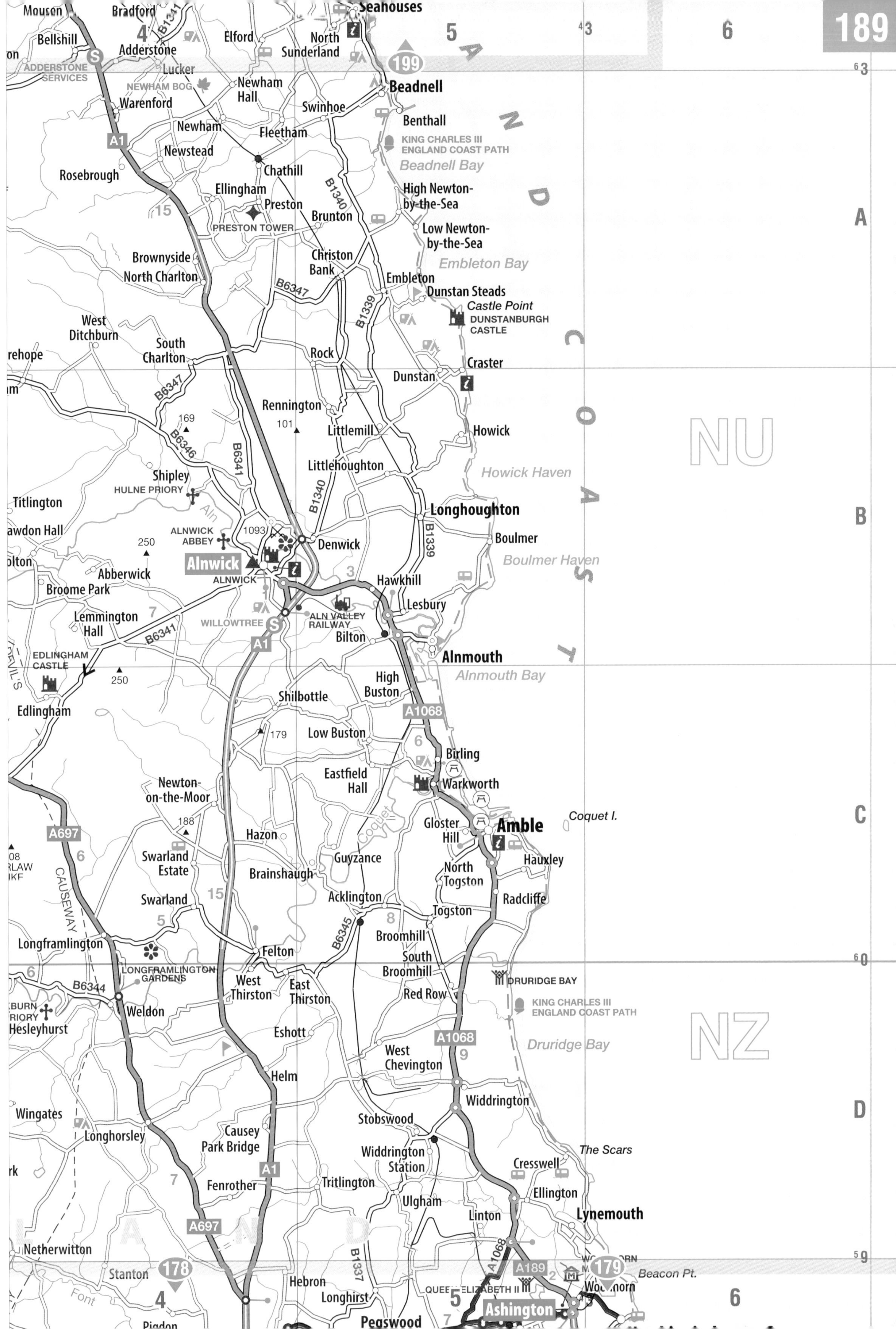
Seahouses
North Sunderland
Beadnell
Bradford
Mouson
Bellshill
Adderstone
ADDERSTONE SERVICES
Lucker
Elford
NEWHAM BOG
Newham Hall
Swinhoe
Warenford
Newham
Fleetham
Benthall
KING CHARLES III ENGLAND COAST PATH
Beadnell Bay
Newstead
Chathill
Rosebrough
Ellingham
Preston
PRESTON TOWER
Brunton
High Newton-by-the-Sea
Low Newton-by-the-Sea
Embleton Bay
Brownyside
North Charlton
Christon Bank
Embleton
Dunstan Steads
Castle Point
DUNSTANBURGH CASTLE
West Ditchburn
South Charlton
Rock
Craster
Dunstan
Rennington
Littlemill
Howick
Littlehoughton
Howick Haven
Shipley
HULNE PRIORY
Titlington
Longhoughton
Boulmer
Boulmer Haven
ALNWICK ABBEY
Alnwick
Denwick
Abberwick
Broome Park
Hawkhill
Lesbury
Lemmington Hall
ALN VALLEY RAILWAY
WILLOWTREE
Bilton
Alnmouth
Alnmouth Bay
EDLINGHAM CASTLE
Edlingham
Shilbottle
High Buston
Low Buston
Birling
Eastfield Hall
Warkworth
Newton-on-the-Moor
Coquet I.
Gloster Hill
Amble
Hazon
Hauxley
Swarland Estate
Brainshaugh
Guyzance
North Togston
Swarland
Acklington
Radcliffe
Togston
Broomhill
Longframlington
Felton
South Broomhill
LONGFRAMLINGTON GARDENS
West Thirston
East Thirston
DRURIDGE BAY
Red Row
Weldon
Hesleyhurst
Eshott
Druridge Bay
West Chevington
Helm
Widdrington
Wingates
Stobswood
Longhorsley
Causey Park Bridge
Widdrington Station
The Scars
Cresswell
Fenrother
Tritlington
Ellington
Ulgham
Linton
Lynemouth
Netherwitton
Stanton
Hebron
Longhirst
Beacon Pt.
Ashington
Pegswood
SANDSTONE COAST
NU
NZ
A1
A697
A1068
A189
B1340
B1339
B6347
B6346
B6341
B6345
B6344
B1337
CAUSEWAY
199
178
179

Gigalum Island
Cara Island
Tayinloan
322 CNOC NAN CRAOBH
CRUACH MHIC-AN T-SAOIR 364
Carradale Water
Grogport
Killean
Beacharr
354 CRUACH NAN GABHAR
Brackley
Clachaig Water
Muasdale
201
202
A83
Carradale
Amod
Glenacardoch Pt.
426 BEINN BHREAC
Port Righ
Belloch
Barr Water
Bridgend
Glenbarr
Torrisdale-Square
454 BEINN AN TUIRC
Carradale Pt.
Carradale Bay
Saddell Glen
Cleongart
Bellochantuy Bay
Saddell
SADDELL ABBEY
Bellochantuy
341 A'CHRUACH
Saddell Bay
Killocraw
Lussa Loch
397 SGREADAN HILL
Ugadale
Tangy Loch
Skeroblingarry
B842
Black Bay
Westport
Kilchenzie
Glenlussa Water
Peninver
Ardnacross Bay
A83
Kilmichael
West Darlochan
Low Smerby
Machrihanish Bay
CAMPBELTOWN
CAMPBELTOWN HERITAGE CENTRE
Campbeltown Loch
Machrihanish
Trodigal
Campbeltown
Island Davaar
DAVAAR ISLAND CAVE PAINTING
Drumlemble
B843
Stewarton
CAMPBELTOWN BUNKHOUSE
Kilkerran
Kildalloig
Knocknaha
Earadale Pt.
352 BEINN GHUILEAN
Achinhoan Hd.
ARDROSSAN (May-Sept)
BRODICK (May-Sept, Sat only)
B842
385 THE SLATE
Woodbank
446 CNOC MOY
BALLYCASTLE
Feochaig
Rubh'a'Mharaiche
Glen Breackerie
277 CNOC ODHAR
Conie Glen
Johnston's Pt.
North Carrine
Keprigan
Strone Glen
Macharioch
Polliwilline Bay
428
Southend
Carskiey
Brunerican Bay
Cove Pt.
MULL OF KINTYRE
Port Mean
Sheep I.
Rubha Chlachan
123
Sanda Island
KINTYRE
KILBRANNAN SOUND
0 1 2 3 miles
0 1 2 3 4 5 km

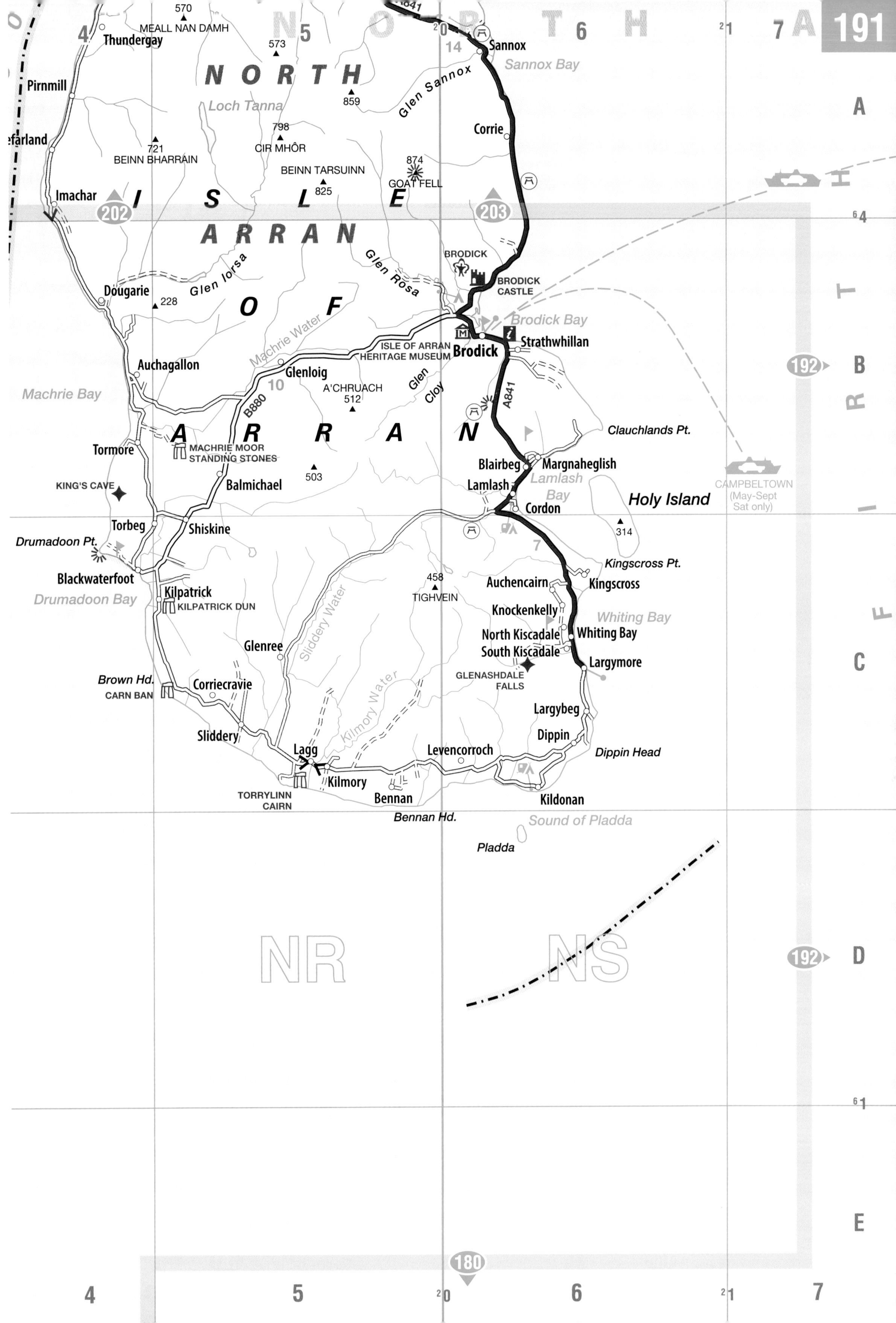
Thundergay
MEALL NAN DAMH
570
573
Pirnmill
NORTH
859
Glen Sannox
Sannox
Sannox Bay
Loch Tanna
798
CIR MHÔR
721
BEINN BHARRAIN
Corrie
874
GOAT FELL
BEINN TARSUINN
825
Imachar
ISLE
ARRAN
OF
ARRAN
Glen Iorsa
Glen Rosa
BRODICK
BRODICK CASTLE
Brodick Bay
Dougarie
228
Machrie Water
ISLE OF ARRAN HERITAGE MUSEUM
Brodick
Strathwhillan
Auchagallon
Glenloig
A'CHRUACH
512
Glen Cloy
A841
B880
Machrie Bay
Clauchlands Pt.
Tormore
MACHRIE MOOR STANDING STONES
Blairbeg
Margnaheglish
Lamlash Bay
Lamlash
Cordon
Holy Island
314
CAMPBELTOWN
(May-Sept Sat only)
KING'S CAVE
Balmichael
503
Torbeg
Shiskine
Drumadoon Pt.
Blackwaterfoot
Drumadoon Bay
Kilpatrick
KILPATRICK DUN
458
TIGHVEIN
Kingscross Pt.
Kingscross
Auchencairn
Knockenkelly
Whiting Bay
North Kiscadale
Whiting Bay
South Kiscadale
Largymore
Glenree
Sliddery Water
GLENASHDALE FALLS
Brown Hd.
CARN BAN
Corriecravie
Kilmory Water
Largybeg
Dippin
Dippin Head
Sliddery
Lagg
Levencorroch
Kilmory
Bennan
Kildonan
TORRYLINN CAIRN
Bennan Hd.
Sound of Pladda
Pladda
NR
NS
FIRTH
202
203
192
180
A
B
C
D
E
4
5
6
7

AYRSHIRE
Seamill
204
Dalgarven
AYRSHIRE MUSEUM OF COUNTRY LIFE & COSTUME
ABBEY
Kilwinning
Torranyard
Chapelhill
Dykesmains
Horse Isle
Ardrossan
NORTH AYRSHIRE HERITAGE CENTRE
Saltcoats
Stevenston
EGLINTON
Benslie
Cunninghamhead
Girdle Toll
Perceton
Irvine
Springside
Knockentiber
SCOTTISH MARITIME MUSEUM
Fullarton
Dreghorn
Irvine Bay
Drybridge
Gatehead
FIRTH
NS
Dundonald
DUNDONALD CASTLE
Earlston
191
Barassie
North Bay
Muirhead
Loans
Bogend
Symington
CAMPBELTOWN
(May-Sept Sat only)
Troon
South Bay
ROYAL TROON
Hansel Village
Lady Isle
Monkton
GLASGOW PRESTWICK
Prestwick
St Quivox
Woodfield
Newton on Ayr
Wallacetown
Whitletts
Ayr
AYR
Seafield
Belston
ROBERT BURNS BIRTHPLACE MUS
Belmont
Masonhill
Heads of Ayr
HEADS OF AYR FARM PARK
Doonfoot
MACLAURIN GALLERY & ROZELLE HOUSE
Alloway
Laigh Glengall
BURNS NATIONAL HERITAGE PARK
Fisherton
Dunure
287
Culroy
Minishant
Dalrymple
ELECTRIC BRAE
182
Culzean Bay
196
CULZEAN CASTLE
270
Whitefaulds
Maybole
CULZEAN
COLLEGIATE CHURCH
Kirkmichael
Maidenhead Bay
Aitkenhead
Loch Spallander
Maidens
CROSSRAGUEL ABBEY
TURNBERRY
Kirkoswald
Crosshill
Turnberry Bay
SOUTER JOHNNIE'S COTTAGE
Turnberry
252
Brest Rocks
Ruglen
180
181
Straiton
Townhead
Wallacetown
Water of Girvan
SOUTH
0 1 2 3 miles
0 1 2 3 4 5 km

Stewarton
Laighmuir
Flow Moss
Lochgoin Reservoir
CORSE HILL
Strathaven
Waterside
Fenwick
Laigh Fenwick
CRINS HILL
Whitelaw
Caldermill
Calder Water
Wallacegill Muir
Moscow
Onthank
Knockinlaw
DEAN CASTLE
Kilmarnock
Stobieside
Gilmourton
Drumclog
Greenholm
Grange
DICK INSTITUTE
Crookedholm
Galston
Newmilns
Darvel
Riccarton
Hurlford
Rough Moss
Shortlees
Crossroads
MILL RIG
Glengavel Reservoir
Sornhill
Craigie
WEDDER HILL
MIDDLEFIELD LAW
Millburn
Auchmillan
Cessnock Water
Netherwood
Mossgiel
BACHELOR'S CLUB
BURN'S HOUSE MUSEUM
SORN CASTLE
Tarbolton
Mauchline
Smallburn
Catrine
Sorn
Failford
AYR GORGE WOODLANDS
Mossblown
Haugh
Airds Moss
Crosshill
Stair
EAST AYRSHIRE
Cronberry
Back Rogerton
Trabboch
Ochiltree
Auchinleck
Lugar
WARDLAW HILL
Glenmuir
Glenmuirshaw
DUMFRIES HOUSE
Holmhead
Logan
Coylton
Coalhall
KEIR HARDIE STATUE
Cumnock
Hillhead
Drongan
BAIRD INSTITUTE MUSEUM
Netherthird
Dalblair
Craigens
Barbieston
Skares
Sinclairston
Hayhill
Littlemill
Rankinston
Pathhead
Mansfield
Water of Coyle
Connel Park
Bankglen
New Cumnock
Nith
Polnessan
KILMEIN HILL
Burnside
THE KNIPE
Patna
Burnfoot
Dalleagles
Afton Water
Waterside
DOON VALLEY RAILWAY
BENBEOCH
Burnton
Dalmellington
ENOCH HILL
BLACKCRAIG HILL
Afton Reservoir
Bogton Loch
Bellsbank
A71
A77
A76
A70
A719
A713
B743
B744
B7037
B730
B705
B7036
B7046
B741
B742
B751
B778
A735

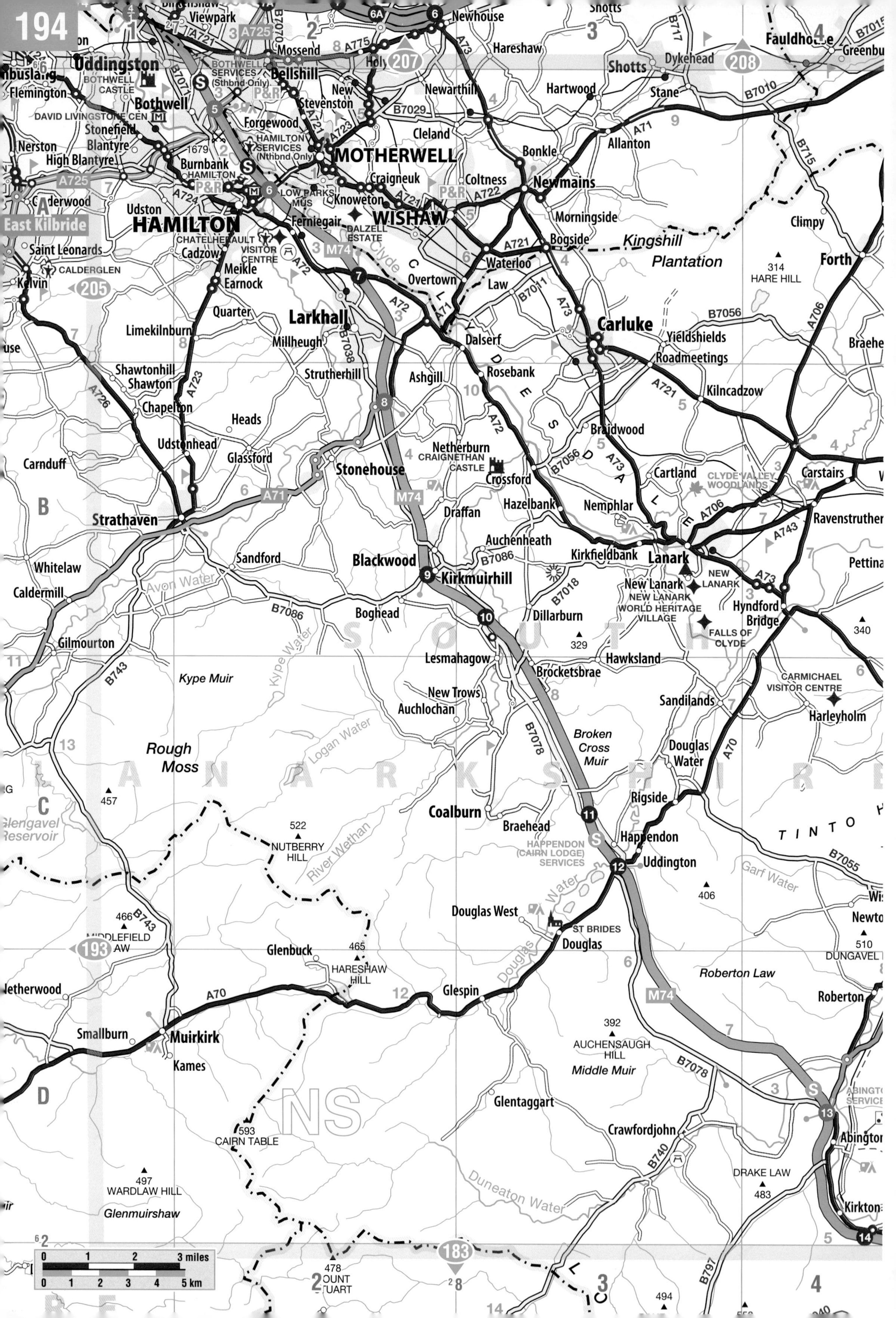
Viewpark
Newhouse
Shotts
Fauldhouse
Greenburn
Uddingston
Mossend
Bellshill
Holytown
207
Hareshaw
Dykehead
208
BOTHWELL SERVICES (Sthbnd Only)
BOTHWELL CASTLE
Flemington
Bothwell
New Stevenston
Newarthill
Hartwood
Stane
DAVID LIVINGSTONE CEN
Stonefield
Blantyre
High Blantyre
Nerston
Forgewood
HAMILTON SERVICES (Nthbnd Only)
Cleland
Allanton
Burnbank
MOTHERWELL
Bonkle
Craigneuk
Coltness
Newmains
Calderwood
Udston
HAMILTON
LOW PARKS MUS
Knowetop
WISHAW
Morningside
Climpy
East Kilbride
Ferniegair
DALZELL ESTATE
Bogside
Kingshill
Plantation
CHATELHERAULT VISITOR CENTRE
Cadzow
Waterloo
Forth
Saint Leonards
CALDERGLEN
314 HARE HILL
Meikle Earnock
Overtown
Law
Kelvin
205
Quarter
Larkhall
Dalserf
Carluke
Yieldshields
Roadmeetings
Braehead
Limekilnburn
Millheugh
Rosebank
Kilncadzow
Shawtonhill
Shawton
Strutherhill
Ashgill
Chapelton
Heads
Braidwood
Udstonhead
Glassford
Netherburn
CRAIGNETHAN CASTLE
Crossford
Cartland
CLYDE VALLEY WOODLANDS
Carstairs
Carnduff
Stonehouse
Strathaven
Draffan
Hazelbank
Nemphlar
Ravenstruther
Auchenheath
Whitelaw
Sandford
Blackwood
Kirkfieldbank
Lanark
Pettinain
Caldermill
Avon Water
Kirkmuirhill
New Lanark
NEW LANARK
NEW LANARK WORLD HERITAGE VILLAGE
Hyndford Bridge
Boghead
Dillarburn
FALLS OF CLYDE
340
Gilmourton
329
Lesmahagow
Hawksland
Brocketsbrae
CARMICHAEL VISITOR CENTRE
Kype Muir
Kype Water
New Trows
Auchlochan
Sandilands
Harleyholm
Rough Moss
Logan Water
Broken Cross Muir
Douglas Water
LANARKSHIRE
457
Glengavel Reservoir
Coalburn
Rigside
522 NUTBERRY HILL
Braehead
HAPPENDON (CAIRN LODGE) SERVICES
Happendon
TINTO
Uddington
River Wetham
Garf Water
406
Douglas West
ST BRIDES
Douglas
466
MIDDLEFIELD LAW
193
Glenbuck
465 HARESHAW HILL
Newton
510 DUNGAVEL HILL
Roberton Law
Netherwood
Glespin
Roberton
Smallburn
Muirkirk
Kames
392 AUCHENSAUGH HILL
Middle Muir
Glentaggart
ABINGTON SERVICES
NS
593 CAIRN TABLE
Crawfordjohn
Abington
497 WARDLAW HILL
Glenmuirshaw
Duneaton Water
DRAKE LAW 483
Kirkton
183
478 MOUNT STUART
494
0 1 2 3 miles
0 1 2 3 4 5 km

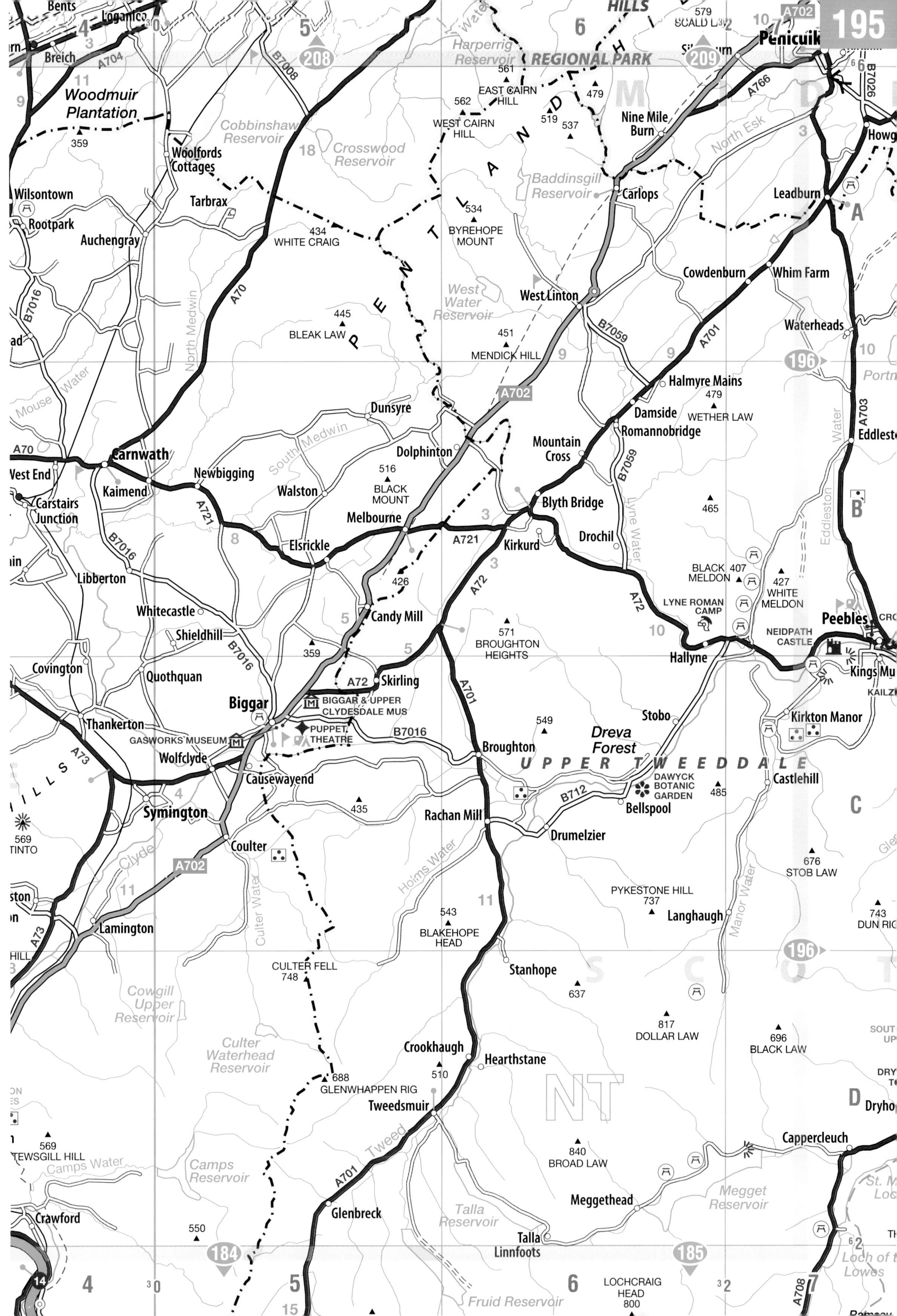
Penicuik
Nine Mile Burn
Carlops
Leadburn
West Linton
Cowdenburn
Whim Farm
Waterheads
Halmyre Mains
Damside
Romannobridge
Mountain Cross
Blyth Bridge
Drochil
Kirkurd
Eddleston
Peebles
Hallyne
Stobo
Kirkton Manor
Castlehill
Dawyck Botanic Garden
Bellspool
Drumelzier
Rachan Mill
Broughton
Skirling
Biggar
Biggar & Upper Clydesdale Mus
Puppet Theatre
Gasworks Museum
Wolfclyde
Causewayend
Symington
Coulter
Lamington
Thankerton
Covington
Quothquan
Shieldhill
Whitecastle
Libberton
Carstairs Junction
Kaimend
Carnwath
West End
Newbigging
Walston
Elsrickle
Melbourne
Dolphinton
Dunsyre
Candy Mill
Wilsontown
Rootpark
Auchengray
Tarbrax
Woolfords Cottages
Woodmuir Plantation
Breich
Bents
Pentland Hills Regional Park
Harperrig Reservoir
Cobbinshaw Reservoir
Crosswood Reservoir
Baddinsgill Reservoir
West Water Reservoir
Upper Tweeddale
Dreva Forest
Crookhaugh
Hearthstane
Tweedsmuir
Glenbreck
Stanhope
Meggethead
Talla Linnfoots
Talla Reservoir
Megget Reservoir
Cappercleuch
Crawford
Cowgill Upper Reservoir
Culter Waterhead Reservoir
Camps Reservoir
Fruid Reservoir
Langhaugh
Neidpath Castle
Lyne Roman Camp
Kings Muir
Tinto
White Craig
Bleak Law
Byrehope Mount
Mendick Hill
Black Mount
Broughton Heights
Culter Fell
Blakehope Head
Glenwhappen Rig
Dollar Law
Broad Law
Black Law
Stob Law
Pykestone Hill
Wether Law
Black Meldon
White Meldon
Dun Rig
Lochcraig Head
Tewsgill Hill
East Cairn Hill
West Cairn Hill
Scald Law
A70
A72
A73
A701
A702
A703
A704
A708
A721
A766
B7008
B7016
B7026
B7059
B712

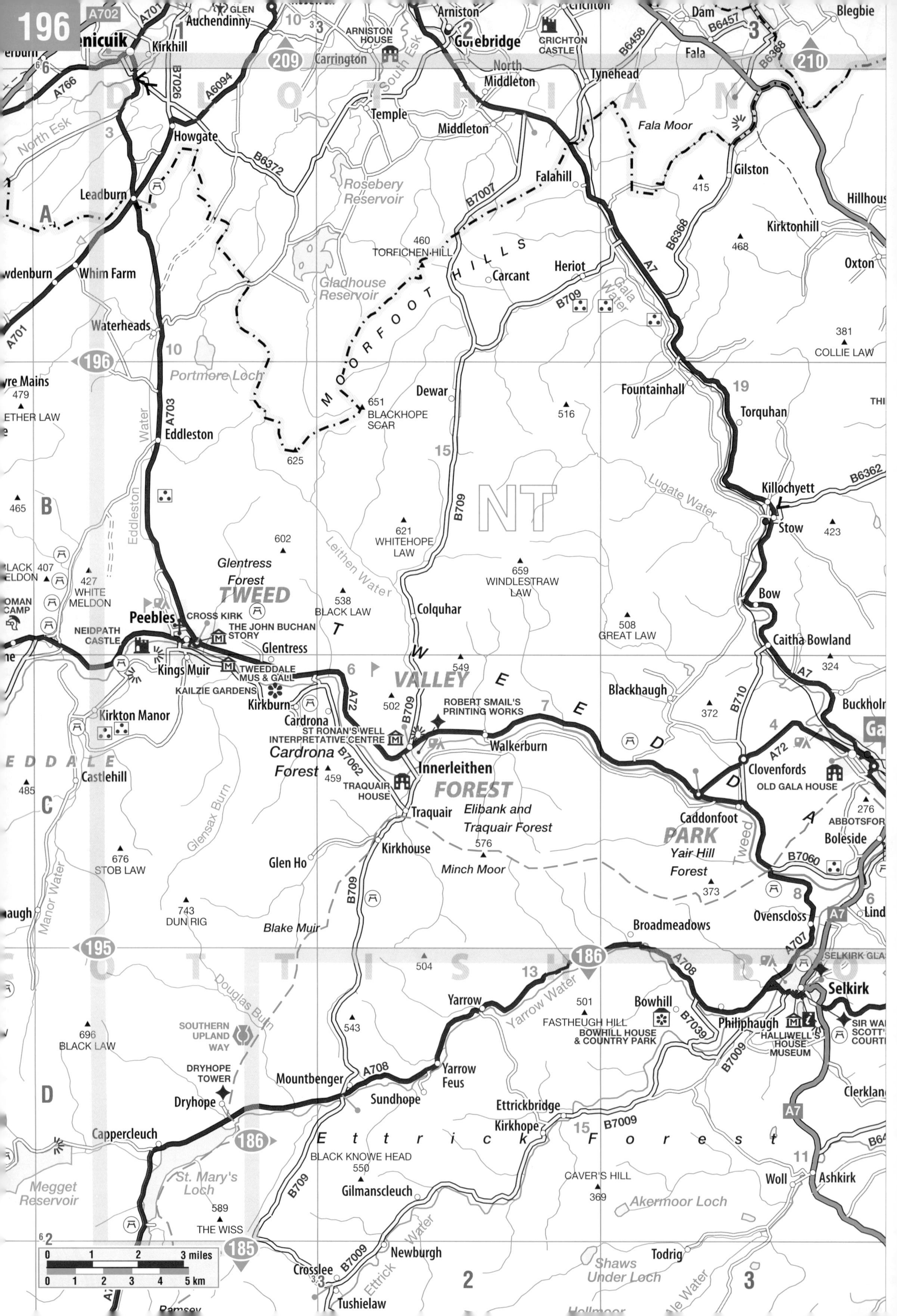
A702
A701
GLEN
Auchendinny
Penicuik
Kirkhill
B7026
A6094
A766
North Esk
Howgate
B6372
Leadburn
Whim Farm
A701
Waterheads
Portmore Loch
A703
Eddleston
Eddleston Water
Arniston
Gorebridge
ARNISTON HOUSE
Carrington
South Esk
CRICHTON CASTLE
Crichton
North Middleton
Temple
Middleton
Rosebery Reservoir
Gladhouse Reservoir
B7007
Falahill
460
TORFICHEN HILL
MOORFOOT HILLS
Carcant
Heriot
Gala Water
B709
651
BLACKHOPE SCAR
625
Dewar
Dam
B6457
Blegbie
Fala
B6458
B6368
Tynehead
Fala Moor
Gilston
415
A7
468
Kirktonhill
Hillhouse
Oxton
381
COLLIE LAW
Fountainhall
Torquhan
516
NT
Lugate Water
Killochyett
B6362
Stow
423
Bow
Caitha Bowland
508
GREAT LAW
324
Blackhaugh
372
B710
Buckholm
A72
Clovenfords
OLD GALA HOUSE
Caddonfoot
276
ABBOTSFORD
Boleside
B7060
Yair Hill Forest
373
Ovenscloss
A7
Lindean
A707
479
ETHER LAW
465
BLACK MELDON
407
427
WHITE MELDON
ROMAN CAMP
NEIDPATH CASTLE
Peebles
CROSS KIRK
THE JOHN BUCHAN STORY
Glentress Forest
TWEED
Glentress
Kings Muir
TWEEDDALE MUS & GALL
KAILZIE GARDENS
Kirkburn
Cardrona
602
538
BLACK LAW
Leithen Water
621
WHITEHOPE LAW
B709
Colquhar
659
WINDLESTRAW LAW
549
VALLEY
502
ROBERT SMAIL'S PRINTING WORKS
ST RONAN'S WELL INTERPRETATIVE CENTRE
Walkerburn
Cardrona Forest
B7062
459
TRAQUAIR HOUSE
Innerleithen
FOREST
Traquair
Elibank and Traquair Forest
576
Minch Moor
Kirkhouse
Glen Ho
Kirkton Manor
EDDALE
Castlehill
485
Glensax Burn
676
STOB LAW
743
DUN RIG
Manor Water
Blake Muir
Broadmeadows
PARK
Tweed
504
SCOTTISH BORDERS
Douglas Burn
Yarrow
Yarrow Water
501
FASTHEUGH HILL
Bowhill
BOWHILL HOUSE & COUNTRY PARK
B7039
A708
Philiphaugh
HALLIWELL'S HOUSE MUSEUM
Selkirk
SIR WALTER SCOTT'S COURTROOM
B7009
Clerklands
696
BLACK LAW
SOUTHERN UPLAND WAY
DRYHOPE TOWER
Dryhope
543
Mountbenger
A708
Yarrow Feus
Sundhope
Ettrickbridge
Kirkhope
B7009
Ettrick Forest
Cappercleuch
BLACK KNOWE HEAD
550
Gilmanscleuch
CAVER'S HILL
369
Akermoor Loch
Woll
Ashkirk
Megget Reservoir
St. Mary's Loch
589
THE WISS
B709
Ettrick Water
Newburgh
B7009
Crosslee
Tushielaw
Todrig
Shaws Under Loch
Ale Water
Ramsey
209
210
196
195
186
185
0 1 2 3 miles
0 1 2 3 4 5 km

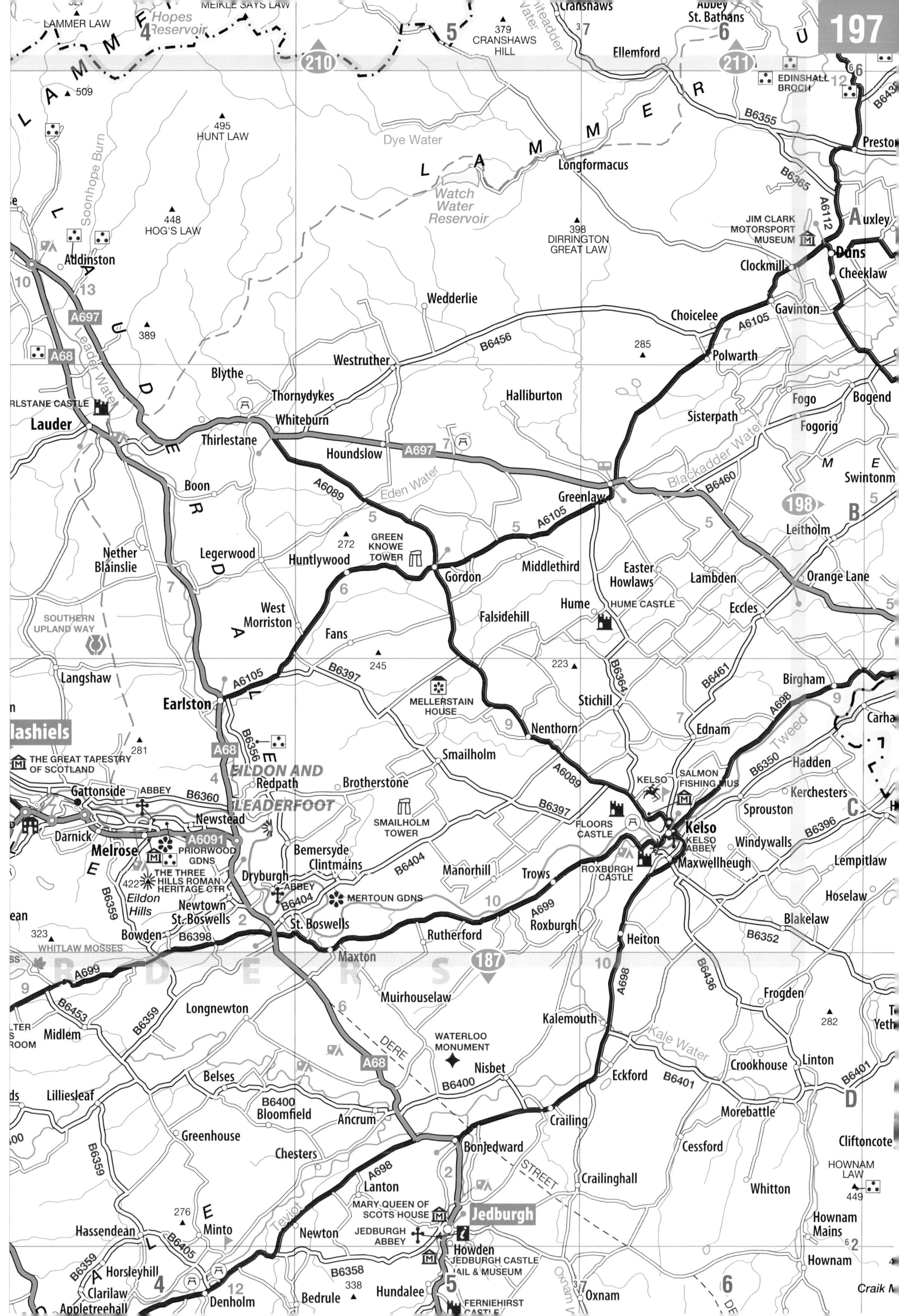
LAMMER LAW
Hopes Reservoir
MEIKLE SAYS LAW
379 CRANSHAWS HILL
Cranshaws
Abbey St. Bathans
Ellemford
210
211
EDINSHALL BROCH
509
495 HUNT LAW
Dye Water
B6355
Preston
L A M M E R M U I R
Longformacus
Soonhope Burn
Watch Water Reservoir
448 HOG'S LAW
398 DIRRINGTON GREAT LAW
B6365
A6112
Auxley
JIM CLARK MOTORSPORT MUSEUM
Duns
Addinston
Clockmill
Cheeklaw
Wedderlie
Choicelee
Gavinton
A697
A6105
A68
389
Leader Water
B6456
285
Polwarth
Westruther
Blythe
Thornydykes
Halliburton
Fogo
Bogend
THIRLESTANE CASTLE
Whiteburn
Sisterpath
Fogorig
Lauder
Thirlestane
Houndslow
Blackadder Water
Swintonm
Boon
Eden Water
A6089
Greenlaw
B6460
198
Leitholm
Nether Blainslie
GREEN KNOWE TOWER
272
Legerwood
Huntlywood
Gordon
Middlethird
Easter Howlaws
Lambden
Orange Lane
SOUTHERN UPLAND WAY
West Morriston
Hume
HUME CASTLE
Eccles
Fans
Falsidehill
245
223
B6397
B6364
B6461
Langshaw
Bingham
Earlston
MELLERSTAIN HOUSE
Stichill
Carha
Galashiels
281
Nenthorn
Ednam
Tweed
Hadden
THE GREAT TAPESTRY OF SCOTLAND
A68
B6356
Smailholm
B6350
Kerchesters
EILDON AND LEADERFOOT
KELSO
SALMON FISHING MUS
Gattonside
ABBEY
Redpath
Brotherstone
Sprouston
B6360
Newstead
SMAILHOLM TOWER
FLOORS CASTLE
Kelso
Darnick
A6091
KELSO ABBEY
Windywalls
B6396
Melrose
PRIORWOOD GDNS
Bemersyde
Clintmains
B6404
Manorhill
Trows
ROXBURGH CASTLE
Maxwellheugh
Lempitlaw
THE THREE HILLS ROMAN HERITAGE CTR
422
Eildon Hills
Dryburgh
ABBEY
MERTOUN GDNS
B6359
A699
Hoselaw
Newtown St. Boswells
St. Boswells
Roxburgh
Blakelaw
323
Bowden
B6398
Rutherford
Heiton
WHITLAW MOSSES
Maxton
187
B6352
B O R D E R S
B6436
Muirhouselaw
Frogden
B6453
Longnewton
282
Midlem
B6359
Kalemouth
Yeth
WATERLOO MONUMENT
DERE
A698
Kale Water
Linton
Crookhouse
Nisbet
Belses
A68
B6400
Eckford
B6401
Lilliesleaf
B6400 Bloomfield
Ancrum
Crailing
Morebattle
Greenhouse
Chesters
Bonjedward
Cessford
Cliftoncote
A698
STREET
HOWNAM LAW
449
Lanton
Crailinghall
Whitton
MARY QUEEN OF SCOTS HOUSE
Jedburgh
276
E
Minto
Hassendean
Teviot
Newton
JEDBURGH ABBEY
Hownam Mains
B6405
Howden
Horsleyhill
JEDBURGH CASTLE JAIL & MUSEUM
Hownam
B6358
338
Clarilaw
Denholm
Bedrule
Hundalee
Oxnam
Craik
Appletreehall
FERNIEHIRST CASTLE

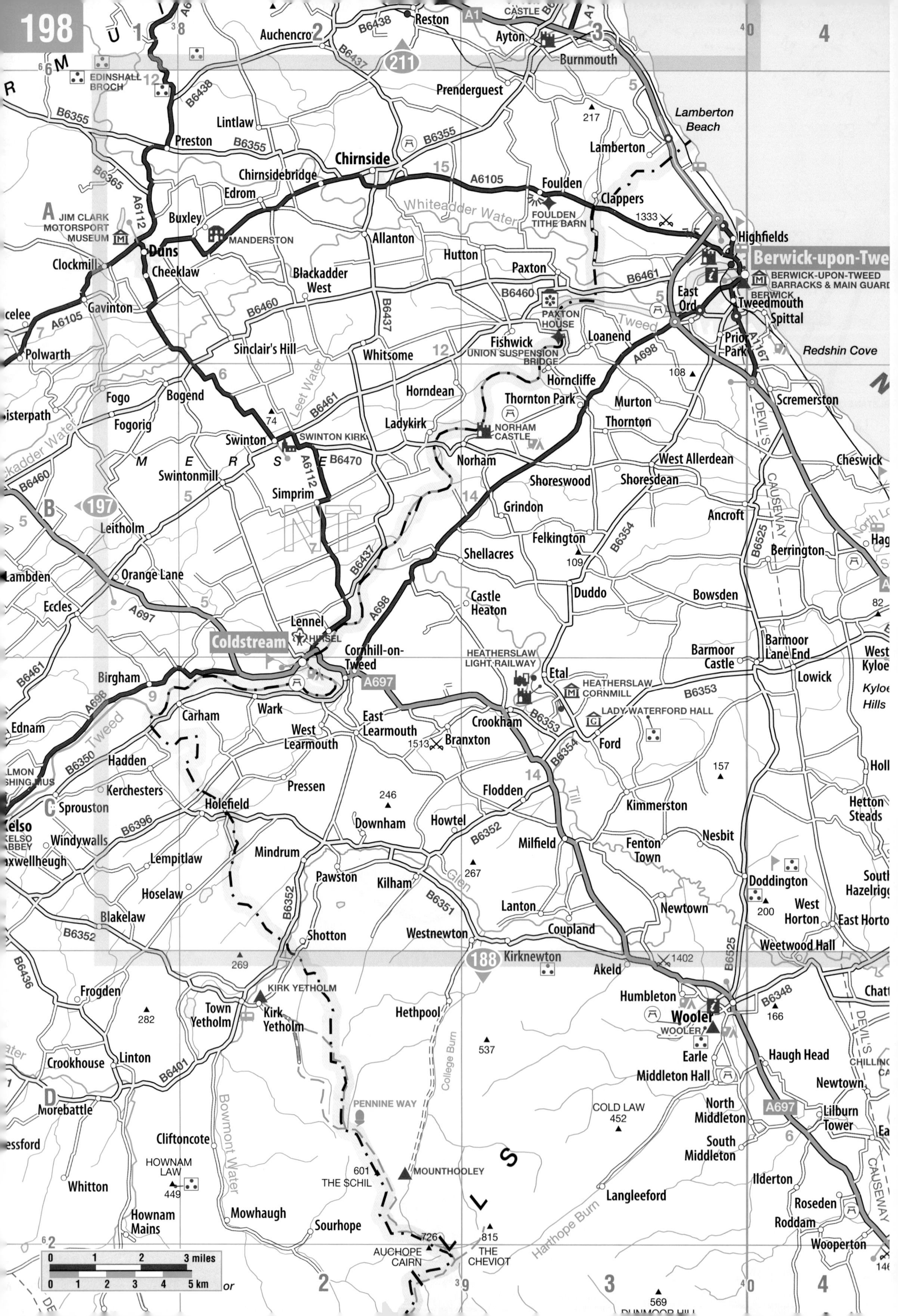
Reston
Auchencrow
Ayton
Burnmouth
211
EDINSHALL BROCH
Prenderguest
Lamberton Beach
Lamberton
Lintlaw
Preston
Chirnside
Chirnsidebridge
Edrom
Foulden
Clappers
Whiteadder Water
FOULDEN TITHE BARN
JIM CLARK MOTORSPORT MUSEUM
Buxley
MANDERSTON
Allanton
Highfields
Berwick-upon-Tweed
Duns
Clockmill
Cheeklaw
Hutton
Paxton
BERWICK-UPON-TWEED BARRACKS & MAIN GUARD
Blackadder West
East Ord
Tweedmouth
Spittal
Gavinton
PAXTON HOUSE
Loanend
Polwarth
Sinclair's Hill
Whitsome
Fishwick
UNION SUSPENSION BRIDGE
Prior Park
Redshin Cove
Horncliffe
Fogo
Bogend
Horndean
Thornton Park
Murton
Scremerston
Fogorig
Ladykirk
NORHAM CASTLE
Thornton
Swinton
SWINTON KIRK
MERSE
Norham
West Allerdean
Cheswick
Swintonmill
Shoreswood
Shoresdean
Simprim
Grindon
Ancroft
197
Leitholm
Felkington
Shellacres
Berrington
DEVIL'S CAUSEWAY
Orange Lane
Lambden
Duddo
Bowsden
Castle Heaton
Eccles
Lennel
Coldstream
HIRSEL
Cornhill-on-Tweed
HEATHERSLAW LIGHT RAILWAY
Barmoor Castle
Barmoor Lane End
West Kyloe
Kyloe Hills
Lowick
Etal
HEATHERSLAW CORNMILL
Birgham
Wark
Carham
East Learmouth
West Learmouth
Crookham
LADY WATERFORD HALL
Ford
Branxton
Ednam
Tweed
Hadden
Kerchesters
Pressen
Flodden
Sprouston
Holefield
Kelso
KELSO ABBEY
Windywalls
Downham
Howtel
Kimmerston
Hetton Steads
Mindrum
Milfield
Fenton Town
Nesbit
Lempitlaw
Pawston
Kilham
Doddington
Hoselaw
Lanton
Newtown
West Horton
East Horton
Blakelaw
Shotton
Westnewton
Coupland
Wetwood Hall
188
Kirknewton
Akeld
Frogden
KIRK YETHOLM
Humbleton
Town Yetholm
Kirk Yetholm
Hethpool
Wooler
WOOLER
Haugh Head
Crookhouse
Linton
Earle
Middleton Hall
Morebattle
PENNINE WAY
COLD LAW 452
North Middleton
Lilburn Tower
Cliftoncote
South Middleton
HOWNAM LAW 449
MOUNTHOOLEY
601 THE SCHIL
Whitton
Langleeford
Ilderton
Roseden
Hownam Mains
Mowhaugh
Sourhope
Roddam
AUCHOPE CAIRN
THE CHEVIOT
815
Wooperton
Bowmont Water
College Burn
Harthope Burn
0 1 2 3 miles
0 1 2 3 4 5 km

NU
NORTHUMBERLAND
Goswick
Beal
Causeway
Holy Island Sands
Holy Island
LINDISFARNE
Emmanuel Hd.
Holy Island (Lindisfarne)
LINDISFARNE CASTLE
Castle Pt.
HERITAGE CENTRE
LINDISFARNE PRIORY
Guile Pt.
Fenham
Fenwick
East Kyloe
Buckton
Elwick
Ross
Budle Bay
Detchant
Middleton
Belford
North Hazelrigg
Easington
B1342
Budle
Waren Mill
BAMBURGH CASTLE
Bamburgh
B1340
Burton
Glororum
Spindlestone
Bradford
B1341
B6349
Mousen
Bellshill
Warenton
Adderstone
ADDERSTONE SERVICES
Lucker
NEWHAM BOG
Newham Hall
Elford
North Sunderland
Seahouses
Farne Islands
Staple Sound
FARNE ISLANDS
Inner Sound
Beadnell
Benthall
KING CHARLES III ENGLAND COAST PATH
Beadnell Bay
Swinhoe
Warenford
B6348
Greendikes
Newham
Fleetham
Newstead
Chathill
Rosebrough
Chillingham
WILD CATTLE OF CHILLINGHAM
Hepburn
Ellingham
Preston
PRESTON TOWER
Brunton
High Newton-by-the-Sea
Low Newton-by-the-Sea
Embleton Bay
Brownyside
North Charlton
Christon Bank
Embleton
Dunstan Steads
Castle Point
DUNSTANBURGH CASTLE
B6347
B1339
Old Bewick
B6346
Harehope
West Ditchburn
South Charlton
Rock
Craster
New Bewick
Eglingham
Dunstan
Rennington
Beanley
Littlemill
Howick
A1
189
A
B
C
D
4
5
6
7

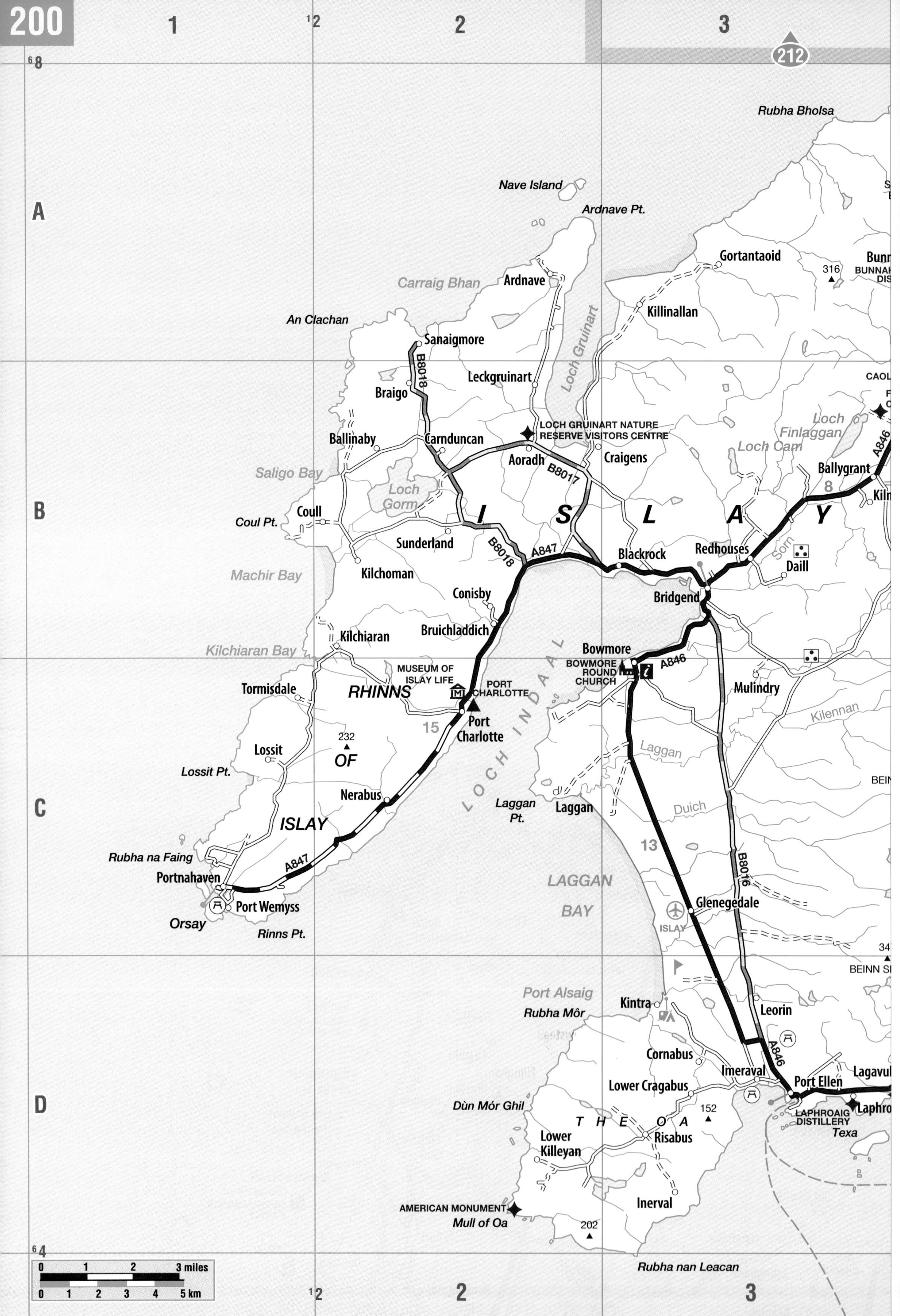

212
Rubha Bholsa
Nave Island
Ardnave Pt.
Gortantaoid
Ardnave
Carraig Bhan
Killinallan
An Clachan
Sanaigmore
Loch Gruinart
Leckgruinart
Braigo
LOCH GRUINART NATURE RESERVE VISITORS CENTRE
Ballinaby
Carnduncan
Aoradh
Craigens
Saligo Bay
Loch Gorm
Loch Finlaggan
Loch Cam
Ballygrant
Coull
Coul Pt.
I S L A Y
Sunderland
Blackrock
Redhouses
Daill
Machir Bay
Kilchoman
Bridgend
Conisby
Kilchiaran
Bruichladdich
Kilchiaran Bay
Bowmore
BOWMORE ROUND CHURCH
MUSEUM OF ISLAY LIFE
PORT CHARLOTTE
Tormisdale
RHINNS
Mulindry
Port Charlotte
Kilennan
Laggan
Lossit
OF
Lossit Pt.
LOCH INDAAL
Nerabus
Laggan Pt.
Laggan
Duich
ISLAY
Rubha na Faing
Portnahaven
Port Wemyss
Orsay
Rinns Pt.
LAGGAN BAY
Glenegedale
ISLAY
Port Alsaig
Rubha Mòr
Kintra
Leorin
Cornabus
Imeraval
Port Ellen
Lower Cragabus
Dùn Mór Ghil
THE OA
Risabus
LAPHROAIG DISTILLERY
Texa
Lower Killeyan
Inerval
AMERICAN MONUMENT
Mull of Oa
Rubha nan Leacan
A847
A846
B8018
B8017
B8016
0 1 2 3 miles
0 1 2 3 4 5 km

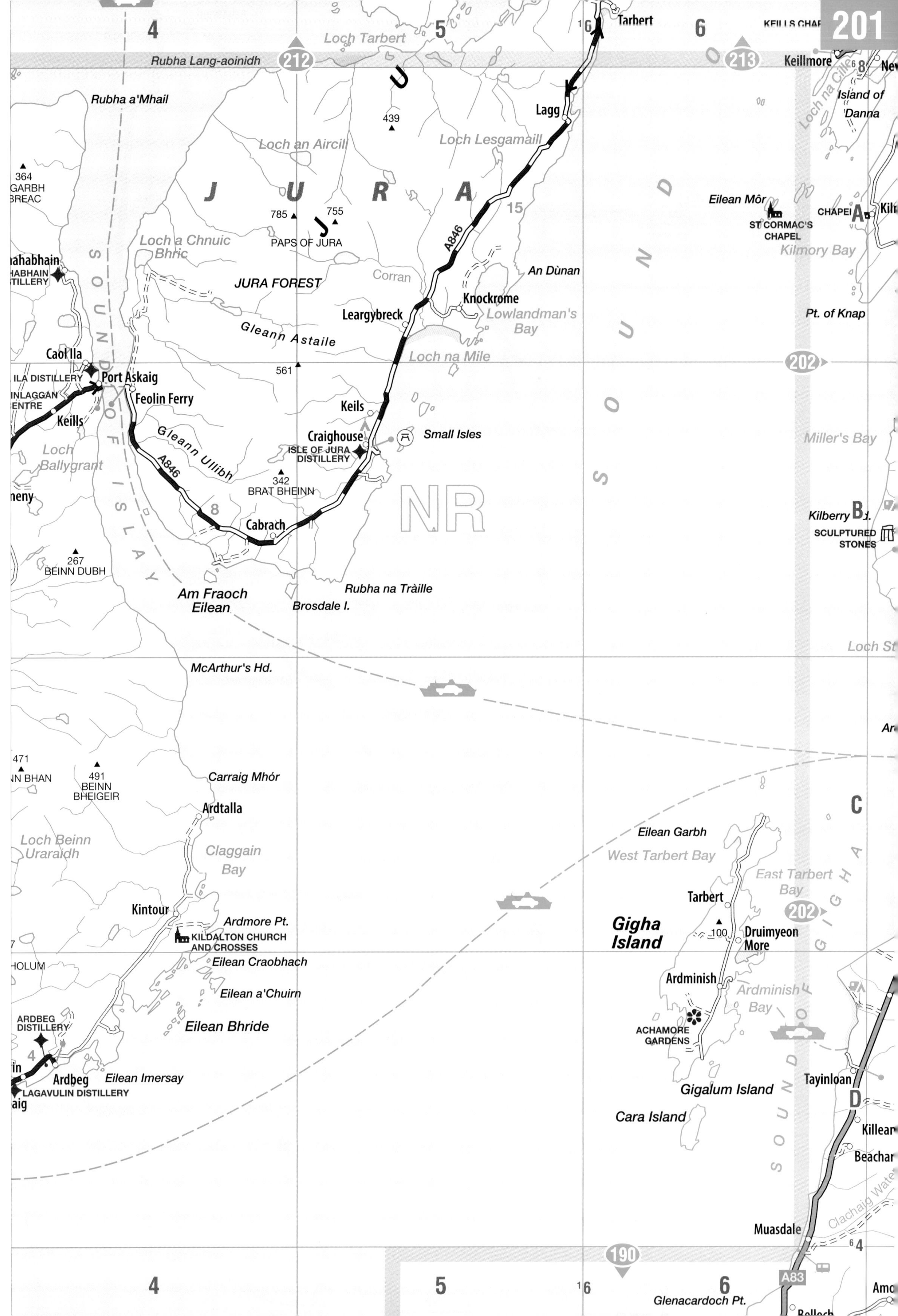

Tarbert
KEILLS CHAP
Loch Tarbert
Rubha Lang-aoinidh
212
213
Keillmore
Island of Danna
Loch na Cille
Rubha a'Mhail
439
Lagg
Loch an Aircil
Loch Lesgamaill
364 GARBH BREAC
JURA
785
755
PAPS OF JURA
15
Eilean Mòr
ST CORMAC'S CHAPEL
CHAPEL
Kilmory Bay
Loch a Chnuic Bhric
A846
JURA FOREST
Corran
An Dùnan
Knockrome
Lowlandman's Bay
Leargybreck
Pt. of Knap
Gleann Astaile
Caol Ila
ILA DISTILLERY
Port Askaig
Feolin Ferry
561
Loch na Mile
202
Keills
Keils
Craighouse
ISLE OF JURA DISTILLERY
Small Isles
Miller's Bay
Loch Ballygrant
Gleann Ullibh
342 BRAT BHEINN
SOUND OF ISLAY
SOUND OF JURA
NR
8
Cabrach
Kilberry
SCULPTURED STONES
267 BEINN DUBH
Am Fraoch Eilean
Brosdale I.
Rubha na Tràille
Loch St
McArthur's Hd.
471
491 BEINN BHEIGEIR
Carraig Mhór
Ardtalla
Loch Beinn Uraraidh
Claggain Bay
Eilean Garbh
West Tarbert Bay
East Tarbert Bay
Kintour
Ardmore Pt.
KILDALTON CHURCH AND CROSSES
Tarbert
Gigha Island
100
Druimyeon More
Eilean Craobhach
Ardminish
Ardminish Bay
Eilean a'Chuirn
ARDBEG DISTILLERY
Eilean Bhride
ACHAMORE GARDENS
SOUND OF GIGHA
Ardbeg
Eilean Imersay
LAGAVULIN DISTILLERY
Tayinloan
Gigalum Island
Cara Island
Killean
Beachar
Clachaig Water
Muasdale
190
A83
Glenacardoch Pt.
4
5
6
B
C
D

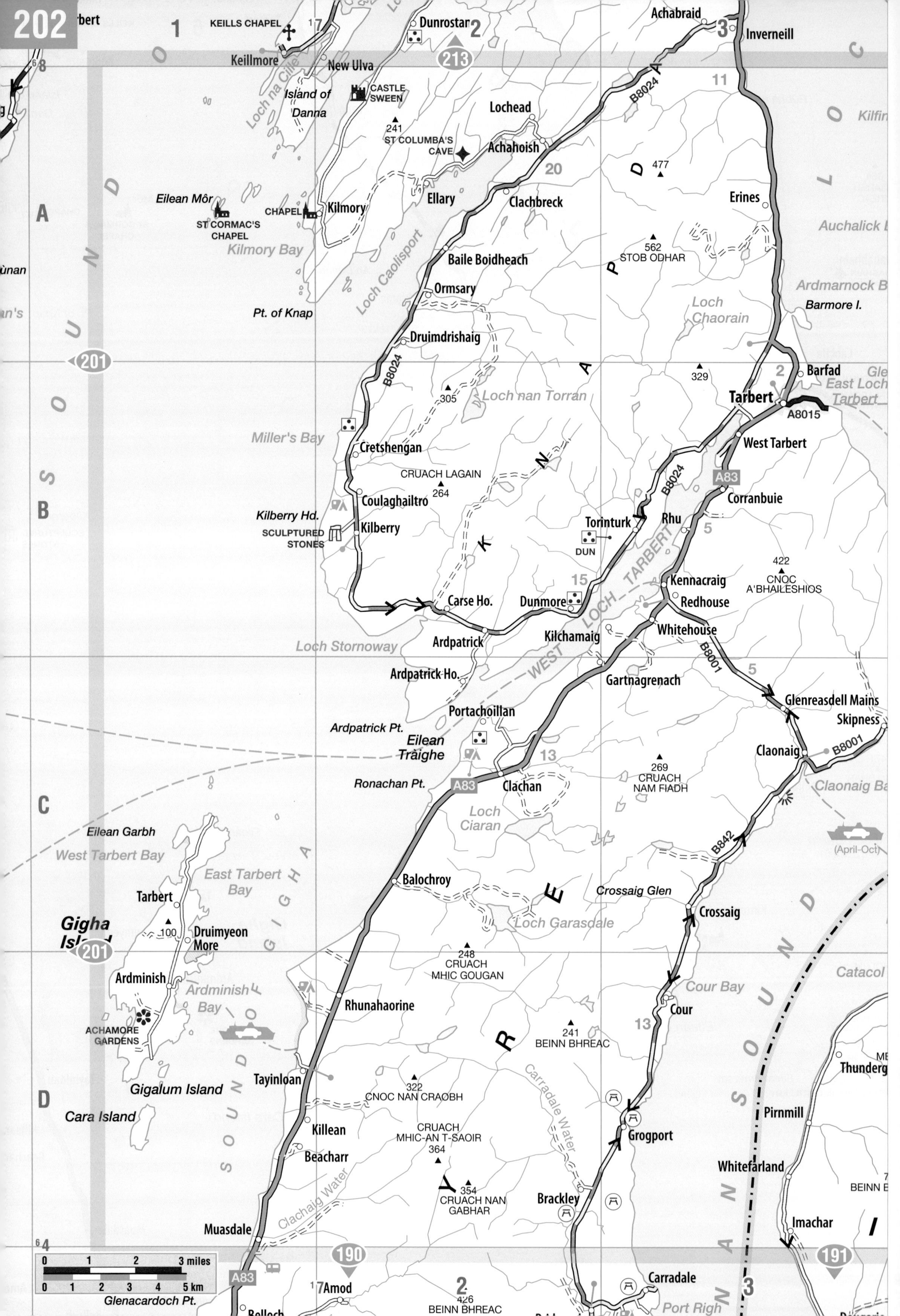
KEILLS CHAPEL
Keillmore
Dunrostan
New Ulva
Island of Danna
Loch na Cille
CASTLE SWEEN
241 ST COLUMBA'S CAVE
Lochead
Achahoish
Achabraid
Inverneill
B8024
Eilean Mòr
ST CORMAC'S CHAPEL
CHAPEL
Kilmory
Kilmory Bay
Ellary
Clachbreck
477
Erines
Loch Caolisport
Baile Boidheach
562 STOB ODHAR
Auchalick
Ardmarnock B
Ormsary
Pt. of Knap
Loch Chaorain
Barmore I.
Druimdrishaig
329
Barfad
East Loch Tarbert
Tarbert
A8015
305
Loch nan Torran
Miller's Bay
West Tarbert
A83
Cretshengan
CRUACH LAGAIN 264
Coulaghailtro
Corranbuie
Kilberry Hd.
SCULPTURED STONES
Kilberry
Torinturk
Rhu
DUN
422 CNOC A'BHAILESHIOS
Kennacraig
Redhouse
Carse Ho.
Dunmore
Whitehouse
Kilchamaig
WEST LOCH TARBERT
Loch Stornoway
Ardpatrick
B8001
Ardpatrick Ho.
Gartnagrenach
Glenreasdell Mains
Skipness
Portachoillan
Ardpatrick Pt.
Eilean Traighe
Claonaig
Claonaig Bay
269 CRUACH NAM FIADH
Ronachan Pt.
Clachan
Loch Ciaran
(April-Oct)
Eilean Garbh
West Tarbert Bay
East Tarbert Bay
B842
Balochroy
Crossaig Glen
Tarbert
Crossaig
Loch Garasdale
Gigha Island
100
Druimyeon More
248 CRUACH MHIC GOUGAN
Catacol
Ardminish
Ardminish Bay
Cour Bay
Rhunahaorine
Cour
ACHAMORE GARDENS
241 BEINN BHREAC
Carradale Water
Thunderg
Tayinloan
322 CNOC NAN CRAOBH
Gigalum Island
Cara Island
Pirnmill
Killean
CRUACH MHIC-AN T-SAOIR 364
Grogport
Beacharr
Clachaig Water
Whitefarland
354 CRUACH NAN GABHAR
Brackley
BEINN B
Muasdale
Imachar
0 1 2 3 miles
0 1 2 3 4 5 km
Glenacardoch Pt.
Amod
426 BEINN BHREAC
Carradale
Port Righ
SOUND OF GIGHA
KNAPDALE
KILBRANNAN SOUND
KYRE
213
201
190
191

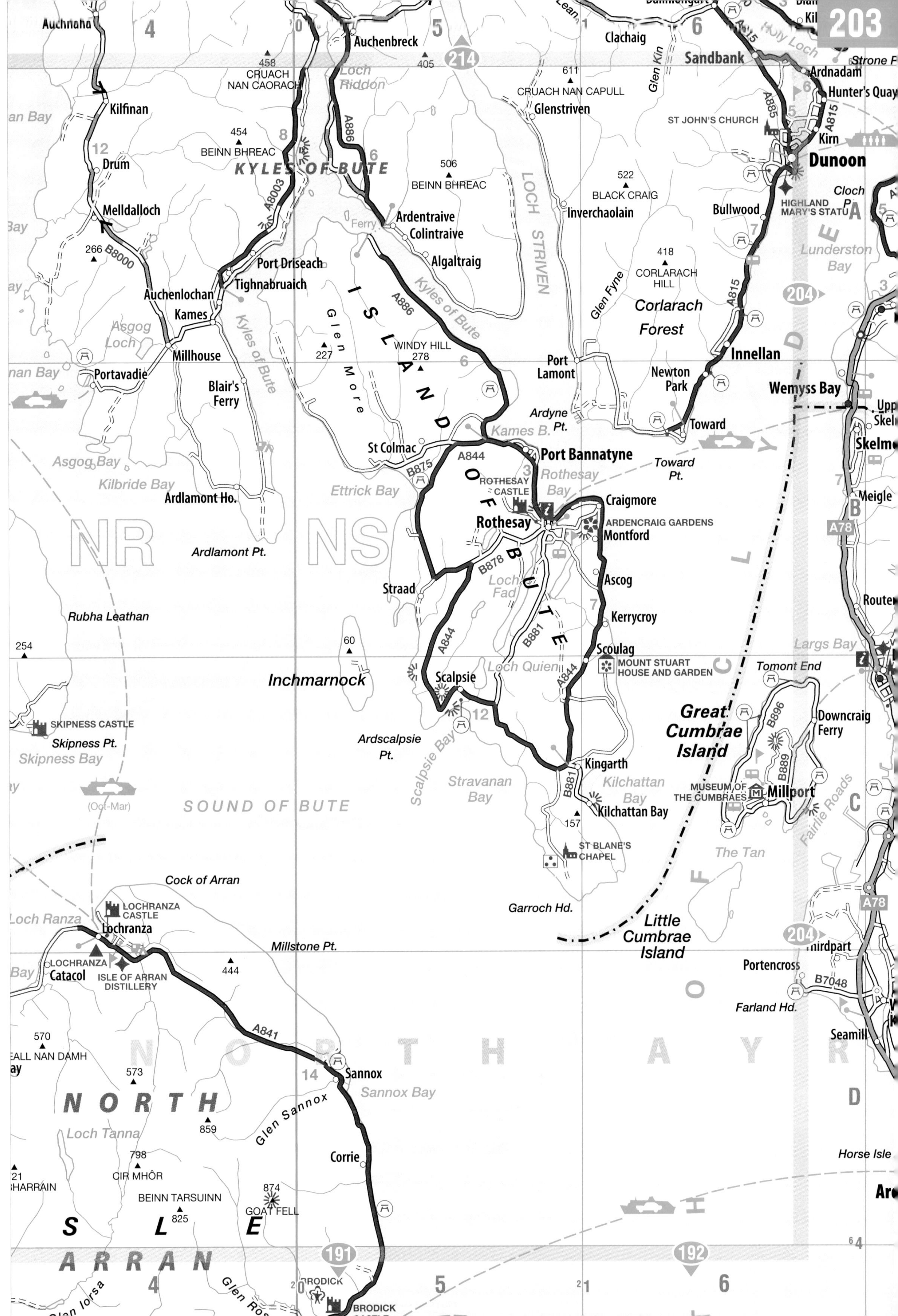
Auchnaha
Kilfinan
Drum
Melldalloch
Auchenbreck
CRUACH NAN CAORACH
458
405
214
Loch Riddon
BEINN BHREAC
454
KYLES OF BUTE
A8003
A886
506
BEINN BHREAC
Clachaig
Sandbank
Glen Kin
611
CRUACH NAN CAPULL
Glenstriven
LOCH STRIVEN
Inverchaolain
522
BLACK CRAIG
Ardnadam
Hunter's Quay
A815
A885
Holy Loch
ST JOHN'S CHURCH
Kirn
Dunoon
Cloch
HIGHLAND MARY'S STATUE
Bullwood
Lunderston Bay
266
B8000
Ferry
Ardentraive
Colintraive
Algaltraig
Port Driseach
Tighnabruaich
Auchenlochan
Kames
Asgog Loch
Millhouse
Portavadie
Blair's Ferry
Kyles of Bute
ISLAND OF BUTE
Glen More
227
WINDY HILL
278
418
CORLARACH HILL
Glen Fyne
Corlarach Forest
204
Port Lamont
Newton Park
Innellan
Wemyss Bay
Ardyne Pt.
Toward
Kames B.
St Colmac
A844
Port Bannatyne
B875
ROTHESAY CASTLE
Rothesay Bay
Toward Pt.
Skelmorlie
Asgog Bay
Kilbride Bay
Ardlamont Ho.
Ettrick Bay
Rothesay
Craigmore
ARDENCRAIG GARDENS
Montford
Meigle
A78
NR
NS
Ardlamont Pt.
B878
Loch Fad
Straad
Ascog
Kerrycroy
Routenburn
Rubha Leathan
254
60
B881
Scoulag
MOUNT STUART HOUSE AND GARDEN
Largs Bay
Tomont End
Inchmarnock
Scalpsie
Loch Quien
SKIPNESS CASTLE
Skipness Pt.
Skipness Bay
Great Cumbrae Island
Downcraig Ferry
B896
B889
Ardscalpsie Pt.
Scalpsie Bay
Stravanan Bay
Kingarth
Kilchattan Bay
MUSEUM OF THE CUMBRAES
Millport
Fairlie Roads
(Oct-Mar)
SOUND OF BUTE
157
ST BLANE'S CHAPEL
The Tan
Cock of Arran
LOCHRANZA CASTLE
Garroch Hd.
Loch Ranza
Lochranza
Little Cumbrae Island
Millstone Pt.
Portencross
B7048
LOCHRANZA
Catacol
ISLE OF ARRAN DISTILLERY
444
Farland Hd.
Seamill
A841
570
NORTH AYRSHIRE
573
Sannox
Sannox Bay
NORTH
Glen Sannox
859
Loch Tanna
798
CIR MHÒR
Corrie
Horse Isle
874
BEINN TARSUINN
GOAT FELL
825
ISLE OF ARRAN
191
192
Glen Iorsa
BRODICK
Glen Rosa

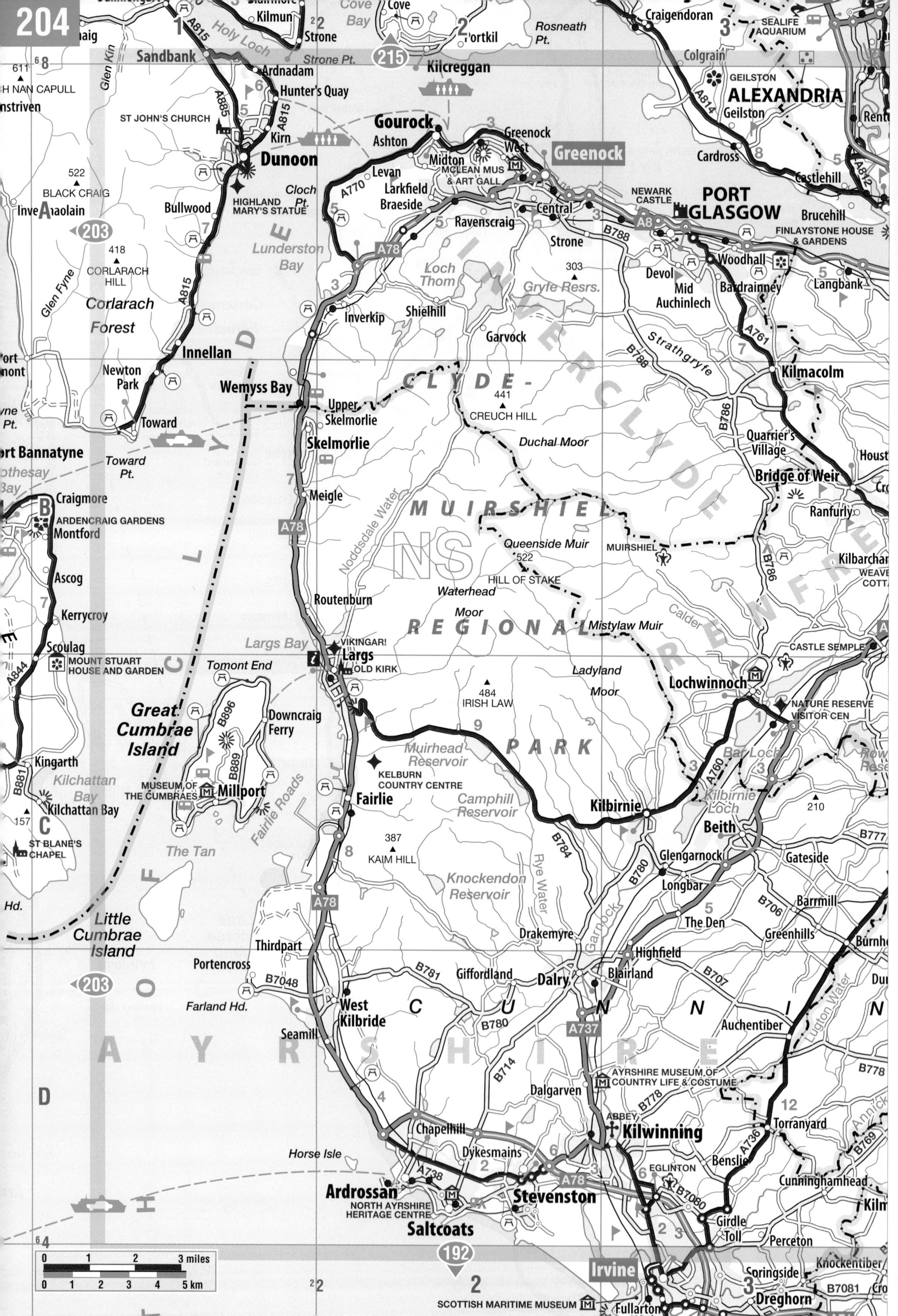
Kilmun
Strone
Cove
Cove Bay
Portkil
Rosneath Pt.
Craigendoran
SEALIFE AQUARIUM
Holy Loch
Sandbank
Strone Pt.
215
Kilcreggan
Colgrain
611
H NAN CAPULL
nstriven
Glen Kin
Ardnadam
Hunter's Quay
A815
A885
ST JOHN'S CHURCH
Kirn
Dunoon
Gourock
Ashton
Greenock West
Greenock
GEILSTON
ALEXANDRIA
Geilston
A814
Cardross
Castlehill
A812
522
BLACK CRAIG
Inverchaolain
203
HIGHLAND MARY'S STATUE
Cloch Pt.
Levan
Larkfield
Braeside
Midton
MCLEAN MUS & ART GALL
A770
Central
NEWARK CASTLE
PORT GLASGOW
Brucehill
FINLAYSTONE HOUSE & GARDENS
A8
Bullwood
Ravenscraig
Strone
B788
418
CORLARACH HILL
Lunderston Bay
A78
Loch Thom
303
Gryfe Resrs.
Devol
Mid Auchinlech
Woodhall
Bardrainney
Langbank
Glen Fyne
Corlarach Forest
Inverkip
Shielhill
Garvock
INVERCLYDE
Strathgryfe
A761
Innellan
Newton Park
Wemyss Bay
CLYDE-
441
CREUCH HILL
Kilmacolm
Upper Skelmorlie
Toward
B786
Quarrier's Village
Duchal Moor
Skelmorlie
Toward Pt.
rt Bannatyne
othesay Bay
Bridge of Weir
Craigmore
ARDENCRAIG GARDENS
Montford
Meigle
Noddsdale Water
MUIRSHIEL
NS
Ranfurly
Queenside Muir
522
HILL OF STAKE
Kilbarchan
Ascog
Waterhead Moor
Routenburn
Kerrycroy
REGIONAL
Mistylaw Muir
Calder
RENFREW
Scoulag
MOUNT STUART HOUSE AND GARDEN
A844
Largs Bay
VIKINGAR!
Largs
OLD KIRK
CASTLE SEMPLE
Tomont End
Ladyland Moor
Lochwinnoch
Great Cumbrae Island
B896
Downcraig Ferry
484
IRISH LAW
NATURE RESERVE VISITOR CEN
PARK
Muirhead Reservoir
Barr Loch
Kingarth
Kilchattan Bay
B881
B889
MUSEUM OF THE CUMBRAES
Millport
Fairlie Roads
KELBURN COUNTRY CENTRE
Fairlie
Camphill Reservoir
Kilbirnie
A760
Kilbirnie Loch
Beith
210
157
ST BLANE'S CHAPEL
The Tan
387
KAIM HILL
B784
Glengarnock
B780
Gateside
B777
Knockendon Reservoir
Rye Water
Longbar
Barrmill
B706
Little Cumbrae Island
Hd.
A78
The Den
Greenhills
Drakemyre
Garnock
Thirdpart
Highfield
Portencross
B7048
B781
Giffordland
Dalry
Blairland
B707
Farland Hd.
West Kilbride
A737
Auchentiber
Lugton Water
Seamill
AYRSHIRE
CUNNINGHAME
B714
AYRSHIRE MUSEUM OF COUNTRY LIFE & COSTUME
B778
Dalgarven
ABBEY
Kilwinning
Torranyard
Chapelhill
Horse Isle
Dykesmains
EGLINTON
A736
Benslie
B769
Cunninghamhead
Ardrossan
A738
NORTH AYRSHIRE HERITAGE CENTRE
Stevenston
B7080
Girdle Toll
Saltcoats
Perceton
192
Irvine
Springside
Knockentiber
SCOTTISH MARITIME MUSEUM
Fullarton
Dreghorn
B7081
3 miles
5 km

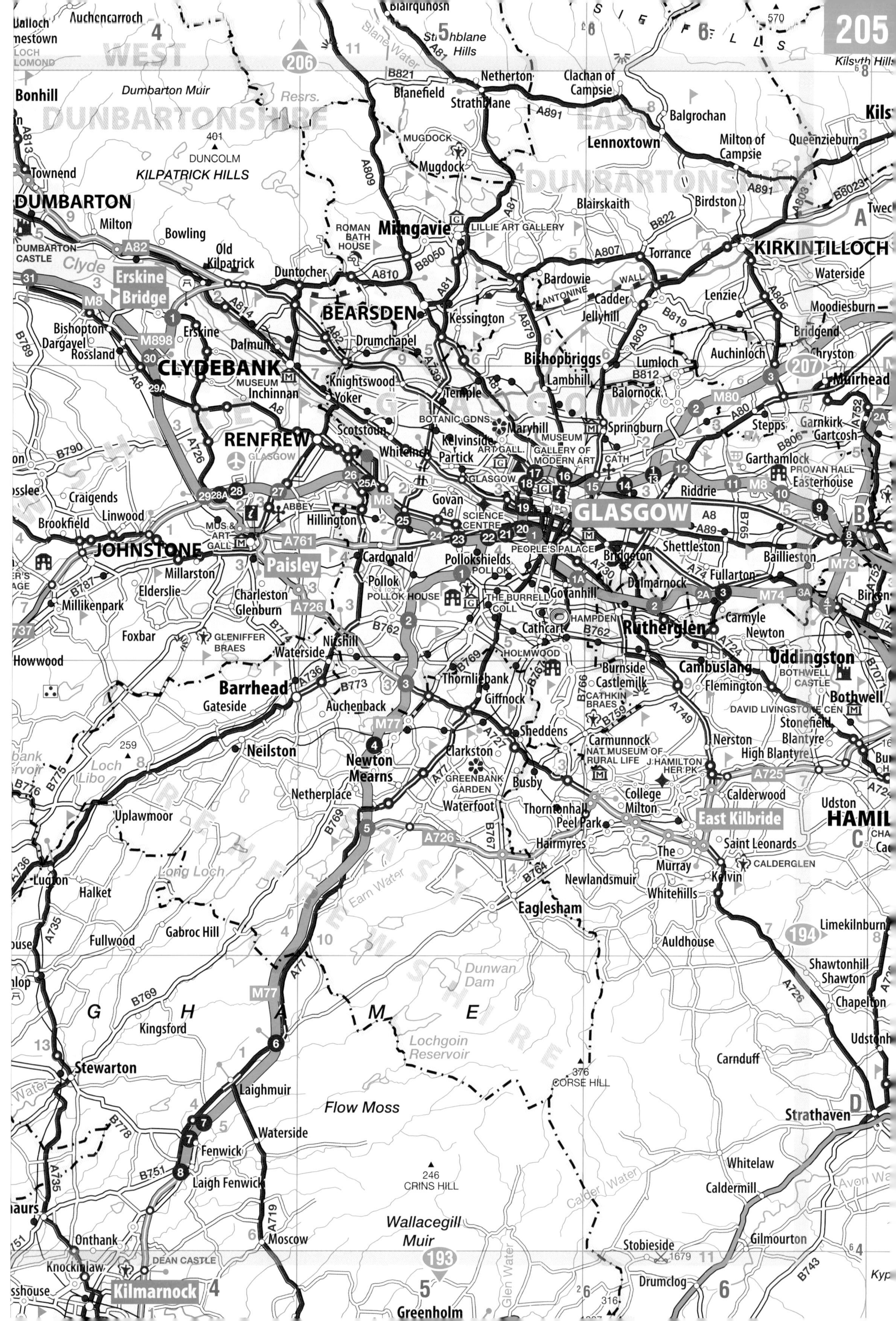
205
Balloch
Jamestown
LOCH LOMOND
Auchencarroch
WEST DUNBARTONSHIRE
Bonhill
Dumbarton Muir
Resrs.
Blane Water
Blairquhosh
Strathblane Hills
Netherton
Clachan of Campsie
Kilsyth Hills
Blanefield
Strathblane
Balgrochan
EAST DUNBARTONSHIRE
Lennoxtown
Milton of Campsie
Queenzieburn
MUGDOCK
Mugdock
401
DUNCOLM
KILPATRICK HILLS
Townend
DUMBARTON
Milton
Bowling
Old Kilpatrick
DUMBARTON CASTLE
Clyde
Erskine Bridge
ROMAN BATH HOUSE
Milngavie
LILLIE ART GALLERY
Blairskaith
Birdston
Torrance
KIRKINTILLOCH
Waterside
Duntocher
Bardowie
ANTONINE WALL
Cadder
Lenzie
Moodiesburn
BEARSDEN
Kessington
Jellyhill
Bishopton
Dargavel
Rossland
Erskine
Dalmuir
Drumchapel
Bishopbriggs
Lumloch
Auchinloch
Bridgend
Chryston
Muirhead
CLYDEBANK
MUSEUM
Inchinnan
Knightswood
Yoker
Temple
Lambhill
Balornock
BOTANIC GDNS.
Maryhill
Springburn
Stepps
Garnkirk
Gartcosh
RENFREW
Scotstoun
Kelvinside
Partick
Whiteinch
ART GALL.
MUSEUM
GALLERY OF MODERN ART
CATH
Garthamlock
PROVAN HALL
Easterhouse
GLASGOW
Craigends
Linwood
Brookfield
ABBEY
MUS.& ART GALL.
Hillington
Govan
SCIENCE CENTRE
GLASGOW
Riddrie
JOHNSTONE
Millarston
Elderslie
Millikenpark
Paisley
Cardonald
Pollok
POLLOK HOUSE
Pollokshields
POLLOK
PEOPLE'S PALACE
Bridgeton
Shettleston
Baillieston
THE BURRELL COLL
Govanhill
Dalmarnock
Fullarton
Birkenshaw
Charleston
Glenburn
Foxbar
GLENIFFER BRAES
Nitshill
HAMPDEN
Cathcart
Rutherglen
Carmyle
Newton
Howwood
Waterside
HOLMWOOD
Burnside
Castlemilk
Cambuslang
Uddingston
BOTHWELL CASTLE
Flemington
Barrhead
Gateside
Auchenback
Thornliebank
Giffnock
CATHKIN BRAES
DAVID LIVINGSTONE CEN
Bothwell
Stonefield
Blantyre
High Blantyre
Neilston
Newton Mearns
Sheddens
Clarkston
Carmunnock
NAT MUSEUM OF RURAL LIFE
J.HAMILTON HER PK
Nerston
Loch Libo
259
Netherplace
GREENBANK GARDEN
Busby
College Milton
Calderwood
East Kilbride
Udston
HAMILTON
Uplawmoor
Waterfoot
Thorntonhall
Peel Park
Hairmyres
Saint Leonards
The Murray
CALDERGLEN
Long Loch
Lugton
Halket
Earn Water
Newlandsmuir
Kelvin
Whitehills
Eaglesham
Fullwood
Gabroc Hill
Auldhouse
Limekilnburn
Dunwan Dam
Shawtonhill
Shawton
Chapelton
EAST RENFREWSHIRE
Kingsford
Lochgoin Reservoir
Udstonhead
Stewarton
376
CORSE HILL
Carnduff
Laighmuir
Flow Moss
Strathaven
Waterside
Fenwick
Whitelaw
246
CRINS HILL
Laigh Fenwick
Calder Water
Caldermill
Avon Water
Onthank
Moscow
Wallacegill Muir
Stobieside
Gilmourton
Knockinlaw
DEAN CASTLE
Kilmarnock
Drumclog
Greenholm
Glen Water
206
207
194
193

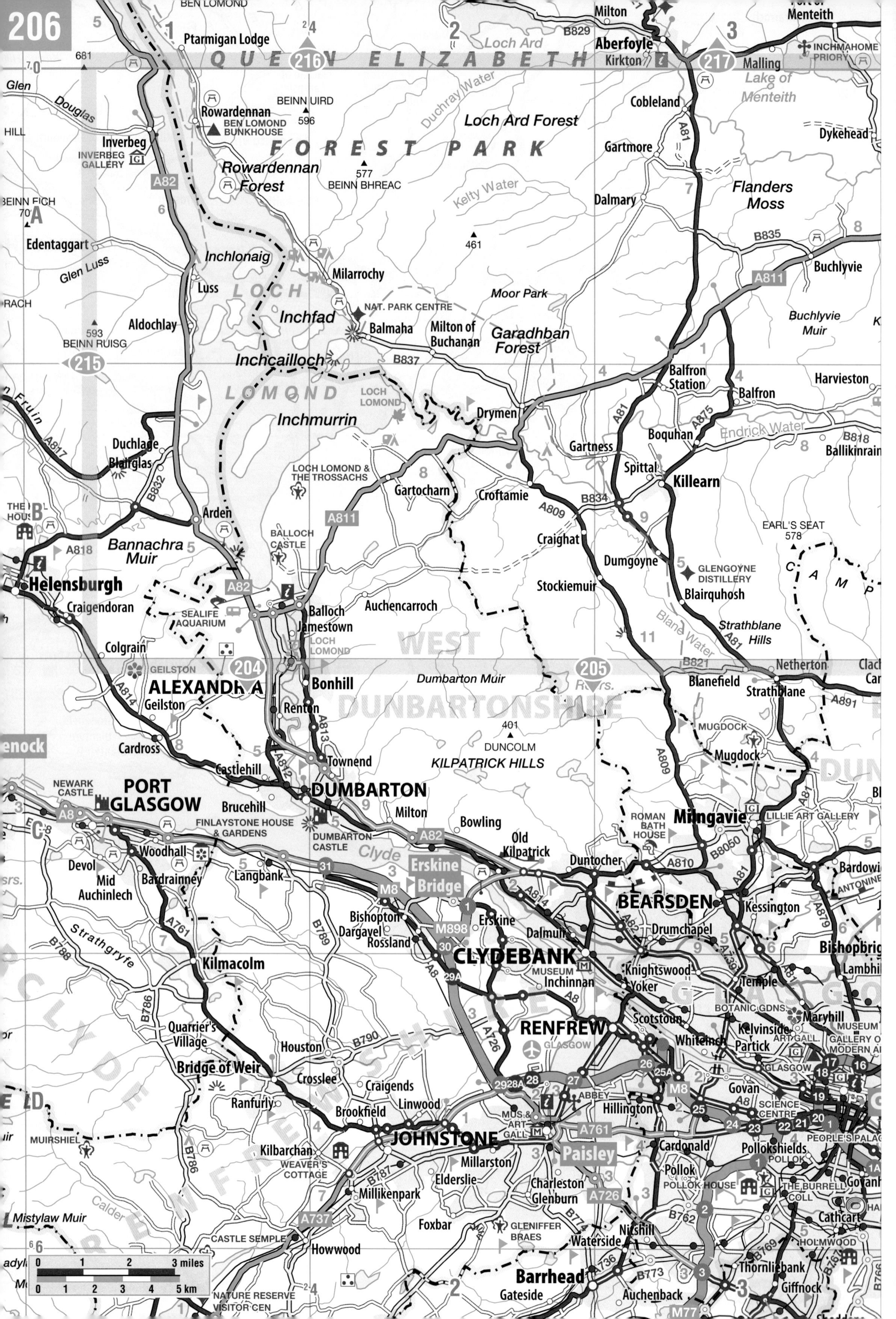

206
Ptarmigan Lodge
QUEEN ELIZABETH
FOREST PARK
216
217
Loch Ard
Milton
Aberfoyle
Kirkton
Menteith
INCHMAHOME PRIORY
Malling
Lake of Menteith
Glen Douglas
Rowardennan
BEN LOMOND BUNKHOUSE
BEINN UIRD
596
Loch Ard Forest
Duchray Water
Cobleland
Inverbeg
INVERBEG GALLERY
Gartmore
Dykehead
Rowardennan Forest
577
BEINN BHREAC
Kelty Water
Dalmary
Flanders Moss
A82
A81
Edentaggart
Inchlonaig
461
B835
Buchlyvie
Glen Luss
Milarrochy
A811
Luss
LOCH
Moor Park
NAT. PARK CENTRE
Inchfad
Aldochlay
Balmaha
Milton of Buchanan
Garadhban Forest
Buchlyvie Muir
593
BEINN RUISG
215
Inchcailloch
B837
LOMOND
LOCH LOMOND
Balfron Station
Balfron
Harvieston
Inchmurrin
Drymen
A875
Endrick Water
B818
Ballikinrain
A817
Duchlage
Blairglas
Gartness
Boquhan
B832
LOCH LOMOND & THE TROSSACHS
Gartocharn
Spittal
Killearn
Croftamie
B834
A809
Arden
EARL'S SEAT
578
Bannachra Muir
BALLOCH CASTLE
Craighat
A818
Dumgoyne
GLENGOYNE DISTILLERY
Helensburgh
Stockiemuir
Craigendoran
Balloch
Auchencarroch
Blairquhosh
SEALIFE AQUARIUM
Jamestown
Strathblane Hills
Colgrain
WEST
Blane Water
GEILSTON
204
205
Netherton
ALEXANDRIA
Bonhill
Dumbarton Muir
B821
Blanefield
Strathblane
A814
Geilston
Renton
DUNBARTONSHIRE
A891
A813
401
DUNCOLM
MUGDOCK
Mugdock
Cardross
KILPATRICK HILLS
Townend
Castlehill
A812
NEWARK CASTLE
PORT GLASGOW
DUMBARTON
Brucehill
Milton
ROMAN BATH HOUSE
Milngavie
LILLIE ART GALLERY
FINLAYSTONE HOUSE & GARDENS
Bowling
DUMBARTON CASTLE
Old Kilpatrick
A8
Clyde
Woodhall
Erskine Bridge
Duntocher
A810
B8050
Devol
Mid Auchinlech
Bardrainney
Langbank
M8
BEARSDEN
Kessington
Bishopton
Dargavel
Erskine
Dalmuir
Drumchapel
A879
Strathgryfe
Rossland
M898
B789
B788
A761
Kilmacolm
CLYDEBANK
MUSEUM
Inchinnan
Knightswood
Yoker
Temple
Lambhill
Bishopbriggs
B786
Scotstoun
BOTANIC GDNS.
Maryhill
Quarrier's Village
RENFREW
Kelvinside
A726
Houston
B790
Whiteinch
Partick
GLASGOW
MUSEUM OF MODERN ART
Bridge of Weir
Crosslee
Craigends
Govan
SCIENCE CENTRE
Ranfurly
ABBEY
Hillington
Linwood
Brookfield
A761
MUS. & ART GALL.
JOHNSTONE
MUIRSHIEL
Kilbarchan
WEAVER'S COTTAGE
Millarston
Paisley
Cardonald
Pollokshields
POLLOK
Pollok
POLLOK HOUSE
THE BURRELL COLL.
Elderslie
B787
Millikenpark
Charleston
Glenburn
A726
Mistylaw Muir
Calder
A737
Foxbar
GLENIFFER BRAES
B774
B762
Nitshill
Cathcart
CASTLE SEMPLE
Waterside
Howwood
HOLMWOOD
B769
Thornliebank
Barrhead
B773
Giffnock
Gateside
Auchenback
M77
NATURE RESERVE VISITOR CEN
0 1 2 3 miles
0 1 2 3 4 5 km

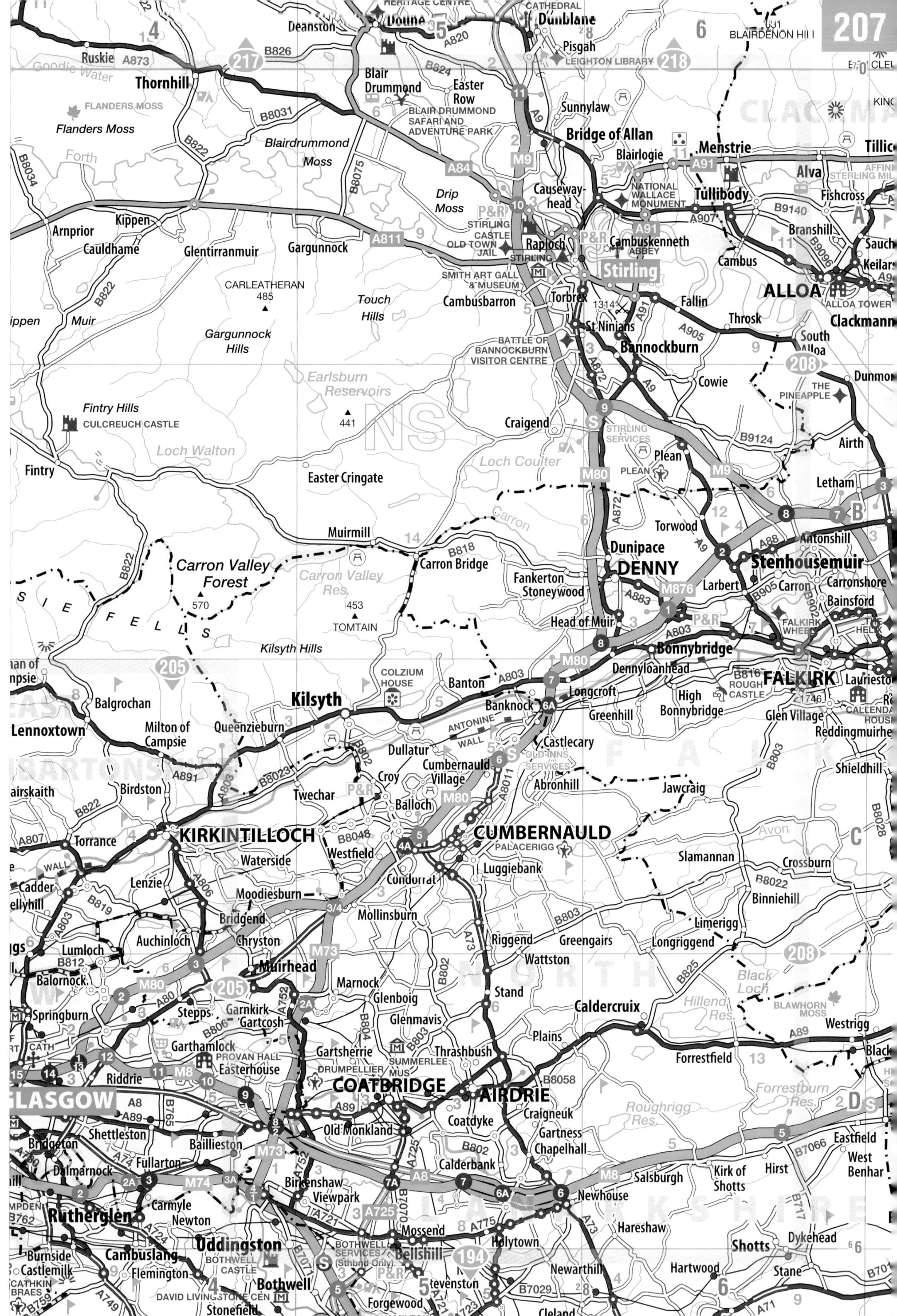
Deanston
Doune
HERITAGE CENTRE
CATHEDRAL
Dunblane
Pisgah
LEIGHTON LIBRARY
BLAIRDENON HILL
217
218
Ruskie
Goodie Water
Thornhill
FLANDERS MOSS
Flanders Moss
Blair Drummond
Easter Row
BLAIR DRUMMOND SAFARI AND ADVENTURE PARK
Blairdrummond Moss
Sunnylaw
Bridge of Allan
Blairlogie
Menstrie
CLACKMANNAN
Tillicoultry
Alva
Forth
Drip Moss
Causewayhead
NATIONAL WALLACE MONUMENT
Tullibody
Fishcross
Arnprior
Kippen
Cauldhame
Glentirranmuir
Gargunnock
STIRLING CASTLE
OLD TOWN JAIL
Raploch
Cambuskenneth ABBEY
Branshill
Sauchie
Cambus
Keilarsbrae
SMITH ART GALL & MUSEUM
Stirling
CARLEATHERAN 485
Touch Hills
Cambusbarron
Torbrex
St Ninians
Fallin
ALLOA
ALLOA TOWER
Throsk
Clackmannan
Muir
Gargunnock Hills
BATTLE OF BANNOCKBURN VISITOR CENTRE
Bannockburn
South Alloa
208
Dunmore
Earlsburn Reservoirs
Cowie
THE PINEAPPLE
Fintry Hills
CULCREUCH CASTLE
441
NS
Craigend
STIRLING SERVICES
Airth
Loch Walton
Loch Coulter
Plean
PLEAN
Fintry
Easter Cringate
Letham
Carron
Torwood
Muirmill
Dunipace
Carron Valley Forest
570
Carron Bridge
Carron Valley Res.
453
TOMTAIN
DENNY
Fankerton
Stoneywood
Antonshill
Stenhousemuir
Larbert
Carron
Carronshore
Bainsford
FALKIRK WHEEL
Head of Muir
Bonnybridge
Kilsyth Hills
FELLS
205
COLZIUM HOUSE
Banton
Dennyloanhead
ROUGH CASTLE
FALKIRK
Laurieston
Balgrochan
Kilsyth
Longcroft
Banknock
High Bonnybridge
Greenhill
Glen Village
CALLENDAR HOUSE
Reddingmuirhead
Lennoxtown
Milton of Campsie
Queenzieburn
ANTONINE WALL
Castlecary
Dullatur
Cumbernauld Village
Croy
OLD INNS SERVICES
Abronhill
Jawcraig
Shieldhill
Birdston
Twechar
Balloch
FALKIRK
Torrance
KIRKINTILLOCH
Westfield
CUMBERNAULD
PALACERIGG
Avon
Waterside
Luggiebank
Slamannan
Crossburn
Lenzie
Condorrat
Binniehill
Moodiesburn
Mollinsburn
Bridgend
Limerigg
Auchinloch
Chryston
Riggend
Greengairs
Longriggend
Lumloch
Wattston
Balornock
Muirhead
Marnock
Glenboig
NORTH
Black Loch
Springburn
Stepps
Garnkirk
Gartcosh
Stand
Caldercruix
Hillend Res.
BLAWHORN MOSS
Glenmavis
Westrigg
Garthamlock
PROVAN HALL
Gartsherrie
Thrashbush
Plains
Riddrie
Easterhouse
SUMMERLEE MUS
DRUMPELLIER
Forrestfield
GLASGOW
COATBRIDGE
AIRDRIE
Craigneuk
Roughrigg Res.
Forrestburn Res.
Shettleston
Old Monkland
Coatdyke
Gartness
Eastfield
Bridgeton
Baillieston
Chapelhall
West Benhar
Dalmarnock
Fullarton
Calderbank
Salsburgh
Kirk of Shotts
Hirst
Birkenshaw
Carmyle
Viewpark
Newhouse
Rutherglen
Newton
LANARKSHIRE
Mossend
Holytown
Hareshaw
Dykehead
Burnside
Cambuslang
Uddingston
BOTHWELL SERVICES (Sthbnd Only)
Bellshill
194
Shotts
Castlemilk
Flemington
BOTHWELL CASTLE
Newarthill
Hartwood
Stane
CATHKIN BRAES
Bothwell
Stevenston
DAVID LIVINGSTONE CEN
Stonefield
Forgewood
Cleland

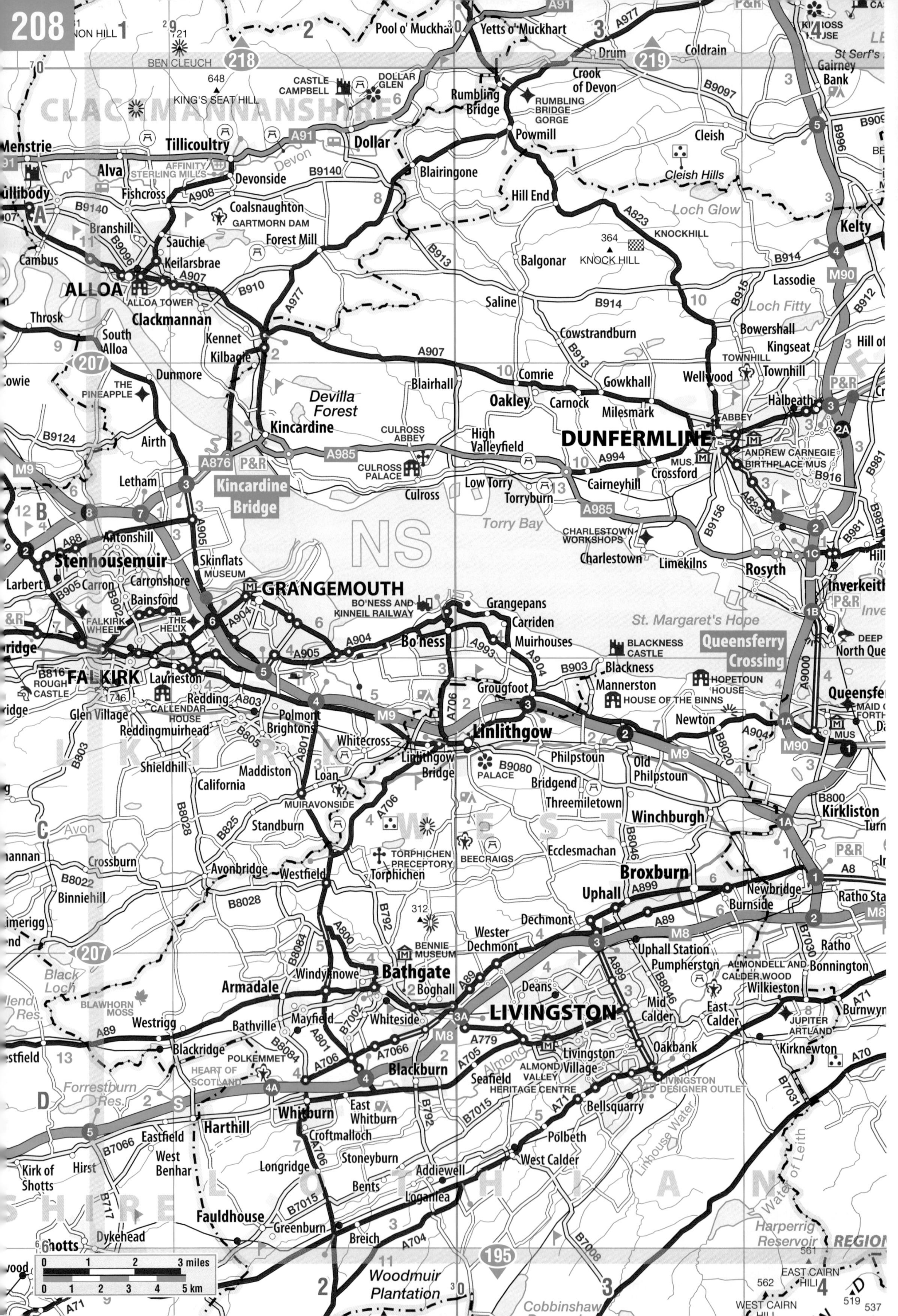
CLACKMANNANSHIRE
BEN CLEUCH
KING'S SEAT HILL
Pool o' Muckhart
Yetts o' Muckhart
Drum
Coldrain
Crook of Devon
Rumbling Bridge
RUMBLING BRIDGE GORGE
CASTLE CAMPBELL
DOLLAR GLEN
Dollar
Tillicoultry
Menstrie
Alva
AFFINITY STERLING MILLS
Devonside
Fishcross
Coalsnaughton
GARTMORN DAM
Branshill
Sauchie
Forest Mill
Keilarsbrae
Cambus
ALLOA
ALLOA TOWER
Clackmannan
Throsk
South Alloa
Kennet
Kilbagie
Dunmore
THE PINEAPPLE
Airth
Letham
Kincardine
Kincardine Bridge
Devilla Forest
Blairingone
Powmill
Cleish
Cleish Hills
Hill End
Loch Glow
KNOCKHILL
KNOCK HILL
Balgonar
Saline
Kelty
Gairney Bank
Lassodie
Loch Fitty
Bowershall
Kingseat
Townhill
TOWNHILL
Wellwood
Halbeath
Cowstrandburn
Comrie
Gowkhall
Oakley
Carnock
Milesmark
Blairhall
DUNFERMLINE
ABBEY
ANDREW CARNEGIE BIRTHPLACE MUS
Crossford
Cairneyhill
High Valleyfield
CULROSS ABBEY
CULROSS PALACE
Culross
Low Torry
Torryburn
Torry Bay
CHARLESTOWN WORKSHOPS
Charlestown
Limekilns
Rosyth
Inverkeithing
St. Margaret's Hope
Queensferry Crossing
NS
Stenhousemuir
Antonshill
Larbert
Carron
Carronshore
Skinflats
Bainsford
GRANGEMOUTH
BO'NESS AND KINNEIL RAILWAY
FALKIRK WHEEL
THE HELIX
FALKIRK
ROUGH CASTLE
Laurieston
Redding
CALLENDAR HOUSE
Glen Village
Reddingmuirhead
Polmont
Brightons
Shieldhill
Maddiston
California
Grangepans
Carriden
Bo'ness
Muirhouses
BLACKNESS CASTLE
Blackness
Mannerston
HOUSE OF THE BINNS
HOPETOUN HOUSE
Grougfoot
Linlithgow
PALACE
Whitecross
Linlithgow Bridge
Philpstoun
Old Philpstoun
Bridgend
Newton
Queensferry
North Queensferry
DEEP
Threemiletown
Winchburgh
Kirkliston
Loan
MUIRAVONSIDE
Standburn
Avon
Crossburn
Avonbridge
Westfield
TORPHICHEN PRECEPTORY
Torphichen
BEECRAIGS
Ecclesmachan
Broxburn
Uphall
Newbridge
Burnside
Ratho
Binniehill
Dechmont
Wester Dechmont
Uphall Station
Pumpherston
ALMONDELL AND CALDER WOOD
Bonnington
Wilkieston
BENNIE MUSEUM
Bathgate
Boghall
Windyknowe
Armadale
Black Loch
BLAWHORN MOSS
Westrigg
Bathville
Mayfield
Whiteside
LIVINGSTON
Deans
Mid Calder
East Calder
JUPITER ARTLAND
Kirknewton
Burnwynd
Blackridge
POLKEMMET
HEART OF SCOTLAND
Forrestburn Res.
Blackburn
Seafield
ALMOND VALLEY HERITAGE CENTRE
Livingston Village
Oakbank
LIVINGSTON DESIGNER OUTLET
Whitburn
East Whitburn
Bellsquarry
Harthill
Eastfield
West Benhar
Kirk of Shotts
Hirst
Croftmalloch
Longridge
Stoneyburn
Addiewell
Polbeth
West Calder
Linhouse Water
Water of Leith
Bents
Loganlea
Fauldhouse
Greenburn
Breich
Dykehead
Shotts
Woodmuir Plantation
Cobbinshaw
Harperrig Reservoir
EAST CAIRN HILL
WEST CAIRN
LOTHIAN
M9
M8
M90
A91
A977
A907
A985
A994
A904
A905
A706
A89
A899
A71
A704
B9097
B914
B915
B912
B913
B910
B9140
B9156
B903
B9080
B8020
B8046
B800
B8028
B792
B7015
B7066
B717
B7030
B7031
B7008
A823
A876
A88
B905
B902
B816
A803
B805
A801
B803
B825
B8022
B8084
B7002
A7066
A705
A779
A800
B996
B981
B916
A8
A70
A9000
207
218
219
195
P&R
0 1 2 3 miles
0 1 2 3 4 5 km

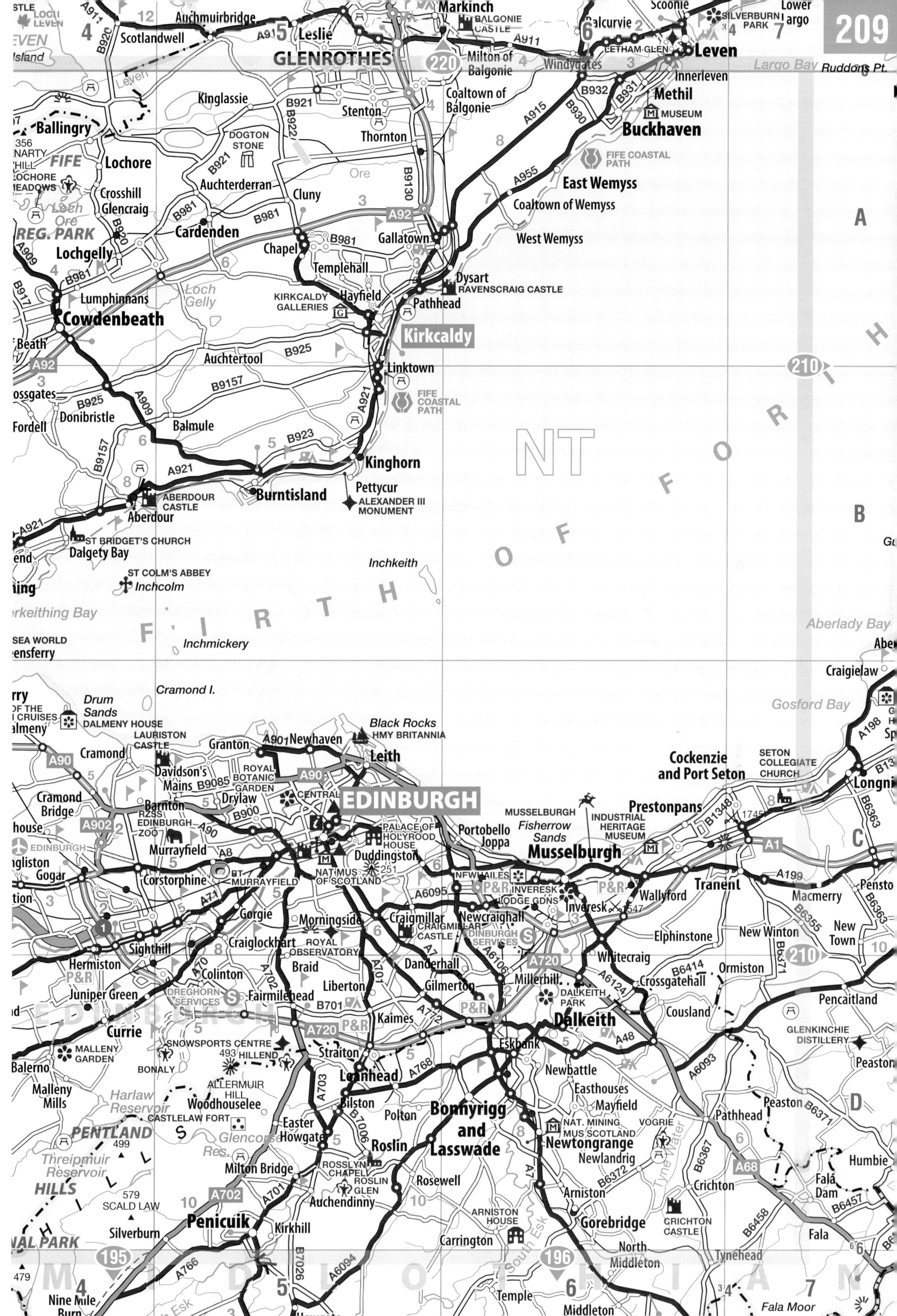
GLENROTHES
Leslie
Markinch
Leven
Methil
Buckhaven
East Wemyss
Kirkcaldy
Cowdenbeath
Lochgelly
Cardenden
Kinghorn
Burntisland
Aberdour
Dalgety Bay
FIRTH OF FORTH
NT
Inchkeith
Inchcolm
Inchmickery
Cramond I.
EDINBURGH
Leith
Musselburgh
Prestonpans
Cockenzie and Port Seton
Tranent
Dalkeith
Bonnyrigg and Lasswade
Loanhead
Penicuik
Newtongrange
Gorebridge
PENTLAND HILLS
MIDLOTHIAN

Lower Largo
St Monans
ST FILLAN'S CAVE
ST MONAN'S WINDMILL
ST MONAN'S CHURCH
221
Largo Bay
Ruddons Pt.
Elie
Earlsferry
Chapel Ness
Sauchar Pt.
Isle of May
ISLE OF MAY
A
209
FORTH
Fidra
Craigleith
Bass Rock
Eyebroughy
North Berwick
SCOTTISH SEABIRD CENTRE
MUSEUM
DIRLETON CASTLE & GARDENS
MUIRFIELD
Dirleton
TANTALLON CASTLE
Auldhame
B
Gullane Bay
Gullane
Scoughall
West Fenton
Kingston
Whitekirk
Fenton Barns
St. Baldred's Cradle
Aberlady Bay
Tyne Mouth
Aberlady
MYRETON MOTOR MUSEUM
Drem
JOHN MUIR BIRTHPLACE
Craigielaw
THE CHESTERS FORT
East Fortune
NATIONAL MUS OF FLIGHT
Tyninghame
JOHN MUIR
Dunbar
Belhaven
West Barns
Gosford Bay
GOSFORD HOUSE
Ballencrieff
Preston
Spittal
Athelstaneford
Peffer Burn
East Linton
SETON COLLEGIATE CHURCH
HOPETOUN MON
PRESTON MILL & PHANTASSIE DOOCOT
Longniddry
Biel Water
Spott
Meikle Pinkerton
Huntington
HAILES CASTLE
Traprain
Pitcox
Elvingston
C
ST MARY'S COLLEGIATE CH
Luggate Burn
Stenton
Tyne
Haddington
Gladsmuir
Halls
Tranent
Penston
Papple
Macmerry
EAST
Garvald
New Winton
New Town
Samuelston
Bolton
209
Dunbar Common
Ormiston
BRANSLY HILL
Carfrae
Pencaitland
LOTHIAN
Gifford
Danskine
GLENKINCHIE DISTILLERY
East Saltoun
West Saltoun
Peastonbank
Gilchriston
Quarryford
Longyester
Long Newton
Bothwell Water
Spartleton Edge
D
Peaston
Pathhead
Whiteadder Reservoir
Humbie
Stobshiel
Birns Water
Fala Dam
Blegbie
LAMMER LAW
Hopes Reservoir
MEIKLE SAYS LAW
LAMMERMUIR HILLS
Whiteadder Water
CRANSHAWS HILL
Fala
196
197
0 1 2 3 miles
0 1 2 3 4 5 km
Fala Moor
HUNT LAW

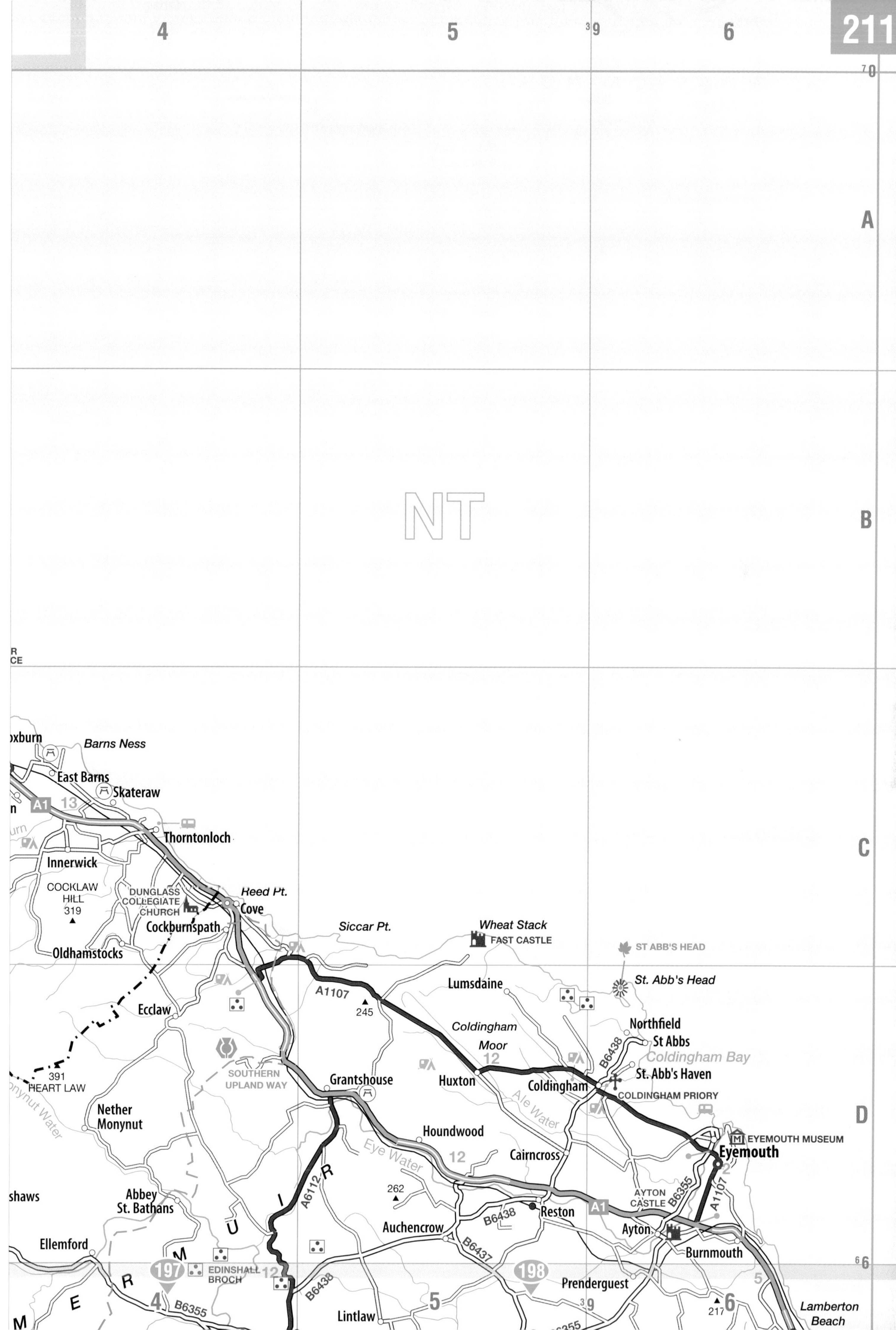
4
5
6
A
B
C
D
NT
Barns Ness
East Barns
Skateraw
A1
13
Thorntonloch
Innerwick
COCKLAW HILL 319
DUNGLASS COLLEGIATE CHURCH
Reed Pt.
Cove
Cockburnspath
Oldhamstocks
Siccar Pt.
Wheat Stack
FAST CASTLE
ST ABB'S HEAD
St. Abb's Head
Lumsdaine
A1107
245
Ecclaw
Coldingham Moor
Northfield
St Abbs
Coldingham Bay
St. Abb's Haven
B6438
391 HEART LAW
Monynut Water
SOUTHERN UPLAND WAY
Grantshouse
Huxton
Coldingham
COLDINGHAM PRIORY
Ale Water
Nether Monynut
Houndwood
EYEMOUTH MUSEUM
Eyemouth
Eye Water
Cairncross
A6112
262
AYTON CASTLE
B6355
Abbey St. Bathans
Reston
Auchencrow
Ayton
Burnmouth
Ellemford
B6437
197
198
EDINSHALL BROCH
Prenderguest
B6438
Lintlaw
B6355
217
Lamberton Beach

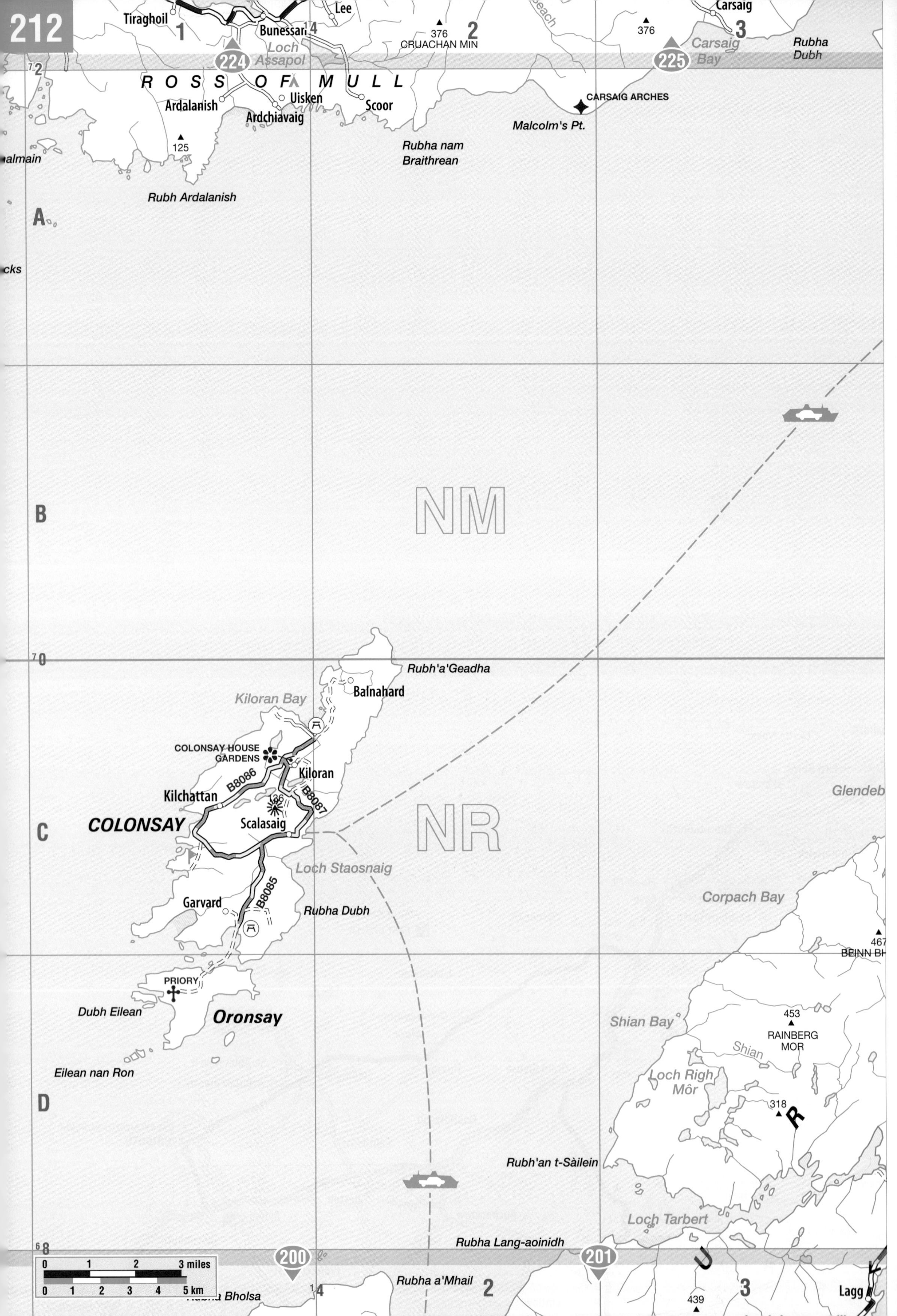
Tiraghoil
1
Bunessan
14
Lee
376
CRUACHAN MIN
2
Beach
376
Carsaig
3
Carsaig Bay
Rubha Dubh
224
225
Loch Assapol
ROSS OF MULL
Ardalanish
Uisken
Ardchiavaig
Scoor
CARSAIG ARCHES
Malcolm's Pt.
125
Rubha nam Braithrean
Rubh Ardalanish
A
B
NM
70
Rubh'a'Geadha
Kiloran Bay
Balnahard
COLONSAY HOUSE GARDENS
Kiloran
B8086
B8087
Kilchattan
136
Scalasaig
COLONSAY
C
NR
Glendeb
Loch Staosnaig
Corpach Bay
Garvard
B8085
Rubha Dubh
467
PRIORY
Dubh Eilean
Oronsay
Shian Bay
453
RAINBERG MOR
Shian
Eilean nan Ron
Loch Righ Mòr
D
318
R
Rubh'an t-Sàilein
Loch Tarbert
68
Rubha Lang-aoinidh
200
201
0 1 2 3 miles
0 1 2 3 4 5 km
Rubha Bholsa
14
Rubha a'Mhail
2
U
439
3
Lagg

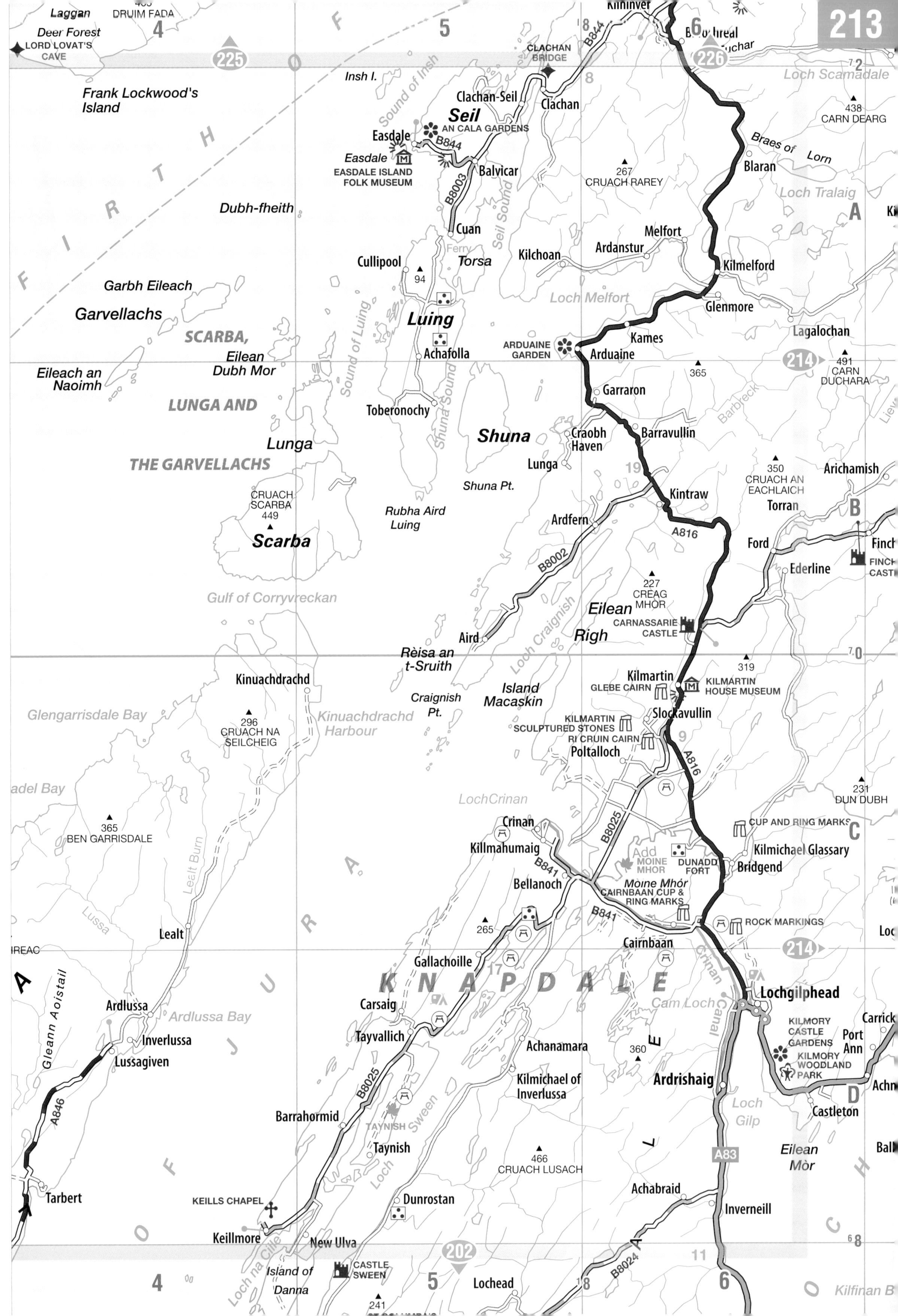

Laggan
Deer Forest
LORD LOVAT'S CAVE
DRUIM FADA
225
226
Kilninver
Frank Lockwood's Island
Insh I.
Sound of Insh
CLACHAN BRIDGE
Clachan-Seil
Clachan
Seil
AN CALA GARDENS
Easdale
B844
Easdale
EASDALE ISLAND FOLK MUSEUM
Balvicar
B8003
Seil Sound
Dubh-fheith
Cuan
Ferry
Torsa
Braes of Lorn
Blaran
267
CRUACH RAREY
438
CARN DEARG
Loch Scamadale
Loch Tralaig
Melfort
Ardanstur
Kilchoan
Kilmelford
Cullipool
94
Garbh Eileach
Garvellachs
Luing
Loch Melfort
Glenmore
Lagalochan
SCARBA,
Eilean Dubh Mor
Eileach an Naoimh
Sound of Luing
Achafolla
ARDUAINE GARDEN
Arduaine
Kames
365
491
CARN DUCHARA
214
LUNGA AND
THE GARVELLACHS
Lunga
Toberonochy
Shuna Sound
Shuna
Garraron
Barbreck
Craobh Haven
Lunga
Barravullin
Shuna Pt.
CRUACH SCARBA
449
Scarba
Rubha Aird Luing
Kintraw
A816
350
CRUACH AN EACHLAICH
Arichamish
Torran
Ford
Ederline
FINCH CASTLE
Ardfern
B8002
227
CREAG MHOR
Gulf of Corryvreckan
Eilean Righ
CARNASSARIE CASTLE
Aird
Rèisa an t-Sruith
Loch Craignish
319
Kinuachdrachd
Kilmartin
GLEBE CAIRN
KILMARTIN HOUSE MUSEUM
Craignish Pt.
Island Macaskin
Glengarrisdale Bay
296
CRUACH NA SEILCHEIG
Kinuachdrachd Harbour
KILMARTIN SCULPTURED STONES
RI CRUIN CAIRN
Slockavullin
Poltalloch
adel Bay
LochCrinan
231
DUN DUBH
365
BEN GARRISDALE
Crinan
Killmahumaig
B8025
Add
MOINE MHOR
DUNADD FORT
CUP AND RING MARKS
Kilmichael Glassary
Bridgend
Lealt Burn
B841
Bellanoch
Moine Mhór
CAIRNBAAN CUP & RING MARKS
B841
Lussa
265
ROCK MARKINGS
Lealt
Cairnbaan
Crinan Canal
Gallachoille
KNAPDALE
Carsaig
Cam Loch
Lochgilphead
Ardlussa
Ardlussa Bay
Gleann Aoistail
Inverlussa
Lussagiven
Tayvallich
Achanamara
KILMORY CASTLE GARDENS
KILMORY WOODLAND PARK
Carrick
Port Ann
360
Kilmichael of Inverlussa
Ardrishaig
A846
B8025
Barrahormid
TAYNISH
Taynish
Loch Sween
Loch Gilp
Castleton
466
CRUACH LUSACH
Eilean Mòr
A83
Achabraid
Tarbert
KEILLS CHAPEL
Dunrostan
Inverneill
Keillmore
New Ulva
202
B8024
Loch na Cille
Island of Danna
CASTLE SWEEN
Lochead
241
Kilfinan B
FIRTH OF LORN
SOUND OF JURA
LOCH FYNE

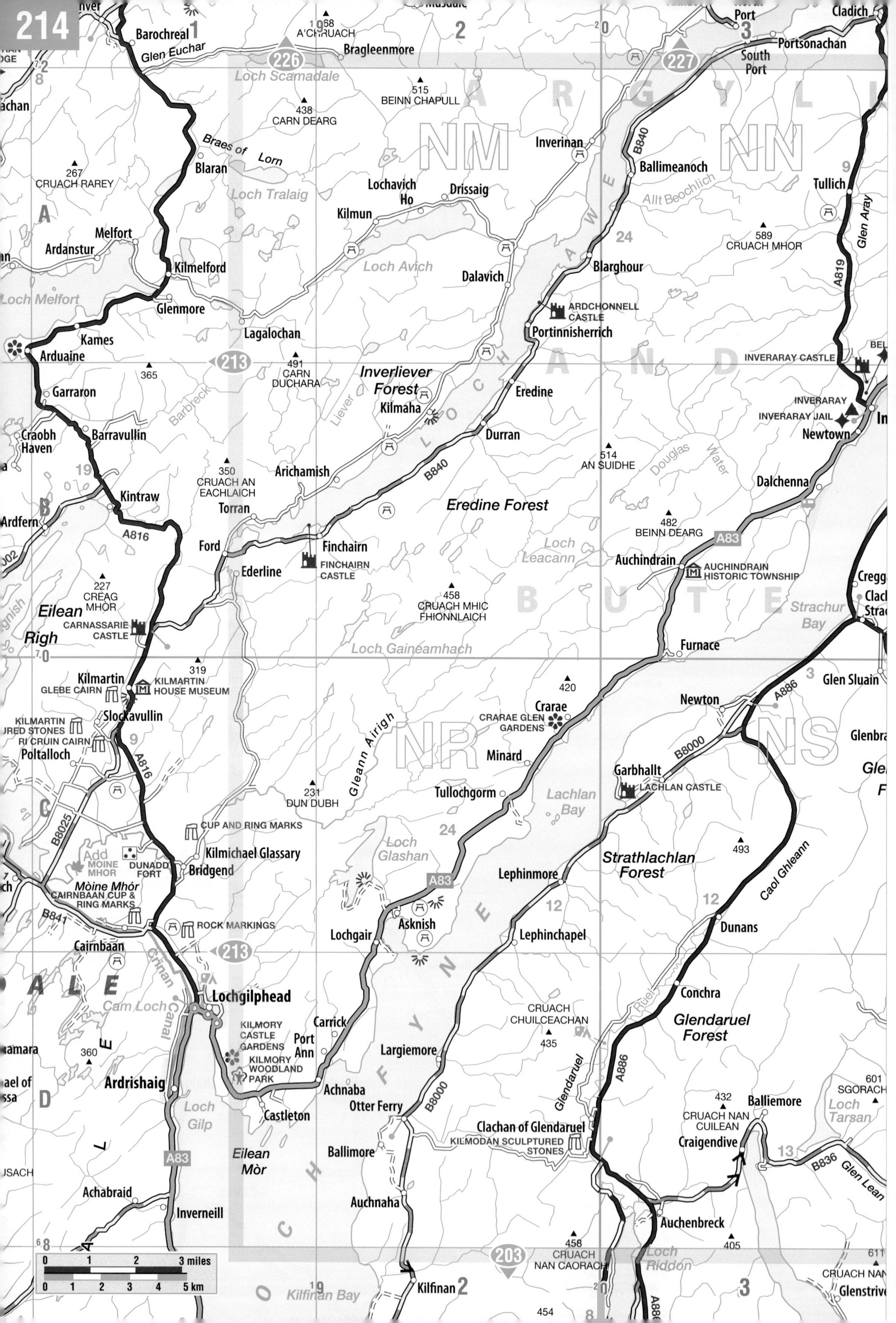
Barochreal
Glen Euchar
A'CHRUACH
Bragleenmore
Port
Cladich
Portsonachan
South Port
226
227
Loch Scamadale
BEINN CHAPULL
CARN DEARG
A R G Y L L
NM
NN
Braes of Lorn
Blaran
Inverinan
B840
Ballimeanoch
Tullich
CRUACH RAREY
Loch Tralaig
Lochavich Ho
Drissaig
Allt Beochlich
Kilmun
Glen Aray
Melfort
Ardanstur
Loch Avich
Dalavich
Blarghour
CRUACH MHOR
A819
Kilmelford
Loch Melfort
Glenmore
ARDCHONNELL CASTLE
Portinnisherrich
Kames
Lagalochan
Arduaine
213
CARN DUCHARA
Inverliever Forest
A N D
INVERARAY CASTLE
Garraron
Barbreck
Liever
Kilmaha
Eredine
INVERARAY
INVERARAY JAIL
Craobh Haven
Barravullin
L O C H
Durran
AN SUIDHE
Douglas Water
Newtown
Arichamish
CRUACH AN EACHLAICH
Dalchenna
Kintraw
Torran
Eredine Forest
Ardfern
A816
Ford
Finchairn
Loch Leacann
BEINN DEARG
A83
Ederline
FINCHAIRN CASTLE
Auchindrain
AUCHINDRAIN HISTORIC TOWNSHIP
CREAG MHOR
CRUACH MHIC FHIONNLAICH
B U T E
Eilean Righ
CARNASSARIE CASTLE
Strachur Bay
Loch Gaineamhach
Furnace
Kilmartin
GLEBE CAIRN
KILMARTIN HOUSE MUSEUM
Glen Sluain
A886
Newton
Crarae
CRARAE GLEN GARDENS
Slockavullin
KILMARTIN STONES
RI CRUIN CAIRN
Poltalloch
Gleann Airigh
NR
NS
Minard
B8000
Garbhallt
LACHLAN CASTLE
Tullochgorm
Lachlan Bay
DUN DUBH
B8025
CUP AND RING MARKS
Loch Glashan
Kilmichael Glassary
Add
MOINE MHOR
DUNADD FORT
Bridgend
Mòine Mhór
CAIRNBAAN CUP & RING MARKS
Strathlachlan Forest
Lephinmore
Caol Ghleann
B841
Asknish
ROCK MARKINGS
Lochgair
Lephinchapel
Dunans
Cairnbaan
Crinan Canal
F Y N E
Cam Loch
Lochgilphead
Conchra
Ruel
KILMORY CASTLE GARDENS
Carrick
Port Ann
CRUACH CHUILCEACHAN
Glendaruel Forest
Largiemore
KILMORY WOODLAND PARK
Ardrishaig
Achnaba
Glendaruel
SGORACH
Otter Ferry
Castleton
CRUACH NAN CUILEAN
Balliemore
Loch Gilp
Loch Tarsan
Clachan of Glendaruel
KILMODAN SCULPTURED STONES
Craigendive
Eilean Mòr
Ballimore
B836
Glen Lean
Achabraid
Auchnaha
Inverneill
Auchenbreck
CRUACH NAN CAORACH
203
Loch Riddon
CRUACH NAN
Glenstriven
Kilfinan
Kilfinan Bay
0 1 2 3 miles
0 1 2 3 4 5 km

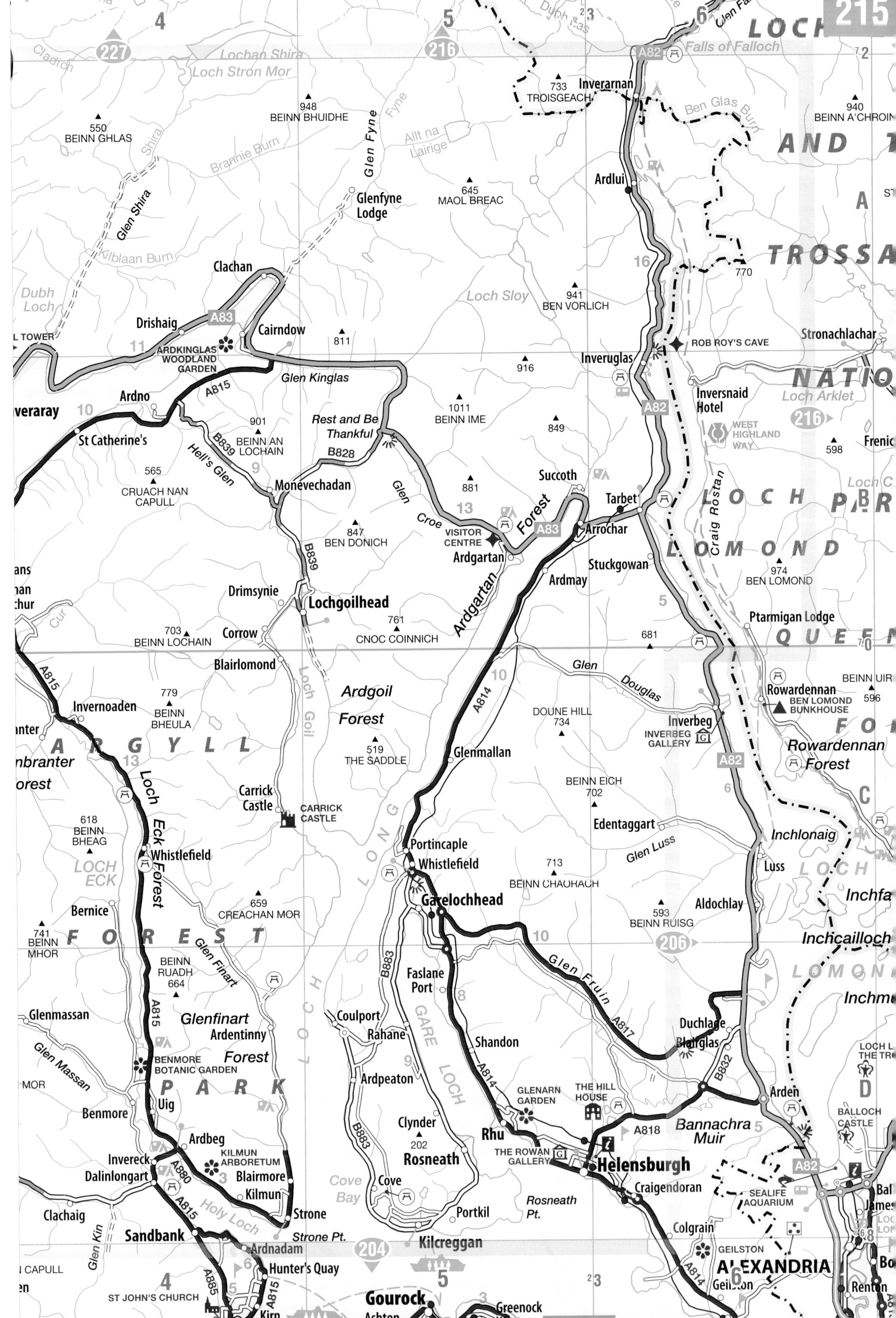
4
227
5
216
6
Glen Fa
LOCH
Falls of Falloch
A82
Lochan Shira
Loch Stron Mor
Cladich
Dubh Las
733
TROISGEACH
Inverarnan
940
BEINN A'CHROIN
948
BEINN BHUIDHE
Fyne
Glen Fyne
Allt na Lairige
Ben Glas Burn
AND
550
BEINN GHLAS
Shira
Brannie Burn
Ardlui
645
MAOL BREAC
Glenfyne Lodge
Glen Shira
A
TROSSA
Kilblaan Burn
16
770
Clachan
Dubh Loch
Loch Sloy
941
BEN VORLICH
A83
Drishaig
Cairndow
L TOWER
811
Stronachlachar
ROB ROY'S CAVE
11
ARDKINGLAS WOODLAND GARDEN
916
Inveruglas
NATIO
Glen Kinglas
Inversnaid Hotel
Loch Arklet
A815
Ardno
1011
BEINN IME
A82
216
veraray
10
901
BEINN AN LOCHAIN
Rest and Be Thankful
849
WEST HIGHLAND WAY
598
Frenic
St Catherine's
B839
B828
Hell's Glen
9
565
CRUACH NAN CAPULL
Monevechadan
Glen Croe
881
Succoth
Tarbet
Craig Rostan
LOCH
13
Loch C
847
BEN DONICH
VISITOR CENTRE
Forest
A83
Arrochar
Ardgartan
LOMOND
B839
Stuckgowan
Ardmay
974
BEN LOMOND
Drimsynie
Lochgoilhead
Ardgartan
5
761
CNOC COINNICH
Ptarmigan Lodge
Cur
703
BEINN LOCHAIN
Corrow
681
QUEEN
Blairlomond
Glen Douglas
A815
10
BEINN UIR
Loch Goil
Ardgoil Forest
A814
Rowardennan
596
779
BEINN BHEULA
Invernoaden
DOUNE HILL
734
BEN LOMOND BUNKHOUSE
Inverbeg
INVERBEG GALLERY
FO
nter
ARGYLL
519
THE SADDLE
Glenmallan
A82
Rowardennan Forest
nbranter
13
Forest
orest
Loch Eck Forest
BEINN EICH
702
Carrick Castle
CARRICK CASTLE
6
C
618
BEINN BHEAG
LONG
Edentaggart
Inchlonaig
Portincaple
LOCH ECK
Whistlefield
Whistlefield
Glen Luss
Luss
713
BEINN CHAORACH
LOCH
Garelochhead
Inchfa
Bernice
659
CREACHAN MOR
593
BEINN RUISG
Aldochlay
741
BEINN MHOR
FOREST
Glen Finart
10
206
Inchcailloch
BEINN RUADH
664
B883
Faslane Port
Glen Fruin
LOMON
A815
Inchm
Glenmassan
Glenfinart Ardentinny Forest
Coulport
Rahane
GARE LOCH
Shandon
A817
Duchlage
Blairglas
Glen Massan
LOCH
LOCH L
THE TR
MOR
9
A814
B832
BENMORE BOTANIC GARDEN
PARK
Ardpeaton
GLENARN GARDEN
THE HILL HOUSE
Arden
D
Benmore
Uig
Clynder
Rhu
A818
Bannachra Muir
5
BALLOCH CASTLE
Ardbeg
B883
202
Rosneath
THE ROWAN GALLERY
Helensburgh
A82
Invereck
KILMUN ARBORETUM
Dalinlongart
A880
Blairmore
Kilmun
Cove Bay
Cove
Craigendoran
SEALIFE AQUARIUM
Bal
James
Clachaig
A815
Holy Loch
Strone
Portkil
Rosneath Pt.
Colgrain
Glen Kin
Sandbank
Strone Pt.
Ardnadam
204
Kilcreggan
GEILSTON
ALEXANDRIA
N CAPULL
Hunter's Quay
A885
A815
5
A814
Geilston
6
Renton
Bo
4
ST JOHN'S CHURCH
Kirn
Gourock
Ashton
3
Greenock

Loch Dochard
Inveroran Hotel
Loch Lyon
BIENN AN DOTHAIDH
1004
228
953
BEINN MHANACH
957
BEINN NAN AIGHENAN
Bridge of Orchy
639
BEINN HEASGARNICH
1076
1076
BEINN DÒRAIN
Allt Chonoghlais
701
Orchy
GLEN ORCHY
A
A82
1047
CREAG MHOR
796
BEINN MHIC-MHONAIDH
6
Arichastlich
Glen Strae
Strae
901
BEINN ODHAR
840
BEINN UDLAIDH
937
BEINN CHEAT
227
B8074
1025
BEN CHALLUM
Glen Lochy
A85
Lochy
Clifton
Tyndrum
Arrivain
13
Cononish
880
Stronmilchan
Strath of Orchy
Achnafalnich
Inverlochy
13
Strath Fillan
Lochdochart House
Dalmally
5
A85
Loch Iubhair
BEN LUI
MCINTYRE MONUMENT
1130
BEN LUI
Inverherive
Loch Dochart
Benmore
Portnellan
B
Eas a'Ghaill
978
BEINN DUBHCHRAIG
Crianlarich
CRIANLARICH
1174
BEN MORE
Allt Fionn Ghlinne
WEST HIGHLAND WAY
739
MEALL NAN TIGHEARN
1165
STOB BINNEIN
Falloch
Glen Falloch
Dubh Eas
LOCH LOMOND
Lochan Shira
A82
Falls of Falloch
Loch Stron Mor
215
733
TROISGEACH
Inverarnan
948
BEINN BHUIDHE
Fyne
Ben Glas Burn
940
BEINN A'CHROIN
Shira
Brannie Burn
Allt na Lairige
Glen Fyne
AND THE
Ardlui
C
Glenfyne Lodge
645
MAOL BREAC
865
STOB A'CHOIN
Clachan
16
770
TROSSACHS
Loch Sloy
941
BEN VORLICH
Strath Gartney
A83
Cairndow
811
ARDKINGLAS WOODLAND GARDEN
ROB ROY'S CAVE
Stronachlachar
916
Inveruglas
Glen Kinglas
NATIONAL
A815
Inversnaid Hotel
1011
BEINN IME
Loch Arklet
Loch Ard Forest
Rest and Be Thankful
A82
901
BEINN AN LOCHAIN
849
WEST HIGHLAND WAY
215
B839
B828
598
Frenich
Hell's Glen
565
9
Monevechadan
Glen Croe
Succoth
881
Craig Rostan
B829
Loch Chon
D
Tarbet
LOCH
PARK
13
847
BEN DONICH
VISITOR CENTRE
Forest
A83
Arrochar
Ardgartan
B839
Stuckgowan
LOMOND
974
BEN LOMOND
Ardmay
Drimsynie
Lochgoilhead
5
761
CNOC COINNICH
Ardgartan
Ptarmigan Lodge
703
Corrow
681
QUEEN ELIZ
0 1 2 3 miles
0 1 2 3 4 5 km
Glen Douglas
Ardgoil Forest
2
10
A814
3
Rowardennan
BEINN UIRD
596
BEN LOMOND BUNKHOUSE
4
BEINN BHEULA
DOUNE HILL
734
Inverbeg

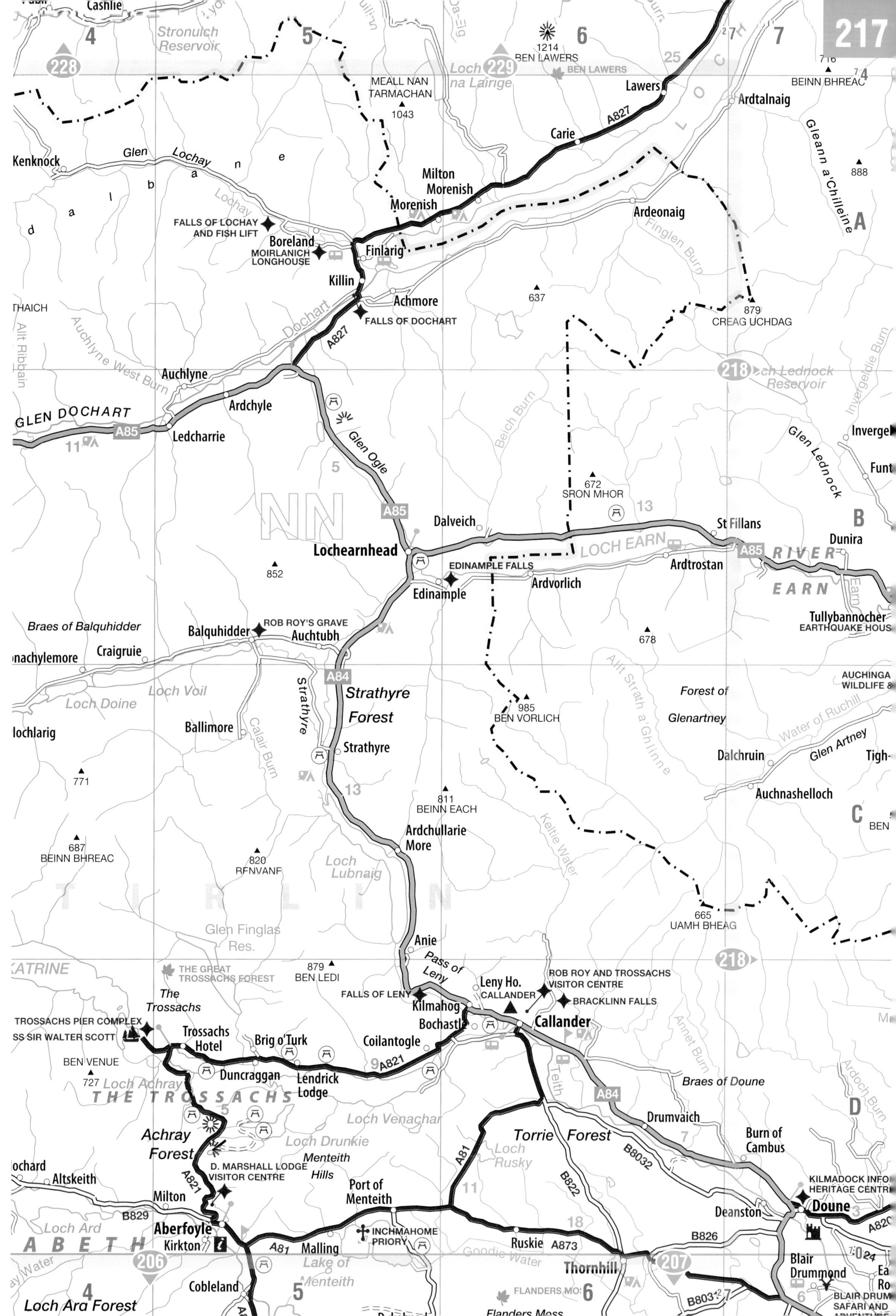
Cashlie
Stronuich Reservoir
228
229
218
206
207
1214 BEN LAWERS
BEN LAWERS
MEALL NAN TARMACHAN
1043
Loch na Lairige
Lawers
A827
Carie
Ardtalnaig
716
BEINN BHREAC
Gleann a'Chilleine
888
Kenknock
Glen Lochay
Milton Morenish
Morenish
Ardeonaig
FALLS OF LOCHAY AND FISH LIFT
Boreland
MOIRLANICH LONGHOUSE
Finlarig
Finglen Burn
Killin
Achmore
637
FALLS OF DOCHART
879 CREAG UCHDAG
Allt Ribbain
Auchlyne West Burn
Dochart
Auchlyne
Loch Lednock Reservoir
Invergeldie Burn
Ardchyle
GLEN DOCHART
A85
Ledcharrie
Glen Ogle
Beich Burn
Glen Lednock
Inverge
Funt
672 SRON MHOR
NN
Dalveich
St Fillans
Dunira
Lochearnhead
LOCH EARN
RIVER EARN
852
EDINAMPLE FALLS
Ardtrostan
Ardvorlich
Edinample
Tullybannocher EARTHQUAKE HOUS
Braes of Balquhidder
Balquhidder
ROB ROY'S GRAVE
Auchtubh
678
Craigruie
A84
Strathyre Forest
Strathyre
Loch Voil
Loch Doine
Ballimore
Calair Burn
985 BEN VORLICH
Allt Strath a'Ghlinne
Forest of Glenartney
AUCHINGA WILDLIFE
Water of Ruchill
Glen Artney
Dalchruin
Tigh-
771
811 BEINN EACH
Auchnashelloch
687 BEINN BHREAC
820 BENVANE
Ardchullarie More
Loch Lubnaig
Keltie Water
665 UAMH BHEAG
STIRLING
Glen Finglas Res.
Anie
KATRINE
THE GREAT TROSSACHS FOREST
879 BEN LEDI
Pass of Leny
Leny Ho.
ROB ROY AND TROSSACHS VISITOR CENTRE
BRACKLINN FALLS
The Trossachs
FALLS OF LENY
CALLANDER
Kilmahog
Bochastle
Callander
TROSSACHS PIER COMPLEX
SS SIR WALTER SCOTT
Trossachs Hotel
Brig o'Turk
Coilantogle
A821
Annet Burn
BEN VENUE
727
Loch Achray
Duncraggan
Lendrick Lodge
Braes of Doune
Teith
THE TROSSACHS
Loch Venachar
Drumvaich
Ardoch Burn
Achray Forest
Loch Drunkie
Torrie Forest
Burn of Cambus
Menteith Hills
Loch Rusky
B8032
A81
B822
D. MARSHALL LODGE VISITOR CENTRE
KILMADOCK INFO HERITAGE CENTR
Altskeith
Port of Menteith
Doune
Milton
Deanston
B829
Loch Ard
Aberfoyle
INCHMAHOME PRIORY
Ruskie
A873
B826
A820
Kirkton
Malling
Goodie Water
Blair Drummond
Lake of Menteith
Thornhill
Cobleland
FLANDERS MOSS
BLAIR DRUM SAFARI AND
Loch Ard Forest
B8031
Flanders Moss

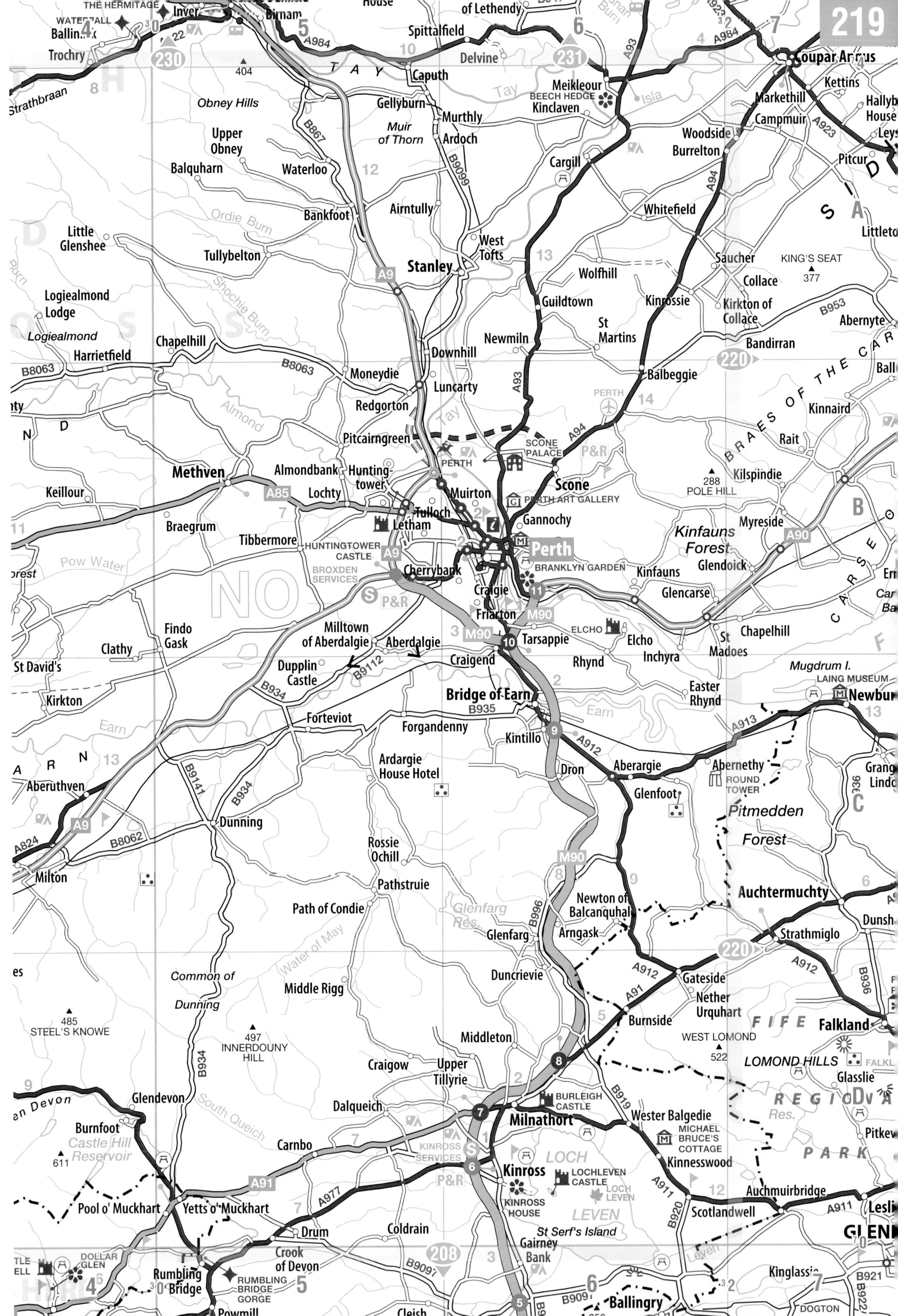
THE HERMITAGE
WATERFALL
Ballinluig
Trochry
Inver
Birnam
of Lethendy
Spittalfield
Delvine
Coupar Angus
Kettins
Strathbraan
404
TAY
Caputh
Obney Hills
Gellyburn
Murthly
Meikleour
BEECH HEDGE
Kinclaven
Isla
Markethill
Hallyburton House
Campmuir
Upper Obney
Muir of Thorn
Ardoch
B867
B9099
Woodside
Burrelton
A923
Balquharn
Waterloo
Cargill
Pitcur
A94
A93
A984
Airntully
Whitefield
Bankfoot
Ordie Burn
Little Glenshee
Tullybelton
West Tofts
Littleton
Saucher
KING'S SEAT
377
Stanley
Wolfhill
Collace
A9
Shochie Burn
Guildtown
Kinrossie
Kirkton of Collace
B953
Logiealmond Lodge
Logiealmond
St Martins
Abernyte
Chapelhill
Newmiln
Bandirran
Harrietfield
B8063
Downhill
Balbeggie
Moneydie
Luncarty
Almond
Redgorton
PERTH
BRAES OF THE CARSE
Kinnaird
Pitcairngreen
SCONE PALACE
Rait
PERTH
P&R
288
POLE HILL
Kilspindie
Methven
Almondbank
Hunting-tower
Scone
Keillour
A85
Lochty
Muirton
PERTH ART GALLERY
Tulloch
Gannochy
Braegrum
Letham
Myreside
Kinfauns Forest
A90
Tibbermore
HUNTINGTOWER CASTLE
Perth
Glendoick
Pow Water
BROXDEN SERVICES
Cherrybank
BRANKLYN GARDEN
Kinfauns
Craigie
Glencarse
Friarton
M90
CARSE OF GOWRIE
Findo Gask
Milltown of Aberdalgie
Aberdalgie
ELCHO
Tarsappie
Elcho
St Madoes
Chapelhill
Clathy
Inchyra
Rhynd
St David's
Dupplin Castle
B9112
Craigend
Mugdrum I.
LAING MUSEUM
Kirkton
B934
Bridge of Earn
Easter Rhynd
Newburgh
B935
Earn
Forteviot
Forgandenny
Kintillo
A912
A913
Aberargie
Abernethy
ROUND TOWER
Ardargie House Hotel
Dron
Glenfoot
Aberuthven
B9141
Dunning
Pitmedden Forest
A824
B8062
Milton
Rossie Ochill
Pathstruie
Auchtermuchty
Path of Condie
Glenfarg Res.
Newton of Balcanquhal
B996
Glenfarg
Arngask
Strathmiglo
Water of May
A912
Common of Dunning
Middle Rigg
Duncrievie
Gateside
Nether Urquhart
B936
A91
Burnside
485
STEEL'S KNOWE
497
INNERDOUNY HILL
Middleton
FIFE
Falkland
WEST LOMOND
522
LOMOND HILLS
Glenfoot
B934
Craigow
Upper Tillyrie
Glasslie
Glendevon
South Queich
BURLEIGH CASTLE
B919
Wester Balgedie
REGIONAL PARK
Burnfoot
Castle Hill Reservoir
Dalqueich
Milnathort
MICHAEL BRUCE'S COTTAGE
611
Carnbo
KINROSS SERVICES
LOCH LEVEN
Kinnesswood
Kinross
LOCHLEVEN CASTLE
A91
A977
KINROSS HOUSE
A911
Auchmuirbridge
Pool o' Muckhart
Yetts o' Muckhart
B920
Scotlandwell
Leslie
Drum
Coldrain
St Serf's Island
Gairney Bank
Crook of Devon
B9097
DOLLAR GLEN
Rumbling Bridge
RUMBLING BRIDGE GORGE
Kinglassie
Ballingry
B909
B921
B922
DOGTON
Powmill
Cleish
230
231
220
208

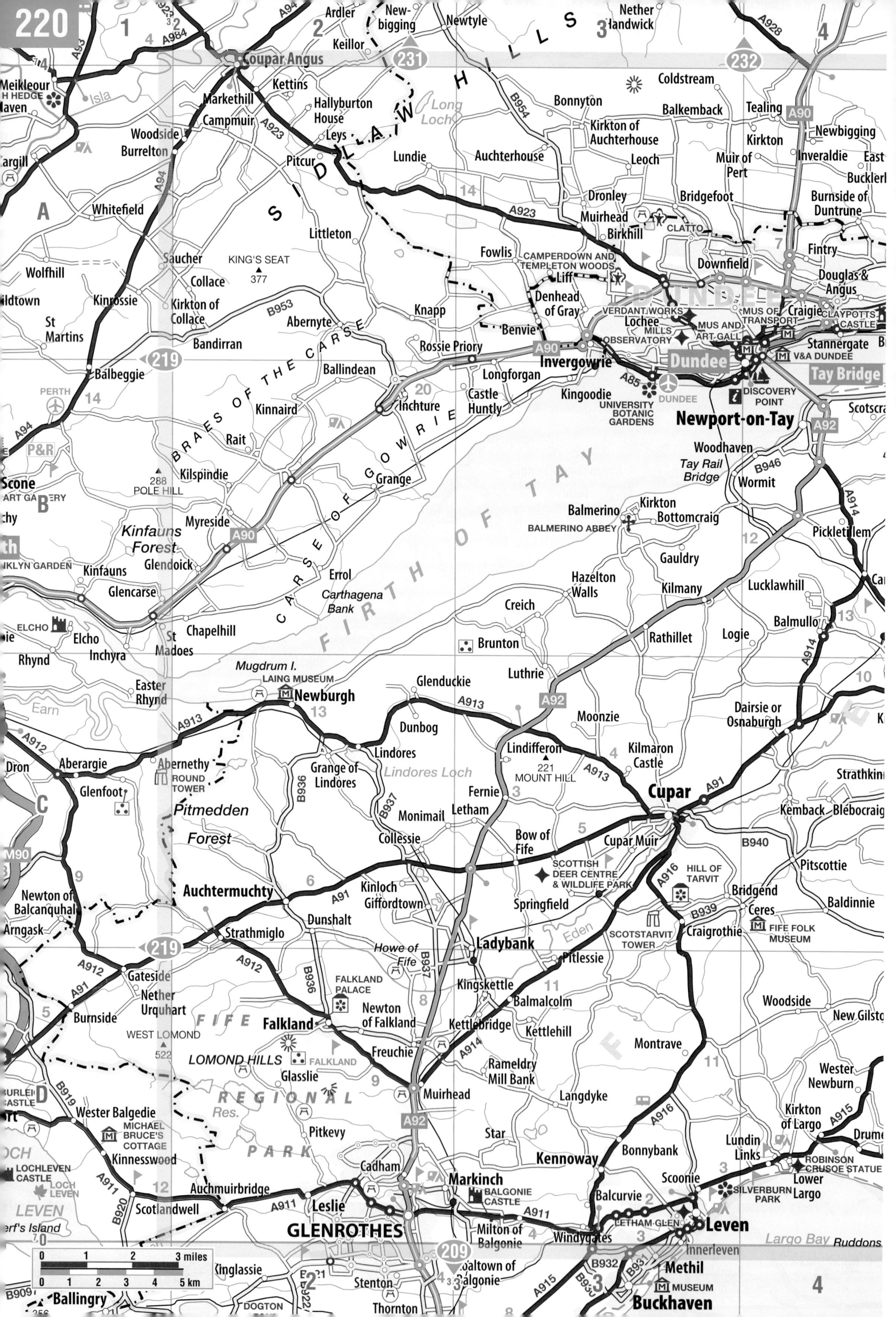
Ardler
New-
bigging
Newtyle
Nether
Handwick
Keillor
231
232
Coupar Angus
Meikleour
Isla
Kettins
Markethill
Hallyburton
House
Long
Loch
Coldstream
Bonnyton
Balkemback
Tealing
Campmuir
Woodside
Burrelton
Leys
Kirkton of
Auchterhouse
Newbigging
Kirkton
Muir of
Pert
Inveraldie
Lundie
Auchterhouse
Leoch
Pitcur
SIDLAW HILLS
Dronley
Bridgefoot
Burnside of
Duntrune
Whitefield
A923
Muirhead
Birkhill
CLATTO
Littleton
Fintry
Fowlis
CAMPERDOWN AND
TEMPLETON WOODS
Downfield
Saucher
KING'S SEAT
377
Wolfhill
Collace
Liff
Douglas &
Angus
Kinrossie
Kirkton of
Collace
Denhead
of Gray
DUNDEE
Craigie
B953
Abernyte
Knapp
VERDANT WORKS
MUS OF
TRANSPORT
CLAYPOTTS
CASTLE
St
Martins
Lochee
MILLS
OBSERVATORY
MUS AND
ART GALL
Benvie
Stannergate
Bandirran
Rossie Priory
A90
Invergowrie
V&A DUNDEE
219
Dundee
Tay Bridge
Balbeggie
Ballindean
Longforgan
A85
PERTH
BRAES OF THE CARSE
20
Inchture
Castle
Huntly
Kingoodie
DUNDEE
DISCOVERY
POINT
Kinnaird
UNIVERSITY
BOTANIC
GARDENS
Newport-on-Tay
A92
A94
Rait
CARSE OF GOWRIE
Woodhaven
P&R
Tay Rail
Bridge
B946
Wormit
288
POLE HILL
Kilspindie
Grange
Scone
B
FIRTH OF TAY
Kirkton
Balmerino
Bottomcraig
A914
BALMERINO ABBEY
Kinfauns
Forest
Myreside
Pickletillem
A90
12
Gauldry
Kinfauns
Glendoick
Errol
Hazelton
Walls
Kilmany
Lucklawhill
Glencarse
Carthagena
Bank
Creich
Balmullo
ELCHO
Elcho
St
Madoes
Chapelhill
Rathillet
Logie
13
Rhynd
Inchyra
Brunton
Luthrie
Mugdrum I.
LAING MUSEUM
Newburgh
Glenduckie
10
Easter
Rhynd
A92
Earn
13
A913
Dunbog
Moonzie
Dairsie or
Osnaburgh
A912
A913
Lindores
Lindifferon
221
MOUNT HILL
Kilmaron
Castle
Aberargie
Abernethy
ROUND
TOWER
Grange of
Lindores
Lindores Loch
Strathkinness
Dron
Glenfoot
B936
Fernie
Cupar
A91
C
Pitmedden
Forest
B937
Monimail
Letham
Kemback
Blebocraig
M90
Collessie
Bow of
Fife
Cupar Muir
B940
SCOTTISH
DEER CENTRE
& WILDLIFE PARK
HILL OF
TARVIT
Pitscottie
Newton of
Balcanquhal
Auchtermuchty
Kinloch
Giffordtown
A916
Bridgend
Baldinnie
Springfield
B939
Ceres
Arngask
Dunshalt
Strathmiglo
Eden
SCOTSTARVIT
TOWER
Craigrothie
FIFE FOLK
MUSEUM
219
Howe of
Fife
Ladybank
A912
Gateside
Pitlessie
FALKLAND
PALACE
11
Kingskettle
Woodside
Nether
Urquhart
Newton
of Falkland
Balmalcolm
A91
Burnside
FIFE
Falkland
Kettlebridge
Kettlehill
New Gilston
WEST LOMOND
522
Montrave
Freuchie
A914
LOMOND HILLS
FALKLAND
Rameldry
Mill Bank
Wester
Newburn
Glasslie
REGIONAL
Muirhead
Langdyke
B919
Wester Balgedie
Res.
A92
A916
Kirkton
of Largo
A915
MICHAEL
BRUCE'S
COTTAGE
Pitkevy
Star
Drum
PARK
Bonnybank
Lundin
Links
Kinnesswood
Kennoway
LOCHLEVEN
CASTLE
Cadham
ROBINSON
CRUSOE STATUE
LOCH
LEVEN
A911
Markinch
Scoonie
Lower
Largo
12
Auchmuirbridge
BALGONIE
CASTLE
SILVERBURN
PARK
Balcurvie
LEVEN
B920
Scotlandwell
A911
Leslie
A911
LETHAM GLEN
Leven
GLENROTHES
Milton of
Balgonie
Windygates
Largo Bay
Ruddons
Innerleven
209
Methil
0 1 2 3 miles
0 1 2 3 4 5 km
Kinglassie
Coaltown of
Balgonie
B932
B931
MUSEUM
A915
B909
Ballingry
Stenton
B933
Buckhaven
DOGTON
Thornton
4

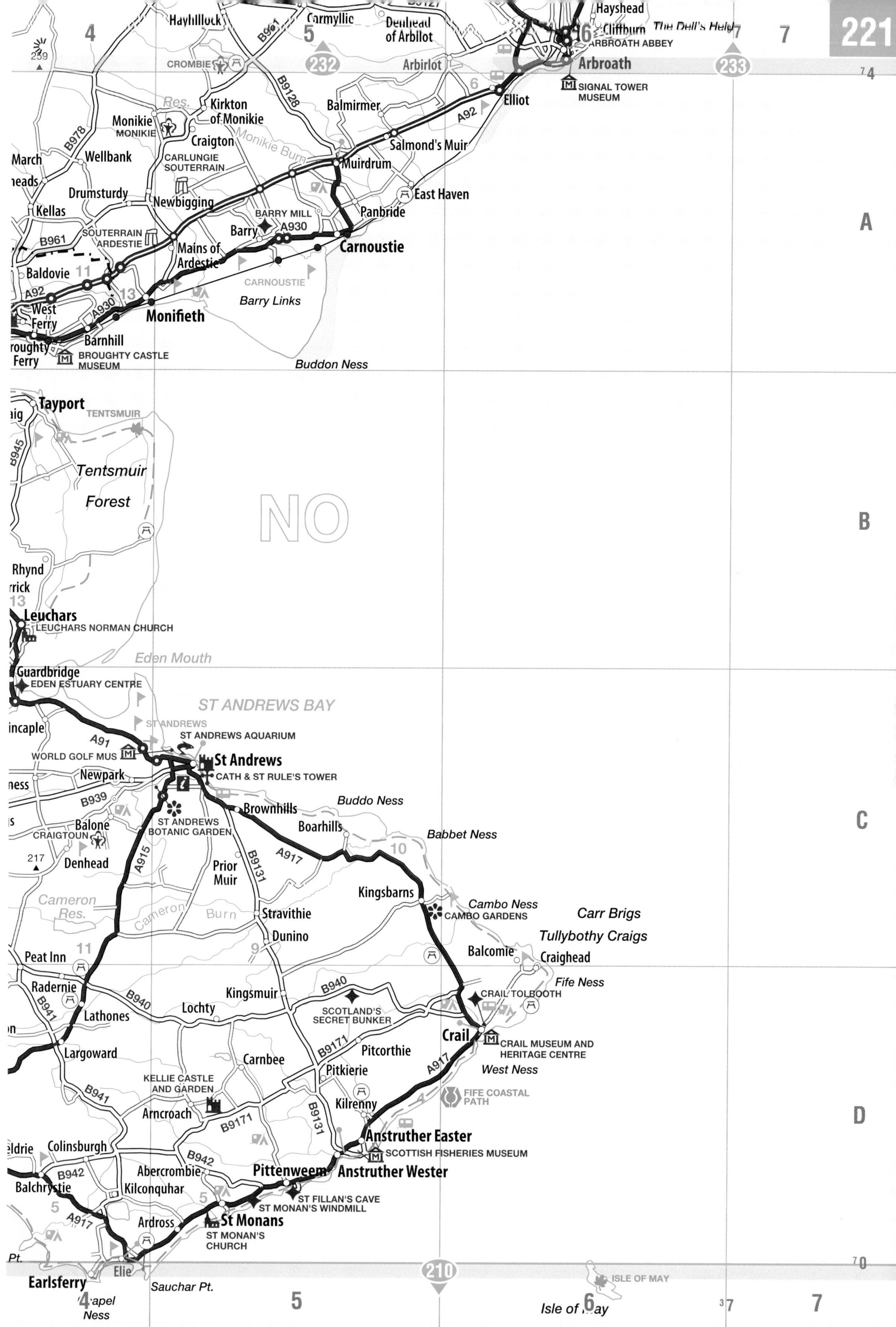
Haylhillock
Carmyllie
Denhead of Arbirlot
Hayshead
Cliffburn
The Deil's Heid
ARBROATH ABBEY
Arbroath
SIGNAL TOWER MUSEUM
CROMBIE
232
233
Arbirlot
B961
B9128
Elliot
Kirkton of Monikie
Monikie
MONIKIE
Res.
Craigton
Monikie Burn
Balmirmer
A92
Salmond's Muir
B978
March
Wellbank
CARLUNGIE SOUTERRAIN
Muirdrum
Drumsturdy
Newbigging
East Haven
Kellas
BARRY MILL
Panbride
Barry
A930
SOUTERRAIN ARDESTIE
B961
Mains of Ardestie
Carnoustie
Baldovie
CARNOUSTIE
A92
West Ferry
A930
Monifieth
Barry Links
Barnhill
Broughty Ferry
BROUGHTY CASTLE MUSEUM
Buddon Ness
Tayport
TENTSMUIR
B945
Tentsmuir Forest
NO
Rhynd
Leuchars
LEUCHARS NORMAN CHURCH
Eden Mouth
Guardbridge
EDEN ESTUARY CENTRE
ST ANDREWS BAY
ST ANDREWS
ST ANDREWS AQUARIUM
A91
WORLD GOLF MUS
St Andrews
CATH & ST RULE'S TOWER
Newpark
B939
Brownhills
Buddo Ness
Balone
ST ANDREWS BOTANIC GARDEN
Boarhills
Babbet Ness
CRAIGTOUN
Denhead
A915
B9131
A917
Prior Muir
Kingsbarns
Cambo Ness
CAMBO GARDENS
Carr Brigs
Cameron Res.
Cameron Burn
Stravithie
Tullybothy Craigs
Dunino
Peat Inn
Balcomie
Craighead
Fife Ness
Radernie
B940
Kingsmuir
B940
CRAIL TOLBOOTH
B941
Lathones
Lochty
SCOTLAND'S SECRET BUNKER
Crail
CRAIL MUSEUM AND HERITAGE CENTRE
Largoward
B9171
Pitcorthie
Carnbee
Pitkierie
A917
West Ness
KELLIE CASTLE AND GARDEN
B941
FIFE COASTAL PATH
Kilrenny
Arncroach
B9171
B9131
Anstruther Easter
Colinsburgh
SCOTTISH FISHERIES MUSEUM
B942
Abercrombie
Pittenweem
Anstruther Wester
B942
Balchrystie
Kilconquhar
ST FILLAN'S CAVE
ST MONAN'S WINDMILL
A917
Ardross
St Monans
ST MONAN'S CHURCH
Earlsferry
Elie
210
Sauchar Pt.
ISLE OF MAY
Isle of May
A
B
C
D
4
5
6
7

286

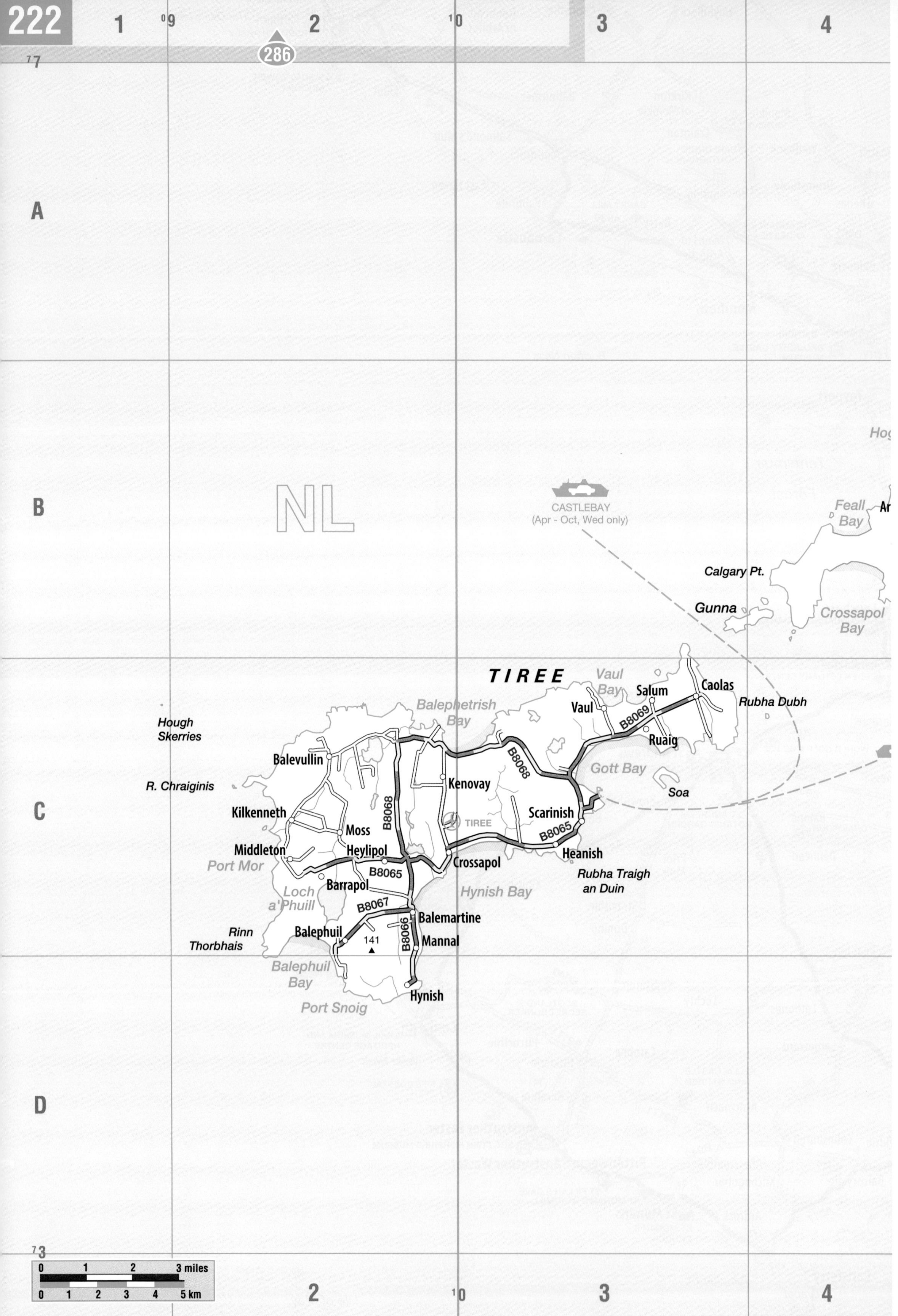
1
2
3
4
A
B
C
D
NL
CASTLEBAY
(Apr - Oct, Wed only)
Feall Bay
Calgary Pt.
Gunna
Crossapol Bay
TIREE
Vaul Bay
Salum
Caolas
Rubha Dubh
Balephetrish Bay
Vaul
B8069
Ruaig
Hough Skerries
Balevullin
B8068
Gott Bay
Soa
R. Chraiginis
Kenovay
Kilkenneth
B8068
TIREE
Scarinish
Moss
B8065
Middleton
Heylipol
Heanish
Port Mor
B8065
Crossapol
Rubha Traigh an Duin
Barrapol
Loch a'Phuill
Hynish Bay
B8067
Balemartine
Rinn Thorbhais
Balephuil
141
B8066
Mannal
Balephuil Bay
Hynish
Port Snoig
0 1 2 3 miles
0 1 2 3 4 5 km

4
5
6
7
CASTLEBAY
LOCHBOISDALE
(Oct - Mar)
Sanna Point
Sanna
Sanna Bay
Portuairk
Point of
Ardnamurchan
ARDNAMURCHAN LIGHTHOUSE
Achosnich
Cairns of Coll
234
Rubha Mor
Eilean Mor
Sorisdale
Bousd
Orms
Ormsaig
An Acairseid
B8072
Cliad Bay
Arnabost
Gallanach
Grishipoll
B8071
73
COLL
Ardmore Ba
Ballyhaugh
B8071
Loch
Cliad
104
Arinagour
Glengorm
Castle
Quinish Pt.
B8070
Totronald
Loch Eatharna
Rubha
an Aird
Quinish
Acha
Caliach Pt.
Eilean
Ornsay
Sunipol
Breachacha
Castle
Friesland
Mornish
Penmore
Mill
Dervaig
Achr
Calgary
THE OLD BYRE
HERITAGE CENT
Soa
Loch Breachacha
Calgary Bay
Ensay
Treshnish Pt.
342
CARN MOR
Bellart
Haunn
Achna
Rubh a'Chaoil
B8073
224
Burg
Kilninian
Achleck
Fanmore
390
Treshnish Isles
Fladda
LOCH TUATH
Ballygown
Eilean Dioghlum
EAS FORS
WATERFALL
Lunga
Gometra
Laggan
Bay
Bearnus
313
Ulva
Ulva House
Sound of Ulva
Bac Mor
LOCH NA
Little
Colonsay
Staffa
STAFFA
INCH KENNETH
CHAPEL
Inch
Kenneth
FINGAL'S CAVE
MACKINNON'S CAVE
Erisgeir
519
ARDMEANAC
224

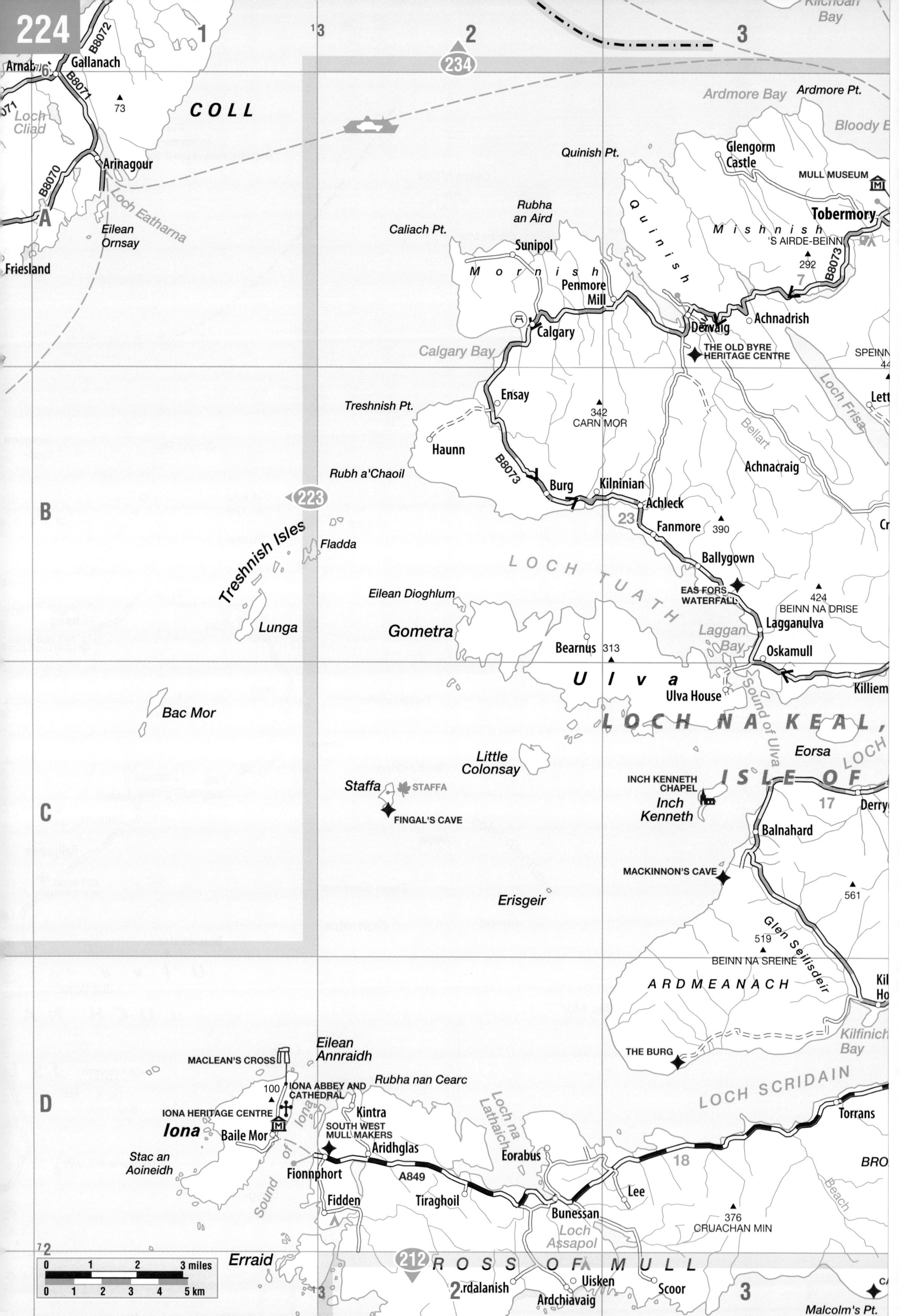
COLL
Gallanach
Arinagour
Friesland
Loch Eatharna
Eilean Ornsay
Quinish Pt.
Glengorm Castle
MULL MUSEUM
Tobermory
Mishnish
Quinish
Mornish
Sunipol
Penmore Mill
Calgary
Calgary Bay
Dervaig
Achnadrish
THE OLD BYRE HERITAGE CENTRE
Treshnish Pt.
Ensay
342 CARN MOR
Haunn
Rubh a'Chaoil
Burg
Kilninian
Achleck
Fanmore
Ballygown
Achnacraig
Treshnish Isles
Fladda
LOCH TUATH
EAS FORS WATERFALL
424 BEINN NA DRISE
Lagganulva
Oskamull
Eilean Dioghlum
Gometra
Lunga
Bearnus
Ulva
Ulva House
LOCH NA KEAL
Bac Mor
Little Colonsay
Eorsa
Staffa
STAFFA
FINGAL'S CAVE
INCH KENNETH CHAPEL
Inch Kenneth
ISLE OF
Balnahard
MACKINNON'S CAVE
Erisgeir
Glen Seilisdeir
519 BEINN NA SREINE
ARDMEANACH
THE BURG
Kilfinichen Bay
LOCH SCRIDAIN
MACLEAN'S CROSS
Eilean Annraidh
IONA ABBEY AND CATHEDRAL
IONA HERITAGE CENTRE
Iona
Baile Mor
Rubha nan Cearc
Kintra
SOUTH WEST MULL MAKERS
Aridhglas
Loch na Lathaich
Eorabus
Torrans
Stac an Aoineidh
Fionnphort
A849
Fidden
Tiraghoil
Bunessan
Lee
376 CRUACHAN MIN
Sound of Iona
Loch Assapol
Erraid
ROSS OF MULL
Uisken
Scoor
Ardchiavaig
Malcolm's Pt.
Ardmore Bay
Ardmore Pt.
Caliach Pt.
Rubha an Aird
Laggan Bay
Sound of Ulva
Loch Frisa
234
223
212
0 1 2 3 miles
0 1 2 3 4 5 km

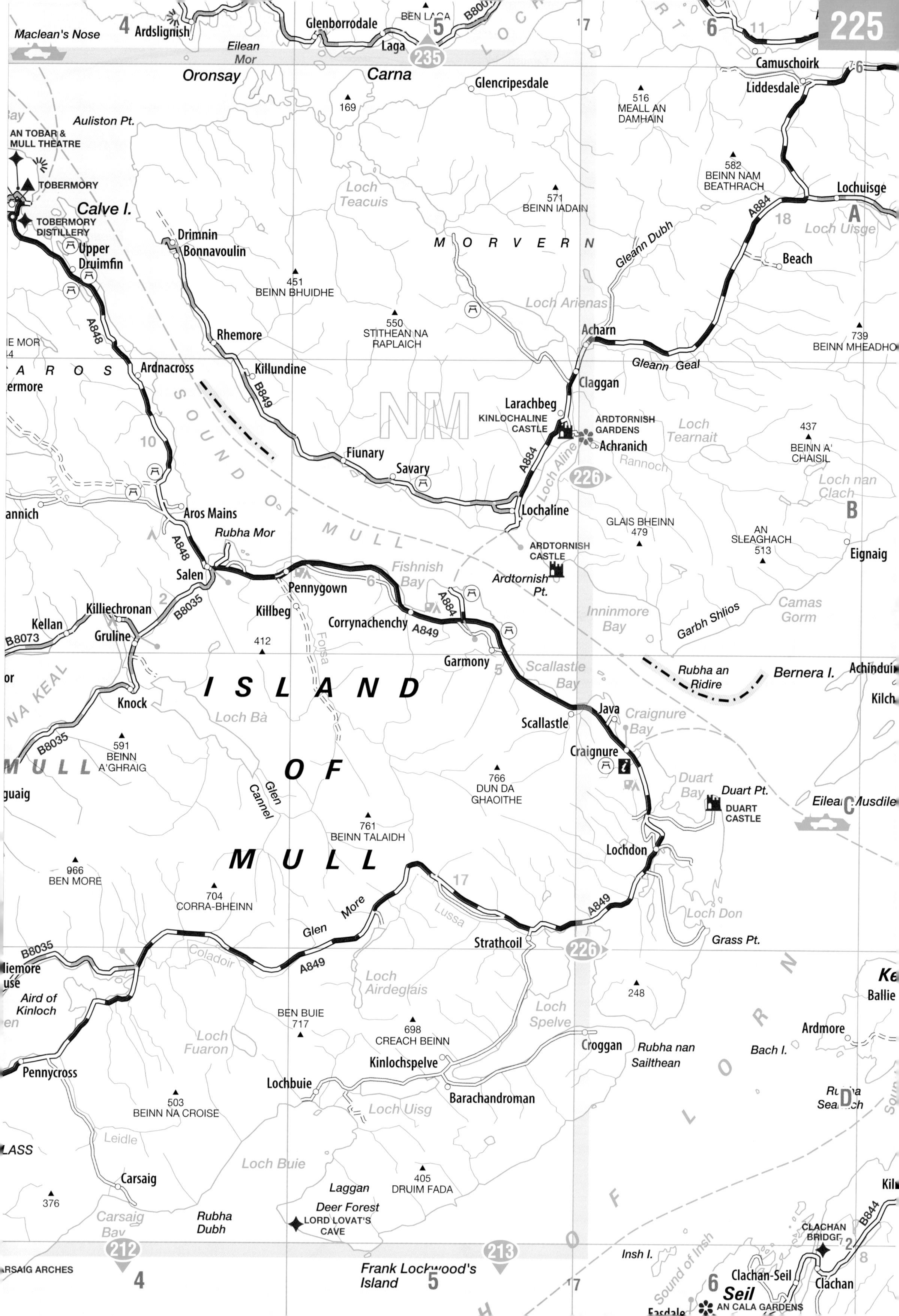

Maclean's Nose
Ardslignish
Glenborrodale
BEN LAGA
Laga
Eilean Mor
Oronsay
Carna
Glencripesdale
516 MEALL AN DAMHAIN
Camuschoirk
Liddesdale
Auliston Pt.
AN TOBAR & MULL THEATRE
TOBERMORY
Calve I.
TOBERMORY DISTILLERY
169
Loch Teacuis
571 BEINN IADAIN
582 BEINN NAM BEATHRACH
Lochuisge
Loch Uisge
Beach
Drimnin
Bonnavoulin
Upper Druimfin
M O R V E R N
Gleann Dubh
451 BEINN BHUIDHE
550 STITHEAN NA RAPLAICH
Loch Arienas
Acharn
739 BEINN MHEADHOI
Rhemore
Ardnacross
Killundine
Gleann Geal
Claggan
A848
B849
A884
NM
Larachbeg
KINLOCHALINE CASTLE
ARDTORNISH GARDENS
Achranich
Loch Tearnait
Rannoch
437 BEINN A' CHAISIL
Loch Aline
Fiunary
Savary
Loch nan Clach
SOUND OF MULL
Aros
Aros Mains
Lochaline
GLAIS BHEINN 479
AN SLEAGHACH 513
Eignaig
Rubha Mor
ARDTORNISH CASTLE
Ardtornish Pt.
Salen
Pennygown
Fishnish Bay
Killiechronan
Kellan
B8073
Gruline
B8035
Killbeg
Corrynachenchy
A849
Forsa
Inninmore Bay
Garbh Shlios
Camas Gorm
412
Garmony
Scallastle Bay
Rubha an Ridire
Bernera I.
Achindui
Kilch
ISLAND OF MULL
Knock
Loch Bà
Java
Scallastle
Craignure Bay
Craignure
591 BEINN A'GHRAIG
766 DUN DA GHAOITHE
Glen Cannel
Duart Bay
Duart Pt.
DUART CASTLE
Eilean Musdile
761 BEINN TALAIDH
Lochdon
966 BEN MORE
704 CORRA-BHEINN
Glen More
Lussa
Loch Don
Grass Pt.
Strathcoil
Coladoir
Loch Airdeglais
248
Aird of Kinloch
BEN BUIE 717
698 CREACH BEINN
Loch Spelve
Croggan
Rubha nan Sailthean
Ballie
Ardmore
Bach I.
Loch Fuaron
Pennycross
Kinlochspelve
Lochbuie
Barachandroman
503 BEINN NA CROISE
Loch Uisg
Leidle
Loch Buie
FIRTH OF LORN
Carsaig
Laggan
405 DRUIM FADA
376
Deer Forest
LORD LOVAT'S CAVE
Carsaig Bay
Rubha Dubh
Insh I.
Sound of Insh
CLACHAN BRIDGE
B844
Clachan-Seil
Clachan
Seil
AN CALA GARDENS
Frank Lockwood's Island
RSAIG ARCHES

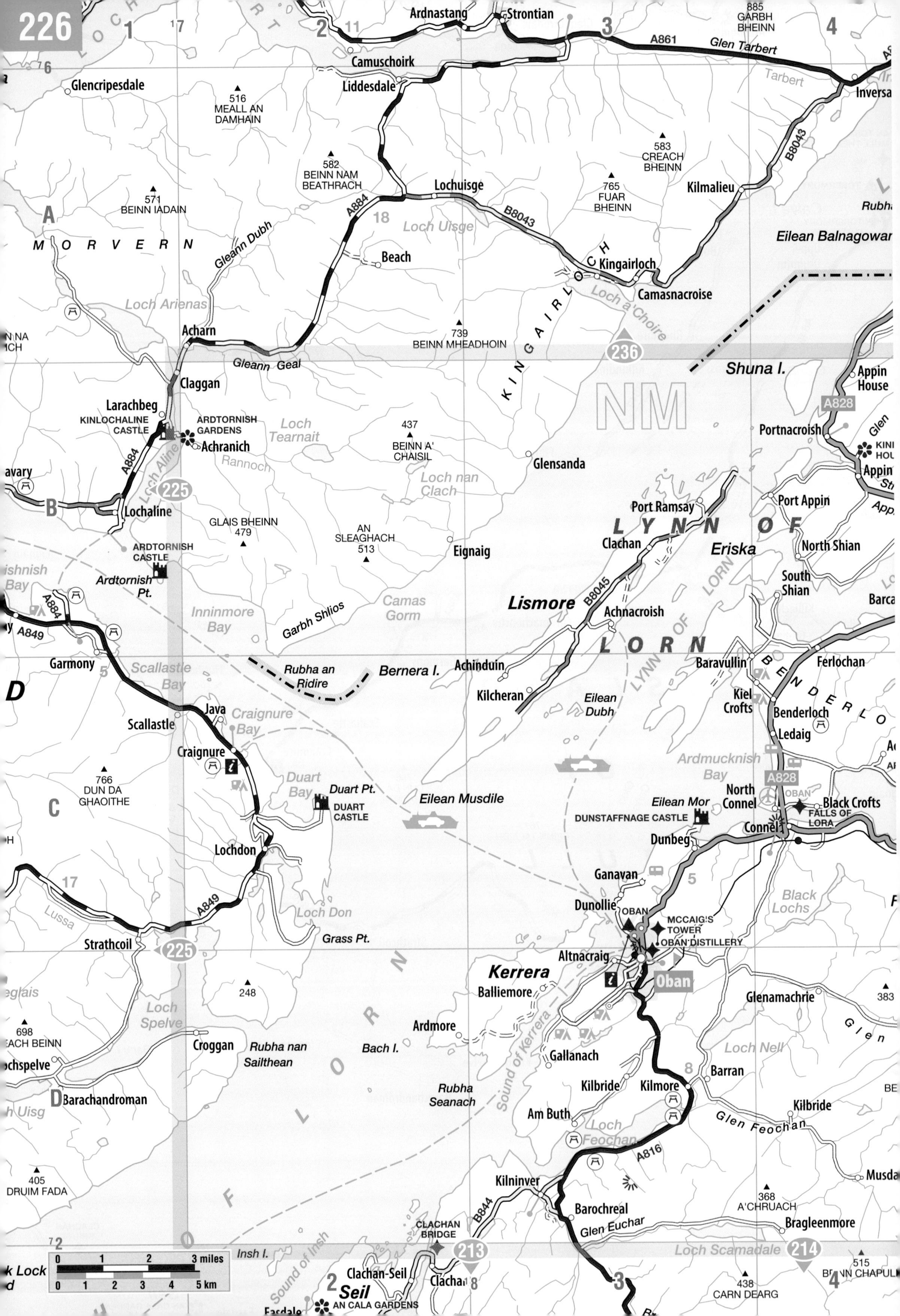
Ardnastang
Strontian
885
GARBH
BHEINN
A861
Glen Tarbert
Camuschoirk
Liddesdale
Tarbert
Inversa
Glencripesdale
516
MEALL AN
DAMHAIN
582
BEINN NAM
BEATHRACH
583
CREACH
BHEINN
765
FUAR
BHEINN
B8043
Kilmalieu
571
BEINN IADAIN
Lochuisge
A884
Loch Uisge
B8043
M O R V E R N
Gleann Dubh
Beach
Kingairloch
Eilean Balnagowan
Camasnacroise
Loch a'Choire
Loch Arienas
Acharn
739
BEINN MHEADHOIN
K I N G A I R L O C H
236
Gleann Geal
Shuna I.
Claggan
Appin
House
Larachbeg
KINLOCHALINE
CASTLE
ARDTORNISH
GARDENS
Achranich
Loch
Tearnait
437
BEINN A'
CHAISIL
NM
A828
Portnacroish
Rannoch
Loch Aline
225
Lochaline
Glensanda
Loch nan
Clach
Port Ramsay
Port Appin
GLAIS BHEINN
479
AN
SLEAGHACH
513
Eignaig
L Y N N O F
Clachan
Eriska
North Shian
ARDTORNISH
CASTLE
Ardtornish
Pt.
South
Shian
A884
A849
Inninmore
Bay
Garbh Shlios
Camas
Gorm
Lismore
B8045
Achnacroish
L O R N
LYNN OF LORN
Garmony
Scallastle
Bay
Rubha an
Ridire
Bernera I.
Achinduin
Baravullin
Ferlochan
B E N D E R L O C H
Kilcheran
Eilean
Dubh
Kiel
Crofts
Benderloch
Java
Craignure
Bay
Scallastle
Ledaig
Craignure
Ardmucknish
Bay
766
DUN DA
GHAOITHE
Duart
Bay
Duart Pt.
DUART
CASTLE
Eilean Musdile
A828
North
Connel
Eilean Mor
Black Crofts
FALLS OF
LORA
DUNSTAFFNAGE CASTLE
Connel
Lochdon
Dunbeg
Ganavan
Black
Lochs
Lussa
A849
Loch Don
Dunollie
OBAN
MCCAIG'S
TOWER
OBAN DISTILLERY
Strathcoil
225
Grass Pt.
Altnacraig
Kerrera
Oban
Balliemore
248
Glenamachrie
383
Loch
Spelve
698
Ardmore
Croggan
Rubha nan
Sailthean
Bach I.
Sound of Kerrera
Gallanach
Loch Nell
Glen
Barran
Kilbride
Kilmore
Barachandroman
Rubha
Seanach
Am Buth
Kilbride
Glen Feochan
Loch
Feochan
A816
L O R N
405
DRUIM FADA
Kilninver
Musda
368
A'CHRUACH
Barochreal
Glen Euchar
Bragleenmore
CLACHAN
BRIDGE
B844
213
Insh I.
Loch Scamadale
214
515
Sound of Insh
Clachan-Seil
Clachan
438
CARN DEARG
Seil
AN CALA GARDENS
Easdale
0 1 2 3 miles
0 1 2 3 4 5 km

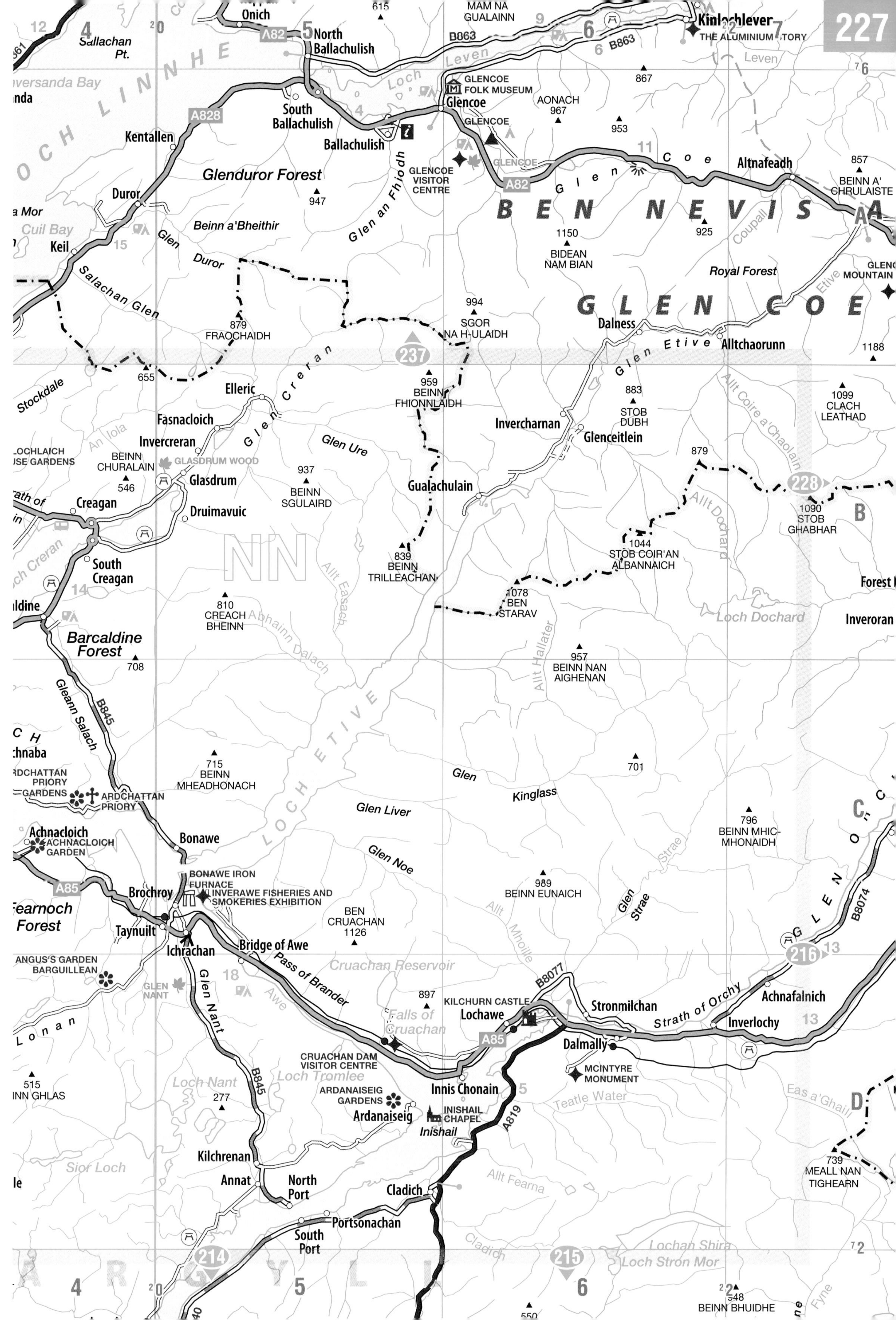
Onich
615
MAM NA GUALAINN
Kinlochleven
THE ALUMINIUM STORY
North Ballachulish
Sallachan Pt.
LOCH LINNHE
A82
B863
Loch Leven
GLENCOE FOLK MUSEUM
Glencoe
867
AONACH 967
South Ballachulish
Ballachulish
A828
Kentallen
GLENCOE
953
Glenduror Forest
Glen an Fhiodh
GLENCOE VISITOR CENTRE
Glen Coe
Altnafeadh
857 BEINN A' CHRULAISTE
Duror
947
BEN NEVIS
Cuil Bay
Keil
Beinn a'Bheithir
Glen Duror
1150 BIDEAN NAM BIAN
925
Coupall
Royal Forest
GLENCOE MOUNTAIN
Salachan Glen
994 SGOR NA H-ULAIDH
GLEN COE
Etive
879 FRAOCHAIDH
Dalness
Glen Etive
Alltchaorunn
655
237
Glen Creran
1188
Stockdale
Elleric
959 BEINN FHIONNLAIDH
883 STOB DUBH
1099 CLACH LEATHAD
Fasnacloich
Invercharnan
Glenceitlein
Allt Coire a'Chaolain
Invercreran
An Iola
Glen Ure
LOCHLAICH HOUSE GARDENS
BEINN CHURALAIN
GLASDRUM WOOD
937 BEINN SGULAIRD
879
546
Glasdrum
Gualachulain
228
Creagan
Druimavuic
1090 STOB GHABHAR
Allt Dochard
B
1044 STOB COIR'AN ALBANNAICH
South Creagan
NN
839 BEINN TRILLEACHAN
Allt Easach
Forest
Loch Creran
1078 BEN STARAV
Loch Dochard
Inveroran
810 CREACH BHEINN
Abhainn Dalach
Allt Hallater
Barcaldine Forest
708
957 BEINN NAN AIGHENAN
Gleann Salach
B845
LOCH ETIVE
715 BEINN MHEADHONACH
701
Glen Kinglass
ARDCHATTAN PRIORY GARDENS
ARDCHATTAN PRIORY
Glen Liver
796 BEINN MHIC-MHONAIDH
C
Achnacloich
ACHNACLOICH GARDEN
Bonawe
Glen Noe
Strae
BONAWE IRON FURNACE
INVERAWE FISHERIES AND SMOKERIES EXHIBITION
989 BEINN EUNAICH
A85
Brochroy
Fearnoch Forest
Glen Strae
BEN CRUACHAN 1126
Allt Mhoille
GLEN ORCHY
B8074
Taynuilt
Ichrachan
Bridge of Awe
216
ANGUS'S GARDEN BARGUILLEAN
Pass of Brander
Cruachan Reservoir
GLEN NANT
Glen Nant
Awe
897
KILCHURN CASTLE
B8077
Stronmilchan
Achnafalnich
Lochawe
Falls of Cruachan
Strath of Orchy
Inverlochy
Lonan
Dalmally
CRUACHAN DAM VISITOR CENTRE
MCINTYRE MONUMENT
515
Loch Nant
Loch Tromlee
Innis Chonain
Teatle Water
Eas a'Ghaill
D
ARDANAISEIG GARDENS
277
Ardanaiseig
INISHAIL CHAPEL
Inishail
A819
Kilchrenan
Sior Loch
Allt Fearna
739 MEALL NAN TIGHEARN
Annat
North Port
Cladich
Portsonachan
South Port
Lochan Shira
Loch Stron Mor
214
215
ARGYLL
Cladich
548 BEINN BHUIDHE
550
Fyne

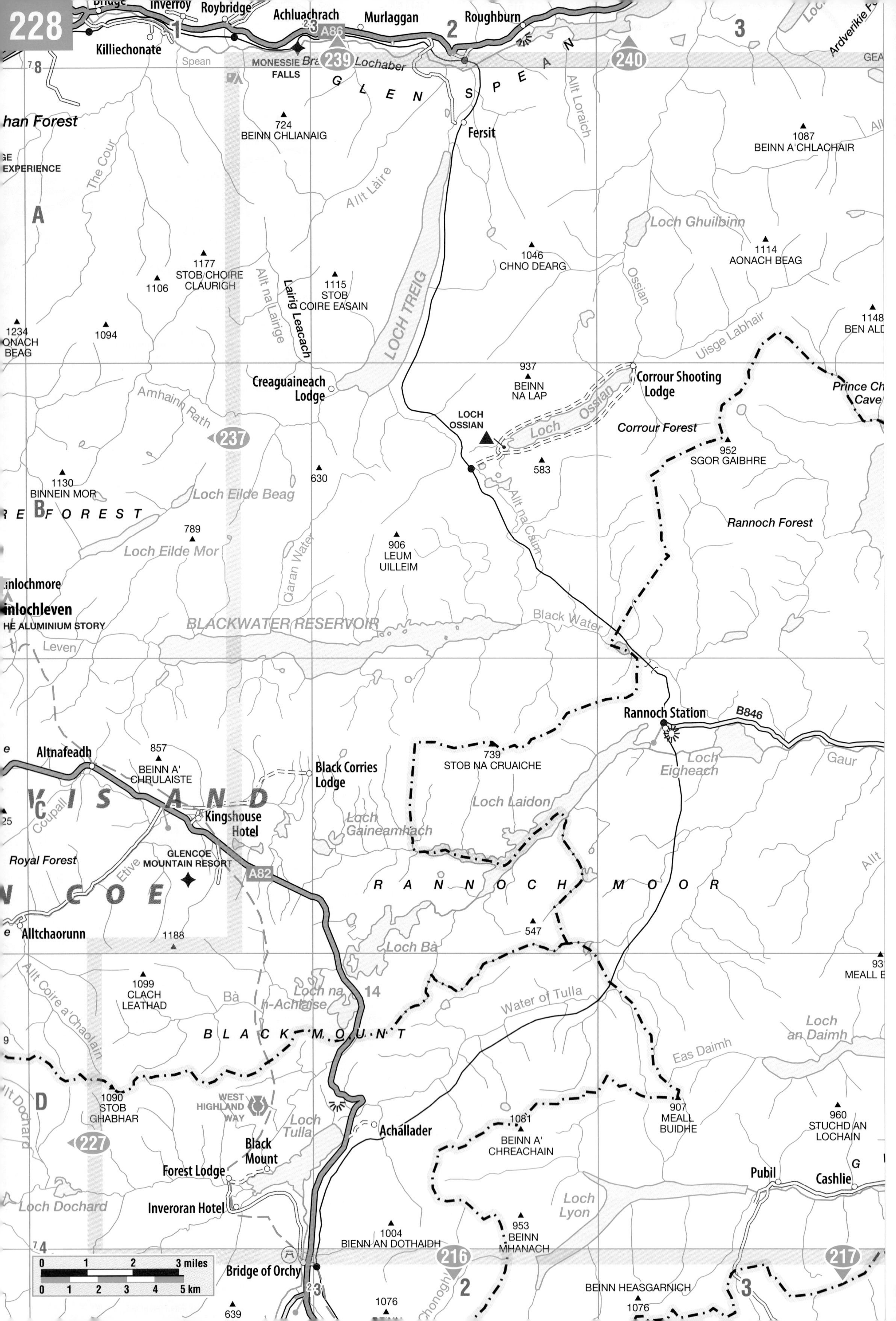

Inverroy
Roybridge
Achluachrach
Murlaggan
Roughburn
Killiechonate
A86
MONESSIE FALLS
Lochaber
GLEN SPEAN
Spean
239
240
724
BEINN CHLIANAIG
Fersit
Allt Loraich
1087
BEINN A'CHLACHAIR
EXPERIENCE
The Cour
Allt Làire
Loch Ghuilbinn
1114
AONACH BEAG
1046
CHNO DEARG
Ossian
1177
STOB CHOIRE CLAURIGH
1106
Allt na Lairige
Lairig Leacach
1115
STOB COIRE EASAIN
LOCH TREIG
1234
1094
1148
Uisge Labhair
937
BEINN NA LAP
Corrour Shooting Lodge
Creaguaineach Lodge
Amhainn Rath
237
LOCH OSSIAN
Loch Ossian
Corrour Forest
952
SGOR GAIBHRE
583
630
1130
BINNEIN MOR
Loch Eilde Beag
FOREST
789
Loch Eilde Mor
906
LEUM UILLEIM
Allt na Càim
Rannoch Forest
Ciaran Water
BLACKWATER RESERVOIR
Black Water
Leven
Rannoch Station
B846
Altnafeadh
857
BEINN A' CHRULAISTE
739
STOB NA CRUAICHE
Black Corries Lodge
Loch Eigheach
Gaur
Loch Laidon
Kingshouse Hotel
Loch Gaineamhach
Coupall
Royal Forest
GLENCOE MOUNTAIN RESORT
A82
Etive
RANNOCH MOOR
547
Alltchaorunn
1188
Loch Bà
1099
CLACH LEATHAD
Bà
Loch na h-Achlaise
14
Water of Tulla
Loch an Daimh
BLACK MOUNT
Allt Coire a' Chaolain
Eas Daimh
1090
STOB GHABHAR
WEST HIGHLAND WAY
Loch Tulla
Achallader
907
MEALL BUIDHE
960
STUCHD AN LOCHAIN
1081
BEINN A' CHREACHAIN
227
Black Mount
Forest Lodge
Pubil
Cashlie
Loch Lyon
Loch Dochard
Inveroran Hotel
1004
BIENN AN DOTHAIDH
953
BEINN MHANACH
216
217
0 1 2 3 miles
0 1 2 3 4 5 km
Bridge of Orchy
BEINN HEASGARNICH
1076
639

4
5
6
240
241
230
217
218
A9
Loch Ericht
1049
L CHARN
Loch Pattack
Ben Alder Lodge
774
CREAGAN MOR
941
CARN NA CAIM
Loch an Duin
Cama Choire
917
Sronphadruig Lodge
Dail-na-Mine Forest
816
SRON A'CHLEIRICH
936
A'BHUIDHEANACH BHEAG
Allt a Chaoil-reidhe
Ben Alder Forest
LOCH ERICHT
934
BEINN UDLAMAIN
803
THE SOW OF ATHOLL
Dalnaspidal Lodge
Dalnacardoch Forest
Edendon Water
Allt Glas Choire
Allt a' Mhuilinn
Allt a' Chireachain
F O R E S T O F
A T H O L L
Loch a' Bhealaich Bheithe
Corrievarkie Lodge
Allt na Glaise
Dalnaspidal Forest
Loch Garry
775
MEALL NA LEITREACH
17
Dalnacardoch Lodge
GLEN GARRY
Garry
855
Talla Bheith Forest
Loch Con
Loch Errochty
Calvine
Dalchalloch
Trinafour
B847
10
Errochty Water
GLEN ERROCHTY
Tummel Forest
841
BEINN MHOLACH
612
NN
R
G
Allt Ghlas
515
SRON BHEAG
Aulich Burn
891
BEINN A'CHUALLAICH
477
Ericht
Killichonan Burn
Craiganor Lodge
Kinloch Rannoch
B846
Dunalastair
Tummel
Tummel Bridge
B8019
LOCH
Bridge of Ericht
Killichonan
19
LOCH RANNOCH
Dunalastair Water
4
Carie
Inverhadden
Foss
Finnart
Bridge of Gaur
Camghouran
Black Wood of Rannoch
Rannoch
Forest
Camghouran
Dall Burn
Allt na Bogair
Innerhadden Burn
Loch Kinardochy
T A Y F O R E S T
1083
SCHIEHALLION
Allt Mor
LOCH RANNOCH AND
GLEN LYON
Keltney Burn
13
Appin of Dull
1042
CARN MAIRG
745
MEALL A'MHUIC
1029
CARN GORM
Keltneyburn
ST FILLAN'S CHURCH &
FORTINGALL YEW
Camserney
Dull
Invervar
Camusvrachan
Lyon
Fortingall
Taymouth Castle
Innerwick
Bridge of Balgie
Glen Lyon
Allt Conait
Gallin
Allt Bail a' Mhuilinn
Allt Gleann Da-Eig
Kenmore
566
A827
Fearnan
THE SCOTTISH CRANNOG CENTRE
Remony
780
1118
Lawers Burn
Acharn
Falls of Acharn
LOCH TAY
Stronuich Reservoir
1214
BEN LAWERS
Loch na Lairige
MEALL NAN TARMACHAN
1043
BEN LAWERS
25
Lawers
716
BEINN BHREAC
Quaich
Ardtalnaig
Carie

UCHD A'CHLARSAIR
Tarf Water
BRAIGH SRON GHORM
BEINN DEARG
Dail-na-Mine Forest
SRON A'CHLEIRICH
Glen Bruar
Bruar Lodge
Loch Loch
FOREST OF ATHOLL
Forest Lodge
Glen Diridh
BEINN A'GHLO
Glen Tilt
CARN LIATH
BEN VUIRICH
Gleann Fearnach
BLAIR CASTLE
Falls of the Bruar
CLAN DONNACHAIDH MUSEUM
Pitagowan
Old Bridge of Tilt
Lude House
Calvine
Blair Atholl
BLAIR ATHOLL MILL
Struan
Ballentoul
Glen Girnaig
TULACH HILL
Errochty Water
GLEN ERROCHTY
ATHOLL COUNTRY LIFE
Aldclune
Killiecrankie
KILLIECRANKIE VISITOR CENTRE
BEN VRACKIE
Dalnavaid
Tarvie
Glen Brerachan
Loch Bhac
Tummel Forest
LOCH TUMMEL
Bonskeid House
Tressait
Queen's View
Tummel Bridge
QUEEN'S VIEW CENTRE
Falls of Tummel
LINN OF TUMMEL
PITLOCHRY
Moulin
Pitlochry
EDRADOUR DISTILLERY
CREAG DHUBH
Loch Faskally
Balmore
Foss
Milton of Edradour
BLAIR ATHOL DISTILLERY VISITOR CENTRE
EXPLORER'S GARDEN
Loch Broom
MEALL REAMHAR
Loch Kinardochy
FARRAGON HILL
Loch Derculich
FOREST PARK
Milton of Dalcapon
Strathtay
Ballechin
Grandtully
Tulliemet
Ballinluig
Edradynate
CLUNY HOUSE GARDENS
Little Ballinluig
Balnaguard
Logierait
Loch Ordie
ST MARY'S CHURCH
CASTLE MENZIES
Weem
Balmacneil
Kindallachan
Camserney
Dull
Keltneyburn
Appin of Dull
DEWAR'S ABERFELDY DISTILLERY
Kincraigie
Guay
Dowally
DEUCHARY HILL
ST FILLAN'S CHURCH & FORTINGALL YEW
WADE'S BRIDGE
Aberfeldy
Falls of Moness
Loch Skiach
Bishopric
Taymouth Castle
BOLFRACKS GARDEN
Dalguise
Craigvinean Forest
Loch Kennard
Kenmore
Urlar Burn
Glen Cochill
STRATH TAY
RIVER
THE SCOTTISH CRANNOG CENTRE
Remony
Balnaguard Burn
Loch Holl
Tombane Burn
Ballinloan Burn
Acharn
Falls of Acharn
Dunkeld
Little Dunkeld
Scotston
THE HERMITAGE
Inver
MEALL DEARG
WATERFALL
Ballinlick
Garrow
Trochry
PERTH
Cablea
Strathbraan
Glen Quaich
Loch Freuchie
3 miles
5 km

4
5
6
7
242
243
CAIRN BANNOCH
998 BROAD CAIRN
Loch Muick
939 AN SOCACH
Clunie Water
Loch Vrotachan
1019 CARN AN TUIRC
958 TOLMOUNT
GLENSHEE SKI CENTRE
THE CAIRNWELL
Devil's Elbow
1068 GLAS MAOL
Caenlochan Forest
832 LAIR OF ALDARARIE
Glen Doll
Glendoll Lodge
Braedownie
Glendoll Forest
CORRIE FEE
905 FINALTY HILL
947 DRIESH
Clova
758
B955
G L E N
A N
BEN GULABIN 806
Glenlochsie
808 MONAMEANACH
Spittal of Glenshee
801 BEN EARB
Loch Beanie
Auchavan
232
Kilburn
Glenprosen Lodge
740 BADENDUN HILL
Glen Prosen
Balnaboth
PROSEN
Glenprosen Village
794 MEALL UAINE
A93
Glen Shee
702 DUCHRAY HILL
Dalnaglar Castle
Meikle Forter
Glenisla Forest
611
Folda
B951
Enochdhu
Cray
744 MOUNT BLAIR
Backwater Res.
Glenhead Farm
Easter Lednathie
STRATHARDLE
Ashintully Castle
Brewlands Bridge
Freuchies
668 CAT LAW
CAPTAIN SCOTT DR WILSON CAIRN
Kirkmichael
Blacklunans
Kirkton of Glenisla
24
Bellaty
497 CREIGH HILL
Balintore
B950
13
520 CAIRN GIBBS
Dykends
KNOCK OF BALMYLE
444
Forest of Alyth
Black Water
NO
409 MILE HILL
Loch of Lintrathen
PEEL FARM NATURE TRAIL
B954
Isla
B951
Kirkton of Kingoldrum
Ballintuim
BALDUFF HILL
425
Bridgend of Lintrathen
LOCH OF KINNORDY NATURE RESERVE
REEKIE LINN WATERFALL
Bridge of Craigisla
561
Ardle
A924
Tullymurdoch
Auchrannie
Netherton
Kirkton of Airlie
Blackcraig Forest
Bamff
A926
Forest of Clunie
Bridge of Cally
Craigton
Loch Benachally
Shanzie
Cochrage Muir
CATERAN ECOMUSEUM
Riemore
Tullyfergus
Ruthven
14
Lornty Burn
Ruthven House
EASSIE SCULPTURED STONE
Alyth
Middleton
New Alyth
308
Riechip
Westfields of Rattray
18
Balhary
Lornty
Castleton
13
A923
Forneth
Achalader
Blairgowrie
Kinloch
Rattray
A926
Leitfie
MEIGLE SCULPTURED STONE MUSEUM
Balkeerie
Eassie
Loch of Lowes
Concraigie
Loch of Clunie
Loch of Drumellie
River Ericht
Kinloch
Meigle
Kirkinch
LOCH OF LOWES NATURE RESERVE
Clunie
Craigie
Muirton of Ardblair
Rosemount
Arthurstone
Wester Denoon
340
Snaigow House
Kirkton of Lethendy
B947
Lunan Burn
A923
A94
Ardler
Newbigging
Newtyle
Spittalfield
A984
A93
Keillor
A984
Delvine
Coupar Angus
SIDLAW HILLS
TAY
Caputh
219
Meikleour
BEECH HEDGE
Kettins
220
Isla
Markethill
Gellyburn
Kinclaven
Murthly
Hallyburton House
Campmuir
Muir
Bonnyton
B954
Kirkton

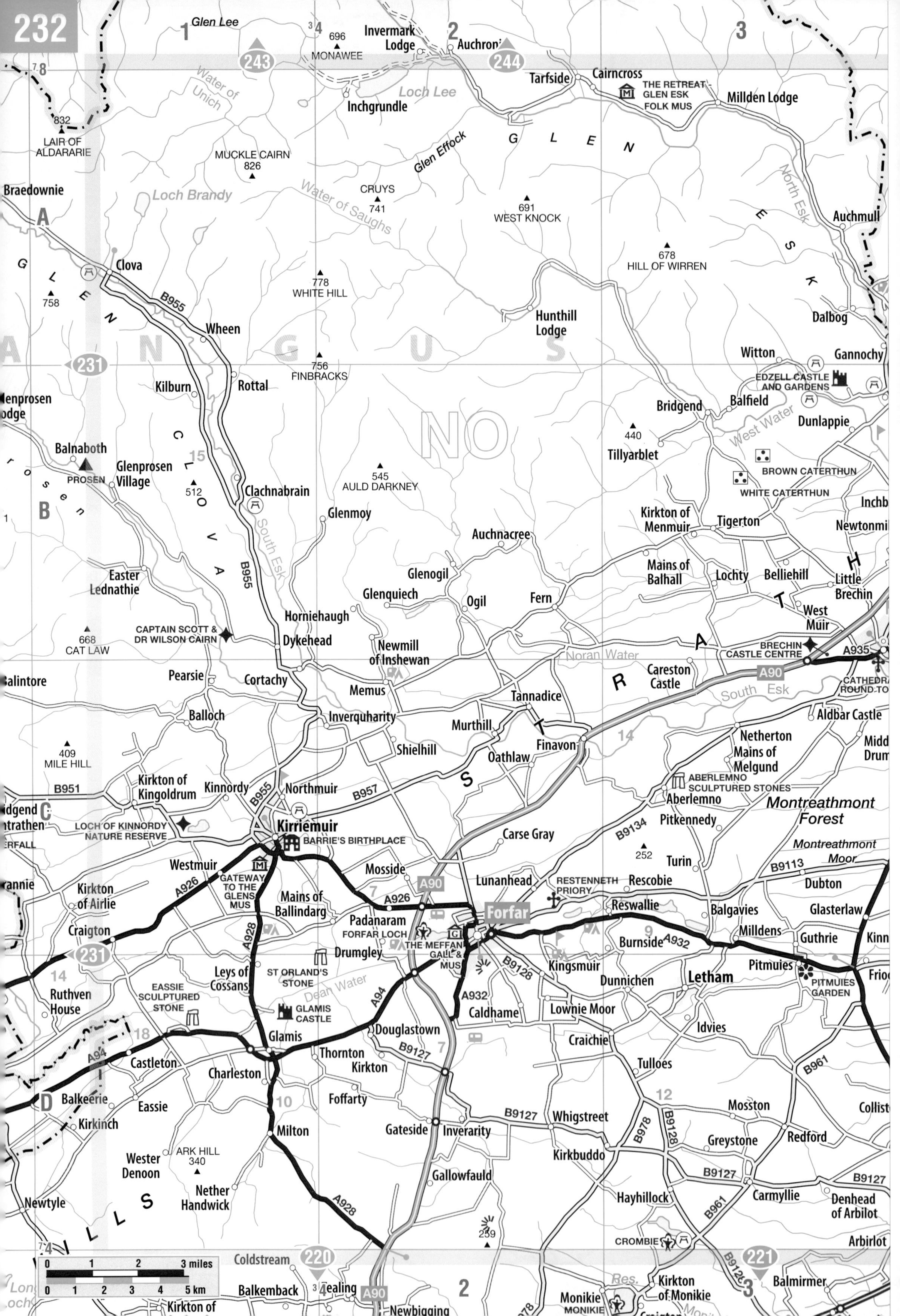
Glen Lee
696
MONAWEE
Invermark Lodge
Auchronie
243
244
Tarfside
Cairncross
THE RETREAT GLEN ESK FOLK MUS
Millden Lodge
Water of Unich
Loch Lee
Inchgrundle
832
LAIR OF ALDARARIE
MUCKLE CAIRN 826
Glen Effock
GLEN ESK
North Esk
Braedownie
Loch Brandy
Water of Saughs
CRUYS 741
691 WEST KNOCK
Auchmull
678 HILL OF WIRREN
Clova
GLEN CLOVA
758
B955
778 WHITE HILL
Hunthill Lodge
Dalbog
Wheen
ANGUS
231
756 FINBRACKS
Witton
Gannochy
EDZELL CASTLE AND GARDENS
Kilburn
Rottal
Glenprosen Lodge
Balfield
Bridgend
Dunlappie
West Water
NO
440
Tillyarblet
Balnaboth
PROSEN
Glenprosen Village
15
512
545 AULD DARKNEY
BROWN CATERTHUN
WHITE CATERTHUN
Prosen
Clachnabrain
Glenmoy
South Esk
Kirkton of Menmuir
Tigerton
Newtonmill
Auchnacree
Mains of Balhall
Lochty
Belliehill
Little Brechin
Easter Lednathie
Glenogil
Glenquiech
Ogil
Fern
STRATHMORE
West Muir
Horniehaugh
668 CAT LAW
CAPTAIN SCOTT & DR WILSON CAIRN
Dykehead
Newmill of Inshewan
BRECHIN CASTLE CENTRE
A935
Noran Water
Balintore
Pearsie
Cortachy
Memus
Careston Castle
A90
CATHEDRAL ROUND TOWER
South Esk
Tannadice
Balloch
Inverquharity
Murthill
Aldbar Castle
409 MILE HILL
Shielhill
Oathlaw
Finavon
14
Netherton
Mains of Melgund
Kirkton of Kingoldrum
Kinnordy
B951
B955
Northmuir
B957
ABERLEMNO SCULPTURED STONES
Aberlemno
Montreathmont Forest
LOCH OF KINNORDY NATURE RESERVE
Kirriemuir
Pitkennedy
BARRIE'S BIRTHPLACE
Carse Gray
B9134
252
Montreathmont Moor
Westmuir
GATEWAY TO THE GLENS MUS
Mosside
Lunanhead
RESTENNETH PRIORY
Rescobie
Turin
B9113
Dubton
Kirkton of Airlie
A926
Mains of Ballindarg
A926
Forfar
Reswallie
Balgavies
Glasterlaw
Craigton
A928
Padanaram
FORFAR LOCH
THE MEFFAN GALL & MUS
Burnside
A932
Milldens
Guthrie
Drumgley
Kingsmuir
Pitmuies
Ruthven House
Leys of Cossans
ST ORLAND'S STONE
EASSIE SCULPTURED STONE
Dean Water
A94
B9128
Dunnichen
Letham
PITMUIES GARDEN
GLAMIS CASTLE
A932
Caldhame
Lownie Moor
Douglastown
Idvies
18
A94
Glamis
Craichie
Castleton
Thornton
Kirkton
B9127
Tulloes
B961
Charleston
Balkeerie
Eassie
10
Foffarty
12
Mosston
Kirkinch
Milton
Gateside
Inverarity
B9127
Whigstreet
B978
B9128
Greystone
Redford
Wester Denoon
ARK HILL 340
Kirkbuddo
Gallowfauld
B9127
B9127
Nether Handwick
Newtyle
SIDLAW HILLS
Hayhillock
Carmyllie
Denhead of Arbilot
B961
A928
259
CROMBIE
Arbirlot
0 1 2 3 miles
0 1 2 3 4 5 km
Coldstream
220
221
Balkemback
Tealing
A90
Newbigging
Kirkton of
Monikie
MONIKIE
Kirkton of Monikie
Res.
Balmirmer

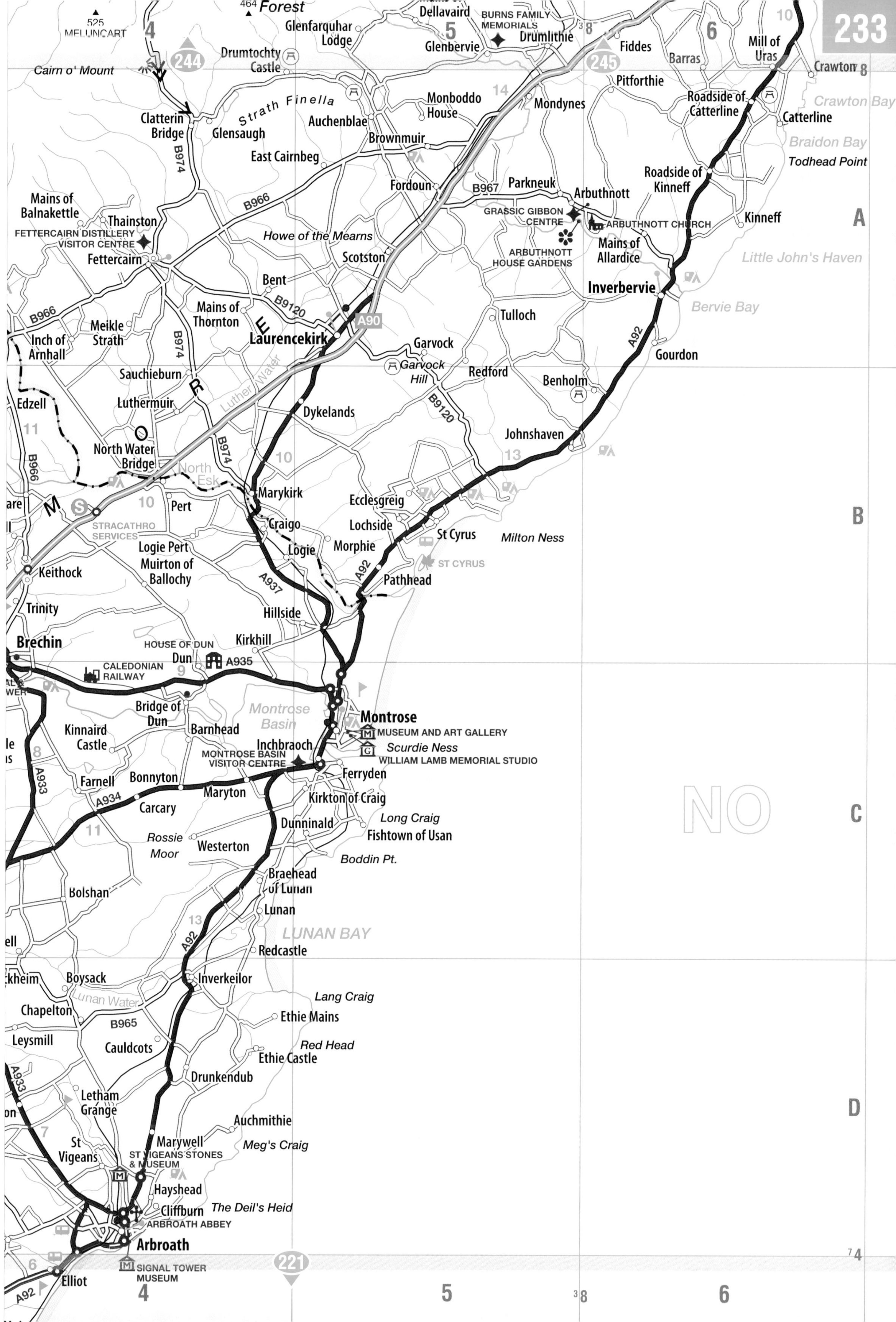
233
Forest
MELUNCART
Cairn o' Mount
Glenfarquhar Lodge
Drumtochty Castle
Dellavaird
BURNS FAMILY MEMORIALS
Glenbervie
Drumlithie
Fiddes
Barras
Mill of Uras
Crawton
Pitforthie
Strath Finella
Monboddo House
Mondynes
Roadside of Catterline
Catterline
Crawton Bay
Clatterin Bridge
Glensaugh
Auchenblae
Brownmuir
Braidon Bay
Todhead Point
East Cairnbeg
Roadside of Kinneff
B974
Fordoun
B967
Parkneuk
Arbuthnott
Mains of Balnakettle
B966
GRASSIC GIBBON CENTRE
ARBUTHNOTT CHURCH
Kinneff
Thainston
FETTERCAIRN DISTILLERY VISITOR CENTRE
Howe of the Mearns
ARBUTHNOTT HOUSE GARDENS
Mains of Allardice
Fettercairn
Scotston
Little John's Haven
Bent
Inverbervie
B9120
Bervie Bay
Mains of Thornton
Tulloch
A90
Meikle Strath
Inch of Arnhall
Laurencekirk
Garvock
A92
Gourdon
Garvock Hill
Sauchieburn
Redford
Benholm
Luther Water
Edzell
Luthermuir
Dykelands
Johnshaven
North Water Bridge
North Esk
Marykirk
Ecclesgreig
Pert
STRACATHRO SERVICES
Craigo
Lochside
St Cyrus
Milton Ness
Logie Pert
Logie
Morphie
ST CYRUS
Muirton of Ballochy
Keithock
A937
Pathhead
Trinity
Hillside
Brechin
HOUSE OF DUN
Kirkhill
Dun
A935
CALEDONIAN RAILWAY
Montrose Basin
Bridge of Dun
Montrose
Kinnaird Castle
Barnhead
MUSEUM AND ART GALLERY
Inchbraoch
Scurdie Ness
MONTROSE BASIN VISITOR CENTRE
WILLIAM LAMB MEMORIAL STUDIO
Ferryden
Farnell
Bonnyton
Maryton
A933
A934
Kirkton of Craig
Carcary
NO
Long Craig
Dunninald
Fishtown of Usan
Rossie Moor
Westerton
Boddin Pt.
Braehead of Lunan
Bolshan
Lunan
LUNAN BAY
Redcastle
Boysack
Inverkeilor
Lunan Water
Lang Craig
Chapelton
Ethie Mains
B965
Leysmill
Cauldcots
Red Head
Ethie Castle
Drunkendub
Letham Grange
Auchmithie
St Vigeans
Marywell
Meg's Craig
ST VIGEANS STONES & MUSEUM
Hayshead
Cliffburn
The Deil's Heid
ARBROATH ABBEY
Arbroath
SIGNAL TOWER MUSEUM
Elliot
244
245
221
A
B
C
D

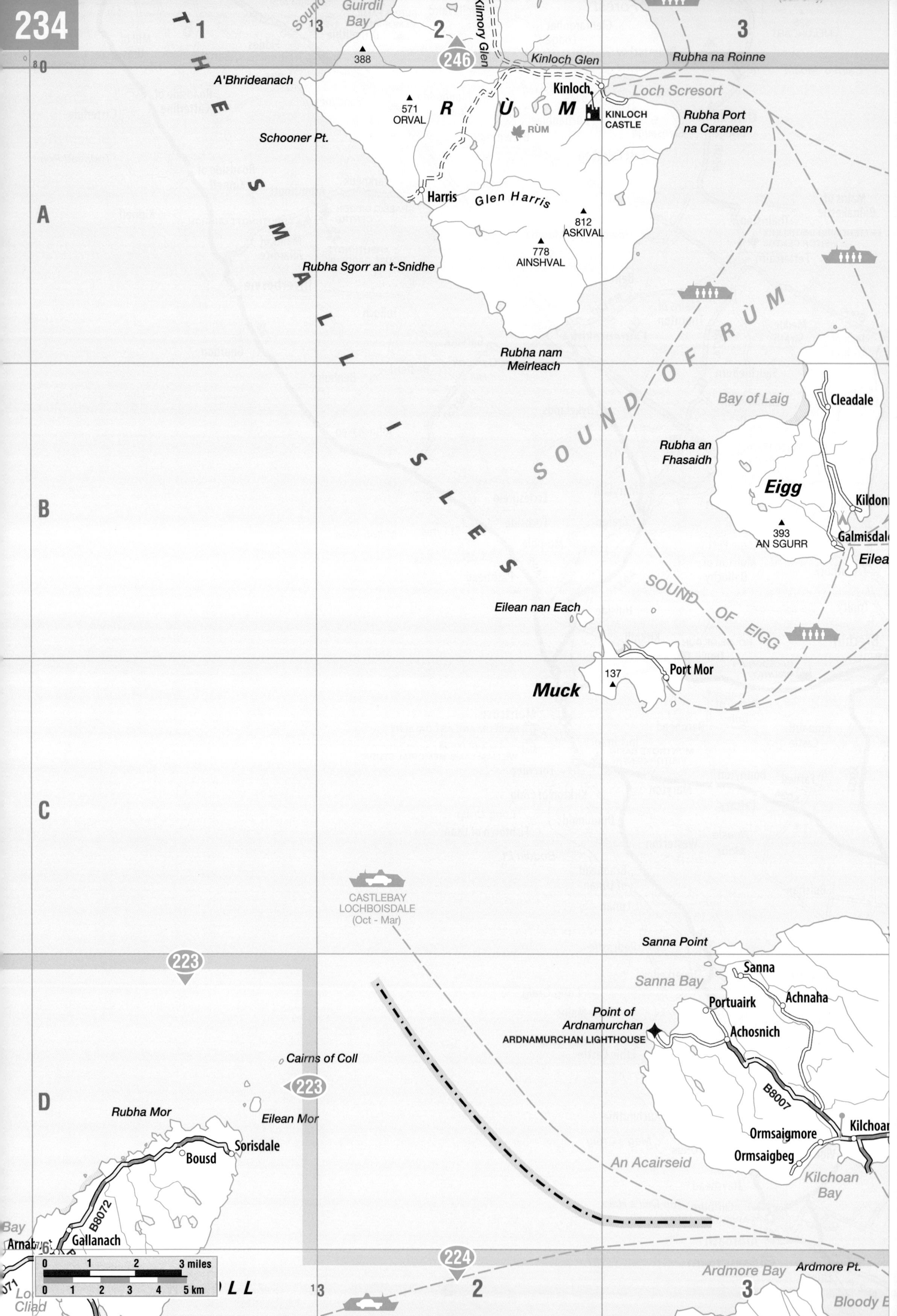

1
2
3
246
Guirdil Bay
Kilmory Glen
Kinloch Glen
Rubha na Roinne
388
A'Bhrideanach
Kinloch
Loch Scresort
571
ORVAL
RÙM
RÙM
KINLOCH CASTLE
Rubha Port na Caranean
Schooner Pt.
THE SMALL ISLES
Harris
Glen Harris
812
ASKIVAL
778
AINSHVAL
Rubha Sgorr an t-Snidhe
SOUND OF RÙM
Rubha nam Meirleach
Bay of Laig
Cleadale
Rubha an Fhasaidh
Eigg
393
AN SGURR
Galmisdale
Eilean nan Each
SOUND OF EIGG
Port Mor
137
Muck
A
B
C
D
CASTLEBAY
LOCHBOISDALE
(Oct - Mar)
223
Sanna Point
Sanna
Sanna Bay
Achnaha
Portuairk
Point of Ardnamurchan
ARDNAMURCHAN LIGHTHOUSE
Achosnich
B8007
Cairns of Coll
Rubha Mor
Eilean Mor
Sorisdale
Bousd
Ormsaigmore
Ormsaigbeg
An Acairseid
Kilchoan Bay
B8072
Gallanach
224
Ardmore Bay
Ardmore Pt.
0 1 2 3 miles
0 1 2 3 4 5 km

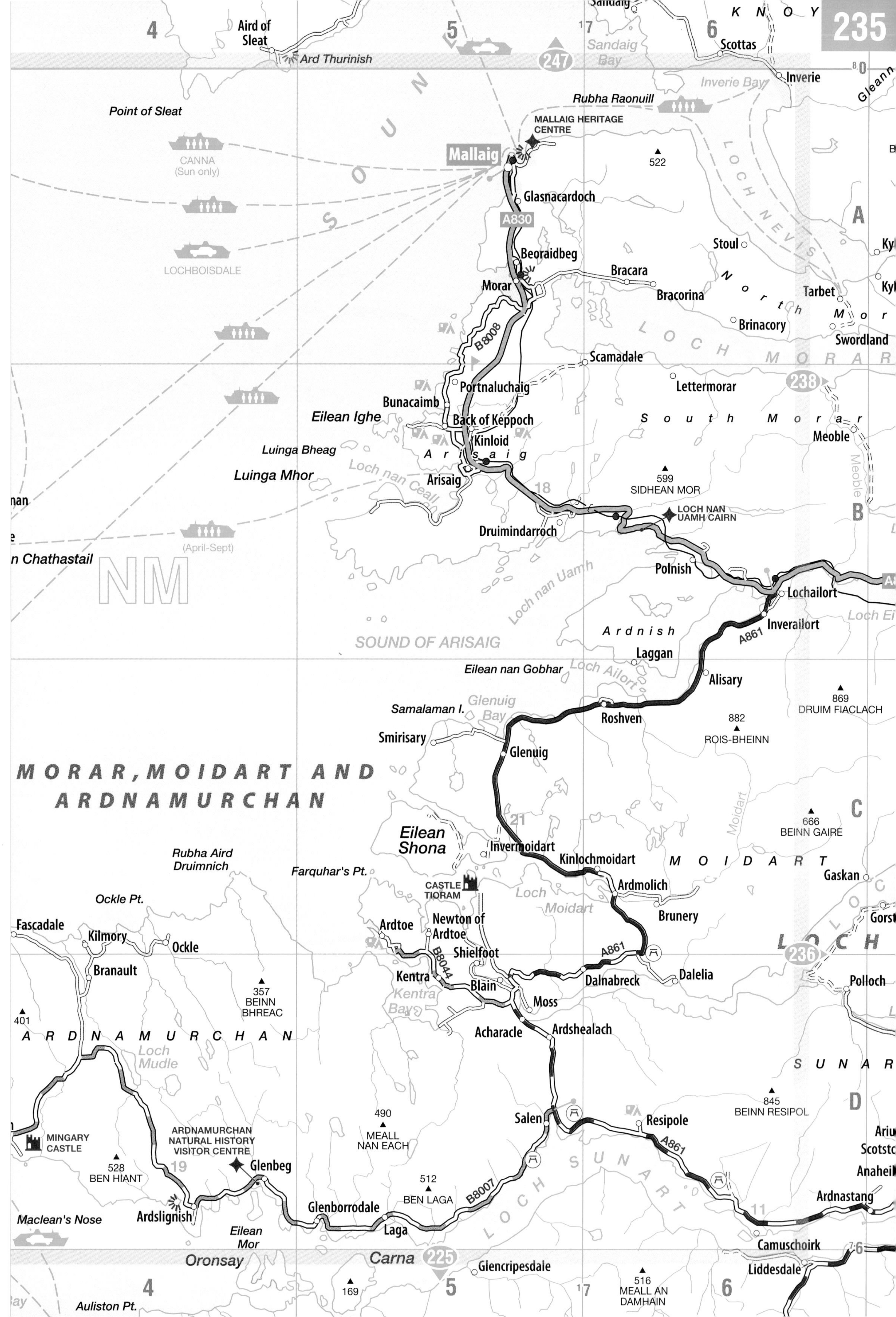


247
238
236
225

235
238
235
225
226

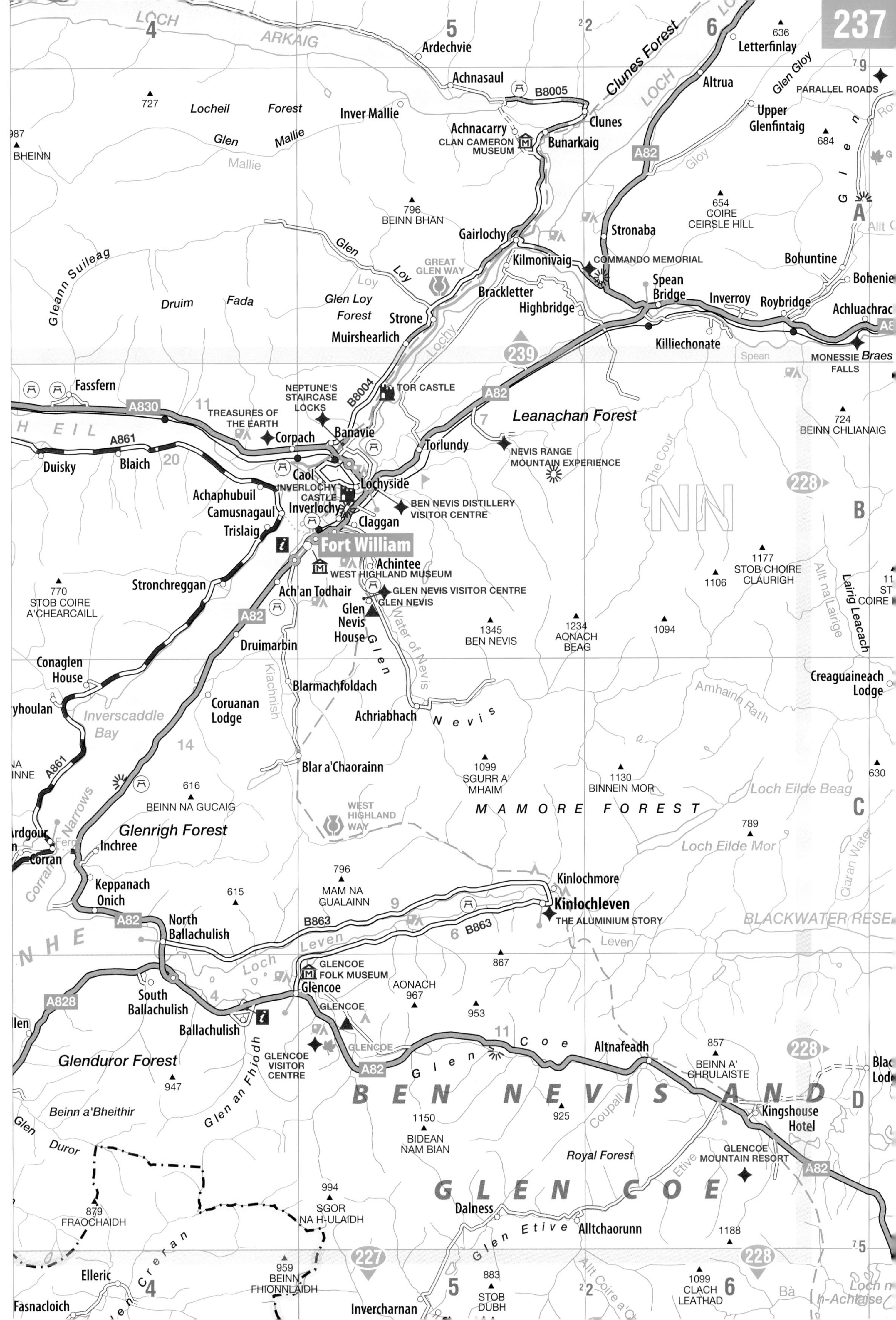
LOCH ARKAIG
Ardechvie
Achnasaul
Clunes Forest
LOCH
Letterfinlay
Altrua
Glen Gloy
PARALLEL ROADS
B8005
Locheil Forest
Inver Mallie
Glen Mallie
Mallie
BHEINN
Achnacarry
CLAN CAMERON MUSEUM
Clunes
Bunarkaig
Upper Glenfintaig
A82
Gloy
684
636
727
987
796
BEINN BHAN
654
COIRE CEIRSLE HILL
Gairlochy
Stronaba
Glen Loy
Loy
GREAT GLEN WAY
Kilmonivaig
COMMANDO MEMORIAL
Bohuntine
Bohenie
Gleann Suileag
Druim Fada
Glen Loy Forest
Strone
Muirshearlich
Brackletter
Highbridge
Spean Bridge
Inverroy
Roybridge
Achluachrac
Killiechonate
Lochy
239
Spean
MONESSIE FALLS
Braes
Fassfern
A830
NEPTUNE'S STAIRCASE LOCKS
B8004
TOR CASTLE
TREASURES OF THE EARTH
Corpach
Banavie
A82
Leanachan Forest
724
BEINN CHLIANAIG
A861
Duisky
Blaich
Torlundy
NEVIS RANGE MOUNTAIN EXPERIENCE
Caol
INVERLOCHY CASTLE
Lochyside
The Cour
228
Achaphubuil
Camusnagaul
Trislaig
Inverlochy
BEN NEVIS DISTILLERY VISITOR CENTRE
Claggan
NN
Fort William
Achintee
WEST HIGHLAND MUSEUM
1177
STOB CHOIRE CLAURIGH
1106
770
STOB COIRE A'CHEARCAILL
Stronchreggan
Ach'an Todhair
GLEN NEVIS VISITOR CENTRE
GLEN NEVIS
Glen Nevis House
Water of Nevis
Glen
1345
BEN NEVIS
1234
AONACH BEAG
1094
Allt na Lairige
Lairig Leacach
Druimarbin
Conaglen House
Kiachnish
Blarmachfoldach
Creaguaineach Lodge
Inverscaddle Bay
Coruanan Lodge
Achriabhach
Nevis
Amhainn Rath
14
Blar a'Chaorainn
1099
SGURR A' MHAIM
1130
BINNEIN MOR
630
616
BEINN NA GUCAIG
Corran Narrows
WEST HIGHLAND WAY
MAMORE FOREST
Loch Eilde Beag
Glenrigh Forest
Inchree
789
Loch Eilde Mor
Corran
Keppanach
Onich
796
MAM NA GUALAINN
615
Kinlochmore
Kinlochleven
THE ALUMINIUM STORY
Ciaran Water
BLACKWATER RESE
North Ballachulish
B863
Leven
Loch Leven
867
A828
South Ballachulish
GLENCOE FOLK MUSEUM
Glencoe
AONACH 967
953
Ballachulish
GLENCOE
GLENCOE VISITOR CENTRE
Glen Coe
Altnafeadh
857
BEINN A' CHRULAISTE
Glen an Fhiodh
Glendurer Forest
947
BEN NEVIS AND
Kingshouse Hotel
Beinn a'Bheithir
Glen Duror
1150
BIDEAN NAM BIAN
925
Coupall
Royal Forest
Etive
GLENCOE MOUNTAIN RESORT
879
FRAOCHAIDH
994
SGOR NA H-ULAIDH
GLEN COE
Dalness
Glen Etive
Alltchaorunn
1188
Glen Creran
227
959
BEINN FHIONNLAIDH
883
STOB DUBH
Allt Coire a'Ch
1099
CLACH LEATHAD
Elleric
Fasnacloich
Invercharnan
Loch na h-Achlaise
A
B
C
D
4
5
6
2
9
5

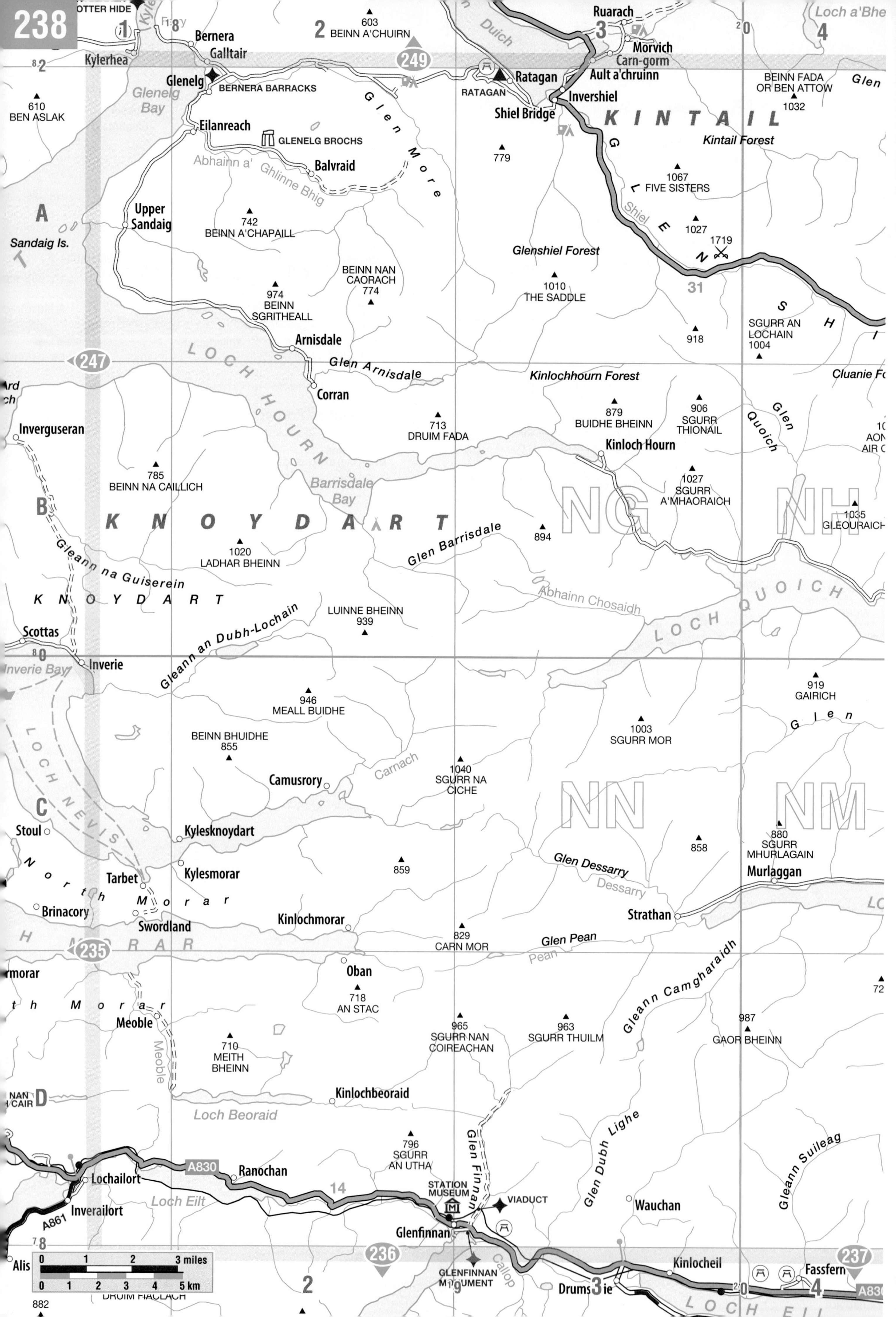
OTTER HIDE
Kylerhea
Bernera
Galltair
Glenelg
BERNERA BARRACKS
Glenelg Bay
610
BEN ASLAK
603
BEINN A'CHUIRN
249
Duich
Ruarach
Morvich
Carn-gorm
Ault a'chruinn
Ratagan
RATAGAN
Inversheil
Shiel Bridge
Loch a'Bhe
BEINN FADA
OR BEN ATTOW
1032
Glen
KINTAIL
Kintail Forest
Eilanreach
GLENELG BROCHS
Glen More
Balvraid
Abhainn a' Ghlinne Bhig
779
1067
FIVE SISTERS
GLEN SHIEL
Shiel
1027
1719
Upper Sandaig
742
BEINN A'CHAPAILL
Sandaig Is.
Glenshiel Forest
BEINN NAN CAORACH
774
974
BEINN SGRITHEALL
1010
THE SADDLE
31
918
SGURR AN LOCHAIN
1004
Arnisdale
247
LOCH HOURN
Glen Arnisdale
Corran
Kinlochhourn Forest
Cluanie Fo
713
DRUIM FADA
879
BUIDHE BHEINN
906
SGURR THIONAIL
Glen Quoich
Inverguseran
Kinloch Hourn
785
BEINN NA CAILLICH
Barrisdale Bay
1027
SGURR A'MHAORAICH
NG
NH
1035
GLEOURAICH
KNOYDART
894
Glen Barrisdale
1020
LADHAR BHEINN
Gleann na Guiserein
Abhainn Chosaidh
LOCH QUOICH
LUINNE BHEINN
939
Gleann an Dubh-Lochain
Scottas
Inverie
Inverie Bay
946
MEALL BUIDHE
919
GAIRICH
Glen
1003
SGURR MOR
BEINN BHUIDHE
855
Carnach
1040
SGURR NA CICHE
Camusrory
NN
NM
LOCH NEVIS
Stoul
Kylesknoydart
858
880
SGURR MHURLAGAIN
859
Glen Dessarry
Dessarry
Murlaggan
Kylesmorar
Tarbet
North Morar
Brinacory
Swordland
Kinlochmorar
Strathan
829
CARN MOR
Glen Pean
Pean
LOCH MORAR
235
Oban
718
AN STAC
Gleann Camgharaidh
Meoble
965
SGURR NAN COIREACHAN
963
SGURR THUILM
987
GAOR BHEINN
710
MEITH BHEINN
Meoble
Kinlochbeoraid
Loch Beoraid
Glen Finnan
Glen Dubh Lighe
Gleann Suileag
796
SGURR AN UTHA
A830
Ranochan
Lochailort
14
STATION MUSEUM
VIADUCT
Loch Eilt
Wauchan
Inverailort
A861
Glenfinnan
236
237
Callop
Kinlocheil
Fassfern
GLENFINNAN MONUMENT
Drumsallie
LOCH EIL
Alis
0 1 2 3 miles
0 1 2 3 4 5 km
882

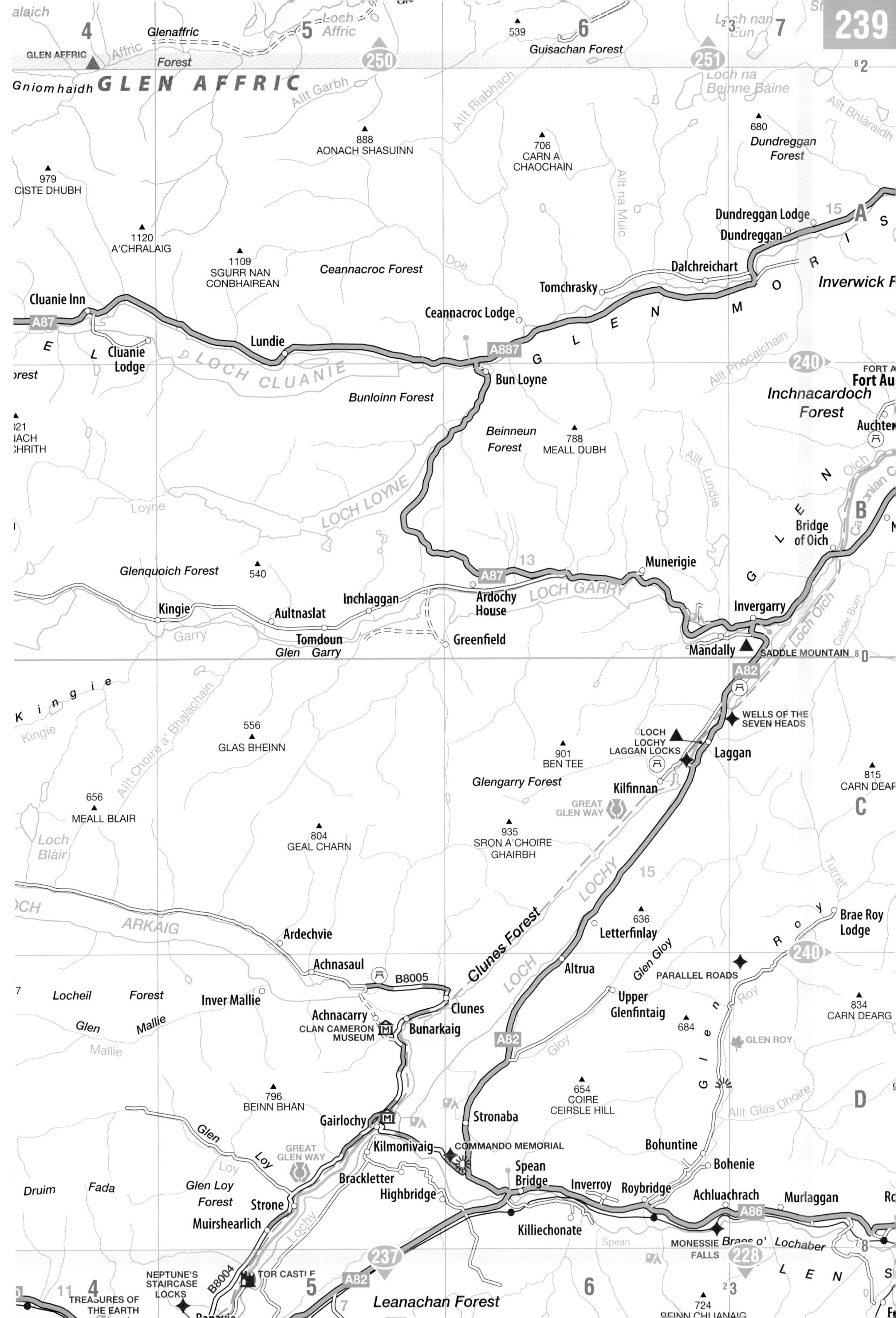
GLEN AFFRIC
Glenaffric
Forest
Loch Affric
Guisachan Forest
Loch nan Eun
Loch na Beinne Bàine
Allt Garbh
Allt Riabhach
Allt Bhlàraidh
888
AONACH SHASUINN
706
CARN A CHAOCHAIN
680
Dundreggan Forest
979
CISTE DHUBH
1120
A'CHRALAIG
1109
SGURR NAN CONBHAIREAN
Ceannacroc Forest
Allt na Muic
Dundreggan Lodge
Dundreggan
Dalchreichart
Tomchrasky
Inverwick
Cluanie Inn
A87
Ceannacroc Lodge
GLEN MORISTON
Cluanie Lodge
Lundie
LOCH CLUANIE
A887
Bun Loyne
Bunloinn Forest
Allt Phocaichain
Inchnacardoch Forest
Fort Augustus
Auchteraw
Beinneun Forest
788
MEALL DUBH
Allt Lundie
LOCH LOYNE
Loyne
Bridge of Oich
GLEN
Glenquoich Forest
540
Munerigie
A87
LOCH GARRY
Kingie
Aultnaslat
Inchlaggan
Ardochy House
Invergarry
Tomdoun
Glen Garry
Greenfield
Mandally
SADDLE MOUNTAIN
Loch Oich
Calder Burn
A82
Kingie
Allt Choire a' Bhalachain
556
GLAS BHEINN
901
BEN TEE
LOCH LOCHY
LAGGAN LOCKS
WELLS OF THE SEVEN HEADS
Laggan
815
CARN DEARG
656
MEALL BLAIR
Glengarry Forest
Kilfinnan
GREAT GLEN WAY
Loch Blàir
804
GEAL CHARN
935
SRON A'CHOIRE GHAIRBH
LOCHY
Turret
LOCH ARKAIG
636
Letterfinlay
Brae Roy Lodge
Ardechvie
Clunes Forest
Glen Gloy
Roy
Achnasaul
B8005
Altrua
PARALLEL ROADS
Locheil Forest
Inver Mallie
Clunes
Upper Glenfintaig
834
CARN DEARG
Glen Mallie
Achnacarry
CLAN CAMERON MUSEUM
Bunarkaig
684
A82
Gloy
GLEN ROY
Glen Roy
796
BEINN BHAN
654
COIRE CEIRSLE HILL
Allt Glas Dhoire
Gairlochy
Stronaba
Glen Loy
GREAT GLEN WAY
Kilmonivaig
COMMANDO MEMORIAL
Bohuntine
Bohenie
Spean Bridge
Druim Fada
Glen Loy Forest
Brackletter
Inverroy
Roybridge
Achluachrach
Murlaggan
Strone
Highbridge
A86
Muirshearlich
Killiechonate
Spean
MONESSIE FALLS
Braes o' Lochaber
NEPTUNE'S STAIRCASE LOCKS
B8004
TOR CASTLE
A82
TREASURES OF THE EARTH
Leanachan Forest
724

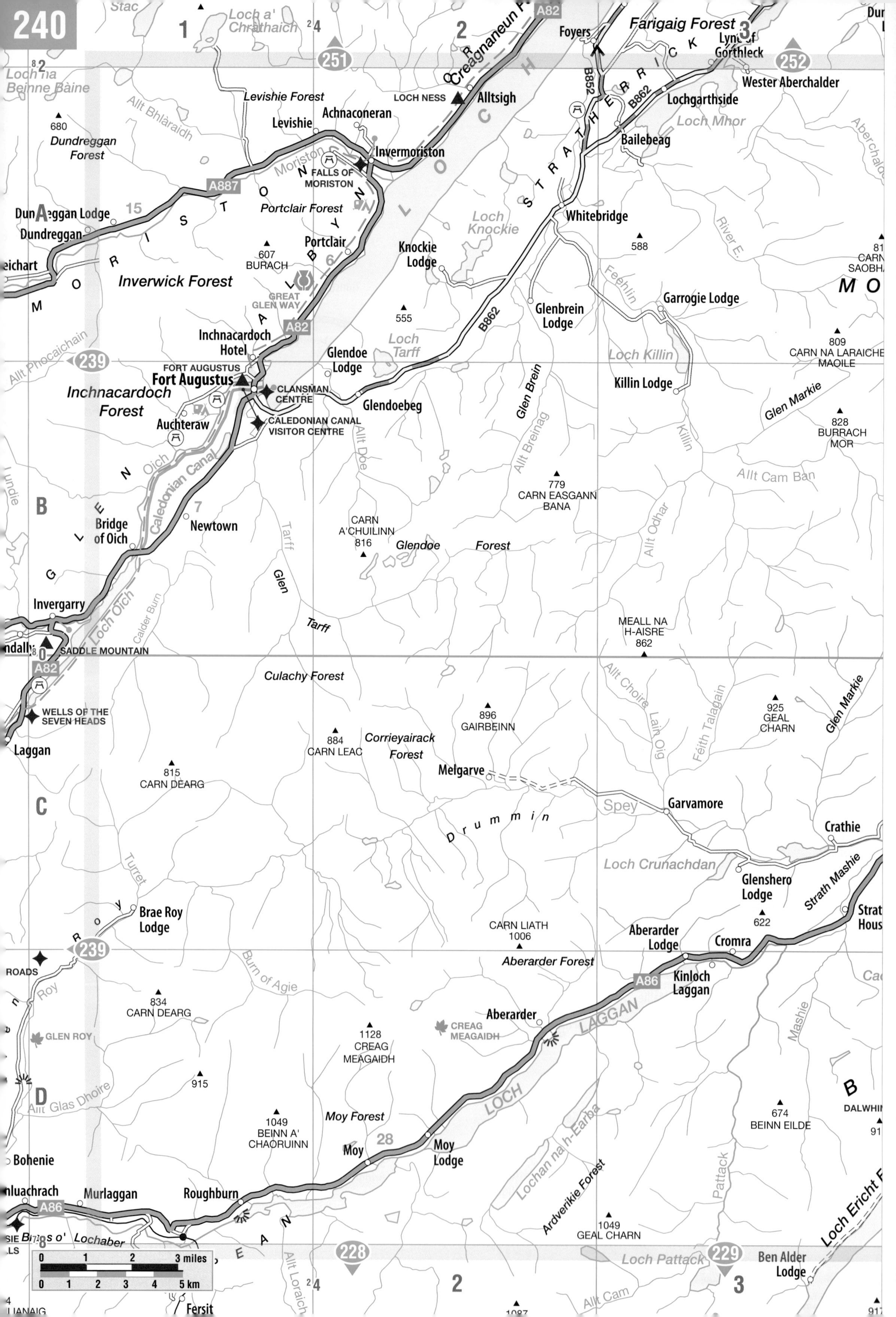
Loch a' Chràthaich
Loch na Beinne Bàine
Levishie Forest
Levishie
Achnaconeran
LOCH NESS
Alltsigh
Creagnaneun F.
A82
251
252
Foyers
Farigaig Forest
Lyne of Gorthleck
Wester Aberchalder
Lochgarthside
Loch Mhor
B852
B862
Bailebeag
STRATHERRICK
Allt Bhlàraidh
680
Dundreggan Forest
Invermoriston
Moriston
FALLS OF MORISTON
A887
GLEN MORISTON
Portclair Forest
Portclair
Dundreggan Lodge
Dundreggan
607
BURACH
Knockie Lodge
Loch Knockie
Whitebridge
588
Inverwick Forest
GREAT GLEN WAY
555
Glenbrein Lodge
Garrogie Lodge
Feehlin
River E.
MO
809
CARN NA LARAICHE MAOILE
Inchnacardoch Hotel
Glendoe Lodge
Loch Tarff
Loch Killin
Killin Lodge
239
Allt Phocaichain
FORT AUGUSTUS
Fort Augustus
CLANSMAN CENTRE
Glendoebeg
Inchnacardoch Forest
Auchteraw
CALEDONIAN CANAL VISITOR CENTRE
Glen Brein
Glen Markie
828
BURRACH MOR
Allt Doe
Allt Breinag
Killin
Allt Cam Ban
Oich
Caledonian Canal
779
CARN EASGANN BANA
Newtown
Bridge of Oich
GLEN
CARN A'CHUILINN
816
Glendoe Forest
Allt Odhar
Tarff
Glen
Invergarry
Loch Oich
Calder Burn
MEALL NA H-AISRE
862
SADDLE MOUNTAIN
Culachy Forest
WELLS OF THE SEVEN HEADS
Allt Choire Lain Oig
Féith Talagain
896
GAIRBEINN
925
GEAL CHARN
884
CARN LEAC
Corrieyairack Forest
Laggan
815
CARN DEARG
Melgarve
Spey
Garvamore
Drummin
Crathie
Loch Crunachdan
Glenshero Lodge
Strath Mashie
Turret
Brae Roy Lodge
622
CARN LIATH
1006
Aberarder Lodge
Cromra
Aberarder Forest
Burn of Agie
ROADS
Roy
A86
Kinloch Laggan
834
CARN DEARG
Aberarder
CREAG MEAGAIDH
1128
CREAG MEAGAIDH
GLEN ROY
LOCH LAGGAN
Mashie
915
Allt Glas Dhoire
B
674
BEINN EILDE
DALWHINNIE
1049
BEINN A' CHAORUINN
Moy Forest
Moy
Moy Lodge
Lochan na h-Earba
Bohenie
Pattack
Ardverikie Forest
Murlaggan
Roughburn
Loch Ericht
1049
GEAL CHARN
Lochaber
LOCH
228
229
Loch Pattack
Ben Alder Lodge
0 1 2 3 miles
0 1 2 3 4 5 km
Allt Loraich
Allt Cam
Fersit

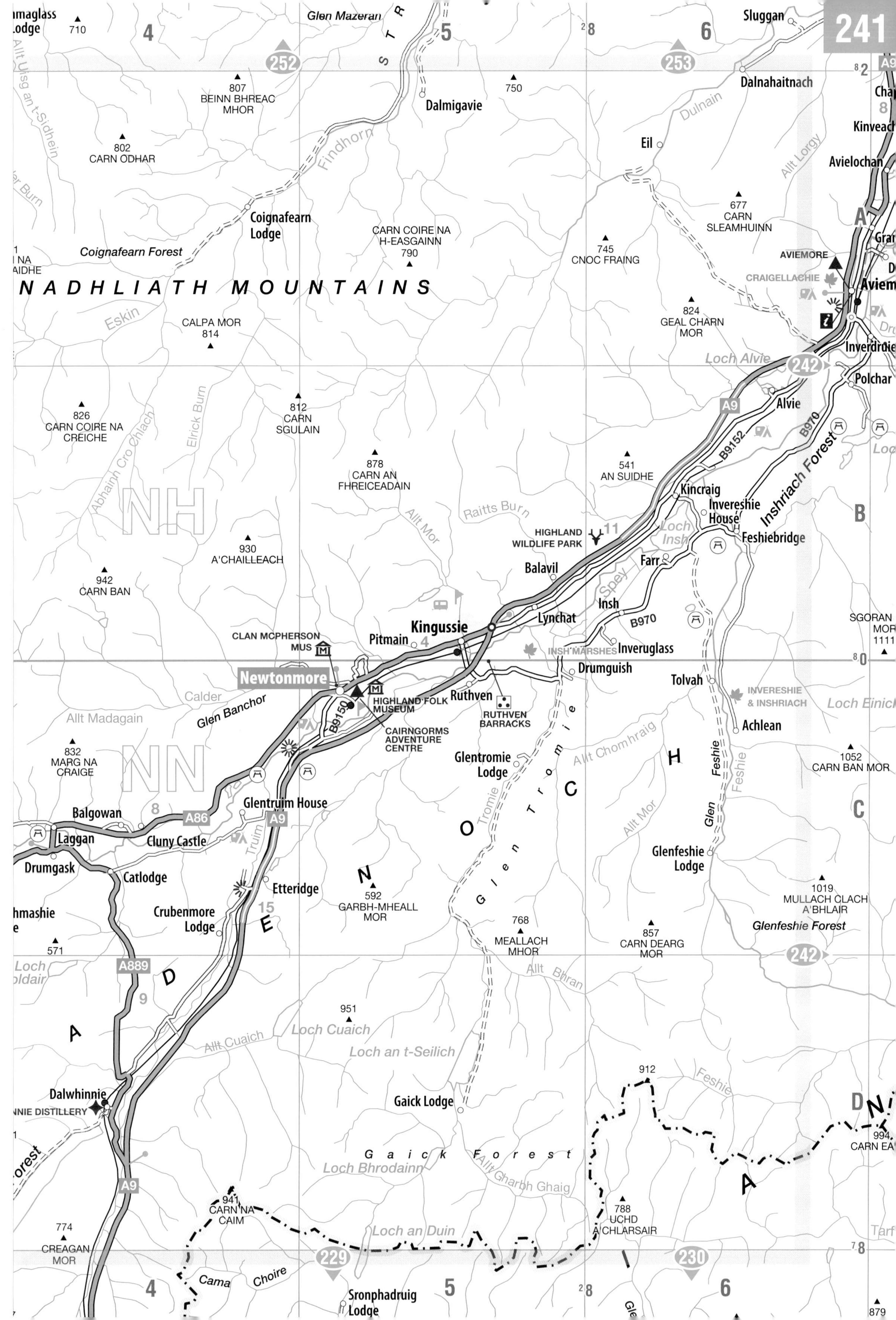
MONADHLIATH MOUNTAINS
Kingussie
Newtonmore
Aviemore
Kincraig
Feshiebridge
Dalwhinnie
Laggan
Balgowan
Cluny Castle
Catlodge
Drumgask
Crubenmore Lodge
Etteridge
Glentruim House
Ruthven
Pitmain
Lynchat
Balavil
Insh
Drumguish
Inveruglass
Tolvah
Achlean
Glentromie Lodge
Glenfeshie Lodge
Gaick Lodge
Sronphadruig Lodge
Coignafearn Lodge
Coignafearn Forest
Dalmigavie
Dalnahaitnach
Sluggan
Eil
Avielochan
Kinveachy
Inverdruie
Polchar
Alvie
Inshriach Forest
Invereshie House
Farr
HIGHLAND WILDLIFE PARK
CLAN MCPHERSON MUS
HIGHLAND FOLK MUSEUM
CAIRNGORMS ADVENTURE CENTRE
RUTHVEN BARRACKS
INSH MARSHES
INVERESHIE & INSHRIACH
CRAIGELLACHIE
AVIEMORE
Glenfeshie Forest
Gaick Forest
Glen Tromie
Glen Feshie
Glen Banchor
Glen Mazeran
CAIRNGORMS NATIONAL PARK
Loch Alvie
Loch Insh
Loch Cuaich
Loch an t-Seilich
Loch Bhrodainn
Loch an Duin
Loch Einich
A9
A86
A889
B9150
B9152
B970
252
253
242
229
230
807 BEINN BHREAC MHOR
802 CARN ODHAR
750
CARN COIRE NA H-EASGAINN 790
745 CNOC FRAING
677 CARN SLEAMHUINN
824 GEAL CHARN MOR
CALPA MOR 814
826 CARN COIRE NA CREICHE
812 CARN SGULAIN
878 CARN AN FHREICEADAIN
541 AN SUIDHE
930 A'CHAILLEACH
942 CARN BAN
832 MARG NA CRAIGE
SGORAN MOR 1111
1052 CARN BAN MOR
1019 MULLACH CLACH A'BHLAIR
592 GARBH-MHEALL MOR
768 MEALLACH MHOR
857 CARN DEARG MOR
951
912
788 UCHD A'CHLARSAIR
941 CARN NA CAIM
774 CREAGAN MOR
571
NH
NN
4
5
6
A
B
C
D

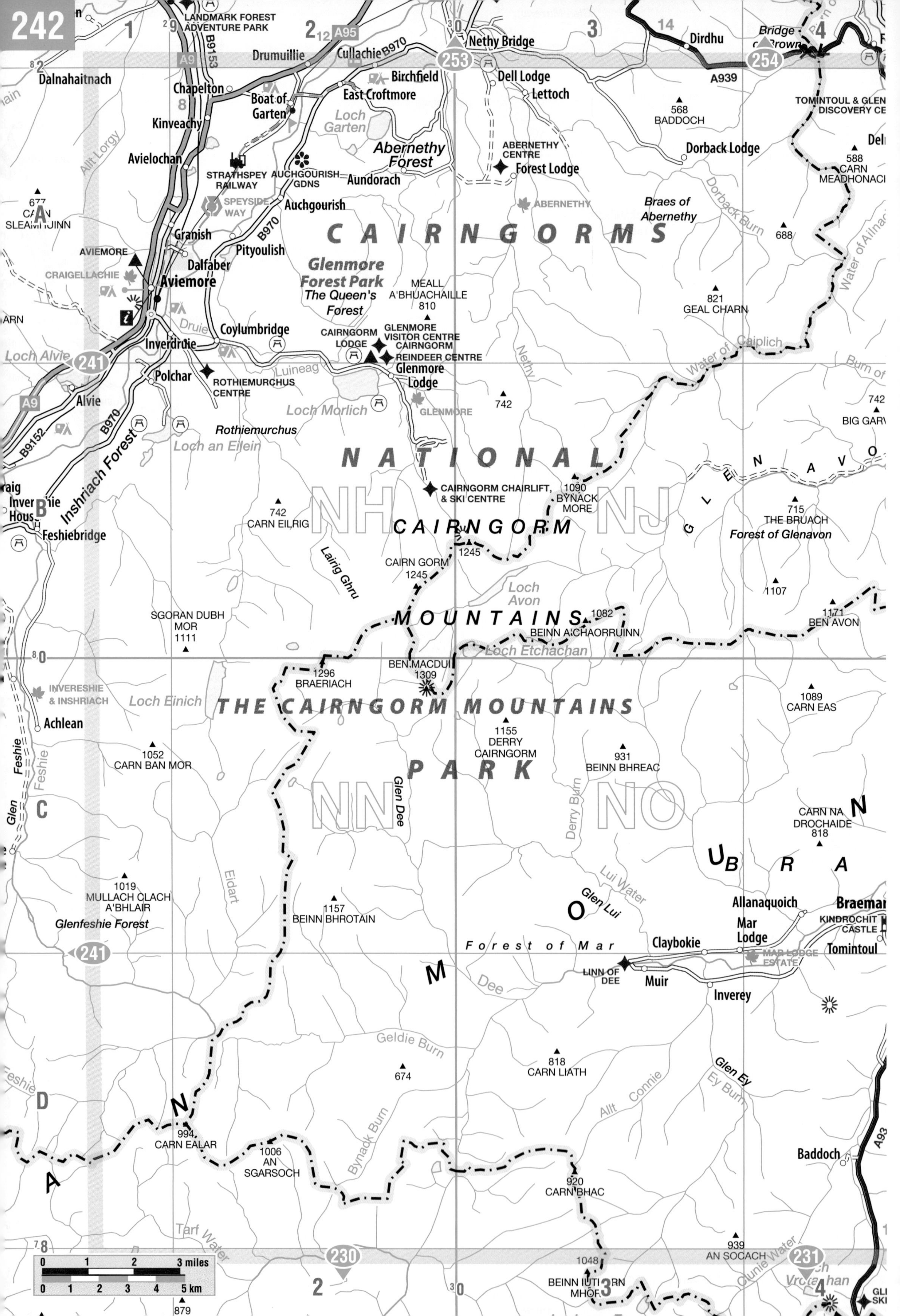
LANDMARK FOREST ADVENTURE PARK
Drumuillie
Cullachie
Nethy Bridge
Dirdhu
Bridge of Brown
Dalnahaitnach
Chapelton
Boat of Garten
Birchfield
East Croftmore
Dell Lodge
Lettoch
568 BADDOCH
TOMINTOUL & GLEN
Kinveachy
Loch Garten
Abernethy Forest
ABERNETHY CENTRE
Forest Lodge
Dorback Lodge
Avielochan
STRATHSPEY RAILWAY
AUCHGOURISH GDNS
Aundorach
588 CARN MEADHONACH
SPEYSIDE WAY
Auchgourish
ABERNETHY
Braes of Abernethy
Dorback Burn
Granish
Pityoulish
CAIRNGORMS
688
AVIEMORE
Dalfaber
Aviemore
CRAIGELLACHIE
Glenmore Forest Park
The Queen's Forest
MEALL A'BHUACHAILLE 810
821 GEAL CHARN
Water of Ailnack
Coylumbridge
CAIRNGORM LODGE
GLENMORE VISITOR CENTRE
CAIRNGORM REINDEER CENTRE
Inverdruie
Loch Alvie
Water of Caiplich
Polchar
ROTHIEMURCHUS CENTRE
Luineag
Glenmore Lodge
Nethy
Alvie
Loch Morlich
GLENMORE
742
742 BIG GARV
Rothiemurchus
Loch an Eilein
Inshriach Forest
NATIONAL
CAIRNGORM CHAIRLIFT, & SKI CENTRE
1090 BYNACK MORE
GLEN AVON
742 CARN EILRIG
715 THE BRUACH
Forest of Glenavon
Feshiebridge
CAIRNGORM
1245
CAIRN GORM 1245
Lairig Ghru
Loch Avon
1107
SGORAN DUBH MOR 1111
MOUNTAINS
1082 BEINN A'CHAORRUINN
1171 BEN AVON
Loch Etchachan
BEN MACDUI 1309
1296 BRAERIACH
INVERESHIE & INSHRIACH
Loch Einich
THE CAIRNGORM MOUNTAINS
1089 CARN EAS
Achlean
1155 DERRY CAIRNGORM
1052 CARN BAN MOR
931 BEINN BHREAC
PARK
Glen Feshie
Glen Dee
Derry Burn
CARN NA DROCHAIDE 818
MAR LODGE
Lui Water
Glen Lui
Eidart
1019 MULLACH CLACH A'BHLAIR
1157 BEINN BHROTAIN
Allanaquoich
Braemar
Glenfeshie Forest
Mar Lodge
KINDROCHIT CASTLE
Forest of Mar
Claybokie
MAR LODGE ESTATE
Tomintoul
LINN OF DEE
Muir
Inverey
Dee
Geldie Burn
674
818 CARN LIATH
Glen Ey
Ey Burn
Allt Connie
Bynack Burn
994 CARN EALAR
1006 AN SGARSOCH
920 CARN BHAC
Baddoch
A93
Tarf Water
939 AN SOCACH
Clunie Water
1048
BEINN IUTHARN MHOR
879
0 1 2 3 miles
0 1 2 3 4 5 km

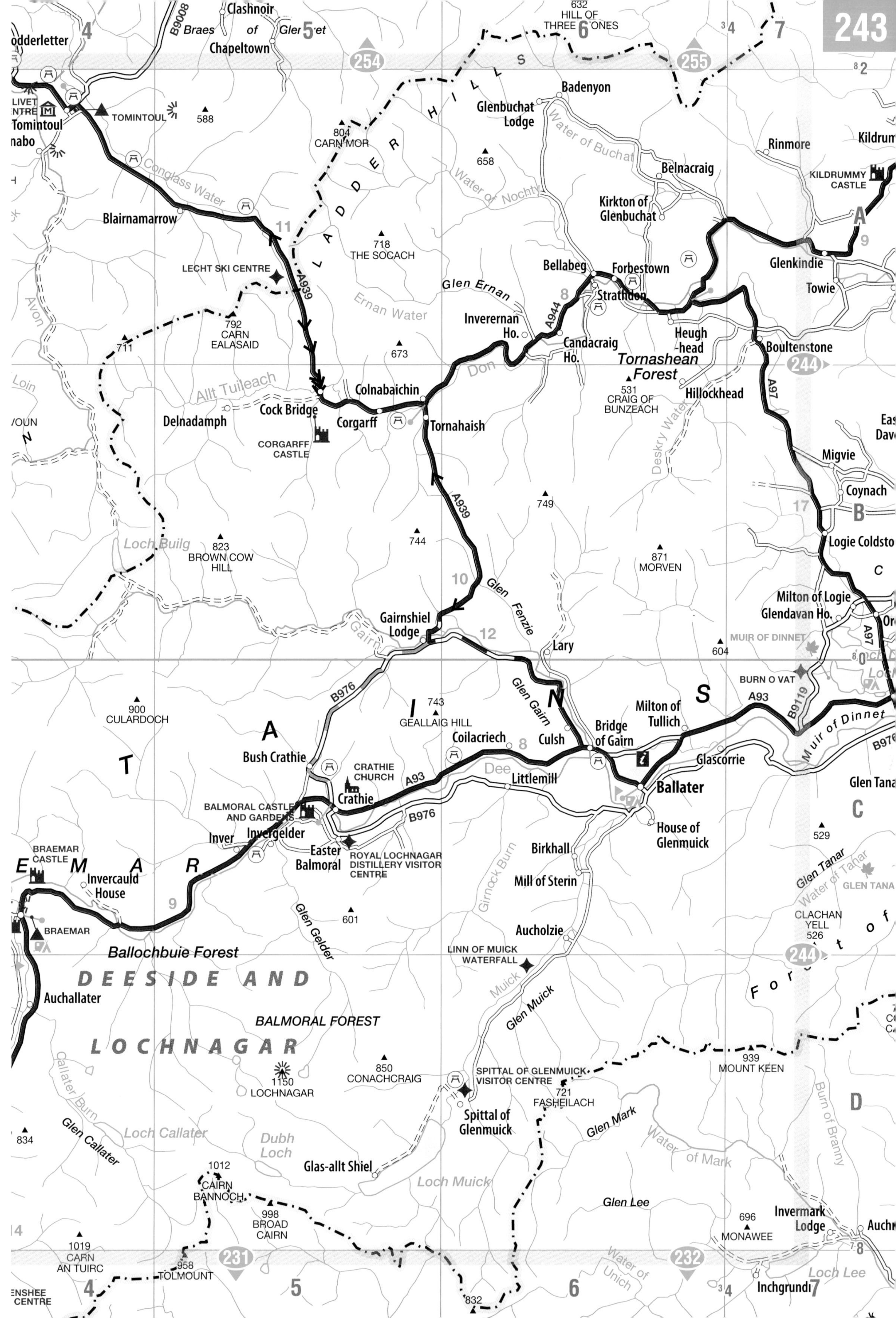
Clashnoir
Braes of Glenlivet
Chapeltown
B9008
632
HILL OF THREE STONES
254
255
odderletter
Tomintoul
TOMINTOUL
588
Conglass Water
Blairnamarrow
804
CARN MOR
LADDER HILLS
Badenyon
Glenbuchat Lodge
Water of Buchat
658
Water of Nochty
Rinmore
Kildrum
Belnacraig
KILDRUMMY CASTLE
Kirkton of Glenbuchat
11
LECHT SKI CENTRE
718
THE SOCACH
A939
Bellabeg
Forbestown
Glenkindie
Towie
Glen Ernan
Strathdon
Ernan Water
Inverernan Ho.
A944
Candacraig Ho.
Heugh-head
Boultenstone
792
CARN EALASAID
711
673
Tornashean Forest
244
Don
531
CRAIG OF BUNZEACH
Hillockhead
A97
Allt Tuileach
Colnabaichin
Cock Bridge
Corgarff
Tornahaish
Delnadamph
CORGARFF CASTLE
Deskry Water
Migvie
Coynach
749
17
Logie Coldsto
Loch Builg
823
BROWN COW HILL
744
871
MORVEN
10
Glen Fenzie
Milton of Logie
Glendavan Ho.
Gairnshiel Lodge
12
MUIR OF DINNET
604
Lary
Gairn
BURN O VAT
B9119
A93
Muir of Dinnet
900
CULARDOCH
B976
743
GEALLAIG HILL
Glen Gairn
Milton of Tullich
Bridge of Gairn
Coilacriech
Culsh
Bush Crathie
CRATHIE CHURCH
Dee
Littlemill
Glascorrie
Ballater
Glen Tana
Crathie
BALMORAL CASTLE AND GARDENS
House of Glenmuick
529
Inver
Invergelder
Easter Balmoral
ROYAL LOCHNAGAR DISTILLERY VISITOR CENTRE
Birkhall
BRAEMAR CASTLE
Invercauld House
Girnock Burn
Mill of Sterin
Glen Tanar
Water of Tanar
GLEN TANA
9
601
Glen Gelder
Aucholzie
CLACHAN YELL
526
BRAEMAR
Ballochbuie Forest
LINN OF MUICK WATERFALL
DEESIDE AND LOCHNAGAR
Auchallater
Muick
Glen Muick
BALMORAL FOREST
939
MOUNT KEEN
850
CONACHCRAIG
SPITTAL OF GLENMUICK VISITOR CENTRE
1150
LOCHNAGAR
721
FASHEILACH
Spittal of Glenmuick
Glen Mark
Callater Burn
Burn of Branny
834
Glen Callater
Loch Callater
Dubh Loch
Water of Mark
Glas-allt Shiel
1012
CAIRN BANNOCH
Loch Muick
Glen Lee
696
MONAWEE
Invermark Lodge
998
BROAD CAIRN
1019
CARN AN TUIRC
231
232
958
TOLMOUNT
Water of Unich
Loch Lee
832
Inchgrundle
ENSHEE CENTRE
4
5
6
7
A
B
C
D

SCOTTISH SCULPTURE WORKSHOP
Lumsden
CORREEN HILLS
Muckleton
Forest
G A R I O C H
255
256
Glenton
Mossat
Tullynessle
Keig
Castle Forbes
Upper Woodend
518 LORD ARTHUR'S CAIRN
A97
Don
A944
Rinmore
Kildrummy
Milltown of Kildrummy
Bridge of Alford
Montgarrie
HAUGHTON
Rorandle
Pitfichie
KILDRUMMY CASTLE
532
Auchintoul
Alford
GRAMPIAN TRANSPORT MUS
Gateside
Pitfichie Forest
HERITAGE MUSEUM
Whitehouse
Pitmunie
Asloun
A980
Todlachie
Monymusk
Glenkindie
Sinnahard
Hillockhead
Little Lynturk
Kirkton of Tough
B993
Towie
Milltown of Towie
Ley
Tillyfourie
Muir of Fowlis
Bridgend
Ordhead
Boultenstone
243
Milton of Cushnie
Tillyfour
Corrennie Moor
Corrennie Forest
Leochel-Cushnie
CRAIGIEVAR CASTLE
Kintocher
Milton of Corsindae
Corsindae
Lockhead
619
494 BENAQUHALLIE
Bankhead
Easter Davoch
B9119
Midmar
Comers
Tillybirloch
Migvie
Douneside
Craskins
476
Tornaveen
Coynach
CULSH SOUTERRAIN
Findrack Ho.
Drumlasie
NJ
Logie Coldstone
Lumphanan
Tarland
PEEL RING OF LUMPHANAN
433 HILL OF FARE
C R O M A R
TOMNAVERIE STONE CIRCLE
Milton of Auchinhove
Burn of Corrichie
Milton of Logie
Coull
Glendavan Ho.
DEESIDE ACTIVITY PARK
Auchlossan
Torphins
Milton of Campfield
Ordie
299 SCAR HILL
MUIR OF DINNET
604
SLUG OF DESS FALLS
Mid Beltie
Loch Davan
B9094
Loch Kinord
BURN O VAT
Aboyne
Kincardine O'Neil
B993
A980
A93
Dinnet
Tillydrine
Brathens
Muir of Dinnet
Dee
Backhill of Trustach
Bridge of Canny
East Mains
Glascorrie
B976
Birsemore
BANCHORY MUSEUM
Birse
GLEN TANAR VISITOR CENTRE
Glen Tanar House
Marywell
Burn of Cattie
Arbeadie
NO
Deebank
310 TOM'S CAIRN
Blackhall Forest
529
Auchattie
Belts of Collonach
525 CARNFERG
Tillygarmond
Glen Tanar
Water of Tanar
GLEN TANAR
Finzean
Strachan
B974
Percie
Forest of Glen Tanar
CLACHAN YELL 526
Forest of Birse
Ballochan
Water of Feugh
617
Water of Aven
727 COCK CAIRN
742 HILL OF CAT
MOUNT SHADE 507
Water of Dye
534 KERLOCH
939 MOUNT KEEN
Glendye Lodge
Bridge of Dye
Burn of Branny
Water of Tarf
Burn of Tennet
778 MOUNT BATTOCK
Glen Dye
Mark
Drumtochty Forest
464
Invermark Lodge
Auchronie
525 MELUNCART
696 MONAWEE
Drumtochty Castle
Cairncross
Tarfside
THE RETREAT GLEN ESK FOLK MUS
Cairn o' Mount
Millden Lodge
232
233
Clatterin Bridge
Glensaugh
Strath Finella
0 1 2 3 miles
0 1 2 3 4 5 km

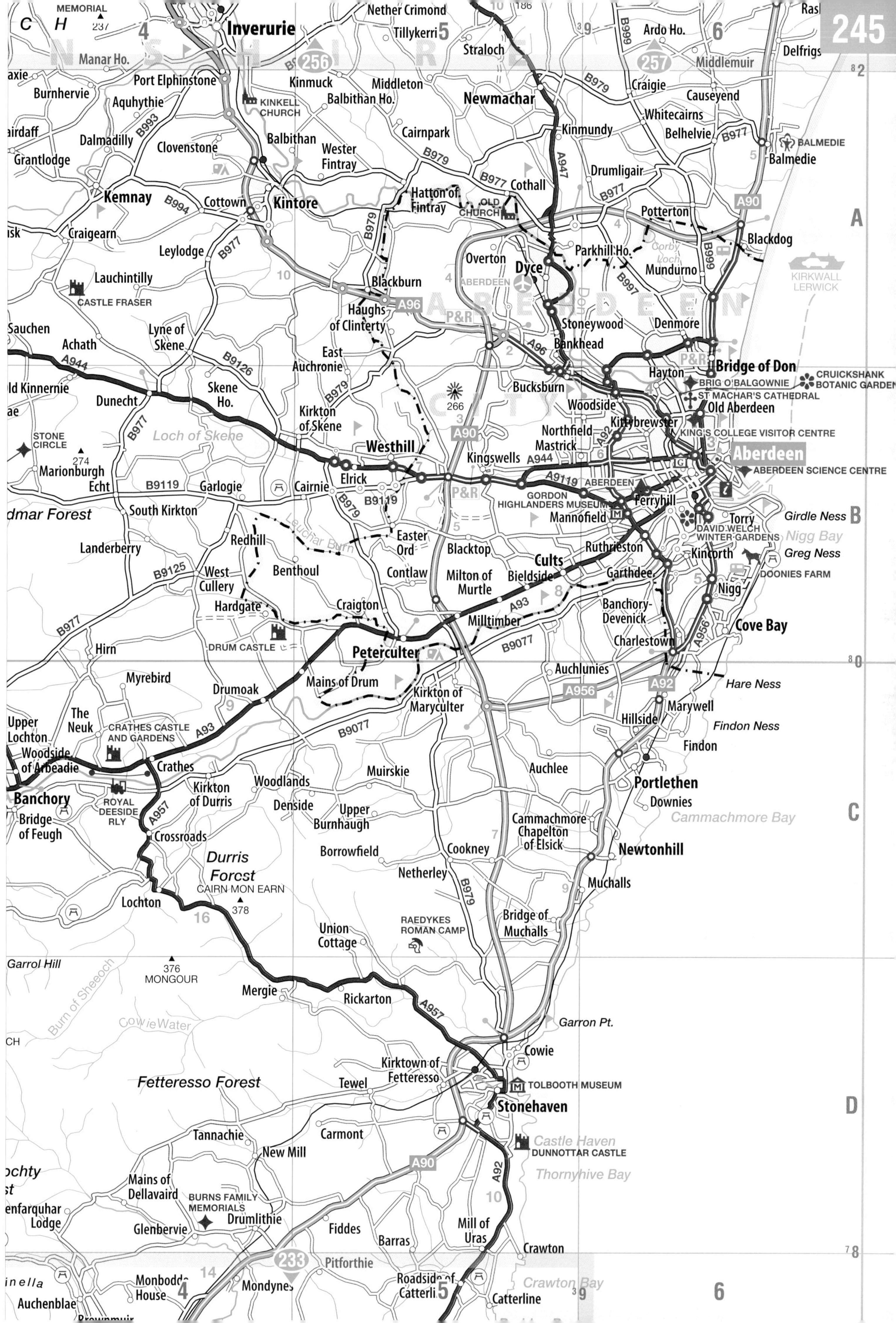
Inverurie
Nether Crimond
Tillykerri
Straloch
Ardo Ho.
Delfrigs
Manar Ho.
Middlemuir
Port Elphinstone
Kinmuck
Middleton
Balbithan Ho.
Newmachar
B979
Craigie
Causeyend
Burnhervie
Aquhythie
KINKELL CHURCH
Whitecairns
Belhelvie
Cairnpark
Kinmundy
B977
BALMEDIE
Balmedie
Dalmadilly
B993
Clovenstone
Balbithan
Wester Fintray
A947
Drumligair
Grantlodge
Cothall
Kemnay
B994
Cottown
Kintore
Hatton of Fintray
OLD CHURCH
Potterton
A90
Craigearn
Leylodge
B977
Overton
Parkhill Ho.
Corby Loch
B999
Blackdog
Lauchintilly
Blackburn
ABERDEEN
Dyce
Mundurno
KIRKWALL LERWICK
CASTLE FRASER
B997
Haughs of Clinterty
A96
P&R
Don
Stoneywood
Denmore
Sauchen
Achath
Lyne of Skene
Bankhead
B9126
East Auchronie
Bridge of Don
Hayton
CRUICKSHANK BOTANIC GARDEN
A944
BRIG O'BALGOWNIE
Old Kinnernie
Dunecht
Skene Ho.
B979
266
Bucksburn
ST MACHAR'S CATHEDRAL
Woodside
Old Aberdeen
Kirkton of Skene
Kittybrewster
KING'S COLLEGE VISITOR CENTRE
STONE CIRCLE
Loch of Skene
B977
Northfield
A92
Westhill
Mastrick
Aberdeen
274
Marionburgh
Echt
Kingswells
A944
ABERDEEN SCIENCE CENTRE
B9119
Garlogie
Cairnie
Elrick
A9119
ABERDEEN
GORDON HIGHLANDERS MUSEUM
Ferryhill
B9119
P&R
Mannofield
Torry
Girdle Ness
Dunecht Forest
South Kirkton
B979
DAVID WELCH WINTER GARDENS
Nigg Bay
Redhill
Leuchar Burn
Easter Ord
Ruthrieston
Greg Ness
Landerberry
Blacktop
Cults
Kincorth
Benthoul
DOONIES FARM
B9125
West Cullery
Contlaw
Milton of Murtle
Bieldside
Garthdee
Nigg
Hardgate
Craigton
A93
Banchory-Devenick
Cove Bay
B977
DRUM CASTLE
Milltimber
A956
Hirn
Peterculter
B9077
Charlestown
Myrebird
Mains of Drum
Auchlunies
Hare Ness
Drumoak
Kirkton of Maryculter
A92
A956
The Neuk
Upper Lochton
CRATHES CASTLE AND GARDENS
A93
B9077
Marywell
Hillside
Findon Ness
Woodside of Arbeadie
Findon
Crathes
Muirskie
Auchlee
Banchory
Kirkton of Durris
Woodlands
Portlethen
ROYAL DEESIDE RLY
Denside
Upper Burnhaugh
Downies
Bridge of Feugh
A957
Cammachmore
Cammachmore Bay
Chapelton of Elsick
Crossroads
Borrowfield
Cookney
Newtonhill
Durris Forest
Netherley
CAIRN MON EARN
Muchalls
B979
Lochton
378
Union Cottage
RAEDYKES ROMAN CAMP
Bridge of Muchalls
Garrol Hill
376
MONGOUR
Burn of Sheeoch
Mergie
Rickarton
A957
Garron Pt.
Cowie Water
Cowie
Kirktown of Fetteresso
Fetteresso Forest
Tewel
TOLBOOTH MUSEUM
Stonehaven
Tannachie
Carmont
Castle Haven
DUNNOTTAR CASTLE
New Mill
A90
Thornyhive Bay
Mains of Dellavaird
A92
BURNS FAMILY MEMORIALS
Drumlithie
Fenfarquhar Lodge
Glenbervie
Fiddes
Mill of Uras
Barras
Crawton
233
Pitforthie
Monboddo House
Mondynes
Roadside of Catterline
Crawton Bay
Auchenblae
Catterline
256
257
A
B
C
D

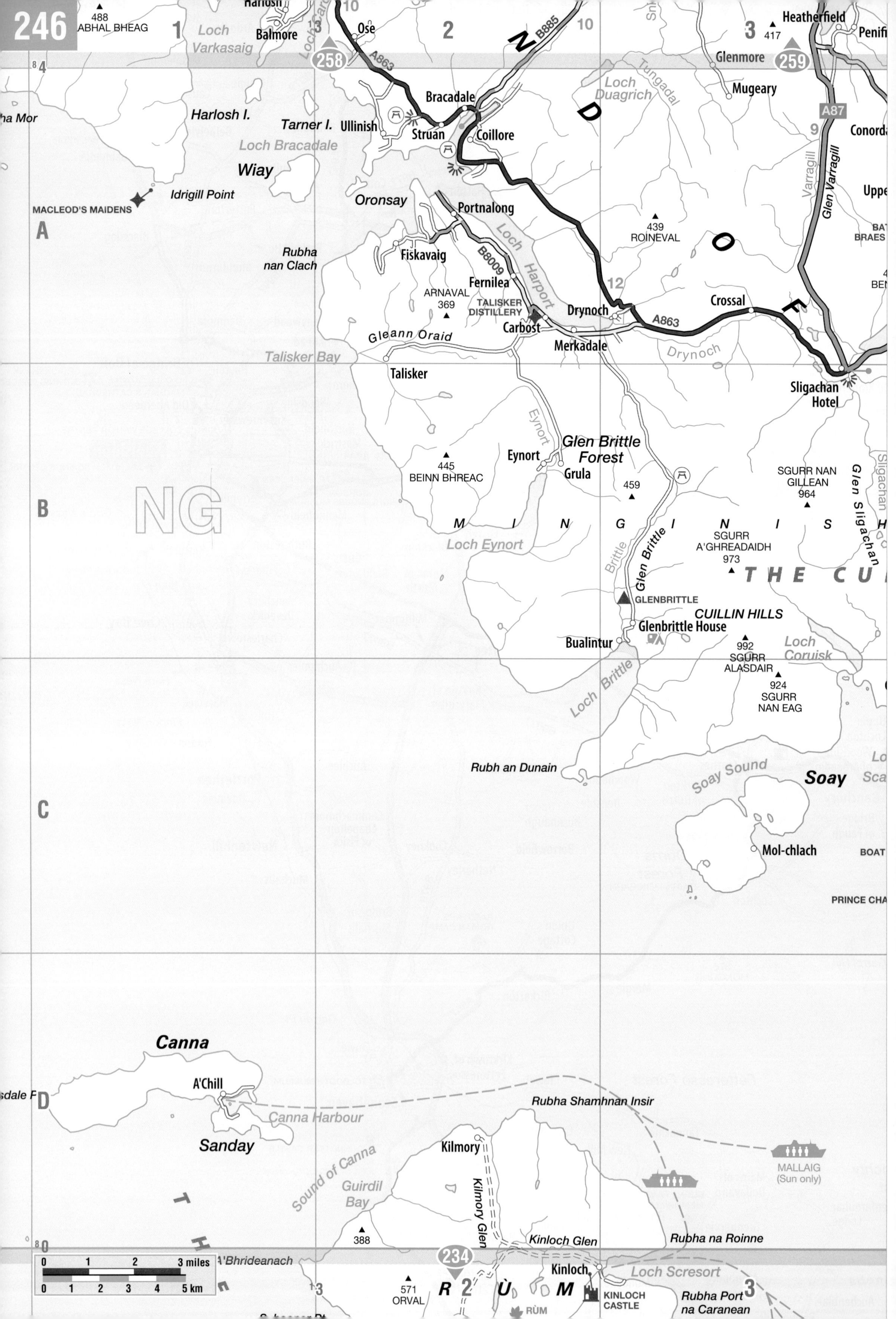

Loch Varkasaig
Balmore
Ose
Bracadale
Struan
Ullinish
Coillore
Harlosh I.
Tarner I.
Loch Bracadale
Wiay
Idrigill Point
MACLEOD'S MAIDENS
Oronsay
Portnalong
Fiskavaig
Rubha nan Clach
Fernilea
ARNAVAL 369
TALISKER DISTILLERY
Carbost
Drynoch
Merkadale
Gleann Oraid
Talisker Bay
Talisker
Loch Harport
Loch Duagrich
Glenmore
Mugeary
Heatherfield
ROINEVAL 439
Crossal
A863
Drynoch
Sligachan Hotel
Glen Varragill
Eynort
Glen Brittle Forest
Eynort
Grula
445 BEINN BHREAC
459
SGURR NAN GILLEAN 964
Glen Sligachan
MINGINISH
Loch Eynort
SGURR A'GHREADAIDH 973
THE CU
Glen Brittle
GLENBRITTLE
CUILLIN HILLS
Glenbrittle House
Bualintur
992 SGURR ALASDAIR
Loch Coruisk
924 SGURR NAN EAG
Loch Brittle
Rubh an Dunain
Soay Sound
Soay
Mol-chlach
BOAT
PRINCE CHA
NG
Canna
A'Chill
Canna Harbour
Sanday
Rubha Shamhnan Insir
Sound of Canna
Kilmory
Guirdil Bay
Kilmory Glen
MALLAIG (Sun only)
388
Kinloch Glen
Rubha na Roinne
A'Bhrideanach
571 ORVAL
RÙM
Kinloch
KINLOCH CASTLE
Loch Scresort
Rubha Port na Caranean
0 1 2 3 miles
0 1 2 3 4 5 km
258
259
234

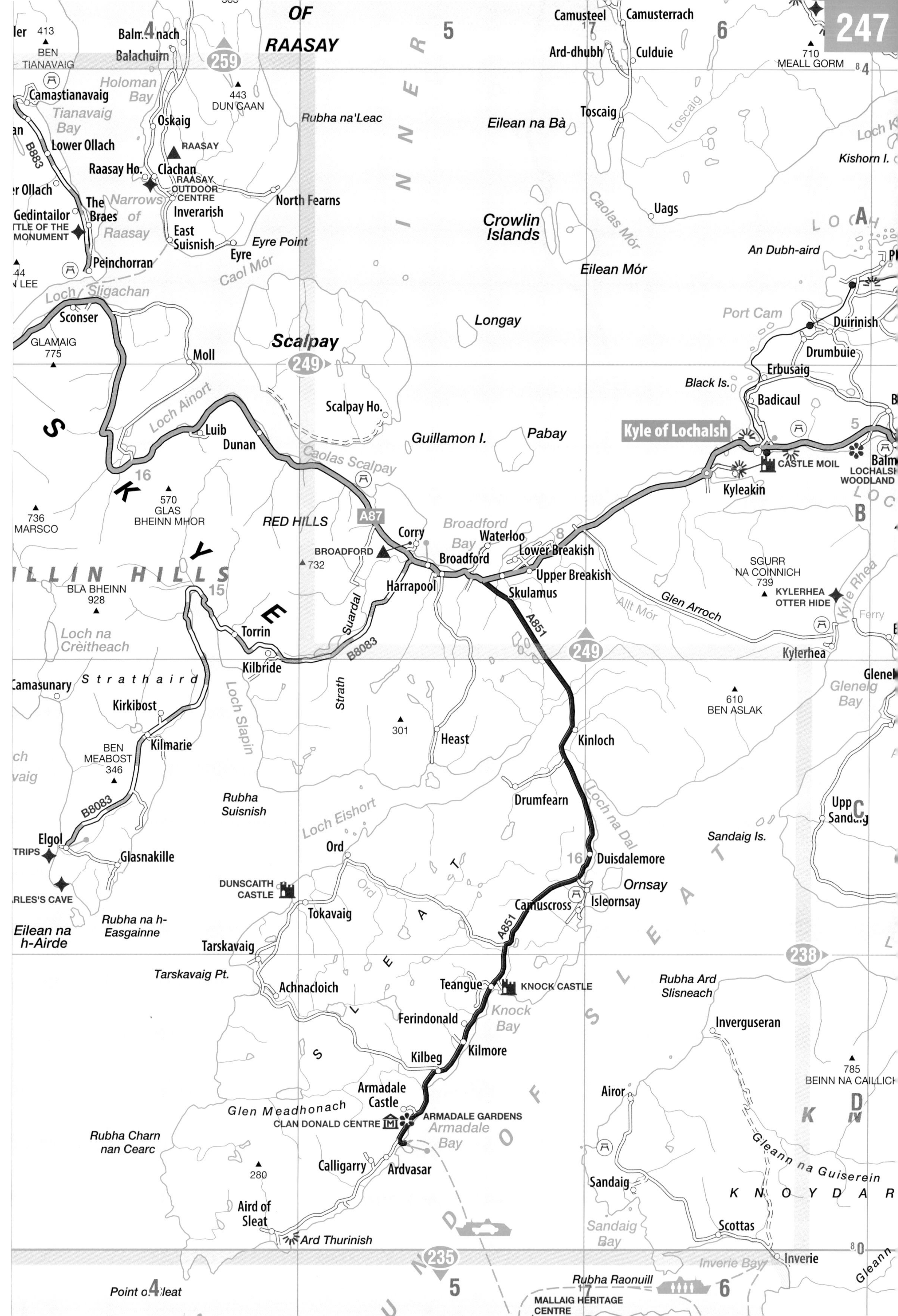

RAASAY
Camastianavaig
Oskaig
Lower Ollach
Raasay Ho.
Clachan
North Fearns
Inverarish
East Suisnish
Eyre
Peinchorran
Sconser
Moll
Scalpay
Luib
Dunan
Broadford
Corry
Harrapool
Waterloo
Lower Breakish
Upper Breakish
Skulamus
Torrin
Kilbride
Kirkibost
Kilmarie
Elgol
Glasnakille
Heast
Kinloch
Drumfearn
Duisdalemore
Isleornsay
Camuscross
Ord
Tokavaig
Tarskavaig
Achnacloich
Teangue
Ferindonald
Kilbeg
Kilmore
Armadale Castle
Calligarry
Ardvasar
Aird of Sleat
Ard Thurinish
Crowlin Islands
Eilean Mór
Longay
Pabay
Guillamon I.
Kyle of Lochalsh
Kyleakin
Castle Moil
Badicaul
Erbusaig
Drumbuie
Duirinish
Kylerhea
Glen Arroch
Uags
Toscaig
Culduie
Ard-dhubh
Camusterrach
Camusteel
Inverguseran
Airor
Sandaig
Scottas
Inverie
Knock Castle
Dunscaith Castle
Armadale Gardens
Clan Donald Centre
Mallaig Heritage Centre
A87
A851
B8083
B883
SKYE
SLEAT
CUILLIN HILLS
RED HILLS

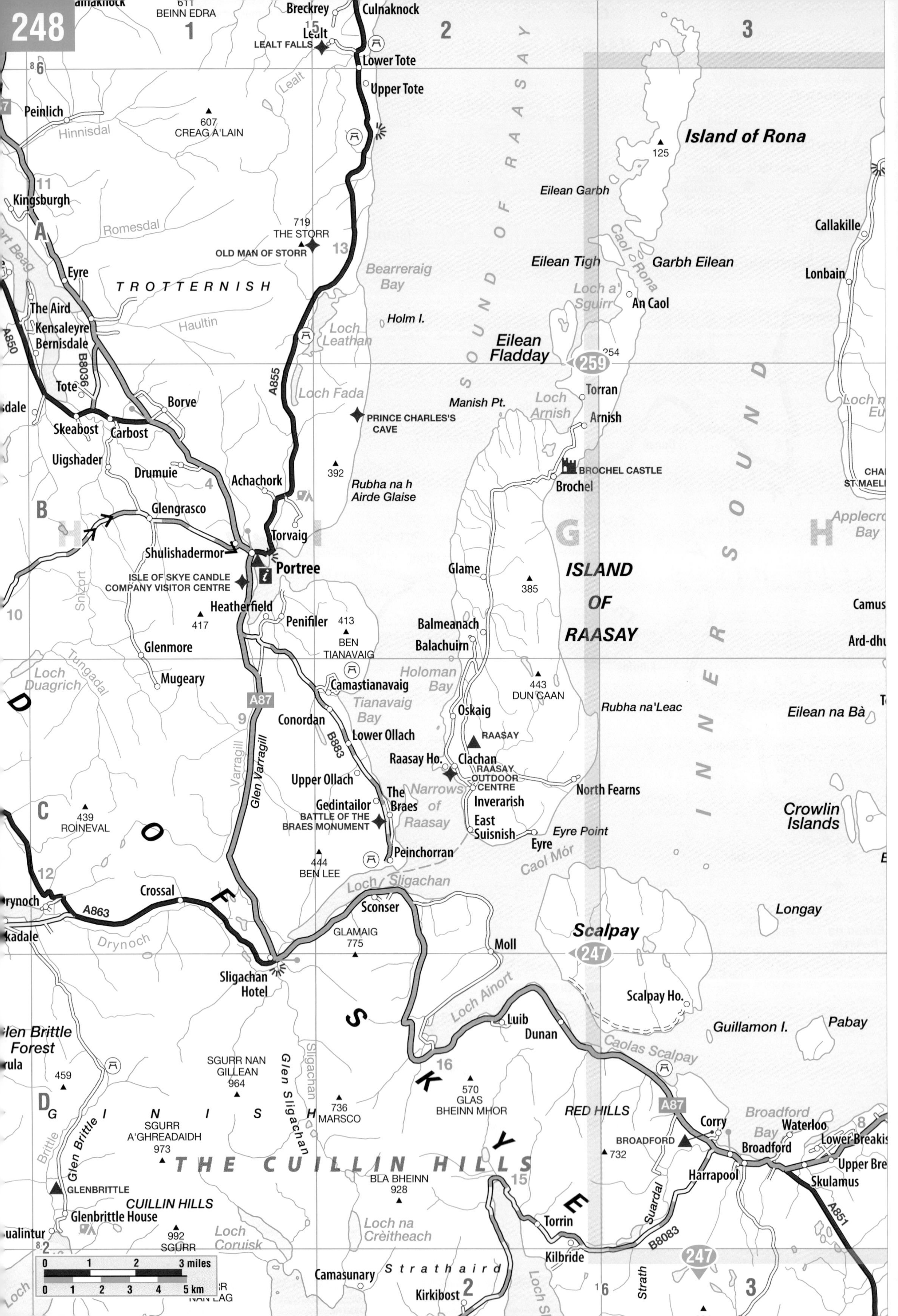
1
2
3
BEINN EDRA
611
Breckrey
Culnaknock
Lealt
LEALT FALLS
Lower Tote
Upper Tote
Lealt
Peinlich
Hinnisdal
607
CREAG A'LAIN
Island of Rona
125
Eilean Garbh
Kingsburgh
Romesdal
719
THE STORR
OLD MAN OF STORR
Callakille
Eyre
TROTTERNISH
Bearreraig
Bay
Eilean Tigh
Caol Rona
Garbh Eilean
Lonbain
Loch a' Sguirr
An Caol
The Aird
Kensaleyre
Bernisdale
Haultin
Holm I.
Loch Leathan
Eilean Fladday
254
259
A850
B8036
Tote
A855
Loch Fada
Torran
Borve
Manish Pt.
Loch Arnish
Arnish
Skeabost
Carbost
PRINCE CHARLES'S CAVE
Uigshader
Drumuie
BROCHEL CASTLE
Brochel
392
Achachork
Rubha na h Airde Glaise
SOUND OF RAASAY
Glengrasco
Torvaig
Applecross Bay
Shulishadermor
Portree
ISLE OF SKYE CANDLE COMPANY VISITOR CENTRE
Glame
385
ISLAND OF RAASAY
Snizort
Heatherfield
417
Penifiler
413
BEN TIANAVAIG
Balmeanach
Balachuirn
Camus
Ard-dhu
Glenmore
Loch Duagrich
Tungadal
Mugeary
Camastianavaig
Holoman Bay
443
DUN CAAN
A87
Tianavaig Bay
Conordan
Oskaig
Rubha na'Leac
Eilean na Bà
B883
Lower Ollach
RAASAY
Raasay Ho.
Clachan
RAASAY OUTDOOR CENTRE
North Fearns
Varragill
Glen Varragill
Upper Ollach
439
ROINEVAL
The Braes
Narrows of Raasay
Inverarish
Gedintailor
BATTLE OF THE BRAES MONUMENT
East Suisnish
Eyre Point
Eyre
Crowlin Islands
Peinchorran
444
BEN LEE
Caol Mór
Loch Sligachan
Crossal
A863
Sconser
Longay
GLAMAIG
775
Moll
Scalpay
247
Drynoch
Sligachan Hotel
Loch Ainort
Scalpay Ho.
Glen Brittle Forest
Luib
Dunan
Guillamon I.
Pabay
Caolas Scalpay
459
SGURR NAN GILLEAN
964
Glen Sligachan
Sligachan
16
570
GLAS BHEINN MHOR
736
MARSCO
RED HILLS
A87
Corry
Broadford Bay
Waterloo
Lower Breakish
Glen Brittle
Brittle
SGURR A'GHREADAIDH
973
THE CUILLIN HILLS
BROADFORD
732
Broadford
Upper Breakish
Harrapool
Skulamus
BLA BHEINN
928
GLENBRITTLE
15
A851
CUILLIN HILLS
Glenbrittle House
Loch na Crèitheach
Suardal
Torrin
992
SGURR
Loch Coruisk
B8083
247
Kilbride
Camasunary
Strathaird
Kirkibost
Loch Slapin
Strath
0
1
2
3 miles
0
1
2
3
4
5 km

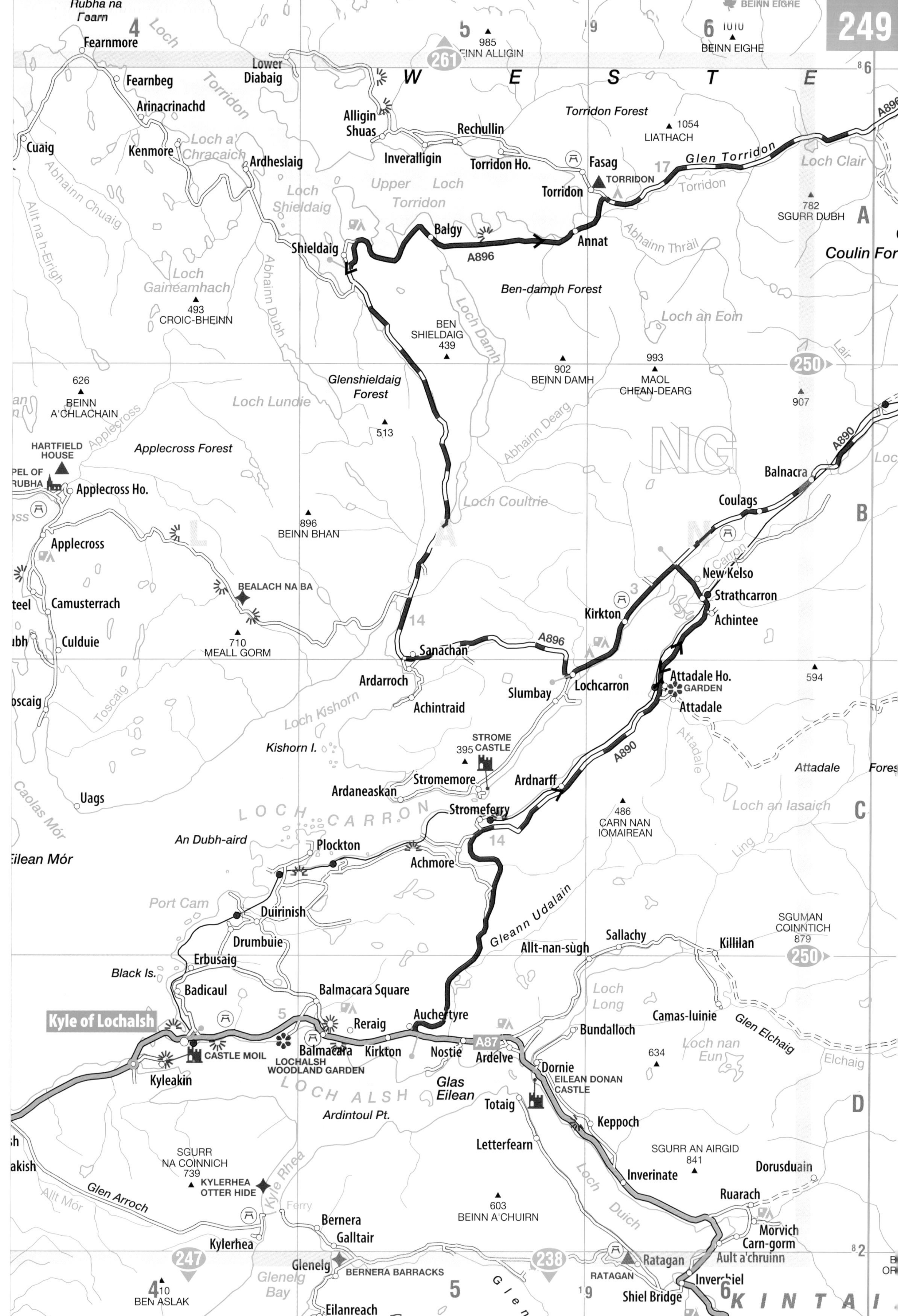
Rubha na Fearn
Fearnmore
Fearnbeg
Arinacrinachd
Cuaig
Kenmore
Loch a' Chracaich
Ardheslaig
Loch Torridon
Lower Diabaig
Alligin Shuas
Inveralligin
Rechullin
Torridon Ho.
Upper Loch Torridon
Loch Shieldaig
Shieldaig
Balgy
A896
Annat
Torridon
Fasag
TORRIDON
Glen Torridon
Torridon Forest
1054
LIATHACH
985
BEINN ALLIGIN
1010
BEINN EIGHE
W E S T E
Loch Clair
782
SGURR DUBH
Coulin Forest
Abhainn Thrail
Ben-damph Forest
Loch an Eoin
Abhainn Chuaig
Allt na h-Eirigh
Loch Gaineamhach
493
CROIC-BHEINN
Abhainn Dubh
BEN SHIELDAIG
439
Loch Damh
902
BEINN DAMH
993
MAOL CHEAN-DEARG
907
Lair
626
BEINN A'CHLACHAIN
Loch Lundie
Glenshieldaig Forest
513
Applecross Forest
HARTFIELD HOUSE
CHAPEL OF RUBHA
Applecross Ho.
Abhainn Dearg
N G
A890
Balnacra
Coulags
Loch Coultrie
896
BEINN BHAN
Applecross
BEALACH NA BA
Camusterrach
Culduie
710
MEALL GORM
New Kelso
Strathcarron
Achintee
Kirkton
Sanachan
Ardarroch
Achintraid
Slumbay
Lochcarron
Attadale Ho.
GARDEN
Attadale
594
Toscaig
Loch Kishorn
Kishorn I.
395
STROME CASTLE
Stromemore
Ardaneaskan
Ardnarff
Attadale Forest
Loch an Iasaich
Uags
Caolas Mór
LOCH CARRON
Stromeferry
486
CARN NAN IOMAIREAN
An Dubh-aird
Plockton
Achmore
Eilean Mór
Ling
Port Cam
Duirinish
Drumbuie
Gleann Udalain
SGUMAN COINNTICH
879
Erbusaig
Allt-nan-sùgh
Sallachy
Killilan
Black Is.
Badicaul
Balmacara Square
Loch Long
Camas-luinie
Glen Elchaig
Kyle of Lochalsh
Reraig
Auchertyre
Bundalloch
CASTLE MOIL
Balmacara
Kirkton
Nostie
A87
Ardelve
Dornie
EILEAN DONAN CASTLE
LOCHALSH WOODLAND GARDEN
Kyleakin
Loch nan Eun
634
Elchaig
LOCH ALSH
Glas Eilean
Totaig
Ardintoul Pt.
Keppoch
Letterfearn
SGURR AN AIRGID
841
Dorusduain
SGURR NA COINNICH
739
KYLERHEA OTTER HIDE
Kyle Rhea
Glen Arroch
Allt Mór
Inverinate
Loch Duich
Ruarach
603
BEINN A'CHUIRN
Ferry
Bernera
Galltair
Morvich
Carn-gorm
Ault a'chruinn
Kylerhea
Glenelg
BERNERA BARRACKS
Ratagan
RATAGAN
Glenelg Bay
Glen
Inverchiel
Shiel Bridge
KINTAIL
610
BEN ASLAK
Eilanreach
261
250
247
238

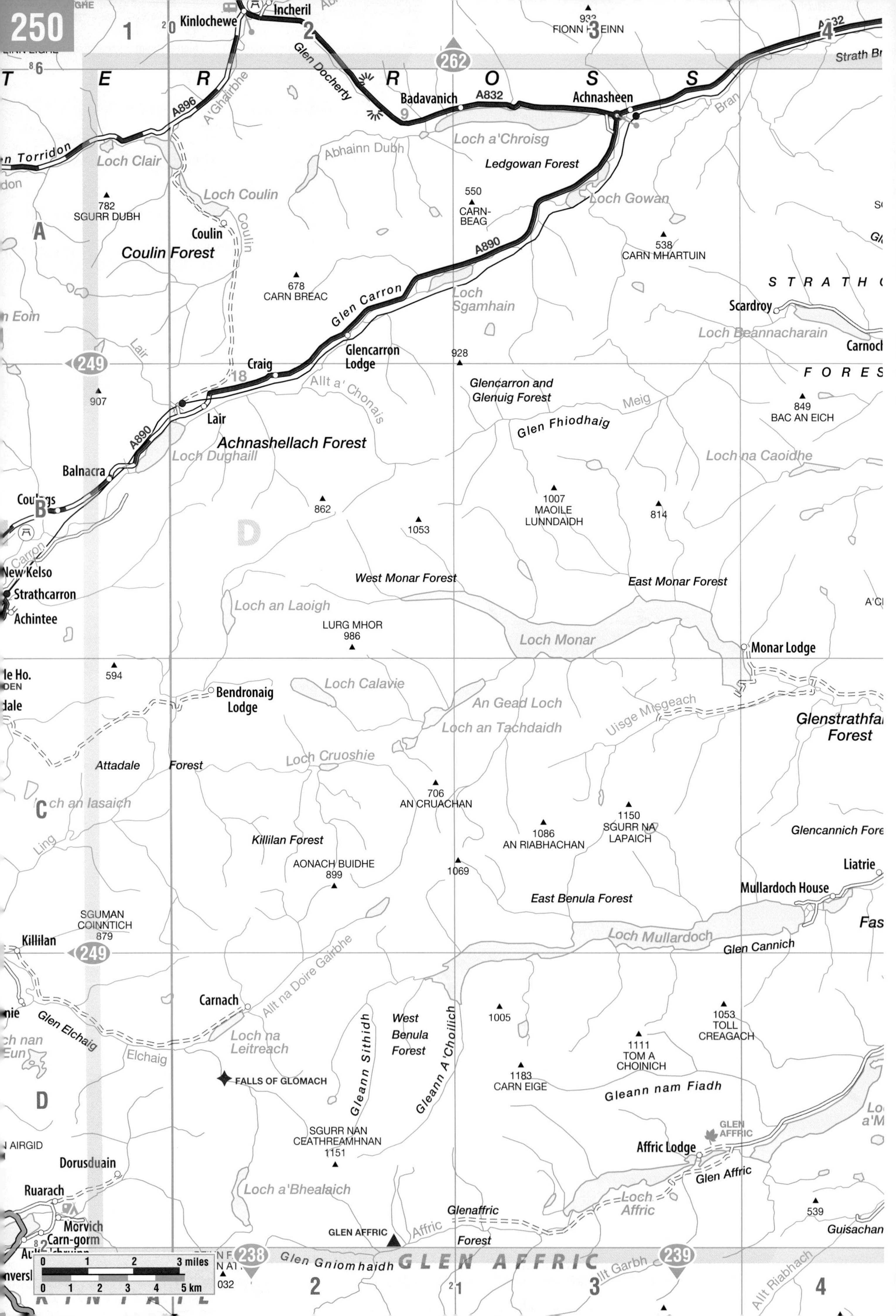


262
249
249
238
239

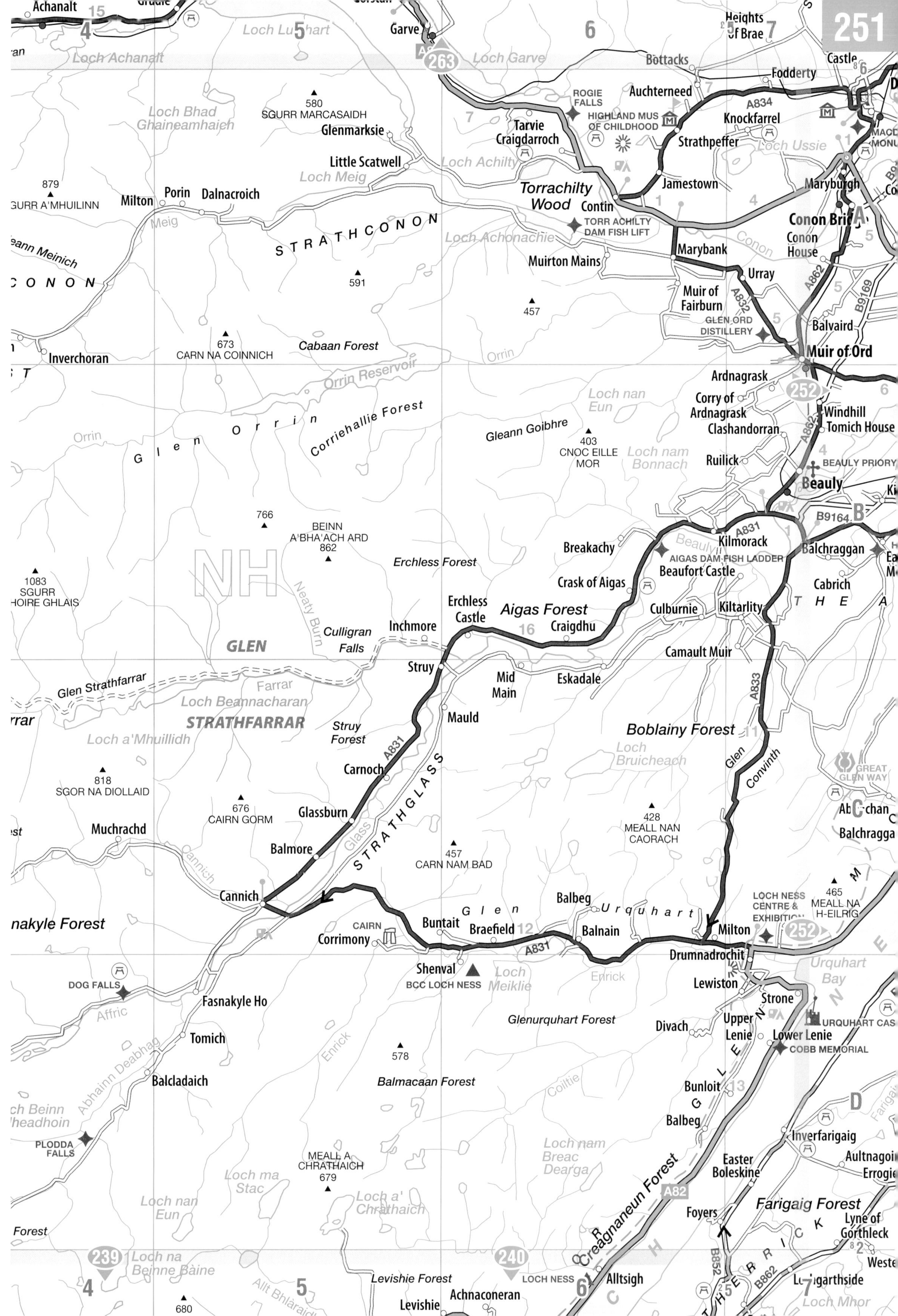
Achanalt
Garve
Loch Luichart
Loch Achanalt
Loch Garve
Heights of Brae
Bottacks
Castle
Fodderty
Auchterneed
ROGIE FALLS
HIGHLAND MUS OF CHILDHOOD
A834
Knockfarrel
Strathpeffer
Loch Ussie
Loch Bhad Ghaineamhaich
580
SGURR MARCASAIDH
Glenmarksie
Tarvie
Craigdarroch
Little Scatwell
Loch Achilty
Loch Meig
Jamestown
Maryburgh
879
SGURR A'MHUILINN
Milton
Porin
Dalnacroich
Meig
Torrachilty Wood
Contin
Conon Bridge
Conon House
TORR ACHILTY DAM FISH LIFT
S T R A T H C O N O N
Loch Achonachie
Marybank
Conon
Muirton Mains
Urray
A862
B9169
Muir of Fairburn
A832
591
457
GLEN ORD DISTILLERY
Balvaird
Muir of Ord
673
CARN NA COINNICH
Cabaan Forest
Inverchoran
Orrin
Orrin Reservoir
Ardnagrask
Corry of Ardnagrask
Clashandorran
Windhill
Tomich House
Loch nan Eun
Corriehallie Forest
G l e n O r r i n
Gleann Goibhre
403
CNOC EILLE MOR
Loch nam Bonnach
Ruilick
BEAULY PRIORY
Beauly
766
BEINN A'BHA'ACH ARD
862
NH
1083
SGURR NA H-DOIRE GHLAIS
Erchless Forest
B9164
A831
Kilmorack
Breakachy
Beauly
AIGAS DAM FISH LADDER
Balchraggan
Beaufort Castle
Crask of Aigas
Cabrich
Neaty Burn
Culligran Falls
Inchmore
Erchless Castle
Aigas Forest
Craigdhu
Culburnie
Kiltarlity
GLEN
Camault Muir
Struy
Mid Main
Eskadale
Glen Strathfarrar
Farrar
Loch Beannacharan
STRATHFARRAR
Stuy Forest
Mauld
A833
Boblainy Forest
Loch a'Mhuillidh
818
SGOR NA DIOLLAID
Carnoch
Loch Bruicheach
Glen Convinth
GREAT GLEN WAY
676
CAIRN GORM
Glassburn
428
MEALL NAN CAORACH
Muchrachd
Glass
Balmore
457
CARN NAM BAD
Cannich
Balbeg
LOCH NESS CENTRE & EXHIBITION
465
MEALL NA H-EILRIG
Milton
Buntait
Glen Urquhart
Braefield
Balnain
Glenakyle Forest
CAIRN
Corrimony
Drumnadrochit
Shenval
Loch Meiklie
Enrick
Urquhart Bay
DOG FALLS
BCC LOCH NESS
Lewiston
Strone
Fasnakyle Ho
Affric
Glenurquhart Forest
Divach
Upper Lenie
URQUHART CASTLE
Lower Lenie
Tomich
COBB MEMORIAL
Abhainn Deabhag
Enrick
578
Balcladaich
Balmacaan Forest
Coiltie
Bunloit
Balbeg
Inverfarigaig
PLODDA FALLS
MEALL A CHRATHAICH
679
Loch nam Breac Dearga
Easter Boleskine
Aultnagoire
Errogie
Loch ma Stac
Creagnaneun Forest
A82
Loch nan Eun
Loch a' Chrathaich
Foyers
Farigaig Forest
Lyne of Gorthleck
239
Loch na Beinne Bàine
240
Levishie Forest
LOCH NESS
Alltsigh
B852
B862
Westerton
Achnaconeran
Levishie
680
Allt Bhlàraidh
Loch Mhor
263
252

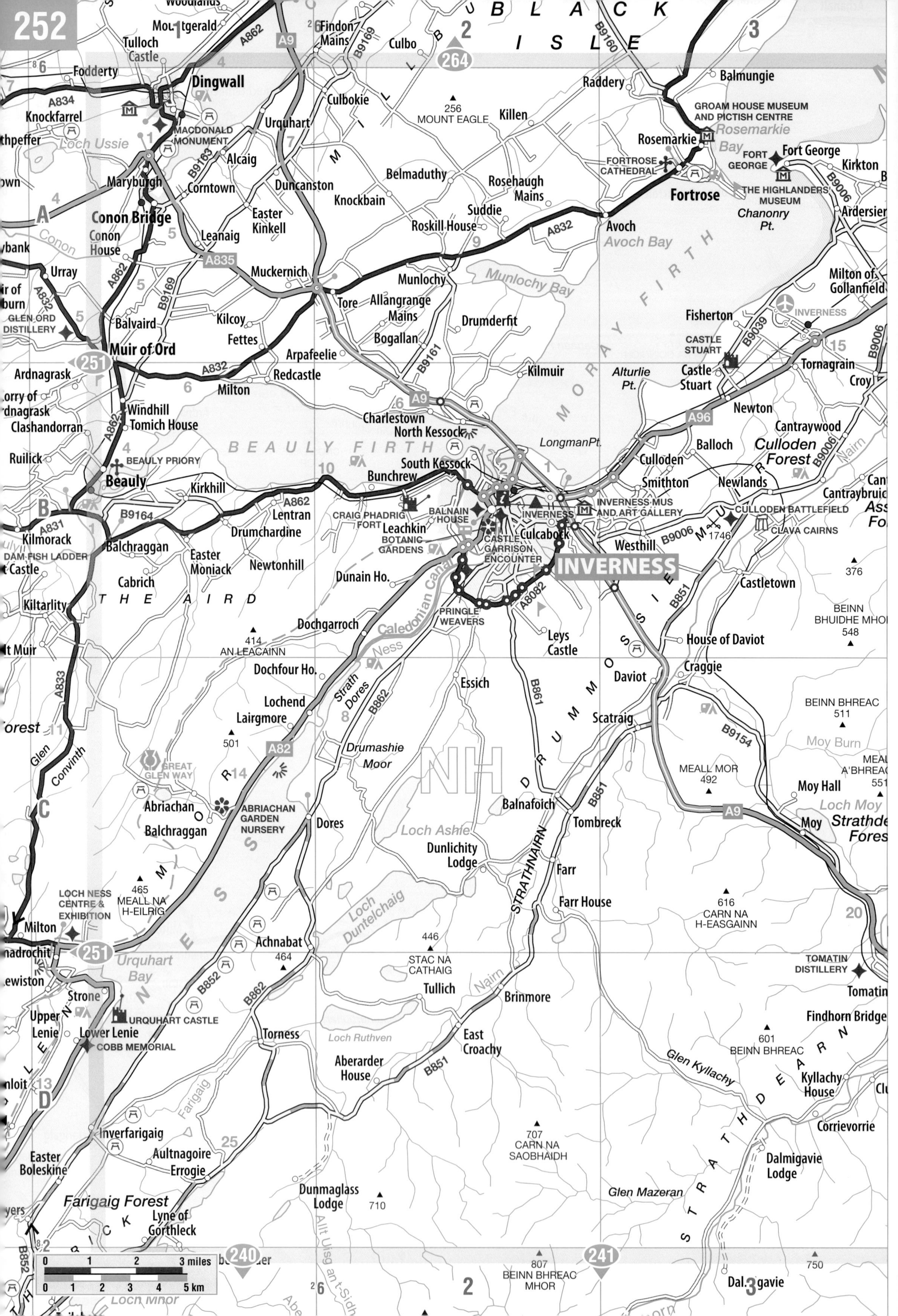
252
BLACK ISLE
Tulloch Castle
Fodderty
Dingwall
Knockfarrel
Loch Ussie
MACDONALD MONUMENT
Maryburgh
Conon Bridge
Conon House
Urray
GLEN ORD DISTILLERY
Muir of Ord
Ardnagrask
Windhill
Tomich House
Clashandorran
Ruilick
BEAULY PRIORY
Beauly
Kilmorack
DAM FISH LADDER
Balchraggan
Cabrich
Kiltarlity
THE AIRD
Findon Mains
Culbo
Culbokie
Urquhart
Alcaig
Corntown
Duncanston
Leanaig
Easter Kinkell
Muckernich
Balvaird
Kilcoy
Fettes
Redcastle
Milton
Arpafeelie
Tore
Allangrange Mains
Bogallan
Knockbain
Belmaduthy
256 MOUNT EAGLE
Killen
Raddery
Rosehaugh Mains
Suddie
Roskill House
Munlochy
Munlochy Bay
Drumderfit
Balmungie
GROAM HOUSE MUSEUM AND PICTISH CENTRE
Rosemarkie
Rosemarkie Bay
FORTROSE CATHEDRAL
Fortrose
Avoch
Avoch Bay
FORT GEORGE
Fort George
Kirkton
THE HIGHLANDERS' MUSEUM
Chanonry Pt.
Ardersier
Milton of Gollanfield
MORAY FIRTH
INVERNESS
Fisherton
CASTLE STUART
Castle Stuart
Tornagrain
Croy
Alturlie Pt.
Kilmuir
Charlestown
North Kessock
BEAULY FIRTH
South Kessock
Bunchrew
Kirkhill
Lentran
Drumchardine
Easter Moniack
Newtonhill
CRAIG PHADRIG FORT
Leachkin
BALNAIN HOUSE
BOTANIC GARDENS
CASTLE GARRISON ENCOUNTER
Culcabock
INVERNESS
INVERNESS MUS AND ART GALLERY
Longman Pt.
Culloden
Smithton
Balloch
Newton
Cantraywood
Culloden Forest
Newlands
Cantraybruich
CULLODEN BATTLEFIELD
1746
CLAVA CAIRNS
Westhill
Castletown
376
BEINN BHUIDHE MHOR 548
Dunain Ho.
Dochgarroch
Caledonian Canal
PRINGLE WEAVERS
Leys Castle
House of Daviot
Daviot
Craggie
414 AN LEACAINN
Dochfour Ho.
Ness
Strath Dores
Essich
Lochend
Lairgmore
501
Scatraig
DRUMMOSSIE
BEINN BHREAC 511
Moy Burn
MEALL MOR 492
MEALL A'BHREAC 551
Moy Hall
Loch Moy
Moy
Strathdearn Forest
Drumashie Moor
NH
GREAT GLEN WAY
Abriachan
ABRIACHAN GARDEN NURSERY
Balchraggan
Dores
Loch Ashie
Balnafoich
Tombreck
Dunlichity Lodge
STRATHNAIRN
Farr
Farr House
616 CARN NA H-EASGAINN
LOCH NESS CENTRE & EXHIBITION
465 MEALL NA H-EILRIG
Milton
Loch Duntelchaig
446 STAC NA CATHAIG
Achnabat
464
Urquhart Bay
Strone
Upper Lenie
Lower Lenie
URQUHART CASTLE
COBB MEMORIAL
Tullich
Nairn
Brinmore
TOMATIN DISTILLERY
Tomatin
Findhorn Bridge
601 BEINN BHREAC
Glen Kyllachy
Kyllachy House
Torness
Loch Ruthven
Aberarder House
East Croachy
STRATHDEARN
Corrievorrie
Inverfarigaig
Farigaig
Aultnagoire
Errogie
Easter Boleskine
707 CARN NA SAOBHAIDH
Dalmigavie Lodge
Farigaig Forest
Lyne of Gorthleck
Dunmaglass Lodge
710
Glen Mazeran
Glen Convinth
Allt Uisg an t-Sidhein
807 BEINN BHREAC MHOR
750
Dalmigavie
0 1 2 3 miles
0 1 2 3 4 5 km

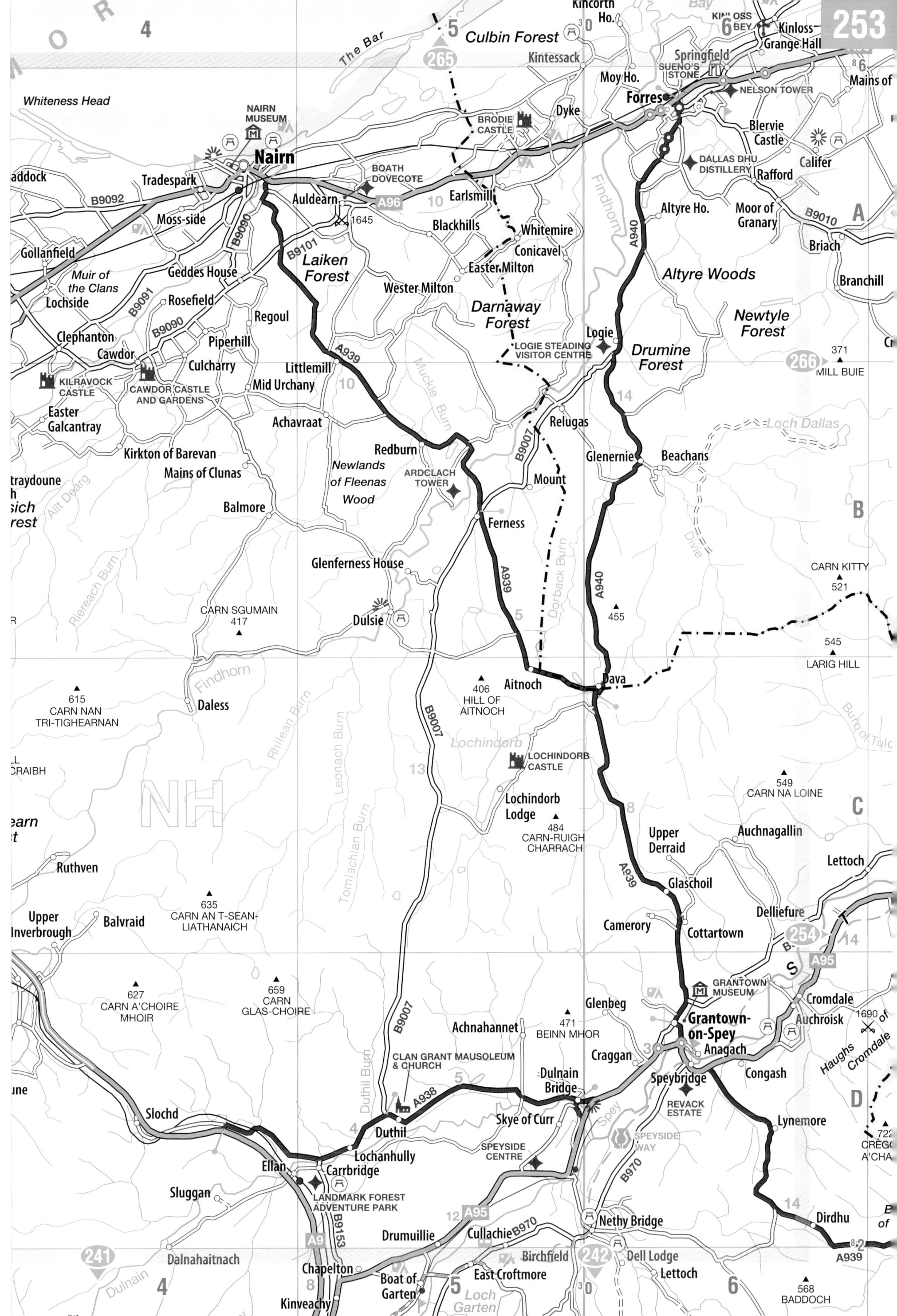
Culbin Forest
The Bar
265
Kincorth Ho.
Kintessack
Kinloss Bey
Kinloss
Grange Hall
Springfield
Sueno's Stone
Moy Ho.
Forres
Nelson Tower
Mains of
Whiteness Head
Nairn Museum
Nairn
Brodie Castle
Dyke
Blervie Castle
Dallas Dhu Distillery
Califer
Rafford
Boath Dovecote
addock
Tradespark
B9092
Auldearn
A96
Earlsmill
Altyre Ho.
Moor of Granary
B9010
Moss-side
1645
Blackhills
Whitemire
Conicavel
B9090
B9101
Laiken Forest
Gollanfield
Easter Milton
A940
Findhorn
Briach
Altyre Woods
Muir of the Clans
Geddes House
Branchill
Lochside
B9091
Rosefield
Wester Milton
Regoul
Darnaway Forest
Newtyle Forest
Clephanton
B9090
Piperhill
Logie
Cawdor
A939
Logie Steading Visitor Centre
Drumine Forest
266
371
Mill Buie
Kilravock Castle
Cawdor Castle and Gardens
Culcharry
Littlemill
Mid Urchany
Muckle Burn
Easter Galcantray
Achavraat
Relugas
Loch Dallas
Redburn
B9007
Glenernie
Beachans
Kirkton of Barevan
Mains of Clunas
Newlands of Fleenas Wood
Ardclach Tower
Mount
traydoune
Alit Dearg
Balmore
Ferness
Glenferness House
Dorback Burn
Divie
Carn Kitty
521
Rieriach Burn
Carn Sgumain
417
Dulsie
455
545
Larig Hill
Findhorn
Aitnoch
Dava
615
Carn nan Tri-Tighearnan
Daless
406
Hill of Aitnoch
Burn of Tulc
Phiilean Burn
Leonach Burn
Lochindorb
Lochindorb Castle
NH
549
Carn na Loine
Lochindorb Lodge
484
Carn-Ruigh Charrach
Upper Derraid
Auchnagallin
Lettoch
Tomlachlan Burn
Ruthven
Glaschoil
635
Carn an t-Sean-Liathanaich
Upper Inverbrough
Balvraid
Camerory
Cottartown
Delliefure
254
A95
Grantown Museum
Cromdale
627
Carn a'Choire Mhoir
659
Carn Glas-Choire
Glenbeg
Grantown-on-Spey
1690
Auchroisk
471
Beinn Mhor
Achnahannet
Anagach
Haughs of Cromdale
Clan Grant Mausoleum & Church
Craggan
Congash
Duthil Burn
Dulnain Bridge
Speybridge
Revack Estate
A938
Slochd
Skye of Curr
Lynemore
Duthil
Spey
Speyside Way
722
Speyside Centre
Lochanhully
Ellan
Carrbridge
B970
Sluggan
Landmark Forest Adventure Park
Dirdhu
A95
Nethy Bridge
B9153
Cullachie
B970
A9
Drumuillie
241
Dalnahaitnach
Birchfield
242
Dell Lodge
A939
Dulnain
Chapelton
Lettoch
Boat of Garten
East Croftmore
568
Baddoch
Kinveachy
Loch Garten
A
B
C
D
4
5
6

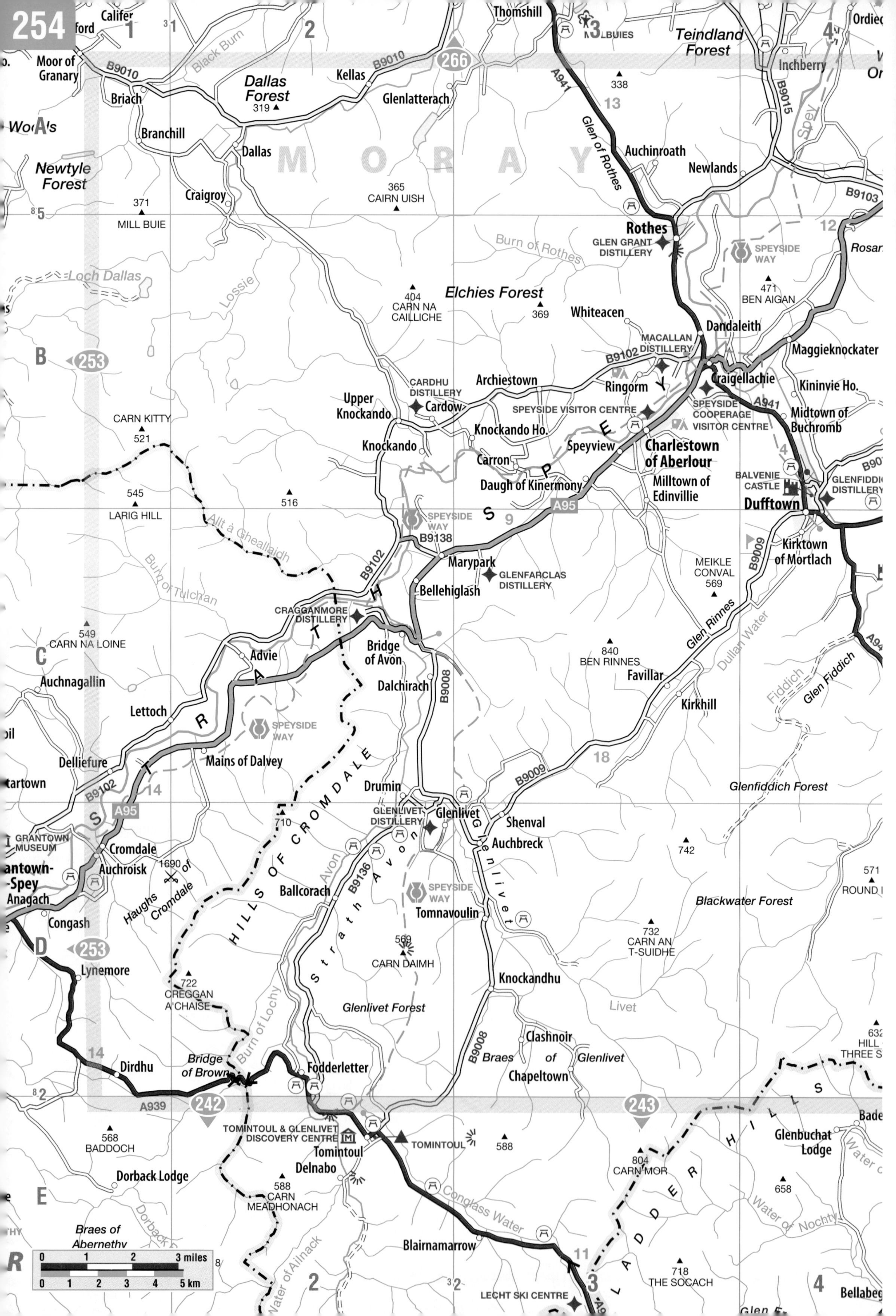

Thomshill
Teindland Forest
Califer
Moor of Granary
Briach
Dallas Forest
319
Kellas
Glenlatterach
266
B9010
Black Burn
338
Inchberry
B9015
Spey
A941
Branchill
Dallas
M O R A Y
Newtyle Forest
Craigroy
365 CAIRN UISH
Auchinroath
Newlands
Glen of Rothes
371 MILL BUIE
Rothes
GLEN GRANT DISTILLERY
SPEYSIDE WAY
Burn of Rothes
B9103
Loch Dallas
Lossie
404 CARN NA CAILLICHE
Elchies Forest
369
Whiteacen
471 BEN AIGAN
Dandaleith
Maggieknockater
253
MACALLAN DISTILLERY
B9102
Archiestown
Ringorm
Craigellachie
Kininvie Ho.
CARDHU DISTILLERY
Upper Knockando
Cardow
SPEYSIDE VISITOR CENTRE
SPEYSIDE COOPERAGE VISITOR CENTRE
Midtown of Buchromb
CARN KITTY 521
Knockando Ho.
Knockando
Speyview
Charlestown of Aberlour
Carron
BALVENIE CASTLE
GLENFIDDICH DISTILLERY
Daugh of Kinermony
Milltown of Edinvillie
Dufftown
545 LARIG HILL
516
A95
SPEYSIDE WAY
B9138
Allt à Ghealláidh
Kirktown of Mortlach
MEIKLE CONVAL 569
Marypark
GLENFARCLAS DISTILLERY
Burn of Tulchan
Bellehiglash
B9009
CRAGGANMORE DISTILLERY
549 CARN NA LOINE
Bridge of Avon
Glen Rinnes
Dullan Water
840 BEN RINNES
Advie
Favillar
Auchnagallin
Dalchirach
B9008
Glen Fiddich
Fiddich
Kirkhill
Lettoch
SPEYSIDE WAY
Dellliefure
Mains of Dalvey
18
HILLS OF CROMDALE
Drumin
Glenfiddich Forest
GLENLIVET DISTILLERY
Glenlivet
Shenval
710
GRANTOWN MUSEUM
Cromdale
Auchbreck
742
Auchroisk
1690
Haughs of Cromdale
Avon
B9136
571 ROUND
Anagach
Ballcorach
SPEYSIDE WAY
Blackwater Forest
Congash
Tomnavoulin
Strath Avon
732 CARN AN T-SUIDHE
569 CARN DAIMH
Lynemore
Knockandhu
722 CREGGAN A'CHAISE
Glenlivet Forest
Livet
Burn of Lochy
Clashnoir
632 HILL THREE S
Braes of Glenlivet
Chapeltown
Dirdhu
Bridge of Brown
Fodderletter
A939
242
243
568 BADDOCH
TOMINTOUL & GLENLIVET DISCOVERY CENTRE
TOMINTOUL
588
Bade
Glenbuchat Lodge
Tomintoul
804 CARN MOR
Delnabo
Dorback Lodge
588 CARN MEADHONACH
658
LADDER HILLS
Conglass Water
Water of Nochty
Braes of Abernethy
Blairnamarrow
Water of Ailnack
718 THE SOCACH
LECHT SKI CENTRE
Bellabeg
0 1 2 3 miles
0 1 2 3 4 5 km

255
4
5
6
7
Mill Stone Hill
B9016
Vood of
rdiequish
Forgie
Broadrashes
Deerhill
Grange Crossroads
267
Mains of Edingight
Edingight Ho.
Gordonstown
20
Knock Hill
430
A95
B9023
Weachyburn
Blacklaw
Finnygaud
Aultmore
Newmill
A96
Crannoch
Bracobrae
B9018
Davoch of Grange
Sillyearn
Knock
Glen Barry
Knowes of Elrick
A97
A
Cranna
Aberchirder
311
Mulben
Keith
A95
Strathisla Distillery
I S L A
Farmtown
Drumnagorrach
B9022
Old Crombie
Knauchland
Marnoch
21
Clunie
5
B9014
366
B9117
265
Deveron
ie Forest
Keith and Dufftown Rly
S T R A T H
Balloch Wood
Milltown of Rothiemay
B9118
Mains of Mayen
Hillbrae
Inverkeithny
Auchin
339
Edintore
Glen of Coachford
Ruthven
Yonder Bognie
Towiemore
Little Pitlurg
Coachford
11
Cairnie
B9022
Bogniebrae
344
Fourman Hill
256
B
Drummuir Castle
B9115
313
The Bin
A97
Glendronach Distillery
Drumblair
Drummuir
A96
The Bin Forest
Corse of Kinnoir
B9001
417
Daugh of Cairnborrow
Nordic Ski Centre
Huntly Castle
Lessendrum
Milltown of Auchindoun
Cairnborrow
A920
Huntly
Drumblade
Corse
Aucharnie
14
Torry
Brander Museum
A920
Deveron
Haugh of Glass
A97
Brideswell
Slioch
259
Auchindoun Castle
Denend
Ythanwells
S T R A T H B O G I E
487
The Scalp
Bailiesward
Thomastown
Bridgend
Hillhead
Tillathrowie
Succoth
Kirkstile
Shanquhar
10
A96
Bainshole
C
381
Ballochford
Glens of Foudland
525
NJ
Coynachie
Blackburn
467
Hill of Foudland
Tomnaven
Culdrain
Clashindarroch Forest
9
Kirkney
Clashindarroch Forest
Colpy
Gartly
Clashindarroch
Largie
Bridgend
Kirkney Water
Cults
434
Knockandy Hill
Inverharroch
Wrangham
Leith Hall
B992
Black Water
The Shevock
18
Milton of Lesmore
Milton of Noth
Kennethmont
Aulton
Oldtown
B9002
Ardlair
Insch
Auchmair
505
A941
Ardoyne
Belhinnie
Cabrach
Rhynie
Cottown
B9002
Aldunie
Clatt
Duncanstone
Wheedlemont
Craig Castle
A97
Leslie
Kirkton
256
D
B9002
Knockespock Ho.
St Mary's Church
Auchleven
721
The Buck
5
Coldwells Croft
Whitehaugh Forest
Clova
Scottish Sculpture Workshop
Lumsden
Correen Hills
Muckletown
G
B992
A B E R D E
Glenton
2
243
244
518
Lord Arthur's Cairn
Tullynessle
Mossat
Keig
Castle Forbes
A97
Kildrummy
Don
6
A944
Bridge of Alford
Montgarrie
Haughton
Rorandle
Rinmore
Milltown of Kildrummy
Grampian Transport Mus
Belnacraig
Kildrummy Castle
532
Auchintoul
Gateside
E
Kirkton of Glenbuchat
Alford
Heritage Museum
A944
Whitehouse
Pitmunie
Asloun
Tillachie
4
Forbestown
Glenkindie
9
5
Sinnahard
Hillockhead
6
Little Lynturk
7
Kirkton of Tough
14

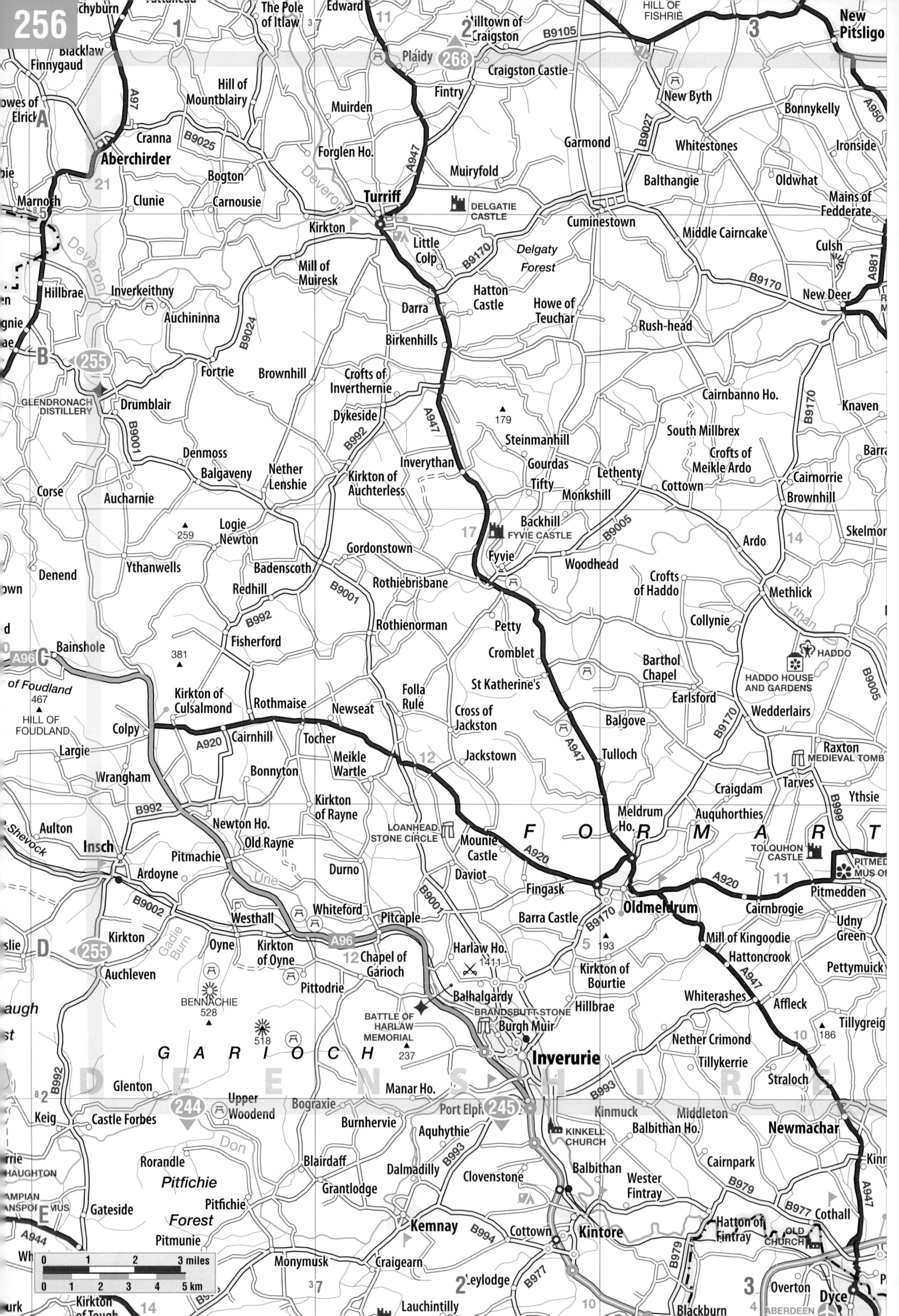
Aberchirder
Turriff
Oldmeldrum
Inverurie
Insch
Kintore
Kemnay
Newmachar
Dyce
New Pitsligo
New Deer
Methlick
Fyvie
FYVIE CASTLE
DELGATIE CASTLE
HADDO HOUSE AND GARDENS
GLENDRONACH DISTILLERY
LOANHEAD STONE CIRCLE
BATTLE OF HARLAW MEMORIAL
TOLQUHON CASTLE
KINKELL CHURCH
BENNACHIE
HILL OF FOUDLAND
F O R M A R T I N E
G A R I O C H
Pitfichie Forest
Delgaty Forest
Cuminestown
Rothienorman
Pitmedden
Tarves
Udny Green
Plaidy
Craigston Castle
0 1 2 3 miles
0 1 2 3 4 5 km

Knowhead
B9093
Strichen
MORMOND HILL
A952
Nether Park
Crimond
Rattray
269
Blackhill
A90
New Leeds
Longhill
Balearn
Adziel
B9093
North Ugie Water
Leys
St Fergus Moss
A981
Little Skillymarno
Backfolds
Kirktown
St Fergus
Scotstown Hd.
Denhead
Hythie
North Kirkton
Fetterangus
Rora Moss
Toux
Rora
Lunderton
Kirkton Hd.
Forest of Deer
A950
DEER ABBEY
Dunshillock
Woodside
Ugie
B U C H A N
Maud
B9029
ADEN
Mintlaw
Water
Newseat
Inverugie
INVERUGIE CASTLE
UGIE SALMON FISH HOUSE
Buchanhaven
MAUD RAILWAY MUSEUM
B9106
Backhill of Clackriach
Old Deer
Longside
Torterston
A982
Peterhead
ABERDEENSHIRE FARMING MUSEUM
South Ugie
Flushing
Stuartfield
Inverquhomery
A950
ARBUTHNOT MUSEUM & ART GALLERY
Drymuir
Keith Inch
Bulwark
Millbreck
Hillhead of Cocklaw
Mains of Crichie
Nether Kinmundy
Peterhead Bay
A948
Crichie
B9030
Invernettie
Nethermuir
Kinnadie
Clola
Little Dens
Sandford Bay
Skelmuir
Blackhill
Millbank
Boddam
Mains of Annochie
Kinknockie
Buchan Ness
Auchnagatt
Backhill of Fortree
Smallburn
Sandfordhill
Stirling
Moss of Cruden
Mains of Inkhorn
Backhill
Stoneygate
Coldwells
Longhaven
Teuchan
Quilquox
Milton Coldwells
A90
North Haven
A952
Hatton
Auchiries
BULLERS OF BUCHAN
Muirtack
Eastertown of Auchleuchries
Twa Havens
Drumwhindle
Arthrath
Cruden Bay
SLAINS CASTLE
A948
Toll of Birness
Port Erroll
Chapel Hill
NJ
Bogbrae
Bay of Cruden
NK
Ythanbank
A975
Hilton
Mains of Birness
Nether Leask
Inverebrie
Whinnyfold
Broomfield
A90
West Kinharrachie
P&R
Artrochie
Auchmacoy
Ellon
Esslemont
I N E
A920
Kirkton of Logie Buchan
VISITOR CENTRE
Kirktown of Slains
Collieston
DEN GDNS & FARMING LIFE
Waterside
St Catherine's Dub
Meikle Tarty
Tipperty
FORVIE
Sands of Forvie
B9000
Hackley Hd. or Forvie Ness
Tarty Burn
B9000
Newburgh
Cultercullen
Foveran
Udny Station
Foveran Burn
A975
Minnes
Drums
Newburgh Bar
Tillycorthie
Rashiereive
B999
Ardo Ho.
Delfrigs
Middlemuir
245
B979
Craigie
Causeyend
Whitecairns
nundy
Belhelvie
B977
BALMEDIE
Balmedie
Drumligair
B977
A90
Potterton
Blackdog
arkhill Ho.
Corby Loch
B999
Mundurno
A
B
C
D
E
4 5 6

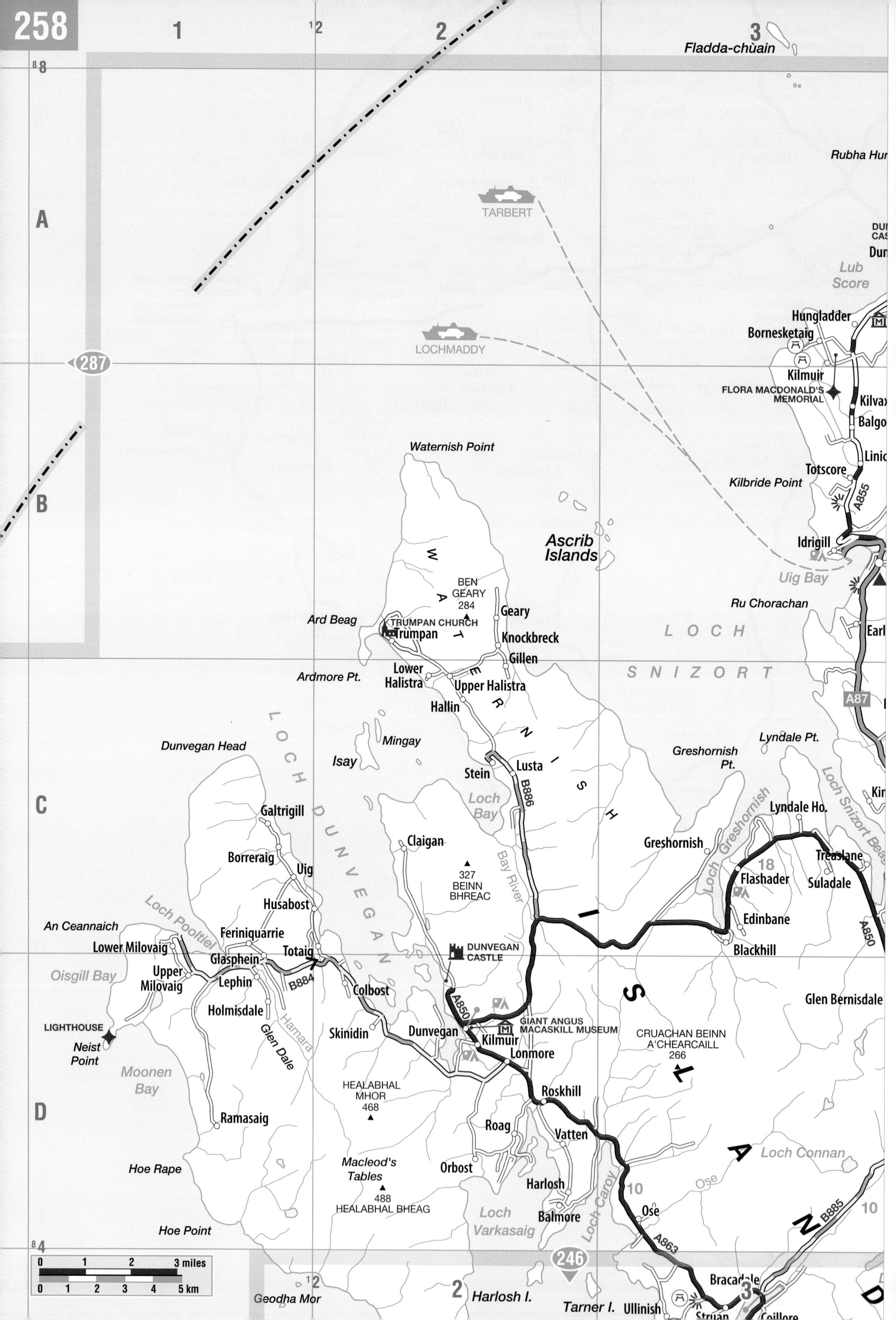

1
2
3
A
B
C
D
Fladda-chùain
Rubha Hur
TARBERT
LOCHMADDY
287
Lub Score
Hungladder
Borneskeitaig
Kilmuir
FLORA MACDONALD'S MEMORIAL
Kilvax
Balgo
Totscore
Kilbride Point
A855
Idrigill
Uig Bay
Ru Chorachan
Earl
Waternish Point
Ascrib Islands
W A T E R N I S H
BEN GEARY 284
Geary
TRUMPAN CHURCH
Trumpan
Knockbreck
Gillen
Ard Beag
Ardmore Pt.
Lower Halistra
Upper Halistra
Hallin
L O C H S N I Z O R T
A87
Lyndale Pt.
Greshornish Pt.
Loch Snizort Beag
Dunvegan Head
LOCH DUNVEGAN
Isay
Mingay
Stein
Lusta
B886
Loch Bay
Galtrigill
Borreraig
Uig
Husabost
Claigan
327 BEINN BHREAC
Bay River
Greshornish
Loch Greshornish
Lyndale Ho.
Treaslane
18
Flashader
Suladale
Edinbane
Blackhill
A850
An Ceannaich
Loch Pooltiel
Feriniquarrie
Lower Milovaig
Glasphein
Totaig
DUNVEGAN CASTLE
Oisgill Bay
Upper Milovaig
Lephin
B884
Colbost
Holmisdale
Hamara
Glen Dale
LIGHTHOUSE
Neist Point
Skinidin
Dunvegan
Kilmuir
GIANT ANGUS MACASKILL MUSEUM
Lonmore
CRUACHAN BEINN A'CHEARCAILL 266
Glen Bernisdale
Moonen Bay
HEALABHAL MHOR 468
Roskhill
I S L A N D
Ramasaig
Roag
Vatten
Loch Connan
Hoe Rape
Macleod's Tables
Orbost
488 HEALABHAL BHEAG
Harlosh
Loch Caroy
10
Ose
B885
A863
Loch Varkasaig
Balmore
Hoe Point
246
0 1 2 3 miles
0 1 2 3 4 5 km
Geodha Mor
Harlosh I.
Tarner I.
Ullinish
Bracadale
Struan
Coillore

Eilean Trodday
Rubha na h-Aiseig
Balmacqueen
Kilmaluag
SKYE MUSEUM OF ISLAND LIFE
Eilean Flodigarry
Flodigarry
MEALL NA SUIRAMACH
543
Digg
Staffin I.
Staffin Bay
THE QUIRAING
Glashvin
Brogaig
Stenscholl
Staffin
TROTTERNISH
Kilt Rock
KILT ROCK & MEALT FALLS
466
BIOD BUIDHE
Elishader
Maligar
Loch Mealt
Valtos
A855
Marishader
Garros
Rubha nam Brathairean
Uig
UIG
Balnaknock
611
BEINN EDRA
Breckrey
Culnaknock
Lealt
LEALT FALLS
Lower Tote
Upper Tote
Peinlich
Hinnisdal
607
CREAG A'LAIN
SOUND OF RAASAY
Island of Rona
125
Eilean Garbh
Romesdal
719
THE STORR
OLD MAN OF STORR
Bearreraig Bay
Eilean Tigh
Caol Rona
Garbh Eilean
Callakille
Lonbain
Eyre
TROTTERNISH
Loch a' Sguirr
An Caol
The Aird
Kensaleyre
Bernisdale
Haultin
Loch Leathan
Holm I.
Eilean Fladday
B8036
Tote
A855
Loch Fada
Manish Pt.
Loch Arnish
Torran
Arnish
Loch nan Eun
Borve
Skeabost
Carbost
PRINCE CHARLES'S CAVE
Uigshader
Drumuie
392
BROCHEL CASTLE
Brochel
CHAPEL OF ST MAELRUBHA
Achachork
Rubha na h Airde Glaise
Glengrasco
Torvaig
Applecross Bay
Shulishadermor
Portree
Glame
ISLAND OF RAASAY
385
Snizort
ISLE OF SKYE CANDLE COMPANY VISITOR CENTRE
Heatherfield
Camusteel
417
Penifiler
413
BEN TIANAVAIG
Balmeanach
Balachuirn
Ard-dhubh
Glenmore
Loch Duagrich
Tungadal
Mugeary
Camastianavaig
Holoman Bay
443
DUN CAAN
Rubha na'Leac
Toscaig
A87
Tianavaig Bay
Oskaig
Eilean na Bà
Conordan
NG
260
261
249
248

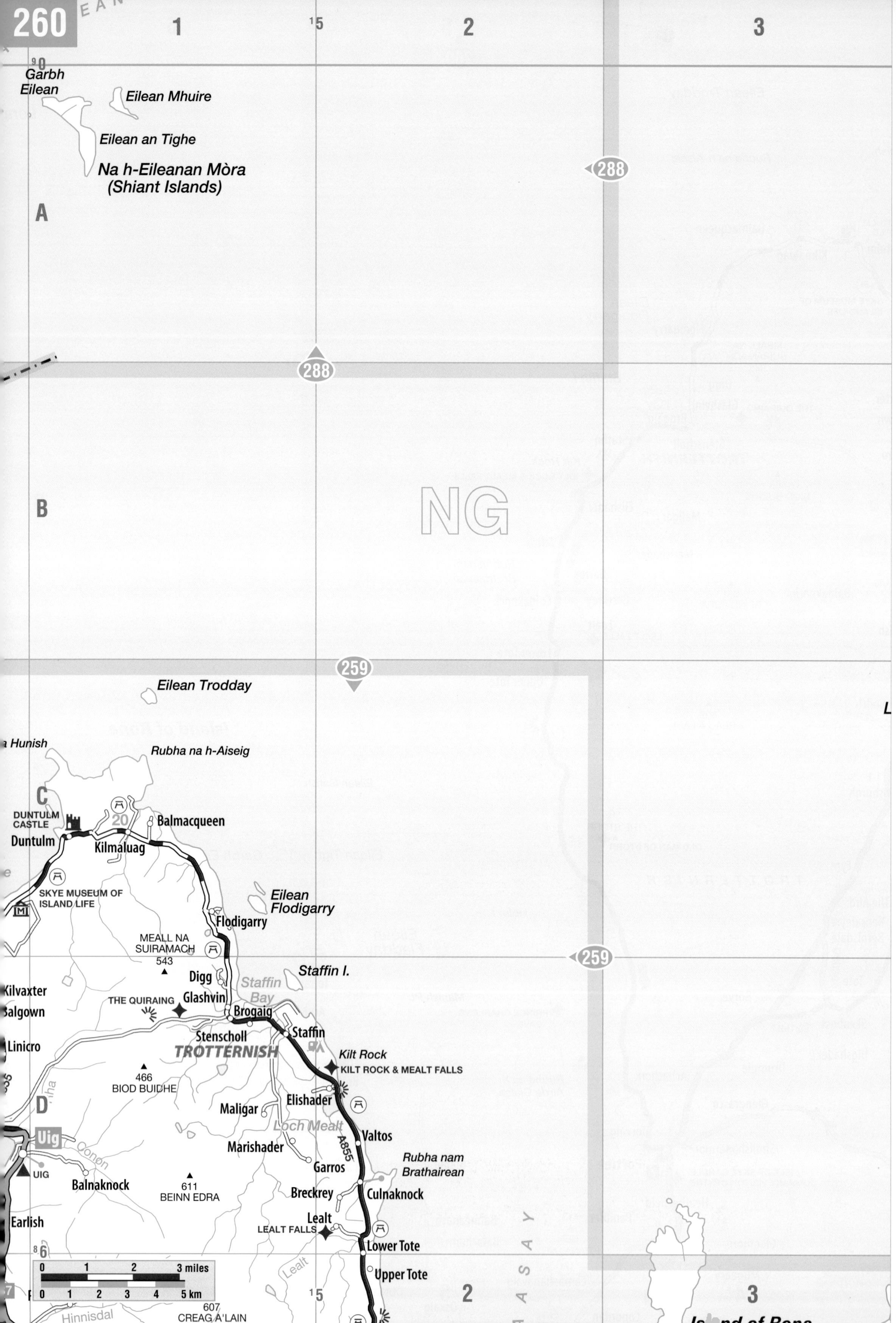
1
2
3
Garbh Eilean
Eilean Mhuire
Eilean an Tighe
Na h-Eileanan Mòra (Shiant Islands)
A
288
288
B
NG
259
Eilean Trodday
Hunish
Rubha na h-Aiseig
C
DUNTULM CASTLE
Duntulm
20
Balmacqueen
Kilmaluag
SKYE MUSEUM OF ISLAND LIFE
Eilean Flodigarry
Flodigarry
MEALL NA SUIRAMACH
543
259
Staffin I.
Digg
Staffin Bay
Kilvaxter
Balgown
THE QUIRAING
Glashvin
Brogaig
Stenscholl
Staffin
Linicro
TROTTERNISH
Kilt Rock
KILT ROCK & MEALT FALLS
466
BIOD BUIDHE
D
Maligar
Elishader
Loch Mealt
Uig
Valtos
Conon
Marishader
A855
Rubha nam Brathairean
UIG
Garros
Balnaknock
611
BEINN EDRA
Breckrey
Culnaknock
Earlish
Lealt
LEALT FALLS
Lower Tote
Lealt
Upper Tote
0 1 2 3 miles
0 1 2 3 4 5 km
607
CREAG A'LAIN
Hinnisdal
2
3
Island of Rona

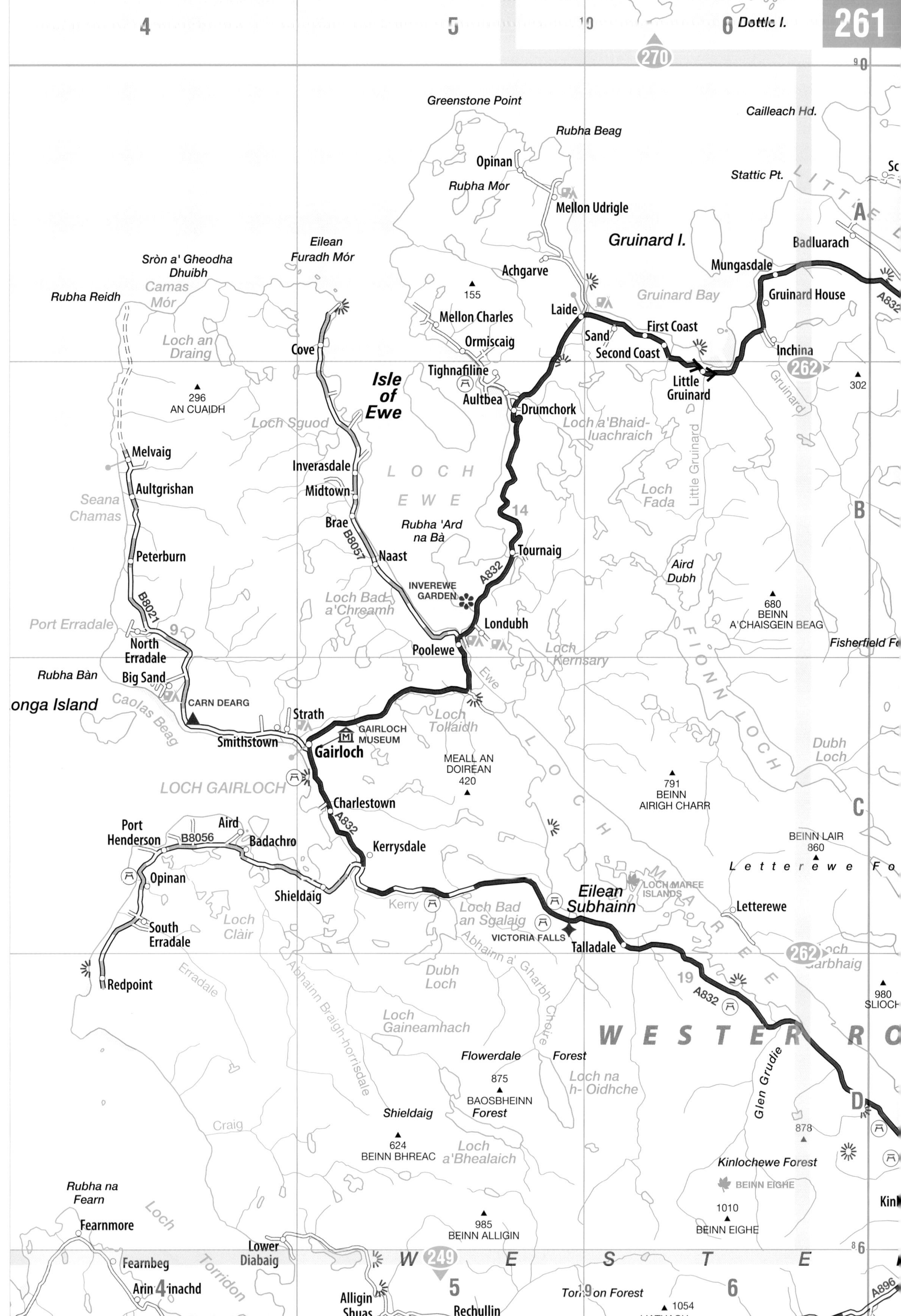

4
5
6
Dottie I.
270
Greenstone Point
Cailleach Hd.
Rubha Beag
Opinan
Rubha Mor
Static Pt.
Mellon Udrigle
Gruinard I.
Badluarach
Mungasdale
Eilean Furadh Mór
Sròn a' Gheodha Dhuibh
Camas Mór
Rubha Reidh
Achgarve
155
Gruinard Bay
Gruinard House
A832
Laide
Mellon Charles
First Coast
Sand
Ormiscaig
Second Coast
Inchina
Loch an Draing
Cove
Tighnafiline
Little Gruinard
262
302
296
AN CUAIDH
Isle of Ewe
Aultbea
Drumchork
Loch Sguod
Loch a'Bhaid-luachraich
Melvaig
Inverasdale
LOCH EWE
Little Gruinard
Loch Fada
Aultgrishan
Midtown
Seana Chamas
14
Brae
Rubha 'Ard na Bà
B8057
Naast
Tournaig
Peterburn
Aird Dubh
A832
INVEREWE GARDEN
B8021
Loch Bad a'Chreamh
680
BEINN A'CHAISGEIN BEAG
Port Erradale
Londubh
9
North Erradale
Poolewe
Loch Kernsary
Fisherfield Fo
Rubha Bàn
Big Sand
Ewe
FIONN LOCH
onga Island
Caolas Beag
CARN DEARG
Strath
Loch Tollaidh
GAIRLOCH MUSEUM
Smithstown
Gairloch
Dubh Loch
MEALL AN DOIREAN
420
791
BEINN AIRIGH CHARR
LOCH GAIRLOCH
Charlestown
Port Henderson
Aird
B8056
A832
Badachro
Kerrysdale
BEINN LAIR
860
Letterewe Fo
Opinan
Shieldaig
Kerry
Loch Bad an Sgalaig
Eilean Subhainn
LOCH MAREE ISLANDS
Letterewe
Loch Clàir
South Erradale
VICTORIA FALLS
Talladale
Abhainn a' Gharbh Choire
262
Loch Garbhaig
Erradale
Dubh Loch
19
A832
980
SLIOCH
Redpoint
Abhainn Braigh-horrisdale
Loch Gaineamhach
WESTER RO
Flowerdale Forest
Loch na h- Oidhche
Glen Grudie
875
BAOSBHEINN
Forest
Craig
Shieldaig
878
624
BEINN BHREAC
Loch a'Bhealaich
Kinlochewe Forest
BEINN EIGHE
Rubha na Fearn
Loch Torridon
1010
BEINN EIGHE
Kin
985
BEINN ALLIGIN
Fearnmore
Lower Diabaig
Fearnbeg
WESTER
249
Arinacrinachd
Alligin Shuas
Rechullin
Torridon Forest
1054
A896

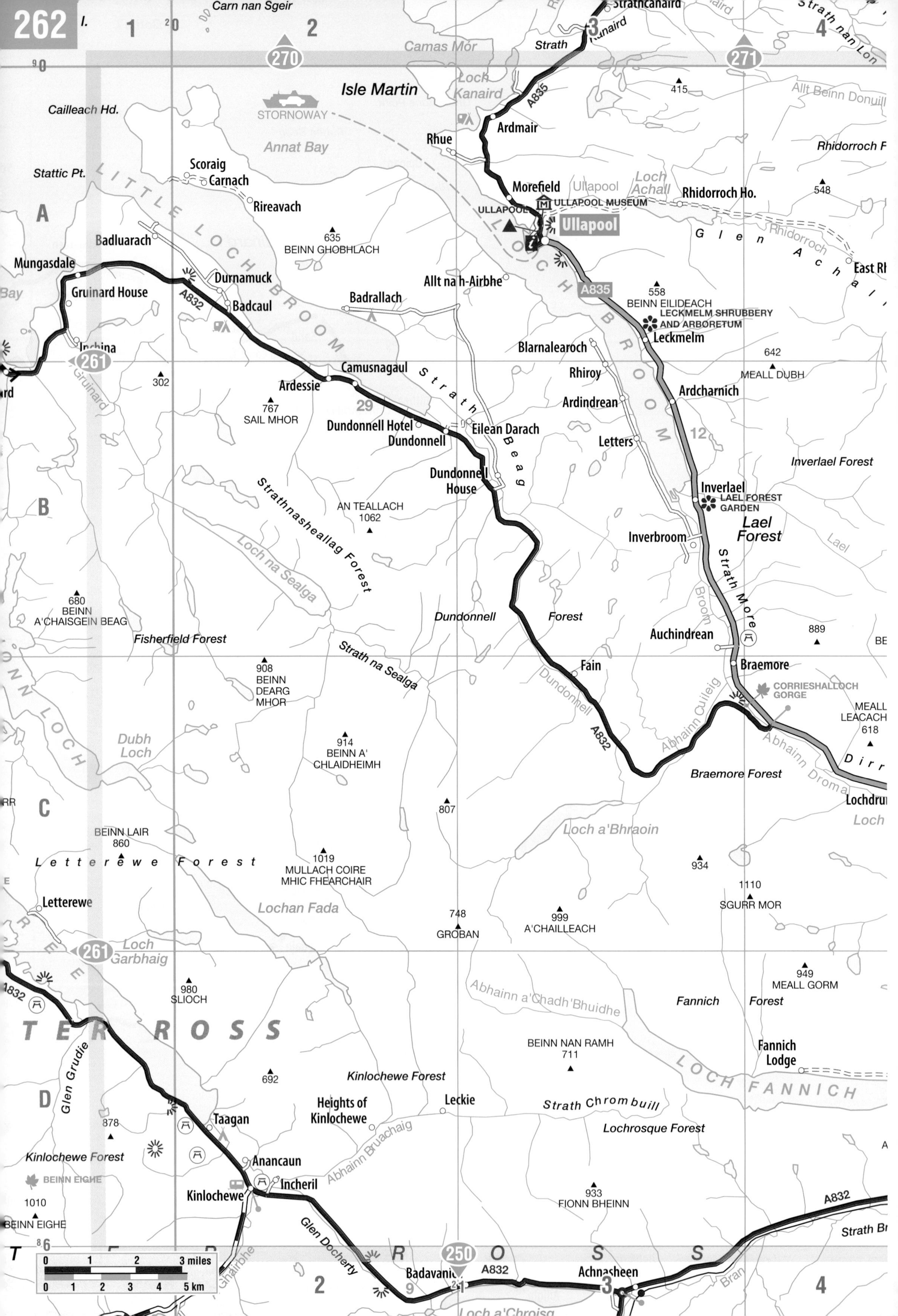
Carn nan Sgeir
Strathcanaird
Camas Mòr
Isle Martin
Loch Kanaird
A835
Ardmair
Cailleach Hd.
STORNOWAY
Annat Bay
Rhue
Scoraig
Carnach
Stattic Pt.
LITTLE LOCH BROOM
Rireavach
Morefield
Ullapool
Loch Achall
Rhidorroch Ho.
ULLAPOOL MUSEUM
Ullapool
Glen Achall
Badluarach
635
BEINN GHOBHLACH
Mungasdale
Durnamuck
Allt na h-Airbhe
Gruinard House
A832
Badcaul
Badrallach
558
BEINN EILIDEACH
LECKMELM SHRUBBERY AND ARBORETUM
Leckmelm
Inchina
Blarnalearoch
642
MEALL DUBH
Camusnagaul
Strath Beag
Rhiroy
302
Ardessie
Ardindrean
Ardcharnich
767
SAIL MHOR
Dundonnell Hotel
Dundonnell
Eilean Darach
Letters
Inverlael Forest
Dundonnell House
Inverlael
LAEL FOREST GARDEN
Strathnasheallag Forest
AN TEALLACH
1062
Lael Forest
Inverbroom
Loch na Sealga
Strath More
680
BEINN A'CHAISGEIN BEAG
Dundonnell Forest
Auchindrean
889
Fisherfield Forest
Strath na Sealga
Braemore
908
BEINN DEARG MHOR
Fain
CORRIESHALLOCH GORGE
MEALL LEACACH
618
Dubh Loch
914
BEINN A' CHLAIDHEIMH
Abhainn Cuileig
Braemore Forest
807
Lochdrum
Loch a'Bhraoin
BEINN LAIR
860
Letterewe Forest
1019
MULLACH COIRE MHIC FHEARCHAIR
934
1110
SGURR MOR
Letterewe
Lochan Fada
748
GROBAN
999
A'CHAILLEACH
Loch Garbhaig
949
MEALL GORM
980
SLIOCH
Abhainn a'Chadh'Bhuidhe
Fannich Forest
ROSS
Fannich Lodge
BEINN NAN RAMH
711
LOCH FANNICH
692
Kinlochewe Forest
Glen Grudie
Heights of Kinlochewe
Leckie
Strath Chrombuill
878
Taagan
Lochrosque Forest
Kinlochewe Forest
Anancaun
BEINN EIGHE
Incheril
Kinlochewe
Abhainn Bruachaig
933
FIONN BHEINN
1010
BEINN EIGHE
A832
Glen Docherty
Badavanich
Achnasheen
Strath Bran
Loch a'Chroisg
0 1 2 3 miles
0 1 2 3 4 5 km

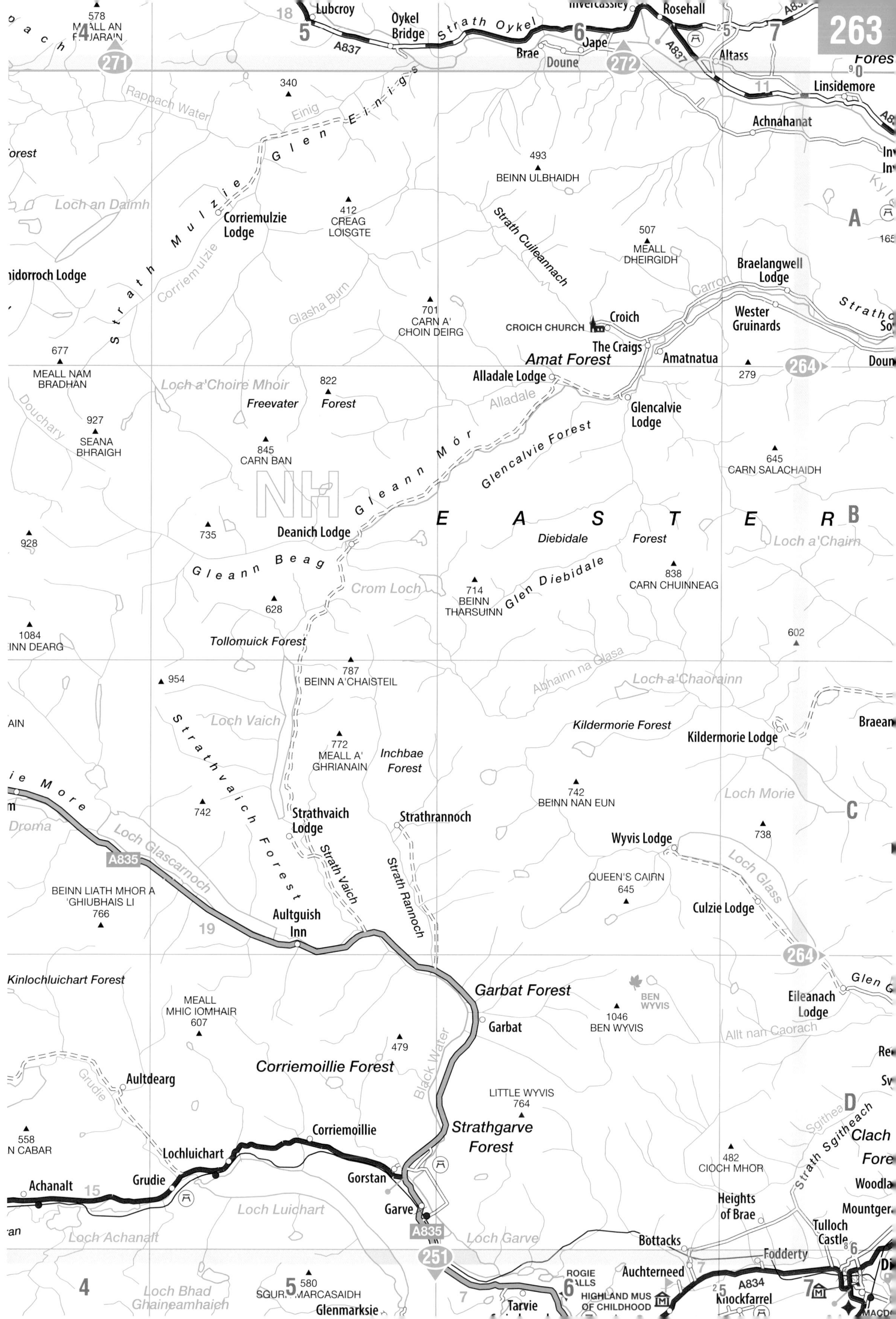
263
Lubcroy
Oykel Bridge
Strath Oykel
A837
Rosehall
Altass
Brae
Doune
Jape
578
MEALL AN F. JARAIN
271
272
Fores
Linsidemore
Achnahanat
Rappach Water
Einig
Glen Einig
340
Loch an Daimh
Corriemulzie Lodge
Strath Mulzie
Corriemulzie
412
CREAG LOISGTE
493
BEINN ULBHAIDH
Strath Cuileannach
507
MEALL DHEIRGIDH
Braelangwell Lodge
Carron
Wester Gruinards
Strath
A
165
idorroch Lodge
Glasha Burn
701
CARN A' CHOIN DEIRG
CROICH CHURCH
Croich
The Craigs
Amatnatua
Amat Forest
279
264
677
MEALL NAM BRADHAN
Loch a'Choire Mhoir
822
Freevater
Forest
Alladale Lodge
Alladale
Glencalvie Lodge
Glencalvie Forest
Douchary
927
SEANA BHRAIGH
845
CARN BAN
Gleann Mór
645
CARN SALACHAIDH
NH
EASTER
Diebidale
Forest
B
Loch a'Chairn
928
735
Deanich Lodge
Gleann Beag
Crom Loch
714
BEINN THARSUINN
Glen Diebidale
838
CARN CHUINNEAG
628
1084
INN DEARG
Tollomuick Forest
602
787
BEINN A'CHAISTEIL
954
Abhainn na Glasa
Loch a'Chaorainn
Loch Vaich
Kildermorie Forest
Kildermorie Lodge
Braean
772
MEALL A' GHRIANAIN
Inchbae Forest
742
BEINN NAN EUN
Loch Morie
Strathvaich Forest
742
Strathvaich Lodge
Strathrannoch
C
Droma
Loch Glascarnoch
A835
Wyvis Lodge
738
Loch Glass
Strath Vaich
Strath Rannoch
QUEEN'S CAIRN
645
Culzie Lodge
BEINN LIATH MHOR A 'GHIUBHAIS LI
766
Aultguish Inn
19
264
Kinlochluichart Forest
Garbat Forest
Glen
MEALL MHIC IOMHAIR
607
Garbat
BEN WYVIS
1046
BEN WYVIS
Eileanach Lodge
Allt nan Caorach
479
Corriemoillie Forest
Black Water
Aultdearg
Grudie
LITTLE WYVIS
764
D
Sgitheach
Strath Sgitheach
Clach Fore
558
N CABAR
Corriemoillie
Strathgarve Forest
482
CIOCH MHOR
Lochluichart
Achanalt
Grudie
15
Gorstan
Garve
Loch Luichart
Woodla
Heights of Brae
Mountger
Loch Achanalt
A835
Loch Garve
Bottacks
Tulloch Castle
251
Fodderty
4
Loch Bhad Ghaineamhaich
580
SGURR MARCASAIDH
5
Glenmarksie
Tarvie
ROGIE FALLS
6
HIGHLAND MUS OF CHILDHOOD
Auchterneed
A834
Knockfarrel
7
MACD

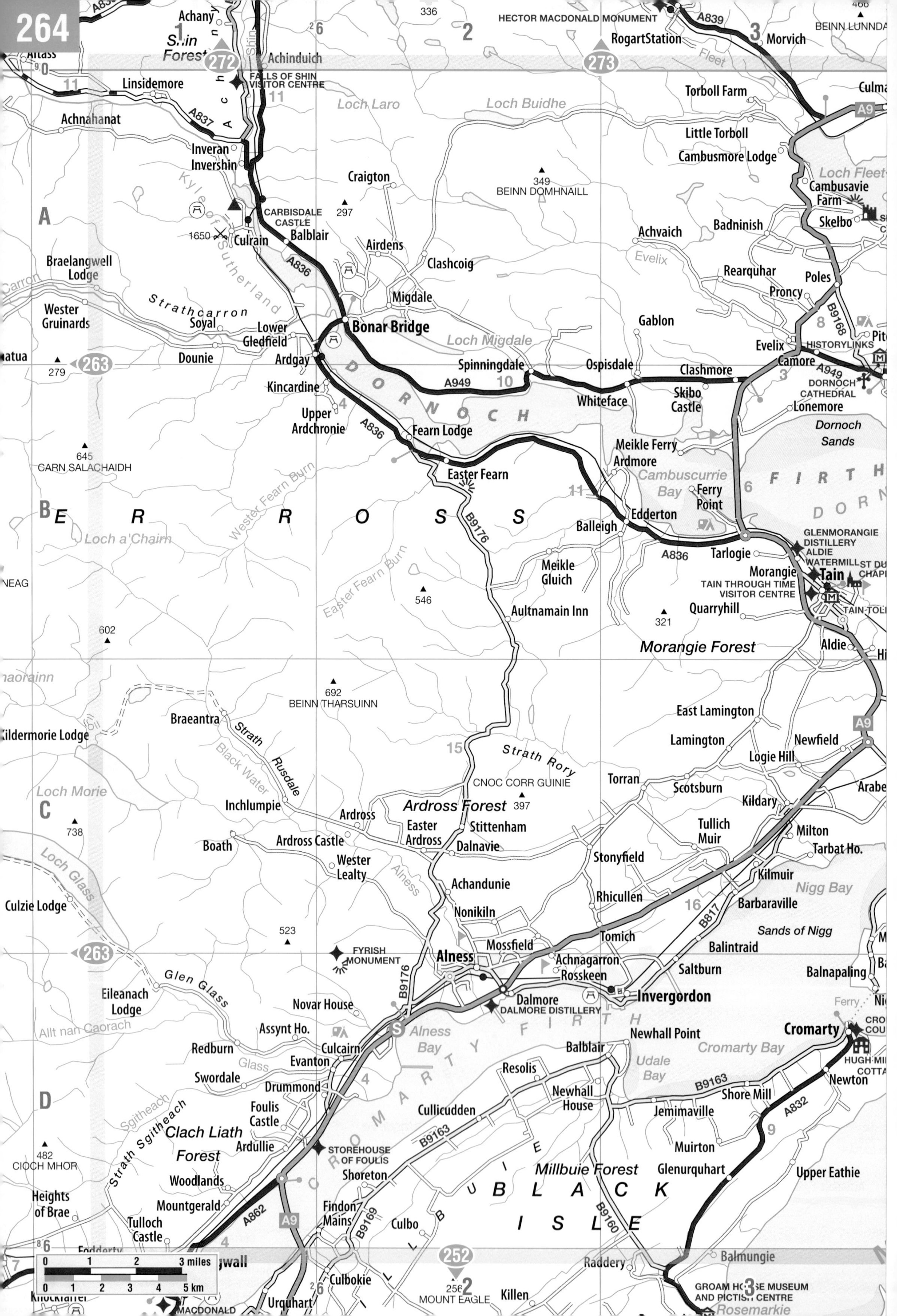
Achany
Shin Forest
272
Achinduich
FALLS OF SHIN VISITOR CENTRE
336
HECTOR MACDONALD MONUMENT
Rogart Station
273
A839
Morvich
BEINN LUNNDA
Altass
Linsidemore
A837
Achnahanat
Loch Laro
Loch Buidhe
Torboll Farm
A9
Little Torboll
Cambusmore Lodge
Loch Fleet
Inveran
Invershin
Kyle of Sutherland
Craigton
349
BEINN DOMHNAILL
Cambusavie Farm
Skelbo
CARBISDALE CASTLE
297
1650
Culrain
Balblair
Airdens
Achvaich
Badninish
Braelangwell Lodge
A836
Clashcoig
Evelix
Rearquhar
Poles
Proncy
Migdale
Wester Gruinards
Strathcarron
Soyal
Lower Gledfield
Bonar Bridge
Gablon
B9168
Loch Migdale
Evelix
HISTORYLINKS
279
263
Dounie
Ardgay
Spinningdale
Ospisdale
Clashmore
Camore
A949
DORNOCH CATHEDRAL
Kincardine
A949
DORNOCH
Whiteface
Skibo Castle
Lonemore
Upper Ardchronie
A836
Fearn Lodge
Dornoch Sands
645
CARN SALACHAIDH
Meikle Ferry
Ardmore
Easter Fearn
Cambuscurrie Bay
FIRTH
Ferry Point
Wester Fearn Burn
Balleigh
Edderton
ROSS
B9176
Loch a'Chairn
GLENMORANGIE DISTILLERY
ALDIE WATERMILL
A836
Tarlogie
Meikle Gluich
Morangie
Tain
TAIN THROUGH TIME VISITOR CENTRE
Easter Fearn Burn
546
Aultnamain Inn
321
Quarryhill
602
Morangie Forest
Aldie
692
BEINN THARSUINN
East Lamington
Braeantra
Strath Rusdale
Kildermorie Lodge
A9
Lamington
Newfield
Black Water
Strath Rory
Logie Hill
CNOC CORR GUINIE
Torran
Scotsburn
Loch Morie
Inchlumpie
Ardross Forest
397
Kildary
738
Ardross
Easter Ardross
Stittenham
Tullich Muir
Milton
Boath
Ardross Castle
Dalnavie
Tarbat Ho.
Loch Glass
Wester Lealty
Alness
Stonyfield
Kilmuir
Achandunie
Nigg Bay
Rhicullen
Culzie Lodge
Nonikiln
B817
Barbaraville
Sands of Nigg
523
Tomich
Balintraid
263
FYRISH MONUMENT
Mossfield
Alness
Achnagarron
Saltburn
Rosskeen
Balnapaling
Glen Glass
Eileanach Lodge
B9176
Dalmore
Invergordon
DALMORE DISTILLERY
Novar House
Ferry
Allt nan Caorach
Assynt Ho.
Alness Bay
CROMARTY FIRTH
Newhall Point
Cromarty
Redburn
Culcairn
Balblair
Cromarty Bay
Evanton
Udale Bay
Swordale
Resolis
Drummond
Newhall House
B9163
Shore Mill
Newton
Foulis Castle
Cullicudden
Jemimaville
A832
Clach Liath Forest
Strath Sgitheach
Ardullie
B9163
STOREHOUSE OF FOULIS
Muirton
482
CIOCH MHOR
Shoreton
Millbuie Forest
Glenurquhart
Upper Eathie
Woodlands
BLACK ISLE
Heights of Brae
Mountgerald
A862
A9
Findon Mains
B9169
Culbo
B9160
Tulloch Castle
Foddertv
252
Raddery
Balmungie
Dingwall
Culbokie
256
MOUNT EAGLE
Killen
GROAM HOUSE MUSEUM AND PICTISH CENTRE
Urquhart
MACDONALD
Rosemarkie
0 1 2 3 miles
0 1 2 3 4 5 km

DUNROBIN CASTLE MUSEUM & GARDENS
274
Golspie
Kirkton
LOCH FLEET
Littleferry
Fourpenny
Embo
Embo Street
WITCHES STONE CARNEGIE
Dornoch
NH
NJ
A
B
C
D
Tarbat Ness
TARBAT NESS LIGHTHOUSE
Wilkhaven
Whiteness Sands
LOCH FIRTH
TARBAT DISCOVERY CENTRE
Bindal
Portmahomack
Rockfield
Inver
Arboll
Balnagall
Tarrel
Lochslin
Loch Eye
Geanies House
Rhynie
Fearn Station
B9165
Fearn
Hill of Fearn
B9166
FEARN ABBEY
Hilton of Cadboll
Loans of Tullich
Balintore
SHANDWICK STONE
Shandwick
B9175
Ankerville
Chapelhill
Pitcalnie
Port an Righ
Nigg
203
King's Cave
Castlecraig
Sutors of Cromarty
MORAY FIRTH
266
Burghead
BURGHEAD BAY
Lower Hempriggs
Findhorn
B9011
Findhorn Bay
Miltonhill
Kincorth Ho.
KINLOSS ABBEY
Kinloss
Culbin Forest
Grange Hall
The Bar
Kintessack
Springfield
A96
SUENO'S STONE
Moy Ho.
Mains of B
253
NELSON TOWER
Forres
Whiteness Head
NAIRN MUSEUM
BRODIE CASTLE
Dyke
Blervie
4
5
6
30
90
31

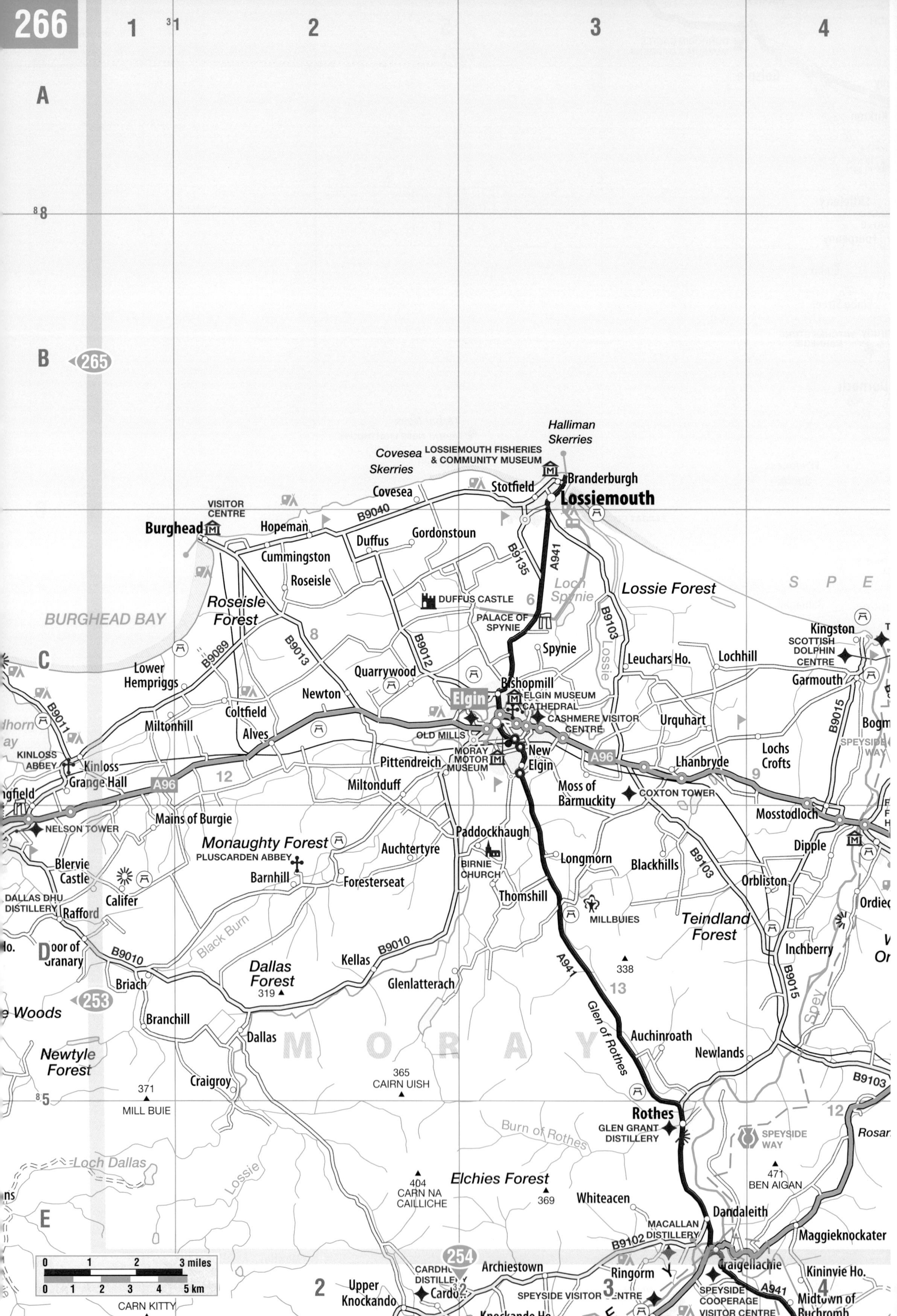
1
2
3
4
A
B
C
D
E
265
253
254
Halliman Skerries
Covesea Skerries
LOSSIEMOUTH FISHERIES & COMMUNITY MUSEUM
Branderburgh
Lossiemouth
Stotfield
Covesea
VISITOR CENTRE
Burghead
Hopeman
B9040
Duffus
Gordonstoun
Cummingston
Roseisle
B9135
A941
Loch Spynie
Lossie Forest
S P E
Roseisle Forest
DUFFUS CASTLE
PALACE OF SPYNIE
BURGHEAD BAY
B9089
B9013
B9012
B9103
Spynie
Lossie
Leuchars Ho.
Lochhill
Kingston
SCOTTISH DOLPHIN CENTRE
Garmouth
Lower Hempriggs
Quarrywood
Newton
Bishopmill
Elgin
ELGIN MUSEUM
CATHEDRAL
CASHMERE VISITOR CENTRE
Urquhart
B9015
Coltfield
Miltonhill
Alves
B9011
Kinloss
KINLOSS ABBEY
Grange Hall
A96
OLD MILLS
MORAY MOTOR MUSEUM
New Elgin
Pittendreich
Miltonduff
Lhanbryde
Lochs Crofts
SPEYSIDE WAY
Moss of Barmuckity
COXTON TOWER
Mosstodloch
NELSON TOWER
Mains of Burgie
Monaughty Forest
PLUSCARDEN ABBEY
Auchtertyre
Paddockhaugh
BIRNIE CHURCH
Longmorn
Blackhills
Dipple
Orbliston
Blervie Castle
Barnhill
Foresterseat
Califer
DALLAS DHU DISTILLERY
Rafford
Thomshill
MILLBUIES
Teindland Forest
Black Burn
B9010
Kellas
Dallas Forest
319
Glenlatterach
338
Inchberry
Briach
A941
13
Glen of Rothes
Branchill
Dallas
M O R A Y
Auchinroath
Newlands
Newtyle Forest
Craigroy
365 CAIRN UISH
371 MILL BUIE
Rothes
GLEN GRANT DISTILLERY
Burn of Rothes
B9103
SPEYSIDE WAY
471 BEN AIGAN
Loch Dallas
Lossie
404 CARN NA CAILLICHE
Elchies Forest
369
Whiteacen
Dandaleith
MACALLAN DISTILLERY
B9102
Maggieknockater
Archiestown
Ringorm
Craigellachie
Kininvie Ho.
Upper Knockando
CARDHU DISTILLERY
SPEYSIDE VISITOR CENTRE
SPEYSIDE COOPERAGE VISITOR CENTRE
A941
Midtown of Buchromb
CARN KITTY
0 1 2 3 miles
0 1 2 3 4 5 km

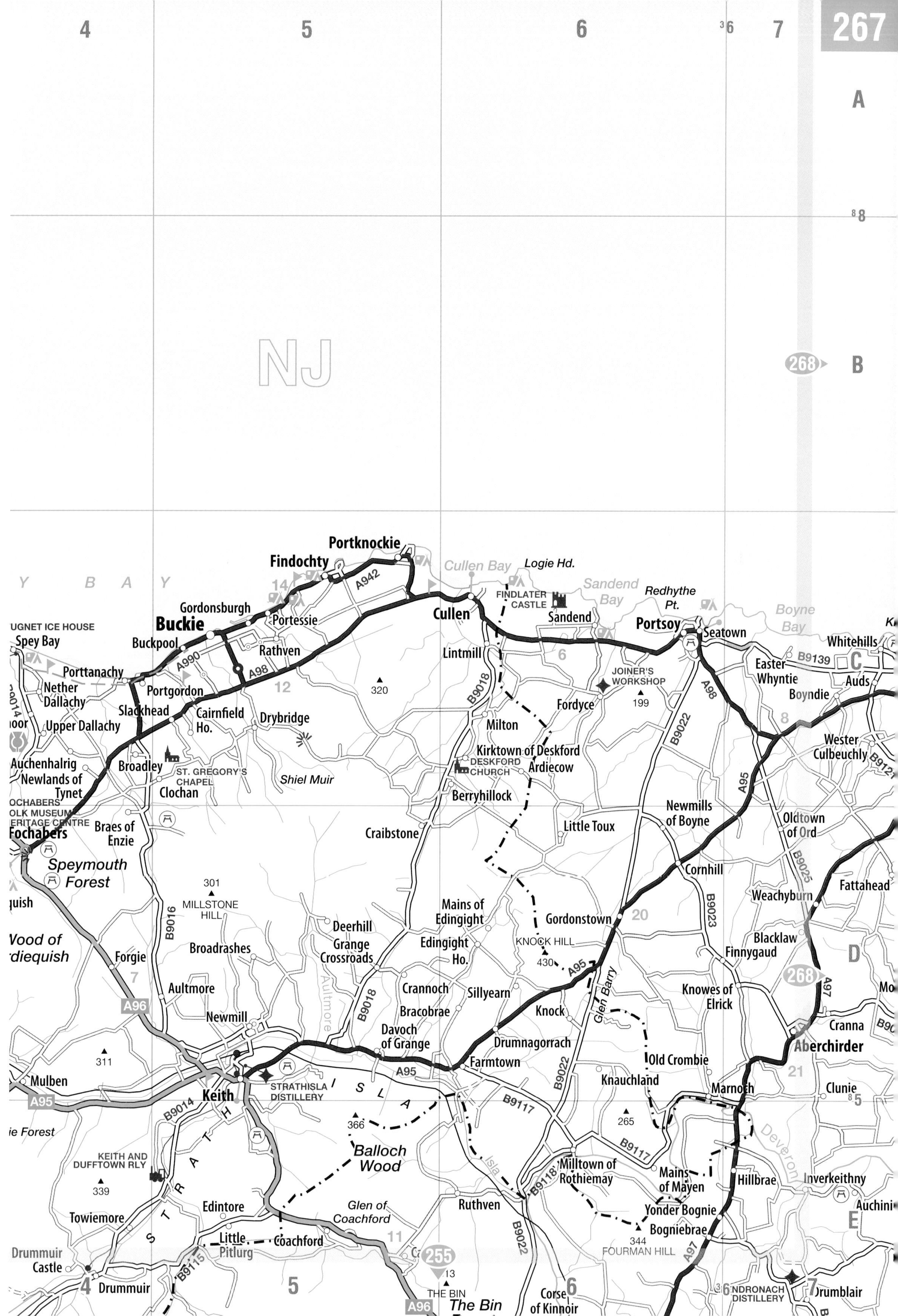

NJ
Portknockie
Findochty
Cullen Bay
Logie Hd.
Sandend Bay
Redhythe Pt.
Boyne Bay
FINDLATER CASTLE
Sandend
Portsoy
Seatown
Gordonsburgh
Buckie
Portessie
Cullen
Buckpool
Rathven
Lintmill
Whitehills
Spey Bay
Porttanachy
Nether Dallachy
Portgordon
Slackhead
Cairnfield Ho.
Drybridge
Upper Dallachy
Milton
Fordyce
JOINER'S WORKSHOP
Easter Whyntie
Boyndie
Auds
Kirktown of Deskford
DESKFORD CHURCH
Ardiecow
Berryhillock
Auchenhalrig
Newlands of Tynet
Broadley
ST. GREGORY'S CHAPEL
Clochan
Shiel Muir
Wester Culbeuchly
Braes of Enzie
Fochabers
Speymouth Forest
Craibstone
Little Toux
Newmills of Boyne
Oldtown of Ord
Cornhill
MILLSTONE HILL
Mains of Edingight
Gordonstown
Weachyburn
Fattahead
Deerhill
Grange Crossroads
Edingight Ho.
KNOCK HILL
Blacklaw
Finnygaud
Broadrashes
Forgie
Aultmore
Crannoch
Sillyearn
Bracobrae
Knock
Glen Barry
Knowes of Elrick
Newmill
Davoch of Grange
Drumnagorrach
Aberchirder
Cranna
Farmtown
Old Crombie
Mulben
Keith
STRATHISLA DISTILLERY
ISLA
Knauchland
Marnoch
Clunie
Balloch Wood
KEITH AND DUFFTOWN RLY
Milltown of Rothiemay
Mains of Mayen
Hillbrae
Inverkeithny
Deveron
Edintore
Glen of Coachford
Ruthven
Yonder Bognie
Towiemore
Bogniebrae
FOURMAN HILL
Little Pitlurg
Coachford
Drummuir Castle
Drummuir
THE BIN
The Bin
Corse of Kinnoir
GLENDRONACH DISTILLERY
Drumblair
A942
A990
A98
A95
A96
A97
B9018
B9022
B9016
B9014
B9115
B9117
B9118
B9023
B9025
B9139
268
255

1
2
3
A
B
C
D
E
267
267
256
Troup Hd.
Pennan Hd.
Quarry Hd
Boyne Bay
Knock Hd.
Boyndie Bay
Gamrie Bay
Head of Garness
Seatown
Whitehills
Macduff
MACDUFF MARINE AQUARIUM
Crovie
Gardenstown
Pennan
Easter Whyntie
B9139
Inverboyndie
Auds
Boyndie
Banff
BANFF MUSEUM
Easter Silverford
B9031
Dubford
Towie
B9031
New Aberdour
DUFF HOUSE
West Greenskares
Longmanhill
Wester Culbeuchly
Doune Park
Cushnie
231 WINDY HEADS HILL
B9121
A97
A95
A98
Montcoffer Ho.
A947
A98
Minnonie
Ladysford
Nether Glasslaw
Oldtown of Ord
Kirktown of Alvah
Keilhill
Netherbrae
Mid Cloch Forbie
Craigmaud
B9025
B9121
Greenlaw
Gorrachie
227 HILL OF FISHRIE
Fattahead
King Edward
New Pitsligo
B9023
Weachyburn
The Pole of Itlaw
Milltown of Craigston
B9105
Blacklaw
Plaidy
Craigston Castle
Hill of Mountblairy
Fintry
New Byth
Bonnykelly
A97
Muirden
A950
B9027
Cranna
B9025
Garmond
Whitestones
Ironside
Aberchirder
Forglen Ho.
A947
Muiryfold
Bogton
Balthangie
Oldwhat
Marnoch
Clunie
Carnousie
Deveron
Turriff
DELGATIE CASTLE
Cuminestown
Mains of Fedderate
Kirkton
Little Colp
Middle Cairncake
Culsh
Deveron
Mill of Muiresk
B9170
Delgaty Forest
B9170
A981
Hillbrae
Inverkeithny
Hatton Castle
Howe of Teuchar
New Deer
Auchininna
Darra
Rush-head
B9024
Birkenhills
Brownhill
Crofts of Inverthernie
Cairnbanno Ho.
Knaven
B9170
Dykeside
179
South Millbrex
0 1 2 3 miles
0 1 2 3 4 5 km

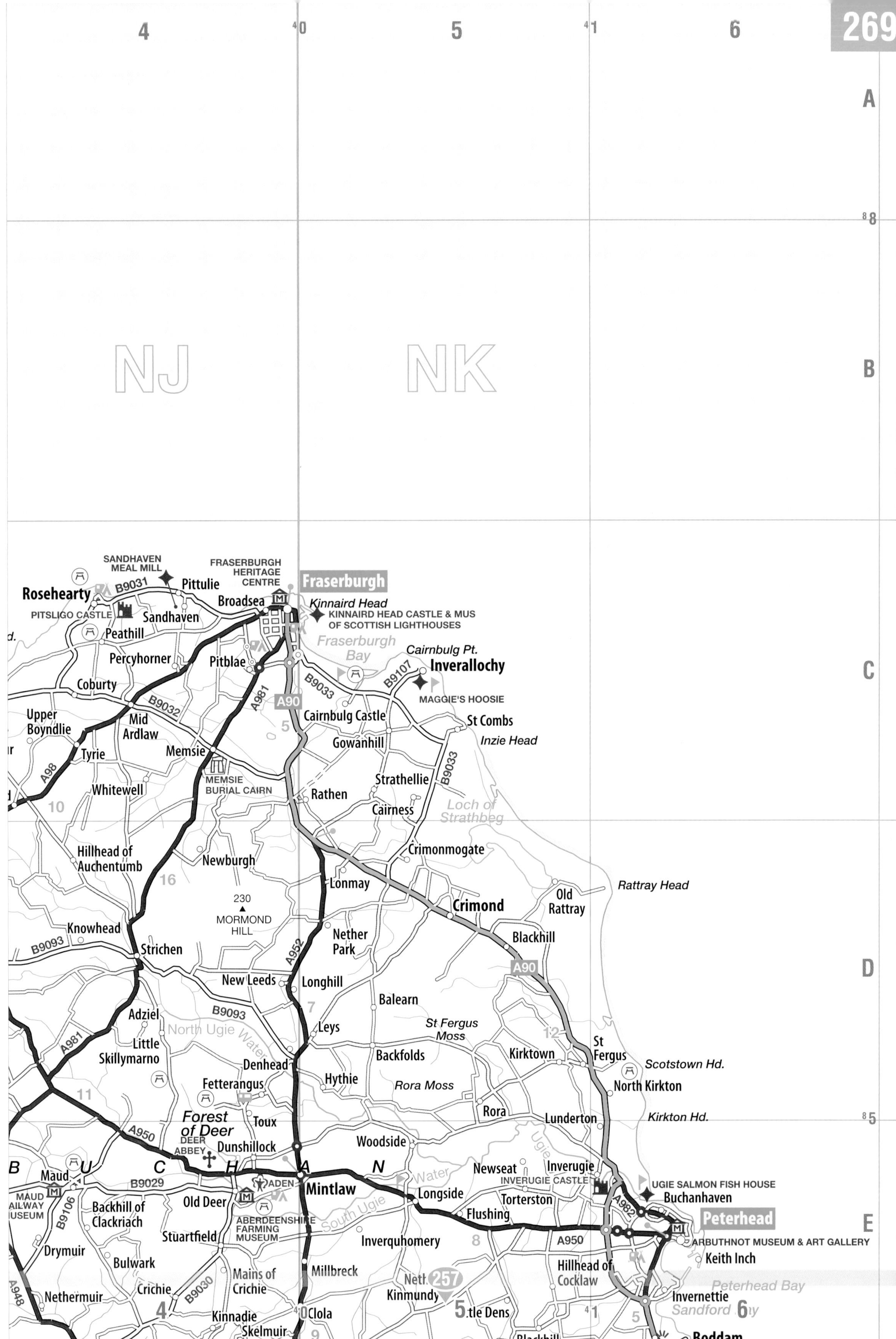

NJ
NK
SANDHAVEN MEAL MILL
FRASERBURGH HERITAGE CENTRE
Fraserburgh
Rosehearty
Pittulie
Broadsea
Kinnaird Head
KINNAIRD HEAD CASTLE & MUS OF SCOTTISH LIGHTHOUSES
PITSLIGO CASTLE
Sandhaven
Peathill
Fraserburgh Bay
Cairnbulg Pt.
Inverallochy
Percyhorner
Pitblae
Coburty
MAGGIE'S HOOSIE
Upper Boyndlie
Mid Ardlaw
Cairnbulg Castle
St Combs
Inzie Head
Tyrie
Memsie
Gowanhill
MEMSIE BURIAL CAIRN
Strathellie
Whitewell
Rathen
Cairness
Loch of Strathbeg
Hillhead of Auchentumb
Newburgh
Crimonmogate
Lonmay
Rattray Head
Old Rattray
Crimond
230
MORMOND HILL
Knowhead
Nether Park
Blackhill
Strichen
New Leeds
Longhill
Balearn
Adziel
North Ugie Water
Leys
St Fergus Moss
Little Skillymarno
Denhead
Backfolds
Kirktown
St Fergus
Scotstown Hd.
Hythie
Rora Moss
North Kirkton
Fetterangus
Forest of Deer
Toux
Rora
Lunderton
Kirkton Hd.
DEER ABBEY
Dunshillock
Woodside
Maud
Newseat
Inverugie
INVERUGIE CASTLE
UGIE SALMON FISH HOUSE
Buchanhaven
MAUD RAILWAY MUSEUM
ADEN
Mintlaw
Longside
Torterston
Peterhead
Backhill of Clackriach
Old Deer
Flushing
ABERDEENSHIRE FARMING MUSEUM
South Ugie Water
ARBUTHNOT MUSEUM & ART GALLERY
Stuartfield
Inverquhomery
Drymuir
Keith Inch
Bulwark
Millbreck
Hillhead of Cocklaw
Mains of Crichie
Peterhead Bay
Nethermuir
Crichie
Kinmundy
Invernettie
Sandford
Kinnadie
Clola
Boddam
Skelmuir
B9031
B9032
B9033
B9107
B9093
B9029
B9106
B9030
A98
A981
A90
A952
A950
A982
A948
257

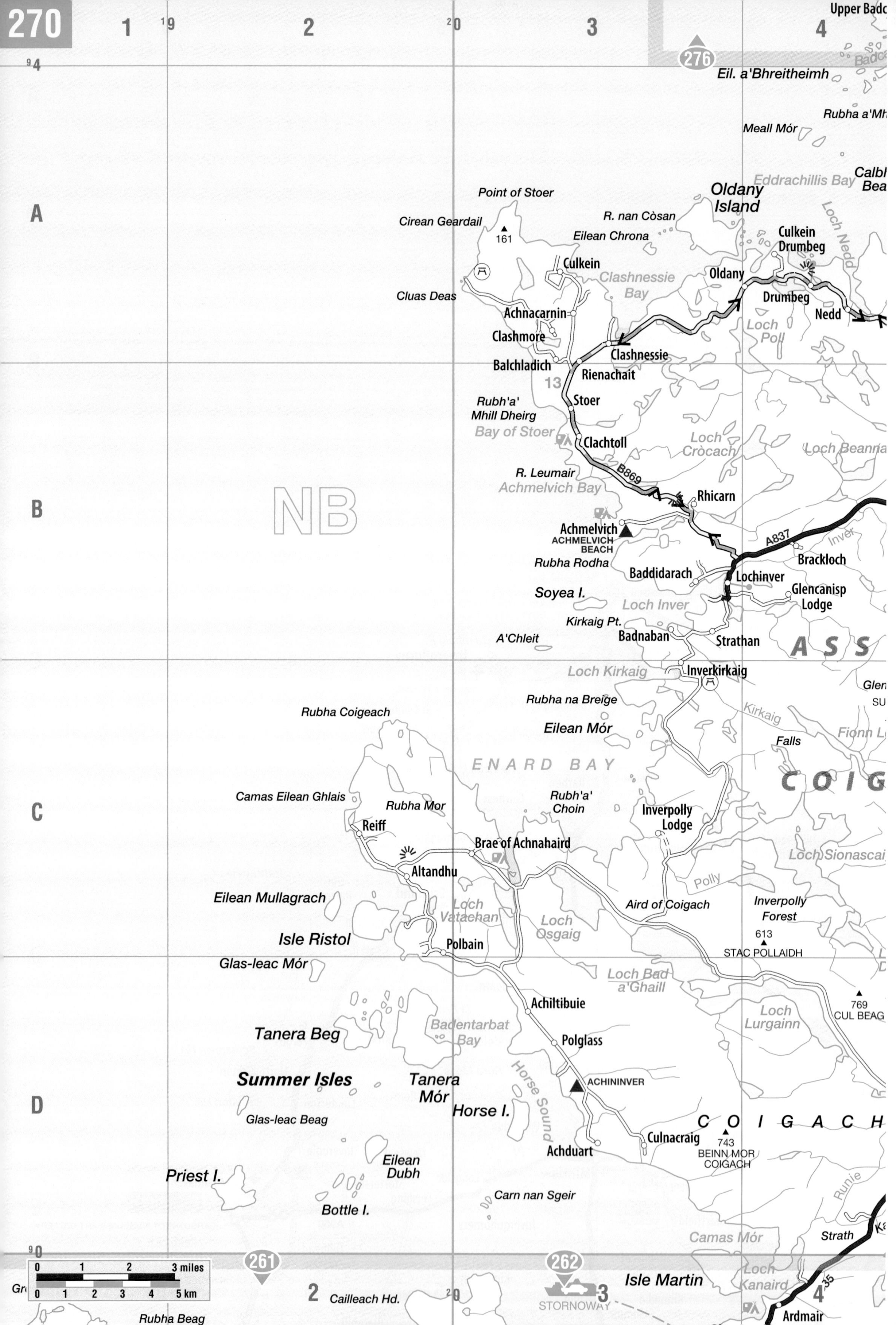

Upper Badc
276
Eil. a'Bhreitheimh
Rubha a'Mh
Meall Mór
Eddrachillis Bay
Calbh Bea
Point of Stoer
Oldany Island
Loch Nedd
R. nan Còsan
Cirean Geardail
161
Eilean Chrona
Culkein Drumbeg
Culkein
Oldany
Clashnessie Bay
Cluas Deas
Drumbeg
Nedd
Achnacarnin
Loch Poll
Clashmore
Clashnessie
Balchladich
Rienachait
13
Rubh'a' Mhill Dheirg
Stoer
Bay of Stoer
Clachtoll
Loch Cròcach
Loch Beanna
R. Leumair
B869
Achmelvich Bay
NB
Rhicarn
Achmelvich
ACHMELVICH BEACH
A837
Inver
Brackloch
Rubha Rodha
Baddidarach
Lochinver
Soyea I.
Glencanisp Lodge
Loch Inver
Kirkaig Pt.
A'Chleit
Badnaban
Strathan
ASS
Loch Kirkaig
Inverkirkaig
Glen
SU
Rubha na Breige
Rubha Coigeach
Kirkaig
Eilean Mór
Falls
Fionn L
ENARD BAY
COIG
Camas Eilean Ghlais
Rubh'a' Choin
Rubha Mor
Inverpolly Lodge
Reiff
Brae of Achnahaird
Altandhu
Loch Sionascai
Polly
Eilean Mullagrach
Loch Vatachan
Aird of Coigach
Inverpolly Forest
Loch Osgaig
Isle Ristol
613
STAC POLLAIDH
Polbain
Glas-leac Mór
Loch Bad a'Ghaill
769
CUL BEAG
Achiltibuie
Loch Lurgainn
Badentarbat Bay
Tanera Beg
Polglass
Horse Sound
Summer Isles
Tanera Mór
ACHININVER
Horse I.
COIGACH
Glas-leac Beag
743
BEINN MOR COIGACH
Culnacraig
Achduart
Eilean Dubh
Priest I.
Runie
Carn nan Sgeir
Bottle I.
Camas Mór
Strath
0 1 2 3 miles
0 1 2 3 4 5 km
261
262
Isle Martin
Loch Kanaird
Cailleach Hd.
STORNOWAY
A835
Rubha Beag
Ardmair

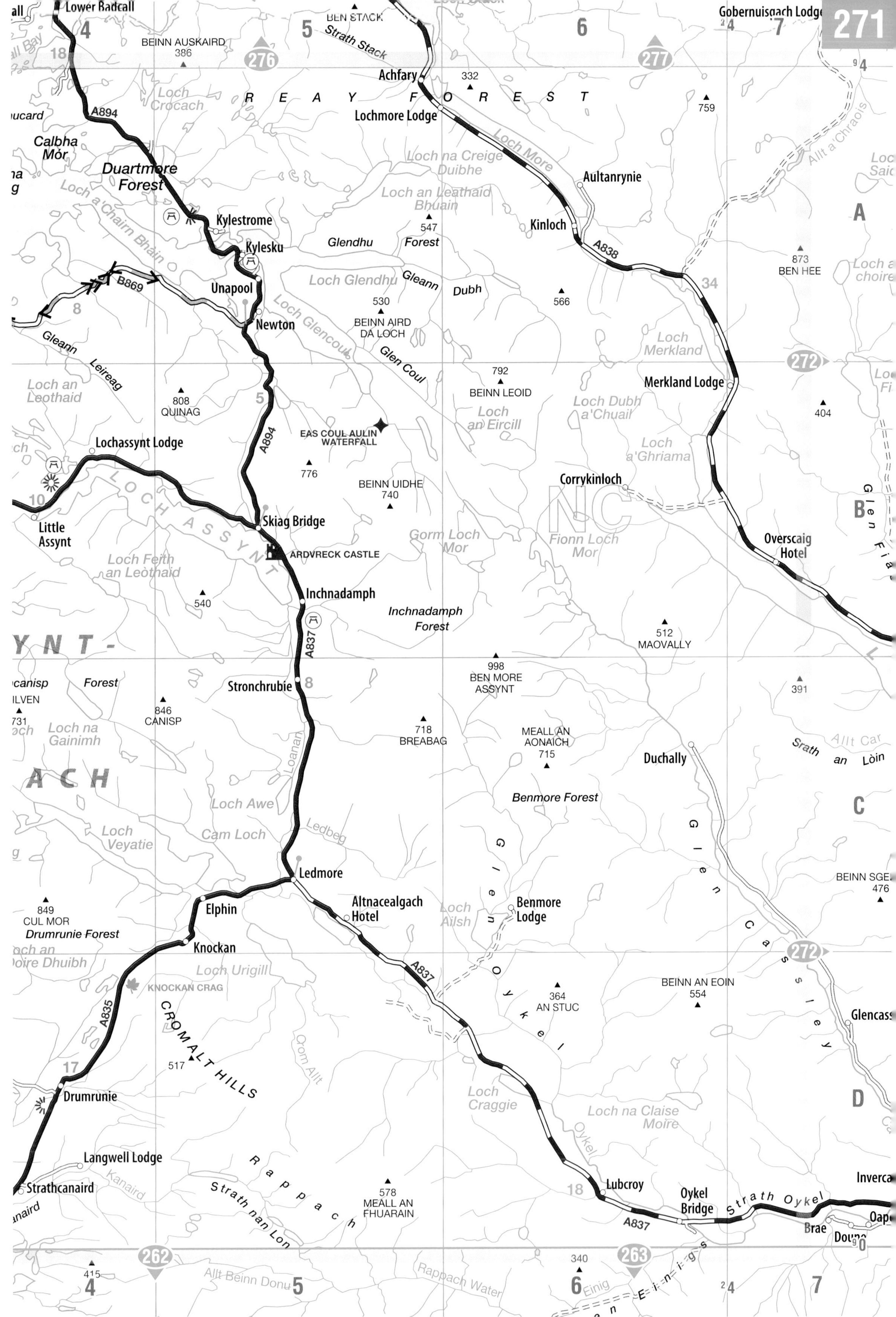
Lower Badcall
BEN STACK
Strath Stack
Gobernuisgach Lodge
BEINN AUSKAIRD
386
276
277
Achfary
332
Loch Crocach
R E A Y F O R E S T
759
A894
Lochmore Lodge
Calbha Mór
Loch More
Loch na Creige Duibhe
Duartmore Forest
Aultanrynie
Loch a'Chairn Bhain
Loch an Leathaid Bhuain
Allt a Chraois
Kylestrome
547
Kinloch
Kylesku
Glendhu
Forest
A838
873
BEN HEE
Unapool
Loch Glendhu
Gleann Dubh
34
B869
530
BEINN AIRD DA LOCH
566
Newton
Loch Glencoul
Loch Merkland
Gleann Leireag
Glen Coul
792
BEINN LEOID
272
Merkland Lodge
Loch an Leothaid
808
QUINAG
Loch an Eircill
Loch Dubh a'Chuail
404
A894
EAS COUL AULIN WATERFALL
Loch a'Ghriama
Lochassynt Lodge
776
BEINN UIDHE
740
Corrykinloch
LOCH ASSYNT
NC
Glen Fiag
Skiag Bridge
Little Assynt
Gorm Loch Mor
Fionn Loch Mor
Overscaig Hotel
Loch Feith an Leòthaid
ARDVRECK CASTLE
Inchnadamph
540
Inchnadamph Forest
A837
512
MAOVALLY
998
BEN MORE ASSYNT
Forest
Stronchrubie
391
846
CANISP
Loch na Gainimh
718
BREABAG
MEALL AN AONAICH
715
Allt Car
Strath an Lòin
Duchally
Loanan
Loch Awe
Benmore Forest
Loch Veyatie
Cam Loch
Ledbeg
Glen Cassley
Ledmore
BEINN SGE
476
849
CUL MOR
Altnacealgach Hotel
Elphin
Loch Ailsh
Benmore Lodge
Glen Oykel
Drumrunie Forest
Knockan
A837
Loch Urigill
KNOCKAN CRAG
364
AN STUC
BEINN AN EOIN
554
A835
CROMALT HILLS
Crom Allt
Glencass
517
Drumrunie
Loch Craggie
Loch na Claise Moire
Oykel
Langwell Lodge
Rappach
Strathcanaird
Kanaird
Strath nan Lon
578
MEALL AN FHUARAIN
Lubcroy
Oykel Bridge
Strath Oykel
Inverca
A837
Brae
Oape
Doune
262
263
415
Allt Beinn Donu
Rappach Water
340
Einig

Gobernuisgach Lodge
Loch Meadie
277
FOREST
Loch More
Aultanrynie
Kinloch
A838
A836
Mudale
Altnaharra
B873
Clebrig
Loch Coire na Saidhe Duibhe
Allt a'Chraois
Meadie Burn
873 BEN HEE
Loch a'Ghorm-choire
566
Dubh
Loch Merkland
Merkland Lodge
271
Loch Fiag
404
473
Strath Vagastie
Klibreck Burn
961 MEALL NAN CON
792 BEINN LEOID
Loch an Eircill
Loch Dubh a'Chuail
Loch a'Ghriama
Corrykinloch
312 CNOC AN ALASKIE
542
Crask Inn
Glen Fiag
Fiag Plantation
Fionn Loch Mor
Overscaig Hotel
Loch Gaineamhach
512 MAOVALLY
Fiag Bridge
Strath Tirry
998 BEN MORE ASSYNT
391
LOCH SHIN
MEALL AN AONAICH 715
Duchally
Srath an Lòin
Allt Car
Rhian
Benmore Forest
Shinness
Glen Cassley
Achnairn
Allt a'Bhunn
BEINN SGEIREACH 476
Benmore Lodge
Loch Ailsh
Glen Oykel
Dalchork
Colaboll
364 AN STUC
BEINN AN EOIN 554
Saval
Sallachy
Glencassley Castle
Lairg Lodge
Lairg
Loch na Fuaralaich
FERRYCROFT VISITOR CENTRE
Loch Craggie
Loch na Claise Moire
Glenrossal
402 CNOC A'CHOIRE
Claonel
Gruids
Grudie Burn
Oykel Forest
Lubcroy
Invercassley
Rosehall
A839
Achany
B864
Oykel Bridge
Strath Oykel
A837
Brae
Oape
Altass
Shin Forest
Doune
263
Achinduich
FALLS OF SHIN VISITOR CENTRE
Linsidemore
Achnahanat
0 1 2 3 miles
0 1 2 3 4 5 km

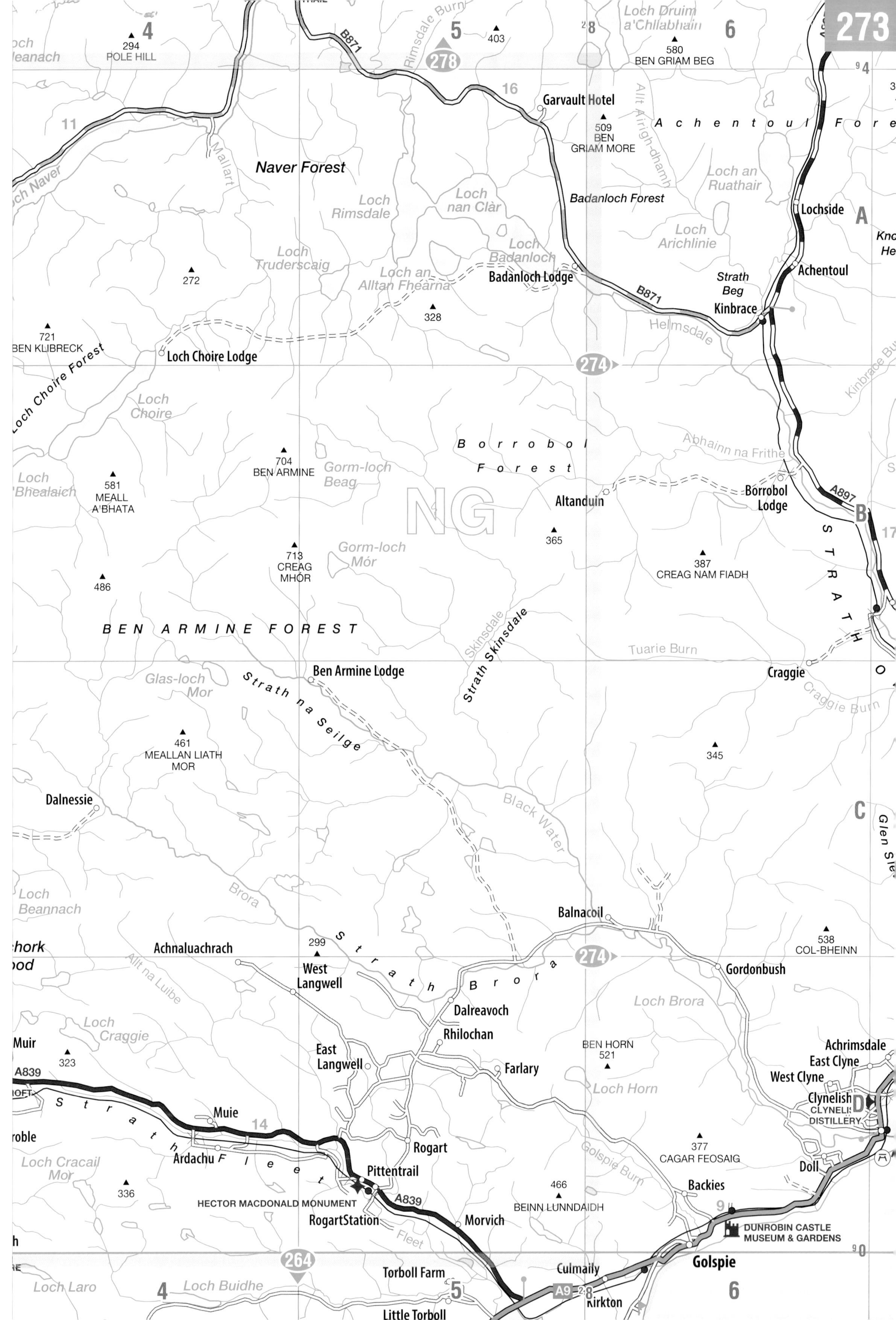
294
POLE HILL
Rimsdale Burn
B871
278
403
Loch Druim a'Chllabhain
580
BEN GRIAM BEG
16
Garvault Hotel
11
509
BEN
GRIAM MORE
Allt Airigh-dhamh
Achentoul Forest
Mallart
Naver Forest
Loch an Ruathair
Loch Rimsdale
Loch nan Clàr
Badanloch Forest
Lochside
A
Loch Arichlinie
Loch Truderscaig
Loch Badanloch
272
Loch an Alltan Fhearna
Badanloch Lodge
Achentoul
Strath Beg
Kinbrace
328
721
BEN KLIBRECK
Helmsdale
Loch Choire Lodge
274
Loch Choire Forest
Loch Choire
Kinbrace Burn
Borrobol Forest
704
BEN ARMINE
Gorm-loch Beag
Abhainn na Frithe
581
MEALL A'BHATA
NG
Altanduin
Borrobol Lodge
A897
B
365
STRATH
713
CREAG MHÓR
Gorm-loch Mór
387
CREAG NAM FIADH
486
BEN ARMINE FOREST
Skinsdale
Strath Skinsdale
Tuarie Burn
Ben Armine Lodge
Craggie
Glas-loch Mor
Strath na Seilge
Craggie Burn
461
MEALLAN LIATH MOR
345
Black Water
Dalnessie
C
Loch Beannach
Brora
Balnacoil
299
Achnaluachrach
Strath Brora
538
COL-BHEINN
West Langwell
Gordonbush
Allt na Luibe
Dalreavoch
Loch Brora
Loch Craggie
Rhilochan
Muir
323
East Langwell
BEN HORN
521
Achrimsdale
East Clyne
A839
Farlary
West Clyne
Loch Horn
Clynelish
CLYNELISH DISTILLERY
D
Strath Fleet
Muie
14
Rogart
377
CAGAR FEOSAIG
Ardachu
Golspie Burn
Loch Cracail Mor
Pittentrail
Doll
336
466
Backies
HECTOR MACDONALD MONUMENT
A839
BEINN LUNNDAIDH
RogartStation
Morvich
DUNROBIN CASTLE MUSEUM & GARDENS
Fleet
264
Torboll Farm
Culmaily
Golspie
Loch Laro
Loch Buidhe
A9
Kirkton
Little Torboll
4
5
6

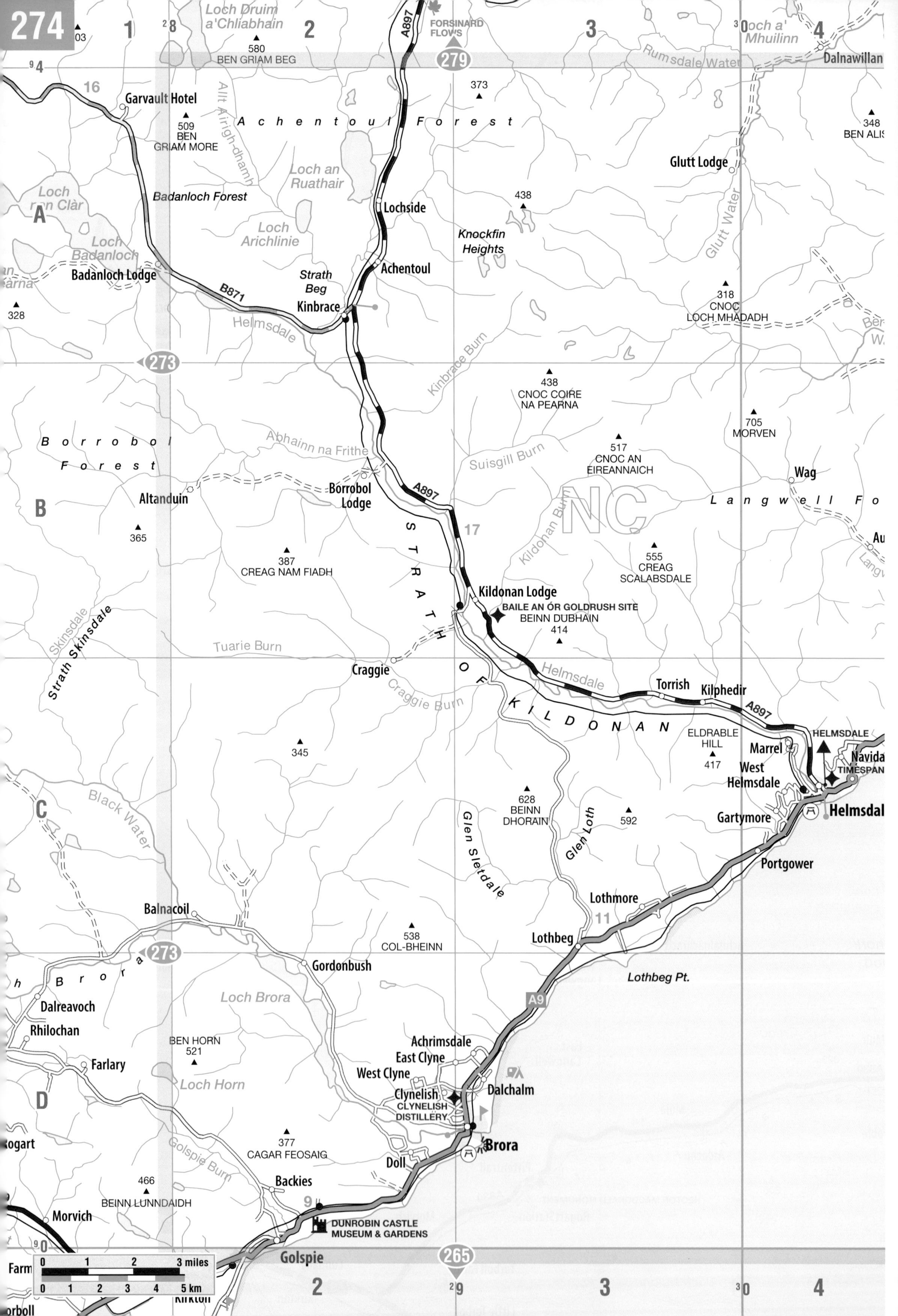
1
2
3
4
A
B
C
D
Loch Druim a'Chliabhain
580
BEN GRIAM BEG
FORSINARD FLOWS
279
A897
Loch a' Mhuilinn
Dalnawillan
Rumsdale Water
16
Garvault Hotel
509
BEN GRIAM MORE
Allt Airigh-dhamh
Achentoul Forest
373
348
BEN ALIS
Glutt Lodge
Loch an Ruathair
Loch nan Clàr
Badanloch Forest
Lochside
438
Knockfin Heights
Glutt Water
Loch Arichlinie
Loch Badanloch
Badanloch Lodge
Achentoul
Strath Beg
Kinbrace
B871
318
CNOC LOCH MHADADH
328
Helmsdale
273
Kinbrace Burn
438
CNOC COIRE NA PEARNA
705
MORVEN
Borrobol Forest
Abhainn na Frithe
517
CNOC AN EIREANNAICH
Suisgill Burn
Wag
Altanduin
Borrobol Lodge
A897
Langwell Fo
NC
17
Kildonan Burn
365
387
CREAG NAM FIADH
555
CREAG SCALABSDALE
STRATH OF KILDONAN
Kildonan Lodge
BAILE AN ÓR GOLDRUSH SITE
BEINN DUBHAIN
414
Skinsdale
Strath Skinsdale
Tuarie Burn
Craggie
Craggie Burn
Helmsdale
Torrish
Kilphedir
A897
ELDRABLE HILL
417
HELMSDALE
Marrel
West Helmsdale
TIMESPAN
345
628
BEINN DHORAIN
592
Gartymore
Helmsdal
Black Water
Glen Sletdale
Glen Loth
Portgower
Lothmore
Balnacoil
11
538
COL-BHEINN
Lothbeg
273
Gordonbush
Lothbeg Pt.
Brora
Dalreavoch
Loch Brora
A9
Rhilochan
BEN HORN
521
Achrimsdale
East Clyne
Farlary
West Clyne
Loch Horn
Clynelish
CLYNELISH DISTILLERY
Dalchalm
Rogart
377
CAGAR FEOSAIG
Brora
Golspie Burn
Doll
466
BEINN LUNNDAIDH
Backies
9
Morvich
DUNROBIN CASTLE MUSEUM & GARDENS
Golspie
265
Farm
0 1 2 3 miles
0 1 2 3 4 5 km
Kirkton
orboll

Loch Sand
Loch Thulachan
Loch Rangag
280
A9
248
STEMSTER HILL
Camster
281
CAIRN OF GET
Ulbster
Whaligoe
Lodge
Roster
Bruan
HILL O' MANY STANES
Crofts of Benachielt
Rumster Forest
Upper Lybster
Mid Clyth
Loch Breac
Braehungie
287
West Clyth
Loch Dubh
269
CNOCAN CONACHREAG
Burn of Houstry
Forse Ho.
Swiney
Reisgill Burn
Houstry
WAG OF FORSE
A99
Lybster
Smerral
Latheron
Forse
CLAN GUNN HERITAGE CENTRE & MUSEUM
Dunbeath Water
Latheronwheel Ho.
Latheronwheel
Braemore
LAIDHAY CROFT MUSEUM
283
Balnabruich
DUNBEATH HERITAGE MUSEUM
Dunbeath
Dunbeath Bay
Knockally
DUNBEATH CASTLE
Ramscraigs
626
SCARABEN
Borgue
Newport
ND
Ceann Leathad nam Bò
Langwell Ho.
Berriedale
BADBEA CLEARANCE VILLAGE
422
A9
Ousdale
Ord Point
HERITAGE CENTRE
A
B
C
D
4
5
6
7

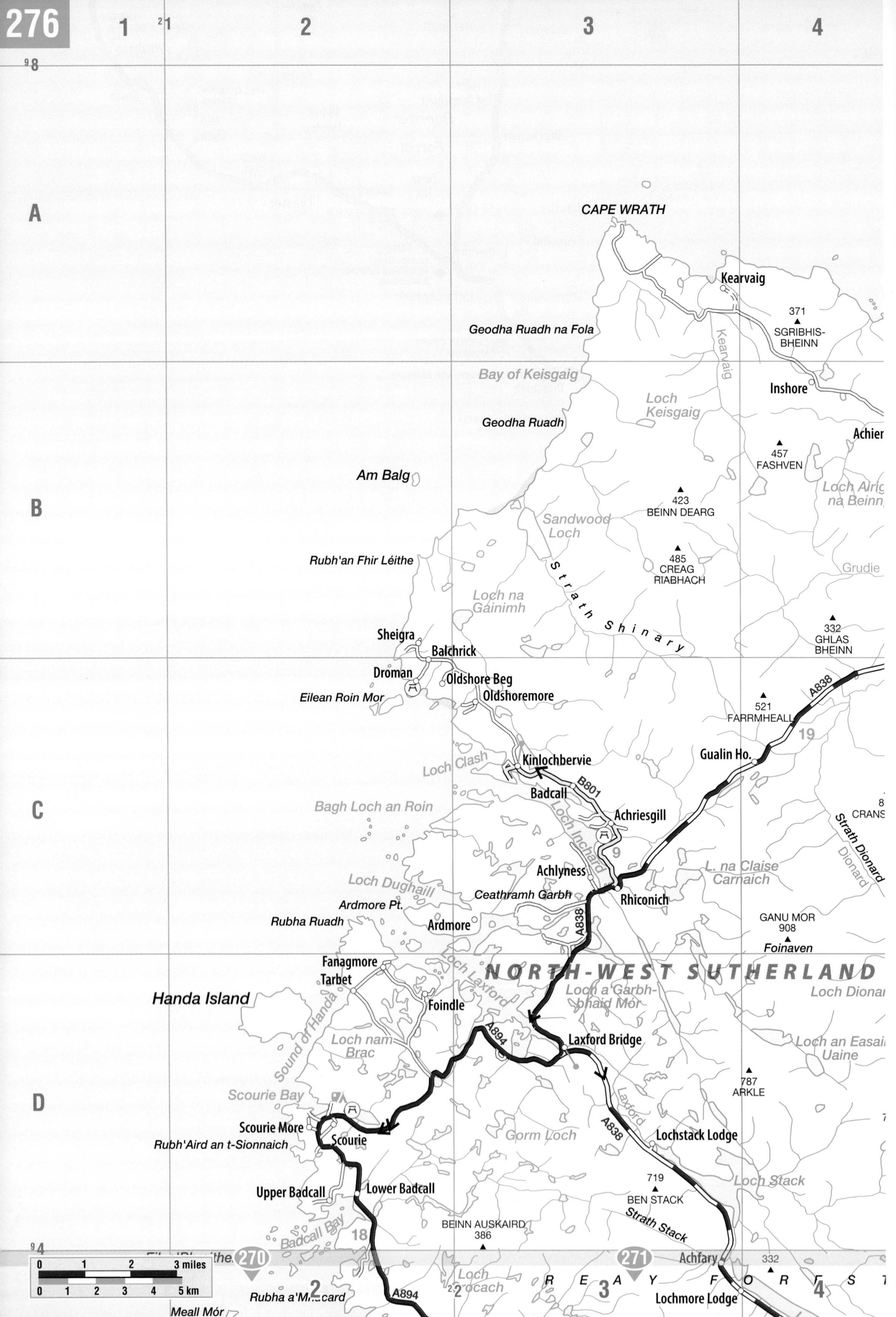

1
2
3
4
A
B
C
D
CAPE WRATH
Kearvaig
371
SGRIBHIS-BHEINN
Geodha Ruadh na Fola
Kearvaig
Bay of Keisgaig
Inshore
Loch Keisgaig
Geodha Ruadh
Achier
457
FASHVEN
Am Balg
Loch Airg na Beinn
423
BEINN DEARG
Sandwood Loch
485
CREAG RIABHACH
Grudie
Rubh'an Fhir Léithe
Loch na Gainimh
Strath Shinary
332
GHLAS BHEINN
Sheigra
Balchrick
Droman
Oldshore Beg
Eilean Roin Mor
Oldshoremore
521
FARRMHEALL
A838
19
Kinlochbervie
Gualin Ho.
Loch Clash
B801
Badcall
Bagh Loch an Roin
Loch Inchard
Achriesgill
CRANS
Strath Dionard
Dionard
9
Achlyness
L. na Claise Carnaich
Loch Dughaill
Ceathramh Garbh
Rhiconich
Ardmore Pt.
GANU MOR
908
Rubha Ruadh
Ardmore
Foinaven
Fanagmore
Tarbet
NORTH-WEST SUTHERLAND
Loch Laxford
Handa Island
Loch a'Garbh-bhaid Mór
Loch Dionard
Sound of Handa
Foindle
A894
Loch nam Brac
Laxford Bridge
Loch an Easain Uaine
787
ARKLE
Scourie Bay
Laxford
A838
Scourie More
Scourie
Gorm Loch
Lochstack Lodge
Rubh'Aird an t-Sionnaich
719
BEN STACK
Loch Stack
Upper Badcall
Lower Badcall
Strath Stack
Badcall Bay
18
BEINN AUSKAIRD
386
270
271
Achfary
332
REAY FOREST
0 1 2 3 miles
0 1 2 3 4 5 km
Loch Crocach
Rubha a'Mhucard
A894
Lochmore Lodge
Meall Mór

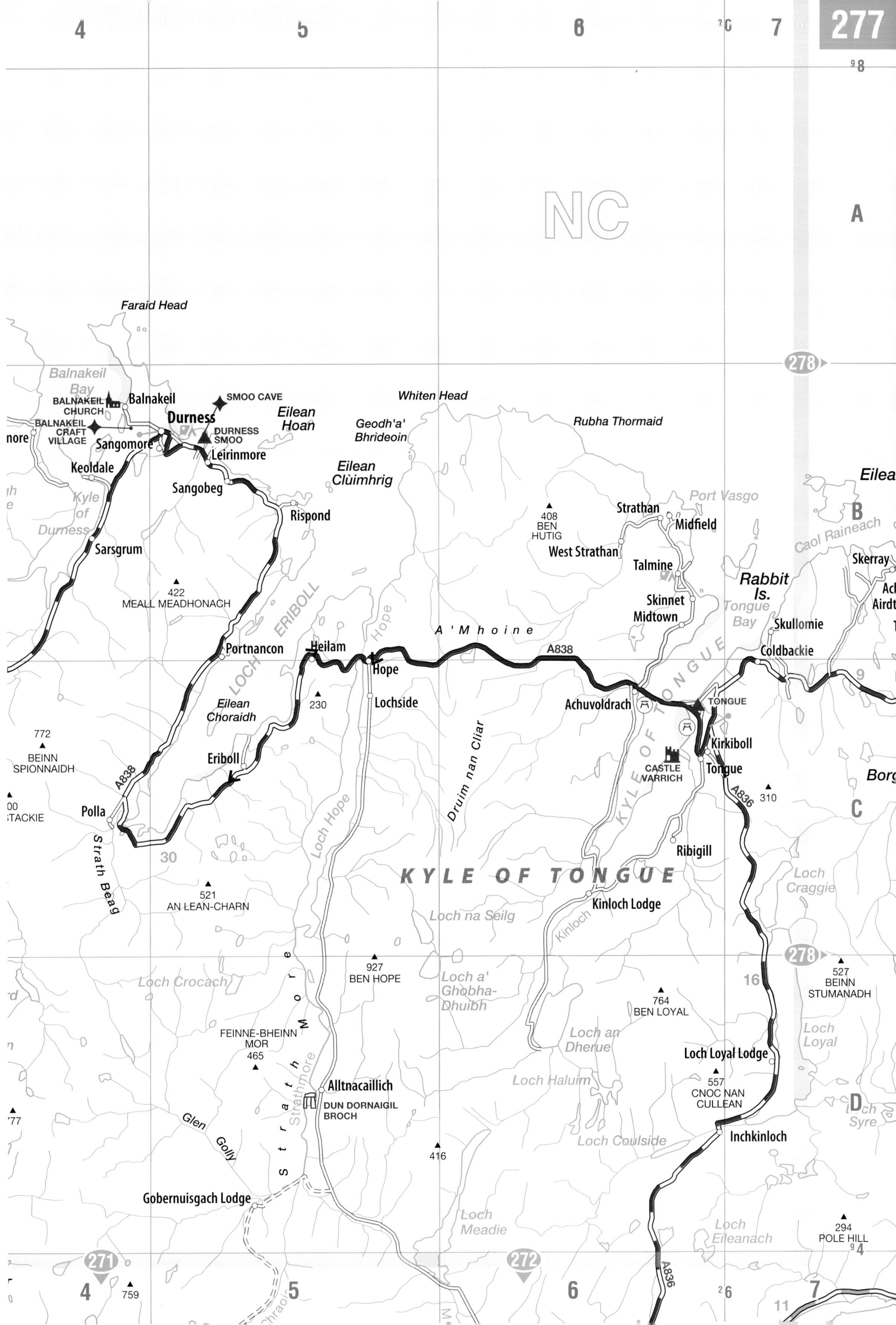
NC
Faraid Head
Balnakeil Bay
BALNAKEIL CHURCH
Balnakeil
BALNAKEIL CRAFT VILLAGE
SMOO CAVE
Durness
DURNESS SMOO
Sangomore
Leirinmore
Keoldale
Kyle of Durness
Sangobeg
Rispond
Sarsgrum
Eilean Hoan
Whiten Head
Geodh'a' Bhrideoin
Eilean Clùimhrig
Rubha Thormaid
Port Vasgo
Strathan
Midfield
408 BEN HUTIG
West Strathan
Talmine
Rabbit Is.
Skinnet
Midtown
Tongue Bay
Skullomie
Coldbackie
Caol Raineach
Skerray
422 MEALL MEADHONACH
LOCH ERIBOLL
Portnancon
Heilam
Hope
A 'M h o i n e
A838
Hope
Lochside
230
Eilean Choraidh
Eriboll
772 BEINN SPIONNAIDH
A838
Polla
Strath Beag
30
521 AN LEAN-CHARN
Achuvoldrach
TONGUE
Kirkiboll
CASTLE VARRICH
Tongue
A836
310
Druim nan Cliar
KYLE OF TONGUE
Loch Hope
Ribigill
KYLE OF TONGUE
Kinloch Lodge
Loch na Seilg
Loch Craggie
Kinloch
Loch Crocach
927 BEN HOPE
Loch a' Ghobha-Dhuibh
278
527 BEINN STUMANADH
16
764 BEN LOYAL
Loch an Dherue
Loch Loyal
Loch Loyal Lodge
FEINNE-BHEINN MOR 465
Strath More
Strathmore
Alltnacaillich
DUN DORNAIGIL BROCH
Loch Haluim
557 CNOC NAN CULLEAN
Inchkinloch
Glen Golly
416
Loch Coulside
Gobernuisgach Lodge
Loch Meadie
Loch Eileanach
294 POLE HILL
271
272
759
A836
11
278
A
B
C
D
4
5
6
7

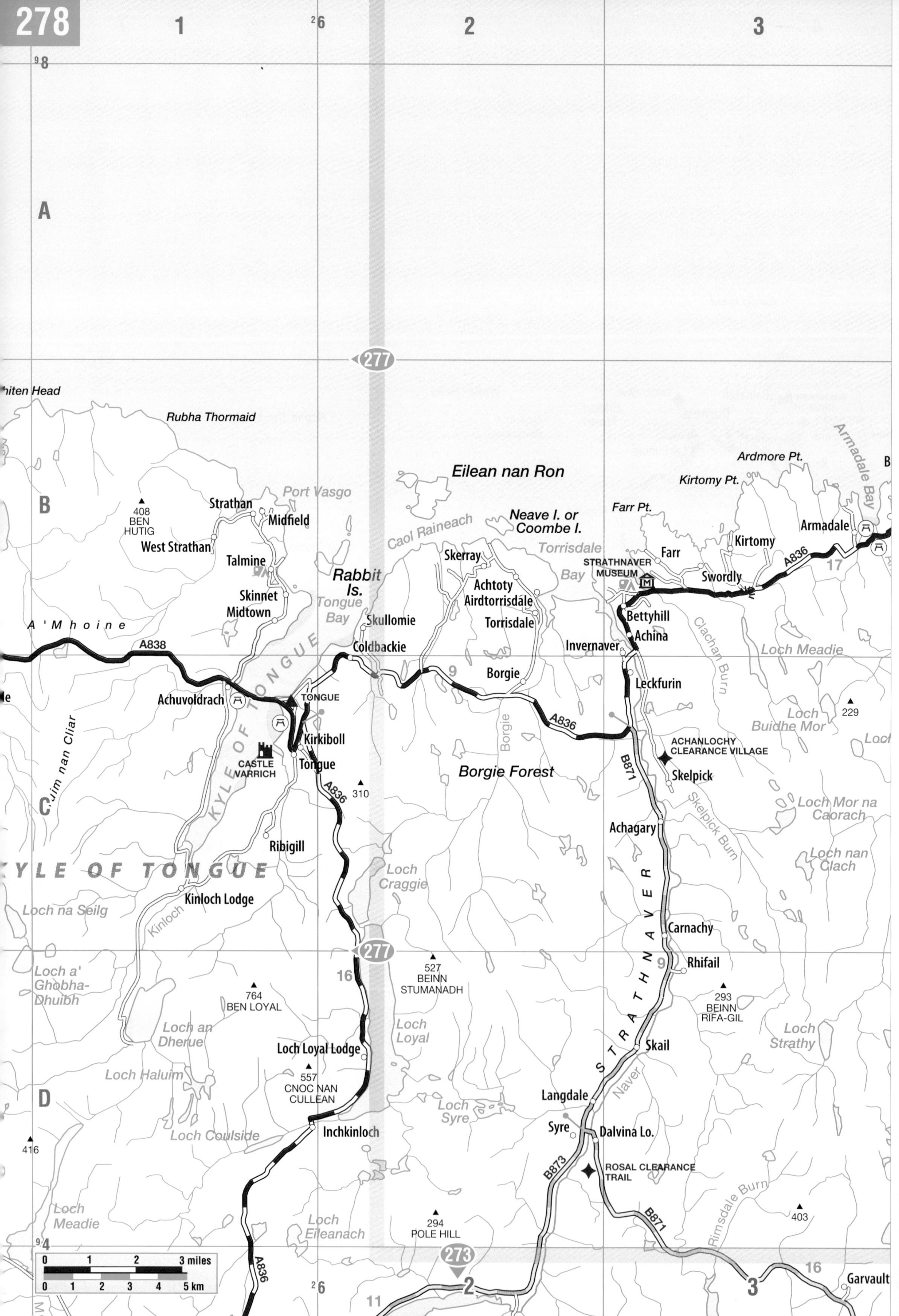
1
2
3
A
B
C
D
277
hiten Head
Rubha Thormaid
Eilean nan Ron
Ardmore Pt.
Armadale Bay
Kirtomy Pt.
Farr Pt.
Port Vasgo
408
BEN
HUTIG
Strathan
Midfield
West Strathan
Talmine
Skinnet
Midtown
Caol Raineach
Neave I. or
Coombe I.
Torrisdale
Bay
Rabbit
Is.
Tongue
Bay
Skerray
Achtoty
Airdtorrisdale
Torrisdale
Skullomie
Coldbackie
Farr
STRATHNAVER
MUSEUM
Kirtomy
Swordly
Armadale
A836
17
A'Mhoine
A838
Bettyhill
Achina
Invernaver
Clachan Burn
Loch Meadie
9
Borgie
Leckfurin
Achuvoldrach
TONGUE
Kirkiboll
CASTLE
VARRICH
Tongue
KYLE OF TONGUE
Borgie
Borgie Forest
A836
B871
ACHANLOCHY
CLEARANCE VILLAGE
Skelpick
Loch
Buidhe Mor
229
Loch Mor na
Caorach
Skelpick Burn
Achagary
Loch nan
Clach
310
Ribigill
YLE OF TONGUE
Loch
Craggie
Kinloch Lodge
Loch na Seilg
Kinloch
STRATHNAVER
Carnachy
Rhifail
Loch a'
Ghobha-
Dhuibh
16
527
BEINN
STUMANADH
764
BEN LOYAL
293
BEINN
RIFA-GIL
Loch an
Dherue
Loch
Loyal
Loch
Strathy
Loch Loyal Lodge
Skail
Loch Haluim
557
CNOC NAN
CULLEAN
Langdale
Naver
Loch
Syre
Syre
Dalvina Lo.
Inchkinloch
416
Loch Coulside
B873
ROSAL CLEARANCE
TRAIL
Rimsdale Burn
B871
403
Loch
Meadie
Loch
Eileanach
294
POLE HILL
273
A836
16
Garvault
11
0 1 2 3 miles
0 1 2 3 4 5 km

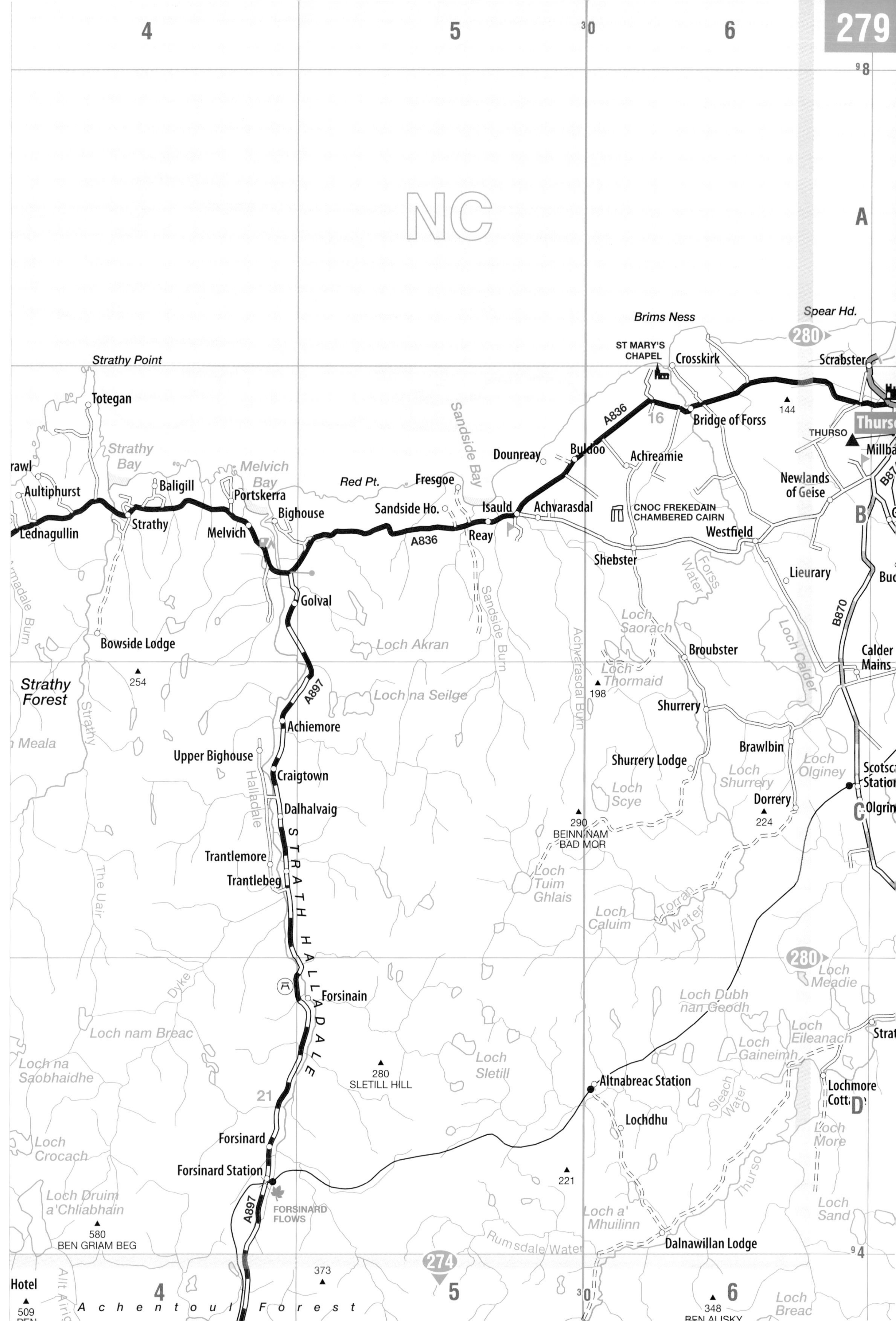

4
5
6
NC
A
B
C
D
Brims Ness
Spear Hd.
280
ST MARY'S CHAPEL
Crosskirk
Scrabster
Strathy Point
Totegan
A836
16
Bridge of Forss
144
THURSO
Strathy Bay
Melvich Bay
Sandside Bay
Dounreay
Buldoo
Achreamie
Newlands of Geise
B874
Aultiphurst
Baligill
Portskerra
Red Pt.
Fresgoe
Sandside Ho.
Isauld
Achvarasdal
CNOC FREKEDAIN CHAMBERED CAIRN
Lednagullin
Strathy
Melvich
Bighouse
Reay
Westfield
Shebster
Forss Water
Lieurary
Golval
Sandside Burn
Achvarasdal Burn
Loch Saorach
B870
Bowside Lodge
Loch Akran
Broubster
Loch Calder
Calder Mains
254
Strathy Forest
Loch Thormaid
198
A897
Loch na Seilge
Shurrery
Achiemore
Strathy
Brawlbin
Upper Bighouse
Shurrery Lodge
Loch Shurrery
Loch Olginey
Halladale
Craigtown
Loch Scye
Dalhalvaig
290
BEINN NAM BAD MOR
Dorrery
224
STRATH HALLADALE
Trantlemore
Trantlebeg
Loch Tuim Ghlais
The Uair
Loch Caluim
Torran Water
280
Loch Meadie
Dyke
Forsinain
Loch Dubh nan Geodh
Loch nam Breac
Loch Eileanach
Loch Gaineimh
Loch na Saobhaidhe
280
SLETILL HILL
Loch Sletill
Altnabreac Station
21
Lochdhu
Sleach Water
Lochmore Cott
Loch More
Loch Crocach
Forsinard
Forsinard Station
221
Thurso
Loch Druim a'Chliabhain
FORSINARD FLOWS
Loch a' Mhuilinn
Loch Sand
580
BEN GRIAM BEG
Rumsdale Water
Dalnawillan Lodge
274
373
Hotel
509
Achentoul Forest
348
Loch Breac

1
2
3
4
A
B
C
D
283
279
275
DUNNET HEAD
Briga Hd.
Brough
Hunspow
The Thirl
MARY ANN'S COTTAGE
St John's Loch
Corsback
Dunnet
SEADRIFT VISITOR CENTRE
DUNNET BAY
FLAGSTONE INTERPRETATIVE TRAIL
Castlehill
STROMNESS
Brims Ness
Spear Hd.
Holborn Hd.
Thurso Bay
THURSO CASTLE
Clardon Hd.
ST MARY'S CHAPEL
Crosskirk
Scrabster
Clardon
Murkle
Greenland
Castletown
CASTLETOWN
Tain
Bridge of Forss
Thurso
THURSO
Millbank
Thurso East
A836
Haimer
Olrig Ho.
Dounreay
Buldoo
Achreamie
Newlands of Geise
Fresgoe
Isauld
Achvarasdal
CNOC FREKEDAIN CHAMBERED CAIRN
Westfield
Reay
Geise
Weydale
Hilliclay
Durran
B876
Shebster
Lieurary
Buckies
Achingills
Stemster
Bowertower
Knockdee
Stemster Ho.
Sordale
Braal Castle
Roadside
Halcro
Broubster
Calder Mains
Loch Calder
Clayock
Gillock
Loch Scarmclate
Loch Saorach
Loch Thormaid
Halkirk
Shurrery
A882
B874
Brawlbin
Banniskirk Ho.
Shurrery Lodge
Loch Shurrery
Loch Olginey
Scotscalder Station
Harpsdale
Loch Watten
Loch Scye
Dorrery
Olgrinmore
BEINN NAM BAD MOR
A9
Spittal
Backlass
B870
Watten
Loch Tuim Ghlais
Mybster
Loch of Toftingall
Acharole
Loch Caluim
Torran Water
Westerdale
Burn of Acharole
Loch Meadie
Loch Dubh nan Geodh
Little River
Loch Eileanach
Strathmore Lodge
Loch Sletill
Loch Gaineimh
Altnabreac Station
Lochmore Cottage
Sleach Water
Lochdhu
Rangag
Loch More
GREY CAIRN OF CAMSTER
Loch Ruard
Achavanich
Loch a' Mhuilinn
Loch Sand
Loch Thulachan
Loch Rangag
STEMSTER HILL
Rumsdale Water
Dalnawillan Lodge
Crofts of Benachielt
Rumster
Upper Lybster
BEN ALISKY
Loch Breac
Sandside Bay
Sandside Burn
Achvarasdal Burn
Forss Water
Camster Burn
Thurso
0 1 2 3 miles
0 1 2 3 4 5 km

PENTLAND FIRTH
Langaton Point
Nethertown
Island of Stroma
Red Head
53
Mell Head
Uppertown
(May-Sept)
Muckle Skerry
Pentland Skerries
Men of Mey
St John's Pt.
Boars of Duncansby
Gills Bay
East Mey
CASTLE OF MEY
Rattar
Mey
Gills
Kirkstyle
Huna
DUNCANSBY HEAD
A836
Canisbay
John o' Groats
Stacks of Duncansby
Barrock
Inkstack
A99
124
Brabster
Skirza
Tofts
Skirza Head
Lochend
Gill Burn
Freswick
Freswick Bay
Slickly
Ness Head
Reaster
BUCHOLLY CASTLE
ND
Alterwall
CAITHNESS BROCH CENTRE
Auckengill
Lyth
LYTH ARTS CENTRE
Sortat
Nybster
Barrock Ho.
Brough Head
Howe
Burn of Lyth
Keiss
KEISS CASTLE
Mireland
Kirk
Loch of Wester
B870
Myrelandhorn
SINCLAIR'S BAY
Killimster
B876
Mains of Watten
CASTLE SINCLAIR
CASTLE GIRNIGOE
Noss Head
Reiss
Winless
60
Ackergill
Sealky Head
Wick
B874
WICK
Staxigoe
Bilbster
WICK HERITAGE CEN & MUS
Papigoe
Strath
A882
Broadhaven
Stirkoke Ho.
Milton
Wick Bay
Achairn Burn
Old Wick
Newton
South Hd.
CASTLE OF OLD WICK
Whiterow
Gote O'Tram
Tannach
Hempriggs House
Loch Hempriggs
Helman Hd.
141
HILL OF OLICLETT
A99
Thrumster
Gansclet
Sarclet
Loch of Yarrows
212
Sarclet Hd.
Ulbster
CAIRN OF GET
Whaligoe
Bruan
HILL O' MANY STANES
Mid Clyth
283
275
A
B
C
D
4
5
6
7

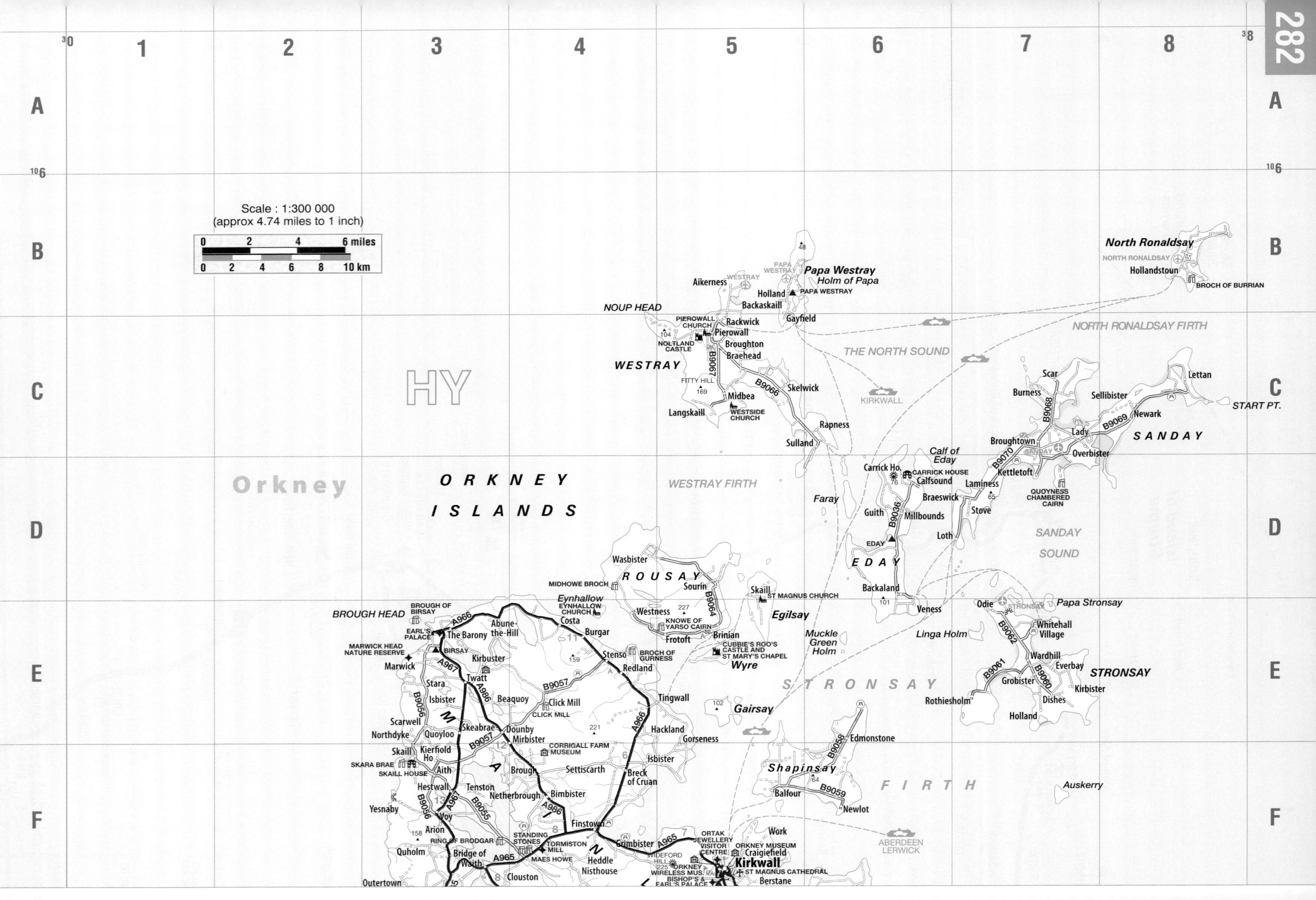

Scale : 1:300 000
(approx 4.74 miles to 1 inch)
0 2 4 6 miles
0 2 4 6 8 10 km
HY
Orkney
ORKNEY ISLANDS
North Ronaldsay
NORTH RONALDSAY
Hollandstoun
BROCH OF BURRIAN
NORTH RONALDSAY FIRTH
Papa Westray
Holm of Papa
PAPA WESTRAY
Holland
Backaskaill
Gayfield
Aikerness
WESTRAY
NOUP HEAD
PIEROWALL CHURCH
Rackwick
Pierowall
NOLTLAND CASTLE
Broughton
Braehead
WESTRAY
B9067
FITTY HILL
169
104
48
B9066
Skelwick
Midbea
WESTSIDE CHURCH
Langskaill
Rapness
Sulland
THE NORTH SOUND
KIRKWALL
Scar
Burness
B9068
Lettan
START PT.
Sellibister
Newark
B9069
SANDAY
Lady
Broughtown
Overbister
B9070
Kettletoft
QUOYNESS CHAMBERED CAIRN
Calf of Eday
Carrick Ho.
CARRICK HOUSE
Calfsound
76
Laminess
65
Braeswick
Stove
Faray
Guith
B9036
Millbounds
Loth
EDAY
SANDAY SOUND
Backaland
101
Veness
WESTRAY FIRTH
Wasbister
ROUSAY
Sourin
B9064
MIDHOWE BROCH
Eynhallow
EYNHALLOW CHURCH
Westness
227
KNOWE OF YARSO CAIRN
Frotoft
Brinian
Skaill
ST MAGNUS CHURCH
Egilsay
Muckle Green Holm
CUBBIE'S ROO'S CASTLE AND ST MARY'S CHAPEL
Wyre
Odie
STRONSAY
Papa Stronsay
Whitehall Village
B9062
Linga Holm
Wardhill
Everbay
STRONSAY
B9061
Grobister
B9060
Kirbister
Rothiesholm
Dishes
Holland
STRONSAY FIRTH
Auskerry
BROUGH HEAD
BROUGH OF BIRSAY
A966
EARL'S PALACE
The Barony
Abune-the-Hill
Costa
Burgar
MARWICK HEAD NATURE RESERVE
BIRSAY
Marwick
A967
Kirbuster
Twatt
159
11
Stenso
BROCH OF GURNESS
Redland
Stara
Isbister
A986
Beaquoy
B9057
Click Mill
CLICK MILL
Tingwall
102
Gairsay
B9056
Scarwell
Northdyke
Quoyloo
Skeabrae
Dounby
Mirbister
B9057
12
221
A966
Hackland
Gorseness
Edmonstone
B9058
CORRIGALL FARM MUSEUM
Skaill
Kierfiold Ho
SKARA BRAE
SKAILL HOUSE
Aith
Brough
Settiscarth
6
Isbister
Breck of Cruan
Shapinsay
64
Balfour
B9059
Newlot
Hestwall
Tenston
Netherbrough
Bimbister
Yesnaby
B9056
13
A967
B9055
A986
Voy
158
Arion
RING OF BRODGAR
STANDING STONES
8
Finstown
Quholm
Bridge of Waith
A965
TORMISTON MILL
MAES HOWE
Heddle
Nisthouse
Clouston
Outertown
Grimbister
A965
7
WIDEFORD HILL
225
ORKNEY WIRELESS MUS.
BISHOP'S & EARL'S PALACE
ORTAK JEWELLERY VISITOR CENTRE
ORKNEY MUSEUM
Craigiefield
Work
Kirkwall
ST MAGNUS CATHEDRAL
Berstane
ABERDEEN LERWICK
MAINLAND

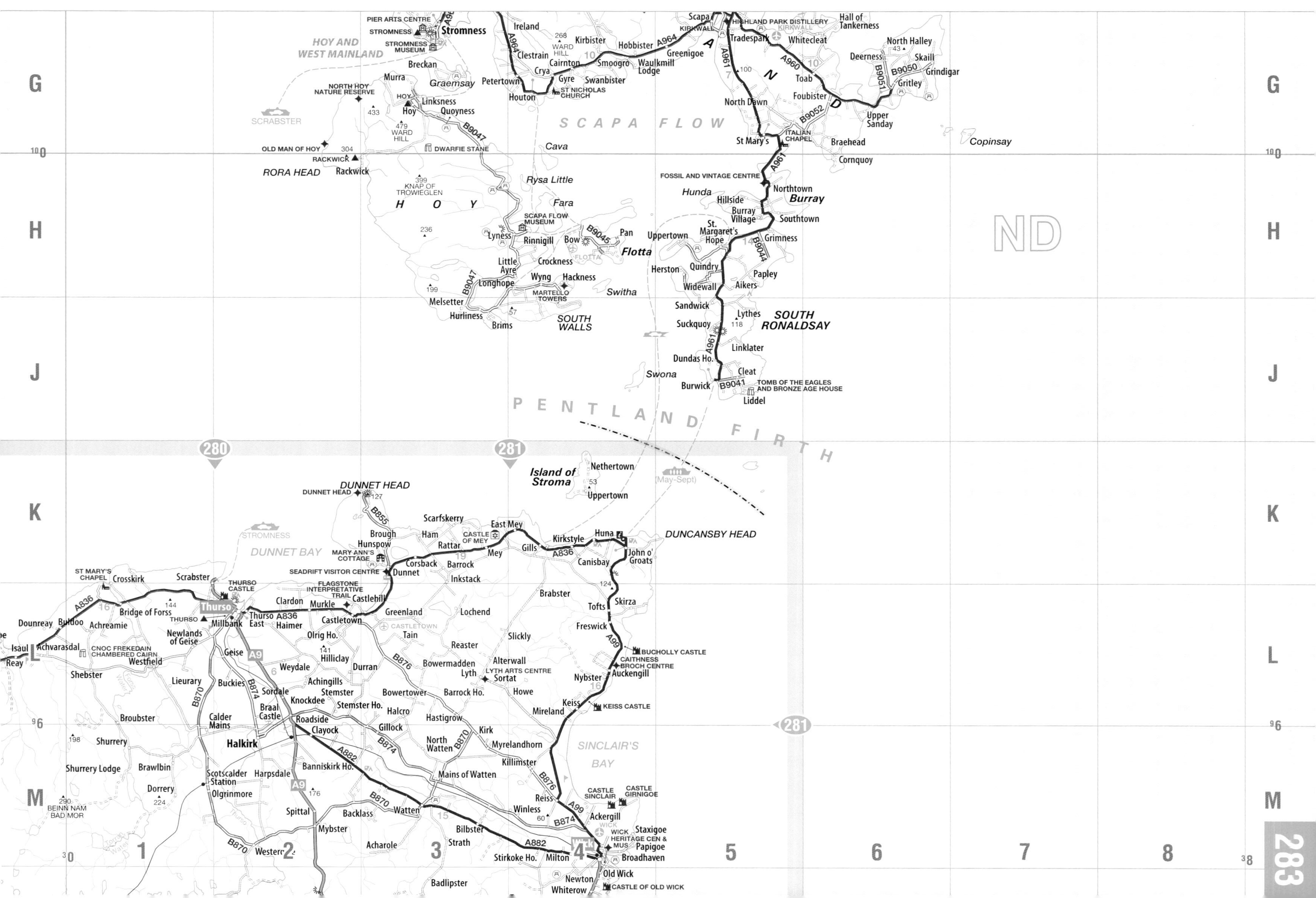
ND
SCAPA FLOW
PENTLAND FIRTH
HOY
SOUTH RONALDSAY
Burray
Flotta
Fara
Rysa Little
Cava
Hunda
Swona
Switha
SOUTH WALLS
Island of Stroma
Copinsay
Graemsay
HOY AND WEST MAINLAND
DUNNET HEAD
DUNCANSBY HEAD
RORA HEAD
DUNNET BAY
SINCLAIR'S BAY
Stromness
Kirkwall
Scapa
St Mary's
St. Margaret's Hope
Thurso
Halkirk
Castletown
Dunnet
John o' Groats
Wick
Keiss
Lyth
Watten
Mey
East Mey
Canisbay
Huna
Gills
Freswick
Auckengill
Nybster
Reiss
Bilbster
Spittal
Westerdale
Scrabster
Reay
Dounreay
Crosskirk
Bridge of Forss
Brough
Ham
Scarfskerry
Rattar
Barrock
Nethertown
Uppertown
Lyness
Longhope
Hoy
Rackwick
Houton
Deerness
Tankerness
A961
A964
A960
A836
A99
A9
A882
B874
B876
B870
B855
B9041
B9044
B9045
B9047
B9050
B9051
B9052
CASTLE OF MEY
MARY ANN'S COTTAGE
ITALIAN CHAPEL
SCAPA FLOW MUSEUM
MARTELLO TOWERS
TOMB OF THE EAGLES AND BRONZE AGE HOUSE
FOSSIL AND VINTAGE CENTRE
HIGHLAND PARK DISTILLERY
DWARFIE STANE
OLD MAN OF HOY
NORTH HOY NATURE RESERVE
ST NICHOLAS CHURCH
PIER ARTS CENTRE
STROMNESS MUSEUM
BUCHOLLY CASTLE
CAITHNESS BROCH CENTRE
KEISS CASTLE
LYTH ARTS CENTRE
CASTLE SINCLAIR GIRNIGOE
WICK HERITAGE CEN & MUS
CASTLE OF OLD WICK
THURSO CASTLE
ST MARY'S CHAPEL
CNOC FREKEDAIN CHAMBERED CAIRN
SEADRIFT VISITOR CENTRE
FLAGSTONE INTERPRETATIVE TRAIL
280
281
(May-Sept)

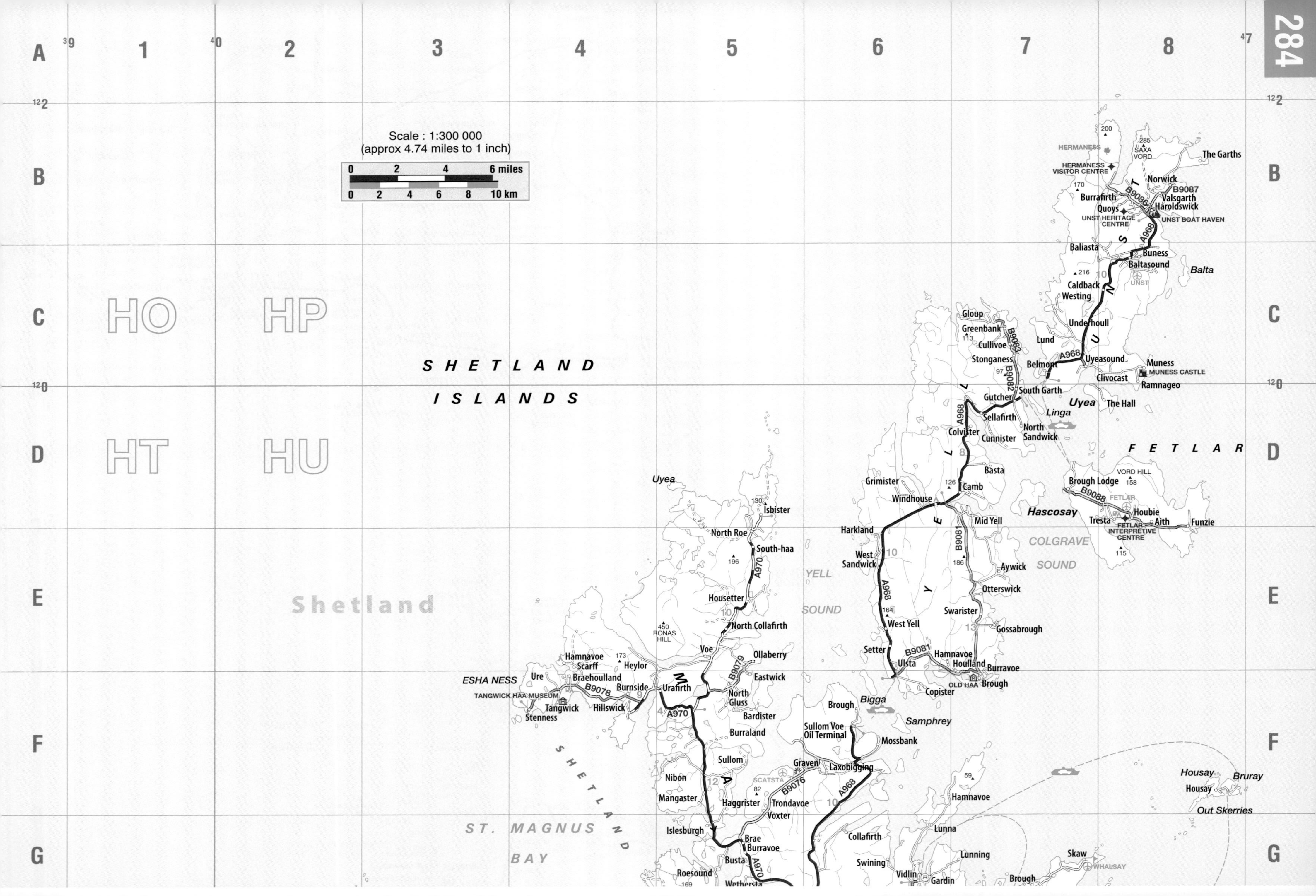
Scale : 1:300 000
(approx 4.74 miles to 1 inch)
0 2 4 6 miles
0 2 4 6 8 10 km
SHETLAND ISLANDS
Shetland
HO
HP
HT
HU
UNST
YELL
FETLAR
YELL SOUND
COLGRAVE SOUND
ST. MAGNUS BAY
SHETLAND
MAINLAND
The Garths
Hermaness
Hermaness Visitor Centre
Saxa Vord
Norwick
B9087
Valsgarth
Haroldswick
Unst Boat Haven
Burrafirth
B9086
Quoys
Unst Heritage Centre
A968
Baliasta
Buness
Baltasound
Balta
Caldback
Westing
Underhoull
Lund
Uyeasound
Muness
Muness Castle
Belmont
Clivocast
Ramnageo
Gloup
Greenbank
Cullivoe
B9083
Stonganess
B9082
South Garth
Gutcher
Uyea
The Hall
Linga
Sellafirth
North Sandwick
Colvister
Cunnister
Basta
Grimister
Camb
Windhouse
Vord Hill
Brough Lodge
B9088
Hascosay
Houbie
Tresta
Aith
Funzie
Fetlar Interpretive Centre
Harkland
Mid Yell
West Sandwick
B9081
Aywick
Otterswick
Swarister
Gossabrough
West Yell
Setter
Hamnavoe
Ulsta
Houlland
Burravoe
Old Haa
Brough
Copister
Uyea
Isbister
North Roe
South-haa
A970
Housetter
North Collafirth
Ronas Hill
Voe
Ollaberry
Hamnavoe
Scarff
Heylor
Eastwick
ESHA NESS
Ure
Braehoulland
Burnside
Urafirth
B9079
North Gluss
Tangwick Haa Museum
B9078
Tangwick
Hillswick
Stenness
Bardister
Brough
Bigga
Samphrey
Burraland
Sullom Voe Oil Terminal
Mossbank
Sullom
Graven
Laxobigging
Nibon
Scatsta
B9076
Mangaster
Haggrister
Trondavoe
Voxter
Hamnavoe
Islesburgh
Brae
Burravoe
Busta
Collafirth
Lunna
Roesound
Wethersta
Swining
Vidlin
Gardin
Lunning
Brough
Skaw
Whalsay
Housay
Bruray
Out Skerries

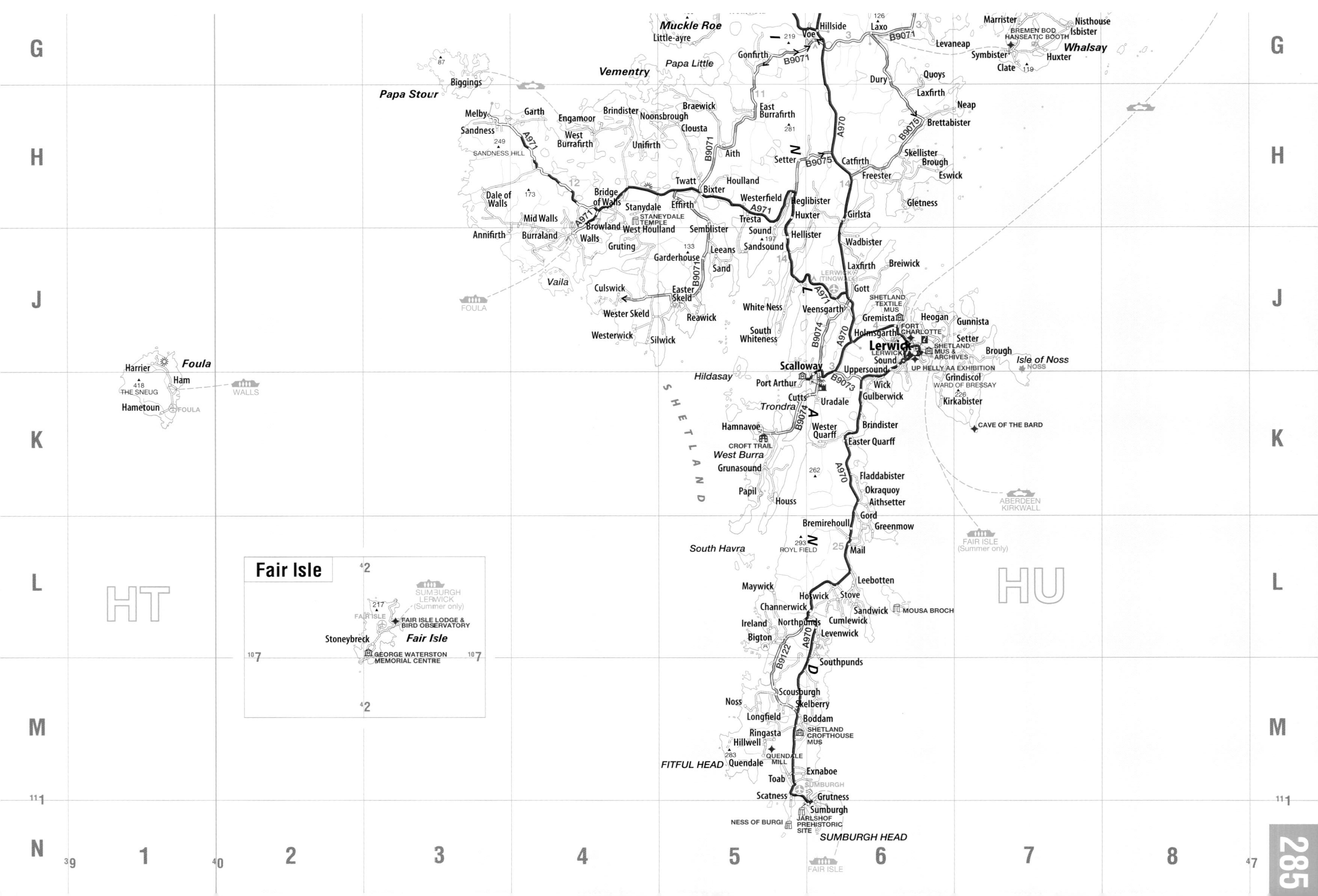
G
H
J
K
L
M
N
1
2
3
4
5
6
7
8
39
40
42
47
107
111
HU
HT
SHETLAND
Muckle Roe
Little-ayre
Hillside
Voe
219
Laxo
126
B9071
Marrister
BREMEN BOD HANSEATIC BOOTH
Nisthouse
Isbister
Whalsay
Levaneap
Symbister
Huxter
Clate
119
Papa Little
Gonfirth
Vementry
Biggings
87
Papa Stour
Dury
Quoys
Laxfirth
Neap
Brettabister
B9075
East Burrafirth
281
A970
Melby
Sandness
249
SANDNESS HILL
Garth
A971
Engamoor
West Burrafirth
Brindister
Noonsbrough
Braewick
Clousta
Unifirth
Aith
Setter
Catfirth
Skellister
Brough
Eswick
Freester
Twatt
Houlland
Bixter
Dale of Walls
173
Mid Walls
Annifirth
Burraland
Bridge of Walls
Browland
Walls
Stanydale
STANEYDALE TEMPLE
West Houlland
Effirth
Westerfield
Weglibister
Huxter
Gletness
Girlsta
Tresta
Sound
197
Sandsound
Semblister
Hellister
Gruting
133
Garderhouse
Leeans
Sand
Wadbister
Laxfirth
Breiwick
LERWICK (TINGWALL)
Vaila
FOULA
Culswick
Easter Skeld
Wester Skeld
Reawick
Westerwick
Silwick
White Ness
Veensgarth
South Whiteness
Gott
SHETLAND TEXTILE MUS
Gremista
Heogan
Gunnista
FORT CHARLOTTE
Holmsgarth
Lerwick
LERWICK
Sound
SHETLAND MUS & ARCHIVES
Setter
Brough
Isle of Noss
NOSS
UP HELLY AA EXHIBITION
Harrier
Foula
Ham
418
THE SNEUG
Hametoun
FOULA
WALLS
Hildasay
Scalloway
Port Arthur
Uppersound
B9073
Wick
Grindiscol
WARD OF BRESSAY
226
Kirkabister
Cutts
Uradale
Gulberwick
Trondra
B9074
Hamnavoe
Wester Quarff
Brindister
Easter Quarff
CAVE OF THE BARD
CROFT TRAIL
West Burra
Grunasound
262
Fladdabister
Okraquoy
Aithsetter
Papil
Houss
ABERDEEN KIRKWALL
Gord
Bremirehoull
Greenmow
293
ROYL FIELD
South Havra
Mail
FAIR ISLE (Summer only)
Fair Isle
SUMBURGH LERWICK (Summer only)
217
FAIR ISLE
FAIR ISLE LODGE & BIRD OBSERVATORY
Stoneybreck
Fair Isle
GEORGE WATERSTON MEMORIAL CENTRE
Maywick
Leebotten
Hoswick
Stove
Channerwick
Sandwick
MOUSA BROCH
Ireland
Northpunds
Cumlewick
Levenwick
Bigton
B9122
Southpunds
Scousburgh
Noss
Skelberry
Longfield
Boddam
Ringasta
SHETLAND CROFTHOUSE MUS
Hillwell
283
QUENDALE MILL
FITFUL HEAD
Quendale
Exnaboe
Toab
SUMBURGH
Scatness
Grutness
Sumburgh
NESS OF BURGI
JARLSHOF PREHISTORIC SITE
SUMBURGH HEAD
FAIR ISLE

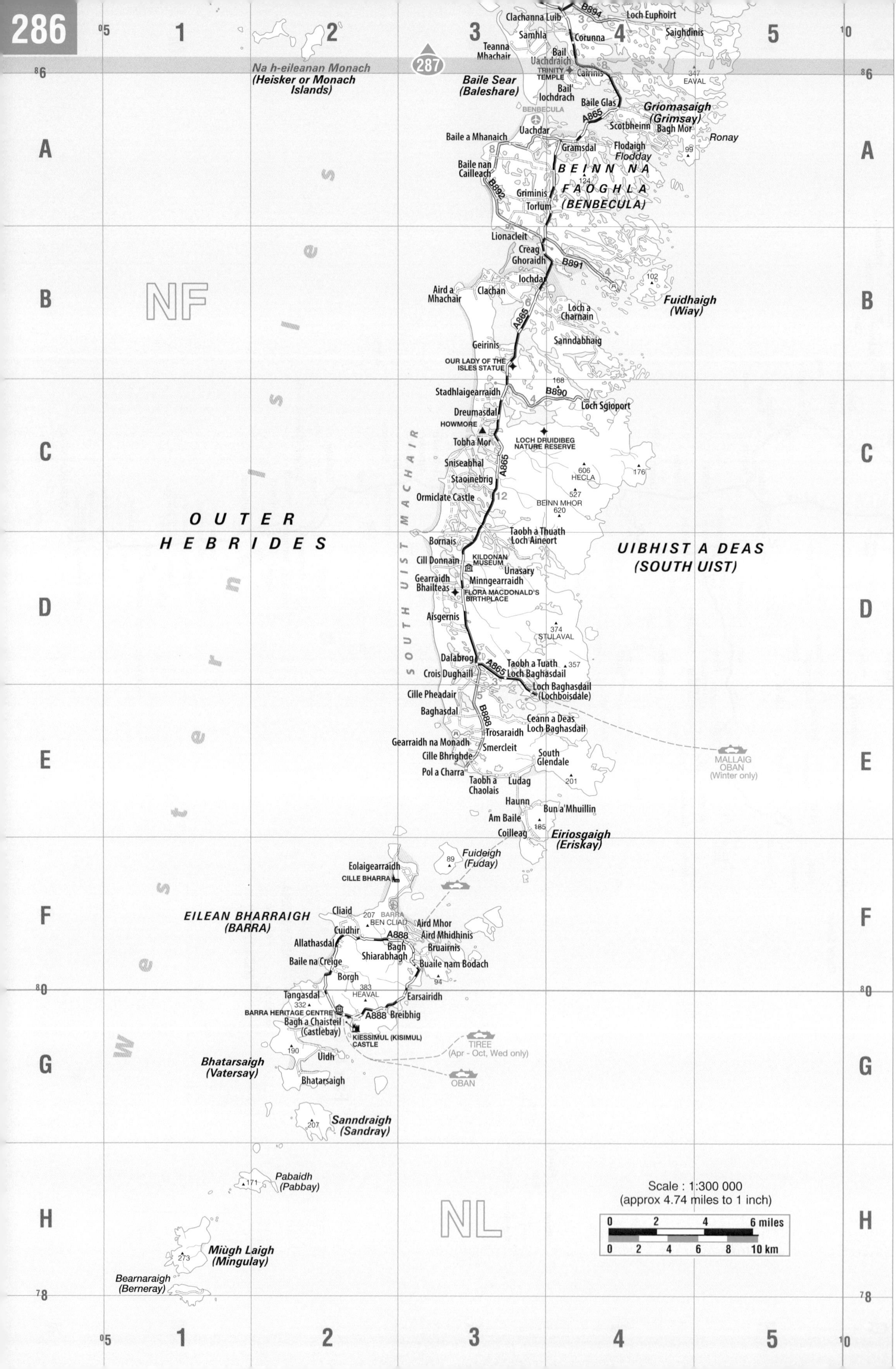

287

Na h-eileanan Monach (Heisker or Monach Islands)

Baile Sear (Baleshare)

Griomasaigh (Grimsay)

Ronay

BEINN NA FAOGHLA (BENBECULA)

Fuidhaigh (Wiay)

NF

OUTER HEBRIDES

UIBHIST A DEAS (SOUTH UIST)

SOUTH UIST MACHAIR

Eiriosgaigh (Eriskay)

Fuideigh (Fuday)

EILEAN BHARRAIGH (BARRA)

Bhatarsaigh (Vatersay)

Sanndraigh (Sandray)

Pabaidh (Pabbay)

Miùgh Laigh (Mingulay)

Bearnaraigh (Berneray)

NL

Sea of the Hebrides (West)

Clachanna Luib, Loch Euphoirt, Saighdinis, Samhla, Corunna, Teanna Mhachair, Bail Uachdrach, Trinity Temple, Cairinis, Eaval 347, Bail Iochdrach, Benbecula, Baile Glas, Uachdar, Scotbheinn, Bagh Mor, Baile a Mhanaich, Gramsdal, Flodaigh Flodday, Baile nan Cailleach, Griminis, Torlum, Lionacleit, Creag Ghoraidh, Iochdar, Aird a Mhachair, Clachan, Loch a Charnain, Geirinis, Sanndabhaig, Our Lady of the Isles Statue, Stadhlaigearraidh, Loch Sgioport, Dreumasdal, Howmore, Tobha Mor, Loch Druidibeg Nature Reserve, Sniseabhal, Hecla 606, Staoinebrig, Ormiclate Castle, Beinn Mhor 620, Taobh a Thuath Loch Aineort, Bornais, Cill Donnain, Kildonan Museum, Unasary, Gearraidh Bhailteas, Minngearraidh, Flora MacDonald's Birthplace, Aisgernis, Stulaval 374, Dalabrog, Taobh a Tuath Loch Baghasdail, Crois Dughaill, Loch Baghasdail (Lochboisdale), Cille Pheadair, Baghasdal, Ceann a Deas Loch Baghasdail, Trosaraidh, Gearraidh na Monadh, Smercleit, Cille Bhrighde, South Glendale, Pol a Charra, Taobh a Chaolais, Ludag, Haunn, Bun a'Mhuillin, Am Baile, Coilleag

Mallaig Oban (Winter only)

Eolaigearraidh, Cille Bhara, Cliaid, Barra, Ben Cliad 207, Aird Mhor, Cuidhir, Aird Mhidhinis, Allathasdal, Bagh Shiarabhagh, Bruairnis, Baile na Creige, Buaile nam Bodach, Borgh, Heaval 383, Tangasdal, Earsairidh, Barra Heritage Centre, Breibhig, Bagh a Chaisteil (Castlebay), Kiessimul (Kisimul) Castle, Uidh, Bhatarsaigh

Tiree (Apr - Oct, Wed only)

Oban

A865, B894, B892, B891, B890, B888, A888

Scale : 1:300 000 (approx 4.74 miles to 1 inch)

0 2 4 6 miles

0 2 4 6 8 10 km

Scale : 1:300 000
(approx 4.74 miles to 1 inch)
St. Kilda
Boreray
Soay
ST KILDA
St Kilda or Hirta (Hiort)
OUTER HEBRIDES
NA HEARADH (HARRIS)
UIBHIST A TUATH (NORTH UIST)
SOUTH LEWIS
HARRIS AND
NORTH UIST
LOCH A SIAR
CAOLAS NA HEARADH
AN CAOLAS MHONACH
Na h-eileanan Monach (Heisker or Monach Islands)
Eilean Bhearnaraigh (Berneray)
Pabaidh (Pabbay)
Tarasaigh (Taransay)
Scarp
Mealasta Island
Vallay
Oronsay
Hermetray
Kirkibost Island
Baile Sear (Baleshare)
Griomasaigh (Grimsay)
Ensay
Killegray
Huisinis
Gobhaig
Abhainn Suidhe
Tairbeart (Tarbert)
An t-Ob (Leverburgh)
Roghadal
Lochportain
Loch nam Madadh (Lochmaddy)
Scolpaig
Solas
Baile Mhartainn
Cairinis
Uig

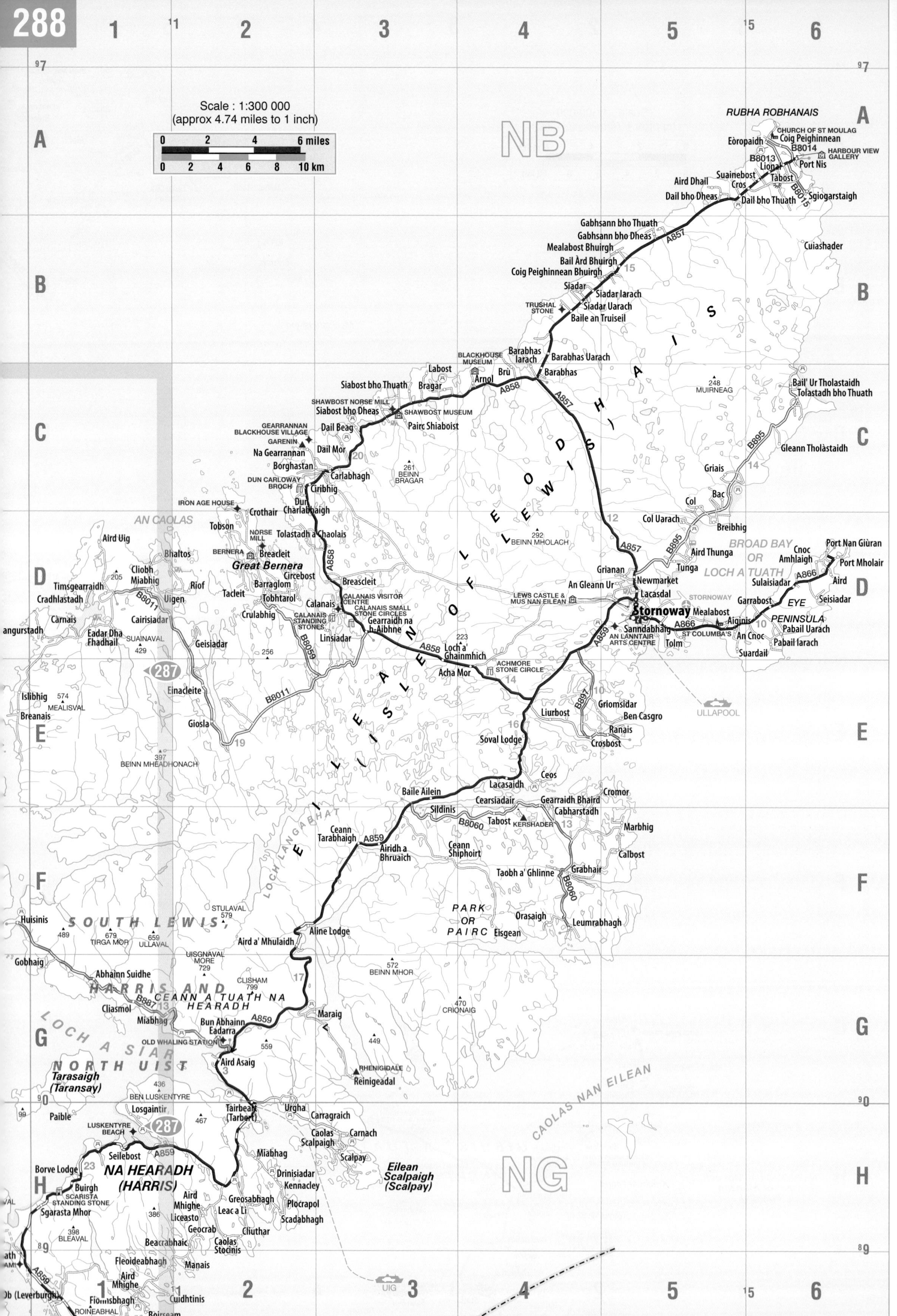
Scale : 1:300 000
(approx 4.74 miles to 1 inch)
0 2 4 6 miles
0 2 4 6 8 10 km
NB
NG
RUBHA ROBHANAIS
CHURCH OF ST MOULAG
Coig Peighinnean
Eòropaidh
B8014
HARBOUR VIEW GALLERY
B8013
Lional
Port Nis
Suainebost
Aird Dhail
Cros
Tabost
B8015
Dail bho Dheas
Dail bho Thuath
Sgiogarstaigh
Gabhsann bho Thuath
Gabhsann bho Dheas
A857
Mealabost Bhuirgh
Cuiashader
Bail Àrd Bhuirgh
Coig Peighinnean Bhuirgh
Siadar
Siadar Iarach
TRUSHAL STONE
Siadar Uarach
Baile an Truiseil
Barabhas Iarach
Barabhas Uarach
BLACKHOUSE MUSEUM
Labost
Brù
Barabhas
Arnol
248 MUIRNEAG
Bail' Ur Tholastaidh
Tolastadh bho Thuath
Siabost bho Thuath
Bragar
A858
SHAWBOST NORSE MILL
Siabost bho Dheas
SHAWBOST MUSEUM
Pairc Shiaboist
GEARRANNAN BLACKHOUSE VILLAGE
GARENIN
Dail Beag
Na Gearrannan
Dail Mor
B895
Gleann Tholàstaidh
Borghastan
Carlabhagh
261 BEINN BRAGAR
Griais
DUN CARLOWAY BROCH
Ciribhig
Bac
IRON AGE HOUSE
Dun Charlabhaigh
Crothair
Col
AN CAOLAS
Col Uarach
Breibhig
Tobson
NORSE MILL
Tolastadh a Chaolais
292 BEINN MHOLACH
Aird Uig
BERNERA
Breacleit
A858
A857
BROAD BAY OR LOCH A TUATH
Port Nan Giùran
Bhaltos
Great Bernera
Aird Thunga
Cnoc Amhlaigh
Port Mholair
Cliobh
Circebost
Tunga
Miabhig
Riof
Barraglom
Breascleit
Grianan
Timsgearraidh
205
B8011
Tacleit
Tobhtarol
An Gleann Ur
Newmarket
A866
Sulaisiadar
Aird
Cradhlastadh
Uigen
Calanais
CALANAIS VISITOR CENTRE
LEWS CASTLE & MUS NAN EILEAN
Lacasdal
STORNOWAY
Garrabost
EYE
Seisiadar
Càrnais
Cairisiadar
Crulabhig
CALANAIS STANDING STONES
CALANAIS SMALL STONE CIRCLES
Gearraidh na h-Aibhne
Stornoway
Mealabost
Aiginis
PENINSULA
Eadar Dha Fhadhail
SUAINAVAL 429
Linsiadar
A866
Pabail Uarach
Geisiadar
B8059
A858
223
Sanndabhaig
AN LANNTAIR ARTS CENTRE
A859
ST COLUMBA'S
An Cnoc
Tolm
Pabail Iarach
256
Loch a' Ghainmhich
Suardail
287
ACHMORE STONE CIRCLE
Acha Mor
Islibhig
574 MEALISVAL
Einacleite
B8011
B897
Griomsidar
Breanais
Liurbost
Ben Casgro
ULLAPOOL
Ranais
Giosla
19
Soval Lodge
Crosbost
397 BEINN MHEADHONACH
Ceos
Lacasaidh
Baile Ailein
Cromor
Cearsiadair
Gearraidh Bhaird
Sildinis
Cabharstadh
LOCH LANGABHAT
B8060
Tabost
KERSHADER
Ceann Tarabhaigh
A859
Marbhig
Airidh a Bhruaich
Ceann Shiphoirt
Calbost
Grabhair
Taobh a' Ghlinne
B8060
PARK OR PAIRC
Orasaigh
STULAVAL 579
Leumrabhagh
Huisinis
SOUTH LEWIS,
Eisgean
489
679 TIRGA MOR
659 ULLAVAL
Aline Lodge
Aird a' Mhulaidh
UISGNAVAL MORE 729
Gobhaig
572 BEINN MHOR
Abhainn Suidhe
CLISHAM 799
HARRIS AND
CEANN A TUATH NA HEARADH
B887
Cliasmol
470 CRIONAIG
Maraig
Miabhag
A859
Bun Abhainn Eadarra
LOCH A SIAR
OLD WHALING STATION
559
449
Aird Asaig
NORTH UIST
RHENIGIDALE
Reinigeadal
Tarasaigh (Taransay)
436
CAOLAS NAN EILEAN
BEN LUSKENTYRE
Paible
Losgaintir
467
Tairbeart (Tarbert)
Urgha
LUSKENTYRE BEACH
287
Carragraich
Caolas Scalpaigh
Carnach
Seilebost
A859
Scalpay
Miabhag
Borve Lodge
NA HEARADH (HARRIS)
Drinisiadar
Eilean Scalpaigh (Scalpay)
Buirgh
Kennacley
SCARISTA STANDING STONE
Aird Mhighe
Greosabhagh
Plocrapol
Sgarasta Mhor
386
Liceasto
Leac a Li
Scadabhagh
398 BLEAVAL
Geocrab
Cluithar
Beacrabhaic
Caolas Stocinis
Fleoideabhagh
Manais
Aird Mhighe
UIG
A859
Ob (Leverburgh)
Fionnsbhagh
Cuidhtinis
ROINEABHAL
Boirseam
EILEAN SIAR (ISLE OF LEWIS)
EILEAN LEODHAIS

# Index to road maps of Britain

## Abbreviations used in the index

| | |
|---|---|
| Aberdeen | **Aberdeen City** |
| Aberds | **Aberdeenshire** |
| Ald | **Alderney** |
| Anglesey | **Isle of Anglesey** |
| Angus | **Angus** |
| Argyll | **Argyll and Bute** |
| Bath | **Bath and North East Somerset** |
| BCP | **Bournemouth, Christchurch and Poole** |
| Bedford | **Bedford** |
| Blackburn | **Blackburn with Darwen** |
| Blackpool | **Blackpool** |
| Bl Gwent | **Blaenau Gwent** |
| Borders | **Scottish Borders** |
| Brack | **Bracknell** |
| Bridgend | **Bridgend** |
| Brighton | **City of Brighton and Hove** |
| Bristol | **City and County of Bristol** |
| Bucks | **Buckinghamshire** |
| Caerph | **Caerphilly** |
| Cambs | **Cambridgeshire** |
| Cardiff | **Cardiff** |
| Carms | **Carmarthenshire** |
| C Beds | **Central Bedfordshire** |
| Ceredig | **Ceredigion** |
| Ches E | **Cheshire East** |
| Ches W | **Cheshire West and Chester** |
| Clack | **Clackmannanshire** |
| Conwy | **Conwy** |
| Corn | **Cornwall** |
| Cumb | **Cumberland** |
| Darl | **Darlington** |
| Denb | **Denbighshire** |
| Derby | **City of Derby** |
| Derbys | **Derbyshire** |
| Devon | **Devon** |
| Dorset | **Dorset** |
| Dumfries | **Dumfries and Galloway** |
| Dundee | **Dundee City** |
| Durham | **Durham** |
| E Ayrs | **East Ayrshire** |
| Edin | **City of Edinburgh** |
| E Dunb | **East Dunbartonshire** |
| E Loth | **East Lothian** |
| E Renf | **East Renfrewshire** |
| Essex | **Essex** |
| E Sus | **East Sussex** |
| E Yorks | **East Riding of Yorkshire** |
| Falk | **Falkirk** |
| Fife | **Fife** |
| Flint | **Flintshire** |
| Glasgow | **City of Glasgow** |
| Glos | **Gloucestershire** |
| Gtr Man | **Greater Manchester** |
| Guern | **Guernsey** |
| Gwyn | **Gwynedd** |
| Halton | **Halton** |
| Hants | **Hampshire** |
| Hereford | **Herefordshire** |
| Herts | **Hertfordshire** |
| Highld | **Highland** |
| Hrtlpl | **Hartlepool** |
| Hull | **Hull** |
| Invclyd | **Inverclyde** |
| IoM | **Isle of Man** |
| IoW | **Isle of Wight** |
| Jersey | **Jersey** |
| Kent | **Kent** |
| Lancs | **Lancashire** |
| Leicester | **City of Leicester** |
| Leics | **Leicestershire** |
| Lincs | **Lincolnshire** |
| London | **Greater London** |
| Luton | **Luton** |
| Mbro | **Middlesbrough** |

| | |
|---|---|
| Medway | **Medway** |
| Mers | **Merseyside** |
| Midloth | **Midlothian** |
| M Keynes | **Milton Keynes** |
| Mon | **Monmouthshire** |
| Moray | **Moray** |
| M Tydf | **Merthyr Tydfil** |
| N Ayrs | **North Ayrshire** |
| Neath | **Neath Port Talbot** |
| NE Lincs | **North East Lincolnshire** |
| Newport | **City and County of Newport** |
| N Lanark | **North Lanarkshire** |
| N Lincs | **North Lincolnshire** |
| N Nhants | **North Northamptonshire** |
| Norf | **Norfolk** |
| Northumb | **Northumberland** |
| Nottingham | **City of Nottingham** |
| Notts | **Nottinghamshire** |
| N Som | **North Somerset** |
| N Yorks | **North Yorkshire** |
| Orkney | **Orkney** |
| Oxon | **Oxfordshire** |
| Pboro | **Peterborough** |
| Pembs | **Pembrokeshire** |
| Perth | **Perth and Kinross** |
| Plym | **Plymouth** |
| Powys | **Powys** |
| Ptsmth | **Portsmouth** |
| Reading | **Reading** |
| Redcar | **Redcar and Cleveland** |
| Renfs | **Renfrewshire** |
| Rhondda | **Rhondda Cynon Taff** |
| Rutland | **Rutland** |
| S Ayrs | **South Ayrshire** |
| Scilly | **Scilly** |
| S Glos | **South Gloucestershire** |
| Shetland | **Shetland** |
| Shrops | **Shropshire** |
| S Lanark | **South Lanarkshire** |
| Slough | **Slough** |
| Som | **Somerset** |
| Soton | **Southampton** |
| Southend | **Southend-on-Sea** |
| Staffs | **Staffordshire** |
| Stirling | **Stirling** |
| Stockton | **Stockton-on-Tees** |
| Stoke | **Stoke-on-Trent** |
| Suff | **Suffolk** |
| Sur | **Surrey** |
| Swansea | **Swansea** |
| Swindon | **Swindon** |
| S Yorks | **South Yorkshire** |
| T&W | **Tyne and Wear** |
| Telford | **Telford and Wrekin** |
| Thurrock | **Thurrock** |
| Torbay | **Torbay** |
| Torf | **Torfaen** |
| V Glam | **The Vale of Glamorgan** |
| W&F | **Westmorland and Furness** |
| Warks | **Warwickshire** |
| Warr | **Warrington** |
| W Berks | **West Berkshire** |
| W Dunb | **West Dunbartonshire** |
| Wilts | **Wiltshire** |
| Windsor | **Windsor and Maidenhead** |
| W Isles | **Western Isles** |
| W Loth | **West Lothian** |
| W Mid | **West Midlands** |
| W Nhants | **West Northamptonshire** |
| Wokingham | **Wokingham** |
| Worcs | **Worcestershire** |
| Wrex | **Wrexham** |
| W Sus | **West Sussex** |
| W Yorks | **West Yorkshire** |
| York | **City of York** |

## How to use the index

Example

**Hovingham** N Yorks **159** D5

- grid square: D5
- page number: 159
- county or unitary authority: N Yorks

## A

## D

## F

## G

## H

## K

## L

## M

## O



## P

## S

## T

## U



## V



## W

## Y



## Z